Mark Levene and George Loizou

A Guided Tour of Relational Databases and Beyond

Springer

Mark Levene, BSc, PhD
Department of Computer Science, University College London,
Gower Street, London WC1E 6BT, UK

George Loizou, BA, PhD
Department of Computer Science, Birkbeck College,
Malet Street, London WC1E 7HX

ISBN 1-85233-008-2 Springer-Verlag London Berlin Heidelberg

British Library Cataloguing in Publication Data

Levene, Mark
    A guided tour of relational databases
    1.Relational databases
    I.Title   II.Loizou, George
    0.05.7'56
    ISBN 1852330082

Library of Congress Cataloging-in-Publication Data
Levene, M. (Mark), 1957-
       A guided tour of relational databases and beyond / Mark Levene and
    George Loizou.
          p.   cm.
       Includes index.
       ISBN 1-85233-008-2 (pbk. : alk. paper)
       1. Relational databases.   2. Database management.   I. Loizou.
    George, 1937-   . II. Title.
    QA76.9.D3L477 1999
    005.75'6--dc21   98-46727

Typesetting: Digital by Design, Cheltenham
Printed and bound at the Athenæum Press Ltd, Gateshead, Tyne and Wear
34/3830-543210 Printed on acid-free paper

A Guided Tour of Relational Databases and Beyond

Springer

London
Berlin
Heidelberg
New York
Barcelona
Hong Kong
Milan
Paris
Santa Clara
Singapore
Tokyo

Contents

Preface

The relational data model, which was first developed in the early 1970's, has gained immense popularity and acceptance in the market place. There are many commercially available relational database products, and there is no doubt that relational database management systems will continue to dominate the database industry for the foreseeable future. A large percentage of the activity in the information technology industry is related to the management of data. The huge number of database-related publications, both academic and commercial, is an indication of how central the database field is in computer science as a whole.

The relational data model is based on a formal and elegant foundation, providing fertile ground for database researchers to investigate the problems associated with database systems. The core theory seems to have stabilised during the early 1990's and the attention of database researchers has subsequently moved to extensions of the relational data model and to newer data models which attempt to solve challenging new problems in database management. Still, the basis of all such developments is core relational database theory. Our book is a timely summary of the state of the art in this field. There is a personal flavour to the book in that we have interleaved into various chapters of the book some of our recent results in database theory, and have chosen to cover in more detail some of the topics which we feel are more important. Overall we have tried to be as unbiased as possible and to cover the spectrum of fundamental topics in database theory. The next section has more detail on the topics covered.

Although there is a large variety of introductory textbooks focusing on relational databases, there are not many textbooks which cater for more advanced courses both at undergraduate and masters levels. We also hope that this book will be useful for new researchers in the field, and as a reference for more established researchers in the database area. Finally, we feel that the book will be relevant to many database practitioners who are interested in a more in-depth understanding of the underlying concepts and results, which are not presented in the more introductory textbooks.

The effect that relational database theory has had on common practice in the information technology industry is immense and there has traditionally been a lot of interplay between theory and practice in the database field. One of the aims of this book is to show that this interplay is carried over to the new developments in database theory. We may now ask why relational database theory has been so successful. The full answer is given in the contents of the book. The relational data model is a relatively simple yet rich model which is appealing to database theorists and practitioners alike. On the one hand, its formal foundations in set theory and logic have provided a firm basis for research, and on the other hand its simple tabular representation has made it possible to popularise the model and make it easy for non-specialists to use.

The Structure of the Book

The book is divided into ten chapters which we now detail. Chapter 1 introduces the fundamental concepts and terminology of the database field. The central notion of a data model is introduced and there follows a review of the main data models from past to present extending into the future. In Section 1.9 we cover the necessary background material from set theory, logic and the theory of computing, so that the book may be self-contained.

Chapter 2 covers the Entity-Relationship model as a meta model for conceptual data modelling. We choose to restrict ourselves to the binary model, since it is the most prevalent in practice. The concepts pertaining to Entity-Relationship modelling will familiarise the reader in an informal manner with concepts that are formalised via the relational data model in Chapter 3.

Chapter 3, which is by far the longest chapter in the book, covers the core material pertaining to the three aspects of the relational data model: its data structure, query and update languages and integrity constraints. Although much of the material in this chapter is by now standard, we have also included some significant recent results bringing the subject up to date.

Chapter 4 covers the all important topic of relational database design and the infamous normal forms. The approach we take in this chapter is novel in the sense that we provide formal justification for normalisation, which includes both functional dependencies (generalising keys) and inclusion dependencies (generalising foreign keys).

Chapters 5, 6 and 7 cover advanced topics building on the core material of Chapter 3. In Chapter 5 we consider the problem of dealing with incomplete information. We feel that this topic has been somewhat neglected by database researchers, to the extent that some fundamental concepts need to be re-examined in the light of incomplete information. Chapter 6 looks at the possibility of enhancing the expressive power of query and update languages for the relational data model. In recent years there has been a steady demand for extending the expressive power of SQL, and thus in this chapter we consider the foundations of such extensions. In Chapter 7 we extend the relational data model to support time. Such a temporal extension of the basic model is of great practical significance due to the growing need for explicit temporal support in database applications, and thus its treatment warrants a full chapter.

Chapter 8 covering concurrency control in relational databases can be considered, alongside Chapters 3 and 4, to be core material. Despite the fact that some recent database textbooks do not cover concurrency control at all, we felt that the book would not be complete without this chapter.

Chapter 9 covers the topic of deductive or logical databases which enhances the relational data model by providing users with an extended relational database query language allowing the specification of recursive queries via a rule-based language, called Datalog. The topic of recursive queries has been the most researched topic in database theory in the last ten years; this has led to cross fertilisation between logicians, database theorists and practitioners. There are many interesting and important results in this chapter which will have a strong impact on current database technology.

The final chapter of the book, Chapter 10, covers various extensions of the relational data model and new data models which are not relational, designed to provide solutions to problems that are not easily solved using the standard relational data model. We also look at current directions and trends in the area of database research such as hypertext databases (the World Wide Web being the most prominent example) and knowledge discovery and data mining. The treatment of the topics in this final chapter cannot be as extensive as in previous chapters, the main reason being that the research into these newer data models has not yet reached a sufficient level of maturity. Despite this proviso, we have attempted to delve into each data model as deeply as possible.

Teaching from the book

The book can be used to teach several database systems courses, from the introductory to the more advanced. We assume that students studying from this book will have done introductory courses in discrete mathematics, data structures and algorithms, and possibly the theory of computation. We also assume some experience in programming. In many cases the proofs of results have been omitted, but in such cases we give the reader enough information about the techniques used in the proofs and provide when appropriate the relevant pointers to the literature where the full proofs can be found.

We mainly recommend teaching from this book on third year undergraduate or masters level courses in computer science. The book could also be used as preparation and reference for graduates wishing to do research in this area. Finally, practitioners who are interested in gaining more insight into the database field in an attempt to understand the foundations of relational databases will find the book very useful.

Four strands for teaching courses from the book are suggested:

1. *The introductory course*: Chapters 1 and 2. An introduction to database systems covering the fundamental concepts. These chapters form a prerequisite of the other courses and provide a brief tour of the subject.

2. *The core relational database theory course*: Chapters 3, 4 and 8. Relational database theory, covering its underlying data structure, i.e. the relation, its query languages and integrity constraints, and also the fundamentals of database design and concurrency control. Chapter 3 forms a prerequisite for the more advanced courses. Chapter 8 can alternatively be taught on a concurrency course. This course forms a detailed tour of the main elements of the subject.

3. *Advanced relational database theory course*: Chapters 5, 6 and 7. This course covers incomplete information, computable queries and temporal databases. It forms an advanced tour for those wishing to explore the subject in more depth.

4. *Extensions of the relational data model course*: Chapters 9 and 10. This course covers deductive databases and recently developed data models. It forms an exotic tour for those wishing to explore the newer data models.

Chapters 1, 2 and 3 should be taught in that order. We would recommend teaching Chapter 4 before any of the more advanced topics are tackled, since some of the central concepts of database design are utilised in later chapters. Chapters 5, 6, 7 and 8 are essentially independent of each other. We would also recommend teaching Chapter 6 before Chapter 9, since much of the research in deductive databases is concerned with the expressive power of its extended query language, Datalog. Chapter 10 can be taught immediately after Chapter 3, to give the student the flavour of recent data models which have been developed as a response to new real-world requirements.

Acknowledgements

When we started writing the book over four years ago, we did not realise what a mammoth task it would be. Now we are wiser! It has been a learning experience and not just in relational database theory and its extensions.

The authors would like to thank the reviewers of the book for their constructive comments. Our special thanks go to Professor Nicholas Spyratos who has provided us with important feedback on the book, and to one of his postgraduate students Yann Loyer who read Chapters 3 and 9 in detail. Any errors or omissions still remaining are, however, the responsibility of the authors. We would like to thank Steve Counsell for drawing the figures in the book and Roger Mitton for linguistic assistance.

We are also grateful to Beverley Ford, who is the computing editor at Springer-Verlag in London, Rebecca Moore the editorial assistant, and Roger Dobbing the production manager, for the efficient manner in which they have dealt with the problems of getting the book through the reviewing and production stages. Finally, we would like to thank St.John Hoskyns from Digital by Design who actually produced the book.

Dedications

Mark Levene would like to dedicate this book to his wife Sara and their children Tamara and Joseph. Being with them has made this project worthwhile. George Loizou would like to dedicate the book to his wife Diane and to his late parents, Loizos and Maritsa, especially the latter who, although illiterate herself, insisted that George be educated.

1. Introduction

A *database* is essentially an organised collection of logically inter-connected *data items*. A computer system which is responsible for the efficient storage and retrieval of the data items in a database is called a *Database Management System* (or simply a database system or a DBMS). Thus the purpose of a DBMS is to organise and manipulate *information*.

Nowadays most medium size to large size organisations use DBMS technology. For example, banks store their customer accounts in a database, libraries keep all their book records and loan information in a database and airline companies keep all their online booking information in a database. The widespread use of Personal Computers (PCs) has also led small organisations such as local video shops and general practitioners to use databases. A brief glance at the available popular computer magazines should be enough to convince you that in the near future we will all have personal databases to organise our day-to-day information. There is at present a very large number of database-related products that are available on the market, which are supported on a wide range of both hardware and software platforms.

How can the potential buyer decide which product to invest in amongst the plethora of available choices? Furthermore, what features should a buyer be looking for apart from a user-friendly and easy-to-use graphical user interface? The problems we face as buyers may actually get worse once a DBMS has been purchased. How do we model the application we are aiming to implement in the most faithful manner to its real-world representation? How do we make sure that all the constraints present in the data are maintained? In addition, how do we make sure that the data is organised in the most efficient manner, and how do we retrieve and update information in the simplest and quickest manner?

The aim of this book is *not* to give you specific product advice but rather to introduce you to the fundamental concepts of databases and their associated systems. In particular, we will concentrate on *data modelling* which provides a high level abstract model of a database. Using data modelling concepts users will be able to design and use their database system at a level compatible with their level of abstraction rather than at the machine level. Each DBMS supports a particular data model, the dominant one currently being the *relational data model* (or simply the relational model). (We will call a DBMS which supports the relational data model a *relational DBMS* [Cha76].) In this book we will mainly concentrate on introducing the various facets of the relational model. As you will discover the relational model has the advantage of being relatively simple to describe and understand but on the other hand it is rich enough to capture most aspects of data modelling. We are convinced that an understanding of the theoretical aspects of the relational model will allow the readers to make a better choice

1

than would otherwise be the case when purchasing a relational product that best suits their needs, on the basis of the DBMS functionality the product offers.

The database concept has been evolving for well over thirty years. During the 1960's databases were viewed as a collection of files and DBMSs were therefore file systems. In the late 1960's and the early 1970's the introduction of the concept of a data model gave rise to the hierarchical data model [TL76] and the network data model [Bac69, Bac73, TF76]. There are today still companies that are using databases based on these models. (Early editions of many of the database books appearing in the bibliography cover the hierarchical and network data models in detail; see also [MMC76, TF76, TL76].)

The relational data model was introduced by Codd in 1970 [Cod70] whilst working for IBM and in 1981 Codd received the Turing award for his important contribution to the theory of databases [Cod82]. During the mid 1970's there was much debate between proponents of the network data model on the one hand and those of the relational data model on the other hand [MMC76, Dat86c]. Joining this debate on the relational side Date has done much to popularise and explain the central features of the relational data model [Dat95]. During the mid 1970's and until the mid 1980's relational database theory dominated the output of database research resulting in a sound mathematical foundation for the relational data model. Commercially, from the mid 1980's until today DBMSs supporting the relational data model have had a dominant position in the DBMS market.

During the late 1980's and the 1990's shortcomings of the relational data model in areas such as scientific and statistical applications, expert systems, text handling, multimedia, office automation, manipulating temporal and spatial data, and computer-aided design, gave rise to several new proposals and extensions to the relational data model. The main extensions to the relational data model include complex objects data models such as the nested relational data model [KK89, Lev92], and the deductive or logical data model [NT89, CGT90]. In addition, several temporal extensions to the relational data model have been put forward [TCG+93]. Some recent proposals suggest object-orientation as a data model [Kim90, KM94] but there is no current agreement on a definitive object-oriented data model. An emerging area, for which several data models are being suggested, is that of hypertext (or more generally hypermedia) [Con87, Nie90, Rad91], which is concerned with organising text in a nonlinear fashion.

The aim of this chapter is to introduce the reader to the basic concepts of data modelling showing how data can be viewed in different ways via different data models starting from the relational model.

The layout of this chapter is as follows. In Section 1.1 we introduce the database concept using an example of a library database. In Section 1.2 we define what a database is. In Section 1.3 we motivate the need for DBMSs. In Section 1.4 we introduce the three levels of data abstraction, which should be supported by any DBMS; these are the physical, conceptual and view levels. In Section 1.5 we detail the components that constitute a DBMS. In Section 1.6 we introduce the fundamental concept of data independence, which allows changes at a lower level of abstraction (say the physical level) without affecting the higher levels (say the conceptual and view levels). In Section 1.7 we define the central concept of a data model and give an intuitive presentation of each of the main existing data models. In Section 1.8 we briefly discuss the trend of extending the relational model and what the future may hold in this respect. In Section 1.9 we present the basic mathematical concepts needed throughout the book.

1.1 An Introductory Example

As an illustration of a small fragment of a library database consider Tables 1.1 and 1.2, which represent information concerning books and loans of these books, respectively.

Table 1.1 The books relation

AUTHOR1	SHORT_TITLE	PUBLISHER	YEAR	ISBN
Atzeni	DB Theory	Benjamin/Cummings	1993	0-8053-0249-2
Date	Introduction to DBs	Addison-Wesley	1990	0-201-52878-9
Korth	DB Concepts	McGraw-Hill	1991	0-07-044754-3
Mannila	The Design of DBs	Addison-Wesley	1992	0-201-56523-4
Ullman	Principles of DBs	Computer Science Press	1988	0-7167-8158-1

Table 1.2 The loans relation

ISBN	LOCATION	QUANTITY	LOAN
0-8053-0249-2	Science	1	0
0-201-52878-9	Main	3	2
0-07-044754-3	Main	1	1
0-201-56523-4	Science	1	0
0-7167-8158-1	Main	2	1

In relational database terminology each such table is called a *relation* and the rows of the relation, which represent the data items, are called *tuples*. Each tuple is seen to model an *entity*, or a thing, relevant to the application; it is also common to refer to an entity as an *object*. The tuples in Table 1.1 represent book entities and the tuples in Table 1.2 represent loan entities. Each relation as a whole represents an *entity set*. We stress that a relation is a set in the mathematical sense (see Subsection 1.9.1), since if we reorder the tuples in any table we will still have the same relation, that is to say, a relation is an *unordered* collection of data items.

The collection of all relations, in this case the books and loans relations, is called a *relational database* (or simply a database). This collection of relations is sometimes referred to as the *extension* of the database.

The header of each column of a relation, which is called an *attribute name* (or simply an attribute), represents a property of the entities being modelled. With each attribute, say A, we associate a set of values, called the *domain* of the attribute, which represents the possible values for the components of tuples appearing in the column headed by A. Attributes furnish a naming mechanism which provides semantics to the components of tuples, which are their *attribute values*. Thus the attribute AUTHOR1 represents the first authors of the books modelled by the relation shown in Table 1.1. Its domain is the set of all possible authors of books. This domain may be the set of all strings over the English alphabet. The attribute LOAN represents the number of books on loan for a particular book. Its domain is the set of all integers between zero and the number of copies of the particular book that is being borrowed. In general, this domain is the (countably infinite) set of all integers and so an integrity constraint must restrict the cardinality of this set to the number of available copies stored in the library.

The first line of a relation is referred to as the header of the relation. The header of a relation is the collection of all attributes of all the columns of a relation and is called a *relation schema* (or simply a schema). In order to avoid ambiguity in naming, it is standard practice to insist that attribute names are distinct. Thus we can consider a schema to be a set of attributes. On the other hand, it is sometimes useful to be able to refer to the attributes in some order and therefore it is common to impose some linear ordering (see Subsection 1.9.2) on the attributes in a schema. For example, in the schema of the books relation we can take AUTHOR1 to be the first attribute, SHORT_TITLE to be the second attribute and so on for the third, fourth and fifth attributes. A relation schema models an *entity type*; it is also common to refer to an entity type as an *object type*.

It is also customary to give names to relation schemas. For example, the books schema could be called BOOKS and the loans schema could be called LOANS. Thus the relation schemas of the library database can be written as: BOOKS(AUTHOR1, SHORT_TITLE, PUBLISHER, YEAR, ISBN) and LOANS(ISBN, LOCATION, QUANTITY, LOAN); this notation emphasises the default order of attributes for these schemas.

The collection of all schemas of all the relations in a database is called *a relational database schema* (or simply a database schema). This collection of relation schemas is sometimes referred to as the *intension* of the database.

1.2   What is a Database?

We use the example of Section 1.1 to give a higher level description of what a database is. Firstly, a database is a collection of *persistent* data. That is, the database relations are stored permanently in the computer rather than being *transient* data of some application program. Secondly, this collection of data, i.e. the database, models part of the real world, called the *enterprise*. For example, the enterprise might be a library and the database models the cataloguing and loaning of books. The fact that a database is modelling an enterprise implies that the data items in the database are logically interconnected. In the library example the books and loans relations are obviously logically connected, while a relation modelling the salaries of library staff for payroll purposes is not logically connected in this case and therefore would not be part of the library database. Thirdly, in many cases a database is a *shared* resource. By sharing we mean that multiple users have access to the database concurrently. A library database for a college will be shared by all members of the college and possibly by other users who can remote login to the database system. An exception to sharing is the use of personal databases on PCs.

1.3   Why do we Need Database Management Systems?

For simplicity let us assume that a DBMS is a software package (in fact this assumption is very close to reality with respect to most commercial DBMSs). So, like any other software package we hope that by using it it will make our life easier in some way.

The main benefit a DBMS can offer is to save programming time and software maintenance by handling all the interactions of an application with the database. This can be viewed as being compatible with one of the main goals of software engineering, which is to make software production as high level as possible. That is, the software package should provide programmers with a variety of functional built-in modules that can be "plugged" into the application software. Such modules may also include application generators and high level database languages. In addition, the DBMS may provide high level graphical user interfaces. These days most PC-based DBMSs will have a window-based user interface. In Section 1.5 we will detail the services that a DBMS should offer the user.

Another important reason for having DBMSs is to provide *data independence*, which is the independence of application programs from the actual organisation of the information in the database. This implies that application programmers and database users do not have to concern themselves with the actual structure of the database as it is stored on external media and as it is manipulated in main memory. Their interaction with the database is on an abstract level and any reorganisation of the way information is stored in the database should not affect their interaction with the database. It follows that data independence will make application programs much easier to maintain. This topic will be discussed in more detail in Section 1.6.

1.4   The Three Levels of Data Abstraction

An important proposal for a generalised framework for the architecture of a DBMS was put forward by the ANSI/X3/SPARC study group on DBMSs [TK78]. The framework emphasises the interfaces that a DBMS should provide and the kind of information that should pass between them. The proposed architecture identifies three distinct levels of abstraction:

- The *physical* (or internal) level comprises the physical schema and the physical database. The physical schema is the description of the storage and access methods used to store the information in the database on the media available within the computer system, and the physical database is the actual data as stored on the storage devices of the computer system.

- The *conceptual* (or logical) level comprises the conceptual database schema (or simply database schema) and the conceptual database (or simply the database). The database schema is the description of the information about the enterprise as it is modelled in the database, and the database is the abstraction of the information being modelled as it is seen by the users.

- The *view* (or external) level comprises a collection of view schemas and a collection of views. Each view schema is a simplified description of the enterprise as seen by an application program (and thus by a group of end users). A view schema has an associated view, which corresponds to the portion of the database being described by the view schema.

A diagrammatic view of the three levels of abstraction is given in Figure 1.1.

The physical level is, in general, dependent on the hardware and software available within the computer system being used. It should be able to reflect current technology. It is possible to make the physical schema machine independent by using device independent storage and access methods but the physical information is normally machine dependent.

The conceptual database schema and the conceptual database are specified by using the data model that is supported by the DBMS. Thus the data model provides a "language" which

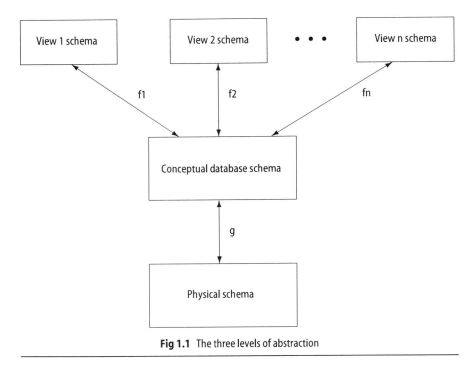

Fig 1.1 The three levels of abstraction

allows us to communicate with the conceptual level of the DBMS. As we have seen in Section 1.1 the relational model provides a simple way of describing the conceptual level.

The external level of a DBMS may provide any number of views, corresponding to different application programs or user groups. For example, in the library database, an application program that checks which books are all out on loan (i.e. books that have a QUANTITY-value equal to their LOAN-value) does not need the detailed book information. An entity type that is represented in a view schema may not be explicitly modelled by the database schema at the conceptual level. For example, the total number of books in the library for a given publisher can be represented in a view but this information is not directly modelled in the library database schema. All the information in views must be derivable from the information present in the database at the conceptual level.

The correspondences between the three levels of abstraction are established through *data mappings* between the view and the conceptual levels, and between the conceptual and the physical levels. The mapping between the view and the physical levels is a composition of the mappings between the view and the conceptual levels, and the mappings between the conceptual and the physical levels. Thus data independence is maintained by insisting that the information at the view level interacts with that of the physical level only through the conceptual level. Assuming that the conceptual level has been defined, the DBMS must then ensure that the mappings to the physical and view levels are consistent with the information at the conceptual level.

An integral part of any DBMS is the *data dictionary*. The data dictionary is a *meta*-database which is a repository of information about the database. It must at least contain the description of the physical, conceptual and view schemas and the mappings between them. It may also contain statistical information on the database usage, recovery information, user login and access information, security information and accounting information. In fact, the data dictionary can be implemented in a relational DBMS as just another relation in the database. Therefore, the data dictionary can be queried and updated, by using the facilities of the DBMS, like any other relation in the database.

1.5   What is a Database Management System?

A DBMS is a computer system which is responsible for storage and maintenance of databases. A DBMS is essentially a software system but it may contain specialised hardware in order to make the management of data more efficient. Such hardware may include special disk drives that support fast access to the data and multiprocessors that support parallelism. From now on we will assume for simplicity that a DBMS is a software package. The DBMS software should provide the following services:

- A *Data Definition Language* (DDL) for defining the schemas of the three levels of abstraction (physical, conceptual and view) and the mappings between them.

- A *Data Manipulation Language* (DML) for querying and updating the information in the database. Updates include inserting new data, deleting existing data and modifying existing data. (A DML is also called a database language, a query and update language or simply a query language.)

- Efficiency in query response time and utilisation of storage space.

- Integrity and consistency. That is, the ability to define and check for integrity constraints, such as an ISBN is associated with a single book and the number of books on loan does not exceed the quantity of books available. It is a fundamental requirement that a database be consistent at all times.

- Concurrency control and data sharing. In a multi-user database environment several processes, such as querying and updating data, may happen concurrently. Concurrency control is the activity of ensuring that these processes do not interfere with each other. A typical example of concurrency control is an airline reservation system which must ensure that two people do *not* book the same seat.

- Transaction management. A transaction is an execution of a program that accesses shared data. The most important operations a transaction can perform are reading data (or querying) and writing data (or updating). If the transaction terminates successfully then it is *committed*, i.e. the changes to the database are made permanent. On the other hand, if the transaction is aborted, that is to say, it does not terminate successfully, then it must be *rolled back*, i.e. all the updates that were made to the database by that transaction have to be undone.

- Recovery from failure. That is, ensuring that system failures, be they software or hardware, do not corrupt the database. The recovery facility should ensure that the database be returned to its most recent consistent state prior to the failure.

- Security. That is, ensuring that users have access only to those parts of the database they are authorised to access. This allows access privileges to be *granted* and *revoked* from users.

- Database administration facilities. These are normally provided as part of the DDL. Thus the DDL must also allow the definition of integrity constraints and security rights. The DBMS might also provide software tools for database design, for monitoring and tuning database performance, for running benchmarks on the database and for generating various reports.

A DBMS has several types of users.

- *End users*, who interact with the external level of the DBMS via interfaces that are generated by application programs. These are the people who *use* the database.

- *Application programmers*, who write the application programs that make use of the database. Application programs may interact with the conceptual and/or the external levels of the DBMS.

- *Database Administrator* (DBA), who is responsible for defining the physical schema and the day-to-day administration of the database. The DBA is also responsible for handling database security, tuning database performance and generating reports concerning the database usage.

- *Enterprise administrator*, who is responsible for defining the conceptual database schema. This involves the important task of database design.

- *Application administrator*, who is responsible for defining the view schemas. This involves defining the view schema relevant to each application. It is possible that each application that is being developed has a separate application administrator.

1.6   The Concept of Data Independence

The concept of *data independence* (or physical data independence) is one of the key factors in the success of the relational model. It means that the physical level of the database may be modified without the need to make any corresponding changes to the conceptual level. This implies that application programs do not require any change when the physical level of the database is restructured. The way data independence is enforced by the DBMS is by modifying the data mapping between the physical and the conceptual levels, when any change to the physical level occurs. With respect to the library example, the conceptual level deals with relations and does not concern itself with their actual physical storage. Therefore, for efficiency reasons, the DBA may decide to restructure the library database, say by changing its physical access method, without affecting the conceptual level at all. The readers can convince themselves that the relational model indeed provides data independence. Data models which preceded the relational model did not provide full data independence.

To summarise, data independence makes maintenance of applications programs easier, gives freedom to the DBA to modify the physical level and frees the users from having to know the many details concerning the physical level when interacting with the database.

A higher level of data independence would be *conceptual data independence*, which is the independence of the view level from the conceptual level. In general, such independence cannot be achieved, since the deletion of a relation or one or more columns of a relation will necessarily disrupt any view that references that relation or those columns. On the other hand, a weaker type of data independence, called *growth independence* [Dat86b], can be achieved in the relational model. Growth independence is the independence of the view level from adding new attributes to relation schemas (and thereafter adding attribute values to the new columns of the relation) and from adding new relation schemas to the database schema (and thereafter adding tuples to the new relations). Such additions to the conceptual level will not require any changes to application programs, due to the fact that these programs do not have references to these new attributes and relation schemas. The way growth independence is enforced by the DBMS is by adding the changes that occur at the conceptual level to the data mapping between the conceptual and view levels without changing the existing part of this data mapping. The readers can convince themselves that growth independence is achieved in the relational model. On the other hand, it is much harder to achieve such independence within the data models that preceded the relational model. With respect to the library example, the DBA may decide to add an attribute called SUBJECT, which represents the subject category of the book, without affecting the view level at all.

1.7 What is a Data Model?

A *data model* (or simply a model) is a combination of three components [Cod82]:

- The structural part: A collection of data structures (or entity types, or object types) which define the set of allowable databases.

- The integrity part: A collection of general integrity constraints, which specify the set of consistent databases or the set of allowable changes to a database.

- The manipulative part: A collection of operators or inference rules, which can be applied to an allowable database in any required combination in order to query and update parts of the database.

Codd [Cod82] claims that the relational model was the first data model to be defined in the above sense. In hindsight the three components of a data model can also be recognised in the hierarchical and network data models. An example of a data model that concentrates mainly on the structural and integrity part of a data model is the *entity-relationship model* (or simply the ER model) [Che76]; this model is discussed in detail in Chapter 2. The reason for this is that the main purpose of the ER model is to provide a conceptual database schema and due to its simple yet powerful graphical representation it is very widely used during database design.

A useful distinction to make between the various data models, with respect to their manipulative part, is whether they are inherently *declarative* or *procedural*.

Declarative database languages are logic-based, i.e. users of such languages specify what data they want to manipulate with respect to the conceptual database schema rather than how to manipulate this schema. On the other hand, procedural database languages are access-path-based, that is, users of such languages specify the access path to the data they want to manipulate with respect to the conceptual database schema.

Declarative database languages are most suitable for end users in the form of easy-to-use graphical interfaces and procedural languages are most suitable for database programmers in the form of well-defined interfaces between the database and a conventional programming language such as COBOL, C or Java. Normally, this interface allows DBMS calls to be embedded in such a programming language but there is an ongoing attempt to extend programming languages with built-in database types and operations over these types [Sch77].

Embedded query languages force application programmers to learn two different formalisms, the formalism of the programming language and the formalism of the query language. These two formalisms are not always fully compatible which leads to a problem known as the *impedance mismatch* problem. Extending programming languages with built-in database types is one way of solving the impedance mismatch problem.

Declarative interfaces may also be provided for database programmers in order to shift the database optimisation issues from the programmer to the DBMS and thus to improve productivity. These declarative interfaces are known as *Fourth Generation Languages* (4GLs). 4GLs which provide full programming capabilities are another way of solving the impedance mismatch problem.

The manipulative part of the relational data model and its extensions naturally allows for declarative query and update languages while that of the hierarchical, network and object-oriented data models naturally allows for procedural query and update languages. This is one reason why object-oriented data models can be regarded as extensions of the hierarchical and network data models.

1.7.1 The Relational Data Model

The *relational data model*, or simply the relational model, is a combination of the following three components:

- Structural part: a database schema is a collection of relation schemas and a database is a collection of relations.

- Integrity part: *primary keys* and *foreign keys*.

- Manipulative part: relational algebra and relational calculus.

For an example of a relational database see Tables 1.1 and 1.2. The relational data model will be discussed in detail from Chapter 3 onwards. We now provide a brief summary of its salient features.

A *candidate key* (or simply a key) for a relation schema is a minimal set of attributes whose values uniquely identify tuples in the corresponding relation. For example, for both the books and loans relation schemas ISBN is a key. Assuming that an author only writes one book a year then the set of attributes {AUTHOR1, YEAR} is also a key for the books relation schema. This key is not as useful as the ISBN, since firstly it assumes that author names are unique, and secondly it is a combination of two attributes and is thus not as concise as the ISBN. For the loans relation schema it may be the case that multiple copies of a book may be held in different locations in which case {ISBN, LOCATION} would be a key for this relation schema. An example of a relation schema with two natural keys is the schema ADDRESS(STREET, CITY, POSTCODE) of addresses. The two keys for this relation schema are {STREET, POSTCODE} and {STREET, CITY}, since both these keys uniquely determine the information conveyed by the other. The *primary key* of a relation schema is a distinguished key designated by the database designer.

In general, it may be that some of the information in a relation may be either unknown or does not exist. Let EMPLOYEE(SSN, ENAME, SALARY, SPOUSE_SSN, ADDRESS, PROJECT_ID) be an employee relation schema with the obvious semantics. It is possible that the address of a given employee is unknown, i.e. this information exists but is not available in the relation at present. It is also possible that an employee is not married in which case there does not exist a social security number for the employee's spouse, i.e. SPOUSE_SSN is inapplicable. In order to represent an unknown or inapplicable value into a relation the domains of attributes are extended with two distinguished values, called *null values* (or simply nulls): *unk* (as an abbreviation of unknown) and *dne* (as an acronym of does not exist).

Now, in order to guarantee that every tuple in a relation is accessible we must ensure that for all tuples in a relation the values of at least one key are not null. Therefore, a constraint is placed on the values of the primary key, namely that these values cannot be null. This constraint is known as *entity integrity*.

A *foreign key* is a set of attributes in a relation schema that forms a primary key of another relation. For example, ISBN in BOOKS and LOANS are both foreign keys of each other. A foreign key of a relation schema is said to *reference* the attributes of another relation schema. Thus, ISBN in BOOKS references ISBN in LOANS and vice versa. Assume a relation schema PROJECT(PROJECT_ID, TITLE, LOCATION, MGR_SSN). Then PROJECT_ID is a foreign key of EMPLOYEE which references PROJECT_ID in PROJECT and MGR_SSN is a foreign key of PROJECT which references SSN in EMPLOYEE. A relation schema may also reference itself; for example, if MGR_SSN were an attribute of EMPLOYEE then it would be a foreign key of EMPLOYEE which references SSN in EMPLOYEE.

In order to guarantee that foreign key values, which are not null, reference existing tuples we place the constraint that if the values of a foreign key are not null then there exists a tuple in the referenced relation having those values as key values. This constraint, known as *referential integrity*, ensures that only valid references are made between tuples in relations.

The relational algebra is a collection of operators which take relations as input and generate a relation as output. It is important to note that the relational algebra processes sets of tuples at a time rather than one tuple at a time. For example, we can generate a relation from the books relation which contains only tuples of books published by Addison-Wesley; such an operation is called a *selection*. We can also generate a relation from the books relation which contains only the ISBN, AUTHOR1 and SHORT_TITLE attribute values of tuples; such an operation is called a *projection*. Moreover, we can combine the books and loans relations to output a relation which contains tuples over the attributes ISBN, SHORT_TITLE and LOCATION; such an operation which combines two or more relations is called a *join*.

The relational calculus is a declarative counterpart of the relational algebra based on first-order logic. The commercial query language SQL (an acronym for *Structured Query Language*), which is the standard query language for relational DBMSs, is based on the relational calculus.

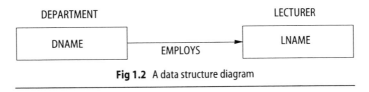

Fig 1.2 A data structure diagram

1.7.2   The Network Data Model

The *network data model*, or simply the network model, is a combination of the following three components:

- Structural part: a database schema in the form of a directed graph, called a *data structure diagram*, and a database is an instance of a data structure diagram.

- Integrity part: *record identity* and *referential integrity*.

- Manipulative part: network traversal.

The nodes of a data structure diagram are called *record types* and its links are called *set types*. Whenever two record types are connected by a link, the source record type is called the *owner record type* (or simply the owner type) and the destination record type is called the *member record type* (or simply the member type). An example of a data structure diagram is shown in Figure 1.2. It has the two record types DEPARTMENT and LECTURER and only one set type EMPLOYS from DEPARTMENT to LECTURER. DEPARTMENT is the owner type of EMPLOYS and LECTURER is the member type of EMPLOYS.

Each record type contains attributes (also called *fields*) in analogy to a relation schema. An instance of a record type is called a *record*. Each record contains attribute values for each of the attributes of its record type, in analogy to tuples of a relation, and, in addition, it has a *record identity*, which is a unique identifier for that record. Record identity can be viewed as a "pointer", which corresponds to the address of the record; it may or may not correspond to the actual physical address of the record. The record identity is generated by the DBMS and is hidden from the user. Thus record identity provides a system-defined key value for each record in the database.

An instance of a set type is called a *set occurrence*. A set occurrence contains one instance of the owner record type together with zero or more instances of the member record type. A set occurrence with no member records is called an *empty set*. The member records are linked together in some order and there are two additional links, one from the owner record to the first member record and one from the last member record to the owner record. An example of an instance of the data structure diagram of Figure 1.2 is shown in Figure 1.3.

A set occurrence is a one-to-many association between owner and members records. It is important not to confuse the use of the word "set" with its set-theoretic meaning. In fact set occurrences in the network model are ordered and the use of the word "set" is unfortunate but historical.

The constraint that a set occurrence must have exactly one owner record is called *referential integrity*. Thus in order for an owner record (for example a department) to have member records (for example lecturers) it must exist.

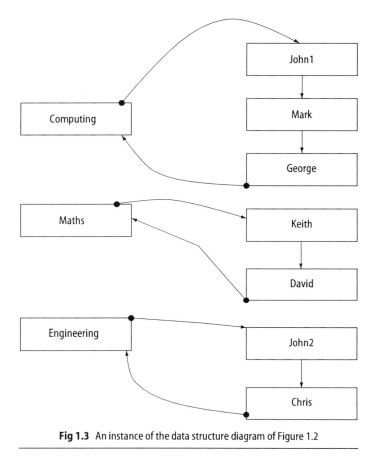

Fig 1.3 An instance of the data structure diagram of Figure 1.2

We can now define a database, which is an instance of a data structure diagram, to be a collection of record instances for each record type in the data structure diagram and a collection of set occurrences for each set type in the diagram.

Another example of a data structure diagram is shown in Figure 1.4. This data structure diagram has two set types TEACHES and TAUGHT_BY, two owner types TEACHER and COURSE, of TEACHES and TAUGHT_BY, respectively, and one member type T_C, where T_C stands for TEACHER_COURSE. An instance of the data structure diagram of Figure 1.4 is shown in Figure 1.5.

In order to discuss the manipulative part of the network model we will assume that all the record types in a data structure diagram are either the owner type or member type of at least one set type in the diagram. There is no loss of generality in this assumption, since if a record type, say R, is isolated (i.e. it is not the owner type or member type of any set occurrence) we can create a new set type, S, and a new record type M, with R being the owner type of S and M being the member type of S.

The fundamental operations of network traversal consist of locating a record in the database and once a record is located following a link (or "chasing a pointer") in order to obtain the next record.

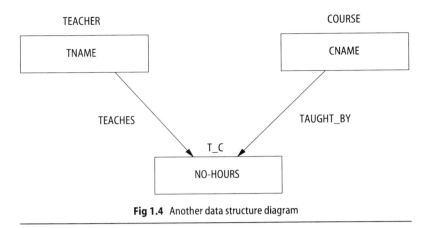

Fig 1.4 Another data structure diagram

For every set occurrence the following operations must be supported:

- Given an owner record process its member records in some order.

- Given a member record process its owner record.

- Given a member record process the other member records in the set occurrence.

Navigation in a network database is done one record at a time. At each stage when the user is navigating through the database several record identities, called *currency pointers*, are maintained by the DBMS. The record identity of the most recently accessed record is referred to as the *current of run unit*. Furthermore, for each record type, R, the record identity of the most recently accessed record of type R is referred to as the *current of* R. Finally, for each set type, S, the record identity of the most recently accessed owner or member record in the most recently accessed set occurrence of type S is referred to as the *current of* S. All the currency pointers are initially null. The actual network traversal query language consists of changing the values of the currency pointers using a sequence of **FIND** statements.

A particular record of a record type can be located by a statement of the form:

FIND *record type* **USING** *record attributes*

where the record attributes are assigned values by assignment statements of the form: *Att* := *val*, where *Att* is an attribute and *val* is a value. If two or more records in the database have the specified attribute values then any one of these records is located. On the other hand, if no records have the specified attribute values then the query fails.

The lecturer record for Mark can be made the current of LECTURER and the department record for Computing can be made the current of DEPARTMENT by the query

> LNAME := 'Mark'
> **FIND** LECTURER **USING** LNAME
> DNAME := 'Computing'
> **FIND** DEPARTMENT **USING** DNAME

The current of run unit will now be the department record for Computing.

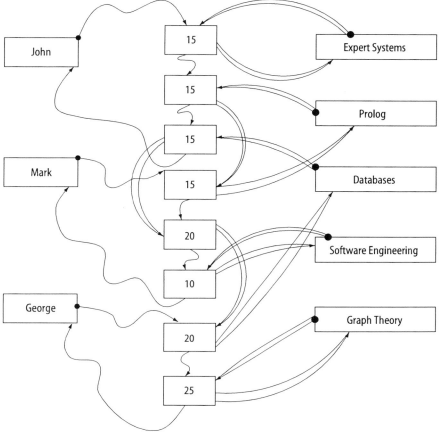

Fig 1.5 An instance of the data structure diagram of Figure 1.4

The first member of a set type can be located by a statement of the form:

FIND FIRST *record type* **IN** *set type*

The first member of the Computing department within EMPLOYS can be located by

FIND FIRST LECTURER **IN** EMPLOYS

The current of EMPLOYS will now be the lecturer record for John1.
The next member of a set type can be located by a statement of the form:

FIND NEXT *record type* **IN** *set type*

The query **FIND NEXT** R **IN** S fails if the current of S is the last member of the current set occurrence being scanned.

The next member of the Computing department within EMPLOYS can be located by

FIND NEXT LECTURER **IN** EMPLOYS

The current of EMPLOYS will now be the lecturer record for Mark.

The owner of a set type can be located by a statement of the form:

FIND OWNER IN *set type*

The owner record of the Computing department can be located by

FIND OWNER IN EMPLOYS

Thus the current of EMPLOYS will now be the department record for Computing.

1.7.3   The Hierarchical Data Model

The *hierarchical data model*, or simply the hierarchical model, is a combination of the following three components:

- Structural part: a database schema in the form of a collection of *tree types*, called a *forest type*, and a database in the form of a collection of *trees*, called a *forest*.

- Integrity part: *record identity* and *referential integrity*.

- Manipulative part: hierarchical navigation.

A rooted tree is a tree which has a single root node and such that each child node in the tree has exactly one parent node (the root node is not a child node). A tree type is a directed graph which is a rooted tree. As in the network model each node in a tree type is called a *record type*. The record type corresponding to the root node is called the *root record type* (or simply the root type). If node, A, is a parent of another node, B, then the record type, say RA, corresponding to A, is the parent record type of the record type, say RB, corresponding to B. Equivalently, RB is a child record type of RA. A record type having no children record types is called a *leaf record type*. A forest type is a collection of tree types. An example of a tree type modelling a university database is shown in Figure 1.6. We also mention the concept of a *virtual record type* which is a pointer to a record type. Virtual record types are useful when we would like to use the same record type in two tree types (or to use the same record twice in a single tree type) without duplicating the record type.

As in the network model each record type contains attributes and the instances of record types are records containing values for each of the defined attributes. Furthermore, as in the network model, each record has a record identity which specifies a unique address to the record. The record identity is generated by the DBMS and is hidden from the user.

An instance of a tree type is a *tree record*, which is a tree whose nodes are records and whose links form one-to-many associations between parent and child records. The root record of a tree record is an instance of the root record type. A parent record may have zero or more children records. On the other hand, a child record must have exactly one parent record; this

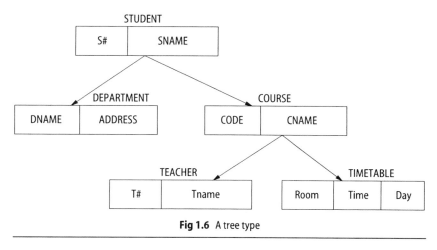

Fig 1.6 A tree type

constraint is called referential integrity. We can now define a database over a forest type to be a collection of tree records over the tree types in the forest. An example of a tree record over the tree type of Figure 1.6 is shown in Figure 1.7.

In order to discuss the manipulative part of the hierarchical model we will assume that the forest type has only one tree type. There is no loss of generality in this assumption, since we can always create a new tree type with a new root record type which combines all the record types in the forest type into a single tree type. Moreover, without loss of generality, we assume that the database consists of a single tree record.

A *hierarchical path* (or simply a path) is a sequence of records starting from a root record and following alternately from a parent record to a child record. For example, STUDENT, COURSE, TEACHER is a path. The fundamental operation of hierarchical navigation is that of traversing tree records by specifying paths starting from a root record to the record we are trying to locate. As in the network model tree traversal is done one record at a time. At each stage when the user is navigating through the database a currency pointer is maintained by the DBMS, which is the record identity of the most recently accessed record.

Traversal of a tree record is performed in a depth-first [Tar72, AHU83] manner as follows, starting by making the root record the current record:

1) visit the current record if it has not already been visited, else

2) visit the leftmost child record not previously visited, else

3) go back to the parent record.

The first record over a record type in depth-first order can be located by a statement of the form:

    GET FIRST *record type* **WHERE** *condition*

where *condition* is a Boolean expression over a record type qualifying the record that should be located.

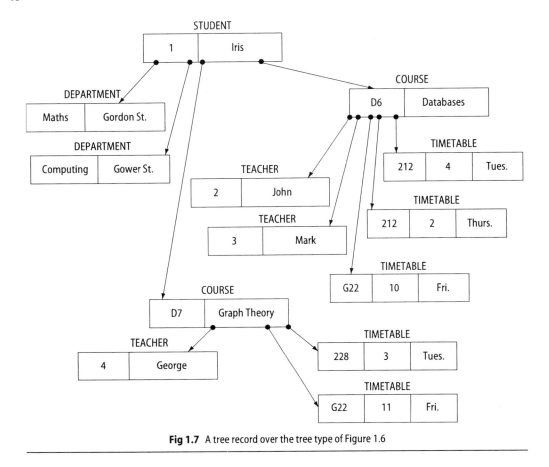

Fig 1.7 A tree record over the tree type of Figure 1.6

The first COURSE record having code D7 can be located by

GET FIRST COURSE **WHERE** CODE = 'D7'

The next record over a record type in depth-first order can be located by a statement of the form:

GET NEXT *record type* **WHERE** *condition*

The next TIMETABLE record in room G22, i.e. the first TIMETABLE record for D7, can be located by

GET NEXT TIMETABLE **WHERE** ROOM = 'G22'

The next sibling record over a record type (i.e. the next record having the same parent record as the current record, if such a record exists) in depth-first order can be located by a statement of the form:

GET NEXT WITHIN PARENT WHERE *condition*

The next TIMETABLE record within the parent record of the current record, i.e. the second TIMETABLE record for D7, can be located by

GET NEXT WITHIN PARENT TIMETABLE

Locating a record independently of the current record is achieved by a statement of the form:

GET UNIQUE WHERE *condition*

The TEACHER record with TNAME John can be located by

GET UNIQUE TEACHER **WHERE** TNAME = 'John'

1.7.4   The Nested Relational Data Model

Relations are often called *flat* relations due to their simple and flat tabular form. The (flat) relational model does not allow attribute values to be sets of values or sets of tuples. In other words, attribute values of (flat) relations cannot themselves be relations. This restriction on the attribute values of relations is known as the *First Normal Form* (or 1NF) assumption. (1NF and higher normal forms will be discussed in detail in Chapter 4 in the context of database design.) The 1NF assumption has the advantage of keeping the tabular structure of relations simple and allowing relational query languages to be able to refer to attribute values in tuples of relations in a straightforward manner.

By relaxing the 1NF assumption we can introduce hierarchical structures into the relational model [Mak77]. A relation which does not necessarily satisfy the 1NF assumption is called a *nested relation* and the resulting data model is called the *nested relational data model*, or simply the nested relational model. Thus an important special case is a nested relation which satisfies the 1NF assumption; such a relation is called a *flat relation* (or simply a relation using our previous terminology). Attributes of nested relation schemas whose values may be nested relations are called *relation-valued attributes*. Many applications have data that can be described naturally in a hierarchical fashion. For example, a family tree, or a parts inventory relation showing parts and their components, are described very naturally by using trees. So the nested relational model generalises the concepts of the (flat) relational model to hierarchical data structures without using record identity and links as was done in the hierarchical model. Thus the nested relational model has the benefits of both the relational and hierarchical models. On the one hand, it builds on over twenty five years of research into the relational model and on the other hand it allows modelling of complex objects which may not be flat. As an example, the flat relation shown Table 1.3 can be restructured into the nested relation shown in Table 1.4 having the relation-valued attribute (CNAME NO_HOURS)*, or the nested relation shown in Table 1.5 having the relation-valued attribute (TNAME NO_HOURS)*. We observe that our notation for describing relation-valued attributes highlights their internal structure by enclosing them with '(' and ')*'. Further nesting such as (CNAME (TNAME NO_HOURS)*)* is possible, for instance if we would like to record the set of courses, teachers and hours that students take. This example highlights the fact that nested relations allow flexibility in presenting the information to the users, which is not present in the relational model. One of the advantages of the nested relational model over the hierarchical model is that it is easy to restructure data according to the users' needs.

Table 1.3 A flat relation

TNAME	CNAME	NO_HOURS
John	Expert Syst	15
John	Databases	15
John	Prolog	15
Mark	Software Eng	10
Mark	Databases	20
Mark	Prolog	15
George	Databases	20
George	Graph Theory	25

The integrity part of the nested relational model generalises that of the relational model. The concepts of key, primary key and foreign key of a nested relation schema must allow for relation-valued attributes. For example, TNAME is a key for the schema of the nested relation shown in Table 1.4, since TNAME attribute values uniquely determine the relation consisting of course and number of hours tuples. Correspondingly, CNAME is a key for the schema of the nested relation shown in Table 1.5, since CNAME attribute values uniquely determine the relation consisting of teacher and number of hours tuples. Let us assume that information about teachers is stored in a further nested relation, over a nested relation schema, say TEACHER, whose primary key is TEACHER_NAME and information about courses is stored in a further nested relation, over a nested relation schema, say COURSE, whose primary key is COURSE_NAME. Then CNAME and TNAME are foreign keys which reference COURSE_NAME in COURSE and TEACHER_NAME in TEACHER, respectively.

Table 1.4 A nested relation

TNAME	(CNAME	NO_HOURS)*
John	Expert Syst	15
	Databases	15
	Prolog	15
Mark	Software Eng	10
	Databases	20
	Prolog	15
George	Databases	20
	Graph Theory	25

The nested relational algebra extends the (flat) relational algebra to nested relations by providing two additional restructuring operators, called NEST and UNNEST. NEST transforms a nested relation into a "more deeply" nested relation and UNNEST transforms a nested relation into a "flatter" nested relation.

Let us call a nested relation over a nested relation schema having only one relation-valued attribute which is not further nested, a *shallow relation*. For simplicity, we will restrict our

Table 1.5 Another nested relation

CNAME	(TNAME	NO_HOURS)*
Expert Syst	John	15
Graph Theory	George	25
Software Eng	Mark	10
Prolog	Mark	15
	John	15
Databases	Mark	20
	George	20
	John	15

attention to shallow relations. For example, the nested relations shown in Tables 1.4 and 1.5 are both shallow relations. Thus NEST transforms a flat relation into a shallow relation and UNNEST transforms a shallow relation into a flat relation. For example, if we NEST Table 1.3 on (CNAME, NO_HOURS) we obtain the shallow relation shown in Table 1.4 and if we NEST Table 1.3 on (TNAME, NO_HOURS) we obtain the shallow relation shown in Table 1.5. On the other hand, if we UNNEST either the shallow relation shown in Table 1.4 or that shown in Table 1.5 we obtain the flat relation shown in Table 1.3. This should not give the reader the false impression that a shallow relation can always be recovered from a flat relation by a NEST operation. For example, consider the shallow relation, shown in Table 1.6, which represents the area of triangles and the x, y coordinates of their vertices. If we UNNEST this relation we obtain the flat relation shown in Table 1.7 and if we then NEST this relation on (X-COORD, Y-COORD) we obtain the different shallow relation shown in Table 1.8.

Table 1.6 A nested relation storing the area of triangles

AREA	(X-COORD	Y-COORD)*
1	0	0
	1	0
	0	2
1	0	0
	2	0
	0	1

Table 1.7 A flat relation obtained by unnesting

AREA	X-COORD	Y-COORD
1	0	0
1	1	0
1	0	2
1	2	0
1	0	1

This problem concerning the loss of information when a nested relation, which has been unnested, cannot be recovered by nesting is called the *1NF normalisability problem*. In order to solve the 1NF normalisability problem, an additional nested relational algebra operator needs to be defined that preserves the key values of nested tuples when unnesting a nested relation. For example, the schema of the shallow relation shown in Table 1.6 has a single key which is the relation-valued attribute (X-COORD, Y-COORD)*. The flat relation shown in Table 1.7 resulting from unnesting this shallow relation does not preserve the two key values. The *keying* operator [JS82] is an operator which adds a new key to the relation schema of a nested relation and maintains a key value for each nested tuple in the nested relation being keyed. For example, keying the nested relation shown in Table 1.6 results in the nested relation shown in Table 1.9. It can be verified that if we UNNEST the shallow relation shown in Table 1.9, then NEST it on (X-COORD, Y-COORD) and finally project the result on AREA and (X-COORD, Y-COORD)* we obtain the original shallow relation shown in Table 1.6.

Table 1.8 A shallow relation obtained by UNNEST and NEST

AREA	(X-COORD	Y-COORD)*
1	0	0
	1	0
	0	2
	2	0
	0	1

The relational calculus and SQL have also been extended to nested relations. (Several of the database books appearing in the bibliography cover such extensions; see also [PT86, RKB87, LL89].)

Table 1.9 A nested relation after keying

NEW_KEY	AREA	(X-COORD	Y-COORD)*
k_1	1	0	0
		1	0
		0	2
k_2	1	0	0
		2	0
		0	1

1.7.5   The Deductive Data Model

Deductive (or logical) databases in their simplest form have the same structural and integrity parts as the relational model. It is common in the deductive database setting to call tuples *facts*, attribute values *constants* and relations *predicates*. In addition, names of relation schemas are called *predicate symbols* and a fixed ordering is imposed on the attributes of relation schemas. For example, the predicate symbol associated with the relation shown in Table 1.1 could be BOOKS with the ordering of attributes as in the header of the relation, and similarly the predicate symbol associated with the relation shown in Table 1.2 could be LOANS with the ordering of attributes as in the header of the relation. This notation allows us to write facts (tuples) in the form, $P(v_1, v_2, \ldots, v_n)$, where P is a predicate symbol and $v_1, v_2, \ldots, v_n$ are its attribute values in the fixed ordering. For example, the third tuple in the books relation can be written as

BOOKS(Korth, DB Concepts, McGraw-Hill, 1991, 0-07-044754-3).

Similarly, the third tuple in the loans relation can be written as

LOANS(0-07-044754-3, Main, 1, 1).

The manipulative part of a deductive database is a logic-based language, the best known example being the rule-based query language *Datalog*. The syntax of Datalog resembles that of the programming language Prolog [MW88a, SS94, Apt97] but its semantics are different, since Prolog processes facts one at a time while Datalog processes sets of facts at a time. In addition, Datalog is a declarative language while Prolog can be viewed as a mixture between a procedural and a declarative programming language. Finally, Datalog is not a fully-fledged programming language and it is thus not computationally complete (see Subsection 1.9.4 for a definition of the important notion of computational completeness).

We briefly describe the basic syntax of Datalog. A statement of the form

$$P(A_1, A_2, \ldots, A_n),$$

where P is a predicate symbol and each A_i, with $i \in \{1, 2, \ldots, n\}$, is either a variable or a constant, is called a *literal*.

Datalog statements are rules of the form

$$P_1(A_1, A_2, \ldots, A_n) :- P_2(B_1, B_2, \ldots, B_k), \ldots, P_m(C_1, C_2, \ldots, C_q),$$

where the P_i's are predicate symbols, the A_i's, B_i's and C_i's are either variables or constants and the variables amongst the A_i's must be a subset of the B_i's, ..., and the C_i's. The symbol ": −" is read as *if* and the commas are read as *and*. The literal to the left of ": −" is called the *head* of the rule and the set of literals to the right of ": −" is called the *body* of the rule. We use the convention that variables are strings beginning with the lowercase letter x, possibly subscripted, and constant values are all other strings.

A Datalog program is now defined to be a finite collection of rules.

Assume that we have a relational database and a Datalog program whose intension is to query that database. A literal is *logically true* in a database if we can find an assignment of constants to its variables that transforms the literal into a fact which is present in the database. Assignments of constants to variables are local to rules and thus we can reuse them, i.e. the same variable can be assigned different constants in different rules.

The intuitive semantics of invoking a Datalog rule is that if all the literals in the body of the rule are *logically true* over the database we are querying, then *derive* a new fact corresponding to the head of the rule and (temporarily) add it to the database. This process is repeated until no further facts can be derived, technically until a *fixpoint* is attained. The result of a query which invokes a rule is the set of facts in the resulting database that have the predicate symbol of the head of the rule. The semantics of running a Datalog program corresponds to invoking all the rules in the program in any order as long as possible, i.e. until a fixpoint is attained for all the rules. Thus the result of running a Datalog program is the set of facts in the original database together with all the new facts derived when a fixpoint is attained. It can be shown that the order in which the rules are processed does not affect the result of running the Datalog program.

Table 1.10 A family relation

PARENT	CHILD
abraham	isaac
sara	isaac
abraham	ishmael
isaac	jacob
rivka	jacob
jacob	joseph
lavan	rachel
lavan	lea
rachel	joseph
jacob	dan

For example, the following rule finds the first author, short title, year and ISBN of books published by Addison-Wesley:

$$\text{ADDISON}(x_1, x_2, x_3, x_4) :- \text{BOOKS}(x_1, x_2, \text{Addison-Wesley}, x_3, x_4).$$

Similarly, the following rule finds the first author, short title, quantity of books in the main library and the number of these books on loan:

$$\text{MAIN}(x_1, x_2, x_6, x_7) :- \text{BOOKS}(x_1, x_2, x_3, x_4, x_5), \text{LOANS}(x_5, \text{Main}, x_6, x_7).$$

The above queries can be expressed in the relational algebra. So in what sense does Datalog extend the relational algebra. The answer is that Datalog supports *recursive* queries, a facility not available in the relational algebra. A Datalog rule is said to be recursive if the predicate symbol of the head of the rule also appears in a literal in the body of the rule. It can be shown that there are recursive rules that are expressible in Datalog but not in the relational algebra [AU79].

Consider the relation shown in Table 1.10 which models a family tree (this relation may be better modelled via a nested relation).

The following nonrecursive rule finds the grandparents relation:

$$\text{GP}(x_1, x_3) :- \text{PAR}(x_1, x_2), \text{PAR}(x_2, x_3).$$

The following nonrecursive rule finds the sibling relation, assuming that a person is a sibling of itself:

$$\text{SIB}(x_1, x_2) :- \text{PAR}(x_3, x_1), \text{PAR}(x_3, x_2).$$

The following two rules, one of which is recursive, find all the ancestors of people in the database:

$$\text{ANC}(x_1, x_2) :- \text{PAR}(x_1, x_2).$$
$$\text{ANC}(x_1, x_3) :- \text{PAR}(x_1, x_2), \text{ANC}(x_2, x_3).$$

The following two rules, one of which is recursive, find all the people in the database which are of the same generation:

$$\text{SAME\_GEN}(x_2, x_3) :- \text{PAR}(x_1, x_2), \text{PAR}(x_1, x_3).$$
$$\text{SAME\_GEN}(x_1, x_2) :- \text{PAR}(x_3, x_1), \text{PAR}(x_4, x_2), \text{SAME\_GEN}(x_3, x_4).$$

Datalog can be extended to handle negation using the *Closed World Assumption* (CWA) [Rei78]. The CWA assumes that the database has complete positive information about the enterprise it is modelling. Thus we can utilise the absence of positive information in order to infer that this information is false. For example, if we assume the CWA with respect to our library database, then we can safely assume that if a book is not recorded in the books relation then it it is not available in the library. Another example is a database containing three relations one for employees, the second for the departments employees can work in and the third recording the assignment of employees to departments. A department may have no employees if it is a newly set up department and a new employee may have not been assigned to a department yet. Thus, we can use the CWA to derive departments that have no employees and employees that have not been assigned to a department. (For more details on the CWA see Chapter 5.)

1.7.6 An Object-Oriented Data Model

The title of this subsection begins with *an* rather than *the* as was the case in the previous subsections. The reason is that there is no wide agreement on what the definitive object-oriented data model should be. The growing field of object-oriented databases lacks the solid theoretical foundation that is characteristic of the relational data model. Thus it is difficult to reach a consensus on the semantics of the various concepts that database practitioners agree should be included in an object-oriented data model. Another source of hindrance is the fact that the development of object-oriented database systems has been application-driven and therefore much experimental work is under way with features being added as necessitated by the demand of the application being developed. Therefore we will restrict ourselves to mentioning the novel concepts that object-oriented databases should possess. It is tempting to define an object-oriented data model as a collection of concepts that have been found to be useful in data modelling but are not directly supported within the relational model.

Object-oriented databases in their simplest form have the same structural and integrity parts as the network model. In object-oriented databases records are called *objects*, record identity is called *object identity* and collections of records are called *classes*. A set occurrence can be modelled by adding an attribute to the member object type, such that for each member object the value of this attribute will be a link to its owner object.

A different approach is to view the concept of a *complex object* as central and to extend the relational model from flat relations to *complex object relations* (cf. [Kim95b]). Such a complex object relation may be a nested relation or, more generally, a *recursive nested relation* [SS90], which uses references to give semantics to nested relations that reference themselves. This approach has the advantage that it builds upon existing relational database technology, but that the simplicity of the flat relational data model is lost.

Class types in an object-oriented database specify the object type of the objects in its class and also the set of operations (also known as *methods*) that can be performed on objects in the class. For example, an EMPLOYEE class type will contain an object type, say EMPLOYEE_SCHEMA, and a set of operations on employees such as *print employee details*, *retrieve salary* and *raise salary*. Both the object type and the operations are stored (or *encapsulated*) in the database. Each operation has an *interface* and an *implementation*. The interface to an operation is the specification of how to call the operation, i.e. the name of the operation and its parameters. For example, in order to call the above-mentioned operations over EMPLOYEE, the user will need as a parameter the record identity of the employee object involved. Encapsulation means that users can access an object only through its interface, with all implementation information of these operations being hidden. Thus encapsulation provides a form of data independence, since the implementation of an operation can be changed without affecting the way users call the operation. One of the problems that arises during query processing is that in order to optimise queries encapsulation must be violated, since in order to perform its task the query optimiser must look inside the implementation of operations. Thus the optimiser must be trusted to access the implementation of operations.

Another useful concept which is adopted in object-oriented databases is that of *inheritance*. As an example, we may have a STUDENT class type whose object type has attributes name, address, age and course description and an EMPLOYEE class type whose object type has attributes name, address, age and salary. Both students and employees are people so we could have an additional class type PERSON whose object type has attributes name, address and age. Thus EMPLOYEE and STUDENT inherit all the attributes and operations of PERSON and are considered to be its *subclasses*. Inheritance is useful, since we can add new class types to the system which reuse existing class types. Thus when we define the class types STUDENT and EMPLOYEE we specify that they are subclasses of PERSON and then define only their new attributes and new operations, so all existing data and code pertaining to PERSON can be reused. Another class type that could be defined for this application is that of RESEARCH_ASSISTANT (RA), which is a subclass of both STUDENT and EMPLOYEE, on the assumption that research assistants are also enrolled as postgraduate students.

The set of all class types is organised in a *class inheritance lattice* (or simply an inheritance lattice). At the top of the inheritance lattice is the class type *object*, which is a superclass of all class types in the lattice. Inheritance can be either *single* or *multiple*. If every class type has a unique superclass then inheritance is single and the inheritance lattice reduces to a *class hierarchy*, i.e. it has the form of a tree. On the other hand, if a class type can have more than one superclass then inheritance is multiple and the lattice has the form of a directed acyclic graph. For example, EMPLOYEE and STUDENT have the single superclass PERSON, while RA has two superclasses, EMPLOYEE and STUDENT. The inheritance lattice for the above example is shown in Figure 1.8.

Single inheritance is simpler than multiple inheritance, since given a class, say STUDENT, there is no ambiguity in determining the superclass PERSON from which STUDENT is to inherit its attributes and operations (or methods). On the other hand, given the class, say RA, it may inherit attributes and operations from both STUDENT and EMPLOYEE. This may lead to naming conflicts; for example, if both STUDENT and EMPLOYEE have an attribute TOPIC, meaning research topic when the research assistant is a student and project topic when the research assistant is an employee, then a naming conflict will arise. It is possible to avoid such naming conflicts in the design phase by insisting

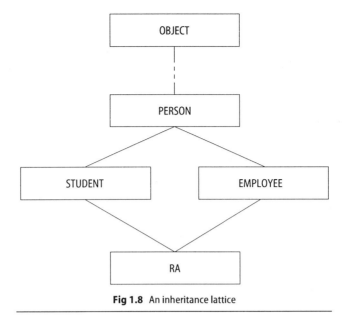

Fig 1.8 An inheritance lattice

that attribute names and operation names are unique (see the universal relation schema assumption in Chapter 2) but this restriction may be hard to enforce if the inheritance lattice is large. The approach taken in many object-oriented systems is to resolve naming conflicts by setting a default superclass for the purpose of inheritance. For example, if STUDENT is the default superclass of RA, then TOPIC from STUDENT will be chosen as the default, whose meaning is the research topic of the research assistant. If multiple inheritance is supported, then a mechanism for overriding the default conflict resolution must also be provided, by allowing the user to explicitly mention the superclasses from which inheritance is to take place in the case of a naming conflict. In our example, if the user is interested in the project topic of a research assistant, then it must be stated explicitly that inheritance is to take place from EMPLOYEE. (A formalisation of multiple inheritance in the context of object-oriented programming languages can be found in [Car88].)

The advantage of the object-oriented approach to databases is that it is compatible with the object-oriented approach to programming and thus the impedance mismatch problem mentioned earlier can be solved by merging an object-oriented data model and an object-oriented programming language. In fact, such a computationally complete database programming language can be used as the manipulative part of an object-oriented data model. The application programmers need only learn one formalism. This approach has the further advantage of providing application programmers with a computationally complete database language [CH80, ABD$^+$89, AV90, Gil94].

It is still important for object-oriented database systems to provide a more limited query language such as the relational algebra. Firstly, it may not be effective or even possible to optimise general programs, written in a computationally complete database programming language, while there are well-known algorithms available for optimising relational algebra queries [KRB85, Ull89]. Secondly, users should be allowed to ask the database system simple queries by using a relatively simple query language such as SQL. This has given rise to several research projects aimed at implementing ad hoc query languages for object-oriented databases. Examples of such query languages are OSQL (*Object SQL*) [AAC+95] and OQL (*Object Query Language*) [Cat96, CB97], both of which can be viewed as extensions of SQL.

1.8   Discussion

The relational data model is currently the dominant data model used in the commercial database market-place and we predict that this dominance will not change in the near future. Although it may seem that object-orientation is threatening to displace the relational approach, advocates of the relational approach are fighting back by extending relational databases with object-oriented features. Thus instead of using the network model for the structural and integrity parts for an object-oriented data model, the structural and integrity parts of the relational model are extended to deal with object identity. The relational algebra is also extended with an operator which caters for the creation of new object identifiers. Such an extension, resulting in what is now called an *object-relational* data model [SM96], is presented in the last chapter of the book in Section 10.2.

Both the nested relational model and the deductive data model are extensions of the relational model and thus fit in well with a trend to support an upwards compatible relational model.

Many applications are naturally expressed as hierarchies and thus even if a flat relational model is maintained at the conceptual level of the DBMS the nested relational model with its hierarchical data structures can enhance the expressiveness of user views. Moreover, the nested relational model can provide a basis for optimising the conceptual flat level at the physical DBMS level. The nested relational model is discussed in more detail in Section 10.1 of Chapter 10.

In the last decade a great deal of effort has gone into theoretical aspects of the deductive database model resulting in several prototype systems being implemented [RU95]. Most of the research has centred around the properties of the rule-based query language Datalog, especially with its ability to express recursive queries. As deductive database technology is reaching maturity we can expect to reap the benefits in the form of extended relational DBMSs supporting Datalog-like query languages. Due to its perceived importance we have devoted the whole of Chapter 9 to the deductive data model.

1.9   Background Material

This section introduces the main mathematical concepts used throughout the book and the notation we have adopted. The reader may skip this section and return to it whenever he or she is in need of the concepts and definitions. We have assumed that the reader has some "mathematical awareness" and therefore it may be necessary to consult one or more of the relevant references for a more fundamental and detailed treatment of any topic. The topics covered include some basic concepts in set theory (Subsection 1.9.1), some basic concepts concerning partially ordered and linearly ordered sets (Subsection 1.9.2), some basic concepts from mathematical logic (Subsection 1.9.3), some basic concepts from the theory of computing and computational complexity (Subsection 1.9.4), and finally a quick introduction to finite-model theory and its impact on database theory (Subsection 1.9.5).

1.9.1 Basic Concepts of Set Theory

Intuitively a set can be viewed as a collection of objects. The objects collected into the set are then called its *members*, or *elements*, and membership is designated by the symbol $\in$ or simply *in*. Thus "a is a member of the set X" or "a is in the set X" is written $a \in X$ or a in X. The members of a set are enclosed by { (begin) and } (end) and ',' (comma) is used as a separator. A set does not contain any duplicates. A relaxation of this condition results in a more general notion of a set which may contain duplicates; such a generalised set is called a *multiset*.

The main principle of set formation is called the *axiom of comprehension*, which says that for any property we can form a set containing precisely those objects with the given property. Thus $\{x \mid \alpha\}$ means the set of all x for which α is true.

The said principle is a very powerful principle and can be used to form a great variety of sets. However, too full an interpretation of the word "property" gives rise to contradictions such as "Russell's Paradox". For example, consider the set $\{x \mid x \notin x\}$.

We next define the principal relations between sets and operations thereon.

Subset: We write $X \subseteq Y$ (or $Y \supseteq X$) to mean that any member of X is also a member of Y, and say that X is a subset of Y, or that X is contained in Y. Alternatively, we say that Y is a superset of X.

Proper subset: Since any set is a subset of itself, if we want to exclude this possibility, then we must talk instead of *proper subsets*. Thus we write $X \subset Y$ (or $Y \supset X$) and say that X is a proper subset of Y, if $X \subseteq Y$ and $X \neq Y$. Alternatively, we say that Y is a proper superset of X.

Another powerful principle in set theory is the *axiom of extensionality*, which tells us that how far a set extends is determined by what its members are. Thus two sets, say S and T, are equal if and only if they have the same members. Symbolically, we write $S = T$ which means that $S \subseteq T$ and $T \subseteq S$.

Intersection: Given any two sets X and Y, their intersection, denoted by $\cap$, is given by

$$X \cap Y = \{z \mid z \in X \text{ and } z \in Y\}.$$

Union: Similarly, the union, denoted by $\cup$, is given by

$$X \cup Y = \{z \mid z \in X \text{ or } z \in Y\}.$$

At times when no ambiguity arises $X \cup Y$ is abbreviated just to XY.

Empty set: The set without any members, i.e. {}, is denoted by $\emptyset$. This could be given by

$$\emptyset = \{x \mid x \neq x\}.$$

That there is only one such set follows vacuously from the axiom of extensionality.

A set with a single element is called a *singleton*, and a singleton, say $\{A\}$, is at times abbreviated simply to A. Note that $\{\emptyset\} \neq \emptyset$.

Power Set: The set of all subsets of a set X, denoted by $\mathcal{P}(X)$, is called its power set. Thus

$$\mathcal{P}(X) = \{Y \mid Y \subseteq X\}.$$

Difference: Given any two sets X and Y, we denote by $X - Y$ the set of all members of X which are not in Y. Thus

$$X - Y = \{z \mid z \in X \text{ and } z \notin Y\}.$$

This is referred to as the *relative* complement of Y in X, and on occasion it is written as $X \backslash Y$.

If all sets under consideration in a certain discussion are subsets of a set $\mathcal{E}$, then $\mathcal{E}$ is called the *universal set* and $\bar{X}$ denotes the complement of X relative to $\mathcal{E}$, namely $\bar{X} = \mathcal{E} - X$.

Disjointness: Two sets X and Y are said to be disjoint if $X \cap Y = \emptyset$, and a set of sets (or collection of sets) is said to be *pairwise disjoint* if any two of its members are disjoint.

If we wish to distinguish the order in which elements are given, we need to use a different notation from { and }. Thus we call (x, y) or $<x, y>$ an *ordered pair*. We refer to x and y as the *coordinates* of the ordered pair (x, y). The basic fact about ordered pairs, over a set X, is that for any $x_1, y_1, x_2, y_2 \in X$

$$(x_1, x_2) = (y_1, y_2) \text{ if and only if } x_1 = y_1 \text{ and } x_2 = y_2.$$

Similarly, we may consider ordered triples, quadruples, or more generally *tuples*. All tuples possess the property that

$$(x_1, x_2, \ldots, x_n) = (y_1, y_2, \ldots, y_n) \text{ if and only if } x_1 = y_1, x_2 = y_2, \ldots, x_n = y_n,$$

where n is a positive (or nonnegative) integer.

The *Cartesian product* of two sets X and Y, denoted by $X \times Y$, is given by

$$X \times Y = \{(x, y) \mid x \in X \text{ and } y \in Y\}.$$

A binary relation, say R, or simply a relation, when no ambiguity arises, is a set of ordered pairs. We write xRy to mean $(x, y) \in R$. We say that R is a binary relation *on* or *in a set* X if $R \subseteq X \times X$. If xRy implies yRx then R is said to be *symmetric*. If $R \subseteq X \times Y$, then we say that R is a relation from X to Y.

A convenient graphical representation of a relation is via an associated *directed graph* or *digraph*. We represent the elements of the underlying set as *nodes* (or *vertices*), and two nodes are joined by a line (straight or curved), called a *directed edge* (or arc), when a relation between them obtains, with the appropriate direction indicated. In such a situation we say that the two nodes are *adjacent*. When R is a relation from X to Y, with $X \cap Y = \emptyset$, then we obtain a *bipartite* digraph, whose node set is $X \cup Y$. Finally, when the relation is symmetric, we may omit the directions in which case we have an *undirected graph* or just a *graph*.

The *first* and *second* coordinates of R are given by

$$\{x \mid \text{ there exists } y \text{ such that } (x, y) \in R\} \text{ and}$$
$$\{y \mid \text{ there exists } x \text{ such that } (x, y) \in R\},$$

respectively, and are known as the *domain* and *range* of R, designated by *dom(R)* and *ran(R)*, respectively. The *inverse relation* is defined by

$$R^{-1} = \{(y, x) \mid (x, y) \in R\}.$$

An *n-ary relation* on a set X is just a subset of $X \times X \times \cdots \times X$, i.e. the Cartesian product of X with n factors, $n \geq 0$, which we denote by X^n; $X^0 = \emptyset$.

Let R be a relation in X. Then R is: *reflexive* if xRx for all $x \in X$; symmetric (defined earlier) if xRy implies yRx; *transitive* if xRy and yRz imply xRz.

If R is reflexive, symmetric and transitive, then R is an *equivalence relation on (in)* X. If R is an equivalence relation, then the equivalence class of x, $x \in X$, with respect to R, is given by

$$R[x] = \{y \mid xRy\}.$$

A *function*, say f, from X to Y or alternatively from X *into* Y (sometimes referred to as a *total* function), is a special relation with $dom(f) = X$ and such that if $(x, y) \in f$ and $(x, z) \in f$ then $y = z$. Alternatively, if $x \in dom(f)$, then there is a unique y in Y such that $(x, y) \in f$; quite often we denote this by $y = f(x)$. We call x an *argument* of f and $f(x)$ is sometimes called the *image* of x under f. Symbolically, we write

$$f : X \to Y,$$

where Y is called the *codomain* of f and $ran(f) \subseteq Y$. If $ran(f) = Y$ then f is a function from X *onto* Y. We say that f is a *partial* function from X into Y if f is a function for which $dom(f) \subseteq X$ and $ran(f) \subseteq Y$.

Let $A \subseteq X$. Then the *characteristic function* of A, denoted by χ_A, is defined by

$$\chi_A : X \to \{0, 1\} \text{ with } \chi_A(x) = 1 \text{ if and only if } x \in A.$$

A function $f : X \to Y$ is 1-1 (*one-to-one*) if every element of X is mapped to a unique element of Y, namely for all $x, y \in X$, if $x \neq y$ then $f(x) \neq f(y)$, or equivalently, if $f(x) = f(y)$, then $x = y$. In this case the *inverse relation* f^{-1} is now a 1-1 and onto function from $ran(f)$ onto $dom(f)$. This is known as the inverse function.

Synonyms for the word "function" include among others *mapping* or *map*, *correspondence*, *transformation*, and *operator*.

The *restriction* of f to A, where $A \subseteq X$, designated by $f|A$, is given by

$$f|A = \{(x, y) \mid (x, y) \in f \text{ and } x \in A\}.$$

A *homomorphism* is a function that preserves structure. Given a binary relation and therefore an underlying digraph we can define homomorphism as follows. Given a digraph, say D, a homomorphism ϕ of D onto a digraph D' is a homomorphic image of D under ϕ, written $\phi(D) = D'$, such that every arc of D' must emanate from some arc of D, namely if u and v are adjacent nodes in D, then there must exist two adjacent nodes u' and v' in D' such that $\phi(u) = u'$ and $\phi(v) = v'$.

If ϕ is a 1–1 mapping then the homomorphism is said to be an *isomorphism*. In addition, if ϕ is an isomorphism of D with itself, then ϕ is called an *automorphism*. Thus each automorphism, say α, of D is a permutation of the node set, say V, of D, which preserves adjacency.

Given two relations R_1 and R_2, the *composition* of R_1 and R_2, symbolised by $R_2 \circ R_1$, is given by

$$R_2 \circ R_1 = \{(x, y) \mid \text{there exists } z \text{ with } (x, z) \in R_1 \text{ and } (z, y) \in R_2\}.$$

Correspondingly, the composition of two functions f and g, $g \circ f$, or simply gf, is also a function. We say that this function exists if $ran(f) \subseteq dom(g)$. If $g \circ f$ exists and $x \in dom(f)$, then $(g \circ f)(x) = g(f(x))$.

Let $f : X \times Y \to X$ be an *onto* function such that for all x in X and for all y in Y, $f(<x, y>) = x$; then f is called the *projection* of $X \times Y$ onto the first coordinate. Similarly, when $f(<x, y>) = y$, then f is called the projection of $X \times Y$ onto the second coordinate.

Let X be a set with a finite number of elements. We use $|X|$ to stand for the number of elements of X; $|X|$ is called the *cardinality* of X. The notion of a 1–1 function enables us to extend the idea of "number of elements" to infinite sets. A 1–1 function from a set X onto a set Y is often called a 1–1 *correspondence* (bijection) between X and Y. We observe then that

1) $|X| = |Y|$ if and only if there is a 1–1 correspondence between X and Y, and

2) $|X| \leq |Y|$ if and only if there is a 1–1 function from X to Y.

We postulate the existence of a "cardinality" function $|X|$ defined for all sets satisfying (1) and (2).

Let ω be the set of natural numbers, namely $\omega = \{0, 1, 2, 3, \ldots\}$. Then an infinite set X is *countable* if it can be put into 1–1 correspondence with ω, and *uncountable* otherwise.

Given a set S, the *size* of S, denoted by $\|S\|$, is the cardinality of some *standard* string encoding of S. Details about the meaning of "standard" can be found in [GJ79]. The concept of size is important when we wish to study the computational complexity of a problem. Any instance of that problem can be viewed as a single finite string of symbols, chosen from a finite input alphabet, which is input to the computer (see Subsection 1.9.4).

We next consider *sets of sets* or (the more frequently used terms) *collection of sets* or *family of sets*. To this end we introduce some further definitions. Suppose that f is a function on a set I into a set Y. Let us call an element i of the domain I an *index*, I itself an *index set*, $ran(f)$ an *indexed set*, and the function f itself a *family*. Denote the value of f at i by f_i and call f_i the ith coordinate of the family. We may write

$$f = \{<i, f_i> \ \in I \times Y \mid i \in I\}.$$

Alternatively, it is common practice to write $\{f_i \mid i \in I\}$ or simply $\{f_i\}_{i \in I}$ or even $\{f_i\}$ when no ambiguity arises.

By definition, a *sequence* is a family on the set of positive (or nonnegative) integers into Y. That is to say, a sequence is a function for which $\omega - \{0\}$ or ω serves as an index set.

By the phrase "a family $\{A_i\}$ of subsets of E" we shall understand a function A on some set I of indices into $\mathcal{P}(E)$. We can now define the union and intersection of a family by

$$\bigcup \{A_i \mid i \in I\} \text{ and } \bigcap \{A_i \mid i \in I\}.$$

Correspondingly, the Cartesian product of a family is given by

$$\bigtimes \{A_i \mid i \in I\}.$$

We are now in a position to define a function of n variables (called an n-place function), namely a function whose domain is

$$\bigtimes_{i \in I} X_i \text{ or } X_1 \times X_2 \times \cdots \times X_n,$$

where I is the index set $\{1, 2, \ldots, n\}$. We write $f(x_1, x_2, \ldots, x_n)$ to mean $f(<x_1, x_2, \ldots, x_n>)$. If $J \subseteq I$, then

$$\bigtimes \{X_i \mid i \in J\} = \{x|J \mid x \in \bigtimes \{X_i \mid i \in I\}\}$$

and we can define a *projection* function

$$f : \bigtimes_{i \in I} X_i \to \bigtimes_{i \in J} X_i \text{ such that } f(x) = x|J.$$

Given a set X, a *partition* of X is a disjoint collection $\mathcal{C}$ of nonempty sets such that

$$\bigcup \{A \mid A \in \mathcal{C}\} = X.$$

If $\mathcal{C}$ is a partition of X, then $\mathcal{C}$ induces the equivalence relation $X/\mathcal{C}$ on X given by

$$X/\mathcal{C} = \{(x, y) \mid \text{ there exists } A \in \mathcal{C} \text{ and } x \in A \text{ and } y \in A\}.$$

Throughout the book we occasionally use the term *class* to mean a subset of a given set whose members are objects of a particular structure.

Two classical books covering set theory are [Hal74] and [Sto79]. The topic of graph theory is covered in many books; we mention [Cha77, Wil85, BH90]. For the more general subjects of discrete mathematics and combinatorics see [VW92, Gri94]. A now classical introduction of the mathematical concepts that computer scientists need to know is Knuth's book [Knu73].

1.9.2 Basic Concepts of Ordered Sets

Let X be a set. A *partial* order on X is a binary relation, say R, on X such that for all $x, y, z \in X$

(i) xRx,

(ii) xRy and yRx imply that $x = y$,

(iii) xRy and yRz imply that xRz.

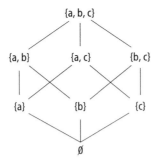

Fig 1.9 Hasse diagram for $\langle \mathcal{P}(\{a, b, c\}), \subset \rangle$

These three conditions are referred to as *reflexivity*, *antisymmetry* and *transitivity*, respectively. A set X equipped with a partial order is said to be a *partially ordered set*.

Let X be a partially ordered set. Then X is a *chain* if, for all $x, y \in X$, either xRy or yRx. A chain is also known as a *linearly ordered set*, or a *totally ordered set*, or simply a *linear ordering*. The *partially ordered* set X is an *antichain* if xRy in X only if $x = y$.

In the following we denote a partial order by the symbol $\preceq$. Let $\langle X, \preceq \rangle$ be a finite partially ordered set. We define the *strict linear order* $\prec$ as follows: for all $x, y \in X$, $x \prec y$ if and only if $x \preceq y$ and $x \neq y$; we say that x is *covered* by y or y *covers* x if $x \preceq y$ and there does not exist $z \in X$ such that $x \prec z \prec y$.

The *covering* (binary) relation for a finite partially ordered set can be conveniently displayed by a Hasse diagram, which is defined as follows. The elements of X are represented as points in the plane. If x is covered by y draw an arrow from x to y. In order to simplify the Hasse diagram further, arrange so that if x is covered by y, then y lies above x on the plane. Thus all arrows point upwards and the arrow heads may be safely omitted. The Hasse diagram for the partially ordered set $\langle \mathcal{P}(\{a, b, c\}), \subset \rangle$ is given in Figure 1.9.

Let X and Y be linearly ordered sets. Then the Cartesian product $X \times Y$ can be linearly ordered as follows:

$$(x, y) \preceq (x', y') \text{ if } x \prec x' \text{ or } x = x' \text{ and } y \preceq y'.$$

This order is known as the *lexicographic* order (or *lexicographical* ordering) of $X \times Y$, since it is similar to the way words are arranged in a dictionary.

Let $\langle X, \preceq \rangle$ be a partially ordered set and assume that $E \subseteq X$. If $x \in X$ then x is a *lower bound* of E if and only if for all $y \in E$, $x \preceq y$. If, in addition, $x \in E$, then x is the *least* element of E. The *greatest lower bound* (glb) of E is the greatest element in the set of lower bounds of E, if such an element exists. That is, x is the glb of E if x is a lower bound of E and for all lower bounds y of E, $y \preceq x$. In general, E may have no, one or many lower bounds; however, E can have at most one glb, which is denoted by glb(E).

Correspondingly, if $x \in X$, then x is an *upper* bound of E if and only if for all $y \in E$, $y \preceq x$. If, in addition, $x \in E$, then x is the *greatest* element of E. The *least upper bound* (lub) of E is the smallest element in the set of upper bounds of E, if such an element exists. That is, x is the lub of E if x is an upper bound of E and for all upper bounds y of E, $x \preceq y$. In general, E may have no, one or many upper bounds; however, E can have at most one lub, which is denoted by $\text{lub}(E)$.

Any partially ordered set X, such that $\text{glb}(x, y)$ and $\text{lub}(x, y)$ exist for any elements $x, y \in X$, is called a *lattice*. If $\text{glb}(E)$ and $\text{lub}(E)$ exist for all $E \subseteq X$, then X is called a *complete lattice*.

Let $\Re$ be the set of real numbers. We define the following subsets of $\Re$:

$$[0, 1] = \{x \in \Re \mid 0 \le x \le 1\}$$

$$(0, 1] = \{x \in \Re \mid 0 < x \le 1\}$$

$$[0, 1) = \{x \in \Re \mid 0 \le x < 1\}$$

$$(0, 1) = \{x \in \Re \mid 0 < x < 1\}.$$

The above subsets of $\Re$ are known as intervals; more specifically they are known as *closed*, *semi-closed* on the right, *semi-closed* on the left and *open* intervals, respectively.

Given $x \in \Re$, we define the ceiling of x, denoted by $\lceil x \rceil$, to be the smallest integer y in ω such that $y \ge x$. Correspondingly, we define the floor of x, denoted by $\lfloor x \rfloor$, to be the greatest integer y in ω such that $y \le x$.

Finally, we mention *topological sort*; this is a process of assigning a linear ordering to the nodes of an acyclic digraph so that if there is an arc from node n_i to node n_j, then n_i precedes n_j in the linear ordering. Topological sort can be accomplished by using depth-first search [Tar72, AHU83]. (For the concept of acyclic digraph see Definition 2.2 in Section 2.1 of Chapter 2.)

An excellent introduction to ordered sets is [DP90], and a classical book on lattice theory is [Grä78].

1.9.3   Basic Concepts of Mathematical Logic

Herein we look at languages that can be used to make *statements* that might reasonably be viewed as true or false. The first language we consider is that of *propositional* calculus. The strings in this language, called formulae, stand for propositions that are either true or false. Formulae are assembled by combining *atomic* formulae with the aid of the *logical connectives*, namely negation ($\neg$), disjunction ($\vee$), conjunction ($\wedge$), conditional ($\Rightarrow$) and biconditional ($\Leftrightarrow$). Atomic formulae are normally represented by small (lower-case) letters such as p, q and r. In the sequel the symbols T and F will stand for *true* and *false*, respectively. These two symbols will be referred to as *truth-values*.

A *truth-assignment* is a function from a set of atomic formulae, say M, to the set $\{T, F\}$. Let F be a formula whose atomic formulae all belong to M. Consider the function $\mathcal{A}: M \to \{T, F\}$, which assigns a unique truth-value to F. We note that $\mathcal{A}$ assigns the natural meaning to formulae which contain logical connectives. Hereafter we will assume that all atomic formulae of F belong to M.

If $\mathcal{A}(F) = \mathsf{T}$ then we write $\mathcal{A} \models F$ and we say that $\mathcal{A}$ *verifies* (or equivalently, satisfies) F; if $\mathcal{A}(F) = \mathsf{F}$ then we write $\mathcal{A} \not\models F$ and we say that $\mathcal{A}$ *falsifies* (or equivalently, does not satisfy) F.

Let S be a set of formulae. If $\mathcal{A}$ verifies each formula in S, then $\mathcal{A}$ is said to verify (or equivalently, satisfy) S; symbolically $\mathcal{A} \models S$. If $\mathcal{A}$ falsifies at least one formula in S, then $\mathcal{A}$ is said to falsify (or equivalently, not to satisfy) S; symbolically $\mathcal{A} \not\models S$. If $\mathcal{A}$ verifies a formula or a set of formulae, then $\mathcal{A}$ is a *model* for that formula or set of formulae.

A formula or a set S of formulae is *satisfiable* if it has at least one model; otherwise it is *unsatisfiable*. A formula F is *valid* if every truth-assignment verifies F, in which case F is called a *tautology*.

In order to determine whether a formula F is valid or satisfiable we can employ the method of *truth* tables. The truth tables of the logical connectives provide the basis upon which appropriate truth-assignments to F are obtained.

As a language for stating mathematical ideas propositional calculus is severely limited, since there is no way of talking about individual objects and neither does there exist a way of making an assertion about all objects in a single formula which covers infinitely many similar cases. The reason for this is the fact that propositional calculus is limited to the structure of sentences in terms of component sentences, namely it does not break a sentence into sufficiently fine constituents for most purposes. To achieve this the structure of sentences must be viewed along the subject-predicate lines employed by classical grammarians.

In *predicate calculus* we can make general statements about all objects in a fixed set, called the *universe*. Atomic formulae are constructed out of names for relations and names for individual objects. Thus $P(x, y)$ is an atomic formula stating that some (binary) relation, designated by P, obtains for the pair of objects (x, y). P is called a *predicate (symbol)* (alternatively, a relation symbol) and x, y are called *variables*. In addition, there are the *universal* and *existential* quantifiers, denoted by $\forall$ and $\exists$, respectively. Besides predicate symbols, there are function symbols and constants. More specifically, we have:

(i) *Terms* are defined inductively as follows:

   (i) Every variable is a term.
   (ii) If f is an n-place function, with $n \geq 0$, and $t_1, t_2, \ldots, t_n$ are terms, then $f(t_1, t_2, \ldots, t_n)$ is a term.

(ii) *Atomic* formulae are defined as follows:

   If P is an n-place predicate, with $n \geq 0$, and $t_1, t_2, \ldots, t_n$ are terms, then $P(t_1, t_2, \ldots, t_n)$ is an atomic formula.

(iii) *Formulae* are defined as follows:

   (i)   Atomic formulae are formulae.
   (ii) If F and G are formulae, then so are $F \vee G, F \wedge G, (F)$ and $\neg F$.
   (iii) If F is a formula and x is a variable, then $\forall x F$ and $\exists x F$ are formulae.

A 0-place function symbol stands for a particular element in the universe and we call such function symbols *constants*. Correspondingly, a 0-place predicate is viewed as a proposition. We sometimes refer to 1-place and 2-place predicates as *unary* and *binary* predicates, respectively.

The *free* variables of a formula are defined inductively as follows:

(i)   In an atomic formula all the variables occurring in it are free.

(ii) The free variables in $F \vee G$ or $F \wedge G$ are the free variables of F and the free variables of G, whilst the free variables of (F) or $\neg F$ are the free variables of F.

(iii) In $\forall x F$ or $\exists x F$ the free variables are the free variables of F, except for x.

An occurrence of a variable x in a formula G is *bound* in G if it is not *free* in G, i.e. it is within a subformula of G of the form $\forall x F$ or $\exists x F$. We say that the indicated occurrence of $\forall$ or $\exists$ *binds* each free occurrence of x in F. A formula F is *closed* if there are no free occurrences of variables in it. A closed formula is also called a *sentence*.

As in the propositional calculus we would like to assign a unique truth-value to any formula F of predicate calculus. However, this task here is much more complicated. The technical details for this can be found, for example, in one of the books we recommend at the end of this subsection. Nevertheless we give the following technical definition in order to facilitate the exposition in Subsection 1.9.5; it is a special case of the more general notion of an interpretation.

Definition 1.1 (Structure)   A structure is a pair $\mathcal{A} = ([\mathcal{A}], \mathcal{F})$, where $[\mathcal{A}]$ is any nonempty set, called the universe of $\mathcal{A}$, and $\mathcal{F}$ is a function whose domain consists of predicate and function symbols. In particular,

(i)   if P is an n-place predicate in the domain of $\mathcal{F}$, then $\mathcal{F}(P)$ is an n-ary relation on $[\mathcal{A}]$, namely a subset of $[\mathcal{A}]^n$;

(ii) if f is an n-place function in the domain of $\mathcal{F}$, then $\mathcal{F}(f)$ is a function from $[\mathcal{A}]^n$ to $[\mathcal{A}]$.
∎

Assume that F is a sentence (closed formula), and that every predicate and function symbol thereof is assigned a value by $\mathcal{F}$. If $\mathcal{A} \models F$ then $\mathcal{A}$ is a model for F. If $\mathcal{A} \models F$ for all structures $\mathcal{A}$ which are appropriate to F, then F is said to be *valid*. (A structure $\mathcal{A}$ is said to be appropriate to F, if each predicate and function symbol of F is assigned a value by the corresponding $\mathcal{F}$.)

A sentence (closed formula) is *satisfiable* if it has at least one model; otherwise it is *unsatisfiable*.

We next describe a *general language* $\mathcal{L}$, which comprises nonlogical symbols and logical symbols. The nonlogical symbols of $\mathcal{L}$ are: propositional constants T, F, propositional variables $p, q, r, \ldots$, (individual) variables $x, y, z, \ldots$, (individual) constants $a, b, c, \ldots$, functions and predicates (also called relations). The logical symbols of $\mathcal{L}$ are: the logical connectives and the two quantifiers; often equality ($=$) is also taken to be a logical symbol, in which case it is interpreted as identity.

An *interpretation* for $\mathcal{L}$ consists of:

(i) a nonempty set D, called the domain;

(ii) for each constant an assignment of an element in D;

(iii) for each n-place function an assignment of a function from D^n to D;

(iv) for each n-place predicate an assignment of an n-ary relation on D^n, or equivalently, a Boolean function from D^n to $\{\mathsf{T, F}\}$.

A *variable assignment* for $\mathcal{L}$ consists of:

(i) for each propositional variable an assignment of T or F;

(ii) for each variable an assignment of an element in D.

The concepts of term, atomic formula, formula and closed formula or sentence carry over from the predicate calculus except that we now have to add constants and propositional variables to terms and to atomic formulae, respectively. We can similarly define free and bound variables and consequently a sentence (closed formula). We observe that for a sentence the variable assignment is irrelevant.

A formula F is *satisfiable* if there is an interpretation and a variable assignment for which it takes the truth-value T. Such an interpretation and variable assignment is a *model* for F. A formula F is *valid* if it takes the truth-value T in any interpretation and any variable assignment. The concepts of satisfiability, model and validity can easily be extended to a set of formulae, say $S = \{F_1, F_2, \ldots, F_n\}$. A formula F is a *logical consequence* of S if every model for S is also a model for F. Symbolically, we write $S \models F$.

Assume that $\mathcal{L}$ admits quantification of individual variables only. Then $\mathcal{L}$ is said to be a *first-order language*. If, in addition, we attach to $\mathcal{L}$ rules of inference such as *modus ponens* (from $\alpha \Rightarrow \beta$ and α infer β), then $\mathcal{L}$ is a *first-order theory*.

A *literal* is an atomic formula or the negation thereof. A *disjunction* of a set of formulae $\{F_1, F_2, \ldots, F_n\}$ is the formula $F_1 \vee F_2 \vee \ldots \vee F_n$ and its *conjunction* is the formula $F_1 \wedge F_2 \wedge \ldots \wedge F_n$.

The *universal closure* of a formula can be obtained by prefixing $\forall x$ for every free variable x in the formula. A *Horn clause* is a formula with no free variables, and is the universal closure of a disjunction of literals. For example, the formula

$$\forall x \forall y (P(x, y) \vee Q(x, x) \vee \neg P(x, f(y)) \vee \neg P(y, x))$$

is a Horn clause.

As in the cases of the propositional and predicate calculi we would like to assign truth-values to any formula or set of formulae over $\mathcal{L}$. However, $\mathcal{L}$ is too general for this to be achieved in a computationally efficient way. So we consider special cases of $\mathcal{L}$.

Let S be a set of formulae. The *Herbrand universe* of S is the set of all terms that contain no variables and contain only the constants and individual functions that occur in S. (Whenever no constants occur in S, then we still allow some constant, say a, to occur in the terms.) The

Herbrand base is the set of all atomic formulae formed by applying predicates that occur in S to the terms in the Herbrand universe.

For example, let
$$S = \{\forall x(P(x) \vee \neg Q(f(x), g(x))), \; \forall y W(y)\}.$$

Then the Herbrand universe is
$$\{a, f(a), g(a), f(f(a)), f(g(a)), g(g(a)), g(f(a)), \ldots\}$$

and the Herbrand base is
$$\{P(a), Q(a, a), W(a), P(f(a)), P(g(a)), Q(a, g(a)), Q(a, f(a)), Q(f(a), a), \ldots\}.$$

A *Herbrand interpretation* is one such that:

(i) the domain D is the Herbrand universe;

(ii) the constants are assigned to themselves;

(iii) the functions are what we normally think they are; for example, f is assigned to the function that maps a to $f(a)$, maps $g(a)$ to $f(g(a))$, maps $f(a)$ to $f(f(a))$ and so on.

There is no restriction on the assignment of predicates, so a set S of formulae will have infinitely many interpretations. Each Herbrand interpretation is characterised by the subset of the Herbrand base consisting of all those base formulae which take the value T in the interpretation. Thus a Herbrand interpretation is a subset of the Herbrand base and vice versa.

A *Herbrand model* for S is a Herbrand interpretation that is a model for S. A Herbrand model, say $\mathcal{M}$, of S is *minimal* if no proper subset of $\mathcal{M}$ is a Herbrand model of S.

The next result signifies the importance of Horn clauses.

Theorem 1.1   If S is a set of Horn clauses and, in addition, S has a model, then S has a Herbrand model. $\qquad\qquad\qquad\qquad\qquad\qquad\qquad\qquad\qquad\qquad\qquad\qquad\qquad\qquad\qquad\qquad\qquad\qquad\square$

We observe that Theorem 1.1 can be extended to general first-order sentences provided that there is an arbitrarily large number of constant symbols available in $\mathcal{L}$ [Fit96]. We further observe that Theorem 1.1 does not necessarily hold if S is merely a set of closed formulae. For example, let $S = \{P(a), \exists x \, \neg P(x)\}$. Let $D = \{0, 1\}$, $a = 0$ and the predicate P be true only on zero, then S has a model but it has no Herbrand model, since the Herbrand universe consists of the singleton $\{a\}$.

A *program clause* is a Horn clause in which every literal, except one, is the negation of an atomic formula. Suppose that S is a set of program clauses. Consider each Herbrand interpretation as a subset of the Herbrand base. The intersection of any number of Herbrand models of S is a Herbrand model. Since the Herbrand base is a Herbrand model, there is always at least one Herbrand model. The intersection of all Herbrand models is a Herbrand model and is called the *least Herbrand model*; evidently the least Herbrand model is a minimal Herbrand model. It consists of just those members of the Herbrand base that are logical consequences of S.

There are numerous introductions to mathematical logic that the reader can consult; we mention [End72, Sto79, Men87, Van89, Fit96]. A more advanced book which covers the interface between logic and computability is [BJ89]. Two books on first-order logic from the point of view of logic programming are [Llo87, Apt97].

1.9.4   Basic Concepts of the Theory of Computing

The pioneering work in this field, and much early work on computers was either done or inspired by Alan Turing and Emil Post. In their seminal papers [Tur36, Pos36, Tur37] they laid the foundations of computable mappings (functions).

In [Tur36, Tur37] Turing defined an idealised kind of machine, nowadays called a "Turing machine", and he argued that it was possible to compute on such a machine any mapping, which it would be reasonable to call "computable". This conjecture is known as the Church-Turing thesis. It was shown that the class of mappings produced in this fashion is identical with the classes of mappings produced by other apparently different methods, proposed by A. Church, K. Gödel, S. Kleene, E. Post and A. Markov.

We begin with "machines" that are less powerful than a Turing machine in terms of the computations they can perform. We then incrementally look at more powerful machines leading to the Turing machine.

A *deterministic finite automaton* consists of an *input tape*, which is divided into squares, and a black box, called *finite control*. The latter can sense what symbol is written at any position on the input tape by means of a movable *reading head* (see Figure 1.10). Initially, the head is placed at the leftmost square of the tape and the finite control is set in a designated *initial state*. At regular intervals the automaton reads one symbol from the input tape and then enters a new state depending on the current state and the symbol just read. After reading an input symbol, the head moves one square to the right (its next square) on the tape and on the next move it will read the symbol in the next square of the tape. This process, namely read a symbol, the head moves to the right, and the state of finite control changes, is carried out repetitively until the head reaches the end of the input string of symbols. The automaton then indicates its approval or otherwise of what it has read by the state it is at the end. If it ends with one of a set of *final states*, the input string is considered to be *accepted* by the automaton; the set of strings accepted by the automaton is the *language accepted* by it.

The formal definition of a deterministic finite automaton follows.

Definition 1.2 (Automaton)   A *Deterministic Finite Automaton* (DFA) is a quintuple $M = (K, \Sigma, \delta, s, F)$, where K is a finite set of *states*, Σ is an alphabet, i.e. a finite set of symbols, $s \in K$ is the *initial state*, $F \subseteq K$ is the set of *final states*, and δ is the *transition function*, i.e. a function from $K \times \Sigma$ to K.   ■

We denote the set of all strings over Σ, i.e. the countably infinite set of all finite sequences of symbols from Σ, by Σ^*. A set of strings over Σ, namely any subset of Σ^*, is called a *language*. Since languages are sets, they can be combined via the set operations of union, intersection and difference. If L is a language, then $\bar{L}$, the complement of L, is given by $\Sigma^* - L$. In addition,

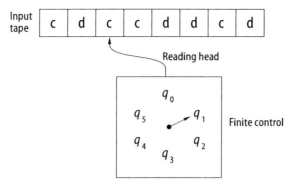

Fig 1.10 A deterministic finite automaton

we can define the *concatenation* of two languages over Σ, that is, if L_1, L_2 are languages over Σ then their concatenation is $L = L_1 \circ L_2$, or simply $L_1 L_2$, defined by

$$L = \{ w \mid w = x \circ y, \text{ or simply } w = xy, \text{ for some } x \in L_1 \text{ and } y \in L_2 \},$$

where $\circ$ stands for the concatenation of strings x and y, namely the leading part of w comes from x and the trailing part from y.

Finally, the *closure* or *Kleene star* of a single language L, denoted by L^*, is the set of all strings obtained by concatenating zero or more strings from L.

The *regular expressions* over Σ are the strings over the alphabet $\Sigma \cup \{ (,), \emptyset, \cup, {}^* \}$ such that

(i) $\emptyset$ and each member of Σ is a regular expression.

(ii) If α and β are regular expressions then so is $(\alpha\beta)$.

(iii) If α and β are regular expressions then so is $(\alpha \cup \beta)$.

(iv) If α is a regular expression then so is α^*.

(v) Nothing is a regular expression unless it follows from (i) through (iv).

The class of *regular languages* (or *regular sets*) over Σ is the minimal set of languages containing $\emptyset$ as well as the singletons $\{a\}$, for all $a \in \Sigma$, and closed under union, concatenation and Kleene star.

It can be shown that a language is regular if and only if it can be described by a regular expression. In addition, a language is regular if and only if it is accepted by a DFA. This fundamental result was proved in a seminal paper by Kleene [Kle56].

The rules according to which a DFA, M, chooses its next state are encoded into δ. They are given in a table, sometimes known as the *state transition table*, or graphically via a *state diagram*. We note that the transition function δ naturally extends to a transition function $\hat{\delta}$ from $K \times \Sigma^*$ to K by composing δ with itself zero or more times.

If when a DFA changes state it has the option of selecting one from a set of possible "next states", then we have a *Nondeterministic Finite Automaton* (NFA). The formal definition is

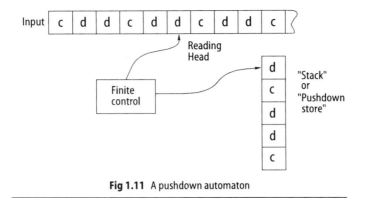

Fig 1.11 A pushdown automaton

as before except that the transition function δ is replaced by the finite *transition relation* $\triangle$, where $\triangle \subseteq K \times \Sigma^* \times K$; as before Σ^* denotes the set of all strings, including the empty string, over the alphabet Σ.

Let $L(M)$ be the *language accepted* by a DFA M. Then DFAs M_1 and M_2 are equivalent if and only if $L_1(M) = L_2(M)$. It can be shown that for each NFA there is an *equivalent* DFA. This result was proved in a seminal paper on finite automata by Rabin and Scott [RS59].

There are languages, however, that are not regular and thus not, in general, accepted by DFAs. In order to recognise such languages via an automaton, we need to increase its memory. To this end we define an automaton that incorporates the idea of a "stack" (see Figure 1.11).

The notion of an automaton with a stack as auxiliary storage is now formalised.

Definition 1.3 (Pushdown automaton)   A *Pushdown automaton* is a sextuple M = $(K, \Sigma, \Gamma, \triangle, s, F)$, where K is a finite set of *states*, Σ is an alphabet (the *input symbols*), Γ is also an alphabet (the *stack symbols*), $s \in K$ is the *initial state*, $F \subseteq K$ is the set of *final states*, and $\triangle$, the *transition relation*, is a finite subset of $(K \times \Sigma^* \times \Gamma^*) \times (K \times \Gamma^*)$.   ■

Intuitively, if $((p, u, \beta), (q, \gamma)) \in \triangle$, then, whenever M is in a state p with β at the top of the stack, it may read u from the input tape, replace β by γ on the top of the stack and then enter state q; such a pair is called a *transition* of M. Since several transitions of M may be applied concurrently, M is nondeterministic in its mode of operation. In addition, a pushdown automaton mimics the *push* and *pop* operations associated with a *stack*.

In essence if a pushdown automaton M reaches a configuration whereby the stack is empty, the input tape has been read and M is in a final state, then M *accepts* the input string. On the other hand, if M detects a mismatch between input and stack symbols, or if the input is exhausted before the stack is emptied, then it does *not accept* the input string.

We next define a class of languages accepted by pushdown automata.

Definition 1.4 (Context-free grammars and languages)   A *context-free* grammar G is a quadruple (N, Σ, R, S), where N is an alphabet, Σ is a subset of N (the set of *terminal symbols*), R is a finite subset of $(N - \Sigma) \times N^*$ (the set of *rules* or *productions*) and S is an element of $N - \Sigma$ (the *start symbol*).

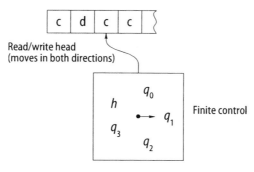

Fig 1.12 A Turing machine

For any $A \in N - \Sigma$ and $u \in N^*$, we often write $A \to u$ whenever $(A, u) \in R$. For any strings $u, v \in N^*$, we write $u \underset{G}{\Longrightarrow} v$ if and only if there are strings $x, y, v' \in N^*$ and $A \in N - \Sigma$ such that $u = xAy$, $v = xv'y$ and $A \to v'$. The language generated by G, designated by $L(G)$, is given by

$$L(G) = \{w \in \Sigma^* \mid S \underset{G}{\overset{*}{\Longrightarrow}} w\},$$

where $\underset{G}{\overset{*}{\Longrightarrow}}$ is the reflexive, transitive closure of $\underset{G}{\Longrightarrow}$. A language L is *context-free* if it is equal to $L(G)$ for some context-free grammar G. ∎

The elements of $N - \Sigma$ are called the *nonterminal symbols*. A string consisting entirely of terminal symbols is termed a *terminal string* (this concept is used in Section 9.3 of Chapter 9).

It can be shown that if a language is accepted by a pushdown automaton, then it is context-free; conversely, each context-free language is accepted by some pushdown automaton. Closure properties of context-free grammars were investigated in a seminal paper by Bar-Hillel et al. [BPS64].

As an epilogue to this particular subarea of the theory of computing we mention the interesting problem of minimising a DFA, M_1, namely finding another DFA, M_2, such that $L(M_1) = L(M_2)$ and with a set of states, whose cardinality is minimum. For a recent application of this idea see [VB92].

We now return to the Turing machine. A *Turing Machine* (TM) is basically composed of a *finite-state control unit* (or simply finite control) and a *tape*. The tape has an infinite (or at any rate arbitrarily large) storage capacity in the simple form of a semi-infinite tape, marked off into squares. Communication between the control unit and the tape is provided by a single read/write head, which reads symbols from the tape and may change symbols on the tape. The control unit operates in discrete steps and at each step it performs the ensuing two functions depending on its current state and the tape symbol which is scanned by the read/write head (see Figure 1.12):

1) The control unit is put in a new state.

2) Either a symbol is written in the tape square, which is currently scanned, thus replacing the one already there or the read/write head is moved one tape square to the left (L) or to

right (R). (If the Turing machine attempts to move its read/write head off the end of the tape, it automatically ceases to operate, in which case we say that the Turing machine *hangs*.)

The input to a TM is a string inscribed on the tape squares at the left end of the tape. The rest of the tape contains a blank symbol, designated by #. A TM can alter its input as it sees fit and can write on the blank portion of the tape situated to the right of the input string. It leaves its answer on the tape (since it can write on its tape) at the end of a computation; a special state, called *halt state*, signals the end of the computation for TMs and is denoted by h.

Definition 1.5 (Deterministic Turing machine)   A *Deterministic Turing Machine* (DTM), referred to simply as a Turing machine, is a quadruple TM $= (K, \Sigma, \delta, s)$, where K is a finite set of *states* such that $h \notin K$, Σ is an alphabet such that $\# \in \Sigma$ and $L, R \notin \Sigma$, $s \in K$ is the *initial state* and δ is the *transition function* (or *next move function*) from $K \times \Sigma$ to $(K \cup \{h\}) \times (\Sigma \cup \{L, R\})$. ■

Sometimes it is advantageous to consider a TM with $k \geq 1$ ($k \in \omega$) one-way infinite tapes. Such a machine is called a *k-tape* TM. Another version for a 1-tape TM is to allow the tape to be two-way infinite. However, these and other variations of TMs are computationally equivalent in the sense that they compute the same class of functions.

In order to specify the status of a TM, it is necessary to specify the state, the contents of the tape, split into three pieces, namely the part (possibly empty) to the left of the tape square being scanned, the symbol currently in the scanned square, and the part (again possibly empty) to the right of the tape square being scanned, and the position of the head. Since no input string ends with the blank symbol #, and in view of the said considerations, we define a *configuration* (also called an *instantaneous description*) to be an element of the set

$$(K \cup \{h\}) \times \Sigma^* \times \Sigma \times (\Sigma^* (\Sigma - \{\#\}) \cup \{\lambda\}),$$

where λ denotes the *empty string*. A configuration whose state component is h will be called a *halt* (or *halting*) configuration. We designate the change from one configuration to another by

$$(q_1, w_1 a_1 u_1) \vdash_{TM} (q_2, w_2 a_2 u_2),$$

incorporating three cases: overwrite the symbol of the scanned tape square without moving the read/write head, TM moves the read/write one square to the left (if it is moving to the left off blank tape the symbol # on the scanned tape square disappears from the configuration) and finally TM moves the read/write head one square to the right (if it is moving onto blank tape, a new blank symbol, #, appears in the configuration as the new scanned tape symbol).

For any Turing machine TM, $\vdash_{TM}^*$ stands for the reflexive, transitive closure of $\vdash_{TM}$. We write $C_1 \vdash_{TM}^* C_2$ to indicate that configuration C_1 yields configuration C_2. Hereafter, the underlined symbol indicates the position of the read/write head.

Henceforth the input string to a Turing machine will be surrounded by # on each side and written on the leftmost squares of the tape. The read/write head is positioned at the symbol #, which marks the right end of the input string, and the Turing machine starts functioning in its initial state. Thus, given a Turing machine TM and $w \in \Sigma^*$, TM is said to *halt on input w* if and only if $(s, \#w\underline{\#})$ yields a halt configuration.

We are now in a position to introduce formally the concept of a *Turing-computable mapping* or *function*.

Definition 1.6 (Turing-computable mapping)   Let Σ_0 and Σ_1 be alphabets not containing #. Let $f: \Sigma_0^* \to \Sigma_1^*$. A Turing machine TM $= (k, \Sigma, \delta, s)$ computes f if $\Sigma_0, \Sigma_1 \subseteq \Sigma$ and for any $w \in \Sigma_0^*$, if $f(w) = u$ then $(s, \#w\underline{\#}) \vdash^*_{\text{TM}} (h, \#u\underline{\#})$. If some such Turing machine TM exists, then f is said to be a Turing-computable mapping (or a Turing-computable function). ■

We note that a function computed by a Turing machine is called a *partially recursive function*. If it happens to be defined for all values of its arguments, then it is also called a *totally recursive function* (or simply a recursive function). In the case of computing a recursive function the Turing machine always halts in state h. The notion of a Turing-computable mapping from strings to strings can be readily extended to mappings from ω to ω.

Turing machines can be viewed as a low-level language for expressing computations; thus they provide a way to measure the expressive power of any programming language.

Definition 1.7 (Computationally complete programming language)   A programming language is said to be *computationally complete* if it can express all Turing-computable mappings. ■

If we allow Turing machines to behave *nondeterministically*, then upon certain combinations of state and scanned symbol such machines might have more than one possible choice of behaviour. Thus in Definition 1.5 δ is replaced by a *transition relation* $\triangle$, which is a subset of $(K \times \Sigma) \times ((K \cup \{h\}) \times (\Sigma \cup \{L, R\}))$. However, $\vdash_{\text{TM}}$ is no longer single-valued, since one configuration may yield several others in a single step (move). It can be shown that for each *Nondeterministic Turing Machine* (NTM) there is an *equivalent* deterministic Turing machine (DTM), i.e. each mapping computed by a nondeterministic Turing machine is Turing-computable.

We next consider the class of *primitive recursive* functions, in other words the smallest class of functions containing the *initial* functions (also called *basis* functions) and closed under composition and *primitive recursion*. Most of the Turing-computable functions arising in practice belong to this class.

The initial functions are primitive recursive and comprise the *successor function* $succ(x) = x+1$, the zero function $zero(x) = 0$, where $x \in \omega$, and the projection functions. If $f_1, f_2, \ldots, f_m$ are primitive recursive functions of n variables and g is a primitive recursive function of m variables, then the function h, obtained via *composition*, where

$$h(x_1, x_2, \ldots, x_n) = g(f_1(x_1, x_2, \ldots, x_n), f_2(x_1, x_2, \ldots, x_n), \ldots, f_m(x_1, x_2, \ldots, x_n)),$$

is primitive recursive.

We next define primitive recursion. If f and g are primitive recursive functions of n and $n + 2$ variables, respectively, then the function h, where

$$
\begin{aligned}
h(x_1, x_2, \ldots, x_n, 0) &= f(x_1, x_2, \ldots, x_n), \\
h(x_1, x_2, \ldots, x_n, y + 1) &= g(x_1, x_2, \ldots, x_n, y, h(x_1, x_2, \ldots, x_n, y)),
\end{aligned}
$$

is primitive recursive.

A function is said to be primitive recursive if it is an initial function or can be generated by a sequence of the operations of composition and primitive recursion.

However, not all functions are primitive recursive. For example, using Cantor's diagonal method [Can55] it can be shown that there is a totally recursive function which is not primitive recursive.

We now look at two derivatives of the important notion of a Turing-computable function, namely that of a Turing-enumerable language and a Turing-decidable language. In this context let Σ_0 be an alphabet which does not contain the blank symbol #.

A Turing machine TM *enumerates* the language $L \subseteq \Sigma_0^*$, denoted as $L = L(\text{TM})$, if and only if, for some fixed state q of TM,

$$
L = \{w \mid \text{for some string } u, (s, \underline{\#}) \vdash_{\text{TM}}^* (q, \#w\underline{\#}u)\},
$$

where s is the initial state of TM.

A language is *Turing-enumerable* (or *recursively enumerable*) if and only if it is enumerated by some Turing machine.

Let $\mathsf{Y}, \mathsf{N} \notin \Sigma_0$ be two distinguished symbols. Then a language $L \subseteq \Sigma_0^*$ is *Turing-decidable* (or *recursively decidable* or simply *recursive* or *decidable*) if and only if the function

$$
\chi_L \colon \Sigma_0^* \to \{\mathsf{Y}, \mathsf{N}\}
$$

is Turing-computable, where for each $w \in \Sigma_0^*$ $\chi_L(w) = \mathsf{Y}$ if $w \in L$ and $\chi_L(w) = \mathsf{N}$ if $w \notin L$.

If χ_L is computed by a Turing machine TM, then we say that TM *decides* (or *accepts*) L, and write $L = L(\text{TM})$. Otherwise, when there is *no* TM that decides L, then L is said to be *undecidable*. It can be shown that a language is Turing-decidable if and only if both it and its complement are recursively enumerable.

The most famous undecidable problem is the *halting problem for Turing machines*, namely to decide (determine), for any arbitrary given Turing machine TM and input w, whether TM will eventually halt on w.

Continuing in this vein we next state Rice's theorem [Ric53], which is utilised in Section 6.4 of Chapter 6.

Theorem 1.2   Assume that C is a proper nonempty subset of the set of recursively enumerable languages. Then the following problem is undecidable: given a Turing machine TM, is the language $L = L(\text{TM})$ enumerated by TM in C? $\square$

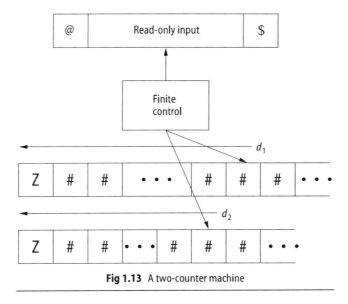

Fig 1.13 A two-counter machine

We next look briefly at another computing device, called the *Two-counter Machine* (or *Register Machine*), which is much simpler than a Turing machine. Such a machine has two counters (or registers), which, at any time during the running of the machine, contain a natural number.

An example of a two-counter machine is shown in Figure 1.13; the symbols @ and $ are used as end markers and Z is the nonblank symbol on each tape. An instance of the two-counter machine can be described by the state, the contents of the input tape, the position of the input head, and the distance of the storage heads from Z (shown in Figure 1.13 as d_1 and d_2). We call these distances the *counts* over the tapes.

Let $\bar{n}$ stand for the contents of the nth counter in some fixed listing, so that $\bar{n} \in \omega$ for $n = 1, 2$. A *two-counter machine program* is a finite sequence $<\hat{1}, \hat{2}, \ldots, \hat{H}>$ of instructions, where $\hat{H}$ stands for the halt instruction. The other $\hat{i}$ are all active instructions; they are of two types, namely (n, j) and (n, j, k), where n is the number of a counter, and j, k are the numbers of instructions. Their meanings follow:

(n, j): add 1 to $\bar{n}$, and then go to instruction $\hat{j}$.

(n, j, k): if $\bar{n} > 0$, subtract 1 from $\bar{n}$, and then go to instruction $\hat{j}$, otherwise go to instruction $\hat{k}$.

We briefly illustrate the way a two-counter machine operates by considering the very simple two-counter machine program:

$$\hat{1}\ (2, 2, 3)$$
$$\hat{2}\ (1, 1)$$
$$\hat{3}\ \text{halt}$$

Starting with, say $(3, 2)$, in the contents of the two counters and at instruction $\hat{1}$, we obtain the following computation:

$$\hat{1}\,(3, 2)\,\hat{2}\,(3, 1)\,\hat{1}\,(4, 1)\,\hat{2}\,(4, 0)\,\hat{1}\,(5, 0)\,\hat{3}\,(5, 0)\ \text{halt}$$

In general, the above two-counter machine program starting at position (m, n), that is, with m and n in the two counters, and at instruction $\hat{1}$, terminates in position $(m + n, 0)$.

It can be shown that a two-counter machine can simulate an arbitrary Turing machine and consequently the corresponding halting problem, that is to say, to decide whether a two-counter machine program, when applied to itself as input, terminates, is undecidable.

In the context of *undecidability*, we state two well-known undecidable problems, namely the *word problem* for *semigroups* and *finite semigroups*, and the *Post correspondence problem*.

We begin with the definition of semigroup and finite semigroup.

Definition 1.8 (Semigroup and finite semigroup) A nonempty set S together with a binary operation, called composition, denoted by the juxtaposition ab for any $a, b \in S$, constitutes a *semigroup* whenever the following two axioms are satisfied:

  (i) (Closure). For any two elements $a, b \in S$, ab is also an element of S.

  (ii) (Associativity). For any three elements $a, b, c \in S$, $(ab)c = a(bc)$.

A semigroup is called a *finite semigroup* if S is a finite set. A semigroup is called a *monoid*, if in addition to (i) and (ii) above, there is a special element ϵ of S, called the *identity*, such that for any $a \in S$, $\epsilon a = a$ and $a\epsilon = a$.   ∎

Let Σ be a finite alphabet and recall that a string over Σ (also called a *word* over Σ) is a finite sequence of symbols from Σ. It is easy to verify that the countably infinite set Σ^* of all words over Σ is a semigroup; the set Σ^* is called the *free semigroup* generated by Σ.

Now, let $E = \{\alpha_i = \beta_i \mid i = 1, 2, \ldots, n\}$ be a finite set of equalities and let e be an additional equality $\alpha = \beta$, with $\alpha_i, \beta_i, \alpha, \beta \in \Sigma^*$. Then E *(finitely) implies* e, if for each (finite) semigroup S and homomorphism $h : \Sigma^* \to S$, the following statement is true:

$$\text{if } h(\alpha_i) = h(\beta_i) \text{ for each } i = 1, 2, \ldots, n, \text{ then } h(\alpha) = h(\beta).$$

The *word problem* for (finite) semigroups is to decide given E and e, whether E (finitely) implies e. The word problem for semigroups was shown to be undecidable by Post [Pos47], and the word problem for finite semigroups was shown to be undecidable by Gurevich [Gur66].

Another powerful result in the theory of computing is the undecidability of Post's correspondence problem [Pos46]. This problem has had many important applications and has been employed to obtain undecidability results in many areas including that of context-free languages. Hereafter we present formally a version of this problem.

A *correspondence pair* is a pair $C = (A, B)$ in which A and B are ordered, finite sets of strings over an alphabet Σ, with

$$A = (\alpha_1, \alpha_2, \ldots, \alpha_n) \text{ and } B = (\beta_1, \beta_2, \ldots, \beta_n),$$

where $n \in \omega$ and $n \geq 1$. We say that the finite sequence of integers $i_1, i_2, \ldots, i_m$, $1 \leq i_j \leq n$, $1 \leq j \leq m$, is a *solution* for the correspondence pair C if and only if the strings

$$u = \alpha_{i_1} \alpha_{i_2} \ldots \alpha_{i_m} \text{ and } v = \beta_{i_1} \beta_{i_2} \ldots \beta_{i_m}$$

are identical. The *correspondence problem* is that of deciding, for any given C, whether C has a solution.

We next turn our attention to the problem of computational complexity. Given an instance of a problem, we can encode it using some *standard string encoding*. We then assess the efficiency of an algorithm for solving the problem by considering the number of primitive steps required to produce an implementation of the algorithm on a computing device; the input to the device is the encoded string version of the problem instance.

The computing device we employ is the nondeterministic Turing machine (NTM) with k tapes. (Recall that NTMs are equivalent to DTMs and that a DTM is just a special case of an NTM.)

We say that an NTM is of *time complexity* $T(n)$ if for every input string of length n there is some sequence of at most $T(n)$ moves leading to the halt state h. Correspondingly, an NTM is of *space complexity* $S(n)$ if for every input string of length n there is some sequence of moves leading to the halt state in which at most $S(n)$ different cells are scanned on any one of the k tapes.

We define PTIME to be the set of all languages which can be accepted by deterministic Turing machines (DTMs) of polynomial-time complexity. In formal terms

PTIME $=$ $\{L \mid$ there exists a deterministic Turing machine, TM, and a polynomial $p(n)$ such that TM is of time complexity $p(n)$ and $L = L(\text{TM})\}$.

Linear-time languages are a special case of polynomial-time languages that are accepted by a TM of time complexity kn ($k \in \omega$), i.e. by a TM that needs to scan its input only a fixed number of times.

Correspondingly, NPTIME (or simply NP) is defined to be the set of all languages which can be accepted by NTMs of polynomial-time complexity.

We next define PSPACE which is a superset of NP. PSPACE is defined to be the set of all languages which can be accepted by polynomial-space-bounded DTMs, namely

PSPACE $=$ $\{L \mid$ there exists a deterministic Turing machine, TM, and a polynomial $p(n)$ such that TM is of space complexity $p(n)$ and $L = L(\text{TM})\}$.

Although it is not known whether PTIME is properly contained in NP, we can show that certain languages are as hard as any in NP, in the sense that if we had a deterministic polynomial-time-bounded algorithm to recognise one of these languages, then we could obtain a deterministic polynomial-time-bounded algorithm to recognise any language in NP.

Let Σ_1 and Σ_2 be two alphabets. A mapping $f: \Sigma_1^* \to \Sigma_2^*$ is a polynomial-time computable transformation (or simply a transformation), if f can be computed in polynomial time on a DTM.

Let $L_1 \subseteq \Sigma_1^*$ and $L_2 \subseteq \Sigma_2^*$ be languages. L_1 is (polynomial, many-to-one) *reducible* to L_2, written $L_1 \propto L_2$, if there is a transformation f such that

$$\text{for all } x \in \Sigma_1^*, x \in L_1 \text{ if and only if } f(x) \in L_2.$$

A language L is *NP-complete*, if $L \in \text{NP}$ and for all $L' \in \text{NP}$, $L' \propto L$.

Historically, the set of satisfiable formulae of the propositional calculus was the first language shown to be NP-complete [Coo71]. There followed a seminal contribution by Karp [Kar72], wherein a large number of problems, many of them graph-theoretic, were shown to be NP-complete.

In a similar vein a language L is *PSPACE-complete*, with respect to polynomial transformability as above, if $L \in \text{PSPACE}$ and for all $L' \in \text{PSPACE}$, $L' \propto L$.

We next define another computational complexity class, designated as co-NP, that deals with complementary problems. As before let Σ be an alphabet. In language terms

$$\text{co-NP} \quad = \quad \{\Sigma^* - L \mid L \text{ is a language over } \Sigma \text{ and } L \in \text{NP}\}.$$

In the context of this book we also employ the computational complexity class *NP-hard* defined by

$$\text{NP-hard} \quad = \quad \{L \mid L \text{ is a language over } \Sigma \text{ and for all } L' \in \text{NP}, \ L' \propto L\}.$$

At this juncture we briefly consider the intriguing problem of the *polynomial hierarchy*. To this end we introduce the *oracle Turing machine* (alternatively, *query Turing machine*), which may be deterministic or nondeterministic. An oracle Turing machine is a Turing machine with an additional distinguished tape, called the *query tape*, and three distinguished states called the *query state*, the *yes state* and the *no state*. The computation of an oracle Turing machine depends on its input and also on a given language over the alphabet Σ, called the *oracle*. The actions of an oracle Turing machine with oracle, say L', are identical to those of a Turing machine with the following exception. If the finite control of the oracle Turing machine enters its query state at some step, then the finite control next enters the machine's *yes* state if the nonblank portion of the query tape contains a string in L'; otherwise the finite control next enters the machine's *no* state.

An oracle Turing machine, OTM, is of time complexity $T(n)$ if and only if, for every input string of length n there is some sequence of at most $T(n)$ moves, relative to *any* oracle, leading to the halt state of OTM. We let $\text{OTM}^{L'}$ denote the oracle Turing machine, OTM, with oracle L', and $L = L(\text{OTM}^{L'})$ denote the language accepted by $\text{OTM}^{L'}$.

We now define two further computational complexity classes as follows, assuming that all languages are over an alphabet Σ.

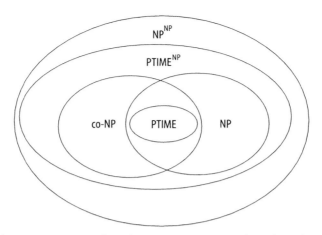

Fig 1.14 Containment relationships amongst computational complexity classes

$$\text{PTIME}^{\text{NP}} \quad = \quad \{L \mid \text{ there exists an oracle Turing machine, } \text{OTM}^{L'}, \text{ with } L' \in \text{PTIME},$$
and a polynomial $p(n)$ such that OTM is of time complexity $p(n)$ and $L = L(\text{OTM}^{L'})\}.$

$$\text{NP}^{\text{NP}} \quad = \quad \{L \mid \text{ there exists an oracle Turing machine, } \text{OTM}^{L'}, \text{ with } L' \in \text{NP},$$
and a polynomial $p(n)$ such that OTM is of time complexity $p(n)$ and $L = L(\text{OTM}^{L'})\}.$

We observe that it is not known whether PTIME^{NP} differs from NP^{NP} or not. Pictorially, assuming that $\text{PTIME} \neq \text{NP}$, the containment relationships amongst PTIME, NP, co-NP, PTIME^{NP} and NP^{NP} are illustrated in Figure 1.14.

On the basis of this figure Stockmeyer [Sto77] observed that this process of defining new computational complexity classes in terms of old ones could be carried out indefinitely, resulting in classes of apparently greater difficulty. We obtain in this manner what is termed the *polynomial hierarchy*. The computational complexity classes in the resulting hierarchy are designated by Σ_k^p, Π_k^p and Δ_k^p, and are defined by

$$\Sigma_0^p = \Pi_0^p = \Delta_0^p = \text{PTIME}$$

and for all $k \geq 0, k \in \omega$,

$$\Delta_{k+1}^p \quad = \quad \text{PTIME}^{\Sigma_k^p}$$
$$\Sigma_{k+1}^p \quad = \quad \text{NP}^{\Sigma_k^p}$$
$$\Pi_{k+1}^p \quad = \quad \text{co-}\Sigma_{k+1}^p,$$

where $\text{co-}\Sigma_{k+1}^p$ denotes the complement of Σ_{k+1}^p in a similar way that co-NP is the complement of NP.

We now look at two further computational complexity classes, namely EXPTIME and EXPSPACE. The former consists of all languages, recognised by a deterministic or nondeterministic Turing machine, with time complexity bounded above by $2^{p(n)}$ for some polynomial p of the input string of length n, whilst the latter consists of all languages recognised by a deterministic or nondeterministic Turing machine, with space complexity bounded above by $2^{p(n)}$.

As above we can define the notions of *EXPTIME-complete* and *EXPSPACE-complete*.

Two further computational complexity classes are LOGTIME, which consists of all languages, recognised by a deterministic or nondeterministic Turing machine, with time complexity bounded above by $\lceil log_2 n + 1 \rceil$, where n is the length of the input string, and LOGSPACE, which consists of all languages, recognised by a deterministic or nondeterministic Turing machine, with space complexity bounded above by $\lceil log_2 n + 1 \rceil$.

A standard way of measuring computational complexity is by introducing the big-O notation, which reads "of the order of". Consider two functions f and g. We say that f is "big oh" of g, written $f = O(g)$ or $f(n)$ is $O(g(n))$, if there exist constants c and n_0 such that $f(n) \leq c\, g(n)$ for all $n \geq n_0$. Thus a polynomial-time algorithm is one whose time complexity is $O(p(n))$, for some polynomial p, where p is a function in the size of the input n to the algorithm. This complexity measure determines the *worst-case* behaviour of the algorithm. Alternatively, we may wish to determine the *average-case* behaviour of an algorithm [Pap94].

Hereafter an algorithm of polynomial-time complexity is meant to be an algorithm of deterministic polynomial-time complexity. In the course of developing the material in this book we shall refer to a problem as *tractable* when there is a polynomial-time algorithm for its solution. The pursuit of efficient polynomial-time algorithms for solving problems is central to computer science [AHU83]. On the other hand, we shall refer to a problem as *intractable* if it is so hard that no polynomial-time algorithm can possibly solve it.

We recommend the now classical books [Min69, Har78, HU79, LP81, Rog87] on the theory of computation and formal languages. A collection of papers dealing with both a historical perspective and contemporary research in the area of computability can be found in [Her88]. The definitive book on computational complexity is [GJ79]; for a recent survey see [Joh90]. A more recent book on computational complexity is [Pap94].

1.9.5   Finite-Model Theory

Model theory is a branch of logic concerned with the study of the properties of mathematical structures. It endeavours to establish the expressive power of a logical language (usually a first-order language) in terms of the class of problems that can be solved by the language. Many of the central results from mathematical logic hinge upon the fact that the universe of a model can be infinite. Finite-model theory is a sub-branch of model theory concerned only with the study of the logical properties of models whose universe is finite. Since, a relational database can be viewed as a finite model, there is an intimate connection between relational database theory and finite-model theory, which has lead to a rich cross-fertilisation of ideas between database theorists and logicians.

Let us consider a first-order language $\mathcal{L}$ having a finite set of relation symbols, $R_1, R_2, \ldots, R_n$, each of which has an arity and a finite set of constant symbols, $c_1, c_2, \ldots, c_m$.

(We assume that equality is a logical symbol of $\mathcal{L}$ interpreted as identity.) A *structure* $\mathcal{A}$ over $\mathcal{L}$ (or simply a structure when $\mathcal{L}$ is understood from context) comprises the following components:

1) a nonempty set $[\mathcal{A}]$, called the *universe* of $\mathcal{A}$;

2) a set of relations $r_1, r_2, \ldots, r_n$ such that each r_i is a relation on $[\mathcal{A}]$ associated with R_i and having the same arity as R_i, for $i = 1, 2, \ldots, n$ (r_i is called the interpretation of R_i); and

3) a set of constants $a_1, a_2, \ldots, a_m$ such that each a_i is a member of $[\mathcal{A}]$ and is associated with c_i, for $i = 1, 2, \ldots, m$ (a_i is called the interpretation of c_i).

We note that the above definition of structure is a special case of the more general Definition 1.1 of Subsection 1.9.3. Given a structure $\mathcal{A}$ and a first-order sentence φ both over the same first-order language $\mathcal{L}$, we write $\mathcal{A} \models \varphi$ to mean that $\mathcal{A}$ *satisfies* φ. We extend the satisfaction relation, $\models$, to a set Σ of first-order sentences over $\mathcal{L}$, where $\mathcal{A} \models \Sigma$ means that $\mathcal{A} \models \varphi$ for all $\varphi \in \Sigma$. A structure $\mathcal{A}$ is a *model* of Σ precisely when $\mathcal{A}$ satisfies Σ.

A *finite structure* is a structure whose universe if finite, and a *finite model* of Σ is a finite structure that satisfies Σ. A first-order sentence over $\mathcal{L}$ is *satisfiable* (*finitely satisfiable*) if it is satisfied in at least one structure (finite structure), i.e. it has at least one model (finite model). A first-order sentence over $\mathcal{L}$ is *valid* (*finitely valid*) if it is satisfied in all structures (finite structures) over $\mathcal{L}$, i.e. every structure (finite structure) is a model (finite model) of the sentence.

An algebraic language operating on structures is presented in Subsection 3.2.1 of Chapter 3 as an alternative to first-order formulae of the first-order predicate calculus, presented in Subsection 3.2.2 of Chapter 3 in the context of the relational data model.

In Subsection 3.3.2 of Chapter 3 it is shown that, on finite structures, the algebraic language is exactly as expressive as its counterpart first-order language. This result is one of the cornerstones of relational database theory.

Many of the classical results from model theory fail for finite models; this in itself justifies the study of finite models as an independent branch of model theory.

In the early 1930's Gödel devised a proof system for first-order sentences which completely characterises the set of valid first-order sentences. This monumental result, known as Gödel's completeness theorem, implies the following result, since we can systematically list all possible proofs with the aid of a Turing machine.

Theorem 1.3   The set of valid first-order sentences over $\mathcal{L}$ is recursively enumerable but not recursive, i.e. its complement is not recursively enumerable.   □

Trakhtenbrot [Tra63] proved the following result which implies the failure of the completeness theorem for finitely valid first-order sentences (the original result in Russian was published earlier in 1950).

Theorem 1.4   The set of finitely valid first-order sentences over $\mathcal{L}$ is *not* recursively enumerable.   □

Turing [Tur36, Tur37] in his seminal paper, defining the notion of computability, proved the following result.

Theorem 1.5 The set of satisfiable first-order sentences over $\mathcal{L}$ is *not* recursively enumerable.
□

On the other hand, the next result holds on using Theorem 1.4 since, given a first-order sentence φ, we can systematically list all finite structures and test whether they satisfy φ.

Theorem 1.6 The set of finitely satisfiable first-order sentences over $\mathcal{L}$ is recursively enumerable but not recursive, i.e. its complement is not recursively enumerable. □

A sentence which is either unsatisfiable or finitely satisfiable is said to be *finitely controllable*. The following result is a direct consequence of Theorems 1.3 and 1.6.

Theorem 1.7 The problem of whether a finitely controllable first-order sentence is satisfiable is decidable. □

The theory of data dependencies, which is central to relational database theory, deals with the investigation of limited subclasses of first-order sentences, which express certain constraints on structures. In particular, the implication problem defined below is central.

Given a set of data dependencies Σ and a data dependency φ both in the same subclass of first-order sentences under consideration, the *implication problem* is the problem of determining the computational complexity of deciding whether for all structures $\mathcal{A}$ over $\mathcal{L}$, the following condition is true:

$$\mathcal{A} \models \Sigma \text{ implies } \mathcal{A} \models \varphi.$$

The reader will find a detailed account of data dependencies in Section 3.6 of Chapter 3.

Another fundamental result of model theory is the *compactness theorem*. It states that if every finite subset of a set of sentences Σ is satisfiable then Σ is satisfiable; the cardinality of Σ may be infinite. To see that the compactness theorem fails for finite models consider the countably infinite set of sentences, $\Phi = \{\phi_1, \phi_2, \ldots, \phi_i, \ldots\}$, where ϕ_i states the existence of at least i distinct elements in the universe. Then it is evident that every finite subset of Φ is finitely satisfiable but Φ itself is *not* finitely satisfiable.

From the above we conclude that the foundations of finite-model theory cannot be built on classical model theory. We will now briefly take a look at the fundamental tools and results of finite-model theory. For the rest of this subsection *we will assume that all structures, and thus all models, are finite* and that all structures and sentences are over a first-order language $\mathcal{L}$. In the following we will often use the term *logic* instead of *language*; thus, for example, we will use the term first-order logic instead of first-order language.

Two structures $\mathcal{A}$ and $\mathcal{B}$ over $\mathcal{L}$ are said to be *elementary equivalent*, denoted by $\mathcal{A} \equiv \mathcal{B}$, if for every sentence φ over $\mathcal{L}$, $\mathcal{A} \models \varphi$ if and only if $\mathcal{B} \models \varphi$. The next theorem implies that two elementary equivalent structures cannot be distinguished by first-order sentences.

Theorem 1.8   Two structures are elementary equivalent if and only if they are isomorphic.

$\square$

Thus in finite-model theory it is more interesting to study *classes* of structures rather than individual structures. Let a class of structures S be a subset of the set of all structures over $\mathcal{L}$, which is closed under isomorphism. A class of structures S can be viewed as expressing some *property* such as being a connected graph (see Section 2.1 which introduces the notion of a graph).

In order for a class of structures S to be *definable* (or *expressible*) in a language $\mathcal{L}$ it must be the case that there is a sentence φ over $\mathcal{L}$ such that if $\mathcal{A} \in S$ then $\mathcal{A} \models \varphi$ and if $\mathcal{A} \notin S$ then $\mathcal{A} \not\models \varphi$. That is, definability means that there is a sentence that is satisfied only by the structures possessing the property.

One of the fundamental tools used to test whether a class of structures is definable is the *Ehrenfeucht-Fraïssè game* [Ehr61, Bar73, Fag97]. The k-round Ehrenfeucht-Fraïssè game, where k is a natural number, is a game consisting of k rounds played on a pair of structures $\mathcal{A}$ and $\mathcal{B}$ by two players the *Spoiler* and the *Duplicator*. At each round the Spoiler makes a move by choosing some constant in the universe of one of the structures and the Duplicator must respond by a move choosing a constant from the universe of the other structure. The game ends after k rounds, with k constants, $a_1, a_2, \ldots, a_k$, chosen from the universe of $\mathcal{A}$ and k constants, $b_1, b_2, \ldots, b_k$, chosen from the universe of $\mathcal{B}$. If the mapping which takes each a_i to b_i, for $i = 1, 2, \ldots, k$, is a partial isomorphism from $\mathcal{A}$ to $\mathcal{B}$ then the Duplicator wins, otherwise the Spoiler wins. (By a partial isomorphism from $\mathcal{A}$ to $\mathcal{B}$ we mean that the respective structures, induced by the restriction of the universe of $\mathcal{A}$ to $a_1, a_2, \ldots, a_k$ together with the interpretation of the constants of $\mathcal{L}$, and the restriction of the universe of $\mathcal{B}$ to $b_1, b_2, \ldots, b_k$ together with the interpretation of the constants of $\mathcal{L}$, are isomorphic.) A *winning strategy* for one of the players is a prescription, for playing the moves of each round of the game, which guarantees that a player wins no matter how the other player moves in each round. The next theorem characterises definability in terms of the Ehrenfeucht-Fraïssè game.

Theorem 1.9   A class of structures S is definable in a first-order language $\mathcal{L}$ if and only if there is a natural number k such that whenever $\mathcal{A} \in S$ but $\mathcal{B} \notin S$ then the Spoiler has a winning strategy in the k-round game over $\mathcal{A}$ and $\mathcal{B}$.

$\square$

As a corollary we can characterise the classes of structures S which are *not* definable in $\mathcal{L}$.

Corollary 1.10   A class of structures S is not definable in a first-order language $\mathcal{L}$ if and only if for all natural numbers k, there exist structures $\mathcal{A} \in S$ and $\mathcal{B} \notin S$ such that the Duplicator has a winning strategy in the k-round game over $\mathcal{A}$ and $\mathcal{B}$.

$\square$

As an example consider a first-order language having no relation symbols and no constant symbols, and two structures $\mathcal{A}_k$ and $\mathcal{A}_{k+1}$, over this language, whose universes have k and $k + 1$ elements, $k \in \omega$, respectively. The reader can verify that the Duplicator has a winning strategy in the k-round game over $\mathcal{A}_k$ and $\mathcal{A}_{k+1}$. It follows that the property of having a universe with an even number of elements is not definable in a first-order language.

As a more complicated example consider a first-order language having a single binary relation symbol $<$, denoting the less than operator, and no constant symbols. A structure $\mathcal{B}_m$ over this language has a universe with m elements and a single relation $1 < 2 < \cdots < m$ modelling a linear order of length m. The reader can verify that the Duplicator has a winning strategy in the k-round game over $\mathcal{B}_{m_1}$ and $\mathcal{B}_{m_2}$ as long as the cardinalities of the two structures are such that $m_1, m_2 \geq 2^k$. Intuitively, after p rounds, with $p \leq k$, the Duplicator can always maintain a large enough gap between any two elements in the smaller cardinality structure which is needed to win the game. A more complex argument is needed to show that the property of being a connected graph is not definable in a first-order language [Fag97].

Viewing the number of variables in a first-order sentence as a logical resource motivates the investigation of the expressiveness of variable-confined logics where variables may need to be reused. This is similar to the situation in programming languages where variables are a memory resource and thus their reuse leads to a more judicious use of space. Let FO^k consist of all the sentences over a first-order language $\mathcal{L}$ having at most k variables, where k is a natural number.

As an example consider a first-order language having a single binary relation symbol E, denoting the edges of a directed graph, and no constant symbols. Then the property asserting the existence of a *path* (see Definition 2.2 in Section 2.1) of length n, where n is a natural number, from a node x to a node y can be expressed in FO^3 by

$$\exists x \, \exists y \, (p_n(x, y)),$$

where $p_1(x, y)$ is defined by

$$p_1(x, y) = E(x, y)$$

and $p_n(x, y)$ is defined inductively by

$$p_n(x, y) = \exists z \, (E(x, z) \wedge (\exists x \, (x = z \wedge p_{n-1}(x, y)))).$$

Two structures $\mathcal{A}$ and $\mathcal{B}$ over $\mathcal{L}$ are said to be *elementary equivalent* in FO^k, denoted by $\mathcal{A} \equiv^k \mathcal{B}$, if for every sentence $\varphi \in FO^k$, $\mathcal{A} \models \varphi$ if and only if $\mathcal{B} \models \varphi$.

It is possible to characterise elementary equivalence in FO^k in terms of an *infinitary k-pebble game*, where k is a natural number, which can be viewed as a variation of the Ehrenfeucht-Fraïssè game defined earlier. The Spoiler and the Duplicator share k pairs of pebbles such that the pebbles in a given pair are said to correspond to each other. The game is played on two structures $\mathcal{A}$ and $\mathcal{B}$ and the players take turns as follows. At each round of the game the Spoiler chooses a pebble and places it on one of the constants in the universe of one of the structures. The Duplicator must respond by placing the corresponding pebble in the pair on one of the constants in the universe of the other structure. At each round the Spoiler may choose a pebble which has so far been unused, i.e. not yet placed on a constant in the universe of one of the structures, or the Spoiler may choose to reuse a pebble already placed on a constant in the universe of one of the structures. In each case the Duplicator must respond by choosing the corresponding pebble and placing it on a constant in the universe of the other structure according to the rules of the game. The game continues indefinitely. After m rounds, $m \geq 0$, we have n pairs $(a_1, b_1), (a_2, b_2), \ldots, (a_n, b_n)$ of constants chosen from the universes of $\mathcal{A}$ and $\mathcal{B}$, respectively, with $n \leq k$, corresponding to the n placed pairs of pebbles. The Spoiler wins the infinitary k-pebble game if after m rounds, for some m, with $m \geq 0$, the mapping which takes each a_i to b_i, for $i = 1, 2, \ldots, n$, is *not* a partial isomorphism from $\mathcal{A}$ to $\mathcal{B}$, otherwise the Duplicator wins. Thus if the Spoiler wins after m rounds the game may be terminated, otherwise the Duplicator can force the game to continue forever. A winning strategy for one of the players is defined as for the Ehrenfeucht-Fraïssé game. The next result characterises elementary equivalence in FO^k [Bar77, IK89, KV92a, KV92b, DLW95].

Theorem 1.11   Let $\mathcal{A}$ and $\mathcal{B}$ be two structures over a first-order language $\mathcal{L}$. Then $\mathcal{A} \equiv^k \mathcal{B}$ if and only if the Duplicator has a winning strategy in the k-pebble game. $\square$

In the above references a further characterisation of elementary equivalence in FO^k is shown in terms of elementary equivalence in the *infinitary logic* $L^k_{\infty\omega}$. The first subscript indicates that conjunctions and disjunctions can be taken over arbitrary, possibly infinite, sets of formulae and the second subscript indicates that only finite quantifier blocks are allowed. The superscript indicates that any formula can have at most k variables. The study of infinitary logics has been instrumental in studying the expressive power of languages which are more expressive than first-order ones.

As we have seen, the expressive power of finite structures over a first-order language is rather limited, since there are many useful properties which are not definable within first-order logic. This has lead researchers to investigate more expressive logics such as fixpoint logic and second-order logic over finite structures. (We refer the reader to Chapter 9 and to Section 6.7 of Chapter 6 for extensions of query languages beyond first-order logic; for example, with the addition of a fixpoint operator.)

A very fruitful subarea of finite-model theory which deals specifically with the expressive power of logical languages is *descriptive complexity* [Imm89, Imm95]. In descriptive complexity we endeavour to capture computational complexity classes in terms of the classes of structures, i.e. properties that are definable in a particular language of logic. The area of descriptive complexity began in 1974 with Fagin's characterisation of the computational complexity class NP as the set of properties that are definable by second-order existential formulae [Fag74]. (The language of second-order logic supersedes first-order logic by also having variables that range over relations such that these variables may be quantified. A second-order existential formula begins with second-order existential quantifiers and is followed by a first-order formula.)

As we have mentioned above the expressive power of first-order logic is limited. More specifically, its descriptive complexity can be seen to be contained in LOGSPACE. The addition of a fixpoint operator to a first-order language increases the expressive power of first-order logic by allowing inductive definitions of relations. In Section 6.7 we present Vardi and Immerman's characterisation of the computational complexity class PTIME as the set of properties that are definable within first-order logic having a linear order relation symbol and augmented with the addition of a fixpoint operator possessing *least fixpoint* semantics [Var82a, Imm86]. We also mention that the computational complexity class PSPACE can be characterised as the set of properties that are definable within first-order logic having a linear order relation symbol and augmented with the addition of a fixpoint operator possessing *partial fixpoint* semantics [Var82a]; partial fixpoint semantics allows the inductive definition to repeat itself an exponential number of times, but using only a polynomial amount of space, when a least fixpoint does not exist.

Descriptive complexity is a significant route one can take in trying to solve hard problems in the area of computational complexity. As an example, Immerman has been able to solve a longstanding open problem using a result in descriptive complexity; specifically he has shown that nondeterministic space is closed under complementation [Imm88].

We now briefly discuss a fascinating connection between the asymptotic probability of a property, which informally measures the probability of a random structure possessing the property, and definability in a language of logic.

Assume a first-order language $\mathcal{L}$ having no constant symbols, and assume that the universe $[\mathcal{A}]$ of a structure $\mathcal{A}$ over $\mathcal{L}$ is always taken to be $\{0, 1, \ldots, n-1\}$ for some natural number n. Also, let C_n be the set of all structures over $\mathcal{L}$, where the universe is the set $\{0, 1, \ldots, n-1\}$ of cardinality n, and let $\mathcal{S}$ be a class of structures over $\mathcal{L}$ defining some property.

The *asymptotic probability* $\mu(\mathcal{S})$ is the limit as n tends to infinity of the fraction of structures over $\mathcal{L}$ whose universe has n elements and are in $\mathcal{S}$. Formally,

$$\mu(\mathcal{S}) = \lim_{n \to \infty} \mu_n(\mathcal{S}),$$

where

$$\mu_n(\mathcal{S}) = \frac{|\mathcal{S} \cap C_n|}{|C_n|}.$$

When the asymptotic probability of the property defined by a class of structures $\mathcal{S}$ over $\mathcal{L}$ is *one* then we say that *almost all* structures over $\mathcal{L}$ have this property, and when the said asymptotic probability is *zero* then we say that *almost no* structures over $\mathcal{L}$ have this property. Many interesting properties of graphs, which can be modelled as structures over a first-order language having a single binary relation symbol, are satisfied by almost all or almost no graphs [BH79]. For example, almost all graphs are connected and almost no graphs are planar. (A *planar* graph is a graph that can be drawn in the plane in such a way that no two edges cross each other.) On the other hand, not all properties have an asymptotic probability of zero or one. Thus, for example, the asymptotic probability of the property of having a universe with an even number of elements is undefined, since it oscillates between zero and one. As another example, suppose we allow $\mathcal{L}$ to have a single constant symbol, c, and that U is a unary relation symbol in $\mathcal{L}$. Then the property $U(c)$ of all structures, which have a tuple whose interpretation is c, has an asymptotic probability of $1/2$.

The asymptotic probability $\mu(\varphi)$ of a sentence φ over $\mathcal{L}$ is the asymptotic probability of the set of all structures which satisfy φ. More formally,

$$\mu(\varphi) = \mu(\{\mathcal{A} \mid \mathcal{A} \models \varphi\}).$$

A language $\mathcal{L}$ is said to have a *zero-one law* if the asymptotic probability of each of its sentences is either zero or one. Fagin [Fag76] and independently Glebskiĭ [GKLT69] proved the remarkable result that first-order logic has the zero-one law. It therefore follows that if the asymptotic probability of a property is *not* zero or one, then it is not definable in first-order logic. Thus for example, the zero-one law for first-order logic implies that the property of having a universe with an even number of elements is not first-order definable. It has been shown that the zero-one law also holds for fixpoint logic [BGK85]. A more general result is that the zero-one law also holds for the infinitary logic $L^k_{\infty\omega}$, where k is a natural number [KV92c].

The reader interested in the finite-model theory of nonclassical logics will also find strong links between such logics and database theory. The foundations, which underpin the treatment of incomplete information in relational databases, presented in Chapter 5, build upon three-valued, modal and fuzzy logics, while the foundations of temporal databases, presented in Chapter 7, build upon temporal logic. Moreover, recent research into deductive databases also known as logical databases, presented in Chapter 9, has made an immense contribution to the advancement of the theories of nonmonotonic and default logics.

The classical reference on model theory, now in its third edition, is [CK90], and a recent introduction to model theory is [Doe96]. Many of the seminal papers which laid the foundations of mathematical logic can be found in [Van67]. A recent book solely devoted to finite-model theory is [EF95]. Gurevich [Gur84] discusses in detail the failure of classical results in model theory, and Fagin [Fag93] presents a very informative perspective on the achievements of finite-model theory from a logician's point of view. A database theorist's point of view is given by Vianu [Via97a]; he surveys the achievements of database theory with the aim of convincing finite-model theorists that database theory provides a rich source of interesting and relevant problems. The reader will find in this book many connections between finite-model theory and database theory.

1.10 Exercises

Exercise 1.1   Assume that we have a relational data model at the conceptual database level. Argue for and against adding a new internal database level between the conceptual and physical levels, whose database schema is either hierarchical or nested relational. Define the notion of internal data independence when such an internal level is added to the DBMS levels [SPS87].

Exercise 1.2   Define relational, network and hierarchical conceptual database schemas for an application which manages exam results.

Exercise 1.3   With the widespread use of personal computers (PCs) it is common for a database system to be used by a single user only. Discuss how this situation eases the tasks the DBMS has to perform.

Exercise 1.4   At the physical level relations are stored as *files* and each tuple in a relation is stored as a *record* in the file. An *index* allows us to locate records in a file in a similar way to locating information in a book via an index. Thus an index to a file consists of the key values of records and their addresses indicating their location in the file. (See [Ull88] for more details on indexed files, and [Com79] for a survey on *B-trees*, which is a well-known technique for organising a file and its index.)

Justify the use of an indexed file for query optimisation purposes, as opposed to a sequential file organisation, where the records in a file are arranged in a particular order and a record can only be accessed when all the records prior to it in the file have been accessed. You must take into account the overhead of maintaining an indexed file compared to a sequential file.

Exercise 1.5   Indexed files allow *random access* to records, in the sense that any record in the file can be accessed independently of accessing any other record. A *hashed* file is a file which allows random access to its records without the need to maintain an index. The basic idea is to compute the location of a record by applying the key value of the desired record to an algorithm, called a *hashing algorithm*. A problem that may arise with a hashing algorithm is that of *collisions*, i.e. the hashing algorithm may map two different key values to the same location. In order to lessen the problem of collisions we can organise the records in a file in *buckets*, which have the capacity to store several records. Then we require that the result of the hashing algorithm return the address of the bucket in which the record is held, so that this bucket can be sequentially searched for the desired record. Still this does not completely solve the problem of collisions, since eventually a bucket may be full, and then an *overflow area* must be designated for new records with the same hashed location. (See [Wie77, Ull88] for more details on hashed files.)

Discuss the issues that determine whether you would choose a hashed file organisation for the physical storage of a relation as opposed to an indexed file organisation.

Exercise 1.6   Suggest how referential integrity may be maintained when primary and foreign key values of tuples in relations are updated [Dat86a, CT88, HR96]. Note that there may be several competing policies for integrity maintenance such as *blocking*, i.e. disallowing the update in certain circumstances, or *propagation* of the update to all tuples in the database which are affected by the update.

Exercise 1.7   Discuss the pros and the cons of having a computationally complete database language as a user query language.

Exercise 1.8   You may have heard of or already used a logic programming language, called Prolog, whose style is similar to that of Datalog. Suggest how a rule-based query language such as Datalog can combine general purpose programming with database programming.

Exercise 1.9   A recent proposal is to extend attribute domains of relation schemas so that they may be specified as user-defined abstract data types. For example, the user may define an abstract data type, ADDRESS, which is composed of the various address components such as house number, street name, city and postcode. Argue for and against calling such an extended relational data model, the *object-relational* data model [SM96].

Exercise 1.10   Suppose that we have available an object-oriented DBMS, which comes equipped with a computationally complete database programming language, called DPLOO, providing the interface between the user and the database. Discuss the validity of the statement that DPLOO queries are harder to optimise than SQL queries.

2. The Entity-Relationship Model

The Entity-Relationship model (abbreviated to ER model) is a data model, which allows us to model the semantics of a conceptual database schema. Actually, the ER model is only a partial data model, since it only caters for the data structure and integrity constraint parts of a data model with no provision being made for a query and update language.

The main motivation for defining the ER model [Che76, Che77] is to provide a high level model for conceptual database design, which acts as an intermediate stage prior to mapping the enterprise being modelled onto a conceptual level of say the relational model. The ER model explicitly incorporates in its constructs important semantic information about the real world, thus easing the task of the database designer. Furthermore, it achieves a high degree of data independence freeing the database designer from the details of the physical structure of the database.

The main semantics modelling constructs of the ER model are: entities, attributes of entities and relationships between entities. For example, we can have employee entities where each employee has the attributes: name, salary, address and phone numbers. Another example is department entities where each department has a name, a manager and a location. This type of abstraction, which forms a class of objects, in this case employee entities or department entities, from its component objects, in this case its set of attributes, is called *aggregation* [SS77, PM88]. An example of a relationship between employees and departments is that of "works in", meaning that an employee works in a department. This is also a type of abstraction, which forms a binary relationship between two types of entity. Another important semantic construct is that of *generalisation* [SS77, PM88] which ignores the differences between similar objects in order to form an object of higher type. For example, employee and student entities can be generalised to person entities. This type of abstraction can be viewed as *specialisation*, since both student and employee entities can be viewed as special cases of person entities. In the ER model generalisation is represented by a built-in relationship, called an *ISA relationship*. For example, an employee ISA person and a student ISA person. This means that both the sets of student and employee entities are a subset of the set of person entities. ISA relationships are useful since they allow *inheritance* of attributes [PM88]. In our example, student entities will inherit all the attributes of person entities. In addition to the inheritance of attributes, student entities may also have specific attributes not present in person entities, such as student id and the course they are taking.

The ER model has proved to be very successful in database design due its simple yet powerful graphical representation via *Entity-Relationship Diagrams* (ERDs). An ERD for describing the conceptual database schema of a computerised book order system is shown in Figure 2.1.

61

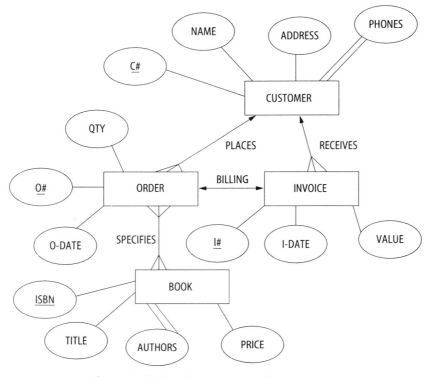

Fig 2.1 An ERD describing a computerised book order system

Intuitively, a Customer places Orders which specify the Books being ordered and each Order is billed by an Invoice, which is received by the Customer who ordered the Books.

The meaning of all the symbols used to represent an ERD will be discussed in Section 2.2 below. We mention that ERDs are widely used in software engineering for doing data analysis [MM85, You89, Pla92], since they provide a high level data independent description of the data involved in the system under development.

The ERD shown in Figure 2.1 represents the database schema, i.e. the types of the objects corresponding to the real world enterprise we are modelling. Our notation differs from the original notation encountered in [Che76, Che77] but is commonly used nowadays in industry [MM85]. On the other hand, there is no accepted notation for the instances of entity types and the relationships amongst relationship types; a conventional approach is the tabular approach as in the relational model. The main disadvantage of this approach is that the semantics which are explicitly represented in the ERD become implicit at the instance level. In Section 2.2 together with the detailed description of ERDs we propose to use a graphical notation in the spirit of the ER model for the actual entities and relationships (cf. [PL94, LL95b]).

The main advantages of ERDs are:

- They are relatively simple.

- They are user-friendly, i.e. they correspond to a natural view of the real world.

- They can be translated into database schemas of different data models such as the relational, network and hierarchical data models and thus can provide a unified view of data [Che76, Che77].

In Section 2.1 we define the concept of a graph. In Section 2.2 we present the building blocks of an ERD. In Section 2.3 we discuss recursive relationships. In Section 2.4 we discuss weak entity types, and in Section 2.5 we describe the steps a database designer should follow when constructing an ERD.

2.1 Graphs

In this section we define the concept of a graph [Cha77, Wil85, BH90], which is the mathematical concept that underpins the notion of a diagram.

Definition 2.1 (Graph and subgraph)   A graph is an ordered pair (N, E), where N is a finite set of *nodes* (also called *vertices*) and E is a set *edges* such that each edge, $e = \{u, v\}$, is an unordered pair of distinct nodes of E.

Both nodes and edges can be *labelled*, i.e. they can be annotated by a number or a string to add meaning to the graph. At times we also label the graph as a whole in order to distinguish it from other graphs.

A directed graph (or simply a digraph) is a special case of a graph (N, E), where E is a set of *arcs* such that each arc, $e = (u, v)$, is an ordered pair of nodes of E. If $(u, v) \in E$, then we say that there is an arc from u to v in E.

A subgraph (or a subdigraph if the graph is directed) of a graph (N, E) is a graph having all of its nodes in N and all of its edges in E. For any subset S of N, the subgraph of (N, E) *induced* by S is the maximal subgraph of (N, E) having S as its node set.   ∎

Definition 2.2 (Acyclic and cyclic graphs)   A *walk* (of length k) from node $u \in N$ to node $v \in$ N in a directed graph (N, E) is an alternating sequence of nodes $n_i \in N$ and arcs $e_i \in E$

$$n_0, e_1, n_1, e_2, n_2, \ldots, e_k, n_k,$$

where $n_0 = u$, $n_k = v$ and $e_i = (n_{i-1}, n_i)$, $1 \le i \le k$. If the graph is undirected then we replace (n_{i-1}, n_i) by the unordered pair $\{n_{i-1}, n_i\}$.

A *path* from u to v is a walk from u to v in which all the nodes n_i, $0 \le i \le k$, are distinct. A *cycle* (from u) is a walk from u to v in which $u = v$ (i.e. it is a closed walk) and such that all the n_i, $1 \le i \le k - 1$, are distinct.

A graph (which is either directed or undirected) is *acyclic* if it does not contain any cycles, otherwise if it contains at least one cycle then it is *cyclic*. In the case when the graph is not directed, a connected acyclic graph is called a *tree*; a graph is *connected* if there is a path joining each distinct pair of its nodes.   ∎

We next give some examples of the usefulness of graphs. In Figure 2.2 we show a graph representing a network of motorways between cities; the labels of the nodes denote the names

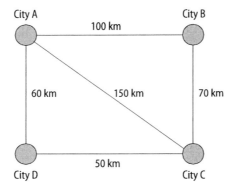

Fig 2.2 Graph representing a network of motorways

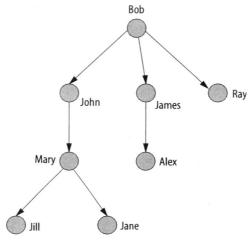

Fig 2.3 Digraph representing a company hierarchy

of the cities and the labels of the edges denote the distance in kilometres between the cities. This type of graph (or digraph) is called a *network*.

In Figure 2.3 we show a digraph representing a company hierarchy between employees. The labels of the nodes denote the employees' names. This type of graph is called a tree (see Definition 2.2) and a collection of trees is called a *forest*.

In Figure 2.4 we show a digraph representing the machine parts supplied to projects. This type of digraph is called a *data structure diagram* [Bac69].

We note that the direction of the arc is represented diagrammatically by an arrow head. If an arc is bidirectional, i.e. both (u, v) and (v, u) are in E, then we can just draw a line between u and v as we would in the case of an edge $\{u, v\}$. Thus a bidirectional arc can be viewed as an edge. At times when the direction of the arc is understood from context we refer to an arc as an edge. We observe that the ERD shown in Figure 2.1 is also a digraph. The exact meaning of the labelling system used for ERDs will be explained in the following sections.

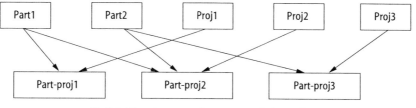

Fig 2.4 Digraph representing parts supplied to projects

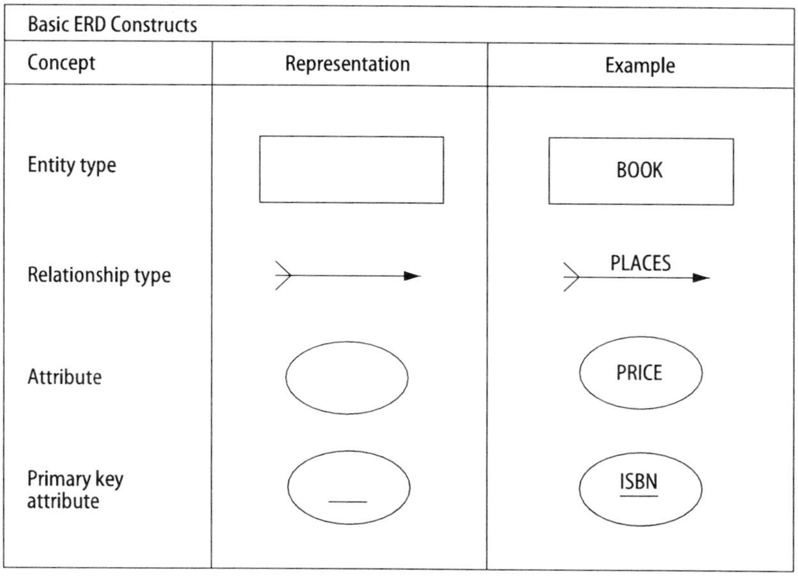

Basic ERD Constructs		
Concept	Representation	Example
Entity type		BOOK
Relationship type		PLACES
Attribute		PRICE
Primary key attribute		ISBN

Fig 2.5 Summary of the basic ERD constructs

2.2 The Building Blocks of an Entity-Relationship Diagram (ERD)

An ERD has only three components:

1) *Entity types* represented by labelled boxes.

2) *Relationship types* represented by labelled arcs, which connect the two entity types participating in the relationship type.

3) *Attributes* represented by labelled ellipses, which are connected to an entity type by an edge.

A summary of the basic ERD constructs is shown in the table of Figure 2.5.

For example, in the ERD shown in Figure 2.1 CUSTOMER and ORDER are entity types, PLACES is a relationship type between CUSTOMER and ORDER and NAME and ADDRESS are attributes of CUSTOMER.

2.2.1   Entities

Definition 2.3 (Entity)   An *entity* (or an object) is a "thing" that exists and is distinguishable, i.e. it can be uniquely identified.   ■

The following are examples of entities:

1) A particular person, say Mark, is an entity.

2) A particular department, say the UCL Computer Science department, is an entity.

3) A particular book, say this book, is an entity.

Definition 2.4 (Entity type)   An *entity type* (sometimes called an entity set) is a collection (or a set) of *similar* entities.   ■

The following are examples of entity types:

1) The entity type of all lecturers in UCL, say LECTURER.

2) The entity type of all students in UCL, say STUDENT.

3) The entity type of all cars in London, say CAR.

Note that, in general, an entity may belong to more than one entity type. For example, Mark may belong to both the entity types PERSON and LECTURER. An instance of an entity type is a set of entities which contains the actual entities of the entity type that are stored in the database. (When no ambiguity arises we also call an instance of an entity type simply an entity set.) We depict an instance of an entity type by a graph which is labelled by the entity type and whose nodes represent the entities in the instance. For some examples of instances of entity types see Figure 2.6.

By convention each node (or entity) in the instance is represented by a string beginning with "$". We observe that since we are dealing with a database system each instance of an entity type can only contain a finite number of entities although the set of possible entities in an entity type may be infinite for all practical purposes.

2.2.2   Relationships and their Functionality

Definition 2.5 (Relationship type)   A (binary) *relationship type* among entity types is an association among two entity types.   ■

The following are examples of relationship types:

1) TEACHES is a relationship type between LECTURER and STUDENT.

2) TUTORS is also a relationship type between LECTURER and STUDENT.

3) ASSIGNED_TO is a relationship type between EMPLOYEE and DEPARTMENT.

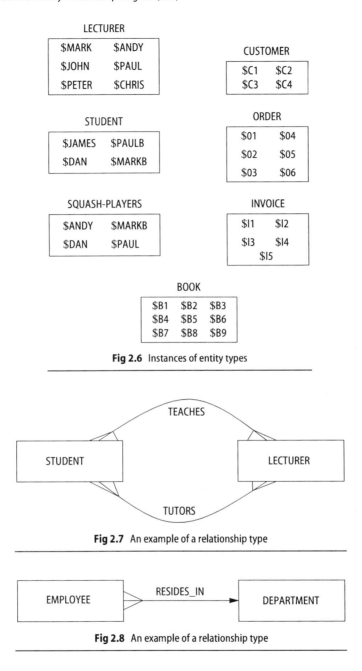

Fig 2.6 Instances of entity types

Fig 2.7 An example of a relationship type

Fig 2.8 An example of a relationship type

We observe that as in TEACHES and TUTORS above there may be more than one relationship type between any two entity types. Relationship types are linked to the entity sets participating in the relationship type by edges whose end points are either arrow heads or crow's feet; the meaning of this notation will be explained below. Some examples of relationship types are shown in Figures 2.7, 2.8, 2.9 and 2.10.

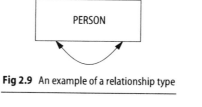

Fig 2.9 An example of a relationship type

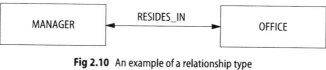

Fig 2.10 An example of a relationship type

We refer to a relationship as the instance of a relationship type, i.e. to the set of pairs of entities that are constructed from the entity types over which the relationship type is defined and that participate in the actual relationship that is stored in the database. In mathematical terms a relationship is just a (binary) set-theoretic relation (see Section 1.9.1). For simplicity of the model we will always assume that any entity in an instance of an entity type may or may not participate in a relationship. Thus, for example, if $John is an entity belonging to an instance of EMPLOYEE, then $John may or may not participate in an ASSIGNED_TO relationship. That is, we are assuming that $John may or may not be assigned to a department. This allows the participation in a relationship of entities, in an entity type of a relationship type, to be *optional* (or *partial*). In general, it is also possible to constrain the participation in a relationship of entities, in an instance of an entity type of a relationship type, to be *mandatory* (or *total*), i.e. if we insist that every entity in the instance of the entity type participates in the relationship. Such a distinction is made in [MM85, BCN92, Teo94]. By default we assume that the participation of entities in relationships is optional.

In the following we will use the term *cardinality* of a set to be the number of elements in that set (see Section 1.9.1). Let R be a relationship type connecting the two entity types E_1 and E_2. We now classify a relationship type according to how many entities in an instance of E_1 can be associated with how many entities in an instance of E_2, within an instance of the relationship type R. That is, we classify relationship types according to the cardinality ratio between the instances of the two participating entity types. Now, let r be a relationship over R and let e_1 and e_2 be entities belonging to instances of E_1 and E_2, respectively, such that e_1 and e_2 participate in r. Then we say that R is

- *many-to-one* if every entity e_1 as defined above is associated in r with at most one entity belonging to an instance of E_2.

- *one-to-many* if every entity e_2 as defined above is associated in r with at most one entity belonging to an instance of E_1.

- *one-to-one* if every entity e_1 as defined above is associated in r with at most one entity belonging to an instance of E_2, and correspondingly every entity e_2 as defined above is associated in r with at most one entity belonging to an instance of E_1.

- *many-to-many* if every entity e_1 as defined above is associated in r with zero or more entities belonging to an instance of E_2, and correspondingly every entity e_2 as defined above is associated in r with zero or more entities belonging to an instance of E_1.

We note that the definitions of many-to-one and one-to-many are symmetric with respect to E_1 and E_2 and that R is one-to-one if and only if it is many-to-one and one-to-many. Furthermore, R is many-to-many if it is neither many-to-one or one-to-many. In mathematical terms a many-to-one relationship type induces a partial *mapping* (or *function*) from instances of E_1 to instances of E_2, and correspondingly a one-to-many relationship type induces a partial mapping from instances of E_2 to instances of E_1 (see Section 1.9.1). Furthermore, a one-to-one relationship type induces a partial one-to-one mapping from instances of E_1 to instances of E_2. Finally, a many-to-many relationship type induces a (mathematical) relation between instances of E_1 and instances of E_2.

Some examples of the functionality of relationship types are now given:

1) The relationship type ASSIGNED_TO between EMPLOYEE and DEPARTMENT is many-to-one.

2) The relationship type EMPLOYS between DEPARTMENT and EMPLOYEE is one-to-many.

3) The relationship type MANAGES between MANAGER and DEPARTMENT is one-to-one.

4) The relationship types TEACHES and TUTORS between LECTURER and STUDENT are many-to-many.

We use the following notation in an ERD to indicate the functionality of a relationship type R from E_1 to E_2:

1) If R is one-to-one then the end points of the edge connecting E_1 and E_2 are both depicted by arrow heads.

2) If R is many-to-one then the end points of the edge connecting E_1 and E_2 are depicted by a crow's foot on the E_1 side and an arrow head on the E_2 side.

3) If R is one-to-many then the end points of the edge connecting E_1 and E_2 are depicted by an arrow head on the E_1 side and a crow's foot on the E_2 side.

4) If R is many-to-many then the end points of the edge connecting E_1 and E_2 are both depicted by crow's feet.

A summary of the constructs for an ERD relationship type is shown in the table of Figure 2.11.

As with instances of entity types, instances of relationship types are also depicted as graphs. In this case the graph is labelled by the relationship type, its nodes represent the entities that participate in the relationship and its edges (or arcs) represent the associations which make up the relationship. As in our representation of instances of entities the nodes in the relationship are represented by strings beginning with a "$". For some examples of instances of relationship types see Figure 2.12.

We note that the graphs that represent instances of relationship types are *bipartite* graphs, i.e. their node set N is partitioned into two subsets, say N_1 and N_2, such that every edge (or arc) in E joins a node in N_1 with a node in N_2, and no node joins with another node of its own subset. Diagrammatically, we can see in Figure 2.12 that the node sets N_1 and N_2 of a bipartite

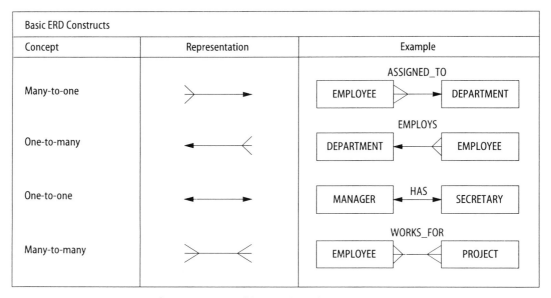

Fig 2.11 Summary of the ERD relationship type constructs

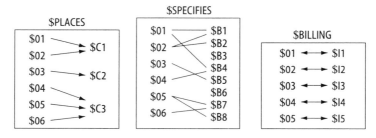

Fig 2.12 Examples of instances of relationship types

graph can be depicted each in a separate column and each edge in E joins a node from one column to the other. The node set N_1 is seen to represent the set of entities E_1 and N_2 is seen to represent the set of entities E_2.

In the formalism we have presented herein we have restricted ourselves to binary relationship types, since they are the most common in practice. In fact this is not a restriction, since any relationship type can always be reduced to a set of binary relationship types. For example, suppose that we have the entity types, SUPPLIER, PART and PROJECT, with a ternary relationship type between these three entity types meaning that a Supplier supplies many Parts to many Projects. In Figure 2.13 we show how this ternary relationship type can be expressed as a set of three binary relationship types, via the new entity type SPP.

We close this section with a bit of controversy. It has been claimed in [Dat92b] that there is no clear distinction between the concepts of entity and relationship, i.e. one person's entity may be another person's relationship. For example, suppose that we are designing an airline's flight database. Then, a FLIGHT may be considered as a relationship type between an entity type ROUTE and an entity type AIRCRAFT or as an entity type in its own right. There are two

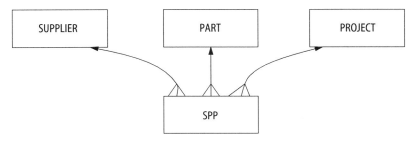

Fig 2.13 A binary relationship type representing a ternary relationship type

answers one can give to such critics of the ER model. The first answer is that the ER model provides the flexibility to model real-world enterprises in several different ways. This is an advantage, since in any case there is always more than one way of viewing the semantics of any application under development and, in general, there is no one definitive design. Furthermore, from the practical point of view the distinction between entity and relationship seems to be very useful and it is clear that without relationship types the semantics of the data model would be greatly reduced. The second answer is that if the relationship type is such that it needs to have attributes then it must be modelled as an entity type, since we do not allow relationship types to have their own attributes. Thus, if we would like to model the flight's date as an attribute of FLIGHT rather than an attribute of ROUTE, then FLIGHT must be modelled as an entity type. We note that in the original ER model of Chen [Che76, Che77] relationship types are allowed to have their own attributes. It follows that the variation of the ER model we have presented herein has the advantage of simplifying the problem of deciding whether to represent some part of the enterprise as an entity or as a relationship.

2.2.3   Attributes and Domains

Definition 2.6 (Attribute)   *Attribute names* (or simply attributes) are properties of entity types. ∎

The following are examples of attributes:

1) SOC#, PNAME, SPOUSE, CNAMES, HEIGHT and ADDRESS are attributes of PERSON.

2) DNAME, COLLEGE, ADDRESS and PHONES are attributes of DEPARTMENT.

3) SERIAL#, MODEL, COLOUR and ENGINE_SIZE are attributes of CAR.

We distinguish between *single-valued* attributes such as PNAME, DNAME and ADDRESS and *multi-valued* attributes such as CNAMES and PHONES. In the ERD we represent the fact that an attribute is single-valued by connecting it to its entity type with a single line and the fact that an attribute is multi-valued by connecting it to its entity type by a double line; see Figure 2.1 for examples of single-valued and multi-valued attributes in an ERD.

The domain of an attribute indicates what values the attribute can take. Domains can be viewed as giving meaning (or semantics) to attributes.

Definition 2.7 (Domain)   The *domain* of an attribute of an entity type is a set of constant values (or simply values) associated with that attribute.   ∎

A domain is *atomic* (or primitive) if its values are nondecomposable, i.e. as far as the database system is concerned they have no internal structure. Examples of atomic domains are the domain of all positive integers, the domain of integers between 10 and 10,000, the domain of all strings over the English alphabet and the domain of all strings of length 20 over the English alphabet. A domain is *set-valued* if its values are finite sets of atomic domains, i.e. a set-valued domain is a subset of the *power set* of an atomic domain. Examples of set-valued domains are the domains of finite sets of integers and the domain of finite sets of strings.

We note that a domain may be finite or countably infinite. (A set is countably infinite if it can be put into a one-to-one correspondence with the set of all natural numbers; see Section 1.9.1.) Furthermore, we observe that we can view domains in terms of *Data Dictionary* (DD) definitions, where atomic domains are specified by primitive DD definitions and set-valued domains are specified by iterated DD definitions [You89].

An attribute for a given entity type, say E, associates with each specific entity in an instance of E, a unique *attribute value* (or simply a value) from its domain. That is, an attribute can be considered as a mapping from an instance of its underlying entity type to its domain.

Let *att* be an attribute of the entity type E and *ent* be an entity in an instance of E. The value that *att* associates with *ent* is denoted by *att(ent)*.

For example, let P1 be an entity in an instance of the entity type PERSON. Then we may have:

    SOC#($P1) = 45671,
    PNAME($P1) = Jack,
    SPOUSE($P1) = Lisa,
    CNAMES($P1) = {Jill, Mary, Mona},
    HEIGHT($P1) = 187 and
    ADDRESS($P1) = "North London".

As another example, let D2 be an entity in an instance of the entity type DEPARTMENT. Then we may have:

    DNAME($D2) = "Computer Science",
    COLLEGE($D2) = "UCL",
    ADDRESS($D2) = "Central London" and
    PHONES($D2) = {3807777, 3877050}.

We depict the attribute values of an entity, say *ent*, as a digraph labelled by *ent* as follows:

1) For each attribute we have a node in the digraph labelled with the name of the attribute, which is denoted by a string of uppercase letters possibly containing the underscore character.

2) For each attribute value we have a node in the digraph labelled with the value of the attribute, which is denoted by a string containing at least one lowercase letter or a string surrounded by double quotes or a natural number.

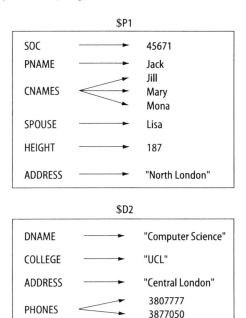

Fig 2.14 Digraphs that depict entities

3) For each single-valued attribute, designated SATT, we draw an arc from SATT to its value, say *val*, representing the fact that SATT(*ent*) = *val*. (That is, for single-valued attributes we have a single arc for the only attribute value.)

4) For each multi-valued attribute, designated MATT, and each value, say *val*$_i$, with *val*$_i$ ∈ MATT(*ent*), we draw an arc from MATT to *val*$_i$. (That is, for multi-valued attributes we may have multiple arcs, one for each attribute value.)

Our graphical representation allows a natural representation of missing information of the type value *does not exist*. For example, if CNAMES($P1) = ∅, i.e. $P1 does not have any children, then in the digraph for $P1 we do not have any arcs emanating from CNAMES. In addition, if SPOUSE($P1) is undefined or inapplicable, i.e. $P1 does not have a spouse, then in the digraph for $P1 we do not have any arcs emanating from SPOUSE. Some examples of the digraphs that depict entities are shown in Figure 2.14.

2.2.4 Keys

Definition 2.8 (Key and superkey)   An attribute or a set of attributes, whose values uniquely identify each entity in an instance of an entity type, is called a *superkey* for the entity type.

If a set of attributes K is a superkey for an entity type E and, in addition, no proper subset of K is a superkey for E (i.e. K is a minimal set of attributes that is a superkey for E) then K is called a *candidate key* (or a *minimal key* or simply a *key*) for E.

A *simple* key for E is a key for E which is composed of a single attribute. ∎

In other words a key is a minimal set of attributes that uniquely determines each entity in an instance of an entity type. From now on we will assume that keys contain at least one attribute, i.e. we disallow keys to be the empty set of attributes.

The following are examples of simple keys:

1) {SOC#} (or simply SOC#) is a simple key for PERSON.

2) {PHONES} (or simply PHONES) is a simple key for DEPARTMENT.

3) {SERIAL#} (or simply SERIAL#) is a simple key for CAR.

A *composite* key is a key composed of two or more attributes. The following are examples of composite keys:

1) {DNAME, COLLEGE} is a composite key for DEPARTMENT.

2) {PNAME, ADDRESS} is a composite key for PERSON.

We now make several observations:

- Every entity type must have at least one key, since we define entities to be distinguishable.

- In the absence of a natural key we can create an artificial simple key such as SERIAL#, EMP# and PROJECT#, which assigns a unique number to each entity in an instance of an entity type. Such artificial simple keys are called *surrogate* keys.

- Simple keys are easier to specify and to maintain than composite keys but may have been artificially created.

- An entity type may have more than one key; for example, the entity types PERSON and DEPARTMENT have multiple keys. Thus for such entity types one of the keys is designated as the *primary* key, and the other keys are called *alternate keys*. The primary key provides a guaranteed logical access to every entity in an instance of an entity type through the attribute values of the entity.

In the ERD we represent the fact that an attribute belongs to the primary key by underlining the attribute; see Figure 2.1 for examples of key attributes in an ERD.

Definition 2.9 (Primary key of a relationship type)   Let E_1 and E_2 be the entity types participating in a relationship type R, with K_1 being the primary key of E_1 and K_2 being the primary key of K_2. The primary key of R is determined according to the following cases:

1) If R is many-to-many then $K_1 \cup K_2$ is the primary key of R.

2) If R is one-to-many then K_2 is the primary key of R.

3) If R is many-to-one then K_1 is the primary key of R.

4) If R is one-to-one then either K_1 or K_2 is the primary key of R.   ■

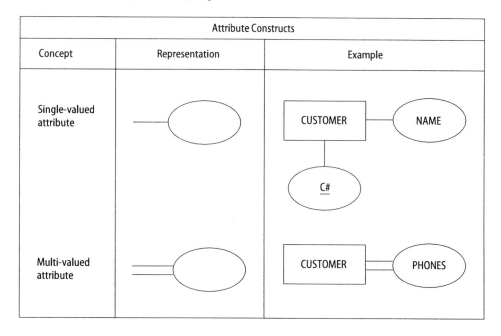

Fig 2.15 Summary of the ERD attribute constructs

In this definition we assume, without loss of generality, that K_1 and K_2 are disjoint; we can always enforce this disjointness by adding to each attribute a *role name* corresponding to the entity type it belongs to; see Section 2.3. We further note that in all cases $K_1 \cup K_2$ is a superkey for R.

The following example gives the primary keys of two relationship types:

1) Assume that there is a many-to-many relationship, SPECIFIES, between ORDER and BOOK, that O# is the primary key of ORDER and that B# is the primary key of BOOK. Then {O#, B#} is the primary key of SPECIFIES.

2) Assume that there is a many-to-one relationship, ASSIGNED_TO, between EMPLOYEE and DEPARTMENT, that {DNAME, COLLEGE} is the primary key of DEPARTMENT and that EMP# is the primary key of EMPLOYEE. Then {EMP#, DNAME, COLLEGE} is a superkey for ASSIGNED_TO and {EMP#} is its primary key.

3) Assume that there is a one-to-one relationship, BILLING, between ORDER and INVOICE, that O# is the primary key of ORDER and that I# is the primary key of INVOICE. Then {O#, I#} is a superkey for BILLING and either O# or I# is the primary key of BILLING.

A summary of the attribute constructs of an ERD is shown in the table of Figure 2.15.

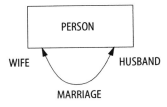

Fig 2.16 Marriage relationship type

2.3   Recursive Relationships

Definition 2.10 (Recursive relationship)   A relationship type between two occurrences of the same entity type is called a *recursive* relationship type (or alternatively a *cyclic* relationship type). ∎

Some examples of recursive relationship types are:

1) MARRIAGE, which is a recursive relationship type between PERSON and PERSON.

2) PARENT-CHILD, which is a recursive relationship type between PERSON and PERSON.

3) PART-SUBPART, which is a recursive relationship type between PART and PART.

In order to uniquely identify a recursive relationship we firstly need to determine the *role* each occurrence of the entity type plays in the relationship.

For example, in MARRIAGE one person plays the role of husband and the other the role of wife. In PARENT-CHILD one person plays the role of the parent and the other the role of the child. On the other hand, in PART-SUBPART one part plays the role of superpart and the other part plays the role of subpart. Thus we create a *role name* for each occurrence of the entity type involved in the recursive relationship type.

In order to create the primary key for a recursive relationship type we first take two copies of the primary key of the entity type involved in the relationship type. We then concatenate the role names of each entity type participating in the relationship type to each attribute in each copy of the primary key and finally take the union of the two resulting sets when appropriate. The resulting set of attributes is the primary key of the recursive relationship type. For example, if in the relationship type MARRIAGE the attached role names are husband and wife, then the primary key of MARRIAGE is either {HUSBAND_SOC#} or {WIFE_SOC#}.

In the ERD we label each end point of the edge connecting the recursive relationship type to itself with the appropriate role name; see Figure 2.16 for the ERD of the MARRIAGE relationship type.

2.4   Weak Entity Types

The existence of an entity in an instance of an entity type may depend on the existence of another entity in an instance of another entity type. The most common example is that of child entities depending on their parent entities; for example, when we record the children of employee entities. Assume that the current database has an instance, say P, of PARENT and an instance, say C, of CHILD. Then in this case a CHILD entity would not be present in C unless its parent entity exists in P. Such an entity type as CHILD is called a *weak* entity type. Another example of a weak entity type arises via the concept of inheritance of attributes. Suppose that we have the entity types PERSON, EMPLOYEE and STUDENT with respective instances P, E and S, where both E and S are subsets of P. Thus, each EMPLOYEE entity is a special case of a PERSON entity and similarly each STUDENT entity is a special case of a PERSON entity. In other words, each person entity can be viewed as a general case of an EMPLOYEE entity and a general case of a STUDENT entity. It follows that the existence of a STUDENT entity depends on the existence of its corresponding PERSON entity and similarly the existence of an EMPLOYEE entity depends on the existence of its corresponding PERSON entity. Such entity types as EMPLOYEE and STUDENT that arise via generalisation are also called *weak* entity types.

Weak entity types can depend on other entity types through two built-in relationship types, the *ID* relationship type and the *ISA* relationship type.

Definition 2.11 (ID relationship type)   An entity type E_1 is related to entity type E_2 via an ID relationship type (or simply E_1 ID E_2) if the primary key of E_1 comprises the primary key of E_2 together with one or more additional attributes of E_1. ∎

For example, suppose that we have a PARENT entity type and a CHILD entity type, where the attributes of PARENT are: SOC#, PNAME, ADDRESS and AGE and the attributes of CHILD are: AGE and CNAME. Furthermore, suppose that the primary key of PARENT is SOC#. Then CHILD ID PARENT holds and the primary key of CHILD is: {SOC#, CNAME}, i.e. in order to uniquely identify a CHILD we need to know the social security number of the child's parent and the child's name. In the ERD we represent an ID relationship, E_1 ID E_2, as a many-to-one relationship from E_1 to E_2 labelled by ID; see Figure 2.17 for the ERD representing the ID relationship type from CHILD to PARENT.

Definition 2.12 (ISA relationship type)   An entity type E_1 is related to entity type E_2 via an ISA relationship type (or simply E_1 ISA E_2) if the primary key of E_1 is the same as the primary key of E_2. In addition, if I_1 and I_2 are the instances of E_1 and E_2, respectively, currently recorded in the database, then I_1 is a subset of I_2 (strictly speaking, the set of primary key values of I_1 is a subset of the set of primary key values of I_2). ∎

For example, suppose we have an EMPLOYEE entity type having attributes: SOC#, PNAME, ADDRESS and SALARY, with primary key SOC#. In addition, suppose we have a MANAGER entity type having the same attributes as EMPLOYEE with the additional attribute DNAME, which indicates the department name the manager is responsible for. Then MANAGER ISA EMPLOYEE holds, and the primary key of MANAGER is the same as the primary key of EMPLOYEE, i.e. SOC#. Furthermore, every MANAGER entity in the current instance of MANAGER recorded in the database is also present in the current instance of EMPLOYEE recorded in the database.

As a consequence of Definition 2.12, if E_1 ISA E_2 then E_1 *inherits* all the attributes of E_2. Thus each entity e_1 in an instance of E_1 derives all the information that is currently available

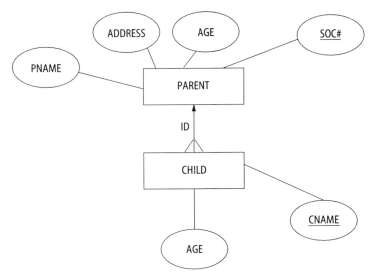

Fig 2.17 ID relationship type from CHILD to PARENT

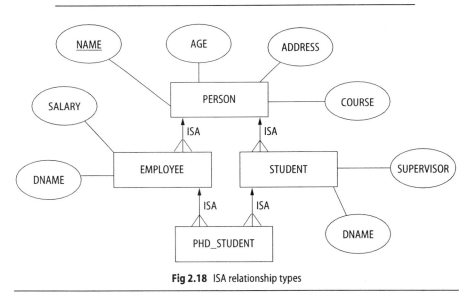

Fig 2.18 ISA relationship types

for its corresponding entity e_2 in an instance of E_2, whenever e_1 and e_2 have the same primary key values.

In the ERD we represent an ISA relationship, E_1 ISA E_2, as a many-to-one relationship from E_1 to E_2 labelled by ISA; see Figure 2.18 for an ERD representing several ISA relationship types. We note that if E_1 ISA E_2 we need not repeat the attributes of E_2 in the ERD representation of E_1 due to the inheritance of attributes.

The situation where an entity type inherits all the attributes of two or more further entity types is called *multiple inheritance*. That is, we have E_1 ISA E_2 and E_1 ISA E_3, where E_2 and E_3 are distinct entity types. In the ERD, shown in Figure 2.18, we have an instance of multiple

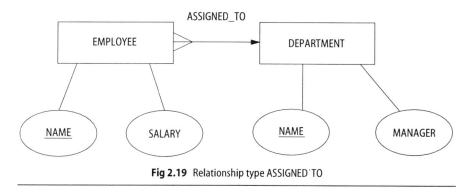

Fig 2.19 Relationship type ASSIGNED TO

inheritance, since PHD_STUDENT ISA EMPLOYEE and PHD_STUDENT ISA STUDENT both hold. Multiple inheritance gives rise to attribute inheritance conflicts whenever an entity type inherits the same attribute name from two or more distinct entity types. In the ERD, shown in Figure 2.18, PHD_STUDENT inherits DNAME from both EMPLOYEE and STUDENT. The problem is that DNAME may have different meanings in EMPLOYEE and STUDENT. That is, DNAME in EMPLOYEE may mean the department an employee works in and DNAME in STUDENT may mean the department the student is enrolled in. Furthermore, in general, a PhD student may work in a different department to that which he/she is enrolled in. There are various ways to deal with multiple inheritance, one being to enforce some preference ordering on inherited attributes in order to resolve conflicts. We prefer to avoid conflicts altogether by requiring attribute names to have a global meaning in the ERD. The following definition formalises this assumption.

Definition 2.13 (Universal relation schema assumption)   An ERD is said to satisfy the *Universal Relation Schema Assumption* (or simply URSA) if each attribute of an entity type plays a unique role in the ERD. That is, all occurrences of an attribute name in an ERD are assumed to have the same meaning. ■

The URSA solves another problem highlighted in the ERD shown in Figure 2.19, which depicts a relationship type ASSIGNED_TO between the EMPLOYEE and DEPARTMENT entity types. Both EMPLOYEE and DEPARTMENT have an attribute, called NAME, meaning employee name and department name, respectively. When we are referring to NAME, there should be no ambiguity as long as it is clear from the context whether we mean employee name or department name. The URSA resolves this ambiguity that may arise when referring to attribute names by insisting that we have two distinct attribute names, say ENAME for employee name, and DNAME for department name.

From now on, we assume that ERDs satisfy the URSA. The URSA can also be viewed as the assumption that the name of an attribute uniquely determines its underlying domain. The URSA is not as restrictive as it may seem, since it can always be enforced by a suitable renaming of attribute names. In our example above, if DNAME does mean two different things in EMPLOYEE and STUDENT, then DNAME in EMPLOYEE can be renamed to WORK_DNAME and DNAME in STUDENT can be renamed to ENROL_DNAME.

There has been some controversy about the validity of the URSA [Ken81, Ken83b]. In particular, it has been claimed that due to the necessity of renaming attributes, some attributes

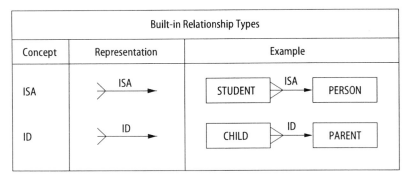

Fig 2.20 Summary of the ERD built-in relationship type constructs

will receive unintuitive names. However, as stated in [Ull83] there is no real practical evidence to that effect, and in particular it does not seem to be true that in practice many attributes have to be renamed. In fact, although the URSA is not always made explicit, it seems to be fundamental in the initial stage of database design and relational database design in particular. We note that the URSA does not involve the stronger assumptions made in the context of the *Universal Relation*, i.e. the unique role assumption and the one-flavour assumption [MUV84, MRW86, Var89b, Lev92], which are harder to justify.

Our approach to defining weak entity types is similar to that taken in [MR92a], which can be viewed as a formalisation of the original approach in [Che76, Che77] in terms of the relationship of the primary keys of the entity types involved in the relationship type. A summary of the ERD built-in relationship type constructs is presented in the table of Figure 2.20.

2.5   The Steps Needed for Constructing an ERD

Constructing an ERD for the enterprise being modelled is a data analysis activity and involves abstracting the semantics of the data being used in the application under development. There are several methodologies a data analyst can use for this purpose with varying degrees of formality (see [BCN92, Teo94] for detailed methodologies). We will content ourselves with outlining the major steps that a database designer ought to take when constructing an ERD:

1) Identify the entity types (including weak entity types) of the enterprise.

2) Draw some instances of the identified entity types.

3) Identify the relationship types (including ISA and ID relationship types) of the enterprise.

4) Classify each relationship type identified in step 3 according to its functionality, i.e. if it is a one-to-one, many-to-one (equivalently one-to-many) or many-to-many.

5) Draw some instances of the identified relationship types.

6) Draw an ERD with the entity types and the relationship types between them.

7) Identify the attributes of entity types and their underlying domains; if you are familiar with DD notation then give the DD definitions of the domains (recall that DD is an abbreviation for data dictionary).

8) Identify a primary key for each entity type.

9) Draw some instances of attribute values of entities.

10) Add the attributes and keys to the ERD drawn in step 6.

The main purpose of steps (2), (5) and (9), which involve drawing example instances, is to verify by example that the previous identification steps faithfully model the enterprise.

Let us assume that we are planning to implement the application under development over a relational DBMS. After the ERD has been finalised, it is possible to convert it into a relational database schema using an algorithmic approach [JNS83a, JNS83b, CA84, DA87, MM90, MR92a, Teo94]. The main benefit of this approach is that data analysts can use the ERDs, which provide us with an intuitive and high level picture of the enterprise being modelled, without worrying themselves, at this stage of the design process, with the details of the relational database schema. We will present such a conversion algorithm in Chapter 4, which deals with relational database design.

2.6 Discussion

The ER approach to data modelling has become a very popular paradigm for conceptual database design. It is widely used in industry during systems analysis and design due to its relative simplicity and its naturalness. We will return to the ER model in Chapter 4 in the context of relational database design, where we will show how to convert an ERD into a relational database schema.

The ER model was pioneered in Chen's seminal paper [Che76] (see also the monograph [Che77]). At the time there was ongoing debate between proponents of the relational model on the one hand and hierarchical and network models on the other hand. The ER model was proposed as a higher level model with the view of translating an ERD into a conceptual schema in any of these three data models. Arguments in favour of the binary relationship concept as the smallest meaningful concept can be found in [Abr74, BPP76]. Some early ideas relating to the semantics of entities and relationships in terms of the relational model can be found in [SS75] and [Ken79]; therein the entity, relationship and attribute approach is advocated. Although the original ER model had no provision for querying instances of entity types and relationship types, there have been several proposals of algebras for the ER model [Che84, PS87]. These algebras are similar to the relational algebra and include operators for: projecting specified attribute values of entities in an instance, selecting entities from an instance which satisfy certain selection criteria, taking the union and difference of two instances of an entity type and joining two instances of two entity types via an instance of a relationship type in order to create an instance of a new entity type. The ER model has also been extended to include concepts such as complex objects [AH87, PS89], incomplete information [ZC86] and view updates [LL96b].

Several books have been solely devoted to the ER model; [BCN92, Teo94] concentrate on data modelling issues and [Pla92] concentrates on system modelling issues. Both [BCN92] and [Pla92] show how functional and data analysis can be done jointly by incorporating ERD information into *Data Flow Diagrams* (DFDs). This highlights the importance of database design in the software engineering process. A recent book [MR92a] makes extensive use of the ER model in the process of relational database design.

The ER model can be viewed as a *visual formalism* which conceptualises part of the real world. Other visual formalisms which were proposed for knowledge representation are: conceptual graphs [Sow76], higraphs [Har87, Har88], concept lattices [Wil92] and hypernodes [PL94, LL95b].

2.7 Exercises

Exercise 2.1   We have presented an ER model in which the relationships are restricted to be binary. Discuss the pros and cons of binary versus general *n*-ary relationships.

Exercise 2.2   In the ER model there are entities and relationships, although it is possible to view a relationship as a special kind of entity. Why do you think the ER model supports entities and relationships as two distinct concepts?

Exercise 2.3   Discuss the statement that the ER model provides an informal foundation for the relational model.

Exercise 2.4   Construct an ERD for an application whereby a company would like to record information about its employees and managers, information about the projects they work on and the various locations of projects.

Exercise 2.5   Discuss the view that the ER model supports the fundamental concepts of an object-oriented data model.

Exercise 2.6   Given an ERD describing the conceptual schema of an application, suggest how ERDs can be used to describe the view schema of the application. In particular, care has to be taken so that the semantics of the view schemas are consistent with those of the conceptual schema.

Exercise 2.7   Data flow diagrams (DFDs) represent a diagrammatic tool that is used in software engineering in order to describe the interconnection of processes for a given application being analysed. Suggest an outline of a proposal for integrating the analysis of the processes and data for a given application using ERDs.

Exercise 2.8   Consider an application where we would like to record the changes to an entity over time; for example, such an entity could represent bank account details. Describe how this could be done in the ER model.

Exercise 2.9   Discuss the merits of a DBMS having an ER-like user interface.

Exercise 2.10 Consider enhancing the ER model with *entity clustering*, which allows us to combine several entity types and their relationships into a higher order entity type [Teo94]. For example, in the ERD of the computerised book order system, shown in Figure 2.1, we can cluster the entity types Order, Invoice and Book to form an entity cluster called Book_Ordering_Interface. How could you use entity clustering to improve an ER-like user interface?

Exercise 2.11 Devise a query language for the ER model with binary relationships [AC83, Che84]. Such a query language must provide at least the following facilities:

1) Locating the entities in an entity set such that their attribute values satisfy a given Boolean condition.

2) Locating the entities that participate in a particular relationship.

3) Chaining queries together by composition of relationships.

3. The Relational Data Model

In this chapter we present the core theory of relational databases. As described in Subsection 1.7.1 of Section 3.1 of Chapter 1 the relational model has three components: a structural part, a manipulative part and an integrity part. Thus we can view this chapter as consisting of three mini chapters one corresponding to each component of the relational model. The data structure of the model, i.e. the relation, and the relation schema over which it is defined, is presented in Section 3.1. In this section the simple tabular form of database relations is given a set-theoretic formalism.

The manipulative part of the relational model is presented in Section 3.2. We present three relational query languages: the relational algebra, which is a procedural language, the relational calculus, which is a declarative query language (SQL is based on the relational calculus) and nonrecursive Datalog, which is a rule-based query language. In Section 3.3 we show that all three query languages are equivalent, i.e. they differ only in style but not in expressive power. This result is fundamental to the theory of relational databases for two main reasons. Firstly, it establishes the robustness of the query formalism for the model, i.e. three languages which on the surface seem to be distinct turn out to be as expressive as each other. Secondly, from a practical point of view we can choose the query language that best fits the application. For example, naive users will, in general, prefer declarative languages such as the relational calculus and Datalog, while system programmers may prefer the relational algebra due to its procedural nature. It is considered beneficial to give users of database systems (or any computerised system) choice of the method of interaction with the information. In Section 3.3 we also present a simple update language for the relational model allowing us to formalise the notion of a transaction. Updates are often not given enough coverage, although the dynamic changes that occur to the current state of the database as a result of updates are an ongoing and fundamental process in the management of the database.

The integrity part of the relational model is introduced in Section 3.4. Integrity constraints restrict the allowable relations in a database to satisfy certain logical conditions, called integrity constraints. Constraints such as functional dependencies (which generalise the notion of keys) and inclusion dependencies (which generalise the notion of foreign keys) are called *data dependencies*. The theory of data dependencies is very rich and there is a multitude of results in this area. It is fair to say that although the core theory can be considered stable, researchers are still refining and extending it. In Section 3.5 we describe the central problem of automating the process of inferring new integrity constraints from a given set of integrity constraints; this problem is known as the *implication problem*. In order to solve it data dependency theorists have investigated the logical notion of a sound and complete axiom system for a particular class of integrity constraints. Such a system, when it exists, provides us with a computational procedure to solve the implication problem. When the implication problem can be solved efficiently, the database designer can use the resulting algorithm to refine his/her constraints over the database. On the other hand, when the database theorist has shown that the implication problem cannot be solved efficiently for a particular class of constraints, then only heuristic algorithms can be used to help the database designer refine his/her constraints. In Section 3.6 we cover the most common data dependencies that are used in practice. We attempt to cover the main achievements in this field but would need several volumes to cover all the results obtained so far. In Section 3.7 we study domain and cardinality constraints, which we feel have been neglected in the database literature despite their importance. We arrive at a novel interpretation of the notion of atomic domain that can pave the way to incorporating the notion of user-defined data types in relational database systems.

Up until now we have concentrated on the conceptual level of the database system. The question arises, however, as to what happens at the view level which is the level at which the interaction between the users and the database systems occurs. In a relational database a view can be defined as any portion of the database that can be retrieved by a relational algebra query. Querying a view does not pose any particular problem, since it only involves composing the query on the view with the definition of the view. On the other hand, updating the view can cause serious problems to the database system, since in general such updates do not unambiguously translate into database updates. We investigate solutions to this problem, called the *view update problem*, in Section 3.8.

3.1   The Data Structure of the Relational Model

The relational model has only one data structure, the *relation*. An informal description and an example of a relation and a relational database were given in Section 1.2 of Chapter 1. A relation is a set of tuples, each tuple representing some entity, and a relational database is a set of relations. The schema of a relation (i.e. a relation schema) is a set of attributes describing the properties of the components of tuples, and the schema of a database (i.e. a database schema) is a set of relation schemas. Notation-wise we give every relation schema a name, say R, and denote the set of attributes of R by schema(R).

The representation of relations as tables is very convenient. The rows of the tables are the tuples and the column headers the attributes of its schema.

We present a further example of a simple university database. In Table 3.1 we show a relation r_1 over a relation schema STUDENT, where schema(STUDENT) = {SNAME, AGE, ADDRESS, DEPT, DEGREE, YEAR}. In Table 3.2 we show a relation r_2 over a relation schema COURSE, where schema(COURSE) = {DEPT, CNAME, TNAME, TEXT}. In Table 3.3 we show a relation r_3 over a relation schema TUTOR, where schema(TUTOR) = {TNAME, DEPT, SALARY, DAY}. Together, the set of relations {r_1, r_2, r_3} is a database d over a database schema UNIVERSITY = {STUDENT, COURSE, TUTOR}.

Recall the definitions of attribute and domain from Subsection 2.2.3 of Chapter 2.

Table 3.1 The relation r_1 over STUDENT

SNAME	AGE	ADDRESS	DEPT	DEGREE	YEAR
Iris	21	Malet St	Computing	BSC	first
Reuven	32	Harold Rd	Maths	BSC	second
Hanna	31	Harold Rd	Linguistics	BA	second
Dan	34	Gower St	Linguistics	BA	second
Hillary	25	Gower St	Computing	BSC	third
Eli	38	Oxford St	Economics	BCOM	third
Naomi	39	Oxford St	Maths	BA	fourth
David	42	Queens Ave	Computing	BSC	first

Table 3.2 The relation r_2 over COURSE

DEPT	CNAME	TNAME	TEXT
Computing	databases	Robert	Date
Computing	databases	Robert	Ullman
Computing	programming	Hanna	Knuth
Computing	programming	Richard	Knuth
Computing	algorithms	Ada	Harel
Maths	logic	Reuven	Mendelson
Maths	graph-theory	Martine	Harary
Linguistics	hebrew	Dan	Bible

Table 3.3 The relation r_3 over TUTOR

TNAME	DEPT	SALARY	DAY
Robert	Computing	2000	Monday
Robert	Computing	2000	Tuesday
Robert	Computing	2000	Thursday
Hanna	Computing	1400	Wednesday
Hanna	Computing	1400	Friday
Richard	Computing	1000	Friday
Martine	Maths	1600	Tuesday
Martine	Philosophy	1600	Friday
Reuven	Maths	1500	Wednesday
Reuven	Maths	1500	Thursday
Dan	Linguistics	1000	Tuesday
Ruth	Linguistics	1100	Monday

Definition 3.1 (Attributes and domains)   We assume that for the purpose of defining relational databases a countably infinite set of attribute names (or simply attributes), $\mathcal{U}$, and a countably infinite set of constant values, $\mathcal{D}$, are available. $\mathcal{U}$ is called the *universe of attributes* and $\mathcal{D}$ is called the *underlying database domain*.

Given an attribute A in $\mathcal{U}$ the *domain* of A, denoted by DOM(A), is a subset of $\mathcal{D}$ (which may be finite or infinite). We will also refer to the constant values in DOM(A) simply as constants or values.   ∎

The following assumption states that if two constants are written differently then they are actually different. For example, 'Robert' and 'Mark' and 1400 are all different but 'Mark' is the same as 'Mark'.

Definition 3.2 (The unique names assumption) The *Unique Names Assumption* (UNA) states that any two constant values $c_1 \in \text{DOM}(A_1)$, $c_2 \in \text{DOM}(A_2)$ are equal if and only if they are syntactically identical, i.e. they have the same name. ∎

Definition 3.3 (Relation schema) A *relation schema* (or simply a schema) is a relation symbol R together with an associated similarity type, denoted by type(R), such that type(R) is a natural number. We refer to such a schema simply as R. We associate with each relation schema R a one-to-one mapping, att: $\{1, 2, \ldots, \text{type}(R)\} \rightarrow \mathcal{U}$, which allows us to attach attribute names to the type(R) components of a relation schema R; we denote the set $\{$att(1), att(2), $\ldots$, att(type(R))$\}$ by schema(R). ∎

The relation symbol R is the name we attach to the relation schema, for example, STUDENT, COURSE and TUTOR are relation symbols. The number of attributes in a relation schema, R, is its similarity type, type(R). For example, type(STUDENT) = 6, type(COURSE) = 4 and type(TUTOR) = 4. Finally, schema(R) is the set of attributes associated with R. For example, schema(TUTOR) = {TNAME, DEPT, SALARY, DAY}. The mapping *att* allows us to refer to the attributes in schema(R) in some fixed order. For example, the mapping att associated with TUTOR gives us att(1) = TNAME, att(2) = DEPT, att(3) = SALARY and att(4) = DAY. This ordering is useful for displaying the columns of a relation in some default ordering.

A database schema is now defined as a set of relation schemas.

Definition 3.4 (Database schema) A *database schema* is a finite set $\mathbf{R} = \{R_1, R_2, \ldots, R_n\}$ such that each $R_i \in \mathbf{R}$ is a relation schema. We denote by schema($\mathbf{R}$) the set of all attributes associated with the relation schemas in $\mathbf{R}$, i.e. schema($\mathbf{R}$) = $\bigcup_{i \in I}$ schema(R_i), where $I = \{1, 2, \ldots, n\}$.

We also refer to a database schema $\mathbf{R}$ as a *decomposition* of a finite set of attributes X $\subset \mathcal{U}$ whenever X = schema($\mathbf{R}$) (or we call $\mathbf{R}$ simply a decomposition if X is understood from context). ∎

In the following uppercase letters (which may be subscripted) appearing at the end of the alphabet such as X, Y, W, Z will be used to denote sets of attributes, whilst those at the beginning of the alphabet such as A, B, C will, in general, be used to denote single attributes. Whenever no ambiguity arises in a particular context we will write schema to mean either relation schema or database schema.

Recall the definition of an atomic domain (i.e. a nondecomposable set of values which has no internal structure as far as the database system is concerned) from Subsection 2.2.3 of Chapter 2. We now formalise a very important structural constraint on relation schemas.

Definition 3.5 (First Normal Form) A relation schema R is in *First Normal Form* (1NF) if all the domains of attributes A_i in schema(R) are atomic. A database schema $\mathbf{R}$ is in 1NF if each relation schema R_i in $\mathbf{R}$ is in 1NF. ∎

Relation schemas (respectively, database schemas) that are in 1NF are also called *normalised relation schemas* (respectively, *normalised database schemas*) or *flat relation schemas* (respectively, *flat database schemas*). From now on throughout the rest of the book *a relation schema will be assumed to be in 1NF unless otherwise stated.* This assumption is known as the *1NF assumption*. We note that Codd defined the concept of 1NF schemas in his seminal paper in 1970 [Cod70]. The main justifications for assuming 1NF schemas are:

1) It is easy to understand the semantics of attributes of 1NF schemas, since the internal structure of atomic attributes is hidden both from the user and the database system.

2) It is simpler to formalise the relational model under this assumption.

As an example with respect to point (1) assume that an address comprises a street number, street name, city and postcode. Then the attribute name ADDRESS, over a nonatomic domain of address values, is ambiguous, since it has a nontrivial internal structure which is not obvious. On the other hand, the four attributes, STREET_NUMBER, STREET_NAME, CITY and POSTCODE, all over atomic domains, collectively describe an address in an unambiguous manner. With respect to point (2), as we have demonstrated in Subsection 1.7.4 of Chapter 1, when we admit attributes over nonatomic or *nested* domains (i.e. we relax the 1NF assumption), we are essentially allowing attribute values themselves to be relations. The formalisation of such a *nested relational model*, which allows hierarchical structures in addition to flat structures, is obviously more complex.

We now rephrase the *Universal Relation Schema Assumption* (URSA), given in Definition 2.13 in Section 2.4 of Chapter 2 in the context of ERDs, in terms of relational database schemas.

Definition 3.6 (Universal relation schema assumption)   A database schema **R** satisfies the URSA if each attribute in schema(**R**) plays a unique role in **R**. That is, all occurrences of any attribute name in the relation schemas of **R** are assumed to have the same meaning.   ■

For the justification of this assumption see Section 2.4 of Chapter 2. The URSA is a semantic assumption which can only be enforced by the database designer if he/she decides on the attributes in schema(**R**) prior to deciding which attributes will belong to any particular schema(R_i), where R_i is in **R**. We observe that the URSA is stronger than the assumption that two attributes with the same name possess the same domain. As an example, let NUMBER be an attribute in an employee schema (meaning employee number) and, in addition, let NUMBER be an attribute in a parts schema (meaning part number). Furthermore, assume that the domain of NUMBER in both schemas is the set of all natural numbers. Obviously, the resulting database schema violates the URSA. We view the URSA as an assumption that makes our life slightly easier (both in theory and in practice) by allowing us to refer to attributes unambiguously without referring to the specific relation schema in which the attribute occurs.

We now give the formal definition of a relation and a database.

Definition 3.7 (Relation and database)   A *tuple* over a relation schema R, with schema(R) = $\{A_1, A_2, \ldots, A_m\}$ and where att(i) = A_i, for $i = 1, 2, \ldots, m$, is a member of the Cartesian product

$$\text{DOM}(A_1) \times \text{DOM}(A_2) \times \cdots \times \text{DOM}(A_m).$$

A *relation* over R is a finite set of tuples over R. A *database* over **R** = $\{R_1, R_2, \ldots, R_n\}$ is a set $d = \{r_1, r_2, \ldots, r_n\}$ such that each $r_i \in d$ is a relation over $R_i \in$ **R**.   ■

It is important to remember that relations are *finite* sets of tuples. Only a finite amount of information can be stored in a computer.

It is also possible to view a tuple t over a relation schema R as a total mapping from schema(R) to the union of the domains DOM(A_i), such that for all $A_i \in$ schema(R), $t(A_i) \in$ DOM(A_i). In this case we can ignore the linear order imposed on the attributes of R by the Cartesian product of the domains in Definition 3.7. This alternative definition of a tuple as a mapping highlights the fact that the ordering of the attributes in the sequence of attributes <att(1), att(2), ..., att(type(R))> is not important; that is, we can choose an alternative linear order without changing the semantics of a relation. On the other hand, when we display a relation as a table we need to choose some ordering of the columns in the displayed table and the definition of a tuple as an element in the Cartesian product of the domains highlights this default ordering.

Due to the 1NF assumption each tuple in a relation is a sequence of atomic values, which have no internal structure as far as the DBMS is concerned. For this reason relations (respectively, databases) are also called *normalised relations* (respectively, *normalised databases*) or *flat relations* (respectively, *flat databases*). As we have demonstrated in Subsection 1.7.4 of Chapter 1 when we relax the 1NF assumption we obtain *nested relations* and *nested databases*, wherein tuples of relations are sequences of values which may either be atomic or nested, nested values being values which are themselves relations. The advantages of normalised (1NF) relations over nested relations are:

1) Normalised relations can be presented in a simple two-dimensional tabular form, where each value in such a table is atomic.

2) Under the 1NF assumption, querying, updating and maintaining the fundamental integrity constraints of a relational database are performed easily and in a straightforward manner.

Let us now continue the formalisation of the relational model under the 1NF assumption. Informally, the projection of a tuple t over R onto a subset Y of schema(R) is the restriction of t to the attributes of Y.

Definition 3.8 (Projection)   The *projection* of a tuple t in a relation r over relation schema R onto the attribute $A_i = $ att(i) in schema(R) is the i-coordinate of t, i.e. $t(i)$.

We extend the notion of projection to a set of attributes, Y = {att(i_1), att(i_2), ..., att(i_k)} $\subseteq$ schema(R), with $i_1 < i_2 < \cdots < i_k$, as follows. The projection of t onto Y (also called the Y-value of t), denoted by $t[Y]$, is defined by $t[Y] = <t(i_1), t(i_2), ..., t(i_k)>$.   ∎

For example, consider the relation r_2 in Table 3.2 and let $t = $ <Computing, databases, Robert, Date>. Then $t[\text{TEXT}] = $ <Date> and $t[\text{DEPT, TNAME}] = $ <Computing, Robert>.

The *active domain* of a relation r over R is the set of constant values that appear in the tuples of r and the *active domain* of a database d over **R** is the union of the active domains of its relations; the formal definition follows.

Definition 3.9 (Active domain)   The *active domain* of a relation r over R, denoted by ADOM(r), is defined by

$$\text{ADOM}(r) = \{v \mid \exists A \in \text{schema}(R) \text{ and } \exists t \in r \text{ such that } t[A] = v\}.$$

The active domain of a database d over $\mathbf{R}$, denoted by $\text{ADOM}(d)$, is defined by

$$\text{ADOM}(d) = \bigcup \{\text{ADOM}(r) \mid r \in d\}. \qquad \blacksquare$$

3.2 Query and Update Languages for the Relational Model

In the previous section we have concerned ourselves with the structural part of the relational model. Here we elaborate on the manipulative part of the relational model, in the form of query and update languages. In Subsection 3.2.1 we present the relational algebra which is a procedural query language for the relational model. In Subsection 3.2.2 we present the domain relational calculus which is the declarative counterpart of the relational algebra and is based on the first-order predicate calculus. The domain relational calculus is the query language which provides the theoretical underpinning of SQL which is the commercial relational query language used in most DBMSs; in fact, many people go further and equate SQL with relational databases. In Subsection 3.2.3 we present Datalog which is a rule-based query language for the relational model and views a relational database in a logical way. In Subsection 3.2.4 we consider an update language for the relational model that takes into account the dynamic aspects of updating a relational database; it complements the query languages we present in Subsections 3.2.1, 3.2.2 and 3.2.3, which can only be used to retrieve information from a relational database.

3.2.1 The Relational Algebra

The relational algebra is a collection of operators; each operator takes as input either a single relation or a pair of relations and outputs a single relation as its result. A relational query is a composition of a finite number of relational operators. In that sense a query is procedural, since it specifies the order in which the operators comprising the query are to be evaluated. The declarative counterpart of the relational algebra, i.e. the domain relational calculus, is defined in Subsection 3.2.2. The relational algebra was first presented in Codd's seminal 1970 paper [Cod70] and a variant of the domain relational calculus was first presented in 1972 in another of Codd's fundamental papers [Cod72b]. Since then the relational algebra has become a yardstick for measuring the expressiveness of any relational query language.

Our style of presentation of the relational algebra operators is: for each operator we give an informal definition of the operator, then we give its formal definition and finally we give an example of its use over the database presented in Section 3.1.

The set-theoretic operators, union, difference and intersection, defined below, are all binary operators which take two relations over a common relation schema, say R, and return a relation over R. It is customary to call two relations *union-compatible* if their corresponding relation schemas have the same attribute set, and are thus effectively the same.

The union of two relations, r_1 and r_2 over relation schema R, is the set of tuples that are either in r_1 or in r_2.

Definition 3.10 (Union)   The union, $\cup$, of two relations r_1 and r_2 over R is defined by

$$r_1 \cup r_2 = \{t \mid t \in r_1 \text{ or } t \in r_2\}. \qquad \blacksquare$$

Let s_1 be the relation over SHORT_STUD with schema(SHORT_STUD) = {SNAME, ADDRESS, DEPT}, shown in Table 3.4, representing students having computing accounts, and let s_2 be the relation over SHORT_STUD, shown in Table 3.5, representing students receiving a grant. The query, "Retrieve the students who either have a computing account or are receiving a grant", can be expressed as the union $s_1 \cup s_2$. The result of this query is shown in Table 3.6.

Table 3.4 The relation s_1 over SHORT_STUD

SNAME	ADDRESS	DEPT
Iris	Malet St	Computing
Reuven	Harold Rd	Maths
Hanna	Harold Rd	Linguistics
Brian	Alexandra Rd	Sociology

Table 3.5 The relation s_2 over SHORT_STUD

SNAME	ADDRESS	DEPT
Iris	Malet St	Computing
Reuven	Harold Rd	Maths
Annette	Harold Rd	Linguistics
Cyril	Oakley Gdns	Medicine

Table 3.6 The result of the query $s_1 \cup s_2$ over SHORT_STUD

SNAME	ADDRESS	DEPT
Iris	Malet St	Computing
Reuven	Harold Rd	Maths
Hanna	Harold Rd	Linguistics
Annette	Harold Rd	Linguistics
Brian	Alexandra Rd	Sociology
Cyril	Oakley Gdns	Medicine

The difference between two relations, r_1 and r_2 over relation schema R, is the set of tuples that are in r_1 but not in r_2.

Definition 3.11 (Difference)   The difference, $-$, of two relations r_1 and r_2 over R is defined by

$$r_1 - r_2 = \{t \mid t \in r_1 \text{ and } t \notin r_2\}. \qquad \blacksquare$$

The query, "Retrieve the students who have a computing account but do not receive a grant", can be expressed as the difference $s_1 - s_2$, where s_1 and s_2 are shown in Tables 3.4 and 3.5, respectively. The result of this query is shown in Table 3.7.

We note that the intersection, $\cap$, of two relations r_1 and r_2 over relation schema R, i.e. the set of tuples that are included in both r_1 and r_2, can be defined in terms of the difference operator by

$$r_1 \cap r_2 = r_1 - (r_1 - r_2).$$

Table 3.7 The result of the query $s_1 - s_2$ over SHORT_STUD

SNAME	ADDRESS	DEPT
Hanna	Harold Rd	Linguistics
Brian	Alexandra Rd	Sociology

The query, "Retrieve the students who have a computing account and are also receiving a grant", can be expressed as the intersection $s_1 \cap s_2$, where s_1 and s_2 are shown in Tables 3.4 and 3.5, respectively. The result of this query is shown in Table 3.8.

Table 3.8 The result of the query $s_1 \cap s_2$ over SHORT_STUD

SNAME	ADDRESS	DEPT
Iris	Malet St	Computing
Reuven	Harold Rd	Maths

The projection of a relation r over relation schema R onto a set of attributes Y included in schema(R) is the set of tuples resulting from projecting each of the tuples in r onto Y.

Definition 3.12 (Projection) The projection, π, of a relation r over relation schema R onto a set of attributes Y $\subseteq$ schema(R) is defined by

$$\pi_Y(r) = \{t[Y] \mid t \in r\},$$

where $t[Y]$ is the restriction of t to Y given in Definition 3.8. ∎

The query, "Retrieve the departments, degrees and years of students", can be expressed as the projection $\pi_{\{DEPT, DEGREE, YEAR\}}(r_1)$, where r_1 is shown in Table 3.1. The result of this query is shown in Table 3.9.

Table 3.9 The result of the query $\pi_{\{DEPT, DEGREE, YEAR\}}(r_1)$

DEPT	DEGREE	YEAR
Computing	BSC	first
Computing	BSC	third
Maths	BSC	second
Maths	BA	fourth
Linguistics	BA	second
Economics	BCOM	third

We note that the cardinality of $\pi_Y(r)$ is less than or equal to the cardinality of r, since two or more tuples in r may have the same projection onto Y. For example, in the above query the tuple <Linguistics, BA, second> is the {DEPT, DEGREE, YEAR}-value of both the tuples, whose SNAME-values are Hanna and Dan in r_1 of Table 3.1. We further note that projection captures the semantics of existential quantification. For example, in the above query we retrieved the {DEPT, DEGREE, YEAR}-values of tuples such that there exist {SNAME, AGE, ADDRESS}-values for these tuples.

Selection of tuples from a relation r with respect to a selection formula F is the subset of tuples from r that satisfy the formula F.

Definition 3.13 (Selection formula)   A *simple selection formula* over a schema R is either an expression of the form A = a or an expression of the form A = B, where A, B ∈ schema(R) and a ∈ DOM(A).

A *selection formula* (or simply a formula whenever no ambiguity arises) over R is a well-formed expression composed of one or more simple selection formulae over R together with the Boolean logical connectives: ∧ (and), ∨ (or), ¬ (not) and parentheses. A selection formula is called *positive* if it does not have any occurrence of ¬. We abbreviate ¬(A = a) by A ≠ a and ¬(A = B) by A ≠ B.   ∎

A simple selection formula of the type A = B is sometimes referred to as *restriction*. For simplicity we have only included equality (=) as a comparison operator but, in general, we can also expect ≤ (less than or equal to) and < (less than) to be available in simple selection formulae.

Informally a tuple, t, logically implies a formula, F, if the tuple satisfies F. In the next definition F_1 and F_2 are also formulae.

Definition 3.14 (Logical implication, ⊨)   Let r be a relation over relation schema R, t be a tuple in r and, in addition, let F be a selection formula over R. Then t *logically implies* F, written $t \models F$, is defined recursively, as follows:

1) $t \models A = a$, if $t[A] = a$ evaluates to true.

2) $t \models A = B$, if $t[A] = t[B]$ evaluates to true.

3) $t \models F_1 \wedge F_2$, if $t \models F_1$ evaluates to true and $t \models F_2$ evaluates to true.

4) $t \models F_1 \vee F_2$, if $t \models F_1$ evaluates to true or $t \models F_2$ evaluates to true.

5) $t \models \neg F$, if $t \models F$ does not evaluate to true, i.e. $t \not\models F$.

6) $t \models (F)$, if $t \models F$.   ∎

We are now ready to formalise selection which, when applied to a relation, r, with respect to a formula, F, returns all the tuples in r that logically imply F.

Definition 3.15 (Selection)   The selection, σ, applied to a relation r over relation schema R with respect to a selection formula F over R is defined by

$$\sigma_F(r) = \{t \mid t \in r \text{ and } t \models F\}.$$ ∎

The following theorem, which easily follows from the definitions of selection and logical implication, shows that the Boolean logical connectives, ¬, ∨ and ∧, present in selection formulae can be expressed in terms of the set operators −, ∪ and ∩, respectively.

Theorem 3.1 The following equalities are all satisfied, where r is a relation over relation schema R, and F, F_1 and F_2 are selection formulae over R.

1) $\sigma_{\neg F}(r) = r - \sigma_F(r)$.

2) $\sigma_{F_1 \vee F_2}(r) = \sigma_{F_1}(r) \cup \sigma_{F_2}(r)$.

3) $\sigma_{F_1 \wedge F_2}(r) = \sigma_{F_1}(r) \cap \sigma_{F_2}(r)$. $\qquad\square$

The query, "Retrieve the students who are either studying in the Linguistics department or whose address is Oxford St", can be expressed as the selection $\sigma_{F_1}(r_1)$, where F_1 is the formula DEPT = 'Linguistics' $\vee$ ADDRESS = 'Oxford St', and r_1 is shown in Table 3.1. The result of this query is shown in Table 3.10.

Table 3.10 The result of the query $\sigma_{F_1}(r_1)$

SNAME	AGE	ADDRESS	DEPT	DEGREE	YEAR
Hanna	31	Harold Rd	Linguistics	BA	second
Dan	34	Gower St	Linguistics	BA	second
Eli	38	Oxford St	Economics	BCOM	third
Naomi	39	Oxford St	Maths	BA	fourth

The query, "Retrieve the students who are not studying Computing and are not in their second year", can be expressed as the selection $\sigma_{F_2}(r_1)$, where F_2 is the formula DEPT $\neq$ 'Computing' $\wedge$ YEAR $\neq$ 'second', and r_1 is shown in Table 3.1. The result of this query is shown in Table 3.11.

Table 3.11 The result of the query $\sigma_{F_2}(r_1)$

SNAME	AGE	ADDRESS	DEPT	DEGREE	YEAR
Eli	38	Oxford St	Economics	BCOM	third
Naomi	39	Oxford St	Maths	BA	fourth

The query, "Retrieve the students who did the same number of courses in their first and second years", can be expressed as the selection $\sigma_{F_3}(s_3)$, where F_3 is the formula FIRST = SECOND, and s_3 is the relation over FST_SND shown in Table 3.12. The result of this query is shown in Table 3.13.

Table 3.12 The relation s_3 over FST_SND

SNAME	FIRST	SECOND
Reuven	5	5
Hanna	4	5
Dan	5	4
Hillary	4	4
Eli	3	6
Naomi	6	5

Informally, the natural join of two relations r_1 over relation schema R_1 and r_2 over relation schema R_2, with schema(R_1) $\cap$ schema(R_2) being the set of attributes X, is the relation

Table 3.13 The result of the query $\sigma_{F_3}(s_3)$

SNAME	FIRST	SECOND
Reuven	5	5
Hillary	4	4

containing tuples that result from concatenating every tuple of r_1 with every tuple of r_2 both of which have the same X-values. The attributes in X are called the *join attributes* of R_1 and R_2.

Definition 3.16 (Natural join)   The natural join (or simply the join), $\bowtie$, of two relations r_1 over relation schema R_1 and r_2 over relation schema R_2 is a relation over relation schema R defined by

$$r_1 \bowtie r_2 = \{t \mid \exists t_1 \in r_1 \text{ and } \exists t_2 \in r_2 \text{ such that } t[\text{schema}(R_1)] = t_1 \text{ and } t[\text{schema}(R_2)] = t_2\},$$

where $\text{schema}(R) = \text{schema}(R_1) \cup \text{schema}(R_2)$.   ∎

Let $s_1 = \pi_{\{CNAME,DEPT,TNAME\}}(r_2)$ be the relation shown in Table 3.14 and $s_2 = \pi_{\{DEPT,TNAME,SALARY\}}(r_3)$ be the relation shown in Table 3.15. The query, "Retrieve the courses given in departments and the salaries of tutors for these courses", can be expressed as the natural join $s_1 \bowtie s_2$.

The result of this query is shown in Table 3.16 We observe that the tuples <Philosophy, Martine, 1600> and <Linguistics, Ruth, 1100> in s_2 did not participate in the join, since their {DEPT, TNAME}-values do not match any corresponding values in s_1. Furthermore, the tuple <algorithms, Computing, Ada> in s_1 did not participate in the join, since its {DEPT, TNAME}-value does not match any corresponding values in s_2. Such tuples are known as *dangling* tuples.

There is a connection between the concept of dangling tuples and referential integrity, which was introduced in Subsection 1.7.1 of Chapter 1. For example, suppose that the set of attributes {DEPT, TNAME} forms the primary key for the schema of relation s_2. In this case the attributes {DEPT, TNAME} of the schema of relation s_1 form a foreign key which references these attributes in the schema of s_2. It follows that the tuple <algorithms, Computing, Ada> is dangling as a result of referential integrity being violated. More specifically, if referential integrity is satisfied then there must exist a tuple t in s_2 such that $t[\text{DEPT}] = \text{Computing}$ and $t[\text{TNAME}] = \text{Ada}$. If, in addition, the set of attributes {DEPT, TNAME} were the primary key for the schema of s_1, then the tuples in s_2 that did not participate in the join are also dangling as a result of referential integrity being violated. (It is unlikely that {DEPT, TNAME} is the primary key for the schema of s_1, since one would expect a teacher to teach more than one course in a given department.)

The query, "Retrieve the courses that students can do in the department they are studying in", can be expressed as the natural join $\pi_{\{CNAME,DEPT\}}(s_1) \bowtie \pi_{\{DEPT,SNAME\}}(r_1)$, where s_1 and r_1 are shown in Tables 3.14 and 3.1, respectively. The result of this query is shown in Table 3.17.

It may be easier to understand the semantics of the natural join algorithmically rather than by the above declarative definition. The pseudo-code of an algorithm, designated JOIN(r_1, r_2), which given the input relations r_1 over R_1 and r_2 over R_2, with $X = \text{schema}(R_1) \cap \text{schema}(R_2)$, returns $r_1 \bowtie r_2$ over R, is presented as the ensuing algorithm.

Table 3.14 The relation $s_1 = \pi_{\{CNAME, DEPT, TNAME\}}(r_2)$

CNAME	DEPT	TNAME
databases	Computing	Robert
programming	Computing	Hanna
programming	Computing	Richard
algorithms	Computing	Ada
logic	Maths	Reuven
graph-theory	Maths	Martine
Hebrew	Linguistics	Dan

Table 3.15 The relation $s_2 = \pi_{\{DEPT, TNAME, SALARY\}}(r_3)$

DEPT	TNAME	SALARY
Computing	Robert	2000
Computing	Hanna	1400
Computing	Richard	1000
Maths	Martine	1600
Philosophy	Martine	1600
Maths	Reuven	1500
Linguistics	Dan	1000
Linguistics	Ruth	1100

Table 3.16 The result of the query $s_1 \bowtie s_2$

CNAME	DEPT	TNAME	SALARY
databases	Computing	Robert	2000
programming	Computing	Hanna	1400
programming	Computing	Richard	1000
graph-theory	Maths	Martine	1600
logic	Maths	Reuven	1500
Hebrew	Linguistics	Dan	1000

Algorithm 3.1 (JOIN(r_1, r_2))
1. **begin**
2.   Result := $\emptyset$;
3.   **for each** tuple $t_1 \in r_1$ **do**
4.   **for each** tuple $t_2 \in r_2$ **do**
5.   **if** $t_1[X] = t_2[X]$ **then**
6.   Joined_tuple := a tuple over R such that
                        Joined_tuple[schema(R_1)] = t_1 and
                        Joined_tuple[schema(R_2)] = t_2;
7.   Result := Result $\cup$ Joined_tuple;
8.   **end if**
9.   **end for**
10.   **end for**
11.   **return** Result;
12. **end.**

We note that if schema(R_1) = schema(R_2), then the natural join operator reduces to the intersection operator, i.e.

$$r_1 \bowtie r_2 = r_1 \cap r_2.$$

Table 3.17 The result of the query $\pi_{\{CNAME,DEPT\}}(s_1) \bowtie \pi_{\{DEPT,SNAME\}}(r_1)$

CNAME	DEPT	SNAME
databases	Computing	Iris
databases	Computing	Hillary
databases	Computing	David
programming	Computing	Iris
programming	Computing	Hillary
programming	Computing	David
algorithms	Computing	Iris
algorithms	Computing	Hillary
algorithms	Computing	David
logic	Maths	Reuven
logic	Maths	Naomi
graph-theory	Maths	Reuven
graph-theory	Maths	Naomi
Hebrew	Linguistics	Hanna
Hebrew	Linguistics	Dan

Furthermore, if schema(R_1) $\cap$ schema(R_2) = $\emptyset$, then the natural join operator reduces to the *Cartesian product* operator, denoted by $\times$. Therefore, in this case,

$$r_1 \bowtie r_2 = r_1 \times r_2.$$

Informally, the Cartesian product of r_1 over R_1 and r_2 over R_2, with schema(R_1) $\cap$ schema(R_2) = $\emptyset$, is the result of concatenating every tuple of r_1 with every tuple of r_2.

The renaming operator allows us to change the name of an attribute in a schema of a relation. Renaming is useful when we want to take the union, difference or intersection of relations over different schemas, and when we want to take the natural join of two relations over a set of attributes other than the set of common ones.

Definition 3.17 (Renaming) Let r be a relation over relation schema R, A be an attribute of schema(R) and B be an attribute in $\mathcal{U}$, which is not in schema(R). The renaming, ρ, of A to B in r, is a relation over relation schema S, where schema(S) = (schema(R) $-$ {A}) $\cup$ {B}, defined by

$$\rho_{A \to B}(r) = \{t \mid \exists u \in r \text{ such that } t[\text{schema}(R) - \{B\}] = u[\text{schema}(R) - \{A\}] \text{ and } t[B] = u[A]\}.$$

■

The query, "Rename SNAME to STUDENT_NAME, ADDRESS to STUDENT_ADDRESS and DEPT to DEPARTMENT in s_1", can be expressed as the renaming

$$\rho_{SNAME \to STUDENT\_NAME}(\rho_{ADDRESS \to STUDENT\_ADDRESS}(\rho_{DEPT \to DEPARTMENT}(s_1))),$$

where s_1 is the relation shown in Table 3.4. The result of this query is shown in Table 3.18. We observe that the only effect of renaming is to change attribute names.

We next define the division operator, which captures the semantics of universal quantification (i.e. for all). Informally, the division of two relations, r over a schema having attributes XY and s over a schema having attributes Y, is the set of X-values, say $t[X]$, of tuples $t \in r$ such that for all tuples $u \in s$, u is included in the set of Y-values of tuples t in r having X-value $t[X]$.

Table 3.18   The result of the query $\rho_{\text{SNAME}\rightarrow\text{STUDENT\_NAME}}$
$(\rho_{\text{ADDRESS}\rightarrow\text{STUDENT\_ADDRESS}}(\rho_{\text{DEPT}\rightarrow\text{DEPARTMENT}}(s_1)))$

STUDENT_NAME	STUDENT_ADDRESS	DEPARTMENT
Iris	Malet St	Computing
Reuven	Harold Rd	Maths
Hanna	Harold Rd	Linguistics
Brian	Alexandra Rd	Sociology

Definition 3.18 (Division)   Let r be a relation over relation schema R, with schema(R) = XY, and s be a relation over relation schema S, with schema(S) = Y. The division, $\div$, of r by s, is a relation over relation schema R_1, where schema(R_1) = X, defined by

$$r \div s = \{t[X] \mid t \in r \text{ and } s \subseteq \pi_Y(\sigma_F(r)), \text{ where } X = \{A_1, A_2, \ldots, A_q\}$$
$$\text{and } F \text{ is the formula } A_1 = t[A_1] \wedge A_2 = t[A_2] \wedge \ldots \wedge A_q = t[A_q]\}. \quad \blacksquare$$

Let s_4 be the relation over TOPICS, shown in Table 3.19, with schema(TOPICS) = TOPIC representing the research topics of the Computing department and let s_5 be the relation over INTERESTS, shown in Table 3.20, with schema(INTERESTS) = {LECTURER, TOPIC} representing the particular topics academic staff are interested in. The query, "Retrieve the lecturers who are interested in all the topics of the Computing department", can be expressed as the division $s_5 \div s_4$. The result of this query is shown in Table 3.21.

Table 3.19 The relation s_4 over TOPICS

TOPIC
databases
software-engineering
distributed-computing

Table 3.20 The relation s_5 over INTERESTS

LECTURER	TOPIC
Jack	databases
Jack	software-engineering
Jack	distributed-computing
Jeffrey	databases
Jeffrey	distributed-computing
Jeffrey	automata-theory
John	expert-systems
John	software-engineering
Jill	databases
Jill	software-engineering
Jill	distributed-computing
Jill	algorithms

Table 3.21 The result of the query $s_5 \div s_4$

LECTURER
Jack
Jill

The following proposition shows that the division operator can be expressed by the relational algebra operators, projection, difference and Cartesian product.

Proposition 3.2 Let r be a relation over relation schema R, with schema(R) $=$ XY, and s be a relation over relation schema S, with schema(S) $=$ Y. Then

$$r \div s = \pi_X(r) - \pi_X((\pi_X(r) \times s) - r). \qquad \Box$$

A relational algebra expression is an expression resulting from composing a finite number of relational algebra operators together, where the operands of the expression are relation schemas.

Definition 3.19 (Relational algebra expressions) A *relational algebra expression* (or alternatively a relational algebra query, or just simply a query whenever no ambiguity arises) is a well-formed expression composed of a finite number of relational algebra operators whose operands are relation schemas which can be treated as input variables to the query. A query Q having as operands the relation schemas $R_1, R_2, \ldots, R_n$ is denoted by $Q(R_1, R_2, \ldots, R_n)$ or simply by Q if $R_1, R_2, \ldots, R_n$ are understood from context.   ∎

Definition 3.20 (An answer to a query) An *answer to a query* $Q(R_1, R_2, \ldots, R_n)$ is obtained by replacing every occurrence of R_i in Q by a relation r_i over R_i and computing the result by invoking the algebra operators present in Q; such an answer to Q will be denoted by $Q(r_1, r_2, \ldots, r_n)$ or simply by Q(d) if d is a database over **R** and for all $i \in \{1, 2, \ldots, n\}, R_i \in$ **R** and $r_i \in d$.   ∎

We will assume that parentheses are present in Q to indicate the priority of evaluation of subexpressions of Q in order to avoid ambiguity when computing $Q(r_1, r_2, \ldots, r_n)$. At times, when no ambiguity arises, we will also refer to an answer to a query simply as a query.

The relational algebra operators defined above are considered to be the core operators of any relational query language. Therefore, in the following we will refer to this set of operators (or any minimal subset which is of the same expressiveness) as *the relational algebra.* For example, it is not hard to show that union, difference, projection, selection and Cartesian product are such a minimal subset of the relational algebra [Bec78].

The set of queries, which are expressible in the relational algebra, is considered to be the minimal set of queries that any query language for the relational model should possess. Thus the relational algebra provides a yardstick for measuring the expressive power of a query language for the relational model independently of any implementation.

Definition 3.21 (Relational completeness of a query language) A query language is said to be *relationally complete* if it is at least as expressive as the relational algebra.   ∎

It is interesting to investigate the independence of the operators comprising the relational algebra. For instance, in Proposition 3.2 we have shown that division is not independent, since it can be expressed with projection, difference and Cartesian product. Furthermore, we have also shown that intersection can be expressed with difference or with join, Cartesian product can be expressed with join and in Theorem 3.1 we have shown that simple selection together with difference, union and intersection can express any selection formula. Another independence result is that join can be expressed with selection, renaming, Cartesian product and projection. It can be shown that projection, union and difference are independent operators of the relational algebra. Projection is the only operator that removes columns from a relation and union is the only operator that adds rows to a relation. It may seem that difference can be expressed with selection formulae that allow negation but this is not the case as evidenced by the following argument.

An operator, τ, from relations to relations is *monotonic*, if whenever r_1 and r_2 are relations over R, with $r_1 \subseteq r_2$, it is also the case that $\tau(r_1) \subseteq \tau(r_2)$; otherwise τ is *nonmonotonic*. We leave it to the reader to verify that selection is a monotonic operator. Now, let r be a relation over R, with schema(R) = $\{A_1, A_2, \ldots, A_m\}$. The *complement* of r, denoted by $\bar{r}$, is given by

$$\bar{r} = (\pi_{A_1}(r) \times \pi_{A_2}(r) \times \cdots \times \pi_{A_m}(r)) - r.$$

We leave it to the reader to show that, in general, the complement operator is nonmonotonic. We therefore conclude that difference cannot be expressed with selection.

Although the relational algebra provides minimal relational capability, in practice, there arises a need for extending the relational algebra in order to enhance its expressive power. We will now introduce two extensions in the form of two additional algebraic operators, which we will not consider as an integral part of the relational algebra.

Table 3.22 A family relation

PARENT	CHILD
p1	p3
p1	p4
p2	p4
p2	p5
p3	p6
p3	p7
p4	p8
p5	p9
p5	p10
p5	p11
p7	p12
p9	p12

The first extension deals with a new operator, called the *transitive closure* operator, which solves the "parts explosion problem" also known as the "bill of materials problem". Consider the relation, which we call family, over the relation schema FAMILY with schema(FAMILY) = {PARENT, CHILD} describing the descendants of the two parents p1 and p2. The acyclic structure of the family relation shown in Table 3.22 is described pictorially as a family tree shown in Figure 3.1. We note that another common example considers a relation, called *parts*, which has attributes SUPER_PART corresponding to PARENT and SUB_PART corresponding to CHILD. In this case the family tree tells us which parts are immediate subparts of a given part and which subparts are indirect subparts of a given part.

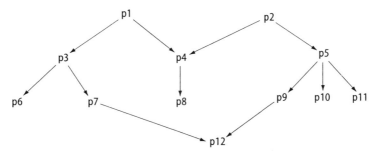

Fig 3.1 The family tree of the family relation in Table 3.22

A query such as "output the parents and their children" is answered easily by just displaying the family relation, and the query "output the parents and their grandchildren" is also easily answered by the query:

$$\pi_{\{GPARENT,GCHILD\}}(\rho_{CHILD\to Jatt}(\rho_{PARENT\to GPARENT}(FAMILY)) \\ \bowtie \rho_{PARENT\to Jatt}(\rho_{CHILD\to GCHILD}(FAMILY))).$$

Let us denote the above query by $Q^g p(FAMILY)$. Using this query we can easily answer queries such as who are the grandchildren of p1 by

$$\pi_{GCHILD}(\sigma_F(Q^g p(FAMILY))),$$

where F is the formula GPARENT = p1, and who are the grandparents of p12 by

$$\pi_{GPARENT}(\sigma_F(Q^g p(FAMILY))),$$

where F is the formula GCHILD = p12.

On the other hand, it can be shown that a query such as "Who are the descendants of a particular parent at all levels?" cannot be expressed as a relational algebra query, in such a way that, for every input relation over FAMILY, we obtain the correct answer. A similar query that, in general, cannot be expressed as a relational algebra query is "Who are the ancestors of a particular child at all levels?" (A formal proof can be found in [AU79] showing that the transitive closure cannot be expressed by using the relational algebra operators we have defined so far.)

In order to understand why the relational algebra is unable to answer such queries, let us first examine the bill of materials for the family relation, shown in Table 3.23. This relation shows the structure of the family tree by indicating the level of a parent-child relationship relative to a given parent at level 1. For example, the tuple <1, p1, p3> indicates that p1 is a parent of p3 at level 1, the tuple <2, p3, p7> indicates that p3 is the parent of p7 at level 2 relative to p1 implying that p1 is a grandparent of p7, and the tuple <3, p7, p12> indicates that p7 is the parent of p12 at level 3 implying that p1 is a great grandparent of p12. Now, informally, the reason that the relational algebra is not powerful enough to express such queries is that we cannot know *a priori* how many levels the bill of materials relation will contain. As we have seen it is easy to answer queries involving parents, grandparents, great grandparents, etc., by joining the family relation as many times as is necessary. However, this technique will not work in general, since if the relational algebra query is to give the correct answer for all possible relations over FAMILY then it would contain an unbounded number of joins. This leads to a contradiction of the definition of a relational algebra query, which states that a query must be composed of a finite number of relational algebra operators.

Table 3.23 The bill of materials for the family relation

LEVEL	PARENT	CHILD
1	p1	p3
2	p3	p6
2	p3	p7
3	p7	p12
1	p1	p4
1	p2	p4
2	p4	p8
1	p2	p5
2	p5	p9
3	p9	p12
2	p5	p10
2	p5	p11
1	p3	p6
1	p3	p7
2	p7	p12
1	p4	p8
1	p5	p9
2	p9	p12
1	p5	p10
1	p5	p11
1	p7	p12
1	p9	p12

We observe that the family tree is actually a directed graph (recall the formal definition of a directed graph given in Section 2.1 of Chapter 2). We now define the transitive closure operation on directed graphs.

Definition 3.22 (Transitive closure of a directed graph)   The *transitive closure* of a directed graph (N, E) is a directed graph (N, E^+) defined by

1) if $(u, v) \in$ E, then $(u, v) \in E^+$,

2) if $(u, v) \in E^+$ and $(v, w) \in$ E, then $(u, w) \in E^+$, and

3) nothing is in E^+ unless it follows from (1) and (2).   ■

The transitive closure of the family tree of Figure 3.1 is shown in Figure 3.2; the new arcs, which were added to the original family tree in order to obtain the transitive closure, are shown as squiggled lines. We are now in a position to define the transitive closure of a relation.

Definition 3.23 (Transitive closure of a relation)   Let R be a relation schema with schema(R) = {A, B} such that att(1) = A and att(2) = B, and where DOM(A) = DOM(B). The transitive closure of a relation r over R is the relation r^+, where r^+ is the set of arcs of the transitive

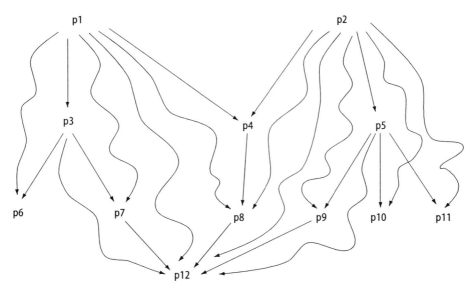

Fig 3.2 The transitive closure of the family tree in Figure 3.1

closure of the directed graph (V, r), with V being the set of values present in the tuples of r, i.e. the active domain of r. ∎

The transitive closure $family^+$ of the family relation, which was shown in Table 3.22, is shown in Table 3.24. We observe that the transitive closure of a relation expresses exactly the *same information* as the bill of materials of the relation (see the bill of materials for the family relation shown in Table 3.23).

It may be easier to understand the semantics of the transitive closure algorithmically rather than by the above declarative definition, namely Definition 3.22. The pseudo-code of an algorithm, designated TR_CL(r), which given the input relation r over R returns r^+ over R, is presented as the algorithm that follows. In the algorithm we let $Q^{join}(R)$ denote the query

$$\pi_{\{A,B\}}(\rho_{B \to Jatt}(R) \bowtie \rho_{A \to Jatt}(R)).$$

Algorithm 3.2 (TR_CL(r))
1. **begin**
2.   Result := r;
3.   Tmp := $\emptyset$;
4.   **while** Tmp $\neq$ Result **do**
5.   Tmp := Result;
6.   Result := Result $\cup$ Q^{join}(Result);
7.   **end while**
8.   **return** Result;
9. **end.**

Table 3.24 The transitive closure of the family relation

PARENT	DESCENDANT
p1	p3
p1	p6
p1	p7
p1	p12
p1	p4
p1	p8
p2	p4
p2	p8
p2	p5
p2	p9
p2	p12
p2	p10
p2	p11
p3	p6
p3	p7
p3	p12
p4	p8
p5	p9
p5	p12
p5	p10
p5	p11
p7	p12
p9	p12

The second extension of the relational algebra we deal with is that of allowing aggregate functions in queries. Aggregate functions allow us to answer queries such as:

Q1 How many tutors work in the college?

Q2 How many tutors are employed by the college in each department?

Q3 What is the overall average salary of tutors?

Q4 What is the average salary of tutors per department?

Q5 What is the maximum, respectively minimum, salary of any tutor?

Q6 What is the sum of money that the college spends on its tutors per department?

The above queries cannot be expressed as relational algebra queries, since the relational algebra treats domain values as uninterpreted objects and does not provide for computations that involve iterating over the tuples in a relation. Informally, an aggregate function computes an operation over the A-values of a set of tuples over relation schema R, where $A \in schema(R)$.

Definition 3.24 (Aggregate functions) An aggregate function f_A over R is a Turing-computable function, with $A \in schema(R)$, which given a finite set of tuples over R returns a natural number. ∎

The most common aggregate functions are:

1) COUNT, which returns the number of tuples in its input set of tuples (in this case the attribute A is irrelevant);

2) MIN, which returns the minimum A-value of its input set of tuples;

3) MAX, which returns the maximum A-value of its input set of tuples;

4) SUM, which returns the sum of the A-values of its input set of tuples; and

5) AVG, which returns the average A-value of its input set of tuples.

The above list of aggregate functions is by no means exhaustive and various relational DBMSs support additional aggregate functions of a statistical nature. For simplicity, we assume that if an aggregate function is not defined over one of the A-values of a tuple in its input set (which may be empty), then it returns the natural number zero.

Definition 3.25 (Aggregate functions in queries)   Let f_A be an aggregate function over R, X $\subseteq$ schema(R) and assume that $A_f \notin$ schema(R) is an attribute in $\mathcal{U}$. The result of applying f_A to a relation r, over R, with the partitioning attribute set X, denoted by $f_A^X(r)$ (or simply f_A if X = $\emptyset$), is a relation over relation schema S, where schema(S) = X $\cup$ {A_f}, defined by

$$f_A^X(r) = \{t \mid \exists t_1 \in r \text{ such that } t[X] = t_1[X] \text{ and } t[A_f] = f_A(\{t_2 \mid t_2 \in r \text{ and } t_2[X] = t[X]\})\}.$$

■

Consider the relation r_3 over TUTOR with schema(R_3) = {TNAME, DEPT, SALARY, DAY}, shown in Table 3.3.

- The answer to Q1, i.e. COUNT($\pi_{\text{TNAME}}(r_3)$), is shown in Table 3.25.
- The answer to Q2, i.e. COUNT$^{\text{DEPT}}(\pi_{\{\text{TNAME,DEPT}\}}(r_3))$, is shown in Table 3.26.
- The answer to Q3, i.e. AVG$_{\text{SALARY}}(\pi_{\{\text{TNAME,SALARY}\}}(r_3))$, is shown in Table 3.27.
- The answer to Q4, i.e. AVG$_{\text{SALARY}}^{\text{DEPT}}(\pi_{\{\text{TNAME,DEPT,SALARY}\}}(r_3))$, is shown in Table 3.28.
- The answer to Q5, i.e. MAX$_{\text{SALARY}}(r_3) \times$ MIN$_{\text{SALARY}}(r_3)$, is shown in Table 3.29.
- The answer to Q6, i.e. SUM$_{\text{SALARY}}^{\text{DEPT}}(\pi_{\{\text{TNAME,DEPT,SALARY}\}}(r_3))$, is shown in Table 3.30.

Table 3.25 The answer to COUNT($\pi_{\text{TNAME}}(r_3)$)

COUNT
7

Table 3.26 The answer to COUNT$^{\text{DEPT}}(\pi_{\{\text{TNAME,DEPT}\}}(r_3))$

DEPT	COUNT
Computing	3
Maths	2
Philosophy	1
Linguistics	2

Table 3.27 The answer to $\text{AVG}_{\text{SALARY}}(\pi_{\{\text{TNAME,SALARY}\}}(r_3))$

AVG_SALARY
1371

Table 3.28 The answer to $\text{AVG}^{\text{DEPT}}_{\text{SALARY}}(\pi_{\{\text{TNAME,DEPT,SALARY}\}}(r_3))$

DEPT	AVG_SALARY
Computing	1467
Maths	1550
Philosophy	1600
Linguistics	1050

Table 3.29 The answer to $\text{MAX}_{\text{SALARY}}(r_3) \times \text{MIN}_{\text{SALARY}}(r_3)$

MAX_SALARY	MIN_SALARY
2000	1000

Table 3.30 The answer to $\text{SUM}^{\text{DEPT}}_{\text{SALARY}}(\pi_{\{\text{TNAME,DEPT,SALARY}\}}(r_3))$

DEPT	SUM_SALARY
Computing	4400
Maths	3100
Philosophy	1600
Linguistics	2100

It may be easier to understand the semantics of the aggregate functions in queries algorithmically rather than by the above declarative definition, namely Definition 3.25. The pseudo-code of an algorithm, designated $\text{AGG}(f_A, X, r)$, which given the aggregate function f_A and a relation r over R with A, X $\subseteq$ schema(R), returns $f_A^X(r)$, is presented as the following algorithm. (A *partition* of a set P is a disjoint collection of nonempty subsets of P whose union is P; each subset B_i in a partition P is called a *block*.)

Algorithm 3.3 ($\text{AGG}(f_A, X, r)$)
1. **begin**
2.   Result $:= \emptyset$;
3.   P $:=$ a partition of r such t_1, t_2 are in the same block in P
       if and only if $t_1[X] = t_2[X]$;
4.   **for each** block B_i in the partition P **do**
5.   Agg_tuple $:=$ a tuple over S such that
          Agg_tuple$[X] = t[X]$ with $t \in B_i$ and Agg_tuple$[A_f] = f_A(\{t \mid t \in B_i\})$;
6.   Result $:=$ Result $\cup$ {Agg_tuple};
7.   **end for**
8.   **return** Result;
9. **end.**

3.2.2   The Domain Relational Calculus

The domain relational calculus (or simply the relational calculus or the domain calculus or even the calculus) is the declarative counterpart of the relational algebra. It is based on the first-order predicate calculus (see Subsection 1.9.3). In this logical approach a relational database is considered to be an *interpretation* of a first-order theory. In particular, the domain of the interpretation is a superset of the active database domain and the relations in the database are the extensions of the relation symbols of the database schema. A query in the domain relational calculus is essentially checking whether the database is a *model* of the first-order formula represented in the query. The importance of the relational calculus is that it is more suitable as a basis of user-oriented query languages due to its high-levelness and closeness to natural language. The equivalence between the relational algebra and the domain relational calculus (suitably restricted so that it only yields finite answers to queries) was first shown in [Cod72b] and is discussed in detail in Section 3.3. We proceed to formalise the relational calculus.

Definition 3.26 (Domain calculus expressions)   A domain calculus expression (or alternatively a domain calculus query or just simply a query whenever no ambiguity arises) has the form:

$$\{x_1 : A_1, x_2 : A_2, \ldots, x_n : A_n \mid F(x_1, x_2, \ldots, x_n)\},$$

where F is a well-formed formula, $A_1, A_2, \ldots, A_n$ are distinct attributes in $\mathcal{U}$ and $x_1, x_2, \ldots, x_n$ are domain variables which occur freely in F, with $n \geq 0$. When $n = 0$ the above query becomes a Boolean query. ∎

We will assume that all the relation symbols mentioned in the well-formed formula F stand for relation schemas which are members of a database schema **R**. (The concepts of a well-formed formula and free occurrence of a variable in a well-formed formula are formalised subsequently; see also Subsection 1.9.3.)

Informally, the answer to a domain calculus query

$$\{x_1 : A_1, x_2 : A_2, \ldots, x_n : A_n \mid F(x_1, x_2, \ldots, x_n)\}$$

with respect to a database $d = \{r_1, r_2, \ldots, r_m\}$ over the database schema $\mathbf{R} = \{R_1, R_2, \ldots, R_m\}$ is a relation r over relation schema R with schema(R) $= \{A_1, A_2, \ldots, A_n\}$ such that a tuple $<v_1, v_2, \ldots, v_n> \in r$ if and only if

1) for all $i \in \{1, 2, \ldots, n\}$, $v_i \in \text{DOM}(A_i)$; and

2) if for all $i \in \{1, 2, \ldots, n\}$, we substitute v_i for x_i in F, then $<v_1, v_2, \ldots, v_n>$ satisfies the formula F with respect to the database d. (The exact meaning of satisfaction of a formula will be explained subsequently.)

If there no free variables in F, i.e. $n = 0$, then the answer to the query is either true if $\{<>\}$ is returned or false if $\emptyset$ is returned.

If Q is a domain calculus query, then we denote the *answer* to Q with respect to a database d by Q(d), or simply as Q whenever d is understood from context.

We now give some example queries so that the reader can get a feel of the style of the relational calculus as opposed to the relational algebra.

Let $d = \{r_1, r_2, r_3\}$ denote the example database given in Section 3.1, where r_1 is shown in Table 3.1, r_2 is shown in Table 3.2 and r_3 is shown in Table 3.3.

The query, "Retrieve all the tuples in the relation over STUDENT", can be expressed as the domain calculus query:

$$\{x_1 : \text{SNAME}, x_2 : \text{AGE}, x_3 : \text{ADDRESS}, x_4 : \text{DEPT}, x_5 : \text{DEGREE}, x_6 : \text{YEAR} \mid$$
$$\text{STUDENT}(x_1, x_2, x_3, x_4, x_5, x_6)\}(d).$$

The query, "Retrieve the departments, degrees and years of students", can be expressed as the domain calculus query:

$$\{x_4 : \text{DEPT}, x_5 : \text{DEGREE}, x_6 : \text{YEAR} \mid$$
$$\exists x_1 : \text{SNAME}(\exists x_2 : \text{AGE}(\exists x_3 : \text{ADDRESS}(\text{STUDENT}(x_1, x_2, x_3, x_4, x_5, x_6))))\}(d).$$

Note the use of the existential quantifier ($\exists$) in this query, which is the way that the domain calculus simulates the relational algebra projection operation.

The query, "Retrieve the names and ages of students who are either studying in the Linguistics department or whose address is Oxford St", can be expressed as the domain calculus query:

$$\{x_1 : \text{SNAME}, x_2 : \text{AGE} \mid \exists x_3 : \text{ADDRESS}(\exists x_4 : \text{DEPT}(\exists x_5 : \text{DEGREE}(\exists x_6 : \text{YEAR}$$
$$(\text{STUDENT}(x_1, x_2, x_3, x_4, x_5, x_6) \wedge (x_4 = \text{'Linguistics'} \vee x_3 = \text{'Oxford St'})))))\}(d).$$

This query is an example of how the calculus simulates the relational algebra selection operation.

In general, there are many ways of posing the same query. An alternative formulation of the above query is:

$$\{x_1 : \text{SNAME}, x_2 : \text{AGE} \mid$$
$$(\exists x_3 : \text{ADDRESS}(\exists x_5 : \text{DEGREE}(\exists x_6 : \text{YEAR}(\text{STUDENT}(x_1, x_2, x_3, \text{Linguistics}, x_5, x_6)))))\vee$$
$$(\exists x_4 : \text{DEPT}(\exists x_5 : \text{DEGREE}(\exists x_6 : \text{YEAR}(\text{STUDENT}(x_1, x_2, \text{Oxford St}, x_4, x_5, x_6)))))\}(d).$$

The query, "Retrieve the names, degrees and departments of students who are not studying in the Computing department and are also not in their second year", can be expressed as the domain calculus query:

$$\{x_1 : \text{SNAME}, x_5 : \text{DEGREE}, x_4 : \text{DEPT} \mid \exists x_3 : \text{ADDRESS}(\exists x_2 : \text{AGE}(\exists x_6 : \text{YEAR}$$
$$(\text{STUDENT}(x_1, x_2, x_3, x_4, x_5, x_6) \wedge (x_4 \neq \text{'Computing'} \wedge x_6 \neq \text{'second'})))\}(d).$$

This query is another example of how the calculus simulates the relational algebra selection operation.

For the following query let s_3 be the relation over FST_SND from Subsection 3.2.1, which is shown in Table 3.12. The query, "Retrieve the names of students who did the same number of courses in their first and second years", can be expressed as the domain calculus query:

$$\{x_1 : \text{SNAME} \mid \exists x_2 : \text{FIRST}(\exists x_3 : \text{SECOND}$$
$$(\text{FST\_SND}(x_1, x_2, x_3) \wedge x_2 = x_3))\}(\{s_3\}).$$

This query is an example of how the calculus simulates the relational algebra restriction operation, which is a special case of selection.

Let SHORT_STUD1 and SHORT_STUD2 be relation schemas with schema(SHORT_STUD1) = schema(SHORT_STUD2) = {SNAME, ADDRESS, DEPT} and let s_1 over SHORT_STUD1 and s_2 over SHORT_STUD2 be the relations from Subsection 3.2.1, shown in Tables 3.4 and 3.5, respectively. The query, "Retrieve the students who either have a computing account or are receiving a grant", can be expressed as the domain calculus query:

$$\{x_1 : \text{SNAME}, x_2 : \text{ADDRESS}, x_3 : \text{DEPT} \mid$$
$$\text{SHORT\_STUD1}(x_1, x_2, x_3) \vee \text{SHORT\_STUD2}(x_1, x_2, x_3)\}(\{s_1, s_2\}).$$

This query is an example of how the calculus simulates the relational algebra union operation.

The query, "Retrieve the students who have a computing account but do not receive a grant", can be expressed as the domain calculus query:

$$\{x_1 : \text{SNAME}, x_2 : \text{ADDRESS}, x_3 : \text{DEPT} \mid$$
$$\text{SHORT\_STUD1}(x_1, x_2, x_3) \wedge (\neg\text{SHORT\_STUD2}(x_1, x_2, x_3))\}(\{s_1, s_2\}).$$

This query is an example of how the calculus simulates the relational algebra difference operation.

The query, "Retrieve the students who have a computing account and are receiving a grant", can be expressed as the domain calculus query:

$$\{x_1 : \text{SNAME}, x_2 : \text{ADDRESS}, x_3 : \text{DEPT} \mid$$
$$\text{SHORT\_STUD1}(x_1, x_2, x_3) \wedge \text{SHORT\_STUD2}(x_1, x_2, x_3)\}(\{s_1, s_2\}).$$

This query is an example of how the calculus simulates the relational algebra intersection operation.

The query, "Retrieve the names of courses and the tutoring days", can be expressed as the domain calculus query:

$$\{x_1 : \text{CNAME}, x_2 : \text{DAY} \mid$$
$$\exists x_3 : \text{DEPT}(\exists x_4 : \text{TNAME}(\exists x_5 : \text{TEXT}(\exists x_6 : \text{SALARY}$$
$$\text{COURSE}(x_3, x_1, x_4, x_5) \wedge \text{TUTOR}(x_4, x_3, x_6, x_2))))\}(d).$$

This query is an example of how the calculus simulates the relational algebra natural join operation.

An alternative formulation of the above query is:

$$\{x_1 : \text{CNAME}, x_2 : \text{DAY} \mid$$
$$\exists x_3^1 : \text{DEPT}(\exists x_3^2 : \text{DEPT}(\exists x_4^1 : \text{TNAME}(\exists x_4^2 : \text{TNAME}(\exists x_5 : \text{TEXT}(\exists x_6 : \text{SALARY}$$
$$(\text{COURSE}(x_3^1, x_1, x_4^1, x_5) \wedge \text{TUTOR}(x_4^2, x_3^2, x_6, x_2) \wedge x_3^1 = x_3^2 \wedge x_4^1 = x_4^2))))))\}(d).$$

Assume that s_1 over SHORT_STUD is the relation of Subsection 3.2.1, shown in Table 3.4 and recall that r_2 is a relation over COURSE, shown in Table 3.2. The query, "Retrieve the courses that students can do in the department they are studying in", can be expressed as the domain calculus query:

$$\{x_1 : \text{CNAME}, x_2 : \text{DEPT}, x_3 : \text{SNAME} \mid \exists x_4 : \text{ADDRESS}(\exists x_5 : \text{TNAME}(\exists x_6 : \text{TEXT}$$
$$(\text{SHORT\_STUD}(x_3, x_4, x_2) \wedge \text{COURSE}(x_2, x_1, x_5, x_6)))))\}(\{s_1, r_2\}).$$

This query is another example of how the calculus simulates the relational algebra natural join operation.

Let s_4 be the relation over TOPICS, shown in Table 3.19, and let s_5 be the relation over INTERESTS, shown in Table 3.20. The query, "Retrieve the lecturers who are interested in all the topics of the Computing department", can be expressed as the domain calculus query:

$$\{x_1 : \text{LECTURER} \mid \forall x_2 : \text{TOPIC}(\exists x_3 : \text{TOPIC}$$
$$(\text{TOPICS}(x_2) \wedge \text{INTERESTS}(x_1, x_3) \wedge x_2 = x_3))\}(\{s_4, s_5\}).$$

This query is an example of how the calculus simulates the relational algebra division operation.

We now formally define the components - which are the symbols allowed in formulae and well-formed formulae built from atomic formulae by using the logical connectives - of domain calculus expressions.

The following symbols are allowed to appear in formulae:

- Constant values (or simply constants), $v, v_1, v_2, \ldots$, which are elements of the set $\mathcal{D}$.

- Domain variables (or simply variables), $x, x_1, x_2, \ldots$, which are members of a countably infinite set of variables $\mathcal{V}$ disjoint from $\mathcal{D}$.

- Relation symbols, R, R_1, R_2, $\ldots$, which are drawn from a countably infinite set of symbols disjoint from $\mathcal{V}$ and $\mathcal{D}$; each relation symbol corresponds to the relation schema associated with that symbol.

- The equality operator, =.

- The quantifiers and logical connectives, $\exists$ (there exists), $\forall$ (for all), $\wedge$ (and), $\vee$ (or), $\Rightarrow$ (implication) and $\neg$ (not).

- Delimiters, () (parentheses), and , (comma).

As in the relational algebra selection formulae we have only included equality (=) as a comparison operator; in general, however, we can expect also to have at least $\leq$ (less than or equal to) and $<$ (less than) available.

Atomic formulae are defined as follows:

1) $R(y_1, y_2, \ldots, y_n)$, where R is a relation symbol with type(R) $= n$ and for all $i \in \{1, 2, \ldots, n\}$, y_i is either a constant or a variable.

2) $x = y$, where x is a variable and y is either a variable or a constant.

Well-formed formulae (or simply formulae) are now defined recursively as follows:

1) An atomic formula is a formula.

2) If F is a formula, then so are $\neg F$ and (F).

3) If F_1 and F_2 are formulae, then so are $F_1 \wedge F_2$, $F_1 \vee F_2$ and $F_1 \Rightarrow F_2$.

4) If F is a formula then $\exists x : A(F)$ and $\forall x : A(F)$ are formulae, where x is a variable and A is an attribute.

5) No other formulae are well-formed formulae.

A *subformula* of a formula F is a substring of F that is also a formula. We omit parentheses in formulae if no ambiguity arises as to the meaning of a formula. In addition, we write $x \neq y$ as an abbreviation for $\neg(x = y)$.

From now on we will assume that all the relation schemas corresponding to the relation symbols that are mentioned in F are included in a database schema **R**.

The *free* occurrences of variables in a formula are defined as follows:

1) All the variables occurring in an atomic formula are free.

2) The free variables occurring in $\neg F$ and F are the same as the free variables occurring in the formula F.

3) The free variables occurring in $F_1 \wedge F_2$, $F_1 \vee F_2$ and $F_1 \Rightarrow F_2$ are the free variables occurring in the formula F_1 together with the free variables occurring in the formula F_2.

4) The free variables occurring in $\exists x : A(F)$ and $\forall x : A(F)$ are the free variables occurring in the formula F except for occurrences of x in F.

We write $F(x_1, x_2, \ldots, x_n)$ for a formula F to indicate that $x_1, x_2, \ldots, x_n$ are all the free variables occurring in F.

Definition 3.27 (Satisfaction of a formula by a tuple)   Let $d = \{r_1, r_2, \ldots, r_m\}$ be a database over the database schema $\mathbf{R} = \{R_1, R_2, \ldots, R_m\}$ and consider the query

$$\{x_1 : A_1, x_2 : A_2, \ldots, x_n : A_n \mid F(x_1, x_2, \ldots, x_n)\}.$$

A tuple $<v_1, v_2, \ldots, v_n>$ *satisfies* the formula F with respect to d, if for all $i \in \{1, 2, \ldots, n\}$, $v_i \in \text{DOM}(A_i)$, and one of the following conditions is satisfied:

1) If F is the atomic formula $R(y_1, y_2, \ldots, y_k)$, then $R \in \mathbf{R}$ and the tuple t, resulting from substituting v_i for each variable $y_i \in \{y_1, y_2, \ldots, y_k\}$, satisfies $t \in r$, where r is the relation over R in d.

2) If F is the atomic formula $x_i = y_j$, then $v_i = v_j$ is satisfied, where v_i is substituted for x_i, and either y_j is a variable and v_j is substituted for y_j or y_j is a constant and $v_j = y_j$.

3) If F is the formula (G), then $<v_1, v_2, \ldots, v_n>$ satisfies the formula F if $<v_1, v_2, \ldots, v_n>$ satisfies G.

4) If F takes one of the forms: $\neg F$, $F_1 \wedge F_2$, $F_1 \vee F_2$ or $F_1 \Rightarrow F_2$, then $<v_1, v_2, \ldots, v_n>$ satisfies F is defined according to the semantics of the corresponding logical connectives. As an example, $<v_1, v_2, \ldots, v_n>$ satisfies $F_1 \Rightarrow F_2$ if either $<v_1, v_2, \ldots, v_n>$ does not satisfy F_1 or $<v_1, v_2, \ldots, v_n>$ satisfies F_2. (See Definition 3.14 of logical implication for the semantics of the rest of the connectives.)

5) If F is the formula $\exists x_i : A (G(x_1, x_2, \ldots, x_i, \ldots, x_n))$, then $<v_1, v_2, \ldots, v_{i-1}, v_{i+1}, \ldots, v_n>$ satisfies F if there exists a constant $v_i \in \text{DOM}(A)$ such that when v_i is substituted for x_i, $<v_1, v_2, \ldots, v_{i-1}, v_i, v_{i+1}, \ldots, v_n>$ satisfies G.

6) If F is the formula $\forall x_i : A (G(x_1, x_2, \ldots, x_i, \ldots, x_n))$, then $<v_1, v_2, \ldots, v_{i-1}, v_{i+1}, \ldots, v_n>$ satisfies F if for all constants $v_i \in \text{DOM}(A)$, when v_i is substituted for x_i, $<v_1, v_2, \ldots, v_{i-1}, v_i, v_{i+1}, \ldots, v_n>$ satisfies G. ∎

Informally, an answer to a query

$$\{x_1 : A_1, x_2 : A_2, \ldots, x_n : A_n \mid F(x_1, x_2, \ldots, x_n)\}$$

with respect to a database d is the set of all tuples satisfying F.

Definition 3.28 (An answer to a domain calculus query) An *answer to a query*

$$\{x_1 : A_1, x_2 : A_2, \ldots, x_n : A_n \mid F(x_1, x_2, \ldots, x_n)\}$$

with respect to a database d over **R**, denoted by

$$\{x_1 : A_1, x_2 : A_2, \ldots, x_n : A_n \mid F(x_1, x_2, \ldots, x_n)\}(d),$$

is a relation r over relation schema R, with schema(R) = $\{A_1, A_2, \ldots, A_n\}$, defined by

$$r = \{t \mid t \text{ satisfies } F\}.$$ ∎

At times we will also refer to an answer to a query simply as a query when no ambiguity arises.

We do not deal with the extension of the domain calculus to incorporate the transitive closure operator or aggregate functions. We mention that an extension of the relational calculus which deals with aggregate functions was given in [Klu82]. On the other hand, we will see that the transitive closure operator can be expressed naturally in Datalog, which is presented in the next section.

We now briefly introduce SQL (Structured Query Language) [AC75, Cha80], which is a relational database query language based on the domain calculus. SQL is in fact more than just a query language, since it also supports updates, data definition of relation schemas, transaction processing and recovery, security of relations, definition of integrity constraints and definition of views. SQL was developed during the 1970's at IBM as part of the System R project. During the 1980's SQL was standardised by ISO and the current ISO SQL standard is its second version, called SQL2 [DD93]. Currently most relational DBMSs support SQL and there is a growing demand from users that these systems support the standard.

In the following we will only cover a small subset of the data manipulation part of SQL. A simple SQL query is a statement, called a *SELECT* statement, having the form:

SELECT $A_1, A_2, \ldots, A_q$
FROM $R_1, R_2, \ldots, R_k$
WHERE F

In the above SELECT statement, $R_1, R_2, \ldots, R_k$ are relation schemas, $A_1, A_2, \ldots, A_q$ are attributes in those relation schemas and F is a selection formula over a relation schema whose attributes comprise the union of the attributes in each schema$(R_j), j \in \{1, 2, \ldots, k\}$.

The semantics of the above SQL query can be best explained in terms of the following relational algebra query:

$$\pi_{\{A_1, A_2, \ldots, A_q\}}(\sigma_F(R_1 \times R_2 \times \cdots \times R_k)).$$

That is, in order to answer a simple SQL query we take the Cartesian product of the relations r_j over R_j in the database which we are querying, then select the tuples that logically imply F and finally project the result onto attributes specified in the SELECT clause. If the WHERE clause is omitted then all the tuples in the Cartesian product are projected onto the specified attributes.

The SQL query

SELECT DEPT, DEGREE, YEAR
FROM STUDENT

is equivalent to the relational algebra query, $\pi_{\{DEPT, DEGREE, YEAR\}}(STUDENT)$.

The SQL query

SELECT *
FROM STUDENT
WHERE DEPT = 'Linguistics' OR ADDRESS = 'Oxford St'

is equivalent to the relational algebra query $\sigma_{F_1}(STUDENT)$, where F_1 is the formula: DEPT = 'Linguistics' $\vee$ ADDRESS = 'Oxford St'. Note that "*" is used to denote the set of all attributes in schema(STUDENT).

The SQL query

SELECT *
FROM STUDENT
WHERE (NOT (DEPT = 'Computing')) AND (NOT (YEAR = 'second'))

is equivalent to the relational algebra query $\sigma_{F_2}(STUDENT)$, where F_2 is the formula: DEPT $\neq$ 'Computing' $\wedge$ YEAR $\neq$ 'second'.

The SQL query

SELECT SNAME, STUDENT.DEPT, CNAME
FROM STUDENT, COURSE
WHERE STUDENT.DEPT = COURSE.DEPT

is equivalent to the relational algebra query $\pi_{\{SNAME,DEPT,CNAME\}}$(STUDENT $\bowtie$ COURSE).
Note that whenever an attribute appears in two or more schemas we use the dot notation R.A
to indicate that we are referring to the attribute A in schema(R).

The SQL query

SELECT DEPT, MAX(SALARY)
FROM TUTOR
GROUP BY DEPT

is equivalent to the relational algebra query $\mathrm{MAX}^{DEPT}_{SALARY}$(TUTOR). Note that the GROUP BY
clause has the effect of partitioning an input relation to the query, over the schema TUTOR,
according to the attribute DEPT.

The final example shows an SQL query in which the formula in the WHERE clause of the
query is an SQL query itself. Such a query in the WHERE clause is called a *subquery*. The
syntax of a subquery, which is nested within the WHERE clause of an SQL query, is the same
as a general SQL query and thus multiple subqueries are allowed.

The SQL query

SELECT TNAME
FROM TUTOR
WHERE EXISTS
    SELECT *
    FROM COURSE
    WHERE TNAME.TUTOR = TNAME.COURSE

is equivalent to the relational algebra query π_{TNAME}(TUTOR $\bowtie$ COURSE). Note that the
subquery is connected to the main query by using the keyword **EXISTS**; informally, this leads
to the selection of only those tuples such that the result of applying the subquery is a nonempty
relation.

3.2.3   Datalog

Datalog is an abbreviation for *Data Logic*. As mentioned in Subsection 1.7.5 of Chapter 1
Datalog is a rule-based declarative query language. The syntax of Datalog is essentially a
subset of the syntax of Prolog [MW88a, SS94]. In Datalog function symbols in predicates
are not allowed and in its purest form there are no extra-logical predicates that operate by
"side-effect" such as input and output predicates and, in addition, there are no procedural
predicates such as the infamous *cut*, which, in general, cannot be interpreted declaratively.
The semantics of Datalog are purely logical as opposed to the semantics of Prolog which

are procedural. Thus, for example, in Prolog the order of the rules in a program and the order of the literals in the body of rules can have an effect on the semantics of a program. Furthermore, the order of facts in a Prolog database can also have an effect on the semantics of a program. In Datalog the order of rules in a program and the order of literals in the body of rules have no effect whatsoever on the semantics of the program. Another important difference between Prolog and Datalog is that Prolog processes one fact at a time while Datalog processes sets of facts at a time. The importance of Datalog is that it adds deductive or inference capabilities to the relational calculus, thus transforming a relational database into a logical database.

We now formally define the syntax of Datalog programs.

The atomic formulae of Datalog are the same as the atomic formulae of domain calculus expressions. As with domain calculus expressions, we write $x \neq y$ as an abbreviation for $\neg(x = y)$. We will distinguish between the following types of atomic formula:

- An atomic formula of the form $R(y_1, y_2, \ldots, y_k)$ is called a *predicate formula* (or simply a predicate); recall that the relation symbol R of the atomic formula corresponds to the relation schema having that symbol (when no ambiguity arises we use the terms relation symbol, predicate and relation schema interchangeably).

- An atomic formula of the form $x = y$ is called an *equality formula* (or simply an equality).

- A predicate formula of the form $R(v_1, v_2, \ldots, v_k)$, where the v_i are constants in DOM(att(i)) for each $i \in \{1, 2, \ldots, k\}$, is called a *ground atomic formula* over R.

A *literal* is either an atomic formula, say L, or the negation of L, namely $\neg L$; L is called a *positive literal* and $\neg L$ is called a *negative literal*. A literal which is a ground atomic formula or the negation of a ground atomic formula is called a *ground literal*.

A *clause* (or alternatively a *rule*) is an expression of the form:

$$L :- L_1, L_2, \ldots, L_n.$$

In a rule such as above $n \geq 0$ is a natural number, for all $i \in \{1, 2, \ldots, n\}$, L_i is a literal and L is a predicate. The sequence of literals, $L_1, L_2, \ldots, L_n$, is called the *body* of the clause and L is called the *head* of the clause. If $n = 0$ then we abbreviate $L : -$ simply to L. In the special case where $n = 0$ and L is a ground atomic formula over R, we call L a *fact* over R (or simply a fact if R is understood from context). A clause which is not a fact is called a *nontrivial rule* (or when there is no confusion, simply a rule). A *Datalog program* P (or simply a program P) is a finite set $C_1, C_2, \ldots, C_m$ of clauses. (When it is convenient then, without any loss of generality, we view P as a sequence of clauses.)

We observe that a relation r over a schema R induces a set of facts all having the relation symbol R. For example, the first two tuples in the relation r_1 over STUDENT, shown in Table 3.1, induce the following two facts:

STUDENT(Iris, 21, Malet St, Computing, BSC, first).
STUDENT(Reuven, 32, Harold Rd, Maths, BSC, second).

Prior to the ensuing definition, we recall the definition of an acyclic and cyclic directed graph from Section 2.1 of Chapter 2.

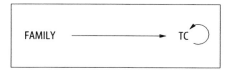

Fig 3.3 The dependency graph of TC

Definition 3.29 (Recursive and nonrecursive Datalog programs)   The *dependency graph* of a Datalog program P is a digraph (N, E), where the set of nodes N is the set of relation symbols that appear in the literals of P, and there is an arc from R_1 to R_2 in E if there is a rule in P whose body contains either the positive literal $R_1(y_1, y_2, \ldots, y_k)$ or the negative literal $\neg R_1(y_1, y_2, \ldots, y_k)$ and whose head is the literal $R_2(z_1, z_2, \ldots, z_q)$.

A Datalog program is said to be *nonrecursive* if its dependency graph is acyclic, otherwise if its dependency graph is cyclic, it is said to be a *recursive* Datalog program.   ∎

An example of a recursive Datalog program, say TC, is:

$TC(x_1, x_2) :- FAMILY(x_1, x_2)$.
$TC(x_1, x_3) :- FAMILY(x_1, x_2), TC(x_2, x_3)$.

The cyclic dependency graph of the above simple Datalog program is shown in Figure 3.3.

After we define the meaning of a Datalog program it will be evident that the Datalog program given above computes the transitive closure of FAMILY, assuming that the program contains some facts over FAMILY (see Definition 3.34 below).

For the rest of this section we will assume that Datalog programs are nonrecursive and refer to them simply as Datalog programs. Although we restrict Datalog programs to be nonrecursive, Definition 3.34, giving the semantics of Datalog programs, does obtain for recursive Datalog programs also. (The definition for recursive Datalog programs will be needed in Chapter 9 on deductive databases).

We now give some examples of Datalog programs so that the reader can get a feel of the programming style of Datalog. In all of the programs we have assumed a relation symbol, RESULT, whose set of facts will contain the result of the query when the Datalog program is evaluated.

The query, "Retrieve all the tuples in the relation over STUDENT", can be expressed as the result of the Datalog program:

$RESULT(x_1, x_2, x_3, x_4, x_5, x_6) :- STUDENT(x_1, x_2, x_3, x_4, x_5, x_6)$.

The query, "Retrieve the departments, degrees and years of students", can be expressed as the result of the Datalog program:

$RESULT(x_4, x_5, x_6) :- STUDENT(x_1, x_2, x_3, x_4, x_5, x_6)$.

Note how the absence of variables in the head of a rule simulates the use of the existential quantifier ($\exists$) in a domain calculus query and thus the relational algebra projection operation.

The query, "Retrieve the names and ages of students who are either studying in the Linguistics department or whose address is Oxford St", can be expressed as the result of the Datalog program:

$\text{RESULT}(x_1, x_2) :- \text{STUDENT}(x_1, x_2, x_3, x_4, x_5, x_6), x_4 = \text{'Linguistics'}.$
$\text{RESULT}(x_1, x_2) :- \text{STUDENT}(x_1, x_2, x_3, x_4, x_5, x_6), x_3 = \text{'Oxford St'}.$

Note how two rules in a Datalog program simulate the use of disjunction ($\vee$) in a domain calculus query. In addition, each rule simulates a relational algebra selection operation.

The query, "Retrieve the names, degrees and departments of students who are not studying in the Computing department and are also not in their second year", can be expressed as the result of the Datalog program:

$\text{RESULT}(x_1, x_5, x_4) :- \text{STUDENT}(x_1, x_2, x_3, x_4, x_5, x_6), x_4 \neq \text{'Computing'}, x_6 \neq \text{'second'}.$

The above program is an example of how Datalog simulates the relational algebra selection operation.

For the following query let s_3 be the relation over FST_SND from Subsection 3.2.1, which is shown in Table 3.12. The query, "Retrieve the names of students who did the same number of courses in their first and second years", can be expressed as the result of the Datalog program:

$\text{RESULT}(x_1) :- \text{FST\_SND}(x_1, x_2, x_3), x_2 = x_3.$

The above program is an example of how Datalog simulates the relational algebra restriction operation, which is a special case of selection.

Let SHORT_STUD1 and SHORT_STUD2 be relation schemas with schema(SHORT_STUD1) = schema(SHORT_STUD2) = {SNAME, ADDRESS, DEPT} and let s_1 over SHORT_STUD1 and s_2 over SHORT_STUD2 be the relations from Subsection 3.2.1, shown in Tables 3.4 and 3.5, respectively. The query, "Retrieve the names of students who either have a computing account or are receiving a grant", can be expressed as the result of the Datalog program:

$\text{RESULT}(x_1, x_2, x_3) :- \text{SHORT\_STUD1}(x_1, x_2, x_3).$
$\text{RESULT}(x_1, x_2, x_3) :- \text{SHORT\_STUD2}(x_1, x_2, x_3).$

The above program is an example of how Datalog simulates the relational algebra union operation.

The query, "Retrieve the names of students who have a computing account but do not receive a grant", can be expressed as the result of the Datalog program:

$\text{RESULT}(x_1, x_2, x_3) :- \text{SHORT\_STUD1}(x_1, x_2, x_3), \neg\text{SHORT\_STUD2}(x_1, x_2, x_3).$

The above program is an example of how Datalog simulates the relational algebra difference operation.

The query, "Retrieve the names of students who have a computing account and are receiving a grant", can be expressed as the result of the Datalog program:

$$\text{RESULT}(x_1, x_2, x_3) :- \text{SHORT\_STUD1}(x_1, x_2, x_3), \text{SHORT\_STUD2}(x_1, x_2, x_3).$$

The above program is an example of how Datalog simulates the relational algebra intersection operation.

The query, "Retrieve the names of courses and the tutoring days", can be expressed as the result of the Datalog program:

$$\text{RESULT}(x_1, x_2) :- \text{COURSE}(x_3, x_1, x_4, x_5), \text{TUTOR}(x_4, x_3, x_6, x_2).$$

The above program is an example of how Datalog simulates the relational algebra natural join operation.

An alternative formulation of the above query is:

$$\text{RESULT}(x_1, x_2) :- \text{COURSE}(x_3^1, x_1, x_4^1, x_5), \text{TUTOR}(x_4^2, x_3^2, x_6, x_2), x_3^1 = x_3^2, x_4^1 = x_4^2.$$

Assume that s_1 over SHORT_STUD is the relation of Subsection 3.2.1, shown in Table 3.4, and recall that r_2 is a relation over COURSE. The query, "Retrieve the courses that students can do in the department they are studying in", can be expressed as the result of the Datalog program:

$$\text{RESULT}(x_1, x_2, x_3) :- \text{SHORT\_STUD}(x_3, x_4, x_2), \text{COURSE}(x_2, x_1, x_5, x_6).$$

The above program is another example of how Datalog simulates the relational algebra natural join operation.

Let s_4 be the relation over TOPICS, shown in Table 3.19, and let s_5 be the relation over INTERESTS, shown in Table 3.20. The query, "Retrieve the lecturers who are interested in all the topics of the Computing department", can be expressed as the result of the Datalog program:

$$\text{RESULT}(x_1) :- \text{INTERESTS}(x_1, x_3), \neg\text{DIFF}(x_1).$$
$$\text{DIFF}(x_1) :- \text{PROD}(x_1, x_2), \neg\text{INTERESTS}(x_1, x_2).$$
$$\text{PROD}(x_1, x_2) :- \text{INTERESTS}(x_1, x_3), \text{TOPICS}(x_2).$$

The above program is an example of how Datalog simulates the relational algebra division operation. The acyclic dependency graph of the above program is shown in Figure 3.4.

A Datalog program makes sense only if the relations that can be derived from executing these programs are finite. The *safety* restriction, defined next, provides a syntactic restriction of programs which enforces the finiteness of derived predicates (or relations).

Definition 3.30 (Safe Datalog program)   A variable x occurring in one of the literals in the head or the body of a rule, say C, *occurs positively* in C if and only if either

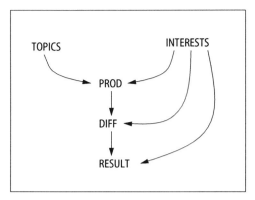

Fig 3.4 The dependency graph of RESULT

1) The variable x appears in a predicate formula $R(y_1, y_2, \ldots, x, \ldots, y_k)$, which is a positive literal in the body of C, or

2) The variable x appears in an equality formula $x = v$, which is a positive literal in the body of C, where v is a constant, or

3) The variable x appears in the equality $x = y$ or $y = x$, which is a positive literal in the body of C, where y is a variable that appears positively in C.

A Datalog rule C is said to be *safe* if all the variables appearing in the literals of C (including the head of C) occur positively in C. A Datalog program P is said to be *safe* if all the rules of P are safe.   ■

We observe that in a safe rule all the variables in the head of a rule must appear in one or more literals in its body. Furthermore, all the variables appearing in negative literals in the body of a safe rule must occur positively in one or more atomic formulae in its body.

Example 3.1   The following rules are not safe:

1) $RESULT1(x) :- COURSE(x_1, x_2, x_3, x_4)$

2) $RESULT2(x_1, x_2, x_3, x_4) :- \neg COURSE(x_1, x_2, x_3, x_4)$

3) $RESULT3(x_1) :- COURSE(x_1, x_2, x_3, x_4), x_5 = x_6$

In the first rule the variable x does not appear in the body of the rule. In the second rule the variables x_1, x_2, x_3, x_4 appear only in the negative literal in the body of the rule. In the third case x_5 and x_6 appear only in the equality $x_5 = x_6$.   ■

The reader can verify that all the examples of Datalog programs given prior to Example 3.1 are safe.

As we will show in Subsection 3.3.2 the class of nonrecursive safe Datalog programs can express exactly the same set of queries that the relational algebra can express. Moreover, we also show in Subsection 3.3.2 that nonrecursive safe Datalog can be viewed as a restricted version of the domain calculus, that is, nonrecursive safe Datalog is exactly as expressive as this restricted version of the domain calculus.

We proceed to define the semantics of general Datalog programs, which may be recursive and unsafe.

Definition 3.31 (The schema of Datalog program)   The database schema of a Datalog program P, denoted by SCHEMA(P), is a set of relation schemas defined by

SCHEMA(P) = {R | R is a relation symbol that appears in a literal of a rule in P}. ◼

Definition 3.32 (Substituting the variables in a clause)   Let C be a clause and $\{x_1, x_2, \ldots, x_q\}$ be the variables appearing in the literals of the body of C. A *substitution* θ for C is a set of assignments $\{x_1/v_1, x_2/v_2, \ldots, x_q/v_q\}$, where for all $i \in \{1, 2, \ldots, q\}$, v_i is in the domain of constants, $\mathcal{D}$. We denote by $\theta(C)$ the clause resulting from applying the substitution θ to the literals in C, i.e. the result of substituting, for each $i \in \{1, 2, \ldots, q\}$, the constant v_i for the variable x_i in each of the literals in C. ◼

We note that all the literals of the clause $\theta(C)$ are ground literals.

Definition 3.33 (Truth of a clause with respect to a database)   A literal L in the body of a clause C in a Datalog program P is true with respect to a substitution θ for C and a database d over SCHEMA(P) if one of the following conditions is satisfied:

1) $\theta(L)$ is a ground atomic formula of the form $R(v_1, v_2, \ldots, v_k)$ and $<v_1, v_2, \ldots, v_k> \in r$, where $r \in d$ is the relation over R.

2) $\theta(L)$ is an equality, $v = v$, where v is a constant.

3) $\theta(L)$ is a ground literal of the form $\neg R(v_1, v_2, \ldots, v_k)$ and $<v_1, v_2, \ldots, v_k> \notin r$, where $r \in d$ is the relation over R.

4) $\theta(L)$ is a negative literal of the form, $\neg(v_i = v_j)$, where v_i and v_j are distinct constants, i.e. such that $v_i \neq v_j$.

A clause C in a program P is true with respect to a substitution θ for C and a database d over SCHEMA(P) if each of the literals in the body of C is true with respect to θ and d. ◼

We observe that the truth of a negative literal with respect to a substitution and a database is consistent with the CWA (closed world assumption) [Rei78], since $\neg R(v_1, v_2, \ldots, v_k)$ is assumed to be true if the tuple $<v_1, v_2, \ldots, v_k>$ is absent from the database. This causes a problem if the Datalog program is unsafe, since infinite relations may be derived due to the fact that the underlying domain is infinite. Thus RESULT2 of Example 3.1 is an infinite relation.

We further note that if the body of the clause is empty, i.e. the clause is a predicate, then C is trivially true with respect to any substitution θ for C and any database d over SCHEMA(P). In particular, if C is a fact then C is trivially true with respect to θ and d.

The meaning of a Datalog program P, denoted by MEANING(P), is informally the database resulting from adding to the initial set of facts recorded in P as many new facts of the form

$\theta(L)$ as possible, where θ is a substitution that makes a rule C in P true and L is the head of C. (A set of facts whose relation symbols are in SCHEMA(P) is naturally associated with a database d over SCHEMA(P), since a fact having the relation symbol R can be viewed as a set of tuples over R.)

Definition 3.34 (The meaning of a Datalog program)   The pseudo-code of an algorithm, which realises MEANING(P), is next presented. (The variable Im is called the *immediate consequence* of the current state of MEANING(P).)   ∎

Algorithm 3.4 (MEANING(P))
1. **begin**
2.   Result := ∅;
3.   Tmp := {<>};
4.   **while** Tmp ≠ Result **do**
5.   Tmp := Result;
6.   Im := ∅;
7.   **for all** clauses C in P and substitutions θ for C
                such that C is true with respect to θ and Result **do**
8.   Im := Im ∪ {$\theta(L)$} where L is the head of C;
9.   **end for**
10.   Result := Result ∪ Im;
11.   **end while**
12.   **return** Result;
13. **end.**

We observe that the current state of Result strictly increases after each iteration of the while loop beginning at line 4, provided the relations in the immediate consequence, Im, of Result are not already included in the respective relations in Result. Thus Im induces an *immediate consequence* operator, say $\mathcal{T}$, such that $\mathcal{T}(\text{Result}) = \text{Result} \cup \text{Im}$. Such an increasing operator is called *inflationary*, and the final output database returned from MEANING(P) is called the *inflationary fixpoint* of the Datalog program P [GS86, KP91]. (We also refer to MEANING(P) as the inflationary meaning of P.)

We will now show how we can optimise Algorithm 3.4.

Let CONST(P) denote the set of all constants appearing in the literals of the clauses in a Datalog program P, and call a substitution $\theta = \{x_1/v_1, x_2/v_2, \ldots, x_q/v_q\}$ for a clause C in P a *safe* substitution if $\{v_1, v_2, \ldots, v_q\} \subseteq \text{CONST(P)}$.

The following proposition, which follows immediately from the definition of a clause being true with respect to a substitution and a database, states that when computing MEANING(P) for a safe Datalog program, P, it is sufficient to consider only safe substitutions.

Proposition 3.3   Let d over SCHEMA(P) be the current state of Result at line 10 of the algorithm MEANING(P) after one or more executions of the while loop beginning at line 4 of the algorithm. Then a clause C in a safe Datalog program P is true with respect to a substitution θ for C and d if and only if θ is a safe substitution for C.   □

The next proposition states that when considering only safe substitutions, then safe and unsafe Datalog are equivalent, since only finite relations can be generated in both cases.

Proposition 3.4   Assume that only safe substitutions θ for C are considered in line 7 of MEANING(P). Then safe and unsafe Datalog are equivalent in the sense that for every unsafe Datalog program P^u, there exists a safe Datalog program P^s such that MEANING(P^u) = MEANING(P^s).

Proof. Let P^u be an unsafe Datalog program. We can then construct a safe Datalog program, denoted by P^c, having a distinguished unary predicate, CONSTANT, which is the head of all the rules in P^c, and such that the set of facts in MEANING(P^c) over CONSTANT is exactly CONST(P^u). First for every rule R^u in P^u whose head is R($x_1, x_2, \ldots, x_i, \ldots, x_k$) such that x_i does not appear in the literals of the body of R^u add CONSTANT(x_i) to the body of R^u. Then for every rule R^u in P^u, and every negative literal in the body of R^u of the form $\neg$R($x_1, x_2, \ldots, x_k$), which causes R^u to be unsafe, add the positive literals, CONSTANT(x_1), CONSTANT(x_2), $\ldots$, CONSTANT(x_k), to the body of R^u. Moreover, for every rule R^u in P^u, and every equality in the body of R^u of the form $x_i = x_j$, which causes R^u to be unsafe, add the positive literals, CONSTANT(x_i) and CONSTANT(x_j) to the body of R^u. Finally, add the rules in P^c to the modified version of P^u, and denote this program by P^s. We leave it to the reader to verify that P^s is indeed a safe Datalog program and that MEANING(P^s) = MEANING(P^u).   □

For the rest of the book *we assume that only safe substitutions are considered at line 7 of* MEANING(P). Therefore, due to the above proposition, we need not distinguish between safe and unsafe Datalog, since under this assumption all Datalog programs can be considered as being *safe*. (At times for clarity we will highlight the fact that a Datalog program is safe.)

Definition 3.35 (The initial database of a Datalog program)   The initial (relational) database of a Datalog program P, over SCHEMA(P) = $\{R_1, R_2, \ldots, R_n\}$, denoted by DB(P), is the set of relations $\{r_1, r_2, \ldots, r_n\}$ such that for all $i \in \{1, 2, \ldots, n\}$, r_i is defined by

$$r_i = \{<v_1, v_2, \ldots, v_k> \mid R_i(v_1, v_2, \ldots, v_k) \text{ is a fact over } R_i \text{ that appears in P}\}. \quad ■$$

We say that a database d_1 over a database schema **R** is *included* in a database d_2 over **R**, written $d_1 \subseteq d_2$, if $\forall r_i^1 \in d_1$ over $R_i \in$ **R**, with $r_i^1 \neq \emptyset$, $\exists r_i^2 \in d_2$ over R_i such that $r_i^1 \subseteq r_i^2$.

The following proposition follows immediately from inspecting Algorithm 3.4 noting that if a clause C is actually a fact, say R($v_1, v_2, \ldots, v_k$), then C is true with respect to any database and the empty substitution $\theta = \emptyset$.

Proposition 3.5   The initial database of a Datalog program P, DB(P), is included in the meaning of P, MEANING(P).   □

Let P be a Datalog program and SCHEMA(P) = $\{R_1, R_2, \ldots, R_n\}$. Now, due to the fact that in this section P is assumed to be nonrecursive, we can order the relation schemas in SCHEMA(P) in such a way that for any $R_i, R_j \in$ SCHEMA(P) if there is a path from R_i to R_j in the dependency graph of P then $i < j$. (We note that such an ordering can be obtained by a topological sort of the dependency graph, as defined in Subsection 1.9.2 of Chapter 1.) Let us assume that the relation schemas in SCHEMA(P) are ordered in this manner.

The pseudo-code of an algorithm, which realises NEW_MEANING(P), taking into account Propositions 3.3, 3.4 and 3.5 and the ordering of the relation schemas in SCHEMA(P), is presented as the algorithm that follows; for the purpose of the algorithm, given a database d over SCHEMA(P), $d \cup R_i(v_1, v_2, \ldots, v_k)$ is the database resulting from inserting $<v_1, v_2, \ldots, v_k>$ into the relation $r_i \in d$ over R_i, where d is a database over SCHEMA(P).

Algorithm 3.5 (NEW_MEANING(P))
1. **begin**
2.   Result := DB(P);
3.   **for** $i := 1$ **to** n **do**
4.   **while** there exists a rule C in P such that R_i is the relation symbol of its head
             and there exists a safe substitution θ for C
             such that C is true with respect to θ and Result **do**
5.   Result := Result $\cup \theta(L)$ where L is the head of C;
6.   **end while**
7.   **end for**
8.   **return** Result;
9. **end.**

We leave the proof of the following theorem to the reader.

Theorem 3.6   Given a Datalog program P (which is assumed to be nonrecursive and safe), MEANING(P) = NEW_MEANING(P).   □

We now show how the meaning of a Datalog program can be used to answer queries.

Definition 3.36 (Datalog query)   A *Datalog query* with respect to a Datalog program P is an expression of the form : $-_P L$, where L is a predicate (or simply : $-L$ whenever P is understood from context).   ∎

Definition 3.37 (The answer to a Datalog query)   Let L be the predicate $R(y_1, y_2, \ldots, y_k)$ and $\{x_1, x_2, \ldots, x_q\}$ be the variables appearing in L. Furthermore, let us call a substitution $\theta = \{x_1/v_1, x_2/v_2, \ldots, x_q/v_q\}$ *safe* for L with respect to a Datalog program P if $\{v_1, v_2, \ldots, v_q\} \subseteq$ CONST(P). Then the answer to the Datalog query, : $-_P L$, is the relation r over R, defined by

$$\{\theta(L) \mid \theta \text{ is a safe substitution for } L \text{ with respect to P, and } \theta(L) \in r,$$
$$\text{where } r \in \text{MEANING(P) is the relation over R} \in \text{SCHEMA(P)}\}.$$ ∎

We note that if R $\notin$ SCHEMA(P), then the answer to : $-L$ is the empty set. The following notation will be useful later on when we discuss the equivalence of the relational algebra, the domain calculus and nonrecursive safe Datalog programs.

Definition 3.38 (Datalog query with respect to a database)   Let P be a Datalog program and d be a database over **R** such that **R** $\subseteq$ SCHEMA(P). The Datalog program P with respect to d, denoted by P(d), is the Datalog program resulting from removing all the facts in DB(P) from P and then adding to P all the facts contained in the relations of the database d. That is, DB(P(d)) = d holds, i.e. the facts in P are replaced by those in d to obtain P(d).

Let Q be the Datalog query $:-_P L$. Then the Datalog query Q with respect to P and d, denoted by Q(d), is defined as the Datalog query $:-_{P(d)} L$. ∎

3.2.4   An Update Language for the Relational Model

So far we have only considered query languages for the relational model, which can only be used to retrieve information from a relational database. In this section we consider the dynamic aspects of updating a relational database resulting in its transition from one state to another. An update can take one of three forms, namely an insertion, a deletion or a modification. Insertion of a tuple into a relation results in the addition of this tuple to the relation. The deletion of a set of tuples from a relation with respect to a condition, C, results in the removal of the set of tuples satisfying C from the relation. The modification of a set of tuples with respect to two conditions, C_1 and C_2, results in replacing the set of tuples satisfying C_1 by the set of tuples satisfying C_2. A transaction can now be defined as the sequential composition of one or more updates. The aim of this section is two-fold. Firstly, to formalise the notion of an update and a transaction, and secondly to show that the equivalence of two transactions can be tested in polynomial time in the size of the transactions being tested. The test for equivalence is an essential ingredient in optimising a transaction, which intuitively means replacing the transaction by an equivalent one which requires less operations. Prior to defining updates we formalise the notion of a condition and a set of tuples satisfying a condition.

Definition 3.39 (Condition)   A *simple condition* over R is either an expression of form A = a or an expression of the form A ≠ a, where A ∈ schema(R) and a ∈ DOM(A).

A *condition* C over R is a conjunction $c_1 \wedge c_2 \wedge \ldots \wedge c_q$ of simple conditions c_i, $i \in \{1, 2, \ldots, q\}$, such that C does not contain two distinct simple conditions of the form A = a and A = b or of the form A = a and A ≠ a, for some A ∈ schema(R).

A *positive condition* over R is a condition of the form

$$A_1 = a_1 \wedge A_2 = a_2 \wedge \ldots \wedge A_q = a_q,$$

where $\{A_1, A_2, \ldots, A_q\} \subseteq$ schema(R) and $a_i \in$ DOM(A_i), for $i \in \{1, 2, \ldots, q\}$.

A *complete condition* over R is a positive condition over R, where $\{A_1, A_2, \ldots, A_q\} =$ schema(R) obtains in the definition of a positive condition. ∎

We observe that disallowing distinct simple conditions of the form A = a and A = b or of the form A = a and A ≠ a, for some A ∈ schema(R), restricts conditions to be *meaningful* by not having mutually exclusive conditions.

Definition 3.40 (Satisfaction of a condition by a tuple)   Let r be a relation over R, let t be a tuple in r and, in addition, let $C = c_1 \wedge c_2 \wedge \ldots \wedge c_q$ be a condition over R. Then t *satisfies* C, written $t \models C$, is defined recursively, as follows:

1) $t \models$ A = a, if $t[A] = a$ is true.

2) $t \models$ A ≠ a, if $t[A] \neq a$ is true.

3) $t \models C$, if $\forall i \in \{1, 2, \ldots, q\}$, $t \models c_i$. ∎

We note that we could extend conditions in a straightforward way to be general Boolean expressions but we prefer to keep the formalism simple. Furthermore, for simplicity we only formalise updates on single relations but we note that the definitions given below can be extended to databases (containing several relations) in a straightforward manner.

Definition 3.41 (An update)   Let r be a relation over relation schema R, with schema(R) = $\{A_1, A_2, \ldots, A_m\}$. An update over R is either an *insertion* over R, a *deletion* over R or a *modification* over R.

An insertion over R is an expression of the form insert(C), where C is a complete condition over R. The *effect* of an insertion insert(C) over R on r is defined by

$$[\text{insert}(C)](r) = r \cup \{t \mid t \models C\}.$$

A deletion over R is an expression of the form delete(C), where C is a condition over R. The *effect* of a deletion delete(C) over R on r is defined by

$$[\text{delete}(C)](r) = r - \{t \mid t \in r \text{ and } t \models C\}.$$

The modification of a tuple t over R with respect to a condition C, denoted by $[\text{modify}(C)](t)$, is defined by

$$[\text{modify}(C)](t) = u, \text{ where } u \text{ is a tuple over R such that}$$
$$\forall A_i \in \text{schema}(R), u[A_i] = a_i \text{ if } (A_i = a_i) \in C, \text{ otherwise } u[A_i] = t[A_i].$$

A modification over R is an expression of the form modify($C_1; C_2$), where C_1 and C_2 are conditions over R such that for each A $\in$ schema(R), if A $\neq a$ is in C_2 for some $a \in$ DOM(A), then A $\neq a$ is also in C_1. The *effect* of a modification modify($C_1; C_2$) over R on r is defined by

$$[\text{modify}(C_1; C_2)](r) = (r - \{t \mid t \in r \text{ and } t \models C_1\}) \cup \{[\text{modify}(C_2)](t) \mid t \in r \text{ and } t \models C_1\}.$$

∎

The definition of a modification can be viewed as a deletion followed by a sequence of insertions whereby each inserted tuple is the result of modifying some deleted tuple. We note that we could restrict condition C_2 above to be positive and the effect of the modification would remain unchanged; however, for the purpose of the normal form introduced in Definition 3.44, we find the above definition convenient.

As a running example for this subsection, suppose that we have a relation schema EMPLOYEE having attributes: ENAME (employee name, abbreviated to EN), DNAME (department name, abbreviated to DN) and SALARY (employee salary, abbreviated to SL). A relation r over EMPLOYEE is shown in Table 3.31.

Table 3.31 The relation r over EMPLOYEE

ENAME	DNAME	SALARY
John	Computing	30K
Jack	Computing	35K
Jake	Biology	30K

Consider the following updates, where ":=" denotes assignment:

1) $r_1 := [\text{insert}(EN = \text{Jill} \wedge DN = \text{Maths} \wedge SL = 25K)](r)$ is shown in Table 3.32.

2) $r_2 := [\text{insert}(EN = \text{Joe} \wedge DN = \text{Maths} \wedge SL = 35K)](r_1)$ is shown in Table 3.33.

3) $r := [\text{delete}(DN = \text{Maths})](r_2)$ is shown in Table 3.31.

4) $r := [\text{delete}(DN \neq \text{Computing} \wedge DN \neq \text{Biology})](r_2)$ is shown in Table 3.31.

5) $r_1 := [\text{delete}(EN = \text{Joe})](r_2)$ is shown in Table 3.32.

6) $r_3 := [\text{modify}(DN = \text{Computing}; DN = \text{Maths})](r)$ is shown in Table 3.34.

7) $r_4 := [\text{modify}(DN \neq \text{Computing}; DN = \text{Maths})](r)$ is shown in Table 3.35.

Table 3.32 The relation r_1 over EMPLOYEE

ENAME	DNAME	SALARY
John	Computing	30K
Jack	Computing	35K
Jake	Biology	30K
Jill	Maths	25K

Table 3.33 The relation r_2 over EMPLOYEE

ENAME	DNAME	SALARY
John	Computing	30K
Jack	Computing	35K
Jake	Biology	30K
Jill	Maths	25K
Joe	Maths	35K

Table 3.34 The relation r_3 over EMPLOYEE

ENAME	DNAME	SALARY
John	Maths	30K
Jack	Maths	35K
Jake	Biology	30K

Table 3.35 The relation r_4 over EMPLOYEE

ENAME	DNAME	SALARY
John	Computing	30K
Jack	Computing	35K
Jake	Maths	30K

Informally a transaction is the composition of several updates. In the following an update will be designated by *upd*.

Definition 3.42 (Transaction)   A *transaction* T over R is a finite sequence of updates over R. The *effect* of a transaction T = $upd_1, upd_2, \ldots, upd_n$, on a relation r over R, where $n \geq 0$ is a natural number, is defined by

$$[T](r) = [upd_n](\ldots([upd_2]([upd_1](r)))\ldots). \qquad \blacksquare$$

We note that according to Definition 3.42, if $n = 0$ then $[T](r) = r$. Consider the following transactions on r:

1) T_1 = insert(EN = Jill $\wedge$ DN = Maths $\wedge$ SL = 25K), modify(EN = Jack; DN = Maths).

2) T_2 = insert(EN = Jill $\wedge$ DN = Maths $\wedge$ SL = 25K), insert(EN = Jack $\wedge$ DN = Maths $\wedge$ SL = 35K), delete(EN = Jack $\wedge$ DN = Computing $\wedge$ SL = 35K).

3) T_3 = modify(EN = John; EN = Jill $\wedge$ DN = Maths $\wedge$ SL = 25K), insert(EN = John $\wedge$ DN = Computing $\wedge$ SL = 30K), modify(EN = Jack; DN = Maths).

4) T_4 = delete(EN = Jack), insert(EN = Jack $\wedge$ DN = Maths $\wedge$ SL = 35K), insert(EN = Jill $\wedge$ DN = Maths $\wedge$ SL = 25K).

5) T_5 = modify(DN $\neq$ Biology; DN = Maths), modify(EN = John; DN = Computing), insert(EN = Jill $\wedge$ DN = Maths $\wedge$ SL = 25K).

It can be verified that $[T_1](r) = [T_2](r) = [T_3](r) = [T_4](r) = [T_5](r) = r_5$, where r is shown in Table 3.31 and r_5 is shown in Table 3.36.

Table 3.36 The relation r_5 over EMPLOYEE

ENAME	DNAME	SALARY
John	Computing	30K
Jack	Maths	35K
Jake	Biology	30K
Jill	Maths	25K

The next definition formalises the intuition that two transactions over R are equivalent if they have the same effect on all relations over R.

Definition 3.43 (Equivalent transactions)   Two transactions, T_1 and T_2, over a relation schema R are said to be *equivalent* if for all relations, r, over R, $[T_1](r) = [T_2](r)$. $\blacksquare$

We next define a normal form for transactions which will be useful in proving that the equivalence of transactions can be decided in polynomial time in the size of the transactions.

Definition 3.44 (Normal form transaction)   Let T be a transaction over R. Then the *active domain* of T with respect to an attribute A $\in$ schema(R), denoted by ADOM(T, A), is the set of all values in DOM(A) that occur in the conditions of the updates of T. The active domain of T with respect to R (or simply the active domain of T when R is understood from context), denoted by ADOM(T), is given by

$$ADOM(T) = \bigcup_{A \in schema(R)} ADOM(T, A).$$

We associate with T and each attribute, $A \in schema(R)$, a set of *normal form conditions*, denoted by NF(T, A), given by

$$NF(T, A) = \{A = a \mid a \in ADOM(T, A)\} \bigcup \left\{ \bigwedge_{a \in ADOM(T,A)} A \neq a \right\}.$$

The set of normal form conditions for T, denoted by NF(T), is the set of all possible conjunctions of normal form conditions having one normal form condition from NF(T, A) for each attribute A in schema(R) such that A appears in T. Formally NF(T) is given by

$$NF(T) = \left\{ \bigwedge_{A \in schema(R)} C_A \mid C_A \in NF(T, A) \right\}.$$

The transaction T is in *normal form* if *every* condition C occurring in T is in NF(T). ∎

It follows that a transaction T is in normal form if for every two conditions C_1 and C_2 occurring in T the set of tuples $\{t \mid t \models C_1\}$ is either disjoint or equal to the set of tuples $\{t \mid t \models C_2\}$. To see this, suppose for example that schema(R) = {A, B}, ADOM(T, A) = {0, 1} and ADOM(T, B) = {1, 2}. Then NF(T) = {A = 0 ∧ B = 1, A = 0 ∧ B = 2, A = 0 ∧ B ≠ 1 ∧ B ≠ 2, A = 1 ∧ B = 1, A = 1 ∧ B = 2, A = 1 ∧ B ≠ 1 ∧ B ≠ 2, A ≠ 0 ∧ A ≠ 1 ∧ B = 1, A ≠ 0 ∧ A ≠ 1 ∧ B = 2, A ≠ 0 ∧ A ≠ 1 ∧ B ≠ 1 ∧ B ≠ 2}.

From Definition 3.44 we have that insertions are always in normal form. On the other hand, transactions consisting of deletions and modifications may not be in normal form. For example, the transaction, delete(DN ≠ Biology ∧ SL = 30K), modify(DN ≠ Maths; DN = Computing), is *not* in normal form, while the transaction, delete(DN ≠ Biology ∧ DN ≠ Maths ∧ DN ≠ Computing ∧ SL = 30K), delete(DN = Maths ∧ SL = 30K), delete(DN = Computing ∧ SL = 30K), modify(DN ≠ Biology ∧ DN ≠ Maths ∧ DN ≠ Computing ∧ SL = 30K; DN = Computing ∧ SL = 35K), modify(DN = Computing ∧ SL = 30K; DN = Computing ∧ SL = 35K), modify(DN = Biology ∧ SL = 35K; DN = Computing ∧ SL = 30K), is in normal form. (We observe that the active domain of EN with respect to both these transactions is empty.)

Given a condition C over R we let the *restriction* of C to the attributes in schema(R)−{A}, denoted by $C \mid_{\neg A}$, to be the condition C with any simple condition of the form A = a or A ≠ a removed from C.

The following two axioms, called the *split* axioms, allow us by their repeated application to transform any transaction into normal form.

Definition 3.45 (Split axioms)   The two split axioms are given by

SPLIT1: delete(C) is transformed into the equivalent transaction:

$$delete(C \wedge A \neq a), delete(C \mid_{\neg A} \wedge A = a),$$

SPLIT2: modify($C; C'$) is transformed into the equivalent transaction:

$$\text{modify}(C \wedge A \neq a; C_1), \text{modify}(C \mid_{\neg A} \wedge A = a; C_2),$$

where $A \in \text{schema}(R)$, $a \in \text{DOM}(A)$, $A \neq a$ is not one of the simple conditions of C, and for each $b \in \text{DOM}(A)$, there is no simple condition in C of the form $A = b$. Moreover, $C_1 = C_2 = C'$ if $A = b$ is a simple condition in C' for some $b \in \text{DOM}(A)$, otherwise $C_1 = C' \wedge A \neq a$ and $C_2 = C' \mid_{\neg A} \wedge A = a$. ∎

Intuitively, when the split axioms transform a condition C the set of tuples satisfying C is partitioned into two complementary sets: the set of tuples satisfying C and $A \neq a$ and the set of tuples satisfying C and $A = a$. This allows us to apply the resulting updates to each one of the two sets of tuples independently.

For example, the SPLIT1 axiom transforms delete(DN = Maths $\wedge$ EN $\neq$ Jack) into the transaction: delete(DN = Maths $\wedge$ EN $\neq$ Jack $\wedge$ EN $\neq$ John), delete(DN = Maths $\wedge$ EN = John). As another example, the SPLIT2 axiom transforms modify(DN $\neq$ Biology; DN = Maths) into the transaction: modify(DN $\neq$ Biology $\wedge$ DN $\neq$ Computing; DN = Maths), modify(DN = Computing; DN = Maths). As a final example, the SPLIT2 axiom transforms modify(EN $\neq$ John; DN = Computing) into the transaction: modify(EN $\neq$ John $\wedge$ EN $\neq$ Jack; DN = Computing $\wedge$ EN $\neq$ Jack), modify(EN = Jack; DN = Computing $\wedge$ EN = Jack). It is now evident that applying the SPLIT axioms repeatedly to a transaction results in an equivalent transaction.

Lemma 3.7   Given a transaction T over R, a normal form transaction T', which is equivalent to T and such that for all $A \in \text{schema}(R)$, $\text{ADOM}(T, A) \subseteq \text{ADOM}(T', A)$, can be found in polynomial time in any finite set of values $\text{ADOM}(T')$ that includes $\text{ADOM}(T)$.

Proof. We assume without loss of generality that T consists of a single update. Otherwise, we can transform each update in T into normal form and then concatenate all of the resulting normal form updates to obtain the desired normal form transaction T'.

In order to transform T into normal form we iteratively apply the relevant split axiom with respect to some value in $\text{ADOM}(T')$ until the current state of T is in normal form. The number of such iterations is bounded by $O(|\text{ADOM}(T')|^{\text{type}(R)})$, since by Definition 3.45 each update can only be split once with respect to a given domain value. The result follows since this transformation is polynomial in $\text{ADOM}(T')$, although we note that it is exponential in type(R). □

The next theorem establishes the central result of this section, namely that transaction equivalence can be decided in polynomial time in the size of the transactions being tested [AV88].

Theorem 3.8   The problem of whether two transactions over a relation schema R are equivalent can be decided in polynomial time in the number of active domain values in the two transactions.

Proof. Let $T = upd_1, upd_2, \ldots, upd_n$ be a transaction over R which is in normal form. We show how to transform T into a pair (f, s), called a *transition* over R, where f is a partial mapping from the set of all tuples over R to themselves and s is a relation over R. The relation s corresponds to the tuples that are inserted by T and is equal to $[T](\emptyset)$. The partial mapping f is defined from the updates, upd_i, as the composition $f_n f_{n-1} \cdots f_2 f_1$ (we denote composition of mappings by juxtaposition), where f_i, $i \in \{1, 2, \ldots, n-1, n\}$, is defined as follows:

1) If upd_i is the insertion update, insert(C), then for all tuples t over R, $f(t) = t$, i.e. in this case f is the identity mapping.

2) If upd_i is the deletion update, delete(C), then for all tuples t over R such that $t \models C, f(t)$ is undefined and for all other tuples t' over R such that $t' \not\models C, f(t') = t'$.

3) If upd_i is the modification update, modify$(C_1; C_2)$, then for all tuples t over R such that $t \models C_1, f(t) = [\text{modify}(C_1; C_2)](\{t\})$ and for all other tuples t' over R such that $t' \not\models C_1$, $f(t') = t'$.

We observe that although the mapping f is defined at the individual tuple level, conceptually we can view the tuples as being grouped into sets of tuples according to the condition C that they satisfy, where C is a normal form condition.

The *effect* of a transition (f, s), as constructed above, on a relation r over R is given by

$$[(f, s)](r) = \{f(t) \mid t \in r \cap dom(f)\} \cup s,$$

where $dom(f)$ denotes the domain of the partial mapping f; we note that if $t \notin r \cap dom(f)$ then $f(t)$ is undefined. It is evident that the effect of a transaction T on a relation r is the same as the effect of the transition, which was constructed from T, on r, i.e. $[(f, s)](r) = [T](r)$.

Next, let T_1 and T_2 be two transactions over R. By Lemma 3.7 we can assume without any loss of generality that T_1 and T_2 are in normal form and that $ADOM(T_1) = ADOM(T_2)$. When T_1 and T_2 are in normal form we can transform them in polynomial time in the sizes of T_1 and T_2 into the transitions (f_1, s_1) and (f_2, s_2), respectively, as described above.

We say that two transitions (f_1, s_1) and (f_2, s_2) over R are *equivalent* if for all relations r over R the effect of (f_1, s_1) on r is the same as the effect of (f_2, s_2) on r, i.e. $[(f_1, s_1)](r) = [(f_2, s_2)](r)$. It, therefore, remains to decide whether (f_1, s_1) and (f_2, s_2) are equivalent.

Now, it can be shown that (f_1, s_1) and (f_2, s_2) are equivalent if and only if the following two conditions obtain:

1) $s_1 = s_2$, i.e. both transitions insert the same tuples, and

2) for each distinct $i, j \in \{1, 2\}$ and for each tuple t over R, if $f_i(t)$ is defined and is not in s_j, then $f_j(t)$ is defined and $f_i(t) = f_j(t)$, i.e. if one transition modifies a tuple t that was not the result of an insertion, then the other transition must also modify this tuple in the same manner.

We observe that if $f_i(t)$ is undefined then $f_j(t)$ must also be undefined, otherwise a contradiction occurs due to the following argument. If $f_j(t)$ is defined and it is not in s_j then by condition (2) $f_i(t) = f_j(t)$, otherwise if $f_j(t) \in s_j$ then $f_j(t) = f_i(t) = t$, since $s_i = s_j$ by condition (1).

Finally, the equivalence of (f_1, s_1) and (f_2, s_2) can be tested in polynomial time in $|ADOM(T_i)|$ as follows. Firstly, we can easily test whether the first condition holds, i.e. $s_1 = s_2$. Secondly, in order to test the second condition we need only consider tuples t such that for all $A \in schema(R)$, $t[A] \in ADOM(T_i, A) \cup \{v_A\}$, where v_A is a distinct value in $DOM(A) - ADOM(T_i, A)$ and there are at most $|ADOM(T_i)+1|^{type(R)}$ such tuples, where $i \in \{1, 2\}$. (The value v_A acts as a representative value not in $ADOM(T_i, A)$.) To conclude the proof, it can be verified by the construction of f_k, for $k \in \{1, 2, \ldots, n\}$, that we can simulate $f(t)$ by $[T](\{t\})$.   □

A survey on update languages can be found in [Abi88], and an algorithm for optimising transactions is presented in [AV88]. An extension of the formalism we have described to parameterised transactions and an investigation on how the consistent states, which satisfy a set of data dependencies, can be expressed in terms of transactions can be found in [AV85, AV89]. (Data dependencies are discussed in detail in Section 3.6.) A sound and complete axiom system (see Definition 3.53) for proving the equivalence of two transactions is given in [KKPV87, KV91]. Finally, an extension of transactions to handle parallel updates is presented in [KV88].

3.3 The Equivalence of Query Languages for the Relational Model

A fundamental result in relational database theory is that of the equivalence of the query languages for the relational model, which we presented in the previous section. Two query languages are equivalent if for all input databases and for each query in the first (respectively the second) query language there is some query in the second (respectively the first) query language such that both queries return the same answer relation. Establishing the equivalence of these query languages is important for several reasons. Firstly, it provides strong evidence that Definition 3.21 of relational completeness is a robust measure of the expressive power we would like a relational database query language to have. Secondly, due to the different styles of the equivalent query languages, it allows for a relational DBMS to support procedural, declarative and rule-based interfaces, all having the same underlying query processing engine. Thirdly, by proving the equivalence we gain a better understanding of the limitations of the relational algebra and how it can be enhanced to deal with recursive queries by using the logical basis of Datalog (see Chapter 9 on deductive databases for details).

In order to prove the equivalence of the three query languages we have presented in the previous section, both the domain calculus and Datalog need to be restricted so that their answer set is always finite, even when the underlying attribute domains may be infinite. A suitable restriction of Datalog is that it be safe (see Definition 3.30 in Subsection 3.2.3), while a suitable restriction of the domain calculus is that it be allowed (see Definition 3.50 in Subsection 3.3.1).

In Subsection 3.3.1 we study the important concept of domain independence which intuitively means that the result of a query over a database depends only on the domain elements in the database and those mentioned in the query and *not* on the rest of the values in the underlying domains. We show that relational algebra and Datalog queries are domain independent but that domain calculus queries are, in general, not domain independent.

When the domain calculus is restricted to the allowed domain calculus it becomes domain independent. In Subsection 3.3.2 we prove the fundamental result that the relational algebra is equivalent to both the allowed domain calculus and to nonrecursive safe Datalog.

3.3.1   Domain Independence

Queries expressed in the relational algebra always yield finite answers, since the operands of such queries are relations which are by definition finite objects. Furthermore, the values present in an answer to a relational algebra query depend only on the values in the input relations together with the constant values that appear in the query itself, and not on the totality of values in the domains, $DOM(A_i)$, from which the relations are built. This characteristic of the relational algebra is important, since attribute domains are, in general, either countably infinite sets or very large finite sets. It follows that an answer to a relational algebra query depends only on the constants present in the query and the active domain of the database with respect to which the query was issued; it does not depend on other constant values in the domains, $DOM(A_i)$. A query language that satisfies this property is called *domain independent*. We show that both the relational algebra and Datalog are domain independent but that the domain calculus is not. We present a domain independent subset of the domain calculus, called the *allowed domain calculus*, which, in the next subsection, will be shown to be equivalent both to the relational algebra and nonrecursive safe Datalog.

In the following when we refer to a query Q it will either be a relational algebra query, a domain calculus query or a Datalog query. We will assume that the arguments of the query are relation schemas in a database schema **R**. In the case of a relational algebra query these arguments are the operands of the query, in the case of a domain calculus query these arguments are the relation schemas mentioned in the well-formed formula of the query, and in the case of a Datalog query with respect to a Datalog program these are the relation schemas over which the initial database of the Datalog program is defined.

In order to formalise the notion of domain independence some definitions follow.

Definition 3.46 (Active domain of a query)   The active domain of a query Q, denoted by $ADOM(Q)$, is the set of constant values appearing in Q. ∎

Example 3.2   Let Q be the query "Retrieve the names of students who are enrolled in the Computing department" and let r_1 be the relation over STUDENT, shown in Table 3.1. Then $ADOM(Q)$ = Computing. The relational algebra query corresponding to Q is:

$$\pi_{\text{SNAME}}(\sigma_F(r_1)),$$

where F is the formula DEPT = 'Computing'.

The domain calculus query corresponding to Q is:

$$\{x_1 : \text{SNAME} \mid \exists x_2(\exists x_3(\exists x_4(\exists x_5(\exists x_6$$
$$(\text{STUDENT}(x_1, x_2, x_3, x_4, x_5, x_6) \wedge x_4 = \text{`Computing'})))))\}(\{r_1\}).$$

The Datalog query corresponding to Q is:

$: -_P$ COMP_STUD(x)

where P is the Datalog program

COMP_STUD$(x_1) : -$ STUDENT$(x_1, x_2, x_3, $ Computing$, x_5, x_6)$.

together with the set of facts that are contained in r_1.   ■

In order to distinguish between various finite or infinite subsets of $\mathcal{D}$ which can be chosen as the domain of an attribute A $\in$ schema$(\mathbf{R})$, we extend the notation, DOM(A), to $DOM_j(A)$, where j is a natural number. Thus, in general, $DOM_j(A) \neq DOM_k(A)$, for $j \neq k$. We will let $DOM_j(\mathbf{R})$ denote the union of $DOM_j(A)$ for all attributes A in schema$(\mathbf{R})$, i.e.

$$DOM_j(\mathbf{R}) = \bigcup \{ DOM_j(A) \mid A \in \text{schema}(\mathbf{R}) \}.$$

We will refer to $DOM_j(\mathbf{R})$ as the *underlying domain of* $\mathbf{R}$ and say that $DOM_j(\mathbf{R})$ is the underlying domain of a database d over $\mathbf{R}$ if DOM_j replaces DOM in Definition 3.7 of a database. (Note that this is equivalent to stating that ADOM$(d) \subseteq DOM_j(\mathbf{R})$.) When we want to emphasise the fact that $DOM_j(\mathbf{R})$ is the underlying domain of d we will refer to d as the pair $(d, DOM_j(\mathbf{R}))$.

We are now ready to define the concept of a domain independent query, which informally means that for all databases d input to a query Q the answers to Q depend only ADOM(Q) $\cup$ ADOM(d).

Definition 3.47 (Domain independent query)   A query Q is *domain independent* if, for all underlying domains of $\mathbf{R}$, $DOM_1(\mathbf{R})$ and $DOM_2(\mathbf{R})$, and for all databases d over $\mathbf{R}$ such that ADOM(Q) $\cup$ ADOM(d) is a subset of both $DOM_1(\mathbf{R})$ and $DOM_2(\mathbf{R})$, the equation

$$Q((d, DOM_1(\mathbf{R}))) = Q((d, DOM_2(\mathbf{R})))$$

holds.   ■

In Exercise 3.12 you are required to show that there is no loss of generality in restricting $DOM_1(\mathbf{R})$ and $DOM_2(\mathbf{R})$ in Definition 3.47 to be finite domains. This result immediately implies that a domain independent query is well-defined for all input databases, in the sense that its answer is always a finite relation.

The following proposition follows from the semantics of answers to relational algebra and Datalog queries (recall from Subsection 3.2.3 that we only consider safe substitutions when computing the meaning of a Datalog program).

Proposition 3.9   All relational algebra and Datalog queries are domain independent. $\square$

Note that the above proposition still holds if we allow safe recursive Datalog programs in addition to nonrecursive safe Datalog programs. On the other hand, domain calculus queries may *not* be domain independent as we now demonstrate with two example queries. Let STUDS and LECTS be two unary relation schemas with schema(STUDS) = schema(LECTS) = {PNAME}, where DOM(PNAME) is the domain of person names. A relation over STUDS contains the names of students currently enrolled in the college and a relation over LECTS contains the names of lecturers currently employed by the college. In addition, let r_1 be a nonempty relation over STUDS, r_2 be a nonempty relation over LECTS and let $d = \{r_1, r_2\}$ be a database over {STUD, LECTS}.

The following domain calculus query asks for the names of people who are not currently enrolled in the college, namely

$$\{x : PNAME \mid \neg STUDS(x)\}. \tag{3.1}$$

According to Definition 3.28 the answer to (3.1) with respect to d includes all the tuples in DOM(PNAME) that are not in r_1. Assuming that DOM(PNAME) is infinite then the answer to (3.1) is infinite. Apart from the fact that the answer is not a relation (which by Definition 3.7 must be finite), it cannot be computed in a finite amount of time. Moreover, even if DOM(PNAME) is finite then increasing DOM(PNAME) by adding elements to it will increase the number of tuples in the answer to (3.1).

The following query asks for the names of people who are either students enrolled in the college or lecturers employed by the college, namely

$$\{x_1 : PNAME, x_2 : PNAME \mid STUDS(x_1) \vee LECTS(x_2)\}. \tag{3.2}$$

The answer to (3.2) according to Definition 3.28 is the set of all possible name pairs <sname, lname> such that either <sname> $\in r_1$ is true or <lname> $\in r_2$ is true but not necessarily both are true. Thus, if <sname> $\in r_1$ and <lname> $\notin r_2$ or if <lname> $\in r_2$ and <sname> $\notin r_1$, <sname, lname> is still in the answer to (3.2). Note that if r_1 and r_2 are both empty then the answer to the query is empty. It follows that if either r_1 or r_2 is nonempty and DOM(PNAME) is infinite then the answer to (3.2) is infinite and therefore not computable in a finite amount of time. Moreover, as in (3.1), even if DOM(PNAME) is finite then increasing DOM(PNAME) by adding elements to it will increase the number of tuples in the answer to (3.2).

The above example highlights the two main problems which cause a domain calculus query to be domain dependent, namely

1) The query has a subformula of the form $\neg F$ such that a variable in F does not occur positively in some atomic formula elsewhere in the query.

2) The query has a subformula of the form $F_1 \vee F_2$ such that the free variables of F_1 are not the same as the free variables of F_2.

The following theorem, which was proved in [DiP69] and [Var81] (see also [Kif88]), implies that, in general, there is no effective algorithm to decide whether a domain calculus query is domain independent or not. The proof relies on a reduction from the finite validity problem, which was stated in Theorem 1.4 of Subsection 1.9.5 of Chapter 1.

Theorem 3.10   The problem of determining whether a domain calculus query is domain independent is undecidable.   □

Despite the negative result stated in Theorem 3.10, we will now define a subclass of domain calculus queries, called *allowed domain calculus queries* [Top87, VT91], which are guaranteed to be domain independent.

Definition 3.48 (Positive occurrence of a variable in a domain calculus formula) A variable *x occurs positively* (or simply *x* is positive) in a domain calculus formula if and only if one of the following cases holds:

1) x is positive in an atomic formula $R(y_1, y_2, \ldots, x, \ldots, y_k)$ in which x appears.

2) x is positive in an atomic formula $x = v$ in which x appears, where v is a constant.

3) x is positive in the formula $\neg F$, if x is negative in F.

4) x is positive in the formula $F_1 \wedge F_2$, if either x is positive in F_1 or x is positive in F_2.

5) x is positive in the formula $F_1 \vee F_2$, if x is positive in F_1 and x is positive in F_2.

6) x is positive in the formula $F_1 \Rightarrow F_2$, if x is negative in F_1 and x is positive in F_2.

7) x is positive in the formula $\exists y : A\ (F)$, if $x \neq y$ and x is positive in F.   ∎

Definition 3.49 (Negative occurrence of a variable in a domain calculus formula) A variable *x occurs negatively* (or simply *x* is negative) in a domain calculus formula if and only if one of the following cases holds:

1) x is negative in the atomic formula $x = y$ in which x appears, where y is a variable.

2) x is negative in the formula $\neg F$, if x is positive in F.

3) x is negative in the formula $F_1 \wedge F_2$, if x is negative in F_1 and x is negative in F_2.

4) x is negative in the formula $F_1 \vee F_2$, if either x is negative in F_1 or x is negative in F_2.

5) x is negative in the formula $F_1 \Rightarrow F_2$, if either x is positive in F_1 or x is negative in F_2.

6) x is negative in the formula $\forall y : A\ (F)$, if $x \neq y$ and x is negative in F.

7) if x does not appear in a formula F, then x is negative in F.   ∎

Definition 3.50 (An allowed domain calculus query) A domain calculus formula F is *allowed* if all of the following conditions hold:

1) For every free variable x of F, x is positive in F.

2) For every subformula $\exists x : A\ (G)$ of F, x is positive in G.

3) For every subformula $\forall x : A\ (G)$ of F, x is negative in G.

A domain calculus query is allowed if its formula is allowed.   ∎

In the following we call the domain calculus, restricted to allowed formulae, the *allowed domain calculus* (or simply the allowed calculus).

We note that an algorithm which decides whether a domain calculus query is allowed or not can easily be devised by a simple recursion on the structure of the domain calculus formula of the query.

The following theorem can be proved by induction on the number of logical connectives in the domain calculus formula of a query.

Theorem 3.11   Every allowed domain calculus formula is domain independent. $\square$

We demonstrate the above theorem with some simple queries, where STUDS and LECTS are the relation schemas defined above and LIVES is a relation schema with schema(LIVES) = {PNAME, ADDRESS}. The following query retrieves the names of people who do not live in London:

$$\{x_1 : \text{PNAME} \mid \text{LIVES}(x_1, x_2) \wedge \neg \text{LIVES}(x_1, \text{London})\}.$$

This query is allowed, since x_1 is positive in $\text{LIVES}(x_1, x_2)$.

The following query retrieves the names of people who either live in Manchester or London:

$$\{x_1 : \text{PNAME} \mid \text{LIVES}(x_1, \text{Manchester}) \vee \text{LIVES}(x_1, \text{London})\}.$$

This query is allowed, since x_1 is positive in both $\text{LIVES}(x_1, \text{Manchester})$ and $\text{LIVES}(x_1,$ London).

The following allowed query returns true if the relation r_1 over STUDS is empty otherwise it returns false if r_1 is not empty:

$$\{x : \text{PNAME} \mid \forall x : \text{PNAME}(\neg \text{STUDS}(x))\}.$$

The above query is actually equivalent to the following query:

$$\{x : \text{PNAME} \mid \neg(\exists x : \text{PNAME}(\text{STUDS}(x)))\}.$$

The query shown in (3.1) is not allowed, since the free variable x is negative (i.e. it is not positive) in $\neg \text{STUDS}(x)$. The query shown in (3.2) is also not allowed, since the free variable x_2 is negative in $\text{STUDS}(x_1)$ and similarly the free variable x_1 is negative in $\text{LECTS}(x_2)$.

The following query is not allowed, since x_1 does not appear in the formula of the query:

$$\{x_1 : \text{PNAME} \mid \text{LIVES}(x_2, \text{Manchester})\}.$$

Another way of restricting domain formulae so as to obtain a subclass of domain independent queries is to restrict the quantifiers $\exists$ and $\forall$ to range over relations, which are by definition finite objects. Let DOMAIN be a unary relation schema with schema(DOMAIN) = {A}, then

$$\forall x \in \text{DOMAIN}(F) \text{ is an abbreviation for } \forall x : A \ (\text{DOMAIN}(x) \Rightarrow F)$$

and

$$\exists x \in \text{DOMAIN}(F) \text{ is an abbreviation for } \exists x : A \ (\text{DOMAIN}(x) \wedge F),$$

where F is a well-formed formula of the domain calculus. Such restricted quantifiers are known in logic as *relativised quantifiers* [Van89].

For the rest of this subsection let us assume that $\text{DOMAIN} \in \mathbf{R}$ holds, and thus any database d, with respect to which a query Q is answered, includes a relation over DOMAIN. In addition, let us assume that the relation r in d over DOMAIN is such that $r = \text{ADOM}(Q) \cup \text{ADOM}(d)$, i.e. r includes all the active domain values in Q and d.

We note that if the underlying domains of different attributes are disjoint (or more generally not equal to each other) then we can partition the relation over DOMAIN accordingly.

The following proposition [Top87] shows that relativised quantifiers can be used to transform a domain calculus query, which may not be domain independent, into a domain independent query.

Proposition 3.12   Let Q be the domain calculus query

$$\{x_1 : A_1, x_2 : A_2, \ldots, x_n : A_n \mid F(x_1, x_2, \ldots, x_n)\}$$

and let $\{y_1, y_2, \ldots, y_m\}$ be the subset of the free variables of Q that are negative in F. Then, provided all of the quantifiers in F are relativised, the query

$$\{x_1 : A_1, x_2 : A_2, \ldots, x_n : A_n \mid F \wedge \text{DOMAIN}(y_1) \wedge \text{DOMAIN}(y_2) \wedge \ldots \wedge \text{DOMAIN}(y_m)\} \quad (3.3)$$

is allowed and thus domain independent.   □

The following theorem taken from [Top87] shows that in most practical cases domain independent queries have an equivalent allowed query.

Theorem 3.13   If Q is domain independent, then for all databases d over $\mathbf{R}$, such that the relation r in d over DOMAIN is nonempty, $Q(d) = Q^r(d)$, where Q is the domain calculus query of Proposition 3.12 and Q^r is given by the relativised query of (3.3).   □

The reader can verify that the condition that DOMAIN be nonempty is necessary in the statement of Theorem 3.13 by considering a database schema $\mathbf{R} = \{R\}$, with schema(R) = $\{A\}$, and taking Q to be the Boolean query

$$\{ \ \mid \forall x : A \ (R(x) \wedge \neg R(x))\},$$

whose result is always empty, representing the fact that Q is false. However, the relativised query Q^r, given by

$$\{ \ \mid \forall x : A \ (\text{DOMAIN}(x) \Rightarrow (R(x) \wedge \neg R(x)))\},$$

returns $\{<>\}$ when DOMAIN is empty, representing the fact that Q^r is true.

From a practical point of view we note that all SQL queries are domain independent, since they effectively maintain the form of the query Q^r of (3.3). Every domain variable declared in an SQL query must range over a projection $\pi_A(R)$, where R is a relation schema mentioned in the FROM-clause of the query.

An alternative approach to dealing with the undecidability result of Theorem 3.10, which does not restrict the domain calculus to a subclass of its queries, is now briefly discussed, assuming that the underlying database domain, $\mathcal{D}$, is *fixed* and *infinite*. In this alternative approach for a given database d over **R** and a domain calculus query Q we solve the *state-safety problem*, which is the problem of deciding whether the answer Q(d) is finite, prior to actually computing the answer to the query. If the solution to the state-safety problem for d and Q is negative, i.e. the answer Q(d) is infinite, then we abandon the query and return a result indicating that the query is undefined for the input database. The next theorem [AGSS86, Kif88] (see also [AH91, ST95]) implies that for the domain calculus a tractable solution exists for the state-safety problem and thus this alternative approach is viable in practice.

Theorem 3.14 The state-safety problem is decidable in polynomial time in the size of the input database.

Proof. Let d be a database and Q be a domain calculus query. We say that the underlying domain $DOM_j(\mathbf{R})$ is *sufficiently large* with respect to Q and d if it is finite, it contains all the elements in ADOM(Q) $\cup$ ADOM(d) and the number of elements in $DOM_j(\mathbf{R}) - (\text{ADOM(Q)} \cup \text{ADOM}(d))$ is at least one plus twice the number of occurrences of equality and inequality terms in Q, which are of the form $x = y$ and $x \neq y$, respectively.

Now, evaluate the query Q($(d, DOM_j(\mathbf{R}))$), where $DOM_j(\mathbf{R})$ is sufficiently large with respect to Q and d, and let r be its answer, which is finite since $DOM_j(\mathbf{R})$ is finite. If r contains a tuple t with an attribute value, say $t[A]$, which is not in ADOM(Q) $\cup$ ADOM(d) then return undefined, otherwise return r. We leave it to the reader as an exercise to verify that we return undefined if and only if Q(d) is infinite. $\square$

3.3.2 The Equivalence of the Algebra, the Calculus and Datalog

Herein we prove one of the most important results concerning query languages for the relational model, i.e. that the relational algebra is equivalent to both nonrecursive safe Datalog and to the allowed domain calculus.

Informally, two queries are *equivalent* if they return the same answer for all input databases, and two query languages are *equivalent* if they express exactly the same set of queries.

Definition 3.51 (Equivalence of queries and query languages) Two queries Q_1 and Q_2, whose arguments are relation schemas in a database schema **R**, are *equivalent*, denoted by $Q_1 \equiv Q_2$, if for all databases d over **R** $Q_1(d) = Q_2(d)$.

A query language L_1 is *contained* in a query language L_2, if for all queries Q_1 in L_1 there exists a query Q_2 in L_2 such that $Q_1 \equiv Q_2$. L_1 is *equivalent* to L_2, if L_1 is contained in L_2 and L_2 is contained in L_1. ∎

We now set out to prove that the relational algebra, nonrecursive safe Datalog and the allowed domain calculus are equivalent query languages for the relational model. We will assume that the arguments of queries are relation schemas in a database schema **R**. We first show that nonrecursive safe Datalog is at least as expressive as the relational algebra.

Lemma 3.15 The relational algebra is contained in nonrecursive safe Datalog.

Proof. We need to show that for every relational algebra query there exists an equivalent Datalog query. The lemma follows by induction on the number of operators present in the relational algebra query, say Q.

Basis. If Q does not contain any operators then it is simply a query of the form R, where $R \in \mathbf{R}$. Then the equivalent nonrecursive safe Datalog query is

$$:-_P R(x_1, x_2, \ldots, x_k)$$

where P is a Datalog query satisfying $R \in \mathrm{SCHEMA}(P)$.

Induction. Assume the result holds for relational algebra queries containing q operators; we then need to prove that the result holds for relational algebra queries Q containing $q + 1$ operators. Without loss of generality we assume that answers to Q result in relations over a relation schema also named Q such that schema(Q) has k attributes. The Datalog query equivalent to Q is

$$:-_P Q(x_1, x_2, \ldots, x_k)$$

where P is a Datalog program satisfying $Q \in \mathrm{SCHEMA}(P)$ such that Q is defined inductively according to the $(q + 1)$th relational algebra operator.

We consider the $(q + 1)$th relational algebra operator to be either union, difference, projection, join or selection.

If Q is the query $Q_1 \cup Q_2$, then the Datalog rules in P that define Q are:

$$Q(x_1, x_2, \ldots, x_k) :- Q_1(x_1, x_2, \ldots, x_k).$$
$$Q(x_1, x_2, \ldots, x_k) :- Q_2(x_1, x_2, \ldots, x_k).$$

where by inductive hypothesis P contains nonrecursive safe Datalog rules that define Q_1 and Q_2.

If Q is the query $Q_1 - Q_2$, then the Datalog rule in P that defines Q is:

$$Q(x_1, x_2, \ldots, x_k) :- Q_1(x_1, x_2, \ldots, x_k), \neg Q_2(x_1, x_2, \ldots, x_k).$$

where by inductive hypothesis P contains nonrecursive safe Datalog rules that define Q_1 and Q_2.

If Q is the query $\pi_X(Q_1)$, where $X = \{x_1, x_2, \ldots, x_k\} \subseteq \{z_1, z_2, \ldots, z_m\}$ and Q_1 results in a relation over a relation schema with m attributes, then the Datalog rule in P that defines Q is:

$$Q(x_1, x_2, \ldots, x_k) :- Q_1(z_1, z_2, \ldots, z_m).$$

where by inductive hypothesis P contains nonrecursive safe Datalog rules that define Q_1.

If Q is the query $Q_1 \bowtie Q_2$, where $\{x_1, x_2, \ldots, x_k\} = \{y_1, y_2, \ldots, y_m\} \cup \{z_1, z_2, \ldots, z_n\}$ and Q_1 and Q_2 result in relations over relation schemas with m and n attributes, respectively, then the Datalog rule in P that defines Q is:

$$Q(x_1, x_2, \ldots, x_k) :- Q_1(y_1, y_2, \ldots, y_m), Q_2(z_1, z_2, \ldots, z_n).$$

where by inductive hypothesis P contains nonrecursive safe Datalog rules that define Q_1 and Q_2.

If Q is the query $\sigma_F(Q_1)$, where F is a selection formula, which by Theorem 3.1 can be assumed to be a simple selection formula, then the Datalog rule in P that defines Q is:

$$Q(x_1, x_2, \ldots, x_k) :- Q_1(x_1, x_2, \ldots, x_k), x = y.$$

where $x = y$ is the appropriate equality formula corresponding to the selection formula F. Now by inductive hypothesis P contains nonrecursive safe Datalog rules that define Q_1. $\square$

We next show that the allowed domain calculus is at least as expressive as nonrecursive safe Datalog.

Lemma 3.16 Nonrecursive safe Datalog is contained in the allowed domain calculus.

Proof. We need to show that for every nonrecursive safe Datalog query Q of the form

$$:-_P R(y_1, y_2, \ldots, y_k)$$

there exists an equivalent allowed domain calculus query, where SCHEMA(R) = $\{A_1, A_2, \ldots, A_k\}$.

In order to simplify the proof we assume, without loss of generality, that the set of variables appearing in any two rules in P are disjoint; if this is not the case then a simple renaming of variables will realise this assumption.

We now create a set of atomic formulae from the predicate $R(y_1, y_2, \ldots, y_k)$ as follows. For each constant $y_i \in \{y_1, y_2, \ldots, y_k\}$ we create an atomic formula $x_i = y_i$, where x_i is a variable which is not in $\{y_1, y_2, \ldots, y_k\}$, and for each repeated variable $y_i \in \{y_1, y_2, \ldots, y_k\}$ in positions i and j we create an atomic formula $y_i = x_j$, where x_j is a variable distinct from y_i. We now define the domain calculus formula

$$af_1 \wedge af_2 \wedge \ldots \wedge af_m$$

which we denote by F_R, where $\{af_1, af_2, \ldots, af_m\}$ is the set of atomic formulae we have created from $R(y_1, y_2, \ldots, y_k)$.

Thus the allowed domain calculus query, which is equivalent to Q, has the form

$$\{x_1 : A_1, x_2 : A_2, \ldots, x_k : A_k \mid (F_R \wedge F_Q)(x_1, x_2, \ldots, x_k)\},$$

where F_Q is a domain calculus formula which will be defined below and $\{x_1, x_2, \ldots, x_k\}$ is a set of k variables containing all the variables in $\{y_1, y_2, \ldots, y_k\}$.

The remaining part of the lemma follows by induction on the number of rules in the nonrecursive safe Datalog program P, with respect to which Q is issued, having the relation symbol R in their head.

Basis. If P does not contain any such rules then the equivalent domain calculus query is

$$\{x_1 : A_1, x_2 : A_2, \ldots, x_k : A_k \mid (F_R \wedge R(x_1, x_2, \ldots, x_k))(x_1, x_2, \ldots, x_k)\}$$

which is allowed, since for each $x_i \in \{x_1, x_2, \ldots, x_k\}$ x_i is positive in the atomic formula $R(x_1, x_2 \ldots, x_k)$.

Induction. Assume the result holds for nonrecursive safe Datalog programs P containing q rules having the relation symbol R in their head; we then need to prove that the result holds for nonrecursive safe Datalog programs P containing $q + 1$ rules having the relation symbol R in their head.

Let us choose a rule C_1 in P having the relation symbol R in its head and assume, for simplicity of the argument, that it has the form

$$R(y_1, y_2, \ldots, y_k) :- R_1(y_1^1, y_2^1, \ldots, y_{m_1}^1), \neg R_2(y_1^2, y_2^2, \ldots, y_{m_2}^2), \ldots,$$

where all the variables in the head of the rule have been appropriately renamed to conform with the variables x_i appearing in $R(x_1, x_2, \ldots, x_k)$. Now, let $\{z_1, z_2, \ldots, z_m\}$ be the set of variables appearing in the body of C_1 but not in its head. We create the following domain calculus formula for C_1:

$$\exists z_1 : A_1(\exists z_2 : A_2(\ldots (\exists z_m : A_m(R_1(y_1^1, y_2^1, \ldots, y_{m_1}^1) \wedge \neg R_2(y_1^2, y_1^2, \ldots, y_{m_2}^2))) \wedge \ldots)),$$

which we denote by F_1. The reader can verify that the domain calculus formula F_1 is allowed, since C_1 is a safe Datalog rule.

We will make a short cut in the proof by assuming that the relation symbols of the literals in the body of C_1 do not appear as the heads of other rules in P. We will leave it to the reader to extend the proof to this more general case. As a hint for solving this case, for each such rule, where a relation symbol of a literal in the body of C_1 appears as the head of another rule in P, we replace the appropriate literal in F_1 by the body of the said rule, renaming the variables and adding existential quantifiers where appropriate, and finally negating the resulting formula if the said literal was negative. If there are several such rules, say n, for a given relation symbol, say R_i, then we create a disjunction $F_1^1 \vee F_1^2 \vee \ldots \vee F_1^n$, where F_1^j is the formula created for the jth rule having the relation symbol R_i in its head.

Finally, the equivalent allowed domain calculus query is

$$\{x_1 : A_1, x_2 : A_2, \ldots, x_k : A_k \mid (F_R \wedge (F_1 \vee F_q))(x_1, x_2, \ldots, x_k)\},$$

where by inductive hypothesis F_q is the allowed domain calculus formula used to obtain an equivalent allowed domain calculus query if C_1 is removed from P. (Note that $F_Q = F_1 \vee F_q$.) $\square$

We finally show that the relational algebra is at least as expressive as the allowed domain calculus.

Lemma 3.17   The allowed domain calculus is contained in the relational algebra.

Proof. We need to show that for every allowed domain calculus query there exists an equivalent relational algebra query.

The lemma follows by induction on the number of logical connectives present in the allowed domain calculus query, say Q, which has the form

$$\{x_1 : A_1, x_2 : A_2, \ldots, x_n : A_n \mid F(x_1, x_2, \ldots, x_n)\},$$

where F is an allowed domain calculus formula.

We can assume without loss of generality that F contains only the logical connectives, $\neg$, $\vee$ and $\exists$. This is due to the fact that the subformula $F_1 \wedge F_2$ is logically equivalent to the subformula $\neg(\neg F_1 \vee \neg F_2)$, the subformula $F_1 \Rightarrow F_2$ is logically equivalent to the subformula $\neg F_1 \vee F_2$ and the subformula $\forall x : A(F)$ is equivalent to the subformula $\neg(\exists x : A(\neg F))$. Furthermore, the reader can verify that if a formula is allowed its logically equivalent formula, containing only $\neg$, $\vee$ and $\exists$, is also allowed. We can also assume that F does not contain subformulae of the form $x = y$, since such subformulae can be simulated by repeated variables or constants in atomic formulae as appropriate. For example, $R(x_1, x_2) \wedge x_1 = x_2$ can be simulated by $R(x_1, x_1)$, where x_1 and x_2 are variables, and $R(x_1, x_2) \wedge x_2 = v$ can be simulated by $R(x_1, v)$, where x_1 is a variable and v is a constant value.

For each relation symbol R_i appearing in F, with $\text{schema}(R_i) = \{A_1, A_2, \ldots, A_m\}$, we create the domain calculus formula

$$\exists z_2 : A_2(\ldots(\exists z_m : A_m(R_i(x, z_2, \ldots, z_m)))\ldots) \vee \ldots \vee$$
$$\exists z_1 : A_1(\ldots(\exists z_{m-1} : A_{m-1}(R_i(z_1, \ldots, z_{m-1}, x)))\ldots),$$

which we denote by $Fdom_i(x)$, with one free variable, x.

Let $\text{ADOM}(Q) = \{v_1, v_2, \ldots, v_p\}$ and assume that the set $\{R_1, R_2, \ldots, R_k\}$ includes all the relation symbols appearing in Q. Then we let $Fdom(x)$ denote the allowed formula

$$x = v_1 \vee x = v_2 \vee \ldots \vee x = v_p \vee Fdom_1(x) \vee Fdom_2(x) \vee \ldots \vee Fdom_k(x).$$

Intuitively, $Fdom(x)$ states the possible values that a variable x can range over (this is similar to the assumption of the unary relation schema DOMAIN encountered towards the end of Subsection 3.3.1).

Thus Q is equivalent to the allowed domain calculus query

$$\{x_1 : A_1, x_2 : A_2, \ldots, x_n : A_n \mid F \wedge Fdom(x_1) \wedge Fdom(x_2) \wedge \ldots \wedge Fdom(x_n)\},$$

since Q is allowed and thus domain independent (see Proposition 3.12).

Now, it can easily be seen that $Fdom(x)$ translates into the equivalent relational algebra expression

$$\{v_1, v_2, \ldots, v_p\} \cup RelDom_1 \cup RelDom_2 \cup \ldots \cup RelDom_k,$$

which we denote by $RelDom(F)$, with $RelDom_i$ being the relational algebra expression

$$\pi_{A_1}(R_i) \cup \pi_{A_2}(R_i) \cup \ldots \cup \pi_{A_m}(R_i).$$

Thus it is sufficient to show that Q translates into an equivalent relational algebra expression:

$$E \cap RelDom(F)^n,$$

where E is a relational algebra expression and $RelDom(F)^n$ denotes the Cartesian product

$$RelDom(F) \times \cdots \times RelDom(F), n \text{ times.}$$

We are now ready to proceed with the induction referred to at the beginning of the proof.

Basis. If F does not contain any logical connectives then it is an atomic formula of the form $R(y_1, y_2, \ldots, y_m)$, where $\{x_1, x_2, \ldots, x_n\} \subseteq \{y_1, y_2, \ldots, y_m\}$ and the set $\{y_1, y_2, \ldots, y_m\} - \{x_1, x_2, \ldots, x_n\}$ consists of constants.

Let ψ be the conjunction of simple selection formulae of the form $A_i = A_j$ whenever a variable y_i is repeated in positions i and j in $R(y_1, y_2, \ldots, y_m)$ and $A_i = y_i$ whenever y_i is a constant value.

Thus the relational algebra expression equivalent to Q is

$$\pi_X(\sigma_\psi(R)),$$

where $X = \{A_1, A_2, \ldots, A_n\}$.

Induction. Assume the result holds for allowed domain calculus queries containing q logical connectives; we then need to prove that the result holds for domain calculus queries Q containing $q + 1$ logical connectives.

If $F(x_1, x_2, \ldots, x_n)$ is the formula $F_1(y_1, y_2, \ldots, y_m) \vee F_2(z_1, z_2, \ldots, z_k)$ then the relational algebra expression equivalent to Q is

$$\pi_X(E_1 \times RelDom(F)^{n-m}) \cup \pi_X(E_2 \times RelDom(F)^{n-k}),$$

where $X = \{A_1, A_2, \ldots, A_n\}$, and by inductive hypothesis E_1 and E_2 are equivalent to the domain calculus queries

$$\{y_1 : A_{y1}, y_2 : A_{y2}, \ldots, y_m : A_{ym} \mid F_1(y_1, y_2, \ldots, y_m)\},$$

and

$$\{z_1 : A_{z1}, z_2 : A_{z2}, \ldots, z_k : A_{zk} \mid F_2(z_1, z_2, \ldots, z_k)\},$$

respectively.

If $F(x_1, x_2, \ldots, x_n)$ is the formula $\neg F_1(x_1, x_2, \ldots, x_n)$, then the relational algebra expression equivalent to Q is

$$RelDom(F)^n - E_1,$$

and by inductive hypothesis E_1 is equivalent to the domain calculus query

$$\{x_1 : A_1, x_2 : A_2, \ldots, x_n : A_n \mid F_1(x_1, x_2, \ldots, x_n)\}.$$

If $F(x_1, x_2, \ldots, x_n)$ is the formula $\exists x_{n+1} : A_{n+1}(F_1(x_1, x_2, \ldots, x_n, x_{n+1}))$, then the relational algebra expression equivalent to Q is

$$\pi_X(E_1),$$

where $X = \{A_1, A_2, \ldots, A_n\}$, and by inductive hypothesis E_1 is equivalent to the domain calculus query

$$\{x_1 : A_1, x_2 : A_2, \ldots, x_n : A_n, x_{n+1} : A_{n+1} \mid F_1(x_1, x_2, \ldots, x_n, x_{n+1})\}.$$

This concludes the proof. $\qquad\square$

The following theorem is implied by the preceding lemmas, since query language containment is transitive.

Theorem 3.18 The following three query languages for the relational model are equivalent:

1) The relational algebra.

2) Nonrecursive safe Datalog.

3) The allowed domain calculus. □

3.4 Integrity Constraints in Relational Databases

In general, we would like to restrict relations so that they satisfy certain conditions, called *integrity constraints* (or simply constraints). Integrity constraints can be viewed as first-order logic statements that restrict the set of allowable relations in a database. For example, stating that EMP_NO is a primary key of a relation schema, EMPLOYEE, is an integrity constraint that specifies that no two distinct tuples in a relation over EMPLOYEE have the same EMP_NO. Primary key constraints are a special case of the more general class of *Functional Dependencies* (FDs), the most studied class of integrity constraints in relational database theory. An example of a functional dependency, which is not necessarily a primary key, is the constraint that an employee's ADDRESS has a unique POSTCODE; it is written as ADDRESS $\rightarrow$ POSTCODE.

As another example, stating that DEPT_NO is a foreign key of a relation over EMPLOYEE referencing the primary key, DEPT_NO, of a relation schema, DEPARTMENT, is an integrity constraint that specifies that if a tuple over EMPLOYEE has a nonnull DEPT_NO-value, say d_i, then there exists a tuple in the relation over DEPARTMENT whose DEPT_NO-value is d_i. Foreign key constraints are a special case of the more general class of *Inclusion Dependencies* (INDs). An example of an inclusion dependency that is not necessarily the result of a foreign key is the constraint that the location in which an employee works is included in the collection of locations of offices of the company the employee works in.

Constraints such as functional and inclusion dependencies, which depend on the equality or inequality of values in tuples of relations, are called *data dependencies*. Another type of integrity constraint restricts the allowable domain values of attributes; such constraints are called *domain dependencies*.

For example, a domain dependency could state that values of an attribute EMP_SALARY range between 15,000 and 40,000 pound sterling. Another domain dependency could state that the values of an attribute EMP_NAME is a string of at most 25 English characters.

Yet another type of integrity constraint restricts the cardinality of a projection of a relation onto a set of attributes; such constraints are called *cardinality constraints*.

For example, a cardinality constraint could state that there are less managers than employees. Another cardinality constraint could state that the number of students doing a particular course should not exceed some specified number.

All the integrity constraints mentioned above are *static*, i.e. their satisfaction in a database can be checked by examining the current database state. There is another class of constraints which are *dynamic* in nature in the sense that two database states need to be examined in order to test their satisfaction; such integrity constraints are called *state transition constraints* [NY78]. As an example we may want to state that the attribute value age of a schema PERSON only increases when a relation over PERSON is updated. Thus in order to check this constraint during an update, we need to examine the person relation before and after the update. Another example of this type of integrity constraint is a constraint which states that salaries of employees increase in time. Such state transition constraints cannot be checked statically only on the relation prior to or after an update took place.

3.5   Inference of Integrity Constraints

The integrity part of a data model is one of its fundamental components. As we have indicated above there are many useful constraints that can be defined over a database schema in order to restrict the set of allowable relations in a database to those that are of interest to the particular application we are dealing with. Given that we have defined a set of integrity constraints, we would like to know what other integrity constraints this set logically implies and also whether there are any redundancies in the set we have specified. For example, if an employee works in a unique department and a department has a unique location we can infer by transitivity that an employee works in a unique location. Thus, there is no need to specify this implied functional dependency as part of our specification. However, how do we know that our inference procedure can derive only and all possible logical implications from the initial set of constraints? If our inference procedure is "sound and complete", then the answer to this question is positive, otherwise, in general, we may not be able to derive an integrity constraint which is indeed logically implied by the original set of constraints. Even if the inference procedure is sound and complete, we need to investigate the computational complexity of deciding whether an integrity constraint is logically implied by a given set of integrity constraints. If the computational complexity of such an inference procedure is polynomial time in the size of the input set of integrity constraints, then we can normally solve this inference problem in reasonable time, otherwise the solution is probably only solvable in exponential time in which case this inference problem is intractable.

A *class* C of integrity constraints refers to a particular set of integrity constraints over a given relation schema or database schema. For example, the set of all FDs over relation schema R is a class of integrity constraints and the set of all FDs and INDs over database schema **R** is another class of integrity constraints. Whenever no ambiguity arises we will refer to a set of integrity constraints, say Σ, which is included in a class of integrity constraints, say C, simply as Σ without explicitly mentioning the class C. In the following we will assume for simplicity that a set of integrity constraints is over a relation schema R; the definition carries over to a database schema **R** in a straightforward way.

We denote the fact that a relation r over schema R *satisfies* an integrity constraint α over R by $r \models \alpha$. If $r \models \alpha$ does not hold, we write $r \not\models \alpha$ and say that r does not satisfy (or *violates*) α. We say that r *satisfies* a set Σ of integrity constraints over R, if for all integrity constraints $\alpha \in \Sigma, r \models \alpha$ holds.

We say that a set of integrity constraints Σ over R *logically implies* a single integrity constraint α over R, written $\Sigma \models \alpha$, whenever for all relations r over R the following condition is true:

$$\text{if } r \models \Sigma \text{ holds then } r \models \alpha \text{ also holds.}$$

We say that a set of integrity constraints Σ over R *logically implies* a set of integrity constraints Γ over R (or Γ is a logical consequence of Σ), written $\Sigma \models \Gamma$, if for all $\alpha \in \Gamma$, $\Sigma \models \alpha$ holds.

The concept of logical implication is very important, since if $\Sigma - \{\alpha\} \models \alpha$, then the integrity maintenance algorithm need only check for the satisfaction of $\Sigma - \{\alpha\}$. For example, {EMP $\rightarrow$ ADDRESS, ADDRESS $\rightarrow$ PHONE} $\models$ {EMP $\rightarrow$ PHONE} holds and thus the fact that an employee has a unique telephone number does not need to be explicitly stored in the database system.

In order that a class of integrity constraints be of any practical use we need to address the problem of the efficiency of mechanising the process of logical implication.

Definition 3.52 (The implication problem) The implication problem for a class of integrity constraints C is the problem of finding the computational complexity of deciding whether $\Sigma \models \alpha$ or $\Sigma \not\models \alpha$, where $\Sigma \subseteq C$ and $\alpha \in C$; if the class of integrity constraints C is understood from context we will not mention it explicitly. ∎

An inference rule (with respect to a class C of integrity constraints) is a rule which allows us to *derive* an integrity constraint from a given set of integrity constraints. More precisely, an *inference rule* is a sentence of the form: *if* certain integrity constraints can be derived from the given set of constraints *then* we can derive an additional constraint. The *if* part of an inference rule is called the *hypothesis* of the rule and the *then* part of the rule is called its *conclusion*. An *axiom* is an inference rule with an empty if part, that is, the additional constraint can be derived unconditionally. An *axiom system* for a class C of integrity constraints is a set of inference rules with respect to C.

For example, if the FDs, EMP $\rightarrow$ ADDRESS and ADDRESS $\rightarrow$ PHONE both hold, then we can infer by the *transitivity rule* that the FD EMP $\rightarrow$ PHONE also holds.

Given an axiom system S (for a class of integrity constraints), a *proof* (in S) of an integrity constraint α from a given set of integrity constraints Σ is a finite sequence of integrity constraints, whose last element is α, such that each constraint in the said sequence is either in Σ or can be derived from a finite number of previous constraints in the sequence by using one of the inference rules of the axiom system S. We denote by $\Sigma \vdash \alpha$ the fact that there exists a proof (in S) of α from Σ in a given axiom system; if the axiom system is understood from context we will not mention it explicitly.

Informally, an axiom system is sound and complete for a class of integrity constraints if the concept of logical implication coincides with the concept of proof within the said axiom system. The benefit of a sound and complete axiom system is as follows. In order to solve the implication problem $\Sigma \models \alpha$ in a naive way, we can test the logical implications $r \models \Sigma$ and $r \models \alpha$ for all relations r over R. In general, this solution is infeasible, since there are, in general, an infinite number of such relations. We therefore need to find a more efficient way to check whether $\Sigma \models \alpha$. Now, if the axiom system is sound and complete then all we need to do is to check whether $\Sigma \vdash \alpha$, i.e. we need to find a proof (which is a finite procedure) of α from Σ. In many cases we can actually devise efficient algorithms which construct proofs for $\Sigma \vdash \alpha$ and thus solve the implication problem efficiently.

Definition 3.53 (Sound and complete axiom system) Let Σ be a set of integrity constraints included in a given class C and let α be a single integrity constraint belonging to C. An axiom system is *sound* (for C) whenever the following condition is true:

$$\text{if } \Sigma \vdash \alpha \text{ holds then } \Sigma \models \alpha \text{ also holds.}$$

An axiom system is *complete* (for C) whenever the following condition is true:

$$\text{if } \Sigma \models \alpha \text{ holds then } \Sigma \vdash \alpha \text{ also holds.} \qquad \blacksquare$$

The following definition will be useful when we investigate the inference structure for integrity constraints.

Definition 3.54 (Closure operator)   Let S be a finite set and recall that $\mathcal{P}(S)$ denotes the finite power set of S. A *closure operator* [BDK87, DP90] is a total mapping C from $\mathcal{P}(S)$ to $\mathcal{P}(S)$ such that $\forall\, X, Y \subseteq S$, the following conditions are satisfied:

1) $X \subseteq C(X)$,

2) if $X \subseteq Y$ then $C(X) \subseteq C(Y)$, and

3) $C(C(X)) = C(X)$. $\blacksquare$

Definition 3.55 (The closure of a set of integrity constraints)   The *closure* of a set of integrity constraints Σ over R (with respect to an axiom system), denoted by Σ^+, is the set of all integrity constraints α over R that can be proved from Σ. Formally,

$$\Sigma^+ = \{\alpha \mid \Sigma \vdash \alpha\}. \qquad \blacksquare$$

We observe that the operator "+" induced by the closure Σ^+ of Σ is a closure operator; the reader can verify that "+" satisfies the three conditions of a closure operator.

A set of integrity constraints Σ is said to be *closed* if $\Sigma^+ = \Sigma$. Also, a set of integrity constraints Σ is said to be a *cover* of another set of integrity constraints Γ if $\Sigma^+ = \Gamma^+$.

As an example, let $\Sigma = \{\text{EMP} \rightarrow \text{ADDRESS}, \text{ADDRESS} \rightarrow \text{PHONE}, \text{EMP} \rightarrow \text{PHONE}\}$. Then as we will see later on $\Gamma = \Sigma - \{\text{EMP} \rightarrow \text{PHONE}\}$ is a cover of Σ. The FD EMP $\rightarrow$ PHONE is called a *redundant* FD, since it can be removed from Σ without loss of information.

Armstrong relations [Fag82a, BDFS84] are relations, which satisfy all and only those integrity constraints which are logically implied by a given set of integrity constraints. The existence of Armstrong relations for FDs holding in relations was first shown in [Arm74]. Such relations have been shown to be important in the process of database design [MR86a]. Various combinatorial results concerning the size of Armstrong relations (which is, in general, exponential for FDs) and algorithms that generate such relations are given in [Fag82a, BDFS84, MR86a, DT93].

Definition 3.56 (Armstrong relations)   An *Armstrong relation* for a given set of integrity constraints Σ over schema R is a relation r over R satisfying the following condition for all integrity constraints α:

$$r \models \alpha \text{ if and only if } \Sigma \models \alpha.$$

We say that a class of integrity constraints *enjoys* Armstrong relations if there exists an Armstrong relation for each set of integrity constraints in the class. $\blacksquare$

The following theorem, whose proof we leave for the reader, shows an elegant connection between sound and complete axiom systems and the property of enjoying Armstrong relations.

Theorem 3.19   Let S be an axiom system for a class of integrity constraints C and consider the following statements:

1) S is sound for C and for all sets Σ of constraints included in C there exists a relation r over R that satisfies the condition

$$r \models \alpha \text{ if and only if } \Sigma \vdash \alpha.$$

2) C enjoys Armstrong relations.

3) S is sound and complete for C.

Then (1) is true if and only if (2) and (3) are both true.   □

3.6   Data Dependencies

Constraints such as functional and inclusion dependencies, which depend on the equality or inequality of values in tuples of relations in a database, are called data dependencies. More specifically, a data dependency is a first-order logic formula defined over a database schema that expresses the constraint that given that certain tuples exist in the database and these tuples satisfy certain equalities or inequalities, then other tuples must also be present in the database and these other tuples must also satisfy certain equalities or inequalities. The theory of data dependencies has been central in the research area of relational databases, since it deals with the foundations of the integrity part of the relational model and generalises the fundamental notions of keys and foreign keys, which were discussed in Subsection 1.7.1 of Chapter 1. The theory of data dependencies also forms the basis of relational database design, which is discussed in detail in Chapter 4.

In Subsection 3.6.1 we introduce *Functional Dependencies* (FD), which generalise keys, and give a sound and complete axiom system for FDs. In Subsection 3.6.2 we show that FDs enjoy Armstrong relations. In Subsection 3.6.3 we discuss the implication problem for FDs and show that it can be solved in polynomial time. In Subsection 3.6.4 we introduce the *chase procedure* for FDs, which acts as a theorem prover that enables us to solve the implication problem of whether a set of FDs logically implies that the relations in a given database can be losslessly joined together. The property of being able to losslessly join relations in a database is a fundamental one, since naturally joining relations is the means in the relational model by which information in several relations is combined. In Subsection 3.6.5 we investigate the issue of finding an appropriate cover of a set of FDs that has less redundancy in it than the original set of FDs. In Subsection 3.6.6 we investigate the problem of whether a relation schema having a subset of attributes of another relation schema, say R, satisfies a given set of FDs defined over R. This problem is very important in database design, since we may define a set of FDs over a relation schema, say R, and then decompose R into two or more relation schemas each having less attributes than R. In Subsection 3.6.7 we introduce *Inclusion Dependencies*

(INDs), which generalise foreign keys, and give a sound and complete axiom system for INDs. In Subsection 3.6.8 we extend the chase procedure, introduced in Subsection 3.6.4, in the presence of FDs and INDs. In this subsection we utilise the chase procedure in order to test whether a given database satisfies a set of FDs and INDs. This highlights the versatility of the chase procedure as a very useful tool for the relational database theorist in his/her investigation of the properties of a class of data dependencies. In Subsection 3.6.9 we show that certain subclasses of FDs and INDs enjoy Armstrong relations. In Subsection 3.6.10 we discuss the implication problem for INDs and show that it is, in general, intractable. In Subsection 3.6.11 we investigate the interaction between FDs and INDs. Studying this interaction is important, since FDs and INDs are the most fundamental integrity constraints that arise in practice in relational databases. The interaction between FDs and INDs turns out to be a complex matter resulting in the negative result that there is *no* sound and complete axiom system for the general class of FDs and INDs, and also that their implication problem is, in general, undecidable. In this subsection we investigate subclasses of FDs and INDs that have a sound and complete axiomatisation and for which the implication problem is decidable. Due to the complex interaction between FDs and INDs, in Subsection 3.6.12 we study subclasses of FDs and INDs that do not interact at all. We exhibit a large and useful class of FDs and INDs that do not interact. FDs express dependencies within a relation schema and INDs express dependencies between relation schemas. It is not at all clear whether FDs are adequate to express the dependencies within a relation schema. In particular, FDs only express single-valued properties while in the "real world" multivalued properties, such as a person may have one or more children, naturally arise. In Subsection 3.6.13 we define *Mulitvalued Dependencies* (MVDs)which express the fact that a relation can be decomposed into two further relations that can be losslessly joined together. This is a special kind of multivalued property that can, for example, express that a person has a set of children and independently a set of hobbies. We present a mixed sound and complete axiom system for FDs and MVDs and study various problems that have intrigued database researchers during the late 1970's until the mid 1980's. The *Join Dependency* (JD), presented in Subsection 3.6.14, generalises the MVD to express the fact that a relation can be decomposed into two or more relations that can be losslessly joined together. As such the JD is fundamental to relational database design since the lossless join property guarantees that we can meaningfully combine relations together in queries using the natural join operator. There is a plethora of results in data dependency theory and in a book such as ours we can only cover the most important results. The reader wishing to further his/her study of this area will discover many additional interesting kinds of data dependencies and results that have made relational database theory the fruitful area in computer science that it is.

3.6.1 Functional Dependencies and Keys

As we have already mentioned, the *Functional Dependency* (FD) generalises the notion of keys and as such it is the most common data dependency that arises in practice. The theory of FDs has been instrumental in providing a solid foundation for the theory of data dependencies and has had a major impact on relational database design, which we detail in Chapter 4. We begin with a motivating example. Let EMPLOYEE be a relation schema describing employees' details, with schema(EMPLOYEE) = {SS#, ENAME, AGE, ADDRESS, POSTCODE, SALARY}. The semantics of EMPLOYEE are that SS# and {ENAME, ADDRESS} are keys for EMPLOYEE and

ADDRESS uniquely determines POSTCODE. Thus the set of FDs specified over EMPLOYEE is: {SS# → schema(EMPLOYEE), {ENAME, ADDRESS} → SS#, ADDRESS → POSTCODE}.

Let STUD_POS be a relation schema describing the students linear ordering in a class, with schema(STUD_POS) = {SNAME, SUBJECT, POSITION}. The semantics of STUD_POS are that {SNAME, SUBJECT} and {SUBJECT, POSITION} are keys, i.e. both these sets uniquely determine all the attributes in the schema; note that this implies that no more than one student can occupy any position. Thus the set of FDs specified over STUD_POS is: {{SNAME, SUBJECT} → POSITION, {SUBJECT, POSITION} → SNAME}.

The formal definition of an FD follows.

Definition 3.57 (Functional dependency) A *functional dependency* over schema R (or simply an FD) is a statement of the form R : X → Y (or simply X → Y whenever R is understood from context), where X, Y ⊆ schema(R).

An FD X → Y is said to be *trivial* if Y ⊆ X; it is said to be *standard* if X ≠ ∅. ∎

An FD R : X → Y is satisfied in a relation r over R if whenever two tuples in r have equal X-values they also have equal Y-values. This implies that every X-value in r has only one corresponding Y-value. The formal definition of satisfaction of an FD in a relation follows.

Definition 3.58 (Satisfaction of an FD) An FD R : X → Y is satisfied in a relation r over R, denoted by $r \models R : X \to Y$, if $\forall t_1, t_2 \in r$, if $t_1[X] = t_2[X]$, then $t_1[Y] = t_2[Y]$. ∎

As defined above an FD X → Y is *nonstandard* if X = ∅. Whenever a relation r over R satisfies the FD ∅ → Y, it must be the case that r can only have at most one Y-value. That is, the cardinality of $\pi_Y(r)$ is less than or equal to one; if $r = ∅$, then the cardinality of $\pi_Y(r)$ is zero, otherwise it must be one. It follows that nonstandard FDs correspond to cardinality constraints. From now on unless otherwise stated *we will assume that FDs are standard*. The justification for this assumption is that nonstandard FDs are rare in practice. Moreover, a nonstandard FD can always be described as a cardinality constraint when it is necessary for the application (see Section 3.7).

When F is a set of FDs over one or more relation schemas R ∈ **R**, where **R** is a database schema, we say that F is a set of FDs over **R**. Usually, all the FDs in F are over a single relation schema R ∈ **R**, in which case we simply say that F is a set of FDs over R.

Definition 3.59 (Inference rules for FDs) Let F be a set of FDs over schema R. We define the following inference rules for FDs:

FD1 Reflexivity: if Y ⊆ X ⊆ schema(R), then F ⊢ X → Y.

FD2 Augmentation: if F ⊢ X → Y and W ⊆ schema(R), then F ⊢ XW → YW.

FD3 Transitivity: if F ⊢ X → Y and F ⊢ Y → Z, then F ⊢ X → Z.

FD4 Union: if F ⊢ X → Y and F ⊢ X → Z, then F ⊢ X → YZ.

FD5 Decomposition: if F ⊢ X → YZ, then F ⊢ X → Y and F ⊢ X → Z.

FD6 Pseudo-transitivity: if F ⊢ X → Y and F ⊢ YW → Z, then F ⊢ XW → Z. ∎

Note that FD1 is an axiom, since it has no hypotheses. We call the inference rules FD1, FD2 and FD3 *Armstrong's axiom system* [Arm74].

Definition 3.60 (The closure of a set of attributes)   We define the closure of a set of attributes $X \subseteq$ schema(R) with respect to a set of FDs F over R, denoted by X^+ (assuming that F is understood from context), by

$$X^+ = \bigcup \{Y \mid F \vdash X \to Y \text{ using Armstrong's axiom system}\}. \qquad \blacksquare$$

The reader can easily verify that the operator "+" induced by the closure X^+ is a closure operator. For our motivating examples we have:

- $\text{SS\#}^+ = \{\text{ENAME, ADDRESS}\}^+ = \text{schema(EMPLOYEE)}$.

- $\text{ADDRESS}^+ = \{\text{ADDRESS, POSTCODE}\}$.

- $\{\text{SNAME, SUBJECT}\}^+ = \{\text{SUBJECT, POSITION}\}^+ = \text{schema(STUD\_POS)}$.

- $\text{SNAME}^+ = \{\text{SNAME}\}$.

Lemma 3.20   Armstrong's axiom system is sound.

Proof. We prove that transitivity (FD3) is sound and leave it to the reader to prove that the other inference rules are also sound.

Let r be a relation over R and $t_1, t_2 \in r$ be tuples such that $t_1[X] = t_2[X]$. We need to show that $t_1[Z] = t_2[Z]$, which implies that $r \models X \to Z$. Now, $t_1[Y] = t_2[Y]$, due to the fact that $F \vdash X \to Y$ and thus by assumption $r \models X \to Y$. The result follows, since $t_1[Y] = t_2[Y]$ implies that $t_1[Z] = t_2[Z]$ due to the fact that $F \vdash Y \to Z$ and thus by assumption $r \models Y \to Z$. $\qquad \square$

The reader can verify that FD4, FD5 and FD6 are also sound inference rules.

Theorem 3.21   Armstrong's axiom system is sound and complete.

Proof. Soundness follows from the previous lemma. It remains to prove the completeness.

In order to prove completeness of Armstrong's axiom system, we need to show that if $F \models X \to Y$, then $F \vdash X \to Y$. Equivalently, we need to show that if $F \not\vdash X \to Y$, then $F \not\models X \to Y$. Thus assuming that $F \not\vdash X \to Y$ it is sufficient to exhibit a counterexample relation, r over R, such that $r \models F$ but $r \not\models X \to Y$.

Let r over R be the relation shown in Table 3.37. We conclude the proof by showing that $r \models F$ but $r \not\models X \to Y$.

Table 3.37 A counterexample relation

X^+	schema(R) $-X^+$
$1 \ldots 1$	$1 \ldots 1$
$1 \ldots 1$	$0 \ldots 0$

Firstly, we show that $r \models F$. Suppose to the contrary that $r \not\models F$ and thus $\exists V \to W \in F$ such that $r \not\models V \to W$. It follows by the construction of r that $V \subseteq X^+$ and $\exists A \in W$ such that $A \in$

schema(R) $-X^+$. Now, $F \vdash X \to V$, since $V \subseteq X^+$ and $F \vdash V \to A$ by the decomposition inference rule (FD5). Thus $F \vdash X \to A$ by the transitivity rule (FD3). This leads to a contradiction, since it follows that $A \in X^+$.

Secondly, we show that $r \not\models X \to Y$. Suppose to the contrary that $r \models X \to Y$. It follows by the construction of r that $Y \subseteq X^+$ and thus $F \vdash X \to Y$. This leads to a contradiction, since $F \not\vdash X \to Y$ was assumed. $\qquad\qquad\square$

A superkey is a set of attributes that determines all the attributes in a relation schema and a key is a superkey whose set of attributes is minimal.

Definition 3.61 (Key and superkey)   A set of attributes $K \subseteq$ schema(R) is a *candidate key* (or a *minimal key* or simply a *key*) for R with respect to a set of FDs F over schema R if the following two conditions hold:

1) *uniqueness*: $K^+ =$ schema(R), and

2) *minimality*: for no proper subset $X \subset K$ is X a key for R with respect to F.

A set of attributes $K \subseteq$ schema(R) is a *superkey* for R with respect to a set of FDs F over schema R if it satisfies condition 1 (but not necessarily condition 2), i.e. $K^+ =$ schema(R).   ∎

For our motivating examples we have:

- SS# and {ENAME, ADDRESS} are keys for EMPLOYEE; any proper superset of one of these is a superkey which is not a key.

- {SNAME, SUBJECT} and {SUBJECT, POSITION} are keys for STUD_POS; the only superkey that is not a key is schema(STUD_POS).

In the following we omit to mention the schema R and the set of FDs F over R if they are understood from context. Given a relation schema R and a set of FDs F over R one of the candidate keys is designated as the *primary key*. The other keys are called *alternate keys*. An attribute in schema(R) that belongs to at least one candidate key for R with respect to F is called a *prime* attribute of R with respect to F; an attribute in schema(R) which is not prime is called *nonprime*. A key is said to be *simple* if it consists of a single attribute; otherwise it is said to be *composite*.

There has been much debate on the merits of simple keys versus composite keys. For example, consider a PERSON schema consisting of attributes NAME, ADDRESS, AGE and OCCUPATION. Obviously, NAME is not, in general, a minimal key since there may be more than one John Smith recorded in the database, so it can be assumed that {NAME, ADDRESS} is a key, which is also the primary key. However, there are several problems with this key. Firstly, we cannot distinguish between two John Smith's that happen to live in the same address. Secondly, it is more cumbersome to refer to composite keys in queries and updates, since such queries and updates are often tedious to specify and therefore more error prone than would otherwise be the case. If a simple key such as social security number (SS#) is available, then it should be chosen as the primary key. Simple keys such as SS# may not always be forthcoming and thus it is often suggested to introduce a new simple key into the schema such as person number (P#), which has no intrinsic meaning; we will call such a simple key a *surrogate* key.

The sole purpose of surrogate keys is to uniquely identify tuples in a relation. The values of a surrogate should be generated either by the database system (if it supports such a mechanism) or by an application program, and it is advisable that they be concealed from the user, since they are not real-world identifiers and thus have no meaning to the user. Although such a solution is viable, there are various overheads in maintaining surrogates and querying in their presence which need to be considered. Still surrogates can be very useful as are, for example, social security numbers, part numbers of various machines and order numbers.

We next present some combinatorial problems relating to keys. The following result, which was shown in [DK93], gives an upper bound on the number of candidate keys that can be satisfied in a relation. In the following theorem $\binom{n}{r}$ denotes the number of combinations of choosing r objects from n objects with no reference to the order in which the r objects are chosen. Recall from Subsection 1.9.2 of Chapter 1 that $\lfloor m \rfloor$ denotes the greatest natural number less than or equal to some real number m.

Theorem 3.22 The number of candidate keys, K_i, for a schema R, with $|\text{schema(R)}| = n$, is at most

$$\binom{n}{\lfloor n/2 \rfloor}$$

and there exists a relation r over R such that for all K_i, $r \models K_i \rightarrow \text{schema(R)}$.   □

It is a well-known combinatorial result that given a set S of cardinality n there are at most $\binom{n}{\lfloor n/2 \rfloor}$ incomparable subsets of S under set inclusion, hence the upper bound (the result was first obtained by Sperner in 1928; see [VW92]). The existence of a relation satisfying the upper bound number of keys follows from the fact that FDs enjoy Armstrong relations (see Theorem 3.28 in the next subsection for a proof of this fact). Firstly, given a set of keys $\mathcal{K}$ it can easily be verified that every distinct pair of keys in $\mathcal{K}$ is incomparable under set inclusion. Secondly, we take F = {K → schema(R) | K ∈ $\mathcal{K}$} and construct an Armstrong relation, r over R, for F.

As an example of a set of FDs with an exponential number of keys let schema(R) = $\{A_1, A_2, \ldots, A_n, B_1, B_2, \ldots, B_n\}$ and let F = $\{A_i \rightarrow B_i, B_i \rightarrow A_i \mid i \in \{1, \ldots, n\}\}$. It can easily be verified that R has 2^n keys with respect to F.

The following lemma shows that finding a single key for a relation schema can be done in polynomial time [LO78, Kun85]. The idea behind an algorithm to compute a key for R is: starting from schema(R), which is a superkey for R, we loop over all the attributes A in schema(R) in some order and remove A from the current state of the output key, say K, if A $\in (K-A)^+$. The loop will be iterated at most type(R) times.

Lemma 3.23 Given a schema R and a set of FDs F over R the problem of finding a single key for R with respect to F can be solved in time polynomial in the sizes of R and F.   □

The following two decision problems concerning keys of relation schemas are unlikely to have efficient solutions; the full proofs can be found in [LO78].

Theorem 3.24 Given a schema R and a set of FDs F over R the following decision problems are NP-complete:

1) The problem of deciding whether R has at least one superkey with respect to F of cardinality less than or equal to k.

2) The problem of deciding whether an attribute A $\in$ schema(R) is prime with respect to F.

Proof. We sketch the main idea of the proof. Showing that the above two problems are in NP is easily done, since testing whether a set of attributes X, with $|X| \leq k$, is a superkey for R with respect to F can be done in polynomial time by testing whether $X^+ = $ schema(R). Moreover, A is prime if X is a key for R, i.e. for all B $\in$ X, X $-$ B is not a superkey for R, and in addition A $\in$ X.

To show that the first problem is NP-hard, a polynomial-time transformation from the vertex cover problem, which is known to be NP-complete [Kar72, GJ79], is given.

The vertex cover problem: Given a graph (N, E) and a natural number k, does there exist a subset M of the node set N, with $|M| \leq k$, such that for each edge $\{u, v\} \in$ E, at least one of u and v belongs to M?

Essentially, we construct a relation schema, R, such that schema(R) has one attribute A_i for each node in N and one attribute B_j for each edge in E. We also construct a set F of FDs which is initially the empty set. We then add to F an FD $A_i \to B_j$ for each node represented by A_i that is in the edge represented by B_j. In addition, an FD X $\to$ Y is added to the set F, where X is the union of the attributes B_j and Y is the union of the attributes A_i; thus X is a key for R with respect to F and Y is a superkey for R with respect to F. It can now be shown that M is a vertex cover for (N, E) if and only if the set of attributes representing M is a superkey for R.

To show that the second problem is NP-hard, a polynomial-time transformation from the superkey of cardinality k problem, shown to be NP-complete in part (1) above, can be given. $\square$

The following result shows that the problem of finding whether a schema R has at least one superkey of cardinality less than or equal to k with respect to the set of FDs that hold in a specific relation over R is also NP-complete. We begin with a definition.

Definition 3.62 (The set of FDs satisfied in a relation)   The set of FDs holding in a relation r over R, denoted by F(r), is defined by F(r) = {X $\to$ Y | X, Y $\subseteq$ schema(R) and $r \models$ X $\to$ Y}.   ∎

The proof of the next theorem follows by a reduction of the vertex cover problem [DT88].

Theorem 3.25   Given a relation r over R, the problem of deciding whether R has at least one superkey of cardinality less than or equal to k with respect to the set of FDs F(r) that is satisfied in r is NP-complete. $\square$

Definition 3.63 (Antikey)   An *antikey* for a relation schema R with respect to a set F of FDs over R is a maximal set of attributes included in schema(R) that is *not* a superkey for R with respect to F.   ∎

The following result shown in [DT87] characterises the set of prime attributes with respect to a set of FDs, F over R, in terms of the set of antikeys for R with respect to F.

Theorem 3.26   An attribute A ∈ schema(R) is prime with respect to a set F of FDs over a relation schema R if and only if A ∉ $\mathcal{A}$, where $\mathcal{A}$ denotes the intersection of all antikeys for R with respect to F.

Proof. If. Suppose that A ∉ $\mathcal{A}$ and thus A ∈ schema(R) − $\mathcal{A}$. Thus for some antikey W for R with respect to F, we have A ∉ W. Therefore, WA is a superkey for R with respect to F due to the fact that W is an antikey for R with respect to F. It follows that A is prime with respect to F.

Only if. Suppose that A is prime and thus there exists a key X for R with respect to F such that A ∈ X. Let Y = X − {A}. Now, since Y is not a superset of any key for R with respect to F, there exists an antikey W for R with respect to F such that Y ⊆ W. Obviously, A ∉ W, otherwise W would be a superkey for R with respect to F. So A ∈ schema(R) − W ⊆ schema(R) −$\mathcal{A}$.   □

The following surprising result shows that if we are interested in finding whether an attribute is prime with respect to the set of FDs that hold in a specific relation over R, then the problem can be solved in polynomial time [DT87]. Its proof relies on Theorem 3.26, since given a relation r over R, it can be shown that the set of antikeys for R with respect to the set F(r) of FDs that holds in r can be computed in polynomial time in the size of r.

Theorem 3.27   Given a relation r over R and a set F of FDs over R the problem of deciding whether an attribute A ∈ schema(R) is prime with respect to the set of FDs F(r) that is satisfied in r can be determined in time polynomial in the size of r.   □

We now motivate foreign keys. Assume a simple database with two relation schemas, EMPLOYEE (storing employee information) with attributes E#, ENAME and D# and DEPT (storing department information) with attributes D#, DNAME and MGR. Let us further assume that E# is the primary key of EMPLOYEE and D# is the primary key of DEPT.

A tuple <E1, John, D1> means that the name of employee E1 is John and E1 works in department D1. A tuple <D1, Computing, E2> means that the name of department D1 is Computing and its manager is employee E2. Thus the values of the attribute D# in EMPLOYEE reference the primary key values of the attribute D# in DEPT and similarly the values of MGR in DEPT reference the primary key values of the attribute E# in EMPLOYEE. Such referencing attributes are called *foreign keys*. Foreign keys are fundamental to the relational model, since they assert that values of tuples in one relation *reference* the primary key values of tuples in another relation. In our motivating example, D1 in an employee tuple references a department tuple with primary key value D1, and E2 in a department tuple references an employee tuple with primary key value E2.

Up until now we have not mentioned how we model situations where the information is missing or incomplete. Suppose that the schema EMPLOYEE contains the attributes ADDRESS and SPOUSE. Furthermore, assume that the address of an employee may be unknown or an employee may not have a spouse. In order to be able to record such information we add a distinguished null value, denoted by *unknown* and abbreviated to *unk*, to the domain of ADDRESS, and a distinguished null value, denoted by *inapplicable* (or alternatively *does_not_exist* which is abbreviated to *dne*), to the domain of SPOUSE. Thus if the attribute value of ADDRESS for a given employee tuple is *unk* then we interpret this as meaning that the address of the employee exists but is unknown, and if the attribute value of SPOUSE is *inapplicable* for a given employee tuple then we interpret this as meaning that the employee does not have a spouse. We will now show how primary and foreign keys relate to the fact that the information in the database may be missing or incomplete.

We begin by formalising the notion of a foreign key in a database.

Definition 3.64 (Foreign key)   Let **R** be a database schema, R_1, R_2 be relation schemas of **R** and let K be the primary key of R_2. In addition, let $d = \{r_1, r_2, \ldots, r_n\}$ be a database over **R**.

A *foreign key* constraint is a specification of a set of attributes $X \subseteq \text{schema}(R_1)$ and a primary key K of R_2. The set of attributes X is called a *foreign key* of R_1 and it is said to *reference* the primary key K of R_2. The foreign key constraint that X references K is satisfied in d if the following condition holds: for all tuples $t_1 \in r_1$, if $t_1[X]$ does not contain any null values, then there exists $t_2 \in r_2$ such that $t_1[X] = t_2[K]$.

If d satisfies the foreign key constraint that X references K then the X-values of tuples in r_1, which are called foreign key values, are said to satisfy the foreign key constraint.   ∎

We now state the two most fundamental integrity constraints that should be enforced in the relational model [Cod79, Cod90].

Entity integrity The primary key values of tuples in a relation should not contain null values.

Referential integrity If a set of attributes in a relation schema is specified as a foreign key
    referencing the primary key of another relation schema then its foreign key values in a
    database must satisfy this foreign key constraint.

The meaning of these two constraints should be clear. Entity integrity guarantees that each tuple in a relation has at least one unique logical access path. On the other hand, referential integrity guarantees that primary key values which are referenced via foreign key values indeed relate to existing tuples.

We close this subsection with two algorithms which enforce entity and referential integrity in a relational database. The first algorithm, given below, checks whether entity integrity is satisfied in a relation r over R with primary key $X \subseteq R$.

Algorithm 3.6 (CHECK_PRIMARY_KEY(r, X))
1. **begin**
2.   **for all** tuples $t \in r$ **do**
3.   **if** $\exists A \in X$ such that $t[A]$ is null **then**
4.   **return** NO;
5.   **end if**
6.   **for all** tuples $u \in r - \{t\}$ **do**
7.   **if** $u[X] = t[X]$ **then**
8.   **return** NO;
9.   **end if**
10.   **end for**
11.   **end for**
12.   **return** YES;
13. **end.**

The second algorithm, given below, checks whether referential integrity is satisfied in a database $d = \{r, s\}$ over a database schema $\mathbf{R} = \{R, S\}$, with foreign key attributes $X \subseteq$ schema(R) which reference the primary key attributes $K \subseteq$ schema(S).

Algorithm 3.7 (CHECK_FOREIGN_KEY(d, X, K))
1. **begin**
2.   **for all** tuples $t \in r$ **do**
3.   **if** $\forall A \in X, t[A]$ is nonnull **then**
4.   **if** $\not\exists u \in s$ such that $t[X] = u[K]$ **then**
5.   **return** NO;
6.   **end if**
7.   **end if**
8.   **end for**
9.   **return** YES;
10. **end.**

3.6.2   Armstrong Relations for Functional Dependencies

Recall Definition 3.56 of Armstrong relations. For FDs this can be restated as follows: a relation r over R is an Armstrong relation for a set of FDs F over R if for all FDs, $X \to Y$ over R, $r \models X \to Y$ if and only if $F \models X \to Y$. An immediate consequence of this definition and the established fact that Armstrong's axiom system is sound and complete is that r is an Armstrong relation for F if for all FDs $X \to Y$ over R, $r \models X \to Y$ if and only if $X \to Y \in F^+$, where $F^+ = \{W \to Z \mid F \vdash W \to Z\}$ is the closure of F with respect to Armstrong's axiom system.

Armstrong [Arm74] was the first to show that FDs enjoy Armstrong relations. We next give a proof of this assertion assuming that all FDs are standard.

Theorem 3.28   FDs enjoy Armstrong relations.

Proof. We first claim that if $F \not\models X \to Y$, then there exists a relation over R, which we denote by $r(X \to Y)$, containing exactly two tuples such that $r(X \to Y) \models F$ but $r(X \to Y) \not\models X \to Y$.

Now, since $F \not\models X \to Y$, there exists a relation r over R such that $r \models F$ but $r \not\models X \to Y$. Thus $\exists t_1, t_2 \in r$ such that $\{t_1, t_2\} \not\models X \to Y$. Therefore, we let $r(X \to Y)$ be $\{t_1, t_2\}$. The claim follows, since $\{t_1, t_2\} \models F$ holds due to the fact that $r \models F$.

We assume that the underlying domains are infinite and also that for two distinct FDs $X \to Y$ and $W \to Z$ the active domains of $r(X \to Y)$ and $r(W \to Z)$ are pairwise disjoint. We take r^{arm} to be the union of all the relations $r(X \to Y)$ such that $X \to Y$ is an FD over R which is not a member of F^+.

It can easily be verified that r^{arm} is an Armstrong relation for F. $\square$

The technique used in the above proof for constructing an Armstrong relation for a set of FDs is called the *disjoint union* technique. Other techniques discussed in [Fag82a] are:

agreement sets (which are sets of *closed attributes*, i.e. sets X of attributes satisfying $X = X^+$), direct products and the chase procedure (see Subsection 3.6.4).

As an example, consider a relation schema, R, having attributes TEACHER (T), COURSE (C) and DAY (D). Following [MR86a] we will illustrate how Armstrong relations can be used as a tool to show users example relations during the relational database design stage. Suppose the user wishes to examine a relation over R prior to specifying any FDs that should be satisfied in this relation. The tool could display an arbitrary relation, say the relation r_1, shown in Table 3.38. It can easily be verified that both $r \models C \rightarrow TD$ and $r \models T \rightarrow CD$ hold. Thus r_1 may mislead the user to suppose that these FDs indeed must be specified.

Table 3.38 The relation r_1 satisfying several FDs

TEACHER	COURSE	DAY
Robert	databases	Monday
Richard	algorithms	Monday

A better example relation to start off with would be the relation r_2, shown in Table 3.39. It can easily be verified that r_2 is an Armstrong relation for the empty set of FDs, that is, no nontrivial FDs are satisfied in r_2. Thus the user can inspect this relation and decide what FDs correspond to the semantics of the application.

Table 3.39 The relation r_2 satisfying no FDs

TEACHER	COURSE	DAY
Robert	databases	Monday
Richard	databases	Monday
Richard	algorithms	Monday
Robert	databases	Tuesday

Suppose the user decided that the only nontrivial FD that should be satisfied in the relation over R is $TC \rightarrow D$. The tool could then display the relation r_3, shown in Table 3.40, which is an Armstrong relation for the set of FDs, $\{TC \rightarrow D\}$.

Table 3.40 The relation r_3 satisfying $TC \rightarrow D$

TEACHER	COURSE	DAY
Robert	databases	Monday
Richard	databases	Monday
Richard	algorithms	Monday
Robert	algorithms	Tuesday

A tool which displays Armstrong relations might also minimise such relations, since the presence of redundant tuples may make it more difficult for the user to understand the semantics embedded in the relation. Some results on the size of Armstrong relations can be found in [BDFS84, MR86a]. In general, the size of Armstrong relations for a given set of FDs is exponential in the number of attributes in the relation schema. Some special cases, when Armstrong relations have polynomial size in the number of attributes, are considered in [DT93, DT95].

3.6.3   The Implication Problem for Functional Dependencies

The implication problem for FDs is the problem of deciding whether $F \models X \to Y$, given a set of FDs F and a single FD $X \to Y$ over R. Now, by the soundness and completeness of Armstrong's axiom system we need only consider the problem of deciding whether $F \vdash X \to Y$. This is equivalent to the problem of deciding whether Y is in the closure of X, or symbolically whether $Y \subseteq X^+$ holds. We now show that the implication problem for FDs can be efficiently solved.

The pseudo-code of an algorithm, designated CLOSURE(X, F), which returns the closure X^+ with respect to a set of FDs F over R, is given below.

Algorithm 3.8 (CLOSURE(X, F))
1. **begin**
2.   Cl := X;
3.   Done := *false*;
4.   **while** *not* Done **do**
5.   Done := *true*;
6.   **for each** $W \to Z \in F$ **do**
7.   **if** $W \subseteq Cl$ and $Z \not\subseteq Cl$ **then**
8. $Cl := Cl \cup Z$;
9.   Done: = *false*;
10.   **end if**
11.   **end for**
12.   **end while**
13.   **return** Cl;
14. **end.**

The computational complexity of CLOSURE(X, F) is $O(|F| \times |R|)$, where |F| is the number of FDs in F (i.e. its cardinality) and |R| is the number of attributes in schema(R). A faster linear time algorithm to compute X^+ in the size of F was shown in [BB79], where the size of F is the sum of the number of attributes in each of the FDs in F.

Example 3.3   Consider a relation schema R, with attributes COURSE (C), TEACHER (T), HOUR (H), ROOM (R), STUDENT (S) and GRADE (G). Let the set of FDs F associated with R be $\{C \to T, HR \to C, HT \to R, CS \to G, HS \to R\}$ with the obvious meaning. The following results returned from CLOSURE(X, F) can be verified:

- $C^+ = CT$.
- $HR^+ = CHRT$
- $CS^+ = CGST$
- $HST^+ = CHGRTS = $ schema(R).   ∎

3.6.4   Lossless Join Decompositions and the Chase Procedure

The (natural) join operator provides the means of combining information in two or more relations together. For example, if we have an employees relation containing every employee's name and the name of the department each employee works in, and a departments relation having department names and their locations, we can obtain the location that an employee works in by joining these two relations together. Thus the join operator allows us to reconstruct a larger relation, say r, from smaller ones that could have been obtained from r via projection. The problem we investigate in this subsection is the characterisation of when the join of two or more relations is meaningful, in the sense that the join operation does not incur any loss of information. The concept of joining relations together without loss of information is a fundamental property of a decomposition, which is a desirable property to attain during the database design stage detailed in Chapter 4 (recall from Definition 3.4 of Section 3.1 that decomposition is just a synonym of database schema).

Consider a relation schema R having the set of attributes, STUDENT (S), COURSE (C) and TEACHER (T). Let r_1 over R be the relation shown in Table 3.41, representing the fact that both Reuven and Hanna are taking the databases course but Reuven is taught by Mark and Hanna by George. Now, let $\mathbf{R} = \{SC, CT\}$ be a decomposition whose aim is to separate the information about students and their courses from the information about courses and their teachers. Suppose that we construct the database $d = \{\pi_{SC}(r_1), \pi_{CT}(r_1)\}$ over the decomposition $\mathbf{R}$. When we join the relations in d together we get $r_2 = \pi_{SC}(r_1) \bowtie \pi_{CT}(r_1)$ shown in Table 3.42. This has created a problem, since $r_1 \neq r_2$ (or more precisely $r_1 \subset r_2$) and thus the database d does not preserve the information of r_1. If this situation occurs we say that the decomposition $\mathbf{R}$ is *lossy*.

<table>
<tr><td colspan="3">Table 3.41 A relation r_1 over R</td></tr>
<tr><th>STUDENT</th><th>COURSE</th><th>TEACHER</th></tr>
<tr><td>Reuven</td><td>databases</td><td>Mark</td></tr>
<tr><td>Hanna</td><td>databases</td><td>George</td></tr>
</table>

<table>
<tr><td colspan="3">Table 3.42 The relation $r_2 = \pi_{SC}(r_1) \bowtie \pi_{CT}(r_1)$ over R</td></tr>
<tr><th>STUDENT</th><th>COURSE</th><th>TEACHER</th></tr>
<tr><td>Reuven</td><td>databases</td><td>Mark</td></tr>
<tr><td>Reuven</td><td>databases</td><td>George</td></tr>
<tr><td>Hanna</td><td>databases</td><td>Mark</td></tr>
<tr><td>Hanna</td><td>databases</td><td>George</td></tr>
</table>

The next definition formalises the notion of losslessness.

Definition 3.65 (Lossless join decomposition) Let $\mathbf{R} = \{R_1, R_2, \ldots, R_n\}$ be a database schema and recall that schema$(\mathbf{R}) = \bigcup_{i \in I}$ schema(R_i), where $I = \{1, 2, \ldots, n\}$. Then $\mathbf{R}$ is a *lossless join decomposition* of schema$(\mathbf{R})$ with respect to a set of FDs F (or simply the decomposition $\mathbf{R}$ is lossless with respect to F) if for all relations, r over schema$(\mathbf{R})$, with $r \models$ F, the equality

$$r = \pi_{R_1}(r) \bowtie \pi_{R_2}(r) \bowtie \cdots \bowtie \pi_{R_n}(r)$$

holds. ∎

In the example above we have shown that $\mathbf{R} = \{SC, CT\}$ is not a lossless join decomposition with respect to the empty set of FDs. Let us assume that a course has only one teacher, that is, $F = \{C \rightarrow T\}$, and let r_3 be the relation over R shown in Table 3.43. It can easily be verified that $r_3 = \pi_{SC}(r_3) \bowtie \pi_{CT}(r_3)$. In fact, the stronger statement that $\mathbf{R}$ is a lossless join decomposition of schema$(\mathbf{R})$ with respect to F holds.

In order to show a sufficient and necessary condition for a decomposition to be lossless with respect to a set of FDs, F over R, we introduce the *chase procedure*.

Table 3.43 A relation r_3 over R

STUDENT	COURSE	TEACHER
Reuven	databases	Mark
Hanna	databases	Mark

We first define the notion of a *tableau*, which is a relation whose active domain contains certain types of variable instead of constant values; we will call the tuples of a tableau *rows*.

The types of variable that can appear in the active domain of a tableau are:

- *distinguished variables* (dv's) denoted by subscripted *a*'s; we assume that for each attribute A $\in$ schema(R), a_i is the dv corresponding to A if and only if att(i) = A.

- *nondistinguished variables* (ndv's) denoted by subscripted *b*'s.

We will now define a partial order, denoted by $\sqsubseteq$, between dv's and ndv's; we take $v_1 \sqsubset v_2$ to mean $v_1 \sqsubseteq v_2$ but $v_1 \neq v_2$.

- for every dv a_i and ndv b_j, $a_i \sqsubset b_j$.
- for every pair of dv's a_i and a_j, $a_i \sqsubseteq a_j$ if and only if $i \leq j$.
- for every pair of ndv's b_i and b_j, $b_i \sqsubseteq b_j$ if and only if $i \leq j$.

In the following let T be a tableau over R and F be a set of FDs over R. We next define a transformation rule with respect to F, called the FD rule, which is applied to a tableau T over R and as a result modifies T by changing the occurrences of a particular variable to another variable.

FD rule: if X $\rightarrow$ Y $\in$ F and $\exists w_i, w_j \in$ T such that $w_i[X] = w_j[X]$ but $w_i[A] \sqsubset w_j[A]$ for some A $\in$ Y, then change all occurrences of the variable $w_j[A]$ in T to $w_i[A]$.

We are now ready to define the implementation of the *chase* procedure of a tableau T over R with respect to F. The chase procedure will be used as a theorem prover to test whether a database schema is a lossless join decomposition with respect to a set of FDs and, in addition, as an alternative way to solve the implication problem for a set of FDs.

The pseudo-code of an algorithm, designated CHASE(T, F), which returns the chase of a tableau T over R with respect to a set of FDs F over R, is given below. The algorithm is nondeterministic, since the FD rule is free to choose any FD in F and any two tuples in T that cause a change in the tableau.

Algorithm 3.9 (CHASE(T, F))
1. **begin**
2.   Result := T;
3.   Tmp := $\emptyset$;
4.   **while** Tmp $\neq$ Result **do**
5.   Tmp := Result;
6.   Apply the FD rule to Result;
7.   **end while**
8.   **return** Result;
9. **end.**

We call an execution of line 6 in Algorithm 3.9 a *chase step* and we say that the chase step *applies* the FD $X \to Y \in F$ to the tuples t_1 and t_2. There are several properties that CHASE(T, F) possesses. Firstly, it is a finite *Church-Rosser* system. That is, the tableau returned by CHASE(T, F) is unique independently of the order in which the FDs in F are chosen and the tuples in T are chosen by the FD rule. Secondly, the tableau returned by CHASE(T, F) satisfies F, since if this were not the case the FD rule could be applied at line 6 of Algorithm 3.9 causing a further modification to the returned tableau. Finally, the chase procedure, which computes CHASE(T, F), terminates after a finite number of steps, since no new values are created by the algorithm. In fact CHASE(T, F) can be computed in time polynomial in the sizes of **R** and F, since each application of a chase step reduces the number of distinct values in the chased tableau by at least one.

We will now utilise the chase to solve two important problems. The first problem is that of testing whether a decomposition is lossless with respect to a set of FDs, and the second one is an alternative method to that presented in Subsection 3.6.3 for solving the implication problem for FDs.

Definition 3.66 A *distinct* ndv b_i appearing in a tableau T over R is a ndv that appears in only one row and column of T.

The tableau T for a database schema $\mathbf{R} = \{R_1, R_2, \ldots, R_n\}$, denoted by T($\mathbf{R}$), is a tableau over R, with schema(R) = schema($\mathbf{R}$), having a row w_i for each $R_i \in \mathbf{R}$. For all attributes $A \in$ schema(R), if $A \in$ schema(R_i), then row w_i has the dv a_j as the value of $w_i[A]$, where att(j) = A, otherwise if $A \in$ schema(R) $-$ schema(R_i), then row w_i has a distinct ndv as the value of $w_i[A]$.

A winning row for CHASE(T($\mathbf{R}$), F) is a row which contains dv's over all the attributes in schema(R).

The tableau T for an FD $X \to Y$ over R, denoted by T($X \to Y$), is a tableau over R containing two rows. Both rows have the dv a_i as the value of $w_i[A]$, $\forall A \in X$, where att(i) = A, and distinct ndv's as the value of $w_i[A]$, $\forall A \in$ schema(R) $-$ XY. The first row, w_1, has the dv a_j as the value of $w_1[B]$, $\forall B \in Y$, where att(j) = B, and the second row, w_2, has distinct ndv's as the value of $w_2[B]$, $\forall B \in Y$.

A winning row for CHASE(T($X \to Y$), F) is a row which contains dv's over all the attributes in XY.   ■

Theorem 3.29 A database schema **R** is a lossless join decomposition with respect to a set of FDs F over R, with schema(**R**) = schema(R), if and only if CHASE(T(**R**), F) contains a winning row.

Proof. Let T = CHASE(T(**R**), F). We need to show that for all relations, r over schema(R), with $r \models F$, $r = \bowtie_{i=1}^{n} \pi_{R_i}(r)$, where $\mathbf{R} = \{R_1, R_2, \ldots, R_n\}$, if and only if T has a winning row.

If. Let r be a relation over R such that $r \models F$ and suppose that $\exists t \in \bowtie_{i=1}^{n} \pi_{R_i}(r)$ such that $t \notin r$. Furthermore, let $s = \{t_1, t_2, \ldots, t_n\}$ be the set of tuples in r satisfying $\{t\} = \bowtie_{i=1}^{n} \pi_{R_i}(\{t_i\})$. We claim that T does not contain a winning row. Let φ be a mapping from T(**R**) to s, with $\varphi(w_i) = t_i$, where w_i are the tuples of T(**R**) and $1 \leq i \leq n$. Now, suppose we apply the FD rule for an FD, say $X \to Y \in F$ with respect to an attribute $A \in Y$, to two tuples, say w_1 and w_2, in the intermediate state of the tableau when computing T = CHASE(T(**R**), F). Then it can be verified that the set of tuples $\{\varphi(w_1), \varphi(w_2)\}$ satisfies $X \rightarrow A$, due to the fact that $r \models F$. Thus, by the construction of t it follows that all the equalities in T must hold in s and therefore φ is a homomorphism from T to s, that is, if $w_1[A] = w_2[A]$, with $w_1, w_2 \in T$, then $\varphi(w_1)[A] = \varphi(w_2)[A]$, where $A \in Y$. The result that T does not contain a winning row follows, since otherwise $t \in r$ would hold contrary to our assumption.

Only if. Suppose that T does not contain a winning row. We create a relation r over R from T by mapping each distinct dv and ndv in T to a distinct constant value. Now, it must be the case that $r \models F$, since $T \models F$. Moreover, let t_i, $i \in \{1, 2, \ldots, n\}$, be the tuple in r corresponding to the tuple in T having dv's as values for all the attributes in schema(R_i). The result follows, since $\bowtie_{i=1}^n \pi_{R_i}(\{t_i\}) \not\subseteq r$, due to the fact that T does not contain a winning row. $\square$

Example 3.4   Let us apply Theorem 3.29 to the database schema $\mathbf{R} = \{SC, CT\}$, with $F = \{C \rightarrow T\}$. The tableau $T(\mathbf{R})$ is shown in Table 3.44 and the tableau CHASE($T(\mathbf{R})$, F)) is shown in Table 3.45. It follows that $\mathbf{R}$ is a lossless join decomposition of SCT with respect to F, since the latter tableau has a winning row.   ■

Table 3.44 The tableau for $\mathbf{R}$

S	C	T
a_1	a_2	b_1
b_2	a_2	a_3

Table 3.45 The tableau CHASE($T(\mathbf{R})$, F)

S	C	T
a_1	a_2	a_3
b_2	a_2	a_3

The following theorem can be proved by using a similar argument to that made in Theorem 3.29.

Theorem 3.30   Given a set of FDs F over R and an FD $X \rightarrow Y \in F$, $F \models X \rightarrow Y$ if and only if both the rows of CHASE($T(X \rightarrow Y)$, F) are winning rows. $\square$

Example 3.5   Let R be a relation schema with attributes EMP (E), ADDRESS (A) and PHONE (P), with a set of FDs $F = \{E \rightarrow A, A \rightarrow P\}$. The tableau $T(E \rightarrow P)$ is shown in Table 3.46 and the tableau CHASE($T(E \rightarrow P)$, F)) is shown in Table 3.47. It follows that $F \models E \rightarrow P$, since the single row of Table 3.47 is a winning row.   ■

Table 3.46 The tableau for $E \rightarrow P$

E	A	P
a_1	b_1	a_3
a_1	b_2	b_3

Table 3.47 The tableau CHASE($T(E \rightarrow P)$, F)

E	A	P
a_1	b_1	a_3

The following corollary, which characterises binary lossless join decompositions with respect to a set of FDs, follows immediately from the above two theorems.

Corollary 3.31   Let $R = \{R_1, R_2\}$, $X = $ schema$(R_1) \cap $ schema(R_2) and F be a set of FDs over R, with schema$(\mathbf{R}) = $ schema(R). Then the decomposition $\mathbf{R}$ is lossless with respect to F if and only if either $F \models X \to $ schema(R_1) or $F \models X \to $ schema(R_2).   □

The reader can find a more detailed account of the chase procedure in [ABU79, MMS79, Hon82].

3.6.5   Minimal Covers for Sets of Functional Dependencies

Recall that a set of FDs, F over R, is a *cover* of another set of FDs, G over R, if $F^+ = G^+$. In other words, the set of FDs that can be derived from F is equal to the set of FDs that can be derived from G. (Note that the concept of a cover of a set of FDs is an *equivalence relation* in the set-theoretic sense.) Thus all the covers of a set of FDs equally describe the semantics of the application in hand. Some covers of a set of FDs are better than others in the sense that they contain less redundancy in them. A set of FDs, say F over R, can have redundancy in it if there is a cover which has less FDs in it, or it has a cover with a smaller size (the size of a set of FDs is the number of attributes appearing in the FD set including repetitions). We are interested in choosing a cover of F which has minimal redundancy in it. This is beneficial, since the algorithms, which we develop that involve processing a set of FDs, such as Algorithm 3.8 for computing the closure of a set of attributes with respect to a set of FDs, will execute faster on a set of FDs which has less redundancy in it. We next give a motivating example.

Example 3.6   Consider a relation schema R with the three attributes EMPLOYEE (E), ADDRESS (A) and PHONE (P).

Now, let $F_1 = \{E \to P, E \to A\}$ and $G_1 = \{EA \to P, E \to A\}$. It is easy to verify that F_1 is a cover of G_1, since $\{E \to P\} \vdash \{EA \to P\}$ by augmentation and decomposition and $G_1 \vdash \{E \to P\}$ by augmentation and transitivity. However, F_1 has less attributes than G_1 and is therefore a more succinct representation of the semantics of the application.

Now, let $F_2 = \{E \to A, A \to P\}$ and $G_2 = \{E \to A, A \to P, E \to P\}$. It is easy to verify that F_2 is a cover of G_2 by using transitivity. However, F_2 has fewer FDs than G_2 and is therefore a more succinct representation of the semantics of the application.   ■

Minimising the cover of a set of FDs has the benefits of reducing the time it takes to test whether a relation satisfies a set of FDs and also reducing the time it takes to compute the closure of a set of attributes. The next definition gives three types of coverfor sets of FDs.

Definition 3.67 (Types of cover)   Three *types of cover* for FDs are given by

1) A set of FDs F is *nonredundant* if there does not exist a cover G of F that is properly contained in F.

2) A set of FDs F is *minimum* if there does not exist a cover G of F that has fewer FDs than F.

3) A set of FDs F is *optimum* if there does not exist a cover G of F that has fewer attributes than F.   ■

The reader can easily verify that a minimum cover is nonredundant and not so easily that an optimum cover is minimum. On the other hand, a cover of a set of FDs may be nonredundant but not minimum. As a counterexample, $F = \{E \to P, E \to A\}$ is nonredundant but not minimum, since $G = \{E \to PA\}$ is a cover of F. Moreover, a cover of a set of FDs may be minimum but not optimum. As a counterexample, let us assume that R of Example 3.6 also has attributes NAME (N) and SALARY (S). Then $F = \{E \to NA, NA \to E, NA \to S\}$ is minimum but not optimum, since $G = \{E \to NA, NA \to E, E \to S\}$ is a cover of F.

The pseudo-code of an algorithm, designated MINIMUM(F), which returns a minimum cover G of a set of FDs F over R, is given below.

Algorithm 3.10 (MINIMUM(F))
1. **begin**
2. $G := \emptyset$;
3.   **for each** $X \to Y \in F$ **do**
4. $G := G \cup \{X \to X^+\}$;
5.   **end for**
6.   **for each** $X \to X^+ \in G$ **do**
7.   **if** $G - \{X \to X^+\} \vdash X \to X^+$ **then**
8. $G := G - \{X \to X^+\}$;
9.   **end if**
10.   **end for**
11.   **return** G;
12. **end.**

The correctness of Algorithm 3.10 relies on the result that if all the FDs in a set G of FDs over R are of the form $X \to X^+$, that is to say, the right-hand sides of FDs are the closures of their left-hand sides, then G is minimum if and only if it is nonredundant [Sho86].

The computational complexity of MINIMUM(F) is $O(|F| \times ||F||)$, where $|F|$ is the cardinality of F and $||F||$ is the size of F, namely the number of attributes appearing in F including repetitions.

The following theorem shows that finding an optimum cover of a set F of FDs over R is most likely intractable. Its proof follows by a reduction from the problem of deciding whether R has at least one superkey with respect to F of cardinality less than or equal to k, which was shown to be NP-complete in part (1) of Theorem 3.24.

Theorem 3.32   Given a set of FDs F over a relation schema R, the problem of deciding whether there exists a set of FDs G, with fewer than k attributes, $k \in \omega$, such that F is a cover of G, is NP-complete.   □

For a detailed account of minimal covers of FDs and full proofs of the results we have presented we refer the reader to [Mai80, MR83]. A recent investigation of minimal covers in a lattice-theoretic framework can be found in [Wil94]. An interesting investigation of minimal covers in the context of FDs and *functional independencies*, which are negations of FDs, can be found in [Jan88, Jan89].

3.6.6 Projection of Functional Dependencies

Given a set of FDs F over R, we are often interested to know which set of FDs is satisfied in a smaller relation schema, S, where schema(S) is a subset of schema(R). This is known as the problem of projecting a set of FDs over R onto S. Its solution is very important during database design, since often, as we shall see in Chapter 4, we need to decompose a relation schema R into two or more smaller relation schemas each having a subset of the attribute set of R. We can only carry out this decomposition if the set of FDs F is *preserved* in the decomposed relation schemas. By FD preservation we mean that the closure of the set of projected FDs is a cover of the original set of FDs F.

Definition 3.68 (Projection of a set of FDs) The *projection* of a set of FDs F over R onto a relation schema S, with schema(S) $\subseteq$ schema(R), denoted by F[S], is given by

$$F[S] = \{X \to Y \mid X \to Y \in F \text{ and } XY \subseteq \text{schema}(S)\}.$$

The FDs in F[S] are said to be *embedded* in S.

A relation schema S is said to *preserve* the set of FDs F over R if F[S] is a cover of $F^+[S]$, i.e. F[S] is a cover of

$$\{X \to Y \mid X \to Y \in F^+ \text{ and } XY \subseteq \text{schema}(S)\}. \qquad \blacksquare$$

We now investigate whether FDs are *closed under projection*, i.e. whether a projection of a relation always satisfies the projection of a set of FDs and vice versa, i.e. whether a relation that satisfies the projection of a set of FDs is a projection of a relation that satisfies the original set of FDs.

The following result follows immediately from the above definition.

Lemma 3.33 Let F be a set of FDs over a relation schema R and r be a relation over R such that $r \models F$. Then $\pi_{\text{schema}(S)}(r) \models F^+[S]$, where S is a relation schema with schema(S) $\subseteq$ schema(R). $\qquad \square$

Surprisingly the converse of this lemma is shown to be false in [GZ82].

Theorem 3.34 There exist relation schemas R and S, with schema(S) $\subset$ schema(R), a set of FDs F over R and a relation s over S such that $s \models F^+[S]$ but there does not exist a relation r over R such that $r \models F$ and $s = \pi_{\text{schema}(S)}(r)$.

Proof. Let R be a relation schema with schema(R) = {A, B, C, D, E, H, I} and S be a relation schema with schema(S) = {A, B, C, D, E}. Furthermore let F = {A $\to$ I, B $\to$ I, C $\to$ H, D $\to$ H, IH $\to$ E}. In addition, let G = {AC $\to$ E, AD $\to$ E, BC $\to$ E, BD $\to$ E}. We leave it to the reader to verify that G is a cover of $F^+[S]$.

Now, let $s = \{t_1, t_2, t_3, t_4\}$ be the relation over S shown in Table 3.48. The reader can verify that $s \models G$ and thus $s \models F^+[S]$. Suppose that there exists a relation r over R such that $r \models$ F and $s = \pi_{\text{schema}(S)}(r)$. It follows that $\exists\ u_1, u_2, u_3, u_4 \in r$ such that for $i \in \{1,2,3,4\}$, $t_i = u_i[\text{schema}(S)]$. Let $u_1[\text{IH}] = <i_1, h_1>$. Then the following equalities can be deduced from F:

- $u_1[I] = u_4[I]$, since $u_1[A] = u_4[A]$ and $A \rightarrow I \in F$.

- $u_2[I] = u_4[I]$, since $u_2[B] = u_4[B]$ and $B \rightarrow I \in F$.

- $u_1[I] = u_2[I]$ follows from the above two equalities.

- $u_1[H] = u_3[H]$, since $u_1[C] = u_3[C]$ and $C \rightarrow H \in F$.

- $u_2[H] = u_3[H]$, since $u_2[D] = u_3[D]$ and $D \rightarrow H \in F$.

- $u_1[H] = u_2[H]$ follows from the above two equalities.

- $u_1[\text{IH}] = u_2[\text{IH}]$ is now implied from the above.

Table 3.48 The counterexample relation

A	B	C	D	E
a_1	b_1	c_1	d_1	e_1
a_2	b_2	c_2	d_2	e_2
a_3	b_3	c_1	d_2	e_3
a_1	b_2	c_3	d_3	e_4

Therefore, $u_1[E] = u_2[E]$ due to the fact that $IH \rightarrow E \in F$ and we have assumed that $r \models$ F. However, this leads to a contradiction, since $t_1[E] \neq t_2[E]$ and thus $u_1[E] \neq u_2[E]$. We must therefore conclude that there does not exist a relation r over R such that $r \models$ F and $s = \pi_{\text{schema}(S)}(r)$.   □

The following result was shown in [BH81]; recall that co-NP is the complement of NP.

Theorem 3.35   The problem of determining whether a relation schema S preserves a set of FDs F over R is co-NP-complete.

Proof. We show that the complement of the problem, that is, to determine whether S does *not* preserve F is NP-complete.

The problem is easily seen to be in NP. Simply guess an FD $X \rightarrow Y$ over S and then verify in polynomial time by using CLOSURE(X, F), which was defined by Algorithm 3.8, that $X \rightarrow$ $Y \in F^+[S]$ but $X \rightarrow Y \notin F[S]$.

To show that the problem is NP-hard we give a polynomial-time transformation from the *hitting set* problem (which was shown to be NP-complete in [Kar72]) to the problem of determining whether S does not preserve F.

The hitting set problem: Given a family $S_1, S_2, \ldots, S_n$ of subsets of a set U, does there exist a subset $W \subseteq U$, such that $\forall i \in \{1, 2, \ldots, n\}$, $|W \cap S_i| = 1$. Such a subset W of U is called a hitting set, in other words W is a hitting set if for each i the cardinality of the intersection of W and S_i is one.

Let R be a relation schema with schema(R) = $U \cup \{B_1, B_2, \ldots, B_n, C\}$, where $\{B_1, B_2, \ldots, B_n, C\} \cap U = \emptyset$, and let schema(S) be a relation schema with schema(S) = $U \cup \{C\}$. We define three sets of FDs, F_1, F_2 and F_3 over R, and let F = $F_1 \cup F_2 \cup F_3$.

1) $F_1 = \{A_j \rightarrow B_i \mid A_j \in S_i$ for some $i \in \{1, 2, \ldots, n\}\}$; this set of FDs captures each membership of the form $A_j \in S_i$.

2) $F_2 = \{A_j A_k \rightarrow C \mid A_j, A_k \in S_i$ for some $i \in \{1, 2, \ldots, n\}$ and $A_j \neq A_k\}$.

3) $F_3 = \{B_1 B_2 \ldots B_n \rightarrow C\}$.

We claim that W is a hitting set if and only if S does not preserve F. That is, W is a hitting set if and only if F[S] is not a cover of $F^+[S]$.

If. Suppose that F[S] is not a cover of $F^+[S]$. Then there exists a nontrivial FD in $F^+[S] - (F[S])^+$. By inspection of F and schema(S) we can deduce that this FD must be of the form W $\rightarrow$ C, where $\forall i \in \{1, 2, \ldots, n\}$, $|W \cap S_i| = 1$. Thus W is a hitting set.

Only if. Suppose that W is a hitting set. Then W $\rightarrow$ C $\in F^+[S]$ can be derived from F_1 and F_3. On the other hand, W $\rightarrow$ C $\notin (F[S])^+$, since $F_3 \not\subseteq F[S]$ and, in addition, we cannot use F_2 to derive W $\rightarrow$ C due to the fact that $\forall i \in \{1, 2, \ldots, n\}$, $(|W \cap S_i| = 1) < 2$. Thus S does not preserve F. $\square$

3.6.7 Inclusion Dependencies

Inclusion Dependencies (or simply INDs) generalise the notion of referential integrity which together with entity integrity form the fundamental integrity contraints of the relational model. In fact, foreign keys can be expressed by a subclass of INDs called key-based INDs. There is a proviso in that we will assume that none of the relations in the database do contain null values. This assumption will be relaxed in Section 5.5 of Chapter 5, where we investigate integrity contraints, including INDs, in the presence of incomplete information.

INDs are different from other data dependencies such as FDs, since they can express interrelational constraints between attributes in two relations. Together FDs and INDs constitute the most fundamental data dependencies that are used in practice.

Intuitively, an IND is an expression of the form $R[X] \subseteq S[Y]$, where R and S are relation schemas and X and Y are equal length sequences of attributes from schema(R) and schema(S), respectively. Such an IND is satisfied in a database having relations r over R and s over S if the projection of r onto X is included in (i.e. is a subset of) the projection of s onto Y.

We now give a motivating example. Let STUDENTS be a relation schema having attributes STUD recording names of students and DEPT recording names of departments. In addition, let HEADS be a relation schema having attributes HEAD recording names of heads of departments and DEPT be as before. Finally, let LECTURERS be a relation schema having attributes LECT recoding names of lecturers and DEPT be as before. A database $d = \{r_1, r_2, r_3\}$ over the database schema containing the relation schemas STUDENTS, HEADS and LECTURERS is shown in Tables 3.49, 3.50 and 3.51, respectively. The semantics of the database schema can be captured by several FDs and INDs. The FDs are: STUD $\rightarrow$ DEPT over STUDENTS, DEPT $\rightarrow$ HEAD over HEADS, and LECT $\rightarrow$ DEPT over LECTURERS, with their obviously intended meaning. The INDs are: STUDENTS[DEPT] $\subseteq$ HEADS[DEPT] meaning that a student only studies in a department which has a head, and HEADS[HEAD, DEPT] $\subseteq$ LECTURERS[LECT, DEPT] meaning that a head of a department is also a lecturer in the department he/she heads. The reader can verify that the specified FDs and INDs are all satisfied in d. There is also some interaction between the FDs and INDs, since the IND HEADS[HEAD, DEPT] $\subseteq$ LECTURERS[LECT, DEPT] together with the FD LECT $\rightarrow$ DEPT over LECTURERS logically imply the FD HEAD $\rightarrow$ DEPT over HEADS. The reader can verify that this implied FD is satisfied in r_2.

Table 3.49 The relation r_1 over STUDENTS

STUD	DEPT
Iris	Computing
Reuven	Computing
Eli	Maths
Naomi	Maths
Susi	Philosophy

Table 3.50 The relation r_2 over HEADS

HEAD	DEPT
Raphael	Computing
Dan	History
Brian	Maths
Annette	Philosophy

Table 3.51 The relation r_3 over LECTURERS

LECT	DEPT
Hanna	Biology
Raphael	Computing
Dan	History
Eli	Maths
Naomi	Maths
Brian	Maths
Annette	Philosophy

Consider another example. Let BOSS be a relation schema having two attributes, EMP and MGR, and let r be the relation over BOSS shown in Table 3.52. The fact that a manager is also an employee is captured by the IND BOSS[MGR] $\subseteq$ BOSS[EMP]. This type of IND gives rise to the notion of *circular* INDs, which leads to the following problem. In order to enforce the satisfaction of this IND over BOSS in a relation without nulls we get into a circular argument implying that a relation that satisfies the IND has an infinite number of tuples (we allow only finite relations), unless we allow employees to manage themselves. As can be verified in Table 3.52 Jill is the manager of herself.

Table 3.52 The relation r over BOSS

EMP	MGR
Jack	John
John	Jill
Jill	Jill

In order to formally define INDs we will introduce notation for sequences of distinct attributes, i.e. sequences which do not repeat any attribute. A sequence of distinct attributes $A_1, A_2, \ldots, A_n$, whose underlying set of attributes, $\{A_1, A_2, \ldots, A_n\}$, is equal to Y, is denoted by $<A_1, A_2, \ldots, A_n>$ or by $<Y>$. Whenever no confusion arises between a sequence and its underlying set, we will refer to the sequence of distinct attributes $<Y>$, simply as Y. We take $A \in <A_1, A_2, \ldots, A_n>$ to mean $A \in \{A_1, A_2, \ldots, A_n\}$ and $<A_1, A_2, \ldots, A_n> \subseteq <B_1, B_2, \ldots, B_m>$ to mean $\{A_1, A_2, \ldots, A_n\} \subseteq \{B_1, B_2, \ldots, B_m\}$. From now on we will refer to a sequence of attributes as a shorthand for a distinct sequence of attributes.

We will denote the concatenation of two sequences X and Y by XY; we will assume that, unless otherwise stated, when we concatenate two sequences of attributes these sequences have no common attributes, i.e. they are disjoint. The difference between two sequences of attributes, denoted by X−Y, is the sequence resulting from removing all the common attributes in X and Y from X while maintaining the original order of the attributes remaining in X. If the sequences X, Y are *not* disjoint we define their concatenation XY to be (X−Y)Y. The intersection of two sequences of attributes, denoted by X ∩ Y, is a shorthand for X − (X − Y). For simplicity, we will not distinguish between the empty sequence of attributes, < >, and the empty set of attributes, ∅.

The projection of a tuple t over a relation schema R onto the sequence of attributes $<Y>$ = $<att(i_1), att(i_2), \ldots, att(i_k)>$, where Y ⊆ schema(R), denoted by $t[<Y>]$ (or simply $t[Y]$ when no ambiguity arises), is defined by $t[<Y>] = <t(i_1), t(i_2), \ldots, t(i_k)>$. We extend projection to a relation r over R onto $<Y>$ in the usual manner, namely

$$\pi_Y(r) = \{t[Y] \mid t \in r\}.$$

Definition 3.69 (Inclusion dependency)   An *Inclusion Dependency* over a database schema **R** (or simply an IND) is a statement of the form $R_1[X] \subseteq R_2[Y]$, where $R_1, R_2 \in \mathbf{R}$ and X, Y are sequences of attributes such that X ⊆ schema(R_1), Y ⊆ schema(R_2) and $|X| = |Y|$.

An IND is said to be *trivial* if it is of the form R[X] ⊆ R[X]. An IND R[X] ⊆ S[Y] is said to be *unary* if $|X| = 1$. An IND R[X] ⊆ S[Y] is said to be *typed* if X = Y.   ∎

An example of an IND which is both typed and unary is STUDENTS[DEPT] ⊆ HEADS[DEPT] and an example of an IND which is neither unary nor typed is HEADS[HEAD, DEPT] ⊆ LECTURERS[LECT, DEPT].

Definition 3.70 (Satisfaction of an IND)   Let d be a database over a database schema **R**, where $r_1, r_2 \in d$ are relations over relation schemas $R_1, R_2 \in \mathbf{R}$. An IND $R_1[X] \subseteq R_2[Y]$ is satisfied in a database d over **R**, denoted by $d \models R_1[X] \subseteq R_2[Y]$, if $\forall t_1 \in r_1, \exists t_2 \in r_2$, such that $t_1[X] = t_2[Y]$. (Equivalently, $d \models R_i[X] \subseteq R_j[Y]$, whenever $\pi_X(r_i) \subseteq \pi_Y(r_j)$.)   ∎

An important subclass of INDs that is utilised in the next subsection is the class of noncircular INDs [Sci86].

Definition 3.71 (Circular and noncircular sets of INDs)   A set of INDs I over **R** is *circular* if either

1) there exists a nontrivial IND R[X] ⊆ R[Y] ∈ I, or

2) there exist m distinct relation schemas, $R_1, R_2, R_3, \ldots, R_m \in \mathbf{R}$, with $m > 1$, such that I contains the INDs: $R_1[X_1] \subseteq R_2[Y_2], R_2[X_2] \subseteq R_3[Y_3], \ldots, R_m[X_m] \subseteq R_1[Y_1]$.

A set of INDs is *noncircular* if it is not circular.   ∎

The reader can verify that the set of INDs {STUDENTS[DEPT] ⊆ HEADS[DEPT], HEADS[HEAD, DEPT] ⊆ LECTURERS[LECT, DEPT]} is noncircular. On the other hand, the single IND {BOSS[MGR] ⊆ BOSS[EMP]} is circular according to part (1) of Definition 3.71. Let us now add an attribute TUTEE to schema(LECTURERS) indicating those students that are in the tutorial group of a lecturer. Then we can add the IND LECTURERS[TUTEE]

⊆ STUDENTS[STUD] specifying that the students in a tutorial group of a lecturer are included in the official list of students. We now have the set of INDs {STUDENTS[DEPT] ⊆ HEADS[DEPT], HEADS[HEAD, DEPT] ⊆ LECTURERS[LECT, DEPT], LECTURERS[TUTEE] ⊆ STUDENTS[STUD]}, which is circular according to part (2) of Definition 3.71.

We can easily test whether a set of INDs, I over **R**, is noncircular as follows: construct a directed graph $G_I = (N, E)$, whose nodes in N are labelled by the relation schemas in the database schema **R** and such that there is an arc in E from R to S if there is a nontrivial IND R[X] ⊆ S[Y] in I (R = S is possible). It follows that I is noncircular if and only if G_I is an acyclic directed graph. Testing whether a directed graph is acyclic can easily be done in polynomial time in the size of G_I by a depth-first search algorithm [Tar72, AHU83].

We next define an important class of INDs where the attributes on the right-hand side of INDs are keys. We remind the reader that when F is a set of FDs over one or more relation schemas R ∈ **R**, we say that F is a set of FDs over **R**.

Definition 3.72 (Key-based INDs) An IND R[X] ⊆ S[Y] over **R** is *superkey-based*, respectively *key-based*, if Y is a superkey, respectively a key, for S with respect to a set of FDs F over **R**.

A set I of INDs is superkey-based, respectively key-based, with respect to a set of FDs F over **R** if every IND in I is superkey-based, respectively key-based. ∎

For example, the IND STUDENTS[DEPT] ⊆ HEADS[DEPT] is key-based, since DEPT → HEAD over HEADS implies that DEPT is a key for HEADS. On the other hand, the IND HEADS[HEAD, DEPT] ⊆ LECTURERS[LECT, DEPT] is superkey-based but not key-based, since the FD LECT → DEPT over LECTURERS implies that LECT is a key for LECTURERS. The reader can verify that the IND HEADS[DEPT] ⊆ LECTURERS[DEPT] is neither superkey-based nor key-based.

An alternative formalisation of referential integrity in terms of key-based INDs is now evident, recalling that we have assumed that relations in the database do not have null values. If R[X] ⊆ S[Y] is a key-based IND and Y is a primary key of S, then the set of attributes X is a *foreign key* of R referencing the primary key Y of S.

The following inference rules allow us to axiomatise INDs.

Definition 3.73 (Inference rules for INDs) Let I be a set of INDs over a database schema **R** = $\{R_1, R_2, \ldots, R_n\}$. We define the following inference rules for INDs:

IND1 Reflexivity: if X ⊆ schema(R), with R ∈ **R**, then I ⊢ R[X] ⊆ R[X].

IND2 Projection and permutation: if I ⊢ $R_1[X]$ ⊆ $R_2[Y]$, where X = $<A_1, A_2, \ldots, A_m>$ ⊆ schema(R_1), Y = $<B_1, B_2, \ldots, B_m>$ ⊆ schema(R_2) and $i_1, i_2, \ldots, i_k$ is a sequence of distinct natural numbers from $\{1, 2, \ldots, m\}$, then I ⊢ $R_1[A_{i_1}, A_{i_2}, \ldots, A_{i_k}]$ ⊆ $R_2[B_{i_1}, B_{i_2}, \ldots, B_{i_k}]$.

IND3 Transitivity: if I ⊢ $R_1[X]$ ⊆ $R_2[Y]$ and I ⊢ $R_2[Y]$ ⊆ $R_3[Z]$, then I ⊢ $R_1[X]$ ⊆ $R_3[Z]$. ∎

Note that IND1 is an axiom, since it has no hypothesis. We call the inference rules IND1, IND2 and IND3 *Casanova et al.'s axiom system* [CFP84]. The next lemma and theorem were first proved in [CFP84].

Lemma 3.36 Casanova et al.'s axiom system is sound.

Proof. We prove that transitivity (IND3) is sound and leave it to the reader to prove that the other inference rules are also sound.

Let r_1, r_2 and r_3 be the relations in d over the relation schemas R_1, R_2 and R_3 in **R**, respectively. Moreover, let $t_1 \in r_1$, so we are required to show that $t_1[X] \in \pi_X(r_3)$. By the fact that $d \models R_1[X] \subseteq R_2[Y]$ we have $t_1[X] \in \pi_Y(r_2)$. The result follows, since $d \models R_2[Y] \subseteq R_3[Z]$ implies that $t_1[X] \in \pi_Z(r_3)$ as required. $\qquad\square$

Theorem 3.37 Casanova et al.'s axiom system is sound and complete for INDs.

Proof. Soundness follows from the previous lemma. It remains to prove completeness. As in Theorem 3.21, in which we proved that Armstrong's axiom system is sound and complete for FDs, we assume that I $\not\vdash$ R[X] $\subseteq$ S[Y]. To conclude the proof it is sufficient to exhibit a counterexample database, d over **R**, such that $d \models$ I but $d \not\models$ R[X] $\subseteq$ S[Y], where X = $<A_1, A_2, \ldots, A_m>$.

Let $r \in d$ be the relation over R that contains a single tuple t such that $t[A_i] = i$, for $i = 1, 2, \ldots, m$, and $t[A_i] = 0$ otherwise. All the other relations in d are initialised to be empty. We insert tuples into the relations in d by applying the following rule until no more tuples can be inserted into the current state of d by a further application of this rule. Let us call the resulting database d' (cf. the chase procedure for INDs, which is defined in the next subsection).

IND tuple insertion rule: If $R_1[W] \subseteq R_2[Z] \in$ I and $\exists t_1 \in r_1$ such that $t_1[W] \notin \pi_Z(r_2)$, then add a tuple t_2 over R_2 to r_2 such that $t_2[Z] = t_1[W]$ and $\forall A \in schema(R_2) - Z$, $t_2[A] = 0$, where r_1 and r_2 in d are the relations over R_1 and R_2 in **R**, respectively.

We observe that the IND tuple insertion rule can only be applied a finite number of times, since this rule does not introduce new values into d'. It follows that $d' \models$ I, since if this were not the case then we could apply the IND tuple insertion rule to d', contradicting the fact that this rule cannot be further applied.

It remains to show that $d' \not\models$ R[X] $\subseteq$ S[Y]. We claim that if $t[X] \in \pi_Y(s)$ then I $\vdash$ R[X] $\subseteq$ S[Y], where $s \in d$ is the relation over S. The claim can be formally proved by induction on the minimal number, say k, $k \in \omega$, of applications of the IND tuple insertion rule. The basis step, when $k = 0$, follows by the reflexivity rule. The induction step follows by the projection and permutation rule and the transitivity rule on using the induction hypothesis. We leave it to the reader to fill in the missing details.

It follows by the above claim that $t[X] \notin \pi_Y(s)$, since we have assumed that I $\not\vdash$ R[X] $\subseteq$ S[Y]. The result now follows by Definition 3.70 of the satisfaction of an IND. $\qquad\square$

In [Mit83] repeated attributes are allowed in inclusion dependencies. For example, if an IND of the form R[A, B] $\subseteq$ R[C, C] is satisfied in a database d, where $r \in d$ is the relation over

R, then for any tuple $t \in r$ we have $t[A] = t[B] = t[C]$. (In [CFP84] such INDs with repeating attributes are called *repeating dependencies*.)

IND4 Substitutivity of equivalents: if $I \vdash R[A, B] \subseteq S[C, C]$ and $I \vdash \alpha$, where $R[X]$ is either the right-hand side or the left-hand side of α, then $I \vdash \beta$, where β is obtained from α by substituting one or more occurrences of B in $R[X]$ with A.

It is shown in [Mit83] that the axiom system consisting of the inference rules IND1, IND2, IND3 and IND4 is sound and complete for INDs which may contain repeated attributes. As we shall see in Subsection 3.6.11 when we consider the interaction between a set F of FDs and a set I of INDs, a repeating dependency α may be logically implied by F and I even if I does not contain any repeating dependencies.

3.6.8 The Chase Procedure for Inclusion Dependencies

In this section we introduce the chase procedure for INDs in order to test the satisfaction of a set of INDs in a database. This highlights the versatility of the chase procedure as a useful tool in relational database theory, recalling that in Subsection 3.6.4 the chase was employed in the context of the implication problem. In the theory of data dependencies it is common to use the chase in both roles, i.e. to test satisfaction of a set of dependencies and to test for implication of dependencies.

Let d be a database over a database schema $\mathbf{R}$, where $r, s \in d$ are, respectively, the relations over the relation schemas $R, S \in \mathbf{R}$.

IND rule: If $R[X] \subseteq S[Y] \in I$ and $\exists t \in r$ such that $t[X] \notin \pi_Y(s)$, then add a tuple u over S to s, where $u[Y] = t[X]$ and $\forall A \in \text{schema}(S) - Y$, $u[A] \notin \text{ADOM}(d)$.

That is, the IND rule adds a new tuple u to the relation s, which has *new values*, not present in s, over all the attributes which are not in Y. For convenience we will assume that the elements in $\text{ADOM}(d)$ are linearly ordered and that the new values, $u[A] \notin \text{ADOM}(d)$, are greater than all the values in the current state of $\text{ADOM}(d)$.

The pseudo-code of an algorithm, designated ICHASE(d, I), which returns the chase of a database d over $\mathbf{R}$ with respect to a set I of INDs over $\mathbf{R}$, is given below. As in the case of the chase of a tableau with respect to a set of FDs the algorithm is nondeterministic.

Algorithm 3.11 (ICHASE(d, I))
1. **begin**
2.   Result := d;
3.   Tmp := $\emptyset$;
4.   **while** Tmp $\neq$ Result **do**
5.   Tmp := Result;
6.   Apply the IND rule to Result;
7.   **end while**
8.   **return** Result;
9. **end.**

As in the case of CHASE(T, F), where T is a tableau over a relation schema R, ICHASE(d, I) is a finite *Church-Rosser* system; the order in which the INDs are chosen by the IND rule in line 6 of the algorithm does not affect the result, up to the particular choice of new values that are added to d. On the other hand, ICHASE(d, I) does *not* always terminate. Consider the relation, r, shown in Table 3.53, and assume that $d = \{r\}$ and I = {R[MGR] $\subseteq$ R[EMP]}, modelling the fact that every manager is an employee. When applying the IND rule to d we will add to r a tuple of the form, <New_value(1), John>. The next application of the IND rule will add to r an additional tuple of the form, <New_value(2), New_value(1)>. In general, the ith application of the IND rule will add to r an additional tuple of the form, <New_value(i), New_value($i-1$)>. Thus, ICHASE(d, I) will not terminate.

Table 3.53 A managers and employees relation

MGR	EMP
John	Jack

It is not hard to see that the following theorem holds.

Theorem 3.38   Let I be a set of noncircular INDs over **R** and d be a database over **R**.

1) The chase procedure, which computes ICHASE(d, I), terminates.

2) ICHASE(d, I) $\models$ I.

3) d = ICHASE(d, I) if and only if $d \models$ I.   □

The reader may think that the chase procedure for INDs terminates if and only if the set I of INDs is noncircular. We next show that this finite chase property holds for a wider class of INDs, which was defined in [Imi91], called *proper circular*.

Definition 3.74 (Proper circular sets of INDs)   A set I of INDs over **R** is *proper circular* if it is either noncircular or whenever there exist m distinct relation schemas, $R_1, R_2, R_3, \ldots, R_m$ $\in$ **R**, with $m > 1$, such that I contains the INDs: $R_1[X_1] \subseteq R_2[Y_2]$, $R_2[X_2] \subseteq R_3[Y_3]$, $\ldots$, $R_{m-1}[X_{m-1}] \subseteq R_m[Y_m]$, $R_m[X_m] \subseteq R_1[Y_1]$, then for all $i \in \{1, 2, \ldots, m\}$ we have $X_i = Y_i$. ∎

Let $r_1, r_2, \ldots, r_m$ be the relations in d over the relation schemas $R_1, R_2, \ldots, R_m$ in **R**, respectively. Then the set of proper circular INDs, $\{R_1[X_1] \subseteq R_2[Y_2]$, $R_2[X_2] \subseteq R_3[Y_3]$, $\ldots, R_{m-1}[X_{m-1}] \subseteq R_m[Y_m]$, $R_m[X_m] \subseteq R_1[Y_1]\}$, is satisfied in d if and only if

$$\pi_{X_1}(r_1) = \pi_{X_2}(r_2) = \cdots = \pi_{X_{m-1}}(r_{m-1}) = \pi_{X_m}(r_m).$$

That is, proper circular INDs extend noncircular INDs by the ability to state that the projections of two sequences of attributes onto two relations are equal. We leave it to the reader to verify that Theorem 3.38 still holds when I is proper circular.

For example, the set of INDs {STUDENTS[DEPT] $\subseteq$ HEADS[DEPT], HEADS[DEPT] $\subseteq$ LECTURERS[DEPT], LECTURERS[DEPT] $\subseteq$ STUDENTS[DEPT]} is proper circular but it is *not* noncircular. This set of INDs states that the projections onto DEPT of the relations in the database over these relation schemas are all equal. On the other hand, the set of INDs {STUDENTS[DEPT] ⊆ HEADS[DEPT], HEADS[HEAD] ⊆ LECTURERS[LECT], LECTURERS[TUTEE] ⊆ STUDENTS[STUD]} is not proper circular.

We now extend the chase procedure to FDs and INDs by introducing an FD rule. Let d be a database over schema **R**, with $r \in d$ being the relation over schema $R \in$ **R**. (We remind the reader that the elements in ADOM(d) are linearly ordered.)

FD rule: If $R : X \to Y \in F$ and $\exists t_1, t_2 \in r$ such that $t_1[X] = t_2[X]$ but $t_1[Y] \neq t_2[Y]$ then, $\forall A \in Y$, change all the occurrences in d of the larger of the values of $t_1[A]$ and $t_2[A]$ to the smaller of the values of $t_1[A]$ and $t_2[A]$.

That is, the FD rule equates values in d whenever an FD $R : X \to Y$ is violated in a relation in d. We now modify the chase procedure to take a set $\Sigma = F \cup I$, where F is a set of FDs and I is a set of INDs over **R**, as input and modify ICHASE(d, Σ) by changing line 6 of Algorithm 3.11 to

6.   Apply the FD rule or the IND rule to Result;

The following theorem extends Theorem 3.38 when considering FDs and INDs together. (In the following we will write $d \models R : X \to Y$ to mean $r \models R : X \to Y$.)

Theorem 3.39 Let $\Sigma = F \cup I$ be a set of FDs and proper circular INDs over **R** and d be a database over **R**.

1) The chase procedure, which computes ICHASE(d, Σ), terminates.

2) ICHASE(d, Σ) $\models \Sigma$.

3) $d =$ ICHASE(d, Σ) if and only if $d \models \Sigma$.

4) (1) to (3) hold when replacing ICHASE(d, Σ) by ICHASE(ICHASE(d, I), F).   □

Part (4) of Theorem 3.39 implies that the chase procedure can be decoupled into two stages: in the first stage we chase d with the INDs on their own, and in the second stage we chase the resulting database with the FDs on their own. In fact, Theorem 3.39 holds for any class of FDs and INDs possessing the finite chase property.

3.6.9   Armstrong Databases for Inclusion Dependencies

An *Armstrong database* for a set of INDs generalises the concept of Armstrong relations as follows: d is an Armstrong database for a set of INDs I over **R** whenever

$$d \models R[X] \subseteq S[Y] \text{ if and only if } I \models R[X] \subseteq S[Y].$$

As demonstrated in Subsection 3.6.2 Armstrong databases can be very useful as a tool to show users example databases satisfying exactly the set of FDs and INDs for a given application.

We prove below that proper circular INDs enjoy Armstrong databases and indicate how this result can be generalised to include both standard FDs and INDs. (Recall that a standard FD is one whose left-hand side is nonempty.)

Theorem 3.40   Proper circular INDs enjoy Armstrong databases.

Proof. Let I be a set of proper circular INDs and d be a database with nonempty relations such that the active domains of distinct relations in d are disjoint, and, in addition, the active domains of distinct columns of the relations in d are also disjoint. We observe that this implies that d does not satisfy any nontrivial IND.

We claim that ICHASE(d, I) is an Armstrong database for I, that is, ICHASE(d, I) $\models$ R[X] $\subseteq$ S[Y] if and only if I $\models$ R[X] $\subseteq$ S[Y].

For the *if* part suppose that I $\models$ R[X] $\subseteq$ S[Y]. By Theorem 3.38 (2), ICHASE(d, I) $\models$ I, and therefore ICHASE(d, I) $\models$ R[X] $\subseteq$ S[Y] as required.

For the *only if* part we need to show that if ICHASE(d, I) $\models$ R[X] $\subseteq$ S[Y], then I $\models$ R[X] $\subseteq$ S[Y]. Assume to the contrary that ICHASE(d, I) $\models$ R[X] $\subseteq$ S[Y] but I $\not\models$ R[X] $\subseteq$ S[Y]. Then there exists a database d' over **R** such that $d' \models$ I but $d' \not\models$ R[X] $\subseteq$ S[Y]. By the definition of the satisfaction of an IND, for some tuple $t' \in r'$, $t'[X] \in \pi_X(r')$ but $t'[X] \notin \pi_Y(s')$, where r' and s' are the relations in d' over R and S, respectively. We can also assume without any loss of generality that for all A $\in$ X the A-values of $t'[X]$ are distinct, since we have assumed that INDs do not have repeated attributes.

Let $r, s \in d$ be the relations over R and S, respectively, and, due to the disjointness of the relations in d and the columns of the relations in d, we assume without loss of generality that $\exists t \in r$ such that $t[X] = t'[X]$ but $\not\exists u \in s$ such that $u[X] = t'[X]$. It follows that $d \not\models$ R[X] $\subseteq$ S[Y]. In order to conclude the proof we show that $d' \neq$ ICHASE(d', I) implying by Theorem 3.38 (3) that $d' \not\models$ I leading to a contradiction.

The result follows by tracing the applications of the IND rule in line 6 of Algorithm 3.11 when computing ICHASE(d, I); denote the ith application of the IND rule by apply(i). In order to show that $d' \neq$ ICHASE(d', I) we check for each i whether apply(i) will cause a modification to the current state of d'. In particular, we take note each time the value, $t'[X]$, is part of a tuple that is added to a relation in the current state of d' as a result of apply(i). Let apply(j) be the application that causes $t'[X]$ to be added to the current state of $\pi_Y(s)$. Now, if apply(j) does not modify the current state of d' in ICHASE(d', I), then $d' \models$ R[X] $\subseteq$ S[Y]; on the other hand if apply(j) modifies the current state of d' in ICHASE(d', I), then $d' \not\models$ I.   □

Armstrong databases have also been investigated in the context of FDs and INDs. It was shown in [MR88] that in the special case when ICHASE(d, I) = ICHASE(d, Σ), standard FDs and noncircular INDs enjoy Armstrong databases. The proof relies on a modification of Theorem 3.40 by requiring that the relations in the database d are Armstrong relations for their respective sets of FDs.

Theorem 3.40 does not give us a general result, since it is restricted to proper circular INDs. In order to obtain a more general result we cannot utilise the chase procedure, since ICHASE(d, I) may not terminate if I is not a proper circular set of INDs. A more general result was obtained in [Fag82b, FV83] using direct products, which shows that standard FDs and the general class of INDs enjoy Armstrong databases.

3.6.10   The Implication Problem for Inclusion Dependencies

The implication problem for INDs is the problem of deciding whether $I \models R[X] \subseteq S[Y]$, given a set I of INDs and a single IND $R[X] \subseteq S[Y]$ over **R**. Now, by the soundness and completeness of Casanova et al.'s axiom system we need only consider the problem of deciding whether $I \vdash R[X] \subseteq S[Y]$. Unfortunately, the implication problem for INDs turns out to be intractable. As we will see the problem gets worse when we consider FDs and INDs together, since their joint implication problem is, in general, undecidable. This has motivated researchers to investigate subclasses of INDs, which have a more tractable implication problem.

The proof of the following theorem can be found in [CFP84].

Theorem 3.41   The implication problem for INDs (which may be circular) is PSPACE-complete.   □

The proof of the following theorem can be found in [Man84, CK86].

Theorem 3.42   The implication problem for noncircular INDs is NP-complete.   □

The next theorem shows that the implication problem for proper circular INDs is not more difficult than that for noncircular INDs.

Theorem 3.43   The implication problem for proper circular INDs is NP-complete.

Proof. The problem is in NP, since any minimal proof of $I \vdash R[X] \subseteq S[Y]$, where I is a proper circular set of INDs, contains at most $|\mathbf{R}|$ INDs. The result follows, since NP-hardness of the problem is a consequence of the NP-completeness of the implication problem for noncircular INDs.   □

The next theorem can easily be verified, since by Theorem 3.37 IND1 (reflexivity) and IND3 (transitivity) are sound and complete for unary INDs [CKV90].

Theorem 3.44   The implication problem for unary INDs is linear-time in the size of the input set of unary INDs.   □

The next theorem shows that the implication problem for typed INDs can also be solved efficiently [CV83].

Theorem 3.45   The implication problem for typed INDs is polynomial-time in the size of the input set of typed INDs.

Proof. Suppose we would like to decide whether $I \vdash R[X] \subseteq S[X]$. We utilise a directed graph representation, $G_X = (N, E)$, of the set of INDs I, which is constructed as follows. Each relation schema R in **R** has a separate node in N labelled by R; we do not distinguish between nodes and their labels. There is an arc (R_1, R_2) in E if and only if there is a nontrivial IND $R_1[W] \subseteq R_2[W] \in I$, with $X \subseteq W$.

We claim that I ⊢ R[X] ⊆ S[X] if and only if either R = S, in which case the IND can trivially be derived, or there is a path from R to S in G_X. The claim can be proved by induction on the minimal length of a proof of R[X] ⊆ S[X] from I. The result now follows from the fact that path reachability is a well-known polynomial-time problem in the size of the input graph [AHU83]. □

3.6.11   Interaction between Functional and Inclusion Dependencies

As we have seen in the example at the beginning of Subsection 3.6.7 the IND HEADS[HEAD, DEPT] ⊆ LECTURERS[LECT, DEPT] together with the FD LECT → DEPT over LECTURERS logically imply the FD HEAD → DEPT over HEADS. This is an example of interaction between FDs and INDs that results in an FD being derived.

Suppose that we add an attribute FACULTY to both the relation schemas HEADS and LECTURERS, indicating the faculty in which a lecturer is employed, together with the IND HEADS[HEAD, FACULTY] ⊆ LECTURERS[LECT, FACULTY]. Then, this IND combined with the IND HEADS[HEAD, DEPT] ⊆ LECTURERS[LECT, DEPT] and the FD LECT → DEPT over LECTURERS logically imply the IND HEADS[HEAD, DEPT, FACULTY] ⊆ LECTURERS[LECT, DEPT, FACULTY]. This is an example of interaction between FDs and INDs that results in an IND being derived.

Furthermore, suppose that we add an additional attribute INSTITUTE to the relation schema HEADS together with the IND HEADS[HEAD, INSTITUTE] ⊆ LECTURERS[LECT, DEPT]. Then, this IND combined with the IND HEADS[HEAD, DEPT] ⊆ LECTURERS[LECT, DEPT] and the FD LECT → DEPT over LECTURERS logically imply the IND HEADS[HEAD, DEPT, INSTITUTE] ⊆ LECTURERS[LECT, DEPT, DEPT] having a repeating attribute DEPT. Now, by IND2 (projection and permutation) we can derive the repeated dependency HEADS[DEPT, INSTITUTE] ⊆ LECTURERS[DEPT, DEPT] indicating that DEPT and INSTITUTE have the same meaning. Such a repeating dependency is not equivalent to any set of FDs and INDs and therefore repeating attributes must be considered when dealing with the interaction of FDs and INDs.

The interaction between FDs and INDs turns out to be a complex matter. In fact, for FDs and INDs we have the negative result that, in general, we cannot find a sound and complete axiom system for FDs and INDs at all. This is a consequence of the important result that the implication problem for FDs and INDs taken together is, in general, undecidable [Mit83, CV85]. In practice this result means that relational database designers should restrict themselves to some meaningful subclass of FDs and INDs whose implication problem is decidable. The most tractable known subclass is that of FDs and unary INDs for which there is an interesting sound and complete axiom system, which is discussed below. In addition, for the subclass of FDs and unary INDs the implication problem can be solved in polynomial time. The implication problem for the subclass of FDs and proper circular INDs is decidable but intractable. Moreover, apart from the subclass of FDs and unary INDs, it is the largest meaningful subclass of FDs and INDs we know of that has a sound and complete axiom system in addition to having a decidable implication problem.

We remind the reader that we assume that relations can only have a finite number of tuples. If we relax this assumption and allow relations to have an infinite number of tuples then we need to consider two kinds of notion of logical implication, one for finite relations and the other for infinite relations. When considering FDs and INDs together it is readily shown that $\{R : A \rightarrow B, R[A] \subseteq R[B]\}$ finitely implies $\{R : B \rightarrow A, R[B] \subseteq R[A]\}$ but not infinitely [CFP84]. To demonstrate the latter case consider the relation, say r_1, shown in Table 3.54, and the relation, say r_2, shown in Table 3.55. For $i = 1, 2$, it can be seen that the infinite relations resulting from ICHASE($\{r_i\}$, $\{R[A] \subseteq R[B]\}$) satisfy $\{R : A \rightarrow B, R[A] \subseteq R[B]\}$ but violate $R : B \rightarrow A$ and $R[B] \subseteq R[A]$, respectively. Thus even for the subclass of FDs and unary INDs finite and infinite logical implication do not coincide.

Table 3.54 A relation having an infinite chase

A	B
1	1
2	1

Table 3.55 Another relation having an infinite chase

A	B
1	0

In [Mit83, CV85] it was shown that the implication problem for FDs and INDs is, in general, undecidable for infinite logical implication as well as for finite logical implication as mentioned above. It is interesting to note that, although we cannot find a sound and complete axiom system for FDs and INDs with respect to finite relations, the axiom system presented in [Mit83], which we call *Mitchell's axiom system*, is sound and complete for FDs and INDs defined to hold in relations which may be infinite. This axiom system is not *attribute bounded* in the sense that new attributes not present in the original database schema may need to be generated during a derivation sequence (see the attribute introduction inference rule for FDs and INDs given below). In fact, due to the undecidability of infinite logical implication for FDs and INDs, there cannot be an attribute bounded axiomatisation of FDs and INDs for infinite relations. On the other hand, for FDs on their own and for INDs on their own it can be shown that finite and infinite logical implication coincide. The largest subclass of FDs and INDs for which we know finite and infinite logical implication to coincide is the subclass of FDs and proper circular INDs. This can formally be proved by using the fact shown above, namely that proper circular INDs possess the finite chase property (see [Man84, Imi91]). It follows that Mitchell's axiom system is sound and complete for the subclass of FDs and proper circular INDs. It remains an open problem to find an attribute bounded axiomatisation for this subclass.

The fact that finite and infinite logical implication coincide for a certain class of data dependencies is not just of pure theoretical interest, since it is not hard to show that this property implies that the implication problem for such a class of data dependencies is decidable.

In this subsection we let F be a set of FDs over $\mathbf{R}$, where each FD in F is of the form $R : X \rightarrow Y$, with $R \in \mathbf{R}$, so the relation schema R distinguishes the schema over which the FD holds. Moreover, we let $F_i = \{R_i : X \rightarrow Y \in F\}$, with $i \in \{1, 2, \ldots, n\}$, be the set of FDs in F over $R_i \in \mathbf{R}$. Finally, we let I be a set of INDs over $\mathbf{R}$ and let $\Sigma = F \cup I$.

The next inference rule takes into account the fact that we are considering sequences of attributes rather than unordered sets of attributes. It states that an FD $X \rightarrow Y$ holds independently of the ordering of X and Y.

FD7 Permutation: if $F \vdash R : X \rightarrow Y$, W is a permutation of X and Z is a permutation of Y, then $F \vdash W \rightarrow Z$.

The next three inference rules capture the basic interaction between FDs and INDs [Mit83].

FD-IND1 Pullback: if $\Sigma \vdash R[VW] \subseteq S[XY]$, with $|V| = |X|$, and $\Sigma \vdash S : X \rightarrow Y$, then $\Sigma \vdash R : V \rightarrow W$.

FD-IND2 Collection: if $\Sigma \vdash R[UV] \subseteq S[XY]$, $\Sigma \vdash R[UW] \subseteq S[XZ]$ and $\Sigma \vdash S : X \rightarrow Y$, then $\Sigma \vdash R[UVW] \subseteq S[XYZ]$.

FD-IND3 Attribute introduction: if $\Sigma \vdash R[X] \subseteq S[Y]$ and $\Sigma \vdash S : Y \rightarrow B$, then $\Sigma \vdash R[XA] \subseteq S[YB]$, where A is an attribute that is newly added to schema(R), i.e. prior to adding A to schema(R), $A \notin$ schema(**R**).

We call the inference rules comprising Armstrong's axiom system, Casanova's et al. axiom system, together with FD7 (permutation), IND4 (substitutivity of equivalents), FD-IND1 (pullback), FD-IND2 (collection) and FD-IND3 (attribute introduction), *Mitchell's axiom system* [Mit83].

The reader can verify that both the pullback and collection inference rules are sound, i.e. if $\Sigma \vdash \alpha$ using either FD-IND1 or FD-IND2 then $\Sigma \models \alpha$, where α is an FD or IND. The attribute introduction inference rule requires some further explanation. Consider a database d containing relations r over R and s over S such that $d \models \{R[X] \subseteq S[Y], S : Y \rightarrow B\}$. Then *after* extending schema(R) with a new attribute A we can add an additional column to r over the new attribute A, resulting in a new relation r' as follows. Each tuple $t \in r$ is extended to a tuple t', with $t = t'[\text{schema}(R) - A]$ and $t'[A] = u[B]$, where u is the tuple in s such that $t[X] = u[Y]$; note that this extension is unique due to the FD $S : Y \rightarrow B$. Thus attribute introduction is a sound inference rule. It is important to note that we do *not* allow Σ^+ to contain any data dependencies having new attributes, so that new attributes may be present in FDs or INDs only during intermediate steps of a derivation of a data dependency α from Σ.

The next example shows that attribute introduction is a nonredundant inference rule for FDs and INDs.

Example 3.7 Let $\mathbf{R} = \{R, S\}$, with schema(R) = $\{A, B, C\}$ and schema(S) = $\{A, B_1, B_2, C_1, C_2\}$. Also, let $\Sigma = F \cup I$, where F = $\{S : A \rightarrow C_1 C_2, S : C_1 C_2 \rightarrow A, S : B_1 \rightarrow C_1, S : B_2 \rightarrow C_2\}$ and I = $\{R[AC] \subseteq S[AB_1], R[AC] \subseteq S[AB_2], R[BC] \subseteq S[AB_1], R[BC] \subseteq S[AB_2]\}$. We leave it to the reader to verify that $\Sigma \vdash R[AB] \subseteq S[AA]$. Moreover, this repeating dependency cannot be derived without the attribute introduction inference rule. ∎

We next direct our attention to whether we can restrict the number of antecedents in inference rules of an axiom system.

Definition 3.75 (k-ary axiomatisation) Given a set of data dependencies Σ over **R**, an inference rule in an axiom system may have the form

$$\text{if } \Sigma \vdash \alpha_1, \Sigma \vdash \alpha_2, \ldots, \text{ and } \Sigma \vdash \alpha_k, \text{ then } \Sigma \vdash \beta,$$

where $\alpha_1, \alpha_2, \ldots, \alpha_k, k \geq 0, k \in \omega$, and β are also data dependencies over **R**. Such an inference rule allows us to derive β from $\alpha_1, \alpha_2, \ldots, \alpha_k$ and is said to have k antecedents.

An axiom system for a certain class of data dependencies is said to be k-ary if all its inference rules have at most k antecedents. ∎

An axiom system which is k-ary is said to be a *finite axiom system*, for the obvious reason that it has a finite set of inference rules. For example, both FDs and INDs on their own have 2-ary axiomatisations. The following negative result shows that FDs and INDs do not have a finite axiomatisation. It was proved in [CFP84] and strengthened in [CK86, CKV90].

Theorem 3.46   For no $k \geq 0$, $k \in \omega$, does there exist a k-ary axiomatisation for FDs and INDs, even if we restrict ourselves to unary INDs.

Proof. Let Γ be a set of data dependencies in a certain class, C, of data dependencies over **R**. We say that Γ is *closed under implication* if whenever (i) $\Sigma \subseteq \Gamma$, (ii) $\alpha \in C$ and (iii) if $\Sigma \models \alpha$ then $\alpha \in \Gamma$. Correspondingly, we say that Γ is closed under k-ary implication, for $k \geq 0$, $k \in \omega$, if whenever (i), (ii) and (iii) hold and, in addition, $|\Sigma| \leq k$ then $\alpha \in \Gamma$.

In [CFP84] it was shown that a class, C, of data dependencies over **R** has a k-ary axiomatisation if and only if whenever a set of data dependencies Σ in C is closed under k-ary implication then Σ is also closed under implication.

In order to prove our result we exhibit, for any $k \geq 0$, $k \in \omega$, a set of FDs and INDs Σ that is closed under k-ary implication but is not closed under implication. Let **R** be a database schema with $k + 1$ relation schemas such that schema$(R_i) = \{A, B\}$, for $i = 0, 1, \ldots k$. In addition, consider the set of FDs and INDs Σ and an IND α defined by

1) $\Sigma = \{R_i : A \rightarrow B, R_i[A] \subseteq R_{i+1}[B]\}$, for $i = 0, 1, \ldots, k$, and

2) $\alpha = R_0[B] \subseteq R_k[A]$,

where we let $k + 1$ be 0, i.e. addition is modulo k. Let Γ be the union of Σ and all the trivial FDs and INDs over **R**. By using a cardinality argument it can be shown that $\Gamma \models \alpha$, but Γ is not closed under implication, since $\alpha \notin \Gamma$.

It remains to show that Γ is closed under k-ary implication. That is, we need to show that if $\Delta \subseteq \Gamma$ contains at most k data dependencies and α is an FD or an IND, then $\Delta \models \alpha$ implies that $\alpha \in \Gamma$. Now, Σ contains $k+1$ INDs and thus some IND $\beta \in \Sigma$ is not in Δ. It can be shown that a database d can be constructed such that d satisfies exactly the set of data dependencies in $\Gamma - \{\beta\}$; we refer the reader to [CFP84] for the details. We observe that d is an Armstrong database for $\Gamma - \{\beta\}$ as defined in Subsection 3.6.9. It follows that $d \models \Delta$, since $\Delta \subseteq \Gamma - \{\beta\}$ and thus $d \models \alpha$ also. The result that $\alpha \in \Gamma - \{\beta\}$ now follows, since by the construction of d we have $d \models \alpha$ if and only if $\Gamma - \{\beta\} \models \alpha$.   □

We now turn our attention to axiomatising FDs and unary INDs. If all the INDs in I are of the form R[X] $\subseteq$ R[Y], then we say that I is a set of INDs over R and abbreviate R[X] $\subseteq$ R[Y] to X $\subseteq$ Y. The *k-cycle* inference rule for a set of FDs and unary INDs Σ over R is defined as follows: for each odd natural number k and attributes $A_0, A_1, \ldots, A_{k-1}, A_k \in$ schema(R),

from $\Sigma \vdash A_0 \rightarrow A_1$ and $\Sigma \vdash A_2 \subseteq A_1$ and $\ldots$ and $\Sigma \vdash A_{k-1} \rightarrow A_k$ and $\Sigma \vdash A_0 \subseteq A_k$
derive $\Sigma \vdash A_1 \rightarrow A_0$ and $\Sigma \vdash A_1 \subseteq A_2$ and $\ldots$ and $\Sigma \vdash A_k \rightarrow A_{k-1}$ and $\Sigma \vdash A_k \subseteq A_0$.

We observe that if we allow relations to have an infinite number of tuples then the k-cycle inference rule will become unsound.

The following inference rule can be derived by the 1-cycle inference rule and Armstrong's axiom system:

1) from $\Sigma \vdash \emptyset \to A$ and $\Sigma \vdash B \subseteq A$ derive $\Sigma \vdash B \to A$ and $\Sigma \vdash A \to B$ and $\Sigma \vdash A \subseteq B$.

The following result was shown in [CKV90].

Theorem 3.47 The axiom system comprising FD1 (reflexivity), FD2 (augmentation), FD3 (transitivity), FD7 (permutation), IND1 (reflexivity), IND3 (transitivity) and the k-cycle inference rule is sound and complete for FDs and unary INDs over a relation schema R.

Proof. We leave it to the reader to establish the soundness of this mixed axiom system. The technique used to prove completeness is already familiar to us. Let Σ be a set F of FDs and a set I of unary INDs over R. We assume that $\Sigma \nvdash \alpha$, where α is an FD or a unary IND over R. To conclude the proof it is sufficient to exhibit a counterexample database, d, containing a single relation r over R, such that $d \models \Sigma$ but $d \nvDash \alpha$. We refer the reader to [CKV90] for the details of the construction of d. $\square$

We observe that the axiom system of Theorem 3.47 has a countably infinite number of inference rules, since for each odd k, $k \in \omega$, we have one k-cycle inference rule.

It was shown in [CKV90, ZO92a] that the implication problem for FDs and unary INDs can be solved in polynomial time in the size of the input dependency set. The technique used to solve the implication problem is to construct a directed graph $G_\Sigma = (N, E)$, where $\Sigma = F \cup I$ is a set of FDs and INDs over R as follows. Each attribute $A \in schema(R)$ has a separate node in N labelled A. G_Σ has two types of arc, *black* and *red*. There is a black arc, (B, A) in E, if there is a nontrivial IND $A \subseteq B \in I$. Correspondingly, there is a red arc, (A, B) in E, if there is a nontrivial FD $A \to B \in F^+$. It follows that the k-cycle inference rule can be used in a derivation if and only if there is a corresponding cycle in G_Σ having $k + 1$ nodes and $k + 1$ arcs such that the arcs alternate between red and black arcs. This problem can be solved in polynomial time in the size of G_Σ. This result is extremely important, since the class of FDs and unary INDs is the largest class of FDs and INDs whose implication problem is known to be tractable.

Theorem 3.47 can be extended to the case where the set of unary INDs are over a database schema rather than just over a single relation schema [CKV90]. To effect this extension cardinality constraints, which are discussed in Subsection 3.7, turn out to be extremely useful.

The next theorem shows that the chase procedure can be utilised as a sound and complete axiom system for FDs and proper circular INDs. This is complementary to the result, mentioned in the introduction to this subsection, that Mitchell's axiom system is sound and complete for FDs and proper circular INDs, since finite and infinite logical implication coincide for this subclass of FDs and INDs. It is interesting to note that Mitchell's axiom system is a finite 3-ary axiomatisation but it is not attribute bounded. Apart from the result of Theorem 3.47 for unary INDs this is the most meaningful subclass of FDs and INDs whose implication problem is decidable and for which a sound and complete axiomatisation exists.

Definition 3.76 (The database for an FD and an IND) Let α be an FD $R : X \to Y$ over **R**. The *database* for α, denoted by d_α, is a database over **R**, where apart from the relation $r_\alpha \in d$ over R all the other relations are empty and such that r_α contains two tuples t_1 and t_2, which are constructed as follows: $t_1[X] = t_2[X]$ and for all $A \in schema(R) - X$, $t_1[A] \neq t_2[A]$. Moreover, for every pair of distinct attributes A and B in $schema(R)$, $t_i[A] \neq t_j[B]$, for $i, j \in \{1, 2\}$, i.e. the columns of r_α are disjoint.

Let β be an IND $R[X] \subseteq S[Y]$ over $\mathbf{R}$. The *database* for β, denoted by d_β, is a database over $\mathbf{R}$, where apart from the relation $r_\beta \in d$ over R all the other relations are empty and such that r_β contains a single tuple t which is constructed as follows: for every pair of distinct attributes A and B in schema(R), $t[A] \neq t[B]$, i.e. as above the columns of r_β are disjoint. ■

Theorem 3.48 Let $\Sigma = F \cup I$ be a set of FDs and proper circular INDs over $\mathbf{R}$, α be an FD R $: X \to Y$ over $\mathbf{R}$ and β be the IND $R[X] \subseteq S[Y]$ over $\mathbf{R}$. The following two inference rules are sound and complete for FDs and proper circular INDs:

Chase FD: $\Sigma \vdash \alpha$, if $t_1'[Y] = t_2'[Y]$, where t_1' and t_1' are the final states of t_1 and t_2 in ICHASE(d_α, Σ).

Chase IND: $\Sigma \vdash \beta$, if $t[X] \in \pi_Y(s')$, where s' is the final state of the relation over S in ICHASE(d_β, Σ).

Proof. In order to prove soundness we consider the chase FD and the chase IND inference rules separately.

Chase FD case. Assume that $t_1'[Y] = t_2'[Y]$ as in the definition of the chase FD inference rule and let d be a database over $\mathbf{R}$ such that $d \models \Sigma$. We need to show that $d \models R : X \to Y$. Let us define a mapping ψ from d_α to d such that $\psi(t_1) = u_1$ and $\psi(t_2) = u_2$, with $u_1[X] = u_2[X]$, where $t_1, t_2 \in r$ and $r \in d$ is the relation over R. (The mapping ψ is called a *containment mapping* from d_α to d.) We claim that $u_1[Y] = u_2[Y]$ by an induction on the number of chase steps, say k, required to compute ICHASE(d_α, Σ), thereby proving the result. Due to the union (FD4) and decomposition (FD5) inference rules for FDs, we assume without loss of generality that $Y = \{A\}$ is a singleton, and due to the reflexivity (FD1) inference rule for FDs we assume without loss of generality that $A \notin X$.

Basis If $k = 1$ then the only chase step executed is an application of the FD rule for an FD $R : W \to Z \in F$, with $W \subseteq X$ and $A \in Z$. It follows that $u_1[A] = u_2[A]$ as required, since $d \models R : W \to Z$.

Induction Assume the result holds when the number of chase steps required to compute ICHASE(d_α, Σ) is k, with $k \geq 1$; we then need to prove that the result holds when the number of chase steps required to compute ICHASE(d_α, Σ) is $k + 1$. Let us consider the last chase step executed to obtain ICHASE(d_α, Σ). There are two cases to consider.

Case 1. The last chase step is an application of the IND rule. The result follows by inductive hypothesis, since this chase step does not change the current states of t_1 and t_2, implying that they are already in their final states, i.e. t_1' and t_2'.

Case 2. The last chase step is an application of the FD rule for an FD $S : W \to Z$. Let w_1 and w_2 be the two tuples in the current state of the relation over S in the current state of d_α such that $w_1[Z]$ and $w_1[Z]$ are equated as a result of this FD rule. It follows that for some $B \in Z$, $t_1'[A] = t_2'[A] = w_1'[B] = w_2'[B]$, where w_1' and w_2' are the final states of w_1 and w_2, respectively. Thus $\psi(w_1'[B]) = \psi(w_2'[B])$ since $d \models S : W \to Z$. The result now follows, since by inductive hypothesis either $u_1[A] = \psi(w_1[B])$ and $u_2[A] = \psi(w_2[B])$ or $u_1[A] = \psi(w_2[B])$ and $u_2[A] = \psi(w_1[B])$.

Chase IND case. Assume that $t[X] \in \pi_Y(s')$ as in the definition of the chase IND inference rule and let d be a database over $\mathbf{R}$ such that $d \models \Sigma$. We need to show that $d \models R[X] \subseteq S[Y]$. Let us define a mapping ψ from d_β to d such that $\psi(t) = u$, where $u \in r$ and $r \in d$ is the relation over R. (The mapping ψ is called a *containment mapping* from d_β to d.) We claim that $u[X] \in \pi_Y(s)$, where $s \in d$ is the relation over S, by an induction on the number of chase steps, say k, required to compute ICHASE(d_β, Σ), thereby proving the result. We assume without loss of generality by the reflexivity (IND1) inference rule for INDs that $R[X] \subseteq S[Y]$ is a nontrivial IND.

Basis If $k = 1$ then the only chase step executed is an application of the IND rule for an IND $R[W] \subseteq R[Z] \in I$, where $R[X] \subseteq S[Y]$ can be obtained from $R[W] \subseteq S[Z]$ by the projection and permutation (IND2) inference rule for INDs. It follows that $u[X] \in \pi_Y(s)$ as required, since $d \models R[W] \subseteq S[Z]$.

Induction Assume the result holds when the number of chase steps required to compute ICHASE(d_β, Σ) is k, with $k \geq 1$; we then need to prove that the result holds when the number of chase steps required to compute ICHASE(d_β, Σ) is $k + 1$. Let us consider the last chase step executed to obtain ICHASE(d_β, Σ). There are two cases to consider.

Case 1. The last chase step is an application of the IND rule for an IND $T[W] \subseteq S[Z]$, with $Y \subseteq Z$. Now, by inductive hypothesis there exists an IND $R[V] \subseteq T[W]$ that is logically implied by Σ, with $X \subseteq V$. It therefore follows that $R[X] \subseteq S[Y]$ can be inferred from $R[V] \subseteq T[W]$ and $T[W] \subseteq S[Z]$ by the transitivity (IND3) and projection and permutation (IND2) inference rules for INDs. Thus by inductive hypothesis there is a tuple w in the relation over T in d such that $u[V] = w[W]$. The result is now evident, since $d \models T[W] \subseteq S[Z]$.

Case 2. The last chase step was an application of the FD rule for an FD $T : W \rightarrow Z$. Let w_1 and w_2 be the two tuples in the current state of the relation over T in d_α such that $w_1[Z]$ and $w_1[Z]$ are equated as a result of this FD rule. Assume without loss of generality that $Z - W = \{B\}$ is a singleton, otherwise the argument below can be repeated for all attributes in $Z - W$. It follows that $t[A] = w'_1[B] = w'_2[B]$, where w'_1 and w'_2 are the final states of w_1 and w_2, respectively. Thus $\psi(w'_1[B]) = \psi(w'_2[B])$ since $d \models S : W \rightarrow Z$. The result now follows, since by inductive hypothesis $u[X - A] = v[Y - C]$, for some attribute $C \in Y$ and tuple $v \in \pi_Y(s)$, and either $u[A] = \psi(w_1[B]) = v[C]$ or $u[A] = \psi(w_2[B]) = v[C]$.

Completeness follows from Theorem 3.38, since both ICHASE(d_α, Σ) $\models$ Σ and ICHASE(d_β, Σ) $\models$ Σ, implying that ICHASE(d_α, Σ) $\models$ α and ICHASE(d_β, Σ) $\models$ β, respectively. $\square$

The following result showing the intractability of the implication problem for FDs and noncircular INDs was established in [CK85]

Theorem 3.49 The implication problem for FDs and noncircular INDs is EXPTIME-complete. $\square$

It was also shown in [CK86] that the implication problem for the class of FDs and typed noncircular INDs is NP-hard; recall from Theorem 3.45 that the implication problem for typed INDs on their own is polynomial-time decidable. The next theorem shows that the implication problem for FDs and proper circular INDs is not more difficult than that for FDs and noncircular INDs.

Theorem 3.50 The implication problem for the class of FDs and proper circular INDs is EXPTIME-complete.

Proof. The problem is in EXPTIME, since the chase procedure for FDs and INDs can be shown to terminate in exponential time when its input set of INDs is proper circular. The result follows, since EXPTIME-hardness of the problem is a consequence of the EXPTIME-completeness of the implication problem for FDs and noncircular INDs.   □

The proof of the following fundamental theorem, which follows by a reduction from the word problem for finite semigroups defined in Subsection 1.9.4, can be found in [Mit83, CV85].

Theorem 3.51   The implication problem for FDs and INDs is undecidable, even if we restrict ourselves to binary INDs, i.e. INDs whose left-hand sides and right-hand sides are restricted to contain only two attributes.   □

3.6.12   The Case of No Interaction Between Functional and Inclusion Dependencies

As we have seen in Subsection 3.6.11 the interaction between FDs and INDs is complex leading, in general, to the undecidability of their joint implication problem. Given a set $\Sigma = F \cup I$ of FDs and INDs over a database schema $\mathbf{R}$ it would be useful if F and I do *not* interact in the sense that we need not apply any mixed FD-IND rules in deciding whether Σ logically implies an FD or an IND, α. The benefit of Σ belonging to such a class of FDs and INDs is that the implication problem is much simpler: for FDs we need only use Armstrong's axiom system while for INDs we need only use Casanova et al.'s axiom system. Unfortunately, the implication problem for INDs on their own is still intractable unless we restrict ourselves to subclasses of INDs such as unary and typed INDs. The next definition formalises the notion of no interaction.

Definition 3.77 (No interaction occurring between FDs and INDs)   A set of FDs F over $\mathbf{R}$ is said *not to interact* with a set of INDs I over $\mathbf{R}$, if

1) for all FDs α over $\mathbf{R}$, for all subsets $G \subseteq F$, $G \cup I \models \alpha$ if and only if $G \models \alpha$, and

2) for all INDs β over $\mathbf{R}$, for all subsets $J \subseteq I$, $F \cup J \models \beta$ if and only if $J \models \beta$.   ■

For example, the set of FDs and INDs, {LECTURERS : LECT $\rightarrow$ DEPT, HEADS[HEAD, DEPT] $\subseteq$ LECTURERS[LECT, DEPT]}, logically implies the FD HEADS : HEAD $\rightarrow$ DEPT by the pullback inference rule and thus the FDs and INDs *do* interact. On the other hand, it can be verified that the set of FDs and INDs, {STUDENTS : STUD $\rightarrow$ DEPT, HEADS : HEAD $\rightarrow$ DEPT, STUDENTS[DEPT] $\subseteq$ HEADS[DEPT]}, is such that the FDs and INDs do *not* interact, since they do not logically imply any additional nontrivial FD or IND.

In the remaining part of this subsection we restrict ourselves to the subclass of FDs and proper circular INDs.

Informally, a reduced set of FDs and INDs is one such that, for each IND R[X] $\subseteq$ S[Y] in the set I of INDs, Y does not contain any nontrivial FDs with respect to the set F of FDs.

Definition 3.78 (Reduced set of FDs and INDs)   The projection of a set of FDs F_i over R_i onto a set of attributes $Y \subseteq schema(R_i)$, denoted by $F_i[Y]$, is given by $F_i[Y] = \{R_i : W \rightarrow Z \mid R_i : W \rightarrow Z \in F_i^+$ and $WZ \subseteq Y\}$.

A set of attributes $Y \subseteq \text{schema}(R_i)$ is said to be *reduced* with respect to R_i and a set of FDs F_i over R_i (or simply reduced with respect to F_i if R_i is understood from context) if $F_i[Y]$ contains only trivial FDs. A set of FDs and INDs $\Sigma = F \cup I$ is said to be *reduced* if $\forall R_i[X] \subseteq R_j[Y] \in I$, Y is reduced with respect to F_j. ∎

The next lemma shows that being reduced is a necessary condition for no interaction between F and I to occur.

Lemma 3.52   If F and I do not interact then Σ is reduced.

Proof. We prove the result by contraposition. Assume that Σ is not reduced and thus for some IND $R_i[Z_i] \subseteq R_j[Z_j] \in I$, Z_j is not reduced with respect to R_j and F_j. It follows that $F_j[Z_j]$ contains a nontrivial FD, say $R_j : X_j \to Y_j$, with $X_j Y_j \subseteq R_j$. Furthermore, we have that $I \models R_i[X_i Y_i] \subseteq R_j[X_j Y_j]$ for some subset $X_i Y_i \subseteq Z_i$, with $|X_i|=|X_j|$, since $X_j Y_j \subseteq Z_j$. Therefore, by the pullback inference rule (FD-IND1) $\Sigma \models R_i : X_i \to Y_i$, where $R_i : X_i \to Y_i$ is a nontrivial FD. The result follows, since $F_j \cup I \models R_i : X_i \to Y_i$ but $F_j \not\models R_i : X_i \to Y_i$. □

The next example shows that being reduced is not a sufficient condition for no interaction to occur between F and I.

Example 3.8   Let $\mathbf{R} = \{R_1, R_2\}$ be a database schema, with $R_1 = \{B_1, B_2, B_3, A\}$ and $R_2 = R_1 \cup \{C\}$. Also, let $d = \{r_1, r_2\}$ be a database over $\mathbf{R}$, with $r_1 = \{<1, 2, 3, 0>\}$ and $r_2 = \emptyset$. Finally, let $\Sigma = F \cup I$ be a set of FDs and typed noncircular INDs. The set of INDs is given by $I = \{R_1[B_2 B_3] \subseteq R_2[B_2 B_3], R_1[B_1 B_3 A] \subseteq R_2[B_1 B_3 A], R_1[B_1 B_2 A] \subseteq R_2[B_1 B_2 A]\}$. The set of FDs is given by $F = F_2 = \{B_1 A \to C, B_2 \to C, B_3 C \to A\}$. It can be verified that $\Sigma \models R_1[B_2 B_3 A] \subseteq R_2[B_2 B_3 A]$, since ICHASE$(d, \Sigma)$ produces a tuple t in r_2, with $t[B_2 B_3 A] = <2, 3, 0>$. So there is interaction between F and I but Σ is reduced. It is interesting to note that the closure of Σ is *not* reduced, since $F \models R_2 : B_2 B_3 \to A$. ∎

The next counterexample shows that even if the closure of Σ is reduced there may still be interaction between F and I.

Example 3.9   Let $\mathbf{R} = \{R_1, R_2, R_3\}$ be a database schema, with $R_1 = R_2 = \{A, B, C\}$ and $R_3 = \{A, B_1, B_2, C_1, C_2\}$. Also, let $d = \{r_1, r_2, r_3\}$ be a database over $\mathbf{R}$, with $r_1 = \{<0, 1, 2>\}$, $r_2 = r_3 = \emptyset$. Finally, let $\Sigma = F \cup I$ be a set of FDs and noncircular INDs as follows. The set of INDs is given by $I = \{R_1[AC] \subseteq R_2[BC], R_1[AC] \subseteq R_3[AB_1], R_1[AC] \subseteq R_3[AB_2], R_1[BC] \subseteq R_3[AB_1], R_1[BC] \subseteq R_3[AB_2]\}$. The set of FDs is given by $F = F_3 = \{A \to C_1 C_2, C_1 C_2 \to A, B_1 \to C_1, B_2 \to C_2\}$. It can be verified that $\Sigma \models R_1[BC] \subseteq R_2[BC]$, since in ICHASE$(d, \Sigma)$ the values 0 and 1 are equated. So there is interaction between F and I but it can be verified that the closure of Σ is reduced. ∎

The next two theorems give two sufficient conditions for no interaction to occur [LL97c] (cf. [MR92a]). An FD of the form $R : X \to Y$ is said to be *n-standard* if $|X| \geq n$ for some natural number $n \geq 1$. (When $n = 1$ then $R : X \to Y$ is a standard FD.) An IND $R[X] \subseteq S[Y]$ is said to be *n-ary* if $|X| \leq n$ for some natural number $n \geq 1$. (When $n = 1$ then $R[X] \subseteq S[Y]$ is a unary IND.)

Theorem 3.53   If F is a set of n-standard FDs and I is a set of proper circular and n-ary INDs then F and I do not interact.

Proof. The proof hinges on the fact that in this case it is true that whenever a database d satisfies F then ICHASE(d, I) = ICHASE(d, Σ), i.e. the FD rule is *not* applied at all during the computation of the chase.

To see why this fact is true consider a tuple, say t, which was newly added to a relation, say s, over S due to the application of the IND rule for an IND, say R[X] $\subseteq$ S[Y]. Then by the definition of the IND rule $t[Y] \notin \pi_Y(s)$. Moreover, since I is n-ary $|Y| \leq n$. However, since F is n-standard then for any FD S : W $\to$ Z we have $|W| \geq n$. So, there can be no tuple in s having that same W-value as the newly added tuple t, due to the fact that for all A $\in$ schema(R)$-$Y the A-value of t is a new value. Thus the FD rule cannot be applied to $s \cup \{t\}$. To conclude the proof there are two cases to consider.

Case 1. We show that when α is an FD over a relation schema R $\in$ **R** and F $\not\models \alpha$ then $\Sigma \not\models \alpha$. Now, since F $\not\models \alpha$ there is a database d_α over **R** such that $d_\alpha \models$ F but $d_\alpha \not\models \alpha$. Let $d' =$ ICHASE(d_α, Σ). Then $d' \not\models \alpha$, since ICHASE(d_α, I) = ICHASE(d_α, Σ). Therefore, $d' \models \Sigma$ but $d' \not\models \alpha$ implying the result that $\Sigma \not\models \alpha$.

Case 2. We show that when β is an IND over **R** and I $\not\models \beta$ then $\Sigma \not\models \beta$. Now, consider the database d_β of Definition 3.76. It is easy to see that $d_\beta \models$ F but $d_\beta \not\models \beta$. Let $d' =$ ICHASE(d_β, Σ). Then by Theorem 3.48, $d' \not\models \beta$, since ICHASE(d_β, I) = ICHASE(d_β, Σ) and I $\not\models \beta$. Therefore, $d' \models \Sigma$ but $d' \not\models \beta$ implying the result that $\Sigma \not\models \beta$. $\square$

For the next theorem we need the definition of Boyce-Codd Normal Form, which is a desirable property in database design, discussed in detail in Subsection 4.4.3 of Chapter 4. A database schema **R** is in *Boyce-Codd Normal Form* (or simply BCNF) with respect to a set of FDs F over **R** if for all $R_i \in$ **R** and for all nontrivial FDs R_i : X $\to$ Y $\in F_i$, X is a superkey for R_i with respect to F_i.

Theorem 3.54   If **R** is in BCNF with respect to F, I is a proper circular set of INDs and $\Sigma =$ F $\cup$ I is reduced, then F and I do not interact.

Proof. The proof hinges on the fact that, as in Theorem 3.53, in this case it is also true that whenever a database d satisfies F then ICHASE(d, I) = ICHASE(d, Σ), i.e. the FD rule is *not* applied at all during the computation of the chase.

To see why this fact is true consider a tuple, say t, which was newly added to a relation, say s, over S due to the application of the IND rule for an IND, say R[X] $\subseteq$ S[Y]. Then by the definition of the IND rule $t[Y] \notin \pi_Y(s)$. Thus, if the FD rule can be applied for an FD S : W $\to$ Z then it must be the case that W $\subset$ Y, i.e. W is a proper subset of Y, due to the fact that for all A $\in$ schema(R)$-$Y the A-value of t is a new value. Assume without loss of generality that Z = {B} is a singleton and B $\notin$ W. So, either B $\in$ Y or B $\in$ schema(R)$-$Y. In the first case we conclude that Σ is not reduced, since **R** is in BCNF, leading to a contradiction. In the second case, assuming that **R** is in BCNF we conclude again, since W $\subset$ Y, that Σ is not reduced leading to a contradiction. Thus we finally conclude that the FD rule cannot be applied to $s \cup \{t\}$. The rest of the proof is identical to the two cases considered in the proof of Theorem 3.53. $\square$

As the next example shows we cannot, in general, extend the above theorems to the case when the set of INDs I is circular.

Example 3.10   Consider a database schema $\mathbf{R} = \{R, S\}$, where $R = S = \{A, B\}$, and a set $\Sigma = F \cup I$, where $F = \{R : A \to B, S : B \to A\}$ and $I = \{R[A] \subseteq S[A], S[B] \subseteq R[B]\}$. It can easily be verified that Σ is reduced and that I is circular. On using the axiom system of Theorem 3.47 extended to relation schemas, it follows by a cardinality argument that $\Sigma \models \{R : B \to A, S : A \to B\}$ and thus F and I do interact.

As another example let $F = \{R : A \to B\}$ and $I = \{R[A] \subseteq R[B]\}$. It can easily be verified that Σ is reduced and I is circular. Again, F and I do interact, since on using the axiom system of Theorem 3.47 $\Sigma \models \{R : B \to A, R[B] \subseteq R[A]\}$.   ∎

Although a syntactic necessary and sufficient condition for no interaction to occur between FDs and proper circular INDs is still an open problem we close this subsection by identifying the two ways of preventing such interaction occurring. Both of them utilise the fact that the chase procedure can be used to solve the implication problem for FDs and proper circular INDs as a consequence of Theorem 3.48. The first way to prevent interaction is to find a condition which prevents any application of the chase FD rule during the computation of the chase. Examples of such conditions are those found in the statements of Theorems 3.53 and 3.54. The second way to prevent interaction is to find a condition which prevents any old value present in the original database, prior to the computation of the chase, to be equated during the computation of the chase to either another old value or to a new value. In this case new values added to the database during the computation of the chase may be equated to each other. Examples of such conditions which are orthogonal to those of Theorems 3.53 and 3.54 can be found in [LL97c], see Exercise 3.31.

3.6.13   Multivalued Dependencies

Schmid and Swenson [SS75] raised the question of whether FDs are adequate for expressing all the knowledge about the "world" we want to model. Consider an employee relation schema, EMP, with schema(EMP) = {ENAME, CNAME, SALARY, YEAR}, meaning that an employee has name ENAME, a child with name CNAME, and a salary history in which the employee's SALARY is recorded together with the YEAR it was awarded. An example relation, say r, over EMP is shown in Table 3.56. It can be seen that, in general, an employee has one or more children and a salary history comprising one or more {SALARY, YEAR}-values. (We can also record the fact that an employee has no children by using a distinguished null value to indicate that no children exist for this employee; we deal with this problem in Section 5.1 of Chapter 5.)

In terms of the induced ERD we have a one-to-many relationship from employee to children and salary history; children may be modelled as an ID relationship in the ERD but this is another issue. Moreover, the children of an employee are *independent* of his/her salary history. Hence, we can see in r that for a given ENAME each CNAME-value appears together with all the {SALARY, YEAR}-values and correspondingly each {SALARY, YEAR}-value appears together with all the CNAME-values for that ENAME. This independence is equivalent to stating that r has the lossless join decomposition given by

$$r = \pi_{\{ENAME, CNAME\}}(r) \bowtie \pi_{\{ENAME, SALARY, YEAR\}}(r).$$

We observe that the losslessness is *not* a consequence of any FDs that hold in r. Thus the semantics of EMP cannot be captured by FDs on their own.

Table 3.56 The relation r over EMP

ENAME	CNAME	SALARY	YEAR
Jeremy	Jill	40	1990
Jeremy	Jill	50	1993
Jeremy	Jack	40	1990
Jeremy	Jack	50	1993
Eva	Emily	30	1994
Eva	Emily	35	1995
Eva	Emily	30	1998
Eva	Andrew	30	1994
Eva	Andrew	35	1995
Eva	Andrew	30	1998
Erol	Emily	40	1994

This type of constraint can be expressed as the *Multivalued Dependency* (or simply MVD) ENAME *multidetermines* CNAME in the *context* of EMP, or equivalently, ENAME multidetermines {SALARY, YEAR} in the context of EMP. These MVDs are written as: ENAME $\rightarrow\rightarrow$ CNAME (EMP) and ENAME $\rightarrow\rightarrow$ {SALARY, YEAR} (EMP), respectively. Both these MVDs can be expressed jointly as: ENAME $\rightarrow\rightarrow$ CNAME | {SALARY, YEAR}, where the sum of attributes in the joint MVD is schema(EMP), which is the context of the MVD. The joint MVD emphasises the fact that CNAME and {SALARY, YEAR} are orthogonal. In fact, ENAME $\rightarrow\rightarrow$ CNAME (EMP) and ENAME $\rightarrow\rightarrow$ {SALARY, YEAR} (EMP) logically imply each other by *complementation*. This is clearly seen when their satisfaction is expressed in terms of the binary lossless join decomposition of r onto {{ENAME, CNAME}, {ENAME, SALARY, YEAR}}.

To see that the context of an MVD is important consider the relation s over PROJECT, shown in Table 3.57. The attributes of PROJECT are: PNAME meaning a project name, ENAME meaning an employee working on a project, COURSE meaning a course that an employee on the project has taken and YEAR indicating the year in which a particular course was taken. We assume that the semantics of PROJECT are that all employees on a project must take all the courses associated with that project but different employees may take these courses in different years.

Table 3.57 The relation s over PROJECT

PNAME	ENAME	COURSE	YEAR
DB	Jill	Databases	1993
DB	Jill	Programming	1994
DB	Jack	Databases	1994
DB	Jack	Programming	1993

Thus it can be seen that s does not satisfy the MVD PNAME $\rightarrow\rightarrow$ ENAME (PROJECT) nor does it satisfy the complementary MVD PNAME $\rightarrow\rightarrow$ {COURSE, YEAR} (PROJECT). Specifically, Jill took the Databases course in 1993 but not in 1994 and Jill took the Programming course in 1994 but not in 1993. On the other hand, let $s' = \pi_{\{PNAME, ENAME, COURSE\}}(s)$ be the relation shown in Table 3.58 and call the relation schema of s' PROJECTED. We call PROJECTED a *restriction* of PROJECT. The reader can verify that both PNAME $\rightarrow\rightarrow$ ENAME (PROJECTED) and PNAME $\rightarrow\rightarrow$ {COURSE} (PROJECTED) are satisfied in s' in the context of PROJECTED. Therefore the context of an MVD is important and cannot be omitted unless it is somehow clear what the context is. Such an MVD that holds in a restricted context is called an *Embedded Multivalued Dependency* (or simply an EMVD). Although EMVDs are not common in practice they have played an important part in the theory of MVDs which flourished during the late seventies and the early eighties.

Table 3.58 The relation s' over PROJECTED

PNAME	ENAME	COURSE
DB	Jill	Databases
DB	Jill	Programming
DB	Jack	Databases
DB	Jack	Programming

MVDs and EMVDs were introduced in [Fag77b] (see also [Del78]). We next give their formal definition.

Definition 3.79 (Multivalued dependency)   An *embedded multivalued dependency* over schema R (or simply an EMVD) is a statement of the form $X \rightarrow\rightarrow Y$ (S), where schema(S) $\subseteq$ schema(R) and X, Y $\subseteq$ schema(S); S is called the *context* of the EMVD.

An EMVD $X \rightarrow\rightarrow Y$ (S) is said to be *trivial* if either $Y \subseteq X$ or XY = schema(S); it is said to be *standard* if $X \neq \emptyset$.

An MVD over R is an EMVD $X \rightarrow\rightarrow Y$ (R) (or simply $X \rightarrow\rightarrow Y$ whenever R is understood from context), i.e. when the context of the EMVD is R then we have an MVD.   ■

We next define the satisfaction of an MVD over R in a relation r over R. Intuitively, an MVD $X \rightarrow\rightarrow Y$ (R) is satisfied in r if each X-value determines a unique set of Y-values and independently each X-value determines a unique set of (schema(R) − XY)-values.

Definition 3.80 (Satisfaction of an MVD)   An MVD $X \rightarrow\rightarrow Y$ (R) is satisfied in a relation r over R, denoted by $r \models X \rightarrow\rightarrow Y$ (R), if $\forall t_1, t_2 \in r$, if $t_1[X] = t_2[X]$, then $\exists t_3, t_4 \in r$ such that

1) $t_1[X] = t_2[X] = t_3[X] = t_4[X]$,

2) $t_3[Y] = t_1[Y]$, $t_3[Z] = t_2[Z]$ and

3) $t_4[Y] = t_2[Y]$, $t_4[Z] = t_1[Z]$,

where $Z = \text{schema}(R) - XY$.   ■

We observe that due to symmetry we can simplify the above definition by dropping t_4 and case (3) from it.

The next proposition shows that the MVD formalises the concept of a binary lossless join decomposition of R, independently of a set of FDs as was specified in Definition 3.65 of Subsection 3.6.4. This fact is important in relational database design, since the MVD provides the necessary and sufficient condition for decomposing a schema into two of its projections without loss of information.

Proposition 3.55   Let $X \rightarrow\rightarrow Y$ (R) be an MVD, with $Z = $ schema(R)$-$ XY. Then $r \models X \rightarrow\rightarrow$ Y (R) if and only if $r = \pi_{XY}(r) \bowtie \pi_{XZ}(r)$.   □

The definition of the satisfaction of an EMVD can be viewed as a special case of the satisfaction of an MVD.

Definition 3.81 (Satisfaction of an EMVD)   An EMVD $X \rightarrow\rightarrow Y$ (S) is satisfied in a relation r over R, where schema(S) $\subseteq$ schema(R), denoted by $r \models X \rightarrow\rightarrow Y$ (S), if the MVD $X \rightarrow\rightarrow Y$ (S) is satisfied in $\pi_{\text{schema(S)}}(r)$.   ■

The next proposition shows that certain EMVDs obtained by projection can be inferred from a set of MVDs.

Proposition 3.56   Let $X \rightarrow\rightarrow Y$ (R) be an MVD, with $Z = $ schema(R)$-$ XY. Also, let S be a relation schema, with schema(S) $=$ XVW, where $V \subseteq Y$ and $W \subseteq Z$. It is true that if $r \models X$ $\rightarrow\rightarrow Y$ (R) then $\pi_{XWV}(r) \models X \rightarrow\rightarrow V$ (S).   □

We call an EMVD such as $X \rightarrow\rightarrow V$ (S), as defined in Proposition 3.56, a *Projected* MVD (or simply PMVD).

We next present a set of inference rule for MVDs.

Definition 3.82 (Inference rules for MVDs)   Let M be a set of MVDs over a relation schema R. We define the following inference rules for MVDs:

MVD1 Reflexivity: if $Y \subseteq X$, then $M \vdash X \rightarrow\rightarrow Y$.

MVD2 Complementation: if $M \vdash X \rightarrow\rightarrow Y$, then $M \vdash X \rightarrow\rightarrow$ schema(R)$-$XY.

MVD3 Augmentation: if $M \vdash X \rightarrow\rightarrow Y$ and $W \subseteq$ schema(R), then $M \vdash XW \rightarrow\rightarrow YW$.

MVD4 Transitivity: if $M \vdash X \rightarrow\rightarrow Y$ and $M \vdash Y \rightarrow\rightarrow Z$, then $M \vdash X \rightarrow\rightarrow Z-Y$.

MVD5 Union: if $M \vdash X \rightarrow\rightarrow Y$ and $M \vdash X \rightarrow\rightarrow Z$, then $M \vdash X \rightarrow\rightarrow YZ$.

MVD6 Decomposition: if $M \vdash X \rightarrow\rightarrow Y$ and $M \vdash X \rightarrow\rightarrow Z$, then $M \vdash X \rightarrow\rightarrow Y \cap Z$, $M \vdash X$ $\rightarrow\rightarrow Y-Z$ and $M \vdash X \rightarrow\rightarrow Z-Y$.

MVD7 Subset: if $M \vdash X \rightarrow\rightarrow Y$, $M \vdash W \rightarrow\rightarrow Z$ and $Y \cap W = \emptyset$, then $M \vdash X \rightarrow\rightarrow Y \cap Z$ and $X \rightarrow\rightarrow Y-Z$.   ■

Often instead of $X \rightarrow\rightarrow Y$ (R) (or $X \rightarrow\rightarrow Y$ when R is understood from context) we write $X \rightarrow\rightarrow Y \mid Z$, where $Z = $ schema(R)$-$XY, to indicate that the context of the MVD or EMVD is R. The justification for this notation being that from $X \rightarrow\rightarrow Y$ we can derive $X \rightarrow\rightarrow Z$ by the complementation inference rule.

The interaction between FDs and MVDs can be described by the following two mixed inference rules.

Definition 3.83 (Mixed inference rules for FDs and MVDs) Let F be a set of FDs over R and M be a set of MVDs over R. We define the following mixed inference rules for FDs and MVDs:

FD-MVD1 Generalisation: if $F \cup M \vdash X \rightarrow Y$, then $F \cup M \vdash X \rightarrow\rightarrow Y$.

FD-MVD2 Mixed pseudo-transitivity: if $F \cup M \vdash X \rightarrow\rightarrow Y$, $Z \subseteq Y$ and for some W disjoint from Y, i.e. $W \cap Y = \emptyset$, $F \cup M \vdash W \rightarrow Z$, then $F \cup M \vdash X \rightarrow Z$. ∎

We call the inference rules FD1, FD2, FD3 (i.e. Armstrong's axiom system) together with the inference rules MVD1, MVD2, MVD3, MVD4 for MVDs and the mixed inference rules MVD-FD1, MVD-FD2 *Beeri et al.'s axiom system* [BFH77]. The next theorem was first shown in [BFH77]; recall that Σ^+ (see Definition 3.55) is the set of all FDs and MVDs that can be derived by using Beeri et al.'s axiom system, where Σ is a set F of FDs together with a set M of MVDs over R.

Theorem 3.57 Beeri et al.'s axiom system is sound and complete for FDs and MVDs. □

Proof. For soundness we restrict ourselves to the proof that FD-MVD2 is sound. Let r be a relation over R such that $r \models X \rightarrow\rightarrow Y$, $Z \subseteq Y$ and for some W disjoint from Y, $r \models W \rightarrow Z$. Let $t_1, t_2 \in r$ be two tuples such that $t_1[X] = t_2[X]$. We are required to show that $t_1[Z] = t_2[Z]$. By the definition of the satisfaction of the MVD $X \rightarrow\rightarrow Y$, $\exists t_3 \in r$ such that

1) $t_1[X] = t_2[X] = t_3[X]$, and

2) $t_3[Y] = t_1[Y]$ and $t_3[\text{schema}(R) - XY] = t_2[\text{schema}(R) - XY]$.

Since $W \cap Y = \emptyset$, we have that $t_2[W] = t_3[W]$. Hence $t_2[Z] = t_3[Z]$, since $r \models W \rightarrow Z$. We also have $t_3[Z] = t_1[Z]$, since $Z \subseteq Y$. It therefore follows that $r \models X \rightarrow Z$ as required.

To prove completeness of Beeri et al.'s axiom system we use the same technique employed to prove the completeness of Armstrong's axiom system. Therefore we need to show that if $\Sigma \models \alpha$, then $\Sigma \vdash \alpha$, where Σ is a set of FDs F together with a set of MVDs M over R and α is an FD or an MVD over R. Equivalently, we need to show that if $\Sigma \nvdash \alpha$, then $\Sigma \nvDash \alpha$. Thus, assuming that $\Sigma \nvdash \alpha$, it is sufficient to exhibit a counterexample relation, r over R, such that $r \models \Sigma$ but $r \nvDash \alpha$.

Assume that $X \subseteq \text{schema}(R)$ is the left-hand side of α. Let $X^* = \{A \mid \Sigma \vdash X \rightarrow A\}$ be the set of all attributes that are functionally determined by X, and let $W_1, W_2, \ldots, W_k$ be the finest partition of $\text{schema}(R) - X^*$ such that $\Sigma \vdash X \rightarrow\rightarrow Y$ if and only if Y is the union of some of the attributes in X^* together with zero or more W_i, $i \in \{1, 2, \ldots, k\}$. The family of subsets of $\text{schema}(R)$, X^*, $W_1, W_2, \ldots, W_k$, is called the *dependency basis* of X with respect to Σ. It is common practice to denote the dependency basis of X by the *full* MVD

$$X \rightarrow\rightarrow X^* \mid W_1 \mid W_2 \mid \cdots \mid W_k.$$

The dependency basis of X is unique, since it is the finest such partition, and by MVD5 and MVD6 it is closed under the Boolean operations, union, intersection and difference. We now construct the relation r. The active domain of r is the set $\{0, 1\}$ and the cardinality of r is 2^k. Each tuple $t \in r$ corresponds to a sequence $<v_1, v_2, \ldots, v_k>$ of zeros and ones as follows. For all $A \in X^*$, $t[A] = 1$ and for all $A \in W_i$, $t[A] = v_i$. For example, if $k = 4$, then the tuple corresponding to the sequence $<0, 1, 0, 1>$ has 1's as its X^*-value, 0's as its W_1-value, 1's as its W_2-value, 0's as its W_3-value and 1's as its W_4-value. We leave the remaining part of the proof, which is to show that $r \models \Sigma$ but $r \not\models \alpha$, as an exercise.   □

Additional inference rules for MVDs and the role of the complementation inference rule are discussed in [Bis78, Men79]. For example, it is shown in [Bis78] that the reflexivity and complementation rules can be replaced by the single inference rule $M \vdash \emptyset \rightarrow\rightarrow$ schema(R) and in [Men79] it is shown that the augmentation rule can be derived from the reflexivity, complementation and transitivity rules. In fact, in [Men79] it is shown that the reflexivity, complementation and transitivity rules are a minimal sound and complete axiom system for MVDs, i.e. removing any one of these inference rules results in an axiom system which is not complete.

The implication problem for FDs and MVDs is the problem of deciding whether $\Sigma \models \alpha$, given a set Σ of FDs and MVDs over R and a single FD or MVD α. The following result was shown in [HITK79, Bee80].

Theorem 3.58   The implication problem for FDs and MVDs can be solved in polynomial time in the size of the input set of FDs and MVDs.   □

Proof. Given a set Σ over R, consisting of a set F of FDs and a set M of MVDs, and an FD or MVD α whose left-hand side is X, let DEP(X, Σ) denote the dependency basis of X with respect to Σ. By the decomposition and union inference rules for FDs, we assume that each FD in F is of the form $W \rightarrow B$, where B is a singleton.

Let $\bar{F}$ be the set of MVDs resulting from replacing each FD $W \rightarrow B \in F$ by the MVD $W \rightarrow\rightarrow B$ and let $\Gamma = M \cup \bar{F}$. It can be shown that an MVD can be derived from Γ if and only if it can be derived from Σ, i.e. $\Gamma \vdash X \rightarrow\rightarrow Y$ if and only if $\Sigma \vdash X \rightarrow\rightarrow Y$. We next compute DEP(X, Γ) as follows.

We initialise DEP(X, Γ) to be the set $\{A \mid A \in X \} \cup$ schema(R)$-X$; we denote the current state of DEP(X, Γ) by B and call the sets of attributes in B *blocks*. While a change can be effected to B do the following: if we can find an MVD $W \rightarrow\rightarrow Z \in \Gamma$ and a block $V \in B$ such that $V \cap W = \emptyset$, $V \cap Z \neq \emptyset$ and $V - Z \neq \emptyset$, then split V into $V_1 = V \cap Z$ and $V_2 = V - Z$, i.e. replace $V \in B$ by V_1 and V_2. It is shown in [Gal82] that the final state of B is the desired DEP(X, Γ) and that this algorithm runs in polynomial time in the size of Γ.

To conclude the proof assume firstly that α is the MVD $X \rightarrow\rightarrow Y$. Then $\Sigma \vdash X \rightarrow\rightarrow Y$ if and only if Y is the union of one or more blocks in DEP(X, Γ). Secondly, assume that α is the FD $X \rightarrow A$. It is shown in [Bee80] that $\Sigma \vdash X \rightarrow A$ if and only if either $A \in X$ or, when $A \in$ schema(R)$-X$, $A \in$ DEP(X, Γ) and there is some nontrivial FD $W \rightarrow A \in F$ (see FD-MVD2). In both cases the required conditions can be checked in polynomial time in the size of Σ.   □

In Galil [Gal82] it was shown that the implication problem for FDs and MVDs can be solved in $O(\|\Sigma\| \log \|\Sigma\|)$ time, where $\|\Sigma\|$, as before, denotes the size of Σ, namely the number of attributes appearing in F and M including repetitions. This is the fastest known algorithm to date for solving this problem.

A set of MVDs M over R is *nonredundant* if for all $X \rightarrow\rightarrow Y \in M$, $(M - \{X \rightarrow\rightarrow Y\})^+$ is a proper subset of M^+. The computation of the dependency basis, presented in Theorem 3.58, can be used to find a nonredundant cover of a set, M, of MVDs over R as follows. M is nonredundant if and only if for each MVD X $\rightarrow\rightarrow$ Y $\in$ M, DEP(X, M) $\neq$ DEP(X, M$-\{$X $\rightarrow\rightarrow$ Y$\})$.

A simple and elegant characterisation of the implication problem for FDs and MVDs was given in [HF86]. Prior to stating this characterisation in the form of Theorem 3.59 we first give a definition.

Definition 3.84 (Closed set of attributes)   A set of attributes W $\subseteq$ schema(R) is said to be *closed* with respect to an FD X $\rightarrow$ Y, if X $\subseteq$ W implies that Y $\subseteq$ W. Correspondingly, a set of attributes W $\subseteq$ schema(R) is said to be *closed* with respect to an MVD X $\rightarrow\rightarrow$ Y, if X $\subseteq$ W implies that either Y $\subseteq$ W or schema(R)$-$XY $\subseteq$ W.

A set of attributes W $\subseteq$ schema(R) is said to be *closed* with respect to a set Σ of FDs and MVDs over R, if W is closed with respect to all the FDs and MVDs in Σ.   ∎

Theorem 3.59   Let Σ be a set of FDs and MVDs over R and α be a single FD or MVD over R. Then $\Sigma \models \alpha$ if and only if every set of attributes W $\subseteq$ schema(R) that is closed with respect to Σ is also closed with respect to α.   □

We next discuss some special kinds of MVDs. Suppose that schema(R) = XYZ, where X, Y and Z are pairwise disjoint subsets of schema(R). Moreover, let s_1 and s_2 be relations over R such that s_1 satisfies the FD X $\rightarrow$ Y and s_2 satisfies the FD X $\rightarrow$ Z. It can be verified that if we let $r = s_1 \cup s_2$, then, in general, r will not satisfy either X $\rightarrow$ Y or X $\rightarrow$ Z. However, if the X-values of s_1 and s_2 are disjoint then r will satisfy the MVDs X $\rightarrow\rightarrow$ Y (R) and X $\rightarrow\rightarrow$ Z (R). Such MVDs are called *degenerate* MVDs [AD80].

The degenerate MVD has an application in the maintenance of user views. Suppose that r_1 over R_1 and r_2 over R_2 are relations in a database, with schema(R_1) = XY and schema(R_2) = XZ, and that $r_1 \models$ X $\rightarrow$ Y or $r_2 \models$ X $\rightarrow$ Z. Furthermore, assume that the natural join $r = r_1 \bowtie r_2$ is a user view over R.

The relation r is said to be *deletion-viable* if whenever $t \in r$ is deleted from r, then

$$r - \{t\} = (r_1 - \{t[XY]\}) \bowtie r_2 \text{ or}$$
$$r - \{t\} = r_1 \bowtie (r_2 - \{t[XZ]\}),$$

i.e. deleting t from r can be realised by deleting $t[XY]$ from r_1 or $t[XZ]$ from r_2 [Cod74].

Correspondingly, the relation r is said to be *insertion-viable* if whenever t is inserted into r, then

$$r \cup \{t\} = (r_1 \cup \{t[XY]\}) \bowtie (r_2 \cup \{t[XZ]\}),$$

provided that $r_1 \cup \{t[XY]\} \models$ X $\rightarrow$ Y or $r_2 \cup \{t[XZ]\} \models$ X $\rightarrow$ Z. That is, inserting t into r can be realised by inserting $t[XY]$ into r_1 and $t[XZ]$ into r_2 [Cod74].

In [AD80] it was shown that in the general case deletion and insertion viability can be characterised by degenerate MVDs.

Theorem 3.60   Let R be a relation schema, where schema(R) = XYZ and X, Y and Z are pairwise disjoint subsets of schema(R), and let r be a relation over R such that $r \models$ X $\rightarrow\rightarrow$ Y (R). If r

is deletion-viable or insertion-viable, then $X \rightarrow\rightarrow Y$ (R) is a degenerate MVD. Conversely, if $X \rightarrow\rightarrow Y$ (R) is a degenerate MVD, then r is deletion-viable and insertion-viable.   □

We refer the reader to Section 3.8 for a comprehensive treatment of the view update problem.

Another special kind of MVD is an MVD of the form $\emptyset \rightarrow\rightarrow Y$ (R), i.e. a nonstandard MVD, that is, an MVD with an empty left-hand side. Let R be a relation schema, where schema(R) = YZ and such that Y and Z are pairwise disjoint sets of attributes. The reader can verify that a relation r over R satisfies $\emptyset \rightarrow\rightarrow Y$ (R) if and only

$$r = \pi_Y(r) \times \pi_Z(r),$$

i.e. r is the Cartesian product of its projections onto Y and Z.

An important class of MVDs, which was investigated in the context of relational database design in the presence of MVDs, is the class of *conflict-free* MVDs [Sci81, Lie82]. One of the main characteristics of a set M of conflict-free MVDs over R is that M is equivalent to an *acyclic join dependency* which has many beneficial properties [BFMY83, Fag83] (see Subsection 3.6.14 for more details).

When we have a nontrivial MVD $X \rightarrow\rightarrow Y$ (R) then it is natural to decompose R into R_1 and R_2, with schema(R_1) = XY and schema(R_2) = XZ, where Z = schema(R)$-$XY. This is due to Proposition 3.55 which guarantees that $\{R_1, R_2\}$ is a lossless join decomposition of R. Given a set of MVDs M over R we can iterate this binary decomposition process on R using nontrivial PMVDs (i.e. projected MVDs) of the form $X \rightarrow\rightarrow Y$ (S) whenever possible with respect to a relation schema S in the current state of the decomposition of R (see Proposition 3.56). The resulting decomposition is lossless but is not unique as the next example shows [Lie81]. One of the benefits of a conflict-free set of MVDs M is that they give rise to a unique lossless join decomposition by iterating the process just described [Sci81, Lie82]. Historically, this was the original motivation in defining the concept of conflict-freeness.

Example 3.11 Let R be a relation schema with schema(R) = {EMP_NO, PROJECT, LOCATION}, where we abbreviate EMP_NO to E, PROJECT to P and LOCATION to L. Let $M = \{E \rightarrow\rightarrow L \mid P, P \rightarrow\rightarrow L \mid E\}$ be a set of MVDs over R; we denote the first MVD in M by m_1 and the second MVD by m_2. The meaning of m_1 is that an employee works in all locations of the projects he/she is involved in. The meaning of m_2 is that a project is associated with all the locations of all the employees in that project.

We can now decompose R losslessly into R_1 and R_2, with either schema(R_1) = {E,P} and schema(R_2) = {E, L} on using m_1, or schema(R_1) = {P, E} and schema(R_2) = {P, L} on using m_2. Thus R does *not* decompose uniquely. The problem here is that $M \models \{E \rightarrow\rightarrow L, P \rightarrow\rightarrow L\}$ but $M \not\models \emptyset \rightarrow\rightarrow L$. Such a problem is called an *intersection anomaly*.   ∎

Definition 3.85 (Intersection property)   A set of MVDs has an intersection anomaly if $M \models \{X \rightarrow\rightarrow Z, Y \rightarrow\rightarrow Z\}$, where Z is disjoint from X and Y but $M \not\models (X \cap Y) \rightarrow\rightarrow Z$.

A set of MVDs M over R possesses the *intersection* property if it does not have any intersection anomalies.   ∎

Example 3.12 Let us add the attribute MANAGER_NO (abbreviated to N) to schema(R) of Example 3.11 and modify M of Example 3.11 to be the set M = {{E, N} →→ L | P, {P, L} →→ E | N} of MVDs over R; we denote the first MVD in the modified version of M by m_3 and the second MVD by m_4. The meaning of m_3 is that an employee and his/her manager work in all the locations of the projects they are involved in. The meaning of m_4 is that a project and its location are associated with all the employees under the jurisdiction of the manager of that project.

We can now decompose R losslessly into R_1 and R_2, with either schema(R_1) = {E, N, P} and schema(R_2) = {E, N, L} on using m_3, or schema(R_1) = {P, L, E} and schema(R_2) = {P, L, N} on using m_4. Thus R does *not* decompose uniquely. The problem here is that m_3 *splits* the left-hand side of m_4, i.e. P ∩ {P, L} ≠ ∅ and L ∩ {P, L} ≠ ∅. Similarly, m_4 splits the left-hand side of m_3. Such a problem is called a *split-lhs anomaly*. ■

Definition 3.86 (Split-freeness property) An MVD X →→ Y *splits* a set of attributes W if it is nontrivial, W ∩ (Y−X) ≠ ∅ and W ∩ (schema(R)−XY) ≠ ∅. A set of MVDs M over R splits W if some MVD in M splits W.

Let M be a set of MVDs over R, and let us denote the set of left-hand sides of nontrivial MVDs in M by LHS(M). A set of MVDs has a split-lhs anomaly if for some W ∈ LHS(M) M splits W.

A set of MVDs M over R is *split-free* if it does not have any split-lhs anomalies. ■

We next define conflict-freeness by combining Definitions 3.85 and 3.86.

Definition 3.87 (Conflict-free set of MVDs) A set M of MVDs over R is *conflict-free* if it is split-free and possesses the intersection property. ■

Example 3.13 Let schema(R) = {EMP_NO, SALARY, YEAR, PROJ, LOC}, where EMP_NO, SALARY, YEAR, PROJ and LOC are abbreviated to E, S, Y, P and L, respectively. Also, let M = {E →→ {S, Y} | {P, L}, P →→ L | {E, S, Y}}, meaning that an employee has a salary history and independently works on projects which have a set of locations, and a project has a set of locations. The reader can verify that M is a conflict-free set of MVDs. ■

Recall that a set of MVDs, M over R, is a *cover* of another set of MVDs, N over R, if $M^+ = N^+$. We next define two properties of MVDs that are related to the concept of cover. This is the theme of Theorem 3.61 below.

Definition 3.88 (Subset property) A set of MVDs M over R possesses the *subset property* if for every pair of nontrivial MVDs in M, X →→ Y | Z, where Z = schema(R)−XY, and U →→ V | W, where W = schema(R)−UV, we have

$$XY \subseteq UV \text{ and } UW \subseteq XZ,$$

up to the renaming of Y by Z and Z by Y, or the renaming of V by W and W by V. ■

Definition 3.89 (Interaction-free sets of MVDs) A set of MVDs M over R possesses the *interaction-free property* if for every pair of nontrivial MVDs in M, X →→ Y | Z, where Z

= schema(R)−XY, and U →→ V | W, where W = schema(R)−UV, and for any relation r over R, we have

$$\pi_{UV}(r_1) \bowtie \pi_{UW}(r_1) = \pi_{XY}(r_2) \bowtie \pi_{XZ}(r_2),$$

where $r_1 = \pi_{XY}(r) \bowtie \pi_{XZ}(r)$ and $r_2 = \pi_{UV}(r) \bowtie \pi_{UW}(r)$.   ◼

Definitions 3.88 and 3.89 were first given in [GT84] and [Van86], respectively. The following theorem was established in [GT84, Van86].

Theorem 3.61   Let M is a set of MVDs over R. Then the following statements are equivalent:

1) A cover of M is conflict-free.

2) A cover of M possess the subset property.

3) A cover of M is interaction-free.   □

The next result was established in [Lak86, ÖY87a].

Theorem 3.62   It can be checked in polynomial time in the size $\|M\|$ of a set of MVDs M over R whether M is conflict-free.

Proof. An MVD X →→ Y ∈ M^+ is said to be *reduced* if it is nontrivial and satisfies the following three conditions:

1) *left-reduced*, i.e. for no proper subset Z ⊂ X, does Z →→ Y ∈ M^+ hold.

2) *right-reduced*, i.e. for no proper subset W ⊂ Y, is X →→ W a nontrivial MVD in M^+.

3) *nontransferable*, i.e. for no proper subset Z ⊂ X, does Z →→ (X−Z)Y ∈ M^+.

A set of MVDs N over R is a *minimal* set of MVDs if each MVD in N is reduced and N is nonredundant. In [ÖY87a] it was shown that a minimal cover, say N, of M can be computed in polynomial time in the size of M. Furthermore, it was shown therein that a set of MVDs has a conflict-free cover if and only if the minimal cover computed by the said polynomial-time algorithm is also conflict-free. The result now follows by computing a minimal cover, say N, of M, and then invoking Definition 3.87 with the help of the algorithm for computing the dependency basis, given in Theorem 3.58.   □

When we have FDs in addition to MVDs we need to extend the definition of a conflict-free set of data dependencies [Kat84, BK86, YÖ92a]. Let Σ = F ∪ M be a set F of FDs over R together with a set M of MVDs over R. Given a set of attributes X ⊆ schema(R), recall that X^* = {A | Σ ⊢ X → A} and assume that the dependency basis of X with respect to Σ is given by DEP(X, Σ) = {X^*, W_1, W_2, . . . , W_k}.

Informally, Σ is extended conflict-free if the set of MVDs, obtained by replacing each nontrivial data dependency, i.e. FD or MVD, in Σ, whose left-hand side is X, by an MVD, whose left-hand side is X^*, is conflict-free according to Definition 3.87. Essentially, an extended conflict-free set of MVDs is obtained by neutralising the effect of the FDs in Σ.

Definition 3.90 (Extended conflict-free sets of FDs and MVDs)   Let us denote the set of left-hand sides of nontrivial FDs and MVDs in Σ by LHS(Σ). We call an MVD of the form $X^* \rightarrow\rightarrow W_1 \mid W_2 \mid \cdots \mid W_k$, where $X \in$ LHS(Σ), a *lhs-closed* MVD.

The set Σ of FDs and MVDs is *extended conflict-free* if the set of all lhs-closed MVDs obtained from the sets of attributes $X \in$ LHS(Σ) is conflict-free. ∎

Example 3.14   Let us alter Example 3.13 be removing the attribute YEAR from schema(R) and by adding the FD E $\rightarrow$ S to the dependency set, meaning that an employee has a unique salary. Thus F = {E $\rightarrow$ S} and M = {E $\rightarrow\rightarrow$ S | {P, L}, P $\rightarrow\rightarrow$ L | {E, S}}. The reader can verify that F $\cup$ M is an extended conflcit-free set of MVDs, since the set of lhs-closed MVDs induced by F $\cup$ M, which is given by the nontrivial MVD P $\rightarrow\rightarrow$ L | {E, S} together with the trivial MVD {E, S} $\rightarrow\rightarrow$ {P, L}, is conflict-free. ∎

In Subsection 3.6.14 we present the result giving the connection between extended conflict-free sets of FDs and MVDs and acyclic join dependencies.

We close this section with the story of the EMVD. As can be seen from Definition 3.81 the EMVD is a generalisation of the MVD where the context of the dependency may be any subset of schema(R). Thus the EMVD is sensitive to the context over which it is defined as opposed to FDs which are *oblivious* to their context. Proposition 3.56, which was given in [Fag77b], shows that certain EMVDs, called PMVDs, can be obtained from a set of MVDs by using projection. It was shown in [ABU79] that the inference rule emanating from Proposition 3.56, called the projection inference rule or simply **EMVD1**, is sound and complete for inferring PMVDs. However, as Fagin observed, and as we have shown in Table 3.57, not all EMVDs are PMVDs. That is, it is possible for a nontrivial EMVD $X \rightarrow\rightarrow Y$ (S) to hold in a projection of a relation r over R, but for the corresponding MVD $X \rightarrow\rightarrow Y$ (R) to be violated in r, where schema(S) is a proper subset of schema(R).

The first negative result for EMVDs was obtained in [PPG80, SW82, CFP84], wherein it was shown that for no $k \geq 0$, $k \in \omega$, does there exist a k-ary axiomatisation for EMVDs (see Theorem 3.46 showing this result for FDs and INDs). That is, there is no finite axiomatisation for EMVDs. In proof let R be a relation schema containing at least $k + 2$ distinct attributes $A_1, A_2, \ldots, A_k, A_{k+1}$, B. Also, let E = {$A_1 \rightarrow\rightarrow A_2 \mid$ B, $A_2 \rightarrow\rightarrow A_3 \mid$ B, $\ldots$, $A_k \rightarrow\rightarrow A_{k+1} \mid$ B, $A_{k+1} \rightarrow\rightarrow A_1 \mid$ B} be a set of EMVDs over R and α be the EMVD $A_1 \rightarrow\rightarrow A_{k+1} \mid$ B. It can be verified that the following three conditions are satisfied: (i) E $\models \alpha$, (ii) if $\beta \in$ E then $\beta \not\models \alpha$ and (iii) if D is a set of at most k EMVDs of E, β is an EMVD over R and D $\models \beta$, then there is an EMVD $\gamma \in$ D such that $\gamma \models \beta$. It was shown in [CFP84] that if these conditions are satisfied then the aforesaid negative result holds.

As we have seen for FDs and unary INDs, the fact that no k-ary axiomatisation exists for a class of data dependencies does not rule out a decision procedure for solving the implication problem. So it remained as an open problem whether the implication problem for EMVDs is decidable or not.

Let E be a set of EMVDs over R, let S be a relation schema, with schema(S) $\subseteq$ schema(R), and let X, V, Y, Y', Z and Z' be sets of attributes in S, with $Y' \subseteq Y$ and $Z' \subseteq Z$. The next inference rule for EMVDs was given in [ITK83].

EMVD2 Embedded union: if $E \vdash X \twoheadrightarrow Y \mid Z$, $E \vdash XY \twoheadrightarrow Z'V$ (S) and $E \vdash XZ \twoheadrightarrow Y'V$ (S) then $E \vdash X \twoheadrightarrow Y'Z'V$ (S).

In [ITK83] EMVD2 together with EMVD1 (the projection inference rule) were used to investigate some subclasses of EMVDs that have decidable solutions to their implication problem. A year later Vardi [Var84a] showed that for a larger class of data dependencies, which properly includes EMVDs, the implication problem is undecidable (see also [CLM81, GL82]). Vardi [Var83] suggested that the solvability of the implication problem for EMVDs is one of the outstanding open questions in data dependency theory. He went further to say: "That question still haunts and baffles us". More than a decade later the answer was given in [Her95]: the implication problem for EMVDS is undecidable both for finite and for infinite logical implication (see the discussion at the beginning of Subsection 3.6.11 about the difference between logical implication for finite and infinite relations). We note that Herrmann's proof utilises a lattice theoretic interpretation of EMVDs. This implies that, as is the case for FDs and INDs, we cannot find a sound and complete (finite or countably infinite) axiom system for EMVDs at all.

3.6.14   Join Dependencies

MVDs formalise the notion of binary lossless join decompositions but there are situations where we require a lossless join decomposition into more than two relation schemas. Aho et al. [ABU79] prove that there are situations where there is a lossless join decomposition into $n \geq 3$ relation schemas but no proper subset of this collection of relation schemas is lossless. For $n = 3$, they give the database schema $\mathbf{R} = \{R_1, R_2, R_3\}$, with schema$(R_1) = \{A_1, A_2\}$, schema$(R_2) = \{A_1, B_1, B_2\}$ and schema$(R_3) = \{A_2, B_1, B_2\}$, together with the set of FDs $F = \{A_1 \to B_1, A_2 \to B_2\}$. Using the chase procedure for FDs given in Subsection 3.6.4 and the result of Theorem 3.29, it can be verified that $\mathbf{R}$ is a lossless join decomposition with respect to F but that no proper subset of $\mathbf{R}$ is lossless with respect to F. The concept of a *Join Dependency* (or simply a JD) allows us to model arbitrary lossless join decompositions, independently of a set of FDs as was specified in Definition 3.65 of Subsection 3.6.4. Lossless join decomposition of a database schema will play an important role as a desirable property to achieve during database design (see Chapter 4 for details).

Consider a relation schema, called SPJ, with attributes SUPPLIER (abbreviated to S), PARTS (abbreviated to P) and PROJECTS (abbreviated to J). A tuple $<s_i, p_i, j_i>$ in a relation over SPJ means that a supplier s_i supplies part p_i to project j_i. In Table 3.59 we show an example relation, say r, over SPJ.

Table 3.59 The relation r over SPJ

SUPPLIER	PART	PROJECT
s_1	p_1	j_1
s_1	p_2	j_1
s_1	p_1	j_2
s_2	p_1	j_1

Let $\mathbf{R} = \{R_1, R_2, R_3\}$ be a database schema, with schema$(\mathbf{R}) = \{S,P,J\}$, where schema$(R_1) = \{S, P\}$, schema$(R_2) = \{P, J\}$ and schema$(R_3) = \{S, J\}$. The reader should verify that r can be decomposed losslessly onto these three relation schemas, since

$$r = \pi_{\{S,P\}}(r) \bowtie \pi_{\{P,J\}}(r) \bowtie \pi_{\{S,J\}}(r).$$

This type of constraint can be expressed by the JD

$$\bowtie [\{S, P\}, \{P, J\}, \{S, J\}].$$

Definition 3.91 (Join dependency) A *Join Dependency* (or simply a JD) over a relation schema R is a statement of the form $\bowtie[\text{schema}(R_1), \text{schema}(R_2), \ldots, \text{schema}(R_n)]$, where $\mathbf{R} = \{R_1, R_2, \ldots, R_n\}$ is a database schema such that schema($\mathbf{R}$) = schema(R). When no ambiguity arises we write $\bowtie[\mathbf{R}]$ instead of $\bowtie[\text{schema}(R_1), \text{schema}(R_2), \ldots, \text{schema}(R_n)]$.

A JD $\bowtie[\mathbf{R}]$ is said to be *trivial* if one of its components is schema(R) (or when no ambiguity arises simply R). ∎

Alternatively, if $\bowtie[\mathbf{R}]$ is a JD over R we say that $\mathbf{R}$ is a *lossless join decomposition* of R. A JD $\bowtie[\mathbf{R}]$ is satisfied in r if there is no loss of information when projecting r onto the relation schemas in $\mathbf{R}$ and then joining the projections together.

Definition 3.92 (Satisfaction of a JD) A JD $\bowtie[\mathbf{R}]$ is satisfied in a relation r over R, denoted by $r \models \bowtie[\mathbf{R}]$, if

$$r = \pi_{\text{schema}(R_1)}(r) \bowtie \pi_{\text{schema}(R_2)}(r) \bowtie \ldots \bowtie \pi_{\text{schema}(R_n)}(r).$$

When no ambiguity arises we write the above equality as

$$r = \pi_{R_1}(r) \bowtie \pi_{R_2}(r) \bowtie \cdots \bowtie \pi_{R_n}(r).$$ ∎

It is evident that if the decomposition $\mathbf{R}$ has a lossless join with respect to a set of FDs F and $r \models F$, then it is also the case that $r \models \bowtie[\mathbf{R}]$. (See Subsection 3.6.4 for details on lossless join decompositions with respect to F.) Also, by Proposition 3.55 we have that an MVD is a special case of a JD when the cardinality of $\mathbf{R}$ is two. That is, the JD $\bowtie[X, Y]$ is equivalent to the MVD $X \cap Y \rightarrow\rightarrow X{-}Y \mid Y{-}X$.

In order to investigate the properties of JDs we next define the project-join mapping.

Definition 3.93 (Project-join mapping) The *project-join mapping* associated with a database schema $\mathbf{R}$ with respect to a relation r over R, denoted by $m_\mathbf{R}(r)$, is given by

$$m_\mathbf{R}(r) = \pi_{\text{schema}(R_1)}(r) \bowtie \pi_{\text{schema}(R_2)}(r) \bowtie \cdots \bowtie \pi_{\text{schema}(R_n)}(r).$$ ∎

It can easily be verified that $r \models \bowtie[\mathbf{R}]$ if and only if $m_\mathbf{R}(r) = r$. The following basic properties of $m_\mathbf{R}(r)$ were shown in [BMSU81].

Lemma 3.63 The following properties are satisfied for all relations r and s over R:

1) $r \subseteq m_\mathbf{R}(r)$.

2) $m_\mathbf{R}(m_\mathbf{R}(r)) = m_\mathbf{R}(r)$.

3) If $r \subseteq s$ then $m_{\mathbf{R}}(r) \subseteq m_{\mathbf{R}}(s)$.   □

We observe that the project-join mapping satisfies the three conditions given in Definition 3.54 and is thus a closure operator.

We next define two database schemas, associated with a relation schema R, to be equivalent if the sets of relations over R that satisfy the JDs induced by these schemas are exactly the same.

Definition 3.94 (Equivalent database schemas)   The set of all relations r over R such that $r \models$ $\bowtie[\mathbf{R}]$, i.e. $m_{\mathbf{R}}(r) = r$, is denoted by JD(**R**). Two database schemas **R** and **S**, with schema(**R**) = schema(**S**) = R, are said to be *equivalent* if JD(**R**) = JD(**S**).   ■

The project-join mapping can now be used to give a syntactic condition which guarantees that two database schemas be equivalent.

Definition 3.95 (Cover of a database schema)   A database schema **R** is said to *cover* a database schema **S**, denoted by **R** $\geq$ **S**, if for all relation schemas S $\in$ **S** there exists a relation schema R $\in$ **R** such that schema(S) $\subseteq$ schema(R).   ■

The next theorem was shown in [BMSU81].

Theorem 3.64   The following statements are equivalent:

1) **R** covers **S**.

2) for all relations r over R, $m_{\mathbf{R}}(r) \subseteq m_{\mathbf{S}}(r)$.

3) JD(**S**) $\subseteq$ JD(**R**).   □

The soundness of the next two inference rules for JDs, where J is a set of JDs over R, is a direct consequence of Theorem 3.64. (See [BV81, Sci82] for more details on inference rules for JDs.)

JD1 Reflexivity: J $\vdash \bowtie[\{R\}]$.

JD2 Covering: if J $\vdash \bowtie[\mathbf{S}]$ and **R** $\geq$ **S** then J $\vdash \bowtie[\mathbf{R}]$.

The next theorem, which was established in [Pet89], shows that JDs do not have a finite axiomatisation.

Theorem 3.65   For no $k \geq 0$, $k \in \omega$, does there exist a k-ary axiomatisation for JDs.   □

A sound and complete infinite axiom system for JDs, which has an *unbounded* inference rule, i.e. an inference rule such as the k-cycle inference rule for FDs and unary INDs, was exhibited in [BV85].

The implication problem for JDs is the problem of deciding whether J $\models \bowtie[\mathbf{R}]$, given a set J of JDs over R and a single JD $\bowtie[\mathbf{R}]$ over R. Firstly, we present two intractability results for the logical implication of JDs from JDs and MVDs.

Theorem 3.66   The following two decision problems are NP-hard:

1) Testing whether a set of JDs and MVDs logically imply a JD.

2) Testing whether a set of MVDs logically implies a JD.   □

We note that the first decision problem was proved in [BV80, MSY81] and the second one was proved in [FT83]. An MVD $X \rightarrow\rightarrow Y$ is unary if Y is a singleton. In [TL86] it was shown that the implication problem, namely whether the set of unary MVDs implied by an arbitrary set of MVDs, say M, logically implies a JD, can be solved in polynomial time in the size of M. The following polynomial-time result was proved in [MSY81, Var83].

Theorem 3.67   Testing whether an FD $X \rightarrow Y$ or an MVD $X \rightarrow\rightarrow Y$ (R) is logically implied by a set $\Sigma = J \cup F$, where J is a set of JDs over R and F is a set of FDs over R, can be done in polynomial time in the size of Σ; more specifically it can be computed in $O(|\text{schema}(R)| \, \| \Sigma \|)$ time.

Proof.   The idea is to replace Σ by a set M of MVDs such that the set of MVDs that is logically implied by M is exactly the same as the set of MVDs that is logically implied by Σ. The set of MVDs M is constructed by replacing each FD $X \rightarrow Y \in F$ by the set of MVDs $\{X \rightarrow\rightarrow A \mid A \in Y-X\}$, and by replacing each JD $\bowtie[R] \in J$, where $R = \{R_1, R_2, \ldots, R_n\}$, by the set of MVDs given by

$$\{\bowtie [X_1, X_2] \mid \{S_1, S_2\} \text{ is a binary partition of } R \text{ with } X_1 = \text{schema}(S_1) \text{ and } X_2 = \text{schema}(S_2)\}.$$

Recall that an MVD is a binary JD and observe that without any loss of generality we can remove any trivial MVDs from M. As an example, consider the JD, $\bowtie[\{A, C\}, \{C, L\}, \{L, B\}, \{B, A\}]$, where A stands for account, C stands for customer, L stands for loan and B stands for bank. Then M consists of the set of nontrivial MVDs given by $\{\bowtie[\{A, C, L\}, \{A, L, B\}], \bowtie[\{A, C, B\}, \{C, L, B\}]\}$, or equivalently, $\{\{A, L\} \rightarrow\rightarrow C \mid B, \{C, B\} \rightarrow\rightarrow A \mid L\}$.

By using this set M of MVDs we can also derive all the FDs that are logically implied by Σ, since as was mentioned in Theorem 3.58 Σ logically implies a nontrivial FD $X \rightarrow A$ if and only if $X \rightarrow\rightarrow A$ is logically implied by M and there is a nontrivial FD $W \rightarrow Z \in F$ with $A \in Z$.

All that remains is to compute the dependency basis of X with respect to M, i.e. DEP(X, M) (see Theorem 3.58). This cannot be done by first computing M, since the size of M may be exponential in the size of Σ. Essentially, we can find the finest partition of schema(R)$-X$ by *refining* a set of attributes, say X_i, in the current state of the partition, when there is an MVD $W \rightarrow\rightarrow Z \in M$ such that $X_i \cap W = \emptyset$ but $X_i \cap Z \neq \emptyset$ and $X_i - Z \neq \emptyset$. In this case we replace X_i by $X_i \cap Z$ and $X_i - Z$. Finding whether there exists in M such an MVD $W \rightarrow\rightarrow Z$ is computed directly from the set J of JDs by considering the JDs $\bowtie[R] \in J$. In order to do so we construct a graph, $G = (N, E)$, whose nodes are the attributes in X_i and such that $\{A, B\}$ is an edge in E if both $A, B \in \text{schema}(R_j) \cap X_i$ for some $R_j \in R$. It was shown in [MSY81] that $\bowtie[R]$ can refine X_i if and only if G is *not* connected, i.e. there exists a pair of nodes in N that do not have a path connecting them. The result follows since G can be constructed in polynomial time in the size of J and the graph connectivity problem is a linear-time problem in the size of the input graph [AHU83].   □

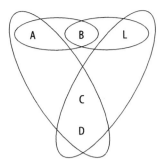

Fig 3.5 The hypergraph represented in Table 3.60

See also [LT87a] for a polynomial algorithm which determines whether a set of MVDs and the subclass of PMVDs induced by a decomposition **R** logically imply the JD $\bowtie[\mathbf{R}]$.

The intractability results of Theorem 3.66 have led researchers to consider the subclass of *acyclic* JDs. The term *acyclic* will be explained by viewing a database schema **R** = $\{R_1, R_2, \ldots, R_n\}$ as a *hypergraph*. A hypergraph is a pair $(\mathcal{N}, \mathcal{E})$, where $\mathcal{N}$ is a finite set of nodes and $\mathcal{E}$ is a set of hyperedges, each hyperedge being a nonempty subset of $\mathcal{N}$. A hypergraph generalises the notion of a graph, since a graph is just a hypergraph where each hyperedge consists of exactly two nodes (assuming there are no loops in the graph, i.e. there are no singleton edges of the form $\{n\}$). The hypergraph induced by a database schema **R** has schema(**R**) as its node set and {schema(R_1), schema(R_2), ..., schema(R_n)} as its hyperedge set. Thus a JD $\bowtie[\mathbf{R}]$ induces a hypergraph. In the following we will not distinguish between a database **R** and the hypergraph, say $\mathcal{H}$, that it induces. We can represent a hypergraph in a table whose columns are the attributes of schema(**R**) and whose rows are the hyperedges; a given cell is nonempty if and only if the attribute of its column is in the hyperedge represented by that row. In Table 3.60 we show the representation of the hypergraph $\mathcal{H}_1 = \{\{A, B\}, \{A, C, D\}, \{B, L\}, \{C, D, L\}\}$, where A, B, C, D and L stand for account, bank, customer, address and loan, respectively; a pictorial representation of this hypergraph is shown in Figure 3.5. In Table 3.61 we show the representation of the hypergraph $\mathcal{H}_2 = \{\{A, B\}, \{B, L\}, \{A, Cb, Db\}, \{L, Cl, Dl\}\}$, where Cb, Db, Cl, and Dl stand for borrowing customer, borrowing address, loan customer and loan address, respectively; a pictorial representation of this hypergraph is shown in Figure 3.6.

We now give a syntactic definition of acyclicity.

Table 3.60 A hypergraph representation of **R**

A	B	L	C	D
A	B			
A			C	D
	B	L		
		L	C	D

We now give a syntactic definition of acyclicity.

Definition 3.96 (Acyclic join dependency) A database schema **R** is *acyclic* if and only if applying the following two operations repeatedly on the hypergraph $\mathcal{H}$, induced by **R**, results

Table 3.61 Another hypergraph representation of **R**

A	B	L	Cb	Db	Cl	Dl
A	B					
	B	L				
A			Cb	Db		
		L			Cl	Dl

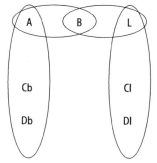

Fig 3.6 The hypergraph represented in Table 3.61

---

in a hypergraph having an empty set of hyperedges:

1) If an attribute A appears in exactly one hyperedge in $\mathcal{H}$ then remove A from that hyperedge; A is called an *isolated* attribute.

2) If S_i and S_j are distinct hyperedges in $\mathcal{H}$ such that $S_i \subseteq S_j$ then remove S_i from the hyperedge set of $\mathcal{H}$; S_i is called a *redundant* relation schema.

A database schema **R** is *cyclic* if it is not acyclic. A JD $\bowtie[\mathbf{R}]$ is said to be acyclic, respectively cyclic, if **R** is acyclic, respectively cyclic. ∎

The algorithm used to determine the acyclicity of a database schema is known as *Graham's reduction algorithm* [BFMY83, Fag83]. The reader can verify that the hypergraph represented in Table 3.60 is cyclic while the hypergraph represented in Table 3.61 is acyclic.

The next theorem gives an alternative, more semantic characterisation of acyclic database schemas [FMU82, BFMY83].

Theorem 3.68 The following statements are equivalent:

1) **R** is an acyclic database schema.

2) The JD $\bowtie[\mathbf{R}]$ over R is logically equivalent to a conflict-free set M of MVDs over R, i.e. $\bowtie[\mathbf{R}] \models M$ and $M \models \bowtie[\mathbf{R}]$. □

The next theorem, which tells us how to infer MVDs from a JD, was established in [FMU82] (see also the proof of Theorem 3.67).

Prior to stating the next theorem we introduce some further notions concerning hypergraphs. A sequence $<e_1, e_2, \ldots, e_k>$, with $e_i \in \mathcal{E}$, $1 \leq i \leq k$, is called a *path* from

e_1 to e_k if $e_i \cap e_{i+1} \neq \emptyset$, $1 \leq i < k$. Two hyperedges of a hypergraph $\mathcal{H}$ are *connected* if there is a path from one to the other. A set of hyperedges in $\mathcal{H}$ is connected if *every* pair of hyperedges in the set is connected. The *connected components* of $\mathcal{H}$ are the maximal connected sets of hyperedges in $\mathcal{H}$.

Theorem 3.69 An MVD $X \twoheadrightarrow Y$ is logically implied by a JD $\bowtie[\mathbf{R}]$ if and only if Y is the union of some of the connected components of the hypergraph induced by $\mathbf{R}$ with the nodes of X removed from the node set of the hypergraph. $\qquad\square$

When $\mathbf{R}$ is acyclic then, by using Theorem 3.69, a set of MVDs, say M over R, which is equivalent to $\bowtie[\mathbf{R}]$, can be found in polynomial time in the size of $\mathbf{R}$. The set M consists of the MVDs whose left-hand side is the intersection of exactly two hyperedges of $\mathbf{R}$. Therefore, by Theorem 3.67 the problem of testing whether a set of JDs and FDs logically implies an acyclic JD can be solved in polynomial time in the size of the input. A variation of this result is that testing whether a set of data dependencies consisting of a single acyclic JD and a set of FDs logically implies any JD can be solved in polynomial time in the size of the input by modifying the chase procedure of Subsection 3.6.4 [Yan81].

Recall Definition 3.90 of an extended conflict-free set of MVDs from Subsection 3.6.13.

Definition 3.97 (Compatibility of a set of FDs with a JD) An FD $X \rightarrow Y$ over R is *compatible* with a JD $\bowtie[\mathbf{R}]$ over R if for some $R_i \in \mathbf{R}$, $XY \subseteq \mathrm{schema}(R_i)$, where $\mathrm{schema}(R) = \mathrm{schema}(\mathbf{R})$.

A set F of FDs over R is *compatible* with a JD $\bowtie[\mathbf{R}]$ over R if every nontrivial FD in F is compatible with $\bowtie[\mathbf{R}]$. A set F of FDs over R is *completely compatible* with a JD $\bowtie[\mathbf{R}]$ over R if F is compatible with $\bowtie[\mathbf{R}]$, and for every FD $X \rightarrow Y \in F$ such that for some $R_i \in \mathbf{R}$, $X \subseteq \mathrm{schema}(R_i)$, then it is also true that $Y \subseteq \mathrm{schema}(R_i)$. $\qquad\blacksquare$

The main result of [Kat84] on extended conflict-free sets of FDs and MVDs is presented in the next theorem; we recall that two sets of data dependencies, Σ and Γ, are logically equivalent if $\Sigma \models \Gamma$ and $\Gamma \models \Sigma$. In the context of the next theorem $\Sigma = F \cup M$, where F and M are, respectively, a set of FDs and a set of MVDs over R.

Theorem 3.70 The following statements are equivalent:

1) Σ is logically equivalent to an extended conflict-free set of FDs and MVDs.

2) Σ is logically equivalent to an acyclic JD and a set of FDs which is compatible with this acyclic JD.

3) Σ is logically equivalent to an acyclic JD and a set of FDs which is completely compatible with this acyclic JD. $\qquad\square$

An immediate corollary of this result is that any set F of FDs over R has an extended conflict-free cover. To show this let $\mathbf{R} = \{R\}$, in which case it is obvious that F is compatible with $\bowtie[\mathbf{R}]$.

We next define the concepts of pairwise and join consistency which are related to the concept of the so called "universal relation". Intuitively, when a database designer chooses a decomposition (or database schema) **R** then it is reasonable to assume that the join of all the relations r_i in a database d over **R** is meaningful. In the universal relation approach meaningful is taken to mean the existence of some "fictitious" relation r such that each $r_i \in d$ is the projection of r onto the attributes of the relation schema R_i of r_i, i.e. schema(R_i). (See Section 2.4 of Chapter 2 for further discussion on the universal relation approach. Also see the monograph [Lev92] for a comprehensive survey of the role of the universal relation and its derivative, the weak instance approach, in relational database theory.)

Definition 3.98 (Pairwise and join consistency) Let r and s be relations over relation schemas R and S, respectively, and let X = schema(R) $\cap$ schema(S). The relations r and s are said to be *consistent* if $\pi_X(r) = \pi_X(s)$. That is, r and s are consistent if their projections onto the common set of attributes of their schemas are the same.

A database d over **R** is *pairwise consistent* if for all $r_i, r_j \in d$, r_i and r_j are consistent. That is, d is pairwise consistent if for each $r_i \in d$ over $R_i \in$ **R** and each $r_j \in d$ over $R_j \in$ **R**,

$$\pi_X(r_i) = \pi_X(r_j),$$

where X = schema(R_i) $\cap$ schema(R_j).

A database d over **R** is *join consistent* if there exists is a relation r over R, with schema(R) = schema(**R**), such that for all $r_i \in d$ over $R_i \in$ **R** we have

$$r_i = \pi_{\text{schema}(R_i)}(r).$$

That is, d is join consistent if there is some "universal relation" r such that each $r_i \in d$ is the projection of r onto the attributes of the relation schema R_i of r_i. ∎

We observe that pairwise consistency of a database over **R** can be expressed via a set of typed INDs over **R** (see Definition 3.69 in Subsection 3.6.7). For example, if we have two schemas EMP and DEPT, with schema(EMP) = {ENAME, DNAME} and schema(DEPT) = {DNAME, ADDRESS}, then pairwise consistency can be expressed by {EMP[DNAME] $\subseteq$ DEPT[DNAME] and DEPT[DNAME] $\subseteq$ EMP[DNAME]. In this case the semantics of pairwise consistency are that employees work in departments and every department has at least one employee.

The next lemma shows that we can test join consistency by joining all the relations in the database [HLY80].

Lemma 3.71 A database $d = \{r_1, r_2, \ldots, r_n\}$ over **R** is join consistent if and only for all $r_i \in d$ we have

$$r_i = \pi_{\text{schema}(R_i)}(r_1 \bowtie r_2 \bowtie \cdots \bowtie r_n).$$

Proof. *If.* The result follows by Definition 3.98, since the join of all the relations in the database d is the relation r, which demonstrates that d is join consistent.

Only if. Let us denote $r_1 \bowtie r_2 \bowtie \cdots \bowtie r_n$ by [$\bowtie d$] and $\pi_{\text{schema}(R_i)}([\bowtie d])$ by $\bar{r}_i$, where $R_i \in$ **R**. Now suppose that d is join consistent and thus there is some relation r over R such that for all $r_i \in d$, $r_i = \pi_{\text{schema}(R_i)}(r)$.

By part (1) of Lemma 3.63 $r \subseteq [\bowtie d]$ and thus $r_i \subseteq \bar{r}_i$. It remains to show that $\bar{r}_i \subseteq r_i$. Now, let t be a tuple in $\bar{r}_i$. It follows that there exists a tuple $u \in [\bowtie d]$ such that $t = u[\text{schema}(R_i)]$. Now suppose that $t \notin r_i$, i.e. $t \notin \pi_{\text{schema}(R_i)}(r)$, then $u \notin [\bowtie d]$ leading to a contradiction. □

Unfortunately, using the result of Lemma 3.71 for checking whether a database is join consistent by joining all the relations in the database leads to an exponential time algorithm in the size of the input database. We observe that by the definitions of pairwise consistency and join consistency, it follows that join consistency implies pairwise consistency. Now, testing whether a database is pairwise consistent can be carried out in polynomial time in the size of the input database. So, if pairwise consistency were to imply join consistency then a polynomial-time test for join consistency would be readily available. This conjecture unfortunately turns out to be false by the following counterexample database d. Let $d = \{r_1, r_2, r_3\}$ be a database over $\mathbf{R} = \{R_1, R_2, R_3\}$, with schema($R_1$) = {A, B}, schema($R_2$) = {B, C}, and schema($R_3$) = {A, C}, where r_1, r_2 and r_3 are shown in Tables 3.62, 3.63 and 3.64, respectively. It can be verified that d is pairwise consistent but not join consistent.

Table 3.62 The relation r_1			Table 3.63 The relation r_2			Table 3.64 The relation r_3	
A	B		B	C		A	C
0	0		0	0		0	1
1	1		1	1		1	0

The next theorem shows that, in general, testing whether a database is join consistent is intractable.

Theorem 3.72   Determining whether a database is join consistent is NP-complete.

Proof. We sketch the main idea of the proof. Showing that the problem is in NP is easily done, since for each tuple t in each relation $r_i \in d$ we can guess whether there are tuples in the other relations $r_j \in d$ such that their join is nonempty.

To show that the problem is NP-hard a polynomial-time transformation from the graph 3-colourability problem, which is known to be NP-complete [Kar72, GJ79], can be given.

The 3-colourability problem: Given a graph G = (N, E) and three colours, red, blue and green, does there exists a function f from N to the three colours such that for each edge $\{u, v\} \in$ E, it is true that $f(u) \neq f(v)$.

We construct a database for G as follows. For each edge $e_k = \{u_k, v_k\} \in$ E we construct a relation schema R_k, with schema(R_k) = $\{u_k, v_k\}$ and a relation r_k consisting of all possible valid 3-colourings of e_k; r_k is shown in Table 3.65. It can then be verified that the constructed database is join-consistent if and only if G is 3-colourable.   □

Table 3.65 The relation r_k for the edge $e_k = \{u_k, v_k\}$

u_k	v_k
red	green
red	blue
blue	green
blue	red
green	blue
green	red

The proof of the next theorem can be found in [BFMY83].

Theorem 3.73   A database schema **R** is acyclic if and only if every pairwise consistent database over **R** is also join consistent.

Proof. We sketch the idea of the proof. A *join tree* for a database schema **R** is a tree (N, E), denoted by Tree(**R**), whose node set N is the set of relation schemas $R_i \in$ **R** and such that

1) each edge $\{R_i, R_j\} \in$ E is labelled by the set of attributes schema(R_i) $\cap$ schema(R_j).

2) For every pair of distinct relation schemas R_i and R_j and for each attribute A $\in$ schema(R_i) $\cap$ schema(R_j), every edge in the unique path from R_i to R_j includes A in its label.

It was shown in [GS83] that **R** is acyclic if and only if **R** has a join tree. To prove this intermediate result, it can be shown that **R** has a join tree if and only if Graham's reduction algorithm results in an empty hypergraph. Essentially the operations of (i) removing an isolated attribute, say A, and (ii) removing a redundant relation schema, say S_i, from the current state of the hypergraph correspond to the operations of (i) removing A from schema(**R**) and (ii) removing S_i from **R**, respectively. Moreover, **R** has a join tree if and only if the database schema, say **S**, resulting from applying the above two operations to **R** any number of times and in any order, also has a join tree. It follows that **R** has a join tree if and only if Graham's reduction algorithm results in a hypergraph having an empty set of hyperedges.

We distinguish a node in Tree(**R**) to be the *root* of the join tree. Given that R_i is the root of the join tree its *children* are relation schemas R_j such that $\{R_i, R_j\}$ is an edge in the said tree; if R_j is a child of R_i then R_i is said to be the *parent* of R_j. Now, given a relation schema R_i in the join tree, which is *not* the root, its children are relation schemas R_j such that $\{R_i, R_j\}$ is an edge in the join tree and R_j is *not* the parent of R_i; in this case the parent of R_j is R_i. If a relation schema has no children then it is called a *leaf*. We define the *level* of a node R_i in the join tree inductively as follows: if R_i is the root node of the tree then its level is zero, otherwise the level of R_i is one plus the level of its *parent* node.

To conclude the proof we are required to show that **R** has a join tree if and only if every pairwise consistent database over **R** is also join consistent. A join tree for **R** induces a *join plan* which tells us in what order to join together the relations in a database d over **R**. Let $r_1, r_2, \ldots, r_n$ be a linear ordering of the relations in d such that if R_i is the parent of R_j then $i < j$; we note that such an ordering can be obtained by a topological sort of the join tree for **R**, as defined in Section 1.9.2 of Chapter 1. (Note that R_1 is the root of the join tree and R_n is a leaf.) This linear ordering induces the following join plan, where parentheses indicate the order in which to join the relations in d, namely

$$(\cdots ((r_1 \bowtie r_2) \bowtie r_3) \cdots \bowtie r_n).$$

Now, if **R** has a join tree and d is pairwise consistent, then d is also join consistent since by induction on $|$**R**$|$ it can be shown that no tuples are lost at any stage of executing the join plan for d. Conversely, if pairwise consistency implies join consistency, then there exists a join plan for d such that no tuples are lost during the execution of the join plan. From this join plan we can construct a join tree for **R**. $\square$

An immediate corollary of Theorem 3.73 is that join consistency can be checked in polynomial time in the size of the input database when **R** is acyclic, since acyclicity can be checked in polynomial time (see Definition 3.96).

Recall that a database schema **R** is also called a *decomposition*. This is meant to indicate that a relation r over R can be replaced by its projections $r_i = \pi_{schema(R_i)}(r)$, where $R_i \in \mathbf{R}$ and schema(R) = schema(**R**). The reasons why we might prefer a decomposition rather than just keeping a single relation schema are to do with database design considerations, which are discussed in detail in Chapter 4. In order for such a decomposition to be useful it must be lossless in the sense that given the projections $\{r_i\}$ we must be able to reconstruct the "universal" relation r over R. An operation that replaces a relation r over R by its projections $\{r_i\}$ over $\{R_i\}$ is called a *decomposition map*. A decomposition map $\Delta_\mathbf{R}$ is said to be one-to-one with respect to a set of data dependencies Σ over R, if whenever r and s are relations over R that satisfy Σ, with $r \neq s$, then $\Delta_\mathbf{R}(r) \neq \Delta_\mathbf{R}(s)$. If a decomposition map is one-to-one then it has an inverse which is called the *reconstruction map*.

The most natural candidate to be the reconstruction map is the (natural) join operator. Thus it is reasonable to conjecture that the join operator is the only possible reconstruction map, but in [Var82b] this conjecture was refuted by showing that for a general class of data dependencies, which includes FDs and JDs, the reconstruction map is not necessarily the join operator. However, when the database schema **R** is acyclic and we consider only FDs and JDs in our dependency set, then the reconstruction map is necessarily the join operator [BV84b] (see also [MMSU80]).

Theorem 3.74 Let **R** be an acyclic database schema, with schema(R) = schema(**R**), and let Σ be a set of FDs and JDs over R. Then the following statements are equivalent:

1) The decomposition map $\Delta_\mathbf{R}$ is one-to-one with respect to Σ.

2) $\Sigma \models \bowtie[\mathbf{R}]$.

3) The reconstruction map is the join operator.

Proof. We sketch the proof.

(1 *implies* 2) Suppose that $\Delta_\mathbf{R}$ is one-to-one but that $\Sigma \not\models \bowtie[\mathbf{R}]$. Then by Theorem 3.68 there is an MVD X $\rightarrow\rightarrow$ Y | Z, logically implied by $\bowtie[\mathbf{R}]$, such that $\Sigma \not\models$ X $\rightarrow\rightarrow$ Y | Z, since R is acyclic. Now by the results given in [SDPF81] there exists a relation r having exactly two tuples such that $r \models \Sigma$ but $r \not\models$ X $\rightarrow\rightarrow$ Y | Z; we assume without loss of generality that the active domains of distinct attributes are disjoint. Let S = $\{S_1, S_2\}$, with schema(S_1) = XY and schema(S_2) = XZ. It follows that there exists a tuple t such that $t \in m_S(r)$ but $t \notin r$. Furthermore, it can be shown that there exists a permutation δ on the active domain of r such that $t \in \delta(r)$ and, in addition, $\Delta_S(r) = \Delta_S(\delta(r))$. We also have $r \neq \delta(r)$, due to the fact that $t \notin r$. Moreover, it can be shown that $\delta(r) \models \Sigma$. Finally, it can be verified that $\Delta_\mathbf{R}(r) = \Delta_\mathbf{R}(\delta(r))$ and thus the decomposition map is not one-to-one with respect to Σ, leading to a contradiction.

(2 *implies* 3) Let r be a relation that satisfies Σ and thus it also satisfies $\bowtie[\mathbf{R}]$. It follows that $r = m_\mathbf{R}(r)$ and thus by Definition 3.93 the reconstruction map is the join operator. (Recall that $m_\mathbf{R}$ is the project-join mapping associated with **R**.)

(3 *implies* 1) If the reconstruction map is the join operator then Δ_R must be one-to-one with respect to Σ.   □

It is interesting to consider how FDs can be used to relax the condition that a database schema **R** is acyclic by considering a set of FDs over **R**. We say that **R** is *FD-acyclic* with respect to F if every pairwise consistent database d over **R** that satisfies F is also join consistent [LMG83, SS89]. The problem with this definition is that we need to give appropriate semantics to the notion of d satisfying F. Such semantics are given by the *weak instance* approach that states that d satisfies F if there exists a relation r over schema(**R**) that satisfies F and such that each $r_i \in d$ is contained in the projection of r onto schema(R_i) [Hon82]. As an example, let **R** be a database schema with three relation schemas TEACHES, TAKES and GIVES, with schema(TEACHES) = {S, T}, schema(TAKES) = {S, C} and schema(GIVES) = {C, T}, where S stands for student, T stands for teacher and C stands for course. In addition, let F = {S → T, C → T, T → C} be a set of FDs over schema(**R**), meaning that a student has a unique teacher, a course is taught by a unique teacher and a teacher teaches a unique course. We next show that **R** is FD-acyclic; assume that d has relations r_1 over TEACHES, r_2 over TAKES and r_3 over GIVES. Let <1, 2> be a tuple in r_1, then by pairwise consistency there is a tuple <1, 3> in r_2 and a tuple <3, 4> in r_3. Since d satisfies F, the FDs S → T and C → T imply that 2 = 4, and thus <1, 2, 3> is in the join of the relations in d. It follows that no tuple in r_1 is lost when the join of the relations in d is computed. Similarly, it can be shown that no tuple in r_2 or in r_3 is lost in the join of the relations in d. Therefore, **R** is FD-acyclic with respect to F.

Other characterisations of acyclic database schemas can be found in [GS82, BFMY83, GS83, MU84], and efficient algorithms in the presence of acyclic database schemas are given in [Yan81]. A method of breaking cycles in a cyclic database schema by using maximal objects, which union together two or more hyperedges in the hypergraph induced by a database schema, is presented in [MU83]. Other types of acyclicity of database schemas, which are more restrictive than that of Definition 3.96, can be found in [Fag83, GR86, Gys86]. Also, see [Sac85, ADS86] for an extension of the hypergraph concept to include directed hyperedges, thus allowing us to model FDs in addition to JDs.

It is possible to define *Embedded Join Dependencies* (or simply EJDs), which generalise the notion of EMVDs, by allowing the attribute set, schema(**R**), of a database schema **R**, to be a proper subset of schema(R). The implication problem for EJDs is undecidable by the corresponding result for EMVDs discussed at the end of Subsection 3.6.13. The implication problem for a subclass of EJDs, called *projected* JDs, which generalise PMVDs, was also shown to be undecidable [Var84a]. Axiomatisation of EJDs is considered in detail in [BV81, Sci82]. The axiom system for EJDs was shown to be sound and complete for the special case when the set of JDs, J over R, contains a single JD over R [MGKL88]. In [BR84] a subclass of EJDs, called *cross dependencies*, are considered, where the relation schemas of **R** have disjoint attribute sets. Therein, a sound and complete axiom system for cross dependencies is exhibited.

For a generalisation of FDs and JDs to *Equality Generating Dependencies* (EGDs) and *Tuple Generating Dependencies* (TGDs), respectively, see [Fag82b], [BV84a, BV84c] and [GMV86]. An EGD says that if some tuples fulfilling certain equalities appear in the database then some values in those tuples must be equal. Correspondingly, a TGD says that if some tuples fulfilling certain equalities appear in the database then some additional tuples must be present in the database. We formalise and further discuss the notions of EGD and TGD in Section 9.6 of Chapter 9 in the context of deductive databases. For comprehensive surveys on data dependencies see [FV84a, Var88b].

3.7   Domain and Cardinality Constraints

The concept of a domain is fundamental to the definition of a relation. With each attribute, A, in a relation schema, R, we associate a set of values which we call the domain of A, denoted by DOM(A) (see Definition 3.1 in Section 3.1). Recall that a relation schema R is in 1NF if all its attribute domains are atomic, i.e. each value in such a domain is a nondecomposable set of values which has no internal structure as far as the database system is concerned.

With the advent of the object-oriented database paradigm we follow Date's proposal and interpret an atomic domain as a *user-defined data type* (or simply a data type) [Dat90]. The concept of a user-defined data type is a well-known concept which is supported by many programming languages; often user-defined data types are called *abstract data types*. To be more specific a user-defined data type has the following characteristics:

1) A data type may be a *simple* data type, which is defined as a *scalar* (or primitive) data type, such as a numeric data type or a string, or a *composite* data type, which is composed of other data types, such as date, being composed of day, month and year, or polygon being composed of a list of (x, y) coordinates.

2) The internal structure of the values of a data type is hidden both from the DBMS and the user; the internal structure of a data type is called its *implementation*.

3) The manipulation of the values of a data type can be carried out only through the operators which are defined for that data type; the set of operators defined for a data type is called its *interface* which includes equality, inequality and comparison operators such as less than and greater than.

Points (2) and (3) above are known as the *encapsulation* principle. The intention is that both the database system and the user manipulate and access the values of a data type in a disciplined manner. The encapsulation principle also guarantees data independence, since the implementation of a data type may change but its interface remains the same. Encapsulation should not be viewed as a restriction but rather as a protection against any misuse of the data type. For example, a data type DATE can be composed of the data types DAY, MONTH and YEAR, with the comparison operators, "=" and "<", which allow us to test whether two dates are equal and whether one date precedes another date, respectively. In addition, the operators DAY, MONTH and YEAR allow us to access the components of a date, for example MONTH(28/6/96) will return 6. As another example, a data type CITY defined as CHAR(15), i.e. a string comprising 15 characters, will normally have various wild card operators to access substrings and the comparison operator "<" could test whether the lexicographical order of one substring is less than that of another substring.

Another advantage of encapsulation is that certain typing errors can be detected by the DBMS through *type checking*. For example, two attributes, WEIGHT and GRADE, may be numeric but defined over distinct domains, so comparing the two should normally be illegal. There are exceptions that can be catered for by *coercion* rules which allow us to convert from one data type to another; for example, we can compare an integer with a real number by coercing the integer to be a real number.

It may seem that the definition of an atomic domain is inconsistent, since we are essentially allowing a domain to be of arbitrary complexity. The crux of the argument is that an atomic domain is nondecomposable by the DBMS. The interpretation of the statement that *as far as the* DBMS *is concerned a data type has no internal structure* is that the DBMS has no access to the implementation of a data type, but there is nothing to stop the DBMS accessing a data type through its interface. This holds both for built-in data types and for data types that were defined by the user; built-in data types could have been defined by the user but it is convenient to have data types such as DATE and TIME built into the system. An interesting implication of viewing domains as data types is that domains can be thought of as *object classes* and domain values can be thought of as *objects*, so relational databases are object-oriented after all ! (See Section 10.2 of Chapter 10 for a comprehensive introduction to relational object-oriented databases.) We note that currently SQL does not support user-defined data types in their full generality but SQL3 promises to deliver these features [DD93].

Under our interpretation of a domain as a data type attributes are just variables ranging over data types. It is common, but not necessary, to use the same name for both a domain and an attribute. For example, we may have two data types, namely EMP_NAME, which is defined as CHAR(25), and DATE which is composed of DAY, MONTH and YEAR. Moreover, the attribute EMP_NAME will be defined over the domain EMP_NAME and the attribute HIRE_DATE will be defined over the domain DATE.

Definition 3.99 (Domain constraint)   A *domain constraint* (or simply a DC) is a statement of the form R[A] $\in \mathcal{S}$, where R is a relation schema, A is an attribute in schema(R) and $\mathcal{S} \subseteq$ DOM(A) is a subset of the domain of A (or equivalently, the user-defined data type of A).

A DC R[A] $\in \mathcal{S}$ is satisfied in a relation r over R, denoted by $r \models$ R[A] $\in \mathcal{S}$ if $\pi_A(r) \subseteq \mathcal{S}$. ∎

There are several ways in which we may specify the subset $\mathcal{S}$ of DOM(A):

1) Enumerating all the values in $\mathcal{S}$. For example, if the domain COLOUR is defined as CHAR(10) then $\mathcal{S}$ could enumerate a finite set of colours, say {"red", "yellow", "blue", "white"}.

2) Specifying a range of values, when DOM(A) is linearly ordered. For example, the range of a day in a month is from 1 to 31, and the range of grades of students could be from A to F.

3) Specifying a conditional expression which must be satisfied in order for the value to be in $\mathcal{S}$. For example, we may specify that a salary is greater than 10,000 as a conditional expression. (Such conditional expressions can be specified as *event-condition-action rules*; see Section 10.4 of Chapter 10 for details.)

Relations are defined as finite sets of tuples, and in practice it is often useful to further restrict their cardinality. For example, if we have a relation schema EMP, with attributes EMPLOYEE# and MANAGER#, it is quite sensible to assume that the number of managers is less than or equal to the number of employees, written as EMP[MANAGER#] $\leq$ EMP[EMPLOYEE#]. As another example, we may want to restrict the number of students taking a particular course, or the number of tickets sold for a particular football match. Despite the practical importance of such cardinality constraints there are very few research papers which explicitly discuss their formalisation.

Definition 3.100 (Cardinality constraint)   A *Cardinality Constraint* (or simply a CC) is a statement of the form $R[X] \leq S[Y]$, where R and S are relation schemas in a database schema **R**, $X \subseteq$ schema(R) and $Y \subseteq$ schema(S). A CC $R[X] \leq S[Y]$ is said to be *unary* if $|X|=|Y|= 1$.

A CC $R[X] \leq S[Y]$ is satisfied in a database d over **R**, denoted by $d \models R[X] \leq S[Y]$, if $|\pi_X(r)| \leq |\pi_Y(s)|$, where r and s are the relations in d over R and S, respectively.   ■

We may also define CCs with bound k to be of the form $R[X] \leq k$, where $k \in \omega$, i.e. k is a natural number. A CC $R[X] \leq k$ is satisfied in a relation r over R, denoted by $r \models R[X] \leq k$, if $|\pi_X(r)| \leq k$. A CC with bound k can always be modelled by a CC by adding a new relation to the database over a new relation schema and inserting exactly k tuples into this new relation.

The following inference rules allow us to axiomatise the restricted subclass of unary CCs.

Definition 3.101 (Inference rules for unary CCs)   Let C be a set of CCs over a database schema **R**, and let R, S, T $\in$ **R**. We define the following inference rules for CCs:

CC1 Reflexivity: if $A \in$ schema(R), then $C \vdash R[A] \leq R[A]$.

CC2 Transitivity: if $C \vdash R[A] \leq S[B]$ and $C \vdash S[B] \leq T[D]$, then $C \vdash R[B] \leq T[D]$.   ■

An FD is *unary* if it is of the form R: $A \to B$, where A, B are single attributes in schema(R). The next two inference rules capture the basic interaction between unary FDs and unary CCs, where Σ is a set of unary FDs and unary CCs over **R**.

FD-CC1 Many-to-one: if $\Sigma \vdash$ R: $A \to B$, then $\Sigma \vdash R[B] \leq R[A]$.

FD-CC2 One-to-one: if $\Sigma \vdash$ R: $A \to B$ and $\Sigma \vdash R[A] \leq R[B]$, then $\Sigma \vdash$ R: $B \to A$.

We now prove soundness and completeness for the class of unary CCs [Ng96].

Theorem 3.75   The axiom system comprising the inference rules CC1 (reflexivity) and CC2 (transitivity) is sound and complete for unary CCs over a database schema **R**.

Proof. We leave it to the reader to verify that the axiom system is sound. It remains to prove its completeness. Without loss of generality, we assume that all the unary CCs in a set of unary CCs C over **R** are of the form $R[A] \leq R[B]$, in which case we say that C is a set of CCs over R, and abbreviate $R[A] \leq R[B]$ to $A \leq B$. (We simply rename attributes in the relation schemas in **R** so that if R_i and R_j are disjoint relation schemas in **R**, then schema(R_i) and schema(R_j) are also disjoint, and then we construct a single relation schema R, whose attribute set is schema(**R**).) Now, as in Theorem 3.21 for example, assume that $C \not\vdash A \leq B$. To conclude the proof it is sufficient to exhibit a counterexample database, $d = \{r\}$ over R, such that $d \models C$ but $d \not\models A \leq$ B.

Let $X = \{D \mid C \vdash D \leq B\}$ and let $Y = $ schema(R)$-X$. Now, let $d = \{r\}$, where r is the relation over R shown in Table 3.66 (see Table 3.37). We conclude the proof by showing that $d \models$ C but $d \not\models A \leq$ B.

Firstly, we show that $d \models$ C. Suppose to the contrary that $A_i \leq B_i \in$ C but $d \not\models A_i \leq B_i$. It follows that $A_i \in$ Y and $B_i \in$ X, and thus $C \vdash B_i \leq$ B by the construction of d. Therefore, on

Table 3.66 A counterexample relation

X	Y
$1\ldots1$	$1\ldots1$
$1\ldots1$	$0\ldots0$

using CC2, we have that $C \vdash A_i \leq B$. However, by the construction of d we must have $A_i \in X$ which leads to a contradiction.

Secondly, we show that $d \not\models A \leq B$. Suppose to the contrary that $d \models A \leq B$. Then by the construction of d, we have that $A \in X$, whence $C \vdash A \leq B$, leading to a contradiction. □

The next result strengthens Theorem 3.75 by considering unary FDs and unary CCs together [Bel95b].

Theorem 3.76 The axiom system, comprising the inference rules FD1 (reflexivity), FD3 (transitivity) for unary FDs, the inference rules CC1 (reflexivity), CC2 (transitivity) for unary CCs, and the mixed inference rules FD-CC1 (many-to-one) and FD-CC2 (one-to-one) for unary FDs and unary CCs, is sound and complete for unary FDs and unary CCs over a database schema **R**.

Proof. We leave the reader to verify that the axiom system is sound and sketch the idea of proving its completeness. Let Σ be a set of unary FDs F over **R** together with a set of unary CCs C over **R**. We are required to show that $\Sigma \models \alpha$ implies that $\Sigma \vdash \alpha$, where α is an FD or a CC.

Firstly, we assume that α is a CC. Define $CC(F) = \{B \leq A \mid A \rightarrow B \in F\}$ to be the set of CCs that can be derived from F on using the inference rule FD-CC1. It can be shown that $\Sigma \models \alpha$ if and only if $C \cup CC(F) \models \alpha$. The result then follows by Theorem 3.75.

We next assume that α is an FD, say $A \rightarrow B$. It can be shown that if $\Sigma \models A \rightarrow B$, then either $F \models A \rightarrow B$ or $F \models B \rightarrow A$. If $F \models A \rightarrow B$ then the result is immediate by Armstrong's axiom system, so assume that $F \models B \rightarrow A$ but $F \not\models A \rightarrow B$. Then by the completeness of Armstrong's axiom system we have $\Sigma \vdash B \rightarrow A$. Moreover, since $\Sigma \models A \rightarrow B$ by the soundness of FD-CC1 we have that $\Sigma \models B \leq A$ and by the first case above we have $\Sigma \vdash B \leq A$. The result now follows, since by FD-CC2 we have $\Sigma \vdash A \rightarrow B$ as required. □

Further investigation on the effects induced by the cardinalities of domains on data dependency satisfaction is carried out in [Kan80, Fag81, CK86, CKV90, Bel95b].

3.8 The View Update Problem

Users interact with a database system through its view (or external) level. A view is a relation comprising a portion of the conceptual level of the database system which provides the interface between the user and the database. Different views of the database may be set up for different groups of users. A view is defined as a relational algebra query over the database and is created by computing the answer to the query. It can be *virtual* (or equivalently *derived*) in which case it is recomputed each time the user accesses the view, or it can be *materialised* in which case the relation is physically stored in the database system. In addition, a view may be required to satisfy a set of integrity constraints such as a set of FDs and INDs. For simplicity, we will assume a user who is interacting with a single view, i.e. with the single relation resulting from computing the view definition. The interaction is carried out via relational algebra queries and updates on the view, as if the view were a relational database consisting of a single relation.

Let $V[\mathbf{R}]$ (or simply V when $\mathbf{R}$ is understood from context) be a view definition over a database schema $\mathbf{R}$, i.e. $V[\mathbf{R}]$ is a query over $\mathbf{R}$. We denote the set of attributes of the relation schema induced by $V[\mathbf{R}]$ by schema($V[\mathbf{R}]$) (or simply schema(V) when $\mathbf{R}$ is understood from context). Given a database d over $\mathbf{R}$ at the conceptual level the result of computing $V[\mathbf{R}]$ with respect to d, i.e. the actual view, is given by $V[\mathbf{R}](d)$ (or simply $V(d)$ if $\mathbf{R}$ is understood from context).

Querying a view $V(d)$ is straightforward from the DBMS's point of view. The user's query is simply composed with $V(d)$ to obtain the output, i.e. it is computed over $V(d)$, which is a relation over the relation schema induced by $V[\mathbf{R}]$. On the other hand updating a view is a difficult problem, called the *view update problem*. We will only consider updates that are insertions or deletions, recalling that a modification can be simulated by a deletion followed by an insertion; see Subsection 3.2.4 for more details on an update language for the relational model.

As a running example for this section, suppose that a database schema $\mathbf{R}$ at the conceptual level has two relation schemas EMPLOYEE (abbreviate to E) and DEPARTMENT (abbreviated to D) such that EMPLOYEE has attributes: ENAME (employee name), DNAME (department name), SALARY (employee salary), and DEPARTMENT has attributes: DNAME, MGR (manager name), and LOC (department location). In addition, we assume a set F of FDs over $\mathbf{R}$, where F = {E: ENAME → {DNAME, SALARY}, D: DNAME → {MGR, LOC}, D: MGR → DNAME}, meaning that employee name is a key for E and, correspondingly, DNAME and MGR are keys for D, and a set I of INDs over $\mathbf{R}$, where I = {E[DNAME] ⊆ D[DNAME], D[DNAME] ⊆ E[DNAME], D[MGR] ⊆ E[ENAME]}, meaning that employees work in established departments and all department have at least one employee, and, in addition, managers are also employees. We let $d = \{r_1, r_2\}$ be a database over $\mathbf{R}$, where r_1 over EMPLOYEE is shown in Table 3.67 and r_2 over DEPARTMENT is shown in Table 3.68; it can be verified that $d \models \Sigma$, where $\Sigma = F \cup I$.

Table 3.67 The relation r_1 over EMPLOYEE

ENAME	DNAME	SALARY
John	Computing	30,000
Jack	Computing	30,000
Jill	Maths	25,000
Joe	Maths	35,000
Jake	Biology	35,000

Table 3.68 The relation r_2 over DEPARTMENT

DNAME	MGR	LOC
Computing	Jack	West London
Biology	Jake	West London
Maths	Jill	East London

We consider another database $d' = \{r_3, r_4\}$ over a database schema $\mathbf{R}'$ containing two relation schemas EMP_WEST and EMP_EAST, where schema(EMP_WEST) = schema(EMP_EAST) = schema(EMPLOYEE). The relation r_3, representing the employees working in West London, is shown in Table 3.69 and the relation r_4, representing the employees working in East London, is shown in Table 3.70. The database d' can be viewed as a distributed database, satisfying $r_1 = r_3 \cup r_4$.

Table 3.69 The relation r_3 over EMP_WEST

ENAME	DNAME	SALARY
John	Computing	30,000
Jack	Computing	30,000
Jake	Biology	35,000

Table 3.70 The relation r_4 over EMP_EAST

ENAME	DNAME	SALARY
Jill	Maths	25,000
Joe	Maths	35,000

Let us consider some views which are defined by the following relational algebra expressions:

V1. $\pi_{\{ENAME, DNAME\}}(r_1)$.

V2. $\pi_{\{DNAME, SALARY\}}(r_1)$.

V3. $r_1 \bowtie r_2$

V4. $\pi_{\{ENAME, LOC\}}(r_1 \bowtie r_2)$

V5. $\sigma_{DNAME = \text{'Computing'}}(r_1)$.

V6. $r_3 \cup r_4$.

The view V1, shown in Table 3.71, is a projection of r_1 giving us a list of the employees and the departments they work in. The view V2, shown in Table 3.72, is also a projection giving us the departments and salaries of employees. The view V3, shown in Table 3.73, is the join of r_1 and r_2 which combines information about employees and departments. The view V4, shown in Table 3.74, tells us in what locations employees work in. The view V5, shown in Table 3.75, tells us the employees who work in the Computing department. Finally, the view V6, shown in Figure 3.67, which is equal to r_1, gives us the list of employees working either in West London or in East London.

As stated above a view may be required to satisfy a set of integrity constraints. Rather than state the integrity constraints separately for the view, we assume that the set of integrity constraints that the view should satisfy is exactly the set of all integrity constraints that can be derived from the underlying set of integrity constraints that are satisfied in the database from which the view is constructed. Assume that we are given a set of data dependencies $\Sigma = F \cup I$ consisting of FDs and INDs over $\mathbf{R}$ defining the valid database states over a database schema $\mathbf{R}$. Then, since the view definition $V[\mathbf{R}]$ is a relational algebra query, the set of data dependencies

Table 3.71 The view V1

ENAME	DNAME
John	Computing
Jack	Computing
Jill	Maths
Joe	Maths
Jake	Biology

Table 3.72 The view V2

DNAME	SALARY
Computing	30,000
Maths	25,000
Maths	35,000
Biology	35,000

Table 3.73 The view V3

ENAME	SALARY	DNAME	MGR	LOC
John	30,000	Computing	Jack	West London
Jack	30,000	Computing	Jack	West London
Jake	35,000	Biology	Jake	West London
Jill	25,000	Maths	Jill	East London
Joe	35,000	Maths	Jill	East London

that should be satisfied in any view over $V[\mathbf{R}]$ is exactly the set of data dependencies that are satisfied in all views $V(d)$, where d is a database over $\mathbf{R}$ that satisfies Σ. Let us denote this set of data dependencies by $V[\Sigma]$. The *membership problem* for data dependencies *in views* is to determine whether a data dependency α is in $V[\Sigma]$ or not.

For the running example of this section we have,

1) $V1[\Sigma] = \{\text{ENAME} \to \text{DNAME}\}$,

2) $V2[\Sigma] = \emptyset$,

3) $V3[\Sigma] = F \cup \{R[\text{MGR}] \subseteq R[\text{ENAME}]\}$, where R is the relation schema of $V[\mathbf{R}]$,

4) $V4[\Sigma] = \{\text{ENAME} \to \text{LOC}\}$,

5) $V5[\Sigma] = \{\text{ENAME} \to \{\text{DNAME}, \text{SALARY}\}\}$ and

6) $V6[\Sigma] = \emptyset$, since, for example, if we add a tuple $<$John, Maths, 29,000$>$ to r_4, then $r_3 \cup r_4$ would violate both ENAME $\to$ DNAME and ENAME $\to$ SALARY.

For the view V6, if we have the additional integrity constraint that employee names in relations over EMP_WEST are disjoint from employee names in relations over EMP_EAST, which can be stated as the *exclusion dependency* [CV83] EMP_WEST[ENAME] $\cap$ EMP_EAST[ENAME] $= \emptyset$, then we have, as is the case in our example, that $V6[\Sigma] = V5[\Sigma]$.

From a practical point of view, if $d \models \Sigma$ then $V(d) \models V[\Sigma]$ and thus we need only maintain the consistency of the database defining the view. However, it may be useful to solve the membership problem for data dependencies in view, so that we can compute $V[\Sigma]$ when designing a view. Knowing $V[\Sigma]$ is useful for update purposes, since apart from the view

Table 3.74 The view V4

ENAME	LOC
John	West London
Jack	West London
Jake	West London
Jill	East London
Joe	East London

Table 3.75 The view V5

ENAME	DNAME	SALARY
John	Computing	30,000
Jack	Computing	30,000

update problem, we may reject an update if the resulting state of the view after the update does not satisfy $V[\Sigma]$. Moreover, the information embedded in $V[\Sigma]$ can be used to validate the view definition. For example, the user of a projection of r_1 may wish to maintain a key for EMPLOYEE with respect to F and thus would accept the view V1 but would reject the view V2.

We briefly survey the results concerning the membership problem for FDs in views, which is the problem of determining whether an FD is in $V[F]$ or not, given a set of FDs over R. In [Klu80] the negative result was shown, namely, that the membership problem for FDs in views is, in general, undecidable. If we consider only views which are constructed from relational algebra expressions, which do not include any difference operations and such that all the formulae of selection operations included in these expressions are simple, then the membership problem for FDs in views in co-NP-complete [IITK84]. Moreover, if the relational algebra expressions that are used to construct the view are further restricted so as not to include any union operations, then the membership problem for FDs in views can be solved in polynomial time in the size of the input [IITK84]. The membership problem for data dependencies in views in the presence of MVDs and JDs, in addition to FDs, is considered in [KP82, IITK84].

We now use the views we have defined above to illustrate some of the problems that arise when we update views. In particular, for each such view we will consider the insertion of a new tuple into the view and the deletion of an existing tuple from the view. We will not consider any update that violates the set of data dependencies $V[\Sigma]$ which should be satisfied by the view.

Consider the insertion of a tuple <Jerome, Computing> into V1. The only reasonable *translation* (see Definition 3.102) of this request is to insert <Jerome, Computing, *unk*> into r_1, where we allow attribute values which are *not* part of the primary key to have null values; we note that ENAME is the only key for EMPLOYEE with respect to F and thus it must also be its primary key.

Consider the deletion of the tuple <John, Computing> from V1. The only reasonable translation of this request is to delete the tuple <John, Computing, 30,000> from r_1.

Consider the insertion of a tuple <Maths, 30,000> into V2. In order to translate this insertion we need to insert a tuple <*unk*, Maths, 30,000> into r_1. However, the primary key value of this tuple will be null thus violating entity integrity. So it is not possible to insert such a tuple into V2.

Consider the deletion of the tuple <Computing, 30,000> from V2. In order to translate this deletion we could delete the first two tuples from r_1. There are several problems with this translation. Firstly, the IND D[DNAME] $\subseteq$ E[DNAME] will be violated, since no employees will remain in the Computing department. Secondly, for the same reason the IND D[MGR] ⊆ E[ENAME] will also be violated. Thirdly, the deletion of a single tuple from the view results in the deletion of several (in this case two) tuples in the underlying database and is thus ambiguous. Fourthly, assume that after the deletion of the tuple <Computing, 30,000> from V2 we request to re-insert this tuple into V2; then since we have no knowledge of the primary key, we cannot insert this tuple and thus we cannot recover the original view. So we should disallow deletion of tuples from V2.

Consider the insertion of a tuple <Jerome, 30,000, Computing, Jack, West London> into V3. The only reasonable translation of this request is to insert <Jerome, Computing, 30,000> into r_1. If instead we request to insert the tuple <Jerome, 30,000, Physics, Jerome, West London> into V3, then we need to insert <Jerome, Physics, 30,000> into r_1 and <Physics, Jerome, West London> into r_2.

Consider the deletion of the tuple <Joe, 35,000, Maths, Jill, East London> from V3. The only reasonable translation of this request is to delete <Joe, Maths, 35,000> from r_1.

Consider the insertion of a tuple <Jerome, West London> into V4. In order to translate this insertion we could either insert <Jerome, Computing, *unk*> into r_1 or we could alternatively insert <Jerome, Biology, *unk*> into r_1. The reason for our uncertainty is that there is an ambiguity as to which department Jerome works in. Next, consider the insertion of a tuple <Jerome, North London> into V4. We can insert the tuple <Jerome, *unk*, *unk*> into r_1, but since no departments are known to be located in "North London" we cannot insert a tuple into r_2 without violating entity integrity. Thus we should, in general, disallow insertions of tuples into V4.

Consider the deletion of the tuple <John, West London> from V4. The only reasonable translation of this request is to delete <John, Computing, 30,000> from r_1.

Consider the insertion of a tuple <Jerome, Computing, 30,000> into V5. The only reasonable translation of this request is to insert this tuple into r_1. Now, consider the insertion of a tuple <Jerome, Physics, 30,000> into V5. This has no effect on V5 and thus it would be *incorrect* to insert this tuple into r_1; the correct approach is to leave r_1 unchanged. Finally, consider the insertion of a tuple <Jill, Computing, 25,000> into V5. There are two approaches to handling this update. Firstly, we can reject this insertion on the grounds that if we insert this tuple into r_1 the FD ENAME → {DNAME, SALARY} will be violated, since Jill will then be working in two departments. Secondly, we can delete the tuple <Jill, Maths, 25,000> from r_1 and then insert <Jill, Computing, 25,000> into r_1 resulting in a relation that satisfies the FD ENAME → {DNAME, SALARY}. Thus in the first approach the insertion has no effect on V5 and r_1 remains unchanged and in the second approach we insert the tuple into V5 and modify the corresponding tuple in r_1. Herein we choose the first approach, since it avoids making an update to tuples that are not involved in the view, but on the other hand the second approach is semantically meaningful. Furthermore, if we take the second approach, there is no way we can re-insert the tuple <Jill, Maths, 25,000> into r_1 via a view update on V5, so in the second approach we cannot cancel the effect of inserting <Jill, Computing, 25,000> into V5.

Consider the deletion of the tuple <John, Computing, 30,000> from V5. The only reasonable translation of this request is to delete this tuple from r_1. Now, consider the deletion of a tuple <Jill, Maths, 25,000> from V5. This has no effect on V5 and thus it would be *incorrect* to delete this tuple from r_1; the correct approach is to leave r_1 unchanged.

Consider the insertion of a tuple <Jerome, Physics, 30,000> into V6. In order to translate this insertion we could either insert <Jerome, Physics, 30,000> into r_3 or we could alternatively insert <Jerome, Physics, 30,000> into r_4. The reason for our uncertainty is that there is an ambiguity as to which location Jerome works in. If we wish to avoid ambiguity we should disallow such insertions into this view.

Consider the deletion of the tuple <Jake, Biology, 30,000> from V6. Then, assuming the database d' satisfies the exclusion dependency, EMP_WEST[ENAME] ∩ EMP_EAST[ENAME] = ∅, the only reasonable translation of this request is to delete this tuple from r_3. In the absence of this exclusion dependency, when this tuple is present in both r_3 and r_4 there is ambiguity as to whether to delete this tuple from r_3 or from r_4; we could just remove it from both these relations. If we wish to avoid ambiguity we should, in some cases, disallow deletions from this view.

We proceed to consider a formalism for dealing with the view update problem. Let U be an update over a view definition $V[R]$ and $v' = U(v)$ be the effect of the update U on the view $v = V(d)$, where d is a database over R. Also, let T be an update over the database schema R and $d' = T(d)$ be the effect of the update T on the database d over R. We assume that we are given a set Σ of integrity constraints comprising a set F of FDs over R together with a set I of INDs over R; Σ defines the set of allowable database states over R.

Informally, a database update $T(d)$ is consistent with respect to a view update $U(v)$ if invoking the view definition V on the updated database results in the updated view, i.e. $V(T(d)) = U(V(d))$, where $v = V(d)$.

For example, the database update which inserts <Jerome, Computing, *unk*> into r_1 is consistent with the view update which inserts <Jerome, Computing> into V1. Similarly the database update which deletes <John, Computing, 30,000> from r_1 is consistent with the view update which deletes <John, Computing> from V1. On the other hand, there is no database update which is consistent with the view update that inserts tuples such as <Maths, 30,000> into V2. Similarly, there is no database update which is consistent with the view update that deletes tuples such as <Computing, 30,000> from V2. The reader can find other examples of consistent database updates for the views V3 and V5, and examples of inconsistent database updates for the views V4 and V6.

A database update $T(d)$ is *acceptable* with respect to a view update $U(v)$ if whenever $U(v)$ is unchanged, i.e. $U(v) = v$, then the database state is unchanged, i.e. $T(d) = d$.

For example, the database update which inserts the tuple <Jerome, Physics, 30,000> into r_1 is not acceptable with respect to the view update that inserts this tuple into V5. On the other hand, the database update that leaves r_1 unchanged is acceptable with respect to the insertion of the above tuple into V5. Similarly, the database update that leaves r_1 unchanged is the only acceptable update with respect to the deletion of the tuple <Jill, Maths, 25,000> from V5.

A final requirement is that, in addition, the resulting state $T(d)$ must satisfy the given set Σ of FDs and INDs over R. For example, the deletion of the tuple <Jake, Biology> from the view V1 cannot be translated by deleting the tuple <Jake, Biology, 35,000> from r_1, since the IND D[DNAME] ⊆ E[DNAME] would then be violated.

Definition 3.102 (Translation) An update $d' = T(d)$ over R is said to be *consistent* with respect to a view update $v' = U(v)$, where $v = V(d)$, if the diagram shown in Figure 3.7 commutes, and is *acceptable* with respect to $U(v)$, if whenever $U(v) = v$ then $T(d) = d$.

An update T over **R** is said to be a *translation* of a view update U over $V[\mathbf{R}]$ with respect to a set Σ of FDs and INDs over **R**, if for all databases d over **R** that satisfy Σ, the following conditions are true:

1) $T(d)$ is consistent with respect to $U(v)$.

2) $T(d)$ is acceptable with respect to $U(v)$.

3) $T(d) \models \Sigma$.   ∎

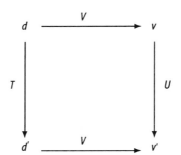

Fig 3.7 Commutative diagram for consistent view updates

Recall that by Definition 3.42 in Subsection 3.2.4 a transaction is the composition of several updates; for the rest of this section we will not distinguish between updates and transactions and refer to both as updates.

Informally, a set of view updates is *complete* if it is closed under composition and for every view update U there exists is another view update U' which cancels the effect of U. Suppose that the translation of the deletion of the tuple <Maths, 35,000> from V2 is the deletion of the tuple <Joe, Maths, 35,000> from r_1. Then we cannot cancel the effect of this deletion by inserting a tuple into the current state of V2 since we have lost knowledge of the primary key of the related tuple in r_1.

Definition 3.103 (Complete view updates)   A set S of view updates over **R** is said to be *complete* with respect to a view definition $V[\mathbf{R}]$ if the following conditions are true:

1) Whenever the updates U_1, $U_2 \in S$, it is also the case that the composed update $U_1 U_2$ is also in S (i.e. the update $U_1 U_2$ resulting from composing U_1 with U_2 is also in S).

2) For all databases d over **R**, whenever $U \in S$, there exists $U' \in S$ such that $U'(U(V(d))) = V(d)$.   ∎

We are now ready to define the notion of a translator which is a mapping from a set of complete view updates to a set of database updates such that

1) each view update in the set is mapped to a translation for that update, and also

2) when we compose two view updates in the set, then the translation of this composition is equal to the composition of the two translations corresponding to the two view updates.

We next formalise this notion.

Definition 3.104 (Translator)   A mapping T from a set of complete view updates S to a set of database updates is said to be a *translator* of S, if the following two conditions are true:

1) For all $U \in S$, $T(U)$ is a translation of U.

2) For all $U_1, U_2 \in T$, $T(U_1 U_2) = T(U_1) T(U_1)$. ∎

So we can now restate the view update problem as the problem of finding a translator of a set of complete updates. The solution we now present is the *constant complement* approach suggested by Bancilhon and Spyratos [BS81b]. Informally a complement of a view with respect to a database d is another view such that together the view and its complement have sufficient information to reconstruct the database d. Given a view and its complement a view update is translatable into a database update if we can find a translation that leaves the complement invariant. Thus a constant complement of a view represents the part of the database that is unaffected by the view update. The importance of translatable view updates is that when they exist then the inverse mapping of the view update is the desired translation which solves the view update problem.

As an example, consider the view V1 defined by: $\pi_{\{ENAME,DNAME\}}(r_1)$. The view $\pi_{\{ENAME,SALARY\}}(r_1) \times r_2$, which we call C1, is a complement view of V1, since $\pi_{schema(E)}($V1 $\bowtie$ C1$) = r_1$, i.e. we can reconstruct r_1 by joining V1 and C1 together and then projecting the result onto schema(E). Now consider an insertion of a tuple $<e, d>$ into V1, where e is a new employee of an existing department d. Then the translation that inserts the tuple $<e, d, unk>$ into r_1 solves the update problem for this insertion. (We assume that tuples whose salary attribute values are null are removed from the projection $\pi_{\{ENAME,SALARY\}}(r_1)$ when constructing the view complement C1, and thus C1 is indeed a constant complement. See Chapter 5 for a comprehensive treatment of null values.) Deletions can be handled similarly.

As another example, consider the view V3 defined by: $r_1 \bowtie r_2$. It is readily seen that the empty relation, which we call C3, is a complement view of V3 due to the inclusion dependencies E[DNAME] $\subseteq$ D[DNAME] and D[DNAME] $\subseteq$ E[DNAME] which ensure that no tuples are lost when joining r_1 with r_2. It is obvious that as long as Σ is satisfied C3 is a constant complement. Now consider an insertion of a tuple $<e, s, d, m, l>$ into V3, where e is a new employee, s is the new employee's salary, d is an existing department, m is its existing manager and l is its existing location. Then the translation that inserts the tuple $<e, d, s>$ into r_1 solves the update problem for this insertion. Deletions can be handled similarly.

As a final example, consider the view V5 defined by: $\sigma_{DNAME='Computing'}(r_1)$. The view $(r_1 - \sigma_{DNAME='Computing'}(r_1)) \times \rho_{DNAME \rightarrow D\_DNAME}(r_2)$, which we call C5, is a complement view of V5, since $\pi_{schema(E)}($C5$) \cup$ V5 $= r_1$, i.e. we can reconstruct r_1 by projecting C5 onto schema(E) and unioning the result with V5. Now consider an insertion of a tuple $<e,$ Computing, $s>$ into V5, where e is a new employee and s is his/her salary. Then the translation that inserts the tuple $<e,$ Computing, $s>$ into r_1 solves the update problem for this insertion. Deletions can be handled similarly.

We now formalise the notion of a complement of a view and how it can be used to solve the update problem. Given a view definition $V[\mathbf{R}]$, a complement of $V[\mathbf{R}]$ is another view definition $C[\mathbf{R}]$ such that for all databases d over $\mathbf{R}$, d can be uniquely reconstructed from the views $V(d)$ and $C(d)$. (As usual we write C for $C[\mathbf{R}]$ whenever $\mathbf{R}$ is understood from context.)

Definition 3.105 (Complement of a view)   A view definition C over **R** is a *complement* of a view definition V over **R**, if for all databases d over **R** the mapping, denoted by $(V \times C)$, that takes d to the pair $(V(d), C(d))$ is one-to-one (that is, $(V \times C)$ has an inverse mapping $(V \times C)^{-1}$). If C is a complement view definition of V and d is a database over **R** then $C(d)$ is said to be the *complement view* to the view $V(d)$.   ■

As can be seen from the above examples, a view definition does not, in general, have a unique complement. Take the view definition V3 assuming that databases over **R** are constrained to be pairwise consistent. Since V3 contains all the information in the database, all possible view definitions are complements of V3. In fact, the database d is always a complement of a view. It is natural to prefer a *minimal* complement, in the sense that there does not exist another complement that has more information in it. As an example consider a database schema **R** having two relation schemas R and S each having a single attribute, where schema(R) = schema(S) = {A}. Consider the simple view definition V = R. Then, obviously S is a complement of V but the symmetric difference, T = (R − S) ∪ (S − R), of R and S is also a complement of V, since S can be reconstructed by the relational algebra expression, (R ∪ T) − (T ∩ R). Both of these complements can be seen to be minimal and thus, in general, a view does not have a unique minimal complement.

We proceed to show how view complements can be used to solve the view update problem. An update U is translatable with respect to a complement C of a view definition V, if for all database states d, we can find a database state d' that reflects the update U on the view $V(d)$ and leaves the complement invariant, i.e. $C(d') = C(d)$.

Definition 3.106 (Translatable with respect to a complement)   A view update U is said to be *translatable* with respect to a complement C of a view definition V over **R**, if for all databases d over **R**, there exists a database d' over **R** such that $V(d') = U(V(d))$ and $C(d') = C(d)$.   ■

When a view update U is translatable with respect to a complement C over V, then we can translate U by using the mapping $\gamma(U)$, which is the mapping that makes the diagram shown in Figure 3.8 commute.

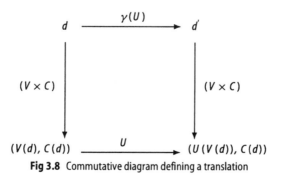

Fig 3.8 Commutative diagram defining a translation

The following result, which is central to the theory of view updates, was shown in [BS81b]. This elegant result states that a set of complete view updates has a translator if and only if there exists a complement C of V such that this translator is induced by $\gamma(U)$.

Theorem 3.77 Let V be a view over $\mathbf{R}$ and let S be a set of complete view updates over $\mathbf{R}$. The following statements are equivalent:

1) $\mathcal{T}$ is a translator of S.

2) V has a complement C such that for all view updates $U \in S$, U is translatable with respect to C and $\mathcal{T}(U) = \gamma(U)$. $\qquad\qquad\square$

By studying the above examples for view definitions V1, V3 and V5, the reader can verify that the following three classes of view definition have translators:

1) Projection views of the form $\pi_X(r)$, where r is a relation over R and F = {K $\rightarrow$ schema(R)} is a singleton set of FDs over R, such that X is a superset of K; that is, the set F of FDs states that K is the primary key of R. We allow attribute values which are *not* part of the primary key to have null values.

2) Selection views of the form $\sigma_M(r)$, where M is a conjunction of simple selection formulae involving only attributes in K, where F = {K $\rightarrow$ schema(R)} is a singleton set of FDs over R, i.e. K is a superkey for R with respect to F.

3) Join views of the form $r_1 \bowtie r_2$, where r_1 is a relation over R_1 and r_2 is a relation over R_2, together with the set F of FDs and the set I of INDs given by

   (i) F consists of one or both of K $\rightarrow$ schema(R_1) or K $\rightarrow$ schema(R_2),

   (ii) I = {$R_1[X] \subseteq R_2[X], R_2[X] \subseteq R_1[X]$}, where X = schema($R_1$) $\cap$ schema(R_2) is a superset of K, i.e. databases over $\mathbf{R} = \{R_1, R_2\}$ are constrained to be pairwise consistent and the intersection of their attribute set includes K.

Furtado and Casanova [FC85] provide a theoretical survey of the various approaches to tackling the view update problem, while Date [Dat86d] provides a discussion of the view update problem, which investigates the viability of updating various kinds of views. It is interesting to note that SQL2's support of view updates is fairly limited and does not cover the class of views that are known to be translatable; for example, join views are not supported at all [DD93]. Some early approaches to the view update problem can be found in [CA79, FSS79, DB82]. The constant view complement approach was initiated by Bancilhon and Spyratos in [BS81b] and was investigated in detail for the case when the view definition is a projection of a single relation database in [CP84b]. In [CP84b] it is shown that finding a minimal view complement is, in general, NP-complete. Keller and Ullman [KU84] consider a restricted class of views, called *independent views*. Informally, two view definitions are independent if any two views over these definitions correspond to some common database state. Thus if two view definitions are both independent and complementary then all possible view updates are translatable with respect to their complement. Suppose that, in addition, we are only interested in *monotonic* views, i.e. views such that when we insert tuples into the database relations no tuples are removed from the view. Then for such a monotonic view there exists a unique complement view. The notion of independent views was also studied in [BS81a] and a characterisation of such database schemes in terms of a single JD $\bowtie[\mathbf{R}]$ and a set F of FDs over $\mathbf{R}$ is given in [CM87]. Hegner [Heg84, Heg90, Heg94] refines the view complement approach by using a lattice theoretic approach. Gottlob and Zicari [GPZ88] generalise the view complement approach by relaxing the constant complement approach so as to allow the content of complement to decrease according to a suitable partial order. Keller [Kel85, Kel86] advocates a more general approach than the constant view complement approach. In particular, Keller proposes various algorithms that translate view updates in which ambiguity can be resolved by a dialogue with the user defining a view. Matsunaga [Mas84] advocates dealing with the view update problem via translation rules, which are invoked recursively, and special purpose translators for solving any ambiguities that arise. Tuchermann et al. [TFC83] and Casanova et al. [CFT91] present an alternative approach to the view update problem based on Abstract Data Types (ADTs). The underlying idea of this approach is to implement the translator of a view update (or a class of view updates) as an ADT whose operations define how to translate the view update into a database update. This approach has the advantage of being general but it requires the programming effort to implement the ADT, while the constant complement approach is completely automatic for the class of updates that can be translated. In addition, such ADTs need to be maintained if the update requirements change.

There is the final issue of materialised views versus virtual views. If the view is materialised then it takes up storage space but querying such a view is more efficient, especially if the view definition includes joins. Another point is that updates on materialised views need to be physically carried out both on the view and the underlying database; this incurs an extra cost factor. A materialised view needs to be updated in one of two situations, either when the view is updated or alternatively when the underlying database relations are updated. In the former case we are confronted with the view update problem and in the latter case we are confronted with the *view maintenance problem*. Let us consider the view maintenance problem further (see [GM95] for a survey of the various approaches taken to solving this problem). Suppose that the underlying database, say d, is updated via an update U. In order to update the materialised view, say V, we could first invoke the update U on d and then recompute V. The overhead in taking such an approach can be prohibitive if d is a very large database and computing V involves one or more joins. Thus we are interested in situations when U can be translated into an update, say U', on V such that when the translated update U' is invoked on V the effect is the same as recomputing the materialised view after updating d. If such a translation producing U' is possible then we say that the view V is *self-maintainable* [GJM96]. If a view is self-maintainable then it can be updated without accessing the underlying database and thus the overhead of updating it is kept to a minimum.

3.9   Discussion

The core of relational database theory has been presented in this lengthy chapter. It is evident that relational database theory is very rich with interesting results that directly affect the practical issues facing database programmers and users. Although the field has matured and the foundations have been established and are well understood, the basic building blocks of relational database theory are still a source for ongoing database theory research. This is especially true with regards to extensions of the basic relational model which will be discussed in later chapters. Not all the contributions to relational database theory have had direct impact on DBMS functionality but there are still issues, especially in the theory of data dependencies, that may still influence future versions of relational DBMSs.

Codd's seminal paper [Cod70] provided the initial impetus for relational database theory, while almost a decade later another seminal paper by Codd [Cod79] provided the basis for extending the relational model with semantic concepts. Codd's proposals are documented in detail in [Cod90]. A summary of the main ideas behind the relational model can be found in Codd's 1981 Turing award lecture [Cod82]. Precursors of the relational data model can be seen in the two papers [LM67, Chi68] which can be found in the reference list of [Cod70]. In [LM67] a database system, called the *relational data file*, is discussed together with a language, called *relational information language*, which is essentially a relational calculus query language. The important idea which is central to the relational model is that a relational database can be viewed as a finite model of a first-order logic language. The undecidability of domain independence with respect to the relational information language was shown in [DiP69], which implies the corresponding result for domain calculus queries (see Theorem 3.10). In [Chi68] a theory of data relations is presented together with a set-theoretic query language, which can be viewed as a relational algebra. Again it was Codd in his seminal paper [Cod72b], who showed the equivalence of the relational algebra and the relational calculus. In the theory of data dependencies Armstrong's seminal paper [Arm74], which presented a sound and complete axiom system for FDs, opened the doors for the plethora of results in this area. The paper by Beeri and Bernstein [BB79] provides a milestone in the development of data dependency theory dealing with the computational complexity of the implication problem. Fagin's seminal paper [Fag77b] is also important, since it instigated the investigation of lossless join decompositions independently of FDs. An interesting account of achievements of database theory up until the late 1980's can be found in [Ull87, Bis98].

3.10 Exercises

Exercise 3.1 In the network and hierarchical data models entities are related to each other (or linked together) via pointers, so querying of related entities is done by "pointer chasing". On the other hand, in the relational model entities are related to each other through their common values, so querying related entities is done by "joining" relations. Discuss the advantages of joining versus pointer chasing as a means of navigating through a database.

Exercise 3.2 Express the natural join using the renaming, Cartesian product, selection and projection operators.

Exercise 3.3 Express the answer to a Datalog query, with respect to a nonrecursive Datalog program P, using the relational algebra. (You may assume by Theorem 3.18 that P can be translated into a relational algebra expression.)

Exercise 3.4 Let r be a relation over schema R, with schema(R) = XY and s be a relation over schema S, with schema(S) = YZ. The *generalised division*, $\div^g$, of r by s, is a relation over schema R_1, where schema(R_1) = XZ, defined by

$$r \div^g s \;=\; \{t[XZ] \mid \exists t_1 \in r \text{ and } \exists t_2 \in s \text{ and } t[X] = t_1[X] \text{ and } t[Z] = t_2[Z] \text{ and }$$
$$\pi_Y(\sigma_{F_2}(s)) \subseteq \pi_Y(\sigma_{F_1}(r))\},$$

where $X = \{A_1, A_2, \ldots, A_p\}$, F_1 is the selection formula given by

$$A_1 = t[A_1] \land A_2 = t[A_2] \land \ldots \land A_p = t[A_p],$$

and correspondingly, $Z = \{B_1, B_2, \ldots, B_q\}$ and F_2 is the selection formula given by

$$B_1 = t[B_1] \land B_2 = t[B_2] \land \ldots \land B_q = t[B_q].$$

For example, if schema(R) = {SUPPLIER, PART} and schema(S) = {PART, PROJECT}, then $r \div^g s$ returns the set of all supplier project pairs of the form $<a, b>$ such that supplier a supplies all the parts used in project b. Give the relational algebra expression for generalised division [DD92a].

Exercise 3.5   Let us denote the fact that two relational algebra expressions, E_1 and E_2, are equivalent by $E_1 \equiv E_2$. Prove the following algebraic equivalences [Ull89]:

1) $E_1 \bowtie E_2 \equiv E_2 \bowtie E_1$.

2) $E_1 \bowtie (E_2 \bowtie E_3) \equiv (E_1 \bowtie E_2) \bowtie E_3$.

3) $\pi_X(\pi_Y(E)) \equiv \pi_X(E)$, if $X \subseteq Y$.

4) $\sigma_{F_1}(\sigma_{F_2}(E)) \equiv \sigma_{F_1 \land F_2}(E)$.

5) $\pi_X(\sigma_F(E)) \equiv \sigma_F(\pi_X(E))$, if the selection formula F involves only the attributes in X.

6) $\sigma_F(E_1 \cup E_2) \equiv \sigma_F(E_1) \cup \sigma_F(E_2)$.

7) $\sigma_F(E_1 - E_2) \equiv \sigma_F(E_1) - \sigma_F(E_2)$.

8) $\sigma_F(E_1 \bowtie E_2) \equiv \sigma_F(E_1) \bowtie \sigma_F(E_2)$, if the selection formula F involves only the common attributes appearing in E_1 and E_2.

9) $\pi_X(E_1 \times E_2) \equiv \pi_Y(E_1) \times \pi_Z(E_2)$, where $Y \subseteq X$ includes all the attributes of X in E_1 and $Z \subseteq X$ includes all the attributes of X in E_2.

10) $\pi_X(E_1 \cup E_2) \equiv \pi_X(E_1) \cup \pi_X(E_2)$.

11) $\pi_X(E_1 - E_2) \not\equiv \pi_X(E_1) - \pi_X(E_2)$.

Exercise 3.6   Physical query optimisation concerns the utilisation of the physical data structures that implement a relational database, and logical query optimisation concerns ordering the execution of the relational algebra operators in a query. Both types of optimisation aim to speed up the processing of queries. Discuss the importance of both types of optimisation with an example.

Exercise 3.7   A simple logical query optimisation rule for queries expressed in the relational algebra is to transform the query into an expression where the projections and selections are processed as soon as possible. Justify this heuristic rule with an example.

Exercise 3.8 Show how a relational algebra expression can be represented by a *query tree*, whose internal nodes are relational algebra operators and leaf nodes are relation schemas. Two query trees are said to be *equivalent* if the relational algebra expressions they represent are equivalent.

Given a query tree, devise an algorithm for logical query optimisation which transforms this query tree into an equivalent query tree by using the heuristic rule of Exercise 3.7 [Ull89].

Exercise 3.9 It is often claimed that the join operator is the bottleneck in relational database query processing. Suggest how indexing relations at the physical level might be used to optimise queries involving joins.

Exercise 3.10 We extend transactions to be *parameterised transactions* as indicated hereafter. Assume that we have available a countably infinite set of *variables* and that conditions may also be parameterised, i.e. they are of the form $A = x$ or $A \neq x$, where $A \in$ schema(R) and x is a variable. For example, if we have a relation schema STUDENT, with attributes NAME and COURSE, we can have a parameterised transaction over STUDENT, called CHANGE_COURSE(x, y, z), which is specified as

$$\text{delete}(\text{NAME} = x \wedge \text{COURSE} = y),$$
$$\text{insert}(\text{NAME} = x \wedge \text{COURSE} = z).$$

A *transaction call* to a parameterised transaction, say P over R, is a transaction, T over R, obtained by replacing all the variables in T by constants. For example, CHANGE_COURSE(John, Programming, Databases) is a transaction call to the parameterised transaction CHANGE_COURSE(x, y, z).

A *transaction schema* **T** over R is a finite set of parameterised transactions over R. The set of relations generated by a transaction schema **T** over R, denoted by GEN(**T**), is the set of all relations that can be generated by the effect, on the the empty relation, of a sequence of transaction calls to one or more of the parameterised transactions in **T**. For example, if **T** = {CHANGE_COURSE} then GEN(**T**) is the set of all possible relations over STUDENT.

Let F be a set of FDs over R and SAT(F) be the set of all relations over R that satisfies F. Show that SAT(F) = GEN(**T**) for some transaction schema **T** over R [AV85, AV89].

Exercise 3.11 Formulate an algorithm which decides whether a domain calculus query is allowed or not (see Definition 3.50 in Subsection 3.3.1).

Exercise 3.12 Prove that a query Q is domain independent if and only if for all *finite* underlying domains of **R**, $DOM_1(\mathbf{R})$ and $DOM_2(\mathbf{R})$, and for all databases d over **R** such that ADOM(Q) $\cup$ ADOM(d) is a subset of both $DOM_1(\mathbf{R})$ and $DOM_2(\mathbf{R})$, the equation

$$Q((d, DOM_1(\mathbf{R}))) = Q((d, DOM_2(\mathbf{R})))$$

holds.

Note that the only difference between the above definition of domain independence and Definition 3.47 is that we require $DOM_1(\mathbf{R})$ and $DOM_2(\mathbf{R})$ to be finite [Kif88]. (Hint: Show that given a database d the answer Q($(d, DOM_j(\mathbf{R}))$) does not depend on $DOM_j(\mathbf{R})$ as long as $DOM_j(\mathbf{R})$ is a superset of some sufficiently large finite domain with respect to Q and d.)

Exercise 3.13   Let Q be a domain calculus query over a database schema **R** whose output is a relation with k attributes. Furthermore, let $ADOM(d, Q)$ denote the set of all constant values, $ADOM(d) \cup ADOM(Q)$, and let $ADOM(d, Q)^k$ denote the Cartesian product of $ADOM(d, Q)$ with itself k times, for $k \geq 0, k \in \omega$.

Show that the following statements are equivalent [HS94c]:

1) Q is domain independent.

2) For all databases d over **R**, $Q(d) = Q(d) \cap ADOM(d, Q)^k$.

3) For all databases d over **R**, $Q(d)$ remains invariant when we replace all the domains, $DOM(A)$, where $A \in schema(\mathbf{R})$, by $DOM(A) \cap ADOM(d, Q)$.

Exercise 3.14   Let R be a relation schema, with $schema(R) = \{A, B, C, D, E, F, G\}$, together with a set of FDs $F = \{A \rightarrow BC, BD \rightarrow E, EC \rightarrow A, FG \rightarrow E\}$. Compute the closure X^+ with respect to F for all sets X of one, two and three attributes of R.

Exercise 3.15   Develop a linear time algorithm in the size of a set F of FDs over R, which computes the closure X^+ of X with respect to F [BB79].

Exercise 3.16   A set of attributes $X \subseteq schema(R)$ is a *subkey* for R with respect to a set F of FDs over a relation schema R if it is a (not necessarily proper) subset of a key for R with respect to F.

A subkey X for R with respect to F can be expanded into a superkey by adding to it attributes $A_1, A_2, \ldots, A_m, m \geq 0$, such that $X \cup \{A_1, A_2, \ldots, A_m\}$ is a superkey for R with respect to F but for each $A_{i+1}, 0 \leq i < m$, we have $A_{i+1} \notin (X \cup \{A_1, A_2, \ldots, A_i\})^+$.

Show that if X is a subkey for R with respect to F and $A_1, A_2, \ldots, A_m$ are chosen as above, then $X \cup A_m$ is also a subkey for R with respect to F. Devise a polynomial-time algorithm which, starting from a subkey for R with respect to F, expands it into a key for R with respect to F [Kun85].

Exercise 3.17   Suppose that for security reasons certain values in a relation are masked from users by presenting them as *null* instead of their true value. For example, managers' salaries may be confidential and thus masked as *null*. Demonstrate how security may be compromised in the presence of FDs and INDs (see [Mic87]).

Exercise 3.18   A *multilevel* relation schema M contains two types of attribute: *data attributes* A_i, which take on values from the domain of A_i extended with a distinguished value, *null*, and *classification* attributes C_i, which take on values from the *security lattice* indicating the security level needed to access A_i-values of tuples; C_i-values cannot be null. Given a relation r over a multilevel relation schema M, a tuple $t \in r$ and a classification attribute $C_i \in schema(M)$, we have that for a user with security level $c \leq t[C_i], t[A_i] = v$, for some data value v distinct from *null*, and for a user with security level $c > t[C_i], t[A_i] = null$. Thus a multilevel relation r over M can be viewed as the union of standard relations, one for each security level in the security lattice, such that users with a certain security level, say c, can view only those relations at levels greater than or equal to c. Define the notion of a primary key for multilevel relations [JS91a, JS91b, SJ91].

Exercise 3.19 Let F be a set of FDs over R and let us denote by $\mathcal{L}(F)$ the family of all *closed* sets of attributes in schema(R) with respect to F, i.e. $X \in \mathcal{L}(F)$ if and only if $X = X^+$.

Show that $\mathcal{L}(F)$ is a lattice ordered by set inclusion, and that it is closed under intersection, i.e. if $X, Y \in \mathcal{L}(F)$, then $X \cap Y \in \mathcal{L}(F)$. Show that $\mathcal{L}(F)$ is cover insensitive, i.e. if G is a cover of F, then $\mathcal{L}(F) = \mathcal{L}(G)$ [DK93].

Exercise 3.20 Let $\mathcal{L}(F)$ be the lattice of closed sets as defined in Exercise 3.19. A closed set $X \in \mathcal{L}(F)$ is *meet-irreducible* if $\forall Y, Z \in \mathcal{L}(F), X = Y \cap Z$ implies that either $X = Y$ or $X = Z$. The family of all meet-irreducible closed sets in $\mathcal{L}(F)$ is denoted by $\mathcal{M}(F)$.

Show that $\mathcal{M}(F)$ is the unique minimal subset of $\mathcal{L}(F)$ such that $X \in \mathcal{L}(F)$ if and only if X is the intersection of all the closed sets in $\mathcal{M}(F)$ that are supersets of X [BDFS84].

Exercise 3.21 We now consider an alternative characterisation of $\mathcal{M}(F)$, which was defined in the Exercise 3.20. Let MAX(F, A) be the family of all the maximal closed sets $\mathcal{L}(F)$ such that $\forall X \in$ MAX(F, A), $A \notin X$. Show that the following equality holds [MR86a]:

$$\mathcal{M}(F) = \bigcup_{A \in \text{schema}(R)} \text{MAX}(F, A).$$

Exercise 3.22 A *Numerical Dependency* over a relation schema R (or simply an ND) is a statement of the form $X \to^k Y$, where $X, Y \subseteq R$ and $k \geq 1, k \in \omega$. An ND $X \to^k Y$ is satisfied in a relation r over R, whenever $\forall t_1, t_2, \ldots, t_k, t_{k+1} \in r$, if $t_1[X] = t_2[X] = \ldots = t_k[X] = t_{k+1}[X]$ then $\exists i, j$ such that $1 \leq i < j \leq k+1$ and $t_i[Y] = t_j[Y]$. A set of NDs N is satisfied in r, denoted by $r \models N$, whenever $\forall X \to^k Y \in N$, r satisfies $X \to^k Y$.

Show that an FD is a special case of an ND, i.e. when $k = 1$, and prove that the following inference rules are sound for NDs, where N is a set of NDs over R [GM85a, GM85b]:

1) If $N \vdash X \to^k Y$ and $W \subseteq$ schema(R), then $N \vdash XW \to^k YW$.

2) If $N \vdash X \to^k YZ$, then $N \vdash X \to^k Y$ and $N \vdash X \to^k Z$.

3) If $N \vdash X \to^k Y$ and $N \vdash Y \to^m Z$, then $N \vdash X \to^{km} YZ$.

4) If $N \vdash X \to^k Y$, then $N \vdash X \to^{k+1} Y$.

Exercise 3.23 The concept of a weak instance defined below allows us to formalise the notion of a set F of FDs over a relation schema R being *globally* satisfied in a database d over a database schema **R**, with schema(**R**) = schema(R).

A relation r over R is a said to be a *weak instance* under F for a database d over **R**, if $r \models F$ and for all $r_i \in d, r_i \subseteq \pi_{\text{schema}(R_i)}(r)$. We say that a database d over **R** satisfies F, written $d \models F$, if there exists a weak instance under F for d.

Give a polynomial-time algorithm in the sizes of d and F that tests whether $d \models F$ or not [Hon82]. (Hint: Pad each relation $r_i \in d$ with unique nondistinguished variables in order to convert r_i to be a relation over R. Then take the union of all the padded relations $r_i \in d$ and invoke the chase procedure with respect to F on the resulting relation, interpreting the constant values in the relations $r_i \in d$ as distinguished variables. The resulting relation, when the chase procedure terminates, can be used to check whether $d \models F$ or not.)

Exercise 3.24 We call an FD of the form K $\to$ schema(R), where K is a key for a relation schema R with respect to a set F of FDs over R a *key dependency* of F. Assume a database schema $\mathbf{R} = \{R_1, R_2, \ldots, R_n\}$, with schema($\mathbf{R}$) = schema(R), and such that with each relation schema, $R_i \in \mathbf{R}$, we associate a set of key dependencies, F_i over R_i, where F = $\{F_1, F_2, \ldots, F_n\}$.

A database d is *locally* satisfying with respect to F, if for all $r_i \in d$, $r_i \models F_i$, and d is said to be *globally* satisfying with respect to F, if $d \models$ F (see Exercise 3.23 for the precise definition of when a database satisfies a set of FDs). We say that $\mathbf{R}$ is *independent* with respect to F if every locally satisfying database with respect to F is also a globally satisfying database with respect to F.

Prove that $\mathbf{R}$ is independent with respect to F if and only if $\mathbf{R}$ satisfies the uniqueness condition with respect to F, which is defined below [Sag83].

A database schema $\mathbf{R}$ satisfies the *uniqueness condition* with respect to F, if for all distinct relation schemas R_i, $R_j \in \mathbf{R}$, there does not exist a key K of R_j with respect to F_j and an attribute $A \in$ schema(R_j) $-$ K such that the closure of schema(R_i) with respect to F $- \{F_j\}$ contains KA.

Exercise 3.25 We extend the definition of independence given in Exercise 3.24 to take into account, both a set F of FDs over R and a set I of INDS over $\mathbf{R}$, as follows. Let G be a cover of the set of FDs that are logically implied by the data dependencies in both F and I. Then $\mathbf{R}$ is said to be *independent* with respect to F and I if every database, which satisfies I and is locally satisfying with respect to F, is also a globally satisfying database with respect to G [AC91].

Give an example of a set F of FDs over R and a set I of INDs over $\mathbf{R}$ such that $\mathbf{R}$ is independent with respect to F but is not independent with respect to F and I. Give a simple condition which guarantees that $\mathbf{R}$ is independent with respect to F if and only if $\mathbf{R}$ is independent with respect to F and I.

Exercise 3.26 A set I of INDs over a database schema $\mathbf{R}$ is *nonredundant* if there does not exist an IND $\alpha \in$ I such that I $- \{\alpha\} \models \alpha$. Devise a polynomial-time algorithm for finding a nonredundant cover of a set of typed INDs over $\mathbf{R}$ [MG90].

Exercise 3.27 Let X $\to\to$ Y be a nontrivial MVD in a set Σ of FDs and MVDs over a relation schema R, and let K be a key for R with respect to the set of FDs in Σ^+. Prove that either X $\to$ Y $\in \Sigma^+$ or that K $\cap$ Y $\neq \emptyset$ [Jaj86].

Exercise 3.28 A set F of FDs over R is said to be *embedded* in a database schema $\mathbf{R}$ if each FD in F is embedded in some relation schema $R_i \in \mathbf{R}$.

Let F be a set of FDs over R that is embedded in a database schema $\mathbf{R}$ and satisfies the following three conditions:

1) We have schema(R) = schema($\mathbf{R}$).

2) For each FD X $\to$ Y $\in$ F, there exists a relation schema $R_i \in \mathbf{R}$ such that X is a superkey for R_i with respect to the set F[R_i] of FDs, where F[R_i] denotes the set of FDs that are embedded in R_i.

3) For some $R_i \in \mathbf{R}$, schema(R_i) is a superkey for R with respect to F.

Show that given a set F of FDs satisfying the above three conditions and a database d over R, a relation r over R that satisfies $\bowtie[R]$ can be constructed by the sequence of joins

$$(\cdots((r_1 \bowtie r_2) \bowtie r_3) \bowtie \cdots \bowtie r_n),$$

where $d = \{r_1, r_2, \ldots, r_n\}$ and $r_i \models F[R_i]$ [Hon80].

Exercise 3.29 Let F be a set of FDs over R, G be a nonredundant cover of F and H be a minimum cover of F. Show that $|G| \leq |H|(\text{type}(R) - 1)$ [Got87].

Exercise 3.30 A database schema R *dominates* another database schema S with respect to a query language, $\mathcal{Q}$, if there exist sets of queries, Q_1 and Q_2 of $\mathcal{Q}$, such that for every database d_1 over R there exists a database d_2 over S such that $\{q_i(d_1) \mid q_i \in Q_1\} = d_2$ and $\{q_j(d_2) \mid q_j \in Q_2\} = d_1$. Intuitively, this means that databases over R can always be restructured into databases over S without any loss of information. Two database schemas R and S are said to be *query-equivalent* with respect to $\mathcal{Q}$, if R dominates S with respect to $\mathcal{Q}$ and S dominates R with respect to $\mathcal{Q}$ [Hul86].

Now, let R and S be two database schemas such that

1) $R = \{R\}$, $S = \{S_1, S_2\}$ and schema(R) = schema(S).

2) F is a set of FDs over R, F_1 is a set of FDs over S_1 and F_2 is a set of FDs over S_2, with $F^+ = (F_1 \cup F_2)^+$. (That is, F is a cover of $F_1 \cup F_2$.)

3) $I = \{S_1[X] \subseteq S_2[X], S_2[X] \subseteq S_1[X]\}$ is a set of INDs over S, where X = schema(S_1) $\cap$ schema(S_2) and $X \neq \emptyset$. (That is, I asserts the pairwise consistency of databases over S.)

4) F^+ contains either the FD X $\to$ schema(S_1) or the FD X $\to$ schema(S_2). (That is, S is a lossless join decomposition of R with respect to F.)

Prove that R and S are query-equivalent with respect to the query language that consists of all possible relational expressions containing only projection and join [AABM82].

Exercise 3.31 We define two subclasses of FDs which have been very useful in characterising desirable properties in the design of incomplete information databases and ask you to prove that when a set of FDs and proper circular INDs is reduced, then restricting the set of FDs to one of these subclasses provides a sufficient condition for no interaction to occur. (See Section 5.5 in Chapter 5 for motivation regarding these subclasses of FDs.)

Firstly, we define the subclass of FDs satisfying the *intersection property*. Two nontrivial FDs of the form R_j: X $\to$ A and R_j: Y $\to$ A are said to be *incomparable* if X and Y are incomparable. A set F of FDs over R satisfies the intersection property if $\forall F_j \in F$, $\forall A \in R_j$, whenever there exist incomparable FDs, R_j: X $\to$ A, R_j: Y $\to$ A $\in F_j^+$, then R_j: X $\cap$ Y $\to$ A $\in F_j^+$.

Secondly, we define the subclass of FDs satisfying the *split-freeness property*. Two nontrivial FDs of the form R_j: XB $\to$ A and R_j: YA $\to$ B are said to be *cyclic*. A set F of FDs over R satisfies the split-freeness property if $\forall F_j \in F$, whenever there exist cyclic FDs, R_j: XB $\to$ A, R_j: YA $\to$ B $\in F_j^+$, then either R_j: Y $\to$ B $\in F_j^+$ or R_j: (X $\cap$ Y)A $\to$ B $\in F_j^+$.

Prove that if I is proper circular, F satisfies either the intersection property or the split-freeness property and $\Sigma = F \cup I$ is reduced, then F and I do not interact.

Exercise 3.32 A *Template Dependency* (TD) is a generalisation of a JD, which intuitively asserts that if in a relation r over R we find tuples, $t_1, t_2, \ldots, t_n$, satisfying certain equalities amongst their attribute values, then r must contain another tuple t, whose attribute values are obtained from certain attribute values of the tuples t_i, for $i = 1, 2, \ldots, n$ [SU82].

Formally, we write a TD over R as $T = t_1, t_2, \ldots t_k/t$, where the t_i's and t are tuples of *variables* over R, and the variables appearing in t are a subset of those appearing in the t_i's. It is assumed that no variable may be both the A_i-value and the A_j-value of any two (not necessarily distinct) tuples, where A_i and A_j are distinct attributes in schema(R). (If this assumption holds for a data dependency, then we say that the data dependency is *typed*, otherwise we say that it is *untyped*. For example JDs are typed dependencies but INDs are untyped dependencies.)

A *homomorphism* h from a TD, T, to a relation, r over R, with type(R) = n, is a mapping from the variables in T to values in r such that $h(<v_1, v_2, \ldots, v_n>) = <h(v_1), h(v_2), \ldots, h(v_n)>$. A relation r over R satisfies a TD, T (i.e. $r \models$ T), if whenever there is a homomorphism h from T to r such that for all $i = 1, 2, \ldots, n$, $h(t_i) \in r$, then $h(t) \in r$ also holds. Satisfaction of a set of TDs in a relation and logical implication of a TD by a set of TDs are defined in the usual manner (see Section 3.5). A TD T over R is *trivial* if it is satisfied by every relation over R.

Show, with an example, how any JD can be expressed as a TD. In addition, prove the following statements about TDs over R [FMUY83]:

1) There exists a TD, T, such that for all other TDs, T', $\{T\} \models T'$ holds, i.e. there is a strongest TD over R.

2) There exists a nontrivial TD, T, such that for all nontrivial TDs, T', $\{T'\} \models$ T holds, where type(R) > 1, i.e. there is a weakest nontrivial TD over R. (Note that all TDs over R, with type(R) = 1, are trivial.)

3) If type(R) = 2, then there are only three distinct TDs over R, up to renaming of variables.

4) TDs are closed under finite conjunction, i.e. if Σ is a finite set of TDs over R, then there exists a single TD, T over R, such that $\Sigma \models$ T and $\{T\} \models \Sigma$.

Exercise 3.33 Assume that the underlying database domain $\mathcal{D}$ is linearly ordered; for example, $\mathcal{D}$ can be the set of natural numbers. Given a relation r over R we let $t_1 \leq t_2$ denote the fact that t_1 is less than or equal to t_2 according to the lexicographical order induced by the underlying linear order of $\mathcal{D}$, where the attributes in schema(R) are linearly ordered, with att(i) $\leq$ att(j) if and only if $i \leq j$. (See Section 1.9.2 of Chapter 1 for the definition of lexicographical order.)

We define an *Ordered Functional Dependency* (OFD) over R to be a statement of the form $X \leadsto Y$, where X, Y $\subseteq$ schema(R). An OFD $X \leadsto Y$ is satisfied in a relation r over R if whenever $t_1, t_2 \in r$ and $t_1[X] \leq t_2[X]$, then it is also true that $t_1[Y] \leq t_2[Y]$.

Give some examples illustrating the usefulness of the OFD. Which inference rules of Armstrong's axiom system are unsound for OFDs? Suggest alternative sound inference rules for OFDs.

Exercise 3.34 Let R be a relation schema and F be a set of FDs over R. Moreover, let $\mathbf{R} = \{R_1, R_2\}$, with schema($\mathbf{R}$) = schema(R), and thus R_1 and R_2 are projection views of R. Show that R_1 and R_2 are complementary views (see Definition 3.105 in Section 3.8) if and only if the decomposition $\mathbf{R}$ is lossless with respect to F [CP84b].

Exercise 3.35   Assume a relation schema R and a singleton set F of FDs over R containing the FD, K $\rightarrow$ schema(R). Show that, when we *disallow* null values in r, the projection view $\pi_X(r)$, where r is a relation over R and X is a superset of K, does *not* have a translator.

Exercise 3.36   Give sufficient conditions for a view containing a selection followed by a projection to have a translator, assuming a database with a single relation r over R and a singleton set F = {K $\rightarrow$ schema(R)} of FDs over R.

Exercise 3.37   It has been proposed to modify the definition of a translator by replacing the condition that the view has a constant complement by the condition that the translation of a view update must be *minimal*, in the sense that there is no transaction having fewer updates (i.e. insertions, deletions and modifications) that realises the translation [Kel85].

Show how this modified definition can be used to give a more intuitive semantics to view updates involving selection. (Hint. Assume a simple selection formula of the form A = yes, where DOM(A) = {yes, no}.)

In addition, show how the modified definition can be used to give semantics for view updates involving the join of two relations over relation schemas R_1 and R_2, respectively, such that the join attributes of R_1 and R_2, i.e. their common attributes, comprise a foreign key of R_1 referencing the primary key of R_2, where, apart from the primary keys of R_1 and R_2, no other data dependencies are specified.

4. Relational Database Design

One of the key activities of an IT department is database design, which is part of the wider activity of software analysis and design. Since the quality of the actual database depends, to a large extent, on the quality of its design, it is important that the methodology and algorithms used are known to be correct with respect to the requirements under consideration. One of the advantages of using relational database systems is that they have a conceptually simple tabular format which is easy to understand. The well-known *normal forms*, which are formally presented in Section 4.4, give the database designer unambiguous guidelines in deciding which databases are "good" in the quest to avoid "bad" designs that have redundancy problems and update anomalies, which are discussed in Section 4.1. The central idea in relational database design is that all the integrity constraints in the database should be describable in terms of keys and foreign keys. As was shown in Section 3.6 of Chapter 3, keys and foreign keys are just special cases of more general classes of data dependencies, i.e. FDs and INDs, respectively. The classical normal forms considered in Section 4.4 all result in a vertical decomposition of the database. That is, assuming that the decomposition $\mathbf{R}$ is lossless this corresponds to being able to recover a relation r over R by projecting r onto $\mathbf{R}$, resulting in a database $\{\pi_{\text{schema}(R_i)}(r)\}$ with $R_i \in \mathbf{R}$, and then joining the projections. In Section 4.5 we consider the possibility of a horizontal decomposition of a relation schema R, resulting in splitting R into two or more union-compatible relation schemas, i.e. schemas having the same attribute set. In this case a relation r over R will be split into two or more disjoint relations using one or more selection operations and can then be recovered by applying the union operator.

Two important criteria that the database designer needs to take into account in order to attain a decomposition with desirable properties are dependency preservation and losslessness with respect to combining the information via the natural join; both of these are discussed in Section 4.2. Moreover, the database designer also needs to take into account query efficiency and to avoid further redundancy caused by choosing a decomposition with too many relation schemas in it. In some cases this may lead the database designer to *denormalise* the database schema, meaning that we sacrifice being in a particular normal form by creating a single new relation schema which replaces two or more existing relation schemas already in normal form. By denormalisation we can enhance query efficiency, since the join operation of combining the information in two or more relations in the database is the largest bottleneck of processing relational queries. It may be the case that although a database schema is in the required normal form, we have replicated information in two or more relation schemas. Such redundancy can be avoided by removing all such replication. On the other hand, in a distributed environment replicated information may be essential for query efficiency.

Apart from the guidelines provided by the normal forms and desirable properties of database schema, relational database technology provides us with the essential algorithms for automating the design process. In Section 4.3 we discuss two fundamental approaches to relational database design: the *synthesis* approach and the *decomposition* approach. (You should not to confuse the decomposition approach with the other usage of the term decomposition which is simply a database schema; the different usages of decomposition will be clear from context). The synthesis approach is a bottom-up approach, i.e. we start from the data dependencies, which in our case will be FDs, in order to obtain a database schema in the required normal form. On the other hand, the decomposition approach is a top-down approach, i.e. we start from the set of attributes schema(R) over which the FDs are defined and *decompose* this set iteratively until the resulting database schema is in the desired normal form. Several algorithms based on these two approaches are presented in Section 4.6. It is important to note that some design problems have been shown to be NP-complete and thus some of the design algorithms provide only heuristic solutions.

When designing a relational database practitioners often use the Entity-Relationship model, described in Chapter 2, as a high level conceptual model. We demonstrate in Section 4.7 how an ERD can be converted into a database schema in a desirable normal form. Thus we view the entity relationship model as a convenient vehicle whose aim is to aid relational database design.

From now on we will assume that R is a relation schema, F is a set of FDs over R and **R** is a decomposition of schema(R) with schema(**R**) = schema(R) (or simply **R** is a decomposition, whenever R is understood from context).

4.1 Update Anomalies in Relational Databases

We have already assumed that relation schemas are in first normal form (1NF) in order to obtain a database model with simple data structures and straightforward semantics. First normal form relation schemas may possess the following two undesirable properties leading to a bad database design:

- Update anomalies.

- Redundancy problems.

We illustrate these problems via three examples.

Example 4.1 Let EMP_1 be a relation schema, with schema(EMP_1) = {ENAME, DNAME, MNAME}, where ENAME stands for employee name, DNAME stands for department name and MNAME stands for manager name. In addition, let F_1 = {ENAME $\rightarrow$ DNAME, DNAME $\rightarrow$ MNAME} be a set of FDs over EMP_1, implying that ENAME is the only key (and thus the primary key) for EMP_1. A relation r_1 over EMP_1 that satisfies F_1 is shown in Table 4.1.

Several problems arise with respect to EMP_1 and F_1. Firstly, due to entity integrity and the fact that ENAME is the primary key we cannot insert a tuple having a null ENAME-value. Thus we cannot add information about a new department unless it has already hired one or more employees. Such a problem is called an *insertion anomaly*.

Secondly, the complement of the first problem arises when we would like to delete all the employees from a department but still maintain the information about this department. Once again this is not allowed, since we cannot have null ENAME-values due to the fact that ENAME is a primary key. Such a problem is called a *deletion anomaly*.

Thirdly, assume that we would like to modify the MNAME-value in the first tuple of r_1 from Peter to Philip. In this case the FD, ENAME $\rightarrow$ {DNAME, MNAME} (resulting from ENAME being a key) is satisfied in the modified relation, but the FD DNAME $\rightarrow$ MNAME (where DNAME is not a key) is violated in the modified relation. Thus when modifying the MNAME-value in a tuple of r_1 it is not sufficient to check that the FDs resulting from the keys for EMP_1 are satisfied in r_1. A similar problem arises if we try to modify the DNAME-value in the first tuple of r_1 to Maths. Such a problem is called a *modification anomaly*.

Fourthly, there is the problem of redundancy of information. In particular, for every employee in a particular department the MNAME-value is repeated. Thus in r_1 the MNAME-value for Computing appears thrice, since there are three employees in the Computing department, and the MNAME-value for Maths appears twice, since there are two employees in the Maths department. Such a problem is called a *redundancy problem*. ■

Table 4.1 The relation r_1 over EMP_1

ENAME	DNAME	MNAME
Mark	Computing	Peter
Angela	Computing	Peter
Graham	Computing	Peter
Paul	Maths	Donald
George	Maths	Donald

Example 4.2   Let EMP_2 be a relation schema, with schema(EMP_2) = {ENAME, CNAME, SAL}, where ENAME stands for employee name, CNAME stands for child name and SAL stands for the employee's salary. In addition, let F_2 = {ENAME $\rightarrow$ SAL} be a set of FDs over EMP_2, implying that {ENAME, CNAME} is the only key (and thus the primary key) for EMP_2. A relation r_2 over EMP_2 that satisfies F_2 is shown in Table 4.2.

As with the previous example several problems arise with respect to EMP_2 and F_2. An insertion anomaly occurs when we try to insert a new employee having no children, since due to entity integrity null values are not allowed over CNAME. A deletion anomaly occurs when we have made a data entry mistake and, for example, we discover that Donald does not really have any children. Again, due to entity integrity we cannot delete all of Donald's children. A modification anomaly occurs when we attempt to modify the SAL-value in the first tuple from 25 to 27. The modified relation still satisfies the FD {ENAME, CNAME} $\rightarrow$ SAL, arising from the key {ENAME, CNAME}, but the FD ENAME $\rightarrow$ SAL will be violated. Finally, a redundancy problem occurs, since for every employee the SAL-value is repeated for each child of that employee. ■

Example 4.3   Let ADDRESS be a relation schema, with schema(ADDRESS) = {S, C, P}, where S stands for STREET, C stands for CITY and P stands for POSTCODE. In addition, let F_3 =

Table 4.2 The relation r_2 over EMP_2

ENAME	CNAME	SAL
Jack	Jill	25
Jack	Jake	25
Jack	John	25
Donald	Dan	30
Donald	David	30

{SC $\rightarrow$ P, P $\rightarrow$ C} be a set of FDs over ADDRESS. Both SC and PS are keys for ADDRESS with respect to F_3, so assume that PS is the primary key. A relation s over ADDRESS that satisfies F_3 is shown in Table 4.3.

As with the previous two examples several problems arise with respect to ADDRESS and F_3. An insertion anomaly occurs when we try to insert a new address which has not yet been assigned a postcode, since due to entity integrity null values are not allowed over POSTCODE.

A deletion anomaly occurs when we would like to delete the postcode of an address, say, due to an erroneous postcode being recorded for a particular address. Again, due to entity integrity we cannot delete the postcode.

A modification anomaly occurs when we attempt to modify the CITY-value in the first tuple of s from London to Bristol. SC and PC are still keys in the modified relation but P $\rightarrow$ C will be violated. Finally, a redundancy problem occurs, since for every postcode the city is repeated for each street in that postcode. ∎

Table 4.3 The relation s over ADDRESS

STREET	CITY	POSTCODE
Hampstead Way	London	NW11
Falloden Way	London	NW11
Oakley Gardens	London	N8
Gower St	London	WC1E
Amhurst Rd	London	E8

In the remaining part of this section we will formalise the notions of update anomalies and redundancy problems.

We call a set F of FDs over R *canonical* if all the FDs in F are nontrivial and of the form X $\rightarrow$ A, with A being a single attribute. For the rest of the chapter, when convenient, we *will assume without any loss of generality that sets of FDs are canonical*; this simplifies some of the definitions and proofs that follow.

Definition 4.1 (Key dependency)   Let R be a relation schema and F be a set of FDs over R. An FD of the form K $\rightarrow$ schema(R), where K is a key for R with respect to F is called a *key dependency* of F. The set of all key dependencies that are logically implied by F is denoted by KEYS(F).

(Recall from Subsection 3.6.1 of Chapter 3 that an attribute A $\in$ schema(R) is prime with respect to F if it is a member of the left-hand side of any FD in KEYS(F).) ∎

We are making the assumption that KEYS(F) contains all the fundamental information a database designer needs to know about the integrity constraints over R. A less general approach, which is subsumed by the above definition, is that KEYS(F) contains only the primary key of R with respect to F.

A compatible tuple with a relation r is a tuple such that if it is inserted in r then the resulting relation does not violate KEYS(F).

Definition 4.2 (Compatible tuple)   Let R be a relation schema, F be a set of FDs over R and r a relation over R. A tuple t over R is *compatible* with r, with respect to F (or simply compatible with r whenever F is understood from context), if $r \cup \{t\} \models$ KEYS(F).   ∎

A relation schema R has an insertion anomaly if there is a relation r over R that satisfies F and a tuple t over R such that t is compatible with r but when we insert t into r the resulting relation violates F.

Definition 4.3 (Insertion anomaly)   A relation r over R has an *insertion violation* with respect to a set F of FDs over R (or simply r has an insertion violation if F and R are understood from context) if

1) $r \models$ F, and

2) there exists a tuple t over R which is compatible with r but $r \cup \{t\} \not\models$ F.

The relation schema R has an *insertion anomaly* with respect to F (or simply R has an insertion anomaly if F is understood from context) if there exists a relation r over R which has an insertion violation.   ∎

A relation schema R has a modification anomaly if there is a relation r over R that satisfies F, a tuple u in r and a tuple t over R such that t is compatible with the relation resulting from deleting u from r but if we delete u from r and insert t into the result, then the resulting relation violates F.

Definition 4.4 (Modification anomaly)   A relation r over R has a *modification violation* with respect to a set F of FDs over R (or simply r has a modification violation if F is understood from context) if

1) $r \models$ F, and

2) there exists a tuple $u \in r$ and a tuple t over R such that t is compatible with $r - \{u\}$ but $(r - \{u\}) \cup \{t\} \not\models$ F.

The relation schema R has a *modification anomaly* with respect to F (or simply R has a modification anomaly if F is understood from context) if there exists a relation r over R which has a modification violation.   ∎

We view a *deletion anomaly* as a special case of a modification anomaly, since in order for such an anomaly to occur we must first remove one or more tuples from the original relation and then insert a new tuple into the resulting relation. For example, with reference to the relation r_1 over EMP_1, in order to record the information about a department having no employees we must first remove all the employee tuples for that department and only then insert the information about the department. This new tuple must have a nonnull ENAME-value, since ENAME is its primary key, and thus this department has at least one employee leading to a contradiction. Straightforward deletion of tuples from a relation does not cause any problems, as it can be verified that if a relation r satisfies F, then the relation resulting from removing a tuple t from r also satisfies F.

A relation schema R has a redundancy problem if there is a relation r over R that satisfies F, there is an FD $X \rightarrow A$ in F and two distinct tuples in r that have equal XA-values.

Definition 4.5 (Redundancy problem)   A relation r over R is *redundant* with respect to a set F of FDs over R (or simply r is redundant if F and R are understood from context) if

1) $r \models F$, and

2) there exists an FD $X \rightarrow A \in F$ and there exist two distinct tuples, $t_1, t_2 \in r$, such that $t_1[XA] = t_2[XA]$.

The relation schema R has a *redundancy problem* with respect to F (or simply R has a redundancy problem if F is understood from context) if there exists a relation r over R which is redundant.   ■

We now show the equivalence of the update anomalies and the redundancy problem [Vin91].

Theorem 4.1   Let F be a set of FDs over a relation schema R. Then the following statements are equivalent:

1) R has an insertion anomaly with respect to F.

2) R has a redundancy problem with respect to F.

3) R has a modification anomaly with respect to F.

Proof. Firstly, we prove that if R has an insertion anomaly then R has a redundancy problem. Suppose that R has an insertion anomaly and as a consequence there exists a relation r over R such that $r \models F$ and t is a tuple which is compatible with r but $r \cup \{t\} \not\models F$. It follows that for some FD $X \rightarrow A \in F$, where X is *not* a superkey for R with respect to F, $r \cup \{t\} \not\models X \rightarrow A$, since $r \cup \{t\} \models \text{KEYS}(F)$. Moreover, for some tuple $t' \in r$, $\{t', t\} \not\models X \rightarrow A$. Let u be a tuple over R, with $u[X^+] = t'[X^+]$, and such that for all attributes $B \in \text{schema}(R) - X^+$, $u[B]$ is a distinct value not appearing in r. (Recall Definition 3.60 given in Subsection 3.6.1 of Chapter 3, namely that X^+ is the closure of X with respect to F and that $Y \subseteq X$ implies that $Y^+ \subseteq X^+$.) Now, $u \notin r$, since X is not a superkey. Thus on replacing r by $r \cup \{u\}$ in Definition 4.5 of a redundancy problem the result follows, since it is evident that $r \cup \{u\} \models F$.

Secondly, we prove that if R has a redundancy problem then R has a modification anomaly. Suppose that R has a redundancy problem and as a consequence there exists a relation r over R such that $r \models F$, and for some FD $X \rightarrow A \in F$ there exist two distinct tuples $t_1, t_2 \in r$ such that $t_1[XA] = t_2[XA]$. It follows that X is not a superkey for R with respect to F and thus each key K for R contains some attribute that is not in X. Now, let t be a tuple over R, with $t[X^+ - A]$ $= t_1[X^+ - A]$, and such that for all attributes B $\in$ schema(R) $-$ $(X^+ - A)$, $t[B]$ is a distinct value not appearing in r. The result follows, since t is compatible with $r - \{t_1\}$ but $(r - \{t_1\}) \cup \{t\} \not\models$ F.

Thirdly, we prove that if R has a modification anomaly then R has an insertion anomaly. Suppose that R has a modification anomaly and as a consequence there exists a relation r over R such that $r \models$ F and t is a tuple over R which is compatible with $r - \{u\}$ but $(r - \{u\}) \cup \{t\} \not\models$ F for some tuple $u \in r$. The result follows by replacing r by $r - \{u\}$ in Definition 4.3 of an insertion anomaly. $\qquad\square$

Recall the definitions of inclusion dependency (Definition 3.69) and its satisfaction (Definition 3.70) given in Subsection 3.6.7 of Chapter 3, which generalise the notion of referential integrity. In particular, the IND R[X] $\subseteq$ S[Y] is satisfied in a database d over **R**, with R, S $\in$ **R**, if $\pi_X(r) \subseteq \pi_Y(s)$, where r and s are the relations in d over R and S, respectively. Also recall the definitions of noncircular INDs (Definition 3.71) and key-based INDs (Definition 3.72) given in Subsection 3.6.7 of Chapter 3. In particular, a set I of INDs over **R** is noncircular if the IND digraph $G_I = (N, E)$ is acyclic. The nodes in N are labelled by the relation schemas in **R** and there is an arc in E from R to S if there is a nontrivial IND R[X] $\subseteq$ S[Y] in I (R = S is possible). In addition, an IND R[X] $\subseteq$ S[Y] is superkey-based, respectively key-based, if Y is a superkey, respectively a key, for S with respect to a set F of FDs over **R**. If R[X] $\subseteq$ S[Y] is key-based and Y is a primary key for S then X is a foreign key for R. Thus when X is a foreign key, then a key-based IND provides a formalisation of referential integrity.

We illustrate the problems that arise with INDs that are not key-based with two examples. It is interesting to observe that there is very little material in the database literature concerning anomalies and redundancy problems that arise as a result of referential integrity constraints (cf. [CA84, MR86b, LG92, MR92a, Mar94, LV99]).

Example 4.4 Let HEAD be a relation schema, with schema(HEAD) = {H, D}, where H stands for head of department and D stands for department, and let LECT be a relation schema, with schema(LECT) = {L, D}, where L stands for lecturer and as before D stands for department. In addition, let $d = \{r_1, r_2\}$ be a database over **R** = {HEAD, LECT}, where r_1 over HEAD is shown in Table 4.4 and r_2 over LECT is shown in Table 4.5. Furthermore, let F = {HEAD : H $\rightarrow$ D, LECT : L $\rightarrow$ D} be a set of FDs over **R** and I = {HEAD[HD] $\subseteq$ LECT[LD]} be a set of INDs over **R**. The reader can verify that d satisfies both F and I. We note that I $\cup$ (F $-$ {HEAD : H $\rightarrow$ D}) $\models$ HEAD : H $\rightarrow$ D by the pullback inference rule and thus the FD HEAD : H $\rightarrow$ D $\in$ F is redundant. (See Subsection 3.6.11 of Chapter 3 for the definition of the pullback inference rule and other interactions between FDs and INDs.) We also note that we have *not* assumed that HEAD : D $\rightarrow$ H is in F and thus a department may have more than one head.

Two problems arise with respect to **R** and F $\cup$ I. Firstly, the interaction between F and I may lead to the logical implication of data dependencies that were not envisaged by the database designer and may not be easy to detect; recall from Subsection 3.6.11 of Chapter 3 that the implication problem for FDs and INDs is in general intractable. In this example the pullback rule implies that an FD in F is redundant.

Secondly, the IND HEAD[HD] $\subseteq$ LECT[LD] combined with the FD LECT : L $\rightarrow$ D imply that the attribute D in HEAD is redundant, since the department of a head can be inferred from the fact that L is a key for LECT. (Formally this inference can be done with the aid of a relational algebra expression which uses renaming, join and projection.) Thus HEAD[HD] ⊆ LECT[LD] can be replaced by HEAD[H] ⊆ LECT[L] and the attribute D in HEAD can be removed without any loss of information. (This point is discussed in [Sci86].) The problem here is that the right-hand side, {L, D}, of the IND HEAD[HD] ⊆ LECT[LD] is a proper superset of a key, namely the key L for LECT.   ∎

Table 4.4 The relation r_1 over HEAD

H	D
Peter	Computing
Donald	Maths
Paul	Maths

Table 4.5 The relation r_2 over LECT

L	D
Peter	Computing
Angela	Computing
Mark	Computing
Donald	Maths
Paul	Maths
Ray	Maths

Example 4.5 Let EMP be a relation schema, with schema(EMP) = {E, P}, where E stands for employee name and P stands for project title, and let PROJ be a relation schema, with schema(PROJ) = {P, L}, where as before P stands for project title and L stands for project location. In addition, let $d = \{r_1, r_2\}$ be a database over **R** = {EMP, PROJ}, where r_1 over EMP is shown in Table 4.6 and r_2 over PROJ is shown in Table 4.7. Furthermore, let F = {EMP : E → P} be a set of FDs over **R** and I = {EMP[P] ⊆ PROJ[P]} be a set of INDs over **R**. The reader can verify that d satisfies both F and I. We note that a project may be situated in several locations and correspondingly a location may be associated with several projects and thus {P, L} is the primary key for PROJ.

Let us assume that an employee working on a project works in one location only. The problem that arises is that the right-hand side, P, of the IND EMP[P] ⊆ PROJ[P] is a proper subset of a key. Thus F ∪ I does not provide us with sufficient information in order to ascertain in what location the employee is actually working in. It follows that a new attribute, say L', must be added to EMP and the IND EMP[P] ⊆ PROJ[P] be replaced by EMP[PL'] ⊆ PROJ[PL].

Even if an employee is assumed to work in all locations of the project he/she is working on a problem arises, which is related to an insertion anomaly. Suppose that an employee is assigned to a project which has not yet been allocated a location. Due to entity integrity such a project cannot be recorded in the relation over PROJ. However, if the project is recorded in the relation over EMP then the IND EMP[P] ⊆ PROJ[P] is violated. Therefore projects are always associated with locations and thus it is sensible to carry out the modifications to the relation schema EMP and the set I of INDs mentioned above.   ∎

Table 4.6 The relation r_1 over EMP

E	P
Mark	Alpha
Naomi	Beta

Table 4.7 The relation r_2 over PROJ

P	L
Alpha	London
Beta	London
Alpha	Paris

We defer the formalisation of the problems exhibited by the above examples that arise in the presence of INDs to Subsection 4.4.4. We now illustrate with an example the problems that arise with sets of INDs that are circular (cf. [Sci86]).

Example 4.6   Let BOSS be a relation schema with schema(BOSS) = {EMP#, MGR#} and let I be the singleton circular IND set {BOSS[MGR#] ⊆ BOSS[EMP#]} asserting that every manager is also an employee. Thus, if r is a relation over BOSS and we insert the tuple $<e, m>$ into r, then we also need to insert a tuple $<m, x>$ for some employee x, who is the manager of m. It follows that r must contain a tuple of the form $<x, x>$ for some employee x, since r must be finite. Thus we must record the fact that at least one employee must be a manager of himself/herself.

We can solve this problem by replacing the relation schema BOSS by the two relation schemas EMPS, with schema(EMPS) = {EMP#}, and BOSSES, with schema(BOSSES) = {MGR#}, and replacing I by the noncircular set {BOSSES[MGR#] ⊆ EMPS[EMP#]}. Moreover, in order not to lose the knowledge of who the manager of a particular employee is, we can safely assume that information pertaining to departments including the MGR# of its manager is contained in a separate department relation schema, say DEPT.   ■

4.2   Desirable Properties of Database Decompositions

The first desirable property of a decomposition **R** is that it be a lossless join decomposition with respect to F. Recall from Subsection 3.6.4 of Chapter 3 that a lossless join decomposition implies that we can project a relation onto a decomposition and then join the projections without loss of information. In order to refresh the reader's memory we repeat the formal definition of lossless join decomposition.

Definition 4.6 (Lossless join decomposition)   Let $\mathbf{R} = \{R_1, R_2, \ldots, R_n\}$ be a database schema and recall that schema(**R**) = $\bigcup_{i \in I}$ schema(R_i), where $I = \{1, 2, \ldots, n\}$. Then **R** is a *lossless join decomposition* of schema(**R**) with respect to a set F of FDs (or simply the decomposition **R** is lossless with respect to F) if for all relations, r over R, with schema(R) = schema(**R**), such that $r \models F$, the following equation holds:

$$r = \pi_{R_1}(r) \bowtie \pi_{R_2}(r) \bowtie \cdots \bowtie \pi_{R_n}(r).$$ ■

Recall from Subsection 3.6.6 of Chapter 3 that the projection of a set F of FDs over R onto a relation schema S is the subset of FDs X → Y ∈ F such that both X and Y are contained in schema(S). In order to refresh the reader's memory we again repeat the formal definition of the projection of a set F of FDs onto a relation schema.

Definition 4.7 (Projection of a set of FDs)   The *projection* of a set F of FDs over R onto a relation schema S, with schema(S) ⊆ schema(R), denoted by F[S], is given by

$$F[S] = \{X \to Y \mid X \to Y \in F \text{ and } XY \subseteq \text{schema}(S)\}.$$

The FDs in F[S] are said to be *embedded* in S. The subset of FDs in F *embedded in a decomposition* **R** of schema(**R**), denoted by F[**R**], is the set F[**R**] = $\bigcup_{i=1}^{m} F[R_i]$.   ■

The second desirable property of a decomposition **R** is that it be dependency preserving with respect to F. Informally, **R** is dependency preserving with respect to F, if the closure of the union of the subsets of F that are embedded in the relation schemas $R_i \in \mathbf{R}$ is equal to the closure of F.

Definition 4.8 (Dependency preserving decomposition)   Let **R** be a decomposition and let F be a set of FDs over R, with schema(R) = schema(**R**). Then **R** is a *dependency preserving decomposition* with respect to F if there exists a cover G of F such that $G[\mathbf{R}]^+ = F^+$, i.e. such that all the FDs in G are embedded in **R**. ∎

We observe that $G[\mathbf{R}]^+ = F^+$ is true if and only if $(F^+[\mathbf{R}])^+ = F^+$.

Example 4.7   Consider a relation schema EMPLOYEE with four attributes: E#, ENAME (N), PROJECT (P) and LOCATION (L) together with the set F of FDs over EMPLOYEE, where F = {E# → schema(R), P → L}.

Let $\mathbf{R} = \{R_1, R_2\}$ be a decomposition of {E#, N, P, L} with schema(R_1) = {E#, N, P} and schema(R_2) = {E#, L}. It can easily be verified that P → L $\notin F^+[\mathbf{R}]$ and thus **R** is not dependency preserving with respect to F.

On the other hand, the decomposition $\mathbf{S} = \{S_1, S_2\}$, with schema($S_1$) = {E#, N, P} and schema(R_2) = {P, L} is easily seen to be dependency preserving with respect to F, i.e. $F[\mathbf{R}]^+ = F^+$.

Let STUD_POS be a relation schema, describing the linear ordering of students in a class, with the three attributes: SNAME (N), SUBJECT (S) and POSITION (P). Let F be a set of FDs over STUD_POS, where F = {NS → P, SP → N}. It can be verified that for no decomposition **R** of {N, S, P}, where for each R_i in **R** schema(R_i) is properly contained in {N, S, P}, is **R** dependency preserving. ∎

The following theorem was proved in [BDB79, LT83, Var84b].

Theorem 4.2   Let **R** be a database schema and F be a set of FDs over R, with schema(R) = schema(**R**). Then the following statements are true:

1) If **R** is a lossless join decomposition of schema(**R**) with respect to F, then there exists S ∈ **R** such that schema(S) is a superkey for R with respect to F.

2) If **R** is a dependency preserving decomposition with respect to F, and there exists a relation schema S ∈ **R** such that schema(S) is a superkey for R with respect to F, then **R** is a lossless join decomposition of schema(**R**) with respect to F.

Proof. Firstly, we prove (1). By Theorem 3.29 given in Subsection 3.6.4 of Chapter 3 concerning lossless join decompositions, we have that CHASE(T(**R**), F) has a winning row. We prove (1) by induction on the minimal number, say k, of chase steps required to produce a winning row in CHASE(T(**R**), F).

Basis. If $k = 0$, then the result follows vacuously, since R ∈ **R**.

Induction. Assume the result holds when the minimal number of chase steps required to produce a winning row is k; we then need to prove that the result holds when the minimal number of chase steps required to produce a winning row is $k + 1$.

Suppose that the last chase step applies the nontrivial FD $X \to A \in F$ to rows w_i and w_j in the penultimate state of $T(\mathbf{R})$ during the execution of CHASE($T(\mathbf{R})$, F) and that w_i is a winning row. By induction hypothesis $F \models$ schema(R_i) $\to$ schema($\mathbf{R}$)$-A$ holds. In particular, $F \models$ schema(R_i) $\to$ X holds by the decomposition and union inference rules. The result that schema(R_i) $\to$ schema($\mathbf{R}$) follows by the transitivity and union inference rules.

Secondly, we prove (2). Suppose that $S \in \mathbf{R}$ is a superkey for R with respect to F and that X denotes the set of attributes schema(S). Also, let G denote a cover of the set $F^+[\mathbf{R}]$ of FDs embedded in $\mathbf{R}$. Then X is also a superkey for R with respect to G, since $G^+ = F^+$ due to the fact that $\mathbf{R}$ is a dependency preserving decomposition. It follows that CLOSURE(X, G) = CLOSURE(X, F) = schema($\mathbf{R}$), where the algorithm CLOSURE that computes X^+ is given as Algorithm 3.8 in Subsection 3.6.3 of Chapter 3.

By inspecting the algorithm CLOSURE it can be verified that there exists a sequence of FDs in G^+, $X_1 \to Y_1, X_2 \to Y_2, \ldots, X_n \to Y_n$, satisfying the following property for $1 \leq i \leq n$: schema(R_0) = schema(S) = X and schema(R_i) = $X_i Y_i$, where $R_{i-1}, R_i \in \mathbf{R}$ and $X_i \subseteq \bigcup_{j=0}^{i-1}$ schema(R_j). The result now follows by induction on the number n of relation schemas in $\mathbf{R}$, recalling that if $\mathbf{R}$ contains two relation schemas then the result follows by Corollary 3.31 given in Subsection 3.6.4 of Chapter 3. $\qquad\square$

4.3 The Synthesis Versus Decomposition Approaches to Relational Database Design

There are two competing approaches to relational database design: the *decomposition* approach [Cod72a] and the *synthesis* approach [Ber76]. Both approaches start from a relation schema R and a set F of FDs over R and obtain a decomposition $\mathbf{R}$ of schema(R) possessing some desirable properties. (There is an unfortunate double meaning in the usage of the word *decomposition*; a decomposition of schema(R) has already been defined as a database schema $\mathbf{R}$, with schema($\mathbf{R}$) = schema(R), while the decomposition approach discussed in this section is a method of obtaining a database schema. The different usages of the term decomposition will be clear from context.)

The decomposition approach is a recursive process which at each step chooses an FD X $\to$ Y $\in$ F satisfying certain conditions and then replaces R with two schemas, R_1 and R_2, such that schema(R_1) = XY and schema(R_2) = schema(R) $-$ (Y$-$X). The set of FDs over R_1 associated with R_1 is $F^+[R_1]$ and the set of FDs over R_2 associated with R_2 is $F^+[R_2]$. The process terminates when each relation schema in the resulting decomposed database schema (or decomposition) possesses the desirable properties the database designer is aiming at.

An inherent difficulty with this approach is that, as shown in Subsection 3.6.6 of Chapter 3, computing a cover of $F^+[R_i]$ is intractable. Thus in order for this approach to be feasible (i.e. polynomial-time computable) the decomposition needs to be carried out together with an efficient computation of a cover of $F^+[R_i]$. Another drawback of the decomposition approach is that if we change the order in which the FDs X $\to$ Y are processed then the resulting database schema may also change and the quality of the decomposition may be affected. For instance changing the order in which the FDs in F are processed may result in one decomposition being dependency preserving and another not being so, or in one decomposition having more relation schemas than another (see [Fag77b, Section 4] for a discussion on these issues).

The main advantage of the decomposition approach is its simplicity. Another advantage is that the resulting decomposition is lossless. This losslessness can be proved by a straightforward induction on the cardinality of the resulting database schema, noting that when the cardinality of the database schema is two then the result follows by Corollary 3.31 given in Subsection 3.6.4 of Chapter 3.

Example 4.8   Let EMP be an employee relation schema, with schema(EMP) = {EN, SAL, CN}, where EN stands for employee name, SAL stands for salary and CN stands for child name. In addition, let F_1 = {EN → SAL} be a set of FDs over EMP.

Using the decomposition approach we obtain the database schema {R_1, R_2}, with schema(R_1) = {EN, SAL} and schema(R_2) = {EN, CN}. This decomposition is lossless and dependency preserving with respect to F_1.   ∎

Example 4.9   Let DEPT be a department relation schema, with schema(DEPT) = {EN, DN, MGR, SEC}, where EN again stands for employee name, DN stands for department name, MGR stands for manager name and SEC stands for the name of the manager's secretary. In addition, let F_2 = {EN → DN, DN → MGR, MGR → SEC} be a set of FDs over DEPT.

If we first choose the FD MGR → SEC and then the FD DN → MGR we obtain the decomposition {R_1, R_2, R_3}, with schema(R_1) = {MGR, SEC}, schema(R_2) = {DN, MGR} and schema(R_3) = {EN, DN}. This decomposition is lossless and dependency preserving with respect to F_2.

On the other hand, if we first choose the FD EN → DN and then the FD MGR → SEC we obtain the decomposition {R_1, R_2, R_3}, with schema(R_1) = {EN, DN}, schema(R_2) = {MGR, SEC} and schema(R_3) = {MGR, EN}. This decomposition is lossless but not dependency preserving with respect to F_2.   ∎

The synthesis approach uses the set F of FDs directly in order to obtain a decomposition of schema(R) possessing the required desirable properties. Normally, a cover G of F is first obtained in polynomial time; such a cover G is more desirable than F, if it removes from F as much redundancy as possible. Then a preliminary decomposition of schema(R) is obtained by creating a relation schema, R_i, with schema(R_i) = XY, for each FD X → Y ∈ G. This decomposition is dependency preserving with respect to F, since G is a cover of F. If the resulting decomposition is not lossless then a key is added to it thus obtaining a lossless decomposition by Theorem 4.2. Finally, improvements are made to the decomposition; for example, by removing attributes [BM87] or adding attributes [Sci83].

The synthesis approach is more complex than the decomposition approach, since heuristics such as adding or removing attributes may have to be used in order to obtain the required desirable properties. On the other hand, it is not always possible to obtain a decomposition which is dependency preserving and also satisfies the required desirable properties (for example being in Boyce-Codd normal form), so the improvements made to the initial decomposition may destroy some desirable property or properties (which may not be required).

Example 4.10   Assume the same relation schema EMP and the set of FDs F_1 over EMP as in Example 4.8. Using the synthesis approach we obtain the same database schema {R_1, R_2}, with schema(R_1) = {EN, SAL} and schema(R_2) = {EN, CN}, as was obtained by using the decomposition approach.   ∎

Example 4.11   Assume the same relation schema DEPT and the set of FDs F_2 over DEPT as in Example 4.9. Using the synthesis approach directly on F_2 we obtain the database schema $\{R_1, R_2, R_3\}$, with schema(R_1) = {EN, DN}, schema(R_2) = {MGR, SEC} and schema(R_3) = {DN, MGR}.   ■

4.4   Normal Forms

Normal forms were introduced in order to solve the anomalies and redundancy problems that may be present in 1NF relation schemas. Each normal form enforces some desirable properties so that, if the relation schema is in that normal form, various problems disappear. We will present several normal forms with respect to functional dependencies and one normal formal form with respect to functional and inclusion dependencies. We will not deal with more general normal forms that take into account other types of integrity constraint. In Subsection 4.4.1 we present *Second Normal Form* (2NF), in Subsection 4.4.2 we present *Third Normal Form* (3NF), in Subsection 4.4.3 we present *Boyce-Codd Normal Form* (BCNF), and in Subsection 4.4.4 we present *Inclusion Dependency Normal Form* (IDNF).

Other normal forms which involve other types of integrity constraint have also been suggested. For example, *Fourth Normal Form* (4NF) has been suggested as a normal form for FDs and MVDs [Fag77a, Fag77b]. *Fifth Normal Form* (5NF), also called *Project-Join Normal Form* (PJNF), has been suggested as a normal form for FDs and JDs [Fag79]. Finally, an ultimate normal form, called *Domain-Key Normal Form* (DKNF), which subsumes all of the above-mentioned normal forms (apart from IDNF), was suggested by Fagin in [Fag81].

All the normal forms incorporate keys and entity integrity into the design process, the underlying idea being that every integrity constraint specified for the application in hand should be logically implied by the set of keys relevant to the application. IDNF is a normal form which incorporates foreign keys and referential integrity into the design process, the underlying idea being that every integrity constraint should be logically implied by the keys and key-based INDs relevant to the application. For semantic reasons, discussed in Example 4.6 of Section 4.1, and computational problems arising with respect to the implication problem in the presence of circular INDs, which are discussed in Subsections 3.6.8 and 3.6.10 of Chapter 3, the set of INDs is restricted to be noncircular.

Relational database design methods that take into account both FDs and MVDs can be found in [ZM81, Lie85, BK86, YÖ92a, YÖ92b].

It is worth mentioning that there may be some conflict between obtaining a decomposition which is in a certain normal form and the performance of query processing. For example, let PARTS be a relation schema, with schema(PARTS) = {PNO, PNAME, QTY} and SUPPLIER be a relation schema, with schema(SUPPLIER) = {SNO, PNO, PRICE}. Suppose also that **R** = {PARTS, SUPPLIER} is a decomposition in a certain normal form. Moreover, let $d = \{r_1, r_2\}$ be a database over **R**, where r_1 is a relation over PARTS and r_2 is a relation over SUPPLIER. Now, suppose that the most common query users are interested in is $r_1 \bowtie r_2$. In this case it may be better to maintain the information in a single relation over a relation schema whose attribute set is schema(PARTS) ∪ schema(SUPPLIER). The act of joining relation schemas together in order to increase response time of query processing is called *denormalisation*. A minimal requirement of denormalising two relation schemas is that they join together losslessly with respect to the specified set of FDs. Another reasonable requirement is that of dependency preservation, i.e. that the denormalised database schema embeds a cover of the projection of the given set of FDs onto the resulting denormalised database schema. Given that the normalised database schema is dependency preserving the resulting denormalised database schema will also preserve the data dependencies. The trade off between normalisation and denormalisation is discussed in [SS82].

4.4.1   Second Normal Form (2NF)

Second normal form was first defined in [Cod72a]. Intuitively, a relation schema is in second normal if it is in first normal form and every nonprime attribute is fully dependent on each key for the relation schema with respect to its set F of FDs.

Definition 4.9 (2NF)   A relation schema R is in *Second Normal Form* (2NF) with respect to a set F of FDs over R (or simply in 2NF if F is understood from context) if for every nontrivial FD $X \rightarrow A \in F$, either X is not a proper subset of a key for R with respect to F or A is a prime attribute.

A decomposition **R** is in 2NF with respect to a set F of FDs over R, with schema(R) = schema(**R**), if each $R_i \in \mathbf{R}$ is in 2NF with respect to $F^+[R_i]$. (When no ambiguity arises we will often say that $R_i \in \mathbf{R}$ is in 2NF with respect to F to mean that $R_i \in \mathbf{R}$ is in 2NF with respect to $F^+[R_i]$.)   ∎

Let us consider the relation schema EMP_2 of Example 4.2 together with its set F_2 of FDs. EMP_2 is *not* in 2NF, since ENAME $\rightarrow$ SAL is a nontrivial FD, where ENAME is a proper subset of the key {ENAME, CNAME} and SAL is not a prime attribute. The reader can verify that the decomposition, $\{EMP_2^1, EMP_2^2\}$, with schema(EMP_2^1) = {ENAME, SAL} and schema(EMP_2^2) = {ENAME, CNAME} is in 2NF with respect to F_2.

We next give an alternative characterisation of 2NF, which is an immediate consequence of Definition 4.9.

Lemma 4.3   A relation schema R is in 2NF with respect to a set F of FDs if and only if for every nontrivial FD $X \rightarrow A \in F$, either X is a superkey for R with respect to F, or at least one of the attributes in X is nonprime, or A is a prime attribute.   □

2NF is not usually employed in practice as an end in itself. Rather it can be viewed as an intermediate step towards achieving 3NF.

4.4.2   Third Normal Form (3NF)

Third normal form was first defined in [Cod72a]. Intuitively, a relation schema is in third normal if it is in second normal form and there is no nonprime attribute that is transitively dependent on a key for the relation schema with respect to its set of FDs.

Definition 4.10 (3NF) A relation schema R is in *Third Normal Form* (3NF) with respect to a set F of FDs over R (or simply in 3NF if F is understood from context) if for every nontrivial FD X → A ∈ F, either X is a superkey for R with respect to F or A is a prime attribute.

A decomposition **R** is in 3NF with respect to a set F of FDs over R, with schema(**R**) = schema(**R**), if each $R_i \in \mathbf{R}$ is in 3NF with respect to $F^+[R_i]$. (When no ambiguity arises we will often say that $R_i \in \mathbf{R}$ is in 3NF with respect to F to mean that $R_i \in \mathbf{R}$ is in 3NF with respect to $F^+[R_i]$.) ∎

Let us consider the relation schema EMP_1 of Example 4.1 together with its set of FDs F_1. The reader can verify that EMP_1 is in 2NF with respect to F_1. On the other hand, EMP_1 is *not* in 3NF, since DNAME → MNAME is a nontrivial FD but DNAME is not a superkey for R with respect to F_1, and, in addition, MNAME is not a prime attribute. The reader can ascertain that the decomposition, $\{EMP_1^1, EMP_1^2\}$, with schema(EMP_1^1) = {ENAME, DNAME} and schema(EMP_1^2) = {DNAME, MNAME}, is in 3NF with respect to F_1.

Lemma 4.4 If a relation schema R is in 3NF with respect to a set F of FDs, then it is also in 2NF with respect to F. □

We next proceed to give an alternative characterisation of 3NF.

Definition 4.11 (Transitively dependent attribute) Let R be a relation schema and F be a set of FDs over R. An attribute A ∈ schema(R) is *transitively dependent* on a set of attributes X ⊆ schema(R) with respect to F (or simply A is transitively dependent on X if F is understood from context) if there exists a set of attributes Y ⊆ schema(R) such that F ⊨ X → Y, F ⊭ Y → X, F ⊨ Y → A, A ∉ X and A ∉ Y (i.e. X → A and Y → A are nontrivial FDs). ∎

Lemma 4.5 A relation schema R is in 3NF with respect to a set F of FDs if and only if every attribute that is transitively dependent on a key is prime.

Proof. We prove the result by contraposition.

If. Suppose that R is not in 3NF. Then there exists a nontrivial FD X → A ∈ F such that X is not a superkey and A is not prime. Let K be any key for R with respect to F. We can deduce that F ⊨ K → X, F ⊭ X → K and F ⊨ X → A. The result follows, since the nonprime attribute A is transitively dependent on the key K.

Only if. Suppose that an attribute A ∈ schema(R) is nonprime and that A is transitively dependent on a key K for R with respect to F. By the definition of transitively dependent it follows that there exists a set of attributes X ⊆ schema(R), such that F ⊨ K → X, F ⊭ X → K (which implies that X is not a superkey for R with respect to F) and F ⊨ X → A, where A ∉ X. By a straightforward induction on the minimal number of inference rules needed to prove X → A from F we can deduce that there exists a nontrivial FD Y → A ∈ F, where A is nonprime and Y is not a superkey. The result that R is not in 3NF with respect to F follows due to the FD Y → A ∈ F. □

The following theorem, which was proved in [JF82], shows that testing whether a relation schema is in 3NF with respect to a set of FDs is NP-complete.

Theorem 4.6   Given a relation schema R and a set F of FDs over R, the problem of deciding whether R is in 3NF with respect to F is NP-complete.

Proof. We first show that the problem is in NP. In order to test whether R is in 3NF with respect to F, we need to check for each nontrivial FD $X \to A \in F$ whether X is a superkey. This can be done in time polynomial in the size of F by using the algorithm CLOSURE, given as Algorithm 3.8 in Subsection 3.6.3 of Chapter 3, to compute X^+. If X is not a superkey, then we need to determine whether A is prime. This problem is in NP, since from part (2) of Theorem 3.24 in Subsection 3.6.1 of Chapter 3 we know that the problem of deciding whether an attribute $A \in$ schema(R) is prime with respect to F is NP-complete.

To show that the problem is NP-hard we present a polynomial-time transformation from the prime attribute problem mentioned above. Thus we would like to decide whether $A \in$ schema(R) is prime with respect to F.

Let B, C and D be new attributes not in schema(R) and let S be a new relation schema, with schema(S) = schema(R) $\cup$ {B, C, D}. In addition, let G be a set of FDs over S consisting of F together with the following FDs, whose left-hand sides are taken to be reduced (i.e. they are minimal with respect to the set G of FDs):

1) $ED \to$ schema(S) for each attribute $E \in$ schema(R),

2) schema(R)$C \to$ schema(S),

3) $BC \to A$, and

4) $D \to B$.

From (1) we can deduce that D and each attribute in schema(R) is prime with respect to G, since ED is a key for S with respect to G. From (2) we can deduce that C is prime, since schema(R)C is a key for S with respect to G. Furthermore, from (4) we can deduce that S is in 3NF with respect to G if and only if B is prime, since D is not a superkey for S with respect to G.

In order to conclude the proof we show that A is prime with respect to F if and only if B is prime with respect to G.

If. Suppose that B is prime with respect to G and thus BY is a key for S with respect to G for some set of attributes $Y \subset$ schema(S) − B. From (4) we can deduce that $D \notin Y$, otherwise BY would not be a key for S. Moreover, $C \in Y$, since no FDs in G apart from those in (1) functionally determine C nontrivially. Therefore, we can rewrite BY as BCZ, with Y = CZ. From (2), (3) and the fact that $D \notin Z$ we can deduce that $Z \subset$ schema(R) − A and thus $G \models BCZ \to$ schema(R) − A, since BCZ is a key for S. It follows that $F \models Z \to$ schema(R) − A, since $G \models BCZ \to D$ can only be derived on using (2). Thus ZA is a key for R with respect to F but Z is not, since CZ cannot be a key for S because of (2). The result that A is prime with respect to F now follows.

Only if. Suppose that A is prime with respect to F and thus XA is a key for R with respect to F for some set of attributes $X \subseteq$ schema(R) − A. From (2) and (3) we can deduce that BCX is a key for S with respect to G and thus B is prime with respect to G as required.   □

Third normal form was defined as a property of the relation schema over which the set F of FDs is specified and is thus independent of any particular relation r over R. We can also define 3NF for a given relation r over R as follows, recalling that $F(r)$ is the set of all FDs that are satisfied in r (see Definition 3.62 in Subsection 3.6.1 of Chapter 3). A relation r over R is in 3NF if R is in 3NF with respect to $F(r)$. The surprising result, not withstanding Theorem 4.6, is that the problem of testing whether a specific relation r over R is in 3NF can be solved in time polynomial in the size of r [DHLM92]. The proof hinges on Theorem 3.27 in Subsection 3.6.1 of Chapter 3, which states that for relations such as r we can test whether an attribute A $\in$ schema(R) is prime with respect to $F(r)$ in time polynomial in the size of r, and on the following observation. Given an attribute A $\in$ schema(R) we can test in polynomial time whether there is a nontrivial FD X $\rightarrow$ A $\in F(r)$ such that X is not a superkey for R with respect to $F(r)$. We conclude this subsection by outlining the proof of this observation. The *equality set* of r is defined as the family of sets of attributes of schema(R) such that Y is in the equality set of r, if there are two distinct tuples in r that agree exactly on Y. It can be shown that the closure of a set of attributes W of schema(R) with respect to $F(r)$ is the intersection of all the sets of attributes that include W in the equality set of r, or schema(R) if no set of attributes in the equality set of r includes W. Thus r violates 3NF if and only if A is nonprime and there is a set of attributes XA in the equality set of r such that A $\notin$ X and A is in the closure of X with respect to $F(r)$.

4.4.3 Boyce-Codd Normal Form (BCNF)

Boyce-Codd Normal Form (BCNF) was first defined in [Cod74]. Intuitively, a relation schema is in BCNF if it is in first normal form and the left-hand side of each nontrivial FD in the given set of FDs is a superkey for the relation schema with respect to this set of FDs. Historically, BCNF should have been called *Fourth Normal Form* (4NF), since it was proposed as an improvement to 3NF. According to Date [Dat92c], in 1973 Boyce had actually called this new normal form 4NF, but Codd [Cod74] called it 3NF viewing it as an improved normal form that supersedes 3NF. Since BCNF is stricter than 3NF database researchers began to refer to this new normal form by its current name, i.e. BCNF. Another interesting anecdote is that, again according to Date [Dat92c], in 1971 Heath defined 3NF in an equivalent manner to BCNF and thus maybe BCNF should have actually been called *Heath Normal Form*. Then, in 1977 Fagin [Fag77b] defined 4NF, a normal form which is stricter than BCNF taking into account both FDs and MVDs. Thus the historical opportunity to call BCNF by its rightful name 4NF was permanently lost. We have also noticed that database designers often confuse 3NF with BCNF and therefore the common statement that practical database design does not go beyond 3NF often means that practical database design actually aims for BCNF.

Definition 4.12 (BCNF) A relation schema R is in *Boyce-Codd Normal Form* (BCNF) with respect to a set F of FDs over R (or simply in BCNF if F is understood from context) if for every nontrivial FD X $\rightarrow$ A $\in$ F, X is a superkey for R with respect to F.

A decomposition **R** is in BCNF with respect to a set F of FDs over R, with schema(R) = schema(**R**), if each $R_i \in$ **R** is in BCNF with respect to $F^+[R_i]$. (When no ambiguity arises we will often say that $R_i \in$ **R** is in BCNF with respect to F to mean that $R_i \in$ **R** is in BCNF with respect to $F^+[R_i]$.) ∎

Let us consider the relation schema ADDRESS of Example 4.3 together with its set of FDs F_3. The reader can verify that ADDRESS is in 3NF with respect to F_3. ADDRESS is *not* in BCNF, since P $\rightarrow$ C is a nontrivial FD but P is not a superkey for R with respect to F_3. The reader can ascertain that the decomposition, {$ADDRESS_1$, $ADDRESS_2$}, with schema($ADDRESS_1$) = {S, C} and schema($ADDRESS_2$) = {P, C}, is in BCNF with respect to F_3.

The following lemma shows that BCNF is insensitive to the particular cover of the given set F of FDs.

Lemma 4.7   A relation schema R is in BCNF with respect to F if and only if for every nontrivial FD X $\rightarrow$ A $\in F^+$, X is a superkey for R with respect to F.

Proof. The if part is immediate from the definition of BCNF, so it remains to show the only if part. Assume that R is in BCNF with respect to F and that X $\rightarrow$ A $\in F^+$. We show that X is a superkey for R with respect to F.

We claim that X $\rightarrow$ A $\in F^+$ if and only if there exists a subset Y $\subseteq$ X such that Y is the left-hand side of a nontrivial FD in F. The claim follows by a straightforward induction on the minimal number of inference rules needed to prove X $\rightarrow$ A from F. The basis case is vacuously true, when no inference rules are needed, since in this case X $\rightarrow$ A $\in$ F. In the induction step there are two cases to consider. In the first case, the last inference rule to be used is decomposition which was preceded by augmentation in which case the result follows by inductive hypothesis. Similarly, in the second case, the last inference rule to be used is transitivity whereupon the result again follows by inductive hypothesis.

Now, by the above claim there exists Y $\rightarrow$ B $\in$ F such that Y $\subseteq$ X and B $\notin$ Y. In addition, Y is a superkey for R with respect to F, since R is in BCNF. The result that X is a superkey follows on using transitivity, since F $\models$ X $\rightarrow$ Y by reflexivity and F $\models$ Y $\rightarrow$ schema(R), since Y is a superkey. $\square$

We leave it to the reader to give a proof similar to the one provided in the above lemma in order to show that both 2NF and 3NF are also insensitive to the particular cover of the given set F of FDs. The following result can be obtained from the definitions of 3NF and BCNF.

Lemma 4.8   If a relation schema R is in BCNF with respect to a set F of FDs, then it is also in 3NF with respect to F. $\square$

The following result taken from [DF92] shows one advantage of having only simple keys.

Lemma 4.9   If a relation schema R is in 3NF with respect to a set F of FDs and every key for R with respect to F is simple then R is also in BCNF.

Proof. Assume that R is in 3NF and let X $\rightarrow$ A $\in$ F be a nontrivial FD. We need to show that X is a superkey for R with respect to F. Now, since R is in 3NF then either X is a superkey for R or A is prime. If X is a superkey then no violation of BCNF occurs, so assume that A is prime. It follows that A is a key for R, since every key for R with respect to F is simple and thus F $\models$ A $\rightarrow$ schema(R). By the transitivity inference rule for FDs we obtain F $\models$ X $\rightarrow$ schema(R) from F $\models$ X $\rightarrow$ A and F $\models$ A $\rightarrow$ schema(R). Thus X is a superkey for R as required and R is in BCNF. $\square$

In fact the above lemma is also a consequence of the stronger result shown in [VS93, Mok97], namely that if a relation schema R is in 3NF with respect to a set F of FDs but is not in BCNF with respect to F, then it must have at least two distinct keys which overlap, i.e. such that their intersection is nonempty.

Recall that we have assumed in Definition 3.57 given in Subsection 3.6.1 of Chapter 3 that all FDs are standard, i.e. we do not allow FDs of the form $\emptyset \rightarrow Y$. The next lemma follows from the fact that if the cardinality of the set of attributes of a relation schema R is two, then the left-hand side of every nontrivial FD in a set F of FDs over R must be a key.

Lemma 4.10 If $|schema(R)| \leq 2$, then R is in BCNF with respect to any set F of FDs over R.
$\square$

A sufficient condition for a relation schema to be in BCNF with respect to a set F of FDs over R is now given [TF82].

Lemma 4.11 If for all pairs of distinct attributes A, B $\in$ schema(R), we have that A $\notin$ $(schema(R) - AB)^+$, then R is in BCNF with respect to F.

Proof. We prove the result by contraposition. Suppose that R is not in BCNF and thus by Lemma 4.7 there exists a nontrivial FD $X \rightarrow A \in F^+$ such that X is not a superkey for R with respect to F. It follows that there exists B $\in$ schema(R) $- XA$, since X is not a superkey. The result follows, since $A \in (schema(R) - AB)^+$ on using the reflexivity and transitivity inference rules.
$\square$

The above lemma can be strengthened to if and only if, when the cardinality of the shortest key for R with respect to F is type(R)-1 [ZO92b].

We next show that R is in BCNF if and only if it is free from update anomalies and redundancy problems.

Theorem 4.12 The following statements, where F is a set of FDs over a relation schema R, are equivalent:

1) R is in BCNF with respect to F.

2) R has no redundancy problems with respect to F.

3) R has no insertion anomalies with respect to F.

4) R has no modification anomalies with respect to F.

Proof. By Theorem 4.1 it is sufficient to show that R is in BCNF with respect to F if and only if R has no redundancy problems with respect to F.

If. Suppose that R is not in BCNF and thus for some $X \rightarrow A \in F$, X is not a superkey. Let t_1 and t_2 be two tuples over R such that $t_1[X^+] = t_2[X^+]$ and for all B $\in$ schema(R) $- X^+$, $t_1[B]$ $\neq t_2[B]$. (Note that schema(R) $- X^+$ is not empty, since X is not a superkey.) The result that R has a redundancy problem follows, since it is evident that $\{t_1, t_2\} \models F$ due to the fact that $Y \subseteq X$ implies that $Y^+ \subseteq X^+$.

Only if. Suppose that R has a redundancy problem and as a consequence there exists a relation r over R such that $r \models$ F, and for some FD $X \rightarrow A \in$ F there exist two distinct tuples $t_1, t_2 \in r$ such that $t_1[XA] = t_2[XA]$. It follows that X is not a superkey for R with respect to F, since $t_1[\text{schema(R)} - X] \neq t_2[\text{schema(R)} - X]$. The result that R is not in BCNF follows immediately. $\square$

A more general definition of redundancy in a relation with respect to a set F of FDs was given in [Vin98]. Informally, a relation has redundancy in it, if it contains a value that is implied by the other values in the relation through its set F of FDs. When a relation has such a redundant value then any change to this value will result in the violation of the set F of FDs.

Consider the relation r over LECTURER shown in Table 4.8, where schema(LECTURER) = {ENAME, DNAME, UNIV}, together with the set of FDs F = {ENAME $\rightarrow$ DNAME, DNAME $\rightarrow$ UNIV}. Then r has redundancy in it, since it satisfies F and changing one of the two occurrences of MIT in r to, say UCL, results in the violation of the FD DNAME $\rightarrow$ UNIV. On the other hand, if we let $r_1 = \pi_{\text{ENAME,DNAME}}(r)$ and $r_2 = \pi_{\text{DNAME,UNIV}}(r)$, then the reader can verify that r_1 and r_2 are free of redundancy. As the ensuing theorem shows it is no coincidence that R is *not* in BCNF with respect to F.

Table 4.8 The relation r over LECTURER

ENAME	DNAME	UNIV
Paul	Computing	MIT
Angela	Computing	MIT

Definition 4.13 (Value redundancy)   Let r be a relation over a relation schema R that satisfies a set F of FDs and let t be a tuple in r. The occurrence of a value $t[A]$, where $A \in$ schema(R), is *redundant* in r with respect to F if for every replacement of $t[A]$ by a distinct value $v \in$ DOM(A) such that $v \neq t[A]$, resulting in the new relation r', we have that $r' \not\models$ F.

A relation schema R is said to be in *Value Redundancy Free Normal Form* (or simply VRFNF) with respect to a set F of FDs over R if there does not exist a relation r over R and an occurrence of a value $t[A]$ that is redundant in r with respect to F.   ∎

The following result, presented in [Vin98], shows that given a set F of FDs VRFNF is equivalent to BCNF.

Theorem 4.13   A relation schema R is in BCNF with respect to a set F of FDs over R if and only if R is in VRFNF with respect to F.

Proof. If. Suppose that R is in VRFNF and let $X \rightarrow A \in F^+$ be a nontrivial FD. Moreover, let r be a relation over R and let t_1 and t_2 be two distinct tuples in r. Now, since $t_2[A]$ is not redundant in r with respect to F, there exists a value, $v \in$ DOM(A), which is distinct from $t_2[A]$, such that replacing $t_2[A]$ by v results in the new relation r', with $r' \models$ F. We claim that $t_1[X] \neq t_2[X]$. There are two cases to consider. In the first case we have in r that $t_1[A] = t_2[A]$. Thus $t_1[X] \neq t_2X]$, otherwise $r' \not\models$ F, since in r', $t_1[A] \neq t_2[A]$. In the second case we have in r that $t_1[A] \neq t_2[A]$. Thus again $t_1[X] \neq t_2X]$, otherwise $r \not\models$ F. The claim is now substantiated implying that X is a superkey for R with respect to F, and thus R must be in BCNF with respect to F as required.

Only if. Suppose that R is in BCNF with respect to F. Let r be a relation over R, $t \in r$ and $A \in$ schema(R). There are two cases to consider. In the first case $A \in K$ for some key dependency K $\to$ schema(R) $\in$ KEYS(F). Then replacing $t[A]$ by a value not in ADOM(r) results in a relation r' that satisfies F. In the second case for all key dependencies K $\to$ schema(R) $\in$ KEYS(F), $A \notin K$, i.e. A is nonprime. Then replacing $t[A]$ by any distinct value $v \in$ DOM(A) such that $v \neq t[A]$ results in a relation r' that satisfies F. $\square$

As a corollary of Theorem 4.13 all the statements of Theorem 4.12 regarding the update anomalies and redundancy problems are equivalent to R being in VRFNF with respect to F. It is interesting to note that Vincent [Vin98] has also shown that, in the presence of FDs and MVDs, VRFNF is equivalent to R being in 4NF. Thus a relation schema being in VRFNF with respect to a set of data dependencies is a robust indication that this relation schema is free of redundancy.

A special case of BCNF, which is important, arises when a relation schema has a unique key with respect to its set of FDs. In this case there is only one choice of primary key and thus database design is made easier. We first define a normal form which requires a relation schema to have a unique key [BDLM91].

Definition 4.14 (UKNF) A relation schema R is in *Unique Key Normal Form* (UKNF) with respect to a set F of FDs over R (or simply in UKNF if F is understood from context) if the cardinality of KEYS(F) is one.

A decomposition **R** is in UKNF with respect to a set F of FDs over R, with schema(R) = schema(**R**), if each $R_i \in \mathbf{R}$ is in UKNF with respect to $F^+[R_i]$. (When no ambiguity arises we will often say that $R_i \in \mathbf{R}$ is in UKNF with respect to F to mean that $R_i \in \mathbf{R}$ is in UKNF with respect to $F^+[R_i]$.) ∎

Let us define LEFT(X) with respect to a set F of FDs over R, where $X \subseteq$ schema(R), to be the set of attributes in X that are either not present in any of the FDs in F, or are included in left-hand sides of FDs in F but not in right-hand sides of such FDs. More formally, assuming that F is understood from context, we have

$$\text{LEFT}(X) = \{A \in X \mid A \notin (X - A)^+\}.$$

Theorem 4.14 A relation schema R is in UKNF with respect to a set F of FDs over R if and only if LEFT(X) is a superkey for R with respect to F, where X = schema(R).

Proof. We first show by contraposition that LEFT(X) $\subseteq$ K, where K is a key for R with respect to F. If for some attribute $A \in$ schema(R), $A \notin K$, then $A \in K^+$ and thus $A \in (X-A)^+$ by the augmentation and decomposition inference rules. It follows that $A \notin$ LEFT(X), and therefore LEFT(X) $\subseteq$ K.

If. Suppose that LEFT(X) is a superkey for R with respect to F. It follows that LEFT(X) is a unique key for R due to the fact that for any key K for R LEFT(X) $\subseteq$ K.

Only if. Suppose that R is in UKNF and K is its unique key. We claim that K = LEFT(X) implying the result. We have already shown that LEFT(X) $\subseteq$ K and thus it only remains to show that $K \subseteq \text{LEFT}(X)$. If $A \notin \text{LEFT}(X)$, then $A \in (X-A)^+$ and thus $X-A$ is a superkey for R. It follows that $A \notin K$ as required, since K is the unique key for R with respect to F. $\qquad\square$

By the above proof if we strengthen the requirement that $\text{LEFT}(X)$ be a key for R with respect to F, instead of just being a superkey, the result still holds. An immediate consequence of the fact that $\text{LEFT}(\text{schema}(R)) \subseteq K$, for any key K for R with respect to F, is that a prime attribute belongs to all the keys for R if and only if it is a member of $\text{LEFT}(\text{schema}(R))$. Another immediate consequence of the above theorem is that UKNF can be checked in time polynomial in the sizes of R and F by using the polynomial-time algorithm given in Algorithm 3.8 in Subsection 3.6.3 of Chapter 3 that computes the closure of a set of attributes with respect to F.

A relation schema may be in UKNF with respect to a set F of FDs but not in BCNF with respect to F. For example, let EMP be a relation schema with $\text{schema}(\text{EMP}) = \{\text{EN, CN, SAL}\}$, where EN stands for employee name, CN stands for child name and SAL stands for the employee's salary. In addition, let $F = \{\text{EN} \rightarrow \text{SAL}\}$ be a set of FDs over EMP implying that $\{\text{EN, CN}\}$ is the unique key (and thus the primary key) for EMP. Thus EMP is in UKNF with respect to F, but EMP is not in BCNF with respect to F, since EN is not a key for EMP with respect to F. Thus, we must strengthen UKNF if we also require a relation schema to be in BCNF [Bis89].

Definition 4.15 (ONF) A relation schema R is in *Object Normal Form* (ONF) with respect to a set F of FDs over R (or simply in ONF if F is understood from context) if it is both in UKNF and BCNF with respect to F.

A decomposition **R** is in ONF with respect to a set F of FDs over R, with $\text{schema}(\textbf{R}) = \text{schema}(\textbf{R})$, if each $R_i \in \textbf{R}$ is in ONF with respect to $F^+[R_i]$. $\qquad\blacksquare$

We can now show that ONF is equivalent to 3NF and UKNF, so 3NF and BCNF are equivalent in this special case.

Theorem 4.15 A relation schema R is in ONF with respect to a set F of FDs over R if and only if it is in 3NF and UKNF with respect to F.

Proof. The only if part of the theorem is an immediate consequence of Lemma 4.8. For the if part suppose that R is in 3NF and UKNF and let $X \rightarrow A$ be a nontrivial FD in F. We claim that A is nonprime thus implying that X is a superkey for R and therefore R is in BCNF as required. Now, by the augmentation and decomposition inference rules $A \in (\text{schema}(R)-A)^+$ and thus there exists a superkey K' for R such that $A \notin K'$. The result that A is nonprime follows, since R is in UKNF and thus $A \notin K$, where $K \subseteq K'$ is the unique key for R. $\qquad\square$

We next consider two theorems pertaining to the computational complexity of testing whether a relation schema is in BCNF. The proof of the first theorem follows directly from algorithm CLOSURE, given as Algorithm 3.8 in Subsection 3.6.3 of Chapter 3, which computes the closure of a set of attributes X with respect to F.

Theorem 4.16 Given a relation schema R and a set F of FDs over R, the problem of deciding whether R is in BCNF with respect to F can be solved in time polynomial in the sizes of R and F. $\qquad\square$

The second theorem, which is proved in [BB79], shows that testing whether a proper subset of a relation schema R is in BCNF with respect to a set F of FDs over R is co-NP-complete; a relation schema S, with schema(S) $\subset$ schema(R), is said to be in BCNF with respect to a set F of FDs over R, if S is in BCNF with respect to $F^+[S]$. This implies that, assuming that P $\neq$ co-NP, testing whether R is in BCNF with respect to F is intractable.

Theorem 4.17   Given a relation schema R and a set F of FDs over R, the problem of deciding whether a relation schema S, with schema(S) $\subset$ schema(R), is in BCNF with respect to F is co-NP-complete.

Proof. We sketch the main idea of the proof. In order to prove the result we show that the complement of the above problem, i.e. the problem of whether S violates BCNF is NP-complete. Showing that the problem is in NP is easily done by testing whether for a guessed nontrivial FD X $\rightarrow$ A over R, XA $\subseteq$ schema(S) and $X^+ \neq$ schema(S).

To show that the problem is NP-hard a polynomial-time transformation from the hitting set problem, which is described in the proof of Theorem 3.35 in Subsection 3.6.6 of Chapter 3, can be given. Recall the description of the hitting set problem.

The hitting set problem: Given a family $S_1, S_2, \ldots, S_n$ of subsets of a set U, does there exist a subset W $\subseteq$ U, such that $\forall i \in \{1, 2, \ldots, n\}$, $|W \cap S_i| = 1$. Such a subset W of U is called a hitting set, in other words W is a hitting set if for each i the cardinality of the intersection of W and S_i is one.

Let R be a relation schema with schema(R) = U $\cup$ $\{B_1, B_2, \ldots, B_n, C, D\}$, where $\{B_1, B_2, \ldots, B_n, C, D\} \cap U = \emptyset$, and let schema(S) be a relation schema with schema(S) = U $\cup$ {C, D}. We define four sets of FDs, F_1, F_2, F_3 and F_4 over R and let F = $F_1 \cup F_2 \cup F_3 \cup F_4$.

1) $F_1 = \{A_j \rightarrow B_i \mid A_j \in S_i$ for some $i \in \{1, 2, \ldots, n\}\}$; this set of FDs captures each membership of the form $A_j \in S_i$.

2) $F_2 = \{A_j A_k \rightarrow CD \mid A_j, A_k \in S_i$ for some $i \in \{1, 2, \ldots, n\}$ and $A_j \neq A_k\}$.

3) $F_3 = \{B_1 B_2 \ldots B_n \rightarrow C\}$.

4) $F_4 = \{CD \rightarrow U\}$.

It can then be shown that W is a hitting set of U if and only if S violates BCNF, where schema(S) = U $\cup$ {C, D}. $\square$

BCNF was defined as a property of the relation schema over which the set F of FDs is specified and is thus independent of any particular relation r over R. We can also define BCNF for a given relation r over R as follows. A relation r over R is in BCNF if R is in BCNF with respect to F(r). The surprising result, not withstanding Theorem 4.17, is that the problem of testing whether the projection of r onto a proper subset X of schema(R) is in BCNF can be solved in time polynomial in the size of r [DHLM92]. The proof of this result is similar to that of the corresponding polynomial-time algorithm for testing whether a relation r is in 3NF (see the discussion at the end of Subsection 4.4.2).

4.4.4   Inclusion Dependency Normal Form (IDNF)

BCNF does not take into account referential integrity which apart from entity integrity is a fundamental constraint of the relational model. In the same manner that FDs generalise the central concept of key, INDs generalise the central concept of foreign key. Herein we consider how INDs can be incorporated into the database design process by considering another normal form, called *Inclusion Dependency Normal Form* (IDNF), that assumes that the semantics of the application are described in terms of a set of FDs and INDs. We will show that when a database schema is in IDNF with respect to a set of FDs and INDs then certain problems that would have otherwise arisen are solved and, in addition, further redundancy is removed.

Definition 4.16 (IDNF)   A database schema $\mathbf{R}$ is in *Inclusion Dependency Normal Form* (IDNF) with respect to a set F of FDs over $\mathbf{R}$ and a set I of INDs over $\mathbf{R}$ (or simply in IDNF if F and I are understood from context) if

- $\mathbf{R}$ is in BCNF with respect to F, and

- the set I of INDs is noncircular and key-based.   ■

In the special case when all the keys are simple then the INDs are all unary.

The justification for insisting that I be noncircular and key-based can be found in Section 4.1, wherein we showed the problems that arise if I were either circular or not key-based. In Example 4.4 we demonstrated that when an IND that is not key-based contains a proper superset of a key then redundancy arises, in Example 4.5 we demonstrated that when an IND that is not key-based contains a proper subset of a key then there is insufficient information to infer key values, and in Example 4.6 we demonstrated that circular INDs give rise to semantic anomalies. We now analyse these three examples in more detail showing how they can be converted into database schemas in IDNF.

In the first example removing a redundant attribute and modifying the set of INDs accordingly solves the problem.

Example 4.12   Consider the database schema $\mathbf{R} = \{$HEAD, LECT$\}$ of Example 4.4 together with its set F of FDs and its set I of INDs. The reader can verify that $\mathbf{R}$ is in BCNF with respect to F and that I is a noncircular set of INDs. On the other hand, $\mathbf{R}$ is *not* in IDNF with respect to F and I, since the IND HEAD[HD] $\subseteq$ LECT[LD] is not key-based. The reader can verify that the decomposition, $\{$NEW_HEAD, LECT$\}$, with schema(NEW_HEAD) = $\{$H$\}$ (i.e. D is removed from schema(HEAD)) is in IDNF with respect to $F' = \{$LECT: L $\rightarrow$ D$\}$ and $I' = \{$NEW_HEAD[H] $\subseteq$ LECT[L]$\}$, since NEW_HEAD[H] $\subseteq$ LECT[L] is key-based.   ■

In the second example adding an attribute and modifying the set of FDs and INDs accordingly solves the problem.

Example 4.13   Consider the database schema $\mathbf{R} = \{$EMP, PROJ$\}$ of Example 4.5 together with its set F of FDs and set I of INDs. The reader can verify that $\mathbf{R}$ is in BCNF with respect to F and that I is a noncircular set of INDs. On the other hand, $\mathbf{R}$ is *not* in IDNF with respect to F and I, since the IND EMP[P] $\subseteq$ PROJ[P] is not key-based. Let us assume that an employee working on a project works in one location only. The reader can verify that the decomposition, {NEW_EMP, PROJ}, with schema(NEW_EMP) = {E, P, L'} is in IDNF with respect to F' = {NEW_EMP : E → PL'} and I' = {NEW_EMP[PL'] ⊆ PROJ[PL]}, since NEW_EMP[PL'] ⊆ PROJ[PL] is key-based. ∎

In the third example adding a relation schema and modifying the set of INDs accordingly solves the problem.

Example 4.14   Consider the database schema **R** = {BOSS}, where BOSS is the schema from Example 4.6 together with an empty set F of FDs and the set of INDs I = {BOSS[MGR#] ⊆ BOSS[EMP#]}. The reader can also verify that **R** is *not* in IDNF, since I is a circular set of INDs. The reader can also verify that the decomposition {EMPS, BOSSES}, with schema(EMPS) = {EMP#} and schema(BOSSES) = {MGR#} is in IDNF with respect to F and I' = {BOSSES[MGR#] ⊆ EMPS[EMP#]}, since I' is noncircular. ∎

Recall the results from Subsection 3.6.11 of Chapter 3 concerning the interaction between FDs and INDs. In particular, we repeat the next definition to refresh the reader's memory.

Definition 4.17 (Interaction between FDs and INDs)   A set F of FDs over **R** is said *not to interact* with of set I of INDs over **R**, if

1) for all FDs α over **R**, for all subsets G ⊆ F, G ∪ I ⊨ α if and only if G ⊨ α, and

2) for all INDs β over **R**, for all subsets J ⊆ I, F ∪ J ⊨ β if and only if J ⊨ β. ∎

If F and I do not interact then the algorithms in database design that use logical implication can be implemented more efficiently than would otherwise be the case. In particular, the implication problem for FDs on their own is linear time and for noncircular INDs on their own it is NP-complete; if the INDs are typed then their implication problem is polynomial time and if the INDs are unary then their implication problem is linear time. Taken together the implication problem for FDs and INDs is, in general, undecidable and the implication problem for FDs and noncircular INDs has a lower bound of exponential time complexity. When the INDs are unary then the implication problem for FDs and unary INDs is polynomial time. (Recall Subsection 3.6.11 of Chapter 3 for more details on the implication problem for FDs and INDs.)

The next result is an immediate consequence of Theorem 3.54 in Subsection 3.6.11 of Chapter 3. It shows that IDNF has an additional desirable property, namely that of no interaction between the sets F and I of FDs and INDs, respectively.

Theorem 4.18   If **R** is in IDNF with respect to a set F of FDs over **R** and a set I of INDs over **R**, then F and I have no interaction. □

Apart from having the desirable property of there being no interaction between the given set of FDs and INDs, we can also justify IDNF in terms of removing attribute redundancy (see Definition 4.18) and satisfying a generalised form of entity integrity (see Definition 4.19).

Let $\Sigma = F \cup I$, where F is a set of FDs over $\mathbf{R}$ and I is a set of noncircular INDs over $\mathbf{R}$. Informally, an attribute A in a relation schema $R \in \mathbf{R}$ is redundant, if whenever d is some database over $\mathbf{R}$, which satisfies the given set Σ of FDs and INDs, the following condition holds. The relation $r \in d$ over R is nonempty and contains an A-value, say $t[A]$ with $t \in r$, that is implied by the other values in the database through the set Σ. When such an attribute as A is redundant then any replacement of the A-value by another value in DOM(A) will result in the violation of the set Σ of FDs and INDs.

Consider the database $d = \{r_1, r_2\}$ over $\mathbf{R} = \{\text{MANAGER, EMPLOYEE}\}$, where r_1 and r_2 are shown in Tables 4.9 and 4.10, respectively, with schema(MANAGER) = {MGR, DEPT} and schema(EMPLOYEE) = {EMP, DEPT}. In addition, let F = {EMPLOYEE : EMP $\rightarrow$ DEPT} be a set of FDs over $\mathbf{R}$, I = {MANAGER[MGR, DEPT] $\subseteq$ EMPLOYEE[EMP, DEPT]} be a set of INDs over $\mathbf{R}$ and $\Sigma = F \cup I$. Note that $F \cup I \models$ MANAGER : MGR $\rightarrow$ DEPT by the pullback inference rule. Then DEPT $\in$ schema(MANAGER) is a redundant attribute, since $d \models \Sigma$ and changing the occurrence of Computing in r_1 to any other value $v \neq$ Computing, say Maths, results in a database that violates the IND MANAGER[MGR, DEPT] $\subseteq$ EMPLOYEE[EMP, DEPT] and thus violates Σ. Even if we were to add the tuple <Peter, Maths> to r_2, then the resulting database, which now satisfies MANAGER[MGR, DEPT] $\subseteq$ EMPLOYEE[EMP, DEPT], will violate the FD EMPLOYEE : EMP $\rightarrow$ DEPT and thus will violate Σ. On the other hand, if we remove the attribute DEPT from schema(MANAGER), then the reader can verify that no attribute in either schema(MANAGER) or in schema(EMPLOYEE) is redundant. Intuitively, DEPT in schema(MANAGER) is redundant, since its values can be inferred from DEPT in schema(EMPLOYEE) due to Σ and the pullback inference rule.

Table 4.9 The relation r_1 over MANAGER

MGR	DEPT
Peter	Computing

Table 4.10 The relation r_2 over EMPLOYEE

EMP	DEPT
Peter	Computing
Paul	Maths

Definition 4.18 (Attribute redundancy)   An attribute A $\in$ schema(R), where R is a relation schema in $\mathbf{R}$, is *redundant* with respect to a set Σ of FDs and INDs over $\mathbf{R}$, if whenever d is a database over $\mathbf{R}$ that satisfies Σ and $r \in d$ is a nonempty relation over R, then for all tuples $t \in r$, if $t[A]$ is replaced by a distinct value $v \in$ DOM(A) such that $v \neq t[A]$, yielding a new database d', then $d' \not\models \Sigma$.

A database schema $\mathbf{R}$ is said to be in *Attribute Redundancy Free Normal Form* (or simply ARFNF) with respect to a set Σ of FDs and INDs over $\mathbf{R}$ if there does not exist an attribute A in a relation schema $R \in \mathbf{R}$ which is redundant with respect to Σ.   ■

Recall the definition of the chase procedure with respect to a set Σ of FDs and INDs from Subsection 3.6.8 in Chapter 3. Intuitively a database schema $\mathbf{R}$ satisfies generalised entity integrity with respect to a set Σ of FDs and INDs over $\mathbf{R}$ if whenever a tuple, say t, is added to a relation over R in a database d over $\mathbf{R}$ as a result of an IND, then prior to t being added to the relation, it must be defined on all the values of at least one key for R.

Definition 4.19 (Generalised entity integrity) Let $\mathbf{R}$ be a database schema, $\Sigma = F \cup I$ be a set of FDs and INDs over $\mathbf{R}$, and let d over $\mathbf{R}$ be a database that satisfies Σ. Suppose that each time we add a tuple t to a relation $r \in d$ over R, we invoke the chase procedure in order to enforce the propagation of insertions of tuples due to the INDs in I.

Then a tuple t that is added to the current state of r during the computation of ICHASE(d, Σ) is *entity-based*, if there exists at least one key K for R with respect to the set of FDs $\{R : X \to Y \mid R : X \to Y \in F\}$ such that for all $A \in K$, $t[A]$ is *not* a new value that is assigned to t as a result of invoking the IND rule.

A database schema $\mathbf{R}$ satisfies *generalised entity integrity* with respect to a set $\Sigma = F \cup I$ of FDs and INDs over $\mathbf{R}$ if for all databases d over $\mathbf{R}$, all the tuples that are added to relations in the current state of d during the computation of ICHASE(d, Σ) are entity-based. ∎

The next theorem gives a complete justification for IDNF in terms of removing redundancy and satisfying generalised entity integrity.

Theorem 4.19 A database schema $\mathbf{R}$ is in IDNF with respect to a set Σ consisting of a set F of FDs and a set I of noncircular INDs over $\mathbf{R}$ if and only if $\mathbf{R}$ is in ARFNF with respect to Σ, all the relation schemas $R \in \mathbf{R}$ are in VRFNF with respect to the set of FDs $\{R : X \to Y \mid R : X \to Y \in F\}$ and $\mathbf{R}$ satisfies generalised entity integrity with respect to Σ.

Proof. We sketch the main ideas behind the proof; the full proof can be found in [LV99].

If. Satisfaction of generalised entity integrity implies that I is a superkey-based set of INDs. Moreover, $\mathbf{R}$ being in ARFNF implies that I must be a key-based set of INDs, otherwise the attributes on the left-hand side of a superkey-based IND that do not belong to a key are redundant in any such superkey-based IND. The result that $\mathbf{R}$ is in IDNF with respect to Σ follows by Theorem 4.13, which implies that when each $R \in \mathbf{R}$ is in VRFNF then $\mathbf{R}$ is also in BCNF with respect to F.

Only if. If $\mathbf{R}$ is in IDNF with respect to Σ then I is a key-based set of INDs implying that $\mathbf{R}$ satisfies generalised entity integrity. Moreover, if $\mathbf{R}$ is in IDNF with respect to Σ then $\mathbf{R}$ is in ARFNF due to the following argument. Let $A \in$ schema(R) be an attribute and d_0 be a database such that the relation $r \in d_0$ over R has a single tuple t over R containing only zeros and all other relations in d are empty. We invoke ICHASE(d_0, Σ) to obtain a database d_1 satisfying Σ. We observe that due to I being noncircular r is not modified by the chase procedure. We then replace $t[A]$ in d_1, which is zero, by one, and invoke ICHASE(d_1, Σ) to obtain the new database d_2 satisfying Σ. Again r remains unmodified by the chase procedure due to I being noncircular. The database d_2 exhibits the fact that A is nonredundant, since by Theorem 4.18 F and I have no interaction and thus changing $t[A]$ in d_2 back to its original value zero results in a new database d_3, where ICHASE$(d_3, \Sigma) = d_3$ and thus $d_3 \models \Sigma$ as required by Definition 4.18. The result now follows by Theorem 4.13 which implies that when each $R \in \mathbf{R}$ is in BCNF with respect to F then each $R \in \mathbf{R}$ is in VRFNF. □

Related normal forms for FDs and INDs and the motivation behind them can be found in [CA84, MR86b, MS89a, LG92, MR92a, Mar94].

4.5   Horizontal Decompositions

All the normal forms discussed in the previous section result in vertical decompositions, i.e. we start with a relation schema R and decompose R into further relation schemas whose attribute sets are subsets of schema(R). Assuming the decomposition **R** is lossless this corresponds to being able to recover a relation r over R by projecting r onto **R** and then joining the projections.

Herein, we briefly discuss the possibility of a horizontal decomposition of a relation schema R, i.e. splitting R into two or more relation schemas each having the same attribute set as R. In this case a relation r over R will be split into two or more disjoint relations using one or more selections and r will be recovered by applying the union operator [Fag79, DP84, GM85b, PDGV89].

Horizontal decompositions are especially useful in situations when there are exceptions to integrity constraints. We will concentrate on the case of exceptions to FDs. Assume a relation r over R and an FD $X \to Y$ over R. If only a few tuples in r cause the FD $X \to Y$ to be violated, then we can partition r into two relations r_1 and r_2, where r_1 satisfies $X \to Y$ and r_2 violates $X \to Y$. In order to formalise the notion of a horizontal partition of r we define the concept of X-complete relations.

Definition 4.20 (X-complete relations)   Let R be a relation schema, X be a set of attributes included in schema(R), and let r be a relation over R. A relation s is X-complete with respect to r (or simply X-complete if r is understood from context) if s is a subset of r and all the X-values of s are disjoint from the X-values of $r - s$. Symbolically, $\forall t_1 \in s, \forall t_2 \in r - s, t_1[X] \neq t_2[X]$. ∎

We next define the afunctional dependency which formalises the notion of an exception to a functional dependency.

Definition 4.21 (Afunctional dependency)   An *Afunctional Dependency* over schema R (or simply an AFD) is a statement of the form $R : X \not\to Y$ (or simply $X \not\to Y$ whenever R is understood from context), where $X, Y \subseteq$ schema(R).

The AFD $X \not\to Y$ is satisfied in r, denoted by $r \models X \not\to Y$, if for all nonempty X-complete relations, s, with respect to r, s violates the FD $X \to Y$, i.e. $s \not\models X \to Y$. ∎

By the definition of an AFD the AFD $X \not\to Y$ is satisfied in a relation r over R if for every X-value of a tuple in r there exist at least two tuples with this X-value which violate the FD $X \to Y$. This motivates partitioning a relation r that violates an FD $X \to Y$ into two relations r_1 and r_2 such that r_1 is the largest X-complete relation with respect to r such that $r_1 \models X \to Y$. It can be deduced that $r_2 = r - r_1$ is the largest X-complete relation with respect to r such that $r_2 \models X \not\to Y$.

Example 4.15   Let PHONE be a relation schema, with schema(PHONE) = {ENAME, EXT}, where ENAME stands for employee name and EXT stands for the extension number of an employee's telephone number. In general, we require that the FD ENAME $\to$ EXT holds. A relation r over PHONE that violates the FD ENAME $\to$ EXT is shown in Table 4.11.

The largest ENAME-complete relation r_1 with respect to r that satisfies the FD ENAME $\rightarrow$ EXT is shown in Table 4.12; the relation schema of r_1 is $PHONE_1$, with schema($PHONE_1$) = schema(PHONE). The relation $r_2 = r - r_1$, shown in Table 4.13, is the largest ENAME-complete relation with respect to r that satisfies the AFD ENAME $\nrightarrow$ EXT; the relation schema of r_2 is $PHONE_2$, with schema($PHONE_2$) = schema(PHONE). ∎

Table 4.11 The relation r over PHONE

ENAME	EXT
Mark	3684
Dan	3685
Reuven	3686
Naomi	3687
Naomi	3688

Table 4.12 The relation r_1 over $PHONE_1$

ENAME	EXT
Mark	3684
Dan	3685
Reuven	3686

Table 4.13 The relation r_2 over $PHONE_2$

ENAME	EXT
Naomi	3687
Naomi	3688

The horizontal decomposition induced by exceptions to FDs can be described as follows. Suppose that we have a relation schema R, an FD X $\rightarrow$ Y over R and assume that the database designer knows that relations r over R will not, in general, satisfy X $\rightarrow$ Y. The decomposition step induced by such an exception is to split R into two relation schemas, R_1 and R_2, with schema(R_1) = schema(R_2) = schema(R) and to associate the FD X $\rightarrow$ Y with R_1 and the AFD X $\nrightarrow$ Y with R_2. This decomposition process generalises to sets of FDs and AFDs.

The important concept of *conflict* between a set F of FDs over R and a set E of AFDs over R needs to be taken into account when decomposing horizontally with respect to exceptions to FDs. For example, ENAME $\rightarrow$ EXT and ENAME $\nrightarrow$ EXT are in conflict, since it cannot be the case that both $r \models$ ENAME $\rightarrow$ EXT and $r \models$ ENAME $\nrightarrow$ EXT. Therefore, this requires that r be decomposed horizontally in order to avoid this conflict. In this particular example the exception could represent employees having more than one telephone.

Definition 4.22 (Conflict between FDs and AFDs) A set F of FDs over R and a set E of AFDs over R are in *conflict* if and only if for some AFD X $\nrightarrow$ Y $\in$ E, F $\models$ X $\rightarrow$ Y. ∎

We briefly describe below the main step in horizontally decomposing a relation schema with respect to a set of FDs and AFDs. It is assumed that at each stage of the decomposition F and E are *not* in conflict and an FD X $\rightarrow$ Y and its counterpart X $\nrightarrow$ Y are considered. Obviously, adding X $\rightarrow$ Y to F and correspondingly adding X $\nrightarrow$ Y to E will result in a conflict, so the idea is to decompose R horizontally into two relation schemas, one with X $\rightarrow$ Y in its set of FDs and the other with X $\nrightarrow$ Y in its set of AFDs, provided that no conflict arises.

Specifically, during a step of the horizontal decomposition process we consider a set F of FDs and a set E of AFDs both over R that are *not* in conflict. In addition, we consider an FD X $\rightarrow$ Y and its counterpart AFD X $\nrightarrow$ Y such that both F $\cup$ E $\not\models$ X $\rightarrow$ Y and F $\cup$ E $\not\models$ X $\nrightarrow$ Y obtain. From this specification it follows that F $\cup$ E $\cup$ {X $\rightarrow$ Y} and correspondingly F $\cup$ E $\cup$ {X $\nrightarrow$ Y} are also not in conflict. Thus as a result of this specification we replace R by two relation schemas R_1 and R_2, with schema(R_1) = schema(R_2) = schema(R), and we replace F $\cup$ E by two sets of data dependencies such that F $\cup$ E $\cup$ {X $\rightarrow$ Y} is associated with R_1 and F $\cup$ E $\cup$ {X $\nrightarrow$ Y} is associated with R_2.

We refer the reader to [DP84, PDGV89] for a sound and complete set of inference rules for FDs and AFDs and for a polynomial-time algorithm which solves the implication problem for FDs and AFDs.

4.6 Algorithms for Converting a Relation Schema into Normal Form

So far we have presented the normal forms and the desirable properties that we aim to achieve in a database which is in a normal form with respect to a given set of data dependencies. We now tackle the problem of how to achieve such a normal form. The solution comes in two stages. In the first stage we present an algorithm that can be used to output a 3NF or BCNF database schema given a set of FDs over a relation schema R. In the second stage we assume that the database schema, say **R**, is already in 3NF or BCNF and we present an algorithm that can be used to transform this database schema into one which is in IDNF given a set of FDs and noncircular INDs over **R** (we can easily relax the definition of IDNF such that **R** is required to be in 3NF rather than the stricter condition of being in BCNF). The success of the process of relational database design is dependent on the quality of the database schema which is output from these algorithms, so we investigate the desirable properties of the database schema output by each algorithm. For 3NF we can achieve a lossless join and dependency preserving decomposition but for BCNF we can only guarantee, in general, that the output database schema is a lossless join decomposition. The algorithm we present for transforming the resulting database schema into IDNF comprises four heuristics which when applied iteratively to the database schema result in an output database schema which is in IDNF.

In Subsection 4.6.1 we present a 3NF synthesis algorithm, in Subsection 4.6.2 we present a BCNF decomposition algorithm, and in Subsection 4.6.3 we present a heuristic algorithm which transforms a decomposition in BCNF into one which is in IDNF.

4.6.1   A 3NF Synthesis Algorithm

We have introduced the synthesis approach to relational database design in Section 4.3. Herein we present the details of a 3NF synthesis algorithm, which given as input a relation schema R and a set F of FDs over R, outputs a database schema **R** which is in 3NF with respect to F and is both lossless and dependency preserving with respect to F. The algorithm consists of three steps: the first step preprocesses the input set of FDs in order to transform it into an appropriate minimum cover, the second step synthesises each FD in the produced cover into a relation schema, and finally the third step ensures that the output database schema is lossless by ensuring that the attribute set of one of its relation schemas is a superkey for R with respect to the input set of FDs.

We first give the pseudo-code of an algorithm, designated MINIMISE(R, F), which returns a cover of F, which is minimum and such that the right-hand sides and left-hand sides of the FDs in the cover are reduced (i.e. they are minimal with respect to F). Recall that

Algorithm 3.10 given in Subsection 3.6.5 of Chapter 3, which was designated MINIMUM(F), returns a minimum cover of F.

Algorithm 4.1 (MINIMISE(R, F))
1. **begin**
2.   Min := MINIMUM(F);
3.   **for each** $X \to Y \in$ Min **do**
4.   W := X;
5.   **for each** $A \in X$ **do**
6.   **if** Min $\models (W-A) \to X$ **then**
7.   W := W $- \{A\}$;
8.   **end if**
9.   **end for**
10.   Min := (Min $- \{X \to Y\}) \cup \{W \to Y\}$;
11.   **end for**
12.   **for each** $X \to Y \in$ Min **do**
13.   W := Y;
14.   **for each** $A \in Y$ **do**
15.   G := (Min $- \{X \to Y\}) \cup \{X \to (W-A)\}$;
16.   **if** $G \models X \to Y$ **then**
17.   W := W $- \{A\}$;
18.   **end if**
19.   **end for**
20.   Min := (Min $- \{X \to Y\}) \cup \{X \to W\}$;
21.   **end for**
22.   **return** Min;
23. **end.**

Next, the pseudo-code of an algorithm, designated SYNTHESISE(R, F), which returns a lossless join and dependency preserving decomposition of schema(R) in 3NF with respect to a set F of FDs over R, is given below.

Algorithm 4.2 (SYNTHESISE(R, F))
1. **begin**
2.   Min := MINIMISE(R, F);
3.   Out := $\emptyset$;
4.   **for each** $X \to Y \in$ Min **do**
5.   **let** S be a relation schema with schema(S) = XY;
6.   Out := Out $\cup \{S\}$;
7.   **end for**
8.   **if** Out is not a lossless join decomposition
9.   of schema(R) with respect to F **then**
10.   **let** S be a relation schema, where schema(S)
                is a key for R with respect to F;
11.   Out := Out $\cup \{S\}$;
12.   **end if**
13.   **return** Out;
14. **end.**

We leave it to the reader to verify that Algorithm 4.2 executes in time polynomial in the sizes of R and F; we note that by the results in Subsections 3.6.5 and 3.6.1 of Chapter 3, respectively, a minimum cover of F and, respectively, a key for R with respect to F can be found in polynomial time in the size of F.

Theorem 4.20   Given a relation schema R and a set F of FDs over R SYNTHESISE(R, F), whose pseudo-code is given in Algorithm 4.2, outputs a lossless join dependency preserving decomposition of schema(R) which is in 3NF.

Proof. Let **R** be the database schema output from SYNTHESISE(R, F) and let G be the output of MINIMISE(R, F). Then **R** is dependency preserving, since G is a cover of F and by line 5 of Algorithm 4.2 we have that for each $X \to Y \in G$ there is a relation schema S, with schema(S) = XY. It follows by part (2) of Theorem 4.2 that **R** is a lossless join decomposition of schema(R) with respect to G and therefore also with respect to F.

It remains to show that **R** is in 3NF with respect to F. Since $F^+ = G^+$ we prove the result with respect to G. Let S be a relation schema in **R** and $X \to Y$ be the FD in $G^+[S]$ that constitutes S in line 5 of Algorithm 4.2. By the for loop in Algorithm 4.1 beginning at line 5 and ending at line 9, it follows that X is a key for S with respect to $G^+[S]$.

Now assume that S is not in 3NF with respect to $G^+[S]$; since S is not in 3NF there exists a nontrivial FD $W \to A \in G^+[S]$, such that W is not a superkey for S and A is nonprime. It follows that $A \in Y$, since X is a key for S with respect to $G^+[S]$. Moreover, $X \not\subseteq W$ and $W \to X \notin G^+[S]$, since W is not a superkey for S. We conclude the proof by arriving at a contradiction of the fact that G is the output of MINIMISE(R, F).

Let $H = (G - \{X \to Y\}) \cup \{X \to Y-A\}$. It follows that $H \models W \to A$, since $G \not\models W \to X$ and $W \to A \in G^+[S]$. Furthermore, since $W \subseteq XY-A$, $H \models X \to W$, and thus by the transitivity inference rule $H \models X \to A$ implying that $H \models X \to Y$. Therefore H is a cover of G. By the for loop in Algorithm 4.1 beginning at line 14 and ending at line 19, it follows that G could not have been output from MINIMISE(R, F), leading to the desired contradiction.   □

We next demonstrate the synthesis algorithm with a nontrivial example.

Example 4.16   Consider a relation schema R, with schema(R) = {A, B, C, D, E, G, H, J, K} together with a set of FDs F = {A → B, B → CD, D → B, ABE → K, E → J, EG → H, H → G} over R. The reader can verify that MINIMISE(R, F) = F; that is, F is a minimum set of FDs and both its left-hand sides and right-hand sides are reduced. Thus SYNTHESISE(R, F) will output $\mathbf{R} = \{R_1, R_2, R_3, R_4, R_5, R_6, R_7, R_8\}$ with schema(R_1) = {A, B}, schema(R_2) = {B, C, D}, schema(R_3) = {B, D}, schema(R_4) = {A, B, E, K}, schema(R_5) = {E, J}, schema(R_6) = {E, G, H}, schema(R_7) = {G, H} and schema(R_8) = {A, E, G}, where AEG is the key for R with respect to F generated at line 10 of Algorithm 4.2. Thus by Theorem 4.20 **R** is a lossless join and dependency preserving decomposition of schema(R) in 3NF with respect to F. We observe that **R** is not in BCNF, since R_6 is not in BCNF due to the fact that the FD H → G is embedded in R_6. Moreover, the relation schemas R_3 and R_7 are redundant, since schema(R_3) $\subset$ schema(R_2) and schema(R_7) $\subset$ schema(R_6). Such redundant relation schemas can easily be removed from **R**. ∎

Improved algorithms which synthesise database schemas in 3NF can be found in [Ber76, BDB79, LTK81, Zan82, BM87]. As an example, if two sets X_1 and X_2 of attributes are equivalent, i.e. $F \models X_1 \rightarrow X_2$ and $F \models X_2 \rightarrow X_1$, then X_1 and X_2 can reside in the same relation schema thus reducing the number of relation schemas in a decomposition. Other improvements deal with removing redundant attributes from relation schemas.

4.6.2   BCNF Decompositions

We have introduced the decomposition approach to relational database design in Section 4.3. Herein we present the details of a BCNF decomposition algorithm which, given as input a relation schema R and a set F of FDs over R, outputs a database schema **R** which is in BCNF with respect to F and is also a lossless join decomposition of schema(R) with respect to F. Whenever a relation schema in the current state of the output database schema violates BCNF, the decomposition algorithm removes the cause for this violation of BCNF by replacing the offending relation schema by two child relation schemas each having fewer attributes than their parent; these two relation schemas can be joined losslessly to reconstruct their parent.

The following example shows that it is not always possible to obtain a BCNF decomposition which is also dependency preserving .

Example 4.17   Recall the relation schema STUD_POS from Example 4.7 together with the set of FDs {N → P, SP → N}, which we denote herein by F_1; we note that we have made a stronger requirement here than in Example 4.7, since we are insisting that SNAME is associated with a unique POSITION. It can easily be verified that there does not exist a decomposition of schema(STUD_POS) = {N, S, P} which is both dependency preserving and in BCNF with respect to F_1.

As another example, recall the relation schema ADDRESS from Example 4.3 together with the set of FDs {SC → P, P → C}, which we denote herein by F_2. It can easily be verified that there does not exist a decomposition of schema(ADDRESS) = {S, C, P} which is both dependency preserving and in BCNF with respect to F_2.   ∎

An exponential time algorithm in the size of F, which decides whether there exists a dependency preserving decomposition of schema(R) that is in BCNF, can be found in [Osb79] (we note that in [TF82] this problem was shown to be co-NP-hard). A method of guaranteeing a dependency preserving decomposition, which is in BCNF, was proposed in [KM80], wherein it was shown that by adding attributes to schema(R) and FDs to F it is always possible to obtain a BCNF dependency preserving decomposition of the augmented schema with respect to the augmented set of FDs. We illustrate the main idea of the augmentation by using the relation schemas and sets of FDs from Example 4.17.

Example 4.18   Let schema(NEW_STUD_POS) = {N, S, P, K} and let G_1 = {K → SP, SP → K, K → N, N → P}. A dependency preserving decomposition of schema(NEW_STUD_POS) into BCNF is the database schema {R_1, R_2, R_3}, with schema(R_1) = {S, P, K}, schema(R_2) = {K, N} and schema(R_3) = {N, P}. Thus by introducing an additional attribute K, which is a simple key, we obtain a dependency preserving decomposition with $G_1^+[STUD\_POS] = F_1^+$.

Similarly, let schema(NEW_ADDRESS) = {S, C, P, K} and let G_2 = {K → SC, SC → K, K → P, P → C}. A dependency preserving decomposition of schema(NEW_ADDRESS) into BCNF is the database schema {R_1, R_2, R_3}, with schema(R_1) = {S, C, K}, schema(R_2) = {K, C} and schema(R_3) = {P, C}. Thus by introducing an additional attribute K, which is a simple key, we obtain a dependency preserving decomposition with G_2^+[ADDRESS] = F_2^+.   ∎

The pseudo-code of an algorithm, designated DECOMPOSE(R, F), which returns a lossless join decomposition of schema(R) in BCNF with respect to a set F of FDs over R, is given below.

Algorithm 4.3 (DECOMPOSE(R, F))
1. **begin**
2.   Out := ∅;
3.   **if** R is in BCNF with respect F **then**
4.   Out := Out ∪ {R};
5.   **else**
6.   let X → Y ∈ F be nontrivial and such that F $\not\models$ X → schema(R);
7.   let R_1 be the relation schema with schema(R_1) = XY;
8.   Out := Out ∪ DECOMPOSE(R_1, F^+[R_1]);
9.   let R_2 be the relation schema with schema(R_2) = schema(R) − (Y−X);
10.   Out := Out ∪ DECOMPOSE(R_2, F^+[R_2]);
11.   **end if**
12.   **return** Out;
13. **end.**

The above algorithm, which outputs a decomposition, can be viewed as building a *binary decomposition tree* whose root is labelled by schema(R) and whose leaves are labelled by the attributes of the relation schemas in the output decomposition. The internal nodes of the tree are the intermediate relation schemas created during the decomposition process.

It is possible to modify Algorithm 4.3 to output a 3NF decomposition with respect to F rather than a BCNF decomposition; we leave this modification to the reader as an exercise. This would give us an alternative to the synthesis approach of Algorithm 4.2.

Example 4.19 Consider a relation schema R, with schema(R) = {A, B, C, D, E, F} together with the set of FDs F = {A → B, A → C, D → A, D → F} over R. The binary decomposition tree associated with the output **R** of DECOMPOSE(R, F) is shown in Figure 4.1. It can be verified that **R** is the collection of labels of the leaf nodes of the decomposition tree and that **R** is a lossless join BCNF decomposition of R with respect to F which is also dependency preserving.

If we replace F by {A → BC, D → AF}, which is a cover of F, we will obtain a more succinct lossless join and dependency preserving BCNF decomposition, i.e. we obtain a decomposition with only two relation schemas. On the other hand, given F, **R** is unique no matter what FD is chosen at line 6 of Algorithm 4.3. The decomposition output from DECOMPOSE(R, F) is *not* always unique as we demonstrate below.   ∎

In general, Algorithm 4.3 does not execute in time polynomial in the sizes of R and F, since as shown in Theorem 3.35 given in Subsection 3.6.6 of Chapter 3 computing a cover of F^+[R_i]

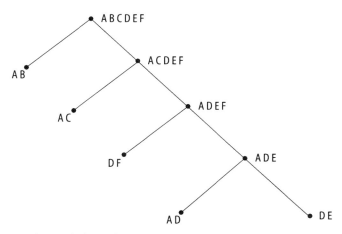

Fig 4.1 The binary decomposition tree associated with Example 4.19

is intractable. This source of inefficiency can easily be removed by changing the computations of $F^+[R_1]$ and $F^+[R_2]$ in lines 8 and 10 of DECOMPOSE, respectively, to the polynomial-time computations of $F[R_1]$ and $F[R_2]$ in the size of F. The problem in this case is that the algorithm may not always output a BCNF decomposition. For example, let F = {A → B, B → C} be a set of FDs over R, with schema(R) = {A, B, C, D}. Then $F[R'] = \emptyset$, where schema(R') = {A, C, D}, but $F^+[R'] = \{A \to C\}$. It follows that if the FD, A → B, is chosen at line 6 of DECOMPOSE, then R', which is not in BCNF with respect to $F^+[R']$, is in the output decomposition. In any case this is not the only problem, since the cardinality of the decomposition returned by DECOMPOSE(R, F) may be exponential in the cardinality of schema(R), i.e. type(R).

A polynomial-time algorithm in the sizes of R and F that outputs a lossless join decomposition of schema(R) in BCNF with respect to F can be formulated by using Lemmas 4.10 and 4.11 in conjunction with Algorithm 4.3 [TF82]. Essentially, if a relation schema, say R, in line 3 of the said algorithm is such that |schema(R)| > 2, then Lemma 4.11 is utilised to remove attributes from schema(R), otherwise Lemma 4.10 is utilised.

Theorem 4.21   Given a relation schema R and a set F of FDs over R, DECOMPOSE(R, F), whose pseudo-code is given in Algorithm 4.3, outputs a lossless join decomposition of schema(R) in BCNF.

Proof. Algorithm 4.3 terminates, since at each recursive call of the algorithm the cardinality of the attribute set of the argument relation schema is strictly smaller than the cardinality of the attribute set of the argument relation schema at the previous call.

Let **R** be the database schema output from DECOMPOSE(R, F). It is easy to verify that **R** is in BCNF with respect to F, since by line 3 of the algorithm a relation schema is added to the output database schema if and only if it is in BCNF.

By Theorem 3.29 given in Subsection 3.6.4 of Chapter 3 concerning lossless join decompositions, we have that **R** is a lossless join decomposition of schema(R) with respect to F if and only if CHASE(T(**R**), F) has a winning row. We leave it to the reader to conclude the proof that **R** is a lossless join decomposition of schema(R) with respect to F by using a straightforward induction on the cardinality of R to show that CHASE($T(R)$, F) indeed has a winning row.   □

Theorem 4.21 shows that we can always find a decomposition R of schema(R) which is lossless and in BNCF with respect to F; as discussed prior to the theorem we can find such an R in polynomial time in the size of the input. It is obvious that we would prefer the cardinality of R to be as small as possible, since this would imply that less joins need to be performed during the processing of queries and also that further redundancy is avoided. For example, let schema(R) = $\{A, B, C\}$ and F = $\{A \rightarrow BC\}$. The database schema $R = \{R\}$ is lossless and in BCNF, while the database schema $S = \{S_1, S_2\}$, with schema(S_1) = $\{A, B\}$ and schema(S_2) = $\{A, C\}$ is also lossless and in BCNF. We would normally prefer R over S due to the above-mentioned reasons. So, an algorithm that minimises the number of relation schemas in R, while maintaining its losslessness and its being in BCNF, would be very useful during database design in order to improve the quality of the resulting database.

We show the negative result that the problem of finding a minimal cardinality database schema that is both lossless and in BCNF is NP-hard. Thus assuming that PTIME $\neq$ NP we cannot find a polynomial-time algorithm to solve this minimisation problem. We begin by defining the concept of redundant relation schemas with respect to a set F of FDs.

Definition 4.23 (Redundant relation schemas)   Let R be a lossless join decomposition of schema(R) with respect to a set F of FDs over R, with schema(R) = schema(R). Then a relation schema S is *redundant* in R with respect to F if $R - \{S\}$ is also a lossless join decomposition of schema(R) with respect to F. A decomposition R is *nonredundant* with respect to F if it does not contain any redundant relation schemas with respect to F.   ■

A similar result to the one stated in the next theorem can be found in [TLJ90].

Theorem 4.22   The problem of finding a lossless join and nonredundant decomposition of schema(R) that is in BCNF with respect to a set F of FDs over R, and such that the number of relation schemas in R is less than or equal to some natural number k, with $k \geq 1$, is NP-hard.

Proof. To show that the problem is NP-hard we give a polynomial-time transformation from the vertex cover problem, which is known to be NP-complete (see part (1) of Theorem 3.24 in Subsection 3.6.1 of Chapter 3 wherein the superkey of cardinality k problem was shown to be NP-complete by using essentially the same reduction). In order to help the reader we repeat the description of the vertex cover problem.

The vertex cover problem: Given a graph (N, E) and a natural number q, does there exist a subset M of the node set N, with $|M| \leq q$, such that for each edge $\{u, v\} \in$ E, at least one of u and v belongs to M?

We construct a relation schema, R, such that schema(R) has one attribute A_i for each node in N and one attribute B_j for each edge in E; in the following we do not distinguish between attributes and the nodes or edges they represent. We then construct a set F of FDs by having an FD $A_i \rightarrow B_j$ for each node represented by A_i that is in the edge represented by B_j. In the following we let X be the union of all the attributes B_j and let Y be the union of all the attributes

A_i. By Theorem 4.14 given in Subsection 4.4.3 it follows that Y is the only key for R with respect to F.

It remains to be shown that M is a vertex cover for (N, E) if and only if schema(R) has a lossless join and nonredundant decomposition **R** which is in BCNF and such that the cardinality of **R** is no more than k, where $k = q + 1$.

If. Suppose that **R** is a lossless join and nonredundant decomposition of schema(R) into BCNF with respect to F with cardinality no more than k. By part (1) of Theorem 4.2 there exists a relation schema $S \in \mathbf{R}$ such that schema(S) is a superkey for R with respect to F. Moreover, since Y is the unique key for R with respect to F, $Y \subseteq$ schema(S) must hold.

Let S be any relation schema in **R** and assume that schema(S) = W. We claim that if there is at least one attribute B_j in W then there is exactly one attribute A_i in W, otherwise S is redundant. To obtain a contradiction if this were not true there are two cases to consider.

Case 1. There is no such A_i in W, i.e. $Y \cap W = \emptyset$. Then by Theorem 3.29 given in Subsection 3.6.4 of Chapter 3 S is redundant in **R** with respect to F, since CHASE(T(**R**), F) contains a winning row if and only if CHASE(T(**R** − {S}), F) contains a winning row. This is due to the fact that no FD in F has an attribute B_j in its left-hand side.

Case 2. There are two distinct attributes A_1 and A_2 in $Y \cap W$. Then due to the fact that no FD in F has an attribute B_j in its left-hand side, neither $A_1 \in B_j^+$ nor $A_2 \in B_j^+$ hold. There are three further subcases to consider. Firstly, suppose that neither $B_j \in A_1^+$ nor $B_j \in A_2^+$. It follows therefore that $B_j \notin (A_1 A_2)^+$, otherwise by the construction of F, $A_1 A_2 = Y$ implying that either $B_j \in A_1^+$ or $B_j \in A_2^+$ leading to a contradiction. (We observe that there are no nontrivial FDs in F^+ of the form $A_1 A_2 \rightarrow A_3$.) Therefore, $Y \not\subseteq$ schema(S) implying that S is redundant in **R** with respect to F, since as in Case 1, we have that CHASE(T(**R**), F) contains a winning row if and only if CHASE(T(**R** − {S}), F) contains a winning row. This is due to the fact that all the FDs in $F^+[S]$ are trivial. Secondly, suppose that either $B_j \in A_1^+$ or $B_j \in A_2^+$ holds. Then S is not in BCNF with respect to F, since neither $A_1 \in A_2^+$ nor $A_2 \in A_1^+$ holds, thus leading to a contradiction. Thirdly, suppose that $B_j \in (A_1 A_2)^+$ but neither $B_j \in A_1^+$ nor $B_j \in A_2^+$. Then by the construction of F we conclude that $A_1 A_2 = Y$ and thus either $B_j \in A_1^+$ or $B_j \in A_2^+$ in which case S is not in BCNF, thus leading to a contradiction. The claim is now proved.

So, we can form a vertex cover for (N, E) with at most q nodes as follows. If **R** contains only one relation schema, say S, then schema(S) = Y, and it must be the case that $E = \emptyset$ implying that $M = \emptyset$. Otherwise, by the above claim **R** contains a single relation schema S with schema(S) = Y and all other relation schemas in **R** have a single attribute A_i in them. We form M by the union of the A_i in the attribute sets of the relation schemas in **R** − {S}. The result follows by the construction of F, since due to the fact that **R** is a lossless join decomposition of schema(R) with respect to F, we have that $X \subseteq M^+$.

Only if. Suppose that $M = \{A_1, A_2, \ldots, A_q\}$ is a vertex cover for (N, E). Let $\mathbf{R} = \{R_1, R_2, \ldots, R_q, R_k\}$ where for all $i \in \{1, 2, \ldots, q\}$, schema$(R_i) = A_i^+ \cap (X \cup \{A_i\})$, i.e. the intersection of the closure of A_i with respect to F with the set of attributes $X \cup \{A_i\}$, and finally schema$(R_k) = Y$. It can be verified that the database schema **R** is in BCNF with respect to F. This relies on the observations that (i) by the construction of F it is true that for all subsets W of X, $W^+ = W$, and (ii) for all proper subsets Z of Y, $Z^+ \cap Y = Z$. Moreover, it is easy to show that **R** is a lossless join decomposition of schema(R) with respect to F on using the chase procedure of Theorem 3.29 given in Subsection 3.6.4 of Chapter 3. □

It is not clear whether the problem stated in Theorem 4.22 is in NP or not. This is due to the fact that we can guess a database schema **R** and check in polynomial time whether **R** is nonredundant with respect to F by using the chase procedure, but as was shown in Theorem 4.17 the problem of deciding whether **R** is in BCNF with respect to a set F of FDs over R is, in general, co-NP-complete.

4.6.3   How to Obtain a Decomposition in IDNF

We present some heuristics for obtaining decompositions which are in IDNF with respect to a set F of FDs and a set I of INDs both over **R**. We assume that **R** is already decomposed into BCNF with respect to F by using the decomposition algorithm given in Subsection 4.6.2.

Our heuristics deal with three problems that can prevent **R** from being in IDNF:

1) I has an IND of the form R[XA] ⊆ S[YB], where Y is a superkey for S with respect to F and B ∉ Y (see Example 4.12 of Subsection 4.4.4); we call this problem the *redundant attribute problem*.

2) I has an IND of the form R[X] ⊆ S[Y], where Y is *not* a superkey for S with respect to F, i.e. the intersection of Y with any key for S with respect to F is a proper subset of a key for S with respect to F (see Example 4.13 of Subsection 4.4.4); we call this problem the *missing attribute problem*.

3) I is a circular set of INDs (see Example 4.14 of Subsection 4.4.4); we call this problem the *circular IND problem*.

Definition 4.24 (BCNF preserving heuristic)   A heuristic is *BCNF preserving* with respect to a database schema **R** and a set F of FDs together with a set I of INDs both over **R** (or simply BCNF preserving if **R**, F and I are understood from context) if after the heuristic is applied, resulting in the modification of **R** to **R'**, F to *F'* and I to *I'*, **R'** is in BCNF with respect to *F'*. ∎

H1 Heuristic for solving the redundant attribute problem, where R[XA] ⊆ S[YB] ∈ I, Y is a superkey for S with respect to F and B ∉ Y. In this case A is redundant in R. Thus we remove A from schema(R) and replace the IND R[XA] ⊆ S[YB] in I with the IND R[X] ⊆ S[Y].

As we showed in Example 4.12, by invoking heuristic H1, we remove the attribute D from schema(HEAD) and transform the IND HEAD[HD] ⊆ LECT[LD] into the key-based IND HEAD[H] ⊆ LECT[L] (in the actual example we renamed the schema HEAD to be NEW_HEAD). The removal of the attribute D from schema(HEAD) does not incur any loss of information, since the original relation schema, which includes D, can be inferred via the relational algebra query

$$\pi_{\{H,D\}}(\sigma_{H=L}(HEAD \times LECT)).$$

H2 Heuristic for solving the missing attribute problem, where R[X] ⊆ S[Y] ∈ I and Y is not a superkey for S with respect to F. Since Y is not a superkey for S with respect to F we can find a nonempty set of attributes W ⊆ schema(S) − Y such that YW is a superkey for R with respect to F. We choose one attribute B ∈ W and add a corresponding new attribute, say A, which is not in schema(**R**), to schema(R). We assume that A is not a prime attribute of R with respect to F and that the keys for R with respect to F remain unchanged, i.e. if K is a key for R prior to adding A to schema(R) then R: K → A ∈ F^+ after adding A to schema(R). Finally, we replace the IND R[X] ⊆ S[Y] in I by the IND R[XA] ⊆ S[YB].

As we showed in Example 4.13, by invoking heuristic H2, we add the new attribute L' to schema(EMP) and transform the IND EMP[P] ⊆ PROJ[P] into the key-based IND EMP[PL'] ⊆ PROJ[PL] (in the actual example we renamed the schema EMP to be NEW_EMP). Moreover, we add the FD EMP: E → L' to F. We note that as a result of invoking H2 we can now losslessly join relations over EMP and PROJ, after renaming L' to L in schema(EMP), since PL is a key for PROJ.

It is evident that repeated application of the heuristics H1 and H2 results in a set of INDs that is key-based. The next lemma shows that these heuristics are also BCNF preserving.

Lemma 4.23   The heuristics H1 and H2 are BCNF preserving.

Proof. H1 is BCNF preserving, since removing an attribute from schema(R) does not affect the property that R is in BCNF with respect to F. H2 is BCNF preserving since the keys for the resulting relation schema remain the same after the new attribute is added to schema(R).   □

The next two heuristics transform I to a noncircular set of INDs by removing cycles from I. Prior to invoking them we assume that we have applied heuristics H1 and H2 repeatedly until I is a set of key-based INDs.

Definition 4.25 (A cycle of INDs)   A *cycle* of INDs in I is either a nontrivial IND R[X] ⊆ R[Y] ∈ I or a sequence of m, with $m > 1$, distinct INDs in I of the form: $R_1[X_1] ⊆ R_2[Y_2], R_2[X_2] ⊆ R_3[Y_3], \ldots, R_m[X_m] ⊆ R_1[Y_1]$, where $R_1, R_2, \ldots, R_m$ are distinct relation schemas in **R**. A cycle of INDs in I is *proper* if for all $i ∈ \{1, 2, \ldots, m\}$ we have $X_i = Y_i$.   ■

Definition 4.26 (Cycle breaking heuristics)   A sequence of heuristics, $H_1, H_2, \ldots, H_k$, is *cycle breaking* with respect to a database schema **R** and a set F of FDs together with a set I of INDs both over **R** (or simply cycle breaking if **R**, F and I are understood from context) if, after applying each heuristic in the sequence a finite number of times such that we always apply H_i before H_j, when $i < j$, resulting in the modification of **R** to **R**′, F to F' and I to I', the set I' is a noncircular set of INDs.   ■

Definition 4.27 (Key-based preserving heuristic)   A heuristic is *key-based preserving* with respect to a database schema **R** and a set F of FDs together with a set I of INDs both over **R** (or simply key-based preserving if **R**, F and I are understood from context) if, after the heuristic is applied resulting in the modification of **R** to **R**′, F to F' and I to I', the set I' is a key-based set of INDs over **R**′ with respect to F'.   ■

H3 First heuristic for solving the circular IND problem, where $R_1[X_1] ⊆ R_2[Y_2], R_2[X_2] ⊆ R_3[Y_3], \ldots, R_m[X_m] ⊆ R_1[Y_1]$ is a proper cycle in I. Collapse R_1 and R_2 into R_1 as follows.

Firstly, we rename all the attributes in schema(R_2) $-$ Y_2 to new attributes that are disjoint from the attributes in schema(**R**); the renaming of the attributes is also carried out in all the data dependencies in which they appear with reference to R_2. Secondly, the attributes in schema(R_2) $-$ Y_2 are added to schema(R_1). Finally, we remove R_2 from **R** and rename all references to the relation schema R_2 and the attributes Y_2 to be to R_1 and X_1, respectively, in all the data dependencies that they appear in.

Example 4.20   Consider a database schema **R** = {EMP, JOB}, with schema(EMP) = {EN, AGE, ADR} and schema(JOB) = {JNO, JDES, DN}, where EN stands for employee name, AGE stands for employee age, JNO stands for job number, JDES stands for job description and DN stands for department name. Moreover, consider a set F of FDs over **R** consisting of the two FDs, EN $\rightarrow$ schema(EMP) and JNO $\rightarrow$ schema(JOB), and a set I of INDs over **R** consisting of the two INDs, EMP[EN] $\subseteq$ JOB[JNO] and JOB[JNO] $\subseteq$ EMP[EN]. When invoking heuristic H3 we add the new attributes, say *JDES'* and *DN'*, to schema(EMP), remove the relation schema JOB from **R** and replace the FD JNO $\rightarrow$ schema(JOB) by the FD EMP: EN $\rightarrow$ {*JDES'*, *DN'*}. We also rename JOB to EMP and JNO to EN in the set I of INDs; thereafter it follows that I is empty since it contains only trivial INDs when the renaming is completed. It can be verified that the resulting database schema is in BCNF and that I is trivially noncircular. We note that each of the two original relation schemas can be inferred from the new one by a relation algebra query involving projection and renaming where appropriate.   ∎

H4   Second heuristic for solving the circular IND problem, where $R_1[X_1] \subseteq R_2[Y_2]$, $R_2[X_2] \subseteq R_3[Y_3], \ldots, R_m[X_m] \subseteq R_1[Y_1]$ is a cycle in I which is not proper. Firstly, we remove the attributes in $X_1 - Y_1$ from schema(R_1), project the set of FDs over the original R_1 onto the resulting relation schema, and remove $R_1[X_1] \subseteq R_2[Y_2]$ from I. Secondly, we add a new relation schema S to **R**, an FD to F and two INDs to I as follows. We set schema(S) = $X_1 Y_1$, noting that since I is key-based we have that Y_1 is a key for R_1 with respect to F, and therefore we add the FD S : $Y_1 \rightarrow X_1$ to F. Lastly, we add the INDs $S[X_1] \subseteq R_2[Y_2]$ and $S[Y_1] \subseteq R_1[Y_1]$ to I.

Example 4.21   Consider a database schema **R** = {EMP}, with schema(EMP) = {EN, MN}, where EN stands for employee name and MN stands for manager name. Moreover, consider a set F of FDs over **R** having the single FD, EMP: EN $\rightarrow$ MN, and a set I of INDs over **R** having the single IND, EMP[MN] $\subseteq$ EMP[EN]. When invoking heuristic H4 we remove the attribute MN from schema(EMP) and add the new relation schema EMP-MGR to **R**, with schema(EMP-MGR) = {EN, MN}. Furthermore, we remove the FD EMP: EN $\rightarrow$ MN from F as a result of the projection in H4 and add to F the FD EMP-MGR : EN $\rightarrow$ MN; we also replace the single IND in I by the two INDs: EMP-MGR[MN] $\subseteq$ EMP[EN] and EMP-MGR[EN] $\subseteq$ EMP[EN] (see also Example 4.14). It can be verified that the resulting database schema is in BCNF and that I is noncircular. Moreover, the original version of the relation schema EMP can be losslessly recovered by a relational algebra expression which joins together EMP and EMP-MGR.

Consider a database schema **R** = {EMP, DEPT}, with schema(EMP) = {EN, DN} and schema(DEPT) = {DN, MN}, where EN stands for employee name, DN stands for department name and MN stands for manager name. Moreover, consider a set F of FDs over **R** consisting of the two FDs, EMP : EN $\rightarrow$ DN and DEPT : DN $\rightarrow$ MN, and a set I of INDs over **R** consisting of the two INDs, EMP[DN] $\subseteq$ DEPT[DN] and DEPT[MN] $\subseteq$ EMP[EN]. When invoking heuristic H4 we remove the attribute DN from schema(EMP) and add the new relation schema EMP-DEPT to **R**, with schema(EMP-DEPT) = {EN, DN}. Furthermore, we remove the FD EMP: EN $\rightarrow$ DN from F as a result of the projection in H4 and add to F the FD EMP-DEPT : EN $\rightarrow$ DN; we also replace the IND EMP[DN] $\subseteq$ DEPT[DN] in I by the two INDs: EMP-DEPT[DN] $\subseteq$ DEPT[DN] and EMP-DEPT[EN] $\subseteq$ EMP[EN]. It can be verified that the resulting database schema is in BCNF and that I is noncircular. Moreover, the original version of the relation schema EMP can be losslessly recovered by a relational algebra expression which joins together EMP and EMP-DEPT. ∎

Lemma 4.24 The heuristics H3 and H4 are BCNF preserving, key-based preserving and the sequence of heuristics H3, H4 is cycle breaking.

Proof. Firstly, we show that H3 and H4 are BCNF preserving. H3 is BCNF preserving, since X_1 and Y_2 are equivalent keys in the sense that in any database d over **R** satisfying F and I we have that $\pi_{X_1}(r_1) = \pi_{Y_2}(r_2)$, where r_1 and r_2 are the relations in d over R_1 and R_2, respectively. Thus the effect of H3 is to merge R_1 and R_2 together by transforming all references to Y_2 to be references to X_1 and the set of keys for the transformed relation schema is just the result of merging together the keys for the old relation schemas R_1 and R_2. H4 is BCNF preserving since we have removed attributes from schema(R_1) and, in addition, schema(S) is a subset of the original schema(R_1) which is known to be in BCNF with respect to F.

Secondly, it is evident that each application of heuristic H3 or H4 results in a set of INDs that is key-based.

Thirdly, we show that the sequence H3, H4 is cycle breaking. This follows directly from the fact that repeated application of H3 or H4 each results in removing a cycle from I. Moreover, no new cycles are introduced by applying either H3 or H4 and the set I of INDs can have only a finite number of cycles in it. □

The next theorem is immediate from Lemmas 4.23 and 4.24 observing that after applying H1 and H2 a sufficient number of times we obtain a key-based set of INDs.

Theorem 4.25 Given a database schema **R** that is in BCNF with respect to a set F of FDs over **R** and a set I of INDs over **R** we can obtain an IDNF database schema by invoking the following two steps:

1) Apply heuristics H1 and H2 repeatedly until I becomes key-based.

2) Apply the sequence of heuristics H3, H4 until I becomes noncircular. □

The problem of achieving a database schema in normal form with respect to a set of FDs and INDs is considered in [CA84, MR86b, MS89a, MM90, MR92a]. In all these references apart from [MR86b] part of the requirement of being in normal form is that each relation schema in **R** also correspond to a particular type of ERD. Thus a database schema which is in such an *Entity Relationship Normal Form* (ERNF) can be readily transformed into an ERD. This approach has the advantage that the semantics of the database schema can be presented in terms of the ER model, whose semantics are easier for users to understand.

4.7   Converting an ERD into a Relational Database Schema in IDNF

It is common practice to produce an ERD as a first step in relational database design. The semantics of the application are more visible in the ERD and many database users find it easier to work with the ERD rather than directly with the attributes of the database schema and the data dependencies over this set of attributes. Herein we present a mapping from an entity relationship diagram, **D**, onto a database schema **R** together with a set of FDs and INDs over **R**. We will show that **R** is in IDNF with respect to the set of data dependencies output from the mapping. Thus given that a database designer prefers to work with ERDs we can automate the process of relational database design once the ERD under consideration is completed.

One of the problems with this approach is that when an entity type is added to the ERD the user needs to specify a primary key (or more generally a set of candidate keys), which has the effect of producing a relation schema already in BCNF. However, in order to specify the candidate keys the user needs to know the set of FDs that are valid for the application in hand. Similarly, the relationship types induce certain key-based INDs but in order for these to be specified correctly the user may need to know more about the INDs that are valid for the application in hand. Thus it may be possible to utilise the algorithms given in Section 4.6 during the process of designing an ERD in order to produce a higher quality result.

For the sake of simplicity of the mapping we will assume that **D** does not contain any recursive relationship types; in fact, a recursive relationship type can always be transformed into a nonrecursive one. This is achieved by replacing the entity type involved in the recursive relationship type by two distinct entity types each denoting one of the two roles the said entity type plays in the relationship type.

Furthermore, we will assume that the set of nonprime (i.e. nonkey) attribute names associated with any two entity types in the ERD are disjoint and that the key attributes of each entity type (including the entity types involved in built-in relationship types) are explicitly represented for each entity type in **D**. We will call this assumption the *disjointness assumption for nonprime attributes*; this assumption can always be enforced by renaming of attribute names. We note that it is still possible for a nonprime attribute of one entity type, say DNAME in EMP, to be the same as a prime attribute of another entity type, say DNAME in DEPT.

With respect to the built-in relationship types we have the following situation. If the relationship type is an ID relationship type from an entity type $\mathcal{E}_1$ to an entity type $\mathcal{E}_2$, then we repeat the primary key attributes of $\mathcal{E}_2$ in the representation of $\mathcal{E}_1$ in **D**. Similarly, if the relationship type is an ISA relationship type from an entity type $\mathcal{E}_1$ to an entity type $\mathcal{E}_2$, then due to the inheritance of attributes we need only repeat the primary key attributes of $\mathcal{E}_2$ in the representation of $\mathcal{E}_1$ in **D**. In the mapping now described we consider the set of attributes associated with an entity type to be the set of attributes explicitly represented in **D** for that entity type.

Another reasonable assumption that we will make concerns the built-in relationship types ID and ISA (see Section 2.4 of Chapter 2). Let **B** denote the ERD resulting from removing from **D** all *non* built-in relationship types, and also all attributes and the corresponding edges connecting these attributes to their entity types. That is, **B** is an ERD describing the entity types and the built-in relationship types present in **D**; we call the subgraph **B**, the *inheritance lattice* induced by **D**. We observe that **B** is directed and that, in general, **B** may not be connected and thus may have islands of connected components. The assumption we make is that the inheritance lattice **B**, which is induced by **D**, does *not* contain any directed cycles (or simply cycles). We justify this assumption by considering two cases when we have a cycle in the inheritance lattice **B** involving two entity types $\mathcal{E}_1$ and $\mathcal{E}_2$. Firstly, suppose that there is an ID relationship type between $\mathcal{E}_1$ and $\mathcal{E}_2$, i.e. $\mathcal{E}_1$ ID $\mathcal{E}_2$. Thus by the transitivity of ID and ISA relationship types we conclude that $\mathcal{E}_2$ ID $\mathcal{E}_1$ or $\mathcal{E}_2$ ISA $\mathcal{E}_1$. This leads to a contradiction since, due to the fact that there is a cycle involving $\mathcal{E}_1$ and $\mathcal{E}_2$, we conclude that the primary keys of $\mathcal{E}_1$ and $\mathcal{E}_2$ are the same contrary to the definition of an ID relationship type. Secondly, suppose that that there is no ID relationship type between $\mathcal{E}_1$ and $\mathcal{E}_2$ and, by symmetry, that there is also no ID relationship type between $\mathcal{E}_2$ and $\mathcal{E}_1$. Thus by the transitivity of ISA relationship types we conclude that $\mathcal{E}_1$ ISA $\mathcal{E}_2$ and $\mathcal{E}_2$ ISA $\mathcal{E}_1$ implying that $\mathcal{E}_1$ and $\mathcal{E}_2$ should be merged, since they do not represent distinct entity types. Therefore, in **D** we can collapse $\mathcal{E}_1$ and $\mathcal{E}_2$ into a single entity type, say $\mathcal{E}$, take the corresponding attribute set E to be the union of the attributes sets of $\mathcal{E}_1$ and $\mathcal{E}_2$, and also adjust the relationship types involving $\mathcal{E}_1$ and $\mathcal{E}_2$ accordingly so that they reference $\mathcal{E}$ instead (see heuristic H3 for solving the proper circular IND problem in Subsection 4.6.3). It follows that we are justified in assuming that the inheritance lattice **B**, which is induced by **D**, does not contain any cycles; we call this assumption the *built-in relationship type assumption*.

Definition 4.28 (Mapping entity types) An entity type $\mathcal{E}$ in **D** is mapped to a relation schema, denoted by $R(\mathcal{E})$, with schema($R(\mathcal{E})$) being equal to the set of attributes associated with $\mathcal{E}$; we will assume that all the attributes of $\mathcal{E}$ are single-valued, so that the resulting relation schema be in 1NF. A singleton set of FDs, denoted by $F(\mathcal{E})$, is associated with $\mathcal{E}$, where ■

$$F(\mathcal{E}) = \{K \to \text{schema}(R(\mathcal{E})) \mid K \text{ is the primary key of } \mathcal{E}\}.$$

We observe that in the above definition we assume that the entity type has a single candidate key, which by default is the primary key. This assumption can be relaxed by allowing additional candidate keys, called *alternate keys*, to be represented in the ERD. Allowing alternate keys to be represented will not affect the translation process.

Definition 4.29 (Mapping cardinality-based relationship types) Let $\mathcal{R}$ in **D** be a relationship type from the entity type $\mathcal{E}_1$ in **D** to the entity type $\mathcal{E}_2$ in **D**, with K_1 being the primary key of $\mathcal{E}_1$ and K_2 being the primary key of $\mathcal{E}_2$; $\mathcal{R}$ may be a many-to-many, a many-to-one or a one-to-one relationship type.

The relationship type $\mathcal{R}$ is mapped to a relation schema, denoted by $R(\mathcal{R})$, with schema($R(\mathcal{R})$) $= K_1 \cup K_2$. We assume without loss of generality that K_1 and K_2 are disjoint; if not we can always enforce this disjointness by adding to each attribute a role name corresponding to the entity type it belongs to; see Definition 2.9 in Subsection 2.2.4 of Chapter 2. The following set of key dependencies, denoted by $F(\mathcal{R})$, is associated with $\mathcal{R}$:

- if $\mathcal{R}$ is a many-to-many relationship type, then $F(\mathcal{R}) = \emptyset$,

- if $\mathcal{R}$ is a many-to-one relationship type, then $F(\mathcal{R}) = \{K_1 \to K_2\}$, or

- if $\mathcal{R}$ is a one-to-one relationship type, then $F(\mathcal{R}) = \{K_1 \to K_2, K_2 \to K_1\}$.

In addition, a set of two key-based INDs, denoted by $I(\mathcal{R})$, is associated with $\mathcal{R}$, where

$$I(\mathcal{R}) = \{R(\mathcal{R})[K_1] \subseteq R(\mathcal{E}_1)[K_1], R(\mathcal{R})[K_2] \subseteq R(\mathcal{E}_2)[K_2]\}. \qquad ■$$

We observe that when the relationship type is many-to-one or one-to-one, there is no need to create an additional relation schema for the relationship type. In the many-to-one case from $\mathcal{E}_1$ to $\mathcal{E}_2$ we can add the primary key attributes of $R(\mathcal{E}_2)$ to $R(\mathcal{E}_1)$, renaming attributes if necessary, and add a key-based IND from these foreign key attributes to the primary key attributes of $R(\mathcal{E}_2)$; the primary key of $R(\mathcal{E}_1)$ remains the same. The construction for the one-to-one case is similar except that it is done in both directions, by considering the one-to-one relationship type as a combination of a many-to-one relationship type from $\mathcal{E}_1$ to $\mathcal{E}_2$ together with another many-to-one relationship type from $\mathcal{E}_2$ to $\mathcal{E}_1$. The problem with this alternative approach is that the resulting set of INDs may be cyclic and thus IDNF will be violated.

Definition 4.30 (Mapping built-in relationship types)   Let $\mathcal{R}$ in $\mathbf{D}$ be a relationship type from the entity type $\mathcal{E}_1$ in $\mathbf{D}$ to the entity type $\mathcal{E}_2$ in $\mathbf{D}$, with K_1 being the primary key of $\mathcal{E}_1$ and K_2 being the primary key of $\mathcal{E}_2$; $\mathcal{R}$ may be an ID or an ISA relationship type. If $\mathcal{R}$ is an ID type then $K_2 \subset K_1$ and if $\mathcal{R}$ is an ISA type then $K_1 = K_2$.

A singleton set of key-based INDs, denoted by $I(\mathcal{R})$, is associated with $\mathcal{R}$, where

$$I(\mathcal{R}) = \{R(\mathcal{E}_1)[K_2] \subseteq R(\mathcal{E}_2)[K_2]\}. \qquad \blacksquare$$

We observe that the INDs produced from mapping relationship types are typed and thus by Theorem 3.45 in Subsection 3.6.10 of Chapter 3 their implication problem is polynomial time decidable. We now summarise the above three mappings as a mapping from an ERD to a database schema together with a set of FDs and INDs.

Definition 4.31 (The mapping from ERDs to database schemas)   We amalgamate the mappings given above to obtain a mapping from an ERD $\mathbf{D}$ to a database schema, $R(\mathbf{D})$, with an associated set of FDs, $F(\mathbf{D})$, and an associated set of INDs, $I(\mathbf{D})$, as follows:

$$
\begin{aligned}
R(\mathbf{D}) \;=\; & \{R(\mathcal{E}) \mid \mathcal{E} \text{ is an entity type in } \mathbf{D}\} \cup \\
& \{R(\mathcal{R}) \mid \mathcal{R} \text{ is a cardinality-based relationship type in } \mathbf{D}\}, \\
F(\mathbf{D}) \;=\; & \{F(\mathcal{E}) \mid \mathcal{E} \text{ is an entity type in } \mathbf{D}\} \cup \\
& \{F(\mathcal{R}) \mid \mathcal{R} \text{ is a cardinality-based relationship type in } \mathbf{D}\}, \text{ and} \\
I(\mathbf{D}) \;=\; & \{I(\mathcal{R}) \mid \mathcal{R} \text{ is a relationship type in } \mathbf{D}\}. \qquad \blacksquare
\end{aligned}
$$

The following theorem shows that the mapping just defined yields a database schema in IDNF (see Definition 4.16 in Subsection 4.4.4 for the definition of IDNF). This has a practical implication, since in many IT departments it is common practice to produce an ERD as a first step in relational database design and then to use the ERD as the basis for constructing a relational database schema.

Theorem 4.26   Let $\mathbf{D}$ be an ERD that satisfies the disjointness assumption for nonprime attributes and the built-in relationship type assumption. Then $R(\mathbf{D})$ is in IDNF with respect to $F(\mathbf{D})$ and $I(\mathbf{D})$.

Proof. Let $R(\mathbf{D}) \in \mathbf{R}$ be a relation schema. If R, where R stands for $R(\mathbf{D})$, is mapped from an entity type then R is in BCNF with respect to $F(\mathbf{D})$, since $F(\mathbf{D})[R]$ contains a single key dependency by the disjointness assumption for nonprime attributes. (If we allow alternate keys to be represented in the ERD, it can be shown that R is still in BCNF with respect to F(D).) On the other hand, if R is mapped from a cardinality-based relationship type, then by construction R is in BCNF with respect to F(D), since K_1 and K_2 are assumed to be disjoint. Furthermore, all the INDs generated from relationship types, whether they be cardinality-based or built-in, are key-based and thus I(D) is a key-based set of INDs. The result that R is in IDNF with respect to F(D) and I(D) follows, since it can be verified that I(D) is noncircular due to the built-in relationship type assumption. □

It can easily be seen that the mappings from R(D), F(D) and I(D) can be carried out in polynomial time in the size of D, and can be viewed as an efficient synthesis algorithm.

Example 4.22 Consider the ERD, D, shown in Figure 2.1 of Chapter 2, concerning a computerised book order system; we will ignore the two multi-valued attributes PHONES of CUSTOMER and AUTHORS of BOOK. The mapping from D results in the following database schema and set of FDs and INDs, where in this case we take R($\mathcal{R}$) = $\mathcal{R}$:

1) R(D) = {CUSTOMER, ORDER, INVOICE, BOOK, PLACES, RECEIVES, BILLING, SPECIFIES}, with schema(CUSTOMER) = {C#, NAME, ADDRESS}, schema(ORDER) = {O#, O_DATE, QTY}, schema(INVOICE) = {I#, I_DATE, VALUE}, schema(BOOK) = {ISBN, TITLE, PRICE}, schema(PLACES) = {C#, O#}, schema(RECEIVES) = {C#, I#}, schema(BILLING) = {O#, I#} and schema(SPECIFIES) = {O#, ISBN}.

2) F(D) = {CUSTOMER : C# → schema(CUSTOMER), ORDER : O# → schema(ORDER), INVOICE : I# → schema(INVOICE), BOOK : ISBN → schema(BOOK), PLACES : O# → C#, RECEIVES : I# → C#, BILLING : O# → I#, BILLING : I# → O#}.

3) I(D) = {PLACES[C#] ⊆ CUSTOMER[C#], PLACES[O#] ⊆ ORDER[O#], RECEIVES[C#] ⊆ CUSTOMER[C#], RECEIVES[I#] ⊆ INVOICE[I#], BILLING[O#] ⊆ ORDER[O#], BILLING[I#] ⊆ INVOICE[I#], SPECIFIES[O#] ⊆ ORDER[O#], SPECIFIES[ISBN] ⊆ BOOK[ISBN]}.

The reader can verify that R(D) is in IDNF with respect to F(D) and I(D). ∎

Jajodia et al. [JNS83a, JNS83b] consider the problem of when an ERD can be mapped to a database schema which is in BCNF without taking INDs into account. They allow general n-ary relationship types, which may have attributes of their own, while we have restricted ourselves to binary relationship types and we do not allow such relationship types to have attributes of their own (see Subsection 2.2.2 of Chapter 2). Several researchers [CA84, DA87, MS89a, MM90, MR92a] have also considered the inverse mapping, namely from a database schema to an ERD. Given that a database schema is in ERNF (see end of Subsection 4.6.3) then it can be mapped to an ERD, which in turn can be mapped back to the database schema. Especially for naive users such a mapping may be very useful as an aid to understanding the semantics of the database schema.

4.8   Discussion

Relational database design has been at the forefront of relational database theory since its inception in Codd's seminal paper [Cod72a], which introduced 2NF and 3NF, and the introduction of BCNF in [Cod74]. An informative summary of the state of the art on the various normal forms, not taking INDs into account, was given by Kent as early as 1983 [Ken83a]. The concepts pertaining to the various normal forms have infiltrated industry and are widely used in practice. Moreover, as we have seen in Section 4.7, relational database design can be combined with the higher-level activity of data modelling by using ERDs. It is our view that relational database design is a good example of how theory can have an important and direct influence on practice. We also feel that recent work on providing semantic justification for the various normal forms is of fundamental importance, since it can provide us with an explanation of what we actually achieve by the process of database design [Vin94, LV99].

We now briefly mention how we can reduce query processing overheads by designing *acyclic* database schemas. It is natural to describe a database schema **R** as a *hypergraph*, where the nodes of the hypergraph correspond to the attributes in the relation schemas of **R** and each hyperedge is the set of attributes of one of the relation schemas in **R**. Fagin [Fag83] investigated various types of *acyclicity* of relational database schemas when viewed as hypergraphs. (See Subsection 3.6.14 in Chapter 3 for the formal definition of an acyclic database schema and its hypergraph representation.) Recall Definition 3.98 in Subsection 3.6.14 of Chapter 3 of pairwise and join consistent databases. Moreover, recall Theorem 3.73 of Subsection 3.6.14 in Chapter 3, where we have shown that a database schema **R** is acyclic if and only if every pairwise consistent database over **R** is also join consistent. Thus in order to check join consistency of a database over an acyclic database schema, we can simply check, in polynomial time in the size of the input database, whether it is pairwise consistent or not. In general, when the database schema is cyclic then, by Theorem 3.72 of Subsection 3.6.14 in Chapter 3, testing for join consistency is an NP-complete problem.

Let us call the query that involves the computation of the natural join of all the relations in the database the *database join query*. The computation of the database join query is said to be *monotone* if it can be computed in a way such that for all the intermediate stages during the computation of the query, the number of tuples in any intermediate result is greater than or equal to the number of tuples in the previous intermediate result, i.e. the number of tuples in the result of the query increases monotonically. In [GS82, BFMY83] it was shown that a database schema is acyclic if and only if the computation of the database join query is monotone assuming that the database is pairwise consistent. Thus the database join query can be computed efficiently when the database schema is acyclic. If the database schema is such that every subset of the database schema is also acyclic then it follows that all natural join queries involving one or more relations in the database can be computed efficiently.

Finally, we refer the reader to [Bis98] for a recent critique on the overall achievements and prospects of database design.

4.9   Exercises

Exercise 4.1   Given a relation schema R, with schema(R) = {A, B, C, D}, together with a set of FDs F = {A → B, A → C, A → D}, is R in 2NF? Is R in 3NF? Is R in BCNF?

Exercise 4.2   Given a relation schema R, with schema(R) = {A, B, C, D}, together with a set of FDs F = {A → B, B → C, C → D}, is R in 2NF? Is R in 3NF? Is R in BCNF?

Exercise 4.3   Given a relation schema R, with schema(R) = {A, B, C}, together with a set of FDs F = {AB → C, AC → B, BC → A}, is R in 2NF? Is R in 3NF? Is R in BCNF?

Exercise 4.4   Given a relation schema R, with schema(R) = {A, B, C}, together with a set of FDs F = {AB → C, C → B}, is R in 2NF? Is R in 3NF? Is R in BCNF?

Exercise 4.5   An FD X → A in a set F of FDs over a relation schema R is *elementary*, if it is nontrivial, A is a single attribute and for no proper subset Y ⊂ X, is it true that Y → A ∈ F^+. A set F of FDs is elementary if all the FDs in F are elementary. Prove that R is in BCNF with respect to a set F of elementary FDs if and only if for every FD X → A ∈ F, X is a key for R with respect to F [Zan82].

Exercise 4.6   Prove that if a relation schema R is in 3NF with respect to a set F of FDs but is not in BCNF with respect to F, then it must have at least two distinct keys for R with respect to F which overlap, i.e. such that their intersection is nonempty [VS93, Mok97].

Exercise 4.7   The definitions of 3NF and BCNF do not mention null values at all, although entity integrity insists that the primary key values of tuples in a relation should not contain any null values. Show how, in the presence of null values, this restriction has an effect on the validity of a 3NF or BCNF decomposition, assuming that the null values are of the type, "value exists but is unknown at the present time" [AC84].

Exercise 4.8   An MVD X →→ Y | Z is *pure* with respect to a set M of FDs and MVDs, if it is nontrivial and neither X → Y nor X → Z are in M^+. Prove that if R is in BCNF with respect to M, i.e. R is in BCNF with respect to the set of FDs in M^+, then for any key K for R with respect to the set of FDs in M^+ and any pure MVD X →→ Y | Z ∈ M^+, YZ ⊆ K [Jaj86].

Exercise 4.9   You are given a relation schema R, with schema(R) = {A, B, C, D, E, G}, together with a set of FDs F = {A → B, CD → A, CB → D, AE → G, CE → D}. Synthesise R into a lossless join and dependency preserving 3NF decomposition with respect to F. Decompose R into a lossless join BCNF decomposition with respect to F.

Exercise 4.10   Let F be a set of FDs over R that is canonical, nonredundant and such that its left-hand sides are reduced. Define an FD digraph G_F = (N, E) for such a set of FDs as follows. The nodes in N are labelled by FDs in F and there is an arc in E from a node labelled X → A to a node labelled Y → B if A ∈ Y. Show that if G_F is an acyclic digraph then R has a lossless join and dependency preserving BCNF decomposition with respect to F [Maj92].

Exercise 4.11   A relation schema R is in *Fourth Normal Form* (4NF) with respect to a set M of FDs and MVDs, if whenever X →→ Y is a nontrivial MVD in M, then X is a superkey for R with respect to the set of FDs in M^+. (Recall that an FD X → Y is a special case of an MVD X →→ Y.) Prove that 4NF is cover insensitive, i.e. that R is in 4NF if and only if whenever X →→ Y is a nontrivial MVD in M^+, then X is a superkey for R with respect to the set of FDs in M^+.

Exercise 4.12   Prove that if a relation schema R is in 4NF with respect to a set of FDs and MVDs M, then it is also in BCNF with respect to the set of FDs in M^+.

Exercise 4.13   Definition 4.13 of value redundancy in Subsection 4.4.3 can be generalised to FDs and MVDs, simply by replacing, in this definition, the set F of FDs by a set M of FDs and MVDs. Generalise Theorem 4.13 to FDs and MVDs, i.e. prove that a relation schema R is in 4NF with respect to a set M of FDs and MVDs over R if and only if R is in VRFNF with respect to M [Vin98].

Exercise 4.14   A decomposition **R** is in 4NF with respect to a set M of FDs and MVDs over R, with schema(**R**) = schema(**R**), if each $R_i \in \mathbf{R}$ is in 4NF with respect to the set of projected MVDs (PMVDs) that hold in the context of R_i. (See Proposition 3.56 of Subsection 3.6.13 in Chapter 3 for the definition of a PMVD.) Propose an algorithm that decomposes a relation schema R into a lossless join decomposition of schema(R) that is in 4NF with respect to M [Fag77a, Fag77b].

Exercise 4.15   Let M be a set of MVDs over R. Devise an algorithm that obtains a lossless join 4NF decomposition of schema(R), whose cardinality is less than or equal to the cardinality of schema(R) [LT87b].

Exercise 4.16   Assume a set M of FDs and MVDs over a relation schema R. Prove that if R is in BCNF with respect to the set of FDs in M^+ and at least one of the keys for R with respect to the set of FDs in M^+ is simple, then R is also in 4NF with respect to M [DF92]. (Recall that a simple key is a key that is a singleton.)

Exercise 4.17   Recall that an Armstrong relation for a set of integrity constraints Σ is a relation which satisfies all the constraints in Σ and violates each constraint not in the closure of Σ (see Definition 3.56 in Section 3.5 of Chapter 3). Discuss how Armstrong relations can be useful in relational database design.

Exercise 4.18   In some applications the stipulation in the definition of IDNF that the set of INDs be noncircular seems to be overly restrictive. Give an example supporting this claim.

Exercise 4.19   A database d over **R** has an *insertion violation* with respect to a set of FDs and INDs $\Sigma = F \cup I$ over **R** if

1) $d \models \Sigma$, and

2) there exists a tuple t over R which is compatible with r, where r is the relation in d over R, but ICHASE($d \cup \{t\}$, I) $\not\models \Sigma$; $d \cup \{t\}$ denotes the database resulting from the insertion of t into r.

A database schema **R** is *free of insertion anomalies* with respect to Σ if there does not exist a database d over **R** which has an insertion violation with respect to Σ.

Prove that if I is noncircular, then **R** is free of insertion anomalies with respect to Σ if and only if Σ is a reduced set of FDs and INDs (see Definition 3.78 in Subsection 3.6.12 of Chapter 3) and **R** is in BCNF with respect to F [LV99].

Exercise 4.20   A database d over **R** has a *modification violation* with respect to a set of FDs and INDs $\Sigma = \text{F} \cup \text{I}$ over **R** if

1) $d \models \Sigma$, and

2) there exists a tuple $u \in r$ and a tuple t over R which is compatible with $r - \{u\}$, where r is the relation in d over R, but $\text{ICHASE}((d - \{u\}) \cup \{t\}, \text{I}) \not\models \Sigma$; $d - \{u\}$ denotes the database resulting from the deletion of u from r.

A database schema **R** is *free of modification anomalies* with respect to Σ if there does not exist a database d over **R** which has a modification violation.

Prove that if I is noncircular, then **R** is free of modification anomalies with respect to Σ if and only if **R** is free of insertion anomalies with respect to Σ [LV99].

Exercise 4.21   Suppose that we have a relational database schema that is in IDNF with respect to a set of FDs. Propose an algorithm to reverse engineer this database schema into an Entity-Relationship Diagram [DA87].

Exercise 4.22   Suggest how you would design a Computer-Aided Software Engineering (CASE) tool for relational database design, which would allow database designers to iteratively improve the quality of their designs.

5. Incomplete Information in the Relational Data Model

Correct treatment of incomplete information in databases is of fundamental importance, since it is very rare that in practice all the information stored in a database is complete. There are several different types of incompleteness that need to be taken into account. In the first case some information in the database may be missing. Missing information generally falls into two categories; applicable information, for example, if the name of the course that Iris is taking is applicable but unknown, and inapplicable information, for example, if Iris does not have a spouse. In both cases the missing information can be modelled by special values, called *null values*, which act as place holders for the information that is missing. Varied interpretations of null values within these two categories were listed in [ANS75]. In the second case information in the database may be inconsistent, for example, if two different ages were recorded for Iris when Iris is only allowed to have one age. Inconsistency can normally be detected during updates to the database and in such cases it can be avoided. In the third case incompleteness involves the modelling of disjunctive information, which is a special case of applicable but unknown information. For example, we may know that Iris either belongs to the Computer Science department or to the Maths department but we do not know for certain to which department she belongs. Disjunctive information can be modelled by a finite set of values, called an *or-set*, one of these values being the true value. That is, Iris's department is a member of the or-set {Computer_Science, Maths}. In the fourth case incompleteness relates to fuzzy information. In this case the membership of an attribute value may be fuzzy; namely, it may be a number in the interval [0, 1] or a linguistic value such as short, medium or tall. For example, Iris's age may be recorded as young and her performance in last year's exam may be recorded as 0.7. Fuzzy sets are also able to model the situation where there is uncertainty about the membership of a tuple in a relation. For example, we may only know with a degree of 0.8 certainty that the tuple recording information about Iris is actually true, i.e. the membership of that tuple is 0.8. Finally, we could use a probabilistic approach to incomplete information by attaching to each attribute value a probability between 0 and 1 according to a known distribution for that attribute domain. This approach allows the use of statistical inference during query processing in order to obtain approximate answers. We will further discuss the use of probability theory in modelling incomplete information at the end of the chapter.

As relational database systems are now widely available in the commercial world there is a growing demand for comprehensive handling of incomplete information within those systems. This has lead researchers to extend the relational model by allowing attribute values of tuples to be incomplete; we shall refer to such relations as *incomplete relations*.

In Section 5.1 we introduce four different types of null value that cover most situations of incompleteness that arise in practice. In Section 5.2 we discuss two fundamental approaches with regards to how complete the information in a database is, namely the open world and closed world assumptions. In Section 5.3 we formalise the notion of an information lattice of types of null value, which allows us to measure the information content of tuples in a relation, and formally define the meaning of an incomplete relation. In Section 5.4 we present an extension of the relational algebra where we allow a single type of null value representing an unknown value from an attribute domain. In Section 5.5 we show how integrity constraints can be extended to hold in incomplete relations; we focus on FDs and INDs (see Subsections 3.6.1 and 3.6.7 of Chapter 3, respectively, for details concerning the satisfaction of FDs and INDs in relations). In Section 5.6 we formalise the notion of an *or-relation*, which allows the representation of a disjunction of a finite set of values, and show how the relational algebra and integrity constraints can be extended within the context of the or-set approach. In Section 5.7 we formalise the notion of a *fuzzy relation*, based on fuzzy set theory, which allows the representation of *vague* information, and show how the relational algebra and integrity constraints can be extended within this approach. In Section 5.8 we discuss the related approach of *rough sets* which addresses *imprecision* and *ambiguity* in data rather than vagueness. In Section 5.9 we present an alternative approach to dealing with incomplete information that uses *default values* rather than null values. Default values have simpler semantics than null values but they do not take into account the information content of a relation and thus may lead users to misinterpret answers to queries. In Section 5.10 we deal with the problem of updating a relational database in the presence of incomplete information by extending the formalism of Subsection 3.2.4 in Chapter 3.

5.1 Different Types of Null Value

In order to model the two categories of missing information referred to earlier we introduce the following types of null value:

1) "value exists but is unknown at the present time" or "value is applicable and missing at the present time", which is denoted in the database by the distinguished value *unk*; for example, if Iris's age is unknown, then the attribute value for age in the tuple recording information about Iris would be *unk*.

2) "value does not exist" or "value is inapplicable", which is denoted in the database by the distinguished value *dne*; for example, if Iris does not have a job, then the attribute value for job in the tuple recording information about Iris would be *dne*; we note that *dne* is very useful when filling in forms where some of the categories in the form may be filled in as inapplicable. As opposed to *unk*, the null value *dne* does not arise due to incompleteness of information. Despite this fact *dne* cannot be treated as just another nonnull value; for example, we can record the fact that a person is unmarried by having *dne* as their spouse attribute value but we cannot say that two unmarried people have the same spouse.

Zaniolo [Zan84] observed that both *unk* and *dne* do not provide the most fundamental type of null value. There are situations when we may not even know if an attribute value exists or not. For example, we may not have any recorded information in the database as to whether Hillary is married or not. Another example is that we may not have any information recorded in the database as to whether Iris has a job or not. This gives rise to the following third basic type of null value.

3) "no information is available for the value", i.e. it is either *unk* or *dne*, which is denoted in the database by the distinguished value *ni*.

In some cases we have contradictory information, which leads to an inconsistency in the database. For this purpose we will make use of the fourth basic type of null value.

4) "value is inconsistent", which is denoted in the database by the distinguished value *inc*; for example, if a student is only allowed to enrol in one department and for some reason we have contradictory information that student number 8 is enrolled both in the Computing and Maths departments, then the attribute value for department in the tuple recording information about student number 8 would be *inc*.

As mentioned before, it is standard practice to detect inconsistencies when the database is updated and thus to avoid inconsistent database states. The actual detection of inconsistencies will be relegated to the algorithms that maintain the integrity constraints which are defined as part of the conceptual database schema.

At times we will refer to a null value in a generic way without specifying its type; we denote such a generic null value by *null*. This will be convenient when we investigate the fundamental semantics which are common to all types of null value.

Prior to giving the formal definition of an incomplete relation we give a motivating example.

Example 5.1 In Table 5.1 we show an incomplete relation, say r, over a relation schema, say R, where type(R) = 6 and schema(R) = {STUD#, NAME, COURSE, SPS, DEPT, HEAD}. The semantics of R are: a student has a unique student number (STUD#), a name (NAME), belongs to one department (DEPT), takes one or more courses (COURSE) and may have at most one spouse (SPS). In addition, a department has one head (HEAD) and each course is given by one department. ∎

Table 5.1 An incomplete relation

STUD#	NAME	COURSE	SPS	DEPT	HEAD
1	Iris	Databases	*dne*	Computing	Dan
2	Iris	Programming	*dne*	Computing	*unk*
3	Reuven	Programming	Hanna	*unk*	*unk*
4	Hillary	Theory	*ni*	Maths	Annette
5	Hillary	*unk*	*ni*	Maths	*unk*
6	Eli	*ni*	Naomi	*ni*	*ni*
7	David	Logic	Rachel	*unk*	*unk*

Informally, the extended domain of an attribute A is the domain of A augmented with the above four types of null value.

Definition 5.1 (Extended domain)   Let R be a relation schema and $A \in$ schema(R) be an attribute, and recall that DOM(A) denotes the countably infinite set of constants that are included in the domain of A. In addition, assume that *unk, dne, ni* and *inc* are not members of DOM(A). Then the *extended domain* of A, denoted by EDOM(A), is defined by

$$EDOM(A) = DOM(A) \cup \{unk, dne, ni, inc\}.$$ ■

Definition 5.2 (Incomplete relation)   An *incomplete tuple* over a relation schema R is a member of the Cartesian product,

$$EDOM(A_1) \times EDOM(A_2) \times \cdots \times EDOM(A_{type(R)}).$$

An *incomplete relation* over R is a finite set of incomplete tuples.

An incomplete tuple is actually a *complete* tuple if none of its attribute values is null; that is, a complete tuple is a special case of an incomplete tuple. Also, an incomplete tuple is *consistent* if none of its attribute values is the null value *inc*; if at least one of its attribute values is the null value *inc* then the incomplete tuple is *inconsistent*.

An incomplete relation is actually complete if all its tuples are complete; note that a complete relation is a special case of an incomplete relation. In addition, an incomplete relation is consistent if all its tuples are consistent; if at least one of its tuples is inconsistent then it is inconsistent.   ■

We note that the definition of the projection of a tuple t onto a set of attributes $Y \subseteq$ schema(R) remains the same for incomplete relations, i.e. $t[Y]$ is the restriction of t to Y.

Whenever no ambiguity arises we will refer to an incomplete tuple simply as a tuple and to an incomplete relation simply as a relation. Furthermore, *from now on we will assume that relations are consistent unless explicitly stated otherwise.*

If we examine the incomplete relation given in Table 5.1 we will notice that we cannot distinguish between different occurrences of a null value in the relation. For example, the *unk* null value appears as the attribute value of the department in the tuples whose student numbers are 3 and 7, but it is not necessarily the case that these two students are studying in the same department. Another example is the multiple occurrence of *ni* as the attribute value of spouse in the tuples with student numbers 4 and 5. In this case we obviously cannot say that these two students are married and even if this were to be the case it would be very unlikely that they would both be married to the same person. On the other hand, the occurrences of *dne* as the attribute value of spouse in the tuples with student numbers 1 and 2 can be considered as conveying exactly the same semantic information, namely that both of these students are not married.

We can classify the above types of null value as being *unmarked nulls*, since we do not distinguish between different occurrences of the null values as attribute values of tuples in an incomplete relation. That is, there is no "mark" to distinguish between different occurrences of the same type of null value. Another possibility is to subscript (or index) each occurrence of a null value, say *null*, by an integer i, resulting in $null_i$, in order to distinguish between different occurrences of the null value. Such null values are classified as *marked nulls*. Consider, for example, the incomplete relation shown in Table 5.2, which consists of incomplete tuples with marked nulls of type *unk*. We can infer from the marked nulls that students 1, 2 and 3 are studying in the same department and that student 5 and student 6 are taking the same course. On the other hand, students 3 and 4 may or may not be studying in the same department and students 6 and 7 may or may not be taking the same course. We observe that it does not make much sense to mark nulls of type *dne*, since the meaning of the fact that students 1 and 2, in the relation shown in Table 5.1, are not married (i.e. that for students 1 and 2 there does not exist a spouse) would not be affected in any way by marking the *dne* null values. In addition, if a relation is inconsistent it will not be meaningful in our context to distinguish between different occurrences of *inc* in the relation, since we are assuming that we are able to avoid any inconsistencies in the database by integrity constraint maintenance.

Thus, as the incomplete relation shown in Table 5.2 indicates, it is most meaningful to mark nulls of type *unk*. Furthermore, marked nulls of type *unk* have a natural logical interpretation as Skolem constants [Fit96], i.e. they are constants that are used to eliminate existential quantifiers in first-order predicate logic proof theory. Now, let us see what the interpretation of marking nulls of type *ni* can be. Suppose that the attribute value of COURSE, for both students 5 and 6 in Table 5.2, is ni_3. We would interpret this situation as meaning that the course value for students 5 and 6 is either *dne* or the same marked null unk_3.

Table 5.2 An incomplete relation with marked nulls

STUD#	COURSE	DEPT
1	Databases	unk_1
2	Databases	unk_1
3	Theory	unk_1
4	Logic	unk_2
5	unk_3	Computing
6	unk_3	Computing
7	unk_4	Computing

For the rest of this section we will only consider marked and unmarked nulls of type *unk*. The next definition formalises the notion of two values having the same information content or being information-wise equivalent; this is known as *symbolic equality*. This notion is important, since semantically, two different occurrences of *unk* may or may not be equal but they definitely convey the same information content.

For example, the head of department in the second and third tuples in the incomplete relation, shown in Table 5.1, may or may not be the same since our information is incomplete, but in both cases the occurrence of *unk* conveys the same information, i.e. that the value exists but is unknown.

Definition 5.3 (Information-wise equivalence)   Let A be an attribute in schema(R) and v_i, v_j be values in EDOM(A). Then v_i is *information-wise equivalence* to v_j, written as $v_i \cong v_j$, if and only if v_i and v_j are syntactically identical, i.e. they have the same name. If v_i is not information-wise equivalent to v_j, then we write $\neg(v_i \cong v_j)$.   ■

Thus, for example, $unk \cong unk$, $unk_2 \cong unk_2$ and Iris $\cong$ Iris, but $\neg$(Iris $\cong$ Hillary), $\neg$(*unk* $\cong$ Iris) and $\neg(unk_1 \cong unk_2)$. We note that if v_i and v_j are nonnull values, i.e. they are both members of DOM(A), then information-wise equivalence reduces to equality. In Section 5.3

we will extend the notion of information-wise equivalence to incomplete tuples and incomplete relations.

In order give a formal treatment of nulls of type *unk*, we adopt a three-valued logic by introducing a third truth-value *maybe* in addition to the standard two truth-values *true* and *false*. In a two-valued world equality is a predicate that evaluates to either true or false. Thus we redefine equality in the presence of incomplete information to be a predicate which evaluates to either true, false or maybe.

Definition 5.4 (Three-valued equality for nulls)   Let A be an attribute in schema(R) and $v_i, v_j \in$ EDOM(A). Then the following cases define the interpretation of equality in a three-valued logic:

1) If v_i and v_j are both nonnull values then $v_i = v_j$ evaluates to true if $v_i \cong v_j$ holds, otherwise it evaluates to false.

2) *unk* = *unk* evaluates to maybe.

3) *unk* = *unk$_i$* evaluates to maybe.

4) *unk$_i$* = *unk$_j$* evaluates to true if $i = j$, otherwise it evaluates to maybe.

5) If v_i is a null value (marked or unmarked) and v_j is a nonnull value, i.e. v_j is in DOM(A), then $v_i = v_j$ evaluates to maybe.   ■

Thus, for example, $unk_{11} = unk_{11}$ evaluates to true, Iris = *unk* evaluates to maybe and Iris = Hillary evaluates to false. From now on, whenever we refer to "$v_i = v_j$" in a sentence of the form "if $v_i = v_j$ then ..." or in the midst of a formula, then we take it to mean $v_i = v_j$ evaluates to true.

We now discuss the advantages and disadvantages of unmarked and marked null values. Marked nulls have the obvious advantage of being more expressive than unmarked nulls, since we can distinguish between different occurrences of them depending on the value of their mark. Furthermore, there may be circumstances when the database system can deduce that two marked nulls are equal and thereby equate their marks. In practice marked nulls add complexity to the database system, which then needs to maintain the marks of nulls globally throughout the database, and to avoid inconsistencies which would arise if two or more marked nulls were inappropriately equated. It is also not clear if the benefit of knowing that two occurrences of a null value are equal outweighs the overhead incurred. Unmarked nulls have the obvious advantage of being conceptually, theoretically and practically simpler than marked nulls. We mention that to date SQL's support for null values includes only the unmarked *unk* null type.

5.2   The Open and Closed World Assumptions

When viewing the database as an *open world* we do not make any assumptions about information that is not stored in the database. Thus when making the *Open World Assumption* (or simply the OWA) we do not utilise the absence of information to infer that this information is false. For example, if we consider the relation shown in Table 5.3, then we cannot infer that Hillary is not taking a database course and we cannot infer that Hillary is not taking a programming course. What we can say is that from the information we have available Hillary may or may not be taking a database course and Hillary may or may not be taking a programming course. Thus under the OWA the database is not expressive enough to infer any negative information.

Table 5.3 A relation illustrating the OWA and CWA

SNAME	COURSE	DEPT
Iris	Databases	Computing
Reuven	Programming	Computing
Hillary	Logic	Philosophy

One possible solution to this problem of negative information is to allow tuples in relations to represent negative data. Let us assume for a moment that we have extended the relational model to store false information in relations. Thus, for example, if we wanted to store the fact that Hillary is not doing a database course, then that fact would be stored explicitly in the relation and tagged as false. The problem with this approach is that in most applications there would be an overwhelming amount of negative data and thus this solution is not very practical. For this reason we will not consider such a solution. Now, in the relation shown in Table 5.3 it is standard practice to record the courses that students are taking and assume that these are in fact the only courses that they are taking. That is, information not recorded in the database is assumed by default to be false. Thus in our example we can infer that Hillary is not taking a database course and also that she is not taking a programming course. In this case we say that we view the database as a *closed world*, meaning that we assume that the database has complete positive information. Thus when making the *Closed World Assumption* (or simply the CWA) we can utilise the absence of information in order to infer that this absent information is false.

The importance of the CWA will become obvious in Chapter 9 when we introduce deductive databases that extend relational databases to allow intentional information, in the form of rules, to be stored as part of the database. For example, we could have a rule stating that if a student is not doing the Programming course in the Computing department, then this student is doing the Theory course in the Maths department. Under the CWA we can infer that Hillary is doing the Theory course in the Maths department and possibly add this fact to the relation shown in Table 5.3. On the other hand, we could not infer this fact under the OWA. We will also utilise the CWA in the next section when we define the relative content of relations.

A generalisation of the CWA, which is meant to solve the inconsistency problem arising from the CWA when disjunctive information is allowed in the database, can be found in [Min88a]. The CWA and its generalisation are further discussed in Chapter 9 in the context of deductive databases.

An interesting suggestion which attempts to merge the CWA and the OWA is given in [GZ88]. This is done by adding another type of null value, denoted by *open*. Consider the relation, *r*, shown in Table 5.4. We interpret *r* under the CWA except for the DEPT-value of the second tuple. Under the CWA we infer that Hillary is the only student taking Logic in the Philosophy department and that she is studying only in this department. In fact, under the

CWA we can derive the stronger fact, namely that Hillary is the only student studying in the Philosophy department and that there is only one department, i.e. the Philosophy department. Under the OWA, due to the occurrence of *open*, we can deduce that Hillary may be taking more courses in the Philosophy department apart from Logic. Thus occurrences of *open* allow us to locally open the database. If we add to a relation a tuple of the form, *<open, ..., open>*, consisting solely of occurrences of *open*, then all the information in the relation is interpreted according to the OWA.

Table 5.4 A relation illustrating the *open* null value

SNAME	COURSE	DEPT
Hillary	Logic	Philosophy
Hillary	*open*	Philosophy

5.3 Introducing Order into the Domain

In this section we will assume that the only types of null that are available are unmarked. It is very natural to view an incomplete relation as containing *less* information than a complete relation, or alternatively, to view a complete relation as containing *more* information than an incomplete relation.

We formalise what we mean by *less informative* and *more informative* by appealing to the theory of ordered sets. Taking this approach we will impose a partial order on the extended domains of attributes, which we will denote by $\sqsubseteq$. Recall from Subsection 1.9.2 of Chapter 1 that a partial order such as $\sqsubseteq$ on a set S is a binary relation on S that is reflexive, antisymmetric and transitive. To convey the fact that a partial order is defined on a set it is customary to consider the partial order together with the set over which it is defined. The resulting ordered pair $\langle S, \sqsubseteq \rangle$ is called *a partially ordered set*.

Thus, if A is an attribute in schema(R) then $\langle EDOM(A), \sqsubseteq \rangle$ is a partially ordered set. The actual ordering is shown pictorially in Figure 5.1, where $DOM(A) = \{v_1, v_2, \ldots, v_n\}$; such a diagram is known as a Hasse diagram. We interpret the diagram as follows: $e_1 \sqsubseteq e_2$ holds if and only if e_1 appears "lower" in the diagram than e_2 and there is a connecting line between e_1 and e_2. Furthermore, if e_1 is not information-wise equivalent to e_2, then it is not the case that $e_2 \sqsubseteq e_1$, which is written as $\neg(e_2 \sqsubseteq e_1)$. Therefore, in Figure 5.1 we have $ni \sqsubseteq unk \sqsubseteq v_i \sqsubseteq inc$ and $ni \sqsubseteq dne \sqsubseteq inc$ and for no other two elements in the diagram does this relationship hold. In the following we will refer to the partially ordered set $\langle EDOM(A), \sqsubseteq \rangle$ as the *information lattice* for A. We note that the information lattice for A is actually as its name suggests a mathematical *lattice*. (We refer the reader to Subsection 1.9.2 of Chapter 1 for the definition of a lattice.)

Definition 5.5 (Less informative and more informative) If $v_1, v_2 \in EDOM(A)$, then v_1 is *less informative* than v_2 (or equivalently, v_2 is *more informative* than v_1) if and only if $v_1 \sqsubseteq v_2$. ∎

We next give an alternative definition of information-wise equivalence for unmarked nulls. That is, v_1 and v_2 are information-wise equivalent, i.e. $v_1 \cong v_2$, if and only if $v_1 \sqsubseteq v_2$ and $v_2 \sqsubseteq v_1$.

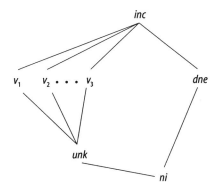

Fig 5.1 The information lattice

We will now continue to develop our order-theoretic approach to incomplete relations.

Definition 5.6 (Less informative and more informative tuples) We extend $\sqsubseteq$ to incomplete tuples as follows: where t_1 and t_2 are incomplete tuples over a relation schema R,

$$t_1 \sqsubseteq t_2 \text{ if and only if } \forall A \in \text{schema}(R), t_1[A] \sqsubseteq t_2[A].$$

If $t_1 \sqsubseteq t_2$, then we say that t_1 is *less informative* than t_2 (or equivalently, that t_2 is *more informative* than t_1).

We extend information-wise equivalence to incomplete tuples as follows: t_1 and t_2 are information-wise equivalent, written $t_1 \cong t_2$, if and only if $t_1 \sqsubseteq t_2$ and $t_2 \sqsubseteq t_1$. ■

We observe that it is also customary in the literature to say that a more informative tuple *subsumes* a less informative tuple. From Definition 5.6 it follows that

$$\langle \text{EDOM}(A_1) \times \text{EDOM}(A_1) \times \cdots \times \text{EDOM}(A_{\text{type(R)}}), \sqsubseteq \rangle$$

is a partially ordered set.

Definition 5.7 (The extended active domain) Let r be an incomplete relation over a relation schema R. Then the *extended active domain* of r with respect to $A \in \text{schema}(R)$, denoted by $\text{EACTIVE}(r, A)$, is defined by

$$\text{EACTIVE}(r, A) = \{t[A] \mid t \in r\} \cup \{unk, dne, ni, inc\}.$$ ■

We observe that the Cartesian product

$$\text{EACTIVE}(r, A_1) \times \text{EACTIVE}(r, A_2) \times \cdots \times \text{EACTIVE}(r, A_{\text{type(R)}})$$

yields a finite set, since $\forall i \in \{1, 2, \ldots, \text{type}(R)\}$, $\text{EACTIVE}(r, A_i)$ is finite. The following proposition is now obvious.

Proposition 5.1 Let r be a relation over a relation schema R. Then

$$\langle \text{EACTIVE}(r, A_1) \times \text{EACTIVE}(r, A_2) \times \cdots \times \text{EACTIVE}(r, A_{\text{type(R)}}), \sqsubseteq \rangle$$

is a partially ordered set. □

Informally a relation r_1 over a relation schema R is less informative than a relation r_2 over R, written $r_1 \sqsubseteq r_2$, if zero or more of the tuples in r_1 can be replaced by (or modified to become) more informative tuples in order to obtain r_2. Prior to giving the formal definition of less informative and more informative relations we provide some motivation. Consider the relations, r_1, r_2 and r_3, shown in Tables, 5.5, 5.6 and 5.7, respectively.

Table 5.5 An incomplete relation r_1

PARENT	CHILD
Jack	Jill
unk	unk
Jack	unk

Table 5.6 An incomplete relation r_2

PARENT	CHILD
Jack	Jill
unk	unk
unk	Jill

Table 5.7 An incomplete relation r_3

PARENT	CHILD
Jack	Jill
unk	unk

First consider r_1 and r_2. The first two tuples in r_1 match with the first two tuples in r_2. Now assume that $r_1 \sqsubseteq r_2$ holds. In this case the tuple <Jack, *unk*> must correspond to a more informative tuple in r_2, i.e. to <Jack, Jill>. However, according to our informal definition of more informative relations we obtain r_3 and not r_2, since the tuple <*unk*, Jill> does not correspond to any tuple in r_1. Nonetheless, there is another possibility to consider. The tuple <*unk, unk*> in r_1 could correspond to the tuple <*unk*, Jill> in r_2. However, then the tuple <*unk, unk*> would correspond to two tuples in r_2. Moreover, this contradicts our informal definition of less informative relations, since <*unk, unk*> would be replaced by two distinct tuples in r_2 which is not possible.

There are two possible solutions to this problem. The first solution is to treat less informative tuples in a way similar to the treatment of duplicate tuples in complete relations. That is, since duplicate tuples are removed from complete relations (recalling that relations are sets), less informative tuples are also removed from incomplete relations. An incomplete relation from which all less informative tuples have been removed is called a *reduced relation*. A reduced relation is an *antichain* (see Subsection 1.9.2 of Chapter 1), since no two tuples in a reduced relation are comparable with respect to $\sqsubseteq$. It is easy to check that in our example all of r_1, r_2 and r_3 reduce to a single tuple <Jack, Jill>. However, it is evident that the process of reduction involves a considerable loss of semantics. The tuple <Jack, *unk*> in r_1 may denote the fact that Jack has another child apart from Jill, the tuple <*unk*, Jill> in r_2 may denote the fact that Jill's mother exists but is unknown and the tuple <*unk, unk*> in either r_1 or r_2 may denote the fact that another unknown parent and a child thereof are stored in the relation. For this reason we will not advocate reduced relations. We mention that the assumption that relations are reduced is common in the database literature mainly due to the fact that, in theory, reduced relations are easier to deal with than non-reduced relations. In practice, there does not seem to be any justification to reduce relations, not to mention the overhead which would be incurred in maintaining such reduced relations.

The second solution is to admit that according to our informal definition $\neg(r_1 \sqsubseteq r_2)$, that is, r_1 is not less informative than r_2. By a similar argument we can deduce that r_2 is not less informative than r_1. Continuing our example we can also deduce that $r_1 \sqsubseteq r_3$ holds, since both <Jack, Jill> and <Jack, *unk*> could have been replaced by <Jack, Jill>. This corresponds to the situation where the occurrence of *unk* in <Jack, *unk*> is replaced by Jill; for example, it may be the case that Jack actually has only one child. In this case <Jack, *unk*> turns out to be a duplicate of <Jack, Jill>. Similarly, we can deduce that $r_2 \sqsubseteq r_3$ holds. Finally, $\neg(r_3 \sqsubseteq r_1)$ and $\neg(r_3 \sqsubseteq r_2)$ can also be verified.

Definition 5.8 (Less informative and more informative relations)   We extend $\sqsubseteq$ to incomplete relations as follows: where r_1 and r_2 are incomplete relations over schema R, $r_1 \sqsubseteq r_2$ if and only if there exists a total and onto mapping θ from r_1 to r_2 such that $\forall t \in r_1, t \sqsubseteq \theta(t)$. (See Subsection 1.9.1 of Chapter 1 for the definition of a total and onto mapping.)

If $r_1 \sqsubseteq r_2$, then we say that r_1 is *less informative* than r_2 (or equivalently, r_2 is *more informative* than r_1).

We extend information-wise equivalence to incomplete relations as follows: r_1 and r_2 are information-wise equivalent, written $r_1 \cong r_2$, if and only if $r_1 \sqsubseteq r_2$ and $r_2 \sqsubseteq r_1$. ■

It can be verified that the formal definition of less informative relations corresponds to the informal definition given earlier. We note that, when $r \sqsubseteq s$, we insist that each tuple in s be more informative than some tuple in r and also that for each tuple $t \in r$ there is some tuple in s that is more informative than t. We make the following interesting observations concerning the boundary cases, where r and s are incomplete relations over R:

1) If $r = \emptyset$ and $s = \emptyset$, then $r \cong s$ holds.

2) If $r = \emptyset$ and $s \neq \emptyset$, then $\neg(r \sqsubseteq s)$, since $\theta = \emptyset$ and thus θ is not an onto mapping.

3) If $r \neq \emptyset$ and $s = \emptyset$, then $\neg(r \sqsubseteq s)$, since θ does not exist in this case.

The following technical definition is now needed.

Definition 5.9 (The set of active incomplete relations)   Let r be an incomplete relation over schema R. Then the set of *active incomplete relations* induced by r, denoted by EAREL(r), is the set of all subsets of the Cartesian product

$$\text{EACTIVE}(r, A_1) \times \text{EACTIVE}(r, A_2) \times \cdots \times \text{EACTIVE}(r, A_{\text{type}(R)}). \qquad ■$$

We note that EAREL(r) is a finite set, since $\forall i \in \{1, 2, \ldots, \text{type}(R)\}$, EACTIVE($r, A_i$) is a finite set. The following proposition states that the set of active incomplete relations induced by an incomplete relation r forms a partially ordered set. Its proof follows from the Definition 5.8 of less informative relations on using composition of mappings.

Proposition 5.2   Let r be a relation over schema(R). Then $\langle \text{EAREL}(r), \sqsubseteq \rangle$ is a partially ordered set. □

In the following we will refer to the partially ordered set $\langle \text{EAREL}(r), \sqsubseteq \rangle$ as the *information ordering*. Our interpretation of a more informative relation is a relation that results from modifying another relation. In particular, our definition directly caters for the replacement (or modification) of tuples, and *not* for the deletion of old tuples from a relation or the insertion of new tuples into a relation. We could amend our definition of less informative in the following two ways:

1) In order to cater for deletions we could relax θ in the definition to be a partial mapping rather than a total mapping.

2) In order to cater for insertions we could relax θ in the definition to be an into mapping rather than an onto mapping.

In the first case the deleted tuples in r would not be mapped to any tuple in the more informative relation s and in the second case the inserted tuples in s would not have any less informative tuples in r mapped to them. Our definition of less informative by using a total and onto mapping can be viewed as an application of the CWA. This is due to the fact that a more informative relation is viewed as the result of modifying existing information and thus each incomplete relation resulting from replacing some null values by nonnull values in a less informative relation will not violate the CWA. For example, in the incomplete relation shown in Table 5.1, say r, on assuming the CWA we can deduce that there are only seven students doing courses at this moment in time. Thus for any incomplete relation s such that $r \sqsubseteq s$ holds there will still be seven tuples, due to our definition being compatible with the CWA.

Our approach to defining the relative information content of an incomplete relation by imposing a partial order on the underlying domains allows us to formalise the notion of the possible worlds relative to an incomplete relation r, denoted by POSS(r). Informally, POSS(r) is the set of all relations, which are more informative than r and do not contain nulls of type ni, unk or inc. On treating dne as having the same information content as some nonnull value, we have that POSS(r) is the set of all complete relations which are more informative than r.

Definition 5.10 (The set of possible worlds relative to a relation)   The set of all *possible worlds* relative to an incomplete relation r over schema R, denoted by POSS(r), is defined by

$$\text{POSS}(r) = \{s \mid r \sqsubseteq s \text{ and } \forall t \in s, \forall A \in \text{schema}(R), t[A] \in \text{EDOM}(A) - \{ni, unk, inc\}\}. \quad \blacksquare$$

We note that r is inconsistent if and only if POSS(r) = $\emptyset$, which fits in with our philosophy that in our context inconsistent relations are not meaningful. The following theorem, which follows from Definition 5.10 above and Definition 5.8 of less informative relations, captures our intuition, namely that an incomplete relation is more informative than another incomplete relation if and only if it has less possible worlds.

Theorem 5.3   The following two statements, where r and s are incomplete relations over schema R, are true:

1) If $r \sqsubseteq s$, then POSS(s) $\subseteq$ POSS(r).

2) If POSS(s) $\subseteq$ POSS(r) and both of POSS(r) and POSS(s) are nonempty, then $r \sqsubseteq s$. $\square$

The next proposition follows directly from the above definition of possible worlds.

Proposition 5.4   An incomplete relation r over schema R is consistent if and only if $r = \emptyset$ or POSS(r) $\neq \emptyset$.
                                                                                                                                      $\square$

Our previous assumption that incomplete relations are consistent unless explicitly stated otherwise is justified by Proposition 5.4, since if inconsistency is introduced it is present in all possible worlds.

We refer the reader to [BJO91, Lib91, Lev92, LL92, LL93a, LL93b, LL94, Lib98] for further investigations into the order-theoretic approach to formalising incompleteness in relational databases. This approach borrows from the theory of denotational semantics of programming languages [Sch86] and from lattice theory [Grä78, DP90].

5.4   Extending the Relational Algebra with Null Values

In this section we will extend the relational algebra so that it is capable of manipulating incomplete relations. With the intention of simplifying the definition of the extended algebra, throughout this section, the only type of null that we will consider being present in incomplete relations will be the unmarked null *unk*.

In order to ascertain that our extended algebra is reasonable we will use the notions of *faithfulness* and *truth-preservation*. An extended operator is faithful if it returns the same result as its corresponding standard operator, when manipulating complete relations. Faithfulness provides us with a reference point as to the expressive power of the extended algebra. An extended operator is truth-preserving if the intersection of the set of relations belonging to all possible worlds induced by the result of applying the said operator to an incomplete relation is the same as the intersection of the set of complete relations resulting from invoking the corresponding standard operator on all possible worlds of this incomplete relation. Thus if an extended operator is truth-preserving then it maintains all the true answers to a query, i.e. all the answers that are true in all possible worlds. We note that we could relax truth-preservation to possibility-preservation if we allow answers that evaluate to maybe to be included in the result of a query. In this case an answer to a query will contain all tuples that evaluate to true in at least one possible world. Herein we will only test for truth-preservation which is the minimal desirable property of an extended operator.

Let *op* be a standard relational algebra operator for complete relations, as defined in Subsection 3.2.1 of Chapter 3, and let op^e be an extended relational algebra operator (or simply an extended operator) for incomplete relations. For simplicity we will assume that *op* and op^e are unary operators but obviously the definitions of faithfulness and truth-preservation also hold when *op* and op^e are binary operators. In the following we will refer to an *extended relational algebra expression* (or equivalently, an extended query) as a well-formed expression composed of a finite number of extended relational algebra operators, whose operands are relation schemas which can be treated as input variables to the extended query. An extended query Q, having operands $R_1, R_2, \ldots, R_n$, is denoted by $Q(R_1, R_2, \ldots, R_n)$ or simply by Q, if $R_1, R_2, \ldots, R_n$ are understood from context. An answer to an extended query $Q(R_1, R_2, \ldots, R_n)$ is obtained by replacing every occurrence of R_i in Q by an incomplete relation r_i over R_i and computing the result by invoking the extended operators present in Q; such an answer to Q will be denoted by $Q(r_1, r_2, \ldots, r_n)$. We will assume that appropriate parentheses are present in Q in order to avoid any ambiguity when computing $Q(r_1, r_2, \ldots, r_n)$. At times we will also refer to an answer of an extended query as an extended query (or simply a query) when no ambiguity arises.

We next formally define faithfulness and truth-preservation for unary operators, leaving it to the reader to define the analogous definitions for binary operators.

Definition 5.11 (Faithful extended operator)   We say that op^e is *faithful* to op if for all complete relations r over schema R, $op(r) = op^e(r)$.   ∎

Definition 5.12 (Truth-preserving extended operator)   We say that an extended operator, op^e, is a *truth-preserving* extension of a standard operator, op, if for all incomplete relations r

$$\bigcap\{s \mid s \in \text{POSS}(op^e(r))\} = \bigcap\{op(s) \mid s \in \text{POSS}(r)\}. \qquad ∎$$

Recall that r is consistent by assumption. We note that in [IL84a, Lip84, Imi89] a more general definition of truth-preservation was given where an operator in the above definition is taken to be a query and an extended operator is taken to be an extended query. This definition is more powerful than Definition 5.12, since although we can obtain truth-preservation for all the extended operators there are still certain subclasses of extended queries that are not truth-preserving. We will illustrate this point later on with examples.

Definition 5.13 (Extended union)   The extended union, $\cup^e$, of two incomplete relations r_1 and r_2 over schema R is defined by

$$r_1 \cup^e r_2 = \{t \mid t \in r_1 \text{ or } t \in r_2\}. \qquad ∎$$

We make the small technical comment that the use of the equality sign, "=", in the definition above should read "is defined as" and is not to be confused with equality between domain values. In some mathematical texts different symbols are used to denote "equals" and "is defined as"; in our case we will use the same symbol, i.e. "=", to denote both meanings since its use is obvious from context.

We note that the definition of extended union is essentially the same as the definition of the standard union. As an example, let r_1 and r_2 be the two incomplete relations over R, where schema(R) = {SNAME, COURSE, DEPT}, shown in Tables 5.8 and 5.9, respectively. The null extended union $r_1 \cup^e r_2$ is shown in Table 5.10.

Table 5.8 An incomplete student relation r_1

SNAME	COURSE	DEPT
Iris	Databases	Computing
Reuven	Theory	*unk*
Hillary	*unk*	Philosophy
Rachel	*unk*	*unk*
Eli	Databases	Computing

Table 5.9 An incomplete student relation r_2

SNAME	COURSE	DEPT
Iris	Databases	Computing
Reuven	*unk*	*unk*
Rachel	Logic	*unk*
David	*unk*	Maths

Table 5.10 The incomplete student relation $r_1 \cup^e r_2$

SNAME	COURSE	DEPT
Iris	Databases	Computing
Reuven	Theory	*unk*
Reuven	*unk*	*unk*
Hillary	*unk*	Philosophy
Rachel	*unk*	*unk*
Rachel	Logic	*unk*
David	*unk*	Maths
Eli	Databases	Computing

We leave the proof of the following theorem to the reader.

Theorem 5.5   Extended union is a faithful and truth-preserving extended operator.   □

We observe that extended union satisfies a stronger property than truth-preservation, which is given by

$$POSS(r_1 \cup^e r_2) = \{s_1 \cup s_2 \mid s_1 \in POSS(r_1) \text{ and } s_2 \in POSS(r_2)\},$$

implying that extended union is also possibility-preserving.

Definition 5.14 (Extended difference)   The extended difference, $-^e$, of two incomplete relations r_1 and r_2 over schema R is defined by

$$r_1 -^e r_2 = \{t \mid t \in r_1 \text{ and } \not\exists u \in r_2 \text{ such that either } u \sqsubseteq t \text{ or } t \sqsubseteq u\}. \qquad ∎$$

As an example, the null extended difference $r_1 -^e r_2$ is shown in Table 5.11, where r_1 and r_2 are the incomplete relations shown in Tables 5.8 and 5.9, respectively.

Table 5.11 The incomplete student relation $r_1 -^e r_2$

SNAME	COURSE	DEPT
Hillary	*unk*	Philosophy
Eli	Databases	Computing

We leave the proof of the following theorem to the reader.

Theorem 5.6   Extended difference is a faithful and truth-preserving extended operator.   □

We note that an alternative definition of the extended difference, denoted by $-^z$ and suggested by Zaniolo [Zan84], is given by

$$r_1 -^z r_2 = \{t \mid t \in r_1 \text{ and } \not\exists u \in r_2 \text{ such that } t \sqsubseteq u\}.$$

Although the definition of $-^z$ may seem intuitively more appealing than that of $-^e$, the reader can verify that $-^z$ is not truth-preserving by setting $r_1 = \{<v>\}$ and $r_2 = \{<unk>\}$. In particular, $r_1 -^z r_2 = r_1$, but $\bigcap\{s_1 - s_2 \mid s_1 \in POSS(r_1) \text{ and } s_2 \in POSS(r_2)\} = \emptyset$.

Definition 5.15 (Extended projection)   The extended projection, π^e, of an incomplete relation r over schema R onto $Y \subseteq$ schema(R) is defined by

$$\pi_Y^e(r) = \{t[Y] \mid t \in r\}. \qquad \blacksquare$$

We note that the definition of extended projection is essentially the same as the definition of the standard projection. As an example, the extended projection $\pi_{\{COURSE,DEPT\}}^e(r_1)$ is shown in Table 5.12, where r_1 is shown in Table 5.8.

Table 5.12   The incomplete student relation $\pi_{\{COURSE,DEPT\}}^e(r_1)$

COURSE	DEPT
Databases	Computing
Theory	unk
unk	Philosophy
unk	unk

We leave the proof of the following theorem to the reader.

Theorem 5.7   Extended projection is a faithful and truth-preserving extended operator. $\square$

Let r be an incomplete relation over R and $Y \subseteq$ schema(R). Then the extended projection satisfies a stronger property than truth-preservation, namely

$$POSS(\pi_Y^e(r)) = \{\pi_Y(s) \mid s \in POSS(r)\},$$

implying that, as well as extended union, extended projection is also possibility-preserving.

We now define extended selection using a three-valued logic approach, as opposed to standard selection which uses the classical two-valued logic approach. Prior to defining the semantics of extended selection we define extended selection formulae.

Definition 5.16 (Extended selection formula)   An *extended simple selection formula* over a relation schema R is either an expression of the form $A = a$ or an expression of the form $A = B$, where $A, B \in$ schema(R) and $a \in$ EDOM(A).

An *extended selection formula* over R is a well-formed expression composed of one or more extended simple selection formulae together with the Boolean logical connectives: $\wedge$ (and), $\vee$ (or), $\neg$ (not) and parentheses. An extended selection formula is called *positive* if it does not have any occurrence of $\neg$. We abbreviate $\neg(A = a)$ by $A \neq a$ and $\neg(A = B)$ by $A \neq B$. $\blacksquare$

We note that an extended simple selection formula of the form $A = B$ is sometimes referred to as an *extended restriction*. We also note that for simplicity we have only included equality ($=$) as a comparison operator but, in general, we can expect to have $\leq$, $<$, $\sqsubseteq$ and $\cong$ available in an extended simple selection formula. We further note that $\sqsubseteq$ and $\cong$ are not truth-preserving, since $unk \cong unk$ evaluates to true while $unk = unk$ evaluates only to maybe.

Definition 5.17 (True logical implication, $\models$)   Let r be an incomplete relation over R, t be a tuple in r and, in addition, let F be an extended selection formula over R. Then t *truly logically implies* F, written $t \models F$, is defined recursively, as follows:

1) $t \models A = a$, if $t[A] = a$ evaluates to true using our three-valued equality for nulls.

2) $t \models A = B$, if $t[A] = t[B]$ evaluates to true using our three-valued equality for nulls.

3) $t \models (F)$, if $t \models F$.

4) $t \models F$, if F evaluates to true by computing the truth-value of F recursively, using (1), (2) and (3) above and the three-valued logic truth tables shown in Tables 5.13, 5.14 and 5.15. ∎

We note that the three-valued truth tables shown in Tables 5.13, 5.14 and 5.15 coincide with those of the three-valued logics defined by Lukasiewicz and Kleene [Res69, BB92].

Table 5.13 The three-valued truth table for conjunction

$\wedge$	true	false	maybe
true	true	false	maybe
false	false	false	false
maybe	maybe	false	maybe

Table 5.14 The three-valued truth table for negation

$\neg$	
true	false
false	true
maybe	maybe

Table 5.15 The three-valued truth table for disjunction

$\vee$	true	false	maybe
true	true	true	true
false	true	false	maybe
maybe	true	maybe	maybe

Definition 5.18 (Extended selection)   The extended selection, σ_F^e, applied to an incomplete relation r over schema R with respect to a selection formula F over R is defined by

$$\sigma_F^e(r) = \{t \mid t \in r \text{ and } t \models F\}.$$

The extended selection is called *positive* if F is a positive extended selection formula. ∎

We give three examples of extended selection. The extended selection $\sigma_{F_1}^e(r_1)$ is shown in Table 5.16, where F_1 is (DEPT = 'Philosophy' or SNAME = 'Rachel') and r_1 is shown in Table 5.8. The extended selection $\sigma_{F_2}^e(r_1)$ is shown in Table 5.17, where F_2 is (DEPT $\neq$ 'Philosophy' and COURSE $\neq$ 'Theory') and r_1 is shown in Table 5.8. The extended selection $\sigma_{F_3}^e(r_4)$ is shown in Table 5.19, where F_3 is FIRST = SECOND and the incomplete relation r_4 indicating the number of courses students did take in their first and second years is shown in Table 5.18.

Table 5.16 The incomplete student relation $\sigma^e_{F_1}(r_1)$

SNAME	COURSE	DEPT
Hillary	*unk*	Philosophy
Rachel	*unk*	*unk*

Table 5.17 The incomplete student relation $\sigma^e_{F_2}(r_1)$

SNAME	COURSE	DEPT
Iris	Databases	Computing
Eli	Databases	Computing

Table 5.18 An incomplete number of courses relation r_4

SNAME	FIRST	SECOND
Iris	5	5
Reuven	5	*unk*
Hillary	6	6
Rachel	*unk*	*unk*
Eli	4	5

Table 5.19 The incomplete student relation $\sigma^e_{F_3}(r_4)$

SNAME	FIRST	SECOND
Iris	5	5
Hillary	6	6

Although all the queries we have just shown are indeed truth-preserving extended selection is not, in general, truth-preserving due to the *tautology* problem. A tautology is a logical formula, in our case an extended selection formula, which evaluates to true, no matter what data values are present in the tuples of the incomplete relation used, when computing the truth-value of the formula. That is, a tautology is an extended selection formula, F over R, such that for all incomplete relations r over R and $\forall t \in r, t \models F$. For example, let F be the formula (COURSE = 'Databases' or COURSE $\neq$ 'Databases'). Then the tuples <Hillary, *unk*, Philosophy> and <Rachel, *unk*, *unk*> will not be included in the answer to the query $\sigma^e_F(r_1)$, where r_1 is the incomplete relation shown in Table 5.8. This is due to the three-valued equality rule which evaluates *unk* = 'Databases' to maybe and thus using the three-valued logic truth table for $\neg$ we obtain that *unk* $\neq$ 'Databases' also evaluates to maybe. Nonetheless in all possible worlds $s \in \text{POSS}(r_1)$ Hillary and Rachel are either doing Databases or not doing Databases, so these tuples ought to be present in the answer to the query. Another example is the formula $\neg(\text{DEPT} = \text{'Computing' and DEPT} \neq \text{'Computing'})$, which evaluates to true for all tuples in all possible worlds but will evaluate to maybe for tuples t such that $t[\text{DEPT}] \cong$ *unk* on using three-valued logic equality with the aid of the three-valued logic truth tables.

It follows that extended selection is not truth-preserving in general. Let us assume for the moment that all the extended domains are finite and thus POSS(r) is also finite; for instance we could assume that POSS(r) is a subset of EAREL(r), where r is an incomplete relation. In this case to obtain a truth-preserving answer to a query involving extended selection we could simply evaluate the selection over all possible worlds, i.e. we could let

$$\sigma^e_F(r) = \{t \mid t \in r \text{ and } \bigcap \{\sigma_F(u) \mid u \in \text{POSS}(\{t\})\} \neq \emptyset\}.$$

However, it is easy to see that this approach is not practical, since the number of possible worlds is exponential in the number of occurrences of *unk* in the incomplete relation, *r*. Furthermore, even if we restrict ourselves to propositional logic (that is, we disallow quantification over formulae), the complement of the problem of deciding whether a formula is a tautology, i.e. the problem of finding whether a formula is satisfiable is known to be NP-complete [GJ79]. This is considered to be an indication that this problem cannot be solved in polynomial time in the size of the formula involved, i.e. that its computation cannot be carried out efficiently. We can still console ourselves by the fact that

$$\bigcap\{s \mid s \in \text{POSS}(\sigma_F^e(r))\} \subseteq \bigcap\{\sigma_F(s) \mid s \in \text{POSS}(r)\},$$

i.e. all the answers to a query involving extended selection are true in all possible worlds but we may not obtain all the true answers. Furthermore, in some special cases it is possible to augment the database query processor with the ability to detect tautologies. We leave the proof of the following theorem to the reader.

Theorem 5.8   The following three statements are true:

1) Extended selection is a faithful extended operator.

2) Positive extended selection is truth-preserving.

3) Extended selection is not, in general, truth-preserving.   □

Definition 5.19 (Extended natural join)   The extended natural join (or simply extended join), $\bowtie^e$, of two incomplete relations r_1, over schema R_1, and r_2, over schema R_2, is an incomplete relation over a schema R, where schema(R) = schema(R_1) $\cup$ schema(R_2), defined by

$$r_1 \bowtie^e r_2 \;=\; \{t \mid \exists t_1 \in r_1 \text{ and } \exists t_2 \in r_2 \text{ such that } t[\text{schema}(R_1)] \cong t_1 \text{ and } t[\text{schema}(R_2)] \cong t_2$$
$$\text{and } t_1[\text{schema}(R')] = t_2[\text{schema}(R')] \text{ evaluates to } true\},$$

where R' is a relation schema with schema(R') = schema(R_1) $\cap$ schema(R_2).   ■

As an example, the null extended join $r_1 \bowtie^e r_5$ is shown in Table 5.21, where r_1 and r_5 are the incomplete relations shown in Tables 5.8 and 5.20, respectively.

Table 5.20   An incomplete department relation r_5

DEPT	HEAD	PHONE
Computing	Dan	7214
Philosophy	*unk*	7116
Maths	Rachel	*unk*
unk	Annette	*unk*

By utilising the extended join we can define the *extended Cartesian product*, denoted as $\times^e$, and the *extended intersection*, denoted as $\cap^e$. The extended join reduces to the extended Cartesian product when schema(R_1) $\cap$ schema(R_2) = ∅ and the extended join reduces to the extended intersection when schema(R_1) = schema(R_2).

We leave the proof of the following theorem to the reader.

Table 5.21 The incomplete relation $r_1 \bowtie^e r_5$

SNAME	COURSE	DEPT	HEAD	PHONE
Iris	Databases	Computing	Dan	7214
Eli	Databases	Computing	Dan	7214
Hillary	*unk*	Philosophy	*unk*	7116

Theorem 5.9 Extended join is a faithful and truth-preserving extended operator. □

Despite the above result there are situations when the extended projection and extended join are combined together to yield a query which is not truth-preserving. Consider the incomplete relation $r = \{<\text{Hillary}, unk, \text{Philosophy}>\}$ over R, where schema(R) = {SNAME, COURSE, DEPT}. Then the reader can verify that $\pi^e_{\{SNAME,COURSE\}}(r) \bowtie^e \pi^e_{\{COURSE,DEPT\}}(r) = \emptyset$, since $unk = unk$ evaluates to maybe. However, the occurrence of unk in $\pi^e_{\{SNAME,COURSE\}}(r) \cong \{<\text{Hillary}, unk>\}$ is the same occurrence of unk in $\pi^e_{\{COURSE,DEPT\}}(r) \cong \{<unk, \text{Philosophy}>\}$. Thus, in this case, the two occurrences of unk should be considered equal and the true result should be r, i.e. $\{<\text{Hillary}, unk, \text{Philosophy}>\}$. Therefore, we can conclude that if we combine extended projection with extended join in queries then the result is not necessarily truth-preserving.

If we examine the result of the extended join $r_1 \bowtie^e r_5$ shown in Table 5.21 we will notice that unmatched tuples are not represented in this relation. For example, both the tuples, <Reuven, Theory, unk> of r_1 and the tuple <Maths, Rachel, unk> of r_5 are not represented in $r_1 \bowtie^e r_5$. In some circumstances we would like to preserve all the information present in the original relations. For example, in the joined relation we would like to maintain a record of all the students and all the departments whether they appear in the result of the extended join or not. Such a generalisation of the extended join operator is called the *outer join* operator. The result of the outer join operator consists of the tuples of the extended join operator unioned with the unmatched tuples padded with null values for the attributes not present in each of the original two relation schemas.

Prior to defining the outer join operator we define the pad operator.

Definition 5.20 (The pad operator) Let r be an incomplete relation over a relation schema R and let S be a relation schema such that schema(R) ⊆ schema(S). The pad, δ, of r with respect to S is defined by

$$\delta(r, S) = \{t \mid \exists u \in r \text{ such that } t[\text{schema}(R)] \cong u \text{ and } \forall A \in \text{schema}(S) - \text{schema}(R),$$
$$t[A] \cong unk\}. \qquad \blacksquare$$

Definition 5.21 (The outer join operator) Let r_1 over schema R_1 and r_2 over schema R_2 be incomplete relations. In addition, let s_1 and s_2 be the incomplete relations over R_1 and R_2, respectively, defined by

1) $s_1 = r_1 -^e \pi^e_{\text{schema}(R_1)}(r_1 \bowtie^e r_2)$.

2) $s_2 = r_2 -^e \pi^e_{\text{schema}(R_2)}(r_1 \bowtie^e r_2)$.

The outer natural join (or simply outer join), $\bowtie$, of r_1 and r_2 is an incomplete relation over a schema R, where schema(R) = schema(R_1) ∪ schema(R_2), defined by

$$r_1 \bowtie r_2 = (r_1 \bowtie^e r_2) \cup^e \delta(s_1, R) \cup^e \delta(s_2, R). \qquad \blacksquare$$

As an example, the outer join $r_1 \bowtie r_5$ is shown in Table 5.22, where r_1 and r_5 are the incomplete relations shown in Tables 5.8 and 5.20, respectively.

Table 5.22 The incomplete relation $r_1 \bowtie r_5$

SNAME	COURSE	DEPT	HEAD	PHONE
Iris	Databases	Computing	Dan	7214
Eli	Databases	Computing	Dan	7214
Hillary	*unk*	Philosophy	*unk*	7116
Reuven	Theory	*unk*	*unk*	*unk*
Rachel	*unk*	*unk*	*unk*	*unk*
unk	*unk*	Maths	Rachel	*unk*
unk	*unk*	*unk*	Annette	*unk*

We conclude the presentation of the extended algebra with the formal definition of the extended renaming operator.

Definition 5.22 (Extended renaming)   Let r be an incomplete relation over schema R, $A \in$ schema(R) and $B \notin$ schema(R) is an attribute in $\mathcal{U}$. The extended renaming, ρ^e, of A to B in r, is an incomplete relation over schema S, where schema(S) = (schema(R) $-$ {A}) $\cup$ {B}, defined by

$$\rho^e_{A \to B}(r) = \{t \mid \exists u \in r \text{ such that } t[\text{schema}(R) - \{A\}] \cong u[\text{schema}(R) - \{A\}] \text{ and } t[B] \cong u[A]\}. \blacksquare$$

We leave the proof of the following theorem to the reader.

Theorem 5.10   Extended renaming is a faithful and truth-preserving extended operator. $\square$

Another criterion for measuring the characteristics of an extended algebra is that of monotonicity of its extended queries.

Definition 5.23 (Monotonic extended queries)   An extended query $Q(R_1, R_2, \ldots, R_n)$ is *monotonic* (with respect to $\sqsubseteq$) when for all incomplete relations r_1 and s_1 over R_1, r_2 and s_2 over $R_2, \ldots, r_n$ and s_n over R_n, if $\forall i \in \{1, 2, \ldots, n\}$, $r_i \sqsubseteq s_i$ is satisfied, then $Q(r_1, r_2, \ldots, r_n)$ $\sqsubseteq Q(s_1, s_2, \ldots, s_n)$ is also satisfied. $\blacksquare$

The intuition behind monotonicity is that the user's view of the database corresponds to queries being evaluated over the current state of the database. Thus monotonicity implies that increasing the information content of the database also increases the information content of the user's view.

Theorem 5.11   All extended queries of the extended algebra are monotonic.

Proof. The length of an extended query is defined to be the number of occurrences of extended algebra operators in the extended query. We now sketch the proof of the result by induction on the length of an extended query, say $Q = Q(R_1, R_2, \ldots, R_n)$.

(*Basis*): If the length of Q is 1, then Q is one of the extended algebra operators: extended union, extended difference, extended projection, extended selection, extended join, pad or extended renaming. The outer join is not included in the list, since it can be considered as a query whose length is greater than one. We next prove that extended difference is a monotonic operator and leave it to the reader to prove that the other extended operators are also monotonic.

Let r_1, r_2, s_1 and s_2 be incomplete relations over schema R satisfying, $r_1 \sqsubseteq s_1$ and $r_2 \sqsubseteq s_2$. We need to show that $(r_1 -^e r_2) \sqsubseteq (s_1 -^e s_2)$. Now let θ_i, for $i = 1, 2$, be the total and onto mapping from r_i to s_i in the definition of $\sqsubseteq$ such that $\forall t \in r_i, t \sqsubseteq \theta_i(t)$.

Suppose that $t \in r_1 -^e r_2$ and thus $\theta_1(t) \in s_1$. It remains to show that $\theta_1(t) \in s_1 -^e s_2$. Suppose to the contrary that in fact $\theta_1(t) \notin s_1 -^e s_2$. Thus by the definition of $-^e$, $\exists u \in r_2$ such that either $\theta_2(u) \sqsubseteq \theta_1(t)$, or $\theta_1(t) \sqsubseteq \theta_2(u)$. It follows that either $u \sqsubseteq \theta_1(t)$, since $u \sqsubseteq \theta_2(u)$, or $t \sqsubseteq \theta_2(u)$, since $t \sqsubseteq \theta_1(t)$, holds.

Now assume that $\neg(u \sqsubseteq t)$ and $\neg(t \sqsubseteq u)$ both hold. Then by the definition of $\sqsubseteq$, $\exists A \in$ schema(R) such that $t[A] = u[A]$ evaluates to false, i.e. $t[A] \neq u[A]$ holds. This leads to a contradiction of the fact that either $u \sqsubseteq \theta_1(t)$ or $t \sqsubseteq \theta_2(u)$ holds and thus we conclude that either $u \sqsubseteq t$ or $t \sqsubseteq u$ must hold contrary to the above assumption. Consequently $t \notin r_1 -^e r_2$ as we have assumed, thus leading to a contradiction of our assumption that $\theta_1(t) \notin s_1 -^e s_2$. The result, namely that the extended difference is monotonic, now follows.

(*Induction*): Assume the result holds when Q is of length k, where $k > 0$. We then need to prove that the result holds when the length of Q is $k + 1$. For simplicity, assume that Q has only one operand, say R, and that $Q = op^e(Q_k(R))$, where $Q_k(R)$ is an extended query of length k. Now let r and s be incomplete relations over R such that $r \sqsubseteq s$. Then by inductive hypothesis, $Q_k(r) \sqsubseteq Q_k(s)$, and thus by the basis step $op^e(Q_k(r)) \sqsubseteq op^e(Q_k(s))$, since op^e was shown to be a monotonic operator. The result that $Q(r) \sqsubseteq Q(s)$ follows.   □

The above result may seem surprising, since as we will see below the extended difference operator is not monotonic with respect to subset. An intuitive explanation of our result is that, as we have already noted, less informative than ($\sqsubseteq$) is compatible with the CWA, which limits the amount of information that can be added to an incomplete relation with respect to $\sqsubseteq$ and thus enforces monotonicity. We observe that if we replace less informative than ($\sqsubseteq$) by subset of ($\subseteq$) in the definition of monotonicity then the above result does not hold, since the extended difference operator is not a monotonic operator with respect to subset. For example, let $r_1 = \{<\text{Hillary}, unk, \text{Philosophy}>\}$ and $r_2 = \emptyset$. It can easily be verified that $r_1 -^e r_2 \cong r_1$. Now, let $s_1 \cong r_1$ and also $s_2 \cong r_1$. Then $r_1 \subseteq s_1$ and $r_2 \subseteq s_2$ both hold. However, $s_1 -^e s_2 = \emptyset$, which implies that $-^e$ is not monotonic with respect to subset.

We comment briefly on our use of unmarked nulls rather than marked nulls in the definition of the extended relational algebra. As we have noted before marked nulls are more expressive than unmarked nulls but would add complexity to the database system. As an example of the added expressiveness of marked nulls we recall that, when we combine extended projection with extended join, extended queries are not necessarily truth-preserving in the presence of unmarked nulls. On the other hand, if we allow marked nulls such extended queries are truth-preserving, since two marked nulls are taken to be equal if their marks are the same. For example, consider the incomplete relation $r = \{<\text{Hillary}, unk_1, \text{Philosophy}>\}$ over R, where schema(R) = {SNAME, COURSE, DEPT}. Then the reader can verify that $\pi^e_{\{SNAME, COURSE\}}(r) \bowtie^e \pi^e_{\{COURSE, DEPT\}}(r) = r$, as expected. On the other hand, in the presence of negation ($\neg$) in extended selection even when we allow marked nulls, extended queries may not be truth-preserving a situation associated with unmarked nulls. The culprit is again the three-valued equality rule. For example, let F be the formula (COURSE = 'Databases' or COURSE $\neq$ 'Databases') and consider the extended query $\sigma_F^e(r)$. Then the answer to this query is empty although F is a tautology.

5.5   Extending Integrity Constraints with Null Values

The problem of extending integrity constraints, so as to take into account the presence of null values, is the problem of redefining the notion of an integrity constraint being satisfied in an incomplete relation. Let r be an incomplete relation over schema R. We will assume throughout this section that both of the unmarked null types, *unk* and *inc*, may be present in incomplete relations. If r is inconsistent then r is taken to violate all integrity constraints; thus our assumption that a database should not contain inconsistent relations is justified. On the other hand, if r is complete then r satisfies an integrity constraint when the standard definition of satisfaction for complete relations obtains. In other words, an extended integrity constraint will always be defined so that it is *faithful* to its standard counterpart. We now discuss the two main approaches to extending the notion of satisfaction of an integrity constraint in r. The first approach insists that the integrity constraint be satisfied in all possible worlds relative to r and is called the *strong satisfaction* approach. The second approach requires that the integrity constraint be satisfied in at least one possible world relative to r and is called the *weak satisfaction* approach. The strong satisfaction approach can be viewed as modal logic *necessity* and the weak satisfaction approach can be viewed as modal logic *possibility*. (For an introduction to modal logic see [Che80].)

We argue that both strong and weak satisfaction arise naturally in the real world. For example, assume that the functional dependency (FD) constraining a student to belong to only one department is satisfied strongly and that the FD constraining a department to have one head is satisfied weakly. We will now show that the difference between strong and weak satisfaction has an effect on integrity constraint maintenance, whose task is to ensure that the database is in a consistent state after an update has taken place. The strong satisfaction of an integrity constraint implies that whenever an occurrence of *unk* is replaced by a nonnull value, the constraint maintenance mechanism *does not* need to recheck the satisfaction of the FD, since the fact that a student belongs to one department holds in all possible worlds. On the other hand, the weak satisfaction of an integrity constraint implies that whenever an occurrence of *unk* is replaced by a nonnull value, the constraint maintenance mechanism *does* need to recheck the satisfaction of the FD, since in the resulting possible world a department may have more than one head in which case the FD is violated, giving rise to inconsistency. Thus strong satisfaction is easier to maintain than weak satisfaction but weak satisfaction allows for a higher degree of uncertainty to be represented in the database.

We will now extend the notion of FD to incomplete relations. Recall that an FD over schema R is a statement of the form R : $X \rightarrow Y$ (or simply $X \rightarrow Y$ whenever R is understood from context), where X, Y $\subseteq$ schema(R). Also recall that an FD $X \rightarrow Y$ is satisfied in a complete relation r over R, denoted by $r \models X \rightarrow Y$, if and only if for all tuples t_1 and t_2 in r, if $t_1[X] = t_2[X]$ then $t_1[Y] = t_2[Y]$.

The following definition formally captures our intuition that an FD is strongly satisfied in an incomplete relation, say r, if and only if it is satisfied in all possible worlds relative to r.

Definition 5.24 (Strong satisfaction of an FD)   An FD $X \rightarrow Y$ is *strongly* satisfied (or simply satisfied whenever no ambiguity arises) in an incomplete relation r over R, denoted by $r \models X \rightarrow Y$, if and only if $\forall s \in POSS(r)$, $s \models X \rightarrow Y$. ∎

The following definition formally captures our intuition that an FD is weakly satisfied in an incomplete relation, say r, if and only if there exists a possible world relative to r in which this FD is satisfied.

Definition 5.25 (Weak satisfaction of an FD)   An FD $X \rightarrow Y$ is *weakly* satisfied (or simply satisfied whenever no ambiguity arises) in an incomplete relation r over R, denoted by $r \approx\!\!\!| X \rightarrow Y$, if and only if $\exists s \in POSS(r)$ such that $s \models X \rightarrow Y$. ∎

We observe that if r is a complete relation then both the definitions of strong satisfaction and weak satisfaction coincide with the standard notion of FD satisfaction, since in this case $POSS(r) = \{r\}$. Thus both strong and weak satisfaction of an FD are faithful to the standard satisfaction of an FD.

As an example of the above definitions let r be the incomplete relation over R, shown in Table 5.23, where schema(R) = {SNAME, COURSE, DEPT, HEAD}, and let F = {SNAME $\rightarrow$ DEPT, COURSE $\rightarrow$ DEPT, DEPT $\rightarrow$ HEAD} be a set of FDs over R. It can be verified that $r \models$ SNAME $\rightarrow$ DEPT, $r \approx\!\!\!|$ COURSE $\rightarrow$ DEPT and $r \approx\!\!\!|$ DEPT $\rightarrow$ HEAD are all satisfied.

Table 5.23 An incomplete relation r

SNAME	COURSE	DEPT	HEAD
Iris	Databases	Computing	Dan
Iris	Theory	Computing	*unk*
Reuven	Theory	*unk*	*unk*
Naomi	Programming	Maths	Annette
Joseph	*unk*	Maths	*unk*
Eli	Logic	*unk*	Brian

Prior to giving a syntactic characterisation of strong and weak satisfaction we define an operator, denoted by lub, which returns the *least upper bound* of two tuples over R with respect to the information lattice. (For the formal definition of the lub of a subset of a partially order set see Subsection 1.9.2 in Chapter 1.)

Definition 5.26 (Least upper bound operator)   The least upper bound of two values $v_1, v_2 \in$ EDOM(A) is defined as follows:

1) if $v_1 \sqsubseteq v_2$ then $lub(v_1, v_2) = v_2$; otherwise

2) if $v_2 \sqsubseteq v_1$ then $lub(v_1, v_2) = v_1$; otherwise

3) if $\neg(v_1 \sqsubseteq v_2)$ and $\neg(v_2 \sqsubseteq v_1)$ then $lub(v_1, v_2) = inc$.

We extend the lub operator to tuples t_1, t_2 over R as follows: $\text{lub}(t_1, t_2) = t$, where t is a tuple over R such that $\forall A \in \text{schema}(R)$, $t[A] = \text{lub}(t_1[A], t_2[A])$. ∎

The following lemma is important, since it gives rise to efficient algorithms for testing whether an FD is strongly or weakly satisfied in an incomplete relation.

Lemma 5.12   The following statements, where r is an incomplete relation over R (which is consistent) and $X, Y \subseteq \text{schema}(R)$, are true:

1) $r \models X \rightarrow Y$ if and only if for all distinct tuples $t_1, t_2 \in r$, if $\text{lub}(t_1[X], t_2[X])$ is consistent, then $t_1[Y{-}X] = t_2[Y{-}X]$ evaluates to true on using three-valued logic equality.

2) $r \approx X \rightarrow Y$ if and only if $\forall t_1, t_2 \in r$, if $t_1[X] = t_2[X]$ evaluates to true on using three-valued logic equality, then $\text{lub}(t_1[Y], t_2[Y])$ is consistent. □

When we are modelling an application under development we will consider a set of FDs that should be satisfied in any instance of the database. Therefore, we now generalise the definition of strong and weak satisfaction of a single FD to a set of FDs. Informally, a set of FDs, say F, is strongly satisfied in an incomplete relation, say r, if all the FDs in F are satisfied in all possible worlds relative to r. Correspondingly, F is weakly satisfied in r if all the FDs in F are satisfied in at least one single possible world relative to r.

Definition 5.27 (satisfaction of a set of FDs)   A set F of FDs over R is satisfied in a complete relation r over R, denoted by $r \models F$, if and only if $\forall X \rightarrow Y \in F, r \models X \rightarrow Y$.

A set F of FDs over R is *strongly* satisfied (or simply satisfied whenever no ambiguity arises) in an incomplete relation r over R, denoted by $r \models F$, if and only if $\forall s \in \text{POSS}(r), s \models F$.

A set F of FDs over R is *weakly* satisfied (or simply satisfied whenever no ambiguity arises) in an incomplete relation r over R, denoted by $r \approx F$, if and only if $\exists s \in \text{POSS}(r)$ such that $s \models F$. ∎

The above definition gives rise to the problem of whether we can test for satisfaction of a set F of FDs over R, in an incomplete relation, r, by testing independently the satisfaction in the relation r of each individual FD in the set F. Obviously a positive answer to this problem is desirable.

Definition 5.28 (Additive satisfaction)   We will say that satisfaction is *additive* for a class of integrity constraints whenever the following condition holds:

for all finite sets of integrity constraints $\Sigma = \{\alpha_1, \alpha_2, \ldots, \alpha_k\}$ in the class, Σ is satisfied in a relation r (which may be incomplete) if and only if $\forall i \in \{1, 2, \ldots, k\}, \alpha_i$ is satisfied in r individually. ∎

Weak satisfaction is defined in terms of possible worlds. Intuitively, if an incomplete relation, r, weakly satisfies a set of data dependencies, Σ, then there exists a sequence of updates, each update modifying a null value to a nonnull value, such that the resulting complete relation satisfies all the data dependencies $\alpha_i \in \Sigma$. The problem that arises is that although there may exist such a sequence of updates for every single data dependency $\alpha_i \in \Sigma$, two or more such sequences may lead to different possible worlds. In particular, there may not exist a single sequence of updates that leads to one possible world that satisfies all of the data dependencies α in Σ. From the user's point of view, when $r \not\approx \Sigma$, it is natural to view such a relation, r, as contradictory. Even if r is a true reflection of the current available information the user may still view Σ as contradictory. We call this problem the *additivity problem*.

If satisfaction is additive for a given class of integrity constraints then the additivity problem does not arise. The following theorem shows the expected result, namely that strong satisfaction is additive and the more surprising result that weak satisfaction is not additive.

Theorem 5.13   The following statements are true:

1) Strong satisfaction is additive.

2) Weak satisfaction is not additive.   □

Proof. Let r be an incomplete relation over R and let F be a set of FDs over R.

(*Part 1*): We need to show that $r \models F$ if and only if $\forall X \to Y \in F, r \models X \to Y$. Now by definition $r \models F$ if and only if $\forall s \in POSS(r), s \models F$, and $s \models F$ if and only if $\forall X \to Y \in F, s \models X \to Y$. Thus $r \models F$ if and only if $\forall X \to Y \in F, \forall s \in POSS(r), s \models X \to Y$. The result now follows by the definition of the satisfaction of an FD, since $\forall s \in POSS(r), s \models X \to Y$ if and only if $r \models X \to Y$.

(*Part 2*): We first observe that, by the definition of weak satisfaction of a single FD and a set of FDs, it follows that if $r \approx F$, then $\forall X \to Y \in F, r \approx X \to Y$. In order to conclude the proof we need to exhibit a counterexample to the statement, if $\forall X \to Y \in F, r \approx X \to Y$ then $r \approx F$. The result follows by setting r to be the incomplete relation r_1 shown in Table 5.24 and by setting F to be the set of FDs $\{A \to B, B \to C\}$.   □

We exhibit two interesting alternatives to setting r and F as in part (2) of Theorem 5.13. Firstly, we can set r to be the incomplete relation r_2, shown in Table 5.25, and F to be the set of FDs $\{A \to C, B \to C\}$. Secondly, we can set r to be the incomplete relation r_3, shown in Table 5.26, and F to be the set of FDs $\{B \to A, AC \to B\}$.

Table 5.24 The counterexample relation r_1

A	B	C
0	unk	0
0	unk	1

Table 5.25 The counterexample relation r_2

A	B	C
0	unk	0
0	0	unk
unk	0	1

Table 5.26 The counterexample relation r_3

A	B	C
0	0	unk
unk	0	0
0	1	0

Let r be an incomplete relation over a relation schema R and F be a set of FDs over R. We now present efficient algorithms for testing whether $r \models F$ or $r \approx F$ hold.

Firstly, the pseudo-code of an algorithm, designated STRONG_SAT(r, F), which given the inputs r and F returns an incomplete relation, is presented as Algorithm 5.1. On inspecting the algorithm the reader can verify that $r \models F$ if and only if STRONG_SAT(r, F) is consistent, on using part (1) of Lemma 5.12 and the fact that by part (1) of Theorem 5.13 strong satisfaction is additive. It can also be seen that the time complexity of Algorithm 5.1 is polynomial in |F| (the cardinality of F), $\|F\|$ (the size of F) and $|r|$ (the cardinality of r).

Algorithm 5.1 (STRONG_SAT(r, F))

1. **begin**
2.   Tmp := r;
3.   **for each** FD X $\rightarrow$ Y $\in$ F **do**
4.   **for each** pair of distinct tuples t_1, $t_2 \in$ Tmp **do**
5.   **if** lub($t_1[X]$, $t_2[X]$) is consistent **and** $t_1[Y] \neq t_2[Y]$ **then**
6. $t_1[Y{-}X] := <inc, \ldots, inc>$;
7. $t_2[Y{-}X] := <inc, \ldots, inc>$;
8.   **return** Tmp;
9.   **end if**
10.   **end for**
11.   **end for**
12.   **return** Tmp;
13. **end.**

Secondly, the pseudo-code of an algorithm, designated WEAK_SAT(r, F), which given the inputs r and F returns an incomplete relation in POSS(r), is presented as Algorithm 5.2. We assume for the purpose of Algorithm 5.2 that UNK = $\{unk_1, unk_2, \ldots, unk_q\}$ is a set of marked nulls of type unk, where $\forall A \in$ schema(R), UNK $\subseteq$ EDOM(A) and q denotes the finite number of distinct occurrences of unk in r. We also extend the partial order, less informative than, i.e. $\sqsubseteq$, in EDOM(A) as follows: $unk_i \sqsubseteq unk_j$ if and only if $i \leq j$ and $\forall v \in$ DOM(A), $\forall unk_i \in$ UNK, $unk_i \sqsubseteq v$ and $\neg(v \sqsubseteq unk_i)$. WEAK_SAT($r$, F) is more complex than STRONG_SAT(r, F), since by part (2) of Theorem 5.13 weak satisfaction is not additive and thus a naive approach whereby each FD in F is tested independently would not not suffice. We note that WEAK_SAT(r, F) is known in the database literature as the *chase procedure* (see Subsection 3.6.4 of Chapter 3). We leave the proof of the correctness of WEAK_SAT(r, F) to the reader; we conclude that $r \not\approx$ F if and only if WEAK_SAT(r, F) is consistent. It can also be seen that the time complexity of Algorithm 5.2 is polynomial in $|F|$, $\|F\|$ and $|r|$.

Algorithm 5.2 (WEAK_SAT(r, F))

1. **begin**
2.   Tmp := r;
3. $i := 1$;
4.   **for each** A $\in$ schema(R) **do**
5.   **for each** $t \in$ Tmp such that $t[A] = unk$ **do**
6. $t[A] := unk_i$;
7. $i := i + 1$;
8.   **end for**
9.   **end for**
10.   **while** $\exists t_1, t_2 \in$ Tmp, $\exists$ X $\rightarrow$ Y $\in$ F such that $t_1[X] = t_2[X]$ **and** $\neg(t_1[Y] \cong t_2[Y])$ **do**
11. $t_1[Y], t_2[Y] := $ lub($t_1[Y]$, $t_2[Y]$));
12.   **end while**
13.   **return** Tmp;
14. **end.**

Example 5.2   Let r be the incomplete relation shown in Table 5.23 and let F = {COURSE $\rightarrow$ DEPT, DEPT $\rightarrow$ HEAD}. WEAK_SAT(r, F) is shown in Table 5.27; it can be verified that WEAK_SAT(r, F) is consistent and that $r \not\approx$ F holds.   ∎

Table 5.27 The relation WEAK_SAT(r, F) of Example 5.2

STUD	COURSE	DEPT	HEAD
Iris	Databases	Computing	Dan
Iris	Theory	Computing	Dan
Reuven	Theory	Computing	Dan
Naomi	Programming	Maths	Annette
Joseph	unk_1	Maths	Annette
Eli	Logic	unk_2	Brian

Recall the notions relating to the inference of integrity constraints, which were defined in Section 3.4 of Chapter 3, and recall the inference rules for FDs which were presented in Subsection 3.6.1 of Chapter 3. We also remind the reader that the set of inference rules FD1, FD2 and FD3 is called Armstrong's axiom system, and herein we call the set of inference rules FD1, FD2, FD4 and FD5 *Lien's and Atzeni's axiom system* [Lie82, AM84]. We now specialise the definition of logical implication with respect to strong and weak satisfaction of FDs.

Definition 5.29 (Strong and weak logical implication)   A set F of FDs over schema R *strongly implies* an FD X $\rightarrow$ Y over R, written F $\models$ X $\rightarrow$ Y, whenever for all incomplete relations r over R the following condition is true:

$$\text{if } \forall \, W \rightarrow Z \in F, r \models W \rightarrow Z \text{ then } r \models X \rightarrow Y.$$

Correspondingly, F *weakly implies* X $\rightarrow$ Y, written F $\not\approx$ X $\rightarrow$ Y, whenever for all incomplete relations r over R the following condition is true:

$$\text{if } \forall \, W \rightarrow Z \in F, r \not\approx W \rightarrow Z \text{ then } r \not\approx X \rightarrow Y.$$ ∎

We note that due to the difference between strong and weak implication we have introduced two different notions of logical implication. Thus in order to avoid confusion in the presentation of the following results, for each result we will explicitly mention whether the result is with respect to weak implication or with respect to strong implication.

The following result is to be expected and its proof follows along the same lines of the proof of Theorem 3.21 given in Subsection 3.6.1 of Chapter 3. (Recall that in Theorem 3.21 we have shown that Armstrong's axioms are sound and complete with respect to logical implication of FDs in complete relations.)

Theorem 5.14   Armstrong's axiom system is sound and complete for FDs with respect to strong implication.   □

We define the closure of a set of attributes X $\subseteq$ schema(R) with respect to a set F of FDs over R and Armstrong's axiom system, denoted as X^{Arm+} (assuming that F in understood from context), by

$$X^{Arm+} = \bigcup \{Y \mid F \vdash X \to Y \text{ using Armstrong's axiom system}\}.$$

We note that the operator "*Arm+*" induced by the closure X^{Arm+} is a closure operator (see Definition 3.54 in Section 3.5 of Chapter 3). Furthermore, $F \vdash X \to Y$ if and only if $Y \subseteq X^{Arm+}$ holds. Finally, from the results presented in Subsection 3.6.1 of Chapter 3 it is immediate that X^{Arm+} can be computed in time linear in $\|F\|$ and thus by Theorem 5.14 it provides an efficient solution to the strong implication problem for FDs.

We now consider soundness and completeness with respect to weak implication. Consider the relation r_1 shown in Table 5.24. This relation proves that the transitivity rule (FD3) is not sound for FDs with respect to weak implication, since both $r_1 \approx A \to B$ and $r_1 \approx B \to C$ hold but $r \approx A \to C$ is violated. Despite this negative result we obtain a sound and complete axiom system by dropping FD3 and adding FD4 (union) and FD5 (decomposition) to the axiom system, thus obtaining Lien's and Atzeni's axiom system. Prior to presenting Theorem 5.15 we define the closure of a set of attributes $X \subseteq schema(R)$ with respect to a set F of FDs over R and Lien's and Atzeni's axiom system, denoted as X^{Lien+} (assuming that F in understood from context), by

$$X^{Lien+} = \bigcup \{Y \mid F \vdash X \to Y \text{ using Lien's and Atzeni's axiom system}\}.$$

We note again that the operator "*Lien+*" induced by the closure X^{Lien+} is a closure operator. Furthermore, $F \vdash X \to Y$ if and only if $Y \subseteq X^{Lien+}$ holds. Finally, F^{Arm+} and F^{Lien+} stand for the closure of F with respect to Armstrong's and Lien's and Atzeni's axiom systems, respectively; this notation for the closure is used only when it is not obvious from context.

Theorem 5.15 Lien's and Atzeni's axiom system is sound and complete for FDs with respect to weak implication.

Proof. We leave it to the reader to prove that Lien's and Atzeni's axiom system is sound with respect to weak implication. We now give the proof of completeness in full, since it is typical of such proofs in database theory and it is both highly elegant and instructive.

We prove completeness by showing that if $F \nvdash X \to Y$, then $F \napprox X \to Y$, where F is a set of FDs over schema R. Equivalently for the latter, it is sufficient to exhibit an incomplete relation, say r, such that $\forall W \to Z \in F, r \approx W \to Z$ but $r \napprox X \to Y$. Let r be the incomplete relation over schema R shown in Table 5.28.

We first show that $\forall W \to Z \in F, r \approx W \to Z$. Suppose to the contrary that there exists an FD, $W \to Z \in F$, such that $r \napprox W \to Z$. It follows by the construction of r that $W \subseteq X$ and that $\exists A \in Z \cap (schema(R) - X^{Lien+})$; this implies that $A \notin X^{Lien+}$. By FD2 (augmentation) it follows that $F \vdash X \to ZX$, and by FD5 (decomposition) it follows that $F \vdash X \to A$. This leads to a contradiction, since it follows that $A \in X^{Lien+}$.

We conclude the proof by showing that $r \napprox X \to Y$. Suppose to the contrary that $r \approx X \to Y$. Thus by the construction of r, $Y \subseteq X^{Lien+}$ holds. Now, $F \vdash X \to X^{Lien+}$ holds by the definition of X^{Lien+}. Therefore, on using FD5 (decomposition) it follows that $\forall A \in Y, F \vdash X \to A$ holds and on using FD4 (union) it follows that $F \vdash X \to Y$ holds. This leads to a contradiction, since we have derived $F \vdash X \to Y$ contrary to our assumption. $\square$

Table 5.28 The incomplete relation used in the proof of Theorem 5.15

X	$X^{Lien+} - X$	schema(R) $-X^{Lien+}$
$0 \ldots 0$	$unk \ldots unk$	$1 \ldots 1$
$0 \ldots 0$	$0 \ldots 0$	$0 \ldots 0$

We now present an efficient algorithm that solves the weak implication problem for FDs. The pseudo-code of the algorithm, designated WEAK_CLOSE(X, F), given inputs X $\subseteq$ schema(R) and a set F of FDs over R, returns X^{Lien+}. We leave it to the reader to verify that WEAK_CLOSE(X, F) is correct and that its time complexity is linear in $\|F\|$.

Algorithm 5.3 (WEAK_CLOSE(X, F))
1. **begin**
2.   CL := X;
3.   **for each** W $\rightarrow$ Z $\in$ F **do**
5.   **if** W $\subseteq$ X **then**
6.   CL := CL $\cup$ Z;
7.   **end if**
8.   **end for**
9.   **return** CL;
10. **end.**

A mixed axiom system for FDs with respect to strong and weak implication was considered in [LL98b]. Therein, each FD, in a set of FDs, is qualified as being either a *strong* FD or a *weak* FD, according to whether its satisfaction in a relation should be strong or weak. For example, one mixed inference rule, which takes into account the interaction between these two types of FDs, states that if a set of FDs logically implies a strong FD X $\rightarrow$ Y then it also logically implies the corresponding weak FD X $\rightarrow$ Y. In modal logic terms, this inference rule states that if the constraint is necessary then it is also possible. In [LL98b] it is shown that the above-mentioned mixed axiom system is sound and complete for a set of strong and weak FDs.

We next introduce two new subclasses of FDs with a view to solving the additivity problem.

Informally, a set F of FDs over R satisfies the intersection property if for each attribute A in schema(R) there exists at most one FD that functionally determines A and the closure of this FD contains all the FDs in the closure of F that functionally determine A. We next formalise this subclass of FDs.

Definition 5.30 (Intersection property)   Two nontrivial FDs X $\rightarrow$ A and Y $\rightarrow$ A (i.e. A $\notin$ X, Y) are *incomparable* if X $\not\subseteq$ Y and Y $\not\subseteq$ X.

A set F of FDs satisfies the *intersection property* if for all attributes A $\in$ schema(R), whenever X $\rightarrow$ A, Y $\rightarrow$ A $\in F^{Arm+}$ are incomparable FDs, then it is also true that X $\cap$ Y $\rightarrow$ A $\in F^{Arm+}$. ∎

We define a set F of FDs over R to be *reduced* if for all FDs X $\rightarrow$ Y $\in$ F, there does not exist a proper subset W $\subset$ X such that W $\rightarrow$ Y $\in F^{Arm+}$.

The next theorem states that if F is reduced and satisfies the intersection property, then the closure of F with respect to Armstrong's axiom system coincides with the closure of F with respect to Lien's and Atzeni's axiom system. Intuitively, this is true due to the fact that the intersection property implies that if $X \to A \in F^{Arm+}$, for some nontrivial FD $X \to A$, then there is an FD $W \to Z \in F$ such that $W \subseteq X$ and $A \in Z$; therefore, it is also true that $X \to A \in F^{Lien+}$. (A full proof of the theorem can be found in [LL97a].) We observe that if F is *not* reduced then the result does not hold; this can be seen by considering the set of FDs, $\{A \to B, AB \to C\}$, which satisfies the intersection property, since $A \to C$ is in F^{Arm+} but not in F^{Lien+}.

Theorem 5.16 If F is reduced and satisfies the intersection property then $F^{Arm+} = F^{Lien+}$.

$\square$

The converse of Theorem 5.16 is, in general, false. For example, let $F = \{A \to C, B \to C\}$ be a set of FDs over R, with schema(R) = $\{A, B, C\}$. It can be easily verified that $F^{Arm+} = F^{Lien+}$ but that F does not satisfy the intersection property, since $\emptyset \to C \notin F^+$.

Informally, a set F of FDs over R satisfies the split-freeness property if there do not exist two FDs in the closure of F such that the right-hand side of one FD splits the left-hand side of the other FD into two parts. We next formalise this subclass of FDs.

Definition 5.31 (Split-freeness property) Two nontrivial FDs of the forms $XB \to A$ and $YA \to B$ are said to be *cyclic*.

A set F of FDs over R satisfies the *split-freeness property*, if whenever there exist cyclic FDs, $XB \to A, YA \to B \in F^{Arm+}$, then it is also true that either $Y \to B \in F^{Arm+}$ or $(X \cap Y)A \to B \in F^{Arm+}$. ∎

Definition 5.32 (Monodependent sets of FDs) A set F of FDs over R is said to be *monodependent* if it satisfies both the intersection property and the split-freeness property. ∎

Let us make a slight modification to Definition 5.28 with respect to FDs by saying that satisfaction is additive for a class **FC** of FDs over R if satisfaction is additive for FC^{red}, where FC^{red} is the result of replacing each set F of FDs in **FC** by a reduced cover of F.

We observe that we cannot relax the condition that the sets of FDs are reduced. Consider the relation r_1, shown in Table 5.24, and let $F = \{A \to B, AB \to C\}$. It can easily be verified that $r_1 \approx A \to B$ and $r_1 \approx AB \to C$ but $r_1 \not\approx F$. On the other hand, if we let $G = \{A \to B, A \to C\}$, i.e. G is a reduced cover of F, then $r_1 \not\approx A \to C$. There is no loss of generality in assuming that sets of FDs, such as F, are reduced, since a reduced cover of F can easily be obtained in polynomial time in the size of F.

The next theorem shows that for FDs the additivity problem is solved when we consider sets of FDs which are monodependent. Assume according to the definition of additive satisfaction for FDs, as modified above, that F is a reduced set of FDs over R.

Intuitively, if for some relation r, we have that $\forall X \to Y \in F$, $r \approx X \to Y$ but $r \not\approx F$, then we can show that F is not monodependent by induction on the minimum number of times the while loop in WEAK_SAT(r, F) is executed in order to ascertain whether WEAK_SAT(r, F) is inconsistent. On the other hand, if F is not monodependent then the counterexamples shown in Tables 5.25 and 5.26 can be generalised to the two cases when F either violates the intersection property, or respectively, the split-freeness property. (A full proof of the theorem can be found in [LL97a].)

Theorem 5.17   Weak satisfaction is additive for a class **FC** of sets of FDs over R if and only if all the sets of FDs in **FC** are monodependent.   □

Many useful properties of monodependent sets of FDs can be found in [Lev95, LL99a]. For example, therein we show that the superkey of cardinality k problem and the prime attribute problem can both be solved in polynomial time in the size of F (see Theorem 3.24 in Subsection 3.6.1 of Chapter 3). In addition, there is a unique optimum cover of F that can be found in polynomial time in the size of F (see Theorem 3.32 in Subsection 3.6.5 of Chapter 3). Moreover, if F is monodependent then every lossless join decomposition **R** of schema(R) with respect to F is also dependency preserving with respect to F (see Section 4.2 of Chapter 4).

In the presence of incomplete information the notions of key, superkey and primary key remain as they were in Subsection 3.6.1 of Chapter 3, the difference being that in the case of weak satisfaction our axiom system has changed. We are now in a position to formalise the notion of entity integrity discussed in Subsection 3.6.1 of Chapter 3. In fact, entity integrity is only really meaningful in the presence of incomplete information. We first quote Codd's definition of entity integrity from [Cod90]:

"No component of a primary key is allowed to have a missing value of any type".

Definition 5.33 (Entity integrity)   Let $K \subseteq$ schema(R) be the primary key of a relation schema R. The entity integrity rule states that: for an incomplete relation, r over R, it is true that for all the tuples $t \in r$, $t[K]$ does not contain any null values.   ■

For example, if the primary key of the student schema, given in Example 5.1, is STUD# then the attribute values of STUD# are not allowed to be null. Thus the relation shown in Table 5.1 satisfies the entity integrity rule. We note that according to the entity integrity rule any attribute value that is not part of the primary key may have a null value. We further note that entity integrity can be viewed as a special case of a more general type of integrity constraint, called a *null-free* constraint, which asserts that certain attributes in schema(R) are not allowed to have null attribute values.

In the presence of incomplete information it can be argued that entity integrity is too strict in practice. Assume for the moment that we restrict ourselves to incomplete relations where the only type of null value that is used is *unk*, modelling the fact that a "value exists but is unknown at the present time".

As a first motivating example consider a relation schema R containing the attributes NAME and ADDRESS, and assume that {NAME, ADDRESS} is the primary key of R. It can easily be seen that the relation, say r, over R shown in Table 5.29 violates entity integrity. Despite this fact all the tuples in r are uniquely identifiable, since the problematic third tuple is the only tuple having the name Sue Jones. Thus all possible worlds of r have three tuples and in all such complete relations, $s \in$ POSS(r), {NAME, ADDRESS} is a superkey in s. (Recall from Definition 3.62 in Subsection 3.6.1 of Chapter 3 that K is a key (superkey) in a complete relation s over R, if K is a key (superkey) for R with respect to the set $F(s)$ of FDs that are satisfied in s.)

Table 5.29 A relation showing that entity integrity is too strict

NAME	ADDRESS
John Smith	Hampstead Way
John Smith	Harold Rd
Sue Jones	*unk*

So as long as each tuple in a relation r is uniquely identifiable as a distinct entity by the nonnull portion of its primary key values, we can consider the relation to satisfy entity integrity. As a second motivating example consider a relation schema R containing the attributes NAME, ADDRESS and DOB (date of birth), and assume that {NAME, ADDRESS, DOB} is the primary key of R. It can easily be seen that the relation, say r, over R shown in Table 5.30 violates entity integrity. Despite this fact all the tuples in r are uniquely identifiable by the nonnull portion of their primary key values. Consider the tuples in r pairwise: the first and second tuples are distinguishable by their NAME, the first and third tuples are distinguishable by their DOB and the second and third tuples are distinguishable by their ADDRESS. As in the previous example all possible worlds of r have three tuples and in all such complete relations, $s \in POSS(r)$, {NAME, ADDRESS, DOB} is a superkey in s.

Table 5.30 Another relation showing that entity integrity is too strict

NAME	ADDRESS	DOB
John Smith	*unk*	13/6/95
Sue Jones	Harold Rd	*unk*
unk	Hampstead Way	17/12/96

The examples given above suggest that in relations, which may be incomplete, the notions of superkey and key can be generalised. We next formalise such a generalisation which was proposed by Thalheim [Tha89a]. (In the following we will make use of the index set $I = \{1, 2, \ldots, n\}$.)

Definition 5.34 (Superkey family) A *superkey family* K for R is a family $K = \{K_1, K_2, \ldots, K_n\}$ consisting of n, $n \geq 1$, subsets of schema(R). ∎

Informally, a superkey family K is satisfied in a relation r over R if all pairs of distinct tuples in r differ on nonnull values with respect to some $K_i \in K$.

Definition 5.35 (Satisfaction of a superkey family) A relation r over R satisfies a superkey family K (alternatively, K is a superkey family in r), written $r \approx K$, if for all pairs of distinct tuples $t_1, t_2 \in r$, there exists $K_i \in K$, $i \in I$, such that $t_1[K_i]$ and $t_2[K_i]$ are complete (i.e. do not contain any null values) and $t_1[K_i] \neq t_2[K_i]$. ∎

The reader can verify that for the boundary cases of a relation, say r, containing no tuples or a single tuple, the superkey family containing the empty set, i.e. {∅}, is always satisfied in r. To avoid these special cases we assume, in the ensuing development of the notion of a superkey family, that relations contain at least two tuples. When r contains two or more tuples, then $\{\emptyset\}$ is not satisfied in r.

Definition 5.36 (Nonredundant, irreducible and minimal key families)   Let K be a superkey family that is satisfied in a relation r over R. We say that K is *nonredundant* in r, if for no proper subset $K' \subset K$, does r satisfy K', i.e. the cardinality of K is minimal. We say that K is *irreducible* in r, if for no proper subset $K_i' \subset K_i$, $i \in I$, with $K_i \in K$, does r satisfy $(K - \{K_i\}) \cup \{K_i'\}$, i.e. the cardinalities of all the elements in K are minimal. Finally, we say that K is *minimal* in r (or alternatively, K is a *key family* in r), if it is nonredundant in r and every $K \in K$ is a singleton, i.e. contains only a single attribute.   ■

By our assumption that r contains at least two tuples, we can deduce that a key family in r is also irreducible in r. The reader can verify the next lemma.

Lemma 5.18   If K is a superkey family in a relation r over R, then there exists a superkey family, $\{\{A_1\}, \{A_2\}, \dots, \{A_m\}\}$, with $m \geq 1$, that is minimal in r and such that $\{A_1, A_2, \dots, A_m\} \subseteq \bigcup_{i \in I} K_i$, with $K_i \in K$.   □

The next proposition states that the notion of a key family is possibility-preserving with respect to the standard notion of a superkey, when we restrict our attention to the class of relations which satisfy at least one key family.

Proposition 5.19   Given a superkey family K and a relation r over R, if K is a superkey family in r, then for all $s \in \text{POSS}(r)$, $\bigcup_{i \in I} K_i$, with $K_i \in K$, is a superkey in s.

Proof. Assume to the contrary that K is a superkey family in r but for some $s \in \text{POSS}(r)$, X is not a superkey in s, where $X = \bigcup_{i \in I} K_i$, with $K_i \in K$. It therefore follows that there are at least two distinct tuples in r that are not uniquely identifiable by the nonnull portion of their superkey values contradicting Definition 5.35.   □

We observe that we cannot strengthen Proposition 5.19 to key families.   As a counterexample, $\{\{\text{NAME}\}, \{\text{ADDRESS}\}\}$ is a key family in the relation shown in Table 5.29 but if we replace *unk* by Asmuns Hill, then ADDRESS is a key in the resulting complete relation. In fact, there are relations which satisfy a key family but in none of their possible worlds is the union of the attributes of the elements of the key family a key. For example, $\{\{\text{NAME}\}, \{\text{ADDRESS}\}, \{\text{DOB}\}\}$ is a key family in the relation shown in Table 5.30. However, $\{\text{NAME}, \text{ADDRESS}, \text{DOB}\}$ is a superkey in all of its possible worlds but a key in none of them. To see this, in order for $\{\text{ADDRESS}, \text{DOB}\}$ *not* to be a key in one of its possible worlds, the *unk* in the first tuple must be replaced by Harold Rd, but then $\{\text{NAME}, \text{ADDRESS}\}$ will be a superkey in all the possible worlds emanating from this replacement.

We are now ready to generalise entity integrity, which is well defined for incomplete relations satisfying key families.

Definition 5.37 (Generalised entity integrity)   A *primary key family* is a superkey family, which is designated by the user. Given a primary key family K, a relation r satisfies *generalised entity integrity* if K is a key family in r.   ■

We now turn our attention to some computational problems related to superkey families. The next result is an immediate consequence of Lemma 5.18, since if **K** is a superkey family in r, then $\{\{A_1\}, \{A_2\}, \ldots, \{A_m\}\}$ must also be a superkey family in r, where schema(R) = $\{A_1, A_2, \ldots, A_m\}$.

Corollary 5.20 The problem of determining, given a relation r over R, whether there exists a superkey family **K** for R such that $r \approx$ **K** can be solved in polynomial time in the sizes of r and R. $\qquad\square$

We next show that the problem of finding a key family in a relation can be computed in polynomial time. The problem of deciding whether a relation satisfies a superkey family of cardinality no greater than some natural number k is NP-complete (see Exercise 5.8).

Proposition 5.21 If there is a superkey family which is satisfied in a relation r over R, then the problem of finding a superkey family **K**, such that **K** is a key family in r, can be solved in polynomial time in the sizes of r and R.

Proof. By Lemma 5.18, **K** = $\{\{A_1\}, \{A_2\}, \ldots, \{A_m\}\}$ is a superkey family in r, where schema(R) = $\{A_1, A_2, \ldots, A_m\}$, with $m \geq 1$. The idea behind an algorithm to compute a key family in r is: starting from **K**, which is a superkey family in r, we loop over all the singleton sets $\{A_i\}$ in **K** in some order and remove $\{A_i\}$ from the current state of the superkey family **K**, if **K** $- \{\{A_i\}\}$ is a superkey family in r. The loop will be iterated at most $m - 1$ times. $\qquad\square$

As a third motivating example for generalising entity integrity, we lift our restriction that *unk* is the only type of null value allowed in incomplete relations by also allowing occurrences of *dne*, modelling the fact that a "value does not exist". Consider a relation schema R containing the attributes SS# (social security number), P# (passport number) and NAME. It is possible that, as in the relation r over R shown in Table 5.31, for some tuples in r, SS# is nonnull but P# is null (see the first tuple in r), and for other tuples in r, P# is nonnull but SS# is null (see the second tuple in r). In this case every tuple in r is distinguishable (by nonnull values) either by SS# or P#, since each is unique, but entity integrity is violated, assuming that both SS# and P# are candidate keys for R and either SS# or P# is the primary key of R. Moreover, on using Definition 5.35 there is no superkey family that is satisfied in r and thus $\{\{SS\#\}, \{P\#\}\}$ is not a superkey family in r. Despite this fact, it is important to observe that, due to the semantics of *dne*, the first and second tuples of r represent distinct entities. Thus if at some later stage, John Smith of the first tuple acquires a P# it cannot be 2, and if at some later stage, John Smith of the second tuple acquires a SS# it cannot be 1. This would not have been the case had the null values in r been of type *unk*, since then there would be a possible world of r in which both the tuples in r represent the same entity. One solution, which is consistent with Definition 5.35, is to treat *dne* as having the same information content as some nonnull value, implying that $<dne>$ is taken to be a complete tuple. To illustrate the problem with this solution, consider the projection of r onto SS# or onto P#. In both cases *dne* will be used for identification purposes, which is contrary to Codd's assertion that tuples should be distinguishable by their nonnull values. This solution can be enhanced by insisting that each tuple in r must be uniquely identified by its nonnull values on some member of the superkey family [LL97b].

Table 5.31 Yet another relation showing that entity integrity is too strict

SS#	P#	NAME
1	*dne*	John Smith
dne	2	John Smith

We now turn our attention to the existence of Armstrong relations, in the presence of null values of type *unk*, with respect to strong and weak implication. Firstly, it is obvious that FDs enjoy Armstrong relations with respect to strong implication by Theorem 3.21 of Subsection 3.6.1 of Chapter 3, since Armstrong's axioms are sound and complete for FDs with respect to strong implication. The following theorem shows the companion result for FDs with respect to weak implication. (Below we still continue to make use of the index set $I = \{1, 2, \ldots, n\}$.)

Theorem 5.22 FDs enjoy Armstrong relations with respect to weak implication.

Proof. Let F be a set of FDs over R and let the power set $\mathcal{P}(\text{schema}(R))$ be the set $\{X_1, X_2, \ldots, X_n\}$. We now construct n tuples as follows: $\forall i \in I$, let t_i be an incomplete tuple such that $t_i[X_i] = <0, \ldots, 0>$, $t_i[X_i^{Lien+} - X_i] = <unk, \ldots, unk>$ and $t_i[\text{schema}(R) - X_i^{Lien+}] = <i, \ldots, i>$. We next construct the incomplete relation r^{Arm} over R defined by

$$r^{Arm} = \bigcup_i \{t_i \mid i \in I\}.$$

We leave it to the reader to show that indeed $r^{Arm} \approx\!\!\!\mid X \to Y$ if and only if $F \models X \to Y$. $\square$

We will now extend the notion of an inclusion dependency (or simply an IND) from Subsection 3.6.7 of Chapter 3 to incomplete relations, containing null values of type *unk*, in order to formalise the notion of referential integrity. Firstly, we will give some preliminary definitions. An *incomplete database* over $\mathbf{R} = \{R_1, R_2, \ldots, R_n\}$ is a collection d of incomplete relations $\{r_1, r_2, \ldots, r_n\}$ such that for all $i \in I$, r_i is an incomplete relation over R_i. An incomplete database is said to be a *complete database* (or simply a database) if for all $i \in I$, r_i is a complete relation.

We can now extend INDs to incomplete relations. Recall that an IND over a database schema $\mathbf{R}$ is a statement of the form $R_1[<X>] \subseteq R_2[<Y>]$, where $R_1, R_2 \in \mathbf{R}$ and $<X>, <Y>$ are sequences of distinct attributes such that $X \subseteq \text{schema}(R_1)$, $Y \subseteq \text{schema}(R_2)$ and $|X| = |Y|$. Whenever no confusion arises between a sequence and its underlying set, we will refer to the sequence of distinct attributes $<Y>$, simply as Y.

Also recall that an IND $R_1[X] \subseteq R_2[Y]$ is satisfied in a complete relation r over R, denoted by $r \models R_1[X] \subseteq R_2[Y]$, if $\forall t_1 \in r_1, \exists t_2 \in r_2$ such that $t_1[X] = t_2[Y]$, i.e. $\pi_X(r_1) \subseteq \pi_Y(r_2)$.

Definition 5.38 (Weak satisfaction of an IND) An IND $R_1[X] \subseteq R_2[Y]$ is satisfied in an incomplete database d over $\mathbf{R}$, denoted by $d \approx\!\!\!\mid R_1[X] \subseteq R_2[Y]$, if $\forall t_1 \in r_1, \exists t_2 \in r_2$ such that $t_1[X] \sqsubseteq t_2[Y]$. ∎

We observe that if d is a complete database then the definition of weak satisfaction of an IND coincides with the standard notion of IND satisfaction. Thus weak satisfaction of an IND is faithful to the standard satisfaction of an IND.

Definition 5.39 (The set of possible worlds of a database) We extend POSS to a database, $d = \{r_1, r_2, \ldots, r_n\}$, as follows:

$$\text{POSS}(d) = \{\{s_1, s_2, \ldots, s_n\} \mid s_1 \in \text{POSS}(r_1) \text{ and } s_2 \in \text{POSS}(r_2) \text{ and } \ldots \text{ and } s_n \in \text{POSS}(r_n)\}.$$

∎

The following proposition gives a semantic characterisation of weak satisfaction of an IND in terms of possible worlds.

Proposition 5.23 Let d_1 be a database over **R** and $R[X] \subseteq S[Y]$ be an IND over **R**. If $d_1 \approx R[X] \subseteq S[Y]$, then $\exists d_2 \in \text{POSS}(d_1)$ such that $\pi_X(r) \subseteq \pi_Y(s)$, where $r \in d_2$ is the relation over $R \in \mathbf{R}$ and $s \in d_2$ is the relation over $S \in \mathbf{R}$. □

We note that the converse of Proposition 5.23 does not hold. For example, let $d_1 = \{r_1, r_2\}$ be a database over $\mathbf{R} = \{R_1, R_2\}$, where $r_1 = \{<a, b>\}$ is the relation over R_1, with schema(R_1) = \{A, B\}, and $r_2 = \{<unk, d>\}$ is the relation over R_2, with schema(R_2) = \{C, D\}. Then $d_1 \not\approx R_1[A] \subseteq R_2[C]$; however, $d_2 \models R_1[A] \subseteq R_2[C]$, where $d_2 = \{r_1, s_2\} \in \text{POSS}(d_1)$ is a database over **R**, with $s_2 = \{<a, d>\}$ being a relation over R_2, and $\pi_A(r_1) \subseteq \pi_C(s_2)$. Thus the existence of a possible world of a database, say d, that satisfies a standard inclusion dependency is not sufficient for a corresponding IND to be weakly satisfied in d.

This leads to an asymmetry between the definition of weak satisfaction for FDs and INDs. We justify our definition of weak satisfaction of an IND by the fact that it faithfully captures the notion of subset in the presence of incomplete information. Suppose that employees work in departments and that we specify the IND, EMP[DNAME] ⊆ DEPT[DNAME], meaning that the information pertaining to the department that an employee works for can be found in the department relation. Now, it could be that the department of an employee is unknown, implying that the DNAME-value could be any value. On the other hand, if the DNAME-value is known then this would indicate the existence of nonnull information about the employee's department in the department relation. Thus a nonnull value, say v, in the DNAME attribute of an employee tuple implies that there must exist a corresponding tuple in the department relation with v as its DNAME-value. In this sense an IND is similar to a *directional link* and thus the definition is asymmetric. (Also see Definition 5.41 of referential integrity, given below.)

Definition 5.40 (Weak logical implication) A set I of INDs over a database schema **R** *weakly implies* an IND $R_1[X] \subseteq R_2[X]$ over **R**, written $I \approx R_1[X] \subseteq R_2[Y]$, whenever for all incomplete databases d over **R** the following condition is true: if $\forall R_i[W] \subseteq R_j[Z] \in I, d \approx R_i[W] \subseteq R_j[Z]$ then $d \approx R_1[X] \subseteq R_2[Y]$. ∎

Now recall the inference rules, IND1, IND2 and IND3, for INDs holding in complete relations, which were given in Subsection 3.6.7 of Chapter 3. The next result shows that in contrast to weak implication of FDs the axiom system for weak implication of INDs remains unchanged.

Theorem 5.24 The axiom system comprising IND1, IND2 and IND3 is sound and complete for INDs with respect to weak implication of INDs.

Proof. We sketch the main idea of the proof. Soundness of the axiom system follows directly from the definition of weak satisfaction of an IND. Now, let I be a set of INDs over a database schema $\mathbf{R}$ and α be a single IND over $\mathbf{R}$ such that I $\not\vdash \alpha$. In order to prove completeness of the axiom system we need to exhibit an incomplete database over $\mathbf{R}$, say d, such that $d \mathrel{\approx\!\!\!|} I$ but $d \mathrel{\not\approx\!\!\!|} \alpha$. By the completeness of the axiom system with respect to standard implication of INDs, shown in Theorem 3.37 in Subsection 3.6.7 of Chapter 3, there exists a complete database, say d' over $\mathbf{R}$, such that $d' \models I$ but $d' \not\models \alpha$. The result now follows since weak implication of INDs is faithful to the standard implication of INDs, which means that for complete databases weak implication and standard implication coincide; thus we can choose d' as the database d showing that $d' \mathrel{\approx\!\!\!|} I$ but $d' \mathrel{\not\approx\!\!\!|} \alpha$. $\square$

We note that, although a significant amount of research has been done on the semantics of FDs in the presence of incomplete information, to our knowledge very little research has been done on the semantics of INDs in the presence of incomplete information. In [LL97d] we have further investigated the interaction between FDs and INDs in the presence of incomplete information. Therein we have shown that the pullback inference rule is sound for weak satisfaction of FDs and INDs but that the collection inference rule is not. We exhibited a sound and complete axiom system for weak satisfaction of FDs and INDs, which replaces the collection inference rule by a new inference rule, called null collection. In contrast to the undecidability result of the implication problem for FDs and INDs for complete relations, we showed that in the presence of incomplete information this decision problem is decidable and EXPTIME-complete. Intuitively, this is due to the fact that when we allow null values the axiom system is weaker mainly as a result of the fact that transitivity for FDs becomes unsound. (See Subsection 3.6.11 of Chapter 3 for details on the interaction of FDs and INDs in complete relations.)

We have also looked into the additivity problem in the context of weak satisfaction for INDs and their interaction with FDs in [LL98a]. We give an example showing why weak satisfaction is not additive for INDs, as is the case with FDs. Let d be an incomplete database over $\mathbf{R}$ and let I be a set of INDs over $\mathbf{R}$. Informally, we need to exhibit a counterexample to the statement, if $\forall R_1[X] \subseteq R_2[Y] \in I, d \mathrel{\approx\!\!\!|} R_1[X] \subseteq R_2[Y]$, then $d \mathrel{\approx\!\!\!|} I$. Let r_1, r_2 and r_3 be the relations shown in Tables 5.32, 5.33 and 5.34, respectively, and let $d = \{r_1, r_2, r_3\}$ be a database over $\mathbf{R}$, with $\mathbf{R} = \{R, S, T\}$ and schema(R) = $<A>$, schema(S) = $<B>$ and schema(T) = $<C>$. Suppose that I = $\{R[A] \subseteq S[B], R[A] \subseteq T[C]\}$. The result follows, since it can easily be verified that $d \mathrel{\approx\!\!\!|} R[A] \subseteq S[B]$ and $d \mathrel{\approx\!\!\!|} R[A] \subseteq T[C]$ but $d \mathrel{\not\approx\!\!\!|} \{R[A] \subseteq S[B], R[A] \subseteq T[C]\}$. In [LL98a] we formalise the additivity problem for INDs and give necessary and sufficient conditions for its solution in the case where the INDs in I are unary. The reader can verify that if we add to the set I of INDs one of the INDs, S[B] $\subseteq$ T[C], T[C] $\subseteq$ S[B], S[B] $\subseteq$ R[A] or T[C] $\subseteq$ R[A] and enforce its weak satisfaction in d, then the additivity problem would not arise in this case.

Table 5.32 The counterexample relation r_1	**Table 5.33** The counterexample relation r_2	**Table 5.34** The counterexample relation r_3
A	B	C
unk	0	1

We are now in a position to formalise the notion of referential integrity discussed in Subsection 3.6.1 of Chapter 3.

Definition 5.41 (Foreign keys and referential integrity)   Let $\mathbf{R}$ be a database schema and R_1, R_2 be relation schemas of $\mathbf{R}$; also let X be a set of attributes in schema(R_1) and K be the primary key of R_2.

A *referential dependency* over $\mathbf{R}$ is an IND of the form $R_1[X] \subseteq R_2[K]$ over $\mathbf{R}$. A *referential dependency* $R_1[X] \subseteq R_2[K]$ is satisfied in a database d over $\mathbf{R}$ if $d \not\approx R_1[X] \subseteq R_2[K]$ holds.

Let RD be a designated set of referential dependencies over $\mathbf{R}$. The referential integrity rule asserts that: for a database d over $\mathbf{R}$, all of the referential dependencies $R_1[X] \subseteq R_2[K] \in$ RD are satisfied in d. The sets of attributes X are called *foreign keys* of $\mathbf{R}$.   ∎

We note that referential dependencies can be generalised to *key-based* INDs, which are INDs of the form $R_1[X] \subseteq R_2[K]$, with K being a candidate key for R_2, which is not necessarily the primary key of R_2.

5.6   The Or-sets Approach

When an incomplete relation has tuples containing the attribute value *unk*, then it has an infinite set of possible worlds assuming that attribute domains are countably infinite. Thus the null value *unk* represents the fact that each value in the domain is possible, or equivalently, it can be viewed as the disjunction of all the possible domain values. As we have seen this approach has the advantage of being relatively simple but in many cases when we have some partial information it may be too vague. For example, suppose we have a tuple <Hillary, *unk*> over schema R with schema(R) = {SNAME, COURSE}. The occurrence of *unk* in this tuple implies that we have no knowledge about the course Hillary is taking. Now, suppose that we know that Hillary is either taking a course on Databases or a course on Programming. We could represent this partial information by a finite set {Databases, Programming} resulting in the tuple <Hillary, {Databases, Programming}>. Next assume that this tuple represents all the information we have about Hillary. Then this new tuple represents an increase of information, since we can now answer the query "Is Hillary taking a Logic course?" with a *no* and the query "Is Hillary taking a Programming course?" with a *maybe*. On the other hand, using the null value *unk* we would have to answer the query "Is Hillary taking a Logic course?" with a *maybe*.

Definition 5.42 (Or-sets)   A finite set of values, one of which is the true value, drawn from a given attribute domain, say DOM(A), is called an *or-set* over A (or simply an or-set).   ∎

In other words an or-set over A is a member of the finite power set of DOM(A). The semantics of an or-set $\{v_1, v_2, \ldots, v_m\}$ are as follows:

1) if $m = 0$, then the or-set is the empty set $\emptyset$ representing an inconsistent value,

2) if $m = 1$, then the or-set is a singleton representing a known value, and

3) if $m > 1$, then the or-set is a set of possible values, where it is unknown which value in the or-set is the true value.

Therefore an or-set can be viewed as a refinement of the unmarked nulls approach, since the unmarked null *unk* can be viewed as the or-set DOM(A) (assuming that DOM(A) is finite) and the unmarked null *inc* can be viewed as the or-set $\emptyset$.

Definition 5.43 (Or-relation) An *or-tuple* over schema R is a member of the Cartesian product,

$$\mathcal{P}(\text{DOM}(A_1)) \times \mathcal{P}(\text{DOM}(A_2)) \times \cdots \times \mathcal{P}(\text{DOM}(A_{\text{type}(R)})),$$

recalling the $\mathcal{P}$ is the finite power set operator. An *or-relation* over R is a finite set of or-tuples.

An or-tuple over R is a *complete* tuple if all its attribute values are singleton or-sets, otherwise the or-tuple is said to be *incomplete*. An or-tuple is *consistent* if none of its attribute values is the empty set; if at least one of its attribute values is the empty set then the or-tuple is *inconsistent*.

An or-relation over R is complete if all its or-tuples are complete. In addition, an or-relation is consistent if all its or-tuples are consistent; if at least one of its tuples is inconsistent then it is inconsistent. ∎

As an example, an or-relation over schema R with schema(R) = {SNAME, COURSE} is shown in Table 5.35. This or-relation is inconsistent due to the second or-tuple being inconsistent; also we observe that the first and fourth or-tuples are incomplete and the third or-tuple is complete.

Table 5.35 A students and courses or-relation

SNAME	COURSE
{Iris}	{Databases, Theory, Graphics}
{Reuven}	$\emptyset$
{Eli}	{Logic}
{Hillary}	{Databases, Programming}

Given a schema R we can specify the constraint that certain attribute values must be complete.

Definition 5.44 (Or-set domain constraints) An *Or-set Domain Constraint* (ODC) over schema R is a total mapping ϕ from schema(R) to {COMPLETE, OR}. An ODC ϕ over R is satisfied in an or-relation r over R, denoted by $r \models \phi$, if for all attributes $A \in$ schema(R) and for all or-tuples $t \in r$, the following condition holds: if $\phi(A) =$ COMPLETE then $t[A]$ is complete. ∎

In the following we will assume that together with a relation schema R we have specified an ODC ϕ over R. We will represent the ODC ϕ explicitly in schema(R) by superscripting the attributes $A \in$ schema(R) such that $\phi(A) =$ OR by "or" (when no ambiguity arises we will superscript a set of attributes by "or" rather than superscripting each attribute separately). At times we will refer to such superscripted attributes as *or-attributes* to distinguish them from other attributes, called *complete attributes*. In addition, on occasion we will abbreviate a singleton such as {v} to v. The or-relation shown in Table 5.35 is depicted again in Table 5.36

using our notation for making the ODC explicit. Finally, from now on we will assume that or-relations are consistent unless explicitly stated otherwise.

Table 5.36 The students and courses or-relation with an explicit ODC

SNAME	$COURSE^{or}$
Iris	{Databases, Theory, Graphics}
Reuven	$\emptyset$
Eli	{Logic}
Hillary	{Databases, Programming}

We now redefine the concept of less informative in the context of or-relations. Intuitively, an or-tuple t_1 over a relation schema R is less informative than another or-tuple t_2 over R if for all attributes A in schema(R) the or-set $t_2[A]$ is a subset of the or-set $t_1[A]$. That is, having less values in an or-set represents having more information, the extreme case being an empty or-set representing inconsistency.

Definition 5.45 (Less informative and more informative or-tuples)   Let t_1 and t_2 be or-tuples over schema R. Then t_1 is *less informative* than t_2 (or equivalently, t_2 is *more informative* than t_1), denoted by $t_1 \sqsubseteq t_2$, if and only if $\forall A \in$ schema(R), $t_2[A] \subseteq t_1[A]$.

If $t_1 \sqsubseteq t_2$, then we say that t_1 is *less informative* than t_2 (or equivalently, t_2 is *more informative* than t_1). ∎

The definition of *less informative* for or-relations remains the same as that for incomplete relations. That is, $r_1 \sqsubseteq r_2$ if and only if there exists a total and onto mapping θ from r_1 to r_2 such that $\forall t \in r_1, t \sqsubseteq \theta(t)$, where r_1 and r_2 are or-relations over R. We are now ready to define POSS(r) in the context of or-relations.

Definition 5.46 (The set of possible worlds relative to an or-relation)   The set of all *possible worlds* relative to an or-relation r over schema R, denoted by POSS(r), is defined by

$$POSS(r) = \{s \mid r \sqsubseteq s \text{ and } \forall t \in s, \forall A \in \text{schema(R)}, t[A] \text{ is a singleton}\}. \quad \blacksquare$$

We note that for or-relations the set POSS(r) is always a finite set, while for incomplete relations (with occurrences of *unk*) POSS(r) is, in general, a countably infinite set. We further note that as is the case with incomplete relations if r is inconsistent then POSS(r) = $\emptyset$ and, in addition, Theorem 5.3 and Proposition 5.4 stated after Definition 5.10 of POSS(r) for incomplete relations in Section 5.3 also hold for or-relations.

We will now briefly discuss two approaches to extending the relational algebra in order to manipulate or-relations. The first approach is to view an or-set whose cardinality is greater than one as the unmarked null value *unk* and an empty or-set as the unmarked null value *inc* (strictly speaking we will not make use of *inc* in the extended algebra, since we have assumed that or-relations are consistent). Thereafter, we can use the extended algebra, as defined in Section 5.4, without change. A slightly different, but equivalent, approach is to assign a unique mark to each occurrence of an or-set (i.e. two occurrences of the same or-set will be given two different marks). In this case we can still use the extended algebra, defined in Section 5.4, by considering *uniquely marked or-sets* simply as different occurrences of *unk.* The advantage of this first approach is its simplicity and computational efficiency, since evaluating an extended algebra expression does not incur a significant overhead compared to evaluating the corresponding standard relational algebra expression. On the other hand, the disadvantage of this approach is that we do not make use, in the extended algebra, of the fact that or-sets are more expressive than the unmarked null *unk.*

The second approach makes use of the fact that POSS(r), where r is an or-relation, is a finite set and thus to obtain the result of a query we directly compute the query over all possible worlds. Let Q($R_1, R_2, \ldots, R_n$) be a standard relational algebra query. Then the result of computing Q with the or-relations, r_1 over R_1, r_2 over $R_2, \ldots, r_n$ over R_n, as its actual parameters, is denoted by $Q^{or}(r_1, r_2, \ldots, r_n)$ and is defined by

$$Q^{or}(r_1, r_2, \ldots, r_n) = \bigcap \{Q(s_1, s_2, \ldots, s_n) \mid s_1 \in \text{POSS}(r_1) \text{ and } s_2 \in \text{POSS}(r_2)$$
$$\text{and } \ldots \text{ and } s_n \in \text{POSS}(r_n)\}.$$

We call a query of the form $Q^{or}(R_1, R_2, \ldots, R_n)$ an *or-query*. The advantage of this approach is that, by definition, the resulting extended relational algebra is both faithful and truth-preserving for all possible or-queries Q^{or}. The disadvantage is that computing answers to such queries may be prohibitively expensive. That is, the additional expressiveness comes at a high computational cost!

The ensuing example adapted from [Imi89, IV89] gives a concrete illustration of an intractable or-query. Let G be a schema with schema(G) = {NODE1, NODE2}, whose instance or-relations represent digraphs, recalling the definition of a digraph from Section 2.1 of Chapter 2. That is, an instance, say *gr*, over G has complete tuples of the form $<n_1, n_2>$ representing an arc in a digraph. We assume without loss of generality that there are no arcs of the form $<n, n>$ in *gr*, i.e. *gr* does not have any loops. Also, let C be a schema with schema(C) = {NODE, *COLOUR^{or}*}, whose instances represent the possible colouring of nodes in a digraph. In particular, let *gr* be an or-relation over G and *co* be an or-relation over C defined by

$$co = \{<n, \{blue, red, green\}> \mid <n, m> \in gr \text{ or } <m, n> \in gr\}.$$

That is, for every node n in the digraph *gr* that participates in an arc, *co* has tuple of the form $< n, \{blue, red, green\}>$ representing the fact that node n can be coloured in three ways. Next, let $G3C^{or}(G, C)$ be the or-query

$$\pi_{\emptyset}(G \bowtie \rho_{\text{NODE}\to\text{NODE1}}(C) \bowtie \rho_{\text{NODE}\to\text{NODE2}}(C)).$$

It can be verified that $G3C^{or}(gr, co) \neq \emptyset$, i.e. $G3C^{or}(gr, co) = \{<>\}$, if and only if the digraph represented by *gr* is *not* 3-colourable, i.e. we cannot find a colouring of *gr*, using only three colours, which assigns different colours to nodes which are contained in the same arc. (This is due to the fact that if the result of the query is nonempty then in all possible worlds, POSS({*gr, co*}), *gr* is not 3-colourable.) However, this is exactly the complement of the graph 3-colourability problem, which is known to be NP-complete [GJ79]. Thus we have a strong indication that this query cannot be answered in polynomial time in the size of the or-relations involved in the above or-query, i.e. that its computation cannot be carried out efficiently.

We are now ready to redefine weak satisfaction of an FD in the context of or-relations; in fact, the definition is identical to that of weak satisfaction of an FD in an incomplete relation but we repeat the definition for the sake of completeness.

Definition 5.47 (Weak satisfaction of an FD in an or-relation) An FD X $\rightarrow$ Y is *weakly* satisfied (or simply satisfied whenever no ambiguity arises) in an or-relation r over R, denoted by $r \approx X \rightarrow Y$, if and only if $\exists s \in POSS(r)$ such that $s \models X \rightarrow Y$.   ∎

For example, it can be verified that the or-relation over schema R, shown in Table 5.37, with schema(R) = {SNAME, $DEPT^{or}$, $HEAD^{or}$}, weakly satisfies the FDs SNAME $\rightarrow$ $DEPT^{or}$ and $DEPT^{or} \rightarrow HEAD^{or}$.

Table 5.37 A students, departments and heads or-relation

SNAME	$DEPT^{or}$	$HEAD^{or}$
Iris	{Computing, Maths}	Dan
Iris	{Computing, Economics}	{Dan, Hanna}
Reuven	{Computing, Philosophy}	{Dan, David}
Naomi	{Maths, Economics}	{Annette}
Naomi	{Maths, Computing}	{Annette, Dan}

Having another look at the or-relation, say r, shown in Table 5.37, we note that the knowledge that the FDs SNAME $\rightarrow$ $DEPT^{or}$ and $DEPT^{or} \rightarrow HEAD^{or}$ are weakly satisfied in r allows us to obtain a more informative or-relation as the following argument demonstrates. The FD SNAME $\rightarrow$ $DEPT^{or}$ implies that there does not exist a possible world where each of Iris, Reuven and Naomi is studying in one department. Thus we can deduce that Iris must be studying in the Computing department and Naomi must be studying in the Maths department. Furthermore, on using the FD $DEPT^{or} \rightarrow HEAD^{or}$ we can deduce that Dan is the head of Computing and that Annette is the head of Maths. This deduction process is a generalisation of the chase procedure mentioned in connection with Algorithm 5.2, which was designated WEAK_SAT(r, F). We now define a similar algorithm in connection with or-relations, where r is an or-relation over schema R and F is a set of FDs over R. We first redefine the least upper bound (lub) operator in the context of or-relations, since it is needed in Algorithm 5.4 given below.

Definition 5.48 (Least upper bound operator) The least upper bound, lub, of two or-sets v_1, v_2 over an attribute A is defined by

$$\text{lub}(v_1, v_2) = v_1 \cap v_2.$$

We extend the lub operator to or-tuples t_1, t_2 over R as follows: lub(t_1, t_2) = t, where t is an or-tuple over R and $\forall A \in$ schema(R), $t[A] = \text{lub}(t_1[A], t_2[A])$.   ∎

Next the pseudo-code of an algorithm, designated OR_CHASE(r, F), which given the inputs r and F returns a more informative or-relation, is presented as Algorithm 5.4. It can be shown that $r \sqsubseteq$ OR_CHASE(r, F) and that if the result of OR_CHASE(r, F) is inconsistent then $\forall s \in$ POSS(r), $s \not\models$ F, i.e. no possible world in r satisfies F. We observe that lines 9 to 11 of the algorithm depart from the standard chase procedure in that it enforces an inequality by a backwards test, when the X-values of two tuples cannot be equal if the FD is to be weakly satisfied. (The reader should verify that if we lift the restriction in line 9 of the algorithm that $|X| = 1$, then, in general, more than two tuples will need to be considered in such a backwards test.) It can also be seen that the time complexity of Algorithm 5.4 is polynomial in $|F|$, $\|F\|$ and $|r|$.

Algorithm 5.4 (OR_CHASE(r, F))
1. **begin**
2.   Result := r;
3.   Tmp := $\emptyset$;
4.   **while** Tmp $\neq$ Result **do**
5.   Tmp := Result;
6.   **if** $\exists$ X $\rightarrow$ Y $\in$ F, $\exists t_1, t_2 \in$ Result such that
                $t_1[X]$ and $t_2[X]$ are complete **and** $t_1[X] = t_2[X]$ **but** $t_1[Y] \neq t_2[Y]$ **do**
7. $t_1[Y], t_2[Y] := \text{lub}(t_1[Y], t_2[Y])$;
8.   **end if**
9.   **if** $\exists$ X $\rightarrow$ Y $\in$ F, with $|X| = 1$, $\exists t_1, t_2 \in$ Result such that
                $t_1[XY]$ and $t_2[Y-X]$ are complete **but** $t_1[Y-X] \neq t_2[Y-X]$ **then**
10. $t_2[X] := t_2[X] - t_1[X]$;
11.   **end if**
12.   **end while**
13.   **return** Tmp;
14. **end.**

Example 5.3   Let r be the or-relation shown in Table 5.37 and let F = $\{$SNAME $\rightarrow$ $DEPT^{or}$, $DEPT^{or} \rightarrow HEAD^{or}\}$. The result of OR_CHASE(r, F) is shown in Table 5.38; it can be verified that the result of OR_CHASE(r, F) is consistent and that both $r \approx$ SNAME $\rightarrow DEPT^{or}$ and $r \approx DEPT^{or} \rightarrow HEAD^{or}$ hold.   ∎

Table 5.38 The result of OR˙CHASE(r, F) of Example 5.3

SNAME	$DEPT^{or}$	$HEAD^{or}$
Iris	{Computing}	{Dan}
Iris	{Computing}	{Dan}
Reuven	{Computing, Philosophy}	{Dan, David}
Naomi	{Maths}	{Annette}
Naomi	{Maths}	{Annette}

We now make two interesting comments regarding the weak satisfaction of FDs in or-relations; these highlight the difference between the weak satisfaction of FDs in incomplete relations and or-relations, respectively. Firstly, let us examine the or-relation, say r_1, shown in Table 5.39, which violates the FD SNAME $\rightarrow COURSE^{or}$. It is interesting to note that any proper subset of r_1 weakly satisfies SNAME $\rightarrow COURSE^{or}$ implying that in order to test weak satisfaction of an FD in an or-relation it is *not* sufficient just to test weak satisfaction with respect to pairs of tuples as can be done in incomplete relations (cf. part (2) of Lemma 5.12

which shows that weak satisfaction of an FD in incomplete relations can be tested with respect to pairs of tuples). We observe that in this case the OR_CHASE is powerful enough to detect the violation of the FD. Secondly, let us examine the or-relation, say r_2, shown in Table 5.40, which violates the FD $DEPT^{or} \to$ HEAD. Yet again we note that any proper subset of r_2 weakly satisfies $DEPT^{or} \to$ HEAD. However, on this occasion the reason for the violation of the FD is due to the fact that the cardinality of the or-set {Computing, Maths}, i.e. two, is less than the cardinality of r_2, i.e. three. All possible worlds in POSS(r_2) have three tuples and thus three attribute values over $DEPT^{or}$ are needed in order for the FD to be satisfied. We observe that in this case the OR_CHASE is not powerful enough to detect the violation of the FD, but if we replace the or-set over $DEPT^{or}$ of the first tuple by {Computing} then the OR_CHASE will indeed detect the violation of the FD with the assistance of the backwards test.

Table 5.39 An or-relation violating SNAME $\to COURSE^{or}$

SNAME	$COURSE^{or}$
Iris	{Databases, Graphics}
Iris	{Databases, Logic}
Iris	{Logic, Graphics}

Table 5.40 An or-relation violating $DEPT^{or} \to$ HEAD

$DEPT^{or}$	HEAD
{Computing, Maths}	Dan
{Computing, Maths}	Annette
{Computing, Maths}	Brian

The following consistency problem is central to detecting weak satisfaction in or-relations.

Definition 5.49 (The consistency problem) Given a set F of FDs over R and an or-relation r over R the *consistency problem* is the problem of deciding whether $r \not\approx F$. ∎

In [VN95] the consistency problem was shown to be intractable.

Theorem 5.25 The consistency problem is NP-complete.

Proof. We provide a sketch of the proof leaving some of the details out. The problem is easily seen to be in NP. Simply guess a possible world $s \in$ POSS(r) and test whether $s \models F$ in polynomial time in the sizes of s and F.

To show that the problem is NP-hard we give a polynomial-time transformation from the *Monotone 3-Satisfiability* (M3SAT) problem, which is known to be NP-complete [GJ79], to the problem of determining whether $r \not\approx F$.

M3SAT problem: Given a finite set U of propositional variables and a collection C of clauses over U such that each clause contains exactly three unnegated variables or exactly three negated variables, is there a satisfying truth-assignment for C (i.e. is C satisfiable)?

For the transformation we choose F to contain the single FD $A^{or} \to$ B over R, with schema(R) = $\{A^{or}, B\}$. We represent each clause $c_i \in C$ by an or-set. If c_i is a positive clause then we represent its three unnegated variables by the or-set $\{p_{i1}, p_{i2}, p_{i3}\}$, and if c_i is a negative clause then we represent its three negated variables by the or-set $\{n_{i1}, n_{i2}, n_{i3}\}$.

We now construct an or-relation r over R containing one tuple for each clause in $c_i \in C$ such that if c_i is positive then we insert the tuple $<\{p_{i1}, p_{i2}, p_{i3}\}, 0>$ into r and if c_i is negative then we insert the tuple $<\{n_{i1}, n_{i2}, n_{i3}\}, 1>$ into r. The reader can verify that C is satisfiable if and only if $r \not\approx F$.   □

In [VN95] it was shown that in the following special case the consistency problem can be solved in polynomial time.

Theorem 5.26   Let F be a set of FDs over R and r be a relation over R. If all the attributes on the left-hand sides of FDs in F are complete attributes (i.e. none of them are or-attributes), then the consistency problem can be solved in polynomial time in the sizes of r and F.

Proof. It can be shown that in this case $r \not\approx F$ if and only if OR_CHASE(r, F) is consistent.   □

Weak implication of FDs in the context of or-relations is just a restatement of Definition 5.29 which replaces incomplete relation by or-relation. The next theorem establishes the fact that for FDs holding in or-relations Lien's and Atzeni's axiom system is sound and complete.

Theorem 5.27   Lien's and Atzeni's axiom system is sound and complete for FDs with respect to weak implication in the context of or-relations.

Proof. We leave it to the reader to prove the soundness of the axiom system. The proof of completeness follows along the same lines as the proof of Theorem 5.15, where the relation used herein to show completeness is that shown in Table 5.41.   □

Table 5.41 The or-relation used in the proof of Theorem 5.27

X	$(X^{Lien+} - X)^{or}$	schema(R) $-X^{Lien+}$
$0 \ldots 0$	$\{0, 1\} \ldots \{0, 1\}$	$1 \ldots 1$
$0 \ldots 0$	$0 \ldots 0$	$0 \ldots 0$

In the presence of or-sets the notions of key, superkey and primary key remain as they were defined in Subsection 3.6.1 of Chapter 3, the difference being that our notion of satisfaction of an FD has changed. We next restate entity integrity in the context of or-relations.

Definition 5.50 (Entity integrity)   Let $K \subseteq$ schema(R) be the primary key of the relation schema R. The entity integrity rule asserts that: for all or-relations, r over R, an ODC ϕ is satisfied, where $\forall A \in K, \phi(A) =$ COMPLETE.   ∎

We note that referential integrity in the context of or-relations can be defined in the same way as in Section 5.5 for incomplete relations by using our definition of less informative for or-relations.

5.7   The Fuzzy Sets Approach

In the real world we often encounter situations where we can only vaguely specify attribute values. Some examples of such vagueness or *fuzziness* are: John's salary is "high", Jeremy's salary is "between 15 to 25 thousand pounds", Jack is "middle aged", Jim's age is "around 35" and Jill is "tall". Such fuzzy data cannot be represented by null values such as *unk* and *dne*, since *unk* is a place holder for a non-fuzzy or *crisp* data value and *dne* is a place holder for the non-existence of a crisp data value.

Given a relation r, each tuple $t \in r$ is taken to be true and each tuple $t \notin r$ is taken to be false. *Fuzzy sets* (originally proposed in [Zad65] and further developed in [Gog67]) generalise the notion of membership in a set by associating with each element in a set a value in the closed interval [0, 1] that denotes its *grade* of membership in the set. The grade of membership is also called the *possibility measure* of a value being in the fuzzy set. We note that the introduction of fuzzy sets has led to the development of *fuzzy logic* which can be viewed as a generalisation of many-valued logic [Res69, BB92]. In turn many-valued logic generalises classical two-valued logic by allowing other truth-values, such as *maybe*, in addition to the standard truth-values *true* and *false* (we observe that three-valued logic is a special case of many-valued logic).

An example of a fuzzy relation r over LIKES, with schema(LIKES) = {SNAME, COURSE}, is shown in Table 5.42. Note that r has an extra column with the heading μ_r representing the *membership function* (or characteristic function) of the fuzzy relation r. More formally, μ_r is a mapping from all possible tuples over LIKES to [0, 1] giving the grade of membership of each possible tuple in the relation r. We note that in accordance with crisp sets (i.e. non-fuzzy sets) it is customary to assume that for all tuples t, which are not represented in r, we have $\mu_r(t) = 0.0$, i.e. we can deduce that they are definitely not members of the fuzzy relation r. Thus μ_r tells us how much each student likes the course he/she is taking. We call the tuples in a fuzzy relation *fuzzy tuples*.

Table 5.42   A fuzzy relation over LIKES

SNAME	COURSE	μ_r
Iris	Databases	0.90
Iris	Graphics	0.45
Reuven	Programming	0.80
Hillary	Logic	1.0

Zadeh [Zad79] utilised the notion of fuzzy sets to introduce the notion of a *possibility distribution* with the aim of representing approximate concepts such as high-salary, tall-person and young-person. For example, small-integer can be described as the fuzzy set

$$\text{small-integer} = \{1.0/0, 0.9/1, 0.8/2, \ldots, 0.3/7, 0.2/8, 0.1/9\}.$$

The notation of the form 0.8/2 for members of the above fuzzy set signifies that the grade of membership of the integer 2 is 0.8. More formally, a member g/v in a fuzzy set $\mathcal{F}$ denotes the fact that the grade of membership of v in $\mathcal{F}$ is g, i.e. $\mu_{\mathcal{F}}(v) = g$. As mentioned before it is assumed that any possible value, say i, that is not represented in the fuzzy set $\mathcal{F}$ has membership grade of 0.0, i.e. $\mu_{\mathcal{F}}(i) = 0.0$. In our example, we can deduce that all integers i greater that nine have a membership grade of 0.0.

A *crisp set* (or simply a set) can now be defined as a fuzzy set of the form $\{1.0/1, 1.0/2, \ldots, 1.0/n\}$, where the membership grade of each of its members is 1.0; in this case we simply represent the set as in the standard way, namely $\{1, 2, \ldots, n\}$. If the crisp set represents a range of values, such as 1 to n, we also represent the set as $1-n$.

Now, suppose that the crisp set $\{10, 15, 20, 25, 30, 35, 40\}$ represents the possible salaries of employees, where the numbers in the set denote the salary in tens of thousands of pounds. Then high-salary can be described as the fuzzy set

high-salary $= \{0.2/10, 0.2/15, 0.3/20, 0.6/25, 0.8/30, 1.0/35, 1.0/40\}$.

Note that the fact that 10 and 15 have the same membership grade of 0.2 and 35 and 40 have the same membership grade of 1.0 does not pose any problems.

We now make the connection between fuzzy sets and the notion of possibility distributions [Zad79]. A fuzzy set $\mathcal{F}$ induces a possibility distribution, which equates the possibility that a variable, say x, taking a value v in the universe of discourse of $\mathcal{F}$, with the grade of membership of v, i.e. with $\mu_{\mathcal{F}}(v)$. That is, we can view a fuzzy set as giving us the possibility that x can take v as its value.

We can now extend fuzzy relations to have fuzzy attribute values, which are fuzzy sets, in addition to having fuzzy tuples. Let r be the fuzzy relation over STUDENT, shown in Table 5.43, where schema(STUDENT) $= \{$SNAME, $AGE^{fuz}\}$. The schema of this relation has a *fuzzy attribute* whose values are fuzzy sets over the domain of AGE; note that fuzzy attributes are indicated by superscripting them with "*fuz*". We now make several observations about r:

1) All the tuples in r are crisp, i.e. their membership grade is 1.0.

2) The age value 25 in the first tuple denotes the singleton crisp set $\{25\}$.

3) The fuzzy set $\{27, 29, 31\}$ is crisp and could also be written as $\{1.0/27, 1.0/29, 1.0/31\}$. Furthermore, this set is actually an or-set, since its interpretation is that Reuven's age is definitely one of 27, 29 or 31. Thus, or-sets are special cases of fuzzy sets.

4) The age values around-35, young and middle-aged are all fuzzy sets.

5) The range 24–27 is a shorthand for the fuzzy set (or equivalently, the or-set) $\{24, 25, 26, 27\}$.

Table 5.43 A fuzzy relation over STUDENT

SNAME	AGE^{fuz}
Iris	25
Reuven	$\{27, 29, 31\}$
Hillary	around-35
Eli	young
Saul	24–27
David	middle-aged

We next introduce *proximity relations*. These set-theoretic relations are utilised in the definition of fuzzy selection as well as the fuzzy satisfaction of an FD.

The concept of equality can also be fuzzified, thus generalising three-valued equality for nulls and giving rise to *proximity relations*. A proximity relation over a fuzzy attribute A $\in$ schema(R) is a fuzzy relation in the domain of A; note that A may be a fuzzy or standard attribute. Thus the membership function of a proximity relation over A is a mapping from DOM(A) $\times$ DOM(A) to $[0, 1]$. Whenever the attribute, say A, over which a proximity relation is defined is understood from context we will denote such a relation by the equality sign "=". Furthermore, if $\mu_=(v_1, v_2) = \alpha$, we will say that the *proximity* between v_1 and v_2 is α. Let us consider the subset of a proximity relation over an attribute, say Att, shown in Table 5.44, whose domain is a subset of the natural numbers. For this table we can deduce, for example, that $\mu_=(one, one) = 1.0$, $\mu_=(one, two) = 0.8$ and $\mu_=(one, three) = 0.6$. In general, a proximity relation is *reflexive*, i.e. for all u in the domain of the attribute, over which the proximity relation is defined, $\mu_=(u, u) = 1.0$, and is *symmetric*, i.e. for all u, v in the said domain, $\mu_=(u, v) = \mu_=(v, u)$. On the other hand, a proximity relation is not, in general, *transitive* (thus differing from two-valued equality), since from the fact that $\mu_=(u, v) = x$ and $\mu_=(v, w) = y$ we cannot, in general, deduce the membership grade of $\mu_=(u, w)$. Thus, in our example, it is not clear how one can deduce that $\mu_=(one, three) = 0.6$ from the other membership grades given in Table 5.44.

Table 5.44 A subset of a proximity relation over Att

$\mu_=$	one	two	three
one	1.0	0.8	0.6
two	0.8	1.0	0.8
three	0.6	0.8	1.0

We will now define an extension of the relational algebra to manipulate fuzzy relations, which may have fuzzy tuples and may also have fuzzy attribute values. The definition of a fuzzy relational algebra operator (or simply a fuzzy algebra operator) extends the definition of a standard algebra operator (see Subsection 3.2.1 of Chapter 3) by characterising the membership function of the fuzzy relation resulting from invoking the fuzzy operator. In the following we let $max(S)$ denote the maximum value of a set of numbers in the unit interval $[0, 1]$ and let $min(S)$ denote the minimum value of a set of numbers in the unit interval $[0, 1]$. In addition, let

$$REL(R) = DOM(A_1) \times DOM(A_2) \times \cdots \times DOM(A_{type(R)})$$

be the countable set of all possible tuples over a relation schema R.

Intuitively, the projection of a fuzzy relation maintains the maximum membership grade of duplicate projected fuzzy tuples.

Definition 5.51 (Fuzzy Projection)   The fuzzy projection of a fuzzy relation r over schema R onto Y $\subseteq$ schema(R), denoted by $\pi_Y^{fuz}(r)$, is a fuzzy relation s over schema S with schema(S) = Y, characterised by the fuzzy membership function μ_s given by

$$\forall t \in REL(S), \mu_s(t) = max(\{\mu_r(u) \mid u \in REL(R) \text{ and } u[Y] = t\}). \qquad \blacksquare$$

We observe that although the sets REL(S) and REL(R) are, in general, countably infinite we need only consider tuples $u \in REL(R)$ such that $\mu_r(u) > 0.0$. As an example, let r be the fuzzy relation shown in Table 5.42. The fuzzy projection $\pi^{fuz}_{SNAME}(r)$ is shown in Table 5.45; μ_r can be interpreted as giving the maximum membership grade referring to how much a student likes his/her courses.

Table 5.45 A projection of the fuzzy relation over LIKES

SNAME	μ_r
Iris	0.90
Reuven	0.80
Hillary	1.0

Intuitively, the union of two fuzzy relations maintains the maximum membership grade of the unioned fuzzy tuples.

Definition 5.52 (Fuzzy union)   The fuzzy union of two fuzzy relations r_1 and r_2 over schema R, denoted by $r_1 \cup^{fuz} r_2$, is a fuzzy relation r over R characterised by the fuzzy membership function μ_r given by

$$\forall t \in \text{REL(R)}, \mu_r(t) = max(\{\mu_{r_1}(t), \mu_{r_2}(t)\}). \qquad \blacksquare$$

As an example, let r_1 and r_2 be two fuzzy relations over LIKES, shown in Tables 5.42 and 5.46, respectively. The fuzzy union $r = r_1 \cup^{fuz} r_2$ is shown in Table 5.47.

Table 5.46 Another fuzzy relation over LIKES

SNAME	COURSE	μ_{r_2}
Iris	Databases	0.95
Reuven	Programming	0.40
Hillary	Logic	0.75
Rachel	Databases	0.8

Table 5.47 The fuzzy relation $r_1 \cup^{fuz} r_2$ over LIKES

SNAME	COURSE	μ_s
Iris	Databases	0.95
Iris	Graphics	0.45
Reuven	Programming	0.80
Hillary	Logic	1.0
Rachel	Databases	0.8

Intuitively, the intersection of two fuzzy relations maintains the minimum membership grade of the intersected fuzzy tuples.

Definition 5.53 (Fuzzy intersection)   The fuzzy intersection of two fuzzy relations r_1 and r_2 over schema R, denoted by $r_1 \cap^{fuz} r_2$, is a fuzzy relation r over R characterised by the fuzzy membership function μ_r given by

$$\forall t \in \text{REL(R)}, \mu_r(t) = min(\{\mu_{r_1}(t), \mu_{r_2}(t)\}). \qquad \blacksquare$$

As an example, the fuzzy intersection $r = r_1 \cap^{fuz} r_2$ is shown in Table 5.48, where r_1 and r_2 are the fuzzy relations over LIKES, shown in Tables 5.42 and 5.46, respectively.

Table 5.48 The fuzzy relation $r_1 \cap^{fuz} r_2$ over LIKES

SNAME	COURSE	μ_{r_2}
Iris	Databases	0.90
Reuven	Programming	0.40
Hillary	Logic	0.75

Intuitively, the difference between two fuzzy relations is defined by the intersection of the first fuzzy relation with the complement of the second fuzzy relation, where the complement of a fuzzy relation complements its membership function.

Definition 5.54 (Fuzzy difference)   The fuzzy complement of a fuzzy relation r over schema R, denoted by $\neg^{fuz}(r)$, is a fuzzy relation s over R characterised by the fuzzy membership function μ_s given by

$$\forall t \in \text{REL}(R), \mu_s(t) = 1 - \mu_r(t).$$

The fuzzy difference of two fuzzy relations r_1 and r_2 over schema R, denoted by $r_1 -^{fuz} r_2$, is a fuzzy relation r over R given by

$$r = r_1 \cap^{fuz} (\neg^{fuz}(r_2)). \qquad \blacksquare$$

As an example, the fuzzy difference $r = r_1 -^{fuz} r_2$ is shown in Table 5.49, where r_1 and r_2 are the fuzzy relations over LIKES, shown in Tables 5.42 and 5.46, respectively.

Table 5.49 Another fuzzy relation over LIKES

SNAME	COURSE	μ_{r_2}
Iris	Databases	0.05
Iris	Graphics	0.45
Reuven	Programming	0.60
Hillary	Logic	0.25

Intuitively, the Cartesian product of two fuzzy relations maintains the minimum membership grade of the fuzzy tuples in the product.

Definition 5.55 (Fuzzy Cartesian product)   Let r_1 be a fuzzy relation over R_1 and let r_2 be a fuzzy relation over R_2, where R_1 and R_2 are relation schemas with schema$(R_1) \cap$ schema(R_2) $= \emptyset$. The fuzzy Cartesian product of the two relations r_1 and r_2, denoted by $r_1 \times^{fuz} r_2$, is a fuzzy relation r over R, where schema(R) = schema$(R_1) \cup$ schema(R_2), characterised by the fuzzy membership function μ_r given by

$$\forall t \in \text{REL}(R), \mu_r(t) = min(\{\mu_{r_1}(t[\text{schema}(R_1)]), \mu_{r_2}(t[\text{schema}(R_2)])\}). \qquad \blacksquare$$

Intuitively, the selection of fuzzy tuples from a fuzzy relation with respect to a selection formula, say *SF*, maintains the fuzzy tuples which fuzzily logically imply *SF* with a threshold of $\alpha \in [0, 1]$.

Definition 5.56 (Fuzzy selection)   Recall that a simple selection formula over a relation schema R is either an expression of the form $A = a$ or an expression of the form $A = B$, where $A, B \in$ schema(R), $a \in$ DOM(A) and "=" is a proximity relation.

Let r be a fuzzy relation over R and t be a tuple in r. We define *fuzzy logical implication* with *threshold* $\alpha \in [0, 1]$, denoted by $(\alpha) \models\approx$, as follows:

1) $t(\alpha) \models\approx A = a$ evaluates to true if $\mu_=(t[A], a) \geq \alpha$;

2) $t(\alpha) \models\approx A = B$ evaluates to true if $\mu_=(t[A], t[B]) \geq \alpha$.

The fuzzy selection applied to a fuzzy relation r over schema R with respect to a simple selection formula SF over R and threshold α, denoted by $(\alpha)\sigma_{SF}(r)$, is a fuzzy relation s over R characterised by the fuzzy membership function μ_s given by

$$\forall t \in \text{REL(R)}, \text{ if } t(\alpha) \models\approx SF \text{ then } \mu_s(t) = \mu_r(t), \text{ otherwise } \mu_s(t) = 0.0. \qquad \blacksquare$$

Fuzzy selection can be extended to well-formed expressions composed of simple selection formulae together with the Boolean logical connectives in a straightforward way, where disjunction corresponds to fuzzy union (i.e. we take the max of the two membership functions), conjunction corresponds to fuzzy intersection (i.e. we take the min of the two membership functions) and negation corresponds to fuzzy complement (i.e. we subtract the membership function from one).

As an example, the fuzzy selection $(0.9)\sigma_{SF}(r)$ over STUDENT, with $SF = AGE^{fuz} = $ young, is shown in Table 5.50, where r is the fuzzy relation over STUDENT shown in Table 5.43. In this example we have *assumed* that anyone, who is possibly 25 or under, qualifies with a threshold of 0.9 as being young (in particular, we assume that $\mu_=$(middle-aged, 25) < 0.9 and that $\mu_=$(around-35, 25) < 0.9).

Table 5.50 The fuzzy relation $(0.9)\sigma_{SF}(r)$ over STUDENT, where SF is $AGE^{fuz} = $ young

SNAME	AGE^{fuz}
Iris	25
Eli	young
Saul	24–27

We observe that fuzzy natural join can now be defined in the standard way by using fuzzy Cartesian product, fuzzy renaming and fuzzy selection. (Fuzzy renaming can be defined in the same way as standard renaming by maintaining the same membership function.)

We note that all the operators of the fuzzy relational algebra are faithful to the standard relational algebra operators. On the other hand, truth-preservation is not relevant in the context of the fuzzy algebra, since we have not defined a possible worlds semantics for fuzzy relations. An alternative measure of the reasonableness of the fuzzy algebra is its faithfulness to fuzzy set theory [Zad65] and fuzzy approximation theory [Zad79], which is immediately evident. The notion of threshold was added to fuzzy selection, since it provides a mechanism for the user to put a filter on the output.

We next discuss the extension of FDs to fuzzy relations. Firstly, we extend the membership function of a proximity relation between tuples as follows:

$$\mu_=(t_1[X], t_2[X]) = min(\mu_=(t_1[A_1], t_2[A_1]), \mu_=(t_1[A_2], t_2[A_2]), \ldots, \mu_=(t_1[A_k], t_2[A_k])),$$

where $X = \{A_1, A_2, \ldots, A_k\}$.

In the following we assume that attributes are fuzzy unless otherwise stated.

Definition 5.57 (Fuzzy satisfaction of an FD in a fuzzy relation)   An FD $X \rightarrow Y$ is *fuzzily* satisfied (or simply satisfied whenever no ambiguity arises) in a fuzzy relation r over R, denoted by $r \mathrel{\rlap{\approx}{\,\vert\!\!\sim}} X \rightarrow Y$, if $\forall t_1, t_2 \in r, \mu_=(t_1[X], t_2[X]) \leq \mu_=(t_1[Y], t_2[Y])$. ∎

We note that if r is a complete non-fuzzy relation, where the proximity relation between domain values is just the standard equality relation, then the definition of fuzzy satisfaction of an FD coincides with the standard notion of FD satisfaction. Thus fuzzy satisfaction of an FD is faithful to standard satisfaction of an FD.

As an example, let r be the fuzzy relation over SALARY-SCALE, shown in Table 5.51, with attributes EXP^{fuz} denoting the (fuzzy) experience of an employee and $SALARY^{fuz}$ denoting the (fuzzy) salary of the employee in thousands of pounds. It can intuitively be verified that $r \mathrel{\rlap{\approx}{\,\vert\!\!\sim}} EXP^{fuz} \rightarrow SALARY^{fuz}$, noting that $\mu_=(10, High)$ and $\mu_=(2, Low)$ are close to 1.0 and $\mu_=(10, Low)$ and $\mu_=(2, High)$ are close to 0.0. (Of course our interpretation of the proximity relation is subjective.)

Table 5.51 A fuzzy relation satisfying the fuzzy FD $EXP^{fuz} \rightarrow SALARY^{fuz}$

EXP^{fuz}	$SALARY^{fuz}$
2	Low
10	High
7–15	around-25
High	High
Low	Low
Moderate	15

Fuzzy implication of FDs in the context of fuzzy relations is just a restatement of Definition 5.29 of weak logical implication with the replacement of incomplete relations by fuzzy relations. The next theorem presented in [RM88] shows that Armstrong's axiom system is still sound and complete in the context of fuzzy relations.

Theorem 5.28   Armstrong's axiom system is sound and complete for FDs with respect to fuzzy implication in the context of fuzzy relations, assuming that for all $A \in schema(R)$ there are at least two values $v_1, v_2 \in DOM(A)$ such that $\mu_=(v_1, v_2) = 0$.

Proof. We leave it to the reader to prove the soundness of the axiom system. The proof of completeness follows along the same lines as the proof of Theorem 3.21 in Subsection 3.6.1 of Chapter 3. □

The reader may be surprised to discover that the transitivity inference rule is sound in the context of fuzzy relations while it is unsound in the context of incomplete relations and or-relations. Consider the fuzzy relation, say r over R, with schema(R) = {A, B, C, D^{fuz}}, which is shown in Table 5.52; assume that $\mu_=(0, 0) = 1.0$, $\mu_=(0, \{0, 1\}) = 0.5$ and $\mu_=(0, 1) = 0.0$. In the context of either incomplete relations, or-relations or fuzzy relations we have that r weakly satisfies the FD A → B but violates the FD A → C. Now, the FD A → D^{fuz} is also weakly satisfied in the context of or-relations, and assuming that we replace {0, 1} in the second tuple by unk, A → D^{fuz} is also weakly satisfied in the context of incomplete relations. This is due to the fact that weak satisfaction in the context of incomplete relations and or-relations is defined in terms of possible worlds, which are induced by substitution semantics. Thus, transitivity is not sound for either incomplete relations or or-relations, since r weakly satisfies both A → D^{fuz} and D^{fuz} → C but it violates A → C. On the other hand, A → D^{fuz} is violated in the context of fuzzy relations, since $(\mu_=(0, 0) = 1.0) > (\mu_=(0, \{0, 1\}) = 0.5)$. Thus fuzzy satisfaction of FDs is defined in terms of proximity of values rather than in terms of possible worlds and therefore the transitivity inference rule is still sound. More specifically, if $\mu_=(t_1[X], t_2[X]) \leq \mu_=(t_1[Y], t_2[Y])$ and $\mu_=(t_1[Y], t_2[Y]) \leq \mu_=(t_1[Z], t_2[Z])$, then due to the transitivity of less than or equal ($\leq$), it follows that $\mu_=(t_1[X], t_2[X]) \leq \mu_=(t_1[Z], t_2[Z])$.

Table 5.52 A fuzzy relation

A	B	C	D^{fuz}
0	0	0	0
0	0	1	{0, 1}

We now discuss two alternative, but related, semantics of fuzzy satisfaction of FDs. We begin by defining the fuzzy implication operator. The fuzzy implication between p and q, denoted by $p \Rightarrow q$, where $p, q \in [0, 1]$, is an operator whose result is given by

$$p \Rightarrow q = \begin{cases} 1 & \text{if } p \leq q \\ q & \text{if } p > q. \end{cases}$$

In the first alternative semantics the degree of fuzzy satisfaction is indicated so Definition 5.57 is strengthened [CKV94].

Definition 5.58 (Fuzzy satisfaction of an FD to degree λ)   An FD $X(\lambda)$ → Y is fuzzily satisfied in a fuzzy relation r over R to the degree $\lambda \in (0, 1]$, denoted by $r(\lambda) \approx X$ → Y, if $\forall t_1, t_2 \in r, (\mu_=(t_1[X], t_2[X]) \Rightarrow \mu_=(t_1[Y], t_2[Y])) \geq \lambda$.   ∎

We note that if $\lambda = 1$, i.e. the degree of fuzzy satisfaction is one, then Definition 5.58 reduces to Definition 5.57.

An interesting inference rule which can be shown to be sound with respect to fuzzy satisfaction of a set F of FDs over R, according to Definition 5.58, is given by

$$\text{if } F \vdash X(\lambda) \to Y \text{ then } F \vdash X(\lambda') \to Y, \text{ where } \lambda' \leq \lambda.$$

It was shown in [CKV94] that Armstrong's axiom system, suitably modified to take the degree of fuzzy satisfaction into account, together with the above inference rule, is sound and complete for FDs with respect to fuzzy implication according to Definition 5.58 of fuzzy satisfaction.

As a simple example illustrating Definition 5.58, consider an FD SS# $\rightarrow$ AGE, meaning that a person's social security number uniquely determines their age. In the context of fuzzy relations the FD $SS\#^{fuz}(0.9) \rightarrow AGE^{fuz}$ means that for any two tuples either the degree of proximity (or closeness) between the AGE^{fuz}-values of the tuples is greater than the degree of proximity between the $SS\#^{fuz}$-values of the tuples, or that the degree of proximity between the AGE^{fuz}-values of the tuples is greater than or equal to 0.9. So, for example, let $r = \{t_1, t_2, t_3\}$ be the fuzzy relation shown in Table 5.53, where t_1, t_2 and t_3 are the first, second and third tuples, respectively, in r. Also assume that $\mu_=(1234, 1234) = 1.0$, $\mu_=(\text{nearly-30}, 27\text{–}29) = 0.9$ and $\mu_=(\text{nearly-30}, 26\text{–}32) = 0.8$. Then $\{t_1, t_2\}(0.9) \approx SS\#^{fuz} \rightarrow AGE^{fuz}$ but $\{t_1, t_3\}(0.9) \not\approx SS\#^{fuz} \rightarrow AGE^{fuz}$. This is due to the fact that the AGE^{fuz}-values of the first two tuples are close enough, i.e. at least 0.9, but the AGE^{fuz}-values of the first and third tuples are not close enough, i.e. less than 0.9.

Table 5.53 A fuzzy relation

$SS\#^{fuz}$	AGE^{fuz}
1234	nearly-30
1234	27–29
1234	26–32

In the second alternative semantics two thresholds are taken into account, so that a constraint such as if any two employees have a similar age then these employees have a similar salary can be expressed [CV94b].

Definition 5.59 (Fuzzy satisfaction of an FD in a fuzzy relation with thresholds (α, β)) An FD $X(\alpha, \beta) \rightarrow Y$ is fuzzily satisfied in a fuzzy relation r over R, with thresholds $\alpha, \beta \in (0, 1]$, denoted by $r(\alpha, \beta) \approx X \rightarrow Y$, if $\forall t_1, t_2 \in r$, whenever $\mu_=(t_1[X], t_2[X]) \geq \alpha$ then it is also true that $\mu_=(t_1[Y], t_2[Y]) \geq \beta$. ∎

An interesting inference rule which can be shown to be sound with respect to fuzzy satisfaction of FDs, according to Definition 5.59, is given by

$$\text{if } F \vdash X(\alpha, \beta) \rightarrow Y \text{ then } F \vdash X(\alpha', \beta') \rightarrow Y, \text{ where } \alpha' \geq \alpha \text{ and } \beta' \leq \beta.$$

It was shown in [CV94b] that Armstrong's axiom system, suitably modified to take into account the thresholds, together with the above inference rule, is sound and complete for FDs with respect to fuzzy implication according to Definition 5.59 of fuzzy satisfaction.

The following example illustrates Definition 5.59. Let r be the fuzzy relation shown in Table 5.56 over a schema with fuzzy attributes $GRADE^{fuz}$ and $SALARY^{fuz}$. Also, suppose that the proximity relation over $GRADE^{fuz}$-values is given in Table 5.54 and the proximity relation over $SALARY^{fuz}$-values is given in Table 5.55. Next let $GRADE^{fuz}(\alpha, \beta) \rightarrow SALARY^{fuz}$ be an FD meaning that employees with similar grades receive similar salaries. The reader can verify that, for instance, $r(0.3, 0.4) \approx GRADE^{fuz} \rightarrow SALARY^{fuz}$ holds according to Definition 5.59, $r \not\approx GRADE^{fuz} \rightarrow SALARY^{fuz}$ is violated according to Definition 5.57, and finally $r(0.6) \not\approx GRADE^{fuz} \rightarrow SALARY^{fuz}$ is violated according to Definition 5.58.

A discussion of the different semantics of fuzzy satisfaction of FDs can be found in [BDP94].

Table 5.54 The proximity relation over $GRADE^{fuz}$

$\mu_=$	analyst	programmer	manager
analyst	1.0	0.8	0.6
programmer	0.8	1.0	0.3
manager	0.6	0.3	1.0

Table 5.55 The proximity relation over $SALARY^{fuz}$

$\mu_=$	medium	28	high
medium	1.0	0.7	0.4
28	0.7	1.0	0.5
high	0.4	0.5	1.0

Table 5.56 A fuzzy relation

$GRADE^{fuz}$	$SALARY^{fuz}$
programmer	medium
analyst	28
manager	high

To conclude this section we show how the notion of an inclusion dependency can be recast in the context of fuzzy relations. We first define a *fuzzy database* over $\mathbf{R} = \{R_1, R_2, \ldots, R_n\}$ in the obvious manner, namely as a collection d of fuzzy relations, $\{r_1, r_2, \ldots, r_n\}$, such that $\forall i \in \{1, 2, \ldots, n\}$, r_i is a fuzzy relation over R_i. Intuitively, an IND $R_1[X] \subseteq R_2[Y]$ is fuzzily satisfied in a fuzzy database, say d, with threshold $\alpha \in (0, 1]$, if for every tuple, say t_1, in the fuzzy relation r_1 over R_1 there exists a tuple, say t_2, in the fuzzy relation r_2 over R_2 such that the proximity between t_1 and t_2 is greater than α and the membership grade of t_1 is less than or equal to the membership grade of t_2.

Definition 5.60 (Fuzzy satisfaction of an IND) An IND $R_1[X] \subseteq R_2[Y]$ is fuzzily satisfied in a fuzzy database d over $\mathbf{R}$ with threshold $\alpha \in (0, 1]$, denoted by $d(\alpha) \models R_1[X] \subseteq R_2[Y]$, if $\forall t_1 \in r_1, \exists t_2 \in r_2$, such that $\mu_=(t_1[X], t_2[Y]) \geq \alpha$ and $\mu_{r_1}(t_1) \leq \mu_{r_2}(t_2)$. ∎

We note that if d is a complete non-fuzzy database, where the proximity relation between domain values is just the standard equality relation and $\alpha = 1.0$, then the definition of fuzzy satisfaction of an IND coincides with the standard notion of IND satisfaction. Thus fuzzy satisfaction of an IND is faithful to standard satisfaction of an IND. Finally, referential integrity in the context of fuzzy relations can be defined in the same way as in Section 5.5 for incomplete relations by using our definition of a fuzzy IND.

We close this section by remarking that the topic of fuzzy relations can be extended to deal with fuzzy normal forms corresponding to the normal forms defined for complete relations in Chapter 4. For further details see [SMF92, CKV96].

5.8   The Rough Sets Approach

An approach related to that of fuzzy sets is that of *rough sets* [Paw82], which addresses the imprecision and ambiguity present in a database rather than addressing vagueness as fuzzy sets do.

Definition 5.61 (Rough relation)   Let r be a complete relation over a relation schema R and $\mathcal{R}$ be an equivalence relation in r. The ordered pair $\langle r, \mathcal{R} \rangle$ is called an *approximation space*.

Let $[t]_{\mathcal{R}}$, where $t \in r$ (or simply $[t]$ whenever $\mathcal{R}$ is understood from context), denote the equivalence class of t with respect to $\mathcal{R}$. The equivalence classes of r with respect to $\mathcal{R}$ are called its *elementary sets* and any finite union of elementary sets is called a *definable set* (or a *composed set*).

The *lower approximation* of a set of tuples $s \subseteq r$ with respect to $\langle r, \mathcal{R} \rangle$, denoted by $\underline{\mathcal{R}}(s)$, is given by

$$\underline{\mathcal{R}}(s) = \{t \mid t \in r \text{ and } [t] \subseteq s\}.$$

The *upper approximation* of a set of tuples $s \subseteq r$ with respect to $\langle r, \mathcal{R} \rangle$, denoted by $\overline{\mathcal{R}}(s)$, is given by

$$\overline{\mathcal{R}}(s) = \{t \mid t \in r \text{ and } [t] \cap s \neq \emptyset\}.$$

The *boundary* of a set of tuples $s \subseteq r$ with respect to $\langle r, \mathcal{R} \rangle$, denoted by $\text{BND}_{\mathcal{R}}(s)$, is the set of tuples in $\overline{\mathcal{R}}(s) - \underline{\mathcal{R}}(s)$.

A set of tuples $s \subseteq r$ is said to be a *rough relation* with respect to the approximation space $\langle r, \mathcal{R} \rangle$ if its lower approximation is different from its upper approximation (i.e. if its lower approximation is properly contained in its upper approximation).

A set of tuples s is said to be a *definable relation* (or a *crisp* relation) with respect to the approximation space $\langle r, \mathcal{R} \rangle$ if its lower approximation is equal to its upper approximation. ∎

As an example, let r be the complete relation shown in Table 5.57 having the attributes PATIENT_NO, DISEASE_NO and SYMPTOM_NOS, with their obvious meaning. Let $\mathcal{R}$ denote the equivalence relation of patients having the same disease, i.e. two tuples are in the same equivalence class if and only if their DISEASE_NO-value is the same. Now, let s consist of the first three tuples, i.e. the patients who have symptom s_2. Then $\underline{\mathcal{R}}(s)$ consists of the first two tuples, while $\overline{\mathcal{R}}(s) = r$. Thus s is a rough relation with respect to the approximation space $\langle r, \mathcal{R} \rangle$, since the set of patients having symptom s_2 cannot be precisely characterised according to the equivalence classes of diseases. If on the other hand, we take s to be the first two tuples, i.e. the tuples representing patients who have symptom s_1, then s is a definable relation with respect to the approximation space $\langle r, \mathcal{R} \rangle$, since in this case s precisely characterises the patients having disease d_1. From this example we see that rough sets are very useful in classifying objects (or tuples) into *indiscernibility classes*.

Table 5.57   A relation recording diseases and their symptoms

PATIENT_NO	DISEASE_NO	SYMPTOM_NOS
p_1	d_1	$\{s_1, s_2\}$
p_2	d_1	$\{s_1, s_2\}$
p_3	d_2	$\{s_3, s_2\}$
p_4	d_2	$\{s_3, s_4\}$

An interesting method of modelling rough relations via the fuzzy membership function of a fuzzy relation was presented in [BP94]; this extends their work on rough relations presented in [BPB95].

Definition 5.62 (Fuzzy rough relation)   A relation r over R is a *fuzzy rough relation* with respect to the approximation space $\langle r, \mathcal{R} \rangle$ and a subset of its tuples $s \subseteq r$, if it is a fuzzy relation whose membership function μ_r is given by

1) $\mu_r(t) = 1$, if $t \in \underline{\mathcal{R}}(s)$,

2) $\mu_r(t) = 0$, if $t \in r - \overline{\mathcal{R}}(s)$, and

3) $0 < \mu_r(t) < 1$, if $t \in \text{BND}_{\mathcal{R}}(s)$.   ∎

The tuples in the lower approximation of s are considered to be certain tuples, the tuples in the boundary of s (i.e. in $\overline{\mathcal{R}}(s) - \underline{\mathcal{R}}(s)$) are considered to be possible tuples whose fuzzy membership value is between zero and one and the set of tuples not in the upper approximation of s are tuples which are not even possible. Under the above interpretation of rough relations, we can use the fuzzy relational algebra of the previous section in order to manipulate fuzzy rough relations.

We next define the rough satisfaction of an FD in a complete relation [Zia91]. Intuitively, given a relation r over R and an FD $X \to Y$ over R, the degree of rough satisfaction measures the degree of functionality of the FD. In the context of rough satisfaction of an FD, the attributes X are called the *condition* attributes and the attributes Y are called the *decision* attributes.

Definition 5.63 (Rough satisfaction of an FD to degree λ)   The X-partition of a complete relation r over R, where $X \subseteq \text{schema}(R)$, is a partition of r, denoted by $[r, X]$, such that $t_1, t_2 \in r$ are in the same element in $[r, X]$ if and only if $t_1[X] = t_2[X]$. In addition, we let $\underline{\mathcal{R}}[X](s)$ be the lower approximation of a set of tuples $s \subseteq r$ with respect to the equivalence relation induced by $[r, X]$ on r.

The *positive region* of the Y-partition of r with respect to the X-partition of r, denoted by $\text{POS}_r(X, Y)$ (or simply $\text{POS}(X, Y)$ whenever r is understood form context), is given by

$$
\begin{aligned}
\text{POS}(X, Y) &= \bigcup_{y \in [r, Y]} \underline{\mathcal{R}}[X](y) \\
&= \bigcup_{y \in [r, Y]} \{x \mid x \in [r, X] \text{ and } x \subseteq y\}.
\end{aligned}
$$

The degree to which a set of attributes Y depends on a set of attributes X in a complete relation r, denoted by $\kappa(r, X \to Y)$, is given by

$$
\kappa(r, X \to Y) = \frac{|\text{POS}(X, Y)|}{|r|}.
$$

An FD $X(\lambda) \to Y$ is *roughly satisfied* in a complete relation r over R to degree $\lambda \in (0, 1]$, denoted by $r(\lambda) \mathrel{\vbox{\hbox{$\approx$}}} X \to Y$, if $\kappa(r, X \to Y) \geq \lambda$.   ∎

Thus $\kappa(r, X \to Y) = 1$ if and only if $X(1) \to Y$ is roughly satisfied in r to degree 1, i.e. X functionally determines Y. We note that $X(1) \to Y$ is roughly satisfied in r if and only if $X \to Y$ is satisfied in r, i.e. $r \models X \to Y$.

As an example, let r be the complete (nested) relation shown in Table 5.57 and denote the four tuples thereof in order of appearance by t_1, t_2, t_3 and t_4. The reader can verify that $r(1) \approx$ SYMPTOM_NOS $\rightarrow$ DISEASE_NO holds. Now, the DISEASE_NO-partition of r is $[r, \text{DISEASE\_NO}] = \{\{t_1, t_2\}, \{t_3, t_4\}\}$ and the SYMPTOM_NOS-partition of r is $[r, \text{SYMPTOM\_NOS}] = \{\{t_1, t_2\}, \{t_3\}, \{t_4\}\}$. Thus, POS(DISEASE_NO, SYMPTOM_NOS) = $\{t_1, t_2\}$ and $\kappa(r, \text{DISEASE\_NO} \rightarrow \text{SYMPTOM\_NOS}) = 0.5$. It follows that the highest degree of rough satisfaction of the FD DISEASE_NO $\rightarrow$ SYMPTOM_NOS is 0.5, i.e. $r(0.5) \approx$ DISEASE_NO $\rightarrow$ SYMPTOM_NOS is the maximal degree for which rough satisfaction holds.

5.9 The Default Values Approach

An approach to missing information that has been put forward by Date in [Dat92a] is that of using *default values* instead of null values as place holders for missing information. As an example, suppose that John's salary is unknown, then instead of representing John's salary by *unk* we represent his salary by a default value, say "minus one". Obviously, "minus one" cannot be a real salary and thus we can interpret "minus one" as an unknown salary. Another common example is that of filling a form. Suppose that we have an application form and we are required to answer whether we are married or not. A default value of "N/A" or a "dash" is normally acceptable as an indication that the question is not applicable in our case. This approach of using default values instead of null values seems to correspond more closely to the way incomplete information is treated in the real world. (In the rest of this section we will only consider default values representing information which is missing but unknown.) The claimed advantages of the default values approach as opposed to the null values approach are: it is simpler to formalise, easier to understand and has a closer correspondence to the real world. Furthermore, we do not not need to depart from the classical two-valued logic to the more complex three-valued logic.

As an example consider the relation over STUDENT, shown in Table 5.58. The value "???", which is a member of the domains DOM(COURSE) and DOM(DEPT), has been distinguished as a default value representing the fact that a course, or department, is unknown. In addition, the value "−1", which is a member of the domain DOM(GRANT), has been distinguished as a default value indicating that the value of a grant is unknown. Thus the default values approach, instead of extending the underlying domain of an attribute, distinguishes a value in the domain as a default value. Note that the tuple <???, ???, Computing, 3750> is meaningful and represents the fact that students who are not recorded in the relation are assumed to be members of the Computing department and to receive a grant of 3750 pounds.

Table 5.58 A student relation with default values

SNAME	COURSE	DEPT	GRANT
Iris	Databases	Computing	−1
Reuven	Theory	???	3500
Hillary	???	Philosophy	4000
Rachel	???	???	−1
Eli	Databases	Computing	4200
???	???	Computing	3750

It follows that, due to the fact that null values are not allowed in the default values approach, the entity integrity rule can simply be dropped. For example, in the above relation if SNAME is the primary key of STUDENT then the default value "???" is a primary key value as are the values "Iris", "Reuven", "Hillary", "Rachel" and "Eli". Thus there can only be one tuple in any relation over STUDENT whose SNAME value is "???". Moreover, since null values are not allowed the referential integrity rule can be simplified by omitting any mention of nulls. Hence, a foreign key value cannot be a null value and must refer to an existing primary key value in the target relation for which it is a foreign key. Furthermore, the relational algebra and integrity constraints remain the same as they were defined in Chapter 3 over relations without null values. It is worth mentioning that when defining domain constraints one has to explicitly take default values into account. For example, if we specify the domain constraint that the value of a grant must range between 3000–5000 pounds, then we would take that to mean that either the value of a grant is -1 (if its true value is unknown) or its value ranges between 3000–5000 (if its value is known).

Although the default values approach as informally explained above is indeed simpler than the null values approach, it has several drawbacks pointed out by Codd in [Cod90], which we now discuss. The main problem with the default values approach is that it is semantically weaker than the null values approach, since it does not take into account the information content of a relation. Let r be the relation over STUDENT shown in Table 5.58 and consider the tuple <Rachel, ???, ???, -1>. The intention is that this tuple has the same meaning as the tuple <Rachel, *unk, unk, unk*>, which uses the null value *unk*. Now, let $Q_1(r)$ be the query $\sigma_{F_1}(r)$, where F_1 = COURSE = 'Databases', and let $Q_2(r)$ be the query $\sigma_{F_2}(r)$, where F_2 = COURSE $\neq$ 'Databases'. A user posing these queries will notice that <Rachel, ???, ???, -1> is not in $Q_1(r)$ but <Rachel, ???, ???, -1> is in $Q_2(r)$. How is the user to interpret these answers when using default values? A sensible interpretation of these answers is that Rachel is definitely not doing the Databases course. This interpretation would be correct if we did not have any missing information but due to the fact that we do not know if Rachel is doing the Databases course this interpretation is incorrect. Now, suppose that we were using null values and extended selection, then in such a case <Rachel, *unk, unk, unk*> is not either in $Q_1(r)$ or in $Q_2(r)$. The interpretation of these answers is that Rachel may or may not be doing the Databases course, i.e. we do not know whether or not she is doing that course. This interpretation is intuitively correct, since a tuple is in the result of an extended query only if the tuple is definitely true. Thus the null values approach is semantically richer than the default values approach precisely for the reason that it formalises the information content of a relation in terms of the partial order, less informative than, leading to the definition of the set of possible worlds relative to a relation. Furthermore, the use of three-valued logic in the null values approach allows us to differentiate between facts which are true, facts which are false and facts which are possible. For example, we can distinguish between the fact that Rachel is not doing the Databases course and the fact that Rachel may or may not be doing that course. Another important point to make is that, unlike the default values approach, the null values approach extends naturally to the semantically richer or-sets and fuzzy sets approaches.

The absence of powerful enough semantics to handle incomplete information can have dire consequences if the handling of incomplete information is relegated to the application programs, since this may lead to an inconsistent and unsystematic treatment of incomplete information. Our conclusion is that the default values approach does not deal comprehensively with the problem of missing and incomplete information; it rather sidesteps the main issues in favour of a simple and realistic solution. As the example above has shown this absence of semantics may lead users to misinterpret the meaning of default values in relations.

The default values approach to incomplete information is not to be confused with default logic [Rei80, Bes89], whose aim is to formalise the common sense reasoning: "in the absence of any information to the contrary assume that ...". For example, if we are given the fact that Tweety is a bird then we can deduce by default reasoning that Tweety can fly unless we have some evidence to the contrary such as the fact that Tweety is actually a penguin. Default reasoning deals nicely with incomplete information, since it relies on the absence of information in order to make deductions. We note that the CWA, discussed in Section 5.2, is a special case of default reasoning where we deduce that a fact does not hold if it is not stored in the database. Default logic relies upon the fact that the real world is far too complex to be represented fully and thus at any given moment in time we can only represent an incomplete fragment of the real world. We rely on the fact that many aspects of the real world, which are not represented, can be inferred by common sense reasoning. With respect to the CWA we rely upon the assumption that if data is not represented then it must be false. It is important to note that default reasoning is tentative in the sense that when our information about the real world increases then conclusions made by default reasoning may be withdrawn. For example, if we add to the relation, shown in Table 5.3, the fact that Hillary is doing a database course in the Computing department, then under the CWA we withdraw our previous conclusion that Hillary is not doing a database course.

Default logic can assist us in dealing with incomplete information in relational databases as the following example shows. Suppose that we have the knowledge that students normally receive grants and that the sum they normally receive is 3750 pounds. Thus, with respect to the relation, say r, shown in Table 5.58, we can use default logic to deduce that Iris and Rachel each receive a grant of 3750 pounds, since we do not have any evidence to the contrary. On the other hand, we cannot use this default rule for the other students recorded in r, since their grant values are already known. As another example suppose that it is normally the case that students are not married; thus in the absence of any other information for a particular student, say Rachel, we can record in the database that Rachel is unmarried. In general, default reasoning allows us to deduce values for attributes that would otherwise be missing or incomplete. This is not always possible or desirable, since the default values are treated by the database system in the same manner as other domain values and thus may lead to a loss of semantics as in Date's default values approach. Thus default logic does not replace the null values approach but rather complements it by allowing us to fill in some gaps in our information whenever this is possible.

5.10   Updating Incomplete Relations

In this section we deal with the problem of updating a relational database in the presence of incomplete information. We will assume the null values approach to incomplete information throughout this section with *unk* being the only available type of null value. Although this approach is less expressive than the or-sets or fuzzy sets approach, it will be sufficient to highlight the main ideas concerning updating incomplete relations. In the formalism we present for updating incomplete relations, we simplify matters by not taking into account any integrity constraints.

We motivate our presentation of updating incomplete relations with several examples, where r is the incomplete relation over STUDENT, shown in Table 5.8. Let our first update be that of inserting the set of tuples $s = \{<$David, Logic, Philosophy$>$, $<$Iris, *unk*, *unk*$>$, $<$Eli, *unk*, Economics$>\}$ into r obtaining the incomplete relation shown in Table 5.59. Thus the updated relation is given by the extended query $r \cup^e s$. It follows that an insert operation is realised via the extended union operator and is, therefore, by Theorem 5.5 both faithful and truth-preserving.

Table 5.59 The incomplete relation of Table 5.8 after some insertions

SNAME	COURSE	DEPT
Iris	Databases	Computing
Reuven	Theory	*unk*
Hillary	*unk*	Philosophy
Rachel	*unk*	*unk*
Eli	Databases	Computing
David	Logic	Philosophy
Iris	*unk*	*unk*
Eli	*unk*	Economics

Now, let our second update be that of deleting the set of tuples $s = \{<$Iris, *unk*, Computing$>$, $<$Reuven, Theory, *unk*$>$, $<$Eli, Databases, *unk*$>\}$ from r obtaining the incomplete relation shown in Table 5.60. Thus the updated relation is given by the extended query $r -^e s$. It follows that a delete operation is realised via the extended difference operator and is, therefore, by Theorem 5.6 both faithful and truth-preserving.

Table 5.60 The incomplete relation of Table 5.8 after some deletions

SNAME	COURSE	DEPT
Hillary	*unk*	Philosophy
Rachel	*unk*	*unk*

Now, let our third update be that of modifying the set of tuples $s_1 = \{<$Reuven, Theory, *unk*$>$, $<$Hillary, *unk*, Philosophy$>$, $<$Rachel, *unk*, *unk*$>\}$, with $s_1 \subseteq r$, to be the set of tuples $s_2 = \{<$Reuven, Quantum, Physics$>$, $<$Hillary, Quantum, Physics$>$, $<$Rachel, Quantum, Physics$>\}$, obtaining the incomplete relation shown in Table 5.61. Thus the updated relation is given by the extended algebra expression $(r -^e s_1) \cup^e s_2$. It follows that a modification operation is realised via the extended difference and extended union operators and it can therefore be shown that it is both faithful and truth-preserving on using Theorems 5.5 and 5.6.

In what follows we formalise our redefinition of update operations, which were originally given in Subsection 3.2.4 of Chapter 3, in the context of incomplete relations. As was done in Subsection 3.2.4 of Chapter 3, for simplicity we allow only conjunctions in conditions rather than general Boolean expressions and, in addition, we only formalise updates on single incomplete relations rather than on incomplete databases, which may contain several incomplete relations.

Table 5.61 The incomplete relation of Table 5.8 after some modifications

SNAME	COURSE	DEPT
Iris	Databases	Computing
Reuven	Quantum	Physics
Hillary	Quantum	Physics
Rachel	Quantum	Physics
Eli	Databases	Computing

The following definition differs from the corresponding one given in Subsection 3.2.4 of Chapter 3 only in the replacement of "=" by "≅". Let us briefly motivate this replacement by a simple example. Suppose the user would like to modify the incomplete tuple <*unk, unk, Philosophy*> over STUDENT to be the complete tuple <Hillary, Logic, Philosophy>. In this case, due to the three-valued equality for nulls the user cannot uniquely select the desired incomplete tuple for modification using true logical implication (assuming the relation in question has more than one student recorded as studying in the Philosophy department). Thus we could either allow *maybe logical implication*, which would select incomplete tuples, whose truth-value evaluates to maybe, or we could opt for the simpler solution which is to use information-wise equivalence instead of equality in the condition which realises the selection. We claim that using information-wise equivalence is better in this case, since the user being aware of the relation's incompleteness is specifically interested in the incomplete tuple <*unk, unk*, Philosophy> rather than tuples such as <Hillary, Many-valued-logic, Philosophy>, which are maybe equal to <*unk, unk*, Philosophy> in three-valued logic.

Definition 5.64 (Extended condition) A *simple extended condition* over R is either an expression of form $A \cong a$ or an expression of the form $\neg(A \cong a)$, where $A \in$ schema(R) and $a \in$ EDOM(A). An *extended condition* is a conjunction $c_1 \wedge c_2 \wedge \cdots \wedge c_n$ of simple extended conditions c_i, $i \in \{1, 2, \ldots, n\}$. A *positive extended condition* over R is an extended condition of the form $A_1 \cong a_1 \wedge A_2 \cong a_2 \wedge \cdots \wedge A_m \cong a_m$, where $\{A_1, A_2, \ldots, A_m\} \subseteq$ schema(R). A *complete extended condition* over R is a positive extended condition over R, with $\{A_1, A_2, \ldots, A_m\}$ = schema(R).

Let r be an incomplete relation over R, let t be an incomplete tuple in r and in addition let $C = c_1 \wedge c_2 \wedge \ldots \wedge c_n$ be an extended condition over R. Then t *satisfies* C, written $t \models C$, is defined recursively, as follows:

1) $t \models A \cong a$, if t[A] $\cong a$ is true.

2) $t \models \neg(A \cong a)$, if $\neg(t[A] \cong a)$ is true.

3) $t \models C$, if $\forall i \in \{1, 2, \ldots, n\}, t \models c_i$. ∎

The following definition differs from the corresponding one given in Subsection 3.2.4 of Chapter 3 only by the replacement of the standard relational algebra operators with their extended counterparts.

Definition 5.65 (Extended update) Let r be an incomplete relation over a relation schema R, with schema(R) = $\{A_1, A_2, \ldots, A_n\}$. An extended update over R is either an *extended insertion* over R, or an *extended deletion* over R or an *extended modification* over R. (In the following we omit to qualify conditions and updates as being "extended" whenever no ambiguity arises.)

An insertion over R is an expression of the form $\text{insert}^e(C)$, where C is a complete condition over R. The *effect* of an insertion $\text{insert}^e(C)$ over R on r is defined by

$$[\text{insert}^e(C)](r) = r \cup^e \{t \mid t \models C\}.$$

A deletion over R is an expression of the form $\text{delete}^e(C)$, where C is a condition over R. The *effect* of a deletion $\text{delete}^e(C)$ over R on r is defined by

$$[\text{delete}^e(C)](r) = r -^e \{t \mid t \in r \text{ and } t \models C\}.$$

Let $X = \{A_1, A_2, \ldots, A_m\}$ and $C = A_1 \cong a_1 \wedge A_2 \cong a_2 \wedge \ldots \wedge A_m \cong a_m$ be a positive condition over R. Then the modification of an incomplete tuple t over R with respect to C, denoted by $[\text{modify}^e(C)](t)$, is defined by

$$[\text{modify}^e(C)](t) = u, \text{ where } u \text{ is an incomplete tuple over R such that } \forall A_i \in X, u[A_i] \cong a_i$$
$$\text{and } \forall A_i \in \text{schema}(R) - X, u[A_i] \cong t[A_i].$$

A modification over R is an expression of the form $\text{modify}^e(C_1; C_2)$, where C_1 is a condition over R and C_2 is a positive condition over R. The *effect* of a modification $\text{modify}^e(C_1; C_2)$ over R on r is defined by

$$[\text{modify}^e(C_1; C_2)](r) = (r -^e \{t \mid t \in r \text{ and } t \models C_1\}) \cup^e \{[\text{modify}^e(C_2)](t) \mid t \in r \text{ and } t \models C_1\}.$$

∎

We note that the notion of a transaction defined in Subsection 3.2.4 of Chapter 3 can be extended in a straightforward way to be a finite sequence of extended updates. For brevity we do not discuss transactions in the context of incomplete information. We now reformulate the example updates given above in terms of the operators we have just defined, where r is the incomplete relation over STUDENT, shown in Table 5.8.

With respect to insertion, let $C_1 = \text{SNAME} \cong \text{David} \wedge \text{COURSE} \cong \text{Logic} \wedge \text{DEPT} \cong \text{Philosophy}$, let $C_2 = \text{SNAME} \cong \text{Iris} \wedge \text{COURSE} \cong unk \wedge \text{DEPT} \cong unk$, and let $C_3 = \text{SNAME} \cong \text{Eli} \wedge \text{COURSE} \cong unk \wedge \text{DEPT} \cong \text{Economics}$, be three complete conditions over STUDENT. The reader can verify that the effect of the extended transaction, $[\text{insert}^e(C_1), \text{insert}^e(C_2), \text{insert}^e(C_3)]$, on r is the incomplete relation shown in Table 5.59.

With respect to deletion, let $C_1 = \text{COURSE} \cong \text{Databases} \wedge \text{DEPT} \cong \text{Computing}$, and let $C_2 = \text{SNAME} \cong \text{Reuven}$. The reader can verify that the effect of the extended transaction, $[\text{delete}^e(C_1), \text{delete}^e(C_2)]$, on r is the incomplete relation shown in Table 5.60.

With respect to modification, let $C_1 = \neg(\text{DEPT} \cong \text{Computing})$, and let $C_2 = \text{COURSE} \cong \text{Quantum} \wedge \text{DEPT} \cong \text{Physics}$. The reader can verify that the effect of the extended transaction, $[\text{modify}^e(C_1; C_2)]$, on r is the incomplete relation shown in Table 5.61.

We leave the formal proof of the following theorem to the reader.

Theorem 5.29   The extended update operators are all faithful and truth-preserving.   □

We complete this section by briefly making a comment on the expressiveness of our update operators. The main problem with incomplete relations is their inability to describe disjunctive information. Or-sets improve upon this situation, since they allow us to express disjunctions of the form <Hillary, {Science, Logic}, Philosophy> meaning that Hillary is taking either Science or Logic in the Philosophy department. Thus by allowing or-sets we could introduce into conditions disjunctions of the form,

$$(COURSE = Science \lor COURSE = Logic),$$

and maintain meaningful update operations for these conditions. Nonetheless, even when taking the or-sets approach we do not get the full expressive power of disjunctions as the following example shows. Suppose that we have a disjunction of the form, <Hillary, Logic, Philosophy> ∨ <Hillary, Set-theory, Maths>, meaning that either Hillary is taking Logic in the Philosophy department or she is taking Set-theory in the Maths department. As the reader can verify such *disjunctive tuples* cannot be represented by or-sets. Therefore, allowing disjunctive tuples in relations would be a natural extension of the or-sets approach. For example, the above disjunctive tuple could be represented as the set, {<Hillary, Logic, Philosophy>, <Hillary, Set-theory, Maths>}.

Therefore, if we extend the or-sets approach to allow disjunctive tuples we could introduce into conditions disjunctions of the form,

$$((COURSE = Logic \land DEPT = Philosophy) \lor$$
$$(COURSE = Set\text{-}theory \land DEPT = Maths)),$$

thereby allowing conditions to be general Boolean expressions and still maintaining meaningful update operations for these conditions.

5.11   Discussion

Incomplete information is one of the most important extensions to the basic relational model due to the growing demand for the correct handling of such information in real-world applications. Most current database systems do not deal with incomplete information in a consistent manner with regard to query processing, integrity constraint maintenance, update transactions and other DBMS facilities. In this chapter we have outlined a consistent theory dealing with either incomplete relations, or or-relations or fuzzy relations. If we include a null value such as *unk* in the database domains then we can model incomplete relations; on the other hand, if we allow values of tuples to be or-sets, i.e. finite disjunctions of domain values, then we can model or-relations. Finally, if we allow attributes and/or tuples to be fuzzy then we can model fuzzy relations. The first of these — incomplete relations — is the easiest route for a database system to manage incompleteness. Although or-relations are more expressive than incomplete relations this comes at a price, since we are faced with the intractability of both query processing and solving the consistency checking problem. Thus if we require general efficiency, only a judicious choice of subclasses of or-relations having polynomial-time querying and consistency checking can be catered for by the database system [IVV95, VN95]. The other option is for the database system to cater for fuzzy relations. In this case we gain expressiveness over incomplete relations, and efficiency of query processing and consistency maintenance because the fuzzy relations approach does not rely upon the possible worlds semantics; but there is the added complexity in the representation and manipulation of fuzzy sets to take into account. The trade-off between higher expressiveness and greater efficiency is a problem that all database system implementers face!

A further extension of the three-valued logic approach to modelling incomplete relations is to use a four-valued logic by adding both the null values *unk* and *dne* to the database domains [Cod90]. The null value *unk* represents missing but applicable information, and correspondingly the null value *dne* represents missing but inapplicable information. The obvious advantage is that we enhance the expressiveness of our modelling of incomplete information but it may be even more onerous on users to understand the four-valued truth tables than to understand the three-valued ones. (See [LL86] for a comprehensive argument in favour of supporting the *dne* null value.)

In this context Belnap's work [Bel77a, Bel77b] is interesting; therein a four-valued logic is proposed with the truth-values: true, false, none (neither true nor false) and both (both true and false). Belnap considers the tuples (or facts) stored in a database as information that the computer has been *told*, and thus when a fact is inserted into the database its logical interpretation is that the computer has been told that this fact is true. The computer can also be told that a fact is false, none or both. Belnap considers truth tables for his four-valued logic, which in fact differ from Codd's truth tables. The truth tables for a four-valued logic depend on their semantics and there is no universal agreement for their specification [Res69, BB92]. Belnap also considers *entailment* between logical sentences, where a logical sentence S_1 entails a logical sentence S_2 if the truth-value of S_1 with respect to the database is less than or equal to the truth-value of S_2 with respect to the same database (cf. Definitions 5.57 and 5.58).

If we relax our assumption that only consistent relations are stored in the database, then a four-valued logic can be useful in dealing with inconsistent relations. Logics which deal with inconsistent information are called *paraconsistent*; Belnap's four-valued logic, mentioned above, is an example of a paraconsistent logic where the truth-value "both" represents inconsistent information. A paraconsistent model for relational databases is presented in [BS95]. In a paraconsistent relation r over R there are two kinds of tuples: those believed to be true, denoted by r^+, and those believed to be false, denoted by r^-, such that $r = r^+ \cup r^-$. If $r^+ \cap r^- = \emptyset$ then r is said to be *consistent* otherwise it is *inconsistent*. If r contains the set of all possible tuples over R (i.e. the Cartesian product of all the attribute domains, assuming attribute domains are finite) then r is said to be *complete* otherwise r is *incomplete*. If r is both consistent and complete then it is said to be *total*. Note that under the CWA we can interpret relations as being total. A relational algebra for paraconsistent relations is defined in [BS95].

Other data dependencies apart from FDs and INDs have been considered in the context of incomplete relations. In particular multivalued dependencies are considered in [Lie79, Lie82] and join dependencies were considered in [LL92]. The more general classes of tuple generating and equality generating data dependencies are considered in [Gra91].

We conclude with a brief discussion of probabilistic relational databases. A probabilistic relation can be defined in the same way as an or-relation (see Section 5.6) with the additional requirement that each value in a nonempty or-set be attached a *weight*; we call such an or-set a *probabilistic or-set*. Thus each value in an or-set is a pair v/w, where v is a domain element and w is a natural number. Given a probabilistic or-set $s = \{v_1/w_1, v_2/w_2, \ldots, v_k/w_k\}$, with

$k \geq 1$, the probability of v_j, $1 \leq j \leq k$, denoted by $P[v_j \mid s]$, is given by

$$P[v_j \mid s] = \frac{w_j}{\sum_{i=1}^{k} w_i},$$

i.e. the proportion of w_j with respect to the sum of the w_i's. Under this interpretation we can view an or-set as a set of equally probable values from a uniform distribution, i.e. such that their weights are equal. The interpretation of an empty or-set is that for any value, v, $P[v \mid \emptyset] = 1$, i.e. with probability one v is inconsistent given the empty or-set.

Thus a *probabilistic relation* is a finite set of tuples whose attribute values are probabilistic or-sets. As an example consider the probabilistic relation, say r, over R, with schema(R) = {SHARE, PRICE}, recording prices of shares obtained from different sources, which is shown in Table 5.62; in r we abbreviate a probabilistic or-set of the form $\{v/1\}$ simply by v, since in this case the probability that the true value is v is one. In this example, the probability of share s_1 having price p_1 is 1/2, having price p_2 is 1/3, and having price p_3 is 1/6. In addition, the probability of share s_2 having price p_1 is 3/4, and having price p_4 is 1/4. Thus tuple-wise, the probabilities are conditional; for example, given the first tuple the probability of price p_1 is 1/2 and given the second tuple the probability of price p_1 is 3/4. Assuming that SHARE is a COMPLETE-attribute, i.e. its probabilistic or-sets are all singletons such that its single value is true with probability one, then SHARE is a key for R which is weakly (probabilistically) satisfied in r with probability one, i.e. this key is satisfied in all possible worlds.

Table 5.62 A probabilistic relation

SHARE	PRICE
s_1	$\{p_1/3, p_2/2, p_3/1\}$
s_2	$\{p_1/3, p_4/1\}$

The possible worlds semantics of or-sets carries over in a straightforward manner to probabilistic relations, assuming stochastic independence between attribute values and tuples in such a relation. As an example consider the probabilistic relation, say r', over R', with schema(R') = {MANAGER, DEPARTMENT}, recording the possible managers of departments; r' is shown in Table 5.63. The probability that Jack is the manager of the Toy department is $2/3 \times 1/3 = 2/9$, and the probability that Jack is the manager of the Carpet department is $2/3 \times 2/3 = 4/9$. Similarly, the probability that Joe is the manager of the Toy department is $1/3 \times 1/3 = 1/9$, and the probability that Joe is the manager of the Carpet department is $1/3 \times 2/3 = 2/9$. Furthermore, the probability that Jill is the manageress of the Toy department is 2/9, and the probability that Jill is the manageress of the Carpet department is 1/9. Similarly, the probability that Jane is the manageress of the Toy department is 4/9, and the probability that Jane is the manageress of the Carpet department is 2/9. What is the probability of a possible world that Jack is the manager of the Toy department and Jill is the manageress of the Carpet department? The answer is: $2/9 \times 1/9 = 2/81$. What is the overall probability that Jack is the manager of the Toy department? The answer is: $(2/9 \times 2/9) + (2/9 \times 1/9) + (2/9 \times 4/9) + (2/9 \times 2/9) = 2/9$, which as expected agrees with the above probability. What is the probability that Joe be a manager of the Carpet department and either Jill or Jane be joint manageresses of the Carpet department. The answer is: $(2/9 \times 1/9) + (2/9 \times 2/9) = 2/27$.

Table 5.63 Another probabilistic relation

MANAGER	DEPARTMENT
{Jack/2, Joe/1}	{Toy/1, Carpet/2}
{Jill/1, Jane/2}	{Toy/2, Carpet/1}

A relational algebra for probabilistic relations can be defined in a manner similar to that of or-sets, with the provision that the probabilities of tuples in the resulting relations be computed according to the stochastic independence assumption. In addition, for selection from a probabilistic relation, r, a threshold value, say $\alpha \in (0, 1]$, can be specified so that tuples appear in the result of a query only if their probability in r is greater than or equal to α. Furthermore, weak (probabilistic) satisfaction of FDs in probabilistic relations can be defined as it was defined for or-relations. Weak probabilistic satisfaction can also be defined to a degree $\lambda \in (0, 1]$, so that a set F of FDs is probabilistically satisfied in a probabilistic relation, r, if there exists one possible world relative to r that satisfies F to a degree whose probability is greater than or equal to λ. Unfortunately, in general, the computational problems relating to the or-sets approach carry over to the probabilistic approach; thus as for or-sets we may need to restrict ourselves to polynomial-time subclasses.

Probabilistic methods can also be utilised for querying relations, which may be incomplete, by viewing a relation as a sample whose distribution may also be unknown [Fuh90]. In this context, given a query, the query processor needs to estimate the probability that a tuple (or an object) is a correct and relevant answer to the query. These probabilities can be used to rank the answer tuples of a query and/or to eliminate tuples below a specified threshold. An early data model which considers a statistical framework for using prior knowledge to query incomplete relations was considered in [Won82].

For a comprehensive survey on the management of probabilistic data see [BGP92] and for an investigation of probabilistic data dependencies see [CP87]. Some fundamental connections between probabilistic and relational concepts are exhibited in [Hil91].

The fuzzy and probabilistic approaches to relational databases can be viewed as complementary. Suppose that we have a tuple in a relational database recording some information about a person named Mary. Then, stating that the probability that Mary is young is 0.5 can be interpreted as saying that Mary is either young or not but she is equally likely to be either. On the other hand, saying that Mary is fuzzily young, where young is a fuzzy set, is taken to mean that the range of possible age values for Mary is restricted and the grade of membership of 20 (years) in this fuzzy set is much higher than the grade of membership of 40 (years) in the same fuzzy set. Consider another example; saying that a cup of tea is hot, with probability 0.6, means that it is more likely to be hot than not, while saying that a cup of tea is fuzzily hot means that it is definitely "hot" and higher temperatures have higher membership grades in this fuzzy set. Probabilities can also be fuzzified by considering statements such as "it is *very likely* that Mary is young" and "it is *unlikely* that the cup of tea is hot". The probabilistic and fuzzy approaches can actually be reconciled if we interpret probabilities as measures of belief.

For interesting discussions on probabilistic versus fuzzy reasoning see [Che86], advocating the probabilistic side of the fence, and [Zad86], advocating the fuzzy side of the fence. A recent survey on different representations and ways of reasoning with imperfect information can be found in [Par96].

5.12 Exercises

Exercise 5.1 Discuss the pros and cons of having marked and unmarked nulls in incomplete relations, with reference to query processing.

Exercise 5.2 Suppose that a bank has a relational database which has, amongst other relations, a master file relation containing all the customer accounts information, and a details file relation containing all the recent transactions of customers such as deposit and withdrawal information. A common activity of the bank's IT department is that of generating a *master-detail* report, which collates for each master file tuple all the transactions that this customer has carried out. Given that some of the customers may not have any transactions recorded in the details file, how can the outer join be useful in generating the report [Bul87] (see Definition 5.21 in Section 5.4).

Exercise 5.3 We say that an extended operator, op^e, is a *possibility preserving* extension of a standard operator, op, if for all incomplete relations r

$$\bigcup \{s \mid s \in \text{POSS}(op^e(r))\} = \bigcup \{op(s) \mid s \in \text{POSS}(r)\}.$$

Redefine all the extended operators of the extended algebra with the intention that they be possibility preserving. If this is not possible for an extended operator justify your claim.

Exercise 5.4 Which of the following equivalences, which are true for complete relations, are also true for incomplete relations:

1) $\sigma^e_{\neg F}(r) \cong r -^e \sigma^e_F(r).$

2) $\sigma^e_{F_1 \vee F_2}(r) \cong \sigma^e_{F_1}(r) \cup^e \sigma^e_{F_2}(r).$

3) $\sigma^e_{F_1 \wedge F_2}(r) \cong \sigma^e_{F_1}(r) \cap^e \sigma^e_{F_2}(r).$

Exercise 5.5 Prove the soundness and completeness of Armstrong's axiom system with respect to strong implication.

Exercise 5.6 Let F be a set of FDs over a relation schema R, and let NF(R) be a subset of schema(R), constraining incomplete relations r over R *not* to have null values in the projection of r onto NF(R). We define the following additional inference rule for FDs holding in incomplete relations:

NFD3 Null-transitivity: if $F \vdash X \to Y$, $F \vdash Y \to Z$ and $Y - X \subseteq$ NF(R), then $F \vdash X \to Z$.

Show that Lien's and Atzeni's axiom system together with NFD3 is sound and complete for FDs with respect to weak implication in the presence of a *null-free* constraint NF(R) [AM84].

Exercise 5.7 Prove that a relation r over R satisfies a superkey family **K** if and only if, where $X = \bigcup_{i \in I} K_i$, with $K_i \in$ **K**, for all relations $s \in$ POSS(r), the cardinality of the projection of s onto X is equal to the cardinality of r, i.e. $|\pi_X(s)| = |r|$.

Exercise 5.8 Prove that the problem of deciding whether a relation r over R satisfies a superkey family of cardinality less than or equal to some natural number k is NP-complete [Tha89a].

Exercise 5.9 Let R be a relation schema such that schema(R) = XYZ, where X, Y and Z are pairwise disjoint sets of attributes in schema(R) and let F be a set of FDs over R. Furthermore, let r be an incomplete relation over R, $r_1 = \pi_{XY}(r)$ and $r_2 = \pi_{YZ}(r)$.

We say that r is *connected*, if r is reduced and for every tuple $t \in r$, t is the outer join of $t[XY]$ and $t[YZ]$. Prove that the following two statements are equivalent [JS90]:

1) For any connected relation r over R that weakly satisfies F, $r = r_1 \bowtie r_2$.
2) Either the FD Y → X or the FD Y → Z, or both, are in F^{Lien+}.

Exercise 5.10 Consider incomplete relations which, apart from nonnull values, have occurrences, only of the null value *dne*. Suppose we have a relation schema PERSON, having three attributes, NAME, ADDRESS and SPOUSE_NAME. Now, since a person may not have a spouse, relations over PERSON may have *dne* in their SPOUSE column. Argue whether it is a good design principle to replace the relation schema PERSON by two relation schemas, one having attributes NAME and ADDRESS and the other having attributes NAME and SPOUSE_NAME [LL86].

Exercise 5.11 Prove that weak satisfaction of FDs in or-relations is not additive.

Exercise 5.12 Consider an or-relation $r = \{<a, \{b_1, b_2\}>\}$ over R, with schema(R) = {A, B}, and a relation $s = \{<b_1, c>, <b_2, c>\}$ over S, with schema(S) = {B, C}. If we naturally join r and s, we would expect either $<a, b_1, c>$ or $<a, b_2, c>$ to be in the result, but not both. Explain why neither of the above tuples is in the answer of the or-query, $r \bowtie s$. How can this problem be alleviated by allowing *or-tuples* in or-relations, i.e. tuples of the form $<a, \{<b_1, c>, <b_2, c>\}>$ representing a disjunction of the subtuples $<b_1, c>$ and $<b_2, c>$ [Imi89].

Exercise 5.13 Prove that if a set F of FDs over a relation schema R satisfies the intersection property, then R is in 2NF with respect to F if and only if it is in 3NF with respect to F [LL99a].

Exercise 5.14 Recall that a relation schema R is in UKNF with respect to a set F of FDs over R, if its set of keys is a singleton (see Definition 4.14 from Subsection 4.4.3 in Chapter 4). Prove that if R is in UKNF with respect to F and F is a monodependent set of FDs, then R is in 2NF with respect to F if and only if R is in 3NF with respect to F if and only if R is in BCNF with respect to F [LL99a].

Exercise 5.15 Prove that if all of the keys for a relation schema R with respect to a set F of FDs over R are simple, i.e. they are singletons, and F is a monodependent set of FDs, then R is in 2NF with respect to F if and only if R is in 3NF with respect to F if and only if R is in BCNF with respect to F [LL99a].

Exercise 5.16 Prove that if a set F of FDs over a relation schema R satisfies the split-freeness property, then all the keys for R with respect to F have the same cardinality [LL99a].

Exercise 5.17   Explain the difference between the *possibility* measure of a value in a fuzzy set and the *probability* of a value in a set with respect to some distribution function.

Exercise 5.18   Define and give an example of the notion of a key being fuzzily satisfied to degree λ [CKV96].

Exercise 5.19   Use your definition from the Exercise 5.18 to define and justify a variant of BCNF, called λ-BCNF, for fuzzy relational databases [CKV96].

Exercise 5.20   Suggest, with a motivating example, how fuzzy sets may be used to enforce security levels to classified information in a relational database [She93].

Exercise 5.21   Explain the difference between vagueness as represented by fuzzy sets and imprecision as represented by rough sets.

Exercise 5.22   Let $X \rightarrow Y$ be an FD over a relation schema(R) and $A \in X$. The attribute A is said to be *superfluous* with respect to $X \rightarrow Y$ and a relation r over R, if $POS(X, Y) = POS(X - \{A\}, Y)$. The *core* of X is the set of attributes given by

$$CORE(X, Y) = \{A \in X \mid POS(X, Y) \neq POS(X - \{A\}, Y)\},$$

i.e. CORE(X) is the set of attributes the are *not* superfluous.

The set of attributes $W \subseteq X$ is *independent* with respect to Y, if for every proper subset Z of W, $POS(Z, Y) \neq POS(X, Y)$. The set of attributes $W \subseteq X$ is a *reduct* of X, if it is independent with respect to Y and $POS(W, Y) = POS(X, Y)$.

Prove that CORE(X) is the intersection of all the reducts of X [Zia91].

6. Computable Database Queries and the Expressiveness of the Relational Algebra

One of the fundamental operations a database system needs to carry out is that of processing queries. The relational algebra was defined in Section 3.2 of Chapter 3 as a yardstick for the expressiveness of a query language for relational databases. The relational algebra on its own is not intended to be used as a general purpose database programming language for developing applications and as such does not provide the application programmer with iteration and recursion facilities. Thus in the context of database application programming the question that arises is: what are the possible queries that such a database language can and should be able to compute? In this chapter we define and investigate a general notion of a computable query in an attempt to answer the question we have just posed. There are essentially two parts to our investigation. The first part involves a categorisation of several subclasses of computable queries and the second part involves the presentation of a database programming language that is complete with respect to computable queries and an investigation of the expressive power of the relational algebra and how it can be made more expressive by adding to it iteration and/or recursion facilities. Since the early 1980's it was realised that the relational algebra is not expressive enough to carry out general database computations. The research into computable queries has been instrumental in motivating the necessity to develop more expressive query languages for relational databases and laying down the fundamental principles which provide the foundations for such development.

6.1 What is a Computable Database Query?

As we have shown in Subsection 3.2.1 of Chapter 3 there are many useful queries that the relational algebra cannot express such as computing the transitive closure of a relation and counting the number of tuples in a relation. In fact, from a computational complexity point of view the relational algebra is equivalent to the set of problems checkable in constant time on a concurrent parallel random access machine [Imm89]. This computational complexity class is very weak and is properly included in the deterministic logspace computational complexity class [Imm81, Var82a, Imm87]. Thus it is natural to investigate extensions of the relational algebra in order to enhance its computational expressiveness. In particular, our aim is to formalise the notion of a *computable query*.

There are two fundamental differences between computable queries and Turing-computable mappings (also known as *partially recursive functions*). The first difference is that Turing-computable mappings are mappings from strings to strings (or alternatively, from natural numbers to natural numbers) whilst computable queries are mappings from finite sets of objects to finite sets of objects (cf. [Gan80]). The second difference is that the objects of computable queries are not strings or numbers but abstract objects (cf. [Fri71]), in our case records (cf. [CM91]), which are defined as total mappings from a finite set of attributes to a set of domain values.

We define the semantics of a computable query as a Turing-computable mapping together with an encoding from finite sets of records (or simply sets) to strings. Consequently, we can evaluate a computable query by encoding the input set into a string, then use this string as an input to a given Turing-computable mapping, and finally decode the resulting output string to obtain the output set, which yields the result of the computable query. This analysis provides clarification of the notion of a computable query by dealing with the problem of how a database language can be implemented on a standard Turing machine that does not cater directly for mappings from sets to sets. Thus, intuitively, a database query language is *computationally query complete* (or simply query complete) if it can express the set of all computable queries.

Once the formal definition of a computable query is established in Section 6.2 we investigate several important subclasses of computable queries in the following section, i.e. Section 6.3. Thereafter in Section 6.4 we further our understanding of computable queries by looking into the Turing-computable mappings that realise a given computable query. In Section 6.5 we define the notion of a database language being query complete, and present the database query language, QL, from [CH80]. In Section 6.6 we present a fundamental characterisation of the expressiveness of the relational algebra. Since the ability to express all the computable queries may be more than is needed from a database query language, in Section 6.7 we describe how the relational algebra can be made more expressive without making it query complete by adding to it a looping mechanism. The motivation for such an extension of the relational algebra is that it may be desirable to enhance the expressiveness of the relational algebra, say to compute queries such as the transitive closure of a relation (see Subsection 3.2.1 in Chapter 3), without making it query complete, since database users rarely require query complete database languages.

6.2 Formalising Computable Database Queries

For the purpose of this chapter we will consider a slightly different model of a relational database. Instead of viewing a database as a set of relations with each relation being a set of tuples, we will view a database as being a set of *records* [CM91].

We first recall from Definition 3.1 in Section 3.1 that $\mathcal{U}$ is the countably infinite universe of attributes and that $\mathcal{D}$ is the countably infinite underlying database domain.

Definition 6.1 (A record and a database)   Let X be a finite subset of the set of attributes $\mathcal{U}$. An X-*record* (or simply a record whenever X is understood from context) is a total mapping, t, from X into $\mathcal{D}$ such that

$$\forall A \in X, t(A) \in \text{DOM}(A).$$

In the case when X = ∅, we take t to be the empty mapping corresponding to the *empty record*, which is denoted by <>. We denote an X-record, t, where X = $\{A_1, A_2, \ldots, A_m\}$ and $\forall i \in \{1, 2, \ldots, m\}$, $t(i) = v_i$, with $v_i \in \text{DOM}(A_i)$, by

$$<(A_1 : v_1), (A_2 : v_2), \ldots, (A_m : v_m)>.$$

In the following we will abbreviate $(A_i : v_i)$ by $A_i : v_i$.

Let RECS denote the countably infinite set of all finite sets of records, where a set of records may contain X-records and Y-records, where X ≠ Y. Then a *database of records* (or simply a database) is a member of RECS. ∎

The reader can verify that every relational database can be translated into a database of records and vice versa; we can assume without loss of generality that whenever R_i and R_j are two distinct relation schemas then schema(R_i) ≠ schema(R_j). The notational advantage of databases of records is that the schema of the database is encoded in the database itself and, in addition, the database can be viewed as a single relation containing variable length records [LL95a].

Example 6.1 In Table 6.1 we show a database of records, say EMP. The translation of EMP into a relational database d comprising three relations r_1, r_2 and r_3 is shown in Tables 6.2, 6.3 and 6.4. The semantics of EMP are: an employee has a NAME, earns a SALary, works in one DEParTment and may have at most one SPouSe. In addition, a DEPT has one ManaGeR and a MGR has one SECretary. ∎

Table 6.1 The database of records EMP

{<DEPT : Computing,	NAME : Iris,	SAL : 20>,	
<DEPT : Computing,	NAME : Reuven,	SAL : 25,	SPS : Hanna>,
<DEPT : Computing,	NAME : Brian,	SAL : 30,	SPS : Annette>,
<DEPT : Maths,	NAME : Naomi,	SAL : 22,	SPS : Sophia>,
<DEPT : Maths,	MGR : Naomi,	SEC : Sophia>,	
<DEPT : Computing,	MGR : Brian,	SEC : Rachel>,	
<DEPT : Philosophy,	MGR : Dan,	SEC : Naomi>}	

Table 6.2 The relation r_1

DEPT	NAME	SAL
Computing	Iris	20

Table 6.3 The relation r_2

DEPT	NAME	SAL	SPS
Computing	Reuven	25	Hanna
Computing	Brian	30	Annette
Maths	Naomi	22	Sophia

Table 6.4 The relation r_3

DEPT	MGR	SEC
Maths	Naomi	Sophia
Computing	Brian	Rachel
Philosophy	Dan	Naomi

We let CHAR be a finite and nonempty set of characters (the alphabet) and STR be the countably infinite set of strings over CHAR. Furthermore, we let TC denote the set of all Turing-computable mappings (also known as *partially recursive functions*) from STR to STR; see Subsection 1.9.4 of Chapter 1 for the necessary background material from the theory of computing. (Recall that we denote the composition of two mappings g and f by the juxtaposition fg of f and g.)

6.2.1 Encodings and Decodings

Herein we investigate in depth the semantics of encodings, an area which has been hitherto neglected in the database literature, and then formally define a computable query by making use of encodings. Informally, an encoding of a set of records consists of two components: an ordering function, which orders the records in the set as well as the values of each record in the set, and an isomorphism, which maps the values in the records of the set to strings. A decoding, which is the inverse of an encoding, also has two components: the inverse of the said isomorphism and a mapping which forgets the order imposed by the aforesaid ordering function used in the encoding. Since, in general, there may not be an algorithm to convert any two encodings into each other, we restrict the set of encodings to a set of *mutually convertible* encodings, which is a set of encodings that are algorithmically convertible to a given standard encoding [GJ79]. It follows that our (restricted set of) encodings are "reasonable" in the sense of [GJ79]. An important class of encodings, called *free encodings*, whose isomorphism maps record values to a corresponding natural string representation, is also defined. In a free encoding the isomorphism has the same semantics as the identity mapping on record values.

Definition 6.2 (Encoding) An encoding is a mapping from RECS which maps each database of records S $\in$ RECS to an (ordered) list of (ordered) lists of ordered pairs.

More specifically, an encoding ϱ is a mapping from RECS to a restricted subset of STR, which is the composition $\theta\phi$ of an *ordering function*, ϕ, together with a *naming function*, θ.

Given an input S the ordering function, ϕ, converts each record in S into a list of ordered pairs and then orders the resulting set of lists of pairs into a further list as follows:

1) if $t = <A_1 : v_1, A_2 : v_2, \ldots, A_m : v_m>$, with $t \in$ S, then $\phi(<A_1 : v_1, A_2 : v_2, \ldots, A_m : v_m>) = [(B_1, w_1), (B_2, w_2), \ldots, (B_m, w_m)]$, such that $A_i = B_j$ and $v_i = w_j$ if and only if $(A_i : v_i)$ is mapped onto the jth ordered pair in $\phi(t)$, where $i, j \in \{1, 2, \ldots, m\}$; and

2) if S $= \{t_1, t_2, \ldots, t_{nj}\}$ then $\phi(S) = [u_1, u_2, \ldots, u_n]$, with $\phi(t_i) = u_j$, is mapped as described in (1), if and only if t_i is mapped onto the jth record in $\phi(S)$, where $i, j \in \{1, 2, \ldots, n\}$.

The naming function, θ, is a one-to-one mapping that converts the attributes and values of records in S into strings in STR which do not contain any delimiters in the fixed set, $\{[,],(,),,,\}$. The mapping θ is extended to $\phi(S)$ as follows:

$$\theta([(A_1, v_1), (A_2, v_2), \ldots, (A_m, v_m)]) = [(\theta(A_1), \theta(v_1)), (\theta(A_2), \theta(v_2)), \ldots, (\theta(A_m), \theta(v_m))].$$

We denote the set of encodings of databases in RECS by ENC and denote the range of ENC by LISTS; we call the elements of LISTS *databases of lists*. ∎

Definition 6.3 (Decoding)   A decoding is a mapping from LISTS to RECS which maps a database of lists in LISTS onto a database of records in RECS.

More specifically, a decoding, ϱ^{-1}, is a mapping from LISTS to RECS, which is the composition $\gamma\theta^{-1}$ of the inverse θ^{-1} of a naming function θ together with the *forgetful function*, γ.

The forgetful function γ maps a database of lists into a set of records simply by ignoring or forgetting the ordering imposed by the list structure representing the records in the database. Furthermore, the inverse mapping θ^{-1} converts all the strings in a database of lists to their original attributes and values, thus yielding an ordered database of records.

We denote the set of decodings of databases of lists in LISTS by DEC. Given an encoding $\varrho = \theta\phi \in$ ENC, $\varrho^{-1} = \gamma\theta^{-1} \in$ DEC is called its decoding. ∎

We now define a special encoding, called a *standard encoding*, which allows us to formalise the notion of what we call a *reasonable encoding*.

Definition 6.4 (A standard encoding)   Assume that χ is an ordering function corresponding to some fixed lexicographical ordering of the set $\mathcal{U} \cup \mathcal{D}$ of attributes and domain values. Furthermore, assume that ι is a naming function that maps the attributes and values in $\mathcal{U} \cup \mathcal{D}$ into some fixed values, which are considered to be their *natural representation*, that is, $\forall A \in \mathcal{U}, \iota(A) = $ "A" and $\forall v \in \mathcal{D}, \iota(v) = $ "v". The encoding $\iota\chi$ is called a *standard encoding*. ∎

We need to restrict the above definition of encodings so that we consider only encodings which can be algorithmically converted to a standard encoding.

Definition 6.5 (Mutually convertible encodings)   An encoding $\varrho \in$ ENC is said to be *mutually convertible* to the encoding $\iota\chi$ if both the compositions $\varrho(\iota\chi)^{-1}$ (observe that $(\iota\chi)^{-1} = \gamma\iota^{-1}$) and $(\iota\chi)\varrho^{-1}$ are Turing-computable mappings. ∎

From now on we will assume that all the encodings in ENC *are mutually convertible to* $\iota\chi$. We leave the proof of the following proposition to the reader.

Proposition 6.1   All encodings $\varrho_1, \varrho_2 \in$ ENC are mutually convertible. □

Thus all encodings are equivalent in the sense that they can all be algorithmically converted into each other. It is also useful to insist that any encoding of a database of records can be converted into another one in polynomial time in the size of the input database of records, but such a restriction is unnecessary in our context. In practice, it is also important that encodings be precise in the sense that naming functions, θ, do not *pad* the input database of records S with extraneous characters.

A free encoding is one which maps attributes and values to their natural representation. Free encodings are useful, since users will easily be able to interpret their output.

Definition 6.6 (Free encoding)   An encoding $\varrho = \theta\phi$ is said to be *free* if $\theta = \iota$. ∎

Example 6.2   In Table 6.5 we show a free encoding of the database of records, EMP, shown in Table 6.1 and in Table 6.6 we show an encoding of EMP which is not free.   ∎

Table 6.5 A free encoding of EMP

[[(DEPT, Computing),	(NAME, Iris),	(SAL, 20)],	
[(DEPT, Computing),	(NAME, Reuven),	(SAL, 25),	(SPS, Hanna)],
[(DEPT, Computing),	(NAME, Brian),	(SAL, 30),	(SPS, Annette)],
[(DEPT, Maths),	(NAME, Naomi),	(SAL, 22),	(SPS, Sophia)],
[(DEPT, Maths),	(MGR, Naomi),	(SEC, Sophia],	
[(DEPT, Computing),	(MGR, Brian),	(SEC, Rachel)],	
[(DEPT, Philosophy),	(MGR, Dan),	(SEC, Naomi)]]	

Table 6.6 An encoding of EMP which is not free

[[(1, COMPUTING),	(2, IRIS),	(3, 20)],	
[(1, COMPUTING),	(2, REUVEN),	(3, 25),	(4, HANNA)],
[(1, COMPUTING),	(2, BRIAN),	(3, 30),	(4, ANNETTE)],
[(1, MATHS),	(2, NAOMI),	(3, 22),	(4, SOPHIA)],
[(1, MATHS),	(5, NAOMI),	(6, SOPHIA)],	
[(1, COMPUTING),	(5, BRIAN),	(6, RACHEL)],	
[(1, PHILOSOPHY),	(5, DAN),	(6, NAOMI)]]	

6.2.2   Definition of Computable Database Queries

We begin this subsection with an example of some computable database queries.

Example 6.3   The following queries over the database of records EMP of Example 6.1, shown in Table 6.1, are intuitively computable.

1) Project EMP onto the set of attributes {DEPT, NAME}.

2) Select from EMP the records whose DEPT-value is Computing.

3) Return the nth record in EMP (with respect to an encoding of EMP) if $|EMP| \geq n$, otherwise return $\{<>\}$.

4) Select from EMP the records, t, where t has n attributes.

5) Return $\{<>\}$ if $|EMP| \geq n$, otherwise return $\emptyset$.

6) Select from EMP all records t_i such that there exists another record t_j in EMP such that $t_i \neq t_j$ and both t_i and t_j contain a common attribute value pair, say $(A : v)$.   ∎

Informally, a computable database query τ is a mapping from RECS to RECS that can be computed via a Turing-computable mapping δ from LISTS to LISTS by encoding the input database of records S to τ via an encoding ϱ and decoding the output database of lists from δ via the decoding ϱ^{-1}. Figure 6.1 shows the commutative diagram describing the semantics of a computable database query, where CQ denotes the set of all computable database queries.

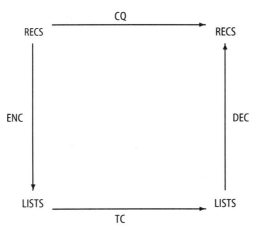

Fig 6.1 Commutative diagram describing the semantics of CQ

Definition 6.7 (Computable database query) A mapping τ from RECS to RECS is a *computable database query* (or simply a computable query or a query) if

$$\exists \delta \in TC, \exists \varrho \in ENC \text{ such that } \tau = \varrho^{-1}\delta\varrho.$$

As an abbreviation to the above equation we say that τ is *realised* via δ and ϱ; at times we simply say that τ is realised via δ meaning that $\exists \varrho \in ENC$ such that τ is realised via δ and ϱ. ∎

Example 6.4 The reader can verify that all the queries given in Example 6.3 are in fact computable according to Definition 6.7. ∎

The next proposition shows that if a computable query τ is realised via δ and ϱ then for any other encoding $\varrho_i \in ENC$ we can effectively find a Turing-computable mapping δ_i such that τ is realised via δ_i and ϱ_i.

Proposition 6.2 Let $\tau \in CQ$. Then $\forall \varrho_i \in ENC, \exists \delta_i \in TC$ such that τ is realised via δ_i and ϱ_i.

Proof. Assume that τ is realised via δ and ϱ. Let $\delta_i = \varrho_i \varrho^{-1} \delta \varrho \varrho_i^{-1}$. By Proposition 6.1 and the fact that TC is closed under composition of mappings it follows that $\delta_i \in TC$. Therefore, τ is realised via δ_i and ϱ_i as required. □

Our definition of a computable query differs from the standard definition given in [CH80] and [AV90], wherein a computable query is defined directly as a computable mapping from sets to sets without detailing the encoding and decoding process. Moreover, another nonstandard feature of a computable query is that, in addition to encoding attribute values of tuples, we also encode the attribute names of values. Research in the area of computable database queries can be found in [CH80, VS89, AV90, AV91a, AV91b, DM92, HS93, Saz93, Van93a, LL96a].

6.3   Subclasses of Computable Database Queries

Herein we define various subclasses of computable queries and investigate the relationships between these subclasses.

6.3.1   Order-Independent Computable Queries

Informally, a computable database query τ that is realised via $\varrho = \theta\phi$ is order-independent if its computation does not depend on the ordering function ϕ. That is, intuitively τ is order-independent if the diagram shown in Figure 6.1 commutes for all encodings $\varrho_i = \theta_i\phi_i \in$ ENC with $\theta = \theta_i$.

Prior to defining order-independent computable queries we define order-independence as a property of the Turing-computable mapping δ that realises τ.

Definition 6.8 (Order-independent Turing-computable mapping)   A   Turing-computable mapping $\delta \in$ TC is *order-independent* if

$$\forall \varrho_i = \theta\phi_i \in \text{ENC}, \forall\varrho = \theta\phi \in \text{ENC}, \delta\varrho_i = \delta\varrho.$$

Hereafter we let OITC denote the set of all order-independent Turing-computable mappings.

∎

We observe that in the above definition $\varrho_i^{-1} = \gamma\theta^{-1} = \varrho^{-1}$ holds and thus it is true that $\varrho_i^{-1}\delta\varrho_i = \varrho^{-1}\delta\varrho$.

Definition 6.9 (Order-independent computable query)   A computable query $\tau \in$ CQ is *order-independent* if $\exists\delta \in$ OITC such that τ is realised via δ.

Hereafter we let OI denote the set of all order-independent computable queries.   ∎

We observe that in Example 6.3 only query (3) is not order-independent and thus OI is a proper subset of CQ.

6.3.2   Isomorphism-Independent Computable Queries

Informally, a computable database query τ that is realised via $\varrho = \theta\phi$ is isomorphism-independent if its computation does not depend on the naming function θ. That is, intuitively τ is isomorphism-independent if the diagram shown in Figure 6.1 commutes for all encodings $\varrho_i = \theta_i\phi_i \in$ ENC with $\phi = \phi_i$.

Prior to defining isomorphism-independent computable queries we define isomorphism-independence as a property of the Turing-computable mapping δ that realises τ.

Definition 6.10 (Isomorphism-independent Turing-computable mapping)   A   Turing-computable mapping $\delta \in$ TC is *isomorphism-independent* if

$$\forall \varrho_i = \theta_i\phi \in \text{ENC}, \forall\varrho = \theta\phi \in \text{ENC}, \theta_i^{-1}\delta\theta_i = \theta^{-1}\delta\theta.$$

Hereafter we let IITC denote the set of all isomorphism-independent Turing-computable mappings. ■

We observe that in the above definition it is true that $\varrho_i^{-1} \delta \varrho_i = \varrho^{-1} \delta \varrho$.

Definition 6.11 (Isomorphism-independent computable query) A computable query $\tau \in$ CQ is *isomorphism-independent* if $\exists \delta \in$ IITC such that τ is realised via δ.

Hereafter we let II denote the set of all isomorphism-independent computable queries. ■

We observe that in Example 6.3 only queries (1) and (2) are not isomorphism-independent and thus II is a proper subset of CQ.

6.3.3 Encoding-Independent Computable Queries

Informally, a computable database query τ that is realised via ϱ is encoding-independent if its computation does not depend on any particular encoding ϱ. That is, intuitively τ is encoding-independent if the diagram shown in Figure 6.1 commutes for all encodings $\varrho \in$ ENC.

In essence encoding-independence with respect to computable queries means that, in practice, the same query executed on two distinct machines, whether they be different or not, will yield the same result irrespective of how the query is represented internally within each machine.

Definition 6.12 (Encoding-independent computable query) A computable query $\tau \in$ CQ is *encoding-independent* if

$$\exists \delta \in \text{TC such that } \forall \varrho \in \text{ENC}, \tau = \varrho^{-1} \delta \varrho.$$

Hereafter we let EI denote the set of all encoding-independent computable queries. ■

We observe that in the above definition it is true that $\forall \varrho_i, \varrho_j \in$ ENC, $\varrho_i^{-1} \delta \varrho_i = \varrho_j^{-1} \delta \varrho_j$. Therefore, EI is a subset of both OI and II. In fact, EI is a proper subset of both OI and II, since in Example 6.3 queries (1) and (2) are in OI but not in EI and query (3) is in II but not in EI. We now show that EI is the intersection of OI and II.

Theorem 6.3 EI = OI ∩ II.

Proof. EI $\subseteq$ OI ∩ II, since EI $\subset$ OI and EI $\subset$ II as noted above.

It remains to show that OI ∩ II $\subseteq$ EI. Let $\tau \in$ OI ∩ II be a computable query which is both order-independent and isomorphism-independent. Now, let $\delta \in$ IITC be a Turing-computable mapping and $\varrho \in$ ENC be an encoding such that τ is realised via δ and ϱ; δ and ϱ exist due to that fact that $\tau \in$ II. Let δ' be the mapping $\delta \varrho \varrho^{-1}$. Now, $\delta' \in$ TC, since by Proposition 6.1 ϱ is mutually convertible to itself. Furthermore, $\delta' \in$ OITC, since the mapping $\varrho \varrho^{-1}$ effectively reorders the encoded input so that it be suitable for δ. Thus τ is realised via δ'.

In order to conclude the proof we need to show that $\forall \varrho_i, \varrho_j \in$ ENC, $\varrho_i^{-1} \delta' \varrho_i = \varrho_j^{-1} \delta' \varrho_j$. That is, we need to show that τ is realised via δ' and any encoding ϱ in ENC. Let $\varrho = \theta \phi$, $\varrho_i = \theta_i \phi_i$

and $\varrho_j = \theta_j\phi_j$; $\varrho_i^{-1}\delta'\varrho_i = \gamma\theta_i^{-1}\delta\theta\phi\gamma\theta^{-1}\theta_i\phi_i = \gamma\theta_j^{-1}\delta\theta\phi\gamma\theta^{-1}\theta_j\phi_i$, since by the definition of IITC $\delta' \in$ IITC due to the fact that $\delta \in$ IITC. Thus, $\gamma\theta_j^{-1}\delta\theta\phi\gamma\theta^{-1}\theta_j\phi_i = \gamma\theta_j^{-1}\delta\theta\phi\gamma\theta^{-1}\theta_j\phi_j = \varrho_j^{-1}\delta'\varrho_j$, since $\delta' \in$ OITC. The result that $\tau \in$ EI follows as required. $\square$

An interesting corollary to the above proof is that any isomorphism-independent computable query τ can be made to be encoding-independent by "hard-wiring" the ordering function into the Turing-computable mapping that realises τ.

A *generic* computable query is one which commutes with every one-to-one mapping from records to records, which is the composition of an encoding and a decoding. The next definition formalises this notion.

Definition 6.13 (Generic computable query)   A computable query τ is generic if $\eta\tau = \tau\eta$, where $\eta = \varrho_1^{-1}\varrho_2$ and $\varrho_1, \varrho_2 \in$ ENC.   ■

The notion of encoding-independence is closely related to the notion of genericity as the following theorem asserts.

Theorem 6.4   A computable query, τ, is encoding-independent if and only if τ is order-independent and generic.

Proof. If. Suppose that τ is realised via δ and $\varrho_1 \in$ ENC, where $\delta \in$ OITC. We need to show that $\tau = \varrho_1^{-1}\delta\varrho_1 = \varrho_2^{-1}\delta\varrho_2$, where $\varrho_2 \in$ ENC.

Let $\eta = \varrho_1^{-1}\varrho_2$. Then $\eta^{-1}\tau\eta = \tau$, since τ is generic. Therefore $\tau = \varrho_2^{-1}\varrho_1\varrho_1^{-1}\delta\varrho_1\varrho_1^{-1}\varrho_2$. Thus $\tau = \varrho_2^{-1}\delta\theta_2\phi$, since $\varrho_2^{-1}\varrho_1\varrho_1^{-1} = \varrho_2^{-1}$ and $\varrho_1\varrho_1^{-1}\varrho_2 = \theta_2\phi$ for some ordering function ϕ, where $\varrho_2 = \theta_2\phi_2$. The result that $\tau = \varrho_2^{-1}\delta\varrho_2$ follows, since $\delta \in$ OITC.

Only if. Suppose that τ is realised by δ and ϱ. Thus, by the definition of encoding-independence $\tau = \varrho^{-1}\delta\varrho = \eta^{-1}\varrho^{-1}\delta\varrho\eta$. The result follows, since $\eta\tau = \eta\eta^{-1}\varrho^{-1}\delta\varrho\eta = \varrho^{-1}\delta\varrho\eta = \tau\eta$. $\square$

We next summarise the benefits of encoding-independent queries.

- The order of records in the database does not influence the result of the query.

- The result of the query is independent of the representation of the attributes and values in the database.

The concept of encoding-independence is related to the concept of data independence discussed in Section 1.6 of Chapter 1. If a database query is in EI, then the result of the query is unaffected by the physical representation of the database.

We close this section by indicating how the concept of encoding-independence can be weakened to allow a finite set C of attributes and values to be mentioned explicitly in a query.

Recall from Definition 6.4 that the naming function ι maps attributes and values to their natural representation. An encoding $\varrho = \theta\phi$ is said to be a C-*encoding* if $\forall c \in$ C, $\theta(c) = \iota(c)$, i.e. any constant in C can be identified by its natural representation. Intuitively, a computable query τ is C-*encoding-independent* if the diagram shown in Figure 6.1 commutes for all

C-encodings. When C = Ø then the notion of C-encoding-independent reduces to the notion of encoding-independent. We denote the set of all C-encoding-independent computable queries by C-EI.

The reader can verify that, with respect to Example 6.3, query (1) is {DEPT, NAME}-encoding-independent and query (2) is {DEPT, Computing}-encoding-independent. In practice we would require C to include at least the attribute names and domain values in the database over which we are querying; that is, with respect to the latter, C should include at least all the constants in the active domain of the database. We leave it to the reader to verify that all the results in Sections 6.2 and 6.3 could be recast in terms of C-encodings rather than general encodings.

6.4 An Equivalence Relation on Computable Queries

The aim of this section is to add to our understanding of computable queries by investigating an equivalence relation on the set CQ of computable queries; two such queries are related if they are realised via the same Turing-computable mapping, say δ. In particular, we are interested in the cardinality of the equivalence class of a computable query, realised via δ and some encoding, with respect to the said equivalence relation; this equivalence class is denoted by Δ_δ. In the case when $|\Delta_\delta| = 0$, there is no computable query τ such that τ is realised via δ and some encoding. On the other hand, when $|\Delta_\delta| = 1$ and τ is realised via δ and all possible encodings in ENC, then τ corresponds to an encoding-independent computable query.

Definition 6.14 (Δ_δ)   Let $\delta \in$ TC. Then $\Delta_\delta = \{\tau \mid \exists \varrho \in$ ENC such that τ is realised via δ and $\varrho\}$. That is, Δ_δ is the set of all computable queries that are realised via δ and some encoding. ∎

The following theorem is proved using Rice's theorem (see Theorem 1.2 in Subsection 1.9.4 of Chapter 1).

Theorem 6.5   The two decision problems: is $|\Delta_\delta| = 0$? and is $|\Delta_\delta| = 1$? are undecidable.

Proof. On using Rice's theorem we need to show that the sets, CL_0 and CL_1, of Turing-computable mappings, δ, such that $|\Delta_\delta| = 0$ and $|\Delta_\delta| = 1$, respectively, are both nontrivial. That is, $CL_i \neq \emptyset$ and $CL_i \neq$ TC, for $i = 0, 1$. We prove the result by exhibiting $\delta_0, \delta_1 \in$ TC, such that $\delta_0 \in CL_0$ and $\delta_1 \in CL_1$.

Let δ_0 be a Turing-computable mapping that removes all the delimiters in the fixed set $\{[,],(,),,\}$ from its input and then halts. It can easily be verified that $|\Delta_{\delta_0}| = 0$, since $\forall \varrho \in$ ENC, $\varrho^{-1}\delta_0\varrho$ is not in RECS.

Let δ_1 be a Turing-computable mapping that returns [[]] (i.e. it returns the string representing the singleton containing the empty record) if its input is an encoding of a set containing an even number of records, and returns [] (i.e. it returns the string representing the empty set of records) otherwise. (We could have also chosen the Turing-computable mapping that realises query (4), (5) or (6) from Example 6.3 to be δ_1.) It can easily be verified that $|\Delta_{\delta_1}| = 1$. ☐

The following theorem shows that either $|\Delta_\delta| = 0$ or $|\Delta_\delta| = 1$ or $|\Delta_\delta| = \omega$ recalling that ω is the set of all natural numbers. Our interpretation of this interesting result is that it is not possible to obtain a finer partition of the class of computable queries with respect to the Turing-computable mappings that realise them, without putting restrictions on the set of encodings.

Theorem 6.6   If $|\Delta_\delta| > 1$, then $|\Delta_\delta| = \omega$.

Proof. Suppose that $|\Delta_\delta| = n$, where $n > 1$, with $n \in \omega$. Then $\exists \varrho_1, \varrho_2, \ldots, \varrho_n \in \mathrm{ENC}$ such that τ_i is realised via δ and ϱ_i and $\forall i, j \in \{1, 2, \ldots, n\}$, $\tau_i \neq \tau_j$. In order to obtain a contradiction to $|\Delta_\delta| = n$, we use a diagonalisation argument to construct a computable query $\tau_{n+1} \in \Delta_\delta$ such that $\forall i \in \{1, 2, \ldots, n\}$, $\tau_{n+1} \neq \tau_i$.

By our assumption that $|\Delta_\delta| = n$, $\exists S_1, S_2, \ldots, S_{n-1} \in \mathrm{RECS}$ such that $\forall i \in \{1, 2, \ldots, n-1\}$, $\tau_i(S_i) \neq \tau_{i+1}(S_i)$. Without loss of generality let $S_n \in \mathrm{RECS}$ be a database of records that satisfies $\varrho_1(S_1) = \varrho_1(S_n)$ and $\varrho_2(S_1) = \varrho_2(S_n)$.

We construct an encoding $\varrho_{n+1} \in \mathrm{ENC}$ such that τ_{n+1} is realised via δ and ϱ_{n+1} as follows. Assume without loss of generality that $\forall i \in \{1, 2, \ldots, n-1\}$, $\varrho_{n+1}(S_i) = \varrho_i(S_i)$, and $\varrho_{n+1}(S_n) = \varrho_2(S_n)$. The result that $\forall i \in \{1, 2, \ldots, n\}$, $\tau_{n+1} \neq \tau_i$ then follows. $\square$

6.5   Computational Query Completeness

We would like to utilise our notion of a computable database query to design expressive query languages. Relational completeness of a query language is only a minimal requirement for such a language, since there are many useful computable queries such as transitive closure and counting the number of tuples in a relation which are not expressible in the relational algebra. (See Definition 3.21 of relational completeness in Subsection 3.2.1 of Chapter 3.) We will further discuss the expressive power of the relational algebra in Section 6.6.

The set of all computable queries, CQ, is too expressive as a measure of the expressiveness of a database query language (or simply a query language), since databases are unordered collections of objects. Thus we should require all expressible queries to be at least order-independent. The class of order-independent computable queries, OI, may also be considered to be overly expressive, since it requires fixing a naming function. On the other hand, the class of encoding-independent computable queries, EI, is not expressive enough, since in practice the user would like to be able to refer to attributes and values which are present in the database. Therefore, we use the notion of C-encoding-independent queries as a measure of the computational completeness of a query language.

Definition 6.15 (Computational query completeness)   A database query language is *computationally query complete* (or simply *query complete*) if it expresses exactly the union of all the classes, C-EI, of all C-encoding-independent computable queries, for some finite set C of attribute names and domain values.

When C is restricted to be a finite set of attribute names only (i.e. C does not include domain values) then we say that the query language is *computationally attribute query complete* (or simply *attribute query complete*).   ∎

In the above definition if we require that C = ∅, then a query language is query complete if it expresses exactly the class, EI, of all encoding-independent computable queries.

In the following let us disregard the differences between relational databases and databases of records recalling that every relational database can be translated into a database of records and vice versa. When a query language is attribute query complete the user can explicitly refer to attribute names in queries. Therefore in this case, without any loss of generality, the naming function used to encode a database can always encode a finite set, $\{A_1, A_2, \ldots, A_m\}$, of attribute names as the finite set of natural numbers, $\{1, 2, \ldots, m\}$, and the ordering function used to encode a database can always order the pair (i, v_i) before the pair (j, v_i) if and only if $i < j$. (See Table 6.6 for such an encoding.) This technicality is useful, since it allows us to view X-records as tuples over a relation schema R, with schema(R) = X. (Recall from Definition 3.3 in Section 3.1 of Chapter 3 that attribute names can be referred to in the fixed order induced by the mapping, att.)

We now describe the query language QL [CH80], where d over **R** is taken to be the input database to a QL program (recall from Definition 3.9 in Section 3.1 of Chapter 3 that ADOM(d) is the active domain of d).

Definition 6.16 (The syntax of QL)   The syntax of QL is defined as follows:

- $\{y_1, y_2, \ldots\}$ is a countable set of *generic variables*.

- The set of *terms* in QL is defined inductively as follows:

    1) The equality relation **E**, a relation rel_i and a generic variable y_i, with i ≥ 1, are terms.

    2) $(e_1 \cap e_2)$, $(\neg e)$, $(e \uparrow)$, $(e \downarrow)$ and $(e \sim)$ are terms, where e, e_1 and e_2 are terms.

- The set of *programs* in QL is defined inductively as follows:

    1) $y_i \leftarrow e$ is a program, where y_i is a generic variable and e is a term.

    2) $(P_1; P_2)$ and **while** $y_i = \emptyset$ **do** P, are programs, where y_i is a generic variable and P, P_1 and P_2 are programs. ∎

Prior to giving the formal semantics of QL programs we give informal descriptions of the operators of QL which appear in the definition of the set of terms:

1) $\cap$ is the intersection operator.

2) $\neg$ is the complementation operator.

3) $\uparrow$ is the extension operator, which extends a relation with an additional column.

4) $\downarrow$ is the projection operator, which projects out the first column of a relation.

5) $\sim$ is the permutation operator, which exchanges the values in the last two columns of a relation.

Definition 6.17 (The semantics of QL)   The semantics of terms are defined as follows:

- $E = \{(v, v) \mid v \in ADOM(d)\}$ is the equality relation.

- rel_i is the relation r_i over a relation schema R_i, if the input database d contains a relation r_i over R_i, otherwise rel_i is the empty set over the relation schema with the empty set of attributes.

- The value of a generic variable y_i is a relation; y_i is initialised to be the empty set over the relation schema with the empty set of attributes. The relation schema of the value of y_i may change during the computation of a QL program.

- Let the value of e be a relation r over R, with type(R) = m, the value of e_1 be a relation r_1 over R_1 and the value of e_2 be a relation r_2 over R_2.

    - If $R_1 = R_2$, then the value of $(e_1 \cap e_2)$ is $r_1 \cap r_2$, otherwise it is the empty set over the relation schema with the empty set of attributes.

    - The value of $(\neg e)$ is $s - r$, where s is the Cartesian product of ADOM(d) with itself m times.

    - The value of $(e \uparrow)$ is the relation $\{<v_1, v_2, \ldots, v_m, v> \mid <v_1, v_2, \ldots, v_m> \in r$ and $v \in ADOM(d)\}$.

    - The value of $(e \downarrow)$ is the relation $\{<v_2, v_3, \ldots, v_m> \mid <v_1, v_2, \ldots, v_m> \in r\}$ if $m \geq 1$, otherwise the value of $(e \downarrow)$ is defined to be the empty relation.

    - The value of $(e \sim)$ is the relation $\{<v_1, v_2, \ldots, v_m, v_{m-1}> \mid <v_1, v_2, \ldots, v_{m-1}, v_m> \in r\}$ if type(R) = $m > 1$, otherwise the value of $(e \sim)$ is r.

The semantics of QL programs are defined as follows:

- The value of $y_i \leftarrow e$ is the result of assigning the value of e to y_i.

- The value of $(P_1; P_2)$ is the result of sequentially composing P_1 and P_2; we omit parentheses whenever no ambiguity arises.

- The value of **while** $y_i = \emptyset$ **do** P is the result of iterating P while the value of y_i is equal to the empty set; if the while loop terminates, then the value of the program P is the value of y_i, otherwise it is undefined.   ∎

The proof of the next theorem can be found in [CH80].

Theorem 6.7   The query language QL is attribute query complete.   □

Using the extension and projection operators we can simulate counting in QL as follows. The term, $((E \downarrow) \downarrow)$, whose value is equal to $\{<>\}$ represents the natural number zero. Let $<i>$ be the representation of the natural number i. Then adding one to $<i>$ is given by $<i> \uparrow$. Similarly, subtracting one from $<i>$ is given by $<i> \downarrow$.

We next give some examples of QL programs.

Example 6.5 Let e_1 and e_2 be terms, where the value of e_1 is a relation r_1 over R_1 and the value of e_2 is a relation r_2 over R_2. If $R_1 = R_2$, then the union of e_1 and e_2, denoted by $e_1 \cup e_2$, is defined by

$$(e_1 \cup e_2) = \neg((\neg e_1) \cap (\neg e_2)).$$

Assume that P_1 and P_2 are programs and that y_1 and y_2 are generic variables that do not appear in P_1 or in P_2. The following program gives the expected semantics to the statement, **if** $y_i = \emptyset$ **then** P_1 **else** P_2:

$$y_1 \leftarrow y_i;$$
$$y_2 \leftarrow (((\mathbf{E} \downarrow) \downarrow) \downarrow);$$
$$\textbf{while } y_1 = \emptyset \textbf{ do } (P_1 ; y_1 \leftarrow \mathbf{E}; \ y_2 \leftarrow \mathbf{E});$$
$$\textbf{while } y_2 = \emptyset \textbf{ do } (P_2 ; y_2 \leftarrow \mathbf{E}).$$

We observe that $(((\mathbf{E} \downarrow) \downarrow) \downarrow) = \emptyset$. Using the above semantics of an if statement we can simulate iterating a program P while $y_i \neq \emptyset$ with the following QL program, where y_1 is a generic variable that does not appear in P:

$$\textbf{if } y_i = \emptyset \textbf{ then } y_1 \leftarrow \mathbf{E} \textbf{ else } y_1 \leftarrow (((\mathbf{E} \downarrow) \downarrow) \downarrow);$$
$$\textbf{while } y_1 = \emptyset \textbf{ do } (P ; \textbf{if } y_i = \emptyset \textbf{ then } y_1 \leftarrow \mathbf{E} \textbf{ else } y_1 \leftarrow (((\mathbf{E} \downarrow) \downarrow) \downarrow)). \qquad \blacksquare$$

Another example of an abstract query language which was shown to be attribute query complete is the *generic machine* [AV91b]. The generic machine is based on extending the relational algebra with Turing-machine capability. An example of a query language which was shown to be query complete is detDL (deterministic transformation language) [AV90]. Finally, another example of a query language which was also shown to be query complete is an extension of Datalog presented in [AV91a], which allows the heads of rules to be negative literals.

An important difference between the semantics of QL and detDL is in the way these query languages simulate counting. As we have seen above QL simulates counting by using the extension operator ($\uparrow$) in order to simulate addition and the projection operator ($\downarrow$) in order to simulate subtraction. On the other hand, detDL simulates counting by generating (or inventing) new values, not in the active domain of the input database, by using a construct called **with new**. The invented values are generated nondeterministically. Furthermore, the invented values are not allowed to appear in the result of a query ensuring that the result of the query is deterministic.

A distinguished value, say v_0, is chosen to represent the natural number zero and another distinguished value, say $v_\star$, is chosen as a placeholder which allows detDL to determine how many natural numbers have already been generated. At any stage during the execution of a detDL program a finite sequence of values, $v_0, v_1, \ldots, v_n$, have already been generated representing the natural numbers $\{0, 1, \ldots, n\}$. In order to indicate the linear ordering $v_0 < v_1 < \ldots < v_n$, these values are stored in a binary relation, r_ω, over a relation schema R_ω, with $\text{schema}(R_\omega) = \{N_1, N_2\}$. The relation r_ω is shown in Table 6.7. Whenever addition is performed on the value, v_n, such that $<v_n, v_\star> \in r_\omega$, then a new value, v_{n+1}, is generated, and r_ω is replaced by $r_\omega - \{<v_n, v_\star>\} \cup \{<v_n, v_{n+1}>, <v_{n+1}, v_\star>\}$.

Table 6.7 The relation r_ω

N_1	N_2
v_0	v_1
v_1	v_2
...	...
v_{n-1}	v_n
v_n	$v_\star$

6.6   The Expressive Power of the Relational Algebra

Let us assume that the relational algebra includes only the basic set of relational operators, that is, union, difference, projection, selection, natural join and renaming. In selection we allow only simple selection formulae of the form A = B, where A and B are attributes. The reader can verify that all queries of the relational algebra are C-encoding-independent computable queries for some finite set C of attributes. As we have already mentioned in Subsection 3.2.1 of Chapter 3 the relational algebra cannot express the transitive closure operation, which is a C-encoding-independent computable query. Furthermore, the relational algebra cannot count the number of tuples in a relation or determine whether the number of tuples in a relation is even or odd; both these queries are encoding-independent computable queries. It therefore follows that the relational algebra is not an attribute complete query language. The fundamental reason for the limited expressiveness of the relational algebra is its lack of a looping mechanism (such as a while loop or a recursion facility) and its inability to simulate counting. Still, the relational algebra has become an important yardstick for measuring the expressiveness of a query language. Thus it is important to pinpoint the expressive power of the relational algebra, which is the objective of this section. In particular, we give a characterisation of the set of relations that can be computed as answers to a relational algebra query with respect to an input database.

Let d be a database over the database schema **R**, let E be a relational algebra expression (or equivalently, a relational algebra query) over the database schema **R** and let $E(d)$ be the answer to E with respect to d (see Definition 3.20 in Subsection 3.2.1 of Chapter 3). We now define the *basic information* of a database to be the set of all relations that can be obtained by a relational algebra query over that database.

Definition 6.18 (The basic information of a database)   The *basic information* of a database d over **R**, denoted by $BI(d)$, is the set of all relations, r, for which there exists a relational algebra expression E such that $E(d) = r$.   ∎

Thus the basic information of d measures the expressive power of the relational algebra with respect to a database d. The operators of the relational algebra (as restricted at the beginning of this section) do not reference explicitly the values in the database, but rather only equality or inequality of values is expressed in relational algebra queries. This motivates us to investigate the connection between the basic information of a database and the mappings from values in the active domain of the database to themselves that leave the database unchanged. Such a mapping that leaves the database unchanged is called an *automorphism* of the database and the set of all automorphisms of a database is called the *cogroup* of the database.

Definition 6.19 (An automorphism of a database)   Let $d = \{r_1, r_2, \ldots, r_n\}$ be a database over R, $r = \{t_1, t_2, \ldots, t_k\}$ be a relation over R ∈ **R** and $t = <v_1, v_2, \ldots, v_m>$ be a tuple in r. An *automorphism* of d is a one-to-one mapping, φ, from V onto V, where V ⊆ $\mathcal{D}$ is a set of domain values, extended to tuples, t, relations, r, and databases, d, as follows:

- $\varphi(t) = \varphi(<v_1, v_2, \ldots, v_m>) = <\varphi(v_1), \varphi(v_2), \ldots, \varphi(v_m)>$.

- $\varphi(r) = \varphi(\{t_1, t_2, \ldots, t_k\}) = \{\varphi(t_1), \varphi(t_2), \ldots, \varphi(t_k)\}$.

- $\varphi(d) = \varphi(\{r_1, r_2, \ldots, r_n\}) = \{\varphi(r_1), \varphi(r_2), \ldots, \varphi(r_n)\}$. ■

Definition 6.20 (The cogroup of a database)   The *cogroup* of a database, d, denoted by CG(d), is the set of all automorphisms of d. ■

The next definition shows how the cogroup of a database can be represented by a relation.

Definition 6.21 (The cogroup relation of a database)   The cogroup of a database, d, can be expressed as a relation, r, over a relation schema R, called the *cogroup relation* of d as follows:

- $|\text{schema}(R)| = |\text{ADOM}(d)| = |\{v_1, v_2, \ldots, v_q\}|$, and

- $<\varphi(v_1), \varphi(v_2), \ldots \varphi(v_q)> \in r$ if and only if $\varphi \in$ CG(d). ■

From now on, for simplicity, we will not distinguish between the cogroup of a database, d, and its cogroup relation; we will denote both by CG(d). Observe that the cogroup relation of d is uniquely defined up to the linear order imposed on ADOM(d) and the attribute names of its database schema.

Example 6.6   The cogroup relation, CG(d), of a database $d = \{r\}$, where the relation r is shown in Table 6.8, is shown in Table 6.9. The latter relation is obtained by applying Algorithm 6.1 to r. ■

Table 6.8 The relation r

EMP	SEC	MGR
John	Jane	John
Jeff	John	Jenny
John	Jill	John
Jenny	John	Jeff

Table 6.9 The cogroup relation of $\{r\}$

A	B	C	D	E
John	Jeff	Jenny	Jane	Jill
John	Jenny	Jeff	Jane	Jill
John	Jeff	Jenny	Jill	Jane
John	Jenny	Jeff	Jill	Jane

We can now prove that the cogroup relation of d is included in the basic information of d.

Lemma 6.8 $CG(d) \in BI(d)$.

Proof. We prove the result when $d = \{r\}$ is a singleton; we leave it to the reader to generalise the result when d may contain more than one relation by constructing a database with a single relation resulting from taking the Cartesian product of all the relations in the database.

Assume that r is a relation over R with $|\text{schema}(R)| = m$, $|r| = k$ and $|ADOM(r)| = q$. The pseudo-code of an algorithm, designated CONSTRUCT_CG(r), which returns the unique cogroup relation of d (up to a permutation of its attribute names) over a relation schema, whose cardinality is q, is presented in the following algorithm. The reader can verify that CONSTRUCT_CG(r) returns a relational algebra expression whose answer with respect to $\{r\}$ is the cogroup relation $CG(\{r\})$ of r.

Algorithm 6.1 (CONSTRUCT_CG(r))
1.   **begin**
2. $r^k := \rho_{A_m \to B_m}(\ldots (\rho_{A_1 \to B_1}(r))\ldots) \times \cdots \times \rho_{A_m \to B_{km}}(\ldots (\rho_{A_1 \to B_{km-m+1}}(r))\ldots)$;
3. $t :=$ the tuple in r^k that is the concatenation of all the tuples in r;
4. $E^{cg} := r^k$;
5.   **for each** $i \in \{1, 2, \ldots, mk - 1\}$ **do**
6.   **for each** $j \in \{i + 1, i + 2, \ldots, mk\}$ **do**
7.   **if** $t[B_j] = t[B_i]$ **then**
8. $E^{cg} := \sigma_{B_i = B_j}(E^{cg})$;
9.   **else**
10. $E^{cg} := \sigma_{B_i \neq B_j}(E^{cg})$;
11.   **end if**
12.   **end for**
13.   **end for**
14.   X := a set of q attributes such that $\exists t \in E^{cg}$ with $\bigcup_{B_i \in X} t[B_i] = ADOM(r)$;
15. $E^{cq} := \pi_X(E^{cg})$;
16.   **return** E^{cg};
17. **end.**   □

Theorem 6.9 $r \in BI(d)$ if and only if $ADOM(r) \subseteq ADOM(d)$ and $CG(d) \subseteq CG(\{r\})$.

Proof. We only sketch the proof.

If. Suppose that $ADOM(r) \subseteq ADOM(d)$ and $CG(d) \subseteq CG(\{r\})$. We then need to show that $r = E(d)$ for some relational algebra expression E. Let t be a tuple in r and let R be the relation schema of r. We know by Lemma 6.8 that $CG(d) \in BI(d)$. Furthermore, for all attributes A $\in \text{schema}(R)$, $t[A]$ is a value in each tuple of $CG(d)$. Thus t is a member of the answer to a relational algebra expression, say E_t, with respect to $CG(d)$. The expression E_t is composed of a Cartesian product for each repeated value in t, appropriate renamings so that the schema of the output corresponds to R and a projection onto the set of attributes schema(R). All the tuples in $E_t(CG(d))$ are of the form $\varphi(t)$, where $\varphi \in CG(d) \subseteq CG(\{r\})$ and thus all the tuples in

$E_t(CG(d))$ are members of r. Thus on letting E be the relational expression $\cup_{t \in r} E_t$, it follows that $E(d) = r$ as required.

Only if. If $r \in BI(d)$, then by Definition 6.18 $r = E(d)$ for some relational algebra expression E. The result that $ADOM(r) \subseteq ADOM(d)$ and $CG(d) \subseteq CG(\{r\})$ follows by induction on the number of relational algebra operators appearing in E. $\square$

The above theorem was first proved in [Ban78, Par78]; a full proof can also be found in [AD93]. An alternative representation of the cogroup relation as a nested relation can be found in [AGV89].

6.7 Adding a Looping Mechanism to the Relational Algebra

The reason that the relational algebra is not expressive enough to express transitive closure queries is its lack of a looping mechanism. One possible extension suggested in [AU79] is to add a *fixpoint operator* to the relational algebra. The fixpoint operates on a relational algebra query, Q, with respect to a database d, by iterating Q with respect to d until no changes occur in the result of the query Q. More formally, we define the result of the fixpoint of Q with respect to d, denoted by $FIX(Q(d))$, by using the auxiliary query Q_i, where $i \geq 0$ is a natural number, as follows:

1) $Q_0(d) = Q(d)$,

2) $Q_{i+1}(d) = Q_i(d) \cup Q(Q_i(d))$; and

3) $FIX(Q(d)) = Q_k(d)$, where $k \geq 0$ is the least natural number such that $Q_k(d) = Q_{k+1}(d)$.

A query of the form $FIX(Q(d))$ is called a *fixpoint query*. We observe that fixpoint queries as we have defined them are *inflationary*, since the intermediate results Q_i are increasing for $i \geq 0$. We show that the cardinality of $FIX(Q(d))$ is polynomial in the size of the input database, d. Let s be the size of d, i.e. the number of symbols needed to encode d, and let m be the number of attributes in the schema of the relation resulting from answering the query. Then $|FIX(Q(d))| \leq s^m$, which is polynomial in the size of the input database.

Let ARC be a binary relation representing the arcs of a digraph. Then the following fixpoint query computes the transitive closure of the digraph:

$$FIX(ARC \cup (\pi_{\{A,B\}}(\rho_{B \to C}(ARC) \bowtie \rho_{A \to C}(ARC)))).$$

Instead of incorporating the fixpoint operator into the relational algebra, it has been suggested that we add an explicit looping mechanism to the algebra such as the while loop of the query language, QL. Such a while loop is *unbounded*, since it is not guaranteed to terminate, resulting in polynomial space computations in the size of the input database. In order to bound the number of iterations of a loop by a polynomial in the size of the input database, a *bounded* looping mechanism can be added to the relational algebra. Adding a bounded looping mechanism, such as the for loop introduced below, provides us with a query language of intermediate expressive power between the relational algebra augmented with the fixpoint operator and QL.

Definition 6.22 (For loop)   Let y_i be a generic variable and P be a QL program. Then the construct

$$\text{for } y_i \text{ do } P,$$

called a *for loop*, is also a QL program.

The semantics of the for loop are defined as follows, where r_i is the value of y_i:

- The program P is executed n times, where n is the cardinality of r_i upon entry to the for loop; when the for loop terminates the value of P is the value of y_i.   ■

We leave it to the reader to verify that the for loop does not add any expressive power to QL, since it can be simulated in QL by a while loop that counts the number of times the for loop is executed and exits the while loop after a specified number of iterations. On the other hand, if we replace the while loop in QL by the for loop, then QL would not be an attribute query complete database query language, since intuitively QL's computations may be unbounded and nonterminating, as opposed to the computations of the for loop restriction of QL which are always bounded and terminating. More precisely it can be shown that the for loop restriction of QL computes exactly the set of primitive recursive queries (see Subsection 1.9.4), which are a proper subset of the set of computable queries [Cha81].

For the purpose of extending the relational algebra with a for loop mechanism we will restrict QL as follows.

Definition 6.23 (ForQL)   A variable is *typed* if the similarity type of its relation schema is fixed and cannot change during the computation of a program. If a typed variable is assigned a relation over a relation schema with a different similarity type then the empty set is assigned to this variable.

ForQL is the query language which restricts QL by assuming that all variables are typed, that the terms of the language are relational algebra expressions (as defined at the beginning of Section 6.6) and that instead of the while loop we have the for loop **for** y_i **do** P, where y_i is a typed variable.   ■

By a similar argument to the fixpoint, it can now be shown that the time complexity of ForQL programs is bounded by a polynomial in the size of the input database. We note that if we lift the restriction that variables be typed, then we cannot, in general, bound the time complexity of such QL programs to a polynomial in the size of the input database, since a nested for loop which uses the same generic variable can lead to a computation which is exponential in the size of the input database.

Assume that r is a relation over R, with schema(R) = {A,B} and that the input database to the next QL program is $d = \{r\}$, i.e. that the value of *rel* in the QL program is r. Also, assume that the schema of the equality relation E is R. The following ForQL program uses a for loop in order to compute the transitive closure of r:

$$y \leftarrow \pi_A(\mathbf{E}) \times \pi_B(\mathbf{E});$$
$$y_1 \leftarrow rel;$$
for y **do**
$$(y_2 \leftarrow y_1 \cup (\pi_{\{A,B\}}(\rho_{B \rightarrow C}(y_1) \bowtie \rho_{A \rightarrow C}(rel))));$$
$$y_1 \leftarrow y_2;$$
$$y \leftarrow y_1).$$

The next ForQL program shows that by using a for loop it is possible to test whether the cardinality of a relation is even. In the ForQL program we assume that $\pi_A(\mathbf{E})$ represents logical truth and $\emptyset$ represents logical falsity:

$$y \leftarrow rel;$$
$$y_1 \leftarrow \pi_A(\mathbf{E});$$
for y **do** $y_1 \leftarrow (\neg y_1).$

When the above program terminates, y_1 is nonempty, i.e. it represents logical truth, if and only if $|r|$ is even. In [CH82] it was shown that testing whether the cardinality of a relation is even cannot be expressed by the relational algebra augmented with the fixpoint operator. It follows that adding a bounded looping mechanism to the relational algebra results in a query language that is strictly more expressive than the language resulting from adding the fixpoint operator to the relational algebra. Still, some natural queries such as checking whether two relations r_1 and r_2 have equal cardinality, i.e. checking whether $|r_1| = |r_2|$, cannot be expressed in ForQL, i.e. it cannot be expressed by the relational algebra augmented with a bounded looping mechanism [Cha88].

In [AV91a] it was shown that Datalog, whose programs may be recursive and contain rules having negative literals in their body (see Subsection 3.2.3 of Chapter 3), is equivalent to the relational algebra augmented with a fixpoint operator, in the sense that they both express exactly the same set of computable queries. This set of computable queries is a proper subset of the set of all polynomial-time computable queries, since as noted above determining whether the cardinality of a relation is even is not amongst such queries.

Definition 6.24 (Ordered relational database)   A relational database d over $\mathbf{R}$ is an *ordered relational database* (or simply an *ordered database*) if $\mathbf{R}$ contains a designated binary relation schema, SUCC, such that the relation r in d over SUCC defines a linear ordering on the set of active domain values, ADOM(d). ∎

We observe that SUCC is isomorphic to a finite fragment of the successor relation on the natural numbers. We further note that an ordered database induces a lexicographical ordering on the tuples of each relation in d. The next fundamental theorem, which characterises the computational expressiveness over ordered databases of the relational algebra augmented with a fixpoint operator, was shown in [Var82a, Imm86] (see also [AHV95b, Chapter 17]).

Theorem 6.10   Over ordered databases, the relational algebra augmented with a fixpoint operator expresses exactly the set of all polynomial-time computable queries.

Proof. We briefly sketch the proof leaving the reader to consult the above references for the full proof. We have already shown that the algebra augmented with a fixpoint can only express computable queries which can be evaluated in polynomial time in the size of the input database, so it suffices to show that it can express all such computable queries.

Let Q be a polynomial-time computable query. The idea is to simulate the Turing machine TM that computes Q with a fixpoint query. Firstly, we can encode TM's input tape by utilising the lexicographical ordering of the tuples of the relations in *d*. Secondly, we can encode an instantaneous description of TM, after the *i*th computation step, by using the lexicographical ordering to encode *i* and by having distinguished attributes whose values encode the current state of TM's finite state control and the current position of its head. The next move function can then be encoded via an algebraic expression, which given the current state and position of the finite state control performs the next computation step of TM. That is, the currently scanned symbol is overwritten, the head of the finite state control moves either left (add one) or right (subtract one) and a transition of state is effected. We assume that TM halts if and only if no more state transitions can be effected or the maximum number of computation steps has been performed. Thus the fixpoint operator is needed in order to repeat the next move function until TM halts.   □

The next corollary follows from the previous theorem and the fact that Datalog, whose programs may be recursive and contain rules having negative literals in their body (see Subsection 3.2.3 of Chapter 3), is equivalent to the relational algebra with a fixpoint and less expressive than the relational algebra with bounded looping; we note that these three query languages can only compute queries whose time complexity is polynomial in the size of the input database.

Corollary 6.11   Over ordered databases, the relational algebra augmented with a fixpoint operator, the relational algebra augmented with a bounded for loop mechanism and Datalog are all equivalent and express exactly the set of all polynomial-time computable queries.   □

As mentioned prior to Definition 6.22 augmenting the relational algebra with a while loop as in QL results in polynomial space computations in the size of the input database. For the purpose of extending the relational algebra with a while loop mechanism, we will restrict QL to allow only typed variables as follows.

Definition 6.25 (WhileQL)   WhileQL is the query language which restricts QL by assuming that all variables are typed, and that the terms of the language are relational algebra expressions (as defined at the beginning of Section 6.6).   ■

Thus WhileQL is the query language resulting from restricting QL in the same manner as the query language ForQL given in Definition 6.23, apart from maintaining the while loop, **while** $y_i = \emptyset$ **do** P, rather than swapping it with a for loop as in ForQL. It can be shown that WhileQL's computational power is included in the set of polynomial space queries [CH82]. (See PSPACE in Subsection 1.9.4 of Chapter 1.) This inclusion is proper, since, for example, WhileQL is not expressive enough to determine whether the cardinality of a relation is even or odd. Moreover, it can be shown that over ordered relational databases WhileQL expresses exactly the set of all polynomial space queries [Var82a].

WhileQL can be further extended with integer arithmetic by augmenting it with the following constructs:

- A countable set $\{c_1, c_2, \ldots\}$ of *counter* variables distinct from typed variables, whose values are natural numbers.

- Assignment statements of the form $c_i \leftarrow c_i + 1$ and $c_i \leftarrow c_i - 1$, which increment and decrement a counter variable c_i, assuming that counter variables are initialised to 0. We assume that if c_i has the value 0, then $c_i \leftarrow c_i - 1$ leaves c_i unchanged.

- Tests of the form **while** $c_i = 0$ **do** P, which terminate when the counter variable c_i has a value other than 0.

Let us call the extension of WhileQL with integer arithmetic as defined above WhileInt. The query language WhileInt is still not attribute query complete, since it still cannot determine whether the cardinality of a relation is even or odd. It can be viewed as providing an interface between a Turing-complete programming language and a first-order query language such as SQL, where SQL statements can be embedded in the statements of the programming language. (See also the recent *Java Database Connectivity* (JDBC) approach for executing SQL statements from within a Java program [HCF97].) It is evident that the expressive power of WhileInt properly includes that of WhileQL, since the ability to manipulate counters gives Turing-machine capability to the language (see Subsection 1.9.4 of Chapter 1) and thus over ordered relational databases WhileInt is attribute query complete.

The class of computable queries that can be expressed by the query language WhileInt is robust as can be seen by its equivalence to the class of computable queries expressed by two other query languages, which we now briefly describe [AV93].

The first query language is called a *relational machine*. Such a machine consists of a Turing machine and a relational store which holds a finite set of relations over a fixed set of relation schemas partitioned into input relations and output relations. The tape of the Turing machine is initially empty. The head of the relational machine can move left and right and can write on the tape in accordance with the state transitions of a standard Turing machine transition function with the following extensions. The machine can check whether the input relations in the relational store satisfy a relational algebra query, i.e. return a nonempty result, and the machine can also assign to an output relation in the relational store the result of computing a relational algebra query on the input relations in this store. In both cases the number of typed variables in any relational algebra query is bounded by some constant. The relational machine accepts its input relations if and only if it reaches its halting state. Its output can then be found in the output relations in the store.

The second query language is an effective fragment of the *infinitary logic* $L^\omega_{\infty\omega}$. The first subscript indicates that conjunctions and disjunctions can be taken over arbitrary, possibly infinite, sets of formulae and the second subscript indicates that only finite quantifier blocks are allowed. The superscript indicates that every formula can only have a finite number k of variables, for some natural number k, with $k \geq 1$.

The formulae of the infinitary logic $L^k_{\infty\omega}$ over a database schema **R** constitute the smallest set of formulae containing relational algebra expressions over **R** having at most k typed variables and closed under the usual logical connectives and quantifiers of first-order logic and, in addition, are closed under conjunction and disjunction of arbitrary sets of formulae. That is, in the infinitary logic $L_{\infty\omega}^k$ the disjunction $\bigvee \Phi$ and the conjunction $\bigwedge \Phi$, where Φ is a set containing an infinite number of formulae, are both well defined. The semantics of the logical connectives including arbitrary conjunctions and disjunctions are the standard ones.

We can now define the formulae of the infinitary logic over a database schema $\mathbf{R}$ by

$$L_{\infty\omega}^\omega = \bigcup_{k=1}^\infty L_{\infty\omega}^k.$$

For more details on the model theory of infinitary logic see [BF85] and for recent research on infinitary logic in finite model theory see [KV92a, KV92b, AVV95, DLW95].

In order to define the effective fragment of the above infinitary logic, we say that a set S of databases over $\mathbf{R}$ is *recursively enumerable* if there exists a recursive enumeration $d_1, d_2, \ldots$ of all databases over $\mathbf{R}$ such that a database d is in S if and only if there is some database which is isomorphic to d and belongs to the enumeration. (See Subsection 1.9.4 of Chapter 1 for an overview of recursively enumerable languages or sets.)

The *effective fragment* of infinitary logic is now defined as the set of formulae in $L_{\infty\omega}^\omega$ whose set of finite models is recursively enumerable. The proof of the next theorem can be found in [AVV95].

Theorem 6.12 The following three query languages express the same class of computable queries over a database schema $\mathbf{R}$:

1) WhileInt.

2) Relational machines.

3) Effective fragment of infinitary logic.

Proof. We only sketch the proof.

The equivalence of (1) and (2) follows from the equivalence between Turing machines and counter machines (see Subsection 1.9.4 of Chapter 1).

To show that part (2) implies part (3), let S be the set of all databases over $\mathbf{R}$ that are accepted by some relational machine M and let $d \in S$. Intuitively, a computation of M that accepts d can be described by a formula in $L_{\infty\omega}^k$ for some natural number k, due to the way in which a relational machine interfaces with the relational algebra. It follows that the set of databases S that are accepted by M can be described by a formula in the effective fragment of infinitary logic, which is a countably infinite disjunction of a recursive set of formulae in $L_{\infty\omega}^k$.

Finally, to show that part (3) implies part (2) suppose that φ is a formula over $\mathbf{R}$ in the effective fragment of infinitary logic. It can be shown that given a relational database d over $\mathbf{R}$, there exists an ordered relational database d' over a database schema $\mathbf{R}'$ and a formula ψ over $\mathbf{R}'$ in the effective fragment of infinitary logic such that d is a model of φ if and only if d' is a model of ψ. We can now use this fact to encode d' on the tape of a relational machine M. The relational machine M utilises its Turing-machine capability to accept d', if and only if d' is a model of ψ, by a recursive enumeration of those databases over $\mathbf{R}'$ which are models of ψ. $\square$

6.8 Discussion

In this chapter we have introduced and developed the fundamental concept of a computable database query, which does not feature prominently in most of the current textbooks on database theory. Although the development is theoretical in nature, the subclass of computable queries implemented has an effect on the degree of portability of the database, in the sense that two queries may yield the same result on different machines if and only if they are C-encoding-independent. The notion of encoding-independence is thus strongly related to the notion of physical data independence, which is one of the fundamental reasons that relational databases are successful in practice. In addition, we have presented the concept of a database language which is *query complete*; such a language allows for both attribute names and domain values to be mentioned in queries. This concept refines the notion of *attribute query complete*, which allows only attribute names to be mentioned in queries.

The notion of computable queries has interested database researchers since the beginning of the 1980's and provides a link between relational database theory and the theory of computing. It also provides a firm basis for developing database programming languages possessing greater computational expressive power than the relational algebra.

Pioneering work on the computational complexity of various query languages can be found in [Fag74, AU79, Cha81, Imm81, CH82, Var82a]. More recent research in this area can be found in [Imm86, BG87, Imm87, Cha88, Imm89, AV90, AV91a, AV91b, AV92, AV93, Fag93, AV95, AVV97].

6.9 Exercises

Exercise 6.1 SQL3 is the emerging standard, which is to replace SQL2 [DD93, Mel96] (see Subsection 3.2.2 of Chapter 3 and Section 10.2 of Chapter 10). One of the features of SQL3 is the addition of procedural constructs to SQL2 including assignment, conditional and looping statements. Thus SQL3 is computationally query complete. Argue for the usefulness of these features of SQL3 and its potential impact on database programming.

Exercise 6.2 Aggregate functions provide an important and useful extension to the basic operators of the relational algebra (see Definition 3.24 in Subsection 3.2.1 of Chapter 3). Suggest how such an extension affects the expressive power of the relational algebra [Klu82, AB95].

Exercise 6.3 It is a standard assumption in relational database theory that domain elements are taken to be unordered. In practice domain elements are defined to be either strings or numbers and thus tuples in relations have a natural lexicographical ordering that can be utilised by the DBMS. Argue whether it is reasonable for the DBMS to use such an ordering when processing queries and how such an ordering can be taken into account in the definition of a computable database query.

Exercise 6.4 Discuss, with a motivating example, the connection between physical data independence and encoding-independent computable queries.

Exercise 6.5   Recall Definition 6.25 of the query language WhileQL. WhileQL is the result of augmenting the relational algebra with an unbounded while loop mechanism as in QL, with the restriction on generic variables that they be typed. Prove that WhileQL cannot determine whether the cardinality of a relation is even or odd [CH82].

Exercise 6.6   Recall that the query language WhileInt extends the query language WhileQL with integer arithmetic. Prove that when all the relation schemas of relations in the input database to a WhileInt program are monadic, i.e. contain a single attribute, then the resulting program is equivalent to a relational algebra query [AV95].

Exercise 6.7   Discuss the significance of Theorem 6.10 and Corollary 6.11 in Section 6.7 with respect to the implementation of database programming languages.

Exercise 6.8   Suggest a parallel model of computation for relational algebra queries, where given an input database d, such a model has available a polynomial number of processors in the size of d in order to speed up the computation [Imm89].

Exercise 6.9   It has been suggested that it is useful to add to query languages an operator that selects a tuple from a relation at random. Discuss this suggestion with a concrete example [ASV90].

7. Temporal Relational Databases

The evolution of a relational database over time is not captured by the standard relational data model we have presented in the previous chapters. For example, the inventory of items in a warehouse changes over time as items are shifted from and to the warehouse, and the details of employees that work in a company change over time as the database is updated with new employees joining the company and old employees leaving the company. Many other scientific, financial and business applications have a substantial temporal element associated with them including applications that involve time series analysis. Although time can be modelled within the standard relational model, this cannot be done in a straightforward and unified manner, since there is no inherent support for temporal data. Thus due to the importance of recording and manipulating temporal information, there is a need for a cohesive and consistent extension of the standard relational model to handle such temporal data. The research into temporal databases has been an active subarea of relational database theory for well over a decade now. In order to merge and encompass the main proposals for temporal relational database query languages, there has been a recent comprehensive specification of a temporal extension of SQL, termed TSQL2. In this chapter we formalise a temporal extension of the relational model, which provides a basis for understanding the way in which time can be seamlessly incorporated into the data structures, the algebra and the fundamental integrity constraints of relational databases.

We now briefly outline the contents of the sections that follow. In Section 7.1 we provide motivation for modelling time in relations through an example. In Section 7.2 we provide a taxonomy of the various interpretations of time and introduce the notions of rollback and historical relations. In Section 7.3 we formalise the notion of a historical relation, which allows us to store the valid time history of tuples in relations. In Section 7.4 we extend the relational algebra so that it can manipulate historical relations and deal with time attribute values that are time intervals. In Section 7.5 we define the notion of historical completeness of a temporal extension of the relational algebra and state the result that the historical relational algebra presented in Section 7.4 is complete. In Section 7.6 we give a brief overview of TSQL2, and in Section 7.7 we extend the fundamental notion of a key so as to hold in historical relations. Finally, in Section 7.8 we briefly discuss the issue of schema evolution when, in addition to the database relations, the schema is also allowed to change over time.

7.1 The Importance of Modelling Time

Suppose that we are storing the information about the current salaries of employees in a relation r_0, over EMP_NOW, with schema(EMP_NOW) = {ENAME, SAL}, as it is shown in

Table 7.1. This relation does not supply us with any past information about employees' salaries or with any future information about these salaries. The relation r_0 provides us only with a *snapshot* of the information about employees' salaries, in particular only the present information is made available. Let us first concern ourselves with past (or historical) and present (or current) information, without referring to the future.

Table 7.1 The relation r_0 over EMP_NOW

ENAME	SAL
Reuven	25
Dan	11
Eli	20
Naomi	20

In order to store past or historical information about employees' salaries we could redesign the relation schema EMP_NOW and obtain a schema EMP, having the attributes of EMP_NOW and an additional attribute called DATE. A relation r_1 over EMP is shown in Table 7.2. Although this relation captures the historical information which is needed it is not sufficient unless direct support for time-based attribute domains is made available. Thus, for example, it is not possible to pose a query asking for the current salary of an employee unless the notion of "current time" is known to the database system. Also, queries such as: in the overlapping years of two employees' salary history, which one of them earned a higher salary and when, are awkward to pose in the relational algebra. Such queries view an employee's salary history as a set of intervals, where each interval such as [1992, 1993] records the years in which an employee earned a particular salary. The relational model does not support interval data; in fact, if we allow intervals into the model then relations would violate 1NF. Support for defining data types involving dates and times and for querying information over these types has been considered important enough for including DATE and TIME as built-in data types in the SQL2 standard (a detailed description of these features can be found in [DD93, Chapter 17]).

Table 7.2 The relation r_1 over EMP

ENAME	SAL	DATE
Reuven	22	1992
Reuven	22	1993
Reuven	25	1994
Dan	8	1991
Dan	8	1992
Dan	11	1994
Eli	20	1990
Eli	20	1993
Eli	20	1994
Naomi	18	1993
Naomi	20	1994

Now, suppose that we extend relation schemas to historical relation schemas so that such schemas contain a special historical attribute, denoted by $\mathcal{T}$, whose domain is interval-based. The semantics of the $\mathcal{T}$-values of a tuple over a historical relation schema are that this interval represents the time points (or dates) when this tuple was valid. A distinguished time point, denoted by *now*, represents the fact that the tuple is valid at the current time. A historical relation r_2 over EMP^H, with schema(EMP^H) = {ENAME, SAL, DATES_INT}, is shown in Table 7.3, where DATES_INT is a historical attribute. There are several advantages in the representation of the historical information in r_2 as opposed to the representation in r_1, shown in Table 7.2. Firstly, r_2 is less redundant than r_1, since the cardinality of r_1 is 11 while the cardinality of r_2 is only 8. Secondly, querying r_2 is easier than querying r_1 assuming that we extend the relational algebra with special purpose comparison operators to deal with intervals. Finally, the current time is made explicit by using the distinguished time point *now*. Thus r_2 need not be updated until a salary changes, while r_1 will have to be updated in 1995 even if all the salaries remain the same.

Table 7.3 The historical relation r_2 over EMP^H

ENAME	SAL	DATES_INT
Reuven	22	[1992, 1993]
Reuven	25	[1994, *now*]
Dan	8	[1991, 1992]
Dan	11	[1994, *now*]
Eli	20	[1990, 1990]
Eli	20	[1993, *now*]
Naomi	18	[1993, 1993]
Naomi	20	[1994, *now*]

Another example of a historical relation r_3 over MGR^H, with schema(MGR^H) = {MNAME, DNAME, DATES_INT}, is shown in Table 7.4. In this relation there is an overlap between the dates when Reuven and Hanna were managers of the Computing department. Time can be considered as adding a third dimension to relations. A standard relation (or a snapshot relation) can be viewed as a two-dimensional table, where its columns represent attributes and its rows represent tuples. A historical relation can be viewed as a three-dimensional cube, the third dimension being time. Thus a snapshot relation can be viewed as a two-dimensional slice of a historical relation.

Table 7.4 The historical relation r_3 over MGR^H

MNAME	DNAME	DATES_INT
Reuven	Computing	[1992, 1993]
Hanna	Computing	[1993, *now*]
Dan	Arts	[1991, 1992]
Eli	Economics	[1990, 1991]
Sara	Economics	[1992, 1992]
Eli	Economics	[1993, *now*]
Naomi	Medicine	[1993, *now*]

In order to benefit from historical relations we extend the relational algebra to cater for interval-based attribute values. The semantics of such an extension are based on *temporal logic*. Temporal logic is an extension of classical logic whose aim is to overcome the awkwardness of classical logic in capturing temporal relationships and giving semantics to statements involving temporal reference [RU71]. Apart from the area of databases temporal logic is widely employed in the area of specification and verification of concurrent programs

[Eme90, MP92]. In addition, temporal logic is employed in the area of artificial intelligence in order to formalise effective temporal reasoning mechanisms [All83]. A more recent application of temporal logic in the area of information systems is in formalising navigation semantics in Hypertext databases [SFR92, LL99c]. A comprehensive survey of the research on the role of time in information systems up until the early 1980's can be found in [BADW82].

7.2   A Taxonomy of Time in Databases

Herein we discuss various interpretations of time. We have already mentioned standard relations as being *snapshots* of information. A snapshot relation represents only the current state or instance of the stored information. When an update transaction takes place such as changing an employee's salary, the state of the snapshot relation changes and the past state becomes inaccessible as soon as the transaction commits (see Section 8.1 of Chapter 8). The time as it is viewed by the database system with respect to the changes that are made to snapshot relations via transactions is called *transaction time*. A relation which allows access to the relation states prior to the commitment of transactions is called a *rollback relation*.

The simplest way to view a rollback relation is via the concept of *timestamping* (see Section 8.7 of Chapter 8). We assume that the system has a *clock* which records the current system time. A rollback relation, say r, is initially empty when it is created. Thereafter, whenever a tuple is inserted into r it is timestamped with the current system time as it is being inserted into r. On the other hand, whenever a tuple is deleted from r it is not physically deleted, but rather it is timestamped with the current system time indicating when it was deleted from r. (Recall from Subsection 3.2.4 of Chapter 3 that a modification of a tuple in a relation can be viewed as a deletion followed by an insertion.)

In a similar way to recording temporal information in a historical relation we can record the timestamps of tuples in a rollback relation by adding a special transaction attribute to the relation schemas of rollback relations, whose domain is interval-based. For simplicity we will represent transaction time by natural numbers. An interval $[i, j]$ over the transaction attribute of a tuple, t, in a rollback relation r, where i and j are transaction times and $i \leq j$, represents the fact that t was inserted into r at transaction time i and was deleted from r at transaction time j. We use the distinguished time point *now* to represent the fact that the tuple is currently present in r. That is, if the interval $[i, now]$ is the value of the transaction attribute of a tuple t in r, then t was inserted into r at transaction time i and is still currently present in r. An example of a rollback relation r over EMP^R, with schema(EMP^R) = {ENAME, SAL, TIMES_INT}, is shown in Table 7.5. The snapshot relation induced by r which contains only the tuples that are currently present in r is shown in Table 7.1.

As opposed to transaction time recorded in rollback relations, historical relations record *valid time*; that is, the time as it is in the real world. To illustrate the difference between valid time and transaction time consider the tuples, t_1 = <Reuven, 22, [1992, 1993]> and t_2 = <Reuven, 25, [1994, *now*]> in the historical relation over EMP^H shown in Table 7.3 and the tuples, t_3 = <Reuven, 22, [1, 2]> and t_4 = <Reuven, 25, [3, *now*]> in the rollback relation over EMP^R shown in Table 7.5. The tuple t_1 indicates that Reuven earned 22 between 1992 and 1993 and the tuple t_2 indicates that Reuven has earned 25 from 1994 up until now. The tuple t_3 indicates that the fact that Reuven earned 22 was inserted at time 1 and deleted at time

Table 7.5 The rollback relation r over EMP^R

ENAME	SAL	TIMES_INT
Reuven	22	$[1, 2]$
Reuven	25	$[3, now]$
Dan	8	$[0, 1]$
Dan	11	$[4, now]$
Eli	20	$[1, now]$
Naomi	18	$[2, 3]$
Naomi	20	$[4, now]$

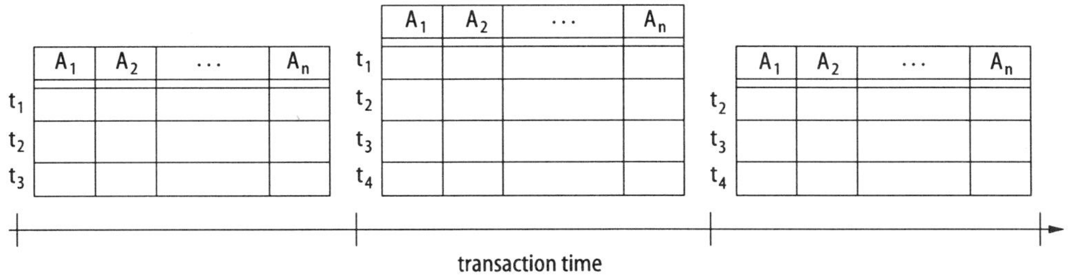

Fig 7.1 The semantics of rollback relations

2 and the tuple t_4 indicates that the fact that Reuven has earned 25 was inserted at time 3 and has not been deleted. It may not be the case that the transaction times 1, 2 and 3 are identical to the valid times, 1992, 1993 and 1994, respectively. This is due to the fact that although Reuven earned a particular salary at a particular valid time the transaction that recorded this information may not have actually happened at identically the same valid time. Thus, for example, the fact that Reuven was earning 22 from 1992 to 1993 may have been actually inserted into the relation in 1993 (which is transaction time 1) and not in 1992, when this salary became the then current salary. On the other hand, the valid time *now* is the same as the transaction time *now*. Thus if the information in both the rollback and historical relations is up-to-date, then the snapshot relation induced by the rollback relation will be identical to the snapshot relation induced by the historical relation.

A relation which supports both valid time and transaction time is called a *temporal relation*. As already mentioned a relation which supports only transaction time is called a *rollback relation* and a relation which supports only valid time is called a *historical relation*. Finally, a relation which supports neither valid time nor transaction time is called a *snapshot relation*. The semantics of rollback relations is depicted in Figure 7.1 and the semantics of historical relations is depicted in Figure 7.2.

With the emergence of new mass media storage technologies, such as optical disks, the cost associated with storage overheads of maintaining temporal relations compared to snapshot relations is becoming affordable. In addition, new implementation techniques for temporal data mean that the physical organisation and query processing of such relations can be carried out efficiently.

Apart from valid time and transaction time there is another type of time, called *user-defined time*. As opposed to valid and transaction time, user-defined time is not interval-based, it simply records a time point such as a date. An example of user-defined time is a birthdate of

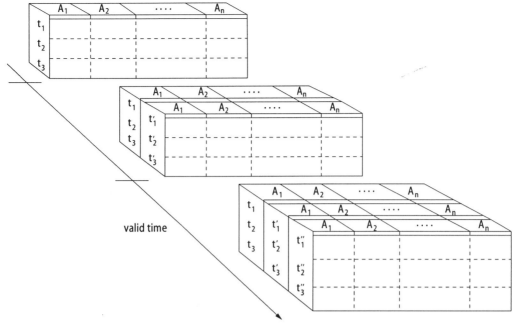

Fig 7.2 The semantics of historical relations

an employee or the date an employee was hired. In order to support user-defined time the database system needs to support the appropriate date types.

From now on we will restrict ourselves to historical relations which record valid time without any reference to the future. We mention that it is also possible to record information that may be valid in the future; for example, if an employee is expected to get a salary rise in a year's time this can be recorded in a way similar to that of recording historical data. The approach that we take is a *tuple-based* one; that is, we record the valid time of tuples in a historical relation. For example, the interval [1992, 1993] in the tuple, <Reuven, 22, [1992, 1993]> of Table 7.3, refers to the whole entity represented by this tuple. A finer-grained approach associates time with individual attributes. For example, we could have historical attributes associated with both DEPT_NAME and SAL for an employee's relation schema containing attributes DEPT_NAME and SAL, recording both the change in time of an employee's department and salary.

An orthogonal issue in representing time is the granularity of time itself. For example, if we are recording the date an employee earned a particular salary, then we can record this date in years only (as we have done in the above examples), but we could be more accurate if we also record the month and even the day together with the year. The granularity of time actually used depends on the application, the finer the granularity the more accurate the information. For example, if we are recording the price of items in a shop, then a granularity which is finer than that of years may be needed.

Finally, we mention that a time-based domain may be *discrete* or *continuous*. In the discrete model such a domain is isomorphic to the set of natural numbers and hence it is a countable domain. Thus in the discrete model time is not dense in the sense that given two times t_1 and t_2 we cannot always find a third time, say t_3, between t_1 and t_2. For most data processing applications such as recording information about employees it is natural to employ a discrete time model. This justifies our choice of using a discrete time model. In the continuous model the time-based domain is isomorphic to the set of real numbers and hence it is an uncountable domain. Thus in the continuous model time is dense in the sense that given two times t_1 and t_2 we can always find a third time, say t_3, between t_1 and t_2. If we are recording physical phenomena such as the weather it may be more appropriate to employ a continuous time model.

7.3   Historical Relations

We now extend snapshot relations to historical relations. The formalisation is based on the extension of a relation schema to contain a historical attribute whose domain is interval-based. Each interval in such a domain is an ordered pair of *time points* contained in a time domain (see Definition 7.1) which is a linearly ordered set.

We recall the definition of chain or equivalently linear order from Subsection 1.9.2 of Chapter 1.

Definition 7.1 (Time domain)   A countable set T is a *time domain* if $\langle T, < \rangle$ is a chain. We call the elements of T *time points* (time points are also referred to in the temporal database literature as *chronons*). We assume that T contains a distinguished *top element*, denoted by *now*, i.e. for all $v \in T - \{now\}$, $v < now$. ∎

We assume that the time points in a time domain are all of the same granularity. The issue of time granularity was discussed in Section 7.2. By refining the granularity, say from years to exact dates and times, we can obtain more accurate historical information. In our examples we have chosen the granularity of time to be years.

Definition 7.2 (Interval)   Let T be a time domain and x and y be time points in T. We denote the set of all consecutive time points between x and y, with respect to the linear order $<$, including x and y by $[x, y]$. Such a set is called a *closed interval* in T (or simply an interval in T when no ambiguity arises). Formally, the interval $[x, y]$ in T is defined by $[x, y] = \{v \mid v \in T$ and $x \leq v \leq y\}$. An interval of the form $[x, x]$ is called a *single-point* interval. We can abbreviate the notation of a single-point interval $[x, x]$ simply to x.

We utilise two operators *from* and *to*, which given an interval $[x, y]$ in T as input return the least value, x, and the greatest value, y, of $[x, y]$, respectively. That is, $from([x, y]) = x$ and $to([x, y]) = y$. ∎

Definition 7.3 (Relationships between intervals)   Let $[x_1, y_1]$ and $[x_2, y_2]$ be two intervals. The following ways in which two intervals can be related were given by Allen [All83]:

1) The interval $[x_1, y_1]$ *overlaps* with the interval $[x_2, y_2]$ if $x_1 \leq x_2 \leq y_1 \leq y_2$; if $x_1 = x_2$ and $y_1 = y_2$ then the intervals are *equal*; on the other hand, if $x_1 = x_2$ but $y_1 < y_2$ then $[x_1, y_1]$ *starts* the interval $[x_2, y_2]$, and finally if $x_1 < x_2$ but $y_1 = y_2$ then $[x_1, y_1]$ is *finished* by the interval $[x_2, y_2]$.

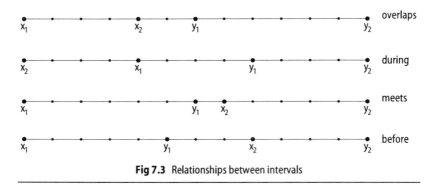

Fig 7.3 Relationships between intervals

2) The interval $[x_1, y_1]$ is *during* the interval $[x_2, y_2]$ if $x_2 < x_1 \le y_1 < y_2$.

3) The interval $[x_1, y_1]$ *meets* with the interval $[x_2, y_2]$ if $x_2 - y_1 = 1$.

4) The interval $[x_1, y_1]$ is *before* the interval $[x_2, y_2]$ if $x_2 - y_1 > 1$.   ▪

A diagram showing the ways in which intervals are related is shown in Figure 7.3.

Definition 7.4 (Historical domain and attribute)   A *historical domain* H over a time domain
T (or simply a historical domain H if T is understood from context) is the set of all intervals I
in T such that *from*(I) $\ne$ *now*.

A *historical attribute* $\mathcal{T}$ is a distinguished attribute, whose domain, DOM($\mathcal{T}$), is a historical
domain.   ▪

The reason for the restriction on historical domains so that their first component cannot
be *now* is to make sure that all intervals have a lower bound; recall that *now* is the top element
of time domains and thus is unbounded if the time domain is infinite. Thus we allow *now* to
extend into the future until it is replaced by another time point. The intervals of time domains
are also referred to in the temporal database literature as *lifespans* indicating a period of time
over which an object (in our case the object will be a tuple) is defined.

Definition 7.5 (Historical relation schema)   A *historical relation schema* is a relation schema,
R^H, where exactly one of the attributes in schema(R^H) is historical. A *historical database
schema* $\mathbf{R^H}$ is a finite set $\{R_1^H, R_2^H, \ldots, R_n^H\}$ of historical relation schemas.   ▪

Historical relation schemas are *not* in 1NF, since historical domains are not atomic. In fact,
the internal structure of intervals allows us to give the desired semantics to historical relations.

From now on we will assume that H is a historical domain over a time domain T.
Furthermore, we will assume that R^H is a historical relation schema, where $\mathcal{T} \in$ schema(R^H)
is a historical attribute, with DOM($\mathcal{T}$) = H, and that $\mathbf{R^H} = \{R_1^H, R_2^H, \ldots, R_n^H\}$ is a historical
database schema, where $\forall R_i^H \in \mathbf{R^H}$, $\mathcal{T}_i \in$ schema(R_i^H) is a historical attribute, with DOM($\mathcal{T}_i$)
= H.

Definition 7.6 (Historical relation)   A *historical tuple* (or simply a tuple) over a historical relation schema R^H with schema$(R^H) = \{A_1, A_2, \ldots, A_m\}$ is a member of the Cartesian product

$$\text{DOM}(A_1) \times \text{DOM}(A_2) \times \cdots \times \text{DOM}(A_m),$$

where $\mathcal{T} = A_i$ for some $A_i \in \text{schema}(R^H)$.

A *historical relation* r^H over R^H is a finite set of historical tuples over R^H. A *historical database* d^H over $\mathbf{R^H}$ is a set $\{r_1^H, r_2^H, \ldots, r_n^H\}$ such that each $r_i^H \in d^H$ is a historical relation over $R_i^H \in \mathbf{R^H}$.

When no ambiguity arises we refer to a historical relation r^H over R^H simply as the relation r over R and to a historical database d^H over $\mathbf{R^H}$ simply as the database d over R. ∎

Examples of historical relations are shown in Tables 7.3 and 7.4.

From now on we will assume that r is a historical relation over R. The above definition of a historical relation and a historical database are the same as the definitions of a relation and a database which are not historical. The difference manifests itself by the fact that each historical tuple in a historical relation, over R, has one attribute value over $\mathcal{T}$ which is an interval. The term historical relation is justified by the semantics of *now* as being the top element of a time domain, on assuming that *now* actually represents the current valid time.

7.4   A Historical Relational Algebra

Let us assume that the (non-historical) relational algebra includes only the basic set of relational operators; that is, union, difference, projection, selection, natural join and renaming. There are two basic approaches to defining a historical relational algebra. In the first approach the historical algebra retains the semantics of the relational algebra treating historical attributes in the same manner as non-historical attributes. The selection operator is then extended with the less than comparison operator, $<$, in order to compare single-point intervals which are linearly ordered. Finally, new historical operators are introduced to deal with time. In the second approach the basic relational operators are extended directly to deal with time.

Herein we take the first approach which retains the semantics of the relational algebra operators and adds new operators to deal with time. In order to motivate the new historical operators we remind the reader of the NEST and UNNEST operators defined in Subsection 1.7.4 of Chapter 1 over nested relations. Assuming only one level of nesting the NEST operator transforms a flat relation into a nested relation and the UNNEST operator transforms a nested relation into a flat relation.

The historical operators *fold* and *unfold* [LJ88, Lor93] are analogous to NEST and UNNEST, respectively. The fold operator transforms a historical relation into a relation whose historical attribute values are maximal intervals, by removing intervals which are during other intervals and unioning intervals which overlap. The motivation for defining fold is to compress the lifespan of a tuple into as few historical tuples as possible, i.e. to remove redundancy in the representation of historical information. On the other hand, the unfold operator transforms a historical relation into a relation whose historical attribute values are single-point intervals. The motivation for defining unfold is to decompress the historical information so that it can be manipulated by selection augmented with $<$ in the same manner as snapshot relations are manipulated (a single-point interval $[x, x]$ can be viewed as the single value x).

We also add another historical operator, called *instantiate*, which replaces the distinguished constant *now* by the current time and its inverse which replaces the current time by *now*. The motivation for defining instantiate is that *now* is unbounded and thus when manipulating historical information we often want to put an upper bound on the attribute values of historical attributes.

We will refer to the historical relational algebra defined in this section as the *Historical Relational Algebra* (or simply the HRA). The reader will find a comprehensive survey on temporal relational algebras in the survey paper by McKenzie Jr. and Snodgrass [MS91].

Let R be a historical relation schema, with historical attribute T, and let X = schema(R) $-$ T. Informally, the unfolding of a historical relation r over R is the set of all tuples t which agree on the X-values of some tuple u in r and such that the T-value of t is a single-point interval contained in the T-value of u. Unfolding a historical relation can be viewed as decompressing the historical information contained in the tuples of that relation.

Definition 7.7 (Unfold operator)   The *unfolding*, $\mu(r)$, of a historical relation r over R is defined by

$$\mu(r) = \{t \mid \exists u \in r, \exists v \in u[T] \text{ such that } u[X] = t[X] \text{ and } to(u[T]) \neq now$$
$$\text{and } t[T] = [v, v]\} \cup \{t \mid t \in r \text{ and } to(t[T]) = now\}. \quad \blacksquare$$

Example 7.1   Let r over DEPT^H, with schema(DEPT^H) = {ENAME, DNAME, T}, be the historical relation shown in Table 7.6. The historical relation $\mu(r)$ is shown in Table 7.7. $\blacksquare$

Table 7.6 The historical relation r over DEPT^H

ENAME	DNAME	T
Reuven	Computing	$[1991, 1992]$
Reuven	Computing	$[1993, now]$
Susi	Computing	$[1994, now]$
Dan	Arts	$[1990, 1992]$
Dan	Languages	$[1993, now]$
Eli	Economics	$[1991, 1992]$
Eli	Economics	$[1994, now]$
Naomi	Medicine	$[1990, 1990]$
Naomi	Medicine	$[1991, 1994]$

Informally, the folding of a historical relation r over R is the result of repetitively removing from r all tuples t_1 whose X-value agrees with that of another tuple t_2 and such that the T-value of t_1 is during the T-value of t_2 as well as replacing the two tuples t_1, t_2, which agree on their X-values and such that the T-value of t_1 overlaps or meets with the T-value of t_2, by a single tuple whose T-value is the union of their intervals. Folding a historical relation can be viewed as compressing the historical information contained in the tuples of that relation.

Table 7.7 The historical relation $\mu(r)$ over DEPT^H

ENAME	DNAME	$\mathcal{T}$
Reuven	Computing	$[1991, 1991]$
Reuven	Computing	$[1992, 1992]$
Reuven	Computing	$[1993, now]$
Susi	Computing	$[1994, now]$
Dan	Arts	$[1990, 1990]$
Dan	Arts	$[1991, 1991]$
Dan	Arts	$[1992, 1992]$
Dan	Languages	$[1993, now]$
Eli	Economics	$[1991, 1991]$
Eli	Economics	$[1992, 1992]$
Eli	Economics	$[1994, now]$
Naomi	Medicine	$[1990, 1990]$
Naomi	Medicine	$[1991, 1991]$
Naomi	Medicine	$[1992, 1992]$
Naomi	Medicine	$[1993, 1993]$
Naomi	Medicine	$[1994, 1994]$

Definition 7.8 (Fold operator)   The *folding*, $\nu(r)$, of a historical relation r over R is defined algorithmically as the output of Algorithm 7.1, designated FOLD(r). The pseudo-code of FOLD(r), which given as input a historical relation r over R returns the unique historical relation $\nu(r)$, is presented as the following algorithm.

Algorithm 7.1 (FOLD(r))
1. **begin**
2.   Result := r;
3.   Tmp := $\emptyset$;
4.   **while** Tmp $\neq$ Result **do**
5.   Tmp := Result;
6.   **for each** t_1, t_2 such that $t_1[X] = t_2[X]$ but $t_1[\mathcal{T}] \neq t_2[\mathcal{T}]$ **do**
7.   **if** $t_1[\mathcal{T}]$ is during $t_2[\mathcal{T}]$ **then**
8.   Result := Result $- \{t_1\}$;
9.   **end if**
10.   **if** $t_1[\mathcal{T}]$ overlaps or meets with $t_2[\mathcal{T}]$ **then**
11. t := a tuple over R with $t[X] = t_1[X] = t_2[X]$,
                        $from(t[\mathcal{T}]) = from(t_1[\mathcal{T}])$ and $to(t[\mathcal{T}]) = to(t_2[\mathcal{T}])$;
12.   Result := (Result $- \{t_1, t_2\}) \cup \{t\}$;
13.   **end if**
14.   **end for**
15.   **end while**
16.   **return** Result;
17. **end.**   ■

Note that $\nu(\mu(r)) = \nu(r)$ but in general $r \neq \nu(r)$.

Example 7.2   The historical relation $\nu(r)$, where r is the historical relation shown in Table 7.6, is shown in Table 7.8.   ■

Table 7.8 The historical relation $v(r)$ over DEPT^H

ENAME	DNAME	$\mathcal{T}$
Reuven	Computing	$[1991, now]$
Susi	Computing	$[1994, now]$
Dan	Arts	$[1990, 1992]$
Dan	Languages	$[1993, now]$
Eli	Economics	$[1991, 1992]$
Eli	Economics	$[1994, now]$
Naomi	Medicine	$[1990, 1994]$

The next historical relational algebra operator allows us to substitute all the occurrences of *now* with the current valid time.

Definition 7.9 (Instantiate operator)   The *instantiation*, $\delta(r)$, of a historical relation r over R, whose historical attribute is $\mathcal{T}$, is defined to be the relation resulting from replacing the occurrence of *now* in an interval of any tuple t in r by the domain value in DOM($\mathcal{T}$) corresponding to the valid current time.

In order for $\delta(r)$ to make sense in the context of a historical relation we must assume that *the current valid time is always greater than or equal to the largest time point in an interval of any tuple in r*.

The inverse of the instantiate operator of a historical relation r over R, denoted by $\delta^{-1}(r)$, is thus also well defined; $\delta^{-1}(r)$ is the historical relation resulting from substituting all occurrences of the current valid time in any tuple in r by the distinguished value *now*.   ■

The reason that the instantiate operator is necessary is that intervals of the form $[v, now]$ are infinite, since we have defined *now* to be the top element of the domain of a historical attribute $\mathcal{T}$. By instantiating a historical relation and then unfolding it we obtain a historical relation such that all its historical attribute values are single-point intervals of the form $[v, v]$ (or simply v), which can easily be manipulated by the standard relational algebra operators defined in Subsection 3.2.1 of Chapter 3.

A recent comprehensive exposition on the semantics of *now* in temporal databases can be found in [CDI$^+$97]. A pessimistic interpretation of *now* will give a negative answer to the query, "Will Reuven be employed in the Computing department next year?". In this approach *now* is a variable which can only refer to the current valid time. In the HRA we can enforce this interpretation by always instatiating a historical relation prior to querying it with a selection. On the other hand, an optimistic interpretation of *now* such as *forever*, will give a positive answer to the above-mentioned query, and to any query on the future employment of Reuven. Our semantics of *now*, as an end point of an interval, are compatible with this optimistic approach. An intermediate approach is to interpret *now* as *until changed* [WJL93]. Using the *until changed* approach we acknowledge the fact that, for example, Reuven will eventually retire or leave the company, and therefore Reuven cannot be employed forever. In order to make this interpretation more precise we could introduce *indeterminate* instants, resulting in intervals such as $[1997, 2000 \sim 2050]$, indicating that one of $[1997, 2000]$, $[1997, 2001]$, ..., $[1997, 2050]$ is the true interval but at the moment we do not know which one.

Example 7.3   Let s be the historical relation over $DEPT^H$, shown in Table 7.8, and assume that the current valid time is 1994. The historical relation $\delta(s)$ over $DEPT^H$ is shown in Table 7.9 and the historical relation $\delta^{-1}(\delta(s))$ over $DEPT^H$ is shown in Table 7.10.   ∎

Table 7.9 The historical relation $\delta(s)$ over $DEPT^H$

ENAME	DNAME	$\mathcal{T}$
Reuven	Computing	[1991, 1994]
Susi	Computing	[1994, 1994]
Dan	Arts	[1990, 1992]
Dan	Languages	[1993, 1994]
Eli	Economics	[1991, 1992]
Eli	Economics	[1994, 1994]
Naomi	Medicine	[1990, 1994]

Table 7.10 The historical relation $\delta^{-1}(\delta(s))$ over $DEPT^H$

ENAME	DNAME	$\mathcal{T}$
Reuven	Computing	[1991, now]
Susi	Computing	[1994, now]
Dan	Arts	[1990, 1992]
Dan	Languages	[1993, now]
Eli	Economics	[1991, 1992]
Eli	Economics	[1994, now]
Naomi	Medicine	[1990, now]

All the standard relational algebra operators defined in Chapter 3 are considered to be part of the historical relational algebra with the provision that when a standard operator is applied to a historical relation then intervals are considered to be *atomic values*. In order to make the historical relational algebra more expressive, we also extend simple selection formulae by allowing expressions of the form $\mathcal{T} < v$ and $\mathcal{T}_1 < \mathcal{T}_2$, where $\mathcal{T}$, $\mathcal{T}_1$ and $\mathcal{T}_2$ are historical attributes. (The expression, $\mathcal{T} \leq v$, is an abbreviation of the selection formula $(\mathcal{T} < v) \vee (\mathcal{T} = v)$, and similarly the expression, $\mathcal{T}_1 \leq \mathcal{T}_2$, is an abbreviation of the selection formula $(\mathcal{T}_1 < \mathcal{T}_2) \vee (\mathcal{T}_1 = \mathcal{T}_2)$.) The comparison operator, $<$, in combination with equality $(=)$ allows us to compare single-point intervals with respect to the linear order on time domains in historical queries. (For simplicity we assume that $<$ and $=$ are generic in the sense that they operate on any time domain.)

When we compare intervals (which may not be single-point) we can only use equality, since we consider intervals to be atomic values. A further extension to simple selection formulae which allows us to compare intervals (which may not be single-point) in a general manner is to allow expressions of the form $\mathcal{T}$ *op* $[v_1, v_2]$ and $\mathcal{T}_1$ *op* $\mathcal{T}_2$, where *op* is one of the relationships: *overlaps, meets, during* or *before*. Such an extension is convenient but does not add expressive power to the algebra, since by using instantiate and unfold we can always reduce any interval to a finite set of single-point intervals.

We now give some examples of historical relational algebra queries which illustrate the above definitions. Let r be the historical relation over $DEPT^H$ shown in Table 7.6.

The query "Retrieve the employees who were working in 1993" is given by

$$\pi_{ENAME}(\sigma_{T=1993}(\mu(\delta(r)))).$$

The query "Retrieve the employees who were working before 1993" is given by

$$\pi_{ENAME}(\sigma_{T<1993}(\mu(\delta(r)))).$$

The query "Retrieve the employees who were working during 1992 and 1993" is given by

$$\pi_{ENAME}(\sigma_{T=1992}(\mu(\delta(r)))) \cap \pi_{ENAME}(\sigma_{T=1993}(\mu(\delta(r)))).$$

Let HUSBAND and WIFE be historical relation schemas with schema(HUSBAND) = {CID, T} and schema(WIFE) = {CID, T}, representing the years during which husbands and their wives were studying for their first degree; the attribute CID is a unique identifier for each husband and wife couple. Furthermore, let r_1 be a historical relation over HUSBAND and r_2 be a historical relation over WIFE. The query "Retrieve the couples and the years in which *both* husband and wife were studying for their first degrees" is given by

$$v(\mu(\delta(r_1)) \bowtie \mu(\delta(r_2))).$$

7.5   Historical Relational Completeness

Herein we briefly discuss the concept of relational completeness of a query language in the context of historical relations. Recall Definition 3.21 in Chapter 3 which stated that a query language is relationally complete if it is at least as expressive as the relational algebra. Thus, the HRA is a relationally complete query language, since it includes the basic relational algebra operators. However, the HRA is not just relationally complete, since it also enables us to manipulate historical information, and thus we need some further criterion to measure its expressiveness.

In order to measure the expressiveness of an algebra with respect to the manipulation of historical information we can give semantics to historical algebra queries in terms of temporal logic. In particular, *linear temporal logic* serves this purpose, where relative to a given time point, the *previous* temporal operator is used to refer to the time point just prior to the present one, and the *since* temporal operator is used to refer to an interval in the past [Eme90, MP92]. Correspondingly, relative to a given time point, the *next* temporal operator is used to refer to the next time point in the future and the *until* temporal operator is used to refer to an interval in the future [Eme90, MP92].

Suppose that A and B are (non-historical) relational algebra queries which are either true (i.e. their answer contains one or more tuples) or false (i.e. their answer is empty) with respect to a snapshot relation at some time point x_j.

- The definition of *previous* A is given by
  previous A is true at time point x_j if A is true at the time point just prior to x_j.

- The definition of *next* A is given by
  next A is true at time point x_j if A is true at the time point just after x_j.

- The definition of A *since* B is given by
  A *since* B is true at time point x_j if B is true at some past time point relative to x_j, say x_i, and A is true throughout the whole interval $[x_i, x_j]$.

- The definition of A *until* B is given by
  A *until* B is true at time point x_j if B is true at some future time point relative to x_j, say x_i, and A is true throughout the whole interval $[x_j, x_i]$.

A historical relational algebra is said to be *historically relationally complete* if it is equivalent to a first-order linear temporal logic with the temporal operators, *previous*, *since*, *next* and *until*. As with the relational calculus the semantics of such a first-order temporal logic must be restricted to finite models. It is interesting to note that in [AHV95a, AHV96, TN96] it was shown that it is not sufficient to enhance the standard relational algebra only with the future temporal operators *next* and *until*, since we then obtain a strictly less expressive relational algebra than the one where, in addition, we have the past temporal operators *previous* and *since*. In particular, the query, "is there a time point, say τ_i, at which a given relation contains exactly the same tuples as it had in the first time point, say τ_1, when the relation became nonempty, and such that $\tau_1 < \tau_i$?", is not expressible with the future temporal operators only but is expressible by using both the past and future temporal operators.

If we enhance the relational algebra with the above temporal operators then all the interaction of the resulting query language with the historical domain of relations is implicit and encapsulated within the temporal operators. In this approach, which we call the *temporal operators approach*, the historical attributes are essentially hidden from the user. As opposed to the temporal operators approach, an alternative approach is to enhance the relational algebra by adding to it a binary less than operator for comparing time points, wherein time is referenced explicitly. The resulting logic is a first-order logic with equality and linear order. This approach, which we call the *linear order approach*, was taken in the HRA defined in Section 7.4, where we use the less than comparison operator, $<$, to explicitly compare two time points.

In [AHV95a, AHV96, TN96] it was shown that a historical relational algebra defined by using the temporal operators approach is strictly less expressive than a historical relational algebra defined by using the linear order approach. In particular, the query, "are there two distinct time points at which a given relation contains exactly the same tuples?", is not expressible in a HRA of the temporal operators approach but is expressible in a HRA of the linear order approach.

We leave it to the reader to verify the following theorem.

Theorem 7.1   The HRA is historically relationally complete.   □

The reader can find more details regarding historically relationally complete query languages, both algebras and calculi, in [TC90, GM91, CCT93] and also in [KSW90]; the latter deals with the problem of representing infinite temporal information. It is interesting to note that historical completeness does not take into account the support needed to manage and analyse time series data [SMDD95] (see [Cha96] for an introduction to time series).

7.6   TSQL2

Herein we give a brief overview of TSQL2 [Sno95], which is an upwards compatible temporal extension of SQL2 [DD93]. The rationale for defining TSQL2 is the growing demand for consistent and cohesive DBMS support for temporal relations. TSQL2 is an attempt to consolidate the main proposals for temporal relational query languages that have been developed. We summarise, mainly through examples, TSQL2's support of temporal data types, its support of specifying time points at different granularities and the ability to change the granularity of time points, its support of both valid and transaction time, and its querying facility over temporal relations.

In TSQL2 dates and times can be specified as one of three temporal data types: DATE, TIME and TIMESTAMP. A literal over one of these data types is called a *datetime*. An example of a datetime literal of type DATE is given by

DATE '1996-08-23'

An example of a datetime literal of type TIME is given by

TIME '12:44:20'

An example of a datetime literal of type TIMESTAMP is given by

TIMESTAMP '1996-08-23 12:44:20'

TSQL2 also supports two data types for specifying intervals. The first data type INTERVAL specifies a duration of time with known length but without any specific starting or ending datetimes. An example of a literal specifying an interval of two months is given by

INTERVAL '2' MONTH

An example of a literal specifying an interval of two hours, two minutes and two seconds is given by

INTERVAL '2:02:02' HOUR TO SECOND

The second data type for specifying an interval is PERIOD, which defines a duration of time with a starting and ending datetime. An example of a literal specifying a period of one month is given by

PERIOD '[1997-08-01 — 1997-09-01]'

An example of a literal specifying a period of one month down to the granularity of seconds is given by

PERIOD '[1996-08-01 01:10:00 — 1996-09-01 23:30:59]'

TSQL2 also supports arithmetic operations, such as addition and subtraction, between datetime literals and between interval and period literals. Moreover, comparison operators between datetimes and between periods, which implement the semantics of Allen's operators, i.e. *overlaps, meets, during* and *before*, are supported in TSQL2 (see Definition 7.3).

Moreover, TSQL2 supports multiple *calendars* such as the Gregorian calendar and the Lunar calendar. In addition, TSQL2 allows users to specify time points in different ways. For example, three different ways of specifying August 1, 1998 are:

```
DATE '1998-08-01'
DATE 'August 1, 1998'
DATE '01/08/98'
```

TSQL2 also supports the distinguished datetime *now*, which is treated as a variable that is assigned the current datetime during query and update processing (see Definition 7.1).

Time points (called *instants* in TSQL2) can be specified at different granularities; for example, salary increases are typically measured to the granularity of years, birthdates are typically measured to the granularity of days and lecture timetables are typically measured to the granularity of minutes. TSQL2 provides two operators SCALE and CAST which allow users to change the granularity of instants. Several examples that illustrate the semantics of SCALE are given below.

```
SCALE(DATE '1996-08-21' AS YEAR) = '1996'
SCALE(DATE '1996-08-21' AS MONTH) = '1996-08'
SCALE(DATE '1996-08-21' AS DAY) = '1996-08-21'
SCALE(DATE '1996-08-21' AS HOUR) = '1996-08-21 00' ~ '1996-08-21 23'
SCALE(DATE '1996-08-21' AS MINUTE) = '1996-08-21 00:00' ~ '1996-08-21 23:59'
SCALE(DATE '1996-08-21' AS SECOND) = '1996-08-21 00:00:00' ~ '1996-08-21 23:59:59'
```

The symbol $\sim$, in the last three examples above, means that the scaling of the datetime to the granularity of hours results in an *indeterminate* instant, with the exact hour being somewhere in between 00 and 23. Several examples that illustrate the semantics of CAST are given below.

```
CAST(DATE '1996-08-21' AS YEAR) = '1996'
CAST(DATE '1996-08-21' AS MONTH) = '1996-08'
CAST(DATE '1996-08-21' AS DAY) = '1996-08-21'
CAST(DATE '1996-08-21' AS HOUR) = '1996-08-21 00'
CAST(DATE '1996-08-21' AS MINUTE) = '1996-08-21 00:00'
CAST(DATE '1996-08-21' AS SECOND) = '1996-08-21 00:00:00'
```

As can be seen from the above examples the behaviour of CAST is the same as that of SCALE when converting from a finer granularity to a coarser granularity or one that has the same granularity. On the other hand, when converting from a coarser granularity to a finer granularity then a determinate instant is produced which is the first instant in the specified granularity.

TSQL2 supports both valid time and transaction time. Herein we concentrate on TSQL2's support of historical relations, i.e. temporal relations which record past valid time only.

In TSQL2 we can define a historical relation over the historical relation schema EMP^H with the TSQL2 create table statement as follows:

        CREATE TABLE EMP
                (ENAME CHAR(30),
                 SALARY DECIMAL(5),
                 PRIMARY KEY (ENAME))
        AS VALID STATE;

The keywords **AS VALID STATE** define the table to be a historical relation recording valid time. In addition, we can define a historical relation over the historical relation schema $DEPT^H$, with the TSQL2 create table statement as follows:

        CREATE TABLE DEPT
                (ENAME CHAR(30),
                 DNAME CHAR(20),
                 PRIMARY KEY (ENAME))
        AS VALID STATE;

We now introduce the flavour of TSQL2 queries over the historical relations we have just created via some examples.

The query asking for the employees who earned more than 15 in any year of their employment is given by

        SELECT SNAPSHOT ENAME
        FROM EMP(ENAME, SAL) (PERIOD) AS E
        WHERE E.SAL > 15

The keyword SNAPSHOT specifies that a snapshot relation, i.e. a standard relation, is returned. The keyword PERIOD specifies that the EMP table should be folded or using TSQL2's terminology that it be *coalesced*. The keyword AS defines a *correlation name* which is an alias for a relation schema; in this case E is an alias for EMP.

The query asking when did Reuven work in the Computing department is given by

        SELECT VALID(D)
        FROM DEPT(ENAME, DNAME) (PERIOD) AS D
        WHERE D.ENAME = 'Reuven' AND D.DNAME = 'Computing'

The keyword VALID specifies that a period representing the valid time of the tuples in the answer relation be returned.

The query asking how many years did employees work and in which departments is given by

        SELECT SNAPSHOT ENAME, CAST(VALID(D) AS INTERVAL YEAR)
        FROM DEPT(ENAME, DNAME) AS D

The CAST operator converts valid time periods into intervals of years and the SNAPSHOT keyword specifies that the resulting relation is a standard one, noting that attributes in standard relations can have a temporal data type.

The query asking for the department that Dan worked in immediately after he left the Arts department is given by

SELECT SNAPSHOT ENAME
FROM DEPT(ENAME, DNAME) (PERIOD) AS E1 E2
WHERE E1.DNAME = 'Arts' AND E2.DNAME <> 'Arts'
AND E1.ENAME = 'Dan' AND E1.ENAME = E2.ENAME
AND VALID(E1) MEETS VALID(E2)

The query asking for the employees of the Computing department who earned more than 10 and when these employees earned such a salary is given by

SELECT E.ENAME, INTERSECT(VALID(E), VALID(D))
FROM EMP(ENAME, SAL) AS E, DEPT(ENAME, DNAME) AS D
WHERE E.ENAME = D.ENAME AND DNAME = 'Computing' AND SAL > 10
AND VALID(E) OVERLAPS VALID(D)

A critical evaluation of TSQL2 is given in [ART95], where clarifications and suggested modifications to TSQL2 are discussed. Issues concerning the completeness of TSQL2 are discussed in [BJS95].

7.7 Historical Key Dependencies

The notion of key dependency is fundamental to the relational model and thus it must be extended to the temporal relational model. (See Definition 3.61 from Subsection 3.6.1 of Chapter 3 for the notion of key in the relational model and Definition 4.1 from Section 4.1 of Chapter 4 for the notion of key dependency.) Herein we will consider the meaning of a historical key dependency being satisfied in a historical relation r over a historical relation schema R with historical attribute $\mathcal{T}$.

Let S be a (non-historical) relation schema such that schema(S) = schema(R) − {$\mathcal{T}$}. A key dependency for R is a statement of the form, K → schema(S), where K is a subset of schema(S). Intuitively, K → schema(S) is satisfied in r if the key dependency K → schema(S) is satisfied in the projection onto schema(S) of all the partitions of the unfolding of r according to its single-point intervals, and K is a minimal set of attributes satisfying this condition. In other words, this means that the key dependency K → schema(S) is satisfied in all snapshot relations induced by the time points recorded in r.

Definition 7.10 (Historical key)   Let r be a historical relation over R, with historical attribute $\mathcal{T}$, S be a relation schema such that schema(S) = schema(R) − {$\mathcal{T}$} and K ⊆ schema(S). Then K → schema(S) is a *historical key dependency* for r if for all $v \in \pi_{\mathcal{T}}(\delta(\mu(r)))$ the following two conditions hold:

1) *uniqueness*: $\pi_{schema(S)}(\sigma_{\mathcal{T}=v}(\mu(r)))$ satisfies the FD K → schema(S); and

2) *minimality*: for no proper subset X ⊂ K is X → schema(S) a historical key dependency for r.

A set of attributes K ⊆ schema(S) is a *historical key* for r over R if K → schema(S) is a historical key dependency for r. ∎

Example 7.4 The unique historical key for the historical relation over EMP^H shown in Table 7.3 is {ENAME}. The unique historical key for the historical relation over MGR^H shown in Table 7.4 is {MNAME}. The unique historical key for the historical relation over $DEPT^H$ shown in Table 7.6 is {ENAME}. ∎

There is an overhead in checking whether a set of attributes K is a historical key for a historical relation compared with checking whether K is a key for a relation which is not historical. The overhead is linear in the number of time points (or equivalently single-point intervals) in $\pi_T(\mu(r))$. (See Check_Primary_Key(r, X), which checks whether X is a primary key of r; the pseudo-code for Check_Primary_Key(r, X) is given as Algorithm 3.6 in Subsection 3.6.1 of Chapter 3.) In practice checking whether K is a historical key can be done incrementally when the historical relation is updated.

Wijsen [Wij95] distinguished between two types of historical key dependency (or more generally historical functional dependency). As an example of the first type consider the historical key ENAME for $DEPT^H$, which states that at all time points an employee works in a single department. Assuming that an employee works in the *same* department at *all times* then we have an example of a *temporal key*. As an example of the second type let us add the attribute RANK to the historical relation schema EMP^H, denoting the rank of an employee in the department he/she works in. Then, stating that at any *two consecutive time points* the {ENAME, SALARY}-value of an employee uniquely determines the employee's RANK and, in addition, that {ENAME, SALARY} is a key at the current time, i.e. *now*, is an example of {ENAME, SALARY} being a *dynamic temporal key*. Intuitively, {ENAME, SALARY} is a dynamic temporal key if the rank of an employee changes only when their salary changes from one time point to the next time point.

The notion of a foreign key can also be extended to historical relations, essentially by asserting that the standard notion of referential integrity is satisfied at all time points recorded in the historical database. More general integrity constraints, which specify that a first-order formula is satisfied at all past time points recorded in the database, are discussed in [Cho94].

We close this section by referring to [Via87, Via88] wherein a dynamic version of the FD is investigated in the context of rollback relations. Let us call the state of a relation prior to the commitment of a transaction an *old* relation and the state of a relation after the transaction is committed a *new* relation. Then a *Dynamic* FD (or simply a DFD) specifies the evolution of an FD from an old relation to a new relation. Let us assume that the EMP_NOW relation schema has an additional attribute PERFORM, which records the current performance of an employee as recorded in the employee's last assessment. Then a DFD from old PERFORM and old SALARY to new SALARY specifies that an employee's new salary is uniquely determined by his/her previous performance and his/her old salary. In the above-mentioned papers Vianu also discusses the effect of the *age* of tuples on a given set of FDs with respect to a set of DFDs, which constrain the transition from old relations to new relations. The *age* of a tuple is defined to be the number of times that the tuple has been modified since it was originally inserted into the relation. This leads to the notion of a set of tuples having *survivability* k if this set of tuples can be validly modified k times, according to a set of DFDs, and still satisfy a given set of FDs and any new FDs which are logically implied by these DFDs.

7.8 Schema Evolution

So far we have not allowed the schema of relations to change over time, but in practice as an application evolves so does its database schema. For the purpose of discussing schema evolution it is more convenient to view a temporal database as a nonempty finite sequence, $k \geq 1$, of indexed pairs, namely

$$\langle (\mathbf{R}_1, d_1)_1, (\mathbf{R}_2, d_2)_2, \ldots, (\mathbf{R}_k, d_k)_k \rangle.$$

Each indexed pair $(\mathbf{R}_i, d_i)_i$, $i \in \{1, 2, \ldots, k\}$, which is called a *version*, consists of a database schema $\mathbf{R}_i$ and a snapshot database (or simply a database) d_i over $\mathbf{R}_i$, with i being the timestamp associated with the pair. The set $\{1, 2, \ldots, k\}$ is the set of timestamps associated with the temporal database; each timestamp represents the transaction time associated with the relevant version. Thus a version denotes the database together with its schema as they are at a particular transaction time during the evolution of the database.

Let us consider two consecutive versions $(\mathbf{R}_i, d_i)_i$ and $(\mathbf{R}_j, d_j)_j$, with $j = i + 1$. If these two versions are identical then no change has occurred between transaction times i and j. On the other hand, if $\mathbf{R}_i = \mathbf{R}_j$ but $d_i \neq d_j$, then the database schema has not changed between transaction times i and j but the database has been updated. Finally, if $\mathbf{R}_i \neq \mathbf{R}_j$ and thus also $d_i \neq d_j$, then the database schema has evolved between transaction times i and j, which implies that the database has also been updated correspondingly. Therefore, a temporal database consisting of a sequence of versions supersedes the notion of a rollback database (i.e. a set of rollback relations) by allowing both the database schema and the database to change over time. In the rest of the section we will concentrate on the situation when the schema evolves, i.e. where $\mathbf{R}_i \neq \mathbf{R}_j$; see Subsection 3.2.4 of Chapter 3 which defines an update language for the relational model, for the situation when $\mathbf{R}_i = \mathbf{R}_j$ but $d_i \neq d_j$. (Hereafter when the database consists of a single relation r over a relation schema R, we will write $(R, r)_i$ as a shorthand for $(\{R\}, \{r\})_i$.)

The following types of schema evolution operations are possible at transaction time i:

1) Change the domain of an existing attribute in a relation schema $R \in \mathbf{R}_i$.

2) Rename the name of an attribute in a relation schema $R \in \mathbf{R}_i$.

3) Add a new attribute to a relation schema $R \in \mathbf{R}_i$.

4) Remove an existing attribute from a relation schema $R \in \mathbf{R}_i$.

5) Add an empty relation over a new relation schema, $R \notin \mathbf{R}_i$, to the database d_i.

6) Remove an existing relation r and its associated relation schema $R \in \mathbf{R}_i$ from the database d_i.

The semantics of the above operations can be formalised in terms of a mapping which transforms $(\mathbf{R}_i, d_i)_i$ into $(\mathbf{R}_j, d_j)_j$, where $j = i + 1$. To illustrate these semantics, consider the relation r over EMP, where schema EMP consists of the attributes ENAME (employee name), SAL (employee salary in pounds sterling) and EXT (employee phone extension). Viewed at transaction time, say 1, we have the version $(EMP, r)_1$, shown in Table 7.11.

Table 7.11 The version $(\text{EMP}, r)_1$

ENAME	SAL	EXT
Reuven	22	6712
Dan	10	6704
Eli	20	3684
Naomi	20	7214

Now, suppose that we would like to change the domain of SAL from pounds sterling to Ecu (*European currency unit*). Then the transformation from $(\text{EMP}, r)_1$ to $(\text{EMP}, r_a)_2$ at transaction time 2 can be defined in terms of an update routine which converts all the salaries of employees in r from pounds sterling to Ecu, resulting in r_a. Next suppose that we would like to rename the attribute ENAME to be called EMP_NAME. Then the transformation from $(\text{EMP}, r_a)_2$ to $(\text{EMP}_a, r_a)_3$ at transaction time 3 renames ENAME in schema(EMP) such that schema(EMP_a) = (schema(EMP) − {ENAME}) ∪ {EMP_NAME}, and leaves r_a unchanged. Next, assume that we would like to add a new attribute, called EMAIL (email address), to EMP_a, so the transformation from $(\text{EMP}_a, r_a)_3$ to $(\text{EMP}_b, r_b)_4$ at transaction time 4 adds this attribute to schema(EMP_a) such that schema(EMP_b) = schema(EMP_a) ∪ {EMAIL}, and then extends r_a by an additional column for this attribute, resulting in r_b, initially having a null value as the EMAIL-value of the extended tuples; the resulting version at transaction time 4 is shown in Table 7.12.

Table 7.12 The version $(\text{EMP}_b, r_b)_4$

EMP_NAME	SAL	EXT	EMAIL
Reuven	26.8	6712	*null*
Dan	12.2	6704	*null*
Eli	24.4	3684	*null*
Naomi	24.4	7214	*null*

Thereafter in further versions, the actual email addresses of employees will replace the null values. Suppose that the company decides to supply each employee with a mobile phone and as a result to remove the attribute EXT from schema(EMP_b). Then the transformation from $(\text{EMP}_b, r_b)_4$ to $(\text{EMP}_c, r_c)_5$ at transaction time 5 deletes EXT from schema(EMP_b) such that schema(EMP_c) = schema(EMP_b) − {EXT}, and replaces r_b by its projection onto schema(R) − {EXT}, thus yielding r_c. The company then decides to create a new relation over a relation schema, MGR, to store information about managers. Then $(\text{EMP}_c, r_c)_5$ is transformed into $(\{\text{EMP}_c, \text{MGR}\}, \{r_c, s\})_6$ at transaction time 6, where s is the new relation in the database over MGR. Initially s is empty, and eventually it will be populated with the relevant information about managers. Finally, the company has decided to fire all of its managers as a result of restructuring and thus $(\{\text{EMP}_c, \text{MGR}\}, \{r_c, s\})_6$ is transformed to $(\text{EMP}_c, r_c)_7$ at transaction time 7.

We refer the reader to [Rod92] for an annotated bibliography on schema evolution and to [Rod96] for a recent survey of the area. Schema evolution in the context of TSQL2, where timestamping attributes are proposed, is discussed in [Sno95, Chapter 22] and in [DGS97], and for schema evolution in the context of object-oriented database systems see [ZCF+97, Part VI]. Finally, the problem of evolving a set of data dependencies, and in particular a set of FDs, was discussed at the end of Section 7.7.

7.9 Discussion

Handling temporal information is a natural extension of the basic relational model capabilities. Although the formalism we have presented deals only with historical data such as maintaining the salary history of employees, it can also cater for future data such as yearly salary increases and bonuses for employees. One of the main current challenges for temporal databases is to solve the physical database problem of efficient storage and retrieval of temporal data. If large volumes of temporal data are to be available online, then it must be organised efficiently. This also has had an impact on logical database design; the effect of temporal databases on normalisation theory is discussed in [JSS92, Wij95]. A comprehensive collection of papers on temporal database issues is [TCG+93]. The field of temporal relational databases is still an active and evolving area of research. For instance, it was recently shown that a point-based approach, which does not use intervals, is expressively equivalent to the interval-based approach [Tom96]. A temporal extension of SQL founded on the point-based approach is proposed in [Tom97].

We did not mention spatial databases [SA95], which are required in *Geographic Information Systems* (GISs), but there is a close connection between temporal and spatial information. See [RU71, Van83] for the logical aspects of spatial information as opposed to temporal information. From a practical point of view spatial databases are mainly concerned with the description and manipulation of geometric data consisting of points, lines, rectangles, polygons and more general surfaces. A recent investigation of the expressive power of queries for spatial databases based on first-order logic over the set of real numbers can be found in [PVV94]. An alternative semantics for spatial databases based on topological relationships between regions such as disjointness, overlap, equality, containment and meet, can be found in [PSV96].

7.10 Exercises

Exercise 7.1 A historical relation r over a historical relation schema R^H is in *First Historical Normal Form* (1HNF) if $r = \nu(\mu(r))$, i.e. r remains unchanged when we unfold r and then fold it. Give an equivalent definition of 1HNF in terms of the relationship between the intervals over H for any two tuples in a historical relation r. Provide justification for the desirability of 1HNF [JSS92].

Exercise 7.2 Generalise Definition 7.10 of a historical key to that of a *Historical Functional Dependency* (HFD).

Exercise 7.3 Use your definition of an HFD from Exercise 7.2 to define a generalisation of BCNF for historical relations [JSS92].

Exercise 7.4 TSQL2 supports the built-in operators BEGIN and END, where BEGIN(P) returns the starting datetime of the period P and END(P) returns the ending datetime of the period P. Show how Allen's *overlaps* operator can be implemented in TSQL2 using BEGIN and END [Sno95, Chapter 8].

Exercise 7.5 TSQL2 supports indeterminate instants such as '1996-03' ~ '1996-11', meaning that the exact month in 1996 is somewhere between March and November. In addition, a probability distribution can be specified for such an indeterminate instant, indicating the likelihood of each possible instant. Suggest, via an example, how this TSQL2 feature can be used to retrieve tuples that are more probable [Sno95, Chapter 18].

Exercise 7.6 Suggest the meaning of the aggregate functions MIN, MAX and COUNT operating on datetime literals [Sno95, Chapter 20]. (See Subsection 3.2.1 of Chapter 3 for a formalisation of aggregate functions in the context of the relational algebra.)

Exercise 7.7 Optimisation of historical queries is more difficult than optimisation of snapshot queries mainly due to the fact that historical relations grow monotonically with the number of transactions. Suggest how the fact that time is linearly ordered can be used by a historical query optimiser [LM93].

Exercise 7.8 A temporal relation, as opposed to a historical relation, can store information about the future, in addition to storing information about the past. Suggest how the data model for historical relations can be extended to cater for temporal relations. For example, it would be useful to be able to store the information that a supervisor meets his project students once a week at a specified time (see [KSW90]).

Exercise 7.9 Suggest how spatial data can be represented via the framework of historical relations by adding the new basic data type *coordinate*, representing a point, say (x, y), in two-dimensional space (see [SA95]).

8. Concurrency Control

So far we have not addressed the problems relating to concurrently accessing a database in a multi-user environment. In the real world single-user databases on microcomputer systems are not adequate to meet the needs of many organisations and companies. Often more than one user may wish to read or update the database simultaneously. This can lead to an inconsistent database. As with any information, if it is not accurate for whatever reason, its value is reduced and it may cause problems for the user. The usefulness of a database system depends on the reliability of its data at all times. For example, a database system which allowed two people to book the same seat on an airline flight, with the resulting confusion and likely customer dissatisfaction, would be of little use indeed, unless of course the airline has a deliberate policy of double booking a certain percentage of seats.

Concurrent access control is required when two or more users have concurrent access to a database system. This requirement is increased when simultaneous access is permitted and where update of data is relatively unrestricted. Modern database systems, such as aircraft reservation systems and banking systems, rely upon fast access to information. Delay in accessing data is simply unacceptable. Hence, serial operation allowing only one user at a time to access data at any given time is not acceptable. Support for concurrent usage of a database system is needed and expected.

The concept of a *transaction* is central to the explanation of concurrency. A transaction is a logical unit of work that transforms a database from one consistent state to another, without being required to preserve consistency at all intermediate points in the transformation. Transactions are required to be *atomic*, which means that either all the operations within a transaction must be executed to completion or none at all. For example, the transfer of money out of one account and into another in a banking database involves two distinct operations, namely debit and credit, within the transfer transaction (see Algorithm 8.1). Yet either both are performed to completion and the transfer is successful, or the transaction is terminated and the transfer fails. The atomicity requirement ensures that one operation of a funds transfer transaction cannot alter the data in one of the two accounts without completing the transfer. This requirement helps to maintain the consistency of the database by ensuring that in the event of a transaction failure, the database is returned to a state such that it could be considered that the transaction never started. In fact, consistency of the database could be maintained in this case via Algorithm 8.2 (in our case for $i = 2$), which should yield the same result prior to the invocation of Algorithm 8.1 and after its successful completion.

In Section 8.1 we describe how the concurrency control problem arises. In Section 8.2 we deal with serialisability and in Sections 8.3, 8.7 and 8.8 we present three different approaches, respectively, for enforcing serialisability, namely locking, timestamp ordering and serialisation graph testing. In Sections 8.4 and 8.5 we deal, respectively, with the corresponding problems of deadlock and lock granularity, and in Section 8.6 we briefly consider the software component of a DBMS that manages locks, i.e. the lock manager.

Algorithm 8.1 (Funds Transfer Transaction)
```
1.  begin
2.     read(Accounts[account1], balance1);
3.     read(Accounts[account2], balance2);
4.     read(amount);
5.     newBalance1 := balance1 − amount;
6.     write(Accounts[account1], newBalance1);
7.     newBalance2 := balance2 + amount;
8.     write(Accounts[account2], newBalance2);
9.     commit;
10. end.
```

Algorithm 8.2 (Total Balance)
```
1.  begin
2.     totalBalance := 0;
3.     for i iterating though all account numbers
4.        read(Accounts[i], balance);
5.        totalBalance := totalBalance + balance;
6.     end for
7.     output(totalBalance);
8.     commit;
9.  end.
```

8.1   Manifestations of Concurrency Control

In the following we assume that the database is partitioned into *data items* (or simply items). The nature and the size of a data item are chosen by the system designer. In the relational model a large data item could be a relation and a small data item could be a single tuple or even a component thereof.

In the context of concurrency control there are only four essential operations pertaining to a transaction; namely *read*, *write*, *commit*, and *abort*. A transaction ends with a commit if all the changes made to a database instance are to become permanent. If a transaction ends up with an abort all the aforesaid changes are to be undone, and we refer to such a situation by saying that the transaction is *rollbacked*. We call this model of transaction operations the *Read/Write* (RW) model.

The justification for employing this low level approach to transactions is that it deals only with the fundamental DBMS operations and thus is independent of the conceptual model, i.e.

the relational model. The RW model is also the most widely accepted model for reasoning about database concurrency issues. An alternative approach is to employ the conceptual model of transactions presented in Subsection 3.2.4 of Chapter 3, which we hereafter call the *Insert/Delete/Modify* (IDM) model [VV92]. The IDM model is semantically richer than the RW model and thus there is more scope for transaction processing optimisation than in the RW model by utilising Theorem 3.8 given in the above-mentioned subsection. On the other hand, the formalisation of concurrency control in the context of the IDM model is more complex.

The following definition formalises transactions by considering only their essential operations.

Definition 8.1 (Transaction) A *transaction* is a sequence T of transaction operations (or simply operations) such that

1) the positions of T are filled with one of: read(T, x), write(T, x), commit(T), abort(T), where x is a data item (when T is understood from context then we abbreviate the above to: read(x), write(x), commit and abort, respectively);

2) commit(T) occurs in T if and only if T is not aborted;

3) if either commit(T) or abort(T) occurs in T, then it occurs in the last position of T.

The operations of a transaction T are often referred to as the *elementary steps* of T. The *readset* of a transaction T is the set of data items T reads, and the *writeset* of T is the set of data items T writes. ∎

A useful yardstick by which transactions can be evaluated is known as the *ACID test*. Transactions pass the ACID test if they possess the following qualities:

- *Atomicity*. Each transaction must have no observable intermediate states. Hence, even if the transaction amends a data item many times to achieve its final update, then these changes should not be visible to any other transaction. This is equally true if the transaction does not alter the database or if it fails.

- *Consistency*. The database is assumed to be in a consistent state at the start of a transaction and at the end of it, whereby consistency refers to the database satisfying a set of integrity constraints.

- *Isolation*. A transaction should not have any unintended side-effects. For example, if the sole action of a transaction is intended to transform data item A into data item B, then it should not transform, as a side-effect, another data item C into data item D. Moreover, a transaction should be seen as if it were in single-user mode.

- *Durability*. If a transaction changes data item A into data item B then this change should also last, i.e. be persistent, until another transaction wishes to update B. In the short term, this means that an update should at least persist until the end of its transaction without being overwritten by another transaction. In the longer term, this guideline means that updates must be written to some form of permanent storage.

The term concurrency should not incline the reader to assume that different transactions are actually being carried out simultaneously. Assuming that there is only one central processing unit in a database system, then only one operation can be carried out during one machine cycle. Many processor operations or machine cycles may be needed to carry out just one database transaction. The execution of two database transactions can however be *interleaved*, with the processing of one transaction being started but not completed before the execution of the other transaction begins. Indeed the execution of a transaction may depend upon the processing of another concurrent transaction. In a multiprogramming environment, with processor time shared among several concurrent transactions, access control is necessary. We next give a succinct yet general definition of concurrency control.

Definition 8.2 (Concurrency control)   Concurrency control is the activity of coordinating the actions of transactions that operate concurrently, access shared data, and therefore potentially interfere with each other.   ■

Transactions interleaving their access to a database can result in interference. The problem of avoiding this interference is termed the *concurrency control problem*. A concurrency control algorithm is used to regulate the interleaving of concurrent transactions. This ensures that all transactions are executed atomically and that no interference takes place between transactions.

We next consider various manifestations of the concurrency control problem. Data held in a database system must be correct and reliable to sustain user confidence. Unless controls are maintained on concurrent access to data, inconsistencies arise which undermine the integrity of the data and render the database virtually useless. Executing concurrent transactions without controls gives rise to classic anomalies which need to be addressed. There now follows an explanation of these anomalies.

The best known of these anomalies is the *lost update* anomaly. This occurs where two concurrent transactions read the same data, modify it, and write a value back to the database. Depending upon the order in which operations are processed, interference between the two transactions may result in one of the updates being ignored by the database system (see Table 8.1). The contents of such a table are referred to as a *transaction history* (cf. *schedule*, Definition 8.3).

Table 8.1 Example of the lost update anomaly

Steps	Transaction T_1	Transaction T_2	Values
1	read(A);		200
2		read(A);	200
3		A := A + 30;	
4		write(A);	230
5	A := A * 2;		
6	write(A);		400
7		commit;	
8	commit;		400

As can be seen from Table 8.1, the net result is incorrect and the work performed by transaction T_2 is lost. The value written by transaction T_2 at step 4 has been lost. At step 8 $A = 400$, whereas it should be 460, on the assumption that T_2 should precede T_1, or 430 if T_1 should precede T_2.

Another anomaly closely related to the lost update anomaly is the *inconsistent retrieval* anomaly (see Table 8.2). In this situation interference between two or more concurrent transactions may result in retrieval of data which is inconsistent with the values held in the database. The data items, A and B, are initialised to 100 and 200, respectively. Transaction T_1 is a transfer of money from A to B, and transaction T_2 calculates the total of A and B.

As can be seen from Table 8.2, the total calculated for A and B at step 12 (A + B = 250) is inconsistent with the values of A and B written to the database at step 11 (A = 50, B = 250).

Table 8.2 Example of the inconsistent retrieval anomaly

Steps	Transaction T_1	Transaction T_2	Values
1	read(A);		100
2	A := A − 50;		
3	write(A);		50
4		read(A);	50
5		read(B);	200
6	read(B);		200
7		C := A + B;	
8		write(C);	250
9	B := B + 50;		
10	write(B);		250
11	commit;		
12		commit;	

The next anomaly is known as the *uncommitted dependency* anomaly. This arises if one transaction T_2 is allowed to retrieve or update data that has been updated by another transaction T_1, where T_1 has not yet been committed. There is always the possibility that T_1 will never be committed, but that it will be rolled back instead. Therefore, transaction T_2 might then process data which do not exist in the database (see Table 8.3). A is initialised to 100. As can be seen from Table 8.3, the value of A written by T_2 was based on processing by T_1, which was subsequently aborted.

Table 8.3 Example of the uncommitted dependency anomaly

Steps	Transaction T_1	Transaction T_2	Values
1	read(A);		100
2	A := A + 50;		
3	write(A);		150
4		read(A);	150
5	abort;		
6		A := A ∗ 2;	
7		write(A);	300
8		commit;	

The final anomaly, known as the *cascading abort* anomaly, arises as a result of aborting transactions. Having started executing a transaction can either run to a natural completion and commit, or terminate its execution and abort. When a transaction is committed, its operations are written to permanent storage in the database and the database system guarantees that the effects of the transaction will not subsequently be nullified. An abort is the premature termination of a transaction, caused either by the user or by the database system.

The issue faced by a database system is what action to take if a transaction is aborted. An abort can vary from only impinging upon one transaction to affecting a large number of transactions. For example, if a transaction has utilised, and is therefore dependent on data values written by an aborted transaction, then the dependent transaction must also be aborted in order to maintain the consistency of the data within the database (see Table 8.4). Again A is initialised to 100.

As can be seen from Table 8.4, transaction T_2 is dependent on a value written by the aborting transaction T_1, consequently T_2 must also be aborted.

Table 8.4 Example of the cascading abort anomaly

Steps	Transaction T_1	Transaction T_2	Values
1	read(A);		100
2	A := A * 2;		
3	write(A);		200
4		read(A);	200
5		A := A + 30;	
6		write(A);	230
7	abort;		
8		. . .	

This type of knock-on effect is caused by a transaction aborting which requires one or more other transactions to also abort. The cascading abort anomaly can be more problematic than might appear from the example of Table 8.5, which shows one of the less obvious knock-on effects, namely that of transaction T_2 being forced to abort notwithstanding the fact that it has not written the data item read from transaction T_1.

Table 8.5 Another example of the cascading abort anomaly

Steps	Transaction T_1	Transaction T_2	Values
1	read(A);		100
2	A := A * 2;		
3	write(A);		200
4		read(A);	200
5		read(B)	100
6		B := B + 30;	
7		write(B);	130
8	abort;		

Whilst the situation in Table 8.5 is somewhat contrived and could have been avoided by a better programming technique, so that transaction T_2 does not read information prematurely, it demonstrates quite clearly the need for a mechanism to closely monitor abort operations.

The database system must be capable of establishing exactly what effect an abort will have on the database. This requirement is part of what is known as the *recovery problem*. It is generally handled by a *recovery algorithm*, which monitors and controls the execution of transactions to ensure that the effects of any aborted transactions are removed from the database. Surprisingly, it is not uncommon to find one fifth of the database system code dedicated to recovery [Cru84].

8.2   Serialisability

In general, it is only safe to allow two transactions to interleave their database operations, if they do not operate on the same data. However, this is not always the case since two transactions can sometimes update the same data without any harmful side-effects. If a transaction update operation is merely incremental (for example, A := A + 2), and another transaction update operation is decremental (for example, A := A − 2), then it would not matter in which order the update operations were performed. These transactions are effectively commutative and are said to be *serialisable*. Consider the following pair of transaction histories, where we abbreviate two consecutive steps such as A := A − 2; write(A) to the single step write(A − 2):

Steps	Transaction T_1	Transaction T_2
1	read(A);	
2	write(A + 2);	
3		read(A);
4		write(A − 2);

Steps	Transaction T_1	Transaction T_2
1		read(A);
2		write(A − 2);
3	read(A);	
4	write(A + 2);	

For each of these transaction histories, at the end of step 4, data item A would have the same value. However, this example of non-conflicting update operations on the same data is an exception rather than a general rule. Consider the case where T_1's operation is, for example, A := A * 3, and T_2's operation is A := A + 3, then the order of execution becomes important. In fact, the transaction history

Steps	Transaction T_1	Transaction T_2
1	read(A);	
2	write(A * 3);	
3		read(A);
4		write(A + 3);

is obviously not equivalent to the transaction history

Steps	Transaction T_1	Transaction T_2
1		read(A);
2		write(A + 3);
3	read(A);	
4	write(A * 3);	

Since interleaving of these operations can yield different results, they are said to be non-serialisable. Read operations on the same data item do not conflict with one another and are always serialisable. However, any transaction history that includes an update operation may not be serialisable, and is treated initially as non-serialisable from the point of view of concurrent access control strategies.

In a multitasking environment several transactions may be executed concurrently. The database system must control the interaction among transactions in order to maintain the consistency of the database. Ideally, to produce the desired result, concurrent transactions should behave as if they were executed in a serial manner. A concurrent execution of transactions is serialisable if interleaved execution of the transactions has the same effect as some sequential execution; see, for example, Table 8.6, where A and B are initialised to 100 and 200, respectively, and the serial execution of T_1 and T_2 has the same effect as their interleaved execution; in fact, the two schedules of Table 8.6 are conflict-equivalent (see Definition 8.6).

Table 8.6 A serial and interleaved execution of two transactions, T_1 and T_2

Steps	Transaction T_1	Transaction T_2	Values
1	read(A);		100
2	A := A + 30		
3	write(A);		130
4	read(B);		200
5	B := B + 50		
6	write(B);		250
7	commit;		
8		read(A);	130
9		A := A + 50;	
10		write(A)	180
11		read(B);	250
12		B := B + 50;	
13		write(B);	300
14		commit;	

Steps	Transaction T_1	Transaction T_2	Values
1	read(A);		100
2	A := A + 30;		
3	write(A);		130
4		read(A);	130
5		A := A + 50;	
6		write(A);	180
7	read(B);		200
8	B := B + 50;		
9	write(B);		250
10		read(B);	250
11		B := B + 50;	
12		write(B);	300
13	commit;		
14		commit;	

The execution sequence of read and write operations in a transaction or a transaction history is called a *schedule*. A schedule represents the chronological order in which transaction operations are executed in a database. We next proceed to define formally a schedule of a set of transactions, and then a serial schedule.

Hereafter we let $T = \{T_1, T_2, \ldots, T_n\}$ be a set of transactions.

Definition 8.3 (Schedule) A *schedule* for T is a sequence, say s, of the elementary steps of the transactions in T satisfying the following conditions:

1) every elementary step of every transaction appears exactly once in s;

2) elementary steps in s occur in exactly the same relative order that they occur in the transactions. ∎

In the following the terms operations and elementary steps (or simply steps) of a transaction will be used interchangeably.

Definition 8.4 (Serial schedule) A schedule s for T is serial if there exists a permutation $T_{i_1}, T_{i_2}, \ldots, T_{i_n}$ of T such that s consists of all the elementary steps of T_{i_1}, followed by all the elementary steps of T_{i_2}, and so on, and ending with all the elementary steps of T_{i_n}. ∎

8.2.1 Serialisability Theory

Serialisability theory allows us to prove whether or not a transaction schedule is serialisable. We begin by introducing the concepts of *conflict* and *conflict-equivalent* schedules.

Definition 8.5 (Conflicting operations) Two operations of two distinct transactions are in *conflict* if both of them involve the same data item and at least one of them is a write operation.

Let T be a set of transactions and let $s \in SCHED(T)$, where $SCHED(T)$ denotes the set of schedules for T. The conflict relation of s, designated by **conf**(s), over $OP(T)$, the set of operations of the transactions in T, is defined by

$$\mathbf{conf}(s) = \{(o, o') \mid o, o' \in OP(T), o \text{ occurs before } o' \text{ in } s, \text{ and } o, o' \text{ are in conflict}\}. \quad ∎$$

Definition 8.6 (Conflict equivalence) Two schedules $s, s' \in SCHED(T)$ are *conflict-equivalent* (or simply equivalent), written $s \equiv_c s'$, if **conf**(s) = **conf**(s'). ∎

Consider the transaction schedules s_1, s_2, s_3 and s_4, presented in Tables 8.7, 8.8, 8.9 and 8.10, respectively. Both A and B are initialised to 200; transaction T_1 debits the balance of A with 50 and credits the balance of B with 100, while transaction T_2 credits the balance of B with 50 and reduces the balance of A by 90%.

On examination of the schedules s_1 and s_2, shown in Tables 8.7 and 8.8, respectively, we observe that both **conf**(s_1) and **conf**(s_2) consist of the set of pairs

$\{(\text{read}(T_1,A), \text{write}(T_2,A)), (\text{write}(T_1,A), \text{read}(T_2,A)), (\text{write}(T_1,A), \text{write}(T_2,A)),$

$(\text{read}(T_1,B), \text{write}(T_2,B)), (\text{write}(T_1,B), \text{read}(T_2,B)), (\text{write}(T_1,B), \text{write}(T_2,B))\}.$

On the other hand, on examination of the schedule s_3, shown in Table 8.9, we see that **conf**(s_3) consists of the set of pairs

$\{(\text{read}(T_2,A), \text{write}(T_1,A)), (\text{write}(T_2,A), \text{read}(T_1,A)), (\text{write}(T_2,A), \text{write}(T_1,A)),$

$(\text{read}(T_2,B), \text{write}(T_1,B)), (\text{write}(T_2,B), \text{read}(T_1,B)), (\text{write}(T_2,B), \text{write}(T_1,B))\}.$

Table 8.7 Schedule s_1

Steps	Transaction T_1	Transaction T_2	Values
1	read(A);		200
2	A := A − 50;		
3	write(A);		150
4	read(B);		200
5	B := B + 100;		
6	write(B);		300
7		read(A);	150
8		A := A ∗ 0.1;	
9		write(A);	15
10		read(B);	300
11		B := B + 50;	
12		write(B);	350

Table 8.8 Schedule s_2

Steps	Transaction T_1	Transaction T_2	Values
1	read(A);		200
2	A := A − 50;		
3	write(A);		150
4		read(A);	150
5		A := A ∗ 0.1;	
6		write(A);	15
7	read(B);		200
8	B := B + 100;		
9	write(B);		300
10		read(B);	300
11		B := B + 50;	
12		write(B);	350

Furthermore, on examination of the schedule s_4, shown in Table 8.10, **conf**(s_4) consists of the set of pairs

$$\{(\text{read}(T_1,A), \text{write}(T_2,A)), (\text{write}(T_1,A), \text{read}(T_2,A)), (\text{write}(T_1,A), \text{write}(T_2,A)),$$

$$(\text{read}(T_2,B), \text{write}(T_1,B)), (\text{write}(T_2,B), \text{read}(T_1,B)), (\text{write}(T_2,B), \text{write}(T_1,B))\}.$$

Thus $s_1 \equiv_c s_2$, $s_1 \not\equiv_c s_3$, and $s_1 \not\equiv_c s_4$ notwithstanding the fact that in schedules s_1 and s_4 the final values produced for A and B are the same.

Definition 8.7 (Conflict-serialisability)   A schedule $s \in SCHED(\mathcal{T})$ is *conflict-serialisable* (or simply serialisable), if there exists a serial schedule $s_0 \in SCHED(\mathcal{T})$ such that $s \equiv_c s_0$.   ■

Prior to establishing the fundamental theorem of conflict-serialisability, we define the conflict digraph of a schedule $s \in SCHED(\mathcal{T})$.

Definition 8.8 (Conflict digraph)   Let $\mathcal{T}$ be a set of transactions. The *conflict digraph* of s is the digraph $\Gamma(s) = (\mathcal{T}, E)$, where $(T_i, T_j) \in E$, if $T_i \neq T_j$ and some operation of T_i is in conflict with some operation of T_j.   ■

Table 8.9 Schedule s_3

Steps	Transaction T_1	Transaction T_2	Values
1		read(A);	200
2		A := A * 0.1;	
3		write(A);	20
4		read(B);	200
5		B := B + 50;	
6		write(B);	250
7	read(A);		20
8	A := A − 50;		
9	write(A);		−30
10	read(B);		250
11	B := B + 100;		
12	write(B);		350

Table 8.10 Schedule s_4

Steps	Transaction T_1	Transaction T_2	Values
1	read(A);		200
2	A := A − 50;		
3	write(A);		150
4		read(B);	200
5		B := B + 50;	
6		write(B);	250
7	read(B);		250
8	B := B + 100;		
9	write(B);		350
10		read(A);	150
11		A := A * 0.1;	
12		write(A);	15

For example, the conflict digraph of both s_1 and s_2 is given in Figure 8.1 (a), while the conflict digraph of s_3 is given in Figure 8.1 (b) and the conflict digraph of s_4 is given in Figure 8.1 (c).

Theorem 8.1   A schedule $s \in SCHED(\mathcal{T})$ is conflict-serialisable if and only if $\Gamma(s)$ is acyclic.

Proof. Assume that $\Gamma(s)$ is acyclic. Since the vertices of an acyclic digraph can be sorted in topological order, we can list the elements of $\mathcal{T}$, i.e. $T_1, T_2, \ldots, T_n$, in such a way that $i < j$ if there exists an arc from T_i to T_j in $\Gamma(s)$. Consider the serial schedule, say s_0, resulting from concatenating the sequence of operations of the set of transactions $\{T_1, T_2, \ldots, T_n\}$ topologically sorted.

We next show that $s \equiv_c s_0$. Let $OP(T_i)$ stand for the set of operations in transaction T_i. If $(o, o') \in \mathbf{conf}\,(s)$, where $o \in OP(T_i)$ and $o' \in OP(T_j)$, then there exists an arc in $\Gamma(s)$ and thus $i < j$. Hence, in s_0 the operations of T_i precede those of T_j and therefore $(o, o') \in \mathbf{conf}(s_0)$. Correspondingly, if $(o, o') \in \mathbf{conf}(s_0)$, then $i < j$. The implication of this is that o, o' are conflicting operations in s and consequently $(o, o') \in \mathbf{conf}(s)$. Since $\mathbf{conf}(s) = \mathbf{conf}(s_0)$, it follows that $s \equiv_c s_0$.

Conversely, assume that s is a conflict-serialisable schedule. Let s_0 be a serial schedule such that $s \equiv_c s_0$. If $\Gamma(s) = (\mathcal{T}, \text{E})$ is cyclic, then there must exist a sequence of transactions, say T_{i_0}, $T_{i_1}, T_{i_2}, \ldots, T_{i_\mu}$, such that $(T_{i_q}, T_{i_{q+1}}) \in \text{E}, 0 \leq q \leq \mu - 1$, and $(T_{i_\mu}, T_{i_0}) \in \text{E}$. This leads to a

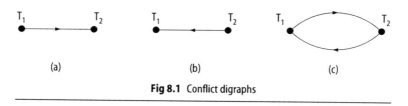

Fig 8.1 Conflict digraphs

contradiction, because in the serial schedule s_0 the operations of T_{i_μ} follow those of T_{i_0} as a result of the path $T_{i_0} \to T_{i_1} \to \dots T_{i_{\mu-2}} \to T_{i_{\mu-1}}$, whilst the operations of T_{i_μ} precede those of T_{i_0} as a result of the arc $(T_{i_\mu}, T_{i_0}) \in E$. Thus $\Gamma(s)$ must be acyclic. $\qquad\square$

A more natural view of schedule serialisability would be based on *view-equivalence*, which is a form of equivalence less stringent than that of conflict-serialisability given in Definition 8.7.

Consider two schedules $s, s' \in SCHED(\mathcal{T})$. The schedules s and s' are said to be *view-equivalent* if the following three conditions are satisfied:

1) For each data item x, if T_i reads the initial value of x in s, then T_i must, in s', also read the initial value of x, namely $IR(s) = IR(s')$ (see Definition 8.9).

2) For each data item x, if T_i executes read(x) in s, and that value was produced by T_j (if any), then T_i must, in s', also read the value of x that was produced by T_j.

3) For each data item x, the transaction (if any) that performs the final write(x) in s must also perform the final write(x) in s', namely $FW(s) = FW(s')$ (see Definition 8.9).

Conditions 1 and 2 ensure that each transaction reads the same values in both schedules s and s' and, therefore, performs the same computation. Condition 3, together with conditions 1 and 2, ensures that both s and s' result in the same final database state.

It is easy to verify that schedules s_1 and s_2 of Tables 8.7 and 8.8, respectively, are view-equivalent, whilst schedules s_1 and s_3 of Table 8.9 are not view-equivalent.

Definition 8.9 (Set of initial reads and final writes)   Given a schedule s, we denote by $IR(s)$, the set of *initial reads*, which comprises the first operations read(T_j, x) for every data item x for which such an operation exists. Correspondingly, $FW(s)$, the set of *final writes*, comprises the final operations write(T_k, x) for every data item x for which such an operation exists.   ∎

In the context of view-equivalence in a schedule s, T_j *reads a data item x from T_i, $i \neq j$*, if read$(T_j, x) \in OP(T_j)$ follows write(T_i, x) and no operation write(T_k, x) exists between write(T_i, x) and read(T_j, x) for any transaction T_k participating in s.

The concept of a transaction reading a data item from another transaction allows us to give a more concise definition of view-equivalence as follows. In essence conditions (1) and (2) above coalesce.

Definition 8.10 (View-equivalence)   Let T_i, $T_j \in \mathcal{T}$ and $s, s' \in SCHED(\mathcal{T})$. The schedules s and s' are view-equivalent, denoted by $s \equiv_v s'$, if

1) T_j reads from T_i in s if and only if T_j does this in s' also; and

2) $FW(s) = FW(s')$. ∎

We observe that a pair of schedules can be view-equivalent but not conflict-equivalent.

Theorem 8.2   For all $s, s' \in SCHED(\mathcal{T})$, if $s \equiv_c s'$ then $s \equiv_v s'$.

Proof. Assume that s and s' are conflict-equivalent. If T_j reads from T_i in s, then for some data item A write$(T_i, A) \in OP(T_i)$, read$(T_j, A) \in OP(T_j)$, with the latter following the former with no write(T_k, A) between them. Hence (write(T_i, A), read$(T_j, A)) \in \mathbf{conf}(s) = \mathbf{conf}(s')$ and in s' there is no write(T_k,A) between write(T_i, A) and read(T_j, A). Consequently, in s' T_j reads from T_i. The reverse can be proved similarly. This proves (1) of Definition 8.10.

Assume that write(T_l, A) is the last write of data item A in s. If in s' the last write of data item A, write$(T_{l'}, A)$, is different, $l \neq l'$, then write$(T_{l'}, A)$ would come after write(T_l, A) in s'. Consequently, (write(T_l, A), write$(T_{l'}, A)) \in \mathbf{conf}(s')$. Since $\mathbf{conf}(s) = \mathbf{conf}(s')$, in s write$(T_{l'}$, A) would follow write(T_l, A), which contradicts the fact that write(T_l, A) is the last write of the data item A in s. This proves (2) of Definition 8.10 □

The concept of view-equivalence leads to the concept of view-serialisability. We say that a schedule $s \in SCHED(\mathcal{T})$ is view-serialisable if it is view-equivalent to a serial schedule. The formal definition now follows.

Definition 8.11 (View-serialisability)   A schedule $s \in SCHED(\mathcal{T})$ is *view-serialisable*, if there exists a serial schedule $s_0 \in SCHED(\mathcal{T})$ such that $s \equiv_v s_0$. ∎

It has been shown by Papadimitriou [Pap79] that testing for view-serialisability is an NP-complete problem. On the other hand, testing for conflict-serialisability is a polynomial-time problem. This is realised by applying Tarjan's depth-first algorithm [Tar72] to $\Gamma(s)$ and then identifying at least one *back* edge (arc), which signifies the existence of a cycle.

A more general notion of serialisability than view-serialisability is that of *final-state serialisability*. We say that two schedules are *final-state equivalent* if they satisfy condition (2) of Definition 8.10, i.e. for any input state of the database the resulting output states from these two schedules, s and s', are identical. A schedule is *final-state serialisable* if there is some serial schedule which is final-state equivalent to it. To verify the generality of this notion, the reader can construct a schedule which is final-state serialisable but *not* view-serialisable. It was shown in [Pap79] that the problem of testing whether a schedule is final-state serialisable is NP-complete.

We motivate the next type of serialisability via an example. Consider the schedule s induced by the transaction history shown in Table 8.11, which is final-state serialisable but neither conflict-serialisable nor view-serialisable. For the sake of simplicity, assume that the database contains only two distinct data items A and B. Moreover, let us partition the database into two *subdatabases* one containing the data item A and the other containing the data item B; for example, in the context of a distributed database each subdatabase may be stored at a physically different site. Let us construct two *subschedules*, s_1 and s_2, which partition the schedule s in accordance with the data items in each respective subdatabase. In this case s_1 contains steps 1 and 2 and s_2 contains steps 3 and 4. It is evident that both s_1 and s_2 are conflict-serialisable. In general, if a situation such as this arises then we say that s is *predicatewise serialisable* [RMB+98].

Table 8.11 A schedule which is final-state serialisable

Steps	Transaction T_1	Transaction T_2
1	write(A);	
2		read(A);
3		write(B);
4	read(B);	

The concept of the execution of a schedule assumes that the database is left in a consistent state. Thus in the case of predicatewise-serialisability the best that we can guarantee is that after the execution of each subschedule the resulting subdatabase is consistent. However, in general, this does not guarantee that the database as a whole is consistent. Thus in order for predicatewise-serialisability to make sense we must impose further conditions so that subdatabase consistency implies database consistency. In [RMB+98] several such conditions are given.

By definition a transaction preserves database consistency, hence a serial execution of transactions also preserves consistency. Since every serialisable execution has the same effect as a serial execution, we conclude that a serialisable execution must indeed preserve database consistency. It makes sense therefore for a database system to permit serialisable executions.

There are various approaches to enforcing serialisability. The two most commonly used approaches are locking mechanisms and timestamp ordering. Other non-locking techniques, such as serialisation graph testing, also merit consideration; this technique is considered in some detail in Section 8.8.

We close this section with a discussion of serialisability in the context of the IDM model, which was mentioned at the beginning of Section 8.1. A schedule is serialisable in the IDM model, if it is equivalent to some serial schedule, i.e. for all input databases the schedule has the same effect on the database as the effect of the execution of the transactions in some serial order. (Recall Definition 3.42 of a transaction and its *effect* on a relation, and Definition 3.43 of equivalent transactions, which were both given in Subsection 3.2.4 of Chapter 3.) It has been shown by Vianu and Vossen [VV92] that testing for serialisability in the IDM model is an NP-complete problem. A polynomial-time testable subclass of schedules are the schedules that are *locally serialisable*. A schedule is locally serialisable if, on repetitive invocation of the commutativity rules for pairs of consecutive updates, we obtain a serial schedule. (The *commutativity rules* for pairs of updates were given in [KKPV87, KV91]; for example, we can insert two tuples in any order, and we can delete two sets of tuples in any order.) Local-serialisability in the IDM model is analogous to conflict-serialisability in the RW model, in the sense that two updates that are *not* commutative can be viewed as conflicting. This observation gives rise to a polynomial-time test for local-serialisability based on the concept of a *local conflict digraph*, which is analogous to the conflict digraph in the RW model. An interesting result, shown in [VV92], is that in the IDM model, if we restrict updates to be only insertions and deletions, i.e. we disallow modifications, then serialisability becomes polynomial-time testable. As a final remark we note that, due to the fact that the IDM model is defined within the relational model, we are also able to use knowledge of integrity constraints, such as functional dependencies, for the purpose of testing serialisability.

8.3 Locking

Building on the serialisability concept that concurrent execution of transactions should have the same result as a serial execution, then some form of control is required to enforce serialisability. By ensuring that access to data is in a mutually exclusive manner, we can guarantee that, while one transaction has access to a data item, no other transaction can modify that particular data item. The most widely used mechanism for enforcing mutually exclusive access to data is locking.

Over time many refinements to the general idea of locking data items have been developed, with a variety of *locking modes* currently in use. These modes of locking are the subject of this section.

Although there are various modes in which data items may be locked, typical locking mechanisms have two basic modes of lock: *shared* and *exclusive*. If a transaction T_1 obtains a lock in shared mode on a data item, then T_1 can read but not update the data item, whilst if T_1 obtains a lock in exclusive mode on a data item, then T_1 can both read and update the data item. In other words a shared lock permits other transactions to read the same data item concurrently, but prevents any updating of this data item.

Definition 8.12 (Well-formed transaction)   A transaction is considered to be *well-formed* if it always locks a data item in shared mode before reading it and in exclusive mode before updating the data item. Two transactions are in *conflict* if they want to lock the same data with two incompatible modes of lock. ■

Locking has a number of problems associated with it. The problem of *deadlock* is perhaps the most undesirable side-effect of locking and its resolution represents an important area of concurrency control theory. Deadlock is caused by a cyclical wait of transactions holding resources required by other transactions and waiting in turn for resources held by these other transactions. Another problem is the *lock granularity* problem, which is the size of the data item (subtuple, tuple, relation, or an entire database) to be locked. Clearly, it is undesirable to lock an entire database or relation when a transaction intends, for example, only to access one value in a particular tuple of that relation. Both of theses important issues will be discussed further in Sections 8.4 and 8.5, respectively.

Whilst locking is the most widely used strategy to prevent undesirable interleaving, it should not be assumed that it is the best approach in all contexts. Clearly, in single-user databases there is no risk of conflicting access, so locking is not needed. Similarly, reference databases such as bulletin boards and technical reference databases allow concurrent read access only. Therefore, the use of locks in such databases would impose an overhead on the DBMS's performance, without being necessary to maintain the integrity of the database. Finally, because data in a distributed database is stored over multiple sites or nodes, the management of access to data items by locking may prove to be an inefficient and expensive approach.

We next consider various types of lock. We begin with *exclusive locks*. The simplest and most commonly used lock strategy to prevent non-serialisable transactions from corrupting one another is the exclusive lock. Exclusive locking gives a transaction an exclusive hold on the data item it wishes to access or update, not allowing any other transaction to access that data item for the duration of the lock. By prohibiting competing updates the transaction knows that its own read or update will be executed safely, and by preventing competing read operations the locking transaction guarantees that other transactions will be unaffected if it decides to update the locked data item.

Exclusive locking works on the idea that a transaction locks a data item on access and that another transaction wanting to access that data item must wait for the lock to be released. So if transaction T_1 holds an exclusive lock on a tuple t, then a request from transaction T_2 for a lock on t will cause T_2 to go into a wait state until T_1 releases its lock on t. When a transaction wishes to update a data item it automatically acquires an exclusive lock on it.

A lock can be thought of as a control block that includes the identity (ID) of the locked data item and the ID of the transaction holding the lock. The locking mechanism in a DBMS is implemented by means of a *lock manager*. The lock manager maintains a lock table where it records the locks that are currently operational on any data item. A transaction begins with the DBMS searching for the required data item in the database. If the data item is already locked then the lock manager instructs a component, called the *transaction scheduler* (see Figure 8.9), to place the requesting transaction in a *wait queue* until the required lock or locks become available. The lock manager then provides the necessary locks for the transaction to proceed. Next the read and write operations are executed. Exclusive locks are retained until the transaction ends with a commit or abort. Early releases of locks can lead to the type of concurrency control problems discussed in Section 8.1.

We now discuss some problems associated with *exclusive locking*. Exclusive locking ensures serialisability and solves the lost update, inconsistent retrieval and cascading abort anomalies (see Table 8.12). In Table 8.12 rx(A) stands for "request exclusive lock on data item A", un(A) stands for "unlock data item A" and A is initialised to 200. As can be seen from this table the lost update problem exemplified in Table 8.1 has been rectified by the use of locks, with a noticeable loss of concurrency.

Unfortunately, if we depend solely on exclusive locking, then all these anomalies are solved at the expense of greatly reducing the level of concurrency. Moreover, the overheads incurred by operating the lock manager may have a detrimental effect on the performance of the DBMS in terms of processing speed and storage space required for the lock table.

We note at this point that the exclusive locking mechanism described above is prone to the following problems:

- Difficulties in ascertaining the appropriate data items to lock.

- Dangers of premature lock release.

- Blocking of resources via deadlock.

- Lack of concurrency because access to data items is restricted to single transactions.

Table 8.12 Illustration of exclusive locking

Steps	Transaction T_1	Transaction T_2	Values
1	rx(A); ...granted		
2	read(A);		200
3		rx(A); ...fail	
4	A := A * 2;	...wait	
5	write(A);	...wait	400
6	un(A);	...wait	
7	commit;	...wait	
8		rx(A); ...granted	
9		read(A);	400
10		A := A + 30;	
11		write(A);	430
12		un(A);	
13		commit;	

It is also worth mentioning at this juncture that many reputable database products make use of exclusive techniques to ensure serialisability.

We next look at *shared locks*. In a database environment transactions that query data items without updating them are common. A shared lock can be applied to a data item when a transaction only wishes to read that data item, with the certain knowledge that another transaction is not going to change the data item during the read operation. No other transaction can gain an exclusive lock to update a data item if another transaction already holds a shared lock on that data item. (We call such modes of lock, in this case shared and exclusive, incompatible.) Two or more transactions can, however, hold shared locks on the same data item simultaneously without any danger of interference between transactions. This helps to alleviate the loss of concurrency resulting from the dependence solely on exclusive locks.

We now define the notion of compatibility matrix in the context of a given set of lock modes.

Definition 8.13 (Compatibility matrix) Assume that a transaction T_i requests a lock of mode, say m_1, on a data item A on which another transaction T_j, $i \neq j$, currently holds a lock of mode, say m_2. If transaction T_i can be granted immediately a lock of mode m_1 on data item A, notwithstanding the fact that T_j has a lock of mode m_2 on A, then we say that mode m_1 is *compatible* with mode m_2, otherwise m_1 is incompatible with m_2. The compatibility relation can be represented by a matrix, called the compatibility matrix. ■

In order to read a data item a transaction must first request a lock on the data item in shared mode. If the data item is already locked by another transaction in an incompatible mode, the requesting transaction must wait until all incompatible locks have been released. While shared locks on the same data item are compatible with each other, neither a shared and an exclusive lock nor two exclusive locks are permitted (see Table 8.13). A shared lock on a data item may require upgrading to an exclusive lock when a read operation needs to progress to an update operation, but can do so only if there are no other shared locks on the data item (see Table 8.14).

In Table 8.14 rs(A) stands for "request shared lock on data item A" and A and B are both initialised to 200; this table illustrates the upgrade from shared lock to exclusive lock at step 8. If there are other shared locks on the said data item, the transaction must wait for the incompatible locks to be released before an upgrade of the lock to exclusive mode can proceed. As a result of this waiting period, deadlock remains a potential problem.

Table 8.13 A lock compatibility matrix of shared and exclusive locks

	SHARED	EXCLUSIVE
SHARED	YES	NO
EXCLUSIVE	NO	NO

As well as being used in conjunction with exclusive locks, shared locks are employed almost exclusively in certain situations. Such a situation might arise, for example, in a statistical database of census data, where many people may wish to query the database simultaneously while few changes to the data will be required. In general, statistical databases allow statistical output only, without permitting the user to access the underlying data. In this situation there is little danger of interference, in which case speed may take precedence over safety, thus allowing the operating system to schedule simultaneous read requests as and when it is required.

Table 8.14 Example showing the use of shared and exclusive locks

Steps	Transaction T_1	Transaction T_2	Values
1	rs(A); ...granted		
2	read(A);		200
3		rs(A); ...granted	
4		read(A);	200
5	rs(B); ...granted		
6	read(B);		200
7		rx(A); ...fail	
8	rx(B); ...granted	...wait	
9	B := B + 100;	...wait	
10	write(B);	...wait	300
11	un(B);	...wait	
12	un(A);	...wait	
13	commit;		
14		rx(A); ...granted	
15		A := A * 3;	
16		write(A);	600
17		un(A);	
18		commit;	

A DBMS using shared locks suffers from a tendency to produce an increased number of deadlocks, while exclusive locking results in a lower degree of concurrency. In an attempt to limit these difficulties some DBMSs employ an additional promotable lock, called the *update lock*. An update lock on a data item indicates that a transaction may want to update the data item on which it has such a lock. Thus any transaction that intends to update a data item must first acquire an update lock on it. Subsequent update of the data item will promote the update lock to an exclusive lock when this is required. This reflects more closely the read/write requirements of many transactions, where a data item is read prior to being updated. Shared locks are compatible with update locks, but update locks are *not* compatible with shared locks; thus in this case compatibility is not symmetric. Neither are update locks compatible with other update locks or exclusive locks (see Table 8.15). A transaction cannot obtain an exclusive lock on a data item which has been locked in update mode by another transaction. We note that a transaction may not be safe from anomalies if it writes data items after reading other data items locked in update mode by another transaction.

Table 8.15 Update lock compatibility matrix

	SHARED	UPDATE	EXCLUSIVE
SHARED	YES	NO	NO
UPDATE	YES	NO	NO
EXCLUSIVE	NO	NO	NO

Once a transaction has acquired an update lock on a data item, the transaction is guaranteed to be able to update that data item eventually. By inspecting Table 8.16, where two concurrent transactions T_1 and T_2, with T_1 using an update lock and T_2 using a shared lock, are accessing the same data item, we see that promotion of the update lock at step 4 is not granted because T_2 holds a shared lock on data item A. When the shared lock is released, the update lock is promoted automatically to an exclusive lock at step 6. In this table ru(A) stands for "request update lock on data item A", update(A) stands for "request to promote update lock to exclusive lock on data item A" and A is initialised to 200.

Table 8.16 Example of update and shared lock modes

Steps	Transaction T_1	Transaction T_2	Values
1	ru(A); ...granted		
2		rs(A); ...granted	
3		read(A);	200
4	update(A);		
5	...wait	un(A);	
6	write(A * 2);		400
7	un(A);		

If a transaction acquires an update lock on a data item, but does not subsequently update that data item, then the update lock can be downgraded to a shared lock. In general, update locking allows slightly more concurrency than direct exclusive locking.

In the context of what follows by database we mean the entire database which is assumed to be composed of exactly a fixed number of *areas*. In essence the areas constitute a partition of the database.

When we change a data item we are implicitly, by association, changing the tuple (record), relation (table/file), area and database containing the data item. The level at which a data item is locked is referred to as *locking granularity* (see Section 8.5). *Fine granularity* is locking, for example, at tuple level, while locking at relation or database level is called *coarse granularity*. It is necessary to control the effects of fine granule locking on coarse granules in order to identify any potential conflicts. To this end we define a hierarchy of granularities whereby small granularities are nested within larger ones. The hierarchy can be defined graphically by a rooted tree, whose highest level, i.e. the root node, represents the entire database, and the lowest level, i.e. the leaf nodes, represent the tuples in the relations of the database.

The aforesaid control can be achieved by giving each higher level lock an associated *intent lock*, in order to indicate where small granules are nested within larger ones. For example, each shared lock at fine granularity acquires an intent shared lock at all higher levels in the database. Thus, the transaction scheduler (see Figure 8.9) in the DBMS can ensure that there are no locks on ancestors of a data item that implicitly lock the data item in a conflicting mode before a request to lock the data item is granted. In Table 8.17 (see [BK91]) we use the abbreviations: S = Shared, X = Exclusive and I = Intent; this table presents the compatibility matrix involving the intent lock.

Table 8.17 Intent lock type compatibility matrix

	X	S	IS	SIX	IX
X	NO	NO	NO	NO	NO
S	NO	YES	YES	NO	NO
IS	NO	YES	YES	YES	YES
SIX	NO	NO	YES	NO	NO
IX	NO	NO	YES	NO	YES

There is an intent lock associated with each shared and exclusive lock. An *Intent Shared* (IS) lock implies that explicit locking is being done at a lower level in the database with shared locks only. Similarly, an *Intent Exclusive* (IX) lock implies that locking with shared or exclusive locks is being done at a lower level. Finally, a *Shared Intent Exclusive* (SIX) lock signifies that within the data item locked explicitly by a shared lock, explicit exclusive locking takes place at a lower level. Prior to granting a shared lock on a data item, say a subtuple, the DBMS must first set an intent shared lock on the database, area, relation, and tuple, for example, that contain the data item (see Table 8.18).

In Table 8.18 we assume a hierarchy (rooted tree) consisting of four levels of nodes. Below the root node (the highest level) are nodes of type area; each area has nodes of type relation as its children and contains exactly those relations which are its children nodes. No relation resides in more than one area. Finally, each relation has nodes of type tuple as its children. As before each relation comprises exactly those tuples that are its children nodes and no tuple resides in more than one relation. It is further assumed that area 1 contains relation 1. Thus, in the context of this table, T_2 and T_4 are attempting incompatible locks at the database level, while T_2 and T_3 are requesting incompatible locks at the relation level. So T_2 must wait for T_3 and T_4 to commit.

The intent locking protocol can be summarised as follows:

1) All locks should be acquired in a top-down (root-to-leaf) order.

2) Prior to requesting a shared or intent shared lock on a node (level), all ancestor nodes must be locked with intent exclusive or intent shared locks.

3) Prior to requesting an exclusive, shared intent exclusive, or intent exclusive lock on a node (level), all ancestors must be locked with intent exclusive or shared intent exclusive locks.

4) All locks should be released in bottom-up (leaf-to-root) order.

Intent locking enables the DBMS to tell whether other transactions are already changing the relation containing the data item being accessed. It also tells the database system

Transaction T_1 := Read tuple 1 in relation 1
          lock the database with intent shared lock
          lock area 1 with intent shared lock
          lock relation 1 with intent shared lock
          lock tuple 1 with a shared lock

Transaction T_2 := Write tuple 2 in relation 1
          lock the database with intent exclusive lock
          lock area 1 with intent exclusive lock
          lock relation 1 with intent exclusive lock
          lock tuple 2 with an exclusive lock

Transaction T_3 := Read all tuples in relation 1
          lock the database with intent shared lock
          lock area 1 with intent shared lock
          lock relation 1 with a shared lock

Transaction T_4 := Read the entire database
          lock the database with a shared lock

Table 8.18 Implementation of intent locking showing the order and levels of locks

whether an ancestor of the data item has an exclusive lock granted to another transaction. This enhanced locking mechanism affords more concurrency and may also reduce locking overheads, particularly in applications that include a mix of short transactions, which access only a few data items, and long transactions, which access an entire relation or a set of relations. Intent locking facilitates relatively simple upgrades from shared to exclusive locks and is employed in DBMSs to alleviate some of the concurrency loss and deadlock problems that are caused by using only shared and exclusive locks.

We next look at the problem of how to allocate locks. We consider three ways of allocating locks, namely:

Transaction scheduling. Transaction scheduling is a static approach to the allocation of locks. The idea is simply that a transaction requests locks on all the data items it may need, before it starts executing. If it is not granted all of its requested locks then it is queued. The problems with this approach are:

- Maintaining the queue and on each commit checking whether any waiting transaction can have its set of desired locks granted.

- Dealing with priority requests and hence the additional overheads of keeping a priority queue.

- The possibility of *livelock*, whereby a transaction may be unlucky enough never to have a high enough priority to be granted its full set of desired locks. Avoiding livelock adds complexity to the DBMS.

- The difficulty of determining in advance of processing which locks are needed. For safety, it may be necessary to lock too much of the database, thereby reducing concurrency.

Transaction rejection. An alternative to transaction scheduling is simply to reject any transaction that cannot immediately obtain the locks it requires and retry at a later time.

Although this approach has less overheads than transaction scheduling in maintaining queues, it is prone to livelock, when several transactions are waiting to access a locked data item and access is granted in a random manner. In order to make a rejection policy workable, a mechanism is required to coordinate retries. Like the transaction scheduling approach, transaction rejection suffers from uncertainty about the set of desired locks and is only viable for batch run tasks.

Dynamic lock allocation. An alternative to the static allocation of locks we have so far considered is to grant locks dynamically on a need to access basis, as the locks are required. The important advantage of this approach is that it increases concurrency and throughput by locking data items only if a lock is required. However, the benefits of dynamic lock allocation are only fully realised if the locks are not prematurely released; this requirement can be met by employing a two-phase locking policy. This locking policy is analysed in the next subsection.

8.3.1   Two-Phase Locking Policy

Any transaction that releases a lock and then goes on to acquire another lock always runs the risk of producing incorrect results (see Table 8.19). Data items A and B are both initialised to 200. As can be seen from Table 8.19 transaction T_2 updates data item A after transaction T_1 releases its lock at step 4. Hence transaction T_1 could be incorrect as it is based on an earlier *out of date* read of data item A. So a transaction should not release any lock until it has acquired all the locks necessary to complete its processing. This strategy is known as *Two-Phase Locking* (2PL), whereby the set of locks of each transaction has a *growing phase* for acquiring locks and a latter *shrinking phase* (or *release phase*) when it is safe to release its locks.

Table 8.19 Two transactions not obeying the two-phase locking policy

Steps	Transaction T_1	Transaction T_2	Values
1	rs(A); ...granted		
2	read(A);		200
3		rx(A); ...fail	
4	un(A);	...wait	
5		rx(A); ...granted	
6		read(A);	200
7		A := A + 100;	
8		write(A);	300
9		un(A);	
10		commit;	
11	rx(B); ...granted		
12	read(B);		200
13	B := B + 150;		
14	write(B);		350
15	un(B);		
16	commit;		

One solution to the problem identified in Table 8.19 is to ensure that all transactions in a schedule follow a set of rules, called a *locking protocol*, which indicates when a transaction may lock and unlock each data item. Basic two-phase locking ensures that a transaction cannot request *any* locks after it has released a lock. During the *growing* phase of this protocol new locks are acquired, while locks are only released during the *shrinking* phase. In order to make basic 2PL work in practice, shared locks may be released at any time during the shrinking phase, but exclusive locks must be held until the transaction commits; these two rules preserve serialisability and guarantee the isolation of transactions.

Theorem 8.3 Every schedule that obeys the basic 2PL protocol is conflict-serialisable.

Proof. Assume that a schedule s, which satisfies the basic 2PL protocol, is not conflict-serialisable. Then there must exist in $\Gamma(s)$ a cycle $T_{i_1}, T_{i_2}, \ldots, T_{i_p}, T_{i_1}$, with $p > 1$. That is to say, two conflicting operations exist in any two consecutive transactions $T_{i_k}, T_{i_{k+1}}, 1 \leq k \leq p - 1$, and in T_{i_p}, T_{i_1}. Consequently an $un(T_{i_k}, x)$ in T_{i_k} is followed by either a read lock on a data item x or a write lock on x in $T_{i_{k+1}}, 1 \leq k \leq p - 1$, and an unlock operation in T_{i_p} is followed by a locking operation in T_{i_1}. Thus $un(T_{i_1}, x)$ is followed by a locking operation in T_{i_1}; however, this contradicts the basic 2PL protocol. □

Two-phase locking is the most widely used of the locking mechanisms employed in DBMSs. Unfortunately, the basic 2PL protocol described above restricts the number of possible transaction schedules and is prone to deadlock. A number of refinements of the protocol have been suggested to overcome these shortcomings, thereby resulting in *aggressive* and *conservative* implementations.

The most aggressive 2PL protocol implementation requires each transaction to request a lock on each data item immediately prior to reading or updating the data item. This approach increases concurrency by liberalising the approach to locking, at the expense of increasing the possibility of conflicting operations. In contrast to the aggressive approach, the most conservative 2PL protocol implementation requires each transaction to request all its locks at the beginning of the transaction. This approach removes the possibility of conflicting locks, but in doing so it decreases the level of concurrency and increases the level of transaction queuing. The requirement to pre-declare all locks means that the full read and write sets of a transaction must be known in advance of any processing.

Determining the most suitable version of 2PL for a particular application depends upon the frequency of conflict between concurrently executing transactions. At low conflict levels aggressive schedules require few operations to be rejected, while conservative schedulers avoid rejecting operations at high conflict levels by deliberately delaying transactions until all required locks are available. There is currently no precise set of rules available for tailoring a scheduler to the performance specification of an application; thus intuition, trial and error, and experience play an important role. In practice, however, a refined version of the basic 2PL, called *strict 2PL*, which requires *all* locks to be released at the commit or abort stage of a transaction, is mostly used.

Locking on its own does not ensure a consistent database or efficient use of resources. The performance of a particular locking mechanism can be evaluated in terms of the ACID test and the following three criteria:

Throughput. The number of transactions that successfully complete, and therefore the average time taken for each successful transaction. This provides a crude guideline to the effectiveness of a database system.

Fig 8.2 Circular wait of transactions resulting in deadlock

Fairness. Does each transaction have an equal chance of completion? If only a subset of all users have successful transactions then the other users will not be very satisfied by the database system.

Cost. A database may exhibit high throughput and fairness, but still be costly in terms of memory and processing overheads.

As an epilogue we mention the recent study of Thomasian [Tho93] pertaining to the performance of 2PL. In this work it is shown that system performance is determined by the fraction of transactions that are blocked, i.e. transactions that are waiting due to the denial of a lock request. In particular, if this fraction exceeds a certain value then *thrashing* occurs, i.e. throughput drops when the number of transactions in the database system is increased.

8.4   Deadlock

Deadlock or *deadly embrace* is an error condition in which processing cannot continue because two elements of the process are waiting for an action from the other. In our context it results from two or more transactions requesting resources, resulting in a circular wait situation (see Figure 8.2).

Deadlock is an undesirable side-effect of locking. The most simple and by far the most common deadlock situation arises when one transaction has locked a data item that is needed by another transaction which has done exactly the same thing with a different data item (see Table 8.20). In this case transaction T_1 is waiting for a data item held by transaction T_2, which in turn is waiting for another data item held by transaction T_1, thus resulting in a circular wait.

Table 8.20 Example of a deadlock situation

Steps	Transaction T_1	Transaction T_2
1	rx(A); ...granted	
2		rx(B); ...granted
3	rx(B); ...fail	
4	...wait	rx(A); ...fail
5	...wait	...wait
6	...wait	...wait

We next consider the conditions that induce deadlock. Four necessary conditions leading to deadlock are presented. All four conditions must obtain for deadlock to occur. The four conditions are: *mutual exclusion, hold and wait, no pre-emption,* and the *circular wait* exhibited above. Mutual exclusion involves at least one data item being held in exclusive mode. For the hold and wait condition to be satisfied there must exist a transaction that is holding at least one data item and is waiting to access additional data items that are being held by other transactions. No pre-emption implies that a data item can only be released voluntarily by the transaction holding it, after the transaction has completed its task. Finally, for the circular wait condition to be satisfied there must exist a set of waiting transactions T_1, $T_2, \ldots, T_n$ such that T_1 is waiting for a data item held by T_2, T_2 in turn is waiting for a data item held by T_3 etc., and finally T_n is waiting for a data item held by T_1. All techniques designed to deal with deadlock attempt to prevent one of these conditions arising, thus eliminating the possibility of deadlock occurring.

Deadlock may occur for different reasons; herein we discuss only four types of deadlock, namely: circular deadlock, conversion deadlock, distributed deadlock, and phantom deadlock.

Circular deadlock. Of the estimated 2% maximum of transactions that result in deadlock [GHOK81] circular deadlock accounts for approximately one in twenty. As a result of a circular wait arising among two or more transactions, processing is brought to a standstill (see Figure 8.2). In fact, this type of deadlock rarely involves more than two transactions. However, if it is not remedied it will eventually bring the whole database system to a halt.

Conversion deadlock. A deadlock may also arise when a single data item is accessed by two transactions and incremental claims are accepted (see Table 8.21). When a read lock is converted to a write lock the read lock must be maintained to satisfy the requirements of 2PL. Conversion deadlock is in turn part of the circular wait type of deadlock, emanating from lock conversion.

It is often unclear in advance of transaction initiation whether a write operation will be required, and it is also undesirable to exclusively lock a data item until this is absolutely necessary. Hence lock conversion and its associated deadlocks are a common occurrence.

Table 8.21 Example of deadlock resulting from lock conversion

Steps	Transaction T_1	Transaction T_2	Values
1	rs(A); ...granted		
2	read(A);		200
3		rs(A); ...granted	
4		read(A);	200
5	rx(A); ...fail		
6		rx(A); ...fail	
7	...wait	...wait	
8	...wait	...wait	

Distributed deadlock. In the context of a distributed database, with data items and processing spread over different sites, deadlock between transactions at different sites cannot be detected from an individual site. Each site has access only to the local *Waits-For-Graph* (WFG) (see next section) which identifies circular wait cycles at that site. A global deadlock detector is required to combine the various local WFGs in order to identify a global deadlock (see Figure 8.3). The global deadlock detector can be run periodically at a chosen site to monitor distributed deadlocks. However, this incurs additional communications overheads resulting from joining together the local WFGs at the different sites.

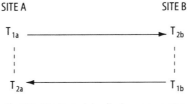

Fig 8.3 Distributed deadlock over two sites

Phantom deadlock. Adding to the complexity of distributed deadlock detection is the possibility of a phantom deadlock being identified. For instance, if transaction T_1 aborts because of a system failure such as a failed buffer, then a deadlock detected between, say, transactions T_1 and T_2, no longer exists. However, the global deadlock detector may not be aware of T_1's abort so it unnecessarily aborts T_2 to break the phantom deadlock between the two transactions.

There are two general approaches to dealing with deadlock: *deadlock prevention* which aims to avoid deadlock by preventing it from occurring in the first place, and *deadlock detection* which aims to identify the deadlocks that have arisen and then force one transaction to release its locks so that the other transactions involved in the deadlock can proceed. This means that one transaction is aborted. In practice, deadlocks rarely involve more than two transactions, so the volume of rollbacks resulting from deadlock detection is limited.

8.4.1   Deadlock Detection

Deadlock detection methods are used in database systems that allow deadlock to occur. The goal of detection is to identify any deadlocks that have occurred, and to determine precisely those transactions and data items involved in a deadlock so that the deadlock can be eliminated from the database system. Two methods of deadlock detection are widely used, namely:

1) *Waits-For-Graphs* (WFGs): data item allocation and request digraphs, and

2) *Timeout Methods*: timeout detection, lock count detection, and deadline detection.

Waits-for-graphs. Detection of deadlock via WFGs involves identifying a cyclical wait in a digraph of transaction interdependence. A detection algorithm can be invoked at different intervals, depending on how frequently we expect deadlocks to occur and how many transactions will be affected. The frequency of deadlock will depend on the degree of interaction among transactions. To maintain a WFG and run a deadlock check for each lock may be too expensive in terms of processor and time overheads. The alternative is to run a less frequent check; for example, once per hour or when CPU utilisation drops below 40% or when a transaction times out [ACL87].

To detect deadlock the database system examines the WFG to identify and eliminate from the digraph of transaction interdependence all transactions that can complete without deadlock (see Figure 8.4). Digraph reduction can be performed in any order. The transactions that cannot be removed from the digraph constitute the deadlocked transactions (see Figure 8.5).

Timeout methods enable the transaction scheduler (see Figure 8.9) to detect delays in processing, so that no transaction is blocked permanently.

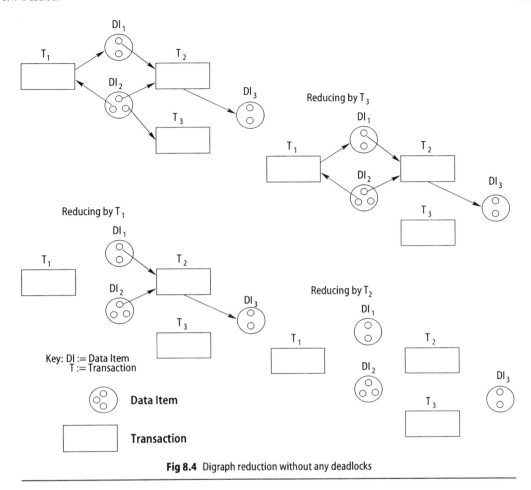

Fig 8.4 Digraph reduction without any deadlocks

Timeout detection. Timeout detection is a commonly used method, and is based on setting a clock on all lock requests by transactions. If a lock exceeds the specified time period, the database system assumes that deadlock may have occurred and action is taken. This action might simply be to assume deadlock and abort the transaction with the result that transactions which are waiting, but not deadlocked, may be aborted (see Figure 8.6). By using a longer timeout period the problem of unnecessary aborts is reduced; deadlocks may build up as timeout detection will take longer. Consequently, the timeout period must be finely tuned so that "must" abort transactions are actually deadlocked and moreover deadlocks are identified without unnecessary delay. A refinement of the basic timeout approach could be, instead of aborting delayed transactions, to check for deadlock by running a WFG.

Lock count detection. This method keeps a count of the number of times a transaction makes an unsuccessful lock request. If the counter reaches a specified limit then deadlock is assumed (see Figure 8.7).

Deadline detection. Deadline detection is another variation on the timeout approach. Each transaction is given a specification of the length of time required to complete processing. If

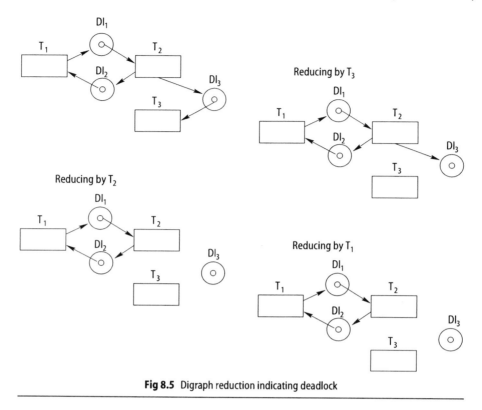

Fig 8.5 Digraph reduction indicating deadlock

this specified time is exceeded, the database system assumes a deadlock has occurred (see Figure 8.8).

The problem with all timeout methods of deadlock detection is tuning the clock or counter. On the one hand, if the timeout period is too short then transactions which are not in deadlock will be aborted unnecessarily. On the other hand, if the timeout period is too long then the response efficiency of the database system will be reduced as deadlocked transactions are left holding data items.

8.4.2   Deadlock Prevention

If one of the four necessary conditions for deadlock is eliminated, then it is impossible for deadlock to occur. Therefore, all techniques employed to prevent deadlock endeavour to eliminate one of these conditions. For example, to prevent deadlock by ensuring that the hold and wait condition never arises, a protocol can be used which requires each process to request and be allocated all of its data items before it starts execution, so a transaction that holds all the data items needed must be allowed to complete; the no pre-emption condition can be eliminated by enforcing the rule that if a transaction is refused access to a data item then it must release all the data items it currently holds, so that only the transaction holding the disputed data item is allowed to proceed. Or a transaction may be aborted and restarted if there is a risk that a deadlock might occur. All of these approaches eliminate the

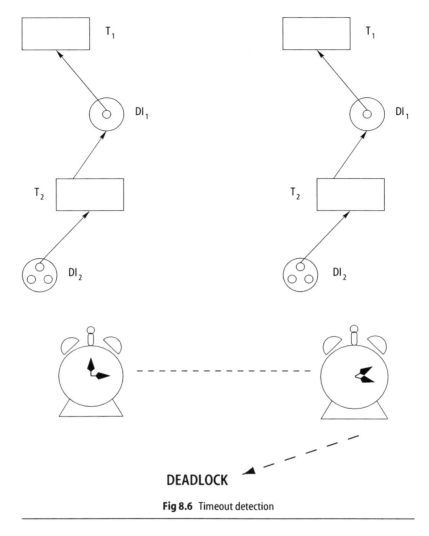

Fig 8.6 Timeout detection

possibility of deadlock arising; thus the problems of deadlock detection and resolution are avoided.

We next consider the implementation of two deadlock prevention strategies:

Transaction scheduling, whereby transactions are scheduled for execution so that two transactions will not be executed concurrently if their data requirements conflict. This requires that each transaction's data requirements are known prior to execution time through explicit declaration or analysis of the program. As the precise requirements of a transaction are not generally known until run-time, this approach to scheduling tends to be unnecessarily pessimistic. Transaction scheduling is in fact a locking mechanism in which the lockable unit is an entire set of tuples and locks are applied at program initiation time instead of during execution.

Transaction rejection, whereby deadlock prevention requires the database system to reject any lock request that could cause deadlock because a lock cannot be granted immediately.

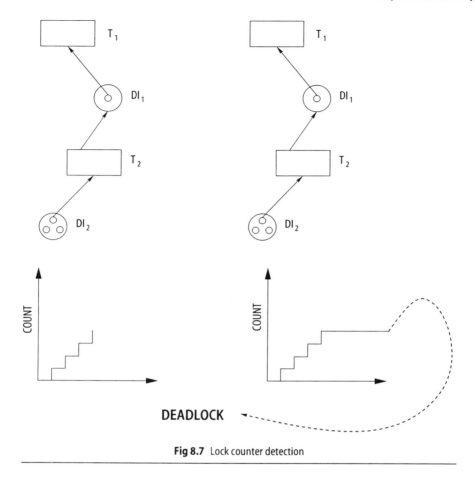

Fig 8.7 Lock counter detection

This approach is more flexible than choosing a transaction for rollback, since the rejected transaction may wait for a short time and then try again. If repeated retries fail, the transaction can then be rolled back in an orderly fashion.

Finally, another way of preventing deadlock is to assign an *arbitrary* linear ordering (see Subsection 1.9.2 of Chapter 1) to the data items, and thereafter require that all transactions acquire their locks according to this ordering. The following theorem establishes this assertion.

Theorem 8.4 Let $\preceq$ be an arbitrary linear ordering imposed on the data items and assume that all transactions acquire their locks according to this ordering. Then no deadlock can occur.

Proof. Let $\mathcal{T} = \{T_1, T_2, \ldots, T_p\}$ be a set of deadlocked transactions and let $A_{i_1} \preceq A_{i_2} \preceq \ldots \preceq A_{i_m}$ be the data items involved in the deadlock, namely each transaction T_i in $\mathcal{T}$ is waiting for some other transaction in $\mathcal{T}$ to unlock a data item, say A_{i_v}, amongst $\mathcal{A} = \{A_{i_1}, A_{i_2}, \ldots, A_{i_m}\}$. We may assume that each T_j in $\mathcal{T}$ holds a lock on at least one of the data items $A_{i_v} \in \mathcal{A}$, $v = 1, 2, \ldots, m$, otherwise we could remove T_j from $\mathcal{T}$ and still have a deadlocked set of transactions. Assume that $T_k \in \mathcal{T}$ is waiting for a lock on A_{i_1}, where A_{i_1} is the least element

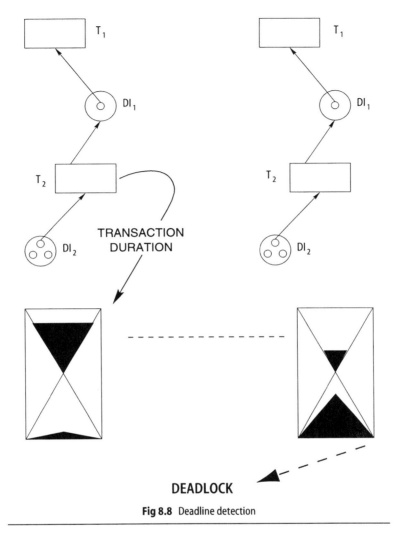

Fig 8.8 Deadline detection

in $\mathcal{A}$. It follows that T_k cannot hold a lock on any of the data items $A_{i_\nu} \in \mathcal{A}$, with $\nu \neq 1$. This leads to a contradiction. □

In a centralised database system preventing deadlock is frequently too costly in terms of resource overheads; thus deadlock detection and resolution is the standard approach. The opposite tends to be the case in the context of a distributed database system. In general, prevention may be used if there is a high probability that the database system will suffer from frequent deadlocks. If there is a low occurrence of deadlock then detection and recovery may be preferred to deadlock prevention.

Deadlock prevention is the ideal theoretical solution to the deadlock problem in the sense that prevention must be considered better than cure. However, the restrictions imposed on the database system by deadlock prevention can be difficult to accept and consequently deadlock avoidance is more acceptable.

The reader is referred to [IM80] for a comprehensive overview of deadlock and its associated problems in the general context of the management of resources in computer systems.

One issue related to the use of timeout methods, which needs to be addressed, is what to do with locks already granted when a transaction times out. It seems unnecessarily wasteful to remove locks on data items that no other transactions wish to access. In fact, only transactions holding data items requested by other transactions merit rollback. All other transactions could be allowed a delayed retry. Such modifications could give timeout methods more flexibility and compensate to some degree for the imprecise approach to deadlock detection.

Finally, when we use WFGs to detect deadlock, all transactions, which remain after digraph reduction, are aborted; however, aborting one transaction may be sufficient to break the deadlock. The detection algorithm, therefore, should be able to identify a *minimum set* of transactions that need to be aborted in order to eliminate deadlock.

8.5   Lock Granularity and Lock Manager

Lock granularity is the size of the data item to be locked. The granularity of locks is significant for the performance of a database system. Locking an entire relation, or a database is viewed as coarse granularity while locking a data item which is a tuple or subtuple is viewed as fine granularity.

The lock granularity required by a transaction will depend on the operation being performed. To update a single tuple, only the relevant tuple need be locked, whilst multiple tuple deletion or update could require a whole relation to be locked. Since different transactions have different characteristics and requirements, it is desirable that the database system provide a range of locking granules, called multi-granularity locking.

Not surprisingly, there is a trade off between providing multi-level granularity and the processing costs involved. We can improve the efficiency of the locking mechanism by considering the granularity of the locks to be applied. However, the overheads incurred by the database system in managing multi-granularity locking can outweigh the performance gains. Moreover, in order to provide multi-granularity locking it is necessary to use a *lock instance graph* so as to control the potential conflict of locks.

The larger the data items locked, the easier it is for the database system to administer the locks. Coarse granularity incurs low locking overheads, since there are fewer locks to manage; however, it reduces concurrency as operations are more likely to conflict. Thus transactions have a better chance of completing successfully at the expense of forcing more transactions to wait.

Locking smaller data items results in less contention among users since there are fewer conflicting lock requests. Fine granularity locks improve concurrency by allowing a transaction to lock only those data items it needs to access. However, it involves higher overheads, since more locks are requested and the lock table is larger (see Table 8.22 and Figure 8.10). The overheads consist of maintaining the lock table and status of locks as well as the I/O time spent on lock setting and releasing. It is interesting to note that the standard unit of update in a database system is a page, so all lock granules will require I/O operations which reflect this.

The RW model of transactions advocates a static view of a database. In reality, when delete and insert operations are supported, a database is dynamic as its size can change over time. Taking a dynamic view of a database the *phantoms problem* may arise.

Consider a database having two relations r_1 and r_2. Relation r_1 stores information about employees including their salary, and relation r_2 stores aggregate information per department about the employees recorded in r_1 such as their average salary. Suppose that a transaction T_1 checks whether the aggregate salary recorded in r_2 for the Computer Science department is consistent with the information about the individual employees recorded in r_1 who work in Computer Science. Moreover, assume that T_1 first locks all the tuples in r_1 of employees who work in Computer Science and thereafter locks the tuple in r_2 referring to Computer Science. Next, suppose that a second transaction T_2 inserts a new tuple into r_1 for an employee who works in Computer Science, and then, prior to T_1 locking the tuple in r_2 referring to Computer Science, T_2 locks this tuple and updates it with the new aggregate value. In this case T_1's aggregate information will be inconsistent, since it did not take the new employee tuple into account. In addition, it can be verified that T_1 and T_2 obey the two-phase locking protocol. The new employee tuple which was inserted into r_1 by T_2 is called a *phantom* tuple, because from T_1's point of view this tuple did not exist but despite this fact its presence affects the consistency of the database.

A solution to the phantoms problem, proposed by Eswaran et al. [EGLT76], is to use *predicate locking*. In our example, T_1 would lock all Computer Science employee tuples over R_1, where R_1 is the relation schema of r_1. Thus all tuples over R_1 whose department value is Computer Science, whether they be in r_1 or not, would be locked and therefore, under 2PL, T_2 would not be able to commence until T_1 has completed. Assuming that the attribute in schema(R_1) which refers to the department in which an employee works is DEPT_NAME, then the predicate (or equivalently, selection formula; see Definition 3.13 in Subsection 3.2.1 of Chapter 3), which locks all the Computer Science employees is: DEPT_NAME = 'Computer Science'. To test whether two predicates conflict we need to test if there exists a tuple that is satisfiable by both predicates. Testing such conflicts is more expensive than testing read/write conflicts. The complexity of maintaining predicate locks was considered in [HR79], wherein it was shown that the problem is in general NP-complete.

Multi-granularity locking allows each transaction to use locking levels that are most appropriate for its mode of operation. In a simple approach this might mean that long transactions use coarse granularity and short transactions use fine granularity. In this way, long transactions do not waste time setting many locks and short transactions do not block others by locking data items that will not be accessed.

Long transactions, also known as *long-duration transactions* or *Long-Lived Transactions* (LLTs), are transactions that by their nature take a substantial amount of computer time relative to other transactions and may lock data items for long periods. For example, one of the features of *Computer Aided Design* (CAD) is that of several groups of designers working on the same project, whose details are stored in a shared database; different groups of designers submit different transactions, which need to cooperate amongst themselves but may also have conflicts [KKB90]. Taken separately the transactions of each group are short-lived but taken together they form a single LLT. As another example, transactions that require human input, as in an airline reservation system, are generally LLTs, since there may be several inputs to the database over a prolonged period of time while the human is logged onto the system. The problem is accentuated, since human interaction considerably slows down the throughput of the database system.

LLTs lead to major performance problems, since they tend to lock large portions of the database, causing other transactions, waiting to access data items locked by LLTs, long delays. There is also potential conflict between an LLT and other transactions, when the LLT writes to many data items, causing additional scheduling and deadlock problems. Thus LLTs are also more likely to abort than short-lived transactions, enhancing the need to relax the atomicity requirement for an LLT.

Considering the airline reservation example, suppose that a human wishes to interactively make several seat reservations on flights in a single transaction T. Each such seat reservation can be viewed as a subtransaction T_i of T. As a whole T may require to lock a large portion of the database, but taken separately each T_i would require locking only the data items related to the flight, say F_i, which is accessed by T_i. Although T can commit only if *all* the T_i's have completed successfully, for scheduling purposes we can allow the subtransactions, say $T_1, T_2, \ldots, T_n$, to be interleaved in any way with other transactions. Such an LLT is called a *saga* [GS87] or, when several levels of subtransactions are allowed, a *nested transaction* [BBG89].

One problem we are now faced with is the situation where the subtransactions $T_1, T_2, \ldots, T_k$, with $k < n$, have all committed and subtransaction T_{k+1} aborts. Since, $T_1, T_2, \ldots, T_k$, have already committed and the database could have been modified in the meanwhile by other transactions we cannot simply rollback these transactions. Instead we execute *compensating transactions*, say $C_1, C_2, \ldots, C_k$, which are transactions whose purpose is to undo the effects of $T_1, T_2, \ldots, T_k$. Each T_i in T must have a compensating transaction C_i attached to it, which was defined prior to scheduling T; compensating transactions are usually user-defined as opposed to rollback which is automatically generated by the system using the log files. As an example, assume that a saga T reserves n seats on flights, F_i, via subtransactions, T_i, $1 \le i \le n$, i.e. each subtransaction reserves a single seat on a flight. In this case, if T_{k+1}, with $k < n$, aborts, then the compensating transactions $C_1, C_2, \ldots, C_k$ will be scheduled, where each C_i cancels the reservation made by T_i, with $1 \le i \le k$.

Two-phase locking, introduced in Subsection 8.3.1, is the most common locking protocol which enforces serialisability. An improvement in the presence of LLTs is the *altruistic* locking protocol proposed by Salem et al. [SGS94]. Intuitively, altruistic locking provides a transaction with a third operation, called *donate*, in addition to the lock and unlock operations. A data item that is locked but no longer accessed by a transaction may be donated by this transaction, thus allowing other transactions to simultaneously lock it. The donating transaction may continue to acquire new locks, and therefore altruistic locking is not necessarily two-phase.

Prior to defining the altruistic locking rules we define the notion of being in the wake of another transaction. A transaction T_1 is *in the wake* of another transaction T_2 with respect to a data item x, if T_1 locks x and x was donated by T_2. A transaction T_1 is *in the wake* of another transaction T_2 if T_1 is in the wake of T_2 with respect to some data item; a transaction cannot be in the wake of itself. A transaction T_1 is *completely in the wake* of another transaction T_2, if T_1 is in the wake of T_2 with respect to all the data items T_1 has locked.

Altruistic locking rule 1. Two transactions may simultaneously hold a lock on the same data item only if one of the transactions has first donated the data item to the other transaction.

Altruistic locking rule 2. If transaction T_1 is in the wake of another transaction T_2, then T_1 must be completely in the wake of T_2 until T_2 executes its first unlock operation.

Exercise 8.9 requires you to prove that a locking protocol based on the altruistic locking rules leads to serialisable schedules. Returning to the airline reservation system, consider an LLT consisting of subtransactions, $T_1, T_2, \ldots, T_n$, where each T_i involves reserving a single seat on a flight F_i, and thus locking all the data items relating to F_i. Furthermore, assume that no two distinct subtransactions access the same flight. In this case T can donate its locks relating to F_i once T_i has completed. When subtransaction T_k, with $k \leq n$, has completed, then a transaction which accesses only flights in $F_1, F_2, \ldots, F_k$ can execute concurrently with T. The altruistic locking rules we have presented do not distinguish between a read lock and a write lock. A generalised altruistic protocol which caters for separate read and write locks is considered in [SGS94].

The level of concurrency is strongly influenced by the size of the data items that can be identified and locked. The choice of locking granularity represents a trade off between concurrency and overheads. That is to say, the increased overheads of maintaining fine granularity versus the possible loss of concurrency due to coarse granule locking. The choice of granularity depends on the type of applications being run and the way applications utilise the database system.

8.6 Lock Manager Implementation

A database system typically comprises a number of interrelated modules designed to satisfy the functional requirements of database operations. These modules will in all likelihood include:

- a transaction manager,

- a lock manager,

- a transaction scheduler (or simply a scheduler),

- a recovery manager and

- a cache memory manager

The above modules appear in the diagram of Figure 8.9. Herein the recovery manager and cache manager together are referred to as the *data manager*.

The lock manager performs lock and unlock operations, while the transaction manager feeds the transaction scheduler. In practice, the transaction scheduler is usually implemented as a combined operation of the lock manager and transaction manager.

When the transaction manager receives a read/write request from a transaction, it sends the appropriate lock instruction to the lock manager. The lock manager sets the lock and acknowledges that it is set, so the transaction manager can send the read/write operation to the data manager.

The lock manager maintains a table of locks to support the lock and unlock operations as shown, for example, in Table 8.22.

In processing a lock, the lock manager attempts to set the specified lock by adding an entry in the lock table. If another transaction holds a conflicting lock, then the lock manager does not add the requested lock to the lock table, but enters it in a queue of waiting requests. An

Database System

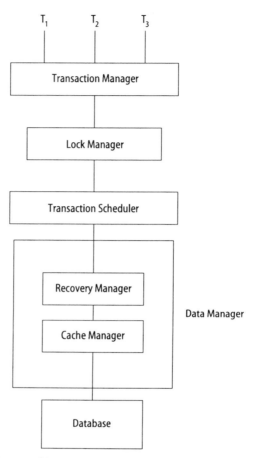

Fig 8.9 Diagram of the core components of a centralised DBMS

Table 8.22 Example of a lock table

TRANSACTION-ID	DATA-ITEM	LOCK-MODE	WAITING TRAN-ID
4846	A	READ	4848
4847	B	WRITE	
. . .	. . .	. . .	. . .

unlock operation releases the specified lock and grants any waiting lock requests that are now unblocked (see Figure 8.10). A locking protocol defines the restricted sequence of steps a lock manager may perform (see Figure 8.11).

Two situations may arise when it is necessary to abort a waiting lock request. Firstly, if a deadlock occurs and the transaction which initiated the waiting lock request is aborted, then the lock request will also be aborted. Secondly, when a timeout parameter facility is provided and a lock request is waiting for longer than the set timeout parameter, then the lock request will be aborted.

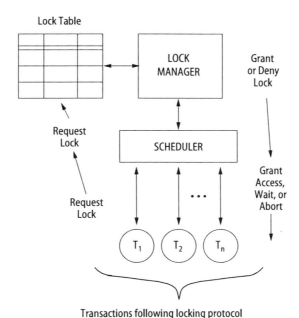

Fig 8.10 Overall relationship between the lock manager, scheduler, and locking protocol

The two main considerations for the lock manager with respect to computational effort are the number of instructions and I/O operations needed to implement lock requests. To increase the speed of locking and unlocking operations the lock manager can be optimised for special cases that occur frequently, such as setting non-conflicting locks or releasing all locks of a transaction simultaneously. This latter optimisation is achieved by linking together all lock entries for each transaction in the lock table. Thus, all locks for a transaction can be released simultaneously as soon as the acknowledgement of commit is received.

In practice, the lock table operates as a temporary file that the database system may keep in main storage while the database is actually used. Often the lock table is implemented as a *hash file* (see Exercise 1.5 from Chapter 1) with the data item identifier as key, because hash files are especially fast for content-based retrievals. The table should be protected against corruption; for example, by including it as part of the operating system, or in a protected area of the database system. In addition, the lock table should only be accessible to those programs that implement lock and unlock instructions.

In conclusion a lock manager provides the facilities necessary to perform locking operations. The implementation of a lock manager will vary from database system to database system. The factors which affect the implementation will include the protocols employed, available lock modes, and lock granularity. Since locking operations are performed with extremely high frequency, it is therefore important to consider carefully how locks are managed.

8.7 Timestamp Ordering

A timestamp is a unique identifier set at the start of a transaction, which allows chronological ordering of transactions to be determined. The timestamp can be as simple as the value of a

PROCESS FLOWCHART

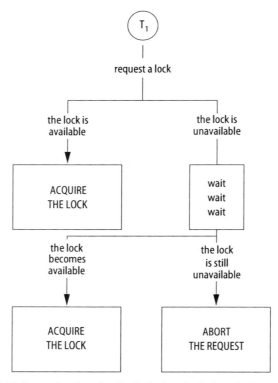

Fig 8.11 Process flowchart showing the logic underpinning a locking protocol

counter, incremented at the start of each transaction. Such a simple implementation, however, suffers from two weaknesses. Firstly, the maximum value of the counter is the maximum integer value of a particular computer. Secondly, in a distributed database environment, transactions initiated at different sites may be granted the same timestamp by the distinct counters of the processors at the different sites.

A more practical approach to timestamp ordering is to employ the values of the computer's clock as timestamps. The computer clock has a finer incremental scale and is also less likely to crash. To produce a unique timestamp in a distributed database system, such systems usually combine the computer's clock value as the major component, together with a site identifier as the minor component. Consequently, although two or more transactions may have the same clock value, the physical requirement that they started from different sites means that the site identifier is different, thus the composite value is unique.

Following this latter approach to timestamp ordering, the values of timestamps are drawn from a totally ordered domain. The following definition of timestamp ordering follows that given in [BG81].

Definition 8.14 (Timestamp ordering)   Timestamp ordering is the method of scheduling whereby each transaction is assigned a unique timestamp and conflicting operations (see Definition 8.5) from different transactions are scheduled to execute in timestamp order.   ■

The next theorem shows that adhering to the timestamp ordering method of Definition 8.14 results in serialisable schedules.

Theorem 8.5   If s is a schedule that obeys the timestamp ordering method of Definition 8.14, then s is conflict-serialisable.

Proof. Assume that a schedule s, which satisfies the timestamp ordering method, is not conflict-serialisable. Then there must exist in $\Gamma(s)$ a cycle $T_{i_1}, T_{i_2}, \ldots, T_{i_p}, T_{i_1}$, with $p > 1$. That is to say, two conflicting operations exist in any two consecutive transactions $T_{i_k}, T_{i_{k+1}}$, $1 \le k \le p - 1$, and in T_{i_p}, T_{i_1}. According to the timestamp ordering method the timestamp of T_{i_k} is strictly less than the timestamp of $T_{i_{k+1}}$, $1 \le k \le p - 1$, and the timestamp of T_{i_p} is strictly less than that of T_{i_1}. Thus the timestamp of T_{i_1} is strictly less than the timestamp of T_{i_1}; however, this contradicts the timestamp ordering method. $\square$

Let T_i, T_j be two transactions with timestamps t_i, t_j, respectively. If $t_i < t_j$ then T_i is said to be *older* than T_j; if $t_i > t_j$ then T_i is said to be *younger* than T_j.

Timestamp ordering is an alternative to locking as a mechanism for concurrency control. It is used primarily but not exclusively in distributed databases. Timestamp ordering allows several users to apparently access the database simultaneously, while maintaining the integrity of the data. As long as no two transactions are accessing the same data item, there is no danger of transaction conflict or data corruption. When conflicting operations are being performed by a database system, then timestamp ordering will prevent anomalies such as the *lost update* by stopping a transaction writing to a data item that has already been read by a *younger* transaction.

Timestamp ordering prevents concurrent access problems by ensuring serialisability of transactions, as was shown in Theorem 8.5. Timestamps are set at transaction start and every operation by the transaction is associated with that *start time*. To maintain the integrity of the database, every time a transaction tries to read or write to a data item, its timestamp is compared to that of the data item being read or written. Depending on the temporal relationship between the two timestamps, the transaction will either be processed or rolled back, and in the latter case the transaction may restart with a new timestamp. That is, a transaction, say T, with timestamp t_1 cannot write to a data item with a read time of t_2, if $t_2 > t_1$. If T makes such an attempt, then it is out of date and therefore must abort and be restarted. Similarly, T cannot read a data item with a write time of t_2, if $t_2 > t_1$. Again if T makes such an attempt, then it is out of date and therefore must abort and be restarted. Only on transaction completion or restart is a timestamp released.

We next present five rules which have been identified for timestamp ordering mechanisms by Ceri and Pelagatti [CP84a]. These rules are:

Rule 1. Every transaction is assigned a globally unique timestamp when it is initiated at its site of origin. (This assumes a distributed computing environment.)

Rule 2. Each data item in the database carries the timestamp of the last transaction to have read it (read timestamp) and the last transaction to have written to it (write timestamp).

Rule 3. Each read and write operation takes the timestamp of its issuing transaction.

Rule 4. For a transaction to read a data item, its timestamp must *not* be less (older) than the last write timestamp of the data item. Otherwise, the transaction is aborted and restarted with a new timestamp. When the transaction has read the data item, the data item then takes the timestamp of that transaction as its latest read timestamp.

Rule 5. For a transaction to write to a data item, its timestamp must not be less than either of the data item's read or write timestamps. Otherwise, the transaction is aborted and restarted with a new timestamp. When the transaction has written to the data item, then the data item takes the timestamp of that transaction as its latest write timestamp.

Rule 4 above ensures that read/write synchronisation is maintained, while Rule 5 ensures write/write synchronisation; in combination these two rules guarantee that conflicting transactions are serialisable. While not enforced by the rules, it is worth stating here that best practice would require that write operations are not written to the physical database until commit is executed. Thus, transaction restart does not require physical rollback of the database.

8.7.1   Timestamp Ordering Implementation

A number of implementation algorithms have been suggested for concurrency control by using the timestamp ordering method, whereby every pair of conflicting operations is executed in timestamp order. We briefly present an overview of three of them. (For algorithmic details the reader is advised to consult [BHG87].)

Basic timestamp ordering. This is essentially the implementation of the five basic rules given above. Although these rules ensure serialisability of transactions, they do not guarantee atomicity. Rules 4 and 5 are usually modified in basic timestamp ordering implementations, so that write operations *pre-write* to a buffer (write-buffer). (See cache manager in Figure 8.9.) The physical update of the database is only executed when the transaction has been committed. Thus, the *two-phase commit* policy is adhered to by modifying these two rules. (Two-phase commit is a protocol that allows a set of autonomous processes or agents to eventually all commit or all abort; see [BHG87, BN97] for details on the two-phase commit protocol.)

Rule 4a. For a transaction to read a data item, its timestamp must not be less (older) than the last write timestamp of the data item. Otherwise the transaction is aborted and restarted with a new timestamp. If a transaction's timestamp is greater (younger) than the data item's last write timestamp, then the read is executed provided there are no outstanding pre-writes of the data item with a timestamp greater (younger) than that of the read operation. If there are pre-writes outstanding, the read operation is placed in a buffer (read-buffer) until the transaction(s) issuing the pre-write(s) is (are) committed.

Rule 5a. For a transaction to pre-write to a data item, the transaction's timestamp must not be less (older) than either of the data item's last read or write timestamps. Otherwise the transaction is aborted and then restarted. If the transaction's timestamp is greater (younger) than both the data item's said timestamps, then the pre-write is executed and the data, with its timestamps, is written to the buffer.

Rule 5b. A transaction's write operation to a data item will always be executed, but if a pre-write on the data item with an older timestamp is still outstanding, the write operation will be buffered until the execution of the outstanding pre-write has been completed.

While basic timestamp ordering completely overcomes the deadlock problem, by never blocking transactions, it can suffer from frequent transaction restarts.

Conservative timestamp ordering. This method, which is applicable in the context of a distributed database, prevents the numerous transaction restarts experienced by the basic timestamp ordering, but at the expense of a lower degree of concurrency. Unfortunately, in solving the problem of restart, the level of concurrency is adversely affected. The method requires that:

- Each transaction has a *home site* from where it was initiated and its execution is controlled.

- All sites must guarantee that transactions will commit in timestamp order; this is done in order to prevent older transactions from attempting to write to a data item after a younger transaction, thus resulting in restart.

- A queue of read and write requests must be maintained, with at least one read and one write operation buffered at all times.

As operation requests are received, the following protocol is employed:

- If the timestamp of a read request is less (older) than that of the first data item in the write-buffer, then the read operation is executed. Otherwise, the read operation is buffered in the read-buffer until that write is executed.

- For a write request to be executed, the buffers must not contain any read or write requests with a lesser (older) timestamp. Otherwise, the new request must be buffered in the write-buffer until the above condition is met.

These rules ensure that all transactions are processed in strict timestamp order, by forcing young requests to wait for older requests to complete. A problem with this conservative timestamp mechanism is that if no read or write requests are sent for a long period of time the buffers (read or write) may become empty, thus causing the database system to *hang*. To prevent this problem from arising, timestamps for null requests must be sent to the buffers periodically to ensure the database system continues to function. Moreover, since transactions are permitted to wait, deadlock may occur.

Thomas's Write Rule (TWR) [Tho79]. This is also known as the *ignore obsolete write* rule; TWR provides an important modification to the basic timestamp ordering technique. The rule allows a write operation to be acknowledged as completed, while ignoring to write the data item to the database, provided that the transaction timestamp is less than that of the last write timestamp of the data item. This is allowable because if the last write timestamp of the data item is after the proposed write operation and the read timestamp of the data item is before the proposed write operation, then the proposed write operation is obsolete and can be ignored.

Prior to stating Thomas's write rule we introduce some relevant notation. Assume that T_i issues the operation write(A). Let $ts(T_i)$ denote a unique fixed timestamp associated with transaction T_i. In addition, we associate with each data item, say x, two timestamp values (referred to earlier), namely $R\_ts(x)$, which denotes the largest (youngest) timestamp of any transaction that has successfully executed read(x), and $W\_ts(x)$, which denotes the largest (youngest) timestamp of any transaction that has successfully executed write(x).

Thomas's write rule states:

1) If $ts(T_i) < R\_ts(x)$, then write(T_i, x) is rejected.

2) If $ts(T_i) < W\_ts(x)$, then T_i is attempting to write an obsolete value of x. Thus the write operation is ignored.

3) Otherwise the write operation is executed and $W\_ts(x) := ts(T_i)$.

After careful consideration it can be seen that Thomas's write rule utilises view serialisability by essentially deleting obsolete write operations from those transactions that issue them [BHG87].

Thomas's write rule deals with the timestamp issue of how to treat unsynchronised write operations. It does, however, give rise to an interesting, counter-intuitive situation; consider the following transaction history, where start T_i, for $i = 1, 2$, stands for "initiate transaction T_i".

Steps	Transaction T_1	Transaction T_2
1	start T_1;	
2		start T_2;
3		write(A);
4		read(A);
5	write(A);	

Under TWR case 1 the write at step 5 must be rejected because it conflicts with the read at step 4, even though there is no direct conflict with the said read as the latter reads the value written at step 3. Moreover, the write operation at step 5 would have been ignored under TWR case 2. There is an implicit priority ordering between these two rules, with the absolute *reject* rule taking precedence over the softer *ignore* rule. If we were to reverse the priority, it would make perfect sense not to *reject* a write which has already been earmarked as an *ignore* write.

Timestamp ordering provides an alternative concurrency control strategy to locking. It ensures that the processing of transactions is equivalent to a specific (time-based) order of execution. In addition, it does not incur the overheads associated with maintaining a lock register. The fact that transactions do not need to wait means that deadlock is not a problem.

On the downside, timestamp ordering may suffer from livelock due to automatic transaction restarts. This problem can be managed by allowing a limited number of restarts before aborting the transaction, with an error message being sent to the user. There is also the substantial overhead of recording the timestamp of each data item. However, since such recording is held in a table and changes constantly, the overhead can be kept to a minimum by purging the table regularly of obsolete data items.

Each timestamp ordering implementation has its advantages and disadvantages, and different system designers will have their own preferences. The choice of implementation is therefore difficult to comment on meaningfully. The end product requirements will, however, have a strong influence on the implementation choice, such as the use of multi-version timestamp ordering [Ree83] for systems with an expected high probability of transaction restarts. More generally, we can safely say that timestamp ordering offers a viable means of ensuring data integrity, whilst not incurring excessive overheads and is particularly cost effective in a distributed database environment.

8.8 Serialisation Graph Testing

We already know that transaction scheduling and serialisability can be achieved by using locking or timestamp ordering. *Serialisation Graph Testing* (SGT) is an alternative approach to transaction scheduling which ensures serialisability.

An SGT scheduler maintains a serialisation digraph (see Definition 8.8) of the transactions it is executing. The node set of this digraph includes nodes for all *active* transactions, namely transactions that have started and have not yet become committed or aborted, and the arcs between the nodes represent dependencies that have been generated by a request to schedule potentially conflicting operations. A cycle in the digraph indicates that the transactions are not serialisable. As the scheduler sends new operations to the data manager, the serialisation digraph is updated by the scheduler. SGT maintains serialisability by preventing any cycles from forming in the serialisation digraph. The digraph has a node for every active transaction, including recently committed transactions.

We next describe briefly two versions of SGT, namely *Basic SGT* and *Conservative SGT*.

Basic SGT. On receiving a request via the transaction manager, a basic SGT scheduler adds, if one does not exist already, a node to the serialisation digraph if the requesting transaction is new. An arc is then added from all the other transactions currently represented by the digraph for every previous operation that conflicts with the scheduled operations of the requesting transaction. A conflict arises if the serialisation digraph becomes cyclic. If the resulting digraph is cyclic, then the scheduling of transactions would be non-serialisable. Therefore, the scheduler rejects the offending transaction by sending an abort instruction to the data manager. All scheduled operations of the offending transaction are removed from the scheduled queue. When the data manager acknowledges the abort, the node of the offending transaction is deleted from the serialisation digraph as well as all arcs incident with it. If the resulting digraph is acyclic, then the new transaction is scheduled once all previous conflicting operations have been acknowledged by the data manager.

We illustrate basic SGT by considering the transaction history

Steps	Transaction T_1	Transaction T_2
1	read(A);	
2		read(A);
3		write(A);
4	write(A);	

At step 1 the digraph consists of a single node labelled by T_1 and the said queue of waiting operations contains $<\text{read}(T_1, A)>$; at step 2 the digraph comprises two nodes T_1 and T_2 and the queue of waiting operations contains $<\text{read}(T_1, A), \text{read}(T_2, A)>$; at step 3 the digraph is as at step 2 together with the arc (T_1, T_2) and the queue of waiting operations contains $<$read(T_1, A), read(T_2, A), write(T_2, A)$>$. The third entry in the queue is a potential read-write conflict; at step 4 the digraph is as at step 3 together with the arc (T_2, T_1). A cycle has arisen, so T_1 is aborted, since it is the transaction that caused the cycle at step 4. After step 4, the digraph consists of a single node labelled by T_2 and the queue of waiting operations contains $<$read(T_2, A), write(T_2, A)$>$.

To detect conflicts with previously scheduled operations the database system maintains the readset and writeset of every transaction (see Definition 8.1). The scheduler can delete information about a terminated transaction only if the transaction could not be involved in a future cycle of the serialisation digraph. A *safe rule* for deleting nodes from the serialisation digraph is one such that information about a transaction may be discarded as soon as that transaction has terminated and its associated node has no incoming arcs in the serialisation digraph.

Conservative SGT. A conservative SGT scheduler does not reject any operations, but delays (or blocks) them as in 2PL and timestamp ordering. It works by having each transaction pre-declare its readset and writeset by attaching them to the start operation. When a transaction start, say start T_i, is received by the scheduler it saves the T_i's readset and writeset. A node labelled by T_i is then created in the serialisation digraph and an arc (T_j, T_i) is added from every node T_j in the serialisation digraph to T_i whenever there exists a conflicting operation between T_j and T_i. The scheduler must also maintain for each data item x, a queue, say queue[x], of delayed operations that access the data item x. All conflicting operations in queue[x] are kept in an order consistent with the order of operations indicated by the arcs in the serialisation digraph. For example, if (T_1, T_2) is an arc in the serialisation digraph, then T_1's operation to read(x) will be closer to the head of the queue than T_2's operation to write(x), so that T_1's read operation will be dequeued before T_2's write operation. The order of non-conflicting operations in queue[x] is not significant.

An operation at the head of a particular queue may only be sent to the data manager by the scheduler if the operation is *ready*. There are two conditions for readiness:

Condition 1. Any operations already sent to the data manager that conflict with the aforesaid operation at the head of the queue must have been acknowledged by the data manager. This condition ensures that the data manager processes conflicting operations in the order that they were scheduled.

Condition 2. For every transaction T_1 that directly precedes a transaction T_2 in the serialisation digraph, with a pair of conflicting operations, T_1's operation has already been sent to the scheduler.

Condition 2 enables the scheduler to avoid abort operations by ensuring that the execution is equivalent to a serial execution of T_1 followed by T_2. So if T_1's read(x) conflicts with T_2's write(x), then the read(x) must be scheduled first. So if T_2's write(x) is received before T_1's read(x) it must be delayed. Otherwise, T_1's read(x) would have to be rejected when it is eventually received, as it would create a cycle in the serialisation digraph involving T_1 and T_2.

When the scheduler receives T_2's write(x) from the transaction manager or an acknowledgement of T_1's read(x) from the data manager, it will check to see if the head of the queue is ready. If so, it dequeues the operation at the head of the queue and sends it to the data manager. The scheduler will then keep repeating this process with the new head of the queue until the queue is emptied or the head thereof is not in a state of readiness.

Finally, we mention that Hadzilacos and Yannakakis [HY89] derived necessary and sufficient conditions for when it is safe to remove a completed, i.e. not active, transaction (which is equivalent to deleting a node from the serialisation digraph) in several versions of conflict-digraph-based schedulers. It is also shown therein that, in general, the problem of deciding whether a transaction cannot be safely removed from the conflict digraph is NP-complete.

8.9 Discussion

Concurrency control is a huge subarea in the context of database systems and research on this topic continues unabated [Kuo96, AJR97, RMB$^+$98]. Specialised textbooks on the subject have been written and we refer the reader to [Cas81, Pap86, BHG87, GR93, BN97]; a recent collection of papers dealing with the practical issues pertaining to performance of concurrency control algorithms is [Kum96]. Herein we have looked at concurrency control primarily from the point of view of the relational model; concurrency control techniques need to be modified when applied to other models such as an object-oriented data model (see for example [GNS93]).

We next briefly indicate the support for concurrency control within SQL2 [DD93]. Transactions are sequences of SQL statements, which terminate either with a **COMMIT** or a **ROLLBACK** statement, with their intended meaning. A transaction is initiated implicitly within an application program when no other transaction is in progress within the same program, and individual SQL statements are the primitive operations of such a transaction. By default SQL transactions are **SERIALIZABLE** but various relaxations of serialisability are possible. A recent critique of SQL's support for concurrency control has raised some serious problems with the standard regarding its ambiguity and lack of support for locking [BBG$^+$95].

We have not considered *recovery*, which is the topic referred to the process of restoring a database to a consistent instance after some system failure, be it hardware or software, rendering the current instance of the database inconsistent. Recovery is an important topic and is closely related to concurrency control. In [Had88] and [AVA$^+$94], respectively, reliability and recovery issues are dealt with in great detail. In this respect we mention ARIES (*Algorithm for Recovery and Isolation Exploiting Semantics*) [MHL$^+$92], which is a relatively new and important recovery algorithm that has been implemented in some current database systems. In [Kuo96] a model and verification of a data manager based on ARIES is presented.

We close the discussion with a brief historical account. The notion of serialisability was introduced by Gray et al. [GLPT75]. In that seminal paper, issues related to lock granularity according to a lock hierarchy from the entire database level down to the tuple level, and the compatibility of various lock modes were also discussed. A central paper to the theory of serialisability and two-phase locking is [EGLT76], where conflict-serialisability and the basic 2PL protocol were introduced, and Theorems 8.1 and 8.3 were proved. In that paper the phantoms problem was also raised and predicate locking was introduced as a solution to the problem. Other early papers dealing with the theory of serialisability and locking are [SLR76, BSW79]. In [PBR77, Pap79] is was shown that testing view-serialisability and final-state-serialisability are both NP-complete problems, strengthening the case of adhering to conflict-serialisability. The technique of detecting deadlock via cycles in the Waits-For-Graph stems from an early paper by Holt [Hol72], who considered the general problem of deadlock detection and prevention in operating systems. Timestamp ordering was introduced by Thomas in his seminal paper [Tho79], and an early investigation of serialisation graph testing was carried out by Casanova in his monograph [Cas81].

We have seen that serialisability can be achieved by the three methods of locking (2PL), timestamp ordering (TO) and serialisation graph testing (SGT). The techniques we have presented are *pessimistic* in the sense that the scheduler checks the possibility of nonserialisability after each operation it receives and makes an immediate decision whether to accept, reject or block the operation. A different *optimistic* approach can be used which, rather than check each operation as it comes, accepts all operations for the time being and makes a final decision regarding whether to commit or abort a transaction at the time when the transaction is ready to commit. Such an optimistic scheduler [KR81] is also called a *certifier*. Optimistic schedulers maximise throughput of transactions when the probability of conflict between any two transactions is low.

We note that we have mainly dealt with the case of concurrency control in a centralised multi-user environment but have occasionally also discussed the case of a distributed database (see Section 10.8 of Chapter 10). An early survey concentrating on concurrency control in distributed database systems can be found in [BG81].

8.10   Exercises

Exercise 8.1   Construct an example of two schedules involving three transactions such that the schedules are view-equivalent but not conflict-equivalent.

Exercise 8.2   Consider a transaction model where each transaction is a sequence of *lock* and *unlock* operations. We denote the operation that a transaction T locks a data item x by lock(T, x), and the operation that T unlocks x by unlock(T, x); whenever T is understood from context we abbreviate these operations to lock(x) and unlock(x), respectively.

Each data item locked must subsequently be unlocked, and whenever a data item is locked by a transaction no other transaction can either read or write it until it is unlocked by the said transaction. Moreover, whenever a transaction locks a data item, say x, it modifies the value of x, and the value that x has when unlocked is essentially unique. Consider the following algorithm.

Input: A schedule s for the set $\{T_1, T_2, \ldots, T_k\}$ of transactions.
Output: Yes if s is serialisable, No otherwise.
Method: Construct a digraph G, where the node set of G is given by $\{T_1, T_2, \ldots, T_k\}$. The set of arcs of G is constructed as follows: (T_i, T_j) is an arc of G, if there exists in s an unlock(T_i, x) followed by a lock(T_j, x). If G has a cycle then s is not serialisable, otherwise perform a topological sort to obtain a serial order for the set transactions.

Prove the correctness of the above algorithm and apply it to the schedule of transactions T_1, T_2, T_3 and T_4 given below.

Steps	T_1	T_2	T_3	T_4
1		lock(A);		
2			lock(A);	
3		lock(B);		
4		unlock(A);		
5			lock(A);	
6		unlock(B);		
7	lock(B);			
8			unlock(A);	
9				lock(B);
10	lock(A);			
11				unlock(B);
12	lock(C);			
13	unlock(A);			
14				lock(A);
15				unlock(A);
16	unlock(B);			
17	unlock(C);			

Exercise 8.3 A *blind write* in a transaction T is a write operation at step, say i, to a data item that is not preceded in T, at any previous step $j < i$, by a read operation to the same data item. Prove that if transactions do not have any blind writes, then a schedule is conflict-serialisable if and only if it is view-serialisable [Pap86].

Exercise 8.4 A *subschedule* s' of a schedule s of a set of transactions $\mathcal{T}$ is the subsequence of the elementary steps of s formed by the elementary steps of a subset of the transactions in $\mathcal{T}$.

Prove that a schedule s is conflict-serialisable if and only if all its subschedules s' are view-serialisable [Yan84].

Exercise 8.5 Use your solution of Exercise 8.4 to prove that a locking policy ensures view-serialisability if and only if it ensures conflict-serialisability [Yan84].

Exercise 8.6 Consider a relational database consisting of N tuples. Assume that there are $n + 1$ transactions and that each transaction comprises $m + 1$ operations. Each operation picks randomly a tuple from the set of N tuples and locks it. At the last step the transaction commits, releasing all its locks. Each step takes one time unit, unless the transaction has to wait for a lock held by another transaction in which case the step completes when the holding transaction commits. Assume that $nm \ll N$ (nm is very small compared to N), i.e. most of the database is unlocked most of the time.

Estimate the probability that a single lock request will wait, and show that the probability a particular transaction, say T, waits in its lifetime is approximately $nm^2/(2N)$. Show that the probability that T participates in a cycle of length two is approximately $nm^4/(4N^2)$, and the probability that any transaction deadlocks is approximately $n^2m^4/(4N^2)$ [GR93].

Exercise 8.7 A schedule of the elementary steps of a set of transactions, such that the rules pertaining to locks are obeyed, is called a *legal* schedule. Consider the transactions T_1 and T_2. Find in how many legal ways they can be scheduled. Identify the serialisable schedules assuming that whenever a data item is locked by a transaction its value is modified.

T_1
lock(A);
lock(B);
unlock(A);
unlock(B);

T_2
lock(B);
unlock(B);
lock(A);
unlock(A);

Exercise 8.8   Show that testing whether a schedule obeys the basic 2PL protocol can be done in polynomial-time [Pap79].

Exercise 8.9   Prove that a schedule which obeys a locking protocol which enforces the altruistic locking rules, given towards the end of Section 8.5, is serialisable.

Exercise 8.10   Discuss the advantages and disadvantages of locking versus timestamp ordering.

Exercise 8.11   Prove that the Ceri and Pelagatti timestamp ordering rules produce serialisable executions.

Exercise 8.12   Construct examples to demonstrate the applicability of Thomas's write rule in all three of its cases.

Exercise 8.13   Consider the transaction history

Steps	Transaction T_1	Transaction T_2
1	start T_1;	
2		start T_2;
3		read(A);
4		write(A);
5	write(A);	

Assume that in TWR Case 2 takes precedence over Case 1. Discuss the implications of such a change with respect to the above transaction history.

Exercise 8.14   Let T be a transaction, whose timestamp is t, attempting to perform an operation X on a data item, whose read time and write time are, respectively, t_r and t_w. Consider the algorithm

Algorithm 8.3
1. **begin**
2.   **if** X = read and $t \geq t_w$ **then**
3.   **if** $t > t_r$ **then** $t_r := t$;
4.   **end if**
5.   **if** X = write and $t \geq t_r$ and $t \geq t_w$ **then**
6.   **if** $t > t_w$ **then** $t_w := t$;
7.   **end if**
8.   **if** X = read and $t < t_w$ or X = write and $t < t_r$ **then** abort(T);
9. **end.**

Show that the above algorithm produces serialisable executions, and apply it to the following schedule

Steps	T_1	T_2	T_3	T_4
1		read(A);		
2			read(A);	
3		write(B);		
4			write(A);	
5	read(B);			
6				read(B);
7	read(A);			
8	write(C);			
9				write(A);

on the assumption that the timestamps of T_1 to T_4 are, respectively,

(a) 310, 320, 330, and 340.
(b) 260, 270, 280, and 290.

The read time and write time of each data item is initialised to zero.

Exercise 8.15 Consider the safe rule for deleting nodes from the serialisation digraph in the context of the basic SGT. Justify the rationale for it.

Exercise 8.16 Show that the conservative SGT scheduler, described in Section 8.8, produces serialisable executions.

Exercise 8.17 In the context of the conservative SGT show that Condition 2 of readiness need only consider transactions T_i which directly precede transaction T_j.

9. Deductive Databases

We have already introduced deductive databases in Subsection 1.7.5 of Chapter 1 and have formalised the rule-based deductive database language, Datalog, in Subsection 3.2.3 of Chapter 3. The investigation of deductive databases, also known as logical databases, has been one of the most significant and prolific strands in database theory in the last decade. We now discuss the motivation for researching deductive databases.

The primary motivation is that logic provides us with a formal and unifying foundation for a data model. In fact, relational databases can be viewed as finite models for a first-order language, whose predicate symbols are the relation symbols of the database schema and whose constants are the domain values. By using a logic formalism the expressive power of relational query languages can be extended with deductive capabilities. In particular, the rule-based language Datalog is a significant extension of the relational algebra and calculus. Logic has the advantage of providing an abstract and high-level declarative specification language for expressing knowledge; it is a precise, well-understood and unambiguous language.

Related to the above motivation for investigating deductive databases is the fact that the relational algebra has limited expressiveness. In particular, the relational algebra has no iteration or recursion facilities. An early result, which was discussed in Subsection 3.2.1 of Chapter 3, is that the transitive closure of a relation *cannot* be expressed within the relational algebra [AU79]. In Section 6.7 of Chapter 6 we discussed how to augment the relational algebra with iteration (the for loop) and with recursion (the fixpoint) so as to gain extra expressive power. The relational algebra is a procedural language and therefore it is natural to investigate an alternative declarative query language such as Datalog in order to achieve this higher expressiveness.

We next recall that due to Proposition 3.4, from Subsection 3.3.2 of Chapter 3, we need only consider safe Datalog programs, which we refer to simply as Datalog programs. Moreover, general Datalog programs may be recursive and may contain rules having negative literals in their body. We further recall Theorem 3.18, from Subsection 3.3.2 of Chapter 3, which shows the equivalence of the relational algebra and nonrecursive Datalog. As a direct consequence of this theorem, the definition of the semantics, MEANING(P), of a Datalog program P, and the definition of the semantics of fixpoint queries, we can state the following fundamental result.

Proposition 9.1 Datalog is equivalent to the relational algebra augmented with a fixpoint operator, i.e. they both express exactly the same set of polynomial-time computable queries.
□

This proposition justifies basing a deductive database model on Datalog. Recall the semantics of Datalog given by Algorithm 3.4 in Subsection 3.2.3 of Chapter 3, i.e. MEANING(P), where P is a Datalog program. Informally, MEANING(P) is the *inflationary fixpoint* of P, which is obtained as follows. As an intermediate step, the immediate consequence of the current state of the result, say I, is computed by concurrently finding all the safe substitutions θ for clauses C in P such that C is true with respect to θ and I, and then all the facts $\theta(L)$ are added to the result, where L is the head of C. This process is iterated until no more facts can be added to the current state of the result by invoking the intermediate step. By Proposition 9.1 the maximum number of iterations necessary in order to obtain the fixpoint is polynomial in the size of CONST(P), namely the set of constants appearing in P.

In addition, recall that SCHEMA(P) is the set of all relation schemas whose relation symbols appear as literals of rules in P, and that DB(P) denotes the initial database of P, i.e. the relations induced by the set of facts in P.

As an example, recall the Datalog program, TC, which computes the transitive closure of a binary relation, FAMILY:

$$TC(x_1, x_2) :- FAMILY(x_1, x_2).$$
$$TC(x_1, x_3) :- FAMILY(x_1, x_2), TC(x_2, x_3).$$

Moreover, assume that the Datalog program also contains some FAMILY facts such as:

FAMILY(Abraham, Isaac).
FAMILY(Isaac, Jacob).

The semantics of the Datalog program TC, obtained by computing MEANING(TC), is a set of FAMILY and TC facts, i.e. a database with two relations over FAMILY and TC, respectively. The FAMILY relation, which comprises the FAMILY facts of TC, is an *extensional relation* (or a conceptual relation), and the TC relation, which comprises the TC facts that can be inferred from TC, is an *intensional relation* (or a view relation).

In general, MEANING(P) of a Datalog program, P, contains both the extensional and intensional relations, where the extensional relations comprise the facts which are present in P and the intensional relations comprise the facts that can be inferred from P.

We now state three implicit assumptions that are made with respect to the underlying data model [Rei84]:

- The *Unique Names Assumption* (UNA), which states that any two constants in CONST(P) are equal if and only if they are syntactically identical, i.e. they are have the same name. (See Definition 3.2 in Section 3.1 of Chapter 3.)

- The *Domain Closure Assumption* (DCA), which states that the only available constants are those that are explicitly mentioned in P, i.e. CONST(P). (This assumption manifests itself in the semantics of Datalog programs, since we consider only safe substitutions when computing MEANING(P).)

- The *Closed World Assumption* (CWA), which states that facts that are not present in the current state of the database are assumed by default to be false. (This assumption manifests itself in the semantics of Datalog programs via the definition of the truth of clauses with respect to safe substitutions.)

It is interesting to note that the CWA as stated above would *not* be valid if we further extend Datalog so as to allow facts which are disjunctions of literals, such as

$$AGE(Jack, 21) \vee AGE(Jack, 23).$$

The reason for this is that given the said disjunction we cannot be certain whether AGE(Jack, 21) is true or whether AGE(Jack, 23) is true, and so under the CWA we are forced to conclude that both AGE(Jack, 21) and AGE(Jack, 23) are false. Thus we have derived a contradiction and the database is deemed to be inconsistent. A generalisation of the CWA which handles disjunctions correctly is given in [Min88a]. In the above example, under the *generalised* CWA we can deduce that either AGE(Jack, 21) is true or that AGE(Jack, 23) is true, which is intuitively what we would expect.

Prior to outlining the contents of the sections that follow, we introduce the important distinction between extensional and intensional database predicates. For a Datalog program P, let us call a predicate which is the head of a nontrivial rule in P an *intensional database* (or IDB) predicate, and all the other predicates in P *extensional database* (or EDB) predicates. In addition, let EDB(P) be the set of facts in P over EDB predicates and IDB(P) be the set of facts in P over IDB predicates together with the nontrivial rules in P, i.e. IDB(P) is given by P − EDB(P). Given a Datalog program P, the set EDB(P) of facts can be considered as the input database to P.

In Section 9.1 we formalise the model-theoretic semantics of Datalog programs. While the semantics of Datalog programs that do not have any negation in them, called *definite* Datalog programs and often referred to as *pure* Datalog programs, are undisputed, when we allow negation in the body of Datalog rules various proposals have been put forward. In the course of Section 9.1 we present these different semantics and discuss their relative merits. In Section 9.2 we investigate the expressive power of Datalog in terms of the set of computable queries that it can express according to the semantics used to compute the meaning of programs. In Section 9.3 we discuss the problem of proving whether two Datalog programs are equivalent in the sense that their meanings coincide for any given input set of facts. The solution to the equivalence problem has implications for query optimisation, since we prefer programs that do not have any redundant clauses in them. In Section 9.4 we investigate an extension of definite Datalog, called Datalog not-equal, that includes equality and inequality as built-in predicates. The significance of Datalog not-equal is that its programs are monotonic, i.e. if we add more facts to the input of such a program P, then the output from P will contain at least as many facts as it did before the inclusion of the extra facts in the input of P. In Section 9.5 we discuss the important issue of updating a deductive database, which can be seen as an extension of the view update problem presented in Section 3.8 of Chapter 3. Finally, in Section 9.6 we discuss another important issue, i.e. that of defining and maintaining integrity constraints in deductive databases.

9.1 Model-theoretic Semantics of Datalog

A natural interpretation of the semantics of a Datalog program is via model theory. (We refer the reader to Subsection 1.9.3 of Chapter 1 for the relevant background in first-order logic.)

Thus we can associate with every Datalog program, P, a first-order language, $\mathcal{L}(P)$, whose constants are those present in CONST(P) and whose relation symbols are those present in SCHEMA(P). We can then associate with P a family $\{\mathcal{M}_i\}$ of finite Herbrand interpretations. Each such interpretation $\mathcal{M}_i$ is a set of facts that can be viewed as a database d_i over SCHEMA(P) such that the active domain, ADOM(d_i), of d_i is a subset of CONST(P). (In the following we write d_i and $\mathcal{M}_i$ interchangeably.) In order to make clear the notion of a Herbrand model for a Datalog program we define the notion of satisfaction.

Definition 9.1 (Satisfaction of a clause by an interpretation) A Herbrand interpretation $\mathcal{M}$ of P, (or equivalently, the database d over SCHEMA(P)), where P be a Datalog program, *satisfies* a clause C, written $\mathcal{M} \models C$ (or equivalently, $d \models C$), if one of the following conditions is true:

1) C is a positive ground literal (or a fact) of the form L and $L \in \mathcal{M}$.

2) C is a negative ground literal of the form $\neg L$ and $\mathcal{M} \not\models L$.

3) C is a rule of the form $L :- L_1, L_2, \ldots, L_n$ and for all safe substitutions θ for C such that for all $i \in I$, where $I = \{1, 2, \ldots, n\}$, $\mathcal{M} \models L_i$, it is also the case that $\mathcal{M} \models L$. ∎

Definition 9.2 (Herbrand model for a Datalog program) A Herbrand interpretation $\mathcal{M}$ of P is a *Herbrand model* of P (or simply a model of P) if for all clauses C in P, $\mathcal{M} \models C$.

A model $\mathcal{M}$ of P is *minimal* if no proper subset of $\mathcal{M}$ is a model of P, and a model $\mathcal{M}$ is *least* if it is included in every other model of P. (Thus if P has a least model then it has a unique minimal model, since a least model is also minimal; on the other hand P may have more than one minimal model and thus no least model.) ∎

In general, a Datalog program has many Herbrand models, since if $\mathcal{M}$ is a Herbrand model of P, then by the definition of satisfaction any superset of $\mathcal{M}$ is also a Herbrand model of P. Our first result states that the inflationary fixpoint of a Datalog program P is a Herbrand model of P.

Lemma 9.2 MEANING(P) is a Herbrand model of P.

Proof. The result follows from the definition of satisfaction of a clause by an interpretation and the definition of MEANING(P). We leave the details to the reader. □

Definition 9.3 (Definite Datalog program) A Datalog program is *definite* if the bodies of all its rules do *not* contain any negative literals or equality formulae. ∎

For example, the Datalog program computing the transitive closure, which was given in the introduction to this chapter, is definite.

There is no loss of generality in allowing equality formulae in the bodies of rules, since the equality formula $x = y$ (written in prefix notation $= (x, y)$) can be defined by the definite Datalog program given by

EQ(x, x).
$= (x, y) :- $ EQ(x, y).

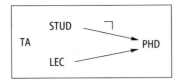

Fig 9.1 The dependency graph of P_1

We note that the rule defining EQ is not safe, but due to Proposition 3.4 of Subsection 3.2.3 in Chapter 3, there exists a safe Datalog program whose meaning is identical. That is, EQ will be defined only with respect to the set of constants in CONST(P).

It is well known that when a Datalog program is definite then it has a least Herbrand model, which is the intersection of all Herbrand models of P [VK76, Apt90, NM90]; this result utilises the celebrated Knaster-Tarski fixpoint theorem [Tar55]. Building upon this result it can be shown that the fixpoint semantics of a definite Datalog program P coincide with the least model semantics of P [VK76, Apt90, NM90] (cf. [KP91]). Thus definite Datalog programs have a very elegant model-theoretic characterisation.

Lemma 9.3   If P is a definite Datalog program then MEANING(P) is the least Herbrand model of P. $\square$

Unfortunately, when negative literals are allowed in the body of a rule then a least model does not always exist. We give several examples that illustrate the problems that arise with the model-theoretic semantics in the presence of negation. Assume a university database having the following entities: people (modelled by the unary predicate PERS), employees (modelled by the unary predicate EMP), lecturers (modelled by the unary predicate LEC), teaching assistants (modelled by the unary predicate TA), students (modelled by the unary predicate STUD) and people having a PhD degree (modelled by the unary predicate PHD).

The following Datalog program, denoted by P_1, states that a typical lecturer who is not a student tends to have a PhD degree.

TA(Wilfred).
LEC(Mark).
$PHD(x) :- LEC(x), \neg STUD(x)$.

The dependency graph of P_1 is shown in Figure 9.1. (We have augmented the construction of the dependency graph by labelling arcs, (R_1, R_2), as being negative whenever the literal R_1 is negative.) P_1 has two minimal Herbrand models. The first model is given by

TA(Wilfred).
LEC(Mark).
PHD(Mark).

In this model Mark has a PhD degree and is therefore not a student. The reader can verify

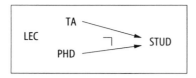

Fig 9.2 The dependency graph of P_2

that MEANING(P) corresponds to the above model. The second model is given by

    TA(Wilfred).
    LEC(Mark).
    STUD(Mark).

In this model Mark is a student and therefore does not have a PhD. The first model seems more natural than the second one, since under the CWA we can deduce that ¬STUD(Mark) is true. Therefore, we should give priority to minimising the STUD facts rather than the PHD facts.

The following Datalog program, denoted by P_2, states that a typical teaching assistant who does not have a PhD degree tends to be a student.

    TA(Wilfred).
    LEC(Mark).
    STUD(x) :− TA(x), ¬PHD(x).

The dependency graph of P_2 is shown in Figure 9.2. P_2 also has two minimal Herbrand models. The first model is given by

    TA(Wilfred).
    LEC(Mark).
    STUD(Wilfred).

In this model Wilfred is a student and therefore does not have a PhD degree. The reader can verify that MEANING(P) corresponds to the above model. The second model is given by

    TA(Wilfred).
    LEC(Mark).
    PHD(Wilfred).

In this model Wilfred has a PhD degree and is therefore not a student. In analogy to the argument that the first model of P_1 is more natural than its second one, we can also argue that the first model of P_2 is more natural than its second model. In this case, we should give priority to minimising the PHD facts rather than the STUD facts. We observe that in P_2 the priorities of the predicates STUD and PHD are reversed.

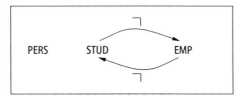

Fig 9.3 The dependency graph of P_3

Fig 9.4 The dependency graph of P_4

The following Datalog program, denoted by P_3, states that a person who is not an employee is a student and a person who is not a student is an employee.

PERS(Dan).
STUD$(x) :- \neg$EMP(x).
EMP$(x) :- \neg$STUD(x).

The dependency graph of P_3 is shown in Figure 9.3. P_3 has two minimal models $\mathcal{M}_1 = \{$PERS(Dan), STUD(Dan)$\}$ and $\mathcal{M}_2 = \{$PERS(Dan), EMP(Dan)$\}$. Both of these models differ from MEANING(P), which is the union of the two asserting that Dan is both a student and an employee. It follows that in this case MEANING(P) is *not* a minimal model. It is not clear, given P_3, which of $\mathcal{M}_1$ or $\mathcal{M}_2$ is a more natural model.

The following Datalog program, denoted by P_4, states that a person who is not recorded as an employee is in fact an employee.

PERS(Dan).
EMP$(x) :- \neg$EMP(x).

The dependency graph of P_4 is shown in Figure 9.4. P_4 has a least model $\mathcal{M} = \{$PERS(Dan), EMP(Dan)$\}$, which coincides with MEANING(P).

The following Datalog program, denoted by P_5, assumes the nonempty binary predicate ARC (modelling the arcs of a digraph), a binary predicate TC (modelling the transitive closure of the digraph) and a binary predicate COMP (modelling the complement of the transitive closure of the digraph). TC and COMP are defined by the following three rules:

TC$(x_1, x_2) :-$ ARC(x_1, x_2).
TC$(x_1, x_3) :-$ ARC(x_1, x_2), TC(x_2, x_3).
COMP$(x_1, x_2) :- \neg$TC(x_1, x_2).

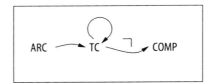

Fig 9.5 The dependency graph of P_5

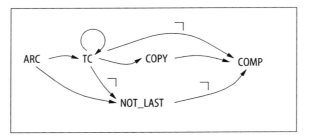

Fig 9.6 The dependency graph of the modified version of P_5

The dependency graph of P_5 is shown in Figure 9.5. Indeed in one of the minimal models of P_5 the predicate COMP stores the complement of the transitive closure TC of the digraph being modelled. This preferred model is the one that gives priority to minimising the TC facts rather than the COMP facts. Unfortunately, the inflationary semantics of P_5, i.e. MEANING(P_5), do not coincide with the intended semantics of P_5. The reader can verify that in MEANING(P_5), COMP is the Cartesian product of the node set of the digraph being modelled. In [AV91a] it was shown how the complement of the transitive closure of a digraph can be computed using inflationary semantics with the aid of two auxiliary predicates, which we call COPY and NOT_LAST. COPY duplicates the TC facts which were added to the resulting database in the previous iteration of the while loop in MEANING(P). On the other hand, NOT_LAST duplicates the same TC facts *unless* all the TC facts that can be added are already in the resulting database, i.e. TC has reached its fixpoint. The modified inflationary version of P_5 is given by the following rules:

$$TC(x_1, x_2) :- ARC(x_1, x_2).$$
$$TC(x_1, x_3) :- ARC(x_1, x_2), TC(x_2, x_3).$$
$$COPY(x_1, x_2) :- TC(x_1, x_2).$$
$$NOT\_LAST(x_1, x_2) :- TC(x_1, x_2), ARC(x_3, x_4), TC(x_4, x_5), \neg TC(x_3, x_5).$$
$$COMP(x_1, x_2) :- \neg TC(x_1, x_2), COPY(x_3, x_4), \neg NOT\_LAST(x_3, x_4).$$

The dependency graph of the modified version of P_5 is shown in Figure 9.6.

The following Datalog program, denoted by P_6, is intended to describe the nodes that are reachable and unreachable from a node, a, in a digraph modelled by the predicate ARC.

$$ARC(a, b).$$
$$ARC(c, d).$$
$$REACHABLE(a).$$

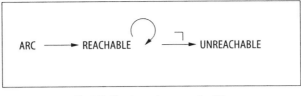

Fig 9.7 The dependency graph of P_6

Fig 9.8 The dependency graph of P_7

REACHABLE(x_2) :— REACHABLE(x_1), ARC(x_1, x_2).
UNREACHABLE(x) :— ¬REACHABLE(x).

The dependency graph of P_6 is shown in Figure 9.7. Indeed, as in P_5, one of the minimal models of P_6 captures the intended semantics. This preferred model is the one that gives priority to minimising the REACHABLE facts rather than the UNREACHABLE facts. As in P_5 the inflationary semantics of P_6, given by MEANING(P_6), does not capture the intended semantics. We leave it to the reader to verify that the intended semantics of P_6 can be captured by modifying P_6 in a way similar to the modification of P_5 by adding to it two predicates COPY and NOT_LAST.

The following Datalog program, denoted by P_7, assumes the nonempty binary predicate MOVE and a unary predicate WIN. It models a two-person perfect information game between two players, where a fact MOVE(a, b) describes a legal move from position a to position b for a player in position a, and a fact WIN(a) asserts that a player in position a wins the game. The rules of the game are such that a player loses if he/she is in a position from which there is no legal move; an example of such a game is *nim* [Bea89]. We observe that MOVE can be viewed as a digraph, and that cycles in this digraph model positions from which neither player can win.

WIN(x) :— MOVE(x, y), ¬WIN(y).

The dependency graph of P_7 is shown in Figure 9.8. For example, consider the four facts describing the legal moves of a game given by

MOVE(a, b).
MOVE(b, c).
MOVE(d, b).
MOVE(d, e).
MOVE(e, e).

The intended semantics of this initial database of P_7 are that position b is winning, positions a and c are losing, while positions d and e are neither winning nor losing, i.e. they are drawing. It is evident that MEANING(P) does not produce this intended meaning. Moreover, since a position may not be winning or losing, we need to allow for facts to be undefined as well as true or false. Thus Herbrand interpretations and models need to be extended so that they be partial, i.e. allow for undefined facts.

We now describe some specific model-theoretic semantics of negation, apart from the inflationary semantics [KP91], which is the semantics we have attached to MEANING(P). A detailed survey of the semantics of negation in Datalog can be found in [Bid91, Via97b]. In particular, we will describe stratified program semantics [CH85, ABW88, Lif88, Van88, Apt90], semipositive program semantics [ABW88], perfect model semantics [Prz88a, Prz88b, AB88, Apt90, PP90], stable model semantics [GL88, Cos95, Sch95], well-founded model semantics [Bry89, Prz89, Ros89, PP90, Prz90, Prz91, VRS91, Prz92, Van93b, Sch95] and default logic semantics [BF91a, BF91b] (see also [CEG94] and cf. [Rei80, Rei87, Bes89]).

For a subset of the clauses C of P, we designate the set of predicates which are heads of the rules in C as the set of the predicates *defined* by C. (Recall that a fact is a trivial rule having an empty body.) Intuitively, a stratification of P is a partition, $\{P_1, P_2, \ldots, P_s\}$, of P into layers P_i, called *strata*, which can be constructed as follows. All the clauses in C which define a given predicate belong to the same stratum. In addition, every rule in P, whose head is H, imposes the following constraints on the stratification of P. Firstly, the clauses in P which define the positive literals in the body of the rule belong to the same or a lower stratum than the stratum of H. Secondly, the clauses in P which define the negative literals in the body of the rule belong to a lower stratum than the stratum of H. It follows that a definite Datalog program has a stratification with a single stratum. The formal definition is now given.

Definition 9.4 (Stratification of a Datalog program)   A *stratification* of a Datalog program P is a partition of P into a number of layers, $\{P_1, P_2, \ldots, P_s\}$, called *strata* as follows.
   For every rule

$$H :- A_1, A_2 \ldots, A_m, \neg B_1, \neg B_2, \ldots, \neg B_q$$

in P, with $m, q \geq 0$, where the A_i's are the positive literals of the rule and the $\neg B_i$'s are the negative literals of the rule, we have that

1) the set of clauses in P which define H all belong to the same stratum;

2) for all $i \in \{1, 2, \ldots, m\}$, $stratum(A_i) \leq stratum(H)$; and

3) for all $i \in \{1, 2, \ldots, q\}$, $stratum(B_i) < stratum(H)$,

where $stratum(L) = i$ if the clauses in P which define a predicate L belong to P_i.   ■

A Datalog program may have zero or more stratifications. The Datalog programs P_3, P_4 and P_7 do not have any stratifications. A stratification for P_5 which has two strata is such that the first stratum consists of the first two rules of P_5 and its ARC facts, and the second stratum consists of the third rule of P_5. Another stratification for P_5 which has three strata is such that the first stratum consists of the ARC facts, the second stratum consists of the first two rules of P_5 and the third stratum consists of the third rule of P_5. Similarly, stratifications for P_1, P_2 and P_6 can also be constructed.

Recall Definition 3.29 of the *dependency graph* of a Datalog program, say P, which was given in Subsection 3.2.3 of Chapter 3. For each rule in P we have an arc from R_1 to R_2 if R_1 is the relation symbol of a literal in the body of the rule and R_2 is the relation symbol of its head. Let us augment the construction of the dependency graph by further labelling arcs as positive or negative according to whether the literal R_1 in the body of the rule is positive or negative.

Definition 9.5 (Stratified Datalog program)   A Datalog program P is *stratified* if the dependency graph of P does *not* have a cycle containing an arc with a negative label.   ■

Note that we can safely assume that stratified Datalog programs do not contain equality formulae, since as we have seen above, equality formulae can be defined by a definite Datalog program containing the predicate EQ and an inequality of the form $x \neq y$ (written in prefix notation $\neq (x, y)$) can defined by using negation, namely

$$\neq (x, y) :- \neg EQ(x, y).$$

On using Definition 9.5 it can be verified that, from the example Datalog programs given above, P_1, P_2, P_5 and P_6 are stratified whilst P_3, P_4 and P_7 are not stratified.

The following theorem was shown in [ABW88].

Theorem 9.4   A Datalog program P is stratified if and only if there exists a stratification of P.
□

The reader can verify that it can be decided in polynomial time in the size of a Datalog program P whether P is stratified or not, and if it is stratified then a stratification of P can also be obtained in polynomial time in the size of P (see [Tar72, AHU83] for efficient digraph algorithms).

Intuitively, the meaning of a stratified Datalog program P is obtained by first stratifying P and then iteratively computing MEANING(Q), where Q is the union of the meaning of the previous strata and the current stratum.

Definition 9.6 (The meaning of a stratified Datalog program)   The pseudo-code of an algorithm, denoted by STRATIFIED_MEANING(P), which realises the meaning of a stratified Datalog program P is presented as the following algorithm.   ■

Algorithm 9.1 (STRATIFIED_MEANING(P))
1. **begin**
2.   Result := ∅;
3.   Compute a stratification $\{P_1, P_2, \ldots, P_s\}$ of P;
4.   **for** $i = 1$ **to** s **do**
5.   CurP := Result ∪ P_i;
6.   Result := Result ∪ MEANING(CurP);
7.   **end for**
8.   **return** Result;
9. **end.**

In order to define the model-theoretic semantics of a stratified Datalog program P we define the concept of a *perfect* model. We first define the relative priorities amongst the relation symbols in P.

Let P be a stratified Datalog program. We say that a relation symbol R_j has a *lower priority* in P than a relation symbol R_i if there is a path in the dependency graph of P from R_j to R_i having at least one negative arc.

For example, in the program P_1 STUD has lower priority than PHD and in P_2 the converse is true. In addition, in P_5 TC has lower priority than COMP and in P_6 REACHABLE has lower priority than UNREACHABLE. In all these programs it is natural to minimise the predicates, whose relation symbols have lower priority, as much as possible, even at the expense of enlarging predicates whose relation symbols have higher priority.

Intuitively, a perfect model for a stratified program P is a Herbrand model that *minimises* the relations over relation schemas whose symbols have a lower priority.

Definition 9.7 (Perfect model)   Let P be a stratified Datalog program and $\mathcal{M}_1$ and $\mathcal{M}_2$ be two distinct Herbrand models of P. We say that $\mathcal{M}_1$ is *preferable* to $\mathcal{M}_2$ with respect to P, if for all facts in $\mathcal{M}_1 - \mathcal{M}_2$ having relation symbol R_1, there exists a fact in $\mathcal{M}_2 - \mathcal{M}_1$ having relation symbol R_2 such that R_2 has a lower priority than R_1.

We say that $\mathcal{M}$ is a *perfect* model of P if $\mathcal{M}$ is a Herbrand model of P and there are no Herbrand models of P which are preferable to $\mathcal{M}$ with respect to P.   ■

The following fundamental result was shown in [Prz88a, Prz88b].

Theorem 9.5   The following statements, where P is a stratified Datalog program, are true:

1) Every perfect model of P is a minimal model.

2) There is a unique perfect model of P.

3) STRATIFIED_MEANING(P) is a perfect model of P.

Proof. For part (1) if $\mathcal{M}_1 \subseteq \mathcal{M}_2$ then it follows that $\mathcal{M}_1$ is preferable to $\mathcal{M}_2$ implying the result.

For part (2) assume that there are two perfect models, $\mathcal{M}_1$ and $\mathcal{M}_2$, such that each is preferable to the other. It follows that $\mathcal{M}_1$ and $\mathcal{M}_2$ are incomparable with respect to subset, since both $\mathcal{M}_1 - \mathcal{M}_2$ and $\mathcal{M}_2 - \mathcal{M}_1$ must be nonempty.

Let R_1 be the relation symbol of a fact in $\mathcal{M}_1 - \mathcal{M}_2$. Then there is a relation symbol R_2 of a fact in $\mathcal{M}_2 - \mathcal{M}_1$ such that R_2 has a lower priority than R_1, since $\mathcal{M}_1$ is preferable to $\mathcal{M}_2$. However, $\mathcal{M}_2$ is also preferable to $\mathcal{M}_1$ and thus there is a relation symbol R_3 of a fact in $\mathcal{M}_1 - \mathcal{M}_2$ such that R_3 has a lower priority than R_2. Moreover, since P is stratified R_1, R_2 and R_3 are pairwise distinct. Continuing this argument it follows that both $\mathcal{M}_1$ and $\mathcal{M}_2$ are infinite Herbrand models having an infinite number of relation symbols, leading to a contradiction, since P has only a finite number of clauses.

For part (3) it can be verified that for every Herbrand model $\mathcal{M}$ of P STRATI-FIED_MEANING(P) is preferable to $\mathcal{M}$, since Algorithm 9.1 minimises relations over relation schemas whose symbols have a lower priority. The result now follows by part (2).   □

We urge the reader to verify the above theorem with respect to the example Datalog programs P_1, P_2, P_5 and P_6 above.

The next corollary follows from the uniqueness of the perfect model semantics.

Corollary 9.6 If P is a stratified Datalog program then STRATIFIED_MEANING(P) is independent of the stratification of P.   □

The class of semipositive Datalog programs is a proper subclass of the class of stratified Datalog programs and a proper superclass of the class of definite Datalog programs.

Definition 9.8 (Semipositive Datalog program) A Datalog program P is *semipositive* if whenever a negative literal appears in the body of a rule in P, then the relation symbol of this literal is *not* the relation symbol of any literal which is the head of a nontrivial rule in P. (We assume that equality formulae of the form $x = y$ and thus inequalities of the form $\neg(x = y)$, which are abbreviated to $x \neq y$, are allowed as literals in the body of rules of semipositive Datalog programs.)   ■

We note that allowing equality formulae as literals in the body of rules of semipositive Datalog programs is equivalent to assuming that EQ is an EDB predicate representing equality such that EQ(v, v) is a fact in the EDB if and only if $v \in$ CONST(P). If we do not allow equality formulae in semipositive Datalog programs, then inequality *cannot* be expressed in semipositive Datalog.

The reader can verify that the stratified Datalog programs P_1 and P_2, given above, are semipositive. On the other hand, the stratified Datalog programs P_5 and P_6 are not semipositive, since TC in P_5 appears in a negative literal in the body of a rule and also in the head of a rule and similarly for REACHABLE in P_6.

It can be verified that each stratum in the stratification of a stratified Datalog program is in fact semipositive. Thus an alternative definition of a stratified program is as a sequence of semipositive programs that partition the original program. We observe that a semipositive Datalog program can be transformed into a program with no negative literals by replacing each negative literal $\neg L$ in P by the complement of L in P with respect to CONST(P). This is consistent with the interpretation of a Datalog program via the CWA (closed world assumption).

The next theorem follows from the fact that a semipositive Datalog program has a stratification consisting of a single stratum.

Theorem 9.7 If P is a semipositive Datalog program then STRATIFIED_MEANING(P) = MEANING(P) is a least Herbrand model of P.   □

We now formalise the notions of Herbrand base and Herbrand program of a Datalog program, both of which will be utilised below.

Definition 9.9 (Herbrand base and Herbrand program) The *Herbrand base* of a Datalog program P, denoted by $\mathcal{B}(P)$, is the set of all facts of the form R$(v_1, v_2, \ldots, v_k)$ such that R is in SCHEMA(P), type(R) $= k$ and $\{v_1, v_2, \ldots, v_k\}$ is a subset of CONST(P). (The set of constants CONST(P) is also known as the *Herbrand universe* of P.)

The *Herbrand program* of P, denoted by $\mathcal{H}(P)$, is the Datalog program resulting from applying all possible safe substitutions θ to the clauses C in P. Formally, $\mathcal{H}(P)$ is a given by

$$\mathcal{H}(P) = \{\theta(C) \mid C \text{ is a clause in P and } \theta \text{ is a safe substitution for C in P}\}. \qquad \blacksquare$$

We observe that although $\mathcal{H}(P)$ does not contain any variables it is still a Datalog program; $\mathcal{H}(P)$ is also known as the *ground instance* of P and the clauses in P are known as the *ground clauses* of P.

Consider the Datalog program P_7 together with a single MOVE fact, given by

MOVE(a, b).
WIN(x) :$-$ MOVE(x, y), $\neg$WIN(y).

Its Herbrand program $\mathcal{H}(P_7)$ is given by

MOVE(a, b).
WIN(a) :$-$ MOVE(a, a), $\neg$WIN(a).
WIN(a) :$-$ MOVE(a, b), $\neg$WIN(b).
WIN(b) :$-$ MOVE(b, b), $\neg$WIN(b).
WIN(b) :$-$ MOVE(b, a), $\neg$WIN(a).

Due to the fact that Datalog programs, such as P_3, P_4 and P_7, are not stratified, there have been proposals to extend the model-theoretic semantics of Datalog to a more general class of programs. We next proceed to define such an extension in the form of stable model semantics for Datalog programs.

Informally, the stable transformation of the Herbrand program of a Datalog program P, with respect to an interpretation $\mathcal{M}$ of P, removes from $\mathcal{H}(P)$ any ground clause that is not satisfied by $\mathcal{M}$ due to a negative ground literal, $\neg L$, in the body of the clause such that $\mathcal{M}$ satisfies L, and then removes all negative literals from the remaining ground clauses in $\mathcal{H}(P)$.

Definition 9.10 (Stable transformation)   For an interpretation $\mathcal{M}$ of a Datalog program P, the *stable transformation* of the Herbrand program $\mathcal{H}(P)$ of P, with respect to $\mathcal{M}$, denoted by $\mathcal{S}(P, \mathcal{M})$, is the Datalog program obtained by

1) deleting each rule in $\mathcal{H}(P)$ that has a negative literal $\neg L$ in its body, where $L \in \mathcal{M}$, and

2) removing all negative literals in the bodies of the remaining rules in $\mathcal{H}(P)$. $\blacksquare$

The stable transformation of $\mathcal{S}(P_7, \{MOVE(a, b), WIN(a)\})$ is given by

MOVE(a, b).
WIN(a) :$-$ MOVE(a, b).
WIN(b) :$-$ MOVE(b, b).

On the other hand, the stable transformation of $\mathcal{S}(P_7, \{MOVE(a, b), WIN(b)\})$ is given by

MOVE(a, b).
WIN(a) :— MOVE(a, a).
WIN(b) :— MOVE(b, a).

The next lemma is an immediate consequence of Lemma 9.3, since $S(P, \mathcal{M})$ is a definite Datalog program.

Lemma 9.8   Given a Datalog program P, MEANING($S(P, \mathcal{M})$) is a least model of $S(P, \mathcal{M})$.
□

A stable model for a Datalog program P is a set of facts $\mathcal{M}$ such that $\mathcal{M}$ is the least fixpoint of the stable transformation of $\mathcal{H}(P)$ with respect to $\mathcal{M}$.

Definition 9.11 (Stable model)   If $\mathcal{M}$ = MEANING($S(P, \mathcal{M})$) for an interpretation $\mathcal{M}$ of a Datalog program P, then we say that $\mathcal{M}$ is a *stable model* of P and that P has *stable model semantics*. If P has a unique stable model then we say that P has *unique stable model semantics*.
∎

We leave it to the reader to verify that the unique stable model of P_7 above is {MOVE(a, b), WIN(a)}, implying that a is the only winning position for this initial database of P_7. The reader can verify that as long as the digraph induced by the MOVE facts describing the game does not have any cycles, then P_7 has a unique stable model semantics. Thus stable model semantics covers only win-lose games, where an outcome of a draw is not possible.

Apart from P_3 and P_4 all the other example Datalog programs given earlier have unique stable model semantics. The reader can verify that P_3 has two stable models {PERS(Dan), EMP(Dan)} and {PERS(Dan), STUD(Dan)} and that P_4 has no stable models, since $S(P_4, \{PERS(Dan)\})$ = {PERS(Dan), EMP(Dan)} and $S(P_4, \{PERS(Dan), EMP(Dan)\})$ = {PERS(Dan)}. Therefore, stable model semantics is *not* defined for all Datalog programs as is the case for inflationary semantics. On the other hand, it is debatable whether programs such as P_3 and P_4 have a "natural" meaning.

The following result, which appeared in [GL88], shows that stable model semantics include perfect model semantics as a special case.

Theorem 9.9   If a Datalog program P is stratified then it has unique stable model semantics and its unique stable model coincides with the unique perfect model of P.   □

We now describe a recent generalisation of the concept of a model to a three-valued formalism, which allows facts to be unknown (or undefined) apart from true and false. This gives rise to an alternative semantics of negation in a Datalog program, thus giving meaning to all Datalog programs.

A Herbrand interpretation, say $\mathcal{M}$, is *two-valued* or *total*, since the facts that are in $\mathcal{M}$ are taken to be true and the facts that are *not* in $\mathcal{M}$ are taken to be false. The underlying idea in generalising the stratified and stable model semantics of Datalog programs is to consider three-valued Herbrand interpretations [Fit85, Kun87].

Definition 9.12 (Three-valued Herbrand interpretations)   A *three-valued* Herbrand interpretation of a Datalog program P (also called a *partial* Herbrand interpretation of P) is a pair (T, F), where T and F are disjoint subsets of the Herbrand base $\mathcal{B}(P)$ of P, called, respectively, the true and false sets of the interpretation. T contains all the facts which are true in the interpretation, F contains all the facts that are false in the interpretation and $U = \mathcal{B}(P) - (T \cup F)$ contains all the facts that are *unknown* (or *undefined*) in the interpretation.

If $U = \emptyset$ then the three-valued interpretation reduces to the standard two-valued Herbrand interpretation (also called *total* Herbrand interpretation), whence $T \cup F = \mathcal{B}(P)$. ∎

We now generalise the concept of satisfaction of a clause in an interpretation to satisfaction in a partial interpretation.

Definition 9.13 (Satisfaction of a clause by a partial interpretation)   A partial Herbrand interpretation $\mathcal{M} = (T, F)$ of P, where P be a Datalog program, *satisfies* a clause C, written $\mathcal{M} \approx C$, if one of the following conditions is true:

1) C is a positive ground literal (or a fact) of the form L and $L \in T$.

2) C is a negative ground literal of the form $\neg L$ and $L \in F$.

3) C is a rule of the form $L :- L_1, L_2, \ldots, L_n$ and for all safe substitutions θ for C such that for all $i \in I$, where $I = \{1, 2, \ldots, n\}$, $\mathcal{M} \approx L_i$, it is also the case that $\mathcal{M} \approx L$. ∎

Definition 9.14 (Three-valued Herbrand model of a Datalog program)   A partial interpretation $\mathcal{M} = (T, F)$ of a Datalog program P is a *three-valued* Herbrand model of P (also called a *partial* Herbrand model of P, or simply a partial model of P) if for all clauses C in P, $\mathcal{M} \approx C$.

A partial model reduces to a *total* model if $U = \emptyset$. ∎

Intuitively, a partial model is minimal if it minimises its true set and maximises its false set.

Definition 9.15 (Minimal partial models of a Datalog program)   We say that a partial model $\mathcal{M}_1 = (T_1, F_1)$ of P is *extended* by a partial model $\mathcal{M}_2 = (T_2, F_2)$ of P if T_1 is a subset of T_2 and F_1 is a superset of F_2.

A partial model $\mathcal{M}$ is *minimal* if it is extended by all other partial models of P. ∎

Prior to defining the well-founded meaning of a Datalog program, we generalise the concept of truth of a clause with respect to a partial interpretation, and correspondingly define the new concept of falsity of a clause with respect to a partial interpretation.

Definition 9.16 (Truth of a clause with respect to a partial interpretation)   A literal L in the body of a clause C in a Datalog program P is true with respect to a substitution θ for C and a partial interpretation $\mathcal{M} = (T, F)$ of P, if one of the following conditions is satisfied:

1) $\theta(L)$ is a ground atomic formula of the form $R(v_1, v_2, \ldots, v_k)$ and $R(v_1, v_2, \ldots, v_k) \in T$.

2) $\theta(L)$ is an equality, $v = v$, where v is a constant.

3) $\theta(L)$ is a ground literal of the form $\neg R(v_1, v_2, \ldots, v_k)$ and $R(v_1, v_2, \ldots, v_k) \in F$.

4) $\theta(L)$ is a negative literal of the form, $\neg(v_i = v_j)$, where v_i and v_j are distinct constants, i.e. $v_i \neq v_j$.

A clause C in a program P is true with respect to a substitution θ for C and a partial interpretation $\mathcal{M}$ of P, if each of the literals in the body of C is true with respect to θ and $\mathcal{M}$. ∎

Definition 9.17 (Falsity of a clause with respect to a partial interpretation)   A literal L in the body of a clause C in a Datalog program P is false with respect to a substitution θ for C and a partial interpretation $\mathcal{M} = (T, F)$ of P, if one of the following conditions is satisfied:

1) $\theta(L)$ is a ground atomic formula of the form $R(v_1, v_2, \ldots, v_k)$ and $R(v_1, v_2, \ldots, v_k) \in F$.

2) $\theta(L)$ is an equality, $v_1 = v_2$, where v_1 and v_2 are distinct constants.

3) $\theta(L)$ is a ground literal of the form $\neg R(v_1, v_2, \ldots, v_k)$ and $R(v_1, v_2, \ldots, v_k) \in T$.

4) $\theta(L)$ is a negative literal of the form, $\neg(v = v)$, i.e. $v \neq v$, where v is a constant.

A clause C in a program P is false with respect to a substitution θ for C and a partial interpretation $\mathcal{M}$ of P, if at least one of the literals in the body of C is false with respect to θ and $\mathcal{M}$. ∎

Intuitively, the well-founded meaning of a Datalog program is a partial model obtained by starting from the empty partial interpretation and iteratively deriving all the facts currently known to be true or false.

Definition 9.18 (The well-founded meaning of a Datalog program)   The pseudo-code of an algorithm, denoted by WELL_FOUNDED_MEANING(P), which realises the well-founded meaning of a Datalog program P is presented as the following algorithm. ∎

Algorithm 9.2 (WELL_FOUNDED_MEANING(P))
1. **begin**
2.   Res_True := ∅;
3.   Res_False := ∅;
4.   Tmp_Res := ({<>}, {<>});
5.   **while** Tmp_Res $\neq$ (Res_True, Res_False) **do**
6.   Tmp_Res := (Res_True, Res_False);
7.   Iter_True := ∅;
8.   Iter_False := $\mathcal{B}(P)$;
9.   Tmp_Iter := ({<>}, {<>});
10.   **while** Tmp_Iter $\neq$ (Iter_True, Iter_False) **do**
11.   Tmp_Iter := (Iter_True, Iter_False);
12.   ImT := ∅;
13.   **for all** clauses C in P and safe substitutions θ for C
                    such that C is true with respect to θ and (Res_True $\cup$ Iter_True, Res_False) **do**
14.   ImT := ImT $\cup$ {$\theta(L)$}, where L is the head of C;
15.   **end for**

```
16.        Iter_True := Iter_True ∪ ImT;
17.        ImF := ∅;
18.        for all facts G ∈ B(P) do
19.            if for all clauses C in P and safe substitutions θ for C
                  such that G = θ(L), where L is the head of C,
                  C is false with respect to θ and (Res_True, Res_False ∪ Iter_False) then
20.                ImF := ImF ∪ {G};
21.            end if
22.        end for
23.        Iter_False := Iter_False ∩ ImF;
24.    end while
25.    Res_True := Res_True ∪ Iter_True;
26.    Res_False := Res_False ∪ Iter_False;
27. end while
28. return (Res_True, Res_False);
29. end.
```

Algorithm 9.2, which was formulated in [Prz88a, PP90], is known as the *iterated least fixpoint* of P. An alternative, yet equivalent, formulation of the well-founded meaning of P, which is known as the *alternating fixpoint*, is given in [Van93b]. WELL_FOUNDED _MEANING(P) outputs a partial model, (Res_True, Res_False), which is constructed iteratively using a temporary partial model (Iter_True, Iter_False). Algorithm 9.2 contains two while loops. The outer while loop beginning at line 5 and ending at line 27 constructs the partial model (Res_True, Res_False), and the inner while loop beginning at line 10 and ending at line 24 constructs the partial model (Iter_True, Iter_False) given the current state of the partial model (Res_True, Res_False).

Intuitively, Iter_True contains new true facts which can be derived from P assuming the current state of (Res_True, Res_False), and Iter_False contains new false facts which can be derived from P also assuming the current state of (Res_True, Res_False). The current state of the partial model (Iter_True, Iter_False) is iteratively extended during each computation of the second while loop (see lines 16 and 23). The current state of the partial model (Res_True, Res_False) increases monotonically after each computation of the second while loop by adding Iter_True to Res_True at line 25, and by adding Iter_False to Res_False at line 26.

As with the inflationary meaning of a Datalog program the well-founded meaning is also defined for all Datalog programs. Thus all the example Datalog programs given earlier have a well-founded meaning. The reader can verify that both WELL_FOUNDED_MEANING(P_3) and WELL_FOUNDED_MEANING(P_4) are equal to ({PERS(Dan)}, ∅). In addition, the well-founded meaning of the rest of the example Datalog programs, apart from P_7, coincide with their unique stable model semantics. With respect to P_7, when we consider games where a draw is *not* possible, i.e. games whose induced digraph is acyclic, then its well-founded meaning coincides with the unique stable model semantics. On the other hand, if we consider games where a draw is possible, i.e. games whose induced digraph may contain cycles, then the well-founded meaning is defined. Its set of true facts contains the winning positions, its set of false facts contains the losing positions and its set of undefined facts contains the set of drawing positions. In contrast, such a game with draws does not have unique stable model semantics.

Part (1) of the next theorem was shown in [Prz89] and parts (2) and (3) were shown in [VRS91].

Theorem 9.10 The following statements, where P is a Datalog program, are true:

1) WELL_FOUNDED_MEANING(P) is a minimal partial model.

2) If P is stratified then WELL_FOUNDED_MEANING(P) = STRATIFIED_MEANING(P).

3) If WELL_FOUNDED_MEANING(P) is a total model, then such a model is a unique stable model. □

The following example program, taken from [VRS91], shows that the converse of part (3) of Theorem 9.10 does not, in general, hold. Thus it may be the case that WELL_FOUNDED_MEANING(P) is not a total model but there exists a unique (total) stable model for P.

Let P_8 be the following Datalog program, where A, B and C are propositions (i.e. zero-place predicates).

$$A :- \neg B.$$
$$B :- \neg A.$$
$$C :- \neg C.$$
$$C :- \neg B.$$

The reader can verify that $(\{A, C\}, \{B\})$ is a total model of P_8 (i.e. A and C are true and B is false), which is a unique stable model of P_8. On the other hand, WELL_FOUNDED_MEANING(P_8) = $(\emptyset, \emptyset)$, i.e. all of A, B and C are undefined.

Intuitively, a preferred model for a Datalog program P is a partial model that *minimises* the true facts of relations over relation schemas whose symbols have a lower priority and *maximises* the false facts of relations over relation schemas whose symbols have a lower priority.

Definition 9.19 (Preferred model) Let P be a Datalog program and $\mathcal{M}_1 = (T_1, F_1)$ and $\mathcal{M}_2 = (T_2, F_2)$ be two distinct partial models of P. We say that $\mathcal{M}_1$ is *preferable* to $\mathcal{M}_2$ with respect to P, if

1) for all true facts in $T_1 - T_2$ having relation symbol R_1, there exists a true fact in $T_2 - T_1$ having relation symbol R_2 such that R_2 has a lower priority than R_1, and

2) for all false facts in $F_2 - F_1$ having relation symbol R_1, there exists a false fact in $F_1 - F_2$ having relation symbol R_2 such that R_2 has a lower priority than R_1.

We say that $\mathcal{M}$ is a *preferred* model of P if $\mathcal{M}$ is a partial model of P and there are no partial models of P which are preferable to $\mathcal{M}$ with respect to P. ∎

The following fundamental result, which shows the connection between preferred models and the well-founded meaning of a Datalog program, P, was shown in [Prz89]. In the theorem we take the intersection of two partial models $(T_1, F_1) \cap (T_2, F_2)$ to be the partial model $(T_1 \cap T_2, F_1 \cap F_2)$.

Theorem 9.11   Let P be a Datalog program and $\mathcal{M}$ = WELL_FOUNDED_MEANING(P). Then $\mathcal{M}$ is a preferred model, which is the intersection of all preferred models of P.   □

The well-founded semantics of a Datalog program is seen to generalise the stable and stratified semantics, whilst giving programs a more "natural" meaning than the inflationary semantics. We note that the stable model semantics can be extended to a three-valued stable model semantics, which coincides with the well-founded semantics of Datalog programs [Prz90, Prz92]. As we shall see in the next section the expressive power of the well-founded semantics is equivalent to that of the inflationary semantics. From a practical point of view the stratified semantics, although less expressive than the well-founded and stable semantics, seems the most "natural" due to its straightforward and elegant formalisation via the unique perfect model.

We close this section with a brief and informal description of an alternative approach whereby negation is viewed via *default logic*. In this approach a Datalog program becomes a *positivist default theory* consisting of a set of facts, a set of *positivist* default rules and a set of *closed world* (or CWA) default rules. Let us transform the example program P_1 into a positivist default theory. The facts TA(Wilfred) and LEC(Mark) remain as they are in the positivist default theory for P_1. The rule

$$\text{PHD}(x) :- \text{LEC}(x), \neg\text{STUD}(x).$$

becomes the positivist default rule

$$\frac{\text{LEC}(x) : M\neg\text{STUD}(x)}{\text{PHD}(x)}.$$

where M is read as "it is consistent to assume".

In this positivist default rule LEC(x) is called the *prerequisite* of the rule, STUD(x) is called the *justification* of the rule and PHD(x) is called the *consequent* of the rule. Informally, the semantics of this rule are as follows. Given a safe substitution θ for the variables in the default rule, we say that the positivist default rule is true in a partial Herbrand interpretation (T, F) for the Datalog program under consideration if PHD($\theta(x)$) $\in$ T whenever LEC($\theta(x)$) $\in$ T and STUD($\theta(x)$) $\notin$ T. In general, a positivist default rule may have a conjunction of prerequisites and a conjunction of justifications. We say that a Herbrand interpretation $\mathcal{M}$ is an *extension* of a positivist default rule, if for all safe substitutions θ for the variables in the rule, the rule is true in $\mathcal{M}$.

In addition, the positivist default theory for P_1 has the following four CWA default rules, one for each predicate in P_1, namely

$$\frac{: M\neg\text{STUD}(x)}{\neg\text{STUD}(x)},$$

$$\frac{: M\neg\text{PHD}(x)}{\neg\text{PHD}(x)},$$

$$\frac{: M\neg\text{LEC}(x)}{\neg\text{LEC}(x)}, \text{ and}$$

$$\frac{: M\neg\text{TA}(x)}{\neg\text{TA}(x)}.$$

Each CWA default rule is of the form

$$\frac{: M\neg\text{PRED}(x_1, x_2, \ldots, x_k)}{\neg\text{PRED}(x_1, x_2, \ldots, x_k)},$$

where PRED is a predicate symbol in the Datalog program under consideration. The occurrence of $\text{PRED}(x_1, x_2, \ldots, x_k)$ in the numerator of the rule is called the *justification* of the rule and the occurrence of $\text{PRED}(x_1, x_2, \ldots, x_k)$ in the denominator of the rule is called the *consequent* of the rule. (We note that CWA default rules are *normal* default rules [Rei80, Bes89].)

Given a safe substitution θ for the variables in a CWA default rule, we say that the CWA default rule is true in a partial Herbrand interpretation (T, F) for the Datalog program under consideration if $\text{PRED}(\theta(x_1, x_2, \ldots, x_k)) \in F$ whenever $\text{PRED}(\theta(x_1, x_2, \ldots, x_k)) \notin T$.

Thus positivist default rules allow us to infer positive facts and CWA default rules allow us to infer negative facts. In [BF91a, BF91b] it was shown that the default logic model semantics of a Datalog program P can be given appropriate stratified program semantics which coincide with the perfect model semantics of P. Moreover, the more general result that the default logic model semantics coincides with the stable model semantics of P was shown in [BF91a, BF91b, SI93].

For extensions of Datalog which add to its expressive power see [Lae90, AV91a]. Moreover, for an extension of Datalog, which allows disjunction ($\vee$) in the heads of rules, see [LMR89, LRM91, EGM97]. The following disjunctive Datalog program solves the 3-colourability problem, which is known to be NP-complete [GJ79], showing that disjunctive definite Datalog is more expressive than definite Datalog under minimal model semantics.

> RED(x) $\vee$ GREEN(x) $\vee$ BLUE(x).
> NOTCOLOURED :− ARC(x_1, x_2), RED(x_1), RED(x_2).
> NOTCOLOURED :− ARC(x_1, x_2), GREEN(x_1), GREEN(x_2).
> NOTCOLOURED :− ARC(x_1, x_2), BLUE(x_1), BLUE(x_2).
> COLOURED $\vee$ NOTCOLOURED.

The intuitive semantics of the above program are described as follows. The first rule assigns each node in the input digraph to one of the three possible colours. The second, third and fourth rules define the situations when the assignment of colours to the nodes of the input digraph is an illegal colouring. Finally, the fifth rule states that the digraph is either coloured or not coloured. Since we are only interested in minimal model semantics, in the result of computing the meaning of this program, with any initial database for the arcs of the input digraph, COLOURED will be true if and only if the input digraph is 3-colourable.

We do not discuss the proof-theoretic semantics of P, where P is a Datalog program; such semantics lead to a top-down approach when we compute the meaning of P in contrast to the bottom-up approach of the fixpoint computation. The reader can consult [VK76, AV82, Apt90, CGT90, NM90] for details of the proof-theoretic approach in the context of logic programming. An extension of the CWA, which specifically caters for stratified databases, leading to a proof-theoretic evaluation of the meaning of P, when P is stratified, can be found in [SI88]. For a more general discussion on the merits of the proof-theoretic approach versus the model-theoretic approach we refer the reader to [NG78, Rei84].

9.2 Expressive Power of Datalog

One of the fundamental motivations for investigating deductive databases is that of enhancing the expressive power of the relational algebra. Herein we measure the expressive power of Datalog in terms of the set of computable queries that it can express under a given semantics. We will not provide full proofs of any of the results in this section but rather refer the reader to the relevant references.

We will use the following terminology to denote the various semantics of Datalog examined in Section 9.1:

1) Definite Datalog denotes the semantics of Datalog programs P in terms of MEANING(P), when P is a definite Datalog program, and is undefined when P is not a definite Datalog program.

2) Inflationary Datalog denotes the semantics of Datalog programs P in terms of MEANING(P).

3) Stratified Datalog denotes the semantics of Datalog programs P in terms of STRATIFIED_MEANING(P), when P is a stratified Datalog program, and is undefined when P is not a stratified Datalog program.

4) Semipositive Datalog denotes the semantics of Datalog programs P in terms of STRATIFIED_MEANING(P), when P is a semipositive Datalog program, and is undefined when P is not a semipositive Datalog program.

5) Stable Datalog denotes the semantics of Datalog programs P in terms of the intersection of all stable models of P if P has at least one stable model, and is undefined when P has no stable models.

6) Well-founded Datalog denotes the semantics of Datalog programs P in terms of WELL_FOUNDED_MEANING(P).

Recall the definition of an ordered relational database, containing a designated binary relation SUCC, which is a successor relation that linearly orders the active domain of the database (see Definition 6.24 in Section 6.7 of Chapter 6). In the context of a Datalog program P the relation SUCC is a predicate which defines a linear order on CONST(P); we will use the *less than* predicate, $x < y$ (or equivalently, $< (x, y)$), with its natural meaning, i.e. $x < y$ if the pair (x, y) is in the transitive closure of SUCC(x, y). (By default we will assume that databases are *unordered*.)

Definition 9.20 (Equivalent Datalog semantics) We say that two Datalog semantics are *equivalent* if they express exactly the same set of computable queries. Correspondingly, we say that a Datalog semantics is *included* in another Datalog semantics if the set of computable queries expressed by the first semantics is included in the set of computable queries expressed by the second semantics. If the inclusion is proper we say that the first semantics is *properly included* in the second semantics. ∎

We observe that inclusion is a partial order on Datalog semantics, and thus one semantics is equivalent to another if and only if they are both included in each other.

The next two theorems establish the inclusion and equivalence relationships that exist amongst the various types of Datalog programs encountered so far.

Theorem 9.12 The following statements concerning Datalog semantics are true over unordered databases:

1) Nonrecursive Datalog is properly included in stratified Datalog. (It is sufficient to assume that EQ is an EDB predicate representing equality.)

2) Definite Datalog is properly included in semipositive Datalog.

3) Semipositive Datalog is properly included in stratified Datalog.

4) Stratified Datalog is properly included in inflationary Datalog.

5) Inflationary Datalog is equivalent to well-founded Datalog.

6) Well-founded Datalog is included in stable Datalog.

Proof. Part (1) is immediate, since the transitive closure of a relation can not be expressed in nonrecursive Datalog.

For part (2) we utilise the fact that definite Datalog programs can only compute monotonic (increasing) computable queries. Let P be a definite Datalog program and r be a relation, over R, in the initial database DB(P) of P such that type(R) = n. Let P' be the semipositive Datalog program resulting from adding the following rule to P.

$$\text{COMP}(x_1, x_2, \ldots, x_n) := \neg R(x_1, x_2, \ldots, x_n).$$

It follows that the complement of a relation in DB(P) can be expressed by a semipositive Datalog program. The result follows, since computing such a complement is a nonmonotonic computable query and thus cannot be expressed by a definite Datalog program.

Let s-stratified Datalog be the subset of stratified Datalog whose programs have stratifications with at most s strata. Part (3) follows from [Dah87, Kol91], where it was shown that if $s_1 < s_2$ then s_1-stratified Datalog is properly included in s_2-stratified Datalog. (See example program P_5, which cannot be expressed by a semipositive Datalog program; P_5 computes the complement of the transitive closure of a digraph.)

For part (4) see [Kol91], where a game-theoretic argument was used to prove the result. (See example program P_7, which is closely related to the game used in [Kol91] in proving the result. Essentially, stratified Datalog is not expressive enough to distinguish between winning and losing positions in the game modelled by P_7.)

Part (5) follows from the fact that both inflationary Datalog and well-founded Datalog are equivalent to the relational algebra augmented with a fixpoint operator by the result in [AV91a, KP91] and [VRS91, Van93b], respectively. (See Section 6.7 of Chapter 6.)

For part (6) see [Sch95]. □

Theorem 9.13 The following semantics of Datalog are all equivalent over ordered databases:

1) Inflationary Datalog,

2) Well-founded Datalog,

3) Stratified Datalog and

4) Semipositive Datalog, together with the additional two unary predicates MIN and MAX, such that $MIN(c)$ is true if and only if $\forall c' \in CONST(P)$ such that $c \neq c', c < c'$ (i.e. c is the minimal element in $CONST(P)$), and $MAX(c)$ is true if and only if $\forall c' \in CONST(P)$ such that $c \neq c', c' < c$ (i.e. c is the maximal element in $CONST(P)$).

Proof. (1) is equivalent to (2) by part (5) of Theorem 9.12; in [Pap85, BG87] it was proved that (4) is equivalent to (1) (see also Theorem 6.10 in Section 6.7 of Chapter 6); (3) is equivalent to (4) by part (3) of Theorem 9.12 and the fact that stratified Datalog over ordered databases can express MIN and MAX by

$$MIN(x) :- \neg PREV(x).$$
$$PREV(x) :- SUCC(y, x).$$
$$MAX(x) :- \neg NEXT(x).$$
$$NEXT(x) :- SUCC(x, y).$$

where PREV and NEXT are unary predicates such that $PREV(x)$ is true if x has a predecessor and $NEXT(x)$ is true if x has a successor. □

It is interesting to note that the semipositive rules given by

$$MIN(x) :- \neg SUCC(y, x).$$
$$MAX(x) :- \neg SUCC(x, y).$$

do *not* define $MIN(x)$ and $MAX(x)$ correctly, since $\neg SUCC(v, v)$ is true for all constants $v \in CONST(P)$.

Corollary 9.14 Inflationary Datalog, well-founded Datalog, stratified Datalog and semipositive Datalog with MIN and MAX predicates (as defined in the statement of Theorem 9.13) are all equivalent over ordered databases and express exactly the set of all polynomial-time computable queries. □

We note that over ordered databases semipositive Datalog, with MIN and MAX, allows us to express universal quantification by iterating over all the constants in $CONST(P)$ from MIN to MAX, which explains the above equivalence between stratified Datalog and semipositive

Datalog. Both semipositive Datalog and stratified Datalog subsume the relational algebra, which is essentially first-order logic defined over finite structures.

Recall from Subsection 1.9.4 of Chapter 1 that co-NP is the complement of NP (NP is the class of all Turing-computable mappings whose time complexity is nondeterministically polynomial in the size of the input). The following result, which characterises the expressive power of stable Datalog, was shown in [Sch95] (see also [MT91]).

Theorem 9.15 Stable Datalog expresses exactly the set of all co-NP computable queries. □

Suppose that we allow function symbols in predicates of rules of Datalog programs and thus Herbrand universes may be infinite. A typical example of the use of function symbols is shown in the following Datalog program, which uses a function symbol $succ$ in order to define the natural numbers:

NAT(0).
NAT($succ(x)$) : $-$ NAT(x).

Another typical example is the following Datalog program, also using the function symbol $succ$, which defines the set of even natural numbers:

EVEN(0).
EVEN($succ(x)$) : $-$ $\neg$EVEN(x).

The following interesting result was shown in [Sch95].

Theorem 9.16 Over the class of infinite Herbrand universes (generated by a finite number of constants and function symbols) stable Datalog and well-founded Datalog have the same expressive power. □

See [AB88, Apt90, MNR92, Sch95] for more results on Datalog programs which may have function symbols in their predicates.

9.3 Equivalence Between Datalog Programs

Informally, two Datalog programs are equivalent if whenever their sets of input facts are equal then their meanings coincide over a designated output relation schema. Thus the set of facts present in a Datalog program P is considered to be its input database and the set of facts generated by the program via MEANING(P) is considered to be its output database. An important issue which we discuss in this section is the problem of deciding whether two Datalog programs are equivalent. This is a significant problem confronted in optimising Datalog programs. On the one hand, we may be able to optimise a Datalog program by finding an equivalent program which is obtained by removing redundant rules and redundant literals from the bodies of rules in the original program; such an optimised program is more compact and thus likely to reduce the computation time of MEANING(P). On the other hand, we may be able to optimise a Datalog program by finding a nonrecursive program which is equivalent to the original program, and thus allowing us to compute its meaning without any recursion via NEW_MEANING(P) instead of via MEANING(P). (For the detailed description of NEW_MEANING(P) see Algorithm 3.5 in Subsection 3.2.3 of Chapter 3.)

It turns out that the equivalence problem is undecidable for the restricted class of nonrecursive Datalog programs (or equivalently, the relational algebra) and also for the restricted class of definite Datalog programs. In addition, it is also an undecidable problem to test whether there exists a nonrecursive Datalog program which is equivalent to a given recursive program. On the positive side there are some useful subclasses of Datalog programs for which the equivalence problem is decidable; we present some of these subclasses below.

Prior to the ensuing definition the reader is advised to recall the definition of the set of extensional database facts EDB(P) and the definition of the set of intensional database facts IDB(P).

Definition 9.21 (The result of applying a Datalog program)   A database d is said to be *compatible* with P, where P is a Datalog program, if it contains a finite set of facts whose relation symbols are those of the EDB predicates of P. We denote by P(d) the Datalog program resulting from replacing EDB(P) in P by d, i.e. P(d) = (P − EDB(P)) ∪ d and thus EDB(P(d)) = d and IDB(P(d)) = IDB(P).

Given a Datalog program P, a predicate R in IDB(P) and a database d which is compatible with P, the *result* for R of *applying* P to d, denoted by P(d, R), is the set of facts in MEANING(P(d)) whose relation symbol is R (or alternatively the relation over R in MEANING(P(d))).   ∎

We now formalise the notion of equivalence.

Definition 9.22 (Equivalent Datalog programs)   Let P and Q be Datalog programs, and let R be an IDB predicate of P and S be an IDB predicate of Q such that type(R) = type(S). We say that P is *equivalent* to Q if for every database d which is compatible with both P and Q, we have that P(d, R) = Q(d, S). The *equivalence problem* for a class of Datalog programs is the problem of deciding whether two Datalog programs in the class are equivalent.   ∎

We next mention some results for subclasses of nonrecursive Datalog programs (or equivalently, the relational algebra). A relational algebra query is said to be *conjunctive* if it is a finite composition of selections with only simple selection formulae, projections and joins (conjunctive queries are also called *select-project-join* expressions). A relational algebra query is *monotonic* if it is a finite composition of unions, selections with only simple selection formulae, projections and joins.

Theorem 9.17   The following statements are true:

1) The equivalence problem for conjunctive queries is NP-complete [CM77, ASU79].

2) The equivalence problem for monotonic relational algebra queries is Π_2^P-complete [SY80]. (Recall from Subsection 1.9.4 of Chapter 1 that Π_2^P is a computational complexity class in the second level of the polynomial hierarchy.)

3) The equivalence problem for nonrecursive Datalog is undecidable [IL84b]. (The result is proved by a reduction from the word problem for finite semigroups, defined in Subsection 1.9.4.) □

In view of the undecidability of the equivalence problem for relational algebra expressions, which may contain the difference operator, it follows that equivalence is also undecidable for stratified Datalog. So we now consider a subclass of definite Datalog programs, called *chain* Datalog programs.

Definition 9.23 (Chain Datalog program)   A Datalog rule is a *chain* rule if it is of the form

$$R(x_1, x_n) :- R_1(x_1, x_2), R_2(x_2, x_3), \ldots, R_{n-1}(x_{n-1}, x_n),$$

where $n \geq 2$ is a natural number. A Datalog program is a *chain* Datalog program (or simply a chain program) if all its nontrivial rules are chain rules. ∎

We observe that a chain rule is equivalent to the $(n-1)$-way project-join query (with a suitable renaming of attributes if necessary) given by

$$\pi_{schema(R)}(R_1 \bowtie R_2 \bowtie \cdots \bowtie R_{n-1}). \tag{9.1}$$

The following theorem establishes an equivalence between a chain Datalog program and a (possibly countably infinite) union of conjunctive queries. Thus given a database d, which is computable with a chain program P, and an IDB predicate R of P, there exists a set $\{P_1, P_2, \ldots\}$ of conjunctive queries such that

$$P(d, R) = P_1(d, R) \cup P_2(d, R) \cup \cdots.$$

Theorem 9.18   A chain program (and in fact any definite Datalog program) is equivalent to a (possibly countably infinite) union of conjunctive queries.

Proof. We sketch the construction of a union of conjunctive queries that is equivalent to P, where P is a chain program. (A similar construction obtains for any definite Datalog program.)

Consider a fact, say $R(v_1, v_2, \ldots, v_q)$, that is generated after the kth iteration of the while loop in Algorithm 3.4 of Subsection 3.2.3 implementing MEANING(P), which is thereafter added to the current state of Result. If $k = 0$ then this fact is already in P, and if $k = 1$ then this fact can be generated by the project-join query shown in (9.1), where $R_1, R_2, \ldots, R_{n-1}$ are all EDB predicates. Inductively, assume that all the facts that are generated before the kth iteration can be output by a union of conjunctive queries.

By the definition of a chain rule it must be the case that $R(v_1, v_2, \ldots, v_q)$ is generated during the kth iteration by the project-join query shown in (9.1), where some of the predicates $R_1, R_2, \ldots, R_{n-1}$ may be IDB predicates. The result now follows by induction hypothesis, since we can replace each such IDB predicate, $R_i(x_i, x_{i+1})$, in this project-join query, where $i \in \{1, 2, \ldots, n-1\}$, by a conjunctive query. □

The next corollary is an immediate consequence of the above proof.

Corollary 9.19 If P is a chain program and $\{P_1, P_2, \ldots\}$ is a set of conjunctive queries whose union is equivalent to P, then each P_i, with $i \in \{1, 2, \ldots\}$, is a chain rule. $\square$

Recall the definition of a context-free grammar from Subsection 1.9.4. Informally, a context-free grammar is a set of production rules of the form $A \rightarrow \alpha$, where A is a nonterminal symbol and α is a (possibly empty) string of terminal and nonterminal symbols; one of the nonterminal symbols is designated as the start symbol. The language generated by a context-free grammar G, with start symbol S, is the set of all terminal strings that can be generated from the production rules of G starting from S.

Definition 9.24 (The context-free grammar of a chain program) Given a chain program P and an IDB predicate, R, of P we convert P into a context-free grammar, denoted by $G(P, R)$, as follows:

1) Replace each EDB predicate by a terminal symbol.

2) Replace each IDB predicate by a nonterminal symbol, with the symbol replacing R being the start symbol S.

3) Replace each chain rule

$$R'(x_1, x_n) :- R_1(x_1, x_2), R_2(x_2, x_3), \ldots, R_{n-1}(x_{n-1}, x_n)$$

by a production rule,

$$S' \rightarrow S_1 S_2 \ldots S_{n-1},$$

where S' is the symbol replacing R' and S_i is the symbol replacing R_i, with $i \in \{1, 2, \ldots, n-1\}$. $\blacksquare$

For example, the chain program computing the transitive closure can be converted into the context-free grammar given by

$$T \rightarrow f,$$
$$T \rightarrow Tf,$$

where T replaces TC and f replaces FAMILY. Another context-free grammar corresponding to an alternative implementation of the transitive closure is given by

$$T \rightarrow f,$$
$$T \rightarrow fT.$$

Finally, the reader can verify that yet another context-free grammar corresponding to another implementation of the transitive closure is given by

$$T \rightarrow f,$$
$$T \rightarrow TT.$$

We can now prove the undecidability of the equivalence problem for definite Datalog programs as a corollary of the undecidability of the equivalence problem for chain Datalog programs [Ull92, Shm93].

Theorem 9.20   The problem of deciding whether two chain Datalog programs are equivalent is undecidable.

Proof. We reduce the problem of whether two context-free grammars are equivalent to the problem of the equivalence of two chain Datalog programs. Let G_1 and G_2 be two context-free grammars. We construct two chain programs P_1 and P_2 by invoking the inverse of the transformation given in Definition 9.24. We note that the inverse of this transformation is well defined, since the variables in a chain rule can be implied once the predicate symbols in the head and the body of the rule are known and, in addition, the variables in a chain rule can always be renamed without altering its meaning. Thus G_1 is equivalent to G_2 if and only if P_1 is equivalent to P_2. The result follows, since the problem of whether two context-free grammars are equivalent, i.e. generate the same formal language, is undecidable [Har78, HU79].   □

We next define a useful subclass of Datalog programs, where the recursion is limited to at most one literal in the body of rules. Such programs often arise in practice.

Definition 9.25 (Linear and bilinear Datalog programs)   A Datalog rule is *recursive* if the relation symbol of the head of the rule is also the relation symbol of one or more literals in the body of the rule. A Datalog program is *recursive* if at least one of its rules is recursive.

A Datalog rule is *linear recursive* if the relation symbol of the head of the rule occurs as the relation symbol of *exactly* one literal in the body of the rule. A Datalog program is *linear* if all of its recursive rules are linear recursive.

Similarly, a Datalog rule is *bilinear recursive* if the relation symbol of the head of the rule occurs as the relation symbol of *exactly* two literals in the body of the rule. A Datalog program is *bilinear* if all of its recursive rules are either bilinear recursive or linear recursive and at least one of its recursive rules is bilinear recursive.   ∎

We note that our use of the term "recursive" rule is sometimes referred to as *directly* recursive rule [ZYT90]. A more general definition of a recursive rule would make use of the dependency graph of the Datalog program under consideration, calling a rule recursive if the relation symbol of the head of the rule is involved in a cycle in the dependency graph. There is no loss of generality in our definition, since the reader can verify that by replacing a literal, which is the head of a rule, by its body with a suitable renaming of variables, we can always transform a recursive rule under the more general definition into a recursive rule according to Definition 9.25.

The rule given by

$$TC(x_1, x_3) :- TC(x_1, x_2), TC(x_2, x_3).$$

is bilinear recursive but not linear recursive, while the rule given by

$$TC(x_1, x_3) :- FAMILY(x_1, x_2), TC(x_2, x_3).$$

is linear recursive.

The next corollary, whose proof is essentially the same as the proof of Theorem 9.20, is an immediate consequence of the fact that the problem of whether two linear context-free grammars are equivalent is undecidable [Har78, HU79]. (A context-free grammar is linear if the right-hand sides of its production rules contain at most one nonterminal symbol.)

Corollary 9.21   The problem of deciding whether two linear chain Datalog programs are equivalent is undecidable. □

   The following result, which implies that given a recursive definite Datalog program the problem of finding whether there exists an equivalent linear recursive definite Datalog program is undecidable, was shown in [FS92].

Theorem 9.22   It is undecidable whether a bilinear recursive definite Datalog program has an equivalent linear recursive definite Datalog program. □

   A simple recursive Datalog program is a definite Datalog program with two nontrivial rules, one which is bilinear recursive and the other, which is not recursive, representing the base case of the recursion.

Definition 9.26 (Simple recursive Datalog program)   A Datalog program P is *simple* recursive if P is definite, has only one IDB predicate R, and only two nontrivial rules of the form

$R(\mathbf{x}) :- S(\mathbf{x}).$
$R(\mathbf{x}) :- R(\mathbf{y_1}), R(\mathbf{y_2}), S_1(\mathbf{z_1}), S_2(\mathbf{z_2}), \ldots, S_k(\mathbf{z_k}).$

where $\mathbf{x}, \mathbf{y_1}, \mathbf{y_2}$ and $\mathbf{z_i}$, for $i \in \{1, 2, \ldots, k\}$, are sequences of variables. The first rule is called the *basis* rule of the simple recursive Datalog program. ∎

   Consider a digraph with coloured arcs. Suppose that there are two relations, *redarc* and *bluearc*, in the initial database (recall Definition 3.35 in Subsection 3.2.3 of Chapter 3); REDARC(x, y) means that the arc from a node x to a node y is red and BLUEARC(x, y) means that the arc from a node x to a node y is blue. The Datalog program P given by

$PATH(x_1, x_2) :- REDARC(x_1, x_2).$
$PATH(x_1, x_2) :- PATH(x_1, x_3), BLUEARC(x_3, x_4), PATH(x_4, x_2).$

is simple recursive, and can be seen to define paths consisting of alternating red and blue arcs and ending in a red arc.

   The following results were shown in [RSUV89, Sar89, Sar95].

Theorem 9.23   The following statements are true:

1) The problem of deciding whether a simple recursive Datalog program has an equivalent linear recursive definite Datalog program is NP-hard.

2) For a simple recursive Datalog program, where in Definition 9.26 $\mathbf{x}$ is a sequence of distinct variables and all of the predicate symbols $S_1, S_2, \ldots, S_k$ are distinct, the problem of deciding whether such a program has an equivalent linear recursive definite Datalog program can be decided in polynomial time in the size of the input program. □

We refer the reader to [Nau88, RSUV89, Sar89, Sar90, ZYT90, IW91, FS92, Sar95] for further results concerning linear recursive definite Datalog programs, and to [CGKV88, AC89, Var89a, GMSV93, Shm93, Shm95] for further results concerning the undecidability and decidability of the equivalence problem for Datalog programs.

For semipositive Datalog programs the following result was obtained in [LMS93].

Theorem 9.24   The following statements are true:

1) The equivalence problem for semipositive Datalog programs whose EDB predicates are all unary is decidable.

2) The equivalence problem for semipositive Datalog programs whose IDB predicates are all unary is undecidable. $\qquad\square$

It is interesting to note that in [CGKV88] it was shown that the equivalence problem for definite Datalog programs, whose IDB predicates are all unary, is decidable. The result of Theorem 9.24 also holds with respect to the related problem of *satisfiability*, which is the problem of determining whether for some IDB predicate R of P the result for R of applying P to a database compatible with P, namely $P(d, R)$, is nonempty [LMS93, MS94].

A variation of the equivalence of Datalog programs in which IDB predicates are also considered to be part of the input is called *uniform equivalence* [Sag87]. That is, when considering uniform equivalence we modify the definition of a database compatible with a Datalog program P to include facts whose relation symbols may be those of either EDB or IDB predicates. Consider the following three rules:

$$TC(x_1, x_2) :- \text{FAMILY}(x_1, x_2).$$
$$TC(x_1, x_3) :- \text{FAMILY}(x_1, x_2), TC(x_2, x_3).$$
$$TC(x_1, x_3) :- TC(x_1, x_2), TC(x_2, x_3).$$

Let TC_1 denote the first and second rule and TC_2 denote the first and third rules. Both TC_1 and TC_2 are equivalent chain programs computing the transitive closure of FAMILY. However, it can be verified that TC_1 and TC_2 are not uniformly equivalent, since we can construct a compatible database (as modified above), d, which contains no FAMILY facts but two TC facts generating a third TC fact using the last rule.

The following result, which can be proved utilising the chase procedure of Subsection 3.6.4 with generalised chase rules, was established in [Sag87].

Theorem 9.25   The problem of deciding whether two definite Datalog programs are uniformly equivalent is decidable. $\qquad\square$

Informally, a Datalog program is bounded if the number of iterations of the while loop invoked when computing its meaning is less than some fixed natural number independently of the input database. Boundedness is a desirable property, since if a Datalog program is bounded then its recursion is independent of the input database and, as will be shown, it is in fact nonrecursive and thus can be computed via a relational algebra expression.

Definition 9.27 (Bounded Datalog program)   A Datalog program P is *bounded* with respect to an IDB predicate R of P (or simply bounded if R is understood from context) if there exists a natural number k depending on P such that for all databases d, which are compatible with P, P(d, R) can be computed with at most k iterations of the while loop in Algorithm 3.4 of Subsection 3.2.3 implementing MEANING(P(d)).   ∎

As a historical note we mention that the notion of boundedness has been introduced in the context of the universal relation model (see discussion at the end of Section 2.4), where it was shown that a universal relation can be constructed via a relational algebra expression if and only if the set of data dependencies associated with the relation schema are bounded [MUV84, Sag88]. (Intuitively a set of data dependencies is bounded if, when they are viewed as a set of production rules, the universal relation can always be constructed with at most k applications of the set of data dependencies to the original database.)

The next proposition shows an important connection between boundedness and nonrecursiveness of Datalog programs.

Proposition 9.26   If a Datalog program is bounded then it is equivalent to some nonrecursive Datalog program.

Proof. We prove the result by contraposition. Assume that for a recursive Datalog program P there does not exist an equivalent nonrecursive Datalog program. Furthermore, assume that for some database d, which is compatible with P, P(d, R) is computed with k iterations of the while loop in Algorithm 3.4 implementing MEANING(P(d)). Then we can always find a database d', which is compatible with P, where d' properly contains d, and such that P(d', R) cannot be computed with less than $k + 1$ iterations of the while loop in Algorithm 3.4 implementing MEANING(P(d')).   □

Consider the linear recursive definite Datalog program given by

$$BUYS(x_1, x_2) :- LIKES(x_1, x_2).$$
$$BUYS(x_1, x_3) :- TRENDY(x_1), BUYS(x_2, x_3).$$

In this case BUYS in the second rule can be replaced by LIKES resulting in a nonrecursive Datalog program which is equivalent to the original program. Now, consider the linear recursive definite Datalog program (which is just the transitive closure program with its relation symbols renamed) given by

$$BUYS(x_1, x_2) :- LIKES(x_1, x_2).$$
$$BUYS(x_1, x_3) :- LIKES(x_1, x_2), BUYS(x_2, x_3).$$

This Datalog program is inherently recursive, i.e. there does not exist a nonrecursive program which is equivalent to it, due to the fact that the transitive closure cannot be expressed within the relational algebra.

The problem of whether a definite Datalog program is bounded or not is called the *boundedness* problem. The next theorem was proved in [GMSV93] by a reduction from the halting problem for two-counter machines defined in Subsection 1.9.4.

Theorem 9.27   The boundedness problem is undecidable.   □

In [Var88a] it was shown that boundedness is still undecidable with respect to linear recursive definite Datalog programs with a single binary IDB predicate (see also [HKMV91]). Furthermore, in [Abi89] it was shown that boundedness is still undecidable with respect to a definite Datalog program with a single recursive rule.

In [GMSV93] a variation of boundedness of definite Datalog programs, in which IDB predicates are also considered as part of the input, called *uniform boundedness*, is considered. It was shown therein that uniform boundedness is also undecidable (see also [HKMV91]). (Contrast this result with that of Theorem 9.25 which states that the problem of deciding whether two definite Datalog programs are uniformly equivalent is decidable.)

We next define another subclass of linear recursive Datalog programs.

Definition 9.28 (Basis linear recursive Datalog program)   A Datalog program P is *basis linear* recursive if P is a linear recursive definite Datalog program, having only one IDB predicate R, and only two nontrivial rules of the form

$$R(\mathbf{x}) :- Q_1(\mathbf{y}_1), Q_2(\mathbf{y}_2), \ldots, Q_m(\mathbf{y}_m).$$
$$R(\mathbf{x}) :- R(\mathbf{y}), S_1(\mathbf{z}_1), S_2(\mathbf{z}_2), \ldots, S_k(\mathbf{z}_k).$$

where $\mathbf{x}, \mathbf{y}, \mathbf{y}_j$ and $\mathbf{z}_i$, with $j \in \{1, 2, \ldots, m\}$ and $i \in \{1, 2, \ldots, k\}$, are sequences of variables. As with simple recursive Datalog programs, the first rule is called the *basis* rule of the basis linear recursive Datalog program. The second rule is the *recursive* rule.   ■

The following decidable cases are of interest.

Theorem 9.28   The following statements are true:

1) The boundedness problem is decidable for definite Datalog programs whose IDB predicates are all unary [GMSV93].

2) The boundedness problem is decidable for chain Datalog programs [Kan90]. (The result follows, since it is decidable whether a context-free grammar is finite [Har78, HU79].)

3) The boundedness problem for basis linear recursive Datalog programs whose only IDB predicate symbol is binary is NP-complete [Var88a].

4) For basis linear recursive Datalog programs, where in Definition 9.28 $\mathbf{x}$ is a sequence of distinct variables, the basis rule has a single literal in its body and the recursive rule has two literals in its body, the boundedness problem can be decided in polynomial time in the size of the input program [Nau89].   □

Further subclasses of definite Datalog programs for which boundedness is decidable were investigated in [Ioa85, Sag88, Cos89, Sar95].

As a special case of Proposition 9.26 we can deduce that if a definite Datalog program is bounded then it is equivalent to some nonrecursive Datalog program (or alternatively, equivalent to some relational algebra query). In [Cos89] it was conjectured that the converse is also true, i.e. if a definite Datalog is equivalent to some nonrecursive Datalog program then it is bounded, or alternatively by contraposition, if a definite Datalog program is unbounded then it is not equivalent to any nonrecursive Datalog program. This result was settled in [AG94].

Theorem 9.29 A definite Datalog program is bounded if and only if it is equivalent to some nonrecursive Datalog program if and only if it is equivalent to a monotonic relational algebra query (i.e. to a finite composition of unions, selections with only simple selection formulae, projections and joins). □

The next corollary follows from Theorem 9.29 and the fact that the transitive closure of a relation can be expressed by an unbounded definite Datalog program.

Corollary 9.30 The transitive closure of a relation cannot be expressed by any relational algebra query. □

Surprisingly, Theorem 9.29 cannot be strengthened to general Datalog programs and thus the converse of Proposition 9.26 does *not* always hold.

Suppose that the input database includes the predicates SUCC, MIN and <, with their intended meaning, and an additional unary predicate INP containing a single constant v. Let Q(INP, SUCC, MIN, <) be a Datalog program which defines a zero-place predicate OUT to be true, if whenever < is a linear order with a minimal element and SUCC is consistent with <, then for every x, with $x < v$, there exists y such that SUCC(x, y). (SUCC is consistent with <, if < is the transitive closure of SUCC.) We leave it to the reader to verify that Q(INP, SUCC, MIN, <) can be defined via a nonrecursive Datalog program (i.e. a relational algebra expression). An unbounded Datalog program, which computes Q(INP, SUCC, MIN, <) but is not equivalent to any definite Datalog program, was exhibited in [AG94].

Another problem of interest is that of determining the equivalence of a given recursive definite Datalog program to a given nonrecursive Datalog program. Let us call this equivalence problem the *definite nonrecursiveness* equivalence problem. The definite nonrecursiveness equivalence problem is different from the boundedness problem for definite Datalog programs, which by Theorem 9.29 is the problem of the *existence* of some equivalent nonrecursive Datalog program, and by Theorem 9.27 its solution is undecidable. In [CV92] it was shown that the definite nonrecursiveness equivalence problem is decidable with a triply exponential time lower bound. (It is claimed in [CV92] that their result also extends to the decidability of determining whether a given Datalog not-equal program is equivalent to a given nonrecursive Datalog program; see Section 9.4.) We note that this decidability result cannot be extended to semipositive Datalog programs, since by part (3) of Theorem 9.17 the equivalence problem for nonrecursive Datalog programs is undecidable.

Due to the high intractability of the definite recursiveness equivalence problem, some special cases of this problem were investigated in [CV92, CV94a], namely the equivalence of a given recursive definite Datalog program to a given union of conjunctive queries. In [CV92] it was shown that for linear recursive Datalog programs the definite nonrecursiveness equivalence problem is EXPSPACE-complete. It was also shown that for linear recursive definite Datalog programs, whose IDB predicates are all unary, the definite nonrecursiveness equivalence problem is PSPACE-complete, and for recursive definite Datalog programs, with a single recursive rule, whose IDB predicates are also all unary, the definite nonrecursiveness equivalence problem is NP-complete.

Despite the above undecidability and intractability results, in practice it is desirable to optimise a Datalog program as far as possible. That is, given an input program we would like to find an equivalent program which can be computed more efficiently than the original input program. Some of the well-known optimisation techniques are semi-naive evaluation [BR86, Ull89, CGT90, AHV95b] and magic sets [Ram88, Ull89, CGT90, BR91, AHV95b]. The underlying idea of the semi-naive evaluation is to avoid duplication in the generation of new facts when computing the meaning of a program. On the other hand, the underlying idea of the magic sets technique is to transform the input Datalog program into a more efficient program by essentially evaluating selection conditions as soon as possible (see [Ull89, CGT90, AHV95b] for more details on optimisation issues).

The connection between context-free grammars and definite Datalog programs has been instrumental in obtaining some of the above results. Of particular interest are Datalog queries that can be implemented efficiently using parallel algorithms. Several classes of definite Datalog programs, such as programs that have the *polynomial fringe property* are discussed in [UV88, Ull92]. A definite Datalog program P has the polynomial fringe property if there is a polynomial $f(n)$, where n is the size of the input database, such that for any fact $p(a_1, a_2, \ldots, a_k)$ that can be derived from P there is a *proof tree* whose *fringe*, i.e. its set of leaves, is not greater that $f(n)$. A proof tree for $p(a_1, a_2, \ldots, a_k)$ with respect to P is a tree whose root is $p(a_1, a_2, \ldots, a_k)$, whose leaves are facts and such that the children of any internal node $p_i(a_{i_1}, a_{i_2}, \ldots, a_{i_k})$ are the facts in the body of a rule in the Herbrand program of P (see Definition 9.9), whose head is $p_i(a_{i_1}, a_{i_2}, \ldots, a_{i_k})$.

9.4 Datalog Not-Equal

As we have seen in the previous sections a great deal of research effort has gone into studying the properties of definite Datalog. Definite Datalog programs are *monotonic*, in the sense that given a definite Datalog program P, an IDB predicate R of P, and two databases d_1 and d_2 which are compatible with P, we have that if d_1 is a subset of d_2 then $P(d_1, R)$ is also a subset of $P(d_2, R)$. Thus any nonmonotonic query such as computing the complement of the transitive closure of a digraph cannot be expressed by a definite Datalog program. (In general, recursive and also nonrecursive Datalog programs are nonmonotonic.)

Definite Datalog does not constitute the largest class of monotonic Datalog programs. So it is natural to extend the expressiveness of definite Datalog without sacrificing monotonicity. In this section we introduce such an extension.

Definition 9.29 (Datalog not-equal program)   A Datalog *not-equal* program is an extension of a definite Datalog program which allows equality and inequality formulae to appear in the bodies of rules. An equality formula has the form $x = y$ and an inequality formula, which is the negation of an equality formulae, has the form $x \neq y$ (this form is an abbreviation of $\neg(x = y)$). ∎

Intuitively, a homomorphism is a mapping between the active domains of two databases which preserves their structure.

Definition 9.30 (Preservation under extensions and homomorphisms)   Let P be a Datalog program and d_1, d_2 be two databases that are compatible with P; as usual we let ADOM(d) denote the active domain of a database d. (We assume without loss of generality that CONST(IDB(P)) is a subset of ADOM(d), i.e. that ADOM(d) contains all the constants in IDB(P).)

The database d_2 is an *extension* of the database d_1, if ADOM(d_1) is a subset of ADOM(d_2) and d_1 is the *restriction* of d_2 to ADOM(d_1) (i.e. if a fact $R_i(v_1, v_2, \ldots, v_k)$ is in d_2 and $\{v_1, v_2, \ldots, v_k\}$ is a subset of ADOM(d_1) then it is also the case that $R_i(v_1, v_2, \ldots, v_k)$ is in d_1).

An IDB predicate R of P is *preserved under extensions* if whenever d_2 is an extension of d_1, we have that P(d_2, R) is a superset of P(d_1, R). A Datalog program is preserved under extensions if all its IDB predicates are preserved under extensions.

A *homomorphism* is a mapping h from ADOM(d_1) to ADOM(d_2) such that for all EDB predicates R_i of P, $R_i(v_1, v_2, \ldots, v_k) \in d_1$ implies that $R_i(h(v_1), h(v_2), \ldots, h(v_k)) \in d_2$. A homomorphism h is one-to-one whenever h is one-to-one. (For the purpose of a homomorphism we include the built-in equality and inequality predicates together with the EDB predicates when appropriate.)

An IDB predicate R of P is *preserved under homomorphisms* if whenever h is a homomorphism, $R(v_1, v_2, \ldots, v_k) \in P(d_1, R)$ implies that $R(h(v_1), h(v_2), \ldots, h(v_k)) \in P(d_2, R)$. A Datalog program is preserved under homomorphisms if all its IDB predicates are preserved under homomorphisms.   ∎

A homomorphism that is not one-to-one is a mapping that identifies constants in the active domain of the database. We observe that a Datalog program is monotonic if and only if it is preserved under extensions and one-to-one homomorphisms. In other words, a Datalog program is monotonic if and only if the result relation does not decrease when adding constants to the active domain of the database and adding facts to the relations in the input database. We leave the proof of the next proposition to the reader.

Proposition 9.31   The following statements are true:

1) Definite Datalog programs are preserved under extensions and homomorphisms.

2) Datalog not-equal programs are preserved under extensions and one-to-one homomorphisms (but do *not* necessarily preserve homomorphisms which are not one-to-one).

3) Semipositive Datalog programs are preserved under extensions (but do *not* necessarily preserve one-to-one homomorphisms).   □

The following Datalog not-equal program, which we denote by P^{TCN}, computes all paths in a digraph, from a node labelled x_1 to a node labelled x_2, which do *not* go through a node labelled by some constant v.

$$\text{TCN}(x_1, x_2, v) :- \text{ARC}(x_1, x_2), x_1 \neq v, x_2 \neq v.$$
$$\text{TCN}(x_1, x_2, v) :- \text{ARC}(x_1, x_3), \text{TCN}(x_3, x_2, v), x_1 \neq v.$$

It can be verified that the Datalog not-equal program P^{TCN} does not preserve homomorphisms that are not one-to-one, since we cannot identify the constant v with any other distinct constant. For example, let $d = \{\text{ARC}(1, 2), \text{ARC}(2, 3)\}$ be a database that is compatible with P^{TCN} and let v be the constant 1. Then $P^{TCN}(d, \text{TCN}) = \{\text{TCN}(2, 3, 1)\}$. Now, let $d' = \{\text{ARC}(1, 1), \text{ARC}(1, 3)\}$ be another database that is compatible with P^{TCN}. It follows that P^{TCN} does not preserve homomorphisms, since the mapping that takes 1 to 1, 2 to 1 and 3 to 3 is a homomorphism, but $\{(1, 3, 1)\}$ is not in $P^{TCN}(d', \text{TCN})$, which is equal to the empty set. We can now deduce by part (1) of Proposition 9.31 that P^{TCN} cannot be computed by any definite Datalog program.

The following semipositive Datalog program, which we denote by $\widehat{P}$, computes the complement of an EDB predicate R (we assume an additional EDB predicate S so that, in general, $\text{CONST}(\widehat{P}) \neq \emptyset$).

$$\text{COMP}(x) :- \neg \text{R}(x).$$

We verify by a counterexample that $\widehat{P}$ does not preserve one-to-one homomorphisms. Let $d = \{\text{S}(1)\}$ be a database that is compatible with $\widehat{P}$. Then $\widehat{P}(d, \text{COMP}) = \{\text{COMP}(1)\}$. Now, let $d' = \{\text{R}(1), \text{S}(1)\}$ be another database that is also compatible with $\widehat{P}$. It follows that $\widehat{P}$ does not preserve one-to-one homomorphisms, since the one-to-one mapping that takes 1 to 1, is a one-to-one homomorphism, but $\text{COMP}(1)$ is not in $\widehat{P}(d', \text{COMP})$, since $\widehat{P}(d', \text{COMP})$ is equal to the empty set. We can now deduce by part (2) of Proposition 9.31 that $\widehat{P}$ cannot be computed by any Datalog not-equal program.

The next result establishes a hierarchy amongst definite Datalog, Datalog not-equal and semipositive Datalog in terms of proper inclusion.

Theorem 9.32   The following statements are true concerning Datalog semantics:

1) Definite Datalog is properly included in Datalog not-equal.

2) Datalog not-equal is properly included in semipositive Datalog.   (It is sufficient to assume that EQ is an EDB predicate representing equality.)   □

It may be conjectured that all monotonic polynomial-time computable queries can be computed by Datalog not-equal programs, but this is not the case. We now exhibit a monotonic query that cannot be expressed in Datalog not-equal.

Given a digraph G and two distinguished nodes m and n in the node set of G, we call the problem of deciding whether G contains a path of even length from m to n the *directed even path* problem. The directed even path problem is monotonic and was shown to be NP-complete in [LM89].

Obviously, if PTIME $\neq$ NP, then the directed even path problem cannot be expressed by a Datalog not-equal program, since only polynomial-time queries can be expressed in Datalog not-equal. However, the proof that the directed even path problem cannot be expressed by any Datalog not-equal program does not depend on the conjecture that PTIME $\neq$ NP. As a note, in [ACY91] a problem known as *linear constraints*, which is a monotonic polynomial-time query, was shown to be inexpressible in Datalog not-equal.

We now describe a pebble game, played on two databases, which can be used to prove that a Datalog program is not expressible as a Datalog not-equal program [LM89, KV95]. In particular, we can apply this technique to prove that the directed even path problem cannot be expressed by a Datalog not-equal program.

For the purpose of the next definition we say that a database d is k-compatible with a Datalog program P, for some natural number k, if the cardinality of ADOM(d) − CONST(IDB(P)) is at least k. (It is possible in this case for the database schema of d to contain IDB relation symbols.)

Definition 9.31 (Existential k-pebble game)   In the existential k-pebble game there are two players I and II, playing on two databases d_1 and d_2, respectively, that are k-compatible with a Datalog program P.

Each player has k distinct pebbles. In particular, $p_1, p_2, \ldots, p_k$ are the pebbles of player I and $q_1, q_2, \ldots, q_k$ are the pebbles of player II.

The game is played on the active domains of d_1 and d_2. Initially no pebbles are placed on ADOM(d_1) and ADOM(d_2). The game consists of several *rounds* and each round proceeds as follows.

In each round player I picks up some pebble, say p_i. If p_i has already been placed on a constant in ADOM(d_1), then player I removes p_i from ADOM(d_1). Player II responds by removing the corresponding pebble q_i from ADOM(d_2). On the other hand, if p_i has not yet been placed on a constant in ADOM(d_1), then player I places p_i on some constant in ADOM(d_1), say a_i. Player II responds by placing the corresponding pebble q_i on some constant in ADOM(d_2), say b_i. It is assumed that the constants a_i and b_i are free, in the sense that currently no pebbles are placed on them.

After each round let ϕ be the mapping that takes each constant a_i in ADOM(d_1), which has a pebble p_i on it, to the constant b_i in ADOM(d_2), which has the corresponding pebble q_i on it. In addition, we require that ϕ maps the constants in CONST(IDB(P)) to themselves (this extra condition allows us to use constants in Datalog programs).

Player I *wins* the round if ϕ is *not* a one-to-one homomorphism between the restriction of d_1 to the domain of ϕ (i.e. to the constants a_i and CONST(IDB(P))) and the restriction of d_2 to the range of ϕ (i.e. to the constants b_i and CONST(IDB(P))). On the other hand, player II wins if the game goes on indefinitely, i.e. player I can never win a round in the game. (In this case player II is said to have a *winning strategy*.) ∎

As noted in [KV95] if we relax the winning condition of player I in an existential k-pebble game so that ϕ is *not* a homomorphism, then we can utilise Lemma 9.33 below in order to show that a Datalog program is not expressible as a definite Datalog program. (In this modified existential k-pebble game player II may sensibly choose, during any round, to place more than one pebble on the same constant.)

For the purpose of the next lemma we say that a database d is k-compatible with a Datalog program P and an IDB predicate R of P, if by removing from d all the facts in d over R we obtain a database that is k-compatible with P, i.e. d is k-compatible with P and R if d is the union of a database that is k-compatible with P together with some facts over the IDB predicate R. Moreover, we say that a database d, which is k-compatible with P and R, *satisfies* P if $r =$ P($d − \{r\}$, R), where r is the set of all facts in d over R, i.e. d satisfies P if, in addition to the EDB facts in d, d contains exactly all the facts over R which are generated by MEANING(P($d − \{r\}$)).

The next result, whose proof can be found in [KV95], states that we can utilise the existential k-pebble game to show that a Datalog program P is not expressible as a Datalog not-equal program.

Lemma 9.33 Let P be a Datalog program having an IDB predicate R. If for every natural number k there are two databases d_1^k and d_2^k, which are k-compatible with P and R, such that d_1^k satisfies P but d_2^k does not satisfy P, and player II can win the existential k-pebble game on d_1^k and d_2^k, then the Datalog program P is not expressible as a Datalog not-equal program.
$\square$

We now apply Lemma 9.33 to the directed even path problem.

Theorem 9.34 The directed even path problem cannot be expressed by any Datalog not-equal program.

Proof. A usual we model a digraph G by a binary predicate ARC, such that $ARC(v_1, v_2)$ means that there is an arc from v_1 to v_2 in the arc set of G. Assume the existence of a Datalog program P which defines a zero-place IDB predicate OUT to be true, if there is a path of even length between two distinguished nodes, say m and n, in the digraph G, which is modelled by ARC. (Thus for the purpose of this proof we assume that PTIME = NP holds contrary to common belief.)

Let d_1^k be a database that is k-compatible with P and OUT such that d_1^k satisfies P, i.e. OUT() is in d_1^k, and the digraph modelled by d_1^k, say G_1^k, has a directed path of even length between nodes m and n, with $m \neq n$. Moreover, let d_2^k be a database that is k-compatible with P and OUT such that d_2^k does not satisfy P, i.e. OUT() is not in d_2^k, and the digraph modelled by d_2^k, say G_2^k, does not have a directed path of even length between m and n.

If $k = 1$ then we can easily construct G_1^1 and G_2^1 as follows. The digraph G_1^1 comprises just a single directed path of length two from m to n, while the digraph G_2^1 comprises just a single directed path of length three from m to n. If player I puts his pebble on m or n, then player II responds by putting his pebble on m or n, respectively. Otherwise, if player I put his pebble on the other node in G_1^1, then player II responds by putting his pebble on one of the two other nodes in G_2^1.

If $k = 2$ then we can construct G_1^2 and G_2^2 as follows. The digraph G_1^2 consists of a single directed path of length eight from m to n. On the other hand, the digraph G_2^2 consists of a single directed path of length five from m to n, together with a cycle of length three starting and ending at the fourth node from m.

The idea behind the construction of G_2^2 is that it has a walk of length eight between m and n, which is not a path. Thus player II can win each round by traversing this walk in the same manner that player I traverses the single directed path of G_1^2. Since each player has only two pebbles player I cannot detect the cycle of length three and thus loses the game.

We leave it to the reader to complete the proof by using a similar construction for each $k > 2$. The result follows on applying Lemma 9.33.
$\square$

More results concerning Datalog not-equal programs can be found in [LM89, ACY91, Afr94, KV95]. As a historical note, pebble games such as that of Definition 9.31 originate from [Ehr61] and are also known as *back-and-forth* games or Ehrenfeucht-Fraïssè games. In the context of database theory such games are normally used to show that a particular computable query is not expressible within a given query language. The original version of the k-pebble game consists of k moves by each player; two moves one by each player constitute a *round*. In each round player I can choose to place a pebble on a constant in either $ADOM(d_1)$ or $ADOM(d_2)$, and player II must place a pebble on a constant in the opposite active domain (i.e. if player I places a pebble on a constant in $ADOM(d_1)$ then player II must respond by placing a pebble on a constant in $ADOM(d_2)$ and vice versa). In the original version of the game the players cannot remove pebbles once they are placed on a constant and a game consists of exactly k rounds. Player II wins the game if the induced mapping between the pebbled constants is an isomorphism between the restrictions of d_1 and d_2, respectively, to the pebbled constants, otherwise player I wins. Player II is said to have a *winning strategy* if this player can always win the game no matter how player I moves. Player I is known as the *spoiler* and player II is known as the *duplicator*.

Let Q be a computable query. A similar result to Lemma 9.33 can be shown for the original pebble game referred to above with respect to the relational algebra. Specifically, if for every natural number k there are two databases d_1^k and d_2^k such that d_1^k satisfies Q but d_2^k does not, and player II has a winning strategy for the game on d_1^k and d_2^k, then Q cannot be expressed within the relational algebra (or equivalently, by any nonrecursive Datalog program). This technique can be used to show that certain queries, such as computing the transitive closure of a graph or testing whether a graph is connected, are not expressible within the relational algebra. The reader should consult Subsection 1.9.5 of Chapter 1 for more details on the use of Ehrenfeucht-Fraïssè games for proving inexpressibility results.

9.5 Updates in Deductive Databases

In Subsection 3.2.4 of Chapter 3 we have defined an update language for relational databases based on the notion of a transaction, which is a composition of one or more update operations. Here we consider only the primitive operations of insertion and deletion of facts, ignoring the modification operation which can be defined as a deletion followed by an insertion. In the context of a Datalog program P, we denote the insertion of a fact f into P by *insert*(f, P), and correspondingly we denote the deletion of a fact f from P by *delete*(f, P).

The update problem is to determine the outcome of $op(f, P)$, where op is either *insert* or *delete*, in terms of the update that has to be effected on the extensional database of P, EDB(P). Logically we view P as a *first-order theory* over the first-order language $\mathcal{L}(P)$ associated with P, and the semantics of P are viewed in terms of the Herbrand model of P generated by the evaluation of the fixpoint of P (i.e. the semantics of P consist of its set of facts together with the set of all IDB facts which can be generated from P when computing MEANING(P)). By viewing a Datalog program in this way we consider both extensional and intensional predicates to be first-class citizens of the database. If we insert or delete a fact over an EDB predicate then the semantics of updating EDB(P) are the same as those considered in Subsection 3.2.4 of Chapter 3, since EDB(P) is essentially a relational database. On the other hand, when we insert or delete a fact over an IDB predicate, then we need to consider two situations.

We say that an IDB predicate R of P is *nonrecursive*, respectively *recursive*, if the restriction of the dependency graph G of P to the predicates R' of P, such that there is a directed path from R' to R in G, is acyclic, respectively cyclic. If we insert or delete a fact over a nonrecursive IDB predicate R of P, then the semantics of updating EDB(P) are the same as those considered in Section 3.8 of Chapter 3, since a nonrecursive Datalog program is equivalent to a relational algebra expression. In this case we are faced with the familiar view update problem for relational databases. On the other hand, the problem of inserting or deleting a fact over a recursive IDB predicate R of P is a new problem. We term the problem of inserting or deleting a fact over an IDB predicate (which may be recursive or nonrecursive) the *view update problem for deductive databases*.

We illustrate the problems that we face in solving the view update problem for deductive databases with two examples. Let EMP be a binary predicate modelling a company's permanent employees and the departments they work in, MGR be a binary predicate modelling the company's departments and their managers and TMP be a binary predicate modelling temporary employees and their direct managers. The definite Datalog program, EMG, which outputs a binary predicate modelling employees and their managers is given by

$$EMG(x_1, x_3) :- EMP(x_1, x_2), MGR(x_2, x_3).$$
$$EMG(x_1, x_2) :- TMP(x_1, x_2).$$

The IDB predicate EMG is nonrecursive and thus defines a view which can be constructed by a relational algebra expression (the union of TMP together with a projection of the join of EMP and MGR).

Assume that the fact MGR(Computing, Steve) is in EDB(P). We can effect an insertion of the IDB fact EMG(Saul, Steve) either by adding the fact EMP(Saul, Computing) to EDB(P) or by adding the single fact TMP(Saul, Steve) to EDB(P). Thus in the absence of any additional information this insertion is ambiguous.

Furthermore, assume that EMP(Saul, Computing) and MGR(Computing, Steve) are in EDB(P). We can effect the deletion of the IDB fact EMG(Saul, Steve) either by deleting the fact EMP(Saul, Computing) from EDB(P) or by deleting the fact MGR(Computing, Steve) from EDB(P). Thus in the absence of any additional information this deletion is ambiguous.

As another example, we again consider the recursive definite Datalog program, TC, which computes the transitive closure of FAMILY:

$$TC(x_1, x_2) :- FAMILY(x_1, x_2).$$
$$TC(x_1, x_3) :- FAMILY(x_1, x_2), TC(x_2, x_3).$$

Assume that FAMILY(Julia, Sara) is an EDB fact. Then inserting the IDB fact TC(Julia, Tamara) can be effected either by inserting FAMILY(Julia, Tamara) into EDB(P) or by inserting FAMILY(Sara, Tamara) into EDB(P). Furthermore, assume that FAMILY(Dan, Iris) and FAMILY(Iris, David) are two EDB facts. Then deleting the IDB fact TC(Dan, David) can be effected either by deleting FAMILY(Dan, Iris) from EDB(P) or by deleting FAMILY(Iris, David) from EDB(P). In both cases, namely the insertion of TC(Julia, Tamara) or the deletion of TC(Dan, David), in the absence of any additional information the update is ambiguous.

Following [AT91, AT92] we provide a declarative semantic framework for such updates on IDB predicates based on the notion of *minimal change*. An equivalent operational semantics for such updates can also be found in [AT91, AT92] (see also [Tom88, Dec90]).

Definition 9.32 (Potential results for insertions and deletions)   Let P be a Datalog program and f be a fact over an IDB predicate R of P. A *potential result* for the insertion $insert(f, P)$ is a Datalog program Q such that

1) f is in MEANING(Q), and

2) MEANING(P) is a subset of MEANING(Q).

A *minimal potential result* Q for the insertion $insert(f, P)$ is a potential result for this insertion such that there is no other potential result Q' for this insertion such that MEANING(Q') is a proper subset of MEANING(Q).

A *potential result* for the deletion $delete(f, P)$ is a Datalog program Q such that

1) f is *not* in MEANING(Q), and

2) MEANING(P) is a superset of MEANING(Q).

A *maximal potential result* Q for the deletion $delete(f, P)$ is a potential result for this deletion such that there is no other potential result Q' for this deletion such that MEANING(Q') is a proper superset of MEANING(Q).   ■

Definition 9.33 (Satisfiable facts)   Let P be a Datalog program and f be a fact over an IDB predicate R of P. The fact f is *satisfiable* by P if there exists a database d, which is compatible with P, such that f is in P(d, R).

The *fact satisfiability problem* is the problem of deciding whether a given fact is satisfiable by a given Datalog program.   ■

Not all facts are satisfiable by a Datalog program as the next example shows. Consider an EDB predicate NEW_EMP, which records the names of new employees in a company database. The IDB predicate DEFAULT_DEPT defined below assigns such new employees by default to the Computing department.

DEFAULT_DEPT(x, Computing) : $-$ NEW_EMP(x).

The reader can verify that for any constant y the fact DEFAULT_DEPT(y, Mathematics) is unsatisfiable by the above Datalog program.

Although by Theorems 9.20 and 9.24 the equivalence problem for semipositive Datalog is undecidable, the following result was shown in [LMS93].

Theorem 9.35   The fact satisfiability problem for semipositive Datalog is decidable.   □

The decidability of the fact satisfiability problem for definite Datalog programs was shown in [Shm93]. In [LMS93] it was shown that, in general, the fact satisfiability problem for Datalog programs is undecidable.

The next proposition shows that the concepts of potential result for insertion and fact satisfiability are equivalent.

Proposition 9.36   There exists a potential result for the insertion $insert(f, P)$ if and only if f is satisfiable by P, where P is a Datalog not-equal program.   □

Although the only if part of Proposition 9.36 is true for general Datalog programs, the if part is false for semipositive Datalog programs when they are nonmonotonic.

Recall the following semipositive Datalog program, denoted by $\widehat{P}$, which computes the complement of an EDB predicate R.

CONSTANT(1).
R(1).
$COMP(x) :- \neg R(x)$.

Due to the nonmonotonicity of $\widehat{P}$ there is *no* potential result for $insert(COMP(1), \widehat{P})$, since as long as R(1) is in $EDB(\widehat{P})$ we cannot insert COMP(1) into $\widehat{P}$. On the other hand, COMP(1) is obviously fact satisfiable by $\widehat{P}$, since COMP(1) is in $\widehat{P}(\{CONSTANT(1)\}, COMP)$.

As the reader can verify from the previous examples, namely those defining the IDB predicates EMG and TC, in general there may be several minimal potential results for an insertion and correspondingly there may be several maximal potential results for a deletion. We define an update to be deterministic if it is not ambiguous in the following sense.

Definition 9.34 (Deterministic updates)   An insertion $insert(f, P)$ is *deterministic* if it has a unique minimal potential result. Correspondingly, a deletion $delete(f, P)$ is *deterministic* if it has a unique maximal potential result.   ∎

Consider any IDB predicate R of a Datalog not-equal program P, which is defined by one nontrivial rule such that all the predicates of the literals in its body are EDB predicates. Then the insertion $insert(R(v_1, v_2, \ldots, v_k), P)$ is deterministic. On the other hand, the insertion $insert(TC(Julia, Tamara), TC)$ is nondeterministic. In fact, the reader can verify that every insertion of a fact into TC is nondeterministic; similarly, every insertion of a fact into EMG is also nondeterministic. These two statements obtain provided the inserted fact is not already in TC and in EMG, respectively.

The deletion $delete(TC(Dan, Iris), TC)$ is deterministic, since the only way it can be effected with a maximal potential result is by deleting the fact FAMILY(Dan, Iris) from the EDB. On the other hand, the deletion $delete(TC(Dan, David), TC)$ is nondeterministic.

We leave it to the reader to verify that if a definite Datalog program allows deterministic updates then it must be bounded. In other words, if a definite Datalog program is not bounded then it does not, in general, allow deterministic updates. On the other, as was shown for the definite Datalog program EMG, the fact that a definite Datalog program is bounded does not imply that it allows deterministic updates. In order to test whether an insertion of a fact into a Datalog program P is deterministic, we need to check whether the intersection over i of $MEANING(P_i)$ of all its potential results P_i for this insertion is a model of some potential result for the insertion. Correspondingly, in order to test whether a deletion of a fact from a Datalog program P is deterministic we need to check whether the union over i of MEANING(P_i) of all its potential results P_i for this deletion is a model of some potential result for the deletion.

The problem of dealing with nondeterministic updates can be solved in several ways. One approach is to provide procedures for disambiguating the update according to some criteria which assign priority to one of the potential results of an update in preference to another. For example, we may prefer to minimise the number of update operations; note that such a criterion on its own does not always disambiguate an update. Another approach is to disambiguate an update with the aid of an appropriate user dialogue. A different approach is to generalise the notion of a fact by allowing disjunctions and negations of facts, and then to add the disjunction of all the potential updates to P as the unique update [RN89]. Using this general semantics deletion of a fact f is interpreted as making $\neg f$ true in MEANING(P). Thus deleting FAMILY(Dan, Iris) or deleting FAMILY(Iris, David) from EDB(P) is represented logically by adding $\neg$FAMILY(Dan, Iris) $\vee$ $\neg$FAMILY(Iris, David) to P. Similarly, inserting FAMILY(Julia, Tamara) or FAMILY(Sara, Tamara) into EDB(P) is represented logically by adding FAMILY(Julia, Tamara) $\vee$ FAMILY(Sara, Tamara) to P.

An overview of different approaches to the problem of updating deductive databases can be found in [Win88a, Win95]. In [FUV83, FKUV86, Var86] a more general framework for updates is considered based on revising the underlying first-order theory of a deductive database. An approach which uses *dynamic logic* [Tha89b] to formalise the update semantics of deductive databases is given in [MW88b, Man89, NT89]. An interesting operational semantics of updates in deductive databases in terms of *abduction* was considered in [KM90]. The underlying idea is that in order to insert a fact f we need to explain f in terms of possible hypotheses on the abductable (i.e. assumable) EDB predicates. Correspondingly, in order to delete f we need to explain the negation, $\neg f$, of f. A recent approach is that of Reiter [Rei92a], who considers the *situation calculus* [MH69] as a basis for database updates. In this context the infamous *frame problem* arises, which is the problem of leaving unchanged the state of the database that is unaffected by a given update. For example, if we update an employee's salary this should not affect the employee's address or the employee's department. Another recent approach to the update problem based on the philosophy of minimal change is that of Katsuno and Mendelzon [KM91a] (see also [KM91b]) in the context of the broader subject of *belief revision* [Gär88a]. Finally, an update semantics tailored specifically for incomplete deductive databases (see Chapter 5) based on the *possible-world* approach is investigated in [AG85, Heg87, Win88b].

9.6 Integrity Constraints in Deductive Databases

In Sections 3.4, 3.5, 3.6 and 3.7 of Chapter 3 we have dealt with integrity constraints in relational databases. In terms of deductive databases a Datalog program consists of an EDB and an IDB and thus it is natural to consider integrity constraints which are defined on both the EDB and the IDB. We take integrity constraints to be first-order sentences (or equivalently, closed first-order formulae), i.e. first-order formulae having *no* free variables.

We do not deal with the problem of inferring whether an integrity constraint holds in an IDB predicate given a set of constraints defined over EDB predicates. Even if we restrict ourselves to nonrecursive Datalog programs (i.e. to the relational algebra) and to FDs as integrity constraints, the problem of deciding whether an FD holds in an IDB predicate is undecidable; if we drop the difference operator from the relational algebra then the problem becomes decidable but it is still intractable (see [Klu80, KP82, IITK84]). Consider next a definite Datalog program P and a set of FDs defined over the EDB predicates of P. The problem of determining whether an FD holds over an IDB predicate of P was proved in [AH88a] to be, in general, undecidable; the proof was obtained by a reduction from the Post correspondence problem defined in Subsection 1.9.4. (In [LMS93] it was shown that satisfiability is undecidable for a Datalog not-equal program P given a set of FDs defined over the EDB predicates of P; recall that satisfiability is the problem of determining whether for some IDB predicate R of P the result of applying P to a database compatible with P, namely P(d, R), is nonempty; see Definition 9.21.)

Hereafter we will mainly restrict ourselves to integrity constraints defined only over EDB predicates, i.e. we consider a relational database d over **R**; d can be viewed as a Datalog program consisting only of EDB facts. Essentially we will study a general type of data dependency, formalised as a first-order sentence; this was briefly mentioned at the end of Section 3.6 of Chapter 3. Recall from Subsection 3.2.3 of Chapter 3 that an *atomic formula* is either a *predicate formula* of the form $R(y_1, y_2, \ldots, y_k)$ or an *equality formula* of the form $y_1 = y_2$. Herein we assume that all the y_i's are variables ranging over the underlying database domain.

Definition 9.35 (Data dependency)   A *data dependency* is a first-order sentence of the form

$$(\forall x_1, x_2, \ldots, x_m)((A_1 \wedge A_2 \wedge \ldots \wedge A_n) \Rightarrow B),$$

where for all $j \in \{1, 2, \ldots, n\}$, A_j is a predicate formula and B is an atomic formula (recall that $\Rightarrow$ stands for logical implication and $\wedge$ stands for logical and, i.e. conjunction).

We assume that for all $i \in \{1, 2, \ldots, m\}$, x_i appears in at least one of the A_j's and that there is at least one A_j, i.e. $n \geq 1$. If B is a predicate formula then the data dependency is called a *Tuple Generating Dependency* (abbreviated to TGD). Correspondingly, if B is an equality formula then the data dependency is called an *Equality Generating Dependency* (abbreviated to EGD).

We say that a data dependency is over a database schema **R**, if for all relation symbols R mentioned in the predicate formulae of the data dependency there is a corresponding relation schema R in **R**. For the rest of this section *we assume that all data dependencies are over a database schema* **R**. ∎

We observe that a TGD can be viewed as a definite Datalog rule. The difference between the two is that a Datalog rule is used to generate an IDB predicate, while a TGD is used to test whether certain tuples have been generated (an EGD is used to test whether some equality is satisfied).

For example, let **R** = {EMP, DEPT} be a database schema modelling employees and the departments they work in. Furthermore, let schema(EMP) = {ENAME, DNAME}, where att(1) = ENAME models an employee's name and att(2) = DNAME models the department's name, and let schema(DEPT) = {DNAME, MNAME}, where att(1) = DNAME models a department's name and att(2) = MNAME models the manager's name of the department. Suppose that the constraints specified over **R** are the FDs: EMP : ENAME → DNAME, DEPT : DNAME → MNAME and DEPT : MNAME → DNAME, and the JD ⋈[EMP, DEPT].

The FD EMP : ENAME $\rightarrow$ DNAME is represented by the EGD

$$(\forall x_1, x_2, x_3)((\text{EMP}(x_1, x_2) \wedge \text{EMP}(x_1, x_3)) \Rightarrow x_2 = x_3).$$

The FD DEPT : DNAME $\rightarrow$ MNAME is represented by the EGD

$$(\forall x_1, x_2, x_3)((\text{DEPT}(x_1, x_2) \wedge \text{DEPT}(x_1, x_3)) \Rightarrow x_2 = x_3).$$

The FD DEPT : MNAME $\rightarrow$ DNAME is represented by the EGD

$$(\forall x_1, x_2, x_3)((\text{DEPT}(x_2, x_1) \wedge \text{DEPT}(x_3, x_1)) \Rightarrow x_2 = x_3).$$

Let ED be an IDB predicate defined by the rule

$$\text{ED}(x_1, x_2, x_3) :- \text{EMP}(x_1, x_2), \text{DEPT}(x_2, x_3).$$

Then the JD $\bowtie$[EMP, DEPT] is represented by the TGD

$$(\forall x_1, x_2, x_3, x_4, x_5)((\text{ED}(x_1, x_2, x_3) \wedge \text{ED}(x_4, x_2, x_5)) \Rightarrow \text{ED}(x_1, x_2, x_5)).$$

Another interesting TGD that can be represented is that of a binary relation being transitively closed. For example, constraining FAMILY to be transitively closed can be represented by the TGD

$$(\forall x_1, x_2, x_3)((\text{FAMILY}(x_1, x_2) \wedge \text{FAMILY}(x_2, x_3)) \Rightarrow \text{FAMILY}(x_1, x_3)).$$

We call such a TGD a *Closure Dependency* (CD); see [GSS89] for an axiom system for FDs and CDs and a discussion on the implication problem for FDs and CDs.

A more general definition of a data dependency is given in [Fag82b, BV84a, BV84c, FV84a, Var88b], which allows existential quantifiers over variables that appear in the atomic formula, B, appearing on the right-hand side of the implication. It is customary to call data dependencies as given in Definition 9.35 having no existential quantifiers *full*. On the other hand, when allowing at least one existential quantifier we call such data dependencies *embedded*.

The definitions of satisfaction and logical implication are essentially identical to those in Section 3.5 of Chapter 3.

Definition 9.36 (Data dependency satisfaction)   Consider a relational database d over **R**; in the context of deductive databases d can be viewed as a Datalog program consisting only of facts. We say that d *satisfies* a data dependency α, written $d \models \alpha$, if d is a Herbrand model of α with respect to the first-order language containing the relation symbols in **R** and the constants in the active domain of d.

As usual, when Σ is a set of data dependencies, we say that d *satisfies* Σ, written $d \models \Sigma$, if $\forall \alpha \in \Sigma, d \models \alpha$. A set of data dependencies Σ over **R** is said to be *satisfiable* if there exists a database d over **R** such that $d \models \Sigma$.   ■

For the sake of completeness we repeat the definition of logical implication for data dependencies.

Definition 9.37 (Logical implication)   We say that a set of data dependencies Σ over R *logically implies* a single data dependency α over R, written $\Sigma \models \alpha$, whenever for all databases d over R the following condition is true:

$$\text{if } d \models \Sigma \text{ holds then } d \models \alpha \text{ also holds.} \qquad \blacksquare$$

Assume that a set Σ of data dependencies is specified by the database designer. This gives rise to a particular class of databases, i.e. the set of all databases that satisfy Σ, which we denote by $SAT(\Sigma)$. On the other hand, suppose that we are given a class of databases, say Γ, satisfying certain *preservation properties* such as the property of closure under intersection or containment. Then it is of interest to know whether there exists a set of data dependencies Σ such that $\Gamma = SAT(\Sigma)$. If such a set Σ exists then we say that Γ is axiomatisable by Σ. Following [MV86] we characterise axiomatisability of a class of databases by the preservation properties it satisfies. (We assume that all classes of databases are closed under isomorphisms; an isomorphism from a database d_1 over R to a database d_2 over R is a homomorphism h from $\text{ADOM}(d_1)$ to $\text{ADOM}(d_2)$ that is one-to-one and onto, implying that its inverse is a homomorphism from $\text{ADOM}(d_2)$ to $\text{ADOM}(d_1)$.)

Definition 9.38 (Axiomatisable classes of databases)   A class Γ of databases is said to be *axiomatisable* by data dependencies (respectively, by TGDs or by EGDs) if there exists a set Σ of data dependencies (respectively, TGDs or EGDs) such that $\Gamma = SAT(\Sigma)$. $\blacksquare$

An important application of axiomatisability relates to user views, which are defined by IDB predicates. Specifically, we would like to know whether the set Σ is still satisfied in the user view, i.e. whether or not the user view is in $SAT(\Sigma)$. By knowing the preservation properties of $SAT(\Sigma)$ we may be able to give a quick answer to such a question.

Definition 9.39 (Empty and trivial databases)   A database is *empty* if all its relations are empty and is *trivial* if all its active domains are singletons and all its relations contain only a single tuple. $\blacksquare$

The reader can verify the next lemma.

Lemma 9.37   Empty and trivial databases satisfy any set of data dependencies. $\square$

Intuitively, a data dependency is domain independent if in order to test its satisfaction by a database, d, only the constants in the active domain of d need to be considered.

Definition 9.40 (Domain independent data dependencies)   Recall that a database d over R has an underlying countably infinite domain, which we denote by $DOM_j(R)$ where j is a natural number; in general, $DOM_j(A) \neq DOM_k(A)$, for $j \neq k$. When we want to emphasise the fact that $DOM_j(R)$ is the underlying domain of d we will refer to d as the pair $(d, DOM_j(R))$.

A data dependency α is *domain independent* whenever $(d, DOM_j(R)) \models \alpha$ if and only if $(d, DOM_k(R)) \models \alpha$. $\blacksquare$

The reader can verify the next lemma, which follows from the fact that if we view data dependencies as rules, then given a database d such values will not generate any new constants which are not in ADOM(d). (See Subsection 3.3.1 of Chapter 3 for the related concept of domain independent queries.)

Lemma 9.38 Data dependencies are domain independent. □

Prior to the next definition the reader is advised to recall Definition 9.30 of an extension of a database.

Definition 9.41 (Preservation under extensions, containment and intersections) A data dependency α is *preserved under extensions* if whenever a database d_1 over **R** is an extension of a database d_2 over **R** and $d_1 \models \alpha$, then it is also the case that $d_2 \models \alpha$.

A database d_1 over **R** *contains* a database d_2 over **R**, if for all R $\in$ **R**, $r_2 \subseteq r_1$, where r_2 and r_1 are the relations over R in d_2 and d_1, respectively.

A data dependency α is *preserved under containment* if whenever a database d_1 over **R** contains a database d_2 over **R** and $d_1 \models \alpha$, then it is also the case that $d_2 \models \alpha$.

The *intersection* of two databases d_1 and d_2 over **R**, denoted by $d_1 \cap d_2$, is the database over **R**, such that for all R $\in$ **R**, $r_1 \cap r_2$ is the relation in $d_1 \cap d_2$ over R, where r_1 and r_2 are the relations over R in d_1 and d_2, respectively.

A data dependency α is *preserved under intersections* if whenever d_1 and d_2 are databases over **R** such that $d_1 \models \alpha$ and $d_2 \models \alpha$, then it is also the case that $d_1 \cap d_2 \models \alpha$. ■

The reader can verify the next lemma by inspecting Definition 9.35 and noting that by Lemma 9.3 the intersection of two Herbrand models for a definite Datalog program P is also a Herbrand model of P.

Lemma 9.39 Data dependencies are preserved under extensions and intersections, and EGDs are preserved under containment. □

Intuitively, a set of data dependencies Σ allows unique minimal insertions if whenever d is a database that satisfies Σ and a set of facts is inserted into d, then there is a unique database d' containing the database resulting from the insertions such that d' satisfies Σ.

Definition 9.42 (Unique minimal insertions) Recall from Section 9.5 that *insert*(f, d) denotes the insertion of a fact (or equivalently, a tuple) into a relation in the database d. Let *insert*($\mathcal{F}, d$), where $\mathcal{F}$ is a finite set of facts, denote the database resulting from a sequence of insertions of the form *insert*(f, d) for all $f \in \mathcal{F}$. (Note that the database *insert*($\mathcal{F}, d$) does not depend on the order in which the facts f are inserted into d.)

A set of data dependencies Σ allows *unique minimal insertions* if for every database d such that $d \models \Sigma$, and for all finite sets of facts $\mathcal{F}$, there exists a unique minimal database d' containing *insert*($\mathcal{F}, d$) such that d' is an extension of d and $d' \models \Sigma$. ■

The reader can verify that the next lemma is a direct consequence of Lemma 9.3, since TGDs can be viewed as definite Datalog rules.

Lemma 9.40 Data dependencies allow unique minimal insertions. □

Intuitively, a data dependency α is preserved under duplicating extensions if whenever a database d satisfies α and d is augmented with an extra copy of itself, where a constant in d is renamed to a new constant in the copy, then the resulting database also satisfies α.

Definition 9.43 (Duplicating extensions) Let d be a database over $\mathbf{R}$, $v_1 \in \text{ADOM}(d)$ be a constant and $v_2 \notin \text{ADOM}(d)$ be another constant. Also, let h be a one-to-one and onto homomorphism, i.e. an isomorphism, from $\text{ADOM}(d)$ to $(\text{ADOM}(d) - \{v_1\}) \cup \{v_2\}$ such that it is the identity on $\text{ADOM}(d) - \{v_1\}$ and $h(v_1) = v_2$.

The database d' over $\mathbf{R}$ is a *duplicating extension* of d if $\text{ADOM}(d') = \text{ADOM}(d) \cup \{v_2\}$ and for all $r \in d$ over R, the relation $r' \in d'$ over R is given by $r' = r \cup h(r)$.

A data dependency α is *preserved under duplicating extensions* if whenever d_1 and d_2 are databases over $\mathbf{R}$ such that $d_1 \models \alpha$ and d_2 is a duplicating extension of d_1, then it is also the case that $d_2 \models \alpha$. ∎

The reader can verify the next lemma.

Lemma 9.41 TGDs preserve duplicating extensions. □

We now define the closure properties of a class of databases Γ corresponding to the preservation properties introduced in Definition 9.41.

Definition 9.44 (Closure properties) Let Γ be a class of databases. Γ is said to be *domain independent* whenever $(d, DOM_j(\mathbf{R})) \in \Gamma$ if and only if $(d, DOM_k(\mathbf{R})) \in \Gamma$. Γ is said to be *closed under extensions* if whenever $d_1 \in \Gamma$ and d_1 is an extension of d_2 then $d_2 \in \Gamma$. Γ is said to be *closed under containment* if whenever $d_1 \in \Gamma$ and d_1 contains d_2 then $d_2 \in \Gamma$. Γ is said to be *closed under intersections* if whenever $d_1, d_2 \in \Gamma$ then $d_1 \cap d_2 \in \Gamma$. Γ is said to be *closed under insertion updates* if whenever $d_1 \in \Gamma$ and $\mathcal{F}$ is a finite set of facts then there exists a unique minimal database d_2 containing $insert(\mathcal{F}, d_1)$ such that d_2 is an extension of d_1 and $d_2 \in \Gamma$, provided there is an extension of d_1 in Γ containing $insert(\mathcal{F}, d_1)$. Γ is said to be *closed under duplicating extensions* if whenever $d_1 \in \Gamma$ and d_2 is a duplicating extension of d_1 then $d_2 \in \Gamma$. ∎

The only if part of the next theorem follows from the preservation properties of data dependencies; the proof of the if part can be found in [MV86].

Theorem 9.42 The following statements are true:

1) A class Γ of databases is axiomatisable by data dependencies if and only if it contains a trivial database, is domain independent and closed under extensions and insertion updates.

2) A class Γ of databases is axiomatisable by TGDs if and only if it contains a trivial database, is domain independent and closed under intersections and duplicating extensions.

3) A class Γ of databases is axiomatisable by EGDs if and only if it contains a trivial database, is domain independent and closed under containment and insertion updates. □

Definition 9.45 (Projection and join of database classes)   We say that a class of databases Γ is over a relation schema R, if it contains only databases having single relations over R; without any loss of generality we will consider a database $d = \{r\}$ simply as the relation r.

If Γ is a class of databases over R, then the *projection* of Γ onto a set of attributes $X \subseteq$ schema(R) is the set of relations $\{\pi_X(r) \mid r \in \Gamma\}$.

If Γ_1 is a class of databases over R_1 and Γ_2 is a class of databases over R_2, then the *join* of Γ_1 and Γ_2 is the set of relations $\{r_1 \bowtie r_2 \mid r_1 \in \Gamma_1 \text{ and } r_2 \in \Gamma_2\}$.   ∎

The next corollary is a direct consequence of part (1) of Theorem 9.42.

Corollary 9.43   The following statements are true:

1) If a class Γ of databases over a relation schema R is axiomatisable by data dependencies, then any projection of Γ is also axiomatisable by data dependencies.

2) If two classes of databases Γ_1, Γ_2 over a relation schema R_1 are axiomatisable by data dependencies, then their join is also axiomatisable by data dependencies.   □

Although a class of databases may be axiomatisable by a set of data dependencies, say Σ, Theorem 9.42 does not guarantee that Σ is a finite set. A further investigation of axiomatisability of a class of databases by a finite set of data dependencies, called *finite axiomatisability*, can be found in [Hul84, MV86] (see also [Mak87]). In particular, it was shown in [Hul84] that both statements of Corollary 9.43 are false when we replace axiomatisability by finite axiomatisability. Intuitively, to formalise finite axiomatisability we need to add the condition that the class of databases Γ is n-local for some natural number n, which implies that the number of variables in any data dependency in Σ is bounded above by n. A class of databases Γ is said to be n-local, if for a given database d_2, whenever Γ contains all the databases d_1 such that d_2 is an extension of d_1 and the cardinality of ADOM(d_1) is at most n, then Γ also contains d_2.

It is possible to generalise further the notion of data dependency given in Definition 9.35 by allowing a data dependency to be any first-order sentence whose basic building blocks are atomic formulae and such that no constants appear in the sentence. Let us call such a generalised data dependency, which is restricted to be domain independent (according to Definition 9.40), an *integrity constraint*. The problem of whether there exists a database which satisfies a set Σ of integrity constraints is called the *satisfiability problem*. In general, the satisfiability problem is undecidable [Man90]; see [BDM88] for an algorithm which tests satisfiability by trying to generate a database satisfying Σ (due to the undecidability of the satisfiability problem this algorithm may not terminate). Due to the said undecidability result it is debatable whether such a generalisation of data dependencies is useful in practice.

The problem of checking whether a particular database satisfies Σ when an update is performed is considered in [Nic82, LST87]. An extension of the approach to the update problem, in the context of a definite Datalog program, to include the specification of a set of FDs, defined over the IDB predicates, is considered in [Tor94]. As was mentioned at the beginning of Section 9.6 the problem of determining whether P(d, R) satisfies a set of FDs is, in general, undecidable given that d satisfies a set of FDs defined over the EDB predicates of a Datalog program, P.

We have implicitly assumed that integrity constraints are *static*, which means that their satisfaction is only determined by the current state of the database. Alternatively, we may wish to consider *dynamic* integrity constraints whose satisfaction is determined by the transition of the database from one state to another during an update operation. For example, we may wish to assert that an employee's salary never decreases, i.e. when a salary is updated its new value is not less than the old value. Maintaining such dynamic integrity constraints can be dealt with naturally within a historical database (see Section 7.7 of Chapter 7) by viewing dynamic integrity constraints as static integrity constraints over historical relations. Alternatively, Nicholas and Yazdanian [NY78] suggest that we augment the database with temporary relations, called *action relations*, which hold the previous state of the database prior to an update, in order that the state transition can be expressed as a static integrity constraint over the augmented database.

We finally mention Reiter [Rei92b] who uses a modal logic formalism [Tha89b] to distinguish between knowledge about the external world (the real world) and what the database knows about the external world. For example, we may know that there exists an employee in the sales department but the database may not know who that employee is. Such an approach is especially useful in the context of incomplete information [Lev84].

9.7 Discussion

Deductive databases enhance the expressive power of relational databases with the ability to express recursion (for example, the transitive closure) and the general facility to define and manipulate views via rules. The Datalog language has been central to the development of the deductive database model as a declarative and logic-based query and update language.

Definite Datalog programs (i.e. programs without negation) have a well-defined semantics in terms of the unique minimal model of the program, which is equivalent to the fixpoint semantics of the program. Definite Datalog also has an equivalent and fairly straightforward proof theory [VK76, Hod93]. (For a novel semantics of Datalog which is based on Petri net theory [Pet81] see [DL91].) When we add negation to Datalog programs the situation is not as straightforward, since we lose the minimal model semantics but we can recover from this difficulty via the perfect model semantics of stratified Datalog programs. As we have seen, further enhancements to the semantics of Datalog have been proposed, since stratified Datalog programs do not give semantics to the full class of Datalog programs.

Most of the deductive database research has concentrated on the query language aspect of the model, stressing various optimisation techniques of queries [Ull88]. An area we have not touched upon is that of giving semantics to aggregate functions in Datalog; several recent such proposals can be found in [RS92, Van92, CM93]. There has been less research in the important areas of updates and integrity constraints in deductive databases. In particular, the area of data dependencies, which has been very instrumental in the broad area of relational database design, may have a similar effect on the design of deductive database.

As deductive database technology is reaching maturity several prototype systems have been implemented [RU95]. Since the basic technology is already available, it seems likely that existing relational database systems will enhance their capabilities with deduction via the provision for defining and executing rules. For a historical perspective on the area of deductive databases see [Min88b].

9.8   Exercises

Exercise 9.1   Consider the following normal form for a deductive database P: P is in *deductive normal form* if none of its rules are redundant and, in addition, none of the literals in the body of its rules are redundant. What is the problem with the definition of deductive normal form in terms of being a database design goal?

Exercise 9.2   Suppose that a Datalog program P has an IDB predicate TC that computes the transitive closure of some binary EDB predicate R. Now, consider transforming P into a program Q by removing TC from the IDB and adding a new predicate TCR to the EDB together with the corresponding closure dependency that asserts that TCR is the transitive closure of R. Discuss the advantages and disadvantages of the Datalog program P versus the Datalog program Q.

Exercise 9.3   Consider the following Datalog program, P, given by

MOVE(a, b).
MOVE(b, c).
MOVE(d, d).
WIN(x) :$-$ MOVE(x, y), $\neg$WIN(y).

What is the well-founded meaning of P? In your answer give the details of the intermediate states of the variables Res_True and Res_False during the computation of WELL_FOUNDED_MEANING(P).

Exercise 9.4   Assume a binary EDB predicate CHILD, where CHILD(Tamara, Mark) means that Tamara is the child of Mark, and a binary IDB predicate SG, where SG(Sara, Mark) means that Sara and Mark are of the same generation. Consider the following rules, which define SG and a unary predicate QUERY:

SG(x_1, x_2) :$-$ CHILD(x_1, x_3), CHILD(x_2, x_4), SG(x_3, x_4).
SG(x, x).
QUERY(x) :$-$ SG(Mark, x).

Let us call the Datalog program, which contains the EDB predicate CHILD and the IDB predicates SG and QUERY, P. Consider the Datalog program Q, consisting of the EDB predicate CHILD and the IDB predicates SGM, MAGIC and QUERY, given below:

SGM(x_1, x_2) :$-$ MAGIC(x_1), CHILD(x_1, x_3), CHILD(x_2, x_4), SGM(x_3, x_4).
SGM(x, x) :$-$ MAGIC(x).
MAGIC(Mark).

$$\text{MAGIC}(x_1) :- \text{MAGIC}(x_2), \text{CHILD}(x_2, x_1).$$
$$\text{QUERY}(x) :- \text{SGM}(\text{Mark}, x).$$

Suppose that we would like to compute the answer to the Datalog query, $:- \text{QUERY}(x)$. Show that the Datalog programs P and Q are equivalent in the sense that for all databases, which contain CHILD facts, the answer to the above query is the same with respect to either P or Q.

The transformation from P to Q is called the *magic set* optimisation method [BR91]. Argue why the magic set method is indeed a query optimisation technique.

Exercise 9.5   Assume that we have two EDB unary predicates STUD and LECT, where STUD(Wilfred) means that Wilfred is a student and LECT(Tony) means that Tony is a lecturer. We can assign each student to a single tutor using the following Datalog program P:

$$\text{TUTOR}(x_1, x_2) :- \text{STUD}(x_1), \text{LECT}(x_2), \text{CHOICE}((x_1), (x_2)).$$

In the above program the predicate CHOICE is a built-in predicate, which nondeterministically chooses a subset of the $<x_1, x_2>$ tuples that are true in the meaning of P such that there is a functional dependency from the x_1 values to the x_2 values, i.e. from students to tutors.

Consider the following Datalog program, which finds the students that are enrolled for at least one course, with ENROL and COURSE being EDB predicates, where ENROL(Wilfred, Databases) means that Wilfred is enrolled in the Databases course and COURSE(Databases, Computing) means that the Databases course is taught in the Computing department:

$$\text{QUERY}(x_1) :- \text{ENROL}(x_1, x_2), \text{COURSE}(x_2, x_3).$$

Suggest how the choice predicate can be used to optimise the above Datalog program, given a query $:- \text{QUERY}(x)$ [NT89, GPSZ91].

Exercise 9.6   Let us define a *term* to be either a variable, a constant or an expression of the form $f(t_1, t_2, \ldots, t_m)$, where each t_i is a term and f is a *function symbol* having m arguments. Furthermore, let us define an atomic formula to be an expression of the form $R(t_1, t_2, \ldots, t_n)$ or of the form $t_1 = t_2$, where each t_i is a term. We also extend a fact to be either an atomic formula of the form $R(c_1, c_2, \ldots, c_n)$, called a *relational* fact, or of the form $f(c_1, c_2, \ldots, c_{n-1}) = c_n$, called a *functional* fact, where each c_i is a constant. Finally, we extend Datalog programs such that atomic formulae are extended as above. For example, an extended Datalog program may contain the following functional facts and rules with their obvious meaning:

EMP(John).
DEPT(John) = Computing.
MGR(Computing) = Jack.
COMP$(x) :- \text{EMP}(x), \text{DEPT}(x) = \text{Computing}.$
MGR$(x_1) = x_2 :- \text{EMP}(x_1), \text{MGR}(\text{DEPT}(x_1)) = x_2.$

A set of facts is said to be *consistent* if whenever it contains two functional facts of the form $f(c_1, c_2, \ldots, c_{n-1}) = c_n^1$ and $f(c_1, c_2, \ldots, c_{n-1}) = c_n^2$, then $c_n^1 = c_n^2$. The meaning of an extended Datalog program P, i.e. MEANING(P), is modified accordingly, so that MEANING(P) is *defined* if the resulting database of facts is consistent, and *undefined* otherwise.

Show that given an extended Datalog program P, the program P can be transformed into a Datalog program Q, having no function symbols, together with a set of FDs F over schema(Q) such that MEANING(P) is consistent if and only if MEANING(Q) satisfies F [AH88a].

Exercise 9.7 Assume that we have a ternary EDB predicate ARC describing a labelled digraph, where $ARC(n_1, n_2, c)$ means that there is is an arc from node n_1 to node n_2 having a cost c, where $c \geq 0$ is a real number. Now, let P be the following Datalog program:

$$PATH(x_1, Direct, x_2, x_3) :- ARC(x_1, x_2, x_3).$$
$$PATH(x_1, x_2, x_3, x_4) :- SHORT(x_1, x_2, x_5), ARC(x_2, x_3, x_6), x_4 = x_5 + x_6.$$
$$SHORT(x_1, x_2, x_3) :- x_3 = MIN(x_4), ARC(x_1, x_2, x_4).$$

We assume that '+' is a built-in operator with its usual meaning of addition, and the aggregate function MIN is a built-in operator that computes the minimum of a multiset of facts (a multiset is a set which may contain duplicates). Thus, intuitively the above program computes the minimum cost path between two nodes in the digraph represented by the predicate ARC.

Give model-theoretic semantics to the above Datalog program, which includes an aggregate function, in terms of its minimal models [RS92, CM93].

Exercise 9.8 Let us extend Datalog with update predicates of the form $+R(y_1, y_2, \ldots, y_n)$, $-R(y_1, y_2, \ldots, y_n)$, where R is an EDB predicate. The meaning of $+R(y_1, y_2, \ldots, y_n)$ is to insert the fact $R(y_1, y_2, \ldots, y_n)$ into the EDB and, correspondingly, the meaning of $-R(y_1, y_2, \ldots, y_n)$ is to delete the fact $R(y_1, y_2, \ldots, y_n)$ from the EDB.

For example, assume a ternary EDB predicate EMP, where EMP(John, Computing, 30) means that John works in the Computing department and earns 30 thousand pounds sterling. The following Datalog program increases all the salaries of employees working in the Computing department by 20%:

$$RAISE(Computing) :- EMP(x_3, Computing, x_1), x_2 = x_1 \times 1.2,$$
$$-EMP(x_3, Computing, x_1), +EMP(x_3, Computing, x_2).$$

Give model-theoretic semantics to the above Datalog program in terms of minimal models, where the $+$ and $-$ operators correspond to *actions* that transform the database from one state to another [NK88, NT89].

Exercise 9.9 Suppose that we extend Datalog by allowing lists as arguments in atomic formulae, as, for example, in the following Datalog program:

$$SIBLING(John, Mary).$$
$$CHILDREN(John, [Jack, Jill, Joe]).$$
$$CHILDREN(Mary, [Mark, Mel, Moe]).$$
$$COUSIN(x_1, x_2) :- CHILDREN(x_3, L_1), CHILDREN(x_4, L_2),$$
$$MEMBER(x_1, L_1), MEMBER(x_2, L_2), SIBLING(x_3, x_4).$$

We assume that MEMBER(x, L) is a built-in predicate which is true if x is a member of the list L (see [NT89] for more details on how lists can be used in Datalog programs).

Discuss the merits and demerits of extending Datalog with lists.

Exercise 9.10   Design a Datalog program to manipulate a family tree, where the EDB contains at least a binary predicate PARENT such that PARENT(Mary, Mel) means that Mary is the parent of Mel, and a predicate PERSON which maintains all the personal information of the people stored in the family tree database [NT89]. You are allowed to use aggregates and lists in your Datalog program rules.

Exercise 9.11   Suggest an architecture for implementing a deductive database system on top of a relational database management system [RU95].

10. Extensions to the Relational Data Model and Recent Directions

So far we have covered the relational data model in detail including an extension to incorporate time into the model. In this final chapter we will briefly survey various extensions of the relational model which have been under development in recent years, and we will briefly overview some new directions that are being researched.

The relational model has already gained acceptance in the market place to such a degree that many database users expect their database systems to be relational by default. With the acceptance of the relational model users are demanding new facilities which are not directly supported by the model. Such facilities include support for deduction mechanisms (see Chapter 9), complex non-first normal form data, object-oriented features and production rules. The availability of database systems on a wide variety of computer platforms has meant that there is a growing demand for the use of databases in non-business applications, such as: office automation, computer-aided design (CAD), multimedia, text retrieval, expert systems and scientific applications such as: geographical and statistical analyses. This demand is a motivating factor for extending the relational model to provide new facilities such as the ones we have just mentioned.

In Section 10.1 we give an overview of nested relational databases, in which relations are *not* necessarily in first normal form. In Section 10.2 we give an overview of object-oriented databases, taking the object-relational approach via an extension of relational databases. In Section 10.3 we give an overview of graph-based databases and present a graph-based model, called the *hypernode* model, which represents objects as labelled nested digraphs. In Section 10.4 we give an overview of active databases, in which production rules, also known as *event-condition-action* rules, are added to the database system.

An emerging field in the broad area of information systems is that of hypertext (or more generally hypermedia), whose aim is to provide database support for networks of "electronic documents" which are logically linked together. Hypertext is concerned with authoring, managing, designing and navigating through the electronic documents of such networks. The vision of virtual electronic libraries is becoming a reality and hence there is a strong need for a formal data model of hypertext. Although it would be naive to consider a data model of such an electronic library to be an extension of the relational model, relational database theory can provide inspiration for the development of such a data model. In Section 10.5 we give an overview of hypertext databases.

A hypertext database can be viewed as an instance of a *semistructured database* in the sense that such a database does not come with a separate schema, since it does not have a regular structure. Although the digraph representing a hypertext database is unstructured, individual pages may have some structure attached to them. For instance, pages which are HTML documents have some structure attached to them in the form of informational tags, but these are insufficient for the purpose of constructing a relation schema over the document space. Semistructured data is often *self-describing* in the sense that its internal structure, when it exists, can be inferred from the data itself. In Section 10.6 we give a brief overview of semistructured databases.

The area of *Knowledge Discovery and Data mining* in databases (KDD) is one of the most exciting and fast growing of the recently developing areas in the database field. The term knowledge discovery refers to the overall process of finding nontrivial and previously unknown knowledge in data whereas the term data mining refers to the application of specific methods and algorithmic techniques which extract patterns from data. KDD brings together the three areas of databases, machine learning and statistics. In Section 10.7 we give an overview of the underlying concepts involved in knowledge discovery and data mining.

In Section 10.8 we briefly mention other important areas in the database field that are being currently researched and in Section 10.9 we conclude that the synergy of the database field with other active areas in computer science will lead to further important advances in database theory.

10.1   Nested Relational Databases

We have already introduced nested relations in Subsection 1.7.4 of Chapter 1. We refresh the reader's memory with an example of a nested relation shown in Table 10.1. The attribute PNAME is *atomic*, while the attributes (HOBBY)* and (CHILD, AGE)* are *relation-valued*. We enclose relation-valued attributes by '(' and ')*', in order to differentiate them from atomic attributes. Thus, PNAME-values are atomic, while (HOBBY)*-values are relations over a relation schema with attribute HOBBY and (CHILD, AGE)*-values are relations over a relation schema with attributes CHILD and AGE. We observe that relation-valued attribute values can be empty, i.e. their value can be the empty set, ∅. For example, Jack does not have any hobbies and Carl does not have any children.

Table 10.1 A nested relation r

PNAME	(HOBBY)*	(CHILD	AGE)*
Jack		Jill	8
		Jacob	10
		John	12
Carl	chess		
	checkers		
	bridge		
Miriam	photography	Maria	6
	reading		

We next extend the notion of an attribute to nested relations.

Definition 10.1 (Attribute, atomic and relation-valued)   An attribute is defined recursively by:

1) An element $A \in \mathcal{U}$ is an attribute, also called an *atomic* attribute.

2) If X is a finite set of attributes then $(X)^*$ is an attribute, also called a *relation-valued* attribute. ∎

The definition of a relation schema and database schema remain unchanged. A relation schema R having a relation-valued attribute $(X)^* \in$ schema(R) is called a *nested relation schema*. Correspondingly, if schema(R) has no relation-valued attributes then R is also called a *flat relation schema*. Moreover, a database schema having no nested relation schemas is also called a *flat database schema*, otherwise it is called a *nested database schema*.

We now extend the notion of the domain of an attribute to nested relations.

Definition 10.2 (Attribute domain, atomic and relation-valued)   The domain of an attribute is defined recursively by:

1) For an atomic attribute, A, the domain of A, denoted by DOM(A), is given by DOM(A) $\subseteq \mathcal{D}$, recalling that $\mathcal{D}$ is the underlying database domain.

2) For a set of attributes, $X = \{A_1, A_2, \ldots, A_n\}$, the domain of X, denoted by DOM(X), is given by
$$DOM(X) = DOM(A_1) \times DOM(A_2) \times \cdots \times DOM(A_n),$$
where $\times$ is the Cartesian product operator.

3) For a relation-valued attribute, $(X)^*$, where X is a set of attributes, the domain of $(X)^*$, denoted by DOM($(X)^*$), is given by DOM($(X)^*$) = $\mathcal{P}$(DOM(X)), where $\mathcal{P}$ is the finite power set operator. ∎

An interesting argument for the inclusion of relation-valued attributes in the relational model is given in [DD92b]. Therein, it is argued that if we interpret a domain as a data type, which can have potentially arbitrary complexity, then we should also allow relation-valued attributes as a special kind of data type. This is quite convincing realising that SQL supports domains such as character strings and dates, which can be viewed as aggregates of simpler data types, i.e. single characters and day, month and year, respectively (see also Section 3.7 of Chapter 3).

The definition of a relation and a database remain unchanged. A relation over a flat relation schema is also called a *flat relation* and a relation over a nested relation schema is called a *nested relation*. Moreover, a database having no nested relation is also called a *flat database*, otherwise it is called a *nested database*.

Retaining the notation of relation schema, relation, database schema and database is convenient since it encapsulates both the flat and nested worlds. It is interesting to note that in Codd's seminal paper, wherein he introduced the relational data model [Cod70], the original definition of a relation does *not* assume that a relation schema is in 1NF. The restriction to first normal form comes after the definition of a relation. Of course, if Codd had not defined 1NF who knows if the relational data model would be as successful as it is? In any case 1NF simplifies the model considerably, and only in the 1980's when relational database theory was already well understood did database researchers tackle the problem of formalising the nested relational model.

The definitions of the relational algebra operators given in Subsection 3.2.1 of Chapter 3 remain valid for both flat and nested relations. The only difference between flat and nested relations with respect to these definitions is that equality of relation-valued attribute values is taken to be equality between relations rather than between atomic values; this difference does not affect the definitions. The *nested relational algebra* extends the relational algebra with three additional operators, NEST and UNNEST, which restructure relations, and *empty*, denoted by λ, which creates a nested relation with a single relation-valued attribute, which is empty. We first define NEST, which transforms a nested relation into a "more deeply" nested relation.

Definition 10.3 (NEST)   Let r be a relation over R and $Y \subseteq$ schema(R). Then $\text{NEST}_Y(r)$ is a relation over S, with schema(S) = (schema(R) $-$ Y) $\cup$ {(Y)*}, which is defined by

$$\text{NEST}_Y(r) = \{t \mid \exists w \in r \text{ such that } t[\text{schema}(R) - Y] = w[\text{schema}(R) - Y] \text{ and}$$
$$t[(Y)^*] = \{u[Y] \mid u \in r \text{ and } u[\text{schema}(R) - Y] = t[\text{schema}(R) - Y]\}\}.$$

∎

We next define UNNEST, which transforms a nested relation into a "flatter" nested relation.

Definition 10.4 (UNNEST)   Let r be a relation over R and $(Y)^* \in$ schema(R). Then $\text{UNNEST}_{(Y)^*}(r)$ is a relation over S, with schema(S) = (schema(R) $-$ {(Y)*}) $\cup$ Y, which is defined by

$$\text{UNNEST}_{(Y)^*}(r) = \{t \mid \exists w \in r \text{ such that } t[\text{schema}(R) - \{(Y)^*\}] = w[\text{schema}(R) - \{(Y)^*\}]$$
$$\text{and } t[Y] \in w[(Y)^*]\}.$$

∎

Some examples of NEST and UNNEST were given in Subsection 1.7.4 in Chapter 1. Let r be the nested relation shown in Table 10.1. The nested relation $\text{UNNEST}_{(\text{HOBBY})^*}(r)$ is shown in Table 10.2 and the nested relation $\text{UNNEST}_{(\text{CHILD,AGE})^*}(r)$ is shown in Table 10.3. The flat relation given by

$$\text{UNNEST}_{(\text{HOBBY})^*}(\text{UNNEST}_{(\text{CHILD,AGE})^*}(r)) = \text{UNNEST}_{(\text{CHILD,AGE})^*}(\text{UNNEST}_{(\text{HOBBY})^*}(r)),$$

is shown in Table 10.4.

The definition of λ now follows.

Definition 10.5 (Empty)   Let R be a relation schema. Then $\lambda_R()$ is a nested relation over a relation schema R', with schema(R') = {(schema(R))*}, containing a single tuple t satisfying $t[(\text{schema}(R))^*] = \emptyset$. (Note that the only parameter of the λ operator is a relation schema.)

∎

Table 10.2 The nested relation UNNEST$_{(HOBBY)^*}(r)$

PNAME	HOBBY	(CHILD	AGE)*
Carl	chess		
Carl	checkers		
Carl	bridge		
Miriam	photography	Maria	6
Miriam	reading	Maria	6

Table 10.3 The nested relation UNNEST$_{(CHILD,AGE)^*}(r)$

PNAME	(HOBBY)*	CHILD	AGE
Jack		Jill	8
Jack		Jacob	10
Jack		John	12
Miriam	photography reading	Maria	6

Table 10.4 The flat relation emanating from r

PNAME	HOBBY	CHILD	AGE
Miriam	photography	Maria	6
Miriam	reading	Maria	6

We can create a tuple for Jack over a schema having the attributes, PNAME and (HOBBY)*, with an empty set component for (HOBBY)* as follows. Let R be a relation schema with schema(R) = {HOBBY}. Then the nested relation $\{<Jack>\} \times \lambda_R()$ is shown in Table 10.5.

Table 10.5 A nested relation with a tuple having no hobbies

PNAME	(HOBBY)*
Jack	

We will refer to the *flat relational algebra* as the basic set of relational operators, that is, union, difference, projection, selection, natural join and renaming. Let us assume that apart from NEST, UNNEST and λ the nested relational algebra includes only the operators of the flat relational algebra.

In [PV88] the following question was posed and answered with respect to the expressive power of the nested relational algebra: are nested relational algebra queries, whose operands are flat relation schemas and such that the schema of answers to such queries is also flat, more expressive than queries expressed in the flat relation algebra?

The following theorem proved in [PV88] shows that the answer to the above question is negative. Thus as long as the input and output to nested relational algebra queries is flat, then the expressive power of the nested relational algebra is equivalent to that of the flat relational algebra. So the power of the nested relational algebra lies in its ability to represent and manipulate nonflat data rather than in its ability to pose additional queries that cannot be expressed in the flat relational algebra.

Theorem 10.1 Let d be a flat database, Q be a nested relational algebra query and Q(d) be the answer to Q such that Q(d) returns a flat relation. Then there exists a flat relational algebra query Q', such that Q(d) = $Q'(d)$. $\square$

We now discuss some of the fundamental properties of the NEST and UNNEST operators. Readers can convince themselves that the UNNEST operator is commutative, i.e.

$$\text{UNNEST}_{(X)^*}(\text{UNNEST}_{(Y)^*}(r)) = \text{UNNEST}_{(Y)^*}(\text{UNNEST}_{(X)^*}(r)),$$

where r is a nested relation over R and $(X)^*$ and $(Y)^*$ are relation-valued attributes in schema(R). Therefore, the nested relation r has a unique flat relation emanating from it, which can be obtained by a sequence of UNNEST operations. Due to the commutativity of UNNEST all such sequences of UNNEST operations result in the same flat relation [TF86, VF88].

The pseudo-code of an algorithm, designated UNNEST*, which given the input nested relation r over R returns the flat relation emanating from r, is presented as the following algorithm.

Algorithm 10.1 (UNNEST*(r))
1. **begin**
2.   Rel := r;
3.   Sch := R;
4.   **while** there exists a relation-valued attribute in schema(Sch) **do**
5.   choose any relation-valued attribute $(Y)^* \in$ schema(Sch);
6.   Rel := UNNEST$_{(Y)^*}$(Rel);
7.   schema(Sch) := (schema(Sch) $- \{(Y)^*\}) \cup$ Y;
8.   **end while**
9.   **return** Rel over Sch;
10. **end.**

We now demonstrate that the NEST operator is *not* commutative. Let s over S be the flat relation shown in Table 10.6, where schema(S) = {A, B, C}. Then the nested relation NEST$_B$(NEST$_C(s)$) is shown in Table 10.7 and the distinct nested relation NEST$_C$(NEST$_B(s)$) is shown in Table 10.8. The following proposition characterises the situation when two NEST operations commute [JS82, FV84b, TF86, VF88].

Proposition 10.2   Let r be a relation over R, with X and Y being disjoint sets of attributes in schema(R) and Z = schema(R) $-$ XY. Then NEST$_Y$(NEST$_X(r)$) = NEST$_X$(NEST$_Y(r)$) if and only if for each distinct pair of tuples, t_1 and t_2 in NEST$_Y$(NEST$_X(r)$) or in NEST$_X$(NEST$_Y(r)$), whenever $t_1[Z] = t_2[Z]$, then $t_1[(X)^*] \cap t_2[(X)^*] = \emptyset$ and $t_1[(Y)^*] \cap t_2[(Y)^*] = \emptyset$.   □

Table 10.6 The flat relation s

A	B	C
0	0	0
0	0	1
0	1	0

Table 10.7 The nested relation NEST$_B$(NEST$_C(s)$)

A	(B)*	(C)*
0	0	0
		1
0	1	0

Table 10.8 The nested relation NEST$_C$(NEST$_B(s)$)

A	(B)*	(C)*
0	0	0
		1
0	0	1

Finally, as was demonstrated in Table 1.6 of Subsection 1.7.4 in Chapter 1, an UNNEST operation cannot always be reversed with a NEST operation and thus we may lose information when unnesting. Recall that this problem was called the *1NF normalisability problem* and it can be solved by introducing the *keying* operator. We give two additional examples of this fact.

Let r over R be the nested relation shown in Table 10.9, where schema(R) = {A, (B)*}. Then the distinct nested relation $\text{NEST}_B(\text{UNNEST}_{(B)*}(r))$, say r', is shown in Table 10.10. Also, let r be the nested relation shown in Table 10.1. Then obviously both $\text{UNNEST}_{(HOBBY)*}(r)$ and $\text{UNNEST}_{(CHILD,AGE)*}(r)$ lose information, since the tuples with empty components over the relation-valued attributes, (HOOBY)* and (CHILD, AGE)*, respectively, are not represented in the unnested relation.

Table 10.9 The nested relation r

A	(B)*
1	0
1	1

Table 10.10 The nested relation r'

A	(B)*
1	0
	1

We assume that the concept of a functional dependency (FD) remains the same as defined in Subsection 3.6.1 of Chapter 3, where relations now may be flat or nested. As mentioned above the only difference between nested and flat relations with respect to their definitions is that equality of relation-valued attribute values is taken to be equality between relations rather than between atomic values; this difference does not affect the definitions. The following proposition characterises the situation when an UNNEST operation does not result in any loss of information [TF86, VF88].

Proposition 10.3   Let r be a nested relation over R, with (Y)* ∈ schema(R). Then

$$r = \text{NEST}_Y(\text{UNNEST}_{(Y)*}(r)),$$

if and only if

1) $\forall t \in r, t[(Y)*] \neq \emptyset$; and

2) r satisfies the FD X → (Y)*, where X = schema(R) − {(Y)*}.   □

An important subclass of nested relations is now defined, wherein the atomic attributes of the schema are superkey values at each level of the nested relation.

Definition 10.6 (Hierarchical relation)   Let r be a relation over R. Then r is a *hierarchical relation* if and only if

1) r satisfies X → schema(R), where X is the set of atomic attributes in schema(R); and

2) for each tuple $t \in r$ and for all relation-valued attributes (Y)* ∈ schema(R), $t[(Y)*]$ is a hierarchical relation over a relation schema whose attribute set is Y.   ■

The reader can verify that the nested relation shown in Table 10.1 is a hierarchical relation. Another example of a hierarchical relation, with two levels of nesting, is shown in Table 10.11.

Hierarchical relations satisfy both the desirable properties formalised in Propositions 10.2 and 10.3, namely the NEST operator is commutative, and the UNNEST operator does not cause any loss of information, provided that all the relation-valued attribute values are nonempty. Hierarchical relations can also be viewed as a normal form for nested relations, in the sense

Table 10.11 A hierarchical relation

A	(B	(C)*)*
1	2	4
		5
	3	5
2	2	4
		6
3	4	
4		

that superkey dependencies are explicitly represented in the nested relation. (More details on the design of nested relational databases can be found in [ÖY87b, AFS89, MNE96].)

Definition 10.7 (The tree induced by schema(R)) The tree induced by R, denoted by TREE(schema(R)), is defined recursively as follows:

1) If schema(R) contains no relation-valued attributes then TREE(schema(R)) consists of a single node labelled by schema(R).

2) If X is the set of atomic attributes in schema(R) and $\{(Y_1)^*, \ldots, (Y_k)^*\}$ = schema(R) − X is the set of relation-valued attributes in schema(R), then the root node, say n, of TREE(schema(R)) is labelled by X, and n has one child node n_i for each $(Y_i)^*$ such that n_i is the root node of TREE(Y_i), $1 \leq i \leq k$.

We assume that the labels of nodes in TREE(schema(R)) are pairwise disjoint; this assumption corresponds to the URSA (see Definition 3.6 in Section 3.1 of Chapter 3). The *path set* of a relation schema R is a family of sets of labels one for each leaf node in TREE(schema(R)); each such set consists of the union of the labels of nodes in one of the paths of TREE(schema(R)) from a leaf node to the root node.   ■

The next theorem characterises hierarchical relations over R in terms of the flat relations satisfying the join dependency induced by the path set of TREE(schema(R)). The proof of the theorem can be found in [ÖY87b, Lev92].

Theorem 10.4 The following two statements are equivalent:

1) r is a hierarchical relation over R, such that the empty set does not occur as a value in r over a relation-valued attribute.

2) UNNEST*(r) satisfies the acyclic JD $\bowtie[P]$, where P is the path set of R.   □

The theorem that follows gives some interesting interactions between nested relations and FDs. (More details on interactions between data dependencies and nested relations can be found in [FSTV85].)

Theorem 10.5 Let r be a relation over R and X, Y, Z $\subseteq$ schema(R). The following statements are true:

1) NEST$_Z$(r) satisfies the FD X → (Z)*, where X = schema(R) − Z.

2) Assuming that $XY \cap Z = \emptyset$, r satisfies the FD $X \to Y$ if and only if $NEST_Z(r)$ satisfies the FD $X \to Y$.

3) Assuming that $X \cap Z = \emptyset$, r satisfies the FD $X \to Z$ if and only if

(i) $NEST_Z(r)$ satisfies the FD $X \to (Z)^*$; and

(ii) $\forall t \in NEST_Z(r)$, $t[(Z)^*]$ is a singleton. $\qquad\square$

One of the reasons the UNNEST operator may cause loss of information is that a nested relation may have empty attribute values over relation-valued attributes. The empty set allows us to model information in situations such as a person having no hobbies or no children. These situations can also be modelled in flat relations provided we extend attribute domains with the following distinguished null value. Let *dne* be a distinguished null value denoting the fact that a "value does not exist"; see Chapter 5 for more details on the semantics of null values. Using *dne* as a HOOBY or CHILD attribute value we can model the fact that a person does not have any hobbies or any children, respectively. Therefore, we can adopt the convention that when we unnest an empty relation-valued attribute value over $(X)^*$, where X is a set of atomic attributes, we obtain a tuple over X whose A-value is *dne* for each A in X. Conversely, when nesting *dne* we obtain $\emptyset$. As an example of this convention the flat relation, shown in Table 10.12; results from unnesting the nested relation shown in Table 10.1. If we modify NEST and UNNEST to adopt this convention then there will be no loss of information during unnest operations due to empty relation-valued attribute values.

Table 10.12 A flat relation with the *dne* null value

PNAME	HOBBY	CHILD	AGE
Jack	*dne*	Jill	8
Jack	*dne*	Jacob	10
Jack	*dne*	John	12
Carl	chess	*dne*	*dne*
Carl	checkers	*dne*	*dne*
Carl	bridge	*dne*	*dne*
Miriam	photography	Maria	6
Miriam	reading	Maria	6

Nested relations can be viewed in the wider context of *complex object types*. It is assumed that a collection of *atomic object types* are available, where the values of each such atomic type are taken from an atomic domain. An object type can now be defined as a tree whose leaves represent atomic object types, and whose internal nodes represent the application of either the *tuple construct*, which aggregates its children object types into a tuple, or the *set construct*, which groups its single child object type into a set. Thus a nested relation type is a special case of a complex object type, where the root of the tree represents a tuple construct, each child node of a node representing a tuple construct either represents a set construct or an atomic object type, and the single child node of a node representing a set construct represents a tuple construct. One aspect of the study of complex object types is that of query and update languages which generalise the nested relational algebra. Another important aspect of the study of complex objects is that of comparing the information capacity of complex object types that may have been obtained as a result of restructuring another complex object type. Intuitively, one object type is *absolutely dominated* by another object type if for all sufficiently large finite subsets $S \subseteq \mathcal{D}$ we can construct at least as many objects of the second type as of the first type, where S is a superset of the active domains of all the constructed objects; the active domain of an object is the set of all atomic values used to construct that object. Moreover, one object type is *query dominated* by another object type if any query over a collection of objects of the first object type can be translated into a query over a collection of objects of the second object type. In [Hul86] it was shown that query dominance implies absolute dominance and thus query dominance is a stronger criterion of information capacity, but the converse implication does not always hold. The information capacity of two object types is *absolutely equivalent* (*query equivalent*) if both object types absolutely dominate (query dominate) each other. Restructuring operations which preserve absolute equivalence were investigated in [HY84, AH88b] and it was shown that two complex object types are absolutely equivalent if and only if they can both be reduced to a normal form complex object type, which is based on some natural restructuring operators (see also [Hul86]).

Recently, it was shown in [VL97] that two nested relation schemas over hierarchical relations are absolutely equivalent and, in this case are also query equivalent, if and only if the sets of MVDs induced by the acyclic JDs of their respective path sets are equivalent. An additional characterisation of absolute equivalence for two nested relation schemas R_1 and R_2 over hierarchical relations, shown in [VL97], is now briefly described. Let *compress* be a restructuring operator which coalesces two nodes n_1 and n_2, when n_2 is the only child of n_1, in TREE(schema(R_1)) or TREE(schema(R_2)). Assume that we apply compress repetitively to the said trees. Then the information capacities of the object types represented by these two trees are absolutely equivalent if and only if, after the aforesaid repetitive application of the compress operator, the resulting trees are isomorphic whenever the corresponding unions of the labels of the nodes in theses two trees, representing the underlying attributes of their nested relation schemas, are identical.

The study of complex object types also lays the foundations for integrating persistent database types into programming languages which allow application programmers to explicitly define and manipulate complex object types. A survey of complex object data types was presented in [Hul87] and a collection of papers on various issues concerning nested relations and complex objects can be found in [AFS89].

10.2   Object-Oriented Databases

We have already introduced object-oriented databases in Subsection 1.7.6 of Chapter 1. Our point of view there was that the structural part of an object-oriented data model can be the same as that of the network data model. Here we take a different view, namely that relational databases and object-oriented databases can be unified by extending the relational model. One possible such extension is to let the data structures of the object-oriented data model to be complex objects or nested relations. This is consistent with the view that the structure of objects should not be restricted in any way. Taking this view the attributes of objects are defined recursively using simple and complex object constructors. Simple object constructors define attributes of type integer, real, string or Boolean, and complex object constructors define attributes of type tuple, set, bag, list or array of objects. In the nested relational model the only complex object constructor is that of a set consisting of tuples of objects, which is sufficient for most applications.

Herein we take a simpler view by extending (flat) relations with explicit object identity. Let us assume that in addition to the set of attributes $\mathcal{U}$ there is a countably infinite set of attributes $\mathcal{I}$, which is disjoint from $\mathcal{U}$. We call the attributes in $\mathcal{I}$ *object attributes* to distinguish them from attributes in $\mathcal{U}$. The domain of all object attributes in $\mathcal{I}$ is a countably infinite set of *object identifiers*, $\mathcal{O}$, which for simplicity is assumed to be the set of natural numbers ω. We next define how to add explicit object identifiers to a relation.

Definition 10.8 (The object identification operator) The *object identification*, $id(s, A)$, of a relation s over S with respect to the object attribute A is a relation over R, with schema(R) = schema(S) $\cup$ {A} such that

1) each tuple in s is extended to be a tuple over R,

2) $id(s, A)$ has the same cardinality as s, and

3) $id(s, A) \models A \rightarrow$ schema(R), i.e. A is a simple key for R.

The attribute A is called an *object identifying attribute* of R. A relation over a relation schema having one or more object identifying attributes is called an *object relation*. A collection of object relations is called an *object database*. ∎

We observe that a relation schema can have more than one object identifying attribute, although in practice one such attribute is sufficient for the purpose of implementing object identity. We assume that when a tuple is added to an object relation r over R, with object identifying attribute A, then an appropriate A-value for this tuple such that A is a simple key for R, i.e. such that $r \models A \rightarrow$ schema(R), is created by the DBMS. Furthermore, once an object identifier is created it *cannot* be modified. We also note that, given an object relation r over R, schema(R) can have object attributes which are *not* object identifying attributes. Such attributes are object identifying attributes of other relation schemas and serve the purpose of referencing tuples (or objects) in the object relations over those relation schemas.

As an example $\{r_1, r_2\}$ is an object database where the object relation r_1 over EMP is shown in Table 10.13 and the object relation r_2 over DEPT is shown in Table 10.14. In this example EID is the object identifying attribute of EMP and DID is the object identifying attribute of DEPT. In addition, DID in EMP is an object attribute referencing DID in DEPT and MID in DEPT is an object attribute referencing EID in EMP. We observe that once a relation schema has an object identifying attribute it can be declared as the primary key of the schema.

Table 10.13 The object relation r_1 over EMP

EID	ENAME	DID
1	Iris	6
2	Reuven	6
3	Brian	7
4	Naomi	7
5	Naomi	8

Table 10.14 The object relation r_2 over DEPT

DID	DNAME	MID
6	Computing	2
7	Maths	4
8	Economics	5

A desirable property of object identifiers is that they allow *sharing*. For example, in the object relation r_1, shown in Table 10.13, the first and the second tuples and the third and fourth tuples share the same department by referencing the same DID. This allows tuples (or objects) to be referenced in a straightforward manner. In addition, any update to a referenced tuple does not have any effect on the reference, since as we noted earlier object identifiers cannot be modified. Sharing through references also highlights the importance of referential integrity constraints.

We now extend Armstrong's axiom system for FDs with an additional inference rule to take object identifying attributes into account.

Definition 10.9 (Identity inference rule for FDs)   Let F be a set of FDs over schema R. The identity inference rule for FDs is given by

FD8 Identity: if A is an object identifying attribute, then $F \vdash A \rightarrow$ schema(R).   ∎

We leave the proof of the next theorem to the reader; it is similar to the proof of Theorem 3.21 in Subsection 3.6.1 of Chapter 3 (see also [LL95a]).

Theorem 10.6   Armstrong's axiom system augmented with FD8 is a sound and complete axiom system for FDs being satisfied in object relations.   □

It is our view that it is straightforward to cater for object identifying attributes within existing relational DBMSs. In [Van93a] it was shown that nested relations can be represented using object relations. It was also shown therein that the relational algebra augmented with object identification operating on object relations can simulate the nested relational algebra operating on nested relations. Therefore, object relations also cater for complex objects.

We have already briefly discussed the notion of an inheritance lattice in Subsection 1.7.6 of Chapter 1 (see the inheritance lattice depicted in Figure 1.8). For simplicity we assume that a class type specifies only an object type, i.e. we ignore any methods associated with the class type. Thus in our context an object type is simply a relation schema, which may contain one or more object attributes. We now formalise the notion of an inheritance lattice.

Definition 10.10 (Inheritance lattice)   We define a partial order in the set of relation schemas, denoted by $\sqsubseteq$, as follows:

$$R_1 \sqsubseteq R_2 \text{ if and only if schema}(R_1) \supseteq \text{schema}(R_2),$$

where R_1 and R_2 are relation schemas. When $R_1 \sqsubseteq R_2$ then we say that R_1 is a *subclass* of R_2, or alternatively, that R_2 is a *superclass* of R_1.

The *inheritance lattice* is a finite set of relation schemas, denoted by $\mathcal{R}$, partially ordered by $\sqsubseteq$ and having a bottom element (i.e. a least element), which we denote by $\perp$.   ∎

It follows that the inheritance lattice is a *lattice* in the sense of the formal definition of a lattice given in Subsection 1.9.2 of Chapter 1. We denote the top element of $\mathcal{R}$ (i.e. its greatest element) by $\top$; normally $\top$ is taken to be the schema with the empty set of attributes. Moreover, the *least upper bound* (or the *join*) of relation schemas $R_1, R_2 \in \mathcal{R}$, denoted by

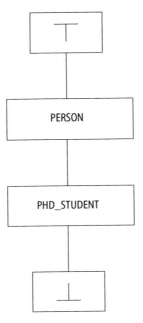

Fig 10.1 An inheritance lattice

$R_1 \sqcup R_2$, is a relation schema R_3 such that schema(R_3) = schema(R_1) $\cap$ schema(R_2); the relation schema $R_3 = R_1 \sqcup R_2$ is called a *generator* of R_1 and R_2.

Example 10.1 Recall the inheritance lattice depicted in Figure 1.8, with $\mathcal{R}$ = {OBJECT, PERSON, STUDENT, EMPLOYEE, RA}. Assume that schema(OBJECT) = $\emptyset$, schema(PERSON) = {NAME, ADDRESS, AGE}, schema(STUDENT) = {NAME, ADDRESS, AGE, DEPARTMENT}, schema(EMPLOYEE) = {NAME, ADDRESS, AGE, SALARY} and schema(RA) = {NAME, ADDRESS, AGE, DEPARTMENT, COURSE, SALARY}. It follows that RA $\sqsubseteq$ EMPLOYEE, RA $\sqsubseteq$ STUDENT, STUDENT $\sqsubseteq$ PERSON, EMPLOYEE $\sqsubseteq$ PERSON and PERSON $\sqsubseteq$ OBJECT. Furthermore, STUDENT $\sqcup$ EMPLOYEE = PERSON, RA = $\bot$ and OBJECT = $\top$. ■

We now give an example of inserting a relation schema into an inheritance lattice.

Example 10.2 Let $\mathcal{R}$ = {$\top$, PERSON, PHD_STUDENT, $\bot$} be an inheritance lattice, where schema(PHD_STUDENT) = schema(STUDENT) $\cup$ {SUBJECT}. Additionally, let BSC_STUDENT be a relation schema, with schema(BSC_STUDENT) = schema(STUDENT) $\cup$ {MAJOR}.

The inheritance lattice $\mathcal{R}$ is shown in Figure 10.1. The result of inserting BSC_STUDENT into $\mathcal{R}$ is shown in Figure 10.2. We note that inserting BSC_STUDENT into the inheritance lattice triggers the additional insertion of STUDENT into the lattice, since STUDENT = PHD_STUDENT $\sqcup$ BSC_STUDENT. ■

We now give an algorithm, designated INSERT($\mathcal{R}$, R), for inserting a relation schema R into an inheritance lattice $\mathcal{R}$, which was presented in [MS89b]. Intuitively, whenever a relation

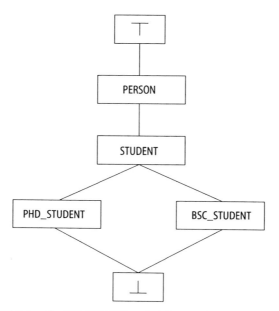

Fig 10.2 Inserting BSC_STUDENT into the inheritance lattice of Figure 10.1

schema, say R, is to be inserted into the lattice $\mathcal{R}$ and the least upper bound of R with another relation schema in the lattice, say S, is not already in the lattice, then a generator $R \sqcup S$ of R and S is also inserted into the lattice. More efficient implementations of INSERT($\mathcal{R}$, R) than Algorithm 10.2 are considered in [MS89b].

Algorithm 10.2 (INSERT($\mathcal{R}$, R))
1. **begin**
2. $\mathcal{R} := \mathcal{R} \cup \{R\}$;
3.   COMP := $\emptyset$;
4.   **for each** $S \in \mathcal{R}$ **do**
5.   **if** $R \sqcup S \notin \mathcal{R}$ **then**
6.   COMP := COMP $\cup$ {S};
7.   **end if**
8.   **end for**
9.   **if** COMP $\neq \emptyset$ **then**
10.   **for each** $S \in$ COMP **do**
11. $T := R \sqcup S$;
12.   INSERT($\mathcal{R}$, T);
13.   **end for**
14.   **end if**
15.   **return** $\mathcal{R}$;
16. **end.**

There are several important data modelling issues that we have not addressed such as the semantics of types and classes, view maintenance, schema evolution, concurrency control, object-oriented database design and object-oriented database programming languages.

Several books have already been written on object-oriented databases [Kim90, ZM90, GKP92, Kho93, KM94] and their number is growing. Moreover, a substantial part of several books is devoted to object-orientation in databases; see [Kim95a, Part IA], [KL89b, Part 3] and [DLR95]. We refer the reader who is interested in furthering their knowledge on object-oriented data models and concepts to the papers [ABD$^+$89, Bee90, LP91, Ban92, Van93a]. Furthermore, articles that are concerned with extending the relational model to cater for object-orientation can be found in [SS90, Van93a, Kim95b]. An interesting proposal to extend values of relations to be queries, which allows modelling of complex objects, is suggested in [SAH87].

A recent book [SM96] specifically explores the marriage of relational databases with object technology resulting in *object-relational* database systems. An object-relational DBMS can be defined as one which supports SQL3 [DD93, Mel96]; SQL3 is discussed below. Since the SQL3 standard is still evolving, four fundamental characteristics of object-relational DBMSs are identified in [SM96]; they are: (i) the ability to add to the database system user-defined data types and functions operating on these types (this can be viewed as an abstract data type facility), (ii) the ability to construct complex object types via general purpose type constructors, (iii) the ability to define supertypes and subtypes together with the support of inheritance from supertype to subtype, and (iv) support for active database rules or alternatively triggers (see Section 10.4).

A recent attempt is to try and merge together the concepts of object-oriented and deductive databases in order to gain the best of both worlds [AK89, KL89a, KW89]. This approach has been encouraged by the formation of a biennial international conference devoted solely to deductive and object-oriented databases.

An interesting comparison between object-oriented and deductive databases can be found in [Ull91]. Ullman essentially argues that deductive database systems will eventually dominate, due to their declarativeness and their upwards compatibility with relational database systems. As we have shown in this section, it is possible to build an object-oriented database system as an extension of a relational database system. Furthermore, as was shown in [AK89, KL89a, KW89], it is possible to give logical foundations to deductive query languages that incorporate object-oriented concepts such as object identity.

We next present some salient features of the support for object-orientation in the emerging SQL3 standard [Kul93, Mat96]. SQL3 has a mechanism that allows database users and application programmers to extend the type system of the DBMS with *User-Defined-Types* (UDTs) and *User-Defined-Functions* (UDFs). We introduce this facility via some examples.

An example of creating a UDT ADDRESS is given by the SQL3 statement:

```
CREATE TYPE ADDRESS
        (number  INTEGER,
        street   CHAR(30),
        city     CHAR(20),
        postcode CHAR(7));
```

An example of creating a UDT PERSON is given by the SQL3 statement:

```
CREATE TYPE PERSON
        (name      CHAR(30),
         home      ADDRESS,
         birthdate DATE,
         text      VARCHAR(512),
         picture   BLOB(1M));
```

We note that DATE and BLOB (*Binary Large Object*) are built-in data types and that the UDT PERSON is a complex object type, since ADDRESS is a UDT.

An example of creating a UDF age, which returns the age of a person, is given by the SQL3 statement:

```
CREATE FUNCTION age (p PERSON) RETURNS INTEGER
        RETURN YEAR(CURRENT_DATE) − YEAR(p.birthdate);
END FUNCTION
```

We have assumed the existence of two built-in functions: CURRENT_DATE, which returns today's date, and YEAR(d), which returns the year, given a date d.

An example of creating an EMPLOYEE UDT as a subtype of PERSON is given by the SQL3 statement:

```
CREATE TYPE EMPLOYEE UNDER PERSON
        (salary    INTEGER,
         project   CHAR(3),
         location  ADDRESS);
```

As a subtype of PERSON, the UDT EMPLOYEE inherits all the attributes and functions which have been defined over PERSON.

The following SQL3 statements define tables (i.e. relations) over PERSON and EMPLOYEE:

```
CREATE TABLE PEOPLE OF PERSON;
CREATE TABLE EMPLOYEES OF EMPLOYEE;
```

Each row in the PEOPLE table is an instance of the UDT PERSON, and correspondingly each row in the EMPLOYEES table is an instance of UDT EMPLOYEE. Moreover, each row in such an instance has a unique object identifier that is assigned to it when the row is created.

We also mention that SQL3 has extensive support for active rules, also referred to as triggers, in order to improve the maintenance of database integrity. Apart from the object-relational extensions in SQL3, procedural language constructs have also been added to SQL, thus making SQL3 a computationally complete database language. Hence using these procedural constructs UDFs can realise any computable database query. In addition, SQL3 supports recursive execution of SQL select statements and thus transitive closure queries can also be formulated naturally in SQL3. It is important to note that SQL3 has been designed in such a way that it is upwards compatible with the current SQL2 standard [DD93].

We close this section with a brief discussion of the *Object Database Management Group* (ODMG) proposal for an *Object-oriented Database Management System* (ODBMS) standard [Cat96, CB97]. The main goal of the standard is to provide a means of source code portability for database application programs through the integration of object-oriented database capabilities with object-oriented programming language capabilities. This is achieved by the ODBMS making database objects appear as programming language objects in existing object-oriented programming languages such as C++, Java and Smalltalk. The proposal is realised via an *Object Definition Language* (ODL) and an *Object Query Language* (OQL). Moreover, the proposal defines the standard binding of both C++, Java and Smalltalk to the ODBMS, showing how ODL and OQL can be invoked from within an application program. OQL has been designed in such a way that its syntax is compatible with that of the SQL standard in the hope that SQL3 and OQL will converge in the future. We next give two examples of data definitions in ODL.

An example of creating a type PERSON is given by the ODL statement:

```
class PERSON
        (extent persons
         key name) {
        attribute string name;
        attribute set<string> nick-names;
        attribute struct Address
                {string street, string city, string postcode} address;
        attribute enum sex {male, female};
        relationship PERSON married_to;
        relationship set<CHILD> children
            inverse CHILD :: parent; };
```

The keyword **class** indicates that a type definition, i.e. schema definition, follows. The class specifies the characteristics of the objects of the type that are visible to users of the objects. The keyword **extent** declares a name given to the current collection of objects of the type in the database. The ODMG object model distinguishes between *literals* which are constants that do not have object identifiers such as the atomic literals **string** and **integer**, and *objects* having unique identifiers which are retained throughout their lifetime. The keyword **key** is followed by a list of candidate keys for the type, whose scope is the extent of the type. The keywords **attribute** and **relationship** allow users to model the state of objects in terms of the properties they possess. An attribute is defined over a single type while a relationship is defined between two types. Attribute types are literals, namely atomic literals, collection literals such as **set<string>**, structured literals having a record format such as Address or an enumeration of literals such as sex; ODL also supports the built-in structured literals **date, interval, time** and **timestamp**. In a relationship the keyword **set** indicates that a set of objects are associated with any object of the defined type. For example, in the relationship children a person may have zero or more children, and in the relationship married_to a person can be married to at most one other person. The keyword **inverse** allows the user to traverse a relationship in the opposite direction; for example, parent is the inverse relationship of children. Operations can also be defined as part of the class; such operations specify the behaviour of objects.

An example of creating a type EMPLOYEE as a subtype of PERSON is given by the ODL statement:

```
class EMPLOYEE extends PERSON
    (extent employees) {
    attribute integer salary;
    attribute string location;
    relationship DEPARTMENT works_in
        inverse DEPARTMENT :: employs;
    relationship set<PROJECT> involved_in
        inverse PROJECT :: has_staff; };
```

As a subtype of PERSON, the type EMPLOYEE inherits all the attributes and relationships which have been defined for PERSON.

Finally, we give some examples of queries in OQL. The OQL query

```
SELECT struct(name: p.name, address: p.address)
FROM persons p
WHERE p.sex = 'male' AND COUNT(p.children) > 1
```

retrieves into a structure the names and addresses of persons who are male and have more than one child. We note the use of the aggregate function COUNT.

The OQL query

```
SELECT p.married_to.address.postcode
FROM persons p
WHERE p.address.city = 'London'
```

retrieves the postcodes of spouses of people who live in London. An expression using the *dot notation* of the form, *p*.married_to.address.postcode, is called a *path expression*. Path expressions provide us with a means to navigate from an object to the data item we are interested in. In this example the path expression, *p*.married_to.address.postcode, results in the postcode of the address of the person married to *p*. We note that in the relational model such a query would involve a join of persons with itself assuming the relationship married_to was modelled by a foreign key attribute in PERSON.

The OQL query

```
SELECT p.name
FROM employees.involved_in p
WHERE p.has_staff.works_in.name = 'Computer Science'
```

retrieves the names of projects of employees working in the Computer Science department, assuming that PROJECT and DEPARTMENT both have an attribute called name.

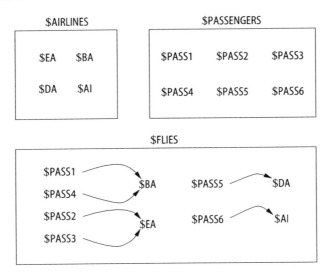

Fig 10.3 Part of a passengers and airlines hypernode database

10.3 Graph-Based Databases

One of the important measures of performance of a database system is user productivity. With the growing demand for complex object databases, as discussed in Sections 10.1 and 10.2, there is a need for database user interfaces which are easier to use and which represent the data in a more intuitive way. This need is accentuated in view of the availability of more sophisticated query languages for complex objects and the ability to express recursion in query languages as in Datalog. One way to address the problem is to base the data model on graph theory in the hope that its visual representation will closely match its intuitive semantics. Such a graph-based data model is built upon the traditional network and hierarchical data models which were presented in Subsections 1.7.2 and 1.7.3 of Chapter 1. Thus in addition to having a natural user interface a graph-based data model can address the problem of representing complex objects.

Here we give a summary of the *hypernode* data model, which supports object identity and arbitrarily complex objects [LPB+93, PL94, LL95b]. Rather than having a single database digraph, a hypernode database consists of a finite set of interconnected digraphs, called hypernodes; see Section 2.1 of Chapter 2 for the definition of a digraph. More specifically, a hypernode is an equation of the form G = (N, E) such that (N, E) is its digraph and G is its unique defining label.

In Figure 10.3 we illustrate part of a simple hypernode database, which models a simple airline reservation system. The hypernode, whose defining label is $AIRLINES, contains the defining labels of other hypernodes which describe the various airlines, and the hypernode, whose defining label is $PASSENGERS, contains the defining labels of other hypernodes which describe the booking information pertaining to passengers. The hypernode with defining label $FLIES represents a relationship telling us with which airline a particular passenger is flying. We note that labels are denoted by strings beginning with "$".

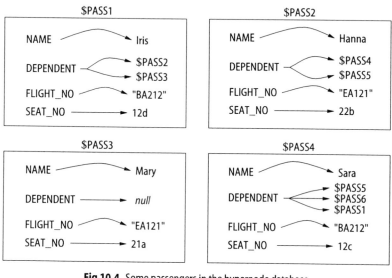

Fig 10.4 Some passengers in the hypernode database

In Figure 10.4 we show the details of some of the passenger hypernodes. Given an arc (u, v) in such a hypernode, we call u the *anchor* of the arc and v its *destination*. The anchor, u, denotes an attribute name and the destination, v, denotes an atomic value (which is an attribute value). We note that attribute names are denoted by strings of uppercase letters possibly containing the underscore character, and atomic values are denoted either by strings containing at least one lowercase letter, or by strings surrounded by double quotes.

We observe that the attribute name DEPENDENT in a passenger hypernode is used to reference other passengers who in some unspecified way depend on this passenger; for example, $PASS2 and $PASS3 may depend on $PASS1 to drive them to the airport. These references between hypernodes can be viewed conceptually as a part-of relationship or alternatively as encapsulating the data represented in the referenced hypernodes. We use the distinguished atomic value *null* to indicate that a "value exists but is unknown". We note that we can also model incomplete information of the type "value does not exist" by isolated attribute names. For example, if we delete the arc (DEPENDENT, *null*) and the node *null* from the digraph of the hypernode, whose defining label is $PASS3, our interpretation changes from "$PASS3 has a DEPENDENT which is unknown" to "there does not exist a DEPENDENT of $PASS3". This interpretation of isolated attribute names corresponds to the *Closed World Assumption* (CWA), which was discussed in Section 5.2 of Chapter 5.

We assume the following two disjoint countable domains of constants are available. Firstly we have a domain of *Labels* L whose elements are denoted by strings beginning with a "$" (when no ambiguity arises we also use the uppercase letter G to denote a label). Secondly we have a domain of *Primitive nodes* **P** which is partitioned into two disjoint domains one of *Atomic Values*, **AV**, and the other of *Attribute Names* (or simply attributes), **AN**. We denote atomic values either by strings containing at least one lowercase letter, or by strings surrounded by double quotes, and we denote attributes by strings of uppercase letters possibly containing the underscore character. We also assume that the domain of atomic values **AV** contains a distinguished value *null* meaning "value exists but is unknown".

Definition 10.11 (Hypernode)   A *hypernode* is an equation of the form

$$G = (N, E),$$

where $G \in L$ is termed the *defining label* of the hypernode (or simply the label of the hypernode when no ambiguity arises) and (N, E) is a digraph, termed *the digraph of the hypernode* (or simply the digraph of G), such that $N \subseteq (L \cup P)$.   ∎

We use the following terminology for a digraph (N, E). An arc $(u, v) \in E$ is said to be *incident* with each of its two nodes u and v. We also say that u is *adjacent to* v and that v is *adjacent from u*. The *indegree* of a node $u \in N$ is the number of nodes adjacent to u and the *outdegree* of u is the number of nodes adjacent from u. A node with no incident arcs is said to be *isolated*.

We impose the following three syntactic restrictions on the arcs of a hypernode, $G = (N, E)$:

E1 the indegree of nodes $u \in (AN \cap N)$, i.e. of nodes that are attributes, is zero;

E2 the outdegree of nodes $u \in (AV \cap N)$, i.e. of nodes that are atomic values, is zero; and

E3 if $(u, v) \in E$ and $u \in (L \cap N)$, i.e. the anchor node of the arc is a label, then $v \in (L \cap N)$, i.e. the destination node of the arc is also a label.

In order to explain the motivation behind the above restrictions we recall the ER model described in Chapter 2, which asserts that the real world can be described by *entities* (or objects which in our case are hypernodes), which are in turn represented by a set of attributes and their values, and by *relationships* between entities.

We observe that an arc set of a digraph can be viewed as a (binary) relation on the nodes which are incident on its arcs. Thus, the semantics of restriction E1 are that attributes cannot be in the range of the relation induced by the arc set. Furthermore, an arc whose anchor is an attribute represents an attribute-value pair (i.e. a property) whose destination node is its value, the value being either an atomic value or a label. Thus, when an arc is incident with an attribute this attribute must be the anchor of the arc. The semantics of restriction E2 are that atomic values cannot be in the domain of the relation defined by the arc set. Thus, when an arc is incident with an atomic value this value must be the destination of the arc. Finally, the semantics of restriction E3 are that when a label (which is an anchor) is in the domain of the relation defined by the arc set, then the destination node of an arc incident with the said anchor is also a label. That is, this arc represents a relationship between two hypernodes, i.e. between two objects. Thus, a relationship between two hypernodes can be represented by an arc which is incident with their defining labels. We observe that conceptually this kind of relationship can be viewed as a *referential* relationship.

It can easily be verified that the hypernodes shown in Figures 10.3 and 10.4 satisfy restrictions E1, E2 and E3. As was discussed above these hypernodes model part of a simple airline reservation system detailing information about passengers and indicating with which airline a particular passenger is flying. We note that each arc in the hypernode with the defining label $FLIES in Figure 10.3 represents a referential relationship and that each arc in the passenger hypernodes of Figure 10.4 represents an attribute-value pair.

Definition 10.12 (Hypernode database)   A *hypernode database* (or simply a database), say HD, is a finite set of hypernodes satisfying the following two conditions:

H1 no two (distinct) hypernodes in HD have the same defining label; and

H2 for any label, say G, in the node set of a digraph of a hypernode in HD there exists a hypernode in HD whose defining label is G.   ∎

We note that condition H1 above corresponds to the *entity integrity* requirement of the relational model, since each hypernode can viewed as representing a real-world entity. In object-oriented terminology labels are unique and serve as system-wide object identifiers, assuming that all of the hypernodes known to the system are stored in a single database. Similarly, condition H2 corresponds to the *referential integrity* requirement of the relational model, since it requires that only existing entities be referenced. This implies that a relationship between two hypernodes can also be represented in terms of a reference from one hypernode to the other (rather than a reference via an arc between two labels in the digraph of a hypernode). We observe that conceptually this kind of relationship can be viewed as a *part-of* relationship, which provides the hypernode model with inherent support for data encapsulation. (See Subsection 3.6.1 of Chapter 3 for the definitions of entity and referential integrity.)

It can easily be verified that the hypernodes shown in Figures 10.3 and 10.4 comprise a portion of a hypernode database (if we add hypernodes for $PASS5, $PASS6, $EA, $BA, $DA and $AI, whose node sets do not include any new labels, we would then have a database satisfying conditions H1 and H2). We note that by condition H1 each hypernode representing one of the objects in the database has a unique label. Furthermore, the defining labels of the passenger hypernodes are part-of the hypernode with the defining label $PASSENGERS. Thus, by condition H2 there must be one hypernode in the database for each passenger.

The *Hypernode Accessibility Graph* (HAG) of a hypernode G = (N, E) ∈ HD (or simply the HAG of G, whenever HD is understood from context) is the digraph telling us which hypernodes in HD are part-of (or encapsulated in) the hypernode with the defining label G, when considering part-of as a transitive relationship.

Definition 10.13 (Hypernode accessibility graph)   The HAG of G, denoted by (N_G, E_G), is the minimal digraph which is constructed from hypernodes in HD as follows:

1) $G \in N_G$, and G is a distinguished node called the *root* of (N_G, E_G), and

2) if $G' \in N_G$ and $G' = (N', E') \in HD$ (such a hypernode must exist by condition H2), then $(L \cap N') \subseteq N_G$ and $\forall u' \in (L \cap N'), (G', u') \in E_G$.   ∎

The HAG of G can be viewed as describing a *composite object* [Kim90]. We note that, in general, the HAG of G may be cyclic. In Figure 10.5 we illustrate the HAG of $PASS1, where the hypernode with defining label $PASS1 is shown in Figure 10.4. We note that the HAG of $PASS1 is cyclic and thus $PASS4 is part-of $PASS1 and $PASS1 is part-of $PASS4, indicating that $PASS1 and $PASS4 depend on each other.

We note that we have assumed that hypernodes are untyped, i.e. we do not put any further constraints on the structure of hypernodes. Thus, hypernodes are dynamic in the sense that nodes and arcs in hypernodes can be updated subject only to all of the above syntactic restrictions. In this approach we do not classify entities according to the entity set to which they belong but rather consider entities to be *classless* (see [Ull91]), i.e. belonging to a single set of entities. In particular, all the available hypernodes are members of a single database.

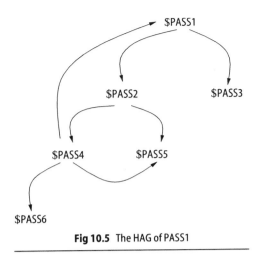

Fig 10.5 The HAG of PASS1

We now briefly illustrate a procedural query and update language for the hypernode model, called *HyperNode Query Language* (HNQL). For this purpose we assume a countable domain of variables denoted by strings beginning with uppercase letters from the end of the alphabet followed by a natural number; the domain of variables is disjoint from the domains of labels and primitive nodes. Variables in HNQL are untyped, i.e. their values range over the union of the domains of labels and primitive nodes. Although variables in HNQL are untyped there is a provision for adding a type checking component to HNQL, whose semantics we now briefly describe. The hypernode model can utilise a typing system based on the structural similarity of graphs. Simply, types of hypernode enforce the allowable structure of hypernodes to be instances of those types. For example, instances cannot contain types of nodes or arcs not contained in their type definitions. More formally, we say that there must exist a homomorphism from nodes in the instance to nodes in the type definition which maps each node in the instance to a node in the type definition, and each arc in the instance to an arc in the type definition, while preserving the adjacency of the nodes in the arcs of the instance. Typing gives us a means of defining database schemas and of enforcing further constraints on the structure and content of hypernodes. A formal investigation of how to declare hypernode types and how to type check hypernodes can be found in [PL94]. For the purpose of this section it is sufficient to assume that if a type is associated with a hypernode in the database then that hypernode must conform to its type.

We introduce the flavour of HNQL via two simple examples but first give the meaning of the relevant HNQL operators and predicates. We assume that HD is a hypernode database and that all the operators we define are to be evaluated with respect to HD. We denote by LABELS(HD) the set of labels appearing in the hypernodes of HD. We also assume that the label $NULL $\notin$ LABELS(HD) is reserved in order to return an error code when necessary. Notationally, we will use strings beginning with the lowercase letter, v, to denote either a label or a primitive node and strings beginning with the uppercase letter G to denote labels only.

The following five operators update hypernodes in HD:

1) insert_node(G, v) returns G if G = (N, E) $\in$ HD, and as a side effect v is inserted into N, i.e. N := N $\cup$ {v}; otherwise $NULL is returned.

2) delete_node(G, v) returns G if G = (N, E) $\in$ HD and $\forall v' \in$ N there is no arc $(v, v') \in$ E or $(v', v) \in$ E, and as a side effect v is deleted from N, i.e. N := N $-$ $\{v\}$; otherwise $NULL is returned.

3) insert_arc(G, v_1, v_2) returns G if G = (N, E) $\in$ HD and v_1, $v_2 \in$ N, and as a side effect (v_1, v_2) is inserted into E, i.e. E := E $\cup$ (v_1, v_2); otherwise $NULL is returned.

4) delete_arc(G, v_1, v_2) returns G if G = (N, E) $\in$ HD and $(v_1, v_2) \in$ E, and as a side effect (v_1, v_2) is deleted from E, i.e. E := E $-$ (v_1, v_2); otherwise $NULL is returned.

5) rename_node(G_{old}, G_{new}) returns G_{new} if $G_{old} \in$ LABELS(HD) and $G_{new} \notin$ LABELS(HD), and as a side effect all occurrences of G_{old} in the hypernodes of HD are replaced with G_{new}; otherwise $NULL is returned.

The following two operators add or remove hypernodes from HD:

1) create() returns an arbitrary new label G such that G $\notin$ (LABELS(HD) $\cup$ {$NULL}), and as a side effect G = ($\emptyset$, $\emptyset$) is added to HD, i.e. HD := HD $\cup$ {G = ($\emptyset$, $\emptyset$)}.

2) destroy(G) returns the label G if G = (N, E) $\in$ HD and for no hypernode G' = (N', E') $\in$ HD is it true that G $\in$ N', and as a side effect G = (N, E) is removed from HD, i.e. HD := HD $-$ {G = (N, E)}; otherwise $NULL is returned.

The following three predicates provide membership tests for a node, an arc or a defining label in HD:

1) $v \in$ nodes(G) returns true if G = (N, E) $\in$ HD and $v \in$ N; otherwise false is returned.

2) $(v_1, v_2) \in$ arcs(G) returns true if G = (N, E) $\in$ HD and $(v_1, v_2) \in$ E; otherwise false is returned.

3) G $\in$ db() returns true if G = (N, E) $\in$ HD; otherwise false is returned.

We also allow the two equality tests: $v_1 = v_2$ for nodes and $(v_1, v_2) = (v_3, v_4)$ for arcs, which return true or false as the case may be.

We define a *simple condition* to be either a membership test or an equality test. A *condition* is now defined to be either a simple condition, the parenthesising of a condition used for grouping purposes, the negation of a condition, say *cond*, denoted by !*cond*, or the conjunction of two conditions, say $cond_1$ and $cond_2$, denoted by $cond_1$&$cond_2$.

The following three nondeterministic operators can be used to arbitrarily choose a node, an arc or a defining label in HD:

1) any_node(G) returns an arbitrary node $v \in$ N if G = (N, E) $\in$ HD and N $\neq \emptyset$; otherwise $NULL is returned.

2) any_arc(G) returns an arbitrary arc $(v_1, v_2) \in$ E if G = (N, E) $\in$ HD and E $\neq \emptyset$; otherwise ($NULL, $NULL) is returned.

3) any_label() returns an arbitrary label G such that G = (N, E) $\in$ HD, if HD $\neq \emptyset$; otherwise $NULL is returned.

We assume that all variables in HNQL have a current value, which is either a label or a primitive node; these are always initialised to have the value $NULL. Thus, we extend our earlier notation to allow strings beginning with the letters *v* or G to denote the current value of a variable when appropriate. We now define an *assignment* statement to be an expression of the form

$$lvalue := rvalue,$$

where *lvalue* is a variable or a pair of variables, and *rvalue* is a constant, or a variable, or any of the possible pairs of these two, or one of the HNQL operators defined so far.

The semantics of an assignment statement are that the current value of *lvalue* becomes the result of evaluating *rvalue* on the current state of the hypernode database, HD (and possibly updating HD as a side effect). We note that evaluating a constant on HD returns the constant itself and that evaluating a variable on HD returns its current value. We assume that if the assignment is undefined, for example, when trying to assign a pair of constants to a variable, or a constant to a pair of variables, then *lvalue* is assigned the value $NULL or ($NULL, $NULL), respectively.

HNQL statements are composed sequentially using the semi-colon symbol as a statement separator. The keywords **TB** and **TE** denote transaction begin and transaction end, respectively. They serve to delimit compound statements in analogy to the *begin* and *end* keywords in Pascal. The for loop, beginning with the keyword **for_all**, provides HNQL with a bounded looping mechanism (see Section 6.7 in Chapter 6 for a discussion on looping constructs). HNQL also has available an unbounded looping mechanism beginning with the keywords **while changes do**, which repeatedly executes a given compound statement on the current state of the hypernode database HD until no further changes are effected on the current state of HD.

The first example is an HNQL program, shown below, that selects the names of passengers who are flying on flight number "BA212" and puts them into a new hypernode whose label is $RESULT.

```
1.   X1 := create();
2.   X2 := rename(X1, $RESULT);
3.   X2 := insert_node($RESULT, NAME);
4.   for_all X1 ∈ nodes($PASSENGERS) do
5.     if (FLIGHT_NO, "BA212") ∈ arcs(X1) then
6.       for_all (Y1, Y2) ∈ arcs(X1) do
7.       TB
8.         if Y1 = NAME then
9.         TB
10.          X2 := insert_node($RESULT, Y2);
11.          X2 := insert_arc($RESULT, NAME, Y2);
12.        TE
13.      TE
```

The second example is an HNQL program, shown below, that modifies flight number "BA212" to "BA345" for all passengers in the database.

```
1.  for_all X1 ∈ nodes($PASSENGERS) do
2.      for_all (Y1, Y2) ∈ arcs(X1) do
3.      TB
4.      if (Y1, Y2) = (FLIGHT_NO, "BA212") then
5.          TB
6.              X2 := delete_arc(X1, Y1, Y2);
7.              X2 := delete_node(X1, Y2);
8.              X2 := insert_node(X1, "BA345");
9.              X2 := insert_arc(X1, Y1, "BA345");
10.         TE
11.     TE
```

The details of the semantics of HNQL programs can be found in [LL95b] and a detailed description of a rule-based counterpart of HNQL, called Hyperlog, can be found in [PL94]. In [LL95b] and [PL94], respectively, it was shown that HNQL and Hyperlog are query complete languages (see Section 6.5 of Chapter 6 for the definition of query completeness).

We next summarise the main features of the hypernode model; it is based on a nested graph structure which is simple and formal. In addition, it has the ability to model arbitrary complex objects in a straightforward manner. Moreover, the hypernode can provide the underlying data structure of an object-oriented data model. Finally, hypernodes can enhance the usability of a complex objects database system via a graph-based user interface.

Apart from the hypernode model there have been several other proposals for graph-based data models. The earliest proposals for graph-based formalisms were the network and hierarchical data models which were presented in Subsections 1.7.2 and 1.7.3 of Chapter 1. These data models were not designed to solve the usability problem for database systems but rather addressed fundamental data modelling issues which were unresolved at the time. As a result, the potential visual representation of these data models was not utilised to the full through the development of user-friendly interfaces for them. Moreover, the network and hierarchical data models are not fully data independent and thus do not have the flexibility that the hypernode model has in modifying the structure of the database. An early proposal for a graph-based data model as a user interface, which incorporates semantic notions into the relational model, can be found in [Bor80].

A digraph can easily be represented in the relational model as a binary relation. An interesting proposal, which builds on this fact, is to extend SQL with the ability to query such binary relations [BRS90]. More specifically, SQL is extended with an appropriate syntax such that the set of all paths in a digraph that satisfy a given condition can be queried.

A recent data model, called *Logical Data Model* (LDM), which caters for arbitrary complex objects through tuple, set and disjoint union type constructors, is described in [KV93]. LDM comes equipped with a query language based on first-order logic which has an equivalent counterpart algebra. LDM can be viewed as an object-oriented generalisation of the relational, network and hierarchical data models.

More recent proposals for graph-based data models are *Graph-Oriented Object Database* (GOOD) [GPV90, PVA+92], GraphLog [CM90, CCM92, CM93] and *Multimedia Object Retrieval Environment* (MORE) [LZ96]. In all of these models the database consists of a

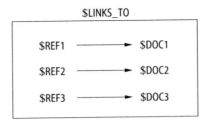

Fig 10.6 Modelling labelled arcs in the hypernode model

single digraph, as opposed to a hypernode database which consists of a finite set of digraphs. This unique feature of the hypernode model permits data encapsulation and the ability to represent each real-world object in the database separately.

GOOD generalises the functional data model [Shi81] by expressing both the database schema and the database instance as a digraph and by the provision of a graph-based query language. GOOD embeds semantics into the nodes and arcs of the database digraph, nodes being printable or non-printable and arcs being single-valued or multi-valued. GOOD's query language is based on the notion of a *pattern*. Patterns are matched against the database digraph and return subgraphs of the database digraph that correspond to the patterns.

Graphlog is a query language operating on a database digraph which corresponds to a semantic network [Gri82]. The arcs in this digraph represent predicates. Graphlog queries are formulated as digraphs whose arcs are annotated with predicates, transitive closures thereof or, more generally, regular expressions. These query digraphs are matched against the database digraph and return subgraphs thereof.

Both GOOD and Graphlog label their arcs. This is a useful facility which allows us to express relationships between nodes. Arc labelling can be modelled in the hypernode model by including all the arcs which have the same label in a single hypernode whose defining label is the common label of the arcs. For example, the set of labelled arcs

$$\$REF1 \rightarrow^{\$LINKS\_TO} \$DOC1$$
$$\$REF2 \rightarrow^{\$LINKS\_TO} \$DOC2$$
$$\$REF3 \rightarrow^{\$LINKS\_TO} \$DOC3$$

are represented by the hypernode shown in Figure 10.6.

We conclude this section by mentioning another graph-based data model, called *Graph Storage System* (GRAS), whose data structure comprises *attribute graphs* [LS88]. Attribute graphs are digraphs whose nodes represent objects which may have attached attributes, and whose labelled arcs represent binary relationships between objects. In GRAS paths in attribute graphs represent derived relations. GRAS comes equipped with a query language, called *Programmed Graph Rewriting System* (PROGRESS), whose semantics are defined in terms of graph transformations [Sch90]. The basic building blocks of graph transformations are *subgraph tests* and *graph rewriting rules*. Subgraph tests are conditions which test the occurrence of a subgraph within the database digraph, and graph rewriting rules are graph transformations which search for certain subgraphs within the database digraph and replace each such subgraph with another one. Subgraph tests and graph rewriting rules are composed into complex graph transformations via *control flow diagrams*.

10.4   Active Databases

So far we have assumed that the database system is *passive*, i.e. queries and updates to the database are submitted to the system via users and application programs. Consider the example of an inventory control system, where items need to be reordered when the stock falls below a critical quantity. In a passive database an application program needs to be written that polls the database periodically to check the various stock levels and to initiate a reordering process when appropriate. Such an application program is *active* in the sense that the program initiates an action when the environment is in a certain state; in the case of the inventory control system when the stock is low. The problems in writing a specific program for each active application are:

- If the polling is frequent then the program may be inefficient, on the other hand if the polling is not frequent enough then the program might not react at the correct time.

- A different program needs to be implemented for each active application, so the maintenance of such software is expensive.

- Active applications have some common semantics, which can be catered for in a uniform and efficient way by the DBMS.

The solution to this problem is to make the database system *active* by adding to it a component which polls the database for certain specified *events* and *acts* when appropriate *conditions* are satisfied. Such *production rules* are known as *Event-Condition-Action rules* (or simply ECA rules or just rules).

An important application for active databases is that of enforcing integrity constraints [CW90]. As an example, suppose that employees' salaries have an upper limit. Then an ECA rule can prevent any update to an employee's salary, which exceeds the limit. Similarly, entity and referential integrity can be efficiently implemented by using appropriate ECA rules. Another significant application is that of incremental maintenance of user views [CW91], which is a proposed solution to the view update problem discussed in Section 3.8 of Chapter 3.

We present an active database model which extends the relational model by adding to it a production rule language. A *program* in this language is a set of ECA rules. We now elaborate on the notions of event, condition and action.

An *event* is a change in the database state which occurs asynchronously, as a result of an update operation (insert, delete or modify; see Subsection 3.2.4 of Chapter 3 for the semantics of updates). The update operation is part of a transaction against the database. Other database operations such as transaction *commit* and transaction *abort* are also considered to be events (see Chapter 8 for the semantics of these operations).

The above events are *primitive* and can be used to form *composite* events by taking the disjunction of two events, the negation of an event and the sequential composition of two events. An *event* can now be either primitive or composite.

Informally, a composite event maps an event history to another event history that contains only the events that are satisfied according to the manner in which the composite event was constructed. An *event history* is a sequence of primitive events, i.e. it is a linear ordering of primitive events.

More specifically, let $\mathcal{H}$ be an event history. The meaning of a disjunction of two events e_1 and e_2 with respect to $\mathcal{H}$ is the largest subset of $\mathcal{H}$ such that either e_1 or e_2 occur in this subset. The meaning of the negation of an event e with respect to $\mathcal{H}$ is the largest subset of $\mathcal{H}$ such that e does not occur in this subset. The meaning of the sequential composition of event e_1 and event e_2 with respect to $\mathcal{H}$ is the largest subset of $\mathcal{H}$ such that e_1 occurs before e_2 in this subset. Thus if the meaning of an event e with respect to $\mathcal{H}$ is $\mathcal{H}$ itself then $\mathcal{H}$ *satisfies e*.

An event is a regular expression and thus a finite automaton can be constructed that accepts an event history if and only if this history satisfies the event. A formal treatment of composite events can be found in [GJS92] (See Subsection 1.9.4 in Chapter 1 for the formal definition of regular expressions and finite automata).

A *condition* is an integrity constraint (specified as a relational algebra expression, or alternatively, an SQL query) that must be satisfied, i.e. be nonempty or equivalently true, with respect to a database state. A mechanism is available which allows the relations in a condition to refer either to the database state prior to the occurrence of an event or after the occurrence of an event; by default it is assumed that the current database state is the state of the database after an event has occurred. Apart from data dependencies, such as functional dependencies and inclusion dependencies, conditions can express transition constraints; for example, stating that an employee's salary always increases with years of service.

An *action* specifies an update operation to be carried out on the current database state. Most production rule languages allow more general actions such as specifying a *rollback* operation to abort the current transaction. Since an action may be an update operation, it may *trigger* other ECA rules, which in turn may trigger further ECA rules.

The syntax of an ECA rule is:

> **ON** *Event occurrence*
> **IF** *database state satisfies Condition*
> **THEN** *execute Action*

The semantics of an ECA rule are that when the event specified in the ON clause occurs, then the rule is *activated*. Thereafter, if the condition specified in the IF clause is satisfied with respect to the database state after the update associated with the event is carried out on the current database state, then the action specified in the THEN clause is executed. In the THEN clause we can refer to the database state prior to the occurrence of the event by using the keyword **previous**. When a rule is activated the process of checking the IF part of the rule and executing the THEN part when appropriate will be referred to as *firing* the rule.

We give several examples, using an informal update syntax and a database comprising two relations the first over EMPLOYEE, with schema(EMPLOYEE) = {ENAME, DNAME, SALARY}, and the second over DEPARTMENT, with schema(DEPARTMENT) = {DNAME, MGR}.

The first example specifies that an employee's salary cannot decrease.

> **ON modify to** EMPLOYEE.SALARY
> **IF** EMPLOYEE.SALARY < **previous** EMPLOYEE.SALARY
> **THEN rollback**

The second example specifies that if a department's name is modified then the corresponding name in the tuples of the employee relation is also changed to the new name.

> **ON modify to** DEPARTMENT.DNAME
> **IF** EMPLOYEE.DNAME = **previous** DEPARTMENT.DNAME
> **THEN** modify EMPLOYEE.DNAME = DEPARTMENT.DNAME

The third example specifies that if an employee who is also a manager is fired then the manager of the department managed by that employee becomes unknown.

> **ON delete from** EMPLOYEE
> **IF** DEPARTMENT.MGR = **previous** EMPLOYEE.ENAME
> **THEN modify** DEPARTMENT.MGR = unk

Let P be a program, i.e. a finite set of ECA rules. In general, the events of different ECA rules are *not* mutually exclusive, so it is possible that two or more rules are activated at any given time. In order to resolve such conflicts the rules in P can either be ordered and then the activated rules are executed according to this predefined order, or alternatively the activated rules can be executed concurrently.

The semantics of processing a program P, with respect to a set of integrity constraints I and a database state d, are presented in the following algorithm.

Algorithm 10.3 (EXE(P, I, d))
1. **begin**
2.   prev := d;
3.   **while** at least one rule in P is activated **do**
4.   **let** S be the set of all the activated rules in P;
5.   deactivate all the rules in S;
6.   fire all the rules in S concurrently;
7.   **if** the current state of d does **not** satisfy I **then**
8.   **return** prev;
9.   **end if**
10.   **end while**
11.   **return** the current state of d;
12. **end.**

We note that, in general, EXE(P, I, d) may not terminate, since, for example, one rule may delete a certain tuple from a relation and another rule may insert the same tuple into this relation. In the special case that none of the actions of any of the rules in P change the active domain of the database and actions involve only insertions then termination is guaranteed, since the current state of d is monotonically increasing towards a fixpoint.

We can construct a digraph for a program P, called the *triggering graph* of P, such that the nodes of the digraph are the rules in P and there is an arc from one rule to another rule if the first rule can trigger the second one. In this case it can be shown that if the triggering graph of P is acyclic then EXE(P, I, d) always terminates [AWH92]. When the triggering graph is cyclic then, in general, we cannot decide whether EXE(P, I, d) will terminate or not.

More details on the semantics of rule evaluation can be found in [HJ91, WCL91, SKdM92].

It is also possible to specify different *coupling modes* for a given ECA rule, which determine the timing of the execution of the rule relative to the database transaction, say T, that caused the event in the ON clause of the rule to be activated. EC-coupling mode determines when the condition specified in the IF clause of the rule is tested for satisfaction relative to T. Correspondingly, CA-coupling determines when the action of the THEN part of the rule is executed relative to T. Two possible coupling modes are:

1) *immediate* — test the condition, respectively execute the action, immediately when the event occurs even if T has not terminated; and

2) *deferred* — test the condition, respectively execute the action, only after T has terminated.

More on the different execution models can be found in [MD89, GJ91, SPAM91] including a third coupling mode in which the condition, respectively the action, is evaluated in transactions which are separate from T.

An important application of production rules is that of integrity constraint maintenance [CW90]. Assume that an update is made to the current database state and that a set of integrity constraints I needs to be enforced. Furthermore, we assume that the database is always required to be in a consistent state. A constraint $\alpha \in I$ may be an FD (for entity integrity maintenance), an IND (for referential integrity maintenance), a domain dependency, or any other type of constraint. Now, if the state of the database, after the update has been carried out, is inconsistent, i.e. α or any other constraint in I is violated, then what actions should the database system initiate in order to "repair" the database state, i.e. to transform it into a consistent state, namely into one that satisfies α and all the other constraints in I. The standard approach is to rollback the database into a consistent state and then abort the transaction which updated the database. An alternative approach, which uses production rules, is to allow the definition of ECA rules whose actions automatically correct the inconsistency by transforming the database into a consistent state.

For example, if we are maintaining entity integrity and a key dependency is violated, for example due to an insertion of a new EMPLOYEE tuple with an existing primary key, then the action can be to delete the offending tuple from the EMPLOYEE relation thus maintaining consistency. As another example, if we are maintaining referential integrity and a key-based IND is violated, for example due to the insertion of a new EMPLOYEE tuple whose department is nonexistent, then the action can be to insert a tuple having the new department name and an unknown manager into the DEPARTMENT relation thus maintaining consistency.

It is shown in [CW90] that for a general class of integrity constraints, defined as SQL queries, *rule templates* can be automatically derived which assist the user in defining the necessary ECA rules needed in order to maintain such integrity constraints. Each rule template enumerates the update operations and conditions that may cause the constraint to be violated, thus forming the ON and IF clauses of a potential ECA rule.

Another important application of production rules is that of incremental view maintenance [CW91]. Assume that a view is a relation that is defined as the result of a relational algebra query (or equivalently, an SQL query); we refer to this query as the *view definition*.

Views may be *materialised*, i.e. they are physically stored in the database, or *virtual*, i.e. they are computed each time the user poses a query over them; we assume that views are materialised. The view maintenance problem is the problem of correctly updating the view when an update is performed on one of the relations of the database (called a *base relation*) that is referenced in the query that forms the view. A simple but inefficient solution is to completely rematerialise the view. Consequently an efficient way of dealing with this problem is to update only those portions of the view that have been changed due to the update carried out on the base relation. In other words, we need to formulate the necessary ECA rules that are activated by updates to the base relations such that when certain conditions are satisfied implying that the view needs to be updated, then the appropriate action, which corresponds to the update of the materialised view, is executed.

Suppose that the user has specified a set of key dependencies over the relation schemas of the base relations in the database and that a view has been defined. Let V be the set of attributes over the relation schema which defines the view. The set of attributes referenced by V, denoted by REF(V), is defined as the largest set of attributes that includes V and all attributes in the view definition that are equated to constants, and such that

1) if in the view definition an attribute A of a relation schema R_i is equated to an attribute in REF(V), then A $\in$ REF(V); and

2) if REF(V) includes a key for R_i, then schema(R_i) $\subseteq$ REF(V).

A base relation schema R_i is said to be *safe* in V if REF(V) includes a key, say K, for R_i.

It can now be shown that if d is a database and $r_i \in d$ is a base relation over R_i then insertions, deletions and modifications carried out on r_i can be reflected incrementally in the view, provided that R_i is safe in V. Consider an insertion of a new tuple t into r_i. Since t is not in r_i prior to the update, then $t[K]$ cannot be in the projection of the view onto K. Thus we insert into the view only the tuples resulting from applying the definition of the view to the database d, where $r_i \in d$ is replaced by $\{t\}$. A similar argument follows when the update is a deletion or a modification.

It follows that when R_i is safe in V, then for every update of a base relation r_i over R_i, an ECA rule can be automatically generated that incrementally reflects the update in the view. When R_i is not safe in V then, in general, only insertions can be updated incrementally, otherwise the view needs to be fully rematerialised.

Assume that ENAME is the primary key of EMPLOYEE and that DNAME is the primary key of DEPARTMENT; it follows that DNAME in EMPLOYEE is a foreign key referencing DNAME in DEPARTMENT and thus inducing a referential integrity constraint. Now, let EMP-MGR be a materialised view which is defined as the projection onto ENAME, DNAME and MGR of the join of EMPLOYEE and DEPARTMENT, i.e.

$$\pi_{\{ENAME, DNAME, MGR\}}(EMPLOYEE \bowtie DEPARTMENT).$$

It follows that REF(EMP-MGR) = {ENAME, DNAME, SALARY, MGR} and thus both EMPLOYEE and DEPARTMENT are safe in the view EMP-MGR. Now, suppose that we insert some new employee tuples. Then the generated ECA rule is given by

ON insert into EMPLOYEE
IF true
THEN insert into EMP-MGR
    where EMP-MGR.ENAME = **inserted** EMPLOYEE.ENAME AND
        EMP-MGR.DNAME = **inserted** EMPLOYEE.DNAME AND
        EMP-MGR.DNAME = DEPARTMENT.DNAME AND
        EMP-MGR.MGR = DEPARTMENT.MGR

where the keyword **inserted** means that we are only referring to the tuples that were inserted into the current state of the database. Note that when we insert a tuple into EMPLOYEE we use the DNAME in order to obtain the MGR of the DEPARTMENT. Next, suppose that a manager of a department is modified. Then the generated ECA rule is given by

ON modify DEPARTMENT.MGR
IF EMP-MGR.DNAME = **modified** DEPARTMENT.DNAME
THEN EMP-MGR.MGR = **modified** DEPARTMENT.MGR

where the keyword **modified** means that we are only referring to the modified tuples in the current state of the database. Note that the IF clause of the rule guarantees that the correct tuples are updated, since DNAME is the primary key of DEPARTMENT. Finally, suppose that an employee is deleted. Then the generated ECA rule is given by

ON delete from EMPLOYEE
IF EMP-MGR.ENAME = **deleted** EMPLOYEE.ENAME
THEN delete EMP-MGR

where the keyword **deleted** means that we are only referring to the tuples that were deleted from the current state of the database. Note that the IF clause of the rule guarantees that the correct tuples are deleted, since ENAME is the primary key of EMPLOYEE.

Overviews of active databases can be found in [Cha89, DD91, Han92, DHW95], and for a recent annotated bibliography of the subject see [JF95]. Finally, a recent collection of papers covering both the theory and applications of active databases can be found in [WC96].

10.5   Hypertext Databases

Traditional text which comes in book form is a linear sequence of words, defining the order in which the text should be read. In order to make the reading easier words are combined into sentences, sentences are combined into paragraphs, paragraphs into sections and sections into chapters. In addition, a table of contents and an index are normally supplied so as to help the reader find quickly some specific piece of information he/she is looking for without the need to read the whole document. It it also common in textbooks for the authors to provide a diagram, which we call a *chapter dependency diagram*, suggesting groups of chapters which should be read together in a certain order, according to a particular topic that they cover. For example, Figure 10.7 depicts a possible chapter dependency diagram for reading this book.

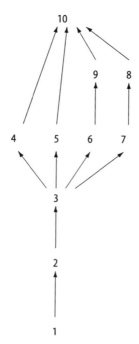

Fig 10.7 Chapter dependency diagram

A dependency diagram is a simple form of hypertext. Hypertext organises documents in a nonsequential (or nonlinear) order. It presents the reader with several different options of reading a document, the choice of how to read the document being made by the reader at the time of reading. Let us call a textual unit of information a *page*. A *hypertext database* consists of a set of pages which are *linked* together according to the author's specification. Thus a hypertext database is a digraph, where the nodes are the pages and the arcs are the links.

For example, Figure 10.8 shows a simple hypertext database consisting of five pages and several links between them. You can start reading (or *browsing*) the text at any page. Say you started at page P1. Once you have browsed through page P1 you have a choice either to go to page P2 or page P3. If you go to page P2, you then have the option of either going to page P4 or page P5. Assume you have chosen to go to page P4. Once you have finished browsing through page P4 you have a single option which is to go back to page P1. The process of traversing links and following a *trail* of information in a hypertext database is called *navigation* (or alternatively *link following*). Every link connects two nodes, the node we start at is called the *anchor* node (or simply the anchor) and the node we finish at is called the *destination* node (or simply the destination). Most hypertext systems will also have a *backtracking* facility which allows the reader to go back to the previously read page. In our example, we could backtrack from page P4 to page P2 and from page P2 back to page P1. Backtracking is useful since it allows the reader to reexamine pages and then to choose a different sequence of pages to follow, i.e. to choose a new trail of information to navigate through.

As another example, consider the *World Wide Web* (WWW), which is undoubtedly the largest hypertext database available [For94]. A lower bound of 320 million WWW pages has been recently estimated which is anticipated to grow ten-fold over the next few years [LG98].

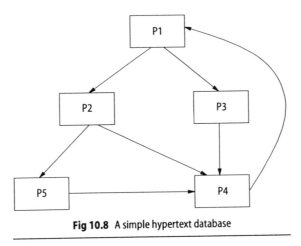

Fig 10.8 A simple hypertext database

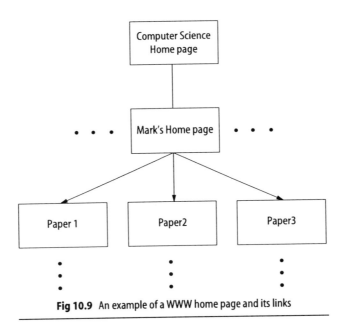

Fig 10.9 An example of a WWW home page and its links

Without going into any detail, each unit of information on the WWW is known as a resource, and each resource has a unique identifier describing where the resource resides and how to retrieve it. (The mechanism used is that of a *Unified Resource Locator*, or simply URL, which specifies the type of resource and a unique path for locating it.) Every WWW user has a *home page*, which is a hypertext page authored by the user, providing information and links created by the user. Thus the home page essentially connects the information provided by the user to the larger body of information available on the WWW, via the links that can be followed from the home page. Any other user *visiting* this home page can follow these links. Figure 10.9 shows how a home page is linked to other pages. In this example, Mark's home page is linked to the Computer Science home page and to several papers.

Authors of WWW pages can create document pages using the *Hypertext Markup Language* (HTML) [Aro94]. HTML provides the facilities for formatting a document, including images in documents, linking a document to other documents and interacting with user input through forms. A recent proposal of a markup language, which supersedes HTML, is the *Extensible Markup Language* (XML) [MFDG98]. XML is a metalanguage that allows you to design your own document types, with their individual structure, as opposed to HTML, which is a regular markup language in the sense that it defines a specific way of describing the information content of document pages. In particular, HTML caters for the report style document type with headings, paragraphs, lists and the like, with some provision for hypertext and hypermedia. XML allows you to customise the information according to the application, in order to cater for many classes of document where the markup is descriptive and the tags are more informative than just for formatting purposes as in HTML. (There is a large amount of online information on the WWW concerning XML and its recommended standard.)

Thus hypertext breaks the traditional view of text as a linear sequence of chapters, sections and paragraphs. In hypertext a document, or more generally a collection of documents, is organised as an arbitrary digraph of interlinked pages. Creating hypertext can be viewed as a dynamic process whereby readers can also take on the role of authors by adding their own pages and links to the database. The example of the WWW is very instructive in this case, since it can be viewed as a continuously evolving hypertext database.

Hypertext nodes are not, in general, restricted to contain text and may contain different multimedia objects such as graphics, sound and video. In this more general context hypertext has been called *hypermedia* but herein we will prefer the original term *hypertext*.

Hypertext is a vastly developing area, which has gained a lot of momentum in the last ten years. As mentioned above the WWW has created some real challenges for hypertext, since the need to efficiently organise and navigate through the rapidly growing volume of available information is quite urgent. Another impetus for hypertext is the current wide availability of CD-ROM (Compact Disk-Read Only Memory) as a hardware device for storing large amounts of text and multimedia data. For example, several encyclopaedias are available on CD-ROM for which hypertext provides the technology for organising and navigating through the information.

We now demonstrate that the hypernode model possesses a number of features which make it a natural candidate for being a formal model for hypertext. In order to do so we slightly extend the hypernode model by allowing arcs (i.e. links) to be labelled. The labels of links allow us to store meta-information about these links in hypernodes having these defining labels.

Firstly, a hypernode is a digraph structure with two built-in link types. The first link type is the arc representing a referential relationship and the second link type is the encapsulating label representing a part-of relationship. Furthermore, attributes allow us to give additional semantics to nodes in the node set of a hypernode, which can be considered to be properties of the hypernode to which the node set belongs. In fact, hypernodes can model arbitrary complex objects. In order to support text directly we can assume that the domain of atomic values is actually a domain of textual fragments over which full-text retrieval operations are possible; the domain of atomic values can readily be extended to accommodate any multimedia object. In Figure 10.10 we show part of a hypertext database, called PAPERS, which stores online papers from scientific journals. In particular, the figure shows an *overview diagram*

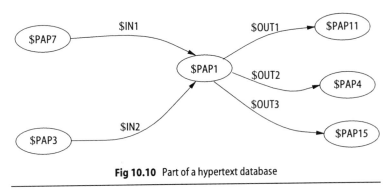

Fig 10.10 Part of a hypertext database

of the papers that are adjacent to $PAP1 (i.e. $PAP7 and $PAP3) and adjacent from $PAP1 (i.e. $PAP11, $PAP4 and $PAP15); we assume that $PAP1 is currently being browsed. The hypernodes encapsulated in $IN1, $IN2, $OUT1, $OUT2 and $OUT3 are *annotations* of links. An annotation of a link provides meta-information about the link such as the name of the creator of the link, the date it was created and the subject matter of the link (see Figure 10.11 for the details of the annotation $OUT1). In addition to the annotation $OUT1, Figure 10.11 shows the hypernode $PAP1, which is currently being browsed and two of its encapsulated hypernodes, $AUTH1 (showing the details of one of the authors of the paper) and $TEXT1 (which contains the actual text of the paper).

Secondly, the hypernode model can provide for browsing and declarative querying facilities via HNQL (more on database browsing in the context of the hypernode model can be found in [PL94]). HNQL can also cater for authoring via its update facilities. Finally, within the context of the hypernode model we can reason about integrity constraints in a hypertext database (in [LL95b] it was shown how functional dependencies can be incorporated into the hypernode model). In summary we view hypertext as a promising application of the hypernode model.

An important aspect of hypertext is that the reader be permitted to customise the presentation of the information in the database [Ash94]. The basic requirement is the ability to create *annotations* to the main text. Annotations are electronic footnotes, which contain some relevant piece of text created by the reader, that are accessed by a link from the main text. A more general requirement is to allow readers to create their own personal links between pages, inducing a personal nonlinear ordering on the database. Such a facility is important, since the built-in links may not be sufficient for the user's purposes.

Links can either be *hard* (equivalently *static*) or *soft* (equivalently *dynamic*). A hard link is one, which given the anchor node, explicitly specifies the address of the destination node. A soft link is one, which given the anchor node, implicitly specifies the address(es) of the destination node(s) via a *script* that computes the set of destination nodes at the time the link is followed. The advantage of soft links is that the addresses of the destination nodes are not fixed and thus the *dangling* link problem is avoided. A dangling link is one which is referencing a page at a nonexistent address.

The *stale URL problem* [Sto95] is the problem of a link pointing to a nonexistent URL, when the URL of a WWW page is modified but the link remains unchanged. In effect a stale URL is a dangling link. Current practice is to manually redirect the reader to the new URL by creating an additional page which contains a link to the new URL. A more attractive approach, suggested by Stotts [Sto95], is to provide the information about the new URL in an HTML file

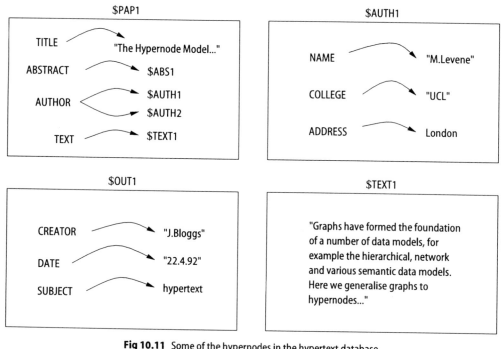

Fig 10.11 Some of the hypernodes in the hypertext database

which is periodically read by the browser instructing it to automatically redirect the link when it is accessed.

An attempt to formally describe the abstractions found in hypertext systems is the *Dexter hypertext reference model* (or simply the Dexter model), so named because it was originally proposed at a workshop which was held in 1988 at the Dexter Inn in New Hampshire [HS94a]. The Dexter model attempts to define a common terminology for hypertext databases and to serve as a reference for the development of hypertext systems.

The architecture of a hypertext system can be described by the following three layers:

- The *run-time* layer, which describes the basic tools for accessing, viewing and manipulating hypertext databases.

- The *storage* layer, which describes the hypertext database (also referred to as the hypertext network) in terms of nodes and links, and the mechanisms whereby the nodes and links are "glued together" to form a hypertext database.

- The *within-component* layer, which describes the contents and structure within the nodes and links of the hypertext database. This layer is actually not elaborated in the Dexter model and it is assumed that other models will deal with the particular document types and data structures needed for the application under consideration.

The Dexter model contains two interfaces:

- The *anchoring* interface between the storage and the within-component layers. This interface provides the mechanisms for addressing (or referring to) the locations or items of individual components.

- The *presentation specifications* interface between the run-time and storage layers. This interface provides the mechanisms for encoding the information about how components in the database are presented to the user.

We briefly elaborate on the layers of the Dexter model. The fundamental entity in the storage layer is the *component*, which is defined recursively as either an atom, a link or a composite entity made out of other components. Atomic components are the nodes of the database and their structure is described in the within-component layer. Links are components that describe relationships between other components. Each component in the database has a *Unique Identifier* (UID), by which it is accessed. UIDs are primitive entities and are assumed to be unique across the whole hypertext database. In order to be able to create a link within a substructure of a component, it is necessary that the anchor of the link has a unique identifier (anchor id), which locates a specific region in that component. An anchor is thus uniquely specified by a UID together with an anchor id. With each component there is an associated *component information*, which describes the properties of the component other than its contents, in the form of attribute-value pairs. The storage layer also includes update operations, which insert, delete and modify a component. In addition, there are operations for retrieving a component, given its UID and anchor id.

The fundamental concept in the run-time layer is the *instantiation* of a component, which determines how the component is to be presented to the user. When a component is instantiated it is assigned a unique instantiation identifier. The anchors of a component are instantiated together with their component; an instantiation of an anchor is known as a *link marker*. Thus a link marker refers to the presentation of the link in the viewed document. The instantiated components are made available to the user for viewing and editing and subsequently they are written back into the storage layer. A hypertext *session* defines the boundaries of a transaction initiated by an instantiation of one or more components.

A formal specification of the Dexter model in the formal specification language Z [Spi88] was undertaken in [PSV94]. Such a specification is a prerequisite to implementing a hypertext system based on the Dexter model. We mention that an earlier reference model for hypertext, called the *Hypertext Abstract Machine* (HAM) model, which is similar to the Dexter model, is described in [CG88].

One of the main unsolved problems confronting hypertext is the navigation problem, namely the problem of having to know where you are in the database digraph representing the structure of a hypertext database, and knowing how to get to some other place you are searching for in the database digraph. In [LL99c] we investigated this problem by defining a formal model for hypertext based on nodes and links and a query language, based on *propositional linear temporal logic* [Eme90], which allows the user to specify a set of trails to be retrieved from the hypertext database. The main result therein is that the computational problem of finding whether there exists a trail in the database which satisfies an arbitrary user query is, in general, NP-complete. This implies that it would be useful to devise approximate solutions to the navigation problem which are computationally feasible. A preliminary investigation of a probabilistic approach, which can utilise statistical information about trails that were traversed in the past in order to speed up query processing, was undertaken in [LL99b]. Other formal models of hypertext, which deal with the navigation problem, can be found in [Gar88b, CM89, AK90, BK90, AS92, SFR92, MW95].

Apart from querying the database users are most often browsing through pages of the hypertext database by following links. During this process they may become "lost in hyper space" [Con87], meaning that they become disoriented in terms of what to do next and how to return to a previously browsed page. In other words, readers may lose the context in which they are browsing and need some orientation tools to assist them in finding their way. The *browser* is the component of a hypertext system that helps users search for the information they are interested in by graphically displaying the relevant parts of the database and by providing contextual and spatial cues with the use of *orientation tools*.

A simple orientation tool is the *link marker* which acts as a signpost to tell the user what links can be immediately followed and what links have just been passed. Maps and webs give the user a more global context by displaying to them links which are at a further distance than just one link from the current position. Maps can be displayed using a *fisheye-view* that selects information according to its *degree-of-interest*, which decreases as the page under consideration is further away from the currently browsed page [TD92]. A set of tools that aid the construction of maps by performing a structural analysis of the database digraph is described in [RBS94]. A more sophisticated orientation tool is the *guided-tour* which actively guides users through the database digraph by suggesting interesting trails that the user can follow [MI89]. Another useful orientation tool is the *book mark*, allowing the reader to mark a page which can be returned to on demand when feeling lost [Ber88]. The reader may also mark pages which were already visited in order to avoid repetition; such marks are called *bread crumbs* [Ber88].

A recent emerging subarea is that of *adaptive hypertext and hypermedia* [Bru96, BKV98], whose aim is to build a model of an individual user using a hypertext system and apply this model for the purpose of adapting the system to that user. A useful distinction is between *adaptive presentation* which deals with adapting the contents of a page according to the user's knowledge and goals, and *adaptive navigational support*, whose aim is to help the user find the most relevant trails to follow by adapting the choice of links that the user can traverse.

Most adaptive presentation techniques deal with *text adaptation* which is concerned with tailoring the contents of a page to a particular user. Thus the content of a page changes according to the user browsing it. An effective technique used to implement adaptive presentation is that of *conditional text*. The text in a page is divided into several chunks, each one being associated with a relevant condition.

The most common techniques for adapting link presentation are: *direct guidance* which aims at suggesting the "best" link to follow, *adaptive ordering* which sorts the links according to some criteria which are useful to the user, *hiding* which restricts the number of allowable links by hiding links that are not relevant to the navigation session, and *annotation* which augments the links with useful comments relating to the pages that can be reached by following them.

The main features that are candidates for adaptation are now outlined:

- The user's knowledge of the subject dealt with in the hypertext page.

- The user's goals; for example, is the user mainly interested in learning about a particular subject, or simply searching for some specific information.

- The user's background, such as the user's profession, and the user's experience regarding the structure of the hypertext system used.

- The user's preferences; for example, the user may prefer certain pages and links and may prefer one presentation mode over another.

A recent challenge for adaptive hypertext research is that of managing *personalised views*, where such a view consists of the subset of the hypertext system relevant to the user. Related to this is the problem of creating *adaptive web sites* [PE98] (see also [JFM97]), where a web site can be viewed as a localised collection of logically interrelated pages. The goal of such adaptive web sites is to automatically improve both their organisation and presentation by using the information from log files of users who have visited the pages of the site under consideration.

Finally, we briefly discuss *Information Retrieval* (IR) issues which are crucial to the efficient querying of a hypertext database. IR is based on a full-text search of the contents of pages in the database for keywords specified by the user. Typically a query is a conjunction (and) of keywords but, in general, a query may contain other Boolean operations such as disjunction (or) and negation (not). Pages which match the query are usually sorted by a *score* which is assigned to each page according to how well they match the query. Matching of a query can be assisted by weighting the keywords according to some statistical relevance properties, and by preferring pages whose links can be followed to reach other *similar pages* relevant to the query. The term *number of hits* in a page indicates the number of keywords that are matched in that page; the number of hits may also include synonyms and related keywords in the page. In the context of hypertext, the integration of query-based retrieval and browsing strategies which include the links was investigated in [CT89]. Their model is based on a Bayesian inference network which includes dependencies between hypertext nodes and between concepts. For a survey on automatic IR techniques for measuring the similarity between textual documents, see [Sal91], and for a recent description of a prototype of a large scale WWW search engine, which incorporates some novel search techniques, see [BP98].

The reader can find surveys dealing with hypertext in [Con87, Hal88, SW88, FC92]. Two recent books on the subject are [Nie90, Rad91].

We close this section with a brief mention of the historical roots of hypertext. The inspiration for Hypertext comes from the *memex* machine proposed by Bush [Bus45] (see also [NK89]). The memex is a "sort of mechanized private file and library" which supports "associative indexing" and allows navigation whereby "any item may be caused at will to select immediately and automatically another". Bush emphasises that "the process of tying two items together is an important thing". In addition, by repeating this process of creating links we can form a *trail* which can be traversed by the user, in Bush's words "when numerous items have been thus joined together to form a trail they can be reviewed in turn". Hypertext can be viewed as the formalisation and realisation of Bush's original vision.

The term "hypertext" was coined by Ted Nelson in 1965 [Nel80]. Nelson considers "a literature" (such as the scientific literature) to be a *system of interconnected writings*. The process of referring to other connected writings, when reading an article or a document, is that of *following links*. The links between documents are not always visible but they exist and can be made concrete.

Nelson's vision is that of creating a repository of all the documents that have ever been written and thus achieving a universal hypertext database. In [Nel80] Nelson discusses the design of this hypertext system, which he calls Xanadu. In Xanadu all documents are potentially interconnected, and thus the fundamental elements of Xanadu are not just documents but links as well. A link is a connection between parts of text and is created by a user of the system. Nelson distinguishes between several types of literary link:

1) the *jump-link*, corresponding to a footnote or a related item,

2) the *quote-link*, corresponding to a quotation from another document,

3) the *correlink*, which places a segment of one document next to a segment of another document in order to structure a document, and

4) the *equilink*, which links two versions of the same document.

Nelson refers to a *document* as containing both text and links. The boundaries of a document are defined by its owner. Xanadu is thus a collection of documents and links between them. It can be viewed as a generalised memex system, which is both for private and public use. In Xanadu all versions of a document are maintained and linked together by equilinks. The system automatically keeps track of equilinks, and thus a full historical record of all versions of any document is made available.

Nelson views his system as a network of distributed documents that should be allowed to grow without any size limit and such that users, each corresponding to a node in the network, may link their documents to any other documents in the network. Nelson's vision is in fact materialised to a large degree in WWW, since he also views his system as a means of publishing material by making it available on the network.

There is also an important connection between hypertext and semantic networks. Semantic networks store factual knowledge in terms of nodes and associative connections between nodes in the form of links. Seminal work by Wood [Woo75] was instrumental in clarifying the notion of a link. Wood distinguishes between *assertional links* which make an assertion about the world, i.e. express a fact, and *structural links* which set up the subparts of a proposition or description. In addition, Wood also distinguishes between *intensional nodes* representing descriptions of the entities as opposed to *extensional nodes* which represent information about the entities themselves. Rada [Rad91] advocates viewing a hypertext database as a semantic network where a link provides the meaning of a relationship between two nodes.

10.6   Semistructured Databases

A hypertext database can be viewed as an instance of a *semistructured database* in the sense that such a database does not come with a separate schema due to its irregular structure.

Although the digraph representing a hypertext database is unstructured, individual pages in the network may have some structure attached to them. For instance, pages which are HTML documents have some structure attached to them in the form of informational tags, but these are normally insufficient for the purpose of constructing a relation schema over the document space. Semistructured data is often *self-describing* in the sense that its internal structure, when it exists, can be inferred from the data itself.

Semistructured data is naturally modelled in terms of digraphs which contain labels giving semantics to its underlying structure. Such databases subsume the modelling power of flat relational databases, nested relational databases and object-oriented databases. For the purpose of this section we will use the hypernode model, defined in Section 10.3, as our data model for semistructured data. The hypernode model is well suited for this task as it is a graph-based data model that supports both complex objects of arbitrary structure and cyclic references between such objects. Moreover, in the hypernode model it is easy to embed the schema information in the database, since appropriate attribute names can be used for this purpose.

Example 10.3 below shows a fragment of a semistructured (hypernode) database. We have chosen to represent the hypernode database textually rather than graphically, since in this case such a representation is more economical and easier to comprehend. We use indentation to represent a part-of relationship between a parent hypernode and the child hypernodes encapsulated in the parent. In object terminology the child hypernodes are subobjects of the parent hypernode object. For example, the contents of the child hypernode labelled $1 follow after the arc COUNTRY $\rightarrow$ $1, which is contained in its parent hypernode labelled $Europe_Hotel_Guide. As another example, the child hypernode labelled $1.1.3 follows after the arc HOTEL $\rightarrow$ $1.1.3, which is contained in its parent hypernode labelled $1.1. We have used the dot notation to make the object subobject relationship more transparent. Using such a convention for labels could be useful for query optimisation and consistency checking purposes. We note that we could represent the database in a more compact manner if we embed semantics into the labels of hypernodes. For example, instead of the arc COUNTRY $\rightarrow$ $1, we could have COUNTRY $\rightarrow$ $U.K. and remove the arc NAME $\rightarrow$ "U.K." after it in the hypernode labelled by $1. However, this approach has the disadvantage that we cannot reuse such labels as $U.K. elsewhere in the database due to the uniqueness of labels. Moreover, we would lose the convenience of the dot notation for labels.

Apart from the need to bring to bear database technology in the organisation, maintenance and querying of hypertext databases or more specifically WWW data, there are several other motivating applications demonstrating the need for semistructured databases.

Data integration is the activity of combining data from several heterogeneous databases. For example, we may want to integrate a relational database with an object-oriented database, both of which store statistical information on student enrolment. The process of integrating the two database schemas, say into a relational database schema, could turn out to be a very time-consuming activity which is fraught with problems due to the incompatibility of the two database systems. In the semistructured approach we do *not* attempt to integrate the two schemas, but rather we embed the schema information in the database itself by using a simple but expressive data model such as the hypernode model. As another example, we may wish to integrate several relational databases storing information about the retail prices of second hand cars. We do not expect that all retailers will use the same database schema; for example, some retailers may store in their database information about

---

Example 10.3 (A semistructured database)

$Europe_Hotel_Guide
  COUNTRY → $1
    NAME → "U.K."
    CITY → $1.1
      NAME → London
      HOTEL → $1.1.1
        NAME → "Hotel Good"
        ADDRESS → "High Street"
        CATEGORY → 5-star
        PRICE → expensive
        NEAR_TO → $1.1.2
      HOTEL → $1.1.2
        NAME → "Hotel Very Good"
        NEAR_TO → $1.1.1
      HOTEL → $1.1.3
        NAME → "Hotel Bad"
        ADDRESS → "Low St."
        CATEGORY → 2-star
    CITY → $1.2
      NAME → Glasgow
      HOTEL → $1.2.1
        NAME → "Hotel Rough"
  COUNTRY → $2
    NAME → France
    CITY → $2.1
      NAME → Paris
      HOTEL → $2.1.1
        NAME → "Hotel Luxury"
        ADDRESS → "Town centre"
        CATEGORY → 5*-plus
    CITY → $2.2
      NAME → Nice
      HOTEL → $2.2.1
        NAME → "Hotel Far"
        ADDRESS → "Far Lane"
        PRICE → cheap   ∎

---

the service history of the car and/or its previous owner, while others may not store such information. In this case the various databases may also use different formats for recording prices and dates, which makes the integration even more difficult. Integrating all these databases, without any loss of information, into a single one with a unified database schema would, as in the previous example, be time-consuming and fraught with problems, so the semistructured approach which essentially maintains the original contents of each database is attractive.

Another motivating example is that of modelling scientific data such as genome data which does not have a regular structure. In such cases it is hard to design a relational or object-oriented database schema that will capture all the semantics of the application. In a semistructured database we can easily adapt to such diversity in the structure of the data by embedding the schema information in the database itself.

Finally we mention the need for browsing through a database without having to know the full details of the database schema. For example a dealer, not knowing the database schema, would like to know which databases record the service history of their cars. As another example, we would like to find all tuples in the database which mention some car manufacturer regardless of any attribute information. Such queries are difficult if not impossible in most conventional database systems but do not pose any problems in a semistructured environment.

Since we use the hypernode model as our model for semistructured data we could simply use HNQL, described in Section 10.3, as our query language. Moreover, since HNQL is query complete, is has the full expressive power needed to query such a database. Despite this fact there are several extensions of HNQL which would enhance its applicability to querying and updating semistructured databases.

In practice primitive nodes should be typed according to a predefined set of primitive data types such as string, integer, real and Boolean. Primitive nodes may also be typed according to more complex types such as date, various measurement units such as kilometres and miles, or pounds sterling and French francs. To ease the querying when data is not strictly typed we perform *coercion* between data types, which for example returns true for equality conditions such as $10.0 = 10$, $10 = $ "10" and $20/11/97 = $ "20 November 1997".

Path expressions provide a navigational tool in a semistructured database, which allow us to query information along a path in the Hypernode Accessibility Graph (abbreviated HAG, see Definition 10.13), rooted by a specified label according to a sequence of attribute names each being present in the hypernode defined by its respective label along the path. Formally, a *path expression* is a sequence, $L.A_1.A_2 \ldots A_n$, where L is a label of a hypernode in a database HD, and $A_1, A_2, \ldots, A_n$ are attribute names. A *data path* matching such a path expression is a sequence, $L_1.L_2 \ldots L_n$, where $L_1, L_2, \ldots, L_n$ are labels of hypernodes in HD, such that

1) $L_1 = L$ and $L_1.L_2 \ldots L_n$ is a walk in the HAG of L (recall that the nodes in a walk may not be distinct; see Definition 2.2 of Section 2.1),

2) A_i is an attribute in the node set of the hypernode labelled by L_i, for $i = 1, 2, \ldots, n$, and

3) $A_i \rightarrow L_{i+1}$ is an arc in the arc set of the hypernode labelled by L_i, for $i = 1, 2, \ldots, n-1$.

For example, the data path $Europe_Hotel_Guide.\$1.\$1.1.\$1.1.1 matches the path expression $Europe_Hotel_Guide.COUNTRY.CITY.HOTEL.PRICE, since COUNTRY $\in$ nodes($Europe_Hotel_Guide), COUNTRY $\rightarrow$ $1 $\in$ arcs($Europe_Hotel_Guide), CITY $\in$ nodes($1), CITY $\rightarrow$ $1.1 $\in$ arcs($1), HOTEL $\in$ nodes($1.1) HOTEL $\rightarrow$ $1.1.1 $\in$ arcs($1.1) and PRICE $\in$ nodes($1.1.1). This demonstrates how we can retrieve the hotel prices from the semistructured database of Example 10.6. Using the style of the *Lorel* query language [AQM+97], we can retrieve from our database of Example 10.6 all the information on expensive hotels in London, by the query

    SELECT $Europe_Hotel_Guide.COUNTRY.CITY.HOTEL
    WHERE $Europe_Hotel_Guide.COUNTRY.CITY.HOTEL.PRICE = 'expensive'
    AND $Europe_Hotel_Guide.COUNTRY.CITY.NAME = 'London'

We can also use wildcards in path expressions, when we do not know at what level in the HAG of, say $Europe_Hotel_Guide, the attribute information for, say CITY, appears. For instance, we can retrieve the names of hotels having a 5-star category, by the query

    SELECT $Europe_Hotel_Guide.*.HOTEL.NAME
    WHERE $Europe_Hotel_Guide.*.HOTEL.CATEGORY = '5-star'

In the above query the wildcard in the select clause causes any data path of the form $Europe_Hotel_Guide.$L_2 \ldots L_{n-1}.L_n$, with HOTEL $\in$ nodes(L_{n-1}), HOTEL $\to L_n \in$ arcs(L_{n-1}) and NAME $\in$ nodes(L_n), to be considered. Similarly, the wildcard in the where clause causes any data path of the form $Europe_Hotel_Guide.$L_2 \ldots L_{n-1}.L_n$, with HOTEL $\in$ nodes(L_{n-1}), HOTEL $\to L_n \in$ arcs(L_{n-1}) and CATEGORY $\in$ nodes(L_n), to be considered.

Path expressions are extended to *generalised path expressions* by allowing a *regular expression* (see Subsection 1.9.4) to replace an attribute name in a path expression. Thus as in the example above, we can also use the wildcard operator, denoted by *, in a generalised path expression; this operator is also called the Kleene closure operator. (We observe that the wildcard operator can lead to an infinite number of data paths being considered and thus in practice cycles in the HAG of the initial label must be detected.) In addition, we can use the union operator, denoted by +, in generalised path expressions, where for example $L.A_0.(A_1 + A_2)$ matches a data path $L.L'$ in the HAG of L such that $A_0 \in$ nodes(L), $A_0 \to L' \in$ arcs(L) and either $A_1 \in$ nodes(L') or $A_2 \in$ nodes(L'). For a more concrete query, we can retrieve either the price or category of hotels in the U.K. by the query

SELECT $Europe_Hotel_Guide.COUNTRY.*.HOTEL.(PRICE + CATEGORY)
WHERE $Europe_Hotel_Guide.COUNTRY.NAME = 'U.K.'

Two recent surveys on the issues in the emerging field of semistructured databases can be found in [Abi97] and [Bun97]. The problems of integrating and querying heterogeneous information in the context of a semistructured database are discussed in [QRS+95] and in a more general context in [Hul97]. The particular problems concerning biological data are discussed in [DOB95]. A solution to the data integration problem in the form of an object-relational extension is given in [LRO96]. The more traditional *multidatabase* approach to schema integration is reviewed in [KCGS95] with respect to relational and object-oriented databases. An overview of the *Lightweight Object Repository Language* (Lorel) query language and its semistructured data model is given in [AQM+97], and details of its rival query language *Unstructured Query Language* (UnQL) and its underlying data model are presented in [BDHS96]. Schema discovery is important for semistructured databases, since it can assist the user in posing meaningful queries and browsing through the database. In addition, the discovered schema can be useful in query optimisation via the creation of *path indices* and the identification of data paths which give empty query results. Foundations of schema discovery in the form of dynamic generation of structural summaries of the information contained in semistructured databases, called *representative objects*, and their implementation, called *DataGuides*, were investigated, respectively, in [NUWC97] and [GW97]. A discussion of several important issues regarding the specification of views for semistructured databases was presented in [AGM+97]. Finally, a recent investigation which formalises a measure which allows us to test whether two semistructured databases have the same information content is presented in [Lev98].

10.7   Knowledge Discovery and Data Mining

The area of knowledge discovery and data mining in databases (KDD) is one of the most exciting recently developing areas in the database field. The term knowledge discovery refers to the overall *process* of finding knowledge in data and the term data mining refers to the application of specific methods and *algorithms* which extract patterns from data. KDD brings together the three areas of databases, machine learning and statistics. In this short section we explain the underlying concepts involved in KDD and give a simple example in the context of mining data dependencies in a relational database. Our treatment of the subject is discursive rather than theoretical, mainly because the theory of KDD is still in its infancy.

The need for KDD arises from the overwhelming number of available databases both in the business and scientific sectors. Examples of business data are: information resulting from bar coding goods, information resulting from credit card purchases and financial market information. Examples of scientific data are: the Humane Genome database project and NASA's Earth Observing System which is predicated to generate vast amounts of remotely sensed image data from satellites. Traditional ad hoc database queries can provide useful and informative answers, but they are not, on their own, capable of extracting knowledge and analysing patterns in the data. KDD provides us with the tools which automatically analyse a database in order to find and mine for *nuggets* of useful knowledge.

Knowledge discovery is defined more precisely as the process of extracting nontrivial, potentially useful and understandable patterns which are implied from a given database.

Fayyad, Piatetsky-Shapiro, Smyth and Uthurusamy further formalise the concept of knowledge discovery [FPSSU96, Chapter 1] using the following notions:

1) A *dataset* (or database) d is defined as a set of facts, or tuples, each over a given relation schema.

2) A *pattern* is an expression E in some language which describes a subset $d[E]$ of a dataset d. A pattern is nontrivial if it is a more concise representation than the simple enumeration of the set $d[E]$ of facts it describes.

3) A *certainty measure* $C(E, d)$ is a measure of how well the pattern E describes $d[E]$.

4) An *interesting* pattern is one which is nontrivial, useful and understandable from the user's point of view; to make the notion of interesting more precise it is possible to attach a measure to it.

A pattern that is *interesting* and whose certainty measure is above some predefined threshold is called *knowledge*. We can now define data mining more precisely as the step in the knowledge discovery process involving the particular methods and algorithms used to extract knowledge.

The KDD process involves the following steps:

1) Understanding the application and collecting the relevant prior knowledge.

2) Creating or selecting the dataset on which knowledge discovery is to be performed.

3) Data cleaning, i.e. removing any detected noise or outliers from the dataset which correspond to errors in the data. Deciding how to handle missing and irrelevant data.

4) Data reduction and projection, i.e. reducing the number of variables under consideration and transforming the data in order to find the useful features which represent the data.

5) Choosing the data mining methods to be used for the chosen data mining tasks and executing them on the input dataset.

6) Interpreting the mined knowledge output from the previous step, and iterating any previous steps if necessary.

7) Consolidating the output discovered knowledge, i.e. using this knowledge to our benefit. This may involve using the discovered knowledge in an application or simply producing a document detailing the results.

The KDD process can be further abstracted in the three main steps of data preparation, data mining operations and data presentation. Data mining methods consist of the following three components:

1) *Model representation*, which is the language for describing the patterns we are mining for; for example, decision trees, rules and Bayesian networks are representation models.

2) *Model evaluation*, which is the estimate on how well an extracted pattern meets the criteria of being knowledge; for example, statistical significance and simplicity with respect to some known patterns can be used for evaluation.

3) *Search*, which is the process of finding a solution, in the form of a pattern, by examining prospective solutions in the search space. Normally, heuristic searching techniques are used, since the search space is, in most KDD applications, too large for an exhaustive search to be computationally feasible. Heuristic search methods include probabilistic algorithms which utilise samples from the data set during their execution.

The main goals of data mining methods are *prediction* and *description*. Prediction involves using some attributes of the database schema to predict certain values of other attributes. Description involves finding patterns which can be considered to be knowledge. The goals of data mining are achieved by the following tasks: classification, regression, clustering, summarisation, dependency modelling and time series modelling.

A related area to KDD that has recently attracted a great deal of attention is that of *On-Line Analytical Processing* (OLAP) [CCS93], rather than the traditional *On-Line Transaction Processing* (OLTP). OLAP concerns the co-existence of transaction intensive databases and decision support systems. OLAP arises from the requirement for multidimensional data analysis tools in order to complement currently available DBMS tools. The activities of such analytic tools against the database constitute a transaction, whose duration may be an order of magnitude longer than a standard database transaction. OLAP transactions interact with historical data in addition to snapshot data and are typically made up of numerous "what-if" and "why" queries. In order to support OLAP the query language must provide facilities for calculation, aggregation and data manipulation across any number of data dimensions. A specific generalisation of the SQL GROUP BY operator, briefly introduced at the end of Subsection 3.2.2 of Chapter 3, is the *data cube* operator [GCB+97]. Given a set of n attributes, the data cube operator computes a GROUP BY query for each of the 2^n possible combinations of the attributes and summarises the results in a single table. Fast algorithms for computing the result of applying the data cube operator are presented in [AAD+96].

The challenge of integrating OLAP into a relational database system can be addressed by developing dedicated OLAP servers that interact with the database in order to store and retrieve data multidimensionally. The database with which an OLAP server interacts is called a *data warehouse* [Inm96, Kim96]. This term broadly refers to a database which contains a collection

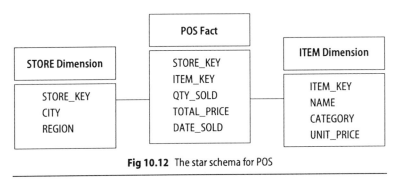

Fig 10.12 The star schema for POS

of subject-oriented, integrated and historical data. Examples of data warehouses are: large collections of scientific data and historical enterprise data such as sales data.

As an example of an OLAP application consider sales data, which has accumulated over a period of time, detailing various products and the stores in which they were sold. A typical OLAP query might ask to find the sales volume of each product type in each store. This query may be refined by asking for a breakdown of the sales per month during the last year. OLAP queries should also be able to analyse relationships which are inherent in the data; for example, we may like to know whether there is a connection between the volume of sales of particular products and the district of the shop in which they were sold. Queries should also be capable of aggregating data according to hierarchical time periods and different perspectives such as sales by product or by district of store. In addition, OLAP queries should be able to carry out complex calculations, which may also be predictive in nature, such as the expected profits per product. (See [CD97] for a recent overview of data warehousing and OLAP technology).

In order to build a data warehouse the database system used should support a multidimensional data model at the conceptual level. Most data warehouses use a *star join schema* (or simply a star schema) [Kim96, Red98] to represent the multidimensional data model. (See [GL97] for a proposal of a higher level mutlidimensional data model and a query language for it, which could in principle be implemented on top of a relational database.) A star schema is a database schema which resembles a star, having a central relation schema, called the *fact table*, and surrounding relation schemas, called the *dimension tables*. For each dimension table in the star schema the fact table contains a distinct foreign key referencing the primary key of the dimension table. The amalgamation of all the foreign keys of the fact table yields its primary key, which is composite assuming that there are at least two dimension tables. In terms of entity-relationship modelling, the fact table expresses a many-to-many relationship amongst the dimension tables. The fact table contains the core information on the data being analysed and the dimension tables contain further properties of the core data. The motivation behind the design of star schemas is that in data warehousing we are primarily interested in efficient query processing rather than in efficient updating via transaction processing [OG95].

As an example of a star schema, consider a point-of-sales data warehouse of a retail business with many outlets, whose fact table is POS, with schema(POS) = {STORE_KEY, ITEM_KEY, QTY_SOLD, TOTAL_PRICE, DATE_SOLD}, and dimension tables are STORE and ITEM, with schema(STORE) = {STORE_KEY, CITY, REGION} and schema(ITEM) = {ITEM_KEY, NAME,

CATEGORY, UNIT_PRICE}; see Figure 10.12. The relation over the fact table of this data warehouse contains one tuple for each item sold on a particular date; the granularity of time is fixed for all such tuples and may be one day in this case. On the other hand, the relation over the store dimension contains one tuple for each store of the business, and the relation over the item dimension contains one tuple for each item supplied. The size of the relation over the fact table is typically much larger than the size of any of the relations over its dimension tables. Assume that the granularity of time is a single day, that the data warehouse stores the point-of-sales information over a year, and that there are 100 stores in the business each selling approximately 1000 different items per day, out of a possible 10,000 items. Then the relation over the fact table contains approximately 36.5 million tuples, the relation over the STORE dimension contains 100 tuples, and the relation over the ITEM dimension contains 10,000 tuples.

Data warehousing has also recently revived the area of view updates, since a data warehouse can be defined as a materialised view [GM95], which may also contain aggregate data [MQM97]. The problem that arises when a view is materialised is the view maintenance problem, which is the problem of consistently updating the materialised view when the underlying database relations are updated (see the discussion at the end of Section 3.8 in Chapter 3). View maintenance of IDB predicates of Datalog programs is considered in [DT92, DR97]. More specifically, the problem of whether a view, which materialises the transitive closure predicate, can be updated via a nonrecursive Datalog program, referred to as the maintenance in first-order problem, is tackled. In [DT92] it is shown that when the updates involve the insertion of edges to the underlying graph then the view can be maintained in first-order, and in [DR97] it is shown that when adding certain constraints on node costs the view can still be maintained in first-order. Monitoring the updates carried out on the underlying database can be done via an active database component (see Section 10.4) as discussed in [ZHKF95].

For surveys elaborating on the issues of KDD we have touched upon, and a wide selection of papers on KDD see [PSF91, CT93, HS94b, FU95, CHY96, FPSSU96, FU96]. A recent introductory book to KDD is [WI98].

As an example of KDD in relational databases we mention the following *functional dependency inference problem* (FD inference problem):

Given a relation r over a relation schema R find a cover of the set of all FDs that are satisfied in r.

More formally, let r be a relation over R and dep(r) be defined by

$$dep(r) = \{X \rightarrow Y \mid X, Y \subseteq schema(R) \text{ and } r \models X \rightarrow Y\}.$$

Then the FD inference problem is the problem of finding a cover of dep(r); note that r is an Armstrong relation for dep(r) (see Subsection 3.6.2 of Chapter 3).

The following naive algorithm solves the FD inference problem.

Algorithm 10.4 (INFER(r, R))
1. **begin**
2.   F := ∅;
3.   **for each** subset X ⊆ schema(R) **do**
4.   **for each** attribute A ∈ schema(R) − X **do**
5.   **if** $r \models$ X → A **then**
6.   F := F ∪ {X → A};
7.   **end if**
8.   **end for**
9.   **end for**
10.   **return** F;
11. **end.**

This algorithm is obviously not practical, since it considers all the subsets of schema(R). Mannila and Räihä have developed several improved algorithms for solving the FD inference problem that can be used in practice [MR86a, MR87, MR94] (see Exercise 10.29 for one such algorithm). In [MR92b] they have shown that, in general, the FD inference problem is exponential in the number of attributes, type(R), of schema(R). Therefore no algorithm exists which in all cases will solve the FD inference problem efficiently. An extension of the inference problem to inclusion dependencies (the IND inference problem) was considered in [KMRS92]. The computational complexity of the IND inference problem is at least NP-complete for general INDs, but can easily be shown to be polynomial in type(R) for unary INDs, since there are at most type(R)^2 possible unary INDs over R.

Example 10.3 Let r be the relation shown in Table 10.15, over R, with ENAME (E), DNAME (D) and MGR (M) being the attributes in schema(R). The reader can verify that F = {D → M, M → D, E → D} is a cover of dep(r). ∎

Table 10.15 A sample relation

ENAME	DNAME	MGR
Miriam	Computing	Eli
Naomi	Computing	Eli
Susi	Mathematics	Cyril

Due to the exponential computational complexity of the FD inference problem the following *approximate* FD inference problem is appropriate:

Given a relation r over a relation schema R find a set of FDs F over R such that, with high probability, F is *close* to a cover of dep(r).

In [AT94, KM95] the approximate FD inference problem is investigated using the framework of *Probably Approximately Correct* (PAC) learning [Val84]. Therein, according to the probability and closeness desired, sample sizes with respect to the input relation and schema are derived which solve this problem. For related approaches to the dependency inference problem see [Zia91, MGB93, PSM93, SF93, Sch93, Bel95a].

Finally, we mention *Inductive Logic Programming* (ILP) which is a subarea of machine learning, whose goal is to induce first-order logic formulae from a set of training examples and background knowledge [MD94, Dže96]. The training examples consist of positive and negative facts, and the background knowledge is expressed in the form of first-order logic formulae. Any induced logic formula in conjunction with the background knowledge should be *complete*, i.e. it should logically imply the positive facts, and it should be *consistent*, i.e. it should not logically imply the negative facts. In other words, an induced logic formula should explain all of the positive facts and none of the negative facts. In the context of KDD, an instantiation of ILP can be viewed as the inference of a nontrivial rule for a Datalog program such that the head of the inferred rule has the same predicate symbol as the training examples. In the context of Datalog, the background knowledge is a Datalog program and the training examples are a separate set of facts, partitioned into positive and negative facts for the purpose of the learning algorithm. As an example, consider a Datalog program with the background knowledge being two unary predicates male and female, and a single binary predicate parent. The ILP task could be to infer the binary predicate daughter given some positive and negative daughter facts. Another more challenging example, which was tackled in [BM94, Mor94], is that of learning playing strategies to solve chess endgames.

In a nonmonotonic setting for ILP the set of positive facts of the training examples is considered to be part of the background knowledge and the set of negative facts of the training examples is empty. Such negative facts, i.e. facts which should be false, are derived via the CWA (closed world assumption).

10.8 Other Areas

There are several important areas in the database field which we would like to mention but have not been covered as such in the book.

Firstly, the issues concerning the presentation of multimedia information are very important, including apart from text, also other media such as graphics, video, sound, and animation. In order to manage such multimedia information, tools need to be developed that store and retrieve such information efficiently. Furthermore, the Human-Computer-Interaction (HCI) problem for multimedia databases poses new problems in the development of user interfaces for databases. A survey on the issues and current approaches to integrating multimedia information into database technology is presented in [CK95]. An interesting approach for giving semantics to query evaluation in a multimedia system, which utilises fuzzy set theory, can be found in [Fag96]. A recent collection of papers on the state of the art in the area of managing multimedia data is [ABH97].

Secondly, the use of high performance parallel computing technology is being utilised in order to speed up processing of large amounts of data. One of the problems confronting the use of such technology is that of devising efficient parallel join algorithms. In particular, such an algorithm needs to partition the relations being joined into *buckets* so that each bucket is processed in parallel. For a survey on parallel relational database systems see [Omi95].

A fundamental area which we did not cover in this book is that of managing distributed relational databases [CP84a, ÖV91, GH95]. A distributed relational database is a collection of relational databases, called *sites*, which are connected via a communication network. Since all the sites share the same data model, i.e. the relational model, the distributed database is *homogeneous*. The fundamental principle underlying a distributed relational database is that as far as the users are concerned the database system behaves exactly like a standard nondistributed relational database system (see [Dat95, Chapter 21]). That is, the fact that the database is distributed should be *transparent* to its users. A common example of a distributed database is that of an airline reservation system, where each individual office has access to part of the reservation information, which is distributed according to the home countries of the airlines. To users of such a reservation system the actual distribution details should be completely transparent.

Two important issues during the design of a distributed relational database are those of *fragmentation* and *replication* of data. Fragmentation is the problem of dividing a relation amongst the various sites at which it is to be stored. For example, in the airline reservation system we may store the information about British Airways flights at the London site and the information about Quantas flights at the Sydney site. From the users' point of view the fragmentation of this relation is transparent. Replication is the problem of duplication of tuples in a relation in two or more sites. For example, we may wish to replicate some of the information concerning Quantas flights in Europe at the London site. Again from the users' point of view the replication of tuples of this relation is transparent. The decisions relating to fragmentation and replication of the data clearly have an effect on the efficiency of query processing. The problems confronting distributed query processing and transaction management are different from those encountered in the nondistributed case, since in many cases the communication costs of transferring data between sites over the network will be the overriding cost that needs to be minimised.

A special type of distributed system which is widely used is that of a *client/server* system. In such a system some of the sites are *clients* (the *frontend*) and others are *servers* (the *backend*). The database resides on the servers and the applications are run on the clients.

Another recent challenge to distributed database systems is that of *mobile computing* [IB92, GH95]. In such an environment users will be operating small portable computers, which will be able to communicate with each other, possibly via a large database server. For example, a minicab firm would like to keep track of all their cabs with the aid of a distributed mobile database, where each minicab is considered to be a site with its own mobile computer and local database. Each local database may contain the current location and destination of the minicab, and information about the customers it has served during the day. In a mobile distributed database the information is rapidly changing and thus it is update-intensive. For example, the current location and passenger information of a minicab is ever changing. Therefore, we may have to accept errors due to the data being out of date, and thus a margin of error may have to be attached to the answer of certain queries. In addition, if the data is being acquired from different sources then there may also arise the problem of dealing with inconsistencies in the database [Lev96].

Database technology has moved a long way since the inception of relational databases in the 1970's. Although the relational data model is currently dominating the database market place there are many operational non-relational database systems which are still in current use. Such systems are either *legacy databases* such as hierarchical or network databases, or newer database systems such as object-oriented databases, whose underlying model is incompatible with the relational one. In order to operate in such a heterogeneous environment, in which several different databases are available, a *multidatabase system* is needed, which provides a unified data model to users of the various databases. Such a database system is also known as a *federated database system*, since each database system in the federation maintains its autonomy, i.e. its local operation remains unchanged, but agrees to share part of its information with other database systems in the federation. For a survey on the problems confronting multidatabase systems and the interoperatability of legacy databases see [Kim95a, Part II].

10.9   What Lies Beyond?

Relational database technology has developed rapidly in the last two decades, and has reached its current maturity by utilising the rich underlying mathematical foundations that were developed in academia. The basic theory of relational databases has reached a relatively stable state but as can be seen from the various extensions presented in this chapter, relational database theory is still a very fluid and active subject. The synergy of database theory with other areas in computer science, such as machine learning and statistics in the knowledge discovery subarea and information retrieval in the hypertext subarea, is leading to important advances in the field.

We expect that relational database theory will continue to be a major influence on the development of DBMSs by providing sound modelling criteria and efficient algorithms for implementing them. The theory also has the role of clearly mapping the boundary between problems that have tractable solutions and problems that do not. In addition to stating which problems are intractable, such as proving NP-completeness for a given problem, the theory has the important role of discovering important subclasses of the problem that can be solved efficiently, i.e. in polynomial time in the size of the input. Moreover, approximation algorithms may be viable in cases where the problem is intractable and we expect that heuristic techniques such as: hill climbing, simulated annealing, tabu search, genetic algorithms, neural networks and probabilistic algorithms will be used.

10.10   Exercises

Exercise 10.1   It has been proposed in [SPS87] that the nested relational model act as an internal level between the conceptual and physical levels of the DBMS, so that relations can be hierarchically clustered as nested relations. Discuss how such an internal level can be useful in the optimisation of flat relational queries at the conceptual level, and how it is related to the concept of denormalising a database schema.

Exercise 10.2   Assume that we extend the definition of a simple selection formula to allow expressions of the form $(X)^* \subseteq (Y)^*$, where $(X)^*$ and $(Y)^*$ are relation-valued attributes in a nested relation schema R. Given a tuple t in a nested relation r over R, t logically implies $(X)^* \subseteq (Y)^*$, if $t[(X)^*] \subseteq t[(Y)^*]$ evaluates to true. Such formulae are called extended simple selection formulae.

Show how the division operator of the relational algebra (Definition 3.18 in Subsection 3.2.1 of Chapter 3) can be expressed in a simpler manner in the nested relational algebra by using one level of nesting and extended simple selection formulae.

Exercise 10.3 The power set algebra comprises the nested relational algebra augmented with a power set operator, which given a nested relation r over R, returns a nested relation r' over R', with schema(R') = {(schema(R))*}, where r' contains the set of all subsets of r.

Show that the power set algebra is strictly more expressive than the nested relational algebra; for example, you can show that the transitive closure can be expressed in the power set algebra but not in the nested relational algebra [Hul87]. In addition, show that either the nest or the difference operator is redundant in the power set algebra, in the sense that the expressiveness of the power set algebra is not diminished when either the nest or the difference operator is removed from it [GV91].

Exercise 10.4 The nest and unnest operators of the nested relational algebra allow us to restructure nested relations according to a suitable schema. For example, we may want to know the set of courses that a given student takes, or alternatively the set of students that take a particular course. Illustrate the problems in restructuring hierarchical relations, when the information content of a hierarchical relation r is represented by the flat relation UNNEST*(r). Suggest how the information content of a hierarchical relation may be better represented by a flat database emanating from r, such that each flat relation in this database can be computed from r via a nested relational algebra expression [AB86, Hul90].

Exercise 10.5 Given a flat relation r over R, where schema(R) = $\{A_1, A_2, \ldots, A_m, B_1, B_2, \ldots, B_n\}$, and a natural number k, prove that the problem of finding a nested relation s over S, where schema(S) = $\{A_1, A_2, \ldots, A_m, (B_1)^*, (B_2)^*, \ldots, (B_n)^*\}$, such that UNNEST*($s$) = r and s has at most k tuples, is NP-complete [Tak89]. (Hint: To establish NP-hardness, give a polynomial-time transformation from the minimum disjunctive normal form problem [GJ79].)

Exercise 10.6 Let r be a relation over a relation schema R, with schema(R) = XYZ, where X ∩ Y = ∅ and Z = schema(R) − XY. Show that the following statements are equivalent [FSTV85]:

1) X →→ Y | Z holds in r.

2) X → (Y)* holds in NEST$_Y$(r).

3) X → (Z)* holds in NEST$_Z$(r).

4) X → (Y)*(Z)* holds in NEST$_Y$(NEST$_Z$(r)).

5) X → (Y)*(Z)* holds in NEST$_Z$(NEST$_Y$(r)).

Exercise 10.7 Let **R** be a nested database schema and let schema(**R**) denote the set of all atomic attributes appearing in the nested relation schemas of **R**. Then **R** is said to be in *Nested Normal Form* (NNF) with respect to a set M of MVDs over schema(**R**), if the path set, P_i, of each nested relation schema $R_i \in \mathbf{R}$ is in 4NF with respect to M, and, in addition, $M \models \bowtie [\{P_i\}]$. (A relation schema R is in *Fourth Normal Form* (4NF) with respect to a set M of MVDs, if every MVD X →→ Y in M is trivial.) Justify the definition of NNF in terms of the FDs that are satisfied in the nested relations in databases over NNF schemas, with reference to BCNF.

Exercise 10.8 The object identity of a tuple can be implemented as the physical address of the tuple, or alternatively, as a *surrogate*, which is a unique identifier that is generated by the

DBMS and is independent of the physical address of the tuple [KC86]. Discuss the advantages of each implementation strategy, and argue that, when using surrogates, object identifiers should be globally unique within the database rather than just locally unique within a relation.

Exercise 10.9   An important feature of an object-oriented database (that we have not delved into) is the facility to introduce user-defined data types as attribute domains, in addition to the standard attribute domains of numbers and strings. Such a facility should allow database programmers to define new data types and the operations on these types [OH86, Sto86]. (See also the discussion in Section 3.7 of Chapter 3.) For example, in a geographic database which needs to manipulate spatial data, we may need to define a data type, called *region*, and operations such as: whether two regions are adjacent and whether one region is contained in another. Assuming that the operations for user-defined data types can be implemented in a computationally complete database query language, suggest how such data types can be used in an extended relational algebra.

Exercise 10.10   Summarise the features that make a database system object-oriented, and discuss the viability of extending a relational database system to support these features [SM96].

Exercise 10.11   Recall the definition of an ISA relationship in the ER model, which was presented in Definition 2.12 in Section 2.4 of Chapter 2. Suggest how the semantics of ISA relationships can provide a basis for extending the relational algebra with an inheritance facility and describe what benefits are gained by such an extension.

Exercise 10.12   Suggest a declarative rule-based query language for the hypernode model [PL94].

Exercise 10.13   Design a user interface for the hypernode model.

Exercise 10.14   Suggest a normal form for hypernodes, wherein a hypernode database is replaced by a single hypernode and such that there is no loss of information in the normal form representation; two hypernodes having the same *information content* should have the same normal form hypernode [Lev98].

Exercise 10.15   A hypernode database HD is said to be *acyclic* if for all defining labels, G, of hypernodes in HD, the HAG of G is acyclic, otherwise HD is *cyclic*. Argue with examples whether cyclic hypernode databases are more expressive than acyclic ones.

Exercise 10.16   A workflow management computer system describes the flow of control between multiple processing steps, which may execute on different servers and such that the duration of the activities being modelled may be long-running. You are given the following outline specification of a workflow management hospital information system. A patient arrives at the hospital and is admitted. Then the patient is examined by a physician and the physician may prescribe several tests to be carried out at certain dates. In addition, the patient may be required to be hospitalised and thus a room must be assigned to this patient and a daily routine be arranged which includes meals and daily checkups. When the results of the tests arrive, then the physician must assess them and reexamine the patient. As a result further tests may be prescribed. When the patient is released, then the administrative records must be updated for billing purposes. Demonstrate how such a system could be implemented by a program of ECA rules [DHL90, DHL91]; you may use pseudo-code where appropriate.

Exercise 10.17 Assume that P is a program consisting of a finite set of ECA rules and let $\sqsupseteq$ be a partial order on the rules in P such that $R_i \sqsupseteq R_j$ implies that the rule R_i has a *higher priority* than the distinct rule R_j, in the sense that if both R_i and R_j are activated at the same time, then R_i is fired before R_j. Two distinct rules R_i and R_j are *non-prioritised* if neither R_i nor R_j has a higher priority than the other.

We say that P is *confluent*, if the final database state resulting from processing the rules in P is independent of the activation order of the set of non-prioritised rules in P. Furthermore, we say that two distinct rules R_i and R_j *commute* if the database state, resulting from activating R_i first and R_j second, is the same as the database state resulting from activating R_j first and R_i second.

Show that if all pairs of distinct rules in P commute then P is confluent. Since some of the rules in P are prioritised, insisting that all pairs of distinct rules commute is too conservative a condition for confluence to hold. Consider the following algorithm, where $T(R)$ is a function which returns the set of all rules, including the rule R, that can be triggered by R.

Algorithm 10.5 (PAIRS(P, R_i, R_j))
1. **begin**
2. $S_1 := \{R_i\}$;
3. $S_2 := \{R_j\}$;
4.   **while** S_1 or S_2 are modified **do**
5. $S_1 := S_1 \cup \{R \in P \mid R \in T(R_1)$ for some $R_1 \in S_1$ and
                      $R \sqsupseteq R_2$ for some $R_2 \in S_2$ and $R \neq R_j\}$;
6. $S_2 := S_2 \cup \{R \in P \mid R \in T(R_2)$ for some $R_2 \in S_2$ and
                      $R \sqsupseteq R_1$ for some $R_1 \in S_1$ and $R \neq R_i\}$;
7.   **end while**
8.   **return** (S_1, S_2);
9. **end.**

Show that P is confluent if for every pair of distinct non-prioritised rules R_i and R_j in P, when (S_1, S_2) is returned by PAIRS(P, R_i, R_j), then every pair of rules $R_1 \in S_1$ and $R_2 \in S_2$ commutes [AWH92].

Exercise 10.18 A *State-Transition Diagram* (STD) [You89] is a diagram used in software engineering analysis, which describes the time-dependent behaviour of a system under design. An STD can be viewed as a finite automaton augmented with the ability to produce an output on change of state; such a finite automaton is called a *Mealy machine* [HU79]. Give an outline of how the semantics of a program consisting of a finite set of ECA rules can be described by using Mealy machines. (See Subsection 1.9.4 in Chapter 1 for a formal definition of a finite automaton.)

Exercise 10.19 Suggest how a hypertext database may be formalised as a finite automaton and how such a formalisation can be used to specify the semantics of browsing [SFR92, LL99c].

Exercise 10.20 Develop a query language for hypertext databases based on temporal logic [BK90, SFR92, LL99c].

Exercise 10.21 In this exercise we investigate the definition of a relevance function for links in a hypertext database, in order to facilitate the computation of fisheye-views [TD92].

Let $G = (N, E)$ be a digraph representing a hypertext database and assume that all links (n, m) in E have a natural number attached to them, denoted by $rel(n, m)$, which represents the relevancy of the arc from the user's point of view; in addition, let max_rel denote the maximal relevance of any link in E. Also, denote the ith path from a node n to a node m in the transitive closure of G by $[n, m]_i$, where the paths from n to m are indexed in some manner.

The *path-dependent a priori relevance* of the ith path, $[n, m]_i$, denoted by $apr([n, m]_i)$, is a real number, defined by

1) $apr([n, n]_i) = 1$.

2) $apr([n, m]_i) = rel(n, m)/max\_rel$, if $[n, m]_i$ is the single arc (n, m) in E.

3) $apr([n, m]_i) = apr([n, p]_j) \times apr([p, m]_k)$, where $([n, p]_j)$ is the path resulting from removing the last arc (p, m) from $[n, m]_i$ and $[p, m]_k$ is the last arc of the path $[n, m]_i$.

(For more details on the transitive closure operation, see Definition 3.22 in Subsection 3.2.1 of Chapter 3).

Finally, we define the *path-independent a priori relevance* of a link (n, m) in the transitive closure of G, denoted by $APR(n, m)$, as follows:

1) $APR(n, n) = 1$.

2) $APR(n, m)$ is the maximum of $apr([n, m]_i)$ over all paths $[n, m]_i$ in G.

3) $APR(n, m)$ is undefined if there is no path from n to m in G.

Prove that $APR(n, m) \leq APR(n, p)$ and $APR(n, m) = APR(n, p) \times APR(p, m)$, where all the paths from n to m contain the node p. What are the shortcomings of the function APR?

Exercise 10.22 Show how a semistructured database can be formalised as a nondeterministic finite automaton, where labels and atomic values correspond to states of the automaton and attribute names correspond to transitions of the automaton from a given state to another state. (See Section 1.9.4 of Chapter 1 for more on deterministic and nondeterministic finite automata.)

A *DataGuide* for a semistructured database represented by a nondeterministic finite automaton, M, is defined as a deterministic finite automaton which is equivalent to M. Give an equivalent definition of a DataGuide in terms of how its path expressions relate to the semistructured database over which it is defined [GW97, NUWC97]. In addition, using an example database, demonstrate the utility of DataGuides as an aid for formulating and processing queries.

A *minimal* DataGuide for a semistructured database represented by a nondeterministic finite automaton M is one which has a minimal number of states. Discuss the desirability of minimal DataGuides by using an example database.

Exercise 10.23 Propose an update language for semistructured databases.

Exercise 10.24 The view maintenance problem is the problem of correctly updating a view when an update is performed on one of the relations of the underlying database (see Section 10.4 and the discussion at the end of Section 3.8 in Chapter 3). A view is *self-maintainable* with respect to an update if it can be maintained without accessing the database relations. We define an SP view to be a view formed from relation algebra expressions involving only selection, projection and renaming over a single relation, and an SPJ view to be a view formed from relational algebra expressions involving only selection, projection, (natural) join and renaming.

1) Show that all SP views are self-maintainable with respect to insertions.

2) Show that an SPJ view that involves the join of two or more distinct relations is not, in general, self-maintainable with respect to insertions.

3) Show that an SP view is self-maintainable with respect to deletions from a relation r_i over R_i, if some key K for R_i is included in the view definition, or K is equated to a tuple of constants in a selection formula defining the view.

4) Show that an SPJ view is self-maintainable with respect to deletions from a relation r_i over R_i, if for each occurrence of R_i in a join in the view definition, either some key K for R_i is included in the view definition, or K is equated to a tuple of constants in a selection formula defining the view.

5) An attribute in a relation schema R_i is *exposed* in a view, if, in the view definition, it is either involved in some selection formula or is a join attribute. Show that an SP view is self-maintainable with respect to modifications of unexposed attribute values of a relation r_i over R_i, if some key for R_i is included in the view definition.

6) Show that an SPJ view is self-maintainable with respect to modifications of unexposed attribute values of a relation r_i over R_i, if for each occurrence of R_i in a join in the view definition, some key for R_i is included in the view definition.

Exercise 10.25 Discuss with an example how historical relations can be utilised in the process of building and maintaining a data warehouse. (See Chapter 7 for details on historical relational databases.)

Exercise 10.26 Argue for the claim that the fact table of a star schema is naturally in a high normal form, i.e. 3NF or BCNF, while it is a waste of time to normalise the dimension tables of a star schema into such a high normal form.

Exercise 10.27 Design a star schema for an electronic mail order book store.

Exercise 10.28 Let r be a relation over R and $X \to Y$ be an FD over R. We say that an FD $X \to Y$ is ϵ-bad in r if

$$\frac{|\ \{t \in r\ |\ \text{there exists } u \in r \text{ such that } t[X] = u[X] \text{ and } t[Y] \neq u[Y]\}\ |}{|r|} > \epsilon,$$

where $0 < \epsilon < 1$, recalling that $|r|$ denotes the cardinality of a relation r.

Show that if the FD $X \rightarrow Y$ is ϵ-bad in r, then algorithm $GOOD(r, X \rightarrow Y, m)$, given below, returns NO with probability of at least $1 - \delta$, where $0 < \delta < 1$ [AT94, KM95]. (In the algorithm we let $m = (1/\epsilon)ln(1/\delta)$, where ln stands for the natural logarithm and $\lceil m \rceil$ denotes the least natural number greater than or equal to m.)

Algorithm 10.6 ($GOOD(r, X \rightarrow Y, m)$)
1. **begin**
2.   **repeat** $\lceil m \rceil$ times
3. $t :=$ random tuple from r;
4.   **if** there exists a tuple $u \in r$ such that $t[X] = u[X]$ and $t[Y] \neq u[Y]$ **then**
5.   **return** NO;
6.   **end if**
7.   **end repeat**
8.   **return** YES;
9. **end.**

Exercise 10.29 In this exercise we investigate an algorithm for mining the FDs in a relation r over a relation schema R [MR94].

Let $lhs(r, A)$, where $A \in schema(R)$, denote the set of all left-hand sides, X, of FDs such that $dep(r) \models X \rightarrow A$ and for no proper subset $Y \subset X$ is it true that $dep(r) \models Y \rightarrow A$. Now, given two tuples t and u in r we define the *agreement* set of t and u, denoted as $agree(t, u)$, by

$$agree(t, u) = \{B \in schema(R) \mid t[B] = u[B]\}.$$

The *disagreement* set of the tuples t and u, denoted as $disagree(t, u)$, is defined by

$$schema(R) - agree(t, u).$$

The *necessary* set of an attribute $A \in schema(R)$ with respect r, denoted as $nec(r, A)$, is defined by

$$nec(r, A) = \{disagree(t, u) - \{A\} \mid t, u \in r \text{ and } A \in disagree(t, u)\}.$$

Finally, we define the collection of all sets X in $nec(r, A)$ that are not supersets of other sets in $nec(r, A)$, denoted by $min\_nec(r, A)$, as

$$min\_nec(r, A) = \{X \in nec(r, A) \mid \text{ there does not exist } Y \in nec(r, A) \text{ such that } Y \subset X\}.$$

A database hypergraph, say $\mathcal{H}$, over a relation schema R is a collection of subsets of $schema(R)$; we assume that $\mathcal{H}$ is *simple*, that is to say, if $X, Y \in \mathcal{H}$ and $X \subseteq Y$ then $X = Y$. A subset T of $schema(R)$ is a *transversal* of $\mathcal{H}$, if for all sets of attributes $X \in \mathcal{H}$, $T \cap X \neq \emptyset$. A *minimal transversal* T of $\mathcal{H}$ is a transversal such that no proper subset $T' \subset T$ is also a transversal of $\mathcal{H}$. The collection of all minimal transversals of $\mathcal{H}$ is denoted by $TRANS(\mathcal{H})$.

Prove that $lhs(r, A) = TRANS(min\_nec(r, A))$.

Exercise 10.30 Argue that due to the additivity problem Algorithm 10.4 is not sufficient for the purpose of inferring the set of FDs that are weakly satisfied in an incomplete relation

[LV97]. (See Section 5.5 of Chapter 5 for the formalisation of the additivity problem for FDs holding in incomplete relations.)

Propose a solution for the FD dependency inference problem in incomplete relations [LV97]. (Hint: consider the maximal subsets G of F^+ with respect to Armstrong's axiom system such that $r \approx\!\!\!| \ G$ if and only if for all $X \to Y \in G$, $r \approx\!\!\!| \ X \to Y$.)

Exercise 10.31   In this exercise we investigate data mining association rules such as 90% of the customers that buy bread and jam also buy butter [AIS93, SON95, AMS$^+$96].

Let R be a relation schema having attributes $\{A_1, A_2, \ldots, A_m\}$ such that the domain of all the attributes $A_i \in$ schema(R) is $\{0, 1\}$. The attributes $A_i \in$ schema(R) are called *items*, and sets of attributes $X \subseteq$ schema(R) are called *itemsets*. A relation r over R is a finite set of tuples over R, which are also called *transactions*. With each transaction $t \in r$ we associate an itemset $X \subseteq$ schema(R), such that for all $i = 1, 2, \ldots, m$, $A_i \in X$ if and only if $t[A_i] = 1$. We say that X is an itemset of r to mean that X is an itemset associated with a transaction $t \in r$.

An *association rule* (or simply a rule) is an implication of the form $X \Rightarrow A$, where X is an itemset, A is an item, and $A \notin X$. The rule $X \Rightarrow A$ is satisfied in a relation r over R with *confidence c*, if at least c% of the itemsets of r that contain X also contain A. The rule $X \Rightarrow A$ has *support s* in the relation r, if at least s% of the itemsets of r contain XA.

The problem of data mining association rules in a relation r over R is to generate all the rules that are satisfied in r with confidence c and support s.

Discuss the significance of the support of a rule in a relation. Show that if $XB \Rightarrow A$ is satisfied in r with support s, then $X \Rightarrow A$ is also satisfied in r with support s, and show that the reverse implication does not necessarily hold. In addition, show that if $X \Rightarrow A$ is satisfied in r with confidence c, then $XB \Rightarrow A$ is not necessarily satisfied in r with confidence c, and show that the reverse implication does not necessarily hold.

Exercise 10.32   Devise an algorithm for data mining association rules, which were defined in Exercise 10.31, with confidence c and support s. (Hint: The *support* of a set of attributes $X \subseteq$ schema(R) in a relation r, over R, is the percentage of itemsets in r that contain X. It follows that $X \Rightarrow A$ is satisfied in r with confidence c, if the support of XA divided by the support of X multiplied by 100 is greater than or equal to c.)

Bibliography

[AABM82]   P. Atzeni, G. Ausiello, C. Batini, and M. Moscarini. Inclusion and equivalence between relational database schemata. *Theoretical Computer Science*, 19:267–285, 1982. [**233**]

[AAC⁺95]   J. Annevelink, R. Ahad, A. Carlson, D. Fishman, M. Heytens, and W. Kent. Object SQL — A language for the design and implementation of object databases. In W. Kim, editor, *Modern Database Systems, The Object Model, Interoperability, and Beyond*, pages 42–68. Addison-Wesley, Reading, Ma., 1995. [**28**]

[AAD⁺96]   S. Agarwal, R. Agrawal, P.M. Deshpande, A. Gupta, J.F. Naughton, R. Ramakrishnan, and S. Sarawagi. On the computation of multidimensional aggregates. In *Proceedings of International Conference on Very Large Data Bases*, pages 506–521, Bombay, 1996. [**562**]

[AB86]   S. Abiteboul and N. Bidoit. Non first normal form relations: An algebra allowing data restructuring. *Journal of Computer and System Sciences*, 33:361–393, 1986. [**569**]

[AB88]   K.R. Apt and H.A. Blair. Arithmetic classification of perfect models of stratified programs. In *Proceedings of International Conference on Logic Programming*, pages 765–779, Seattle, Wa., 1988. [**468, 483**]

[AB95]   S. Abiteboul and C. Beeri. The power of languages for the manipulation of complex objects. *The VLDB Journal*, 4:727–794, 1995. [**383**]

[ABD⁺89]   M.P. Atkinson, F. Bancilhon, D.J. DeWitt, K.R. Dittrich, D. Maier, and S.B. Zdonik. The object-oriented database system manifesto. In *Proceedings of International Conference on Deductive and Object-Oriented Databases*, pages 223–240, Kyoto, 1989. [**27, 529**]

[ABH97]   P.M.G. Apers, H.M. Blanken, and M.A.W. Houtsma, editors. *Multimedia Databases in Perspective*. Springer-Verlag, London, 1997. [**566**]

[Abi88]   S. Abiteboul. Updates, a new frontier. In *Proceedings of International Conference on Database Theory*, pages 1–18, Brüges, Belgium, 1988. [**132**]

[Abi89]   S. Abiteboul. Boundedness is undecidable for Datalog programs with a single recursive rule. *Information Processing Letters*, 32:281–287, 1989. [**491**]

[Abi97]   S. Abiteboul. Querying semi-structured data. In *International Conference on Database Theory*, pages 1–18, Delphi, 1997. Invited talk. [**560**]

[Abr74]   J.R. Abrial. Data semantics. In J.W. Klimbie and K.L. Koffeman, editors, *Data Base Management*, pages 1–59. North-Holland, Amsterdam, 1974. [**81**]

[ABU79]   A.V. Aho, C. Beeri, and J.D. Ullman. The theory of joins in relational databases. *ACM Transactions on Database Systems*, 4:297–314, 1979. [**165, 199, 200**]

[ABW88]   K.R. Apt, H.A. Blair, and A. Walker. Towards a theory of declarative knowledge. In J. Minker, editor, *Foundations of Deductive Databases and Logic Programming*, pages 89–148. Morgan Kaufmann, San Francisco, Ca., 1988. [**468, 469**]

[AC75]   M.M. Astrahan and D.D. Chamberlin. Implementation of a structured English query language. *Communications of the ACM*, 18:580–588, 1975. [**113**]

[AC83]   P. Atzeni and P.P.-S. Chen. Completeness of query languages for the entity-relationship model. In P.P.-S. Chen, editor, *Entity-Relationship Approach to Information Modelling and Analysis*, pages 109–122. North-Holland, Amsterdam, 1983. [**83**]

[AC84]   A.K. Arora and C.R. Carlson. Normalization could be useful. *The Computer Journal*, 27:57–61, 1984. [**283**]

[AC89]   F. Afrati and S.S. Cosmadakis. Expressiveness of restricted recursive rules. In *Proceedings of ACM Symposium on Theory of Computing*, pages 113–126, Seattle, Wa., 1989. [**489**]

[AC91]   P. Atzeni and E.P.F. Chan. Independent database schemes under functional and inclusion dependencies. *Acta Informatica*, 28:777–799, 1991. [**232**]

[ACL87]   R. Agrawal, M.J. Carey, and M. Livny. Concurrency control perfomance modeling: Alternatives and
            implications. *ACM Transactions on Database Systems*, 12:609–654, 1987. [**434**]

[ACY91]   F. Afrati, S.S. Cosmadakis, and M. Yannakakis. On Datalog vs. polynomial time. In *Proceedings of ACM
            Symposium on Principles of Database Systems*, pages 13–25, Denver, Co., 1991. [**495, 497**]

[AD80]   W.W. Armstrong and C. Delobel. Decomposition and functional dependencies in relations. *ACM Transactions
            on Database Systems*, 5:404–430, 1980. [**195**]

[AD93]   P. Atzeni and V. De Antonellis. *Relational Database Theory*. Benjamin/Cummings, Redwood City, Ca., 1993.
            [**377**]

[ADS86]   G. Ausiello, A. D'atri, and D. Saccà. Minimal representation of directed hypergraphs. *SIAM Journal on
            Computing*, 15:418–431, 1986. [**211**]

[Afr94]   F. Afrati. Bounded arity Datalog (≠) queries on graphs. In *Proceedings of ACM Symposium on Principles of
            Database Systems*, pages 97–106, Minneapolis, Mn., 1994. [**497**]

[AFS89]   S. Abiteboul, P.C. Fischer, and H.-J. Schek, editors. *Nested Relations and Complex Objects in Databases*,
            volume 361 of *Lecture Notes in Computer Science*. Springer-Verlag, Berlin, 1989. [**522, 524**]

[AG85]   S. Abiteboul and G. Grahne. Update semantics for incomplete databases. In *Proceedings of International
            Conference on Very Large Data Bases*, pages 1–12, Stockholm, 1985. [**502**]

[AG94]   M. Ajtai and Y. Gurevich. Datalog vs first-order logic. *Journal of Computer and System Sciences*, 49:562–588,
            1994. [**492**]

[AGM⁺97]   S. Abiteboul, R. Goldman, J. McHugh, V. Vassalos, and Y. Zhuge. Views for semistructured data. In
            Proceedings of Workshop on Management of Semistructured Data, Tucson, Az., 1997. [**560**]

[AGSS86]   A.K. Ailamazyan, M.M. Gilula, A.P. Stolboushkin, and G.F. Schwartz. Reduction of a relational model with
            infinite domains to the finite-domain case. *Soviet Physics Doklady*, 31:11–13, 1986. [**139**]

[AGV89]   S. Abiteboul, M. Gyssens, and D. Van Gucht. An alternative way to represent the cogroup of a relation in the
            context of nested relations. *Information Processing Letters*, 32:317–324, 1989. [**377**]

[AH87]   S. Abiteboul and R. Hull. IFO: A formal semantic data model. *ACM Transactions on Database Systems*,
            12:525–565, 1987. [**81**]

[AH88a]   S. Abiteboul and R. Hull. Data functions, Datalog and negation. In *Proceedings of ACM SIGMOD Conference
            on Management of Data*, pages 143–153, Chicago, Il., 1988. [**503, 512**]

[AH88b]   S. Abiteboul and R. Hull. Restructuring hierarchical objects. *Theoretical Computer Science*, 62:3–38, 1988.
            [**524**]

[AH91]   A. Avron and J. Hirshfeld. On first-order database query languages. In *Proceedings of IEEE Symposium on
            Logic in Computer Science*, pages 226–231, Amsterdam, 1991. [**139**]

[AHU83]   A.V. Aho, J.E. Hopcroft, and J.D. Ullman. *Data Structures and Algorithms*. Addison-Wesley, Reading Ma.,
            1983. [**17, 35, 52, 172, 179, 203, 469**]

[AHV95a]   S. Abiteboul, L. Herr, and J. Van den Bussche. Temporal connectives versus explicit timestamps in temporal
            query languages. In *Recent Advances in Temporal Databases, Proceedings of the International Workshop on
            Temporal Databases*, pages 43–57, Zurich, 1995. [**399**]

[AHV95b]   S. Abiteboul, R. Hull, and V. Vianu. *Foundations of Databases*. Addison-Wesley, Reading, Ma., 1995. [**379,
            493**]

[AHV96]   S. Abiteboul, L. Herr, and J. Van den Bussche. Temporal versus first-order logic to query temporal databases.
            In *Proceedings of ACM Symposium on Principles of Database Systems*, pages 49–57, Montreal, 1996. [**399**]

[AIS93]   R. Agrawal, T. Imielinski, and A. Swani. Mining associations rules between sets of items in large databases. In
            Proceedings of ACM SIGMOD Conference on Management of Data, pages 207–216, Washington, D.C., 1993.
            [**575**]

[AJR97]   P. Ammann, S. Jajodia, and I. Ray. Applying formal methods to semantic-based decomposition of
            transactions. *ACM Transactions on Database Systems*, 22:215–254, 1997. [**453**]

[AK89]   S. Abiteboul and P.C. Kanellakis. Object identity as a query language primitive. In *Proceedings of ACM
            SIGMOD Conference on Management of Data*, pages 159–173, Portland, Oregon, 1989. [**529**]

[AK90]   F. Afrati and C.D. Koutras. A hypertext model supporting query mechanisms. In *Proceedings of European
            Conference on Hypertext*, pages 52–66, France, 1990. INRIA. [**554**]

[All83]   J.F. Allen. Maintaining knowledge about temporal intervals. *Communications of the ACM*, 26:832–843, 1983.
            [**388, 391**]

[AM84]   P. Atzeni and N.M. Morfuni. Functional dependencies in relations with null values. *Information Processing
            Letters*, 18:233–238, 1984. [**314, 355**]

[AMS⁺96]   R. Agrawal, H. Mannila, R. Srikant, H. Toivonen, and A.I. Verkamo. Fast discovery of association rules. In U.M. Fayyad, G. Piatetsky-Shapiro, P. Smyth, and R. Uthurusamy, editors, *Advances in Knowledge Discovery and Data Mining*, pages 307–328. AAAI Press, Menlo Park, Ca., 1996. [**575**]

[ANS75]   ANSI/X3/SPARC. Study group on database management systems, interim report. *Bulletin of ACM SIGFIDET*, 7(2), 1975. [**287**]

[Apt90]   K.R. Apt. Logic programming. In J. Van Leeuwen, editor, *Handbook of Theoretical Computer Science*, volume B, chapter 10, pages 493–574. Elsevier Science Publishers, Amsterdam, 1990. [**463, 468, 479, 483**]

[Apt97]   K.R. Apt. *From Logic Programming to Prolog*. Prentice Hall, Englewood Cliffs, NJ, 1997. [**23, 40**]

[AQM⁺97]   S. Abiteboul, D. Quass, J. McHugh, J. Widom, and J.L. Wiener. The Lorel query language for semistructured data. *International Journal on Digital Libraries*, 1:68–88, 1997. [**559, 560**]

[Arm74]   W.W. Armstrong. Dependency structures of data base relationships. In *Proceedings of IFIP Congress*, pages 580–583, Stockholm, 1974. [**148, 152, 158, 227**]

[Aro94]   L. Aronson. *HTML, Manual of Style*. Ziff-Davis Press, Emeryville, Ca., 1994. [**550**]

[ART95]   I. Androutsopoulos, R.D. Ritchie, and P. Thanisch. Experience using TSQL2 in a natural language interface. In *Recent Advances in Temporal Databases, Proceedings of the International Workshop on Temporal Databases*, pages 113–132, Zurich, 1995. [**403**]

[AS92]   B. Amann and M. Scholl. Gram: A graph data model and query language. In *Proceedings of ACM Conference on Hypertext*, pages 201–211, Milano, Italy, 1992. [**554**]

[Ash94]   H. Ashman. What is hypermedia? *ACM SIGLINK Newsletter*, 3:6–8, 1994. [**551**]

[ASU79]   A.V. Aho, Y. Sagiv, and J.D. Ullman. Equivalences among relational expressions. *SIAM Journal on Computing*, 8:218–246, 1979. [**484**]

[ASV90]   S. Abiteboul, E. Simon, and V. Vianu. Non-deterministic languages to express deterministic transformations. In *Proceedings of ACM Symposium on Principles of Database Systems*, pages 218–229, Nashville, Te., 1990. [**384**]

[AT91]   P. Atzeni and R. Torlone. Solving ambiguities in updating deductive databases. In *Proceedings of Symposium on Mathematical Foundations of Database Systems*, pages 104–118, Rostock, Germany, 1991. [**500**]

[AT92]   P. Atzeni and R. Torlone. Updating intensional predicates in Datalog. *Data and Knowledge Engineering*, 8:1–17, 1992. [**500**]

[AT94]   T. Akutsu and A. Takasu. On pac learnability of functional dependencies. *New Generation Computing*, 12:359–374, 1994. [**565, 574**]

[AU79]   A.V. Aho and J.D. Ullman. Universality of data retrieval languages. In *Proceedings of ACM Symposium on Principles of Programming Languages*, pages 110–120, San-Antonio, Texas, 1979. [**24, 102, 377, 383, 459**]

[AV82]   K.R. Apt and M.H. Van Emden. Contributions to the theory of logic programming. *Journal of the ACM*, 29:841–862, 1982. [**479**]

[AV85]   S. Abiteboul and V. Vianu. Transactions and integrity constraints. In *Proceedings of ACM Symposium on Principles of Database Systems*, pages 193–204, Portland, Oregon, 1985. [**132, 229**]

[AV88]   S. Abiteboul and V. Vianu. Equivalence and optimization of relational transactions. *Journal of the ACM*, 35:70–120, 1988. [**130, 132**]

[AV89]   S. Abiteboul and V. Vianu. A transaction-based approach to relational database specification. *Journal of the ACM*, 36:758–789, 1989. [**132, 229**]

[AV90]   S. Abiteboul and V. Vianu. Procedural languages for database queries and updates. *Journal of Computer and System Sciences*, 41:181–229, 1990. [**27, 365, 373, 383**]

[AV91a]   S. Abiteboul and V. Vianu. Datalog extensions for database queries and updates. *Journal of Computer and System Sciences*, 43:62–124, 1991. [**365, 373, 379, 383, 466, 479, 482**]

[AV91b]   S. Abiteboul and V. Vianu. Generic computation and its complexity. In *Proceedings of ACM Symposium on Theory of Computing*, pages 209–219, New Orleans, Lo., 1991. [**365, 373, 383**]

[AV92]   S. Abiteboul and V. Vianu. Expressive power of query languages. In J.D. Ullman, editor, *Theoretical Studies in Computer Science*, pages 207–252. Academic Press, Boston, 1992. [**383**]

[AV93]   S. Abiteboul and V. Vianu. Computing on structures. In *Proceedings of International Colloquium on Automata, Languages and Programming*, pages 606–620, Lund, Sweden, 1993. [**381, 383**]

[AV95]   S. Abiteboul and V. Vianu. Computing with first-order logic. *Journal of Computer and System Sciences*, 50:309–335, 1995. [**383, 384**]

[AVA⁺94]   G. Alonso, R. Vingralek, D. Agrawal, Y. Breitbart, A. El Abbadi, H.-J. Schek, and G. Weikum. Unifying concurrency control and recovery transactions. *Information Systems*, 19:101–115, 1994. [**453**]

[AVV95]   S. Abiteboul, M.Y. Vardi, and V. Vianu. Computing with infinitary logic. *Theoretical Computer Science*, 149:101–128, 1995. [**382**]

[AVV97]   S. Abiteboul, M.Y. Vardi, and V. Vianu. Fixpoint logics, relational machines, and computational complexity. *Journal of the ACM*, 44:30–56, 1997. [**383**]

[AWH92]   A. Aitken, J. Widom, and J.M. Hellerstein. Behavior of database production rules: Termination, confluence, and observable determinism. In *Proceedings of ACM SIGMOD Conference on Management of Data*, pages 59–68, San Diego, Ca., 1992. [**545, 571**]

[Bac69]   C.W. Bachman. Data structure diagrams. *Data Base*, 1:4–10, 1969. [**2, 64**]

[Bac73]   C.W. Bachman. The programmer as a navigator. *Communications of the ACM*, 16:653–658, 1973. [**2**]

[BADW82]   A. Bolour, T.L. Anderson, L.J. Dekeyser, and H.K.T. Wong. The role of time in information processing: A survey. *ACM SIGART Newsletter*, 80:28–48, 1982. [**388**]

[Ban78]   F. Bancilhon. On the completeness of query languages for relational data bases. In *Proceedings of Conference on Mathematical Foundations of Computer Science*, pages 112–123, Zakopane, Poland, 1978. [**377**]

[Ban92]   F. Bancilhon. Understanding object-oriented databases. In *Proceedings of International Conference on Extending Database Technology*, pages 1–9, Vienna, Austria, 1992. [**529**]

[Bar73]   J. Barwise. Back and forth through infinitary logic. In M.D. Morley, editor, *Studies in Model Theory*, volume 8, pages 5–34. The Mathematical Association of America, Washington, D.C., 1973. [**55**]

[Bar77]   J. Barwise. On Moschovakis closure ordinals. *The Journal of Symbolic Logic*, 42:292–296, 1977. [**57**]

[BB79]   C. Beeri and P.A. Bernstein. Computational problems related to the design of normal form relational schemas. *ACM Transactions on Database Systems*, 4:30–59, 1979. [**160, 227, 230, 259**]

[BB92]   L. Bolc and P. Borowik. *Many-Valued Logics 1: Theoretical Foundations*. Springer-Verlag, Berlin, 1992. [**303, 333, 352**]

[BBG89]   C. Beeri, P.A. Bernstein, and N. Goodman. A model for concurrency in nested transactions systems. *Journal of the ACM*, 36:230–269, 1989. [**442**]

[BBG+95]   H. Berenson, P.A. Bernstein, J. Gray, J. Melton, E.J. O'Neil, and P.E. O'Neil. A critique of ANSI SQL isolation levels. In *Proceedings of ACM SIGMOD Conference on Management of Data*, pages 1–10, San Jose, Ca., 1995. [**453**]

[BCN92]   C. Batini, S. Ceri, and S.B. Navathe. *Conceptual Database Design: An Entity-Relationship Approach*. Benjamin/Cummings, Redwood City, Ca., 1992. [**68, 80, 82**]

[BDB79]   J. Biskup, U. Dayal, and P.A. Bernstein. Synthesizing independent database schemes. In *Proceedings of ACM SIGMOD Conference on Management of Data*, pages 143–151, Boston, Ma., 1979. [**246, 269**]

[BDFS84]   C. Beeri, M. Dowd, R. Fagin, and R. Statman. On the structure of Armstrong relations for functional dependencies. *Journal of the ACM*, 31:30–46, 1984. [**148, 159, 231**]

[BDHS96]   P. Buneman, S. Davidson, G. Hillebrand, and D. Suciu. A query language and optimization techniques for unstructured data. In *Proceedings of ACM SIGMOD Conference on Management of Data*, pages 505–516, Montreal, 1996. [**560**]

[BDK87]   G. Burosch, J. Demetrovics, and G.O.H. Katona. The poset of closures as a model of changing databases. *Order*, 4:127–142, 1987. [**148**]

[BDLM91]   J. Biskup, J. Demetrovics, L.O. Libkin, and I.B. Muchnik. On relational database schemes having unique minimal key. *Journal of Information Processing and Cybernetics*, 27:217–225, 1991. [**257**]

[BDM88]   F. Bry, H. Decker, and R. Manthey. A uniform approach to constraint satisfiability in deductive databases. In *Proceedings of International Conference on Extending Database Technology*, pages 488–505, Venice, 1988. [**508**]

[BDP94]   P. Bosc, D. Dubois, and H. Prade. Fuzzy functional dependencies — an overview and a critical discussion. In *Proceedings of IEEE International Conference on Fuzzy Systems*, pages 325–330, Orlando, Florida, 1994. [**341**]

[Bea89]   J.D. Beasley. *The Mathematics of Games*. Oxford University Press, Oxford, U.K., 1989. [**467**]

[Bec78]   L.L. Beck. On minimal sets of operations for relational database sublanguages. Technical Report CS 7802, Department of Computer Science, Southern Methodist University, Dallas, 1978. [**100**]

[Bee80]   C. Beeri. On the membership problem for functional and multivalued dependencies in relational databases. *ACM Transactions on Database Systems*, 5:241–259, 1980. [**194**]

[Bee90]   C. Beeri. New direction in database management systems. In *Proceedings of Jerusalem Conference on Information Technology*, pages 500–506, Jerusalem, Israel, 1990. [**529**]

[Bel77a]   N.D. Belnap. How a computer should think. In G. Ryle, editor, *Contemporary Aspects of Philosophy*, pages 30–56. Oriel Press, Stocksfield, 1977. [**352**]

[Bel77b]   N.D. Belnap. A useful four-valued logic. In J.M. Dunn and G. Epstein, editors, *Modern Uses of Multiple-Valued Logic*, pages 8–37. Reidel, Dordrecht, Netherlands, 1977. [**352**]

[Bel95a]   S. Bell.   Discovery and maintenance of functional dependencies by independencies.   In *Proceedings of International Conference on Knowledge Discovery and Data Mining*, pages 27–32, Montreal, 1995. **[565]**

[Bel95b]   S. Bell. The expanded implication problem of data dependencies. Technical Report LS-8 Report 16, Informatik VIII, University of Dortmund, 1995. **[215]**

[Ber76]   P.A. Bernstein. Synthesizing third normal form relations from functional dependencies. *ACM Transactions on Database Systems*, 1:277–298, 1976. **[247, 269]**

[Ber88]   M. Bernstein.   The bookmark and the compass: Orientation tools for hypertext users.   *SIGOIS Bulletin*, 9:34–45, 1988. **[554]**

[Bes89]   P. Besnard. *An Introduction to Default Logic*. Springer-Verlag, Berlin, 1989. **[347, 468, 479]**

[BF85]   J. Barwise and S. Feferman, editors. *Model-Theoretic Logics*. Perspectives in Mathematical Logic. Springer-Verlag, Berlin, 1985. **[382]**

[BF91a]   N. Bidoit and C. Froidevaux.   General logical databases and programs: Default logic semantics and stratification. *Information and Computation*, 91:15–54, 1991. **[468, 479]**

[BF91b]   N. Bidoit and C. Froidevaux. Negation by default and unstratifiable logic programs. *Theoretical Computer Science*, 78:85–112, 1991. **[468, 479]**

[BFH77]   C. Beeri, R. Fagin, and J.H. Howard. A complete axiomatization for functional and multivalued dependencies. In *Proceedings of ACM SIGMOD Conference on Management of Data*, pages 47–61, Toronto, Canada, 1977. **[193]**

[BFMY83]   C. Beeri, R. Fagin, D. Maier, and M. Yannakakis. On the desirability of acyclic database schemes. *Journal of the ACM*, 30:479–513, 1983. **[196, 205, 209, 211, 282]**

[BG81]   P.A. Bernstein and N. Goodman.   Concurrency control in distributed database systems.   *ACM Computing Surveys*, 13:185–221, 1981. **[446, 454]**

[BG87]   A. Blass and Y. Gurevich. Existential fixed-point logic. In E. Borger, editor, *Computation Theory and Logic*, volume 270 of *Lecture Notes in Computer Science*, pages 20–36. Springer-Verlag, Berlin, 1987. **[383, 482]**

[BGK85]   A. Blass, Y. Gurevich, and D. Kozen. A zero-one law for logic with a fixed-point operator. *Information and Control*, 67:70–90, 1985. **[59]**

[BGP92]   D. Barbará, H. Garcia-Molina, and D. Porter. The management of probabilistic data. *IEEE Transactions on Knowledge and Data Engineering*, 4:487–502, 1992. **[354]**

[BH79]   A. Blass and F. Harary. Properties of almost all graphs and complexes. *Journal of Graph Theory*, 3:225–240, 1979. **[58]**

[BH81]   C. Beeri and P. Honeyman.   Preserving functional dependencies.   *SIAM Journal on Computing*, 10:647–656, 1981. **[168]**

[BH90]   F. Buckley and F. Harary. *Distance in Graphs*. Addison-Wesley, Redwood City, Ca., 1990. **[33, 63]**

[BHG87]   P.A. Bernstein, V. Hadzilacos, and N. Goodman. *Concurrency Control and Recovery in Database Systems*. Addison-Wesley, Reading, Ma., 1987. **[448, 450, 453]**

[Bid91]   N. Bidoit. Negation in rule-based database languages: a survey. *Theoretical Computer Science*, 78:3–84, 1991. **[468]**

[Bis78]   J. Biskup. On the complementation rule for multivalued dependencies in database relations. *Acta Informatica*, 10:297–305, 1978. **[194]**

[Bis89]   J. Biskup.   Boyce-Codd normal form and object normal forms.   *Information Processing Letters*, 32:29–33, 1989. **[258]**

[Bis98]   J. Biskup. Achievements of relational database schema design theory revisited. In B. Thalheim and L. Libkin, editors, *Semantics in Databases*, pages 29–54. Springer-Verlag, Berlin, 1998. **[227, 282]**

[BJ89]   G.S. Boolos and R.C. Jeffrey. *Computability and Logic*. Cambridge University Press, Cambridge, U.K., third edition, 1989. **[40]**

[BJO91]   P. Buneman, A. Jung, and A. Ohori.   Using powerdomains to generalize relational databases.   *Theoretical Computer Science*, 94:23–55, 1991. **[299]**

[BJS95]   M.H. Böhlen, C.S. Jensen, and R.T. Snodgrass. Evaluating the completeness of TSQL2. In *Recent Advances in Temporal Databases, Proceedings of the International Workshop on Temporal Databases*, pages 153–172, Zurich, 1995. **[403]**

[BK86]   C. Beeri and M. Kifer.   An integrated approach to logical design of relational database schemes.   *ACM Transactions on Database Systems*, 11:134–158, 1986. **[198, 249]**

[BK90]   C. Beeri and Y. Kornatzky. A logical query language for hypertext systems. In *Proceedings of European Conference on Hypertext*, pages 67–80. INRIA, France, 1990. **[554, 572]**

[BK91]   N.S. Barghouti and G.E. Kaiser.   Concurrency control in advanced database applications.   *ACM Computing Surveys*, 23:269–317, 1991. **[428]**

[BKV98]   P. Brusilovsky, A. Kobsa, and J. Vassileva, editors. *Adaptive Hypertext and Hypermedia*. Kluwer, Dordrecht, 1998. [**554**]

[BM87]   J. Biskup and R. Meyer. Design of relational database schemes by deleting attributes in the canonical decomposition. *Journal of Computer and System Sciences*, 35:1–22, 1987. [**248, 269**]

[BM94]   M. Bain and S. Muggleton. Learning optimal chess strategies. In K. Furukawa, D. Michie, and S. Muggleton, editors, *Machine Intelligence*, volume 13, pages 291–309. Clarendon Press, Oxford, U.K., 1994. [**566**]

[BMSU81]   C. Beeri, A.O. Mendelzon, Y. Sagiv, and J.D. Ullman. Equivalence of relational database schemes. *SIAM Journal on Computing*, 10:352–370, 1981. [**201, 202**]

[BN97]   P.A. Bernstein and E. Newcomer. *Principles of Transaction Processing for the Systems Professional*. Morgan Kaufmann, San Francisco, Ca., 1997. [**448, 453**]

[Bor80]   S.A. Borkin. The semantic relation data model: Foundation for a user interface. In *Proceedings of International Conference on Data Bases*, pages 47–64, Aberdeen, 1980. [**540**]

[BP94]   T. Beaubouef and F.E. Petry. Fuzzy set quantification of roughness in a rough relational database model. In *Proceedings of IEEE International Conference on Fuzzy Systems*, pages 172–177, Orlando, Florida, 1994. [**343**]

[BP98]   S. Brin and L. Page. The anatomy of a large-scale hypertextual web search engine. In *Proceedings of International World Wide Web Conference*, Brisbane, 1998. [**555**]

[BPB95]   T. Beaubouef, F.E. Petry, and B.P. Buckles. Extension of the relational database and its algebra with rough set techniques. *Computational Intelligence*, 11:233–245, 1995. [**343**]

[BPP76]   G. Bracchi, P. Paolini, and G. Pelagatti. Binary logical associations in data modelling. In G.M. Nijssen, editor, *Modelling in Data Base Management Systems*, pages 125–148. North-Holland, Amsterdam, 1976. [**81**]

[BPS64]   Y. Bar-Hillel, M. Perles, and E. Shamir. On formal properties of simple phrase structure grammars. In Y. Bar-Hillel, editor, *Language and Information: Selected Essays on their Theory and Applications*, pages 116–150. Addison-Wesley, Reading, Ma., 1964. [**43**]

[BR84]   F. Bancilhon and P. Richard. A sound and complete axiomatization of embedded cross dependencies. *Theoretical Computer Science*, 34:343–350, 1984. [**211**]

[BR86]   F. Bancilhon and R. Ramakrishnan. An amateur's introduction to recursive query processing strategies. In *Proceedings of ACM SIGMOD International Conference on Management of Data*, pages 16–52, Washington, D.C., 1986. [**493**]

[BR91]   C. Beeri and R. Ramakrishnan. On the power of magic. *Journal of Logic Programming*, 10:255–299, 1991. [**493, 511**]

[BRS90]   J. Biskup, U. Räsch, and H. Stiefeling. An extension of SQL for querying graph relations. *Computer Languages*, 15:65–82, 1990. [**540**]

[Bru96]   P. Brusilovsky. Methods and techniques of adaptive hypermedia. *User Modeling and User-Adapted Interaction*, 6:87–129, 1996. [**554**]

[Bry89]   F. Bry. Logic programming as constructivism: a formalization and its applications to databases. In *Proceedings of ACM Symposium on Principles of Database Systems*, pages 34–50, Philadelphia, Pa., 1989. [**468**]

[BS81a]   F. Bancilhon and N. Spyratos. Independent components of data bases. In *Proceedings of International Conference on Very Large Data Bases*, pages 398–408, Cannes, 1981. [**225**]

[BS81b]   F. Bancilhon and N. Spyratos. Update semantics of relational views. *ACM Transactions on Database Systems*, 6:557–575, 1981. [**223–225**]

[BS95]   R. Bagai and R. Sunderraman. A paraconsistent relational data model. *International Journal of Computer Mathematics*, 55:39–55, 1995. [**352**]

[BSW79]   P.A. Bernstein, D.W. Shipman, and W.S. Wong. Formal aspects of serializability in database concurrency control. *IEEE Transactions on Software Engineering*, 5:203–216, 1979. [**453**]

[Bul87]   W.I. Bullers Jr. A processing algorithm for master-detail records in a relational database. *Software-Practice and Experience*, 17:701–717, 1987. [**355**]

[Bun97]   P. Buneman. Semistructured data. In *Proceedings of ACM Symposium on Principles of Database Systems*, pages 117–121, Tucson, Az., 1997. Invited talk. [**560**]

[Bus45]   V. Bush. As we may think. *Atlantic Monthly*, 76:101–108, 1945. [**555**]

[BV80]   C. Beeri and M.Y. Vardi. On the complexity of testing implications of data dependencies. Research Report, Department of Computer Science, The Hebrew University of Jerusalem, Jerusalem, Israel, 1980. [**203**]

[BV81]   C. Beeri and M.Y. Vardi. On the properties of join dependencies. In H. Gallaire, J. Minker, and J.-M. Nicholas, editors, *Advances in Database Theory*, volume 1, pages 25–72. Plenum Press, New York, 1981. [**202, 211**]

[BV84a]   C. Beeri and M.Y. Vardi. Formal systems for tuple and equality generating dependencies. *SIAM Journal on Computing*, 13:76–98, 1984. [**211, 504**]

[BV84b]   C. Beeri and M.Y. Vardi. On acyclic database decompositions. *Information and Control*, 61:75–84, 1984. [**210**]

[BV84c]   C. Beeri and M.Y. Vardi. A proof procedure for data dependencies. *Journal of the ACM*, 31:718–741, 1984. [**211, 504**]

[BV85]   C. Beeri and M.Y. Vardi. Formal systems for join dependencies. *Theoretical Computer Science*, 38:99–116, 1985. [**202**]

[CA79]   C.R. Carlson and A.K. Arora. The updatability of relational views based on functional dependencies. In *Proceedings of IEEE International Conference on Computer Software and Applications*, pages 415–420, Chicago, Il., 1979. [**225**]

[CA84]   M.A. Casanova and J.E. Amaral de Sa. Mapping uninterpreted schemes into entity-relationship diagrams: Two applications to conceptual schema design. *IBM Journal of Research and Development*, 28:82–94, 1984. [**81, 243, 263, 277, 281**]

[Can55]   G. Cantor. *Contributions to the Founding of the Theory of Transfinite Numbers*. Dover, New York, 1955. [**46**]

[Car88]   L. Cardelli. A semantics of multiple inheritance. *Information and Computation*, 76:138–164, 1988. [**27**]

[Cas81]   M.A. Casanova. *The Concurrency Control Problem for Database Systems*, volume 116 of *Lecture Notes in Computer Science*. Springer-Verlag, Berlin, 1981. [**453, 454**]

[Cat96]   R.G.G. Cattell, editor. *The Object Database Standard, ODMG-93: Release 1.2*. Morgan Kaufmann, San Francisco, Ca., 1996. [**28, 531**]

[CB97]   R.G.G. Cattell and D.K. Barry, editors. *The Object Database Standard: ODMG 2.0*. Morgan Kaufmann, San Francisco, Ca., 1997. [**28, 531**]

[CCM92]   M.P. Consens, I.F. Cruz, and A.O. Mendelzon. Visualizing queries and querying visualizations. *ACM SIGMOD Record*, 21:39–46, 1992. [**540**]

[CCS93]   E.F. Codd, S.B. Codd, and C.T. Salley. Providing OLAP (On-Line Analytical Processing) to user-analysts: An IT mandate. White Paper, E.F Codd & Associates, 1993. [**562**]

[CCT93]   J. Clifford, A. Croker, and A. Tuzhilin. On the completeness of query languages for grouped and ungrouped historical data models. In A.U, Tansel, J. Clifford, S. Gadia, S. Jajodia, A. Segev, and R. Snodgrass, editors, *Temporal Databases, Theory, Design, and Implementation*, pages 496–533. Benjamin/Cummings, Redwood City, Ca., 1993. [**399**]

[CD97]   S. Chaudhuri and U. Dayal. An overview of data warehousing and OLAP technology. *ACM SIGMOD Record*, 26:65–74, 1997. [**563**]

[CDI+97]   J. Clifford, C. Dyreson, T. Isakowitz, C.S. Jensen, and R.T. Snodgrass. On the semantics of "now" in databases. *ACM Transactions on Database Systems*, 22:171–214, 1997. [**396**]

[CEG94]   M. Cadoli, T. Eiter, and G. Gottlob. Default logic as a query language. In *Proceedings of Principles of Knowledge Representation and Reasoning*, pages 99–108, Bonn, Germany, 1994. [**468**]

[CFP84]   M.A. Casanova, R. Fagin, and C.H. Papadimitriou. Inclusion dependencies and their interaction with functional dependencies. *Journal of Computer and System Sciences*, 28:29–59, 1984. [**173, 174, 178, 180, 182, 199**]

[CFT91]   M.A. Casanova, A.L. Furtado, and L. Tucherman. A software tool for modular database design. *ACM Transactions on Database Systems*, 16:209–234, 1991. [**226**]

[CG88]   B. Campbell and J.M. Goodman. Ham: A general purpose hypertext abstract machine. *Communications of the ACM*, 31:856–861, 1988. [**553**]

[CGKV88]   S.S. Cosmadakis, H. Gaifman, P.C. Kanellakis, and M.Y. Vardi. Decidable optimization problems for database logic programs. In *Proceedings of ACM Symposium on Theory of Computing*, pages 477–490, Chicago, Il., 1988. [**489**]

[CGT90]   S. Ceri, G. Gottlob, and L. Tanca. *Logic Programming and Databases*. Springer-Verlag, Berlin, 1990. [**2, 479, 493**]

[CH80]   A.K. Chandra and D. Harel. Computable queries for relational data bases. *Journal of Computer and System Sciences*, 21:156–178, 1980. [**27, 360, 365, 371, 372**]

[CH82]   A.K. Chandra and D. Harel. Structure and complexity of relational queries. *Journal of Computer and System Sciences*, 25:99–128, 1982. [**379, 380, 383, 384**]

[CH85]   A.K. Chandra and D. Harel. Horn clause queries and generalizations. *Journal of Logic Programming*, 1:1–15, 1985. [**468**]

[Cha76]   D.D. Chamberlin. Relational data-base management systems. *ACM Computing Surveys*, 8:43–66, 1976. [**1**]

[Cha77]   G. Chartrand. *Introductory Graph Theory*. Dover, Mineola, NY, 1977. [**33, 63**]

[Cha80]   D.D. Chamberlin. A summary of user experience with the SQL data sublanguage. Research Report RJ2767 (35322), IBM Research Laboratory, San Jose, Ca., 1980. [**113**]

[Cha81]   A.K. Chandra. Programming primitives for database languages. In *Proceedings of ACM Symposium on Principles of Programming Languages*, pages 50–62, Williamsburg, Virginia, 1981. [**378, 383**]

[Cha88]   A.K. Chandra. Theory of database queries. In *Proceedings of ACM Symposium on Principles of Database Systems*, pages 1–9, Austin, Texas, 1988. [**379, 383**]

[Cha89]   S. Chakravarthy. Rule management and evaluation: An active DBMS perspective. *ACM SIGMOD Record*, 18:20–28, 1989. [**547**]

[Cha96]   C. Chatfield. *The Analysis of Time Series: An Introduction*. Chapman & Hall, London, fifth edition, 1996. [**399**]

[Che76]   P.P.-S. Chen. The entity-relationship model – toward a unified view of data. *ACM Transactions on Database Systems*, 1:9–36, 1976. [**9, 61–63, 71, 80, 81**]

[Che77]   P.P.-S. Chen. *The Entity-Relationship Approach to Logical Database Design*. QED Information Sciences, Wellesley, Ma., 1977. [**61–63, 71, 80, 81**]

[Che80]   B.F. Chellas. *Modal Logic: An Introduction*. Cambridge University Press, Cambridge, U.K., 1980. [**309**]

[Che84]   P.P.-S. Chen. An algebra for a directional binary entity-relationship model. In *Proceedings of IEEE International Conference on Data Engineering*, pages 37–40, Los Angeles, 1984. [**81, 83**]

[Che86]   P. Cheesman. Probabilistic versus fuzzy reasoning. In L.N. Kanal and J.F. Lemmer, editors, *Uncertainty in Artificial Intelligence*, pages 85–102. North-Holland, Amsterdam, 1986. [**354**]

[Chi68]   D.L. Childs. Feasibility of a set-theoretic data structure, a general structure based on a reconstituted definition of a relation. In *Proceedings of IFIP Congress*, pages 162–172, Geneva, 1968. [**227**]

[Cho94]   J. Chomicki. Temporal integrity constraints in relational databases. *IEEE Data Engineering Bulletin*, 17:33–37, 1994. [**404**]

[CHY96]   M.-S. Chen, J. Han, and P.S. Yu. Data mining: An overview from a database perspective. *IEEE Transactions on Knowledge and Data Engineering*, 8:866–883, 1996. Guest Editors, Special issue. [**564**]

[CK85]   S.S. Cosmadakis and P.C. Kanellakis. Equational theories and database constraints. In *Proceedings of ACM Symposium on Theory of Computing*, pages 273–284, Providence, RI, 1985. [**185**]

[CK86]   S.S. Cosmadakis and P.C. Kanellakis. Functional and inclusion dependencies: A graph theoretic approach. In P.C. Kanellakis and F. Preparata, editors, *Advances in Computing Research*, volume 3, pages 163–184. JAI Press, Greenwich, 1986. [**178, 182, 185, 215**]

[CK90]   C.C. Chang and H.J. Keisler. *Model Theory*. Elsevier Science Publishers, Amsterdam, third edition, 1990. [**59**]

[CK95]   S. Christodoulakis and L. Koveos. Multimedia information systems: Issues and approaches. In W. Kim, editor, *Modern Database Systems, The Object Model, Interoperability, and Beyond*, pages 318–337. Addison-Wesley, Reading, Ma., 1995. [**566**]

[CKV90]   S.S. Cosmadakis, P.C. Kanellakis, and M.Y. Vardi. Polynomial-time implication problems for unary inclusion dependencies. *Journal of the ACM*, 37:15–46, 1990. [**178, 182, 183, 215**]

[CKV94]   G. Chen, E.E. Kerre, and J. Vandenbulcke. A computational algorithm for the FFD transitive closure and a complete axiomatization of fuzzy functional dependencies (FFD). *International Journal of Intelligent Systems*, 9:421–439, 1994. [**340**]

[CKV96]   G. Chen, E.E. Kerre, and J. Vandenbulcke. Normalization based on fuzzy functional dependency in a fuzzy relational data model. *Information Systems*, 21:299–310, 1996. [**342, 357**]

[CLM81]   A.K. Chandra, H.R. Lewis, and J.A. Makowsky. Embedded implicational dependencies and their inference problem. Research Report RC8757 (38352), IBM Research Center, Yorktown Heights, NY, 1981. [**200**]

[CM77]   A.K. Chandra and P.M. Merlin. Optimal implementation of conjunctive queries in relational data bases. In *Proceedings of ACM Symposium on the Theory of Computing*, pages 77–90, Boulder, Co., 1977. [**484**]

[CM87]   E.P.F. Chan and A.O. Mendelzon. Independent and separable database schemes. *SIAM Journal on Computing*, 16:841–851, 1987. [**225**]

[CM89]   M.P. Consens and A.O. Mendelzon. Expressing structural hypertext queries in GraphLog. In *Proceedings of ACM Conference on Hypertext*, pages 269–292, Pittsburg, Pa., 1989. [**554**]

[CM90]   M.P. Consens and A.O. Mendelzon. GraphLog: a visual formalism for real life recursion. In *Proceedings of ACM Symposium on Principles of Database Systems*, pages 404–416, Nashville, Te., 1990. [**540**]

[CM91]   L. Cardelli and J.C. Mitchell. Operations on records. *Mathematical Structures for Computer Science*, 1:3–48, 1991. [**360**]

[CM93]   M.P. Consens and A.O. Mendelzon. Low-complexity aggregation in GraphLog and Datalog. *Theoretical Computer Science*, 116:95–116, 1993. **[509, 512, 540]**

[Cod70]   E.F. Codd. A relational model of data for large shared data banks. *Communications of the ACM*, 13:377–387, 1970. **[2, 89, 91, 227, 517]**

[Cod72a]   E.F. Codd. Further normalization of the data base relational model. In R. Rustin, editor, *Data Base Systems*, pages 33–64. Prentice Hall, Englewood Cliffs, NJ, 1972. **[247, 250, 282]**

[Cod72b]   E.F. Codd. Relational completeness of data base sublanguages. In R. Rustin, editor, *Data Base Systems*, pages 65–98. Prentice Hall, Englewood Cliffs, NJ, 1972. **[91, 108, 227]**

[Cod74]   E.F. Codd. Recent investigations in relational data base systems. In *Proceedings of IFIP Congress*, pages 1017–1021, Stockholm, 1974. **[195, 253, 282]**

[Cod79]   E.F. Codd. Extending the database relational model to capture more meaning. *ACM Transactions on Database Systems*, 4:397–434, 1979. **[157, 227]**

[Cod82]   E.F. Codd. Relational database: A practical foundation for productivity. *Communication of the ACM*, 25:109–117, 1982. **[2, 9, 227]**

[Cod90]   E.F. Codd. *The Relational Model for Database Management: Version 2*. Addison-Wesley, Reading, Ma., 1990. **[157, 227, 318, 346, 352]**

[Com79]   D. Comer. The ubiquitous B-tree. *ACM Computing Surveys*, 11:121–137, 1979. **[59]**

[Con87]   J. Conklin. Hypertext: An introduction and survey. *IEEE Computer*, 20:17–41, 1987. **[2, 554, 555]**

[Coo71]   S.A. Cook. The complexity of theorem-proving procedures. In *Proceedings of ACM Symposium on Theory of Computing*, pages 151–158, Shaker Heights, Ohio, 1971. **[50]**

[Cos89]   S.S. Cosmadakis. On the first-order expressibility of recursive queries. In *Proceedings of ACM Symposium on Principles of Database Systems*, pages 311–323, Philadelphia, Pa., 1989. **[491]**

[Cos95]   S. Costantini. Contributions to the stable model semantics of logic programs with negation. *Theoretical Computer Science*, 149:231–255, 1995. **[468]**

[CP84a]   S. Ceri and G. Pelagatti. *Distributed Databases: Principles and Systems*. McGraw-Hill, New York, 1984. **[447, 566]**

[CP84b]   S.S. Cosmadakis and C.H. Papadimitriou. Updates of relational views. *Journal of the ACM*, 31:742–760, 1984. **[225, 234]**

[CP87]   R. Cavallo and M. Pittarelli. The theory of probabilistic databases. In *Proceedings of International Conference on Very Large Data Bases*, pages 71–81, Brighton, 1987. **[354]**

[Cru84]   R.A. Crus. Data recovery in IBM Database 2. *IBM Systems Journal*, 23:178–188, 1984. **[415]**

[CT88]   M.A. Casanova and L. Tucherman. Enforcing inclusion dependencies and referential integrity. In *Proceedings of International Conference on Very Large Data Bases*, pages 38–49, Los Angeles, Ca., 1988. **[60]**

[CT89]   W.B. Croft and H. Turtle. A retrieval model for incorporating hypertext links. In *Proceedings of ACM Conference on Hypertext*, pages 213–224, Pittsburg, Pa., 1989. **[555]**

[CT93]   N. Cercone and M. Tsuchiya. Special issue on learning and discovery in knowledge-based databases. *IEEE Knowledge and Data Engineering*, 5(6), 1993. Guest Editors, Special issue. **[564]**

[CV83]   M.A. Casanova and V.M.P. Vidal. Towards a sound view integration methodology. In *Proceedings of ACM Symposium on Principles of Database Systems*, pages 36–47, Atlanta, 1983. **[178, 218]**

[CV85]   A.K. Chandra and M.Y. Vardi. The implication problem for functional and inclusion dependencies is undecidable. *SIAM Journal on Computing*, 14:671–677, 1985. **[179, 180, 186]**

[CV92]   S. Chaudhuri and M.Y. Vardi. On the equivalence of recursive and nonrecursive Datalog programs. In *Proceedings of ACM Symposium on Principles of Database Systems*, pages 55–66, San Diego, Ca., 1992. **[492]**

[CV94a]   S. Chaudhuri and M.Y. Vardi. On the complexity of equivalence between recursive and nonrecursive Datalog programs. In *Proceedings of ACM Symposium on Principles of Database Systems*, pages 107–116, Minneapolis, Mn., 1994. **[492]**

[CV94b]   J.C. Cubero and M.A. Vila. A new definition of fuzzy functional dependency in fuzzy relational databases. *International Journal of Intelligent Systems*, 9:441–448, 1994. **[341]**

[CW90]   S. Ceri and J. Widom. Deriving production rules for constraint maintenance. In *Proceedings of International Conference on Very Large Data Bases*, pages 566–577, Brisbane, 1990. **[542, 545]**

[CW91]   S. Ceri and J. Widom. Deriving production rules for incremental view maintenance. In *Proceedings of International Conference on Very Large Data Bases*, pages 577–589, Barcelona, 1991. **[542, 546]**

[DA87]   K.H. Davis and A.K. Arora. Converting a relational database model into an entity-relationship model. In *Proceedings of International Conference on the Entity Relationship Approach*, pages 271–285, New York, 1987. **[81, 281, 285]**

[Dah87]   E. Dahlhaus. Skolem normal forms concerning the least fixpoint. In E. Borger, editor, *Computation Theory and Logic*, volume 270 of *Lecture Notes in Computer Science*, pages 101–106. Springer-Verlag, Berlin, 1987. **[481]**

[Dat86a]   C.J. Date. Referential integrity. In *Relational Database: Selected Writings*, pages 41–63. Addison-Wesley, Reading, Ma., 1986. **[60]**

[Dat86b]   C.J. Date. The relational and network approaches: Comparison of the application programming interfaces. In *Relational Database: Selected Writings*, pages 179–202. Addison-Wesley, Reading, Ma., 1986. **[9]**

[Dat86c]   C.J. Date. *Relational Database: Selected Writings*. Addison-Wesley, Reading, Ma., 1986. **[2]**

[Dat86d]   C.J. Date. Updating views. In *Relational Database: Selected Writings*, pages 367–395. Addison-Wesley, Reading, Ma., 1986. **[225]**

[Dat90]   C.J. Date. What is a domain? In *Relational Database Writings 1985-1989*, pages 27–57. Addison-Wesley, Reading, Ma., 1990. **[212]**

[Dat92a]   C.J. Date. The default values approach to missing information. In *Relational Database Writings 1989-1991*, pages 343–354. Addison-Wesley, Reading, Ma., 1992. **[345]**

[Dat92b]   C.J. Date. Entity/relationship modeling and the relational model. In *Relational Database Writings 1989-1991*, pages 357–364. Addison-Wesley, Reading, Ma., 1992. **[70]**

[Dat92c]   C.J. Date. Will the real fourth normal form please stand up? In *Relational Database Writings 1989-1991*, pages 437–443. Addison-Wesley, Reading, Ma., 1992. **[253]**

[Dat95]   C.J. Date. *An Introduction to Database Systems*. Addison-Wesley, Reading, Ma., sixth edition, 1995. **[2, 567]**

[DB82]   U. Dayal and P.A. Bernstein. On the correct translation of update operations on relational views. *ACM Transactions on Database Systems*, 8:381–416, 1982. **[225]**

[DD91]   K.R. Dittrich and U. Dayal. Active database systems, tutorial notes. In *International Conference on Very Large Data Bases*, Barecelona, 1991. **[547]**

[DD92a]   C.J. Date and H. Darwen. Into the great divide. In *Relational Database Writings 1989-1991*, pages 155–168. Addison-Wesley, Reading, Ma., 1992. **[228]**

[DD92b]   C.J. Date and H. Darwen. Relation-valued attributes or will the real first normal form please stand up? In *Relational Database Writings 1989-1991*, pages 75–98. Addison-Wesley, Reading, Ma., 1992. **[517]**

[DD93]   C.J. Date and H. Darwen. *A Guide to the SQL Standard*. Addison-Wesley, Reading, Ma., third edition, 1993. **[113, 213, 225, 383, 386, 400, 453, 529, 530]**

[Dec90]   H. Decker. Drawing updates from derivations. In *Proceedings of International Conference on Database Theory*, pages 437–451, Paris, 1990. **[500]**

[Del78]   C. Delobel. Normalization and hierarchical dependencies in the relational data model. *ACM Transactions on Database Systems*, 3:201–222, 1978. **[191]**

[DF92]   C.J. Date and R. Fagin. Simple conditions for guaranteeing higher normal forms in relational databases. *ACM Transactions on Database Systems*, 17:465–476, 1992. **[254, 284]**

[DGS97]   C. De Castro, F. Grandi, and M.R. Scalas. Schema versioning for multitemporal relational databases. *Information Systems*, 22:249–290, 1997. **[406]**

[DHL90]   U. Dayal, M. Hsu, and R. Ladin. Organizing long-running activities with triggers and transactions. In *Proceedings of ACM SIGMOD Conference on Management of Data*, pages 204–214, Atlantic City, NJ, 1990. **[571]**

[DHL91]   U. Dayal, M. Hsu, and R. Ladin. A transactional model for long-running activities. In *Proceedings of International Conference on Very Large Data Bases*, pages 113–122, Barcelona, 1991. **[571]**

[DHLM92]   J. Demetrovics, G. Hencsey, L. Libkin, and I.B. Muchnik. Normal form relations schemes: A new characterization. *Acta Cybernetica*, 10:141–143, 1992. **[253, 259]**

[DHW95]   U. Dayal, E. Hanson, and J. Widom. Active database systems. In W. Kim, editor, *Modern Database Systems, The Object Model, Interoperability, and Beyond*, pages 434–456. Addison-Wesley, Reading, Ma., 1995. **[547]**

[DiP69]   R.A. DiPaola. The recursive unsolvability of the decision problem for the class of definite formulas. *Journal of the ACM*, 16:324–327, 1969. **[135, 227]**

[DK93]   J. Demetrovics and G.O.H. Katona. A survey of some combinatorical results concerning functional dependencies in database relations. *Annals of Mathematics and Artificial Intelligence*, 7:63–82, 1993. **[154, 231]**

[DL91]   M. Dahr and K. Lautenbach. Towards a formal theory of Datalog nets. Research Report 20/91, Computer Science Department, University of Koblenz-Landau, 1991. **[509]**

[DLR95]   C. Delobel, C. Lècluse, and P. Richard. *Databases: From Relational to Object-Oriented Systems*. International Thomson, London, 1995. **[529]**

[DLW95]   A. Dawar, S. Lindell, and S. Weinstein. Infinitary logic and inductive definability over finite structures. *Information and Computation*, 119:160–175, 1995. [**57, 382**]

[DM92]   E. Dahlhaus and J.A. Makowsky. Query languages for hierarchic databases. *Information and Computation*, 101:1–32, 1992. [**365**]

[DOB95]   S.B. Davidson, C. Overton, and P. Buneman. Challenges in integrating biological data sources. *Journal of Computational Biology*, 2:557–572, 1995. [**560**]

[Doe96]   K. Doets. *Basic Model Theory*. Studies in Logic, Language and Information. CSLI Publications and FoLLI, Stanford, Ca., 1996. [**59**]

[DP84]   P. De Bra and J. Paredaens. Horizontal decompositions for handling exceptions to functional dependencies. In H. Gallaire, J. Minker, and J.-M. Nicholas, editors, *Advances in Database Theory*, volume 2, pages 123–141. Plenum Press, New York, 1984. [**264, 266**]

[DP90]   B.A. Davey and H.A. Priestly. *Introduction to Lattices and Order*. Cambridge University Press, Cambridge, U.K., 1990. [**35, 148, 299**]

[DR97]   G. Dong and K. Ramamohanarao. Maintaining constrained transitive closure by conjunctive queries. In *Proceedings of International Conference on Deductive and Object-Oriented Databases*, pages 35–51, Montreux, Switzerland, 1997. [**564**]

[DT87]   J. Demetrovics and V.D. Thi. Keys, antikeys and prime attributes. *Annales Univ. Sci. Budapest, Sect. Comp*, 8:35–52, 1987. [**155, 156**]

[DT88]   J. Demetrovics and V.D. Thi. Relations and minimal keys. *Acta Cybernetica*, 8:279–285, 1988. [**155**]

[DT92]   G. Dong and R. Topor. Incremental evaluation of Datalog queries. In *Proceedings of International Conference on Database Theory*, pages 282–296, Berlin, 1992. [**564**]

[DT93]   J. Demetrovics and V.D. Thi. Algorithms for generating an Armstrong relation and inferring functional dependencies in the relational datamodel. *Computers and Mathematics with Applications*, 26:43–55, 1993. [**148, 159**]

[DT95]   J. Demetrovics and V.D. Thi. Some observations on the minimal Armstrong relations for normalized relation schemes. *Computers and Artificial Intelligence*, 14:455–467, 1995. [**159**]

[Dže96]   S. Džeroski. Inductive logic programming and knowledge discovery in databases. In U.M. Fayyad, G. Piatetsky-Shapiro, P. Smyth, and R. Uthurusamy, editors, *Advances in Knowledge Discovery and Data Mining*, pages 117–152. AAAI Press, Menlo Park, Ca., 1996. [**566**]

[EF95]   H.-D. Ebbinghaus and J. Flum. *Finite Model Theory*. Springer-Verlag, Berlin, 1995. [**59**]

[EGLT76]   K.P. Eswaran, J.N. Gray, R.A. Lorie, and I.L. Traiger. The notions of consistency and predicate locks in a database system. *Communications of the ACM*, 19:624–633, 1976. [**441, 453**]

[EGM97]   T. Eiter, G. Gottlob, and H. Mannila. Disjunctive Datalog. *ACM Transactions on Database Systems*, 22:364–418, 1997. [**479**]

[Ehr61]   A. Ehrenfeucht. An application of games to the completeness problem for formalized theories. *Fundamenta Mathematicae*, 49:129–141, 1961. [**55, 497**]

[Eme90]   E.A. Emerson. Temporal and modal logic. In J. Van Leeuwen, editor, *Handbook of Theoretical Computer Science*, volume B, chapter 16, pages 997–1072. Elsevier Science Publishers, Amsterdam, 1990. [**388, 398, 553**]

[End72]   H.B. Enderton. *A Mathematical Introduction to Logic*. Academic Press, New York, 1972. [**40**]

[Fag74]   R. Fagin. Generalized first-order spectra and polynomial-time recognizable sets. In R.M. Karp, editor, *SIAM-AMS Proceedings, Complexity of Computation*, volume 7, pages 43–73. American Mathematical Society, Providence, RI, 1974. [**57, 383**]

[Fag76]   R. Fagin. Probabilities on finite models. *The Journal of Symbolic Logic*, 41:50–58, 1976. [**58**]

[Fag77a]   R. Fagin. The decomposition versus the synthetic approach to relational database design. In *Proceedings of International Conference on Very Large Data Bases*, pages 441–446, Tokyo, 1977. [**249, 284**]

[Fag77b]   R. Fagin. Multivalued dependencies and a new normal form for relational databases. *ACM Transactions on Database Systems*, 2:262–278, 1977. [**191, 199, 227, 247, 249, 253, 284**]

[Fag79]   R. Fagin. Normal forms and relational database operators. In *Proceedings of ACM SIGMOD Conference on Management of Data*, pages 153–160, Boston, Ma., 1979. [**249, 264**]

[Fag81]   R. Fagin. A normal form for relational databases that is based on domains and keys. *ACM Transactions on Database Systems*, 6:387–415, 1981. [**215, 249**]

[Fag82a]   R. Fagin. Armstrong databases. Research Report RJ3440 (40926), IBM Research Laboratory, San Jose, Ca., 1982. [**148, 158**]

[Fag82b]   R. Fagin. Horn clauses and database dependencies. *Journal of the ACM*, 29:952–985, 1982. [**177, 211, 504**]

[Fag83]   R. Fagin. Degrees of acyclicity for hypergraphs and relational database schemes. *Journal of the ACM*, 30:514–550, 1983. [**196, 205, 211, 282**]

[Fag93]   R. Fagin. Finite-model theory – a personal perspective. *Theoretical Computer Science*, 116:3–31, 1993. [**59, 383**]

[Fag96]   R. Fagin. Combining fuzzy information from multiple systems. In *Proceedings of ACM Symposium on Principles of Database Systems*, pages 216–226, Montreal, 1996. [**566**]

[Fag97]   R. Fagin. Easier ways to win logical games. In P.G. Kolaitis and N. Immerman, editors, *Descriptive Complexity and Finite Models*, volume 31 of *DIMACS series in Discrete Mathematics and Computer Science*, pages 1–32. American Mathematical Society, Providence, RI, 1997. [**55, 56**]

[FC85]   A.L. Furtado and M.A. Casanova. Updating relational views. In W. Kim, D.S. Reiner, and D.S. Batory, editors, *Query Processing in Database Systems*, pages 127–142. Springer-Verlag, Berlin, 1985. [**225**]

[FC92]   M.F. Frisse and S.B. Cousins. Models for hypertext. *Journal of the American Society for Information Science*, 43:182–192, 1992. [**555**]

[Fit85]   M. Fitting. A Kripke-Kleene semantics for logic programs. *Journal of Logic Programming*, 2:295–312, 1985. [**473**]

[Fit96]   M. Fitting. *First-order Logic and Automated Theorem Proving*. Springer-Verlag, Berlin, second edition, 1996. [**39, 40, 291**]

[FKUV86]   R. Fagin, G.M. Kuper, J.D. Ullman, and M.Y. Vardi. Updating logical databases. In P.C. Kanellakis and F. Preparata, editors, *Advances in Computing Research*, volume 3, pages 1–18. JAI Press, Greenwich, 1986. [**502**]

[FMU82]   R. Fagin, A.O. Mendelzon, and J.D. Ullman. A simplified universal relation assumption and its properties. *ACM Transactions on Database Systems*, 7:343–360, 1982. [**205**]

[FMUY83]   R. Fagin, D. Maier, J.D. Ullman, and M. Yannakakis. Tools for template dependencies. *SIAM Journal on Computing*, 12:36–59, 1983. [**234**]

[For94]   A. Ford. *Spinning the Web: How to Provide Information on the Internet*. International Thomson Computer Press, London, 1994. [**548**]

[FPSSU96]   U.M. Fayyad, G. Piatetsky-Shapiro, P. Smyth, and R. Uthurusamy, editors. *Advances in Knowledge Discovery and Data Mining*. AAAI Press, Menlo Park, Ca., 1996. [**561, 564**]

[Fri71]   H. Friedman. Algorithmic procedures, generalized Turing machines and elementary recursion theory. In *Proceedings of Logic Colloquium '69*, pages 361–389, Manchester, U.K., 1971. [**360**]

[FS92]   T. Feder and Y. Saraiya. Decidability and undecidability of equivalence for lienar Datalog, with applications to normal-form optimizations. In *Proceedings of International Conference on Database Theory*, pages 297–311, Berlin, 1992. [**488, 489**]

[FSS79]   A.L. Furtado, K.C. Sevcik, and C.S. Dos Santos. Permitting updates through views of databases. *Information Systems*, 4:269–283, 1979. [**225**]

[FSTV85]   P.C. Fischer, L.V. Saxton, S.J. Thomas, and D. Van Gucht. Interactions between dependencies and nested relational structures. *Journal of Computer and System Sciences*, 31:343–354, 1985. [**522, 569**]

[FT83]   P.C. Fischer and D.-M. Tsou. Whether a set of multivalued dependencies implies a join dependency is NP-hard. *SIAM Journal on Computing*, 12:259–266, 1983. [**203**]

[FU95]   U.M. Fayyad and R. Uthurusamy, editors. *Proceedings of International Conference on Knowledge Discovery and Data Mining*, Menlo Park, Ca., 1995. AAAI Press. [**564**]

[FU96]   U.M. Fayyad and R. Uthurusamy. Data mining and knowledge discovery in databases. *Communications of the ACM*, 39:24–68, 1996. Guest Editors, Special issue. [**564**]

[Fuh90]   N. Fuhr. A probabilistic framework for vague queries and imprecise information in databases. In *Proceedings of International Conference on Very Large Data Bases*, pages 696–707, Brisbane, 1990. [**354**]

[FUV83]   R. Fagin, J.D. Ullman, and M.Y. Vardi. On the semantics of updates in databases. In *Proceedings of ACM Symposium on Principles of Database Systems*, pages 352–365, Atlanta, Georgia, 1983. [**502**]

[FV83]   R. Fagin and M.Y. Vardi. Armstrong databases for functional and inclusion dependencies. *Information Processing Letters*, 16:13–19, 1983. [**177**]

[FV84a]   R. Fagin and M.Y. Vardi. The theory of data dependencies – a survey. Research Report RJ4321 (47149), IBM Research Laboratory, San Jose, Ca., 1984. [**211, 504**]

[FV84b]   P.C. Fischer and D. Van Gucht. Weak multivalued dependencies. In *Proceedings of ACM Symposium on Principles of Database Systems*, pages 266–274, Waterloo, Ontario, 1984. [**520**]

[Gal82]   Z. Galil. An almost linear-time algorithm for computing a dependency basis in a relational database. *Journal of the ACM*, 29:96–102, 1982. [**194**]

[Gan80]   R. Gandy. Church's thesis and the principles for mechanisms. In *Proceedings of Kleene Symposium*, pages 123–148, Madison, Wisc., 1980. [**360**]

[Gär88a]   P. Gärdenfors. *Knowledge in Flux: Modeling the Dynamics of Epistemic States*. MIT Press, Cambridge, Ma., 1988. **[502]**

[Gar88b]   P.K. Garg. Abstraction mechanisms in hypertext. *Communications of the ACM*, 31:862–870, 1988. **[554]**

[GCB$^+$97]   J. Gray, S. Chaudhuri, A. Bosworth, A. Layman, D. Reichart, M. Venkatrao, F. Pellow, and H. Pirahesh. Data cube: A relational aggregation operator generalizing group-by, cross-tab, and sub-totals. *Data Mining and Knowledge Discovery*, 1:29–53, 1997. **[562]**

[GH95]   H. Garcia-Molina and M. Hsu. Distributed databases. In W. Kim, editor, *Modern Database Systems, The Object Model, Interoperability, and Beyond*, pages 477–493. Addison-Wesley, Reading, Ma., 1995. **[566, 567]**

[GHOK81]   J. Gray, P. Homan, R. Obermarck, and H.F. Korth. A straw man analysis of probability of waiting and deadlock. Research Report RJ3066 (38102), IBM Research Laboratory, San Jose, Ca., 1981. **[433]**

[Gil94]   M.M. Gilula. *The Set Model for Database and Information Systems*. Addison-Wesley, Reading, Ma., 1994. **[27]**

[GJ79]   M.R. Garey and D.S. Johnson. *Computers and Intractability: A Guide to the Theory of NP-Completeness*. W.H. Freeman, New York, 1979. **[32, 52, 155, 208, 305, 328, 331, 362, 479, 569]**

[GJ91]   N.H. Gehani and H.V. Jagadish. Ode as an active database: Constraints and triggers. In *Proceedings of International Conference on Very Large Data Bases*, pages 327–336, Barcelona, 1991. **[545]**

[GJM96]   A. Gupta, H.V. Jagadish, and I.S. Mumick. Data integration using self-maintainable views. In *Proceedings of International Conference on Extending Database Technology*, pages 140–144, Avignon, France, 1996. **[226]**

[GJS92]   N.H. Gehani, H.V. Jagadish, and O. Shmueli. Composite event specification in active databases: Model & implementation. In *Proceedings of International Conference on Very Large Data Bases*, pages 327–338, Vancouver, 1992. **[543]**

[GKLT69]   Y.V. Glebskiĭ, D.I. Kogan, M.I. Liogoñkiĭ, and V.A. Talanov. Range and degree of realizability of formulas in the restricted predicate calculus. *Kibernetika*, 5:17–27, 1969. **[58]**

[GKP92]   P.M.D. Gray, K.G. Kulkarni, and N.W. Paton. *Object-Oriented Databases: A Semantic Data Model Approach*. Prentice-Hall, Hemel Hempstead, Hertfordshire, 1992. **[529]**

[GL82]   Y. Gurevich and H.R. Lewis. The inference problem for template dependencies. *Information and Control*, 55:69–79, 1982. **[200]**

[GL88]   M. Gelfond and V. Lifschitz. The stable model semantics for logic programming. In *Proceedings of International Conference on Logic Programming*, pages 1070–1080, Seattle, Wa., 1988. **[468, 473]**

[GL97]   M. Gyssens and L.V.S. Lakshmanan. A foundation for multi-dimensional databases. In *Proceedings of International Conference on Very Large Data Bases*, pages 106–115, Athens, 1997. **[563]**

[GLPT75]   J.N. Gray, R.A. Lorie, G.R. Putzolu, and I.L. Traiger. Granularity of locks and degrees of consistency in a shared data base. Research Report RJ1654 (24264), IBM Research Laboratory, San Jose, Ca., 1975. **[453]**

[GM85a]   J. Grant and J. Minker. Inferences for numerical dependencies. *Theoretical Computer Science*, 41:271–287, 1985. **[231]**

[GM85b]   J. Grant and J. Minker. Normalization and axiomatization for numerical dependencies. *Information and Control*, 65:1–17, 1985. **[231, 264]**

[GM91]   D. Gabbay and P. McBrien. Temporal logic & historical databases. In *Proceedings of International Conference on Very Large Data Bases*, pages 423–430, Barcelona, 1991. **[399]**

[GM95]   A. Gupta and I.S. Mumick. Maintenance of materialized views: Problems, techniques, and applications. *IEEE Data Engineering Bulletin*, 18:3–18, 1995. **[226, 564]**

[GMSV93]   H. Gaifman, H. Mairson, Y. Sagiv, and M.Y. Vardi. Undecidable optimization problems for database logic programs. *Journal of the ACM*, 40:683–713, 1993. **[489–491]**

[GMV86]   M.H. Graham, A.O. Mendelzon, and M.Y. Vardi. Notions of dependency satisfaction. *Journal of the ACM*, 33:105–129, 1986. **[211]**

[GNS93]   P. Goyal, T.S. Narayanan, and F. Sadri. Concurrency control for object bases. *Information Systems*, 18:167–180, 1993. **[453]**

[Gog67]   J.A. Goguen. L-fuzzy sets. *Journal of Mathematical Analysis and Applications*, 18:145–174, 1967. **[333]**

[Got87]   G. Gottlob. On the size of nonredundant FD-covers. *Information Processing Letters*, 24:355–360, 1987. **[233]**

[GPSZ91]   F. Giannotti, D. Pedreschi, D. Saccà, and C. Zaniolo. Non-determinism in deductive databases. In *Proceedings of International Conference on Deductive and Object-Oriented Databases*, pages 129–146, Munich, 1991. **[511]**

[GPV90]   M. Gyssens, J. Paredaens, and D. Van Gucht. A graph-oriented object database model. In *Proceedings of ACM Symposium on Principles of Database Systems*, pages 417–424, Nashville, Te., 1990. **[540]**

[GPZ88]   G. Gottlob, P. Paolini, and R. Zicari. Properties and update semantics of consistent views. *ACM Transactions on Database Systems*, 13:486–524, 1988. [**225**]

[GR86]   G. Grahne and K.-J. Räihä. Characterizations for acyclic database schemes. In P.C. Kanellakis and F. Preparata, editors, *Advances in Computing Research*, volume 3, pages 19–41. JAI Press, Greenwich, 1986. [**211**]

[GR93]   J. Gray and A. Reuter. *Transaction Processing: Concepts and Techniques*. Morgan Kaufmann, San Francisco, Ca., 1993. [**453, 455**]

[Grä78]   G. Grätzer. *General Lattice Theory*. Academic Press, New York, 1978. [**35, 299**]

[Gra91]   G. Grahne. The problem of incomplete information in relational databases. In *Lecture Notes in Computer Science*, volume 554, pages 1–156. Springer-Verlag, Berlin, 1991. [**352**]

[Gri82]   R.L. Griffith. Three principles of representation for semantic networks. *ACM Transactions on Database Systems*, 7:417–442, 1982. [**541**]

[Gri94]   R.P. Grimaldi. *Discrete and Combinatorical Mathematics: An Applied Introduction*. Addison-Wesley, Reading, Ma., third edition, 1994. [**33**]

[GS82]   N. Goodman and O. Shmueli. Tree queries: A simple class of relational queries. *ACM Transactions on Database Systems*, 7:653–677, 1982. [**211, 282**]

[GS83]   N. Goodman and O. Shmueli. Syntactic characterization of tree database schemas. *Journal of the ACM*, 30:767–786, 1983. [**209, 211**]

[GS86]   Y. Gurevich and S. Shelah. Fixpoint extensions of first-order logic. *Annals of Pure and Applied Logic*, 32:265–280, 1986. [**122**]

[GS87]   H. Garcia-Molina and K. Salem. Sagas. In *Proceedings of ACM SIGMOD Conference on Management of Data*, pages 249–259, San Francisco, Ca., 1987. [**442**]

[GSS89]   G. Gottlob, M. Schrefl, and M. Stumptner. On the interaction between transitive closure and functional dependencies. In *Proceedings of Symposium on Mathematical Fundamentals of Database Systems*, pages 187–206, Visegrád, Hungary, 1989. [**504**]

[GT84]   N. Goodman and Y.C. Tay. A characterization of multivalued dependencies equivalent to a join dependency. *Information Processing Letters*, 18:261–266, 1984. [**198**]

[Gur66]   Y. Gurevich. The word problem for certain classes of semigroups. *Algebra and Logic*, 5:25–35, 1966. In Russian. [**48**]

[Gur84]   Y. Gurevich. Toward logic tailored for computational complexity. In M.M. Richter, E. Börger, W. Oberschelp, B. Schnizel, and W. Thomas, editors, *Computation and Proof Theory*, volume 1104 of *Lecture Notes in Mathematics*, pages 175–216. Springer-Verlag, 1984. [**59**]

[GV91]   M. Gyssens and D. Van Gucht. A comparison between algebraic query languages for flat and nested databases. *Theoretical Computer Science*, 87:263–286, 1991. [**569**]

[GW97]   R. Goldman and J. Widom. Dataguides: Enabling query formulation and optimization in semistructured databases. In *Proceedings of International Conference on Very Large Data Bases*, pages 436–445, Athens, 1997. [**560, 572**]

[Gys86]   M. Gyssens. On the complexity of join dependencies. *ACM Transactions on Database Systems*, 11:81–108, 1986. [**211**]

[GZ82]   S. Ginsburg and S.M. Zaiddan. Properties of functional-dependency families. *Journal of the ACM*, 29:678–698, 1982. [**167**]

[GZ88]   G. Gottlob and R. Zicari. Closed world databases opened through null values. In *Proceedings of International Conference on Very Large Data Bases*, pages 50–61, Los Angeles, Ca., 1988. [**293**]

[Had88]   V. Hadzilacos. A theory of reliability in database systems. *Journal of the ACM*, 35:121–145, 1988. [**453**]

[Hal74]   P.R. Halmos. *Naive Set Theory*. Springer-Verlag, New York, 1974. [**33**]

[Hal88]   F.G. Halasz. Reflections on notecards: Seven issues for the next generation of hypermedia systems. *Communications of the ACM*, 31:836–852, 1988. [**555**]

[Han92]   E.N. Hanson. An overview of production rules in database systems. Research Report RJ9023 (80483), IBM Research Laboratory, San Jose, Ca., 1992. [**547**]

[Har78]   M.A. Harrison. *Introduction to Formal Language Theory*. Addison-Wesley, Reading, Ma., 1978. [**52, 488, 491**]

[Har87]   D. Harel. Statecharts: A visual formalism for complex systems. *Science of Computer Programming*, 8:231–274, 1987. [**82**]

[Har88]   D. Harel. On visual formalisms. *Communications of the ACM*, 31:514–530, 1988. [**82**]

[HCF97]   G. Hamilton, R. Cattell, and M. Fisher. *JDBC^{TM} Database Access with Java^{TM}: A Tutorial and Annotated Reference*. The Java Series. Addison Wesley Longman, Reading, Ma., 1997. [**381**]

[Heg84]   S.J. Hegner. Canonical view update support through Boolean algebras of components. In *Proceedings of ACM Symposium on Principles of Database Systems*, pages 163–172, Waterloo, Ontario, 1984. [**225**]

[Heg87]   S.J. Hegner. Specification and implementation of programs for updating incomplete information databases. In *Proceedings of ACM Symposium on Principles of Database Systems*, pages 146–158, San Diego, Ca., 1987. [**502**]

[Heg90]   S.J. Hegner. Foundations of canonical update support for closed database views. In *Proceedings of International Conference on Database Theory*, pages 422–436, Paris, 1990. [**225**]

[Heg94]   S.J. Hegner. Unique complements and decompositions of database schemata. *Journal of Computer and System Sciences*, 48:9–57, 1994. [**225**]

[Her88]   R. Herken, editor. *The Universal Turing Machine: A Half-Century Survey*. Oxford University Press, Oxford, U.K., 1988. [**52**]

[Her95]   C. Herrmann. On the undecidability of implications between embedded multivalued database dependencies. *Information and Computation*, 112:221–235, 1995. [**200**]

[HF86]   Y. Hanatani and R. Fagin. A simple characterization of database dependency implication. *Information Processing Letters*, 22:281–283, 1986. [**195**]

[Hil91]   J.R. Hill. Relational databases: A tutorial for statisticians. In *Proceedings of Symposium on the Interface between Computer Science and Statistics*, pages 86–93, Seattle, Wa., 1991. [**354**]

[HITK79]   K. Hagihara, M. Ito, K. Taniguchi, and T. Kasami. Decision problems for multivalued dependencies in relational databases. *SIAM Journal on Computing*, 8:247–264, 1979. [**194**]

[HJ91]   R. Hull and D. Jacobs. Language constructs for programming active databases. In *Proceedings of International Conference on Very Large Data Bases*, pages 455–467, Barcelona, 1991. [**545**]

[HKMV91]   G.G. Hillebrand, P.C. Kanellakis, H.G. Mairson, and M.Y. Vardi. Tools for Datalog boundedness. In *Proceedings of ACM Symposium on Principles of Database Systems*, pages 1–12, Denver, Co., 1991. [**491**]

[HLY80]   P. Honeyman, R.E. Ladner, and M. Yannakakis. Testing the universal instance assumption. *Information Processing Letters*, 10:14–19, 1980. [**207**]

[Hod93]   W. Hodges. Logical features of Horn clauses. In D.M. Gabbay, C.J. Hogger, and J.A. Robinson, editors, *Handbook of Logic in Artificial Intelligence and Logic Programming, Logical Foundations*, volume 1, pages 449–503. Clarendon Press, Oxford, U.K., 1993. [**509**]

[Hol72]   R.C. Holt. Some deadlock properties of computer systems. *ACM Computing Surveys*, 4:179–196, 1972. [**454**]

[Hon80]   P. Honeyman. Extension joins. In *Proceedings of International Conference on Very Large Data Bases*, pages 239–244, Montreal, 1980. [**233**]

[Hon82]   P. Honeyman. Testing satisfaction of functional dependencies. *Journal of the ACM*, 29:668–677, 1982. [**165, 211, 231**]

[HR79]   H.B. Hunt III and D.J. Rosenkrantz. The complexity of testing predicate locks. In *Proceedings of ACM SIGMOD Conference on Management of Data*, pages 127–133, Boston, Ma., 1979. [**441**]

[HR96]   T. Härder and J. Reinert. Access path support for referential integrity in SQL2. *The VLDB Journal*, 5:196–214, 1996. [**60**]

[HS93]   R. Hull and J. Su. Algebraic and calculus query languages for recursively typed complex objects. *Journal of Computer and System Sciences*, 47:121–146, 1993. [**365**]

[HS94a]   F.G. Halasz and M. Schwartz. The Dexter hypertext reference model. *Communications of the ACM*, 37:30–39, 1994. edited by K. Grønbæk and R.H. Trigg. [**552**]

[HS94b]   M. Holsheimer and A.P.J.M. Siebes. Data mining: the search for knowledge in databases. Technical Report CS-R9406, Computer Science/Department of Algorithmics and Architecture, Centrum voor Wiskunde en Informatica (CWI), 1994. [**564**]

[HS94c]   R. Hull and J. Su. Domain independence and relational calculus. *Acta Informatica*, 31:513–524, 1994. [**230**]

[HU79]   J.E. Hopcroft and J.D. Ullman. *Introduction to Automata Theory, Languages, and Computation*. Addison-Wesley, Reading, Ma., 1979. [**52, 488, 491, 571**]

[Hul84]   R. Hull. Finitely specifiable implicational dependency families. *Journal of the ACM*, 31:210–226, 1984. [**508**]

[Hul86]   R. Hull. Relative information capacity of simple relational database schemata. *SIAM Journal on Computing*, 15:856–886, 1986. [**233, 524**]

[Hul87]   R. Hull. A survey of theoretical research on typed database complex objects. In J. Paredaens, editor, *Databases*, pages 193–256. Academic Press, Boston, 1987. [**524, 569**]

[Hul90]   G. Hulin. On restructuring nested relations in partitioned normal form. In *Proceedings of International Conference on Very Large Data Bases*, pages 626–637, Brisbane, 1990. [**569**]

[Hul97]   R. Hull. Managing semantic heterogeneity in databases: A theoretical perspective. In *Proceedings of ACM Symposium on Principles of Database Systems*, pages 51–61, Tucson, Az., 1997. Invited talk. [**560**]

[HY84]   R. Hull and C.K. Yap. The format model: A theory of database organization. *Journal of the ACM*, 31:518–537, 1984. [**524**]

[HY89]   T. Hadzilacos and M. Yannakakis. Deleting completed transactions. *Journal of Computer and System Sciences*, 38:360–379, 1989. [**453**]

[IB92]   T. Imielinski and B.R. Badrinath. Querying in highly mobile environments. In *Proceedings of International Conference on Very Large Data Bases*, pages 41–52, Vancouver, 1992. [**567**]

[IITK84]   M. Ito, K. M. Iwasaki, K. Taniguchi, and T. Kasami. Membership problems for data dependencies in relational expressions. *Theoretical Computer Science*, 34:315–335, 1984. [**219, 503**]

[IK89]   N. Immerman and D. Kozen. Definability with bounded number of bound variables. *Information and Computation*, 83:121–139, 1989. [**57**]

[IL84a]   T. Imielinski and W. Lipski Jr. Incomplete information in relational databases. *Journal of the ACM*, 31:761–791, 1984. [**300**]

[IL84b]   T. Imielinski and W. Lipski Jr. On the undecidability of equivalence problems for relational expressions. In H. Gallaire, J. Minker, and J.-M. Nicolas, editors, *Advances in Database Theory*, pages 393–409. Plenum, New York, 1984. [**485**]

[IM80]   S.S. Isloor and T.A. Marsland. The deadlock problem: An overview. *IEEE Computer*, 13:58–78, 1980. [**440**]

[Imi89]   T. Imielinski. Incomplete information in logical databases. *IEEE Data Engineering Bulletin*, 12:29–40, 1989. [**300, 328, 356**]

[Imi91]   T. Imielinski. Abstraction in query processing. *Journal of the ACM*, 38:534–558, 1991. [**175, 180**]

[Imm81]   N. Immerman. Number of quantifiers is better than number of tape cells. *Journal of Computer and System Sciences*, 22:384–406, 1981. [**359, 383**]

[Imm86]   N. Immerman. Relational queries computable in polynomial time. *Information and Control*, 68:86–104, 1986. [**57, 379, 383**]

[Imm87]   N. Immerman. Languages that capture complexity classes. *SIAM Journal on Computing*, 16:760–778, 1987. [**359, 383**]

[Imm88]   N. Immerman. Nondeterministic space is closed under complementation. *SIAM Journal on Computing*, 17:935–938, 1988. [**58**]

[Imm89]   N. Immerman. Descriptive and computational complexity. In J. Hartmanis, editor, *Proceedings of Symposia in Applied Mathematics, Computational Complexity Theory*, volume 38, pages 75–91. American Mathematical Society, Providence, RI, 1989. [**57, 359, 383, 384**]

[Imm95]   N. Immerman. Descriptive complexity: a logician's approach to computation. *Notices of the American Mathematical Society*, 42:1127–1133, 1995. [**57**]

[Inm96]   W.H. Inmon. *Building the Data Warehouse*. John Wiley & Sons, Chichester, second edition, 1996. [**562**]

[Ioa85]   Y.E. Ioannidis. A time bound on the materialization of some recursively defined views. In *Proceedings of International Conference on Very Large Data Bases*, pages 219–226, Stockholm, 1985. [**491**]

[ITK83]   M. Ito, K. Taniguchi, and T. Kasami. Membership problem for embedded multivalued dependencies under some restricted conditions. *Theoretical Computer Science*, 22:175–194, 1983. [**200**]

[IV89]   T. Imielinski and K.V. Vadaparty. Complexity of query processing in databases with or-objects. In *Proceedings of ACM Symposium on Principles of Database Systems*, pages 51–65, Philadelphia, Pa., 1989. [**328**]

[IVV95]   T. Imielinski, R. Van der Meyden, and K.V. Vadaparty. Complexity tailored design: A new design methodology for databases with incomplete information. *Journal of Computer and System Sciences*, 51:405–432, 1995. [**351**]

[IW91]   Y.E. Ioannidis and E. Wong. Towards an algebraic theory of recursion. *Journal of the ACM*, 38:329–381, 1991. [**489**]

[Jaj86]   S. Jajodia. Recognizing multivalued dependencies in relation schemas. *The Computer Journal*, 29:458–459, 1986. [**232, 283**]

[Jan88]   J.M. Janas. On functional independencies. In *Proceedings of Conference on Foundations of Software Technology and Theoretical Computer Science*, pages 487–508, 1988. [**167**]

[Jan89]   J.M. Janas. Covers for functional independencies. In *Proceedings of Symposium on Mathematical Fundamentals of Database Systems*, pages 254–268, Visegrád, Hungary, 1989. [**167**]

[JF82]   J.H. Jou and P.C. Fischer. The complexity of recognizing 3NF relation schemes. *Information Processing Letters*, 14:187–190, 1982. [**251**]

[JF95]   U. Jaeger and J.C. Freytag. An annotated bibliography on active databases. *ACM SIGMOD Record*, 24:58–69, 1995. [**547**]

[JFM97]   T. Joachims, D. Freitag, and T. Mitchell. WebWatcher: A tour guide for the World Wide Web. In *Proceedings of International Joint Conference on Artificial Intelligence*, pages 770–775, Nagoya, Japan, 1997. [555]

[JNS83a]   S. Jajodia, P.A. Ng, and F.N. Springsteel. Entity-relationship diagrams which are in BCNF. *International Journal of Computer and Information Sciences*, 12:269–283, 1983. [81, 281]

[JNS83b]   S. Jajodia, P.A. Ng, and F.N. Springsteel. The problem of equivalence for entity-relationship diagrams. *IEEE Transactions on Software Engineering*, 9:617–630, 1983. [81, 281]

[Joh90]   D.S. Johnson. A catalog of complexity classes. In J. Van Leeuwen, editor, *Handbook of Theoretical Computer Science: Algorithms and Complexity*, volume A, chapter 2, pages 67–161. Elsevier Science Publishers, Amsterdam, 1990. [52]

[JS82]   G. Jaeschke and H.-J. Schek. Remarks on the algebra of non first normal form relations. In *Proceedings of ACM Symposium on Principles of Database Systems*, pages 124–138, Los Angeles, 1982. [22, 520]

[JS90]   S. Jajodia and F.N. Springsteel. Lossless outer joins with incomplete information. *BIT*, 30:34–41, 1990. [356]

[JS91a]   S. Jajodia and R.S. Sandhu. A novel decomposition of multilevel relations into single-level relations. In *Proceedings of IEEE Symposium on Security and Privacy*, pages 300–313, Oakland, Ca., 1991. [230]

[JS91b]   S. Jajodia and R.S. Sandhu. Toward a multilevel secure relational data model. In *Proceedings of ACM SIGMOD Conference on Management of Data*, pages 50–59, Denver, Co., 1991. [230]

[JSS92]   C.S. Jensen, R.T. Snodgrass, and M.D. Soo. Extending normal forms to temporal relations. Technical Report TR 92-17, Department of Computer Science, University of Arizona, Tucson Az., 1992. [407]

[Kan80]   P.C. Kanellakis. On the computational complexity of cardinality constraints in relational databases. *Information Processing Letters*, 11:98–101, 1980. [215]

[Kan90]   P.C. Kanellakis. Elements of relational database theory. In J. Van Leeuwen, editor, *Handbook of Theoretical Computer Science: Formal Models and Semantics*, volume B, chapter 17, pages 1073–1156. Elsevier Science Publishers, Amsterdam, 1990. [491]

[Kar72]   R.M. Karp. Reducibility among combinatorical problems. In R.E. Miller and J.W. Thatcher, editors, *Complexity of Computer Computations*, pages 85–103. Plenum, New York, 1972. [50, 155, 168, 208]

[Kat84]   H. Katsuno. An extension of conflict-free multivalued dependency sets. *ACM Transactions on Database Systems*, 9:309–326, 1984. [198, 206]

[KC86]   S.N. Khoshafian and G.P. Copeland. Object identity. In *Proceedings of Object-Oriented Programming Systems, Languages, and Applications*, pages 406–416, Portland, Oregon, 1986. [570]

[KCGS95]   W. Kim, I. Choi, S. Gala, and M. Scheevel. On resolving schematic heterogeneity in multidatabase systems. In W. Kim, editor, *Modern Database Systems, The Object Model, Interoperability, and Beyond*, pages 521–550. Addison-Wesley, Reading, Ma., 1995. [560]

[Kel85]   A. Keller. Algorithms for translating view updates to database updates for views involving selections, projections and joins. In *Proceedings of ACM Symposium on Principles of Database Systems*, pages 154–163, Portland, Oregon, 1985. [226, 235]

[Kel86]   A. Keller. The role of semantics in translating view updates. *IEEE Computer*, 19:63–73, 1986. [226]

[Ken79]   W. Kent. Limitations of record-based information models. *ACM Transactions on Database Systems*, 4:107–131, 1979. [81]

[Ken81]   W. Kent. Consequences of assuming a universal relation. *ACM Transactions on Database Systems*, 6:539–556, 1981. [79]

[Ken83a]   W. Kent. A simple guide to five normal forms in relational database theory. *Communications of the ACM*, 26:120–125, 1983. [282]

[Ken83b]   W. Kent. Technical correspondence: The universal relation revisited. *ACM Transactions on Database Systems*, 8:644–648, 1983. [79]

[Kho93]   S. Khoshafian. *Object-Oriented Databases*. John Wiley & Sons, New York, 1993. [529]

[Kif88]   M. Kifer. On safety, domain independence, and capturability of database queries. In *Proceedings of International Conference on Data and Knowledge Bases: Improving Usability and Responsiveness*, pages 405–415, Jerusalem, Israel, 1988. [135, 139, 229]

[Kim90]   W. Kim. *Introduction to Object-Oriented Databases*. MIT Press, Cambridge, Ma., 1990. [2, 529, 536]

[Kim95a]   W. Kim, editor. *Modern Database Systems, The Object Model, Interoperability, and Beyond*. Addison-Wesley, Reading, Ma., 1995. [529, 568]

[Kim95b]   W. Kim. Object-oriented database systems: Promises, reality, and future. In W. Kim, editor, *Modern Database Systems, The Object Model, Interoperability, and Beyond*, pages 255–280. Addison-Wesley, Reading, Ma., 1995. [25, 529]

[Kim96]   R. Kimball. *The Data Warehouse Toolkit*. John Wiley & Sons, Chichester, 1996. [562, 563]

[KK89]   H. Kitagawa and T.L. Kunii. *The Unnormalized Relational Data Model for Office Form Processor Design.* Computer Science Workbench. Springer-Verlag, Tokyo, 1989. [2]

[KKB90]   H.F. Korth, W. Kim, and F. Bancilhon. On long-duration CAD transactions. In S.B. Zdonik and D. Maier, editors, *Readings in Object-Oriented Database Systems*, pages 408–431. Morgan Kaufmann, San Francisco, Ca., 1990. [441]

[KKPV87]   A. Karabeg, D. Karabeg, K. Papakonstantinou, and V. Vianu. Axiomatization and simplification for relational transactions. In *Proceedings of ACM Symposium on Principles of Database Systems*, pages 254–259, San Diego, Ca., 1987. [132, 422]

[KL89a]   M. Kifer and G. Lausen. F-logic: A higher-order language for reasoning about objects, inheritance and scheme. In *Proceedings of ACM SIGMOD Conference on Management of Data*, pages 134–146, Portland, Oregon, 1989. [529]

[KL89b]   W. Kim and F.H. Lochovsky, editors. *Object-Oriented Concepts, Databases, and Applications.* ACM Press, New York, 1989. [529]

[Kle56]   S.C. Kleene. Representation of events in nerve nets and finite automata. In C.E. Shannon and J. McCarthy, editors, *Automata Studies*, volume 34 of *Annals of Mathematics Studies*, pages 3–41. Princeton University Press, Princeton, NJ, 1956. [41]

[Klu80]   A. Klug. Calculating constraints on relational databases. *ACM Transactions on Database Systems*, 5:260–290, 1980. [219, 503]

[Klu82]   A. Klug. Equivalence of relational algebra and relational calculus query languages having aggregate functions. *Journal of the ACM*, 29:699–717, 1982. [113, 383]

[KM80]   P. Kandzia and M. Mangelmann. On covering Boyce-Codd normal forms. *Information Processing Letters*, 11:218–223, 1980. [269]

[KM90]   A.C. Kakas and P. Mancarella. Database updates through abduction. In *Proceedings of International Conference on Very Large Data Bases*, pages 650–661, Brisbane, Australia, 1990. [502]

[KM91a]   H. Katsuno and A.O. Mendelzon. On the difference between updating a knowledge base and revising it. In *Proceedings of International Conference on Principles of Knowledge Representation and Reasoning*, pages 387–394, Cambridge, Ma., 1991. [502]

[KM91b]   H. Katsuno and A.O. Mendelzon. Propositional knowledge base revision and minimal change. *Artificial Intelligence*, 52:263–294, 1991. [502]

[KM94]   A. Kemper and G. Moerkotte. *Object-Oriented Database Management: Applications in Engineering and Computer Science.* Prentice Hall, Englewood Cliffs, NJ, 1994. [2, 529]

[KM95]   J. Kivinen and H. Mannila. Approximate inference of functional dependencies from relations. *Theoretical Computer Science*, 149:129–149, 1995. [565, 574]

[KMRS92]   M. Kantola, H. Mannila, K.-J. Räihä, and H. Siirtola. Discovering functional and inclusion dependencies in relational databases. *International Journal of Intelligent Systems*, 7:591–607, 1992. [565]

[Knu73]   D.E. Knuth. *The Art of Computer Programming*, volume 1. Addison-Wesley, Reading, Ma., second edition, 1973. [33]

[Kol91]   P.G. Kolaitis. The expressive power of stratified logic programs. *Information and Computation*, 90:50–66, 1991. [481]

[KP82]   A. Klug and R. Price. Determining view dependencies using tableaux. *ACM Transactions on Database Systems*, 7:361–380, 1982. [219, 503]

[KP91]   P.G. Kolaitis and C.H. Papadimitriou. Why not negation by fixpoint? *Journal of Computer and System Sciences*, 43:125–144, 1991. [122, 463, 468, 482]

[KR81]   H.T. Kung and J.T. Robinson. On optimistic methods for concurrency control. *ACM Transactions on Database Systems*, 6:213–226, 1981. [454]

[KRB85]   W. Kim, D.S. Reiner, and D.S. Batory, editors. *Query Processing in Database Systems.* Springer-Verlag, Berlin, 1985. [27]

[KSW90]   F. Kabanza, J.-M. Stevenne, and P. Wolper. Handling infinite temporal data. In *Proceedings of ACM Symposium on Principles of Database Systems*, pages 392–403, Nashville, Te., 1990. [399, 408]

[KU84]   A. Keller and J.D. Ullman. On complementary and independent mappings on databases. In *Proceedings of ACM SIGMOD Conference on Management of Data*, pages 143–148, Boston, 1984. [225]

[Kul93]   K.G. Kulkarni. Object-orientation and the SQL standard. *Computer Standards and Interfaces*, 15:287–300, 1993. [529]

[Kum96]   V. Kumar, editor. *Performance of Concurreny Control Mechanisms in Centralized Database Systems.* Prentice Hall, Englewood Cliffs, NJ, 1996. [453]

[Kun85]   S. Kundu. An improved algorithm for finding a key of a relation. In *Proceedings of ACM Symposium on Principles of Database Systems*, pages 189–192, Portland, Oregon, 1985. [**154, 230**]

[Kun87]   K. Kunen. Negation in logic programming. *Journal of Logic Programming*, 4:289–308, 1987. [**473**]

[Kuo96]   D. Kuo. Model and verification of a data manager based on ARIES. *ACM Transactions on Database Systems*, 21:427–479, 1996. [**453**]

[KV88]   D. Karabeg and V. Vianu. Parallel update transactions. In *Proceedings of International Conference on Database Theory*, pages 307–321, Brüges, Belgium, 1988. [**132**]

[KV91]   D. Karabeg and V. Vianu. Simplification rules and complete axiomatization for relational update transactions. *ACM Transactions on Database Systems*, 16:439–475, 1991. [**132, 422**]

[KV92a]   P.G. Kolaitis and M.Y. Vardi. Fixpoint logic vs. infinitary logic in finite-model theory. In *Proceedings of IEEE Symposium on Logic in Computer Science*, pages 46–57, Santa Cruz, Ca., 1992. [**57, 382**]

[KV92b]   P.G. Kolaitis and M.Y. Vardi. Infinitary logic for computer science. In *Proceedings of International Colloquium on Automata, Languages and Programming*, pages 450–473, Vienna, 1992. [**57, 382**]

[KV92c]   P.G. Kolaitis and M.Y. Vardi. Infinitary logics and 0-1 laws. *Information and Computation*, 98:258–294, 1992. [**59**]

[KV93]   G.M. Kuper and M.Y. Vardi. The logical data model. *ACM Transactions on Database Systems*, 18:379–413, 1993. [**540**]

[KV95]   P.G. Kolaitis and M.Y. Vardi. On the expressive power of Datalog: Tools and a case study. *Journal of Computer and System Sciences*, 51:110–134, 1995. [**495–497**]

[KW89]   M. Kifer and J. Wu. A logic for object-oriented logic programming (Maier's O-logic revisited). In *Proceedings of ACM Symposium on Principles of Database Systems*, pages 379–393, Philadelphia, Pa., 1989. [**529**]

[Lae90]   E. Laenens. *Foundations of Ordered Logic*. PhD thesis, Department of Mathematics and Computer Science, University of Antwerp, 1990. [**479**]

[Lak86]   V.S. Lakshmanan. Split-freedom and MVD-intersection: A new characterization of multivalued dependencies having conflict-free covers. In *Proceedings of International Conference on Database Theory*, pages 221–241, Rome, 1986. [**198**]

[Lev84]   H.J. Levesque. The logic of incomplete knowledge bases. In M.L. Brodie, J. Mylopoulos, and J.W. Schmidt, editors, *Conceptual Modelling: Perspective from Artificial Intelligence, Databases and Programming Languages*, pages 165–189. Springer-Verlag, Berlin, 1984. [**509**]

[Lev92]   M. Levene. *The Nested Universal Relation Model*, volume 595 of *Lecture Notes in Computer Science*. Springer-Verlag, Berlin, 1992. [**2, 80, 207, 299, 522**]

[Lev95]   M. Levene. A lattice view of functional dependencies in incomplete relations. *Acta Cybernetica*, 12:181–207, 1995. [**318**]

[Lev96]   M. Levene. Maintaining consistency of imprecise relations. *The Computer Journal*, 39:114–123, 1996. [**567**]

[Lev98]   M. Levene. On the information content of semi-structured databases. *Acta Cybernetica*, 13:257–275, 1998. [**560, 570**]

[LG92]   T.-W. Ling and C.H. Goh. Logical database design with inclusion dependencies. In *Proceedings of the International Conference on Data Engineering*, pages 642–649, Tempe, Az., 1992. [**243, 263**]

[LG98]   S. Lawrence and C.L. Giles. Searching the world wide web. *Science*, 280:98–100, 1998. [**548**]

[Lib91]   L. Libkin. A relational algebra for complex objects based on partial information. In *Proceedings of Symposium on Mathematical Foundations of Database and Knowledge Base Systems*, pages 29–43, Rostock, Germany, 1991. [**299**]

[Lib98]   L. Libkin. A semantics-based approach to design of query languages for partial information. In B. Thalheim and L. Libkin, editors, *Semantics in Databases*, pages 170–208. Springer-Verlag, Berlin, 1998. [**299**]

[Lie79]   Y.E. Lien. Multivalued dependencies with null values in relational databases. In *Proceedings of International Conference on Very Large Data Bases*, pages 61–66, Rio de Janeiro, 1979. [**352**]

[Lie81]   Y.E. Lien. Hierarchical schemata for relational databases. *ACM Transactions on Database Systems*, 6:48–69, 1981. [**196**]

[Lie82]   Y.E. Lien. On the equivalence of database models. *Journal of the ACM*, 29:333–362, 1982. [**196, 314, 352**]

[Lie85]   Y.E. Lien. Relational database design. In S.B. Yao, editor, *Principles of Database Design, Logical Organizations*, pages 211–254. Prentice Hall, Englewood Cliffs, NJ, 1985. [**249**]

[Lif88]   V. Lifschitz. On the declarative semantics of logic programs with negation. In J. Minker, editor, *Foundations of Deductive Databases and Logic Programming*, pages 177–192. Morgan Kaufmann, Los Altos, Ca., 1988. [**468**]

[Lip84]   W. Lipski Jr. On relational algebra with marked nulls. In *Proceedings of ACM Symposium on Principles of Database Systems*, pages 201–203, Waterloo, Ontario, 1984. [**300**]

[LJ88]   N.A. Lorentzos and R.G. Johnson. Extending relational algebra to manipulate temporal data. *Information Systems*, 13:289–296, 1988. [**393**]

[LL86]   N. Lerat and W. Lipski Jr. Nonapplicable nulls. *Theoretical Computer Science*, 46:67–82, 1986. [**352, 356**]

[LL89]   M. Levene and G. Loizou. NURQL: A nested universal relation query language. *Information Systems*, 14:307–316, 1989. [**22**]

[LL92]   M. Levene and G. Loizou. Inferring null join dependencies in relational databases. *BIT*, 32:413–429, 1992. [**299, 352**]

[LL93a]   M. Levene and G. Loizou. A fully precise null extended nested relational algebra. *Fundamenta Informaticae*, 19:303–342, 1993. [**299**]

[LL93b]   M. Levene and G. Loizou. Semantics for null extended nested relations. *ACM Transactions on Database Systems*, 18:414–459, 1993. [**299**]

[LL94]   M. Levene and G. Loizou. The nested universal relation data model. *Journal of Computer and System Sciences*, 49:683–717, 1994. [**299**]

[LL95a]   M. Levene and G. Loizou. A correspondence between variable relations and three-valued propositional logic. *International Journal of Computer Mathematics*, 55:29–38, 1995. [**361, 526**]

[LL95b]   M. Levene and G. Loizou. A graph-based data model and its ramifications. *IEEE Transactions on Knowledge and Data Engineering*, 7:809–823, 1995. [**62, 82, 533, 540, 551**]

[LL96a]   M. Levene and G. Loizou. Categorisation of computable database queries. *Fundamenta Informaticae*, 27:319–348, 1996. [**365**]

[LL96b]   T.-W. Ling and M.L. Lee. View update in entity-relationship approach. *Data & Knowledge Engineering*, 19:135–169, 1996. [**81**]

[LL97a]   M. Levene and G. Loizou. The additivity problem for functional dependencies in incomplete relations. *Acta Informatica*, 34:135–149, 1997. [**317**]

[LL97b]   M. Levene and G. Loizou. A generalisation of entity and referential integrity in relational databases. Research Note RN/97/84, Department of Computer Science, University College London, 1997. [**321**]

[LL97c]   M. Levene and G. Loizou. How to prevent interaction of functional and inclusion dependencies. Research Note RN/97/129, Department of Computer Science, University College London, 1997. [**187, 189**]

[LL97d]   M. Levene and G. Loizou. Null inclusion dependencies in relational databases. *Information and Computation*, 136:67–108, 1997. [**324**]

[LL98a]   M. Levene and G. Loizou. The additivity problem for data dependencies in incomplete relational databases. In B. Thalheim and L. Libkin, editors, *Semantics in Databases*, pages 136–169. Springer-Verlag, Berlin, 1998. [**324**]

[LL98b]   M. Levene and G. Loizou. Axiomatisation of functional dependencies in incomplete relations. *Theoretical Computer Science*, 206:283–300, 1998. [**316**]

[LL99a]   M. Levene and G. Loizou. Database design for incomplete relations. *ACM Transactions on Database Systems*, 24, 1999. To appear. [**318, 356**]

[LL99b]   M. Levene and G. Loizou. A probabilistic approach to navigation in hypertext. *Information Sciences*, 114: 165–186, 1999. [**554**]

[LL99c]   M. Levene and G. Loizou. Navigation in hypertext is easy only sometimes. *SIAM Journal on Computing*, 1999. To appear. [**388, 553, 571, 572**]

[Llo87]   J.W. Lloyd. *Foundations of Logic Programming*. Springer-Verlag, New York, second edition, 1987. [**40**]

[LM67]   R.E. Levien and M.E. Maron. A computer system for inference execution and data retrieval. *Communications of the ACM*, 10:715–721, 1967. [**227**]

[LM89]   V.S. Lakshmanan and A.O. Mendelzon. Inductive pebble games and the expressive power of Datalog. In *Proceedings of ACM Symposium on Principles of Database Systems*, pages 301–310, Philadelphia, Pa., 1989. [**495, 497**]

[LM93]   T.Y.C. Leung and R.R. Muntz. Stream processing: Temporal query processing and optimisation. In A.U. Tansel, J. Clifford, S. Gadia, S. Jajodia, A. Segev, and R. Snodgrass, editors, *Temporal Databases, Theory, Design, and Implementation*, pages 329–355. Benjamin/Cummings, Redwood City, Ca., 1993. [**408**]

[LMG83]   K. Laver, A.O. Mendelzon, and M.H. Graham. Functional dependencies on cyclic database schemes. In *Proceedings of ACM SIGMOD Conference on Management of Data*, pages 79–91, San Jose, Ca., 1983. [**211**]

[LMR89]   J. Lobo, J. Minker, and A. Rajasekar. Extending the semantics of logic programs to disjunctive logic programs. In *Proceedings of International Conference on Logic Programming*, pages 255–267, Lisbon, 1989. [**479**]

[LMS93]   A.Y. Levy, I.S. Mumick, and Y. Sagiv. Equivalence, query-reachability, and satisfiability in Datalog extensions. In *Proceedings of ACM Symposium on Principles of Database Systems*, pages 109–122, Washington, D.C., 1993. [**489, 500, 503**]

[LO78]   C.L. Lucchesi and S.L. Osborn. Candidate keys for relations. *Journal of Computer and System Sciences*, 17:270–279, 1978. [**154**]

[Lor93]   N.A. Lorentzos. The interval-extended relational model and its application to valid–time databases. In A.U. Tansel, J. Clifford, S. Gadia, S. Jajodia, A. Segev, and R. Snodgrass, editors, *Temporal Databases, Theory, Design, and Implementation*, pages 67–91. Benjamin/Cummings, Redwood City, Ca., 1993. [**393**]

[LP81]   H.R. Lewis and C.H. Papadimitriou. *Elements of the Theory of Computation*. Prentice-Hall, Englewood Cliffs., NJ, 1981. [**52**]

[LP91]   M. Levene and A. Poulovassilis. An object-oriented data model formalised through hypergraphs. *Data & Knowledge Engineering*, 6:205–224, 1991. [**529**]

[LPB+93]   M. Levene, A. Poulovassilis, K. Benkerimi, S. Schwartz, and E. Tuv. Implementation of a graph-based data model for complex objects. *ACM SIGMOD Record*, 22:26–31, 1993. [**533**]

[LRM91]   J. Lobo, A. Rajasekar, and J. Minker. Semantics of Horn and disjunctive logic programs. *Theoretical Computer Science*, 86:93–106, 1991. [**479**]

[LRO96]   A.Y. Levy, A. Rajaraman, and J.J. Ordille. Querying heterogeneous information sources using source descriptions. In *Proceedings of International Conference on Very Large Data Bases*, pages 251–262, Bombay, 1996. [**560**]

[LS88]   C. Lewerentz and A. Schürr. GRAS, a management system for graph-like documents. In *Proceedings of International Conference on Data and Knowledge Bases: Improving Usability and Responsiveness*, pages 91–131, Jerusalem, Israel, 1988. [**541**]

[LST87]   J.W. Lloyd, E.A. Sonenberg, and R.W. Topor. Integrity constraints checking in stratified databases. *Journal of Logic Programming*, 4:331–343, 1987. [**508**]

[LT83]   G. Loizou and P. Thanisch. Testing a dependency-preserving decomposition for losslessness. *Information Systems*, 8:25–27, 1983. [**246**]

[LT87a]   G. Loizou and P. Thanisch. Losslessness and project-join constructibility in relational databases. *Acta Informatica*, 24:131–144, 1987. [**204**]

[LT87b]   G. Loizou and P. Thanisch. On finding a worst-case optimal fourth normal form database decomposition. *BIT*, 27:157–162, 1987. [**284**]

[LTK81]   T.-W. Ling, F.W. Tompa, and T. Kameda. An improved third normal form for relational databases. *ACM Transactions on Database Systems*, 6:329–346, 1981. [**269**]

[LV97]   M. Levene and M.W. Vincent. Recovery from inconsistency in incomplete relations. Research Note RN/97/81, Department of Computer Science, University College London, 1997. [**575**]

[LV99]   M. Levene and M.W. Vincent. Justification for inclusion dependency normal form. *IEEE Transactions on Knowledge and Data Engineering*, 1999. To appear. [**243, 263, 282, 284, 285**]

[LZ96]   D. Lucarella and A. Zanzi. A visual retrieval environment for hypermedia information systems. *ACM Transactions on Information Systems*, 14:3–29, 1996. [**540**]

[Mai80]   D. Maier. Minimal covers in the relational database model. *Journal of the ACM*, 27:664–674, 1980. [**166**]

[Maj92]   M.E. Majster-Cederbaum. Ensuring the existence of a BCNF-decomposition that preserves functional dependencies in $O(N^2)$ time. *Information Processing Letters*, 43:95–100, 1992. [**283**]

[Mak77]   A. Makinouchi. A consideration on normal form of not-necessarily-normalized relation in the relational data model. In *Proceedings of International Conference on Very Large Data Bases*, pages 447–453, Tokyo, 1977. [**19**]

[Mak87]   J.A. Makowsky. Why Horn formulas matter in computer science: Initial structures and generic examples. *Journal of Computer and System Sciences*, 34:266–292, 1987. [**508**]

[Man84]   H. Mannila. On the complexity of the inference problem for subclasses of inclusion dependencies. In *Proceedings of Winter School on Theoretical Computer Science*, pages 182–193, Lammi, Finland, 1984. [**178, 180**]

[Man89]   S. Manchanda. Declarative expression of deductive database updates. In *Proceedings of ACM Symposium on Principles of Database Systems*, pages 93–100, Philadelphia, Pa., 1989. [**502**]

[Man90]   R. Manthey. Satisfiability of integrity constraints: reflections on a neglected problem. In *Proceedings of Workshop on Foundations of Models and Languages for Data and Objects*, pages 169–179, Aigen, Austria, 1990. [**508**]

[Mar94]   V.M. Markowitz. Safe referential integrity and null constraint structures in relational databases. *Information Systems*, 19:359–378, 1994. [**243, 263**]

[Mas84]   Y. Masunaga. A relational database view update translation mechanism. In *Proceedings of International Conference on Very Large Data Bases*, pages 309–320, Singapore, 1984. **[226]**

[Mat96]   N.M. Mattos. An overview of the SQL3 standard. Research Report, IBM Technology Institute, Santa Teresa Lab., San Jose, Ca., 1996. **[529]**

[MD89]   D.R. McCarthy and U. Dayal. The architecture of an active data base management system. In *Proceedings of ACM SIGMOD Conference on Management of Data*, pages 215–224, Portland, Oregon, 1989. **[545]**

[MD94]   S. Muggleton and L. De Raedt. Inductive logic programming: Theory and methods. *Journal of Logic Programming*, 19,20:629–679, 1994. **[566]**

[Mel96]   J. Melton. An SQL3 snapshot. In *Proceedings of IEEE Conference on Data Engineering*, pages 666–672, New Orleans, Lo., 1996. **[383, 529]**

[Men79]   A.O. Mendelzon. On axiomatizing multivalued dependencies in relational databases. *Journal of the ACM*, 26:37–44, 1979. **[193, 194]**

[Men87]   E. Mendelson. *Introduction to Mathematical Logic*. Wadsworth & Books/Cole, Monterey, Ca., third edition, 1987. **[40]**

[MFDG98]   S. Mace, U. Flohr, R. Dobson, and T. Graham. Weaving a better web. *Byte*, 23:58–68, 1998. **[550]**

[MG90]   R. Missaoui and R. Godin. The implication problem for inclusion dependencies: A graph approach. *ACM SIGMOD Record*, 19:36–40, 1990. **[232]**

[MGB93]   R. Missaoui, R. Godin, and A. Boujenoui. Extracting exact and approximate rules from databases. In *Proceedings of International Workshop on Incompleteness and Uncertainty in Information System*, pages 209–221, Montreal, 1993. **[565]**

[MGKL88]   L.L. Miller, S.K. Gadia, S. Kothari, and K.C. Liu. Completeness issues for join dependencies derived from the universal relation join dependency. *Information Processing Letters*, 28:269–274, 1988. **[211]**

[MH69]   J. McCarthy and P.J. Hayes. Some philosophical problems from the standpoint of artificial intelligence. In B. Meltzer and D. Michie, editors, *Machine Intelligence*, volume 4, pages 463–502. Edinburgh University Press, Edinburgh, 1969. **[502]**

[MHL⁺92]   C. Mohan, D. Haderle, B. Lindsay, H. Pirahesh, and P. Schwartz. ARIES: A transaction recovery method supporting fine-granularity locking and partial rollbacks using write-ahead logging. *ACM Transactions on Database Systems*, 17:94–162, 1992. **[453]**

[MI89]   C.C. Marshall and P.M. Irish. Guided tours and on-line presentations: How authors make existing hypertext intelligible for readers. In *Proceedings of ACM Conference on Hypertext*, pages 15–26, Pittsburg, Pa., 1989. **[554]**

[Mic87]   Z. Michalewicz. Functional dependencies and their connection with security of statistical databases. *Information Systems*, 12:17–27, 1987. **[230]**

[Min69]   M.L. Minsky. *Computation: Finite and Infinite Machines*. Prentice-Hall, Englewood Cliffs, NJ, 1969. **[52]**

[Min88a]   J. Minker. On indefinite databases and the closed world assumption. In M.L. Ginsberg, editor, *Readings in Nonmonotonic Reasoning*, pages 326–333. Morgan Kaufmann, Los Altos, Ca., 1988. **[293, 461]**

[Min88b]   J. Minker. Perspectives in deductive databases. *Journal of Logic Programming*, 5:33–60, 1988. **[510]**

[Mit83]   J.C. Mitchell. The implication problem for functional and inclusion dependencies. *Information and Control*, 56:154–173, 1983. **[173, 174, 179–181, 186]**

[MM85]   J. Martin and C. McClure. *Diagramming Techniques for Analysts and Programmers*. Prentice-Hall, Englewood Cliffs, NJ, 1985. **[62, 68]**

[MM90]   V.M. Markowitz and J.A. Makowsky. Identifying extended entity-relationship object structures in relational schemas. *IEEE Transactions on Software Engineering*, 16:777–790, 1990. **[81, 277, 281]**

[MMC76]   A.S. Michaels, B. Mittman, and C.R. Carlson. A comparison of the relational and CODASYL approaches to data-base management. *ACM Computing Surveys*, 8:125–151, 1976. **[2]**

[MMS79]   D. Maier, A.O. Mendelzon, and Y. Sagiv. Testing implications of data dependencies. *ACM Transactions on Database Systems*, 4:455–469, 1979. **[165]**

[MMSU80]   D. Maier, A.O. Mendelzon, F. Sadri, and J.D. Ullman. Adequacy of decompositions of relational databases. *Journal of Computer and System Sciences*, 21:368–379, 1980. **[210]**

[MNE96]   W.Y. Mok, Y.-K. Ng, and D.W. Embley. A normal form for precisely characterizing redundancy in nested relations. *ACM Transactions on Database Systems*, 21:77–106, 1996. **[522]**

[MNR92]   W. Marek, A. Nerode, and J. Remmel. How complicated is the set of stable models of a recursive logic program? *Annals of Pure and Applied Logic*, 56:119–135, 1992. **[483]**

[Mok97]   W.Y. Mok. On keys and normal forms. *Information Processing Letters*, 62:255–258, 1997. **[255, 283]**

[Mor94]   E. Morales. Learning patterns for playing strategies. *ICCA Journal*, 17:15–26, 1994. [566]

[MP92]   Z. Manna and A. Pnueli. *The Temporal Logic of Reactive and Concurrent Systems*. Springer-Verlag, New York, 1992. [388, 398]

[MQM97]   I.S. Mumick, , D. Quass, and B.S. Mumick. Maintenance of data cubes and summary tables in a warehouse. In *Proceedings of ACM SIGMOD Conference on Management of Data*, pages 100–111, Tucson, Az., 1997. [564]

[MR83]   H. Mannila and K.-J. Räihä. On the relationship of minimum and optimum covers for a set of functional dependencies. *Acta Informatica*, 20:143–158, 1983. [166]

[MR86a]   H. Mannila and K.-J. Räihä. Design by example: an application of Armstrong relations. *Journal of Computer and System Sciences*, 33:126–141, 1986. [148, 159, 231, 565]

[MR86b]   H. Mannila and K.-J. Räihä. Inclusion dependencies in database design. In *Proceedings of IEEE Conference on Data Engineering*, pages 713–718, Los Angeles, Ca., 1986. [243, 263, 277]

[MR87]   H. Mannila and K.-J. Räihä. Dependency inference. In *Proceedings of International Conference on Very Large Data Bases*, pages 155–158, Brighton, U.K., 1987. [565]

[MR88]   H. Mannila and K.-J. Räihä. Generating Armstrong databases for sets of functional and inclusion dependencies. Research Report A-1988-7, Department of Computer Science, University of Tampere, Tampere, Finland, 1988. [177]

[MR92a]   H. Mannila and K.-J. Räihä. *The Design of Relational Databases*. Addison-Wesley, Reading, Ma., 1992. [80–82, 187, 243, 263, 277, 281]

[MR92b]   H. Mannila and K.-J. Räihä. On the complexity of inferring functional dependencies. *Discrete Applied Mathematics*, 40:237–243, 1992. [565]

[MR94]   H. Mannila and K.-J. Räihä. Algorithms for inferring functional dependencies from relations. *Data & Knowledge Engineering*, 12:83–99, 1994. [565, 574]

[MRW86]   D. Maier, D. Rozenshtein, and D.S. Warren. Window functions. In P.C. Kanellakis and F. Preparata, editors, *Advances in Computing Research*, volume 3, pages 213–246. JAI Press, Greenwich, 1986. [80]

[MS89a]   V.M. Markowitz and A. Shoshani. On the correctness of representing extended entity-relationship structures in the relational model. In *Proceedings of ACM SIGMOD Conference on Management of Data*, pages 430–439, Portland, Oregon, 1989. [263, 277, 281]

[MS89b]   M. Missikoff and M. Scholl. An algorithm for insertion into a lattice: Application to type classification. In *Proceedings of International Conference on Foundations of Data Organization and Algorithms*, pages 64–82, Paris, 1989. [527, 528]

[MS91]   L.E. McKenzie Jr. and R.T. Snodgrass. Evaluation of relational algebras incorporating the time dimension in databases. *ACM Computing Surveys*, 23:501–543, 1991. [394]

[MS94]   I.S. Mumick and O. Shmueli. Universal finiteness and satisfiability. In *Proceedings of ACM Symposium on Principles of Database Systems*, pages 190–200, Minneapolis, Mn., 1994. [489]

[MSY81]   D. Maier, Y. Sagiv, and M. Yannakakis. On the complexity of testing implications of functional and join dependencies. *Journal of the ACM*, 28:680–695, 1981. [203]

[MT91]   W. Marek and M. Truszczynski. Autoepistemic logic. *Journal of the ACM*, 38:588–619, 1991. [483]

[MU83]   D. Maier and J.D. Ullman. Maximal objects and the semantics of universal relation databases. *ACM Transactions on Database Systems*, 8:1–14, 1983. [211]

[MU84]   D. Maier and J.D. Ullman. Connections in acyclic hypergraphs. *Theoretical Computer Science*, 32:185–199, 1984. [211]

[MUV84]   D. Maier, J.D. Ullman, and M.Y. Vardi. On the foundations of the universal relation model. *ACM Transactions on Database Systems*, 9:283–308, 1984. [80, 490]

[MV86]   J.A. Makowsky and M.Y. Vardi. On the expressive power of data dependencies. *Acta Informatica*, 23:231–244, 1986. [505, 507, 508]

[MW88a]   D. Maier and D.S. Warren. *Computing with Logic: Logic Programming with Prolog*. Benjamin/ Cummings, Menlo Park, Ca., 1988. [23, 115]

[MW88b]   S. Manchanda and D.S. Warren. A logic-based language for database updates. In J. Minker, editor, *Foundations of Deductive Databases and Logic Programming*, pages 363–394. Morgan Kaufmann, Los Altos, Ca., 1988. [502]

[MW95]   A.O. Mendelzon and P.T. Wood. Finding regular simple paths in graph databases. *SIAM Journal on Computing*, 24:1235–1258, 1995. [554]

[Nau88]   J.F. Naughton. Compiling separable recursions. In *Proceedings of ACM SIGMOD Conference on Management of Data*, pages 312–319, Chicago, Il., 1988. [489]

[Nau89]   J.F. Naughton. Data independent recursion in deductive databases. *Journal of Computer and System Sciences*, 38:259–289, 1989. [491]

[Nel80]   T.H. Nelson. Replacing the printed word: A complete literary system. In *Proceedings of IFIP Congress*, pages 1013–1023, Tokyo, 1980. [556]

[NG78]   J.-M. Nicolas and H. Gallaire. Data base: theory vs. interpretation. In H. Gallaire and J. Minker, editors, *Logic and Data Bases*, pages 33–54. Plenum Press, New York, 1978. [480]

[Ng96]   W. Ng. Personal communication. Department of Computer Science, University College London, 1996. [214]

[Nic82]   J.-M. Nicolas. Logic for improving integrity checking in relational databases. *Acta Informatica*, 18:227–253, 1982. [508]

[Nie90]   J. Nielsen. *Hypertext and Hypermedia*. Academic Press, Boston, 1990. [2, 555]

[NK88]   S. Naqvi and R. Krishnamurthy. Database updates in logic programming. In *Proceedings of ACM Symposium on Principles of Database Systems*, pages 251–262, Austin, Texas, 1988. [512]

[NK89]   J.M. Nyce and P. Kahn. Innovation, pragmaticism, and technological continuity: Vannevar Bush's memex. *Journal of the American Society for Information Science*, 40:214–220, 1989. [555]

[NM90]   U. Nilsson and J. Maluszyński. *Logic Programming and Prolog*. John Wiley & Sons, Chichester, 1990. [463, 479]

[NT89]   S. Naqvi and S. Tsur. *A Logical Language for Data and Knowledge Bases*. Computer Science Press, New York, 1989. [2, 502, 511–513]

[NUWC97]   S. Nestorov, J.D. Ullman, J. Wiener, and S.S. Chawathe. Representative objects: Concise representations of semistructured, hierarchical data. In *Proceedings of IEEE International Conference on Data Engineering*, pages 79–90, Birmingham, 1997. [560, 572]

[NY78]   J.-M. Nicholas and K. Yazdanian. Integrity checking in deductive data bases. In H. Gallaire and J. Minker, editors, *Logic and Data Bases*, pages 325–344. Plenum, New York, 1978. [146, 509]

[OG95]   P.E. O'Neil and G. Graefe. Multi-table joins through bitmapped join indices. *ACM SIGMOD Record*, 24:8–11, 1995. [563]

[OH86]   S.L. Osborn and T.E. Heaven. The design of a relational database system with abstract data types for domains. *ACM Transactions on Database Systems*, 11:357–373, 1986. [570]

[Omi95]   E. Omiecinski. Parallel relational database systems. In W. Kim, editor, *Modern Database Systems, The Object Model, Interoperability, and Beyond*, pages 494–512. Addison-Wesley, Reading, Ma., 1995. [566]

[Osb79]   S.L. Osborn. Testing for the existence of a covering Boyce-Codd normal form. *Information Processing Letters*, 8:11–14, 1979. [269]

[ÖV91]   M.T. Özsu and P. Valduriez. *Principles of Distributed Database Systems*. Prentice-Hall, Englewood Cliffs, NJ, 1991. [566]

[ÖY87a]   M. Özsoyoğlu and L.-Y. Yuan. Reduced MVDs and minimal covers. *ACM Transactions on Database Systems*, 12:377–394, 1987. [198]

[ÖY87b]   Z.M. Özsoyoğlu and L.-Y. Yuan. A new normal form for nested relations. *ACM Transactions on Database Systems*, 12:111–136, 1987. [522]

[Pap79]   C. H. Papadimitriou. The serializability of concurrent database updates. *Journal of the ACM*, 26:631–653, 1979. [421, 453, 456]

[Pap85]   C.H. Papadimitriou. A note on the expressive power of Prolog. *Bulletin of the EATCS*, 26:21–23, 1985. [482]

[Pap86]   C.H. Papadimitriou. *The Theory of Database Concurrency Control*. Computer Science Press, Rockville, Md., 1986. [453, 455]

[Pap94]   C.H. Papadimitriou. *Computational Complexity*. Addison-Wesley, Reading, Ma., 1994. [52]

[Par78]   J. Paredaens. On the expressive power of the relational algebra. *Information Processing Letters*, 7:107–111, 1978. [377]

[Par96]   S. Parsons. Current approaches to handling imperfect information in data and knowledge bases. *IEEE Transactions on Knowledge and Data Engineering*, 8:353–372, 1996. [354]

[Paw82]   Z. Pawlak. Rough sets. *International Journal of Computer and Information Sciences*, 11:341–356, 1982. [342]

[PBR77]   C.H. Papadimitriou, P.A. Bernstein, and J.B. Rothnie Jr. Some computational problems related to database concurrency control. In *Proceedings of Conference on Theoretical Computer Science*, pages 275–282, Waterloo, Ontario, 1977. [453]

[PDGV89]   J. Paredaens, P. De Bra, M. Gyssens, and D. Van Gucht. *The Structure of the Relational Database Model*, volume 17 of *EATCS Monographs on Theoretical Computer Science*. Springer-Verlag, Berlin, 1989. [264, 266]

[PE98]   M. Perkowitz and O. Etzioni. Adaptive web sites: Automatically synthesizing web pages. In *Proceedings of National Conference on Artificial Intelligence*, Madison, Wisconsin, 1998. [555]

[Pet81]   J.L. Peterson. *Petri Net Theory and the Modeling of Systems*. Prentice Hall, Englewood Cliffs, NJ, 1981. [509]

[Pet89]   S.V. Petrov. Finite axiomatization of languages for representation of system properties: Axiomatization of dependencies. *Information Sciences*, 47:339–372, 1989. [**202**]

[PL94]   A. Poulovassilis and M. Levene. A nested-graph model for the representation and manipulation of complex objects. *ACM Transactions on Information Systems*, 12:35–68, 1994. [**62, 82, 533, 537, 540, 551, 570**]

[Pla92]   R. Planche. *Data Driven Systems Modeling*. Prentice-Hall/Masson, Exeter, 1992. [**62, 82**]

[PM88]   J. Peckman and F. Maryanski. Semantic data models. *ACM Computing Surveys*, 20:153–189, 1988. [**61**]

[Pos36]   E.L. Post. Finite combinatory processes. Formulation I. *The Journal of Symbolic Logic*, 1:103–105, 1936. [**40**]

[Pos46]   E.L. Post. A variant of a recursively unsolvable problem. *Bulletin of the American Mathematical Society*, 52:264–268, 1946. [**48**]

[Pos47]   E.L. Post. Recursive unsolvability of a problem of Thue. *The Journal of Symbolic Logic*, 12:1–11, 1947. [**48**]

[PP90]   H. Przymusinska and T. Przymusinski. Semantic issues in deductive databases and logic programs. In R.B. Banerji, editor, *Formal Techniques in Artificial Intelligence: A Sourcebook*, pages 321–367. Elsevier Science Publishers, Amsterdam, 1990. [**468, 476**]

[PPG80]   D.S. Parker Jr. and K. Parsaye-Ghomi. Inferences involving embedded multivalued dependencies and transitive dependencies. In *Proceedings of ACM SIGMOD Conference on Management of Data*, pages 52–57, Santa Monica, 1980. [**199**]

[Prz88a]   T.C. Przymusinski. On the declarative semantics of deductive databases and logic programs. In J. Minker, editor, *Foundations of Deductive Databases and Logic Programming*, pages 193–216. Morgan Kaufmann, Los Altos, 1988. [**468, 470, 476**]

[Prz88b]   T.C. Przymusinski. Perfect model semantics. In *Proceedings of International Conference on Logic Programming*, pages 1081–1120, Seattle, Wa., 1988. [**468, 470**]

[Prz89]   T.C. Przymusinski. Every logic program has a natural stratification and an iterated least fixed point model. In *Proceedings of ACM Symposium on Principles of Database Systems*, pages 11–21, Philadelphia, Pa., 1989. [**468, 477**]

[Prz90]   T.C. Przymusinski. Well-founded semantics coincides with three-valued stable semantics. *Fundamenta Informaticae*, 13:445–464, 1990. [**468, 478**]

[Prz91]   T.C. Przymusinski. Well-founded completions of logic programs. In *Proceedings of International Conference on Logic Programming*, pages 726–744, Paris, 1991. [**468**]

[Prz92]   T.C. Przymusinski. Two simple characterizations of well-founded semantics. In *Proceedings of Conference on Mathematical Foundations of Computer Science*, pages 451–462, Prague, 1992. [**468, 478**]

[PS87]   C. Parent and S. Spaccapietra. A model and an algebra for entity-relation type databases. *Technology and Science of Informatics*, 6:623–642, 1987. [**81**]

[PS89]   C. Parent and S. Spaccapietra. Complex objects modeling: An entity-relationship approach. In S. Abiteboul, P.C. Fischer, and H.-J. Schek, editors, *Nested Relations and Complex Objects*, pages 272–296. Springer-Verlag, Berlin, 1989. [**81**]

[PSF91]   G. Piatetsky-Shapiro and W.J. Frawley, editors. *Knowledge Discovery in Databases*. AAAI Press, Menlo Park, Ca., 1991. [**564**]

[PSM93]   G. Piatetsky-Shapiro and C.J. Matheus. Measuring data dependencies in large databases. In *Proceedings of Workshop on Knowledge Discovery in Databases*, pages 162–173, Washington, D.C., 1993. [**565**]

[PSV94]   W. Penzo, S. Sola, and F. Vitali. Further modification to the Dexter hypertext reference model: A proposal. Technical Report UBLCS-94-1, Laboratory of Computer Science, University of Bologna, 1994. [**553**]

[PSV96]   C.H. Papadimitriou, D. Suciu, and V. Vianu. Topological queries in spatial databases. In *Proceedings of ACM Symposium on Principles of Database Systems*, pages 81–92, Montreal, 1996. [**407**]

[PT86]   P. Pistor and R. Traunmueller. A database language for sets, lists and tables. *Information Systems*, 11:323–336, 1986. [**22**]

[PV88]   J. Paredaens and D. Van Gucht. Possibilities and limitations of using flat operators in nested algebra expressions. In *Proceedings of ACM Symposium on Principles of Database Systems*, pages 29–38, Austin, Texas, 1988. [**519**]

[PVA+92]   J. Paredaens, J. Van den Bussche, M. Andries, M. Gemis, M. Gyssens, I. Thyssens, D. Van Gucht, V. Sarathy, and L. Saxton. An overview of GOOD. *ACM SIGMOD Record*, 21:25–31, 1992. [**540**]

[PVV94]   J. Paredaens, J. Van den Bussche, and D. Van Gucht. Towards a theory of spatial databases queries. In *Proceedings of ACM Symposium on Principles of Database Systems*, pages 279–288, Minneapolis, Mn., 1994. [**407**]

[QRS+95]   D. Quass, A. Rajaraman, Y. Sagiv, J.D. Ullman, and J. Widom. Querying semistructured heterogeneous information. In *Proceedings of International Conference on Deductive and Object-Oriented Databases*, pages 319–344, Singapore, 1995. [**560**]

[Rad91]   R. Rada. *Hypertext: From Text to Expertext.* McGraw-Hill, New York, 1991. [2, 555, 556]

[Ram88]   R. Ramakrishnan. Magic templates: a spellbinding approach to logic programs. In *Proceedings of International Conference on Logic Programming*, pages 140–159, Seattle, Wa., 1988. [493]

[RBS94]   E. Rivlin, R. Botafogo, and B. Shneiderman. Navigating in hyperspace: Designing a structure-based toolbox. *Communications of the ACM*, 37:87–96, 1994. [554]

[Red98]   Red Brick Systems. Star schema processing for complex queries. White Paper, Red Brick Systems, Los Gatos, Ca., 1998. [563]

[Ree83]   D.P. Reed. Implementing atomic actions on decentralized data. *ACM Transactions on Computer Systems*, 1:3–23, 1983. [451]

[Rei78]   R. Reiter. On closed world databases. In H. Gallaire and J. Minker, editors, *Logic and Data Bases*, pages 55–76. Plenum, New York, 1978. [25, 121]

[Rei80]   R. Reiter. A logic for default reasoning. *Artificial Intelligence*, 13:81–132, 1980. [347, 468, 479]

[Rei84]   R. Reiter. Towards a logical reconstruction of relational database theory. In M.L. Brodie, J. Mylopoulos, and J.W. Schmidt, editors, *Conceptual Modelling: Perspective from Artificial Intelligence, Databases and Programming Languages*, pages 191–233. Springer-Verlag, Berlin, 1984. [460, 480]

[Rei87]   R. Reiter. Nonmonotonic reasoning. *Annual Review of Computer Science*, 2:147–186, 1987. [468]

[Rei92a]   R. Reiter. On formalizing database updates: preliminary report. In *Proceedings of International Conference on Extending Database Technology*, pages 10–20, Vienna, Austria, 1992. [502]

[Rei92b]   R. Reiter. What should a database know? *Journal of Logic Programming*, 14:127–153, 1992. [509]

[Res69]   N. Rescher. *Many-valued Logic.* McGraw-Hill, New York, 1969. [303, 333, 352]

[Ric53]   H.G. Rice. Classes of recursively enumerable sets and their decision problems. *Transactions of the American Mathematical Society*, 74:358–366, 1953. [46]

[RKB87]   M.A. Roth, H.F. Korth, and D.S. Batory. SQL/NF: A query language for ¬1NF relational databases. *Information Systems*, 12:99–114, 1987. [22]

[RM88]   K.V.S.V.N. Raju and A.K. Majumdar. Fuzzy functional dependencies and lossless join decomposition of fuzzy relational database systems. *ACM Transactions on Database Systems*, 13:129–166, 1988. [339]

[RMB⁺98]   R. Rastogi, S. Mehrotra, Y. Breitbart, H.F. Korth, and A. Silberschatz. On correctness of nonserializable executions. *Journal of Computer and System Sciences*, 56:68–82, 1998. [422, 453]

[RN89]   F. Rossi and S.A. Naqvi. Contributions to the view update problem. In *Proceedings of International Conference on Logic Programming*, pages 398–415, Lisbon, 1989. [502]

[Rod92]   J.F. Roddick. Schema evolution in database systems – an annotated bibliography. *ACM SIGMOD Record*, 21:35–40, 1992. [406]

[Rod96]   J.F. Roddick. A survey of schema versioning issues for database systems. *Information and Software Technology*, 37:383–393, 1996. [406]

[Rog87]   H. Rogers Jr. *Theory of Recursive Functions and Effective Computability.* MIT Press, Cambridge, Ma., 1987. Original edition published by McGraw-Hill, New York, 1967. [52]

[Ros89]   K.A. Ross. A procedural semantics for well founded negation in logic programs. In *Proceedings of ACM Symposium on Principles of Database Systems*, pages 22–33, Philadelphia, Pa., 1989. [468]

[RS59]   M.O. Rabin and D. Scott. Finite automata and their decision problems. *IBM Journal of Research and Development*, 3:114–125, 1959. [42]

[RS92]   K.A. Ross and Y. Sagiv. Monotonic aggregation in deductive databases. In *Proceedings of ACM Symposium on Principles of Database Systems*, pages 114–126, San Diego, Ca., 1992. [509, 512]

[RSUV89]   R. Ramakrishnan, Y. Sagiv, J.D. Ullman, and M.Y. Vardi. Proof-tree transformation theorems and their applications. In *Proceedings of ACM Symposium on Principles of Database Systems*, pages 172–181, Philadelphia, Pa., 1989. [488, 489]

[RU71]   N. Rescher and A. Urquhart. *Temporal Logic.* Springer-Verlag, New York, 1971. [387, 407]

[RU95]   R. Ramakrishnan and J.D. Ullman. A survey of deductive database systems. *Journal of Logic Programming*, 22:125–145, 1995. [28, 509, 513]

[SA95]   H. Samet and W.G. Aref. Spatial data models and query processing. In W. Kim, editor, *Modern Database Systems, The Object Model, Interoperability, and Beyond*, pages 338–360. Addison-Wesley, Reading, Ma., 1995. [407, 408]

[Sac85]   D. Saccà. Closures of database hypergraphs. *Journal of the ACM*, 32:774–803, 1985. [211]

[Sag83]   Y. Sagiv. A characterization of globally consistent databases and their access paths. *ACM Transactions on Database Systems*, 8:266–286, 1983. [232]

[Sag87]   Y. Sagiv. Optimizing Datalog programs. In *Proceedings of ACM Symposium on Principles of Database Systems*, pages 349–362, San Diego, Ca., 1987. [**489**]

[Sag88]   Y. Sagiv. On bounded database schemes and bounded Horn-clause programs. *SIAM Journal on Computing*, 17:1–22, 1988. [**490, 491**]

[SAH87]   M. Stonebraker, J. Anton, and E. Hanson. Extending a database system with procedures. *ACM Transactions on Database Systems*, 12:350–376, 1987. [**529**]

[Sal91]   G. Salton. Developments in automatic text retrieval. *Science*, 253:974–980, 1991. [**555**]

[Sar89]   Y.P. Saraiya. Linearizing nonlinear recursions in polynomial time. In *Proceedings of ACM Symposium on Principles of Database Systems*, pages 182–189, Philadelphia, Pa., 1989. [**488, 489**]

[Sar90]   Y.P. Saraiya. Hard problems for simple logic programs. In *Proceedings of ACM SIGMOD Conference on Management of Data*, pages 64–73, Atlantic City, NJ, 1990. [**489**]

[Sar95]   Y.P. Saraiya. On the efficiency of transforming database logic programs. *Journal of Computer and System Sciences*, 51:87–109, 1995. [**488, 489, 491**]

[Saz93]   V.Y. Sazanov. Hereditarily-finite sets, data bases and polynomial-time computability. *Theoretical Computer Science*, 119:187–214, 1993. [**365**]

[Sch77]   J.W. Schmidt. Some high level language constructs for data of type relation. *ACM Transactions on Database Systems*, 2:247–261, 1977. [**10**]

[Sch86]   D.A. Schmidt. *Denotational Semantics: A Methodology for Language Development*. Allyn and Bacon, Inc., Newton, Ma., 1986. [**299**]

[Sch90]   A. Schürr. PROGRESS: A VHL-language based on graph grammars. In *Proceedings of International Workshop on Graph Grammars and Their Application to Computer Science*, pages 641–659, Bremen, 1990. [**541**]

[Sch93]   J.C. Schlimmer. Efficiently inducing determinations: A complete and systematic search algorithm that uses optimal pruning. In *Proceedings of International Conference on Machine Learning*, pages 284–290, Amherst, Ma., 1993. [**565**]

[Sch95]   J.S. Schlipf. The expressive powers of the logic programming semantics. *Journal of Computer and System Sciences*, 51:64–86, 1995. [**468, 482, 483**]

[Sci81]   E. Sciore. Real world MVD's. In *Proceedings of ACM SIGMOD Conference on Management of Data*, pages 121–132, Ann Arbor, 1981. [**196**]

[Sci82]   E. Sciore. A complete axiomatization of full join dependencies. *Journal of the ACM*, 29:373–393, 1982. [**202, 211**]

[Sci83]   E. Sciore. Improving database schemes by adding attributes. In *Proceedings of ACM Symposium on Principles of Database Systems*, pages 379–383, Atlanta, 1983. [**248**]

[Sci86]   E. Sciore. Comparing the universal instance and relational data models. In P.C. Kanellakis and F. Preparata, editors, *Advances in Computing Research*, volume 3, pages 139–162. JAI Press, Greenwich, 1986. [**171, 244, 245**]

[SDPF81]   Y. Sagiv, C. Delobel, D.S. Parker Jr., and R. Fagin. An equivalence between relational database dependencies and a fragment of propositional logic. *Journal of the ACM*, 28:435–453, 1981. [**210**]

[SF93]   I. Savnik and P. Flach. Bottom-up induction of functional dependencies from relations. In *Proceedings of Workshop on Knowledge Discovery in Databases*, pages 174–185, Washington, D.C., 1993. [**565**]

[SFR92]   P.D. Stotts, R. Furata, and J.C. Ruiz. Hyperdocuments as automata: Trace-based browsing property verification. In *Proceedings of ACM Conference on Hypertext*, pages 272–281, Milano, Italy, 1992. [**388, 554, 571, 572**]

[SGS94]   K. Salem, H. Garcia-Molina, and J. Shands. Altruistic locking. *ACM Transactions on Database Systems*, 19:117–165, 1994. [**442, 443**]

[She93]   S. Shenoi. Multilevel database security using information clouding. In *Proceedings of IEEE International Conference on Fuzzy Systems*, pages 483–488, 1993. [**357**]

[Shi81]   D.W. Shipman. The functional data model and the data language DAPLEX. *ACM Transactions on Database Systems*, 6:140–173, 1981. [**541**]

[Shm93]   O. Shmueli. Equivalence of Datalog queries is undecidable. *Journal of Logic Programming*, 15:231–341, 1993. [**486, 489, 500**]

[Shm95]   O. Shmueli. A single recursive predicate is sufficient for pure Datalog. *Information and Computation*, 116:91–97, 1995. [**489**]

[Sho86]   R.C. Shock. Computing the minimum cover of functional dependencies. *Information Processing Letters*, 22:157–159, 1986. [**166**]

[SI88]   H. Seki and H. Itoh. A query evaluation method for stratified programs under the extended CWA. In *Proceedings of International Conference on Logic Programming*, pages 195–211, Seattle, Wa., 1988. [**480**]

[SI93]   C. Sakama and K. Inoue. Relating disjunctive logic programs to default theories. In *Proceedings of International Workshop on Logic Programming and Nonmonotonic Reasoning*, pages 266–282, Lisbon, 1993. [**479**]

[SJ91]   R.S. Sandhu and S. Jajodia. Honest databases that can keep secrets. In *Proceedings of National Computer Security Conference*, pages 267–282, Washington, D.C., 1991. [**230**]

[SKdM92]   E. Simon, J. Kiernan, and C. de Maindreville. Implementing high level active rules on top of a relational DBMS. In *Proceedings of International Conference on Very Large Data Bases*, pages 315–326, Vancouver, 1992. [**545**]

[SLR76]   R.E. Stearns, P.M. Lewis II, and D.J. Rosenkrantz. Concurrency control for database systems. In *Proceedings of IEEE Symposium on Foundations of Computer Science*, pages 19–32, Houston, Texas, 1976. [**453**]

[SM96]   M. Stonebraker and D. Moore. *Object-Relational DBMSs: The Next Great Wave.* Morgan Kaufmann, San Francisco, Ca., 1996. [**28, 60, 529, 570**]

[SMDD95]   D. Schmidt, R. Marti, A.K. Dittrich, and W. Dreyer. Time series, a neglected issue in temporal database research? In *Recent Advances in Temporal Databases, Proceedings of the International Workshop on Temporal Databases*, pages 214–232, Zurich, 1995. [**399**]

[SMF92]   S. Shenoi, A. Melton, and L.T. Fan. Functional dependencies and normal forms in the fuzzy relational database model. *Information Sciences*, 60:1–28, 1992. [**342**]

[Sno95]   R.T. Snodgrass, editor. *The TSQL2 Temporal Query Language.* Kluwer, Dordrecht, 1995. [**400, 406–408**]

[SON95]   A. Savasere, E. Omiecinski, and S. Navathe. An efficient algorithm for mining association rules in large databases. In *Proceedings of International Conference on Very Large Data Bases*, pages 432–444, Zurich, 1995. [**575**]

[Sow76]   J.F. Sowa. Conceptual graphs for a data base interface. *IBM Journal of Research and Development*, 20:336–357, 1976. [**82**]

[SPAM91]   U. Schreier, H. Pirahesh, R. Agrawal, and C. Mohan. Alert: an architecture for transforming a passive DBMS into an active DBMS. In *Proceedings of International Conference on Very Large Data Bases*, pages 469–478, Bareelona, 1991. [**545**]

[Spi88]   J.M. Spivey. *Understanding Z, A Specification Language and its Formal Semantics.* Cambridge University Press, Cambridge, U.K., 1988. [**553**]

[SPS87]   M.H. Scholl, H.-B. Paul, and H.-J. Schek. Supporting flat relations by a nested relational kernel. In *Proceedings of International Conference on Very Large Data Bases*, pages 137–146, Brighton, 1987. [**59, 568**]

[SS75]   H.A. Schmid and J.R. Swenson. On the semantics of the relational data model. In *Proceedings of ACM SIGMOD Conference on Management of Data*, pages 211–223, Boston, Ma., 1975. [**81, 189**]

[SS77]   J.M. Smith and D.C.P. Smith. Database abstractions: aggregation and generalization. *ACM Transactions on Database Systems*, 2:105–133, 1977. [**61**]

[SS82]   M. Schkolnick and P. Sorenson. The effects of denormalization on database performance. *The Australian Computer Journal*, 14:12–18, 1982. [**250**]

[SS89]   Y. Sagiv and O. Shmueli. A characterization of finite FD-acyclicity. *Journal of Computer and System Sciences*, 38:380–404, 1989. [**211**]

[SS90]   M.H. Scholl and H.-J. Schek. A relational object model. In *Proceedings of International Conference on Database Theory*, pages 89–105, Paris, 1990. [**25, 529**]

[SS94]   L. Sterling and E. Shapiro. *The Art of Prolog.* MIT Press, Cambridge, Ma., second edition, 1994. [**23, 115**]

[ST95]   A.P. Stolboushkin and M.A. Taitslin. Finite queries do not have effective syntax. In *Proceedings of ACM Symposium on Principles of Database Systems*, pages 277–285, San Jose, Ca., 1995. [**139**]

[Sto77]   L.J. Stockmeyer. The polynomial-time hierarchy. *Theoretical Computer Science*, 3:1–22, 1977. [**51**]

[Sto79]   R.R. Stoll. *Set Theory and Logic.* Dover, New York, 1979. [**33, 40**]

[Sto86]   M. Stonebraker. Inclusion of new types in relational database systems. In *Proceedings of IEEE International Conference on Data Engineering*, pages 262–269, Los Angeles, Ca., 1986. [**570**]

[Sto95]   P.D. Stotts. Timed links solve the "stale url" problem. *ACM SIGLINK Newsletter*, 4:6–7, 1995. [**551**]

[SU82]   F. Sadri and J.D. Ullman. Template dependencies: A large class of dependencies in relational databases and its complete axiomatization. *Journal of the ACM*, 29:363–372, 1982. [**234**]

[SW82]   Y. Sagiv and S.F. Waleca. Subset dependencies and a completeness result for a subclass of embedded multivalued dependencies. *Journal of the ACM*, 29:103–117, 1982. [**199**]

[SW88]   J.B. Smith and S.F. Weiss. An overview of hypertext. *Communications of the ACM*, 31:816–819, 1988. [**555**]

[SY80]   Y. Sagiv and M Yannakakis. Equivalences among relational expressions with union and difference operators. *Journal of the ACM*, 27:633–655, 1980. [**484**]

[Tak89]   K. Takeda. In the uniqueness of nested relations. In S. Abiteboul, P.C. Fischer, and H.-J. Schek, editors, *Nested Relations and Complex Objects in Databases*, volume 361 of *Lecture Notes in Computer Science*, pages 139–150. Springer-Verlag, Berlin, 1989. [**569**]

[Tar55]   A. Tarski. A lattice-theoretic fixpoint theorem and its applications. *Pacific Journal of Mathematics*, 5:285–309, 1955. [**463**]

[Tar72]   R.E. Tarjan. Depth-first search and linear graph algorithms. *SIAM Journal on Computing*, 1:146–160, 1972. [**17, 35, 172, 421, 469**]

[TC90]   A. Tuzhilin and J. Clifford. A temporal relational algebra as a basis for temporal completeness. In *Proceedings of International Conference on Very Large Data Bases*, pages 13–24, Brisbane, Australia, 1990. [**399**]

[TCG⁺93]   A.U. Tansel, J. Clifford, S. Gadia, S. Jajodia, A. Segev, and R. Snodgrass, editors. *Temporal Databases Theory, Design, and Implementation*. Benjamin/Cummings, Redwood City, Ca., 1993. [**2, 407**]

[TD92]   K. Tochtermann and G. Dittrich. Fishing for clarity in hyperdocuments with enhanced fisheye-views. In *Proceedings of ACM Conference on Hypertext*, pages 212–221, Milano, Italy, 1992. [**554, 572**]

[Teo94]   T.J. Teorey. *Database Modeling & Design: The Entity-Relationship Approach*. Morgan Kaufmann, San Francisco, Ca., second edition, 1994. [**68, 80–83**]

[TF76]   R.W. Taylor and R.L. Frank. CODASYL data-base management systems. *ACM Computing Surveys*, 8:67–103, 1976. [**2**]

[TF82]   D.-M. Tsou and P.C. Fischer. Decomposition of a relation schema into Boyce-Codd normal form. *ACM SIGACT News*, 14:23–29, 1982. [**255, 269, 271**]

[TF86]   S.J. Thomas and P.C. Fischer. Nested relational structures. In P.C. Kanellakis and F. Preparata, editors, *Advances in Computing Research*, volume 3, pages 269–307. JAI Press, Greenwich, 1986. [**520, 521**]

[TFC83]   L. Tucherman, A.L. Furtado, and M.A. Casanova. A pragmatic approach to structured database design. In *Proceedings of International Conference on Very Large Data Bases*, pages 219–231, Florence, 1983. [**226**]

[Tha89a]   B. Thalheim. On semantic issues connected with keys in relational databases permitting null values. *Journal of Information Processing Cybernetics*, 25:11–20, 1989. [**319, 356**]

[Tha89b]   A. Thayse, editor. *From Modal Logic to Deductive Databases*. John Wiley & Sons, Chichester, 1989. [**502, 509**]

[Tho79]   R.H. Thomas. A majority consensus approach to concurrency control for multiple copy databases. *ACM Transactions on Database Systems*, 4:180–209, 1979. [**449, 454**]

[Tho93]   A. Thomasian. Two-phase locking performance and its thrashing behavior. *ACM Transactions on Database Systems*, 18:579–625, 1993. [**432**]

[TK78]   D. Tsichritzis and A. Klug. The ANSI/X3/SPARC DBMS framework report of the study group on database management systems. *Information Systems*, 3:173–191, 1978. (Guest editors). [**5**]

[TL76]   D.C. Tsichritzis and F.H. Lochovsky. Hierarchical data-base management: A survey. *ACM Computing Surveys*, 8:105–123, 1976. [**2**]

[TL86]   P. Thanisch and G. Loizou. A polynomial-time dependency implication algorithm for unary multi-valued dependencies. In *Proceedings of International Conference on Database Theory*, pages 397–408, Rome, 1986. [**203**]

[TLJ90]   P. Thanisch, G. Loizou, and G. Jones. Succinct database schemes. *International Journal of Computer Mathematics*, 33:55–69, 1990. [**272**]

[TN96]   D. Toman and D. Niwiński. First-order queries over temporal databases inexpressible in temporal logic. In *Proceedings of International Conference on Extending Database Technology*, pages 307–324, Avignon, Frnace, 1996. [**399**]

[Tom88]   A. Tomasic. View update translation via deduction and annotation. In *Proceedings of International Conference on Database Theory*, pages 338–352, Brüges, Belgium, 1988. [**500**]

[Tom96]   D. Toman. Point vs. interval-based query languages for temporal databases. In *Proceedings of ACM Symposium on Principles of Database Systems*, pages 58–67, Montreal, 1996. [**407**]

[Tom97]   D. Toman. A point-based temporal extension of SQL. In *Proceedings of International Conference on Deductive and Object-Oriented Databases*, pages 103–121, Montreux, Switzerland, 1997. [**407**]

[Top87]   R.W. Topor. Domain-independent formulas and databases. *Theoretical Computer Science*, 52:281–306, 1987. [**136, 138**]

[Tor94]   R. Torlone. Update operations in deductive databases with functional dependencies. *Acta Informatica*, 31:573–600, 1994. [**508**]

[Tra63]   B.A. Trakhtenbrot. Impossibility of an algorithm for the decision problem in finite classes. *American Mathematical Society Traslations, Series 2*, 23:1–5, 1963. [53]

[Tur36]   A.M. Turing. On computable numbers, with an application to the Entscheidungsproblem. *Proceedings of the London Mathematical Society*, 42:230–265, 1936. [40, 54]

[Tur37]   A.M. Turing. On computable numbers, with an application to the Entscheidungsproblem. A correction. *Proceedings of the London Mathematical Society*, 43:544–546, 1937. [40, 54]

[Ull83]   J.D. Ullman. Technical correspondence: On Kent's "consequences of assuming a universal relation". *ACM Transactions on Database Systems*, 8:637–643, 1983. [80]

[Ull87]   J.D. Ullman. Database theory: past and future. In *Proceedings of ACM Symposium on Principles of Database Systems*, pages 1–10, San Diego, Ca., 1987. [227]

[Ull88]   J.D. Ullman. *Principles of Database and Knowledge-Base Systems*, volume 1. Computer Science Press, Rockville, Md., 1988. [59, 60, 509]

[Ull89]   J.D. Ullman. *Principles of Database and Knowledge-Base Systems*, volume 2. Computer Science Press, Rockville, Md., 1989. [27, 229, 493]

[Ull91]   J.D. Ullman. A comparison between deductive and object-oriented database systems. In *Proceedings of International Conference on Deductive and Object-Oriented Databases*, pages 263–277, Munich, 1991. [529, 536]

[Ull92]   J.D. Ullman. The interface between language theory and database theory. In J.D. Ullman, editor, *Theoretical Studies in Computer Science*, pages 133–151. Academic Press, Boston, 1992. [486, 493]

[UV88]   J.D. Ullman and A. Van Gelder. Parallel complexity of logical query programs. *Algorithmica*, 3:5–42, 1988. [493]

[Val84]   L.G. Valiant. A theory of the learnable. *Communications of the ACM*, 27:1134–1142, 1984. [565]

[Van67]   J. Van Heijenoort, editor. *From Frege to Gödel: A Source Book in Mathematical Logic, 1879-1931*. Harvard University Press, Cambridge, Ma., 1967. [59]

[Van83]   J.F.A.K. Van Benthem. *The Logic of Time*. D. Reidel, Dordrecht, Holland, first edition, 1983. [407]

[Van86]   D. Van Gucht. Interaction-free multivalued dependencies. In *Proceedings of International Conference on Database Theory*, pages 410–420, Rome, 1986. [198]

[Van88]   A. Van Gelder. Negation as failure using tight derivations for general logic programs. In J. Minker, editor, *Foundations of Deductive Databases and Logic Programming*, pages 149–176. Morgan Kaufmann, Los Altos, Ca., 1988. [468]

[Van89]   D. Van Dalen. *Logic and Structure*. Springer-Verlag, Berlin, 1989. [40, 138]

[Van92]   A. Van Gelder. The well-founded semantics of aggregation. In *Proceedings of ACM Symposium on Principles of Database Systems*, pages 127–138, San Diego, Ca., 1992. [509]

[Van93a]   J. Van den Bussche. *Formal aspects of object identity in database manipulation*. PhD thesis, Department of Mathematics and Computer Science, University of Antwerp, 1993. [365, 526, 529]

[Van93b]   A. Van Gelder. The alternating fixpoint of logic programs with negations. *Journal of Computer and System Sciences*, 47:185–221, 1993. [468, 476, 482]

[Var81]   M.Y. Vardi. The decision problem for database dependencies. *Information Processing Letters*, 12:251–254, 1981. [135]

[Var82a]   M.Y. Vardi. The complexity of relational query languages. In *Proceedings of ACM Symposium on Theory of Computing*, pages 137–146, San Fancisco, Ca., 1982. [57, 359, 379, 380, 383]

[Var82b]   M.Y. Vardi. On decomposition of relational databases. In *Proceedings of IEEE Symposium on Foundations of Computer Science*, pages 176–185, Chicago, Il., 1982. [210]

[Var83]   M.Y. Vardi. Inferring multivalued dependencies from functional and join dependencies. *Acta Informatica*, 19:305–324, 1983. [200, 203]

[Var84a]   M.Y. Vardi. The implication and finite implication problems for typed template dependencies. *Journal of Computer and System Sciences*, 28:3–28, 1984. [200, 211]

[Var84b]   M.Y. Vardi. A note on lossless database decompositions. *Information Processing Letters*, 18:257–260, 1984. [246]

[Var86]   M.Y. Vardi. Issues in logical databases. In *Proceedings of International Conference on Very Large Data Bases*, pages 103–127, Kyoto, 1986. [502]

[Var88a]   M.Y. Vardi. Decidability and undecidability results for boundedness of linear recursive queries. In *Proceedings of ACM Symposium on Principles of Database Systems*, pages 341–351, Austin, Texas, 1988. [491]

[Var88b]   M.Y. Vardi. Fundamentals of dependency theory. In E. Börger, editor, *Trends in Theoretical Computer Science*, chapter 5, pages 171–224. Computer Science Press, New York, 1988. [**211, 504**]

[Var89a]   M.Y. Vardi. Automata theory for database theoreticians. In *Proceedings of ACM Symposium on Principles of Database Systems*, pages 83–92, Philadelphia, Pa., 1989. [**489**]

[Var89b]   M.Y. Vardi. The universal-relation model for logical independence. *IEEE Software*, 5:80–85, 1989. [**80**]

[VB92]   C.R. Vela and A. Bahamonde. An algorithm to minimize representation of finite order relations. *International Journal of Computer Mathematics*, 41:139–150, 1992. [**43**]

[VF88]   D. Van Gucht and P.C. Fischer. Multilevel nested relational structures. *Journal of Computer and System Sciences*, 36:77–105, 1988. [**520, 521**]

[Via87]   V. Vianu. Dynamic functional dependencies and database aging. *Journal of the ACM*, 34:28–59, 1987. [**404**]

[Via88]   V. Vianu. Database survivability under dynamic constraints. *Acta Informatica*, 25:55–84, 1988. [**404**]

[Via97a]   V. Vianu. Databases and finite-model theory. In P.G. Kolaitis and N. Immerman, editors, *Descriptive Complexity and Finite Models*, volume 31 of *DIMACS series in Discrete Mathematics and Computer Science*, pages 97–148. American Mathematical Society, Providence, RI, 1997. [**59**]

[Via97b]   V. Vianu. Rule-based languages. *Annals of Mathematics and Artificial Intelligence*, 19:215–259, 1997. [**468**]

[Vin91]   M.W. Vincent. Equivalence of update anomalies in relational databases. In *Proceddings of International Conference on Management of Data, COMAD*, pages 251–264, Bombay, 1991. [**242**]

[Vin94]   M.W. Vincent. *The Semantic Justification for Normal Forms in Relational Database Design*. PhD thesis, Department of Computer Science, Monash University, 1994. [**282**]

[Vin98]   M.W. Vincent. Redundancy elimination and a new normal form for relational database design. In B. Thalheim and L. Libkin, editors, *Semantics in Databases*, pages 247–264. Springer-Verlag, Berlin, 1998. [**256, 257, 284**]

[VK76]   M.H. Van Emden and R.A. Kowalski. The semantics of predicate logic as a programming language. *Journal of the ACM*, 23:733–742, 1976. [**463, 479, 509**]

[VL97]   M.W. Vincent and M. Levene. Restructuring partitioned normal form relations without information loss. In *Proceedings of International Conference on Management of Data, COMAD*, pages 111–124, Bombay, 1997. [**524**]

[VN95]   K. Vadaparty and S. Naqvi. Using constraints for efficient query processing in nondeterministic databases. *IEEE Transactions on Knowledge and Data Engineering*, 7:850–864, 1995. [**331, 351**]

[VRS91]   A. Van Gelder, K.A. Ross, and J.S. Schlipf. The well-founded semantics for general logic programs. *Journal of the ACM*, 38:620–650, 1991. [**468, 477, 482**]

[VS89]   D.A. Varvel and L. Shapiro. The computational completeness of extended database query languages. *IEEE Transactions on Software Engineering*, 15:632–638, 1989. [**365**]

[VS93]   M.W. Vincent and B. Srinivasan. A note on relation schemes which are in 3NF but not in BCNF. *Information Processing Letters*, 48:281–283, 1993. [**255, 283**]

[VT91]   A. Van Gelder and R.W. Topor. Safety and translation of relational calculus queries. *ACM Transactions on Database Systems*, 16:235–278, 1991. [**136**]

[VV92]   V. Vianu and G. Vossen. Conceptual level concurrency control of relational update transactions. *Theoretical Computer Science*, 95:1–42, 1992. [**411, 423**]

[VW92]   J.H. Van Lint and R.M. Wilson. *A Course in Combinatorics*. Cambridge University Press, Cambridge, U.K., 1992. [**33, 154**]

[WC96]   J. Widom and S. Ceri, editors. *Active Database Systems: Triggers and Rules for Advanced Database Processing*. Morgan Kaufmann, San Francisco, Ca., 1996. [**547**]

[WCL91]   J. Widom, R.J. Cochrane, and B.G. Lindsay. Implementing set-oriented production rules as an extension to Starburst. In *Proceedings of International Conference on Very Large Data Bases*, pages 275–285, Barcelona, 1991. [**545**]

[WI98]   S.M. Weiss and N. Indurkhya. *Predictive Data Mining: A Practical Guide*. Morgan Kaufmann, San Francisco, Ca., 1998. [**564**]

[Wie77]   G. Wiederhold. *Database Deisgn*. McGraw-Hill, Tokyo, 1977. [**60**]

[Wij95]   J. Wijsen. Design of temporal relational databases based on dynamic and temporal functional dependencies. In *Recent Advances in Temporal Databases, Proceedings of the International Workshop on Temporal Databases*, pages 61–76, Zurich, 1995. [**404, 407**]

[Wil85]   R.J. Wilson. *Introduction to Graph Theory*. Longman, Essex, third edition, 1985. [**33, 63**]

[Wil92]   R. Wille. Concept lattices and conceptual knowledge systems. *Computers and Mathematics with Applications*, 23:493–515, 1992. [**82**]

[Wil94]   M. Wild. A theory of finite closure spaces based on implications. *Advances in Mathematics*, 108:118–139, 1994. [167]

[Win88a]   M. Winslett. A framework for comparison of update semantics. In *Proceedings of ACM Symposium on Principles of Database Systems*, pages 315–324, Austin, Texas, 1988. [502]

[Win88b]   M. Winslett. A model-based approach to updating databases with incomplete information. *ACM Transactions on Database Systems*, 13:167–196, 1988. [502]

[Win95]   M. Winslett. Epistemic aspects of databases. In D.M. Gabbay, C.J. Hogger, and J.A. Robinson, editors, *Handbook of Logic in Artificial Intelligence and Logic Programming, Epistemic and Temporal Reasoning*, volume 4, pages 133–174. Clarendon Press, Oxford, U.K., 1995. [502]

[WJL93]   G. Wiederhold, S. Jajodia, and W. Litwin. Integrating temporal data in a heterogeneous environment. In A.U, Tansel, J. Clifford, S. Gadia, S. Jajodia, A. Segev, and R. Snodgrass, editors, *Temporal Databases, Theory, Design, and Implementation*, pages 563–579. Benjamin/Cummings, Redwood City, Ca., 1993. [396]

[Won82]   E. Wong. A statistical approach to incomplete information in database systems. *ACM Transactions on Database Systems*, 7:470–488, 1982. [354]

[Woo75]   W.A. Wood. What's in a link: Foundations for semantics networks. In D.G. Bobrow and A.M. Collins, editors, *Representation and Understanding: Studies in Cognitive Science*, pages 35–82. Academic Press, New York, 1975. [556]

[Yan81]   M. Yannakakis. Algorithms for acyclic database schemes. In *Proceedings of International Conference on Very Large Data Bases*, pages 82–94, Cannes, 1981. [206, 211]

[Yan84]   M. Yannakakis. Serializability by locking. *Journal of the ACM*, 31:227–244, 1984. [455]

[YÖ92a]   L.-Y. Yuan and M. Özsoyoğlu. Design of desirable relational database schemes. *Journal of Computer and System Sciences*, 45:435–470, 1992. [198, 249]

[YÖ92b]   L.-Y. Yuan and M. Özsoyoğlu. Unifying functional and multivalued dependencies for relational database design. *Information Sciences*, 59:189–211, 1992. [249]

[You89]   E. Yourdon. *Modern Structured Analysis*. Prentice-Hall, Englewood Cliffs, NJ, 1989. [62, 72, 571]

[Zad65]   L.A. Zadeh. Fuzzy sets. *Information and Control*, 8:338–353, 1965. [333, 338]

[Zad79]   L.A. Zadeh. A theory of approximate reasoning. In J.E. Hayes, D. Michie, and L.I. Mikulich, editors, *Machine Intelligence*, volume 9, pages 129–194. Ellis Horwood, Chichester, 1979. [333, 338]

[Zad86]   L.A. Zadeh. Is probability theory sufficient for dealing with uncertainty in AI: A negative view. In L.N. Kanal and J.F. Lemmer, editors, *Uncertainty in Artificial Intelligence*, pages 103–116. North-Holland, Amsterdam, 1986. [354]

[Zan82]   C. Zaniolo. A new normal form for the design of relational database schemata. *ACM Transactions on Database Systems*, 7:489–499, 1982. [269, 283]

[Zan84]   C. Zaniolo. Database relations with null values. *Journal of Computer System Sciences*, 28:142–166, 1984. [289, 301]

[ZC86]   A. Zvieli and P.P.-S. Chen. Entity-relationship modeling and fuzzy databases. In *Proceedings of IEEE Conference on Data Engineering*, pages 320–327, Los Angeles, 1986. [81]

[ZCF+97]   C. Zaniolo, S. Ceri, C. Faloustos, R.T. Snodgrass, V.S. Subrahmanian, and R. Zicari. *Advanced Databases Systems*. Morgan Kaufmann, San Francisco, Ca., 1997. [406]

[ZHKF95]   G. Zhou, R. Hull, R. King, and J.-C. Franchitti. Data integration and warehousing using H2O. *IEEE Data Engineering Bulletin*, 18:29–40, 1995. [564]

[Zia91]   W. Ziarko. The discovery, analysis, and representation of data dependencies in databases. In G. Piatetsky-Shapiro and W.J. Frawley, editors, *Knowledge Discovery in Databases*, pages 195–209. AAAI Press, Meno Park, Ca., 1991. [344, 357, 565]

[ZM81]   C. Zaniolo and M.A. Melkanoff. On the design of relational database schemata. *ACM Transactions on Database Systems*, 6:1–47, 1981. [249]

[ZM90]   S.B. Zdonik and D. Maier, editors. *Readings in Object-Oriented Database Systems*. Morgan Kaufmann, San Francisco, Ca., 1990. [529]

[ZO92a]   Y. Zhang and M.E. Orlowska. The effect of unary inclusion dependencies on relational database design. *Computers and Mathematics with Applications*, 24:49–59, 1992. [183]

[ZO92b]   Y. Zhang and M.E. Orlowska. A new polynomial time algorithm for BCNF relational database design. *Information Systems*, 17:185–193, 1992. [255]

[ZYT90]   W. Zhang, C.T. Yu, and D. Troy. Necessary and sufficient conditions to linearize doubly recursive programs in logic databases. *ACM Transactions on Database Systems*, 15:459–482, 1990. [487, 489]

Index

609